BUSINESS JETS INTERNATIONAL 2000

by

Terry Smith, Peter Simmonds, Steven Sowter and Barrie Towey

First edition - February 1971

Second edition - June 1987

Third edition - August 1988

Fourth edition - June 1989

Fifth edition - May 1990

Sixth edition - May 1991

Seventh edition - May 1992

Eighth edition - June 1993

Ninth edition - May 1994

Tenth edition - April 1995

Eleventh edition - May 1996

Twelfth edition - June 1997

Thirteenth edition - May 1998

Fourteenth edition - May 1999

Fifteenth edition - May 2000

Published by: Air-Britain (Historians) Limited

Registered Office: 12 Lonsdale Gardens, Tunbridge Wells, Kent TN1 1PA

Sales Department: 19 Kent Road, Grays, Essex RM17 6DE

Membership Enquiries: 1 Rose Cottage, 179 Penn Road, Hazlemere, Bucks HP15 7NE

ISBN 0 85130 297 1
ISSN 1468-3202

Cover photographs:

Front cover: The final production CL-600S Challenger OE-HET c/n 1086 wearing Grossmann titles, landing at Manchester on 12.6.98. (Denis Norman)

Rear cover:

Top: IAI 1125A Astra SPX N97FL c/n 110 in Lay's titles. (Darren Metherell)

Bottom: CL-601 Challenger c/n 3004 of Pizza Hut, with hard-to read company-style registration N45PH on the engine cowling. (Darren Metherell)

CONTENTS

INTRODUCTION

When we look back at the last twelve months, and if we had kept records from previous years, we believe it has probably seen record numbers of new aircraft being registered and older aircraft being re-registered. Given that the rate of new aircraft being built is greater than those being taken out of service, for whatever reason, then with a larger corporate fleet there is bound to be an increased number of changes. These levels of change give the editorial team a bigger task each month. As compensation it also means that those readers who only buy the book once every two or three years should consider buying it more frequently. If they do this sales will increase and in turn the unit cost per book goes down as we print more copies and hence the price Air-Britain can sell them to you our loyal readership.

Regular readers will know we have never covered airliners that are in corporate service - they are of course superbly covered in our sister publication, Jet Airliners of the World. (As this editorial is penned a new edition is being prepared for publication a little later this year.) Last year we floated the suggestion of including the new Airbus A319CJ and the Boeing 737BBJ as although they are "airliners" they have been significantly modified for business use. On balance the readers who responded voted for their inclusion and we have decided to include them this year, as an experiment. But as there is a considerable body of opinion, including from within the editorial team, which was against their inclusion we reserve the right to exclude them next year! At the end of the day it is already becoming difficult to ascertain what is a real BBJ or CJ and not just a 737NG or A319 in corporate use and this could just be the final determining factor. Of course they will continue to be included in Jet Airliners of the World, whatever we do.

The monograph follows its now-established format and includes the c/ns of the next 12 months' expected production of each type which is still in current production. This feature should enable readers, if they so wish, to update the book with new production aircraft, details of which may be found in Air-Britain News.

It is our policy, unlike some other publications, to always differentiate between "full" marks and assigned or reserved marks. We do this by placing an asterisk against such entries. In addition those marks which have only been requested have the symbol "^" against such registrations.

The production listings and the index have again been fully updated; once again, new data which has not been previously published, in particular some initial test registrations, has come into our possession and has duly been incorporated into the text. A list of registration sightings where, at the time of publication, the identities of the aircraft are not yet known to us has again been included. In response to readers' requests, all current registrations are highlighted in the text of the Master Index which contains over 46,000 entries.

In a work of this nature there are bound to be some errors and data omitted; the editorial team (whose address appears below) would welcome notification of any such errors and omissions. The most troublesome area undoubtedly remains Mexico, and any official data from that country would be very helpful.

Those interested in current ownership data should refer to other publications such as Jet & Prop Jet, published by our friends AvCom International, whilst those in the aviation industry are recommended to contact Avdata Inc at PO Box 913, Wichita, Kansas 67201, USA; the latter can be commissioned to supply ownership and other data from their comprehensive databases.

Finally, the next edition of this Monograph is scheduled for a similar time next year.

Terry Smith, Pete Simmonds and Steven Sowter, Barrie Towey
Editorial address: 28 Summerfields, The Limes, Ingatestone, Essex CM4 0BS, United Kingdom
e-mail address: Terry_J_Smith@compuserve.com

May 2000

ACKNOWLEDGMENTS

Business Jets International has been produced with the valued past and present assistance of, and from information provided by, the following companies and individuals:

Aerospatiale
Atlantic Aviation
Aviation Data Service of Wichita
British Aerospace plc
Beech Aircraft Co
Canadair Limited
Canadair Challenger Limited
Cessna Aircraft Co
Gulfstream Aerospace
Israeli Aircraft Industries
Lockheed Aircraft Co
Mitsubishi Aircraft Co
Raytheon Aircraft Co
Rockwell International
Sabreliner Corp

INDIVIDUALS

Barry Ambrose
Joseph Anckner
Steve Bailey
H W Barrett
Colin Berry
Bill Blanchard
Mike Brown
David C Buck
B J Burt
Lyn Buttifant
Jim Cain
Russell Carter
Nick C Challoner
Chris Chatfield
Alan E Clark
Colin Clark
Dennis Clement
John Davies
J F Elliott
Robert D Elliott
David England
Brian Gates
S Graham
Nigel Green
Andrew Griffiths
Kay Hagby
Richard Hill
Mike Holdstock
Gerry Hollands
Carolos Hopkins
Nigel Howarth
Heinz Kasmanhuber
John Kim
Bruce Leatherborrow
John MacMaster
Stephen L Mart
J A Newton
Terry Noss
Pierre Parvaud
Nigel Prevett
Brian Print
Mark Reavey
Ian Sant
M Schofield
Simon Scott-Kemball
D Sheldon
Graham Slack
Claude Soussi
Neville Spalding
David Thompson
Peter Thompson
Barrie Towey
Richard Urbeck
D F Walsh
Pete Watson
Tony Wheeler

Plus the many regular contributors to the BIZ-JETS section of Air-Britain News. Due acknowledgment is also given to the "Le Morane-Saulnier Paris MS760" monograph by Pierre Parvaud and Pierre Gailland, published by Le Trait d'Union (the French branch of Air-Britain) and to the article in the Winter 1989 Air-Britain Digest by the same two authors on the HFB320 Hansa. We must also thank the Air-Britain Gulfstream specialist, Alain Jeneve, for his review of the Gulfstream 1 section.

REVIEW OF YEAR 1999-2000

The past 12 months have again proved extremely successful for the world's executive aircraft manufacturers, helped by burgeoning growth in the fractional ownership market. The pre-owned market has again been buoyant as a result.

In the fractional ownership market, the domination of the NetJets, Flexjet and Raytheon Travel Air schemes - all three of which continued to receive and order new aircraft throughout the year - is now being challenged by the Flight Options programme based on pre-owned rather than brand-new aircraft. The latter has steadily added to its fleet of Beechjets, BAe125s, Citation IIs and Challenger 601s, as well as adding a new type - the Falcon 50 - from the beginning of year 2000. The NetJets Europe fleet has added new Hawker 800XPs and was due to receive its first Falcon 2000 as we went to press and the NetJets Middle East programme received a second leased Gulfstream IV while its own aircraft (three known of to date) were undergoing completion. Bombardier Business Jet Solutions set up Flexjets Europe using Learjet 31As, Learjet 60s and a Challenger 601, all under Danish registry and managed by Execujet Scandinavia. In California, a new shared ownership scheme - to be known as XJETS - is hoping to commence operation in the western USA this summer with up to 8 refurbished Citation IIs.

Bombardier

Bombardier had delivered 42 Global Expresses for completion by the end of its 1999-2000 financial year. Completion capacity was increased thanks to agreements reached with Marshall Aerospace at Cambridge, The Jet Center at Los Angeles/Van Nuys and BFGoodrich at Everett in Washington state - three aircraft were at Cambridge at the time of writing. Although less than 10 aircraft were in customer service, these included examples in Malaysia, Korea and Switzerland. Significant orders announced during the year were 5 for the Royal Air Force, 20 for the Flexjets fractional ownership fleet, one for Sweden's EF Aviation, one for Seagrams and one for Japan's CAB.

Challenger 604 production had reached 150 units by April. The Royal Danish Air Force has received its second aircraft and, also in Denmark, Maersk Air received one. The first aircraft for a UK customer was delivered at the beginning of April. Three aircraft were delivered to Germany and other non-US export deliveries were made to Brazil, the Philippines and Bermuda. The government of Jordan received its first of two aircraft, which was delivered to Amman via Farnborough at the beginning of April - Jordan had been on the verge of accepting two Gulfstream IVs but opted very late for the Challengers instead.

Learjet 31 production advanced past the 200 total, but 1999-2000 deliveries included a number of aircraft for Bombardier's own Flexjet shared ownership scheme. Export deliveries were made to Venezuela, Mexico and the Philippines.

Learjet 45 production and deliveries continued apace, including the first delivery to the Flexjets fleet. The four Singapore Air Lines aircraft finally left Wichita in December on delivery to Changi, three of them routing via Glasgow and the other via Shannon. Two Lear 45s were delivered to TAG Aeroleasing SA in Switzerland and other export deliveries were made to Brazil, Canada, South Africa, Egypt and Germany - the latter with Cayman marks.

Learjet 60 production approached the 190 mark, with registration allocations indicating that production will continue until at least number 208. Export deliveries during the past year have included a significant number to Europe - 5 to Germany, 2 to Denmark and one each to Luxembourg and Austria. Other export deliveries were made to Mexico and the United Arab Emirates and an ex-company demonstrator was awaiting delivery to Egypt as we went to press. In the US itself, the Flexjets fleet was a major beneficiary.

First metal for the super-midsize Continental was cut in October 1999 on the back of 54 orders for the type.

Cessna

Cessna enjoyed a record year in 1999, delivering 224 Citations of all models and receiving 353 orders, creating a backlog of 650 units by year-end. A number of significant landmarks have been reached in the past 12 months: the 3000th Citation (a Citation X) was delivered, as were the 50th Excel, the 350th CitationJet, the 500th Citation V, the 100th Bravo, the 100th Citation VII and the 100th Citation X. The 100th Excel rolled off the production line this April.

The CJ1 upgraded version of the CitationJet received its US type certification in February, allowing the first of the type to be delivered at the end of March. Germany continued to be fertile sales territory for the CitationJet with at least 8 of the type, both new and pre-owned, having found homes there since our last book. Other export deliveries in the past year include examples to Austria, Spain, Brazil, Holland, Belgium, Italy, Bermuda, Panama and the UK.

Certification work on the CJ2 stretched CitationJet continued, with the first few production examples coming off the production line in readiness for delivery as quickly as possible after type certification is achieved next year.

Deliveries of the Citation II Bravo passed the 100 mark and included export deliveries to Austria, Germany, Italy, Brazil, Guatemala, Kenya, Australia and Canada along with two to the UK (with a third imminent), albeit with Irish registrations.

The last Ultra version of the Citation V was delivered, to the US Army. Two examples were delivered to the US Marines and, needless to say, the NetJets fleet also received several. Notable export deliveries were a couple to the UK and one each to Japan and Angola.

Certification work continued on the Ultra's replacement, the Encore. The first production example was rolled out in early March and customer deliveries are slated for this coming Autumn, with two of the first 10 aircraft being destined for the US Army.

Excel deliveries continued apace, including the first for the NetJets fleet. In the UK, Nigel Mansell received one to replace his Bravo and two have been delivered to Switzerland. Exports were also made to Brazil, Germany, Saudi Arabia, Sweden, Canada, Cayman Islands, Greece and Italy.

Production of the Citation VII continued but is likely to end this year. The NetJets Europe fleet received a fourth aircraft and deliveries were also made to Germany and Australia. The US NetJets fleet inevitably received several examples, although one aircraft destined for it was damaged beyond repair in a ground accident at Wichita before it could be delivered. Two examples were sold to Wendy's International, the hamburger restaurant company, to replace Falcon 10s.

Total Citation X production easily passed the 100 mark, assisted by numerous additions to the NetJets fleet. Export deliveries were made to the UK (later resold in Sweden), Germany, South Africa, Brazil and the Cayman Islands - the latter for Russian tennis star Yevgeny Kafelnikov. An example for Finland was due for delivery soon after these words were typed, to replace a leased example. In the USA, Pennzoil purchased a Citation X to replace a Gulfstream IV and several operators upgraded to the type from smaller (and slower) Citations. The X's high speed was ably demonstrated when Steve Fossett - better known for his several failed attempts to circumnavigate the globe by balloon - flew his Citation X N377SF around the world from and to Los Angeles in a new record time of 41 hours, 13 minutes and 11 seconds in mid-February. Registrations reserved for the NetJets fleet suggest that orders received to date will take production to some 170 units.

Dassault Aviation

Significant production landmarks in the past year here, too: the 300th Falcon 50 (including the 50th 50EX) built, the 50th Falcon 900EX delivered and the 100th Falcon 2000 delivered.

Of the dozen or so Falcon 50EXs built since our last book, those delivered to non-US customers have included examples to Sweden (with Cayman marks), Bermuda and South Africa. A pair of aircraft currently being completed at Le Bourget are also likely to be for non-US buyers. In the USA, Weyerhauser Corp bought two Falcon 50EXs to replace Citation IIIs and Kellett Aviation bought one to replace a Beechjet.

Dassault also delivered the first of 4 reworked, pre-owned Falcon 50s to the French Navy with the designation Falcon 50M. The other three aircraft are scheduled to enter Aeronavale service later this year.

The Falcon 900C obtained French certification in June 1999 and US certification in August. The first examples are now in service, including one with launch customer Sony Aviation and one with Evergreen. Falcon 900Bs delivered in the past 12 months include examples for Mexico, Portugal and Nigeria - the latter registered in Bermuda.

Falcon 900EX production reached 70 units and deliveries were made to the Italian Air Force (two aircraft), the UK (two aircraft - although one was later resold in the USA), Mexico and Switzerland as well as several to the USA.

Falcon 2000s comfortably passed the 100 total and an order for an additional 6 by Executive Jet International for its NetJets fleets took that company's total commitment to 60 aircraft. Notable recent deliveries have included 2 for Volkswagen - one for their US operation, the other for Germany under Cayman marks - one to Belgium and the first for the NetJets Europe fleet managed by Air Luxor in Portugal. Two aircraft for Italy were nearing fit-out completion at Le Bourget at the time of writing.

Gulfstream Aerospace

The 400th Gulfstream IV was rolled out in February, destined for an Asian customer. Although the majority of the year's deliveries were to US customers, including a number replacing Gulfstream IIIs and no less than 10 for the NetJets fleet, the Governments of Bahrain and Japan also received a new aircraft apiece. Three aircraft were registered in Saudi Arabia for the NetJets Middle East fleet but appeared to still be awaiting service entry at the time of writing. The Egyptian Air Force ordered two GIVs for VIP transport.

The 100th Gulfstream V out of more than 150 ordered has now been delivered for outfitting - it too is destined for a customer in Asia. Two more GVs have entered US military service, with two more to follow this year, and Kuwait Airways' three aircraft have all now been delivered. New GVs are now flying with Mexican, Swiss and Saudi customers, the latter with Bermudan marks. The first NetJets example is due to enter service later this year - in fact, Executive Jet International converted options for 5 GIVs and 5 GVs into firm orders for the NetJets programme in December.

Elsewhere in the USA, the computer world created two sets of Gulfstream V headlines in the last year: firstly, Mark Cuban (one of the co-founders of broadcast.com) used the Internet to buy a GV and secondly, the Apple Computers board of directors awarded a GV to CEO Steve Jobs in recognition of his performance.

Israeli Aircraft Industries

Ten Galaxies have been delivered to the completion centre at Fort Worth/Alliance since our last book and the first three of the type entered customer service in the first three months of the year 2000, two in the USA and one in Switzerland. IAI and Galaxy Aerospace were given a Flight International Aerospace Industry 2000 award in recognition of the type having created the new 'super-midsize' biz-jet market segment. Galaxy Aerospace intends a delivery rate of two per month to be achieved by this June.

Astra SPX production continued steadily and a delivery rate of one a month is Galaxy Aerospace's intention. Arguably the most significant delivery in the last year was one heavily-modified aircraft to Taiwan, for use as a target-towing, special mission and scientific research aerial platform throughout Asia and the Pacific region. The year was however marred by severe damage caused to Lions Air's second Astra SPX, c/n 113, shortly after it had been delivered to Switzerland when engine bleed air leaked into the tailcone assembly during a flight. Galaxy Aerospace had to donate their own demonstrator to Lions Air as a replacement and c/n 113 has reportedly been ferried back to IAI's Tel Aviv factory.

Raytheon Aircraft

Raytheon delivered 45 Beechjets in 1999, including the 500th of the type last October and the 10th aircraft for the Japan Air Self Defence Force. The company's own Travel Air fractional ownership fleet was a major beneficiary, however, and only Turkey and Mexico have received new civil Beechjets outside the USA in the last 12 months.

Hawker 800XP production continues to impress and 14 aircraft were ordered by Executive Jet International for the NetJets Middle East programme, the first due for delivery this year. Exports to Brazil, Turkey, Italy, South Africa, Bermuda, China, Germany and Spain and military deliveries to the Republic of Korea, Japan and Brazil were achieved. Five aircraft were added to Air Luxor's Portuguese-registered NetJets Europe fleet, while the US NetJets and the Raytheon Travel Air fleets also received several new aircraft each. In a 'coals to Newcastle' situation, the first US-built Hawker for a UK customer was delivered to Blackpool in early April.

Certification of the Premier was imminent as we went to press. The second aircraft first flew on 4 June 1999 and the third made the type's first public appearance at the NBAA Convention last October in Atlanta. Over two hundred Premiers have been ordered by customers in at least 26 countries.

Assembly of the first Hawker Horizon continues with certification and first deliveries due in 2001. More than 150 aircraft have been ordered, with Executive Jet International having ordered 50 and placed options for a further 50.

EXPLANATORY NOTES

The following abbreviations have been used in the text:

A/P	Airport	ff	first flight
AFB	Air Force Base	Inds	Industries
Avn	Aviation	Inst	Institute
b/u	broken up	TL	total landings
c/s	colour scheme	TT	total time
cvtd	converted	wfs	withdrawn from service
cx/canx	cancelled	wfu	withdrawn from use
dbr	damaged beyond repair	w/o	written off
exp	expired		

* An asterisk following the last registration indicates that at the time of compilation these marks were only reserved or assigned. Reserved means that the marks in question are offically listed on the FAA reservation fiche. Assigned marks are those which the owner/operator of the aircraft have requested. In both cases, on many occasions, such marks will never actually be taken up.

( ) Brackets around a registration indicate that these marks were not taken up.

NOTE: When an aircraft has been sold to another country and the new marks are not known at the time of compilation, the country prefix only is shown. A number of aircraft which have been sold in Brazil and Mexico where no marks were known at the time of compilation are shown in the production list respectively as PT- and XA-, even though they may eventually carry other prefixes used by those countries..pa

BRITISH AEROSPACE (RAYTHEON) 125 SERIES

The majority of the series 3, 400 and 700 aircraft which were exported to North America were allocated an additional number in the NA... range, and these numbers are quoted as the c/n. This practice was reintroduced on production 800 and 1000 series aircraft but has since ceased. The production list is in the normal c/n order, and a cross-reference of the two sets of numbers follows the production list. 800 series aircraft above c/n 258208 and 1000 series aircraft above c/n 259024 are known by the nomenclature Corporate Jets BAe125. Following the sale of Corporate Jets by BAe to Raytheon, owner of Beechcraft, yet another nomenclature change took place to Hawker 800 (at c/n 258255) and Hawker 1000 (at c/n 259043).

Only the first use of the UK class B marks are given from G-5-501 onwards as these are only used (and re-used!) by one aircraft.

C/n	Series	Identities
25001	1	G-ARYA ff 13Aug62 CofA exp 01Oct65; wfu Kelsterton College, UK
25002	1	G-ARYB CofA exp 22Jan68; wfu BAe Hatfield, UK cx 04Mar69 - Midland Air Museum, Coventry, UK
25003	1	G-ARYC CofA exp 01Aug73; wfu Mosquito Museum, Hatfield, UK
25004	1/521	G-ASEC G-FIVE wfu by Jun83; cx 14May85, used for spares - wings to c/n 25008
25005	1	G-ASNU (D-CFKG) D-COMA G-ASNU wfu by Dec82; impounded Lagos, Nigeria; cx 18Nov91
25006	1	HB-VAG I-RACE CofA exp Nov87; wfu
25007	1	(G-ASSH) HB-VAH G-ASTY HB-VAH F-BKMF w/o 05Jun66 Nice, France
25008	1	G-ASSI 5N-AWD wfu by Dec83; at Luton, UK - to Staggenhoe Farm, Whitwell Beds - for use by emergency services in crash exercises 10Sep98
25009	1	G-ATPC XW930 wfu, scrapped Jordan's scrapyard, Portsmouth, UK by Jun97
25010	1	G-ASSM 5N-AMK wfu by Dec83; to Science Museum, Kensington, London, UK, painted as G-ASSM
25011	T1	G-37-65 XS709 coded M
25012	T1	XS710 coded O stored RAF Cosford, UK as 9259M circa 1997
25013	1A	G-ASSJ N125J N2426 N7125J N4646S N88MR wfu prior to Jun82; remains to White Inds, Bates City, MO
25014	1A/522	G-ASSK N125G N734AK N621ST (N125WC) XA-JUZ N621ST wfu by Dec82; b/u 1985
25015	3B	VH-CAO (9M-AYI) VH-CAO cx May91; wfu N750D* for spares use by Dodson Int'l Parts
25016	1A	G-ASSL CF-RWA CF-OPC C-FOPC C6-BPC N4997E N222NG
25017	1A/522	G-ASSH N3060 N3060F N306MP N123JB N495G N333M XA-RSR
25018	731	CF-DOM C-FDOM N125LM C-GXPT N125PT N118TS N218TJ
25019	1A	G-ASYX N1125G N1135K w/o 25Feb66 Des Moines, IA
25020	731	G-ASZM N167J N959KW N2KW N2KN N365DJ N711WM (N128TJ) N55RF
25021	1A/522	G-ASZN N575DU N2504 N228G N228GL N125BT N125KC (N575D) N711WJ N300HW wfu; remains to White Industries, Bates City, MO
25022	1A/522	G-ASZO CF-SDA N505PA N100GB N50HH w/o 02Aug86 Bedford, IN
25023	731	G-ASZP N1125 N338 N125BW N125BM N58BT N284DB N584DB
25024	T1	XS711 coded L
25025	1B	D-COME HB-VAR F-BOHU (F-OCGK) 5N-AWB wfu by early 87
25026	1A	G-5-11 G-ATAY N225KJ N225K N225LL N4400E (N40AD) wfu by Apr86; used for spares early 86
25027	1A	CF-SEN C-FSEN N227DH N125BH
25028	1B	Ghana G.511 (N48172) C-GLFI N48172 N50SS XA-ESQ N29977 w/o 14Dec81 as XA-ESQ and parted out; last allocated US marks, N29977, were not worn; cx Apr91; remains to White Inds, Bates City, MO
25029	1A/522	G-ATAZ N10122 N391DA N10D
25030	1A	G-ATBA N413GH N123VM (N97VM) XB-MBM XA-MBM
25031	1A	G-ATBB N1923M N43WJ N79AE N105HS
25032	731	G-ATBC N65MK (N657K) N90WP N692FC N98TJ N942DS
25033	1A/522	G-ATBD N125G N1125G N111AG N111AD (N111AX) (N700AB) N63BL (N32HE) N125LC N125AL N125LL RP-C125
25034	1A	CF-HLL C-FHLL wfu Quebec City by Jun83; possibly following accident 18Apr83 at Gashe, PQ, Canada; fuselage noted at Montreal-St.Hubert Oct95; wings used on c/n 25027; cx Dec90
25035	1A/522	G-ATCO N1515P N1515E N151SG (N57TS)
25036	1A	CF-PQG C-FPQG N136DH cx Jul95 as destroyed/scrapped
25037	1A	G-ATFO D-CAFI N787X N26T N26TL (N26WJ) (N389DA) b/u for spares; cx Jly92
25038	731	G-ATCP N926G N125G (N900KC) N66KC (N15UB) N27RC N301CK (N417TF) (N28MM) N28M N42CK
25039	1A	CF-SIM C-FSIM N125TB N911AS (Freighter)
25040	T1	XS712 coded A
25041	T1	XS713 coded C
25042	731	CF-ANL C-FANL N79TS N42FD*
25043	1A/522	G-ATGA N125J N1230V N3007 N300R N70HB N522BW N522ME N65TS (N165AG)
25044	T1	XS726 coded T stored RAF Cosford, UK circa 1997
25045	T1	XS727 coded D
25046	1A/S-522	G-ATGS N48UC N4886 N125P N666AE N812TT N125AD LV-YGC
25047	1A/522	G-ATGT N778SM N580WS N75CT N800DA (N717GF)
25048	T1	XS728 coded E
25049	T1	XS729 coded G wfu in 1996; stored at RAF Cosford, UK
25050	T1	XS730 coded H
25051	731	G-ATGU N9300 N9300C N125HD C6-BEY N77VK wfu 18Dec85; cx Jan87, used for spares
25052	1A/522	G-ATIK N816M N816MC N812M N812N N388WM N125JR
25053	1A/522	CF-IPG CF-IPJ C-FIPJ N4465N N125TB N254JT N250JT N25JT
25054	TI	XS714 coded P wfu; to RAF Manston, UK for fire training use 9246M
25055	T1	XS731 coded J

BAe 125

C/n	Series	Identities
25056	T1	XS732 coded B wfu Jan91 due to fuselage corrosion; fuselage to Research Establishment, Fort Halstead, Kent, UK 27Mar91; TT 11,955.20, TL 9,067
25057	1A/522	G-ATIL N188K N125AW cx 02Apr86; b/u for spares Pontiac, MI
25058	1B	D-COMI N9308Y N215G N470R N632PB N632PE (EC-) believed used for spares
25059	T1	XS733 coded Q wfu in 1996; stored at RAF Cosford, UK
25060	1A/522	G-ATIM N2601 N26011 N2728 N22DL N22DE XB-FIS XB-EAL XA-BOJ XA-HOU XB-CXZ N96SG reported to be parted out for spares
25061	T1	XS734 coded N stored RAF Cosford, UK as 9260M circa 1997
25062	3B	VH-ECE wfu 21Jly81; to Camden Airport Museum, NSW; TT 13936, TL 53882; derelict at The Oaks, NSW by May97
25063	1B	HB-VAN G-BAXG G-ONPN 5N-ASZ wfu 03Jun86 Southampton, UK; used for spares
25064	1A/522	G-ATKK N230H N125JG N33BK N222G XA-RYW N222G XB-GGK XA-TAL w/o 09Jly99 Toluca A/P, Mexico
25065	1A/522	G-ATKL N631SC N631SQ N1YE XA-KOF
25066	731	G-ATKM N925CT N369JB (N374DH) N373DH
25067	1B/522	9J-RAN ZS-MAN 9J-SAS 9J-EPK Z-TBX ZS-MAN
25068	1A/522	XB-BEA XA-BEM XB-VUI XA-MIR XB-SBC (reported Oct89 with dual marks XA-MIR/XB-SBC) N5274U to Dodson Avn for spares use at Rantoul, KS
25069	3B	VH-ECF G-BAXL G-OBOB w/o 31Jan90 Concordia, MO; remains to White Inds, Bates City, MO
25070	1A/522	G-ATKN N520M N214JR N2148R N84W N51V N470TS N333GZ
25071	T1	XS735 coded R wfu; ground instructional airframe at RAF Cranwell, UK
25072	T1	XS736 coded S
25073	1A/522	G-ATLI N372CM N372GM N36MK w/o 28Dec70 Boise, ID
25074	1A/522	G-ATOV N400NW N400UW N300GB N411FB
25075	731	G-ATLJ N666M CF-MDB C-FMDB N9124N N750GM N731BW N600EG
25076	T1	XS737 coded K
25077	T1	XS738 coded U stored RAF Cosford, UK circa 1997
25078	1A/522	G-ATLK N40DC N448DC N125NT (N770BC) N16PJ*
25079	731	G-ATLL N440DC N448DC N40DC N425DC N425FD N79TJ N425FD (N79TJ) N942Y N942WN
25080	1B/522	VQ-ZIL 3D-AAB G-BDYE EI-BGW C-GLEO N23KL EC-EGT wfu Jan93 with Dodson Avn, Ottawa, KS
25081	T2	XS739 coded F
25082	1A/522	G-ATNM N909B N2125 N125CA N1MY N17SL wfu; cx Dec92; remains to White Inds, Bates City, MO
25083	1A/522	G-ATOW N16777 N435T N437T N533 N538 N50AS wfu for spares 1988 by OK Aircraft, Gilroy, CA; cx Sep92
25084	1A/522	G-ATNN N1125G N453CM N154TR N30EF N784AE (N745HG) N71BL N890RC N888CJ
25085	1B/522	G-ATPD 5N-AGU G-ATPD
25086	1A/522	CF-DSC N3699T XA-COL w/o 11Oct73 Acapulco, Mexico
25087	731/S	G-ATOX CF-ALC C-FALC N66AM N330G
25088	1A/522	G-ATNO N1230B 5B-
25089	1B/522	G-ATPB OO-SKJ 5N-ALH
25090	1B/S522	HB-VAT G-AWYE N102TW N429DA
25091	1A/522	G-ATNP N1230G N20RG N90RG N65FC XA-RSP
25092	1B/522	G-ATPE canx 14Mar90 as wfu (CofA exp 01Apr87)
25093	1A/522	G-ATSN N77D N306L N3MF w/o 26Jan79 New Mexico, USA
25094	1B/R522	G-ATWH HZ-BO1 G-ATWH G-YUGO cx 29Mar93 as wfu
25095	1A/522	G-ATSO N125Y CF-SHZ N1923G N5001G N5012P N80CC N61BL N25AW N831LC w/o 16Mar91 nr San Diego, CA
25096	1A/522	G-ATNR N235KC w/o 21Nov66 Grand Bahama
25097	1A/S522	G-ATSP LN-NPE N125V N12KW N21MF N89HB N67TS
25098	731	G-ATNS N10121 N666SC N57G N11AR N45SL N926LR N29CR YV-815CP N77LJ^
25099	1B/522	HB-VAU 5N-AER (N2246) (N121AC) wfu; located at aircraft trades school Zaira, Nigeria
25100	1A/522	G-ATNT N125J N952B N7SZ N104 N44TG N44TQ N6SS
25101	731/S	G-5-11 G-ATXE N142B N124BM XA-RUX XA-RCH N251LA N78AG
25102	1A/522	G-ATUU N756 N756M XB-AKW N3274Q to spares Houston, TX circa 1995 (cx Feb96) reported marks N3274Q were never carried
25103	1A/522	G-ATUV N533 N210M (N700UU) N601UU N60HU N402AC
25104	1A/522	G-ATUW N257H N140AK C-FMTC derelict Nov97 Vancouver, Canada; hulk removed to Lakeland FL circa Mar00
25105	1B/522	(D-CKOW) D-CKCF G-AYRY HZ-FMA reported wfu
25106	1B/522	HZ-BIN G-AWUF 5N-ALY G-AWUF G-DJMJ G-OMCA G-BOCB wfu 1994 for spares Luton, UK; cx 22Feb95; wfu
25107	1A/522	G-ATUX N7125J N2426 C-GFCL N107BW N694JC XA-GOC XA-HFM
25108	731	G-ATUY N1025C N901TC N901TG N31B C-FTAM N11QD N25LA C-GTTS
25109	1A/S522	G-ATUZ N201H N4CR
25110	1A/522	G-5-11 G-ATZE N3125B N125E w/o 30Jun83 Houston Hobby, TX
25111	3A	G-ATYH N1041B N125GC C-GKRL N31AS N177GP N900CD w/o 30May94 Waukegan Regional A/P, Waukegan, IL; remains to White Inds, Bates City, MO
25112	3A	G-ATYI N2525 N252V XB-AXP XA-LFU XB-FFV XA-SLR
25113	3B/RA	G-5-13 G-AVDX 5N-AVZ noted semi-derelict Dec96 Lagos, Nigeria
25114	3A	G-ATYJ N425K N44K N44KG N78RZ N25PM XA-SGP N114WD
25115	731	G-ATYK N229P N333ME N333MF N317EM N111DT N180ML N21GN N429AC (N750WC) N249BW N249MW N420JC N48DD
25116	3A	G-ATZN N93TC N136LK N345DA (N90SR) N345CT N726CC SX-BSS

BAe 125

C/n	Series	Identities
25117	3B	5N-AET 5N-AKT G-BSAA G-DBAL cx 16Apr93; wfu
25118	731	G-ATYL N743UT N45PM N731KC N300KC N227HF N14HH
25119	731	G-5-11 G-AVAD N213H N500XY
25120	3B	G-AVGW w/o 23Dec67 Luton, UK
25121	731	G-AVAE N795J N307G N807G N200PB N200PF XA-SKZ XB-GHC N125TJ N125LK*
25122	3A	G-AVAF N12225 N555CB N255CB (N123AG) N123AC parted out 1992 San Jose, CA; remains to OK Aircraft, Gilroy, CA
25123	3A	G-AVAG N700M N706M N77C N77CD N46TG N44PW N125FD
25124	3A	G-AVAH N125J N552N N912AS
25125	F3B/RA	G-AVAI LN-NPA G-AVAI F-GFMP 5N-AAN
25126	3B	G-5-11 G-AVDL N510X N66HA w/o 13Aug89 Houston, TX - remains to Aviation Warehouse film prop company warehouse at El Mirage CA
25127	F3B	G-AVPE G-5-623 G-KASS N125GK
25128	3B	G-AVOI F-GECR ZS-SMT
25129	3A	G-5-12 G-AVDM N521M w/o 12Dec72 Findlay, OH
25130	3B	G-5-14 G-AVRD HB-VAZ F-BSIM TR-LXO F-BSIM TR-LFB
25131	3B	G-5-11 G-AVRE F-BPMC G-FOUR I-RASO F-GFDB 3A-MDB F-GJDE 3A-MDE 7T-VVL
25132	3B	OY-DKP G-AZVS G-MRFB G-OCBA EI-WDC G-OCBA EI-WDC
25133	3B	G-AVRF G-ILLS VT-EQZ
25134	3A/RA	G-5-11 G-AVHA N514V N514VA N338 N366MP N366BR N117TS N725DW N946FS N230TS
25135	3B	G-5-14 HB-VAY G-AXPS w/o 20Jly70 Edinburgh, UK
25136	3A/RA	G-AVHB N501W N506N N505W N605W N700RG N700RD N700RG N125HS Brazil VU93-2113 (full prefix not confirmed)
25137	3A/RA	G-5-11 G-AVJD CF-AAG CF-KCI C-FKCI N13MJ N813PR C-GMEA N813PR
25138	3B	(G-5-12) G-5-16 G-AVVA HB-VBN I-BOGI 5N-AVV
25139	3A/RA	G-5-11 G-AVOJ N612G N2G N22GE N140JS
25140	3B/RA	(G-5-16) G-5-17 G-AVVB G-DJLW C6-MED
25141	3A/RA	G-5-12 G-AVOK N75C N55G N208H N14GD N14GQ (N90WP) N888WK C-GSKV N132RL
25142	731	G-AVOL N7055 N9040 N688CC N744CC N744OC N822CC N770DA (N60AM) N25MJ N705EA
25143	3B/RA	G-5-18 G-AVXK D-CHTH G-AVXK 5N-AOG wfu before Jun93; b/u for spares Hurn, UK
25144	3B/RA	G-5-12 G-AVRG G-OHEA cx Jun94; wfu to Cranfield Inst of Technology, Cranfield, UK, as instructional airframe
25145	3B	G-5-20 G-AVXL LN-NPC G-AVXL I-SNAF CofA exp 1983; derelict 1989 Milan-Linate; cx 1990
25146	3A/RA	G-AVRH N77167 N214JR N214TC (N711SW) N114PC N21AR N999SA (N899SA) N777GA XA-
25147	3B/RA	G-5-14 PK-PJR PK-DJW CofA expired 20Oct86; wfu derelict in yard near Jakarta - Halim circa 99
25148	3A/R	G-5-13 G-AVRI N8125J N450JD (N100TT) XB-ERN N814P
25149	3A/R	G-AVRJ N1125E N99SC N99GC N99KR wfu 09Sep80; donated Northrop University nr Los Angeles A/P, CA; cx Apr91 - moved to a technical college in Malaysia in 1998
25150	F3B	G-5-13 G-AWMS N511BX VR-BKY VP-BKY N42AS
25151	3A/RA	G-AVTY N125F
25152	3A/RA	G-AVTZ CF-QNS C-FQNS N45793 N123RZ XA-IIT N28686 N50MJ N23CJ
25153	731	G-5-19 G-AVXM N30F N30FD N731G N336MB N676PC N88DJ
25154	3B/RA	G-5-11 EP-AHK G-AZCH b/u Luton Dec82 due to corrosion; TT 4261, TL 4695, CofA exp 16Aug81; rear fuselage/fin used on c/n 25270
25155	3A/RA	G-AVXN N32F N466MP (N411MF) N999LF N333CJ N77BT N158AG+ current on USCAR since Aug98 but still painted as N77BT circa Feb00
25156	3A/RA	G-AVZJ N522M N10LN b/u 1993 Lakeland, FL; fuselage remains only
25157	3B/RA	D-CAMB VR-BGD G-GGAE G-JSAX wfu Dec82; cx 10Jan86 - at Eastleigh UK minus outer wings
25158	3A/RA	G-AVZK XB-PUE N702GA^
25159	731	G-5-19 G-AVZL CF-WOS C-FWOS N4767M N511WM N511WN N67TJ N600SV
25160	3A/RA	G-5-15 G-AWKH N350NC N873D N873G N627CR SE-DHH N160AG
25161	3A/RA	G-AWKI N9149 N756N N75GN XA-RPT
25162	3B/RC	Brazil VC93-2120
25163	731	G-5-16 G-AWMV N208H N55G (N2G)
25164	3B/RC	Brazil EC93-2125
25165	3B/RC	Brazil VC93-2121
25166	3B/RC	Brazil VC93-2122 w/o 19Jun79 Brasilia, Brazil
25167	3B/RC	Brazil VC93-2123
25168	3B/RC	Brazil VC93-2124
25169	3A/RA	G-5-17 G-AWWL VH-BBJ N3AL G-AWWL N84TF (N9300P) N9300C N99SC (N711SC) N122AW N163AG
25170	3A/RA	G-AWMW N1259K N226G N228G N223G C-GKCO N500YB C-FMKF N322TP
25171	F3B/RA	G-5-19 HB-VBT G-AXPU G-IBIS G-AXPU G-BXPU (N171AV) G-OPOL G-IFTC
25172	F3B/RA	G-AXEG ZS-CAL G-AXEG ZS-CAL
25173	400A	G-AWMX N125J N3711L (N610HC) N711AQ N601JJ*
25174	400A	G-AWMY N1199M N1199G N511WP N60JC N496G N7777B N712VS N713SS
25175	731	G-AWPC N217F YV-825CP N272B N773AA
25176	731	G-AWPD C-FNER N176TS N311JA
25177	400B	G-AWXN S Africa 02 w/o 26May71 Devils Peak, S Africa
25178	400B	G-AWXO 5N-BUA G-OOSP 5N-WMA
25179	731	G-AWPE N778S N200CC N400CC N800CB N800QB N22EH N629P N824TJ N284DB
25180	400A	G-AWPF N196KC N196KQ N888CR N400PH w/o 05Dec87 Blue Grass Field, Lexington, KY

BAe 125

C/n Series Identities

25181 400B (G-5-13) G-AXLU S Africa 01 w/o 26May71 Devils Peak, S Africa
25182 400B G-AXLV S Africa 03 w/o 26May71 Devils Peak, S Africa
25183 731 G-5-18 G-AWXB N162A N162D N100HF (N984HF) w/o 07Nov85 Sparta, TN still as N100HF
25184 400B G-AXLW S Africa 04 ZS-LPE wfs - stored at Waterkloof AFB
25185 400A G-AWXE N140C N4PN N7LG XA-GUB XB-DSQ XA-RMN XB-FRP XA-FRP
25186 731 G-AWXF N125G N93BH N933 N40SK N666JT N668JT (N105EJ) N99CK HR-AMD
N12YS (N999NM) N186NM
25187 731 G-AWXC N600L N600LP N600JA N900DS (N7WG) N16WG N50SL N141JL XA-SSV
N250DH
25188 731 G-AWXD N545S
25189 400B G-5-20 (G-AXFY) Malaysia FM1200 FM1801 M24-01 wfs stored at Subang AFB
25190 400A G-AXDO N1393 N75CS N75QS N75TJ N51MN N209NC N38TS
25191 731 G-AXDP N511YP N900KC N100T N723TS N401JR N444HH
25192 731 CF-SDH C-FSDH N724TS
25193 400A CF-CFL w/o 11Nov69 Newfoundland, Canada
25194 400B G-AXDM
25195 731 G-AXDR N111MB N949CW N949CV N60B N60BD N731G N31VT YV-141CP N922RR
25196 731 G-AXDS N814M N114B N81RR N117RH N100RH XA-TNY
25197 400B G-5-11 PP-EEM PT-LHK
25198 731 G-AXJD N24CH N400KC N320JJ N410PA N32GM
25199 400B G-AXLX HB-VBW G-AXLX (HB-VGU) HB-VBW N3118M (N905Y) to spares 1994 by Dodson
Avn, Ottawa, KS
25200 400A G-AXJE N702S N1C N702SS Brazil VU93-2118
25201 731 G-AXJF N220T N56BL N125MD N800JC N810MC N730TS N101HS N730TS
25202 400A G-AXJG N65LT N700CC N300LD N31TJ (N700PG) (N600DP) XA-JRF
25203 400A G-AXOA N500AG N73JH N44CN N21ES N100LR N109LR N2020 N70JC N732TS
25204 731 G-AXOB N380X N31GT (N125RT)
25205 731 G-AXOC N125J N111RB N621L N621S N6218 N99ST (N38TS)
25206 400A G-AXPX VP-BDH N125AJ N400AG N11SQ XA-ROJ N165AG N800GE
25207 400A G-AXOD N30PR N30PP N112M (N400HF) N800AF
25208 400A G-AXOE N2500W N65EC N65DW (N165AG) (N400JL) N643JL N400KD
25209 400B Malaysia FM1201 FM1802 M24-02 wfs stored at Subang AFB
25210 400A G-AXOF N702D Brazil VU93-2117
25211 731 G-AXTR N125DH N820MC N820MG
25212 400A G-AXTS N702P Brazil VU93-2114
25213 400A(C) G-AXTT CF-CFL C-FCFL w/o 09Dec77 Newfoundland, Canada
25214 731 G-AXTU N40PC N60PC N60QA G-AXTU G-5-20 N731HS N12BN N12AE N369CS
N569CS (N87DC) N74RT N843B
25215 403B HB-VBZ G-BHFT 9M-SSB G-BHFT Z-VEC ZS-NPV D2-EXR
25216 400A G-AXTV N9138 XC-GOB Mexico TP0206 TP108; callsign XC-UJH N125JW
HP-125JW HP-1128P N400D HK-3653X HK-3653 N400LC
25217 403B G-5-14 G-AXYJ 9Q-CGM 9Q-CHD G-5-651 G-BRXR G-OLFR 5N-EAS
25218 400A G-AXTW N575DU N575 (N382DA) N711BP N440BC
25219 F400B G-5-14 G-AYEP 4W-ACA 9K-AEA G-5-12 N5594U N292GA (N292RC) N128DR N219EC
RA-02805 N219EC
25220 731 G-AXYE N41BH N125AR N125AP N427DA N745TS
25221 731 N42BH CF-BNK C-FBNK N468LM N62CH N74WF N103RR ZS-OIF
25222 731 G-AXYF N43BH N125EH N900EL N400FE N590CH N125NW
25223 403B G-5-15 G-AYIZ PJ-SLB F-BSSL G-AYIZ G-TACE canx 09Jan90; wfu
25224 731 G-AXYG N44BH N22DH N222RB N222RG N144PA N189B N199B N143CP N728KA
N777SA YV-1111CP N748TS N601KK
25225 731 G-AXYH N45BH N81T N119CC N583CM N100HF N100HE N45NC N45NQ (N45ND)
SE-DVS N498R N498RS
25226 400A G-AXYI N46BH N300P N304P XA-DIW XB-CCM N3933A N20RG N251AB XA-RWN
N131LA
25227 F403B G-AYFM G-MKOA 5N-AMY N227MS
25228 731 N47BH N640M G-BCLR N640M G-BCLR N120GA N120GB N75RD N75RN N125GH
N79B HC-BTT
25229 731 N48BH N914BD N61MS N61MX N731HS N700PL N700FA N602JR
25230 731 N49BH N400BH N840H N345GL
25231 731 D-CBVW G-BEME 5N-AQY G-BEME N125GC N707EZ N707SH (N125TJ) N832MR (N832MB)
N831NW
25232 731 CF-TEC C-FTEC C-GVQR N62TF N125VC N125EC N60RE N711HL
25233 400A N50BH N711SD N755GW (N5MW) XB-AXP XB-LXP XB-AXP N755WJ
25234 731 N51BH N701Z N7NP N100MT C-GFCD N40Y N400JK
25235 731 G-5-18 HB-VCE G-AYNR G-BKAJ G-5-19 N235AV N227LA N297JD
25236 731 N52BH N125BH N10C N154 (N44BH) N999RW N499SC N50NE (N745WG) N900WG
25237 400A N56BH N125BH N1924L N500MA N580MA XA-RIL N814D
25238 731 G-AYER 9K-ACR G-AYER G-TOPF N125GC N808V VR-BKK VP-BKK
25239 731 G-5-19 N53BH N6709 N731MS
25240 400B G-5-11 G-AYLI I-GJBO VR-BKN VR-BMB stripped of spares - to fire section at Stansted,
A/P UK circa Apr99
25241 400A G-5-20 N54BH N6702 N702M N702MA N810CR N127CM N125CF (N400MR)
25242 403B G-5-20 VH-TOM G-BDKF 3D-ABZ ZS-LME wfs stored at Waterkloof AFB
25243 F400B G-5-14 (G-AYOI) PT-DTY N243TS VP-CTS N4ES
25244 400A G-5-12 N55BH N731X N70LY N456WH
25245 731 N57BH N523M N400GP N125DH
25246 403B G-AYOJ 9Q-COH (G-5-16) G-AYOJ G-LORI derelict Nigeria for many years; cx 21Apr93; wfu

BAe 125

C/n	Series	Identities									
25247	403B	G-AYRR	9Q-CCF	G-5-672	G-AYRR	9Q-CSN	reportedly to 9Q-CPR				
25248	F403B	D-CFCF	G-5-707	G-BTUF	G-SHOP	N792A	G-TCDI				
25249	731	G-5-16	G-AZAF	N51993	N72HT	N72HA	N107AW	N125KC	N200KC	N200VT	N711VT
		N54JC									
25250	731	G-AYOK	TR-LQU	G-AYOK	N20S	N24S	N300CC	N300QC	N125G	N125HG	(N125SJ)
		N7SJ									
25251	400B	Argentina 5-T-30/0653			LV-AXZ						
25252	400B	G-5-17	XX505	G-BAZB	N48US	P4-AMB					
25253	F400B	G-5-18	OY-APM	G-BROD	N731HS	N333B	N50EB	N50FC	N610HC	XA-SKE	N253MT
25254	F400B	G-AYLG	3D-AVL	G-AYLG	G-5-624	G-VJAY	VT-UBG	G-5-624	VT-UBG		
25255	CC1A/400A	XW788	G-BVTP	(N255TS)	N4QB						
25256	600B	G-AYBH	RP-C111	G-5-13	G-AYBH	Ireland IAC236		w/o 27Nov79 Dublin, Ireland			
25257	403B	G-5-19	G-BATA	9M-HLG	wfu Jun93						
25258	400F	(G-AYRR)	G-AZHS	G-BFAN	VR-CJP	VP-CJP	G-OJPB				
25259	400B	G-AZEK	S Africa 05		ZS-JBA	wfs - stored at Waterkloof AFB					
25260	400B	G-AZEL	S Africa 06		ZS-JIH	D2-EFM					
25261	731	N58BH	(N91BH)	N246N	N46B	(N68BW)	N246N	N55B	N125MT	N62TC	N19H
		N1QH*									
25262	400A	N59BH	XB-CUX	N55RZ							
25263	400A	N62BH	N125PA	N700BW	N708BW	N61MS	N68CB	N765TS			
25264	CC1A/400A	XW789	G-BVTR	N264TS	N7171	(N264WD)	(N731WB)	(N264TS)	N93TS*		
25265	731	N63BH	N711YP	N711YR	N300LD	N200CC	N125MD	VH-PAB	N150SA		
25266	CC1A/400A	XW790	G-BVTS	(N266TS)	N135CK	N125CK					
25267	400A	N64BH	N92BH	N28GP	N28GE	N125CM	used for spares Oct94 at Spirit of St Louis A/P,				
		MO; canx Jun95 - remains to Av-Mats, Paynesville, MO									
25268	CC1A/400A	XW791	G-BVTT	(N268TS)	N41953	extensively damaged 07Apr95 Santo Domingo-Herrera Intl A/P					
		- for spares use?									
25269	400B	G-AZEM	S Africa 07		ZS-LPF	wfs - stored at Waterkloof AFB					
25270	731	G-5-13	G-BBGU	G-BKBA	N270AV	N400GP					
25271	400B	G-5-14	G-BABL	XX506	G-BABL	EC-CMU	N37516	N103CJ	N365DA	N400DP	N70AP
		N810HS									
25272	F400B	G-5-15	G-BAZA	N4759D	N121VA	N121VF	N800JT	N63EM			
25273	400A	G-5-20	N65BH	N125BH	N69KA	XA-DIN	N11FX	N7WC	XA-SFQ	N2155P	XA-SFQ
25274	403B	G-5-20	Brazil EU93-2119								
25275	400A	N66BH	N872D	N972D	N125PP	N42BL	N369JH				
25276	731	G-5-11	N67BH	N88GA	N300CF	N74B	N7170J	N38LB			
25277	403B	G-5-11?	Brazil VU93-2126								
25278	731	N68BH	CF-AOS	C-FAOS	N731H	VR-BVI	N298NM	N4WC			
25279	400A	G-5-12	N69BH	XA-CUZ	w/o 27Dec80 Cancun, Mexico						
25280	731	N70BH	C-FPPN	N32KB							
25281	731	N71BH	N1BG	N18GX	N125DB	EI-BRG	N70338	N774EC	RA-02804	G-5-821	RA-02804
		N774TS									
25282	731	N72BH	N5V	N7HV	N17HV	N333DP					
25283	400A	N73BH	G-BACI	XA-LOV	XA-SGM	XB-GNF					
25284	731	N74BH	N571CH	N571GH	N228GC	N125FM	N125MD	N101AD	(N425JF)	w/o 06May91	
		Shreveport, LA; cx Sep91 - fuselage remains at Tulsa OK circa Oct99									
25285	731	N75BH	N555CB	N733K	C-GCEO	N2694C	N67EC	N89SR	N88AF	N778JA	
25286	731	N76BH	N88SJ	N33CP	N84CP	N400WT	N408WT	N808CC			
25287	731	N78BH	N72HC	N65DL	N265DL						
25288	403B	Brazil VU93-2127									
25289	403B	G-5-16	Brazil VU93-2128								
25290	403B	Brazil VU93-2129		w/o 08Sep87 Carajas, Brazil							

Production complete

SERIES 600

C/n	Series	Identities
256001	FA	G-AZUF N82BH N711AG G-BEWW N711AG N82RP N82PP N444PE N444PD N700R N709R N561RP N61TS
256002	A	G-5-15? N79BH N925BH N631SC N631SQ N915JT N61SB N602MM XA-SLP
256003	A	N80BH CF-HSS C-FHSS N256FC N42TS N91KH N91KP
256004	A	N81BH N94BD N94BB N19HH N19HE VR-BRS N4TS (N103RA) N399GA N5AH
256005	B	G-BART (G-BJUT) G-CYII EC-EAC N4253A reported b/u for spares by Western A/C Parts; to White Inds, MO; canx Jun95
256006	CC2A	G-5-15? XX507 N606TS N21SA
256007	A	N21BH N125BH N125KR N3007 N317TC
256008	CC2A	XX508 N256WJ
256009	A	N22BH N3PW N219ST (N210ST) N183RD (N183RM)+ N28TS +marks carried but ntu
256010	A	N23BH N40PC w/o 28Apr77 McLean, VA
256011	A	N24BH N6001H N555CB N555GB VR-BGS N42622 N81D EC-EHF used for spares Oct94 at Spirit of St Louis A/P, MO unmarked - remains to Dodson Int'l Parts, Ottawa, KS circa 1998
256012	B	G-5-17 G-BAYT 5N-ALX G-BAYT G-BNDX G-BAYT EC-272 EC-EOQ N8000Z to spares at Houston, TX circa 95; canx Feb96; reported never carried N8000Z
256013	A	N25BH N25BE N505W (N65GB) N218AC N627HS N80TS VR-CDG 5N-YET
256014	A	N26BH N922CR N922GR N5SJ N47HW N47HV
256015	FA	G-5-19 G-BBCL G-BJCB G-BBCL 9K-ACZ G-BBCL Ireland 239 G-BBCL G-5-11 (D-CCEX) G-BBCL N600AV N917K N777SA (N74TJ) (N615TJ) N777TK N700XJ
256016	A	N27BH N99SC XA-SAI
256017	B	G-5-18 G-BBAS PK-PJD N600WJ
256018	A	N28BH N500GD (N780SC) N880SC N125E N600AW N93TS N288MW XA-JRF N16GA XA-TNX
256019	B	G-BARR HZ-AA1 (G-FANN) cx 29Mar93; wfu; fuselage on fire dump Dunsfold, UK; still marked as HZ-AA1
256020	A	N29BH N125CU N334JR C-GDUP N334JR N5NG XA-NTE N5NG derelict Monterrey, Mexico
256021	B	G-5-11 HB-VDL C-GSTT N125HS N125JJ (N128JJ) N125JA XA-SNH N37SG C-GKHR
256022	A	N34BH N701Z N701A N1515P N757M N757P XA-XET N2114E reported to spares; marks N2114E not carried
256023	A	N35BH N514V EC-121 EC-EGL N523MA N702HC
256024	B	G-BBMD N50GD G-BBMD G-BSHL G-OMGA YR-DVA N731TC*
256025	A	N36BH C-GTPC N721LH
256026	FA	N37BH G-5-16 N124GS N699SC N818TP XA-SWK N125NA
256027	FB	D-CJET G-5-585 D-CJET OE-GIA N693TJ
256028	A	G-5-12 VP-BDH C6-BDH C-GDHW XA-KUT w/o 19Jan88 Houston-Hobby, TX; remains Jan93 to Dodson Avn, Ottawa, KS
256029	FB	G-BBRT PK-PJE PK-HMG N629TS N35WP
256030	B	G-BBEP G-BJOY G-BBEP 5N-ARD G-BBEP G-TOMI N217A
256031	B	G-5-14 9Q-CFW
256032	A	N38BH N4BR (N14BR) G-DBOW C-GLBD N332TA EC-EAV N921RD N801BC N334PS
256033	B	F-BUYP G-DMAN HZ-YA1 N330G G-PJWB G-HALK N6033 XB-FMF N303MW N600HS N514AJ*
256034	A	N39BH N90B N90BL N600FL N600SB EC-115 EC-EGS used for spares Oct94 at Spirit of St Louis A/P, MO; fuselage to Elsberry, MO by Apr96
256035	B	F-BKMC G-BETV G-SUFC VP-BCN
256036	B	(G-BBRT) used paint-spraying trials Chester (a/c not completed)
256037	B	(VH-ARJ) AN-BPR YN-BPR VH-NJA RP-C1600 VP-BBW (N16VT) N63810
256038	A	N40BH N77C N77CU SE-DKF N199SG XA-ACN
256039	B	G-BCCL G-BKBM N61TF N410AW G-BKBM EC-EAO EC-183 EC-EAO G-OMGB wfu Oct94; TT 6,944 hrs; to spares at Houston, TX
256040	A	N41BH C-GJCM N4224Y N125GS N601BA N621BA N16VT
256041	B	G-5-13 G-BCJU VR-CBD N450DA N888PM N273K N42TS N808RP
256042	B	G-BBRO G-BKBU G-5-505 5N-AWS w/o 15Dec86 Casablanca, Tunisia
256043	B	G-BCUX w/o 20Nov75 Dunsfold, UK
256044	A	N42BH N600MB N46B (N46BE) C-GKCC N848W N992SF XA-CAH N9282Y N116DD N454DP N453DP
256045	FB	G-5-18 EC-CQT G-5-11 G-BGYR
256046	FA	N43BH N91HR (N401HR) N402HR N117EM XA-AGL N299BW N299GA N299TJ N299DG*
256047	A	G-5-16 (N44BH)+ (C-GBNS) "N4203S" carried in error N4203Y N400NW N400NE N600TT XA-JEQ N47EX N47WU XA-RYK N68GA +No mention of these marks in official files
256048	B	G-5-15 HB-VDS G-BHIE YU-BME N6567G TC-COS
256049	B	G-BCXL ZS-JHL G-BCXL HZ-KA5
256050	B	G-5-12 5N-ANG G-BLOI 5N-AOL wfu believed scrapped in 1997
256051	A	N45BH C-GBNS N22DL N5DL N35DL N601PS N601JJ N616PA N600AL N95TS N601JA
256052	B	G-5-11 G-BDJE G-BKBH TR-LAU G-BKBH G-5-698 G-BKBH G-5-698 5N-NBC 5N-DNL G-5-698 5N-DNL G-BKBH cx Jly99 wfu Southampton, UK
256053	B	D-CFSK (N) HC-BUR N125WJ N5NR
256054	B	G-5-17 G-BCXF 9K-AED G-BCXF 5N-YFS+ 5N-RNO +incorrectly painted late Mar/early Jun93 as G-BKFS, which is c/n 257172
256055	A	G-5-19 G-BDOP N94B N94BF N777SA N100QR N100QP N125GS N20FM
256056	B	G-5-13 G-BDOA G-BKCD 5N-ARN G-BKCD G-OMGC wfu Sep94; TT 6,404 hrs; to spares at Houston, TX circa 1995
256057	B	G-5-17 HZ-KA2 G-FFLT VR-BNW VP-BNW N602CF N11AF

BAe 125-600

C/n	Series	Identities									
256058	FA	G-5-18	G-BGKN	N9043U	N701Z	N129BA	(N429BA)	(N658TS)	N200XR	N658TS	N658KA
256059	B	G-5-19	HZ-DAC	HZ-SJP	G-BLUW	ZF130					
256060	B	G-5-12	HZ-MF1	G-BFIC	5N-AYK	N660TC	N422TK				
256061	FA	G-5-14	G-BDOB	N125HS	N5253A	N8253A	N707WB	N169B	N189B	N169B	N331DC
		N701MS									
256062	B	G-5-15	G-MFEU	G-TMAS	EC-319	EC-ERX	G-TMAS	5N-MAY			
256063	B	G-5-13	A6-RAK	G-BSPH	N484W	EC-349	EC-ERJ	5N-OPT	N9AZ		
256064	A	G-5-17	HZ-AMM	N105AS	N666LC	N500MA	N580MA	N600SN	N125HF		
256065	B	G-5-16	G-BJCB	XA-MAH	N73JA	N59JR	VR-CSF	V2-LSF	N125SF		
256066	FA	G-5-15	G-BDZH	N32RP	N800JP	N600G					
256067	A	G-BEIN	N522X	N522C	N270MC	N270MQ	N1884	N67MR	XA-SKH	N822BL	
256068	FA	G-5-20	G-BDZR	N33RP	N90WP	G-5-16	N90WP	N14GD	N54GD	N500R	N501R
		N600AE									
256069	A	G-BEIO	N350MH	N600AG	N369TS	(5N-)	N369TS	5N-EMA			
256070	FA	G-5-11	G-BEDT	N322CC	G-5-15	N322CC	N319MF	(N411TC)	N411TP	N83TJ	N365SB
256071	A	G-5-14	G-BEFS	N91884	N571DU	N571E	N121SG	N171TS			

Production complete

SERIES 700

C/n	Series	Identities									
257001	B	G-BEFZ	VP-HIM	G-BEFZ	N4555E	N700SV	N101SK	N101XS	N80KA	N189GE	N97TS
		(9M-???)	VH-LYG	N257AJ	N193TA	N701CW					
257002	A	G-5-20	N700HS	N40WB	N40GT	N700NY	N886GB	VR-BNB	G-IECL	N701TS	
257003	A	G-5-19	G-BERP	N64688	N333ME	N727TA					
257004	A	G-5-15	G-BGDM	G-5-15	N37975	N222RB	N700RJ	N546BC	N746BC	N648WW	N704CW
257005	A	G-BERV	N620M	N104AE							
257006	A	G-5-18	G-BERX	N724B							
257007	B	HB-VFA	D-CADA	G-5-721	D-CADA	G-BUNL	RA-02800	G-5-721	RA-02800	(N307TC)	N257TH
		N257WJ	N54WJ								
257008	A	G-5-11	(G-BEWV)	C-GYYZ	N333PC						
257009	A	G-5-12	G-BEYC	N813H	(N20GT)	N986H	XA-SNN	N701NW			
257010	B	HZ-MMM	LX-MJM	G-5-631	N700WH	N700ER	N3399P	(N339BW)	(N41CC)	N977CC	
257011	A	G-5-13	G-BFAJ	N255CT	(N255QT)	N255TT	N500FC	N33RH	N70X		
257012	A	G-5-14	G-BFBI	N125HS	N700HS	N162A	N700FS	N622AB	N622AD	N37PL	N38PA
257013	B	G-CBBI	N219JA	N75ST	N101HF						
257014	A	G-5-17	G-BFDW	N46901	N120GA	N60MS	N453EP	N586JR	N74B		
257015	A	G-5-18	G-BFFL	N37P	SE-DPZ	(N725WH)	OY-JPJ	N418RD			
257016	A	G-BFFH	N72505	N800CB	N23SB	N23SK	(N23SN)	N999JF			
257017	A	G-5-19	G-BFFU	N62MS	N454EP	N757M	N757C	(I-DRVM)	I-DVMR	HB-VLH	
		RA02806	N211WZ	N411PA							
257018	A	G-BFGU	N733H	N662JB	N125CS						
257019	A	(G-BFGV)	N370M	N370RR							
257020	B	(G-BFTP)	(G-BFVN)	G-EFPT	VR-BHE	(N2634B)	N125HM	N818	N311JD	N777EH	
257021	A	N34CH	N900KC	N1868M	N1868S	N926ZT	N926TC				
257022	B	(G-5-11)	F-GASL	G-5-17	N34RE	N92RP	N109AF				
257023	A	G-BFLF	N54555	N125GP	N6JB	N6UB	N35LM	N195XP	N215RS		
257024	A	G-BFLG	N94BD	N94BE	N7005	N7006	(N6960)				
257025	B	G-5-12	G-BFPI	VR-HIN	G-BFPI	N93TC	N7782	N886S			
257026	A	G-BFMO	N1230A	N372BC	N372BD	N685FM	N685EM	N788WG	N428AS	N428FS	N219TS
257027	A	G-BFMP	C-GPPS	N705CC	N725CC	XA-SAU					
257028	B	G-BFSO	G-5-534	N700TL	N603GY	N7728	N899DM				
257029	A	N465R	N700PD	(N248JH)	N705JH	C-GTOR					
257030	A	G-BFSI	C-GSCL	C-FFAB	HB-VLJ	C-GNAZ					
257031	B	G-BFSP	G-PRMC	G-BFSP	G-5-701	D-CBAE	G-BFSP	G-5-701	N89TJ	HB-VLA	N703TS
257032	A	G-5-14	G-BFUE	N700BA	N353WC	N853WC	N154JS	(N158JS)	N154JD	N720PT	
257033	A	N50JM	N50TN	N200GX	N200GY						
257034	B	G-5-14	G-BFXT	N7007X	(XA-)	N7007X	N510HS	G-PLGI	N402GJ	N34GG w/o 19Oct99	
		Fayetteville NC cx Mar00									
257035	A	G-5-16	N36NP	SE-DPY	N486MJ	N995SK	(N995SL)	N995SA	N137WR		
257036	A	G-5-17	N60JM	N60TN	N600HC	N902RM	N902PM	N47TJ	N42SR	(N42SE)	N7WC
257037	B	G-5-18	G-BFVI	G-IFTE							
257038	A	G-5-19	N10CZ	N81KA							
257039	A	G-5-11	N555CB								
257040	B	HZ-RC1	G-OWEB	EC-375	EC-ETI	N47TJ	VR-BPE	VP-BPE	HB-VMD	G-BYFO	G-OWDB
257041	A	G-5-12	N700BB	N400NW	N400NU	(N601UU)	N700LS	N825CT			
257042	A	G-5-13	N360X	N360DE*							
257043	A	G-BFYV	(N300LD)	N900CC	N500ZB	N22EH	N22KH				
257044	A	G-5-17	G-BFYH	N35D	N5735	N125G	(N125GB)	N225BJ			
257045	A	G-BFZJ	N130BA	N700HH							
257046	B	4W-ACE	G-BKJV	VH-JCC	VH-LRH	N7465T	XA-LEG	N746TS	N55MT	(painted as N55TS	
		for marketing purposes)			N746TS	LV-ZRS					
257047	A	G-BFZI	C-GABX								
257048	A	G-5-16	N711YP	N205BS	N731DL						
257049	A	G-5-17	G-BGBL	N33BK	C-GKPM						
257050	A	G-5-18	N700GB	N10C							
257051	A	G-5-11	N700UK	N14JA	N64HA	N236BN					
257052	A	G-5-19	G-BGBJ	N737X	N697NP	N511GP	N511KA				
257053	A	G-5-20	N700AR	N33CP	N130MH	N120MH					
257054	B	C6-BET	G-BVJY	RA-02802	G-BVJY	G-NCFR					
257055	B	G-5-16	HZ-RC2	N876JC	G-5-598	G-BOXI	F-WZIG	F-GHHG	N46PL	(N696JH)	(N755TS)
		N47PB									
257056	A	G-5-13	N700NT	N492CB	N6VC	N25MK	N300BS				
257057	A	G-5-14	N700UR	N60HJ	(N60HU)	C-GPCC	N125BW	N701CF	(N988GA)	N418BA	
257058	A	G-5-15	N125HS	N700BA	N354WC	N854WC	N750GM	N8PL	N810V	N81QV	
257059	A-II	G-5-17	N130BH	N20S	N20SK	N702BA (first 700-II)			XA-JRF	N104JG	
257060	A	G-5-18	N130BG	N1103	N1183	N230DP	N414RF				
257061	A	G-5-19	G-BGGS	G-OJOY	N700SS	N700SF	N810GS				
257062	B	G-5-16	HB-VGF	G-5-708	HB-VGF	G-5-708	N7062B	G-5-708	(G-BWJX)	RA-02809	N62EA
		N416RD									
257063	A	G-5-20	N130BB	N79HC	N700NW						
257064	B	HZ-NAD	HZ-OFC	G-BMOS	G-5-519	VH-JFT	N395RD				
257065	A	G-5-11	N130BC	N30PR	N530TL	(N530TE)	N87AG	N120JC			
257066	A	G-5-13	G-BGSR	C-GKCI	C-FBMG						
257067	B	HZ-DA1	N9113J	(N115RS)	N360N	N144DJ	HB-VKJ	N267TS	N42TS		
257068	A	G-5-14	N130BD	N31LG	N799SC	XB-FMK					
257069	A	G-5-15	N130BE	N29GP	N29GD	N308DD					
257070	B	HB-VGG	G-5-604	HB-VGG	G-5-604	G-BWCR	G-JETG+	G-BWCR	G-DEZC		

+ not offically regd as such but were painted on the aircraft

BAe 125-700

C/n	Series	Identities									
257071	A	G-5-17	N130BF	N514B	N396U	N810CR					
257072	A	G-5-18	N700HS	N900MR	N401GN	N513GP	N895CC				
257073	B	G-5-12	G-BGTD	N7788	(N59TJ)	N701TA					
257074	A	G-5-19	N422X	(N831CJ)							
257075	A	G-5-13	(G-BHKF)	N125AM	N125TR	N124AR	N125XX				
257076	B	G-5-17	7Q-YJI	MAAW-J1	G-5-524	G-BMWW	G-5-571	XA-LML	N111ZN	N111ZS	N180CH
		(N776TS)	N111ZS								
257077	A	G-5-14	N125AJ	N540B							
257078	A	G-5-15	N125AK	N571CH							
257079	A	G-5-16	XA-JIX	N74JA	(N74JE)	N501MM	XA-SON				
257080	A	G-5-18	N125HS	N611MC							
257081	A	G-5-19	(N125AM)	N700CU	N711CU	N809M	N812M	N193RC			
257082	B	Ireland 238		(N98AF)	XA-TCB	N70HF					
257083	A	G-5-12	(N150RH)	N125AH	N100Y	N128CS	N941CE				
257084	A	G-5-14	N130BK	N202CH	N965JC	N184TB					
257085	B	G-5-15	G-BHIO	RP-C1714	N10TN						
257086	A	G-5-17	N125AL	N277CT	N500EF	N983GT					
257087	A	G-5-16	+(N130BL)	C-GKRS	N3234S	N404CB	(N601JR)	N908JE	N988JE	N350DH	N711WM
		+Marks not confirmed									
257088	B	HZ-DA2	G-5-531	N29RP	N222HL	N224EA					
257089	A	G-5-18	N130BL	N151AE	(N130AE)	N101FC					
257090	A	G-5-19	N299CT	N88MX	N264WC	(N160WC)	N161WC				
257091	B	G-BHLF	G-OCAA								
257092	A	G-5-20	N733M	N783M	N91CM						
257093	A	G-5-11	G-BHMP	C-GBRM	N7UJ	N86MD	N497PT				
257094	B	G-OBAE	HB-VEK	G-5-16	N49566	N80KM	N713KM	N713K	D-CKIM	(G-)	9M-STR
		N415RD	N483FG								
257095	A	G-5-12	N125L	N215G	N352WC	N852WC	N427MD	N745TH	N36GS	N267JE	
257096	A	G-5-14	XA-KEW	w/o 01May81 Monterrey, Mexico							
257097	B	(G-BHTJ)	G-HHOI	G-BRDI	G-BHTJ	RA-02801	G-5-810	RA-02801			
257098	A	G-5-15	N125Y	N89PP	N70SK	N50HS	XA-NTE	N702NW	N972LM	N438PM	
257099	A	G-5-16	G-BHSK	C-GDAO	N621JH	N621JA	PK-CTC				
257100	B	G-5-19	D-CLVW	G-5-549	G-BNFW	N858JR					
257101	A	G-5-17	(N700E)	N89PP	(N700E)	N109JM	N14SY	N77D	N89GN		
257102	A	G-5-18	XA-KIS	N700CN	N700K	N810M	XA-TCR	N280AJ	N280VC*		
257103	B	G-5-12	G-BHSU	G-LTEC	VR-BOJ	VP-BOJ	YL-VIP				
257104	A	G-5-20	N10PW	N411SS	N46TJ	N110EJ					
257105	A	G-5-11	N125BA	N125TA	N44BB	N700DE	HB-VLL	N560SB			
257106	A	G-5-13	N125V	N661JB	N664JB	N404CE	N404CF	N125SJ			
257107	B	G-BHSV	G-5-808	N90AR	VR-CVD	N71MA					
257108	A	G-5-14	XA-KON	N45500	N6GG	N6GQ	N86WC	N700FE			
257109	B	G-BHSW	VR-BPT	VR-BTZ	VP-BTZ						
257110	A	G-5-15	XA-KAC	N277JW	N177JW						
257111	A	G-5-16	N125AF	N324K	N824K	N500	N509	(N799FL)	N509QC		
257112	B	D-CMVW	G-5-536	G-BNBO	G-5-553	9M-SSL	(D-CLUB)	G-SVLB	RA-02850		
257113	A	G-5-17	N125AD	N204R	N204N	N5511A	N1VQ				
257114	A	G-5-18	N125AN	N533	C-GXYN	N169TA	N403DP				
257115	B	HZ-DA3	G-5-502	G-BMIH	5N-AMX	G-5-502	G-BMIH				
257116	A	G-5-19	N125AP	N1982G	N120YB						
257117	A	G-5-20	N125AS	N90B	(N90BN)	N220FL	N93CR	N93GR	N26SC		
257118	B	(G-BIHZ)	5N-AVJ	G-BWKL	VP-BBH	VP-CRA	C-GNND				
257119	A	G-5-11	N125AE	N326K	N826K	N125AR	N125AP	N10UC			
257120	A	G-5-13	N125AT	N40CN	(N14WJ)	N130YB					
257121	A	G-5-14	N125AU	N20FX	N700SB	N301PH	(N156K)	N150CA			
257122	A	G-5-15	N125U	N77LP	N299FB	N3444H	(N731GA)	N564BR			
257123	A	G-5-16	N125AH	N700BW	N198GT						
257124	B	HZ-DA4									
257125	A	G-5-17	N125AJ	N125CG	N62WH	N62WL	N369G	N27KL	N302PC		
257126	A	G-5-18	N700AC	N246VF							
257127	B	G-TJCB	OY-MPA	(F-GNDB)	F-GODB	HB-VLC	N795A				
257128	A	G-5-19	N125BC	N126AR	XA-MSH	N45AF	N947CE				
257129	A	G-5-20	N125AK	(N256MA)	N256EN	N805M	N728JW	N748FB	N48FB		
257130	B	G-DBBI	G-CCAA	G-BNVU	N700FR	G-5-588	N700FR	G-RJRI	RP-C235	N130TS	N499GA
		(regd as a 700A)		N405DP	N405TP						
257131	A	G-5-11	N700BA	N80G	N520M	N52LC	N7CT	N7WG	N700NB		
257132	A	G-BIMY	C-FIPG	N925WC	N925WG	N925DP					
257133	B	G-5-14	LV-PMM	LV-ALW	w/o 11Apr85 Salta, Argentina						
257134	A	G-5-13	N671D	N371D	N888SW	N89MD					
257135	A	G-5-15	N490MP	N31AS	N28GP	N28GG*					
257136	B	G-BIRU	G-5-545	OH-JET							
257137	A	G-5-16	N125BD	N78CS	(N78QS)	N589UC	N945CE				
257138	B	G-5-17	N125G	N80K	N298TS						
257139	B	G-5-18	(G-GAIL)	G-BKAA	G-MHIH	RA02803					
257140	A	G-5-19	N125BE	VR-BHH	N125BE	N555RB	N703JP	N700NY			
257141	A	G-5-20	N70PM	N80PM	N80PN	N700SA	N943CE				
257142	B	G-5-12	G-BJDJ	G-RCDI	G-BJDJ						
257143	A	G-5-20	N700HA	N26H	C-GOGM						
257144	A	G-5-11	N522M	N70AR	N94SA	(N702TJ)	N164WC				

BAe 125-700

C/n	Series	Identities									
257145	A	G-5-18	N70FC	N125BJ	PT-ORJ	N700SA					
257146	A	G-5-13	N700HB	N711RL	N713RL	N744DC	N421SZ	N107LT			
257147	A	G-5-14	N125P	N70PM	N70PN	N67PW	N678W	N900JT			
257148	A	G-5-17	N700BB	N707DS	C-GTDN	N99JD	N96PR	N700NH			
257149	A	G-5-19	N700AA	N700HA	N290PC	N795HE	(N795HL)	C-GEPF			
257150	A	G-5-11	N700HS	N73G	N730H	N305TH					
257151	B	G-5-12	N161MM	N161G	N613MC						
257152	A	G-5-17	N700DD	N270MH	C-FEXB	N400WP	N800MP				
257153	A	G-BJOW	XB-CXK	N18G	PK-CTA	N419RD					
257154	A	G-5-18	N700GG	N270MC	N270KA						
257155	A	G-5-19	N700KK	N1620	C-GYPH	N1843S	N10CN				
257156	A	G-5-17	N15AG	N700MK	N529DM	N526DM	N309WM				
257157	A	G-5-20	N700LL	N64GG	N2640	N18SH					
257158	A	G-5-14	G-BJWB	N45KK	XB-DZN	N700VT					
257159	A	G-5-15	N91Y	N50JR	(N620CC)	(N502R)	VR-CKP	N311NW	N425WN	N700LP	
257160	B	G-5-19	5N-AVK								
257161	A	G-5-17	N700RR	C-GZZX	N700RR	N2630	N2830	VT-AAA			
257162	A	G-5-18	N700NN	N1896T	N1896F	N176RS	N500GS	N412DP			
257163	B	G-5-12	7T-VCW								
257164	A	G-5-11	N152AE	(N106AE)	N53GH						
257165	A	G-5-14	N869KM	N26ME							
257166	B	G-5-18	F-BYFB	F-GRON							
257167	A	G-5-15	N700PP	N125BA	N2989	N640PM	N63PM	N73PM	N333NR	(N501F)	N18BA
257168	A	G-5-20	N700SS	N612MC							
257169	B	G-5-21	(VH-SOA)	VH-HSS	B-HSS+	VR-HSS	B-HSS				
		+ not offically regd as such but painted on the aircraft									
257170	A	G-5-14	N819M	N80CL	EI-RRR						
257171	A	G-5-15	N710BP	(N168H)	N120MH	N128MH	N319NW	XB-MLC			
257172	B	5H-SMZ	G-BKFS	5H-SMZ	G-5-568	5H-SMZ	G-5-765	G-BKFS	VT-MPA		
257173	A	G-5-17	N710BN	N500LS	N300LS	N300HB	N100LR	(N100FF)	N320GP	N700HW	N7490A
257174	A	G-5-18	N710BL	N469JR	C-GTLG	N165DL	N65DL				
257175	B	(C9-TTA)	C9-TAC	N770TJ	VP-CEK						
257176	A	G-5-20	N109G								
257177	A	G-5-11	N710BJ	N711TG	N2000T	N1996F	(N1996E)	N69SB	(N880CR)		
257178	B	G-5-14	4W-ACM	G-5-530	G-BMYX	G-5-570	VH-LMP	G-5-747	N700CJ	N621S	EI-COV
257179	A	G-5-15	N810SC	C-GAAA							
257180	A	G-5-16	N710BG	N2HP							
257181	CC3	G-5-16	ZD620								
257182	A	G-5-17	N710BF	(N277CB)	N1824T	N18243	N756N	N512GP	N190WC		
257183	CC3	G-5-20	N710BD	G-5-20	ZD703						
257184	B	G-5-12	9K-AGA	YI-AKG	9K-AGA	G-OMGD					
257185	A	G-5-12	N700BA	N900BL	XB-JTN						
257186	A	G-5-11	N710BC	N400CH	N400QH	N16GS	XA-STX	N332WE			
257187	B	G-5-14	9K-AGB	YI-AKH	dest 1991 during Gulf War, Muthenna AFB, Iraq; wreckage advertised						
		for sale Jly92									
257188	A	G-5-15	N523M	N125DP	(N301AS)	(N301LX)	N125AS				
257189	B	G-BKHK	(G-OBSM)	G-OSAM	N700BA	N94B	N81HH	N8KG	N45KG		
257190	CC3	ZD621									
257191	A	G-5-17	N710BA	N677RW	(N477RW)	N11TS	VT-SRR	N770HS			
257192	A	G-5-14	N125MT	N2015M	N201PM	N300TW					
257193	A	G-5-15	N710BZ	N710AG	(N797EM)	N797FA					
257194	CC3	ZD704	G-5-870	ZD704							
257195	A	G-5-18	N710BY	N702M	N93GC	N46WC					
257196	B	G-5-11	5N-AXO	G-5-693	5N-AXO	G-5-766	5N-AXO	w/o 17Jan96 Kano, Nigeria			
257197	A	G-5-12	N790Z	N207PC	N207RC	N3GL	N2QL*				
257198	A	G-5-18	N710BX	N702E	C-GJBJ						
257199	A	G-5-12	N710BW	N702W	VR-BKZ	N921RD	XA-SSY	N23BJ	N23EJ		
257200	B	G-5-14	G-MSFY	VR-BMD	VP-BMD						
257201	A	G-5-19	N710BV	N2KW	I-CIGH						
257202	A	G-5-17	N710BU	N518S	N65LC	N8400E	N93FR	N230R			
257203	B	G-5-14	5N-AXP	w/o 31Dec85 Kaduna, Nigeria							
257204	A	G-5-15	N524M	N949CE*							
257205	CC3	G-5-19	ZE395								
257206	A	G-5-16	N710BT	N1C	N502S	C-FWCE	C-GMBA	N11YR			
257207	A	G-5-18	N710BS	N774GF	N686SG	N686FG	N21NY	N21NT	N913V	N313VR+	N913V
		+ marks painted on a/c but ntu									
257208	B	N710BR	G-5-19	(G-BLMJ)	G-BLSM						
257209	B	G-5-20	VR-BHW	VP-BHW	N127SR						
257210	B	N710BQ	G-5-18	(G-BLMK)	G-BLTP						
257211	CC3	ZE396									
257212	B	G-5-12	G-RACL	N81CH	N81CN	G-IJET	G-5-659	OH-BAP	G-5-659	OH-BAP	LY-
257213	B	G-5-16	G-BLEK	N213C							
257214	B	G-5-17	HZ-SJP	G-UKCA	G-OMID	VR-BCF	VP-BCF	P4-CMP			
257215	B	G-5-20	VH-HSP	VT-OBE							

Production complete

SERIES 800 (HAWKER 800)

* after the c/n indicates US assembled aircraft.

C/n	Series	Identities									
258001	B	G-5-11	ff 26May83		"N800BA"+	G-BKTF	G-5-522	G-UWWB	G-5-557	ZK-TCB	N785CA
		OH-JOT	N801CR								
		+These marks never officially allocated									
258002	B	(G-5-16)	G-DCCC	(VH-CCC)	VH-III	G-DCCC	VH-NJM	G-DCCC	N800RY	(N1169D)	
		(N802CW)	N882CW								
258003	A	G-5-20	G-BKUW	N800BA	N800N	N454JB					
258004	A	G-5-15	G-BLGZ	N800EE	N94BD	(N98DD)	N94SD	XA-SEH	XA-RET		
258005	A	(G-5-12)	(G-5-19)	G-5-15	G-BLJC	N800GG	(N219JA)	N601UU	N800FL		
258006	A	G-5-17	N800WW	N800S	N70SK	N861CE	N886CW				
258007	B	G-5-20	G-GAEL	G-5-554	C-GKRL	C-GYPH					
258008	A	G-5-11	N722CC								
258009	A	G-5-15	N400AL	N408AL	N45Y	N48Y					
258010	A	G-5-19	(G-BLKS)	(G-OVIP)	N84A	N810BG					
258011	A	G-5-20	N800VV	N1BG	N186G						
258012	A	G-5-18	N800TT	N400NW	N80BF	N80BR	N106JL	N644JL	N801CW		
258013	B	G-5-14	G-OCCC	N334	(N500RH)+	N300RB					
		+marks painted on a/c at 1994 NBAA show but not on USCAR as such									
258014	A	G-5-15	N800MM	N294W	N800BS	N94WN	N298AG				
258015	A	G-5-17	G-BLPC	C-FTLA	C-GWFM						
258016	B	G-5-18	F-GESL	N415PT	N904SB	N906SB	N816CW				
258017	A	G-5-16	N800LL	N801G	N801P	(N801R)	N217RM	N888ZZ			
258018	A	G-5-12	N800PP	N818TG	N350WC	N350WG	N601RS				
258019	B	G-5-12	VH-SGY	VH-LKV	N900MD	G-5-704	N799SC	N799S	(N800NW)		
258020	A	G-5-14	N800ZZ	N270HC	(N251TJ)						
258021	B	G-5-15	G-GEIL	VR-CEJ	G-RCEJ						
258022	B	G-5-16	G-JJCB	G-5-569	HZ-KSA	EC-193	EC-ELK				
258023	A	G-5-15	N810AA	(N10AA)	N1910H	N1910J					
258024	A	G-5-18	N811AA	N800DP	N802DC	N802D	N337RE				
258025	B	G-5-14	3D-AVL	G-5-742	G-BUIY	N7C	C-GMLR				
258026	A	G-5-18	N800HS	N6TM	N6TU	N826CW					
258027	A	G-5-12	N812AA	(N100PM)	N800PM	(N553US)	N553M	N558M	(N80CC)	N880M	
258028	B	G-5-12	G-TSAM								
258029	A	G-5-16	(N600TH)	N813AA	N600HS	N77LA					
258030	A	G-5-14	N600TH	N6GG	N10WF	N91CH					
258031	B	G-5-15	PT-ZAA	PT-LHB							
258032	A	G-5-11	N815AA	N526M							
258033	A	G-5-19	N157H	N57FF	I-CASG	N24RP	N673TM				
258034	B	G-5-12	G-HYGA	G-5-595	G-HYGA	G-5-595	N85DW	N125HH			
258035	A	G-5-20	N816AA	N30F	HB-VKM	PT-ORH	(N)	HB-VKM	PT-WIA	N835TS	N835CW
258036	A	G-5-18	N817AA	N31F	HB-VKN	D-CFRC	N621MT				
258037	B	G-5-15	G-5-501	4W-ACN	70-ADC						
258038	A	G-5-20	N800TR	N206PC	N206WC	N550RH	D-CHEF	C-GTNT	C-FDDD		
258039	A	G-5-19	N818AA	N400TB	N200KF	N193TR	N173TR				
258040	B	G-5-15	VH-IXL	G-5-697	I-IGNO	N832MJ	N832MR				
258041	A	G-5-18	N819AA	N71NP	N626CG						
258042	A	G-5-11	N820AA	N20S	N112K						
258043	B	G-5-12	(D-CAZH)	N319AT	N313CC						
258044	A	G-5-12	N821AA	N72NP	N833JP						
258045	A	G-5-16	N822AA	N800TF	N845CW*						
258046	A	G-5-20	N823AA	N800BA	N125SB						
258047	A	G-5-11	N824AA	N84BA	N84FA	N324SA					
258048	A	G-5-16	G-BMMO	(N125BA)	C-GCIB						
258049	A	G-5-19	N825AA	N800EX	N24SB	N24SP	N93CT				
258050	B	G-5-503	HZ-OFC	G-BUCR	I-OSLO	N9LR	G-ICFR				
258051	A	G-5-18	N826AA	N889DH	N888DH	N258SR	N851CW				
258052	A	G-5-20	N360BA	N87EC	N68DA	N233KC	N221HB*				
258053	A	G-5-11	N361BA	N5G	N484RA						
258054	A	G-5-15	N527M								
258055	A	G-5-504	N528M								
258056	B	G-5-509	G-JETI								
258057	A	G-5-508	N362BA	N300GN	N800GN						
258058	B	G-5-510	(ZK-EUR)	ZK-EUI	VH-NMR	N125JW	G-5-637	N125JW	G-OMGG		
258059	A	G-5-506	N363BA	N400GN	N355RB	N255RB					
258060	A	G-5-511	N364BA	N686CF	N330X	N330DE*					
258061	A	G-5-515	N365BA	N161MM	N611MM	N611CR*					
258062	A	G-5-516	N366BA	N961JC							
258063	A	G-5-518	N367BA	N684C	N74ND						
258064	B	G-5-514	Malawi MAAW-J1								
258065	A	G-5-520	N368BA	N77CS							
258066	A	G-5-521	N369BA	N75CS							
258067	B	G-5-525	D-CEVW	G-BUZX	G-5-807	N801MM	N801MB	N801MM			
258068	B	G-5-539	HZ-SJP	G-5-653	HZ-SJP	G-5-738	G-BUIM	N68GP	N68HR		
258069	A	G-5-526	N519BA	(N743UP)	N746UP	N364WC	N160WC				
258070	A	G-5-527	N520BA	N528AC							
258071	A	G-5-528	N521BA	N890A	N789LT						
258072	A	G-5-529	N522BA	(N745UP)	N747UP						

BAe 125-800

C/n	Series	Identities								
258073	B	G-5-532	D-CFVW	G-BVBH	N802MM	VR-BSI	VP-BSI			
258074	B	G-5-541	ZK-MRM	N800MD	G-5-640	N800MD	N800MN	N300BW	N850SM	
258075	A	G-5-533	N518BA	N189B	N533P	XA-GFB				
258076	B	G-5-535	D-CGVW	G-BVAS	RA-02807					
258077	A	G-5-538	N523BA	N509GP	N877CW	N897CW*				
258078	B	G-5-544	G-BNEH	G-5-713	G-BNEH	ZS-FSI	OE-GHS			
258079	B	G-5-542	G-GJCB	G-BVHW	SE-DRV	9M-DDW	N800LL			
258080	A	G-5-540	N524BA	N800BP	N800WH					
258081	A	G-5-543	N525BA	N650PM	N700PM	N196MC	N196MG			
258082	B	G-5-548	ZK-RJI	N499SC	N90ME	N601BA				
258083	A	G-5-546	N526BA	(N800HS)	N5C	N8UP				
258084	A	G-5-547	N527BA	N780A	N877RP					
258085	B	G-5-551	G-WBPR							
258086	A	G-5-550	N528BA	N125BA	N523WC					
258087	A	G-5-552	N529BA	N800TR	C-GAWH					
258088	B	G-5-563	(ZK-RHP)	G-BOOA	G-BTAB					
258089	A	G-5-555	N530BA	N125JB	N862CE					
258090	A	G-5-556	N531BA	N2SG	N2YG	N410US	N8090	N800FJ		
258091	B	G-5-560	HB-VIK							
258092	A	G-5-558	N532BA	N2MG	N3007	N3008*				
258093	A	G-5-559	N533BA	N331SC	N800S	(A6-HMK)	N358LL	N317CC		
258094	B	G-5-576	D-CFAN							
258095	A	G-5-561	N534BA	N200LS	(N500LL)	C-FPCP				
258096	A	G-5-562	N535BA	N800UP	N10TC	N596SW				
258097	B	G-5-567	HB-VIL							
258098	A	G-5-564	N536BA	N300LS	N181FH					
258099	A	G-5-565	(G-BNUB)	N537BA	C-FAAU	OY-MCL	N10YJ			
258100	A	G-5-566	N538BA	N108CF	N815CC	N810NE*				
258101	A	G-5-572	N539BA	N1125	N757M					
258102	A	G-5-573	N540BA	N89K	(N89KT)	N89NC				
258103	A	G-5-574	N541BA	N916PT	N494AT					
258104	A	G-5-575	N542BA	N527AC						
258105	A	G-5-577	(N551BA)	G-BNZW	C-GKLB	C-FSCI				
258106	B	G-5-580	PK-WSJ	PK-RGM	(N107CF)	N888SS	G-OLDD			
258107	A	G-5-578	N552BA	N70NE						
258108	A	G-5-579	N553BA	N61CT	N309G					
258109	B	(N554BA)	G-5-581	5N-NPC						
258110	B	(N555BA)	G-5-584	D-CMIR	N710A					
258111	A	(N556BA)	G-5-582	N554BA	N800TR	N375SC	N875SC	XA-TKQ		
258112	B	G-5-583	Botswana OK-1/Z-1		G-5-664	PT-OBT	N112NW	N331DC		
258113	A	G-5-587	N555BA	N683E						
258114	A	G-5-586	N556BA	N600LS	N800EC					
258115	B	G-5-599	(G-BPGR)	Saudi Arabia 104		G-5-665	Saudi Arabia 104		G-5-599	G-TCAP
258116	B	G-5-592	PT-LQP							
258117	A	G-5-589	N557BA	N825PS	N826CT					
258118	B	(G-5-590)	G-5-605	(G-BPGS)	Saudi Arabia 105					
258119	A	G-5-591	N558BA	N203R	N221RE	N239R				
258120	B	G-5-606	G-POSN	HB-VLI	VT-EAU	N120AP				
258121	A	G-5-593	(N559BA)	G-BOTX	C-FRPP	N4361Q	N800WA			
258122	A	G-5-594	N560BA	N800VC						
258123	A	G-5-600	N561BA	N353WC	N353WG	C-GCGS				
258124	A	G-5-596	N562BA	N800BA	N376SC	N876SC	N801NW	C-GCRP	C-GRGE	N824CW
258125	A	G-5-601	N563BA	N802X						
258126	A	G-5-597	N564BA	(N82BL)	HZ-BL2					
258127	A	G-5-602	N565BA	N803X						
258128	A	G-5-603	N566BA	N804X						
258129	C-29A	G-5-622	N269X	USAF 88-0269		N94				
258130	B	G-5-620	G-FDSL	G-TPHK	G-BVFC	G-ETOM	D-CPAS			
258131	C-29A	G-5-611	(N271X)	N270X	USAF 88-0270		N95			
258132	A	G-5-607	N567BA	N125TR	N222MS					
258133	B	G-5-616	G-GSAM	G-5-642	N800FK	G-JETK	N800FK	HP-1262	PT-WAU	
258134	C-29A	G-5-634	(N270X)	N271X	USAF 88-0271		N96			
258135	A	G-5-608	N568BA	N801AB	N801RJ	(N241SM)	N204SM			
258136	A	G-5-609	N569BA	N452SM	I-SDFG					
258137	A	G-5-610	N570BA	N733K	(N100MH)	N110MH				
258138	A	G-5-614	N582BA	N244JM						
258139	A	G-5-612	N580BA	N125BA	(VR-BPA)	VR-BLP	N47VC	N49VG	(N47TJ)	N795PH
258140	A	G-5-613	N581BA	N45Y						
258141	A	G-5-615	N583BA	N72K	C-FGLF	N106GC	N73WF			
258142	A	G-5-617	N584BA	N1903P	N850BM	N149VB	N149VP	N50BN		
258143	B	G-5-656	5N-NPF	5N-AGZ						
258144	A	G-5-618	N585BA	N682B						
258145	A	G-5-619	N586BA	N540M						
258146	B	G-5-629	(G-BPYD)	HZ-109+	G-5-703	HZ-109				
		+Marks painted on a/c but delivered with "HZ" taped over								
258147	A	G-5-621	N587BA	N919P	N9UP					
258148	B	G-5-630	(G-BPYE)	HZ-110	Saudia Arabia 110					
258149	B	G-5-635	G-FASL	N155T	N577T					

BAe 125-800

C/n	Series	Identities
258150	A	G-5-625 N588BA N77W N432AC*
258151	1000	G-EXLR prototype BAe125-1000; ff 16Jun90; last flight 10Jly92; wfu Nov93; shipped to Wichita 27Sep95 remains located in scrapyard, Wichita, KS circa Mar96 to Raytheon Svs hangar, Wichita KS circa Sep99 to train South Korean Hawker 800XP engineers
258152	B	G-5-626 HB-VHU (N42US) N800WG
258153	B	G-5-627 HB-VHV
258154	C-29A	G-5-655 N272X USAF 88-0272 (N272X) N97
258155	A	G-5-628 N800BM D-CBMW+ N800BM D-CBMW N159RA N238AJ N300BL
		+Marks painted on a/c ca 28Sep89 but reverted to US marks by Nov89
258156	C-29A	G-5-661 N273X USAF 88-0273 (N273X) N98
258157	A	G-5-632 N589BA N800BA C-GMTR
258158	C-29A	G-5-667 N274X USAF 88-0274 (N274X) N99
258159	1000	G-OPFC second prototype BAe125-1000; ff 25Nov90; cx 19Jan96 sold in USA for ground tests; to N10855
258160	A	G-5-633 N590BA N354WC N354WG N369BG N389BG N160NW
258161	A	G-5-636 G-BPXW C-FFTM N17DD
258162	A	G-5-638 N591BA N753G N800PA
258163	A	G-5-639 G-BRCZ C-GMOL C-FWCE
258164	B	G-5-654 Botswana OK1 code Z2 Botswana OK2 G-OBLT (VR-BND) G-5-654 Saudi Arabia 130
258165	B	G-5-657 VR-BPG ZS-BPG
258166	A	G-5-641 N592BA N74PC
258167	A	G-5-662 N125AS VR-CAS VP-CAS
258168	A	G-5-643 N593BA N74NP
258169	B	G-5-644 N47CG N526AC
258170	A	G-5-645 N594BA N75NP
258171	A	G-5-646 N595BA N754G N4444J N707PE
258172	A	G-5-647 N596BA N290EC
258173	A	G-5-648 N599BA N95AE N82XP
258174	A	G-5-649 N597BA N174A N174NW
258175	A	G-5-650 N598BA (VR-BPB) VR-BLQ N204JC HB-VMF
258176	B	(N610BA) G-5-652 HB-VJY N176WA XA-TPB
258177	A	G-5-668 PT-OJC N411RA N217AL
258178	B	G-5-658 N611BA
258179	A	G-5-660 N610BA N125BA N60TC
258180	B	G-5-675 G-XRMC
258181	A	G-5-663 N612BA N355WC N355WG C-GAGU
258182	B	G-5-676 (VR-B) G-PBWH G-5-676 N128RS N12F
258183	A	G-5-666 N613BA N50PM N90PM N63PM N599EC CS-DNI
258184	B	G-5-678 (PT-WAW) PT-OSW
258185	A	G-5-669 N614BA N207PC (N207RC) XA-SIV
258186	B	G-5-683 G-BSUL VR-BPM G-BSUL N8186
258187	A	G-5-670 N615BA N60PM N750RV
258188	A	G-5-671 N616BA N1910A
258189	A	G-5-673 N617BA N6JB N6UB N195KC
258190	B	G-5-684 G-BTAE PT-OHB PT-JAA
258191	A	G-5-674 N618BA N152NS
258192	B	TR-LDB G-5-691 TR-LDB
258193	A	G-5-677 N619BA N300PM N699EC CS-DNH
258194	B	G-5-692 PT-OTC
258195	A	G-5-679 N630BA N800BA N800GX N100GX N940HC N941HC
258196	A	G-5-680 N631BA N125TR N511WM N511WD N929WG
258197	B	G-5-696 G-BTMG G-OMGE
258198	B	G-5-694 PT-WAL
258199	A	G-5-681 N632BA N4402
258200	A	G-5-682 N633BA N461W
258201	B	G-5-699 (D-C) G-OCCI G-BWSY
258202	A	G-5-685 N634BA N200GX N800DR
258203	A	G-5-686 N635BA YV-735CP N228G N453TM
258204	A	G-5-687 N636BA N341AP
258205	A	G-5-689 N637BA N805X
258206	A	G-5-688 N638BA (N800BJ) PT-OMC N638BA N466CS
258207	A	G-5-690 N639BA N600KC (N48DD) N2BG
258208	B	G-5-670+ G-5-700 (PT-) G-BUID TC-ANC
		+painted 15May91 as G-5-670 in error; corrected 20May91
258209	A	G-5-695 N670BA YV-800CP N168BA N693C N410BT
258210	B	G-5-705 G-RAAR HB-VMI
258211	B	G-5-724 PT-OSB N91DV
258212	B	G-5-710 G-BUCP D-CSRI RP-C8008 N323L*
258213	B/XP	G-5-709 D-CWBW G-BURV N10857
258214	B	G-5-706 VR-CCX PT-OOI
258215	A/U-125	G-5-727 G-JFCX Japan 29-3041 code 041
258216	A	G-5-714 N671BA N500J
258217	A	G-5-715 N672BA N600J
258218	A	G-5-725 N673BA N57PM N118K
258219	B	G-5-740 (9M-WCM) 9M-AZZ
258220	A	G-5-728 N674BA N58PM
258221	A	G-5-731 N675BA N25W
258222	B	G-5-745 G-VIPI

BAe 125-800

C/n	Series	Identities						
258223	A	G-5-733	N677BA	N800BA	N622AB	N622AD	N44HH	
258224	B	G-5-763	ZS-NJH	N827RH	N847RH	N618JL		
258225	A	G-5-739	N682BA	N800BA	N800CJ	N935H		
258226	B	G-5-755	(9M-)	G-BVCU	D-CSRB	RP-C1926	N709EA	N800MJ
258227	A/U-125	G-5-769	G-BUUW	Japan 39-3042 code 042				
258228	A	G-5-758	HB-VKV	N130LC				
258229	A	G-5-744	N683BA	PT-OTH	N229RY	TC-TEK		
258230	A	G-5-748	N678BA	N71MT				
258231	A	G-5-750	N685BA	N75MT				
258232	A	G-5-752	N686BA	N900KC	XA-NGS			
258233	B	G-5-770	D-CAVW	F-WQCD	(VR-BQH)	VR-BTM	VP-BTM	G-BYHM
258234	B	G-5-757	VR-CDE	YV-814CP	VR-CDE	VP-CDE		
258235	B	G-5-774	D-CBVW	G-BWVA	OY-RAA	N258SA	D-CWOL	PH-WOL*
258236	A	G-5-764	N162BA	N80PM	N800TJ	(N39BL)	N58BL	
258237	B	G-5-775	D-CCVW	G-BWRN	9M-DRL	VP-BAW	N237RA	
258238	A	G-5-767	N163BA	N70PM	N100AG			
258239	A	G-5-768	N164BA	VR-BPN	N904H	N62TC	(N262CT)	N84CT
258240	B	G-5-772	G-BUWC	G-SHEA	HB-VLT	G-HCFR		
258241	A	G-5-777	N165BA	N125CJ	N94NB	N540BA		
258242	A/U-125	G-5-793	G-BVFE	Japan 49-3043				
258243	B	G-5-778	(G-BUWD)	G-SHEB	VH-XMO			
258244	A	G-5-780	N166BA	N800CJ	N95NB	N530BA		
258245	A/U-125A	G-JHSX	Japan 52-3001 code 001					
258246	A	G-5-782	N387H	HB-VKW				
258247	A/U-125A	G-5-813	G-BVRF	Japan 52-3002 code 002				
258248	A	G-5-784	N388H	N789LB				
258249	A	G-5-786	N933H	N326SU	(N826SU)	N500HF		
258250	A/U-125A	G-5-815	G-BVRG	Japan 52-3003 code 003				
258251	A	G-5-787	N937H	N194JS				
258252	A	G-5-788	N938H					
258253	A	G-5-790	N942H	N801CE				
258254	A	G-5-791	N943H	N2015M				
258255		G-5-792	N946H	N127KC	first Hawker 800			
258256		G-5-795	N947H	N256BC	N256FS*			
258257		G-5-796	N951H	N802DC				
258258	B	G-5-798	G-BVJI	(N953H)	G-BVJI	N54SB	N910JD	N910JN
258259		G-5-799	N954H	(N966L)				
258260		G-5-800	N957H					
258261		G-5-802	N958H	PT-GAF				
258262		G-5-803	N959H					
258263		G-5-804	N961H	N826GA				
258264		G-5-806	N805H	HB-VLF				
258265		G-5-809	N806H	HB-VLG				
258266	XP	G-5-811	(N293H)	G-BVRW	(N293H)	N800XP	(N800GT)	N414XP
258267		G-5-812	N294H	N811CC	N980DC			
258268	U-125A	G-5-829	G-BVYV	Japan 62-3004		N809H	Japan 62-3004	
258269		G-5-814	N295H	N380X	N380DE*			
258270		G-5-816	N297H	N802CE				
258271		G-5-818	N298H	N803CE				
258272		G-5-819	N299H	N2426				
258273		G-5-820	N803H	N967L	N258RA			
258274		G-5-822	N804H	N2428				
258275		G-5-823	N905H	N77TC				
258276		G-5-824	N667H	N126KC				
258277	XP	G-BVYW	N97SH					
258278	XP	G-BVZK	N872AT					
258279	XP	G-BVZL	(N817H)	4X-CZM				
258280	XP	G-BWDC	N351SP					
258281	XP	G-BWDD	N914H	VH-ELJ	N281XP	N781TA		
258282	XP	G-5-827	G-BWDW	N916H	PT-WHH	N782TA		
258283	XP	G-5-828	G-BWGB	N918H	(N283XP)	4X-COV		
258284	XP	G-5-830	G-BWGC	N919H	PT-WNO			
258285	XP	G-5-831	G-BWGD	N808H	(N800XP)	N285XP		
258286	XP	G-5-832	G-BWGE	N807H	N501F			
258287	XP	G-5-833	N668H	(N287XP)	N801WB			
258288	U-125A	G-5-848	N816H	Japan 72-3005				
258289	XP	G-5-834	N669H	N515GP	N863CE			
258290	XP	G-5-835	N670H	N348MC				
258291	XP	"G-5-837"	G-5-836	N672H	N291XP	N291SJ	N791TA	
258292	XP	G-5-838	N673H	N33BC				
258293	XP	G-5-839	N679H	N404CE				
258294	XP	G-5-840	N682H	N404BS				
258295	XP	G-5-841	N683H	VH-LAW				
258296	XP	G-5-842	N685H	N801JT	N707TA			
258297*	XP	first US-assembed aircraft			N297XP	N725TA		
258298	XP	G-5-843	N298XP	N880SP				
258299	XP	G-5-844	N299XP	(N32BC)	N601DR^			
258300	XP	G-5-845	N689H	N800VF				

BAe 125-800

C/n	Series	Identities			
258301*	XP	N1105Z	P1-WMA		
258302	XP	G-5-847	N302XP	XA-RUY	
258303	XP	G-5-849	N303XP	N876H	
258304*	XP	N802JT	N5734		
258305	U-125A	G-5-864	N305XP	Japan 72-3006 code 006	
258306*	U-125A	N1103U	Japan 82-3007 code 007		
258307	XP	G-5-850	N307XP	N109TD	
258308	XP	G-5-851	N308XP	(N11WC)	N345BR
258309*	XP	N803JT	N5735		
258310	XP	G-5-852	N310XP	PT-WMG	
258311*	XP	N804JT	N800RD		
258312	XP	G-5-853	N312XP	PT-WMD	
258313*	XP	N2159X	N313XP	N84BA	
258314	XP	G-5-854	N314XP	OM-SKY	N800NJ
258315*	XP	N2169X	N9292X		
258316	XP	G-5-855	N316XP	N516GP	
258317*	XP	N2173X	N9NB	N520BA	
258318	XP	G-5-856	N318XP	N1910H	
258319*	XP	N2291X	C-FIPE		
258320*	XP	N2322X	N720TA		
258321	XP	G-5-857	N691H	N32BC	
258322*	XP	N722TA			
258323	XP	G-5-858	N323XP	N877S	
258324	XP	G-5-860	N324XP	N303BC	
258325*	U-125A	N1112N	Japan 82-3008 code 008		
258326*	XP	N326XP	N1897A		
258327	XP	G-5-861	N327XP	N111ZN	
258328	XP	G-5-866	N328XP	VH-SGY	
258329	XP	G-5-862	N329XP	N901K	
258330	XP	G-5-869	N330XP	N139M	
258331*	XP	N10NB	N510BA		
258332	XP	G-5-865	N332XP	N36H	
258333*	U-125A	N3261Y	Japan 82-3009 code 009		
258334*	XP	N334XP	N399JC		
258335	XP	G-5-867	N335XP	OY-RAC	
258336*	XP	N336XP	N2286U	N745UP	
258337	XP	G-5-868	N337XP	last to be assembled at Chester - rolled out 22Apr97, ff 29Apr97, del'd to USA	
		08May97	(9M-VVV)	N337XP	N733TA

US Production

C/n	Series	Identities			
258338	XP	N838QS			
258339	XP	N23395	SE-DVD		
258340	XP	N840QS			
258341	U-125A	N3251M	(incorrectly painted as N2351M) for JASDF		
258342	XP	N2320J	South Korean AF	(US marks cx Feb00)	
258343	XP	N1102U	for South Korean AF		
258344	XP	N29GP			
258345	XP	N1135A	D-CBMV	D-CBMW	
258346	XP	N23204	for South Korean AF		
258347	XP	N1115G	N40PL		
258348	U-125A	N2175W	Japan 92-3011 code 011		
258349	XP	N723TA	VP-BHL		
258350	XP	N23207	for South Korean AF		
258351	XP	N23208	South Korean AF	(US marks cx Feb00)	
258352	XP	N2321S	South Korean AF	(US marks cx Feb00)	
258353	XP	N2321V	for South Korean AF		
258354	XP	N2G			
258355	XP	N855QS			
258356	XP	N550H			
258357	XP	N2321Z	South Korean AF	(US marks cx Feb00)	
258358	XP	N240B			
258359	XP	N25WX			
258360	U-125A	N3189H	Japan 92-3012 code 012		
258361	XP	N861QS			
258362	XP	N862QS			
258363	XP	N726TA			
258364	XP	N728TA			
258365	XP	N865SM			
258366	XP	N1133N	(CS-MAI)	N894CA	
258367	XP	N3263E	N367DM		
258368	XP	N804AC			
258369	XP	N800PC			
258370	U-125A	N23556		Japan 92-3013 code 013	
258371	XP	N848N			
258372	XP	N1251K	N372XP	LV-ZHY	
258373	XP	N3270X	N168BF		
258374	XP	N729TA			

BAe 125-800

C/n	Series	Identities		
258375	XP	N875QS		
258376	XP	N1640		
258377	XP	N1251K	N984GC	(1,000th HS/BAe/Raytheon 125 sale)
258378	XP	N494RG		
258379	XP	N879QS		
258380	XP	N8SP		
258381	U-125A	N23566	for JASDF	
258382	XP	N23451	SE-DYE	
258383	XP	N730TA		
258384	XP	N23455	TC-MDC	
258385	XP	N23466	SE-DYV	
258386	XP	N23479	N61DF	
258387	XP	N887QS		
258388	XP	N23488	TC-OKN	
258389	XP	N23493	I-DDVA	
258390	XP	N23509	(N800SG)	N800FD
258391	XP	N391XP		
258392	XP	N23569	LX-BYG (painted in error)	LX-GBY
258393	XP	N893QS		
258394	XP	N394XP	N800DW	
258395	XP	N23577	PT-WVG	
258396	XP	N23585	N21EL	
258397	XP	N752TA		
258398	XP	N168HH		
258399	XP	N899QS	CS-DNJ	
258400	XP	N404JC		
258401	XP	N23592	for Brazilian AF	
258402	XP	N729AT		
258403	XP	N23550	ZS-DCK	
258404	XP	N30289	VP-BCM	
258405	XP	N405XP	N866RR	
258406	XP	N754TA		
258407	U-125A	N30562	for JASDF	
258408	XP	N30319	B-3990	
258409	XP	N30337	PT-WPF	
258410	XP	N755TA	N322LA	
258411	XP	N617TM		
258412	XP	N30682	N590HC	
258413	XP	N760TA		
258414	XP	N30742	N800XP	
258415	XP	N31016	TC-BHD	TC-STR
258416	XP	N816QS		
258417	XP	N747NG	N246V	
258418	XP	N31046	N806XM	
258419	XP	N419XP	N508BP	
258420	XP	N31340	N910JD	
258421	XP	N31820	for Brazilian AF	
258422	XP	N822QS	CS-DNM	
258423	XP	N925JF		
258424	XP	N1899K		
258425	XP	N825XP	N800VA	N59BR
258426	XP	N426XP	N27FL	
258427	U-125A	N31833	for JASDF	
258428	XP	N772TA		
258429	XP	N88HD		
258430	XP	N31590	CS-DNK	
258431	XP	N144HM		
258432	XP	N432XP	N1650	
258433	XP	N833QS		
258434	XP	N40027	for Brazilian AF	
258435	XP	N835QS	CS-DNN	
258436	XP	N836QS		
258437	XP	N780TA		
258438	XP	N40113	VP-BHZ	
258439	XP	N31596	CS-DNL	
258440	XP	N40488	N801MB	
258441	XP	N800PE		
258442	XP	N40202	PT-XDY	
258443	XP	N310AS		
258444	XP	N40489	EC-HJL	
258445	U-125A	N40708	for JASDF	
258446	XP	N529M		
258447	XP	N40310	for Brazilian AF	
258448	XP	N41280	N532PJ	
258449	XP	N41431	N365AT	
258450	XP	N41441	D-CTAN	
258451	XP	N41534	N475HM	
258452	XP	N852QS		

BAe 125-800

C/n	Series	Identities		
258453	XP	N802TA	N68CB	
258454	XP	N41093		
258455	XP	N803TA		
258456	XP	N800EM	N41762	G-JMAX
258457	XP	N41984		
258458	XP	N42685	N228TM	
258459	XP	N43259	N939LE	
258460	XP	N81SN		
258461	XP	N804TA		
258462	XP	N43230		
258463	XP	N863QS		
258464	XP	N41964		
258465	XP	N43265	ZS-DDT*	
258466	XP	N805TA		
258467	XP	N5732		
258468	XP	N43436		
258469	U-125A	N43079	for JASDF	
258470	XP	N42830		
258471	XP	N43642		
258472	XP	N44722		
258473	XP	N73UP		
258474	XP	N874QS		
258475	XP	N43675		
258476	XP	N44676		
258477	XP	N44767		
258478	XP	N44648		
258479	XP	N44779		
258480	XP	N4403		
258481	XP	N43926		
258482	XP	N43182		
258483	XP	N44883		
258484	XP	N84UP		
258485	XP	N44515		
258486	XP	N886QS		
258487	XP			
258488	XP			
258489	XP			
258490	XP			
258491	XP			
258492	XP			
258493	XP			
258494	XP			
258495	XP			
258496	XP			
258497	XP			
258498	XP			
258499	XP			
258500	XP			
258501	XP			
258502	XP			
258503	XP			
258504	XP			
258505	XP			
258506	XP			
258507	XP			
258508	XP			
258509	XP			
258510	XP			
258511	XP			
258512	XP			
258513	XP			
258514	XP			
258515	XP			
258516	XP			
258517	XP			
258518	XP			
258519	XP			
258520	XP			
258521	XP			
258522	XP			
258523	XP			
258524	XP			
258525	XP			
258526	XP			
258527	XP			
258528	XP			
258529	XP			
258530	XP			

C/n	Series	Identities
258531	XP	
258532	XP	
258533	XP	
258534	XP	
258535	XP	
258536	XP	
258537	XP	
258538	XP	
258539	XP	
258540	XP	
258541	XP	
258542	XP	
258543	XP	
258544	XP	
258545	XP	
258546	XP	
258547	XP	
258548	XP	
258549	XP	
258550	XP	

SERIES 1000 (BAe 1000) (HAWKER 1000)

C/n	Series	Identities
259001	B	built as c/n 258151 G-EXLR ff 16Jun90; reported wfu Nov93; see c/n 258151
259002	B	built as c/n 258159 G-OPFC N10855 q.v. c/n 258159
259003	B	G-5-702 G-ELRA (built between c/ns 258195-6) N503QS
259004	B	G-LRBJ G-5-779 VR-CPT VP-CPT
259005	A	G-BTTX G-5-735 N1AB N81AB N410US N505QS
259006	A	G-BTTG "N1000U"+ N100U
		+These marks painted on a/c but not regd with FAA; also original Bill of Sale showed N100UT as regn
259007	A	G-BTSI N84WA N119PW
259008	B	G-5-720 HZ-OFC HZ-OFC2 N195L
259009	A	G-5-716 G-BTYN N229U
259010	A	G-5-722 (HZ-) N125CJ N52SM
259011	A	G-5-717 G-BTYO N14GD N208R
259012	B	G-5-726 HZ-SJP2 N512QS
259013	A	G-5-711 G-BTYP N125BA N513QS
259014	A	G-5-712 G-BTYR N680BA N125CJ N514QS
259015	A	G-5-718 G-BTYS N1000E N515QS
259016	B	(D-BJET) G-5-732 G-BULI (5N-) G-5-732 N291H N678SB
259017	B	G-5-719 ZS-NEW ZS-AVL N963H N204R
259018	B	G-5-741 5N-FGR
259019	A	G-5-730 N125CA N792H N2SG N600LS
259020	A	G-5-723 N676BA N520QS
259021	B	G-5-736 G-BUKW XA-GRB N5794J VR-CMZ VP-CMZ
259022	B	G-5-734 VH-LMP
259023	A	G-5-729 (VH-) N679BA N523QS
259024	B	G-5-737 G-BUIX (C-) N5ES N263R
259025	B	G-5-759 (5N-) G-BVDL N292H N525QS
259026	B	G-5-743 ZS-CCT+ ZS-ACT N9026 G-GDEZ
		+Del 29Nov92 with these marks but current at that time on PA-22-150 Tri-Pacer (22-3642)
259027	B	G-5-746 5H-BLM G-BVLO "N333RL"+ N333RU N333RL
		+Painted on a/c in error
259028	B	G-5-749 D-CBWW
259029	B	G-5-751 G-BUNW EK-B021+ EZ-B021
		+Marks EK- were not allowed by ICAO; used EZ- instead
259030	B	G-5-753 G-BUPL G-DCCI N530QS
259031	B	G-5-754 G-BUUY G-HJCB N301PH
259032	B	G-5-760 ZS-NHL F-WQAU G-BWCB VR-CXX VP-CXX N401LS N300LS (regd as a 1000A)
259033	A	G-5-756 N684BA N850BL N533QS
259034	B	G-5-761 G-BUWX N290H N81HH
259035	A	G-5-773 N160BA N535QS
259036	A	G-5-762 N161BA N1AB N127RP
259037	B	G-5-771 G-SCCC G-SHEC XA-TGK XA-RGG
259038	A	G-5-776 N167BA N125GM N107RP
259039	A	G-5-781 N169BA N539QS
259040	A	G-5-783 N22UP N540QS
259041	A	G-5-785 (N937H) N936H N541QS
259042	A	G-5-789 N941H N542QS
259043		G-5-794 N948H first Hawker 1000 (N543QS) TC-AKH (N881JT) XA-RYB
259044		G-5-797 N956H N544QS
259045		G-5-801 (N296H) N545QS
259046		G-5-805 N962H N546QS
259047		G-5-817 N296H N547QS
259048		G-5-826 N802H N548QS
259049		G-5-837 N679H (painted in error) N549QS
259050		G-5-846 N550QS
259051		G-5-859 N551QS
259052		G-5-863 N552QS

Production complete

125 NA NUMBER DECODE

NA	C/N
NA700	25134
NA701	25136
NA702	25137
NA703	25139
NA704	25141
NA705	25142
NA706	25146
NA707	25160
NA708	25161
NA709	25163
NA710	25170
NA711	25173
NA712	25174
NA713	25175
NA714	25176
NA715	25179
NA716	25180
NA717	25183
NA718	25187
NA719	25188
NA720	25185
NA721	25186
NA722	25190
NA723	25191
NA724	25192
NA725	25193
NA726	25195
NA727	25196
NA728	25198
NA729	25200
NA730	25201
NA731	25202
NA732	25203
NA733	25204
NA734	25205
NA735	25206
NA736	25207
NA737	25208
NA738	25210
NA739	25211
NA740	25212
NA741	25213
NA742	25214
NA743	25216
NA744	25218
NA745	25220
NA746	25221
NA747	25222
NA748	25224
NA749	25225
NA750	25226
NA751	25228
NA752	25229
NA753	25230
NA754	25232
NA755	25233
NA756	25234
NA757	25236
NA758	25239
NA759	25241
NA760	25244
NA761	25237
NA762	25245
NA763	25261
NA764	25262
NA765	25263
NA766	25265
NA767	25267
NA768	25273
NA769	25275
NA770	25276
NA771	25278
NA772	25279
NA773	25280
NA774	25281
NA775	25282
NA776	25283
NA777	25284
NA778	25285
NA779	25286
NA780	25287

NA	C/N
NA0201	257002
NA0202	257003
NA0203	257005
NA0204	257006
NA0205	257008
NA0206	257009
NA0207	257011
NA0208	257012
NA0209	257014
NA0210	257015
NA0211	257017
NA0212	257018
NA0213	257019
NA0214	257021
NA0215	257023
NA0216	257016
NA0217	257024
NA0218	257004
NA0219	257026
NA0220	257027
NA0221	257029
NA0222	257030
NA0223	257032
NA0224	257033
NA0225	257035
NA0226	257036
NA0227	257038
NA0228	257039
NA0229	257041
NA0230	257042
NA0231	257044
NA0232	257043
NA0233	257047
NA0234	257048
NA0235	257050
NA0236	257051
NA0237	257052
NA0238	257053
NA0239	257049
NA0240	257045
NA0241	257056
NA0242	257057
NA0243	257059
NA0244	257060
NA0245	257058
NA0246	257063
NA0247	257065
NA0248	257066
NA0249	257068
NA0250	257069
NA0251	257071
NA0252	257072
NA0253	257074
NA0254	257075
NA0255	257077
NA0256	257078
NA0257	257080
NA0258	257081
NA0259	257083
NA0260	257084
NA0261	257086
NA0262	257087
NA0263	257089
NA0264	257090
NA0265	257092
NA0266	257093
NA0267	257095
NA0268	257079
NA0269	257098
NA0270	257099
NA0271	257110
NA0272	257101
NA0273	257104
NA0274	257105
NA0275	257106
NA0276	257096
NA0277	257111
NA0278	257108
NA0279	257113

NA	C/N
NA0280	257102
NA0281	257114
NA0282	257116
NA0283	257117
NA0284	257119
NA0285	257120
NA0286	257121
NA0287	257122
NA0288	257123
NA0289	257125
NA0290	257126
NA0291	257128
NA0292	257129
NA0293	257131
NA0294	257132
NA0295	257134
NA0296	257135
NA0297	257137
NA0298	257138
NA0299	257140
NA0300	257141
NA0301	257146
NA0302	257149
NA0303	257147
NA0304	257148
NA0305	257150
NA0306	257152
NA0307	257154
NA0308	257155
NA0309	257156
NA0310	257157
NA0311	257159
NA0312	257162
NA0313	257153
NA0314	257164
NA0315	257165
NA0316	257167
NA0317	257168
NA0318	257170
NA0319	257171
NA0320	257173
NA0321	257174
NA0322	257176
NA0323	257161
NA0324	257177
NA0325	257143
NA0326	257144
NA0327	257179
NA0328	257180
NA0329	257182
NA0330	257183
NA0331	257185
NA0332	257186
NA0333	257188
NA0334	257195
NA0335	257198
NA0336	257191
NA0337	257192
NA0338	257193
NA0339	257145
NA0340	257199
NA0341	257201
NA0342	257202
NA0343	257204
NA0344	257206
NA0345	257207
NA0346	257208
NA0347	257210
NA0401	258100
NA0402	258101
NA0403	258102
NA0404	258103
NA0405	258104
NA0406	258105
NA0407	258107
NA0408	258108
NA0409	258111
NA0410	258113

NA	C/N
NA0411	258114
NA0412	258117
NA0413	258119
NA0414	258121
NA0415	258122
NA0416	258123
NA0417	258124
NA0418	258125
NA0419	258126
NA0420	258127
NA0421	258128
NA0422	258132
NA0423	258135
NA0424	258136
NA0425	258137
NA0426	258139
NA0427	258140
NA0428	258138
NA0429	258141
NA0430	258142
NA0431	258144
NA0432	258145
NA0433	258147
NA0434	258150
NA0435	258157
NA0436	258160
NA0437	258161
NA0438	258162
NA0439	258166
NA0440	258168
NA0441	258170
NA0442	258171
NA0443	258163
NA0444	258172
NA0445	258174
NA0446	258175
NA0447	258173
NA0448	258179
NA0449	258178
NA0450	258181
NA0451	258183
NA0452	258185
NA0453	258187
NA0454	258188
NA0455	258189
NA0456	258191
NA0457	258193
NA0458	258195
NA0459	258196
NA0460	258199
NA0461	258200
NA0462	258202
NA0463	258203
NA0464	258204
NA0465	258205
NA0466	258206
NA0467	258207
NA0468	258209
NA0469	258216
NA0470	258217
NA0471	258218
NA0472	258220
NA0473	258221
NA0474	258223
NA0475	258225
NA1000	259005
NA1001	259006
NA1002	259009
NA1003	259011
NA1004	259013
NA1005	259014
NA1006	259015
NA1007	259019
NA1008	259020
NA1009	259010
NA1010	259023

BEECHJET 400

* Denotes aircraft originally manufactured by Mitsubishi as MU300-2s and then converted to Beechjet 400 standard. The c/n shown in brackets in these cases is the old Mitsubishi c/n. C/n RJ-12 is the first pure Beechjet 400.

C/n	Series	Identities						
*RJ-1 (A1001SA)	400	N64VM						
*RJ-2 (A1002SA)	400	N103AD	N402FB					
*RJ-3 (A1003SA)	400	N508DM	N203BA					
*RJ-4 (A1004SA)	400	N504DM	N92RW	(N401TJ)	N8YM			
*RJ-5 (A1005SA)	400	N77GA						
*RJ-6 (A1006SA)	400	N106DM	N18JN	YV-737CP	YV-738CP	YV-838CP	N406TS	
*RJ-7 (A1007SA)	400	N507DM	N207BA	N106VC	N25BN	N85BN		
A1008SA	2	N411BW	reportedly w/o at unknown location in Mar97; to Dodson Avn, KS Oct97, for spares use					
*RJ-9 (A1009SA)	400	N109DM	N209BA	(N248PA)	N42SR	N242SR	N800FT	N65RA
*RJ-10 (A1010SA)	400	N499DM	N410BA	I-ALSE	N131AP			
*RJ-11 (A1011SA)	400	N114DM	N111BA					
RJ-12	400	N3112B	N129DB	N3112K	N106CG			
RJ-13	400	N3113B						
RJ-14	400	N3114B	N208R	N208D	N58AU	N672AT	(N770TB)	N599JL
RJ-15	400	N3115B	N25W	N25WA	N73BL	N73BE		
RJ-16	400	N165F	N512WP	N803E	N440MP^			
RJ-17	400	N417BJ	N877S	N400T	N94BJ	N84BJ	N486MJ	N1CG
RJ-18	400	N3180T	I-STAP	N940GA	ZS-NOD	N595PT		
RJ-19	400	N3119W	N800HM	(N700HM)	N880HM	PJ-SOL	N24BA	N101CC N598JL*
RJ-20	400	N3120Y	I-ONDO	(N20CV)	N901P	N455DW		
RJ-21	400	N3121B						
RJ-22	400	N3122B	9M-ATM	N992GA	(VR-BLG)	I-INCZ	OY-JAT	N724AA N48CK
RJ-23	400	N3123T	rebuilt using parts of RK-11, following accident					(I-ALSU) N400GJ
RJ-24	400	N3124M	N510WS	N512WS*				
RJ-25	400	N3025T	I-MPIZ	N125RJ	I-OTTY			
RJ-26	400	N3026U	N88WG	N90SR	N388DA	N426MD	N91MT	N401GJ
RJ-27	400	N3127R	N484CC	N427CW^				
RJ-28	400	N31428	I-ACIF	N48GA	N700LP	N51EB		
RJ-29	400	N3129E	N503EB	N193TR	(N597N)	XA-OAC	N129BT	
RJ-30	400	N3130T	(N815BS)	N486MJ	N777FE			
RJ-31	400	N545GM	N5450M	I-ALSI	N5450M	I-ALSI	N114AP	N499P
RJ-32	400	N31432	XA-RAR					
RJ-33	400	N31733	(N233BJ)	XA-JJA	XA-BNG			
RJ-34	400	N3134N	I-ALSO	N96WW	(N41TJ)			
RJ-35	400	N3035T	N85TT	I-SAMI	N71GA	N737MM		
RJ-36	400	N3236Q	G-RSRS	N3236Q	G-MARS	I-RDSF	VR-BNV	N52GA
RJ-37	400	N31437	LV-PAM	LV-RCT	N31437			
RJ-38	400	N3238K	N147CC	N447CC	VT-OAM			
RJ-39	400	N3239K	N48SR					
RJ-40	400	N3240M	PK-ERA	N3240M				
RJ-41	400	N3141G	(N441EE)	(N270BJ)	N241BJ			
RJ-42	400	N3142E	N31542	N400PL	I-FTAL	N735GA	N444WB	
RJ-43	400	N3143T	N401CG					
RJ-44	400	N3144A	HB-VJE	N3144A	I-GCFA	N22WJ	I-TOPJ	
RJ-45	400	N3145F	N58AU	N218RG+	N58AU	N218RG	N241TR	
		+ painted on aircraft but only reserved						
RJ-46	400	N1546T	N146JB	VT-TEL				
RJ-47	400	N1547B						
RJ-48	400	N1548D	XB-JHE					
RJ-49	400	N1549J						
RJ-50	400	N1550Y	G-OTMC	N56GA	N102MC			
RJ-51	400	N1551B	converted to RK-1 (qv)					
RJ-52	400	N196KC	(N196KQ)	(N52EB)	N196JH			
RJ-53	400	N195KC	N195KA	N711EC	N53EB	N520WS		
RJ-54	400	N1554R	XB-FDH	N418MG				
RJ-55	400	N1555P	(VH-)	N711FG	N711FC	N780GT		
RJ-56	400	N1556W	G-BSZP	OK-UZI				
RJ-57	400	N1557D	N25BR	w/o 11Dec91 Lavender Mt, NW of Rome Airport, GA; cx Jun92				
RJ-58	400	N1558F	XA-RNG	XA-MII				
RJ-59	400	N1559U	ZS-MHN					
RJ-60	400	N1560T	G-BRBZ	N89GA	N400FT	XA-LEG		
RJ-61	400	N1561B	XA-RNE	N701LP				
RJ-62	400	N89KM	N89KK	N333RS	N424BT			
RJ-63	400	N848C						
RJ-64	400	N1564B	N195JH					
RJ-65	400	N1565B						

End of production from Japanese components; production continues with US-built components from c/n RK-1

BEECHJET

C/n	Series	Identities						
RK-1	400A	N1551B	converted from c/n RJ-51			N294FA	N294AW	N401CW*
RK-2	400A	N1902W	N272BC	N272BQ	N402CW			
RK-3	400A	N400A	XA-CLA	N640AC	N400VG	N400VK		
RK-4	400A	N147CC	N147CG	N400BE	N777FL	N771EL	N494CW	
RK-5	400A	N501BG						
RK-6	400A	N56576	I-IPFC	N3119H	N600CC	(N401FF)	N401EE	N406CW
RK-7	400A	VR-COG	N416RP	N631RP	(N631RR)	N401AB	N9PW	
RK-8	400A	N440DS						
RK-9	400A	N8152H	N315R					
RK-10	400A	N2842B	(D-CLSG)	D-CEIS				
RK-11	400A	N2843B	N5680Z	I-ALSU	w/o 27Nov91 Parma, Italy; remains to Dodson Avn, Ottawa, KS - parts used to rebuild RJ-23 (N3123T) q.v.			
RK-12	T-1A	T-1A Jayhawk c/n TT-1; for USAF						
RK-13	400A	N56BE						
RK-14	400A	N28..B	N81709	(F-GKCJ)	F-GLYO	(N414RK)	N81TJ	
RK-15	T-1A	T-1A Jayhawk c/n TT-2; for USAF						
RK-16	400A	N8163G	N71FE	N46FE	N416CW			
RK-17	400A	N505EB	N877S	N877Z	N417CW			
RK-18	400A	N5598Q	N717DD	N717DW	N418CW			
RK-19	400A	N1901W	N11GE	(N8ME)	N41ME	N419CW		
RK-20	400A	N82628	I-UNSA	N82628	N870P	N703LP		
RK-21	400A	(N401TC)	N1904W	N1881W	N717VL	N717VA	N1920	
RK-22	400A	N56616	N51ML	N85CR	N422CW			
RK-23	400A	N107BJ	N200BL	N960AJ*				
RK-24	400A	N8073R						
RK-25	400A	N81918	(VR-CDA)	D-CLBA				
RK-26	400A	N8097V	VH-BBJ	VH-IMP	N700GB	N8097V	N80DX	
RK-27	400A	N10FL	N10FQ					
RK-28	400A	N42SK	N411SK	PT-WLM	(N902PC)	N400NS		
RK-29	400A	I-IPIZ	N15693	I-IPIZ				
RK-30	400A	N205R	N430CW*					
RK-31	400A	N10J	N10JX	N431CW				
RK-32	400A	N999GP	N998GP	N553PF	N432CW			
RK-33	400A	N1878C	N60B	N197PF	N197BE			
RK-34	400A	N400A	N700GM	N74VF	N232BJ	N511JP	N511JF	N721SS
RK-35	400A	N81661	VH-BJD	VH-LAW	VH-BJD	VH-LAW	VH-BJD	N435CW
RK-36	400A	XA-RZG	N56327	N57B				
RK-37	400A	(F-GLPD)	N8014Q	(F-GLOR)	SE-DRS			
RK-38	400A	N5685X	N522EE					
RK-39	400A	N400Q	N34VP	N70BJ				
RK-40	400A	N8252J	N496EE	N440CW				
RK-41	400A	N8265Y	I-FSJA	N920SA	N546BZ			
RK-42	400A	N8253Y	N442CW					
RK-43	400A	N56400	N45RK					
RK-44	400A	N8249Y	N404VP	N908R				
RK-45	400A	N56423	N490TN	(N8051H)	N445E	(N600CC)	N445CC	
RK-46	400A	N8239E						
RK-47	400A	N8053V	N400FT	N408PC				
RK-48	400A	N8060V	N94HT	N48SE				
RK-49	400A	N8060Y	N54HP	N54HD				
RK-50	400A	N80KM	N750AB					
RK-51	400A	N8085T						
RK-52	400A	N709JB	(N709EW)	N709EL				
RK-53	400A	N62KM	N200GP					
RK-54	400A	N80938	PT-WHG					
RK-55	400A	N400Q						
RK-56	400A	N89KM	N456CW					
RK-57	400A	N8157H	ZS-NZO					
RK-58	400A	N56356	(PT-)	N56356	PT-WHC			
RK-59	400A	N80544	N50KH					
RK-60	400A	N8260L	(N794SM)	N61SM				
RK-61	400A	N82378	G-RAHL	N461CW				
RK-62	400A	N8083N	N462CW					
RK-63	400A	N2792B	N82412	PT-JQM				
RK-64	400A	N8164M	N53MS					
RK-65	400A	N39HF	(N97TT)	(N81TT)				
RK-66	400A	N400A	(N400DT)	N400Y	HB-VLM			
RK-67	400A	N8167Y						
RK-68	400A	N8280J	N295FA					
RK-69	400A	N8169Q	N877S	N877J				
RK-70	400A	C-FOPC	N750T	N73HM				
RK-71	400A	N82497	I-IFPC	N777ND	N73BL	N402GS*		
RK-72	400A	N8210W	N709JB	(N72BJ)	N910SH	N428WE		
RK-73	400A	N8070Q	PT-WHB					
RK-74	400A	N8146J	N26JP					
RK-75	400A	(N275PC)	N82400					
RK-76	400A	N8166A	N261JP					
RK-77	400A	N8277Y	PT-WHD					

BEECHJET

C/n	Series	Identities			
RK-78	400A	N8278Z	N611PA		
RK-79	400A	N8279G	(N30SF)	OH-RIF	N8279G
RK-80	400A	N8180Q	AP-BEX		
RK-81	400A	N8167G	PT-WHE		
RK-82	400A	N8282E	PT-WHF		
RK-83	400A	N8283C	XA-SNP		
RK-84	400A	N8138M	D-CHSW		
RK-85	400A	N8299Y	N419MS	N419MB	
RK-86	400A	N1563V	N777GC		
RK-87	400A	N1567L	N702LP		
RK-88	400A	N1549W			
RK-89	400A	N1560G	N94HE		
RK-90	400A	N1570L	N165HB		
RK-91	400A	N1545N	N296FA		
RK-92	400A	N3240J	N555KK		
RK-93	400A	N3038V			
RK-94	400A	N3051S	HB-VLN	N585G	
RK-95	400A	N3114X	HS-UCM	N747RR	
RK-96	400A	N3196N			
RK-97	400A	N3197Q			
RK-98	400A	N3210X	N400A	N866BB	
RK-99	400A	N3199Q	N95FA		
RK-100	400A	N1570B	N400SH		
RK-101	400A	N3221T	ZS-JRO	N400FT	
RK-102	400A	N3232U			
RK-103	400A	D-CIGM	HB-VLW		
RK-104	400A	N3224X	LV-PLT	LV-WPE	
RK-105	400A	N3235U	(N8252J)		
RK-106	400A	N3246H	N1HS		
RK-107	400A	N3227X	N733MK		
RK-108	400A	N3218L			
RK-109	400A	N3269A			
RK-110	400A	N1090X	N400VP	(N400A)	
RK-111	400A	N42SK	N411SK		
RK-112	400A	N3272L			
RK-113	400A	N3263N	N400VG		
RK-114	400A	N1084D	N363K	N698PW	
RK-115	400A	N3265A			
RK-116	400A	N1116R			
RK-117	400A	N1117S	N97FB	N97FF	
RK-118	400A	N1118Y	LV-PMH	LV-WTP	
RK-119	400A	N1119C	N456JG		
RK-120	400A	N3261Y	TC-MDJ		
RK-121	400A	N1121Z	N419MS	N473JE	
RK-122	400A	N1102B	PT-WJS		
RK-123	400A	N1123Z	N110TG	N740TA	
RK-124	400A	N1124Z	TC-MSA		
RK-125	400A	N1105U	N400KP		
RK-126	400A	N3226B	N197SD		
RK-127	400A	N1127U	N696TR	N686TR	
RK-128	400A	N1108Y	N912SH		
RK-129	400A	N1129X	N129MC		
RK-130	400A	N1130B	TC-NEO		
RK-131	400A	N1083Z			
RK-132	400A	N1087Z	N106KC		
RK-133	400A	N1133T	VP-BMR	N133BP	
RK-134	400A	N1094D	N134BJ		
RK-135	400A	N135BJ			
RK-136	400A	N1136Q	N780TP		
RK-137	400A	N1117Z	N400AJ		
RK-138	400A	N40PL	N48PL		
RK-139	400A	N1099S	VH-PNL		
RK-140	400A	N1094N	ZS-OCG		
RK-141	400A	N1027S	N974JD		
RK-142	400A	N142BJ	(N223DK)	YV-	
RK-143	400A	N191NC			
RK-144	400A	N134CM			
RK-145	400A	N745TA			
RK-146	400A	N146TA	N746TA		
RK-147	400A	N147BJ			
RK-148	400A	N1108T	TC-SMB		
RK-149	400A	N149TA	N749TA		
RK-150	400A	N1135U	N100AG	N100AW	
RK-151	400A	N1126V	PT-MAC		
RK-152	400A	N2252Q	N97FB		
RK-153	400A	N153BJ	N500HY		
RK-154	400A	N2354B	VH-BJC		
RK-155	400A	N2355T	N627RP	N631RP	

BEECHJET

C/n	Series	Identities			
RK-156	400A	N2056E	N400PU		
RK-157	400A	N397AT	N897AT	ZS-ONP	
RK-158	400A	N2358X	PT-MPL		
RK-159	400A	N2159P	N3337J		
RK-160	400A	N2360F	N54HP		
RK-161	400A	N761TA			
RK-162	400A	N2362G	ZS-PDB		
RK-163	400A	N2363A	XA-JET		
RK-164	400A	N2164Z	TC-MDB		
RK-165	400A	N2225Y	N224MC		
RK-166	400A	N2299T	N975CM		
RK-167	400A	N2267B	N711EC		
RK-168	400A	N2168G	N768TA		
RK-169	400A	N2329N	N757WS		
RK-170	400A	N2289B	TC-MCX	TC-MSB	
RK-171	400A	N2201J	PT-WUF*		
RK-172	400A	N2272K			
RK-173	400A	N2273Z			
RK-174	400A	N2204J			
RK-175	400A	N175BJ			
RK-176	400A	N476BJ			
RK-177	400A	N2277G			
RK-178	400A	N708TA			
RK-179	400A	N2279K	N75GF	N75GK	
RK-180	400A	N709TA			
RK-181	400A	N2235V			
RK-182	400A	N2322B	N234DK		
RK-183	400A	N710TA			
RK-184	400A	N2314F	N141DR		
RK-185	400A	N2298L	N140GB		
RK-186	400A	N712TA			
RK-187	400A	N2298S	N400TE		
RK-188	400A	N2298W	TC-VIN		
RK-189	400A	N715TA			
RK-190	400A	N2290F	TC-YRT		
RK-191	400A	N2291T	N960JJ	N960JA	
RK-192	400A	N492BJ	N272BC		
RK-193	400A	N13US	N914SH		
RK-194	400A	N194BJ	N909ST		
RK-195	400A	N718TA			
RK-196	400A	N2283T	XA-MEX		
RK-197	400A	N3197A	N214WM		
RK-198	400A	N798TA			
RK-199	400A	N739TA	N446M		
RK-200	400A	N200NA	VP-CKK		
RK-201	400A	N741TA			
RK-202	400A	N742TA			
RK-203	400A	N2359W	B-3989		
RK-204	400A	N2357K	I-ASER		
RK-205	400A	N3030D	N143HM		
RK-206	400A	N3014R	N30046	N982AR	
RK-207	400A	N3015F	N717DD		
RK-208	400A	N3101B	N890BH		
RK-209	400A	N799TA			
RK-210	400A	N111CX			
RK-211	400A	N3028U	TC-NNK		
RK-212	400A	N3029F	N299AW		
RK-213	400A	N3033A	N175PS*		
RK-214	400A	N79EL			
RK-215	400A	N3038W	N515WA		
RK-216	400A	N3050P	N213BK		
RK-217	400A	N217MB			
RK-218	400A	N3068M	N48MF		
RK-219	400A	N3059H	N511JP		
RK-220	400A	N220BJ	N799SM		
RK-221	400A	N221BJ	N18BR		
RK-222	400A	N748TA			
RK-223	400A	N3223R	N777FL		
RK-224	400A	N3224N	N51NP		
RK-225	400A	N751TA			
RK-226	400A	N3226Q	N59BR	N59BP	N750TA*
RK-227	400A	N3197K	N362KM		
RK-228	400A	N3228V	N12WF		
RK-229	400A	N3129X	N515TJ		
RK-230	400A	N753TA			
RK-231	400A	N781TP			
RK-232	400A	N2355N	N674SF		
RK-233	400A	N2293V	N233MW		

BEECHJET

C/n	Series	Identities		
RK-234	400A	N783TA		
RK-235	400A	N695BK		
RK-236	400A	N2349V	N11WF	
RK-237	400A	N784TA		
RK-238	400A	N23525		
RK-239	400A	N785TA		
RK-240	400A	N3240J		
RK-241	400A	N3241Q	N993H	
RK-242	400A	N2322B		
RK-243	400A	N782TP		
RK-244	400A	N428HR	N793TA	
RK-245	400A	N3199Z	N744TA	
RK-246	400A	N500TH		
RK-247	400A	N40252	N20FL	
RK-248	400A	N786TA		
RK-249	400A	N4249K	N611WM	
RK-250	400A	N2293V	N250HP	
RK-251	400A	N3106Y	N705LP	
RK-252	400A	N790TA		
RK-253	400A	N4053T		
RK-254	400A	N3254P	TC-BYD	
RK-255	400A	N988JG	N3255B	N960JJ
RK-256	400A	N3079S	N397AT	
RK-257	400A	N739TA		
RK-258	400A	N40215		
RK-259	400A	N3259Z		
RK-260	400A	N787TA		
RK-261	400A	N3261A	N51B	
RK-262	400A	N300GB		
RK-263	400A	N724MH	N724KW	
RK-264	400A	N792TA		
RK-265	400A	N797TA		
RK-266	400A	N3166Q	N41283	N10FL
RK-267	400A	N4467X		
RK-268	400A	N789TA		
RK-269	400A	N400MV		
RK-270	400A	N3231H		
RK-271	400A	N743TA		
RK-272	400A	N3237H	N701CP*	
RK-273	400A	N731TA		
RK-274	400A	N735TA		
RK-275	400A	N4275K		
RK-276	400A	N775TA		
RK-277	400A			
RK-278	400A	N4378P		
RK-279	400A	N773TA		
RK-280	400A			
RK-281	400A			
RK-282	400A			
RK-283	400A			
RK-284	400A			
RK-285	400A			
RK-286	400A			
RK-287	400A			
RK-288	400A			
RK-289	400A			
RK-290	400A			
RK-291	400A			
RK-292	400A			
RK-293	400A			
RK-294	400A			
RK-295	400A			
RK-296	400A			
RK-297	400A			
RK-298	400A			
RK-299	400A			
RK-300	400A			
RK-301	400A			
RK-302	400A			
RK-303	400A			
RK-304	400A			
RK-305	400A			
RK-306	400A			
RK-307	400A			
RK-308	400A			
RK-309	400A			
RK-310	400A			
RK-311	400A			

C/n	Series	Identities
RK-312	400A	
RK-313	400A	
RK-314	400A	
RK-315	400A	
RK-316	400A	
RK-317	400A	
RK-318	400A	
RK-319	400A	
RK-320	400A	
RK-321	400A	
RK-322	400A	
RK-323	400A	
RK-324	400A	
RK-325	400A	
RK-326	400A	
RK-327	400A	
RK-328	400A	
RK-329	400A	
RK-330	400A	

T-1A JAYHAWK

C/n	Identities			
TT-1 (RK-12)	N2886B	to be 91-0077		
TT-2 (RK-15)	N2887B	90-0412	N2887B	90-0412
TT-3	N2892B	90-0400		
TT-4	90-0405			
TT-5	N2876B	89-0284		
TT-6	N2872B	90-0404		
TT-7	N2896B	90-0401		
TT-8	N2868B	90-0402		
TT-9	90-0403			
TT-10	90-0407			
TT-11	90-0406			
TT-12	90-0408			
TT-13	90-0409			
TT-14	90-0410			
TT-15	90-0411			
TT-16	90-0413			
TT-17	91-0076			
TT-18	91-0075			
TT-19	91-0078			
TT-20	91-0079			
TT-21	91-0080			
TT-22	91-0081			
TT-23	91-0082			
TT-24	91-0083			
TT-25	91-0084			
TT-26	91-0085			
TT-27	91-0086			
TT-28	91-0087			
TT-29	91-0088			
TT-30	91-0089			
TT-31	91-0090			
TT-32	91-0091			
TT-33	91-0092			
TT-34	91-0093			
TT-35	91-0094			
TT-36	91-0095			
TT-37	91-0096			
TT-38	91-0097			
TT-39	91-0098			
TT-40	91-0099			
TT-41	91-0100			
TT-42	91-0101			
TT-43	91-0102			
TT-44	92-0330			
TT-45	92-0331			
TT-46	92-0332			
TT-47	92-0333			
TT-48	92-0334			
TT-49	92-0335			
TT-50	92-0336			
TT-51	92-0337			
TT-52	92-0338			
TT-53	92-0339			
TT-54	92-0340			
TT-55	92-0341			
TT-56	92-0342			
TT-57	92-0343			
TT-58	92-0344			
TT-59	92-0345			
TT-60	92-0346			
TT-61	92-0347	wears code 470G		
TT-62	92-0348			
TT-63	92-0349			
TT-64	92-0350			
TT-65	92-0351			
TT-66	92-0352			
TT-67	92-0353			
TT-68	92-0354			
TT-69	92-0355			
TT-70	92-0356			
TT-71	92-0357			
TT-72	92-0358			
TT-73	92-0359			
TT-74	92-0360			
TT-75	92-0361			
TT-76	92-0362			
TT-77	92-0363			
TT-78	93-0621			

JAYHAWK

C/n	Identities	
TT-79	93-0622	
TT-80	93-0623	
TT-81	93-0624	wears code 86FTS
TT-82	93-0625	N2830B
TT-83	93-0626	
TT-84	93-0627	
TT-85	93-0628	
TT-86	93-0629	
TT-87	93-0630	
TT-88	93-0631	
TT-89	93-0632	
TT-90	93-0633	
TT-91	93-0634	
TT-92	93-0635	
TT-93	93-0636	
TT-94	93-0637	
TT-95	93-0638	wears code 92FTS
TT-96	93-0639	
TT-97	93-0640	
TT-98	93-0641	
TT-99	93-0642	
TT-100	93-0643	
TT-101	93-0644	
TT-102	93-0645	
TT-103	93-0646	
TT-104	93-0647	
TT-105	93-0648	
TT-106	93-0649	
TT-107	93-0650	
TT-108	93-0651	
TT-109	93-0652	
TT-110	93-0653	
TT-111	93-0654	
TT-112	93-0655	
TT-113	93-0656	
TT-114	94-0114	
TT-115	94-0115	
TT-116	94-0116	
TT-117	94-0117	
TT-118	94-0118	
TT-119	94-0119	
TT-120	94-0120	
TT-121	94-0121	
TT-122	94-0122	
TT-123	94-0123	
TT-124	94-0124	
TT-125	94-0125	
TT-126	94-0126	
TT-127	94-0127	
TT-128	94-0128	
TT-129	94-0129	
TT-130	94-0130	
TT-131	94-0131	
TT-132	94-0132	
TT-133	94-0133	
TT-134	94-0134	
TT-135	94-0135	
TT-136	94-0136	
TT-137	94-0137	
TT-138	94-0138	
TT-139	94-0139	
TT-140	94-0140	
TT-141	94-0141	
TT-142	94-0142	
TT-143	94-0143	
TT-144	94-0144	
TT-145	94-0145	
TT-146	94-0146	
TT-147	94-0147	
TT-148	94-0148	
TT-149	95-0040	
TT-150	95-0041	
TT-151	95-0042	
TT-152	95-0043	
TT-153	95-0044	
TT-154	95-0045	
TT-155	95-0046	
TT-156	95-0047	

JAYHAWK

C/n	Identities	
TT-157	95-0048	
TT-158	95-0049	
TT-159	95-0050	
TT-160	95-0051	
TT-161	95-0052	
TT-162	95-0053	
TT-163	95-0054	
TT-164	95-0055	
TT-165	95-0056	
TT-166	95-0057	
TT-167	95-0058	
TT-168	95-0059	
TT-169	95-0060	
TT-170	95-0061	
TT-171	95-0062	
TT-172	95-0063	
TT-173	95-0064	
TT-174	95-0065	
TT-175	95-0066	
TT-176	95-0067	
TT-177	95-0068	
TT-178	95-0069	
TT-179	95-0070	
TT-180	95-0071	wears code 71-FTW

JAYHAWK

C/n	Identities			
TX-1	N82884	Japan 41-5051	code 051	
TX-2	N82885	Japan 41-5052	code 052	
TX-3	N82886	Japan 41-5053	code 053	
TX-4	N3195K	Japan 41-5054	code 054	
TX-5	N3195Q	Japan 41-5055	code 055	
TX-6	N3195X	Japan 51-5056	code 056	
TX-7	N3228M	Japan 51-5057	code 057	
TX-8	N3228V	Japan 51-5058	code 058	
TX-9	N1069L	Japan 71-5059	code 059	
TX-10	N3221Z+	N32212	Japan 91-5060	code 060
	+entered into USCAR in error by FAA and painted on aircraft - there marks were current on Piper PA-22 (c/n 22-7162) at the time			
TX-11		for Japan Self Defence Force		
TX-12		for Japan Self Defence Force		
TX-13		for Japan Self Defence Force		
TX-14		for Japan Self Defence Force		
TX-15		for Japan Self Defence Force		
TX-16		for Japan Self Defence Force		
TX-17		for Japan Self Defence Force		
TX-18		for Japan Self Defence Force		
TX-19		for Japan Self Defence Force		
TX-20		for Japan Self Defence Force		

BOMBARDIER CONTINENTAL

Bombardier launched its new midsize, 8-seat Continental at the 1998 NBAA Convention in Las Vegas. The aircraft will compete with the Citation X, Falcon 50 EX, Galaxy and Hawker Horizon. 54 orders have been reported including one for the United Arab Emirates and one in Germany.

BOMBARDIER BD700 GLOBAL EXPRESS

The Global Express received its FAA type certification on 13Nov98.

C/n	Identities				
9001	C-FBGX	rolled out 26Aug96,	ff 13Oct96		
9002	C-FHGX				
9003	C-FJGX				
9004	C-FKGX				
9005	C-GEGX	(VP-CPC)	N700HX		
9006	C-GCGY	N1TM			
9007	C-GCRW	Malaysia M48-01		C-GCRW	Malaysia M48-01
9008	C-GDBG	N9008	(N90005)		
9009	C-GDGO	N816SR	N816SQ		
9010	C-GDGQ	N701WH			
9011	C-GDGW	N700KJ			
9012	C-GDGY	N70PS			
9013	C-GDXU	HB-IUR			
9014	C-GDXV	N700GX	C-FGGX	N700GX	
9015	C-GDXX	N700KS			
9016	C-GEIM	N700AH	N16GX		
9017	C-GEIR	VP-BDD			
9018	C-GEVO				
9019	C-GEVU	N600CC	HL7576		
9020	C-GEVV	N700GK			
9021	C-GEYY	N8VB			
9022	C-GEYZ	N700HG	N622AB^		
9023	C-GEZD	N324SM			
9024	C-GEZF	N700BH			
9025	C-GEZJ				
9026	C-GEWV				
9027	C-GEZX				
9028	C-GEZY				
9029	C-GEZZ				
9030	C-GFAD				
9031	C-GFAE	N700VN			
9032	C-GFAK	N700HE			
9033	C-GFAN				
9034	C-GFAP	N700HF			
9035	C-GFAQ	(D-AFLW)	N817LS		
9036	C-GFAT	N777GX			
9037	C-GFJQ	N777SW			
9038	C-GFJR				
9039	C-GFJS	N700GT			
9040	C-GFJT	N22BH			
9041	C-GFKT	N195WM			
9042	C-GFKV	N700WL			
9043	C-GFKW	N700BU			
9044	C-GFKX	N700BP			
9045	C-GFKY				
9046	C-GFLS	N700BV			
9047	C-GFLU				
9048	C-GFLW	N700BY			
9049	C-GFLX	N471DG			
9050	C-GFLZ				
9051	C-GFWI	N			
9052	C-GFWP				
9053	C-GFWX				
9054	C-GFWY				
9055	C-GFWZ				
9056	C-GCGY	N			
9057	C-GGIR				

BD700 GLOBAL EXPRESS

C/n	Identities
9058	C-GGJA
9059	C-GGJF
9060	C-GGJH
9061	C-GGJJ
9062	C-GGJR
9063	C-GGJS
9064	C-GGJU
9065	C-GGKA
9066	C-GGKC
9067	
9068	
9069	
9070	
9071	
9072	
9073	
9074	
9075	
9076	
9077	
9078	
9079	
9080	
9081	
9082	
9083	
9084	
9085	
9086	
9087	
9088	
9089	
9090	
9091	
9092	
9093	
9094	
9095	
9096	
9097	
9098	
9099	
9100	
9101	
9102	
9103	
9104	
9105	
9106	
9107	
9108	
9109	
9110	
9111	
9112	
9113	
9114	
9115	
9116	
9117	
9118	
9119	
9120	

CANADAIR CL600 CHALLENGER

C/n	Series	Identities									
1001		C-GCGR-X	ff 08Nov78 w/o 03Apr80 Mojave, CA, flight testing								
1002	S	C-GCGS-X	Canada 144612 coded "X"			displayed Heritage Park, Air Command HQ, Winnipeg, Canada					
1003/3991	S	C-GCGT-X	C-GCGT								
1004	S	C-GXKQ	N2677S	N227CC	N600BP	N640TS	N50PA				
1005	S	C-GBDH	N600CL	C-GBCC	N444WA	D-BJET	N600CL	N605TS	N180CH^		
1006	S	C-GCSN	N110KS	HZ-A04	C-GCSN	Canada 144603					
1007	S	C-GBKC	HZ-TAG	C-GBKC	Canada 144604						
1008	S	C-GBEY	(D-BBAD)	Canada 144605							
1009	S	C-GBFY	N606CL	C-GCVQ	Canada 144606						
1010	S	C-GCIB	N909MG	N802Q							
1011	S	C-GBHS	N42137	N510PC	N510PS	N601JR	N678ML	N116RA			
1012	S	C-GBKE	N600KC	(N78499)	N750PM	N750BM	N121VA	N8KG			
1013	S	C-GBHZ	N2428	N601SA	N129BA	N72SR					
1014	S	C-GBLL-X	N97941	HZ-TAG	C-GBLL	Canada 144607					
1015	S	C-GBLN	N37LB	N604CL	C-GBLN	Canada 144608					
1016	S	C-GWRT	EI-GPA	VR-BKJ	N757MC	N16TS	N920RV				
1017	S	C-GBPX	N4247C	N777XX	C-GBPX	Canada 144609					
1018	S	C-GLWR	N1812C	N198CC	N375PK	N875PK	N771WW				
1019	S	C-GLWT	N9071M	N603CL	N600FF	ZS-NER	3B-GFI				
1020	S	C-GLWV	N36LB	N602CL	N600MG	N600PD					
1021	S	C-GLWX	N914X	N914XA	N63HJ						
1022	S	C-GLWZ	C-GOGO	Canada 144610							
1023	S	C-GLXB	N630M	N680M	N90UC	(N610TS)	N920DS				
1024	S	C-GLXD	N637ML	N567ML	N326MM	N810MT	N811MT				
1025	S	C-GLXF	N2636N	N111G	N111J	HB-ILH	N888LW	N620SB			
1026	S	C-GLXH	N507CC	N507HC	N507WY*						
1027	S	C-GLXK	N420L	N420TX	(N456CG)	N678CG					
1028	S	C-GLXM	HB-VHC	N600ST	5B-CHX	N600BZ	YV-1111CP				
1029	S	C-GLXO	HB-VGA	D-BMTM	(N205A)	OH-WIH					
1030	S	C-GLXQ	N1622	N604CL	C-GCZU	Canada 144611					
1031	S	C-GLXS	N620S								
1032	S	C-GLXU	N455SR	N200CN	N11AZ	(N31DC)	N1884				
1033	S	C-GLXW	N2642F	VR-CKK	N600YY	N101SK	N101ST	N357RT			
1034		C-GLXY	N2634Y	N153SR	(N151SR)	N209WF	(N209WE)	N481JT	LV-YLB		
1035	S	C-GLYA	N122TY	N122WF	N64FC	C-FEAQ	(EI-BYD)	VR-BLD	N700CL		
1036	S	C-GLYC	C-GBOQ	N80AT	N88AT	N66MF	N900DP				
1037		C-GLYE	N805C	w/o 03Jan83 Sun Valley Friedman Memorial, ID							
1038	S	C-GLYH	N8010X	N1045X	N65HJ						
1039	S	C-GLYK	N26640	N1868M	N1868S	N722HP	damaged 02Feb98 Opa Locka, FL				
1040	S	C-GLYM	Canada 144601								
1041	S	C-GLYO	N733K	N733CF	N193DQ	(N95DQ)	N141TS				
1042	S	C-GLWV	N770CA	N999SR	N999TF						
1043	S	C-GLWX	N229GC	C-GJPG	C-FSXG	N43NW	N100QR				
1044	S	C-GLWZ	N541MM	N205MM	N55AR	N800BT					
1045	S	C-GLXB	N55PG	N900FC	C-GBKB						
1046		C-GLXD	C-GTXV	N46SR	N246JL						
1047	S	C-GLXH	C-GBSZ	N2741Q	N601WW	N818LS	N555WD	N556WD	(N500EX)	N315MK	
1048	S	C-GLXK	N29687	N600TT	N500LS	N600LS	N601LS	(EI-BXN)	C-FSIP	C-GDDR	
1049	S	C-GLXM	N2720B	HB-VFW	N491DB	N491TS	N39RE				
1050	S	C-GLXO	N600MK	N82CW	N82CN						
1051	S	C-GLXQ	N27341	N20CX	(N601CR)	N601SR	N91UC	N27BH			
1052	S	C-GLXS	N3330M	N3330L	N110M	N110TD	N409KC	N600LG			
1053	S	C-GLYA	HB-VHO	N4424P	N32BC	N32BQ	N397BE				
1054	S	C-GLYC	N80TF	N7008	N9008	VR-CLI	N602AS				
1055		C-GLYE	N2707T	N1FE	N55SR	N271MB	N643CR				
1056	S	C-GLYH	N26895	N600CC	N600TE						
1057	S	C-GLXU	C-GBTK	N605CL	(VH-OZZ)	N508CC	N508HC	XA-RAP	XA-TIV	XA-ISR	N78SR
1058	S	C-GLXW	N4000X	N60HJ							
1059	S	C-GLXY	N227G	N227GL	(C-FRST)	(C-GFCD)	N3HB				
1060	S	C-GLYK	N29984	N22AZ	N74JA						
1061	S	C-GLYO	N600JW	VH-MXX	VH-MCG	N770JC					
1062	S	C-GLWV	C-GBTT	Malaysia M31-01		N4FE	N62BL	N68SD			
1063	S	C-GLWX	N31240+	N102ML	PT-LXW	N102ML	XA-SOA	N8260D	(N74TJ)	(N711AJ)	(N88TJ)
		(N98TW)	N409CC	N457HL							
		+Recorded for a while in error on FAA files as N32140									
1064	S	C-GLWZ	C-GBUB	Malaysia M31-02		N14FE	N64GL	N75B	N100LR		
1065	S	C-GLXB	C-GBVE	Canada 144602							
1066	S	C-GLXD	N67B	N721SW	N701QS	N701GA	N51TJ	D-BSNA			
1067	S	C-GLXH	VR-CBP+	C-GLXH	C-GBZE	N50928	N800AB	N205EL	N240AK		
		+Marks allocated by Cayman CAA and painted on aircraft but never officially registered nor flown with these marks									
1068	S	C-GLXK	N215RL	N938WH	N160LC						
1069	S	C-GLXM	N203G	N816PD	I-LPHZ	N74LM	(N100LR)	N500RH	N788WG	N818TH	(N818E)
		N455BE									
1070	S	C-GLXO	N3237S	HZ-MF1	N70DJ	N24JK	N670CL	D-BUSY			

CL600 CHALLENGER

C/n	Series	Identities									
1071	S	C-GLXQ	N607CL	N523B	N588UC	N121DF	N127DF	N671SR	N711DB	N220LC	
1072	S	C-GLXW	N82A	(N137FP)	N331FP	N125AC	N10PN				
1073	S	C-GLXY	N234RG	N234MW	N31WT	(N331WT)	N661JB	N888KS	VH-NKS	N600BP	(VR-BBP)
		(N512AC)	N125AN	(N600EC)	N673TS						
1074		C-GLYK	N317FE	N1FE	N10FE	HZ-SAA	HZ-WT2	HZ-WBT1	HZ-RFM		
1075		C-GLXO	N600CP	N2FE	N25SR	N751DB					
1076	S	C-GLXK	N8000	N7SP	I-BLSM	N601WW					
1077	S	C-GLXM	N994TA	(N778XX)	C-GBZK	N152SM	N71M	N500R			
1078	S	C-GLYO	N600DL	N600CF	I-MRDV	N53SR	N1500				
1079	S	C-GLWV	N46ES	N125N	N601Z	N888FW	N600RE	N601SA			
1080	S	C-GLWX	N800CC	N3JL							
1081	S	C-GLWZ	N19HF	(N54PA)	(N681TS)	N456DK					
1082	S	C-GLXB	N3854B	N600ST	I-PTCT	N700KK	N777KK				
1083	S	C-GLXD	N47ES	N471SP	N471SB	N399FL					
1084	S	C-GLXH	N730TL	(N10MZ)	N175ST	N550CW					
1085	S	C-GLXQ	N20G	N20GX	N600ST	OE-HET					
1086		marks C-GLXS reserved 29Mar83 but aircraft not built									

Production complete

CANADAIR CL601 CHALLENGER

C/n	Identities								
3001	C-GBUU-X	ff 17Sep82	N601CL	N601AG	N789DR	N74GR			
3002	C-GBXH	(N509PC)	N4449F	N273G	N601SR	N750GT	N602CW*		
3003	C-GLXU	N500PC	N500TB	N500TD	C-GESR				
3004	C-GLXK	N509PC	N967L	N501PC	N45PH				
3005	C-FAAL	N601TX							
3006	C-GLXY	N372G	(N3728)	HB-IKX	N372G	(EI-TAM)	P4-TAM	N606BA	ZS-ONL
3007	C-GLYE	N711SR	N711SX						
3008	C-GLYK	N733A	N783A	N61AF	(N999SW)	N38SW	N608CW		
3009	C-GLYO	N373G	N873G	N651AC*					
3010	C-GLWV	C-GBLX	N80CS	N601UT	N601SQ	N601BD			
3011	C-GLWX	C-GBYC	N601AG	N399WW	N899WW	N700MK	N7788	N205EL	N205EE
3012	C-GLXB	N226GL	N226G	C-GMII	VR-BMA	N6165C	XA-SHZ	N603GJ	N23BJ
3013	C-GLXD	N601TG	VR-BLA	VP-BLA	N124BC	N633CW			
3014	C-GLXH	N14PN	N292GA						
3015	C-GLXM	N374G	XA-KIM						
3016	C-GLWV	N4562Q	N1107Z	N601CL	VP-BIE				
3017	C-GLWX	N778XX	(HZ-AMA)	HZ-SFS	N778YY	VR-CAR	C-GJPG		
3018	C-GLWZ	C-GBXW	N779XX	w/o 07Feb85 Milan, Italy; cx May91					
3019	C-GLXB	N375G	N875G						
3020	C-GLXO	C-GCFI							
3021	C-GLXQ	N5069P	(N711SP)	N711SJ	N967L	N503PC	N966L	N150MH	
3022	C-GLXS	C-GCFG							
3023	C-GLXY	N778YY	N100WC	N967L	N501PC	N524PC	N601KF		
3024	C-GLYA	N711ST	HB-ILM	N98CR	N93CR	N888AZ			
3025	C-GLWV	N1620	N529DM						
3026	C-GLWX	N5373U	N927A	N601GL	N300S	N80RP	N716HP		
3027	C-GLWZ	N5402X	N17CN	(N401NK)	N627CW				
3028	C-GLXB	C-FBEL							
3029	C-GLXD	N5491V	N1824T	N629TS					
3030	C-GLXH	N611CL	N34CD	N39CD					
3031	C-GLXK	C-GCTB	N607CL	C-GCTB	Germany 1201				
3032	C-GLXM	N779YY	HZ-AK1	N7011H	N111G	N111GX	N392FV		
3033	C-GLXQ	N601TJ	HB-ILK						
3034	C-GLXU	N374BC	N372BC	N372BG	N372PG	N120MP	C-GSAP		
3035	C-GLXW	C-GCUN	Canada 144613		w/o 24Apr95 Shearwater AFB, Nova Scotia, Canada				
3036	C-GLXY	C-GCUP	Canada 144614						
3037	C-GLXB	C-GCUR	Canada 144615						
3038	C-GLYA	C-GCUT	Canada 144616						
3039	C-GLYH	C-GPGD	C-GPCC	N639CL	N500PG				
3040	C-GLYK	N608CL	Germany 1202						
3041	C-GLWV	C-GRBC	N610MS	N600MS	N169TA				
3042	C-GLWX	N613CL	N900CC	N333GJ					
3043	C-GLWZ	N609CL	Germany 1203						
3044	C-GLXD	N921K	N125N	N955DB					
3045	C-GLXH	N914BD	N914BB	N601RP	OE-HCL	N3045	N998JR	N601PR	
3046	C-GLXK	C-GDBX	B-4005	N601HJ	N601TJ	LX-AEN	N46SR		
3047	C-GLXM	C-GBZQ	B-4006	N602HJ	N602TJ	OE-HLE			
3048	C-GLXO	N35FP	N601JM	N628WC^					

CL601 CHALLENGER

C/n	Identities									
3049	C-GLXQ	N610CL	C-FQYT	Germany 1204						
3050	C-GLXS	(N9680N)	N9680Z	N62MS	N62MU	N95SR	N601AE			
3051	C-GLWR	N445AC	N60MS	N60MU	N4415D	N95SR	N651CW			
3052	C-GLWT	C-GDCQ	B-4007	N603HJ	(N601GF)	N801GC	VP-CRX			
3053	C-GLWV	N604CL	Germany 1205							
3054	C-GLWX	N605CL	VH-MZL	N54PR	N601PR	N601TP	N601ZT	N375PK	N315SL	N50TG
3055	C-GLWZ	N100HG	N608RP							
3056	C-GLXB	N612CL	Germany 1206							
3057	C-GLXD	N19J	9J-RON							
3058	C-GLXU	N125PS								
3059	C-GLXW	N614CL	Germany 1207							
3060	C-GLXY	(N601SN)	N601S							
3061	C-GLYO	N9708N	N999JR	N597FJ	N601AA					
3062	C-GLYK	N601HP	N601GT							
3063	C-GLYH	C-FURG								
3064	C-GLYC	N566N	N356N	N224N	N224F	(N224HF)	N224U	(N424JM)	N664CW	
3065	C-GLYA	N602CC	N1623	(N128PE)	N500PE	N601JP	(N603TS)+	N601JP		
		+ marks were painted on the aircraft								
3066	C-GLXQ	N609CL	N144SX	VR-CLE	VP-CLE	N105UP				

Production complete

MODEL 601-3A

C/n	Identities									
5001	C-GDDP	ff 28Sep86	N245TT	N245TL						
5002	C-GDEQ	N611CL	C-GDEQ	N611CL	N585UC	N43PR				
5003	C-GDHP	N778XX	HB-IKT							
5004	C-GDKO	N100KT	N180KT	N618DC	N504TS					
5005	C-GLWR	N613CL	N101PK	HB-IKU	N14GD					
5006	C-GLWT	C-FLPC	C-GENA	N506TS						
5007	C-GLWV	N60GG	N607CL	(N607CZ)	N17TE	N17TZ*				
5008	C-GLWX	N601CC	N601EG							
5009	C-GLWZ	N399SW	N699CW*							
5010	C-GLXB	N57HA	(N57HK)	N1812C						
5011	C-GLXD	N603CC	JA8283	N611MH	N602UK	VR-CIC	VP-CIC			
5012	C-GLXU	N107TB	N1868M	N500LR						
5013	C-GLXW	N711PD	I-CTPT	N604MC						
5014	C-GLXY	N21CX	N31WH	N311G	N311GX	N888DH				
5015	C-GLXH	N601KR	N200DE	N514RB*						
5016	C-GLXQ	N604CC	N49UR	N622AB	(N622AD)	N868CE				
5017	C-GLWX	N700KC								
5018	C-GLWV	N606CC	C-FBHX	9Q-CBS	C-FBHX	N601HH	N618DB	(D-AMTM)	N601GS	(N601DR)
	(N601GR)	N893AC								
5019	C-GLWT	N915BD	N915BB	(N247GA)	N237GA	N602BD				
5020	C-GLYA	C-FBKR	I-BEWW							
5021	C-GLYC	N64F	N122WF	N48FU	(N305M)					
5022	C-GLYK	N449ML								
5023	C-GLYO	N608CC	EI-LJG	N601CJ	N175ST	N623CW				
5024	C-GLYH	C-FCDF	B-4010	N604HJ	N601NB					
5025	C-GLWR	C-FCGS	B-4011	N605HJ	N1TK					
5026	C-GLWT	N601WM								
5027	C-GLWV	N244BH	N64BH	N421SZ	N420SZ					
5028	C-GLWX	N601TL	N601RL	(N601EA)						
5029	C-GLWZ	C-FDAT	N602CC	VR-BMK	N67MR	N83LC				
5030	C-GLXB	N312CT	N816SQ	N816SP						
5031	C-GLXD	N900CL	N908CL	N721MC						
5032	C-GLXF	N604CC	N667LC	N667CC	4X-COT	N601ER	N950SW			
5033	C-GLXH	VH-ASM	N32GG	N397J						
5034	C-GLXK	C-GIOH								
5035	C-GLXU	N606CC	N333MG							
5036	C-GLXW	N225N	N468KL							
5037	C-GLXY	N608CC	(JA8360)	N707GG	N353TC	N212LM				
5038	C-GLXQ	C-GBJA	(N602CN)	N1271A	N78RP	(N220LC)	N78PP	N91KH		
5039	C-GLWX	N811BB	N811BP	N811BR	N765WT					
5040	C-GLWV	N652CN	N807Z							
5041	C-GLWT	C-FETZ	G-FBMB	C-FTIE	N641CL	N352AF	N352AE			

CL601 CHALLENGER

C/n	Identities
5042	C-GLYA C-FEUV HB-IKS
5043	C-GLYC N779YY VR-COJ N601BH N601VH
5044	C-GLYK C-FFBY I-NNUS N901BM VR-CMC VP-CMC
5045	C-GLXS C-FFSO N616CC N500GS N601AF
5046	C-GLXW N6SG N818TH
5047	C-GLXD N140CH
5048	C-GLXY N2004G N716RD N907WS
5049	C-GLXF N721EW N721SW N721BW D-AGKG N628VK VR-CVK VP-CVK N888JA
5050	C-GLXK N826JP N831CJ N881CJ*
5051	C-GLXM N1903G N190GG N300KC N190SB C-GQBQ
5052	C-GLXO N4PG N652CW
5053	C-GLXU N5PG N553CW N653CW*
5054	C-GLXB N619FE N3FE
5055	C-GLXH N601HC N46F
5056	C-GLXQ N614CC N153NS
5057	was to have been first CL601S with c/n 6001 but built as 601-3A C-GLWR N900NM N830CB N830CD N733CF
5058	C-GLWZ N404SK N101SK N527JA
5059	C-GLWV XA-GEO XA-JFE
5060	C-GLYO N5060H N630M ZS-NKD
5061	C-GLYH C-FHHD 9Q-CBS N661CL (N575MA)
5062	C-GLWX N60FC N540W N548W N142B
5063	was to have been second CL601S with c/n 6002 but built as 601-3A, last Cartierville-built airframe C-GLXS N612CC N79AD N78AD N611JW N811JW N801FL (N315FX) N304FX
5064	first Dorval-built airframe C-GLXW C-FIOB VH-BRG N564TS N601EC
5065	C-GLXD N601BF N882C
5066	C-GLXY N506TN N100KT N3PC
5067	C-GLXF N603CC 9A-CRO 9A-CRT
5068	C-GLXK N609CC N88WG JA8361 N602WA D-AOHP N113WA C-FNNT
5069	C-GLXM C-FIGR I-FIPP VR-BNF N655CN N324B
5070	C-GLXO N980HC N780HC N305FX (D-AAFX) OY-CLD
5071	C-GLWT+ N500PC +shown in Canadian DoT files as C-FLWT; this is assumed to be an error
5072	C-GLYC N609K N88HA w/o 20Mar94 Bassett, NE; cx Apr95; remains to Executive Aircraft Corp, KS
5073	C-GLYK N60KR PK-HMK N5073 (VR-CKC) (N400KC)
5074	C-GLXH N23SB
5075	C-GLXU N65357 N810D VR-CCV PT-OSA N601Z N409KC
5076	C-GLXB N5TM
5077	C-GLXQ N1622 N64YP^
5078	C-GLWR N601MG N601MD N53DF
5079	C-GLWV C-FJDF VR-CCR VP-CCR
5080	C-GLYO C-FJGR N601DB N135BC
5081	C-GLYH+ N619CC HL7202 N601ST +also reported as C-GLXH
5082	C-GLWX C-GBJA N611NT N611GS N6BB
5083	C-GLYA N189K
5084	C-GLWT+ N399CF +also reported as C-GLWZ
5085	C-GLXD C-FJPI N618CC D-ACTU
5086	C-GLXS N353K N343K
5087	C-GLXW N601CC C-FLUT XA-RZD
5088	C-GLXH N601CD N601HC C-GPOT
5089	C-GLXY N968L N516SM^
5090	C-GLXF N601CB N404CB N818LS N818TH N400KC VP-CAM
5091	C-GLXM N915BD
5092	C-GLXQ+ C-FKIY HB-IKV N300CR +also reported as C-GLXO
5093	C-GLYA N302EC N601CH N875H
5094	C-GLWT C-FKNN TC-OVA TC-DHB
5095	C-GLYC N95FE N2FE
5096	C-GLYK C-FKTD HB-IKW C-GSQI
5097	C-GLXK C-FKVW XA-JJS XA-TLM
5098	C-GLXH N812GS N808G
5099	C-GLXU N509W N504M N801P N801R N601DW
5100	C-GLXB N510 N505M
5101	C-GLXQ N604CC N105BN
5102	C-GLWR C-FLYJ (HS-TDL) HS-TVA VR-CHK VP-CHK N604AC (N983CE) N494LC
5103	C-GLWV N76CS
5104	C-GLYO N777XX VR-COJ VR-CEG N145ST (N233SG) 9M-SWG N233SG (N604TS) N212CT
5105	C-GLYH C-FMVQ OK-BYA Czech Republic 5105
5106	C-GLWX (N601PR) N106PR N523JM
5107	C-GLWZ N417CL
5108	C-GLXD N428CL N224N
5109	C-GLXS N439CL N721S
5110	C-GLXU N392PT N308FX
5111	C-GLXH C-GBJA N46SG N4SG N502F
5112	C-GLXF N112NC N109NC
5113	C-GLXM N605CC N163M N163MR N733EY

C/n	Identities						
5114	C-GLYA	C-FOSK	VR-BOA	VP-BOA			
5115	C-GLYC	N25SB					
5116	C-GLXW	N841PC	N1904P				
5117	C-GLXY	N606CC	N80BF				
5118	C-GLXK	N824JK	N24JK				
5119	C-GLXO	VR-BNG	VP-BNG				
5120	C-GLWT	N400TB	(N500TB)				
5121	C-GLYK	N502PC					
5122	C-GLXS	N908CL	N7046J	N900CL			
5123	C-GLWR	N601UP					
5124	C-GLXD	C-FBOM					
5125	C-GLWZ	C-FPIY	HB-IKY	N512BC	N604WB		
5126	C-GLXU	N21CL	N21NY	N99UG			
5127	C-GLXB	N718P	N718R				
5128	C-GLWX	C-FPOX	XA-GME				
5129	C-GLXH	N129RH	(N603AF)	N129TF			
5130	C-GLXQ	N603KS	N601GB	VR-BQA	N601SR		
5131	C-GLWV	N602JB	N6JB				
5132	C-GLYO	N610DB	N289K				
5133	C-GLYH	N53DF	N121DF				
5134	C-GLXS	N43R	N43RK	N511WM	N511WN		

MODEL 601-3R

C/n	Identities							
5135	C-GLWR	N1902J	N1902P					
5136	C-GLXW	N51GY	N20G					
5137	C-GLWZ	N137CL	N90AR					
5138	C-GLXF	N138CC	N85					
5139	C-GLXK	N139CD	N34CD					
5140	C-GLXM	N1061D	N79AD					
5141	C-GLXO	N312AT	N601ER	N601TM				
5142	C-GLWT	C-FRGV	VR-CJJ	N330TP				
5143	C-GLYA	built as CL604 prototype with c/n 5991 (qv)						
5144	C-GLYC	N616CC	N347BA	N601CV*				
5145	C-GLYK	C-GPGD	C-GDPF					
5146	C-GLXW	C-FRQA	LX-MMB					
5147	C-GLWR	C-FRJX	XA-SOR					
5148	C-GLXD	N793CT						
5149	C-GLXY	N601GR	XA-GRB	N63ST				
5150	C-GLXU	N602CC	N601BW					
5151	C-GLXB	C-GBJA	VR-BWB	VP-BWB				
5152	C-GLWX	N777XX	VR-COJ	VP-COJ	N605BA	N18RF	(N933PG)	N388PG
5153	C-GLXH	N601EB	VR-CHA	N604BA	OY-APM			
5154	C-GLXQ	N602DP	9M-TAN	N154BA	4X-COY	N601VF		
5155	C-GLWV	N342TC						
5156	C-GLYO	C-FSXH	VR-BAA	N255CC	N601TP			
5157	C-GLYH	N512DG	N471SP	N800KC				
5158	C-GLXS	C-FSYK	XA-ZTA	XA-MKY	XA-MKI			
5159	C-GLWR	C-FTNN	EI-SXT					
5160	C-GLXW	N710HM	N94BA					
5161	C-GLWZ	N994CT						
5162	C-GLXF	C-FTNE	VR-BCC	VP-BCC	N850FL	N850FB		
5163	C-GLXK	N709JM	N980HC	N224F				
5164	C-GLXM	N715BG	N7008					
5165	C-GLXO	C-FTOH	VR-CPO	VP-CPO				
5166	C-GLWT	N618CC	9M-NSK	N601A	HB-IVS			
5167	C-GLYA	N151CC	N86					
5168	C-GLYC	C-GRPF						
5169	C-GLYK	N773A	N154NS					
5170	C-	N166A	N888WS					
5171	C-GLXW	N213MC						
5172	C-GLXD	N601FS	C-FUND					
5173	C-GLXY	N181JC						
5174	C-GLXU	N605CC	N477DM	N877DM	N47HR			
5175	C-GLXB	N601FR	N306FX					
5176	C-GLWX	N142LL	ZS-CCT	N600DR	N600DH	N779AZ		
5177	C-GLXH	N602MC	N757MC					
5178	C-GLXQ	(N602AN)	C-FWGE	CS-MAC				
5179	C-GLWV	(N604CC)	N608CC	N307FX				
5180	C-GLYO	N518CL						
5181	C-GLYH	N602D						
5182	C-FVZC	HL7577						
5183	C-GLWR	N601HF	N55HF					
5184	C-GLXW	N605RP	N607RP					
5185	C-	N611CC	N914X					

CL601 CHALLENGER

C/n	Identities				
5186	C-	N612CC	N9700X		
5187	C-GLXK	N601KJ			
5188	C-GLXM	N614CC	HS-JJA	N575CF	N10FE
5189	C-FXCK	PT-WLZ			
5190	C-GLWT	N190EK	N87		
5191	C-GLYA	N191BE	N605T		
5192	C-GLYC	N354TC			
5193	C-GLYK	N604D	VR-BCI	VP-BCI	
5194	C-FXIP	EI-MAS	N601R		

CL601 production complete, continues as CL604

Note: C/ns beginning 6001 were earmarked for the abortive CL601S programme

CANADAIR CL604 CHALLENGER

C/n	Identities				
5991	C-GLYA	ff 18Sep94	C-FTBZ	marks N604CC applied during 1994 NBAA Show at New Orleans, LA	C-FTBZ
5301	C-FVUC	N604CC	N608CC		
5302	C-GLXD	C-GBJA	N355CC	N255CC	
5303	C-GLXY	C-FXKE	HL7522	N604BD	
5304	C-GLXU	C-FXHE	I-MILK		
5305	C-GLXB	N604B	N747		
5306	C-GLWX	N309FX			
5307	C-GLXH	C-FXUQ	VR-BHA	VP-BHA	
5308	C-GLYO	N604KS	N604TS	N982J	
5309	C-GLYH	C-FXZS	VR-BAC	VP-BAC	
5310	C-GLXS	C-FCCP	C-GPGD	C-GPFC	
5311	C-GLWR	N225LY			
5312	C-GLXW	N604KC	N312AM		
5313	C-GLXD	N605KC	N312AT		
5314	C-GLWZ	N604CT			
5315	C-GLXF	N604LS	N818LS		
5316	C-GLXK	N604BB	N411BB	N1848U	N200UL*
5317	C-FYXC	D-AMIM			
5318	C-GLXO	C-FYYH	(TC-DHE)	HB-IKQ	HB-IVR
5319	C-GLWT	N604KR	N14R		
5320	C-GLXQ	N605CC	HZ-AFA2		
5321	C-GLYA	C-FZDY	PT-WXL		
5322	C-GLXY	N604CL	9A-CRO		
5323	C-GLXU	N604DS			
5324	C-GLXB	N601CC	N667LC		
5325	C-GLWX	N60CT	N331TH		
5326	C-GLYC	N908G	N1903G		
5327	C-GLYK	N609CC	HB-IKJ	D-AJAB	
5328	C-GLXH	N712DG	ZS-AVL		
5329	C-GLWV	N8MC	N1GC	N1QF	
5330	C-GLYO	N812G			
5331	C-GLYH	N810D			
5332	C-GLXS	C-FZRR	VP-BNF		
5333	C-GLWR	N603CC	N811BB	N600MS	N991TW
5334	C-GLXU	N604RC	N43R		
5335	C-GLXB	C-FZVN	VP-CAN	N8206S	N801P
5336	C-GLXW	N310FX			
5337	C-GLXD	N270RA	N990AK		
5338	C-GLWZ	N604PL	N913JB	N78RP	
5339	C-GLXF	C-GBJA	N604CU		
5340	C-GLXK	N606CC	N194WM		
5341	C-GLXM	C-GBJA			
5342	C-GLXO	N311FX			
5343	C-GLWT	C-GAUK	C-GHKY		
5344	C-GLXQ	N344BA			
5345	C-GLYA	N345BA			
5346	C-GLXS	N604JP	HZ-SJP3		
5347	C-GLXW	C-GBDK	PT-MKO	N747TS	
5348	C-GLWR	N881TW			
5349	C-GLXY	N312FX			
5350	C-GLXU	N331TP			
5351	C-GLXB	N374G	N372G		
5352	C-GLWX	C-GBKE	4X-COE		
5353	C-GLXH	C-GRIO			
5354	C-GLYC	N604PM			
5355	C-GLWV	N555WD			
5356	C-GLYO?	N605PM			
5357	C-GLYH	N604FS	XA-AST		
5358	C-GLXS	C-GBRQ	TC-DHE		
5359	C-GLWR	N497DM			
5360	C-GLXW	N606PM			
5361	C-GLXD	N346BA			
5362	C-GLWZ	N607PM			
5363	C-GLXF	N964H			
5364	C-GLXK	C-FBNS			
5365	C-GLXM	N604DC	N618DC		
5366	C-GLXO	N604DD	Denmark C-066		
5367	C-GCCZ	EI-TAM	VP-COJ		
5368	C-GLXQ	N368G	N374G		
5369	C-GCQB	(D-AZPP)	HB-IVP		
5370	C-GLXS	(N370CL)	N320CL		
5371	C-GLYK	N371CL			
5372	C-GLWR	N314FX			
5373	C-GCVZ	HB-ILL			
5374	C-GLXU	N98FJ	N97FJ		
5375	C-GLXB	N604HP	(D-ASTS)	XA-GRB	

CL604 CHALLENGER

C/n	Identities				
5376	C-GLXW	N604CR	N604CC		
5377	C-GLXH	N315FX			
5378	C-GLYC	C-GDBZ	D-ASTS		
5379	C-GLWV	N604CA	C-GQPA		
5380	C-GLYO	C-GDFA	N604DE	C-GEGM	Denmark C-080
5381	C-GLYH	N900ES			
5382	C-GLXS	N604HJ			
5383	C-GLYK	N383DT			
5384	C-GLXW	C-GDLH	HB-IVV		
5385	C-GLXD	N72NP			
5386	C-GLWZ	N315DG	N1DG		
5387	C-GLXF	N316FX			
5388	C-GLXK	C-GDVM	4X-CMY		
5389	C-GLXM	N604JE	D-AUKE		
5390	C-GLXO	N604KG	ZS-DGB	N541DE	
5391	C-GLWT	N604PA	VP-BCA	N2409W	N818SL*
5392	C-GLXQ	C-GDZE	C-FLPC		
5393	C-GLYA	N355CC			
5394	C-GLXS	N604CH	HB-IVT		
5395	C-GLYK	N606CC	N82CW		
5396	C-GLWR	N604SH	N273S	N604SH	N273S
5397	C-GLXY	N605PA	VP-BCB		
5398	C-GLXU	N597DM	N477DM		
5399	C-GLXB	N604GM			
5400	C-GLWX	N604S	(N237G)	N237GA	
5401	C-GLXH	N98FJ			
5402	C-GLYC	N603JM	RP-C5610		
5403	C-GLWV	N604DC	D-ADND		
5404	C-GLYO	VP-BGO			
5405	C-GLYH	N311BP	N811BP		
5406	C-GLXS	N604MU			
5407	C-GLWR	N317FX			
5408	C-GLXW	N898R			
5409	G-GLXD	C-GETU	N401NK		
5410	C-GLWZ	N191BA	N199BA		
5411	C-GLXF	N604JJ	PP-OSA		
5412	C-GLXK	N99FJ			
5413	C-GLXM	C-FSJR			
5414	C-GLXO	N604AG	N90AG*		
5415	C-GLWT	N318FX			
5416	C-GLXQ	N604MG	N161MM		
5417	C-GLYA	N605MP	D-AETV		
5418	C-GLXS	N319FX			
5419	C-GLYK	N500			
5420	C-GLWR	N603CC	VP-BCO		
5421	C-GLXY	N200JP	N604JP		
5422	C-GLXU	N605DC	D-ADNE		
5423	C-GLXB	N238SW	N38SW		
5424	C-GLWX	N604CR	G-DAAC		
5425	C-GLXH	N320FX			
5426	C-GLYC	N604JA	JY-ONE		
5427	C-GLWV	N321FX			
5428	C-GLYO	N640CH			
5429	C-GLYH	N604KM	HL		
5430	C-GLXS	(N604MA)	C-GFOE	OY-MMM	
5431	C-GLWR	N276GC			
5432	C-GLXM	C-FDRS	C-GPGD		
5433	C-GLXD	N433FS			
5434	C-GLXY	N322FX			
5435	C-GLWZ	N604PN			
5436	C-GLXF	N604LA			
5437	C-GLXK	N437FT			
5438	C-GLXM	N609CC			
5439	C-GLXQ	N600ES			
5440	C-GLXU	N500PE			
5441	C-GLXB	N641CA			
5442	C-GLWR	N604PS			
5443	C-GLWT	N605JA			
5444	C-GLWV	N604VF			
5445	C-GLWX	N604HD			
5446	C-GLWZ	N604CE			
5447	C-	N323FX			
5448	C-	N604CB			
5449	C-	N604GT			
5450	C-GLXH	N450DK			
5451	C-GLXK	N816CC			
5452	C-GLXM	N452WU			
5453	C-GLXO	N453AD			

CL604 CHALLENGER

C/n	Identities
5454	C-
5455	C-
5456	C-
5457	C-
5458	C-
5459	C-
5460	C-
5461	C-
5462	C-
5463	C-
5464	C-
5465	C-
5466	C-
5467	C-
5468	C-
5469	C-
5470	C-
5471	C-
5472	C-
5473	C-
5474	C-
5475	C-
5476	C-
5477	C-
5478	C-
5479	C-
5480	C-
5481	C-
5482	C-
5483	C-
5484	C-
5485	C-
5486	C-
5487	C-
5488	C-
5489	C-
5490	C-

CESSNA CITATION I

This production list is presented in order of the Unit Number which was used and allocated by Cessna rather than by the normally used c/n. A c/n-Unit Number cross-reference follows the production list.

Unit No	C/n	Identities
	669	N500CC ff 15Sep69; cx Jan78; scrapped
	701	N501CC (a model 501 converted from c/n 670, a model 500) ff 23Jan70
001	500-0001	(N510CC) N502CC N20SM N38SM N501RM N501KG N715JS
002	500-0002	N8202Q CF-CPW C-FCPW ZS-ONE
003	500-0003	N503CC
004	500-0004	N504CC N500GS N500GE N5005 N505K (N22CA)
005	500-0005	N505CC N501PC N981EE N815HC PT-OIG
006	500-0006	N506CC OE-FGP N506CC N506TF N500MX N506MX N506SR N500AD (N500AH) cx May91; scrapped for spares
007	500-0007	N507CC N500LF N555AJ w/o 19Nov79 Denver, CO
008	500-0008	N508CC HB-VCX N502CC N11TC N11QC ZP-TYO ZP-TYP PT-WBY
009	500-0009	N509CC N500JD N700JD N147DA N147DB (N147DA) N147WS N55FT
010	500-0010	N510CC XC-FIT XC-SCT XC-DGA
011	500-0011	N511CC N227H N13UR N18UR N20FM C-GJEM N700VC
012	500-0012	N6563C N512CC XC-FIU N512CC
013	500-0013	N513CC XC-FIV
014	500-0014	N514CC N6563C N766FT N900W N800W N18FM
015	500-0015	N515CC N5867 N58CC N979EE (N332GJ) N14JL PT-LPZ
016	500-0016	N516CC N3JJ N15FS N711CR N711OK N9AX C-GPLN
017	500-0017	N517CC (N317AB) N500PB N508PB N49E N49EA N565SS
018	500-0018	N518CC N5Q N5QZ (N58AN) N978EE N222MS C-FDJQ N70841 C-FSKC substantially damaged 25Jly98 at Rawlings, WY
019	500-0019	N519CC USCG 519 N519CC N11DH N11DQ N256WN N111QP OB-S-1280 OB-1280 N397SC
020	500-0020	N520CC CF-BAX C-FBAX N556AT scrapped for spares Jun87; canx Feb93
021	500-0021	N521CC JA8421 N5B N550CC N208N (N133N) XA-JLV N7GJ
022	500-0022	N522CC N522JD N800JD C-GESZ parted out Montreal/Saint Hubert, Canada; canx Mar97
023	500-0023	N523CC N523JD N900JD I-ALBS N523CC N50FT
024	500-0024	N524CC N524CA N33TH VH-ICN N94AJ
025	500-0025	N525CC D-IMAN N70703 N745US N976EE N220W N57LL
026	500-0026	N526CC N501GP w/o 21Jan81 Bluefield, WV
027	500-0027	N527CC N502GP N51B N777AN PT-OVK
028	500-0028	N528CC N10DG N103WV N284AM N133JM
029	500-0029	N529CC N31ST C-GDWN N424DA
030	500-0030	N530CC N52AN reported wfu for spares
031	500-0031	N531CC YU-BIA N81883 N666SA YV-646CP stored La Carlotta, Venezuela circa Apr98
032	500-0032	N532CC N536V C-GXFZ (N5364U) w/o 26Sep84 Orillia A/P, Ontario, Canada
033	500-0033	N533CC N533BF N65MA N58PL N20RT N20RF N990AL (N130AL)
034	500-0034	N534CC N25HC N980EE N500DN (N111FS) N11HJ
035	500-0035	N535CC N10108 YV-2479P N35SE XA-JOV
036	500-0036	N536CC OY-DVL SE-DEU D-IEXC N18HJ OO-LCM
037	500-0037	N537CC N109AL SE-DPL N109AL N407SC EC-GTS
038	500-0038	N538CC HB-VCU N2EL N81BA N777FC (N207L) N27L
039	500-0039	N539CC N555CC PT-OOK
040	500-0040	N540CC JA8422 N714US D-IKAN OY-ARP N2170J N600WM N98Q
041	500-0041	N541CC N541AG N50AS N50AM
042	500-0042	N542CC CF-BCL C-FBCL N - aircraft scrapped circa 1997
043	500-0043	N543CC N104UA N34UT N5072L N5072E PT-KXZ N5072E N32DD N502RL N96EJ*
044	500-0044	N544CC N942B N712US N892CA VR-CWW N501WW OO-ATS PH-CTY
045	500-0045	N545CC N4VF N6VF N7KH N11AQ N31MW N666ES N666BS N628BS (N628FS)
046	500-0046	N546CC N50SK N50SL N109AP N109BL N929CA N929RW PT-OTQ
047	500-0047	N547CC N180PF PT-WAB N7281Z (N60181)
048	500-0048	N548CC N727LE N727EE N11DH N5500S N44BW N67JR N911GM
049	500-0049	N549CC PP-FXB PT-FXB PT-LDH
050	500-0050	N550CC N471MM N471MH N471HH N333PP VH-HKX N565GW
051	500-0051	N551CC N51BP N51BR N61BR N4646S VH-ICX VH-EMM
052	500-0052	N552CC N52MA N52FP YV-2267P YV-2477P YV-2628P
053	500-0053	N553CC I-CITY N90WJ I-KUNA HB-VGO I-AEAL
054	500-0054	N554CC N54SK N98MB (N28U) (N54FT)
055	500-0055	N900KC N900MP N999SF N716CB
056	500-0056	N556CC N777JM N500DB C-GCTD N360DA N956S N52FT N52ET
057	500-0057	N557CC PT-ILJ w/o 03Jly97 Guanabara Bay/Rio-Santos Dumont A/p, Brazil - to Dodson Int'l Parts for spares
058	500-0058	N558CC N11WC N11WQ N46RB C-GJLQ N6145Q YV-901CP
059	500-0059	N559CC N559BC N40RD N40PD N913RC
060	500-0060	N560CC N712J N712G XA-SEN XA-PAZ N712G PT-OOL
061	500-0061	N561CC XC-GAD XC-ASA N490EA N52AJ N916RC (Wears US Navy colours with Code 01 and Squadron VT-86 and the legend "T-27A serial 061" where the USN serial would normally appear
062	500-0062	N562CC N4CH N4KH N334RC
063	500-0063	N563CC SE-DDE N70451 OO-RST N70MG
064	500-0064	N564CC N27SF

CITATION I

Unit No	C/n	Identities
065	500-0065	N565CC (N565TW)
066	500-0066	N566CC N66CC C-GQCC
067	500-0067	N567CC N3PC XB-DBA N5301J C-FADL N567EA (F-GIHT)
068	500-0068	N568CC N568CM PT-LAY N53MJ N92FA XB-FDN XA-RYE
069	500-0069	N569CC PT-IQL N969SE
070	500-0070	N570CC N500TD N600MT YV-707CP VR-CMO VP-CMO
071	500-0071	N571CC CF-BCM C-FBCM ZS-AMB D2-EDC
072	500-0072	N572CC N49R N491 XC-BEZ N590EA N103AJ PT-OYA N114LA N72DJ
073	500-0073	N573CC N720C (N881M) C-FKMC
074	500-0074	N574CC N574W N8JG PT-OOF
075	500-0075	N575CC (N600TT) N575RD*
076	500-0076	N576CC N801SC N801SG C-GIAC N90CC N500CV N65WS
077	500-0077	N577CC N342AP N869K ZS-OAM N147SC
078	500-0078	N578CC N2HD ZS-IYY TL-AAW N54531 N21TV N429RC N110CK N269RC
079	500-0079	N579CC D-INHH N31088 N40JF PT-LBN
080	500-0080	N580CC N50CC N419K C-GJAP N59019 N222KW N767PC N10JP N10UP ZS-NGR
081	500-0081	N581CC N5B HB-VDA I-PEGA
082	500-0082	N582CC EC-CCY HB-VGD N4434W N103JA N911JD N500CV N178HH N173HH N482RJ
083	500-0083	N583CC N10UC N10UQ N800KC CP-2131 N50602 CP-2131 N50602 (painted as "50602") VR-CCP VR-BMT N50602 VR-BMO VR-CHH VP-CHH
084	500-0084	N584CC N10 N2 N25 N4 N7 N935GA XB-FPK XA-SMH w/o 25Mar95 Vera Cruz, Mexico
085	500-0085	N585CC N51MW N515AA (N64AJ) 5N-BCI
086	500-0086	N586CC N503GP C-FMAN LX-YKH
087	500-0087	N587CC N85AT (N64792) N700RY N500CP (N911A) (N911CJ) N633AT
088	500-0088	N588CC PH-CTA (OO-FAY) G-HOLL PH-CTA N170MD
089	500-0089	N589CC EC-EBR N39LH
090	500-0090	N590CC N590RB XB-EFR Mexico ETE-1329
091	500-0091	N591CC N76RE (PT-LAW) N50PR C-FCHJ (N1899) N500AD
092	500-0092	N592CC Venezuela 0222
093	500-0093	N593CC PH-CTB OO-FBY N611SW G-OXEC G-OCPI N62BR (conv to Citation Long Wing)
094	500-0094	N594CC N94DE VR-CEB N80GB N96FB
095	500-0095	N595CC N2200R (N578WB) YV-15CP N4294A N500KP I-AMAW N950AM
096	500-0096	N596CC N222SL N202VS N202VV C-GXPT N202VV N837MA (N187AP)
097	501-0446	N597CC N14CF N63CF N888MJ
098	500-0098	N598CC PH-CTC G-BNVY PH-CTC N500GR
099	500-0099	N599CC N21CC to spares circa 1999
100	500-0100	N69566 HB-VDC D-ICPW OE-FNL HB-VDC OE-FNP D-IFAI N80AJ (N58BT)
101	500-0101	N601CC N12MB N101CD N1HM N6JL N6JU N15CC N15CQ
102	500-0102	(N602CC) N800PL N400K N491BT
103	500-0103	(N603CC) N103CC PT-KIR
104	500-0104	(N604CC) N200KC N200KQ C-GPJW N40HP N3030C
105	500-0105	N105CC N105JJ N32W N234UM
106	500-0106	N606CC ZS-RCC
107	500-0107	(N607CC) N107CC N107SC C-GWVC N230JS N40RW N79RS
108	500-0108	N108CC EC-CGG w/o 22Nov74 Barcelona, Spain
109	500-0109	N44SA G-RAVY I-AMCU N221AM
110	500-0110	(N610CC) N500AB N154G (N52WS) N500Y N363K N368K N172MA
111	500-0111	N111CC N11A XA-SHO XA-SLQ w/o 06Feb96 Ensenada A/P, Mexico
112	500-0112	N512CC VH-DRM N3LG C-GRJC N29858 N515DC N500TM
113	500-0113	(N613CC) N113CC N684HA N684H N500NJ
114	500-0114	(N614CC) N999JB N899N (G-BNZP) N899N I-AMCT N65SA
115	500-0115	YV-T-AFA YV-21CP
116	500-0116	N116CC EC-CJH D-IATC
117	500-0117	N617CC N90BA N161WC N442JB
118	500-0118	(N618CC) N220CC N221CC N972JD (N10BF) N972GW N50MM to spares circa 1999
119	500-0119	N619CC N111SU N11KA N95Q
120	500-0120	(N620CC) N120CC N10DG N141DR N141DP N999TC N500NX*
121	500-0121	D-IANE N9871R N939SR OY-SUJ N3QE N661AC*
122	500-0122	N122CC CF-ENJ C-FENJ N122LM N122AP
123	500-0123	N123CC (PI-C7777) N523CC RP-C7777 RP-C102 N123CX N947CC VH-LJL ZK-LJL VH-ECD
124	500-0124	N124CC N300HC N300HQ N303PC N8FC N92SM
125	500-0125	CF-CFP C-FCFP XA-SFE
126	500-0126	(N626CC) HB-VDM D-IDWH N404MA
127	500-0127	N701AS N701AT N22DN N500R N580R
128	500-0128	D-INCC N53584 N40HL N501AR N3490L
129	500-0129	D-IMLN N8114G N500SK
130	500-0130	VH-CRM N4LG OY-ARW N4LG N130G ZS-MCP N800AB N130CE
131	500-0131	D-IDAU N1045T N745DM (N725DM) N457CA PT-OJF
132	500-0132	(N632CC) N35LT N80CC (N10GR) N888JD N888GA N881CA N132BP N501RB N713SA
133	500-0133	N133CC F-BUYL OO-SEL N2070K N1270K PT-LXH
134	500-0134	N134CC PT-JMJ

CITATION I

Unit No	C/n	Identities
135	500-0135	N135CC N135BC N900T N902T N975EE N111AM N220MT (N500EN) YV-717CP (modified with winglets) HK-3885 reportedly crashed 07Mar97 into mountains in NW Colombia
136	500-0136	(N136CC) F-BUUL N136SA XA-JRV
137	500-0137	N137CC N12MB N12ME ZS-MCU N922BA*
138	500-0138	N3056R N138SA
139	500-0139	(N5353J) OE-FDP N3771U N15AW
140	500-0140	N140CC N300PX N111AT (N777SC) N977EE XA-EKO N135JW N2FA N4LK N4ZK N441TC
141	500-0141	N141CC XA-PIC XB-EWQ N727TK engineless at Salt Lake City, UT; presumed wfu
142	500-0142	N142CC VH-UCC N650TF N200GM
143	500-0143	N143CC XC-GUQ XB-CXF N3W N14JZ N14T N787BA SE-DUZ
144	500-0144	(N644CC) N332H OH-CAR w/o 19Nov87 Tuusula, Helsinki, Finland
145	500-0145	N145CC N145FC N145TA N415FC*
146	500-0146	N194AT N111ME
147	500-0147	N404G N494G N688CF
148	500-0148	(N100JC) N718VA N748VA N410GB N225DC LV-PMP LV-WXJ
149	500-0149	N4TL N4TE (N43TC) N100RG (N100FF) N149PJ ZS-TMG
150	500-0150	N150CC N5B VH-WRM N5LG OE-FAU N501JG (N78MC) N9V N914CD
151	500-0151	N151CC N6CD cx Nov91; parted out for spares by White Inds, Bates City, MO
152	500-0152	N152CC (N194AT) I-FERN N53J N152CC XB-AMO N2782D XB-AMO
153	500-0153	9J-ADU N153WB N153JP
154	500-0154	C-GOCM N54MC PT-WFT
155	500-0155	(N655CC) N920W N5ZZ N88GJ
156	500-0156	PT-KBR
157	500-0157	PH-CTD N190AB CS-DCA EC-HFY
158	500-0158	N999CM N910Y N910N (N158TJ) OY-TAM N233DB
159	500-0159	N36MC N165BA N50AC N831CW N881JT N97DD
160	500-0160	N146BF (N146BE) N146JC N1951E N59TS C-GNSA
161	500-0161	(C-GTEL) C-GHEC N161CC
162	500-0162	PT-JXS w/o 16Mar75 Belem, Brazil
163	500-0163	N192G (N94ZG) N8KH
164	500-0164	N164CC D-IHSV N4209K F-GEPL N382JP N334PS (N164GJ) N73MP
165	500-0165	N19M N19MQ G-PNNY VR-CSP VP-CSP N501LB
166	500-0166	N500WR N313JL (N29MW) N8DE N511AT
167	500-0167	PH-CTE N191AB N246RR
168	500-0168	N91BA N918A N135BK N135MA N891CA (N46JA)
169	500-0169	N20FL N19CM XC-CON XC-BOC XA-SJW N676CW (N676WE) N75GM
170	500-0170	N60MS N90237 N818R N66LE
171	500-0171	N171CC YV-370CP N728US PT-LIX PP-LEM
172	500-0172	N172CC PT-KIU w/o 12Nov76 Aracatuba, Brazil
173	500-0173	N77CP N59CL N500EL
174	500-0174	N26HC N21NA N211DB N14MH N931CA N19AJ N16LG
175	500-0175	N175CC XA-HOO XB-CCO XA-SIG N175CC N1DK w/o 06Jan98 Pittsburgh/Allegheny County A/p, PA
176	500-0176	G-BCII G-TEFH N150TT
177	500-0177	PH-CTF N192AB N888XL N883XL*
178	500-0178	D-IKFJ I-FBCK (HB-VJP) HB-VKK
179	500-0179	N444J N111KR N427DM (N997S) EI-BYM N179EA PT-OMT
180	500-0180	N180CC I-AMBR N31079 SE-DDO HB-VFH N31079 PT-LAZ N61MJ N772C N500ET
181	500-0181	N181CC PT-KPA
182	500-0182	D-IABC N525GA C-FNOC N590EA N13HJ OO-DCM
183	500-0183	N183CC (VH-FRM) N1VC (N721CC) N1880S N112CP
184	500-0184	N77RC N71RC N67SF N67BE N67BF
185	500-0185	N22EH N22FH N500JB N500WP N500AZ C-GIAD N500AZ ZP-TZH
186	500-0186	N186MW N186SC
187	500-0187	(HB-VDR) (TI-ACB) N187MW N20VP (N75KC) N99MC N345KC N99BC (N95TJ) N5FW
188	500-0188	N5223J PT-KPB
189	500-0189	XC-GOV XA-SJV N189CC N500HH
190	500-0190	N190CC (N424RD) N99BC N99MC N500HK N602BC
191	500-0191	N5600M N448EC N23WK N155CA N701BR LV-YRB
192	500-0192	N4TK N508S N220S N100JJ I-AMCY (N70WA)
193	500-0193	XC-GOW XA-SQZ N293S OY-JAI
194	500-0194	D-IMSM OY-ASR N310U PT-LAX
195	500-0195	N14JA N100AC N100AQ N440EZ N500LJ N502BE
196	500-0196	N74FC C-GENJ N499BA (N969ZS) (N711FW) N270PM
197	500-0197	XC-GOX XA-SRB N297S
198	500-0198	G-BCKM G-JETE N9UJ N700MP N997CA
199	500-0199	N199SP C-FGAT
200	500-0200	N520CC N200MW N250AA N96G N96EA CS-DBM
201	500-0201	XC-GUO N690EA (F-GIHU)
202	500-0202	N202MW N240AA N500JK N500VK N500WJ
203	500-0203	N95DR (N724CC) N101HF N101HB CC-PZM
204	500-0204	C-GBCK N204Y TG-OZO N204Y N928RD
205	500-0205	N520N (N541NC) N700CW w/o 01Apr83 Eagle Pass, TX
206	500-0206	N33NH N946CC VH-LGL N771HR

CITATION I

Unit No	C/n	Identities
207	500-0207	N92BA N929A N39J N107SF
208	500-0208	N82JT N22JG (N520SC) N501AT (N508CC) N515WE
209	500-0209	N209MW (N919AT) N800AV
210	500-0210	TR-LTI N9011R N210MT N716GA YV-625CP modified with winglets but removed for resale in USA N501TK XA-...
211	500-0211	N990CB N999CB N999CV parted out at Bates City MO circa 2000
212	500-0212	N1LB N222LB N223LB N223AS N223MC N92B N74LL
213	500-0213	N62HB N355H N741JB N73WC N100UF N100UH N101HG (N213CE)
214	500-0214	N214CC N371HH (N371W) N214CA
215	500-0215	N215CC YV-T-000 YV-55CP
216	500-0216	(N216CC) N314TC N99CK N199CK (N612CA)
217	500-0217	N217CC N500GA N560GA N625GA XA-ODC N2201U XA-SOX N217S N55GR
218	500-0218	(N218CC) N4AC N271AC
219	500-0219	N219CC N25CS N101KK (N161KK) N408CA PT-LIY
220	500-0220	N5220J N93WD N932HA G-BOGA G-OBEL N619EA G-ORHE
221	500-0221	N221CC XC-GUH N24AJ
222	500-0222	N222CC N636SC N52PM
223	500-0223	N223CC N444LP N444KV N400SA OH-COC N223P I-CLAD
224	500-0224	(N224CC) N77RE N3ZD N5FG N145CM
225	500-0225	N5225J N5B PH-SAW OO-GPN D-IDFD VH-FSQ VH-OIL RP-C1500 w/o 01Feb97 Mount Balakukan, Mindanao Island, Philippines
226	500-0226	N5226J JA8418 N100AD PT-LTI
227	500-0227	(N227CC) G-BCRM N423RD C-GMMO N227HP
228	500-0228	(N228CC) N6365C N769K wfu; parted out for spares by White Inds, Bates City, MO
229	500-0229	N22FM w/o 26Apr83 Wichita, KS
230	500-0230	N5230J N230CC HB-VEH I-PLLL N92AJ N24S (N300TB) N299TB N200CG
231	500-0231	(N5231J) N99TD N2TN C-GMAT N500SJ
232	500-0232	N5232J N500PB N126R N999AM
233	500-0233	N5233J N233CC N233VM N223S N228S
234	500-0234	(N5234J) PH-CTG N70CA
235	500-0235	N5235J N235CC N12AM
236	500-0236	N5236J N236CC N24PA N2801L N801L N801K N600SR N337TV N236TS N1X N742K
237	500-0237	(N5237J) N14TT VH-FSA w/o 20Feb84 Proserpine, Queensland, Australia
238	500-0238	(N5238J) N3Q N3QZ OO-IBI N68AG N53FT VP-CON
239	500-0239	(N5239J) N239CC N6034F PT-LOS
240	500-0240	N5240J N240CC N234AT
241	500-0241	(N9AT) N5241J XA-DAJ N9060Y XB-EPN N288SP
242	500-0242	N5242J RP-C1964
243	500-0243	N5243J XC-GOY XC-BEN XA-SQY N53AJ N243SH
244	500-0244	(N5244J) (SE-DMM) SE-DDM N244WJ N400BH N91LS (N91BS) N46RD N516AB PT-OQD
245	500-0245	N5245J (TI-AHE) TI-AHH XC-BUR N2019V 9M-FAZ (N245MG) (N245BC) D-IAJJ
246	500-0246	(N5246J) N50WM N227VG PT-LQR
247	500-0247	(N5247J) N4110S N9065J XA-JUA C-GMAJ
248	500-0248	(N5248J) N75PX (N70PB) N111BB
249	500-0249	N5249J N27PA N411DR PT-LPF (N789DD) N501SE
250	500-0250	(N5250J) N250CC N25PA N25CK XA-JEL N444RP C-GRJQ N160JS (N413KA) (N200BA) N251P
251	500-0251	N5251J I-COKE (HB-VGI) N500LP XC-QEO XC-ASB N790EA PT-OMS
252	500-0252	N5252J N10PS N200WN C-GZXA N244WJ N501JC
253	500-0253	N5253J YV-T-MMM YV-19P YV-07P N722US N8TG N592WP
254	500-0254	N5254J N26PA C-GJTX N29991 N79DD w/o 24Sep90 San Luis Obispo, CA
255	500-0255	N5255J D-INCI N37643 N877BP N885CA XA-SAM XB-HND
256	500-0256	N256CC SE-DDN N83TF N73TF N456GB N73HB PT-OZT N131SB N676DG
257	500-0257	N5257J N75MN N75FN N75GW
258	500-0258	(N5258J) TI-AFB N80639 (N76AM) N66GE N886CA N125DS
259	500-0259	N5259J N410ND JA8247 RP-C1299 N259DH
260	500-0260	(N5260J) N260CC OK-FKA N50RD ZS-OGS
261	500-0261	N5261J N261CC N55HF N55LF N711SE N711SF (N124DH) N58TC
262	500-0262	N5262J N44JF N111MU N110AF N110AB (N642CT)
263	500-0263	N126KR (N126KP) N819H (N90WA) I-DUMA N263AL VH-AQR VH-AQS VH-ZMD
264	500-0264	N5264J N205FM F-GLJA G-BWFL G-OEJA
265	500-0265	N5265J N504GP XA-VYF N38MH LV-ZPU
266	500-0266	N5266J N5TK N751CC N424AD N7543H (N40RF) N11MN
267	500-0267	N5267J N28PA N1UT N626P OY-CPK N70704 N41SH (N4090P) N401RD parted out Rantoul KS circa 2000
268	500-0268	N5268J ZS-JKR 3D-ACR VH-NEW A6-RKH N900G
269	500-0269	N5269J (D-IKUC) D-ICCC PH-CTW*
270	500-0270	N5270J N712J N712N N72BC N68CB N4238X G-SWET G-OSCA
271	500-0271	N5271J N168RL N4403 N53FB PT-LQG canx Dec97, status?
272	500-0272	N5272J N505GP N30SB N30JN
273	500-0273	N5273J N273RC XA-LEO XB-OBE XA-RUR XB-GBF
274	500-0274	(N5274J) N111TH N140H XA-IIX N111TH XB-ETE N225BC N70TF
275	500-0275	(N5275J) N600SR N40MM (N38MM) N352WC N352WG N102HF N71HB ZP-TZY N275GK
276	500-0276	(N5276J) N276CC N100CM N473LP N473LR SE-DEG
277	500-0277	(N5277J) N277CC N67MP N67MA N652ND

CITATION I

Unit No	C/n	Identities								
278	500-0278	(N5278J)	N278CC	N278SP	(N278SR)	ZS-LYB	N278SP	XB-FQO	XB-UAG	
279	500-0279	(N5279J)	D-IMEN	OY-AJV	SE-DEX	N70454	VH-NMW	N120S	N501KG	
280	500-0280	(N5280J)	N280CC	N100HP	N102AD					
281	500-0281	N5281J	N49R	N72WC	N144JP	(N721TB)	N62TW			
282	500-0282	(N5282J)	N282CC	N26WD	N520RB	N501SS	N501CW	N510RC		
283	500-0283	N5283J	N10UC	N18AF	VH-ANQ	w/o 11May90 Mt Emerald, Cairns, Australia				
284	500-0284	(N5284J)	N284CC	YV-43CP	N8508Z	N37DW	PT-LOG			
285	500-0285	N5285J	(N285CC)	N2U	N86SS	N113SH				
286	500-0286	N5286J	N286CC	5N-APN						
287	500-0287	(N5287J)	N287CC	N73LL	N57MB	OY-CGO	N31LH	PT-WHZ	N287AB	
288	500-0288	(N5288J)	N288CC	D-IDWN	OY-ASD	N9013S	N5TR	(N502BA)	N1DA	
289	500-0289	N5289J	YV-50CP	N5591A	XA-KAH	N939KS	OE-FAN			
290	500-0290	(N5290J)	N290CC	D-ICFA	N4246Y	N826RD	N88AF	(N390S)	N896MA	N896MB
291	500-0291	N5291J	ZS-JOO	N291DS	OE-FGN					
292	500-0292	N5292J	N10FM	N255LJ	C-FSUN	N18BG	SE-DDX	N501RL	N501HK	N333JH
293	501-0643	(N5293J)	N8RF	N54CM	N54TS					
294	500-0294	N5294J	HL7226	(N501LG)	N924AS	SE-DVB				
295	500-0295	N5295J	EP-PAO	EP-KIA	N2274B	N44HC	N10FG			
296	500-0296	(N5296J)	N98DM	N882CA	ZS-NHF	(N245BC)	N296BF			
297	500-0297	N5297J	(N818CD)	YV-62CP	N48DA	N38SA				
298	500-0298	N5298J	N900GC							
299	500-0299	N5299J	HB-VEO	N3JJ	N66TR	N55AK	ZS-MGH	N5133K	YV-940CP	PT-OZX
		N80364	(OY-EBD)	N80364	OY-TKI					
300	500-0300	(N5300J)	OE-FAP	(N500CX)	wfu - b/u for spares following accident 06Oct84 in Greece;					
		cx Jun90;	remains to Dodson Avn, Ottawa, KS still as OE-FAP							
301	500-0301	N5301J	EP-PAP	N81MJ	N747WA	OE-FNG	N305S			
302	500-0302	N5302J	N302CE	N469PW	(N777QE)					
303	500-0303	(N5303J)	N19M	N19U	C-GDWS	N8DX				
304	500-0304	N5304J	N304CC	N5253A	N5253E	N70U	N10UH			
305	500-0305	(N5305J)	N305BB	N805BB	C-GMLC	N137WC				
306	500-0306	N5306J	N36CJ	N36SJ	N606KK					
307	500-0307	N5307J	N2607	N2613	N777SL					
308	500-0308	(N5308J)	N308CC	N38CJ	N70TG	N6525J	(F-GIRS)	F-GMLH	F-GSMC	
309	500-0309	N5309J	(N1GB)	N1JN	N1UG	N1382C	N57LC	SE-DKM	N791MA	N88NW
310	500-0310	(N5310J)	N510CC	N1851T	N1851N	N820FJ	N820	XA-STT	N998AA	N222VV
		N941JC								
311	500-0311	N5311J	N818CD	OH-COL	N501RL	N39RE	SE-DRT	(OY-VIP)	LN-AAF	
312	F500-0312	N5312J	N33ME	(N233ME)	N33MQ	N82AT	F-GJDG			
313	500-0313	(N5313J)	N76GT	XA-KUJ	XB-DYF	XA-SDS	N313BA	HB-VLE		
314	500-0314	N5314J	(N314CC)	N501SC	N100UF	N180UF	N66ES	N668S		
315	500-0315	N5315J	N55SK	N55SH	SE-DRZ					
316	500-0316	N5316J	N398RP	N97SK	N711MT					
317	500-0317	N53MJ	D-ICCA	N37489	C-GPCO	N317VP				
318	500-0318	N5318J	N518CC	N944B	VR-COM	VP-COM				
319	500-0319	N5319J	HZ-NC1	N5319J	N22LH	D-ICUW	N94MA	F-GKIL (taped marks)		F-GKID
320	500-0320	(N5320J)	N320CC	N341CC	N299WV	N341CC	I-NORT	N74WA	N70WA	
321	500-0321	N5321J	JA8438	cx Sep96 as WFU						
322	500-0322	N5322J	N1AP	N108MC						
323	500-0323	N5323J	N300PB	N474L	N523CC	N307EW	(N268GM)			
324	500-0324	(N5324J)	N324C	N52TC						
325	500-0325	(N5325J)	N25CJ	N50TR	N60MP	PT-OSD				
326	500-0326	N5326J	N45LC	G-UESS	w/o 08Dec83 Stornoway, Scotland					
327	500-0327	N5327J	HL7277							
328	500-0328	(N5328J)	N328CC	(N571K)	PT-LSF					
329	500-0329	N5329J	ZS-JOK	N5329J	XC-IPP	XC-PPM	N4999H	OY-CEV		
330	500-0330	(N5330J)	N330CC	(N82CF)	I-JESE	N270BH	(N237JP)	N141SG		
331	500-0331	(N5331J)	N331CC	N86RE	N96RE	N40AC	LN-NAT	EC-500	EC-FUM	LN-NAT
		G-LOFT								
332	500-0332	N5332J	LV-PUY	LV-LZR	N332SE					
333	500-0333	(N5333J)	N275AL	VH-SOU						
334	500-0334	N5334J	N500DD	N44RD	(N527TA)	ZS-MPI	N334JC	canx Apr98 as scrapped		
335	500-0335	N5335J	ZP-PNB	ZP-PUP	N2937L	PT-LDI				
336	500-0336	(N5336J)	N336CC	YV-O-MAC-1		w/o Jun79 Caracas, Venezuela				
337	500-0337	N5337J	N873D	N22MB	(F-GNAB)	N17KD				
338	500-0338	N5338J	(N868D)	HB-VEX	N8499B	N3300M	N92LA	N97LA	N73WC	(N404JW)
		N41HL								
339	500-0339	(N5339J)	G-JEAN	N707US	N300EC	G-JEAN	G-DJAE			
340	500-0340	(N5340J)	N2630	(N2610)	N505AM	HB-VIV	VR-BTQ	ZS-MBS	N340DN	PT-WOD
		(N340RL)	N26NS							
341	500-0341	(N5341J)	N2650	N505JC	C-GVKL					
342	500-0342	(N5342J)	N530TL	N711TE	N501DR	N501LH				
343	500-0343	(N5343J)	N525AC	C-FRHL	N91D	HB-VJR	N91DZ	C-FOSM		
344	500-0344	(N5344J)	N632SC	HB-VHI	VR-BLV	VP-BLV				
345	500-0345	(N5345J)	N23ND	N410NA	N410N	VR-BUB	N345TL	N747RL	(N747KL)	XA-TOF
346	500-0346	N5346J	D-IJON	N4234K	(N99WB)	N82SE	N56DV	PT-LUA		
347	500-0347	(N5347J)	N500XY	N876WB						
348	500-0348	(N5348J)	N300HC	N301HC	C-GCLQ					
349	500-0349	(N5349J)	N888AC	(N988AC)	N888GZ	VH-HVM				

CITATION I

Unit No	C/n	Identities
350	501-0027	N5350J N350CC N10EH N54DS JA8380
351	501-0001	N5351J N51CJ N506TF
352	501-0261	N5352J N52CC N7NE N501VP
353	501-0002	N5353J OE-FPO N165CB XA-LUN N39301 N501WJ (N501WK) N88TB
354	501-0263	N5354J N948N N501BE (N501BF)
355	501-0003	N5355J N55CJ N781L N81EB
356	501-0004	N5356J N88JJ N86JJ N142DA
357	501-0005	N5357J N661AA N665JB N143EP N284RJ
358	501-0006	(N5358J) N358CC N121JW N121UW (N1236P) N5016P N93TJ I-ERJA
359	500-0353	(N5359J) 9J-AEJ N353WB N27WW
360	501-0007	N5360J N222WA
361	500-0361	N5361J D-IKPW N5361J C-GOIL N5361J N90EB F-GKIR
362	501-0008	N5362J N362CC N6HT (N501DB) N900PS
363	500-0354	(N5363J) G-BEIZ N51GA G-CCCL G-TJHI
364	501-0011	N36842 (N1UB) N36JG N770MH N650AC
365	501-0267	N36846 G-DJBB D-IAEV N944TG N565VV N565V
366	500-0356	N5366J N36848 Argentina AE-185
367	501-0009	N36850 N67CC N715EK (N715JM) N505BC N505RJ
368	501-0269	N5368J N36854 YV-120CP N120RD N545GA (N545G) XB-GVY N501JJ
369	501-0012	N36858 N190K N999RB N99XY N99GC N8P N8PJ HI-527 HI-527SP N4196T N501GS
370	501-0010	N36859 N7WF EP-PBC N7WF (N500MD) VH-POZ EC-EDN
371	501-0014	N36860 N22TP N888FL
372	501-0013	N36861 (N622SS) VR-BJK N501TJ
373	501-0015	N36862 N1823B N18328 XA-MAL N4446P N454AC
374	501-0270	N36863 N300WK N893CA
375	501-0016	N36864 N517A C-GHOS N501DL N38DA (N58DT) N58BT N38DA (N38DL) N255TS N17TJ N45TL
376	501-0017	N36869 N877C N100WJ
377	500-0358	N36870 (EP-PAQ) N82MJ SE-DEP I-UUNY
378	501-0018	N36871 N378CC N18BG N550TG N501GR N228AK N228AJ N228FS
379	501-0272	N36872 N5072L N700JR N700JA
380	501-0020	N36873 N32JJ N123EB
381	501-0041	N36880 N50MC N173SK N120ES w/o 24Apr95 San Salvador Intl A/P, remains to Dodson Avn, Ottawa, KS for spares
382	501-0273	N36881 (I-CCCB) XA-HEV N46106 D-IDPD N333PD N333PE N501MD (N273DA) N501JF (N501EM) N302TS
383	501-0019	N36882 (N301MC) N501SP
384	501-0021	N36883 (YV-135CP) YV-166CP XA-IEM N121SJ N203LH ZS-MGL N151SP
385	501-0022	N36884 N385CC N11DH N110H (N995AU) N10GE w/o 21May85 Harrison Airport, AR
386	501-0023	N36885 N56MC N56MT (N501FB) N56MK
387	501-0024	N36886 (N10CA) N1CA N711NR Z-WSY N724EA N70BG
388	501-0032	N36887 N388CJ N33AA N377KC N690MC N550T N550L N85WP N642BJ
389	501-0025	N36888 N389CC N21BS N20RM
390	501-0030	N36890 N301MC N301MG N100CJ C-GSLL N96BA N911MM (N911MU)
391	501-0026	N36891 N92C N92CC
392	500-0364	N36892 HB-VFF N221AC (N221JB) N20WP N40DA G-OKSP G-ORJB
393	501-0275	N36893 YV-159CP N31AJ ZS-MPN (N41AJ) N40AJ
394	501-0028	N36895 N1234X N501PV
395	501-0031	N36896 N395SC XA-SDI
396	500-0370	N36897 SE-DEY
397	501-0262	N36898 YV-O-SID-3 YV-79CP N9712T LN-AFC N50WJ N794EZ (N58T) N20CC
398	501-0050	N36901 N20SP N880CM N750LA N59MA
399	500-0367	N36906 YV-52CP
400	501-0033	N36908 N400GB N300PB (N715DG) N517BA (N101HC) N411DS N411ME N700LW*
401	501-0034	N36911 N444MW N444MV
402	500-0368	N36912 G-BFAR ZS-LPH G-BFAR A6-SMH G-BFAR A6-SMH G-BFAR G-DANI N104AB N53RG
403	501-0039	N36914 N403CC N800DC N800BH N432DG N808BC N507DS
404	501-0035	N36915 (N800M) N500WN N112MC N25MH (N35K) N35JF N501DD
405	501-0046	N36916 N405CC N5VP
406	501-0036	N36918 N406CJ N36CC HI-493 N360MC
407	501-0279	N36919 SE-DEZ (N371GP) (N371GA) N371GP N43BG SE-DEZ
408	501-0037	N36922 N10J N19J N234JW
409	501-0038	N36923 N315S (N315P)
410	501-0042	N87185 N773FR I-TOSC (N120DP) N420AM
411	501-0029	N87253 (N411CJ) N411WC (N411RJ) N816LL N31JM (N45AQ) XA-TKY
412	501-0040	N87258 N85FS I-KWYJ N501E N21EP
413	501-0047	N87496 HB-VFI N1021T N550T N550U
414	501-0048	N87510 N414CC (I-DAEP) I-OTEL
415	500-0373	N98449 YU-BKZ current status uncertain
416	501-0045	N98468 N833 N833JL
417	501-0043	N98510 N10NL N16NL
418	501-0053	N98528 N59PC YV-253P YV-253CP N14EA N52TL
419	501-0054	N98563 N2BT
420	501-0049	N98586 N2ZC (N36WS) (N347DA) OY-SVL
421	501-0062	N98599 D-IBWB N208W N900DM N980DM
422	501-0051	N98601 N422CC N150TJ N303CB N422DA

CITATION I

Unit No	C/n	Identities								
423	501-0281	N36943	LV-PZI	LV-MGB	N501SJ	N501CB*				
424	501-0044	N98675	N5TC	N944JD	(N122LG)	N131SY	N50US	N600RM		
425	501-0055	N98682	N552MD	N400PC	N400PG	N145DF	N145AJ	N223LC		
426	501-0056	N98688	(N426CC)	(N501SF)	N55WH	CC-CTE	N56WE			
427	501-0052	N98715	N900MC							
428	501-0282	(N98718)	N36949	XC-PMX	XA-SQX	N82AJ				
429	501-0283	N98749	C-GPTC	N204CA						
430	501-0057	N98751	N500JC	N505BG	N577VM	N577JT				
431	501-0059	N2079A	N431CC	N13RC	ZS-EHL	N16HL				
432	501-0066	N2098A	D-IHEY	N501BG	N501CX	C-GHRX	N945AA	VR-CTB	VP-CTB	N501CD
433	501-0284	N2131A	N115K	N409AC	VR-BBY	N788SS	N284PC	N729PX	N45AF	
434	501-0058	N2627A	N44MC	N444AG	N36GC	N32MJ	N65RA	(N400PG)	N501FT	N211EF
		N211X	N501EZ	w/o 02Dec98 Grannis, AR						
435	501-0060	N2741A	N435CC	N500ZC	N5737	N573L	N11TM			
436	501-0061	N2757A	N436CC	N34DL	N1401L	N202CF				
437	501-0064	N2768A	(N33KW)	N9TK	N96DS	N12WH				
438	501-0068	N2841A	N438CC	N9GT	N50GT	N68EA				
439	501-0285	N2887A	N100BX	N13ST						
440	501-0065	N2888A	N33WW							
441	501-0069	N2906A	N501EF	N636N						
442	501-0067	N2959A	SE-DEO	D-IGMB	HB-VJB	VR-BLW	HB-VJB			
443	501-0063	N2991A	N305M	N408MM	N408MW	F-GESZ	N501BA	N555KW		
444	501-0070	N3062A	(N444CW)	N78AB	N21HJ	N96G	N96GT	N70VP	HC-BTQ	(N277RW)
		N628ZG	N45MM							
445	500-0381	N3104M	N445CC	I-ROST	(N789AA)	N381BJ				
446	501-0071	N3105M	N501SR	N501KR						
447	501-0072	N3110M	N1HA							
448	501-0073	N3117M	N100SV	N299RP	(N840MC)					
449	501-0074	N3118M	YV-232CP	N888DS	N717RB	N28GC				
450	501-0075	N3120M	N773LP	N773LR	N325BC	(N325PM)	N51ET			
451	501-0076	N3122M	N451CJ	N315MR	N315MP	N150RM				
452	501-0077	(N3124M)	N15PR	N42HM	N678JD	(N678JG)				
453	501-0078	(N3127M)	N13BT	ZS-MZO	N13BT	N501EK				
454	500-0369	N3132M	C-GVER							
455	500-0374	N3141M	C-GRQA	N501SS	(N501BB)	N505BB*				
456	501-0079	N3144M	N555EW	N33CX	VP-CFF					
457	501-0080	N3145M	N51CC	N51CG	N347DA	N37LA	N800BF			
458	501-0081	N3146M	N12DE	N12CQ	N12CV					
459	501-0289	N3147M	LV-PAT	LV-MMR	N501NA	N1KC	(N501SK)	N501NZ*		
460	501-0082	N3150M	N460CC	N84CF	C-GEVF	N6RF	(N386DA)	XB-ERX	N5WF	
461	500-0378	N3156M	C-GBNE							
462	501-0083	N3158M	N462CC	N5YP	N420PC	N420RC	(N83TJ)	N101LD		
463	501-0084	N3160M	(N463CJ)	(N11JC)	G-CITI	VR-CDM	VP-CDM	G-CITI		
464	501-0098	N3161M	N44RD	N144AR	(N144AB)	HB-VIC	N92BE			
465	501-0093	N3163M	N88CF	N31RC	N623LB	N501RM				
466	501-0090	N3165M	XC-CIR	N41JP	N3GN					
467	501-0099	N3170A	I-FLYA							
468	501-0101	N3170M	C-GDDM	N100TW	N106EA	(N501GS)	N323JB*			
469	501-0095	N3172M	N612DS	XA-AGA						
470	500-0386	N3173M	LV-PAX	LQ-MRM						
471	501-0089	(N3175M)	N471H	N106WV	N588CA	VH-LJG				
472	501-0292	N3180M	YV-O-MTC-2	YV-2295P	N456R					
473	501-0088	(N3181A)	N473CC	N31MT	N22TS	N22TY	N86MT	N23YZ		
474	501-0087	(N3183M)	N501SE	C-GVVT	(N22508)	N501SJ	N501BB			
475	501-0085	N3189M	N575CC	N475CC	N34AA	N25DD	N707W			
476	501-0091	N3194M	(N887DM)	(N55BE)	N33BE	N39BE	(JA8361)	I-OMEP	N2158U	HB-VKY
		N2158U								
477	501-0086	N3195M	N8LG	N88CF	(N711AE)	N583MP	N32SX	N501CW	N501JP	N11SQ
		(N864TT)	N554T	N11SQ	N554T*					
478	501-0092	N3197M	(HB-VGD)	N112WC	(N78BT)	LV-PLM	LV-WOI	N501X		
479	501-0097	N3198M	N479CC	N479JS	N501RS					
480	501-0096	N3202A	N660AA	(N480CC)	N660KC	N501HS				
481	501-0293	N3202M	Ecuador ANE-201		HC-BVP	N850MA	N597CS			
482	501-0107	N3204M	(N333BG)	(N33VV)	N1UL	N107CC	N501LS	N54TB	3A-MTB	(N75471)
		EC-GJF								
483	501-0294	N3205M	N2LN	N38TM	N8EH	N80SL				
484	500-0387	N3206M	N484KA							
485	501-0100	(N3207M)	N485CC	N41ST	(N26MW)	C-GSUN	C-GSUM	N54FT		
486	501-0102	(N2646X)	N486CC	(N223RE)	I-AIRV	N501CG				
487	501-0120	N2646Y	N487HR	N487LS	OY-CPW	N71LP				
488	501-0094	(N2646Z)	N488CC	N103PC	N59CC	N159LC				
489	500-0392	N26461	I-FLYB	D-ISSS						
490	501-0103	(N2647U)	N49WC	N611AT						
491	501-0109	(N2647Y)	N30RL	N30RE	N567WB					
492	501-0104	(N2647Z)	N312GK	N81CC	N29CA	N33HC				
493	501-0105	N2648X	(N231LC)							
494	501-0297	(N2648Y)	VH-SWC	N32DA	N35LD	N41GT				
495	501-0108	(N2648Z)	(N56CJ)	N777AJ	N777GG					

CITATION I

Unit No	C/n	Identities
496	501-0110	(N26481) N15NY w/o 02Aug79 Akron, OH
497	501-0119	(N26486) N35AA N35TM N53RC N77GJ N53EZ
498	501-0111	N2649D N140WC (N333RB) N777FE I-FOMN N94SL N59WP N79BK
499	501-0112	N2649E (N900LL) N350M N14TV (N84TV) N74PM (N74PN) N112EB
500	501-0127	N2649H N500K N88BM N96SK
501	501-0106	(N2649J) (N1234F) OE-FYF D-IANE N793AA
502	501-0113	(N2649S) (N515CC) N502CC N200ES N502CC
503	501-0114	N2649Y N673LP N673LR N485RP N711HL (N725RH) N811HL
504	501-0118	N2649Z I-DECI N61572
505	501-0126	N26492 N505SP N505JH
506	501-0117	N26493 LV-PDW LV-MZG N91AP
507	501-0115	N26494 N501GF (N26540) N501GK N95RE N728MC
508	501-0122	(N26495) N275CC N275CQ N400DB N501HC (N501MD) N501MB
509	501-0116	(N26496) N500XX N7CJ N7QJ (N90MT) N7TK
510	501-0239	N26497 LV-PDZ LV-MYN N164CB OE-FMS
511	501-0298	N26498 (PH-JOB) I-GERA OE-FIW N65M VR-CMS N501D
512	501-0129	(N26499) (N50WP) N70WP PT-LQQ
513	501-0123	N2650C N513CC N627L N627E
514	501-0249	N2650M RP-C237 N4263X ZS-LOW N133DM G-OHLA I-DIDY N249AS N851BC XA-OAC
515	501-0124	N2650N N95RE OE-FFK w/o 26Oct88 nr Salzburg, Austria
516	501-0134	N2650S N501LW N501EM
517	501-0130	(N2650V) N148JB N148JS (N726BB) (N300RN) N102HS N505CF
518	501-0131	N2650X N490WC YV-301P N301PP YV-2605P
519	501-0135	N2650Y N77TW N711GL N49MP N63CG
520	501-0136	(N26502) N66AT N66AG
521	501-0137	N26503 N46SC N14VA
522	501-0128	(N26504) N522CC N900MM N501CF
523	501-0121	N26506 D-IANO HB-VID D-IANO OE-FHW
524	501-0142	N26507 HB-VHA N310AF N880M I-SATV YV-688CP
525	501-0138	(N26509) 8P-BAR 8P-BAB C-GBTB N501CE N74FH
526	501-0139	N2651B N526CC N1LQ (N3UG) N108JL N888BH N501AF
527	501-0132	N2651G N50US N91WZ N717JL
528	501-0133	N2651J (N955WP) N51WP
529	501-0140	(N2651R) (N99TD) N96TD N96CF OE-FDM
530	500-0395	N2651S XA-JEX
531	501-0125	(N2651Y) (N2DP) (N501DP) N45MC N96TC N69EP N125EA
532	501-0141	N26510 N166CB VR-BJN N841MA N501GG
533	500-0396	N26514 (XA-JEW) XC-GTO
534	501-0156	N26517 N123FG N44FM
535	501-0143	N26523 D-IGGK OY-ONE
536	501-0144	N2652U N270SF N270NF
537	501-0159	N2652Y D-IGLU N666JJ N308AT N1AT w/o 11Jun97 Chub Cay, Bahamas; canx Jun97 N8189J
538	501-0145	N2652Z (ZS-KGF) VH-LCL (N2652Z) w/o 22Apr90 Norfolk Island while regd VH-LCL; remains to Dodson Avn, Ottawa, KS still marked VH-LCL; US marks cx Jly94
539	501-0163	N1354G (I-AGIK) I-CIGB
540	500-0403	N1710E G-BPCP w/o 01Oct80 Jersey, Channel Is, UK
541	501-0147	N1728E N254TW CP-2105 N392DA N27TS N551MS
542	501-0148	N1758E (OO-ECT) N167CB N700ER N500DL I-GJMA N148EA N148ED
543	501-0149	(N1772E) N104CF N97FD
544	501-0302	(N1779E) (G-BHIW) XA-JFE XB-ELU XA-RLE XA-JCE N301EL
545	501-0146	(N1782E) N545CC N54MH N61CD N1VU N194RC N53BB
546	501-0151	(N1820E) N269MD N269CM N2690M
547	501-0152	(N1874E) N547CC N501FM N501ED N40FJ N48FJ N15CV (N15UJ) VP-C reported
548	501-0153	(N1930E) N105CF (N118AT) N99CK (N484CS)
549	501-0160	N1951E (N58BD) N60PR C-GAAA N999PW
550	501-0161	N1955E OY-CYD N5UM XB-FXO XB-GRE N501FP
551	500-0397	(N1958E) N6563C OH-CIT OY-FFC SE-DVA
552	501-0162	N1959E N455H N55H N44SW
553	501-0157	N2052A (N88BR) N16VG
554	500-0399	N2069A YU-BML current status unclear
555	501-0175	N2072A EI-BJN VR-BKP VP-BKP
556	501-0158	N2611Y N1MX N501WB
557	501-0165	N2612N (N20KW) N557CC N165NA N501RC
558	501-0154	N2613C N80MF CC-CWW N154SC
559	501-0166	N2614C N476X I-CIPA (N30AF) OY-INI N166FA
560	500-0404	N2614H G-BHTT G-ZAPI N789DD
561	501-0185	N2614K N653DR N72787 N111RB N1CR N501LL
562	501-0150	N2616G N95MJ N73FW N405PC
563	501-0167	(N2616L) N563CC N323CB N38RT N900TW N723JM N501FJ
564	501-0155	N2617B (N108CT) N110TV N110TP N800DW VR-CJB VP-CJB N299D
565	500-0401	N2617K N2651 I-FARN
566	501-0169	N2617U D-IBWG C-GFEE
567	501-0183	N6777V ZS-KPA CS-AYY (N8NC)
568	501-0168	(N6777X) N39LL PT-LNV N168EA N601WT N328NA
569	501-0188	N6778C N1JB N93JM N61DT

CITATION I

Unit No	C/n	Identities								
570	501-0164	(N6778L)	N570CC	N223GC	N750LA	N50DS	N170JS	N286PC		
571	501-0193	N6778T	N164CB	XA-LIM	N39300	N45MK				
572	501-0173	(N6778V)	OE-FPH	N25GT						
573	501-0170	(N6778Y)	N501HP	G-GENE	G-MTLE	N170EA	N610TT			
574	501-0171	N67780	VH-BNK	N171WJ						
575	501-0184	N67786	N90CF	N433MM						
576	501-0187	N6779D	N576CC	(N414CB)	N21EH	N23EH	(N576CC)	N137GK	(N600DH)	N900DH
		N900DL	N713AL	N7MC	N70CG	(N614DD)				
577	501-0176	N6779L	N44LC	N49LC	(VR-CIA)	VR-CFG	VP-CFG			
578	501-0177	N6779P	(N999RB)	N22SD	N501DG	N501NC	N501GW	N457CS		
579	501-0174	N6779Y	N20GT	N721US	N702NC	N702NY	(N174CF)	N50JG	N454DQ	
580	501-0178	N67799	LV-PML	N4246A	N83ND	G-FLVU				
581	501-0186	(N6780A)	N95EW	N37HW	N999WS					
582	501-0189	N6780C	N80SF							
583	501-0182	N6780J	N360DJ	I-PALP	N535GA	(N125CA)	D-ISIS	VP-CAP		
584	501-0190	(N6780M)	N584CC	N333MS	N393DA	N40AW	N723JR			
585	501-0191	N6780Y	N98ME	N64RT						
586	500-0410	N6780Z	XC-GAW							
587	500-0408	N67805	XA-LUD	XB-DVF						
588	501-0181	N6781C	N250SP	N250SR	N501KK					
589	501-0179	(N6781D)	N589CJ	N414CB	HB-VLD	N718SA				
590	501-0192	(N6781G)	N190K							
591	501-0194	N6781L	N28JG	N65WW						
592	501-0222	N6781R	N25HS							
593	501-0180	(N6781T)	(N593CC)	N695CC	N593DS	N9NE	N180VP	N650MW		
594	501-0197	N6781Z	N100SN	N324L						
595	501-0195	N67814	N161CB	N7111H	N109DC	(N123KD)				
596	500-0409	N67815	XC-FEZ							
597	501-0196	N6782B	(N597JV)	N575SR	N311TP	(N311TT)				
598	500-0412	N6782F	XA-LUV	XB-GDJ						
599	501-0172	(N6782P)	N907KH	HI-581SP						
600	501-0311	(N6782T)	SE-DES	OY-JEY	N311VP					
601	501-0199	N6782X	N501MM	N441JT	N62RG					
602	501-0198	N67822	(N602CC)	N105TW	N500LE	N500LH	N198VP	N800DT		
603	500-0406	N67829	SE-DET	OY-FFB						
604	501-0231	N6783C	N55WG	N29HE	N501BP					
605	501-0200	N6783L	7Q-YTL	N47TL						
606	501-0201	N6783U	N801L	N130JS	N123SF	N55BM	N417RC			
607	501-0202	N6783V	N520RP	N607CJ	(XA-PEV)	XA-BOA	N202VP	N477KM	N501G	
608	500-0413	N6783X	(PT-LBZ)	PT-LCC						
609	501-0203	N67830	D-IAEC	w/o 31May87 Blankensee A/P, Luebeck, Germany						
610	501-0207	N67839	N968DM	(N207CF)	OE-FYC	VP-BHO				
611	501-0204	N6784L	(N123HP)	N345N						
612	501-0208	N6784P	N54MJ	I-LAWN	N208EA	N82P				
613	501-0205	N6784T	PT-LVB							
614	501-0209	N6784X	N56MJ	N501CR	N111DT	N36FD	N98RG			
615	501-0206	N6784Y	N501HM	N795MA	OE-FBA	N314EB	N943LL			
616	501-0210	N67848	N32FM							
617	501-0211	N6785C	N617CC	cx Jun96, parted out						
618	501-0213	N6785D	I-AUNY							
619	501-0212	N6785L	N67GM	N70AA	N2243					
620	501-0314	N6887M	N56MC	N56LW						
621	501-0214	N6887R	N567L	I-JUST	(N794WB)	N3312T	N2296S	N2298S	N340AC*	
622	501-0215	N1354G	N50MM	ZS-LXT						
623	501-0217	N1710E	N623RM	N600SS	N500TW					
624	501-0216	N1758E	N57MJ	(N65T)	N57TW	TG-RIF	TG-RIE			
625	501-0219	N1772E	N25CJ	N678DG	N625CH	N625J	N58BT	N501BW	N12RN	N18RN
		N510GA	N56PB							
626	501-0218	N1958E	I-KODE	N218AM	N218JG					
627	501-0223	N1959E	N18HC	(N26HA)						
628	501-0220	N2052A	N628CH	N100CH	N100QH	N100LX				
629	500-0415	N2072A	JA8474							
630	501-0224	N2611Y	N630CE	N456CE	N825PS					
631	501-0228	N2612N	(N999CB)	N501CM	JA8284	N228EA	XA-SEY			
632	501-0260	N2613C	N224RP	N500GA	N7UF					
633	501-0225	N2614C	N49BL	TG-MIL	TG-KIT	N412SE				
634	501-0227	(N2614Y)	N2614H	N374GS	N47CF	N83DM				
635	501-0226	(N2615D)	N29AC	N226VP	N501JM					
636	501-0229	(N2615L)	N636CC	N57MC						
637	501-0232	(N2616G)	N2616C	N853KB	N35TL	VR-CHF	VR-CAT	VP-CAT		
638	501-0230	(N2617B)	N2616G	N653F	N5RL	G-ICED	N505CC	HB-VLB	9A-DVR	N999MS
639	501-0234	N2617B	N61PR	N711RP	PT-LIZ	N643RT	N77PA			
640	501-0237	(N2617K)	N640BS	N237SC	N831CB	N29UF				
641	501-0235	N2617U	(N31CF)	(N13BN)						
642	501-0236	N26227	N711VF							
643	501-0221	(N26228)	N643MC	N217RR	N389JP	HB-VKD	N555HR	N221EB	N107GM	
644	501-0240	N26232	N13BK	N711BT	OY-JET	N62864	N77UB	N501DY		
645	500-0411	N6784Y	G-BIZZ	G-NCMT	SE-DLZ					

CITATION I

Unit No	C/n	Identities								
646	501-0242	N2623B	N40PL	N500BK	N71L					
647	501-0241	(N2624L)	N174CB	N207G	C-GSTR	N101RR				
648	501-0243	N2624Z	N43SP							
649	501-0238	N2626A	N238JS	I-DVAL	(N501EZ)	N995PA	N737RJ			
650	501-0244	N2626J	N650CJ	(N711VF)	N701VF	N418R	N244SL	N176FB		
651	501-0317	N2626Z	5N-AVL							
652	501-0245	N26263	(N678DG)	ZS-LDO	A2-AGM					
653	501-0233	N26264	5N-AVM							
654	501-0246	N2627N	N85RS	N26LC	OE-FHH					
655	501-0247	N2627U	(N24CH)	w/o 12Nov82 Wichita, KS						
656	500-0418	N2628B	ZS-LDV							
657	501-0252	N2628Z	N825HL	N574CC	I-TOIO					
658	501-0254	N2629Z	N84CF							
659	501-0256	N2631N	D-ILLL	I-PAPE	N256P					
660	501-0257	N2631V	(N992NW)	N500NW	OE-FLY	N12NM				
661	501-0255	N661TV	N661TW	N501MR	N707WF	G-SBEC	N400LX	N901NB		
662	501-0248	N2633N	N7700T	(N711EG)						
663	501-0250	N77FD								
664	501-0258	N664CC	N900RB	N900RD	N87FL	VR-BHI	VP-BHI	N16KW	N599BR	
665	501-0319	N124KC	N60EW							
666	501-0251	N30BK	N945BC	N400LX	N501RG					
667	501-0320	N2649D	ZS-LHP	3D-ADH	N70467	N401G				
668	501-0321	OE-FHP	N321VP	N550MH						
669	501-0322	N2663J	N374GS	N314GS	(N669DM)	(N769EW)	N527EW			
670	501-0253	N2650Y	N501JE							
671	501-0323	N2651B	N55HL	N501RF	N501LE	(N142AL)				
672	501-0324	N2651J	JA8493							
673	501-0325	N1710E	(D-IFGP)	N501LM	N64BH					
674	501-0259	N1758E	(N77111)	(N261WB)	N261WR	N261WD	VR-BJW	N501MS	D-IEIR	N225WT^
675	501-0675	N8900M	N501MT							
676	501-0676	N1958E	N676CC	(N76JY)						
677	501-0677	(N1958E)	N727MC	(N184SC)	C-GAAA	N54CG				
678	501-0678	N2052A	N3FE	N678CF	PT-ODC	(N26AA)				
679	501-0679	N2611Y	N200GF	N679CC	N2611Y	VR-BLF	VP-BLF	N73SK		
680	501-0680	N2614C	PT-LFR	PP-EIF						
681	501-0681	N2616G	N82LS							
682	501-0682	N2617B	N3951	N19GB	N55TK	N682DC	N682HC			
683	501-0683	N501BK	N501FR	N170HL	(N49TA)	N96LC				
684	501-0684	N3683G	N501TP							
685	501-0685	N5346C	N400SR	N501TB	(N243AB)	N501EG				
686	501-0686	N6763M	N750PP							
687	501-0687	N321FM	N154CC	N361DB	N361DE					
688	501-0688	D-IMRX								
689	501-0689	N46MT	N689CC	(N88MT)	N88MM	N75TJ	N88MM			

Production complete

CITATION 500 UNIT NUMBER CROSS REFERENCE

Note: From c/n 500-0001 to 500-0349 unit numbers match the last three digits of the c/n, then the tie-ups are as follows:

C/n	Unit	C/n	Unit	C/n	Unit	C/n	Unit	C/n	Unit	C/n	Unit
500-0353	359	500-0368	402	500-0381	445	500-0396	533	500-0404	560	500-0411	645
500-0354	363	500-0369	454	500-0386	470	500-0397	551	500-0406	603	500-0412	598
500-0356	366	500-0370	396	500-0387	484	500-0399	554	500-0408	587	500-0413	608
500-0358	377	500-0373	415	500-0392	489	500-0401	565	500-0409	596	500-0415	629
500-0361	361	500-0374	455	500-0395	530	500-0403	540	500-0410	586	500-0418	656
500-0364	392	500-0378	461								

CITATION 1 CONVERSIONS

The following a/c have been converted from Model 500s to Model 501s (and, in one example, back again):

500-0097 to 501-0446
500-0293 to 501-0643
500-0350 to 501-0027
500-0351 to 501-0261
500-0352 to 501-0263
500-0355 to 501-0267
500-0357 to 501-0269
500-0359 to 501-0270
500-0360 to 501-0272
500-0361 to 501-0265 to 500-0361
500-0362 to 501-0275
500-0363 to 501-0273
500-0365 to 501-0262
500-0366 to 501-0285
500-0371 to 501-0279
500-0372 to 501-0281
500-0375 to 501-0289
500-0376 to 501-0282
500-0377 to 501-0283
500-0379 to 501-0284
500-0383 to 501-0292
500-0389 to 501-0293
500-0391 to 501-0294
500-0393 to 501-0239
500-0394 to 501-0297
500-0398 to 501-0298
500-0400 to 501-0249
500-0402 to 501-0302
500-0405 to 501-0311
500-0414 to 501-0314
500-0416 to 501-0260
500-0417 to 501-0317
500-0476 to 501-0063
500-0667 to 501-0320

CITATION 501 UNIT NUMBER CROSS REFERENCE

C/n	Unit
501-0001	351
501-0002	353
501-0003	355
501-0004	356
501-0005	357
501-0006	358
501-0007	360
501-0008	362
501-0009	367
501-0010	370
501-0011	364
501-0012	369
501-0013	372
501-0014	371
501-0015	373
501-0016	375
501-0017	376
501-0018	378
501-0019	383
501-0020	380
501-0021	384
501-0022	385
501-0023	386
501-0024	387
501-0025	389
501-0026	391
501-0027	350
501-0028	394
501-0029	411
501-0030	390
501-0031	395
501-0032	388
501-0033	400
501-0034	401
501-0035	404
501-0036	406
501-0037	408
501-0038	409
501-0039	403
501-0040	412
501-0041	381
501-0042	410
501-0043	417
501-0044	424
501-0045	416
501-0046	405
501-0047	413
501-0048	414
501-0049	420
501-0050	398
501-0051	422
501-0052	427
501-0053	418
501-0054	419
501-0055	425
501-0056	426
501-0057	430
501-0058	434
501-0059	431
501-0060	435
501-0061	436
501-0062	421
501-0063	443
501-0064	437
501-0065	440
501-0066	432
501-0067	442
501-0068	438
501-0069	441
501-0070	444
501-0071	446
501-0072	447
501-0073	448
501-0074	449
501-0075	450
501-0076	451
501-0077	452
501-0078	453
501-0079	456
501-0080	457
501-0081	458
501-0082	460
501-0083	462
501-0084	463
501-0085	475
501-0086	477
501-0087	474
501-0088	473
501-0089	471
501-0090	466
501-0091	476
501-0092	478
501-0093	465
501-0094	488
501-0095	469
501-0096	480
501-0097	479
501-0098	464
501-0099	467
501-0100	485
501-0101	468
501-0102	486
501-0103	490
501-0104	492
501-0105	493
501-0106	501
501-0107	482
501-0108	495
501-0109	491
501-0110	496
501-0111	498
501-0112	499
501-0113	502
501-0114	503
501-0115	507
501-0116	509
501-0117	506
501-0118	504
501-0119	497
501-0120	487
501-0121	523
501-0122	508
501-0123	513
501-0124	515
501-0125	531
501-0126	505
501-0127	500
501-0128	522
501-0129	512
501-0130	517
501-0131	518
501-0132	527
501-0133	528
501-0134	516
501-0135	519
501-0136	520
501-0137	521
501-0138	525
501-0139	526
501-0140	529
501-0141	532
501-0142	524
501-0143	535
501-0144	536
501-0145	538
501-0146	545
501-0147	541
501-0148	542
501-0149	543
501-0150	562
501-0151	546
501-0152	547
501-0153	548
501-0154	558
501-0155	564
501-0156	534
501-0157	553
501-0158	556
501-0159	537
501-0160	549
501-0161	550
501-0162	552
501-0163	539
501-0164	570
501-0165	557
501-0166	559
501-0167	563
501-0168	568
501-0169	566
501-0170	573
501-0171	574
501-0172	599
501-0173	572
501-0174	579
501-0175	555
501-0176	577
501-0177	578
501-0178	580
501-0179	589
501-0180	593
501-0181	588
501-0182	583
501-0183	567
501-0184	575
501-0185	561
501-0186	581
501-0187	576
501-0188	569
501-0189	582
501-0190	584
501-0191	585
501-0192	590
501-0193	571
501-0194	591
501-0195	595
501-0196	597
501-0197	594
501-0198	602
501-0199	601
501-0200	605
501-0201	606
501-0202	607
501-0203	609
501-0204	611
501-0205	613
501-0206	615
501-0207	610
501-0208	612
501-0209	614
501-0210	616
501-0211	617
501-0212	619
501-0213	618
501-0214	621
501-0215	622
501-0216	624
501-0217	623
501-0218	626
501-0219	625
501-0220	628
501-0221	643
501-0222	592
501-0223	627
501-0224	630
501-0225	633
501-0226	635
501-0227	634
501-0228	631
501-0229	636
501-0230	638
501-0231	604
501-0232	637
501-0233	653
501-0234	639
501-0235	641
501-0236	642
501-0237	640
501-0238	649
501-0239	510
501-0240	644
501-0241	647
501-0242	646
501-0243	648
501-0244	650
501-0245	652
501-0246	654
501-0247	655
501-0248	662
501-0249	514
501-0250	663
501-0251	666
501-0252	657
501-0253	670
501-0254	658
501-0255	661
501-0256	659
501-0257	660
501-0258	664
501-0259	674
501-0260	632
501-0261	352
501-0262	397
501-0263	354
501-0267	365
501-0269	368
501-0270	374
501-0272	379
501-0273	382
501-0275	393
501-0279	407
501-0281	423
501-0282	428
501-0283	429
501-0284	433
501-0285	439
501-0289	459
501-0292	472
501-0293	481
501-0294	483
501-0297	494
501-0298	511
501-0302	544
501-0311	600
501-0314	620
501-0317	651
501-0319	665
501-0320	667
501-0321	668
501-0322	669
501-0323	671
501-0324	672
501-0325	673
501-0675	675
501-0676	676
501-0677	677
501-0678	678
501-0679	679
501-0680	680
501-0681	681
501-0682	682
501-0683	683
501-0684	684
501-0685	685
501-0686	686
501-0687	687
501-0688	688
501-0689	689

CESSNA 525 CITATIONJET

C/n	Identities					
702	N525CJ	prototype; ff 29Apr91 - cx Mar99 re-engineered to serve as the Cessna 525A Citation Jet CJ-2 prototype with c/n 708 q.v.				
0001	N525CC	ff 20Nov91; pre-production prototype + painted on aircraft but ntu	N444RH	N444RF+	N444RH	N800VT
0002	N1326B	N25CJ	N137AL	N46JW		
0003	N1326D	N44FJ				
0004	N1326G	N4YA	N24CJ	N7CC		
0005	N1326H	(N1326D)	N56K	N58KJ	N521PF	
0006	N1326P	N106CJ				
0007	(N1327E)	N525KN				
0008	N1327G					
0009	N1327J	(N529CC)				
0010	(N1327K)	N210CJ	ZS-MVX			
0011	(N1327N)	N525AL				
0012	(N1327Z)	N12PA				
0013	N1328A	N550T				
0014	N1328D	N70TR	N620TC			
0015	(N1328K)	N115CJ	PT-MPE			
0016	N1328M	N216CJ	D-IKOP			
0017	(N1328Q)	N525AE				
0018	(N1328X)	N525MC				
0019	(N1328Y)	N19CJ	N63HB	(N525SP)	N525KA	
0020	N1329D	(OO-LFU)+	N1329D			
	+Marks were carried					
0021	(N1329G)	N793CJ				
0022	N1329N	G-BVCM				
0023	(N1329T)	N525RF				
0024	N13291	F-GNCJ	N525DJ			
0025	(N1330D)	N9LR	D-IOBO			
0026	(N1330G)	N525FS				
0027	N1330N	N825GA	N861PD			
0028	N1330S	G-OICE				
0029	N13308	D-IWHL				
0030	N1331X	(PT-MPE)+	N177RE			
	+Marks were carried					
0031	(N13312)	(N131CJ)	N31CJ	N831S		
0032	(N13313)	N532CJ	N95DJ			
0033	N1354G	ZS-NHE	N526CA	N472SW		
0034	N1772E	N96G				
0035	N1779E	N525HS				
0036	N1782E	N525MB				
0037	N1820E	HB-VKB				
0038	N1874E	N135MM	N600HR			
0039	N1958E	N39CJ				
0040	N1959E	D-ISCH	VP-CCC			
0041	N2098A	N525GG	HB-VJQ	D-IAMM		
0042	N26105	N96GD	PH-MGT			
0043	N2616L	N525PL				
0044	N2617K	XA-SKW	N55DG	D-IDBW		
0045	N2617P	N525AP				
0046	N26174	N123JN				
0047	N2621U	N47TH	(N47VP)	N47FH		
0048	N2621Z	N500HC	N525NA			
0049	N2633Y	N49CJ				
0050	N2634E	N70KW				
0051	N2637R	N800HS	N808HS			
0052	N26379	N252CJ	N52PK			
0053	N2638A	N53CJ	N66ES	N60ES	(N603JC)	
0054	N2638U	N54CJ				
0055	N2639Y	N923AR				
0056	N2646X	N56NZ	JA8420			
0057	N525DG					
0058	N2647Y	N525CK				
0059	N2647Z	N71GW				
0060	N2648Y	XA-SOU	XA-TRI	N525WW		
0061	N26481	N61CJ	N525PS			
0062	N26486	C-FRVE	C-GINT			
0063	N2649J	N55SK				
0064	N2649S	D-IHEB				
0065	N2649Y	N5259Y	EC-704	EC-FZP		
0066	N26495	N420CH				
0067	N26499	N594JB	N525TF			
0068	N2650V	N68CJ	N303LC	N888KU		
0069	N26502	N169CJ	N20FL	N20VL		
0070	N26504	(N70HW)	D-ISGW			
0071	N26509	N940SW				
0072	N2651R	(TG-FIL)	TG-RIF			
0073	N2656G	(D-IHEB)	N77794			

CITATIONJET

C/n	Identities					
0074	N26581	N511TC				
0075	N5076K	N719L				
0076	N5079V	N80TF	N4TF			
0077	N50820	N1000E				
0078	N5085E	N525CH				
0079	N5086W	N179CJ	N525WB			
0080	N5090A	N80CJ	N33DT			
0081	N5090V	N181JT				
0082	N5090Y	D-IHHS				
0083	N5091J	N34TC	(N121CP)			
0084	(N5092D)	D-ITSV				
0085	N5093D	VR-CDN	PT-MJC			
0086	(N5093L)	PT-MIL				
0087	(N5093Y)	N175PS	(N717DA)	N926CH		
0088	(N50938)	N188CJ	N722SG			
0089	N5135K	N189CJ	N920MS			
0090	N5136J	N8288R				
0091	N5138F	N295DS				
0092	N51396	N525AS	N523AS			
0093	N5151S	I-IDAG				
0094	(N51522)	N94MZ				
0095	N5153K	N61SH				
0096	N5153X	(EC-)	D-ICEE			
0097	(N5153Z)	N234WS	N130MR	w/o 26Mar00 near Buda TX		
0098	N5156D	N511AC				
0099	N5156V	N525SC	N525CP	N526CP*		
0100	N51564	N525CC	(N808HS)	N800HS	VH-CIT	
0101	(N5157E)	F-GPFC				
0102	N52038	N202CJ	TC-CRO			
0103	N5204D	(N203CJ)	D-IVHA	OE-FLG		
0104	N5207A	N606MM				
0105	N52081	N305CJ	(D-IAFD)			
0106	N5211A	N21VC				
0107	N5211F	N525WC				
0108	N5211Q	N108CJ				
0109	N52113	N37DG				
0110	N5213S	N195ME				
0111	N52136	N776DF				
0112	N5214J	N1006F	VT-OPJ			
0113	N5214K	N111AM				
0114	N5214L	N96GM				
0115	N52141	OO-PHI				
0116	N5201M	N41EB				
0117	N5203J	N217CJ	(N349CB)	N26CB	N26QB	
0118	N5203S	N52178	(N61TF)	N118AZ	D-IRWR	
0119	(N5264E)	N47TH				
0120	N5264M	PT-WGD				
0121	N5264S	TC-EMA	D-ICSS			
0122	N5264U	N102AF				
0123	(N52642)	N5223P	D-IRKE			
0124	N5090A	N525JH	VP-CWW	ZS-BSS*		
0125	N5090V	N525PE				
0126	N5090Y	N1264V	N14TV	D-IFUP	VP-CFP	D-IHGW
0127	N5091J	N127CJ	N63LB	N63LF		
0128	N5092D	N535LR				
0129	N5093D	N52642	N229CJ			
0130	N5093L	N416KC				
0131	N5093Y	(N577SD)	N577SV			
0132	N50938	N132AH	(N132RP)			
0133	N52038	EC-261	EC-GIE			
0134	N5204B	N234CJ	N525JM	N525TL*		
0135	N5207A	N888RA				
0136	N52081	N525KL	w/o 09Dec99 Branson-Point Lookout MO			
0137	N5211A	N810SS				
0138	N5211F	VH-MOJ				
0139	N52457	N76AE				
0140	N5246Z	N725L				
0141	N5250E	N774CA	N237DG	N525TA		
0142	N5068R	N815MC	N5068R	N815MC		
0143	N51993	D-IOMP	D-IALL			
0144	N5200R	D-IDAG				
0145	N52141	N145CJ				
0146	N5100J	N1329G	(OE-FGG)			
0147	N52178	N996JR				
0148	N52144	N148CJ				
0149	N5218R	N67GH				
0150	N5090V	ZS-NUW				
0151	N5086W	N1015B	9A-CGH	(9A-CAD)	(N151TT)	N7EN	N400RL
0152	N5112K	N152KC	N152KV			
0153	N5090V	N551G	N551Q	(N525EF)	VP-CNF	

CITATIONJET

C/n	Identities					
0154	N51246	N401LG				
0155	N5132T	N155CJ	I-EDEM			
0156	N156ML					
0157	N51817	N1115V	N57HC			
0158	N5093D	N749CP	N800RL			
0159	N51872	N131RG				
0160	N5076J	N66AM				
0161	N5076K	N525BT				
0162	N5122X	N1XT	N525JW			
0163	N5138F	N51CD				
0164	N51444	D-ICGT	N204J			
0165	N5148B	D-IJYP				
0166	N5148N	N343PJ	F-GRRM			
0167	N5151S	(N4EF)	N1EF	N525RA		
0168	N51522	D-IRON				
0169	N5153K	N68CJ				
0170	N5153X	N170BG				
0171	N5153Z	N97VF				
0172	N5156B	N172CJ	D-IAVB	N350GM	VP-CTA	
0173	N51564	N970SU				
0174	N5157E	N817CJ	N417C			
0175	N175CP	N41PG				
0176	N5161J	PT-WLX				
0177	N5163C	N1280A	(RP-C717)	G-OCSB		
0178	N525RC					
0179	N5166U	N377GS				
0180	N5168F	N123AV	(N133AV)	VP-BDS		
0181	N5180K	N181CJ	N88LD			
0182	N5183U	(N740JB)	N177JB	N177JF		
0183	N5185J	(N97CJ)	N399G			
0184	N5185V	N525J				
0185	N5187B	N51176	N1241N	(RP-C8288)	N83TR	N13FH
0186	N51246	N186CJ	N92ND			
0187	N5130J	N696ST				
0188	N51342	(D-IVID)	D-IVIN			
0189	N189CM					
0190	N51396	N41NK	N701TF			
0191	N5145P	N525BF	(N525BL)	C-FIMA		
0192	N51444	N84FG				
0193	N5132T	N193CJ	D-ILCB			
0194	N5148B	N81RA				
0195	N5138F	N525DC	(N525ST)			
0196	N5135A	D-IURH				
0197	N5151S	N525KH	EC-HIN			
0198	N51522	N315MR				
0199	N5153K	N1216K	9A-CAD	N524AF		
0200	N5153Z	N1276J	N226B			
0201	N5156D	N525HV				
0202	N5120U	N202CJ	N747AC			
0203	N5122X	N525GP	N33FW			
0204	N5133E	N1293G	(N323LM)	B-4108		
0205	N5156V	N550MC				
0206	N5136J	N17VB				
0207	N51872	N31SG				
0208	N5153X	N208JV	N211GM			
0209	N5162W	D-ILAT				
0210	N5157E	N210CJ	N999EB			
0211	N	D-IMMD				
0212	N51176	N67VW				
0213	N5168F	N525WM				
0214	N51743	D-IFAN				
0215	N5166U	N28GA				
0216	N5183V	N18GA				
0217	N5202D	(5Y-TCI)	D-IEWS			
0218	N51881	N64LF				
0219	N5197A	N219CJ				
0220	N220CJ	C-GHPP				
0221	N5203S	D-IWIL				
0222	N52038	N111LR	w/o 04Apr98 Roswell, GA			
0223	N5211Q	D-IGAS				
0224	N52038	N224CJ				
0225	N5211F	N525RM				
0226	N5214J	N1216N	TC-LIM			
0227	N5214K	N741CC				
0228	N5216A	N668VP				
0229	N5218R	D-IHOL				
0230	N5218T	N323LM				
0231	N5223D	N606JR				
0232	N5223Y	N525PF				
0233	N5235G	N233CJ	N53CG			

CITATIONJET

C/n	Identities		
0234	N900P	N950P	
0235	N5246Z	VP-BZZ	I-ESAI
0236	N	D-ISWA	
0237	N237CJ		
0238	N5203S	PT-WQI	
0239	N5188N	(PT-WQJ)	PT-XJS
0240	N525GM		
0241	N52081	N241WS	N207BS
0242	N242LJ		
0243	CC-PVJ		
0244	N66ES		
0245	N5214J	N33CJ	
0246	N525EC		
0247	N533JF		
0248	N248CJ		
0249	N5214L	N909M	
0250	N250CJ	HB-VMT	
0251	N50ET		
0252	(N5223P)	N740JV	VP-CIS
0253	N5223P	N8940	
0254	N5183V	OE-FGI	
0255	N514DS		
0256	(N196DR)	N196HA	
0257	N9003	N116DK	N26DK
0258	N5203J	N108CR	
0259	N5235G	PT-MSP	
0260	N5197A	D-IGZA	
0261	N31HD		
0262	N52457	N262BK	
0263	N263CT		
0264	(D-IKHV)	VP-CHV	EC-HBC
0265	N198JH		
0266	N52081	N266CJ	
0267	N5201J	PT-XMM	
0268	N850DG		
0269	N5219T	N607DB	
0270	N5194J	N525HC	
0271	N860DD		
0272	N4GA		
0273	(N525HC)	N911NP	
0274	N	PT-XDB	
0275	N700GW		
0276	N800GW		
0277	N277CJ	OY-JMC	
0278	N5145V	N1127K	N100SM
0279	N	D-IGME	
0280	N5151D	PT-XAC	
0281	N5154J	N1280S	N41NK
0282	N625PG		
0283	N95BS		
0284	N256JB		
0285	N55PZ		
0286	N51666	D-ICEY	
0287	N73PM		
0288	N288AG		
0289	N	D-ISHW	
0290	N808WA		
0291	N51744	F-GPLF	
0292	N117W		
0293	N1127K		
0294	N294AT		
0295	N5209E	N295CM	OE-FJU
0296	N296DC		
0297	N316MJ		
0298	N	G-RSCJ	
0299	N525BE	N711BE	
0300	N300CQ	N881KS	
0301	N27CJ		
0302	N302CJ	N326B	
0303	N51612	D-IMMI	
0304	N1128G	EC-HBX	
0305	N826HS		
0306	(N525BE)	N4RH	
0307	N114FW	N114FG^	
0308	N72SG	N525DR	
0309	N	D-IBMS	
0310	N	D-IVBG	D-IIJS
0311	N523BT		
0312	N	F-GTMD	
0313	N525MP		

CITATIONJET

C/n	Identities		
0314	N5154J	N428PC	
0315	N	(D-IIRR)	D-IAME
0316	N5136J	N187DL	N316EJ
0317	N51444	N317CJ	
0318	N5145P	N525DP	
0319	N5148N	PT-FNP	
0320	N150BV		
0321	N	D-IAAS	PH-ECI
0322	N52LT		
0323	N900GW		
0324	(N428PC)	N5163C	G-IUAN
0325	N464C		
0326	N5183U	N23KG	
0327	N398EP		
0328	N328CJ		
0329	N	XA-DGP	
0330	N5153K	N330CJ	N331MS*
0331	N888RK		
0332	N5161J	OO-FNL	
0333	N5185J	N99CJ	
0334	N51872	N44FE	N525M
0335	N5156D	N335CJ	N335CT
0336	N51564	N105P	
0337	N5241Z	PT-FJA	
0338	N51575	N525RL	
0339	N5225K	N339B	
0340	N5165T	N392RG	
0341	N341AR		
0342	N5216A	N342AC	N918OK
0343	N5244F	D-IURS	
0344	N77VR		
0345	N5185V	G-ZIZI	
0346	N5153J	N5136J	PP-CRS
0347	N5145P	N1133G	I-DAGF
0348	N348KH		
0349	N	D-ICWB	
0350	N51444	HP-1410HT	
0351	N5246Z	VP-BRJ	
0352	N5185V	N99JB	
0353	N5211Q	D-ICOL	
0354	N5225K	N821P	
0355	N51396	N205FH	
0356	N5213S	PP-YOF	
0357	N5214J	N357JV	
0358	N51564	G-HMMV	
0359	N	F-GTRY	
0360	N5156D	N31CJ	(First production CJ1 model)
0361	N5183U	N361RB	
0362	N5214L	N362CJ	
0363	N5161J	N525AS	
0364	N5211F	N525DL	
0365	N651CJ		
0366	N5223Y	D-IRMA*	
0367	N525MD	N525FT	
0368	N820CE		
0369	N5200U	N629DM	
0370	N5145P	N525MW	
0371	N5165T	N175SB	
0372	N372CP		
0373	N415CS		
0374	N12GS		
0375	N5225K	N375KH	
0376	N52352	N802JH	
0377	N5241Z	N15C	
0378	N525CP^		
0379			
0380	N381CJ		
0381	N856BB		
0382	N525LF		
0383			
0384			
0385			
0386	N45MH		
0387			
0388	N525MH		
0389	N389CJ		
0390			
0391			
0392			
0393	N	D-IBIT*	

CITATIONJET

C/n	Identities
0394	N64PM
0395	
0396	
0397	
0398	
0399	
0400	
0401	
0402	N525ML
0403	
0404	
0405	
0406	
0407	
0408	
0409	
0410	
0411	
0412	
0413	
0414	
0415	
0416	
0417	
0418	
0419	
0420	
0421	
0422	
0423	
0424	
0425	
0426	
0427	
0428	
0429	
0430	
0431	
0432	
0433	
0434	
0435	
0436	
0437	
0438	
0439	
0440	
0441	
0442	
0443	
0444	
0445	
0446	
0447	
0448	
0449	
0450	

CESSNA 525A CITATIONJET CJ2

Note: The CJ2 is a 525 with two additional fuselage plugs and a new wing section.

C/n	Identities	
708	N2CJ	ff 27Apr99 McConnell AFB Wichita KS - converted from original 525 prototype c/n 702 q.v.
0001	N525AZ	
0002	N5252	N765CT*
0003	N5148N	N132CJ
0004	N52136	N142CJ
0005	N5235G	N552CJ
0006		
0007		
0008		
0009		
0010		
0011		
0012		
0013		
0014		
0015		
0016		
0017		
0018		
0019		
0020		
0021		
0022		
0023		
0024		
0025		
0026		
0027		
0028		
0029		
0030		
0031		
0032		
0033		
0034		
0035		
0036		
0037		
0038		
0039		
0040		
0041		
0042		
0043		
0044		
0045		
0046		
0047		
0048		
0049		
0050		

Notes: Cessna developed a military jet trainer from the Model 525 for the US JPATS contract evaluation. It was given the model number 526 and, while it used many 525 parts, it bore no resemblance to the CitationJet. For the record, the two prototypes were c/n 704 N526JT, ff 20Dec93, and c/n 705 N526JP, ff 02Mar94.

CESSNA CITATION II/BRAVO

This production list is presented in order of the Unit Number which was used and allocated by Cessna rather than by the normally used c/n. A c/n-Unit Number cross-reference follows the production list.

Unit No	C/n	Identities
	686	N550CC ff 31Jan77 cvtd to S550 standards cx Apr91; presumed wfu
001	550-0001	(N98751) (N551CC) N5050J N560CC (converted to Model 560)
002	551-0027	N98753 N552CC N44GT N552CC N522CC
003	551-0004	N98784 N553CJ YV-19CP N19CP
004	F550-0004	N98786 C-GPAW N312GA F-GNCP
005	550-0005	N98817 OE-GKP N77ND
006	550-0006	N98820 N2 N6 N152GA N725RH
007	550-0007	N98830 N300PB (N447FM) N650WC N650WG (N550TY)
008	550-0008	N98840 N575W OE-GIW (N108AJ) N550JF N70X N70XA
009	550-0009	N98853 N744SW N744DC N656PS
010	550-0010	N98858 OE-GEP N550PL N806C PT-LPK
011	550-0021	N98871 N296AB (N171CB) N900LJ N52RF
012	550-0011	(N99876) Venezuela 0002
013	550-0012	N3208M N513CC C-GHOL N11FH
014	551-0002	N3210M YV-140CP N20FM N700AS XA-SLD N39ML N502CL
015	550-0014	N3212M N702R N780GT (N94FS) N780CF
016	550-0013	N3216M YV-151CP N3952B N21SW N21SV PT-LML cx Aug97 status?
017	550-0016	N3221M N276AL (N216VP) HC-BTJ N204MC
018	551-0007	N3223M YV-169CP (N169CP) YV-169CP YV-05CP N60FJ
019	550-0018	(N3225M) N752CC
020	551-0006	N3227A YV-06CP YV-O-CVG-2
021	550-0017	N3230M VH-MAY P2-RDZ N771ST
022	550-0019	N3232M N1851T N1851D (HI-530) HI-534 HI-534CA N1851D (N200GP) N900AF N7RC
		w/o 26Apr95 Walkers Cay, Bahamas; cx Oct95 - remains to Dodson Avn, KS
023	551-0071	N3236M PH-HES OO-RJT PH-HES N4578F N79CD N790D N551DS N551HH
024	551-0003	N3237M YV-205CP N4445N N72RC I-MESK
025	550-0025	N3239M (EP-KID) EP-KIC N9014S N664JB N664J N78PH N78PR 9H-ACR
026	550-0026	N3240M N256W (N2231B) N30AV
027	550-0027	N3245M N527CC G-BFRM
028	550-0028	(N3246M) (G-BFLY) OE-GAU N501BL N888MW N100CX (F-GHUA) 5Y-HAB N310AV
029	550-0029	(N3247M) G-JEEN N502AL N718VA N202PB N7CC N550TJ N524MA
030	551-0077	(N3249M) G-DJBI G-FERY G-MSLY N64CA VR-CSS N507AB N501KC (N200G) N601KK
		N4TS N16TS
031	550-0031	N3250M RP-C550 RP-C296 N22GA
032	550-0032	N3251M N810SC N810SG N55BP N66ES N50US N905EM N112JS N232CW
033	550-0033	(N3252M) TR-LYE N59MJ N755CM N46DA F-GPLT F-WPLT LX-GDL
034	550-0034	N3258M N771A N697A N60CC N922SL
035	550-0219	(N3261M) N108WG HB-VGK N4457A N108WG VH-ORE N12AC YV-606CP N550RP N550PM
036	550-0036	(N3262M) N58AN N5Q (N54DA) N36CE N711BP (N789RR) N789BR
037	550-0037	(N3268M) N37HG N361DJ XA-SDV (N551NA) N535MA N829NL N237CW
038	550-0038	(N3271M) N526AC N526AG C-FLDO N642CC (N842CC)
039	551-0084	(N3273M) G-BJHH EI-BJL N78FA ZP-TYO N848D
040	550-0040	(N3274M) N220CC N277CJ N900LC HK-3607X N554BA N550SC (N551GA) N545GA
041	550-0024	N3276M N533M N85MG N313CK XA-SJZ N313CK N413CK
042	550-0035	N3278M N8417B N50XX N333X N74G (N50GG)
043	550-0041	N3279M N8418B N341AG N985BA N177HH OE-GCI
044	550-0042	N3283M N666RC N57MB N66AT C-FPEL
045	550-0045	N3284M N4CH N4CR 5N-AMR w/o 21May91 private airstrip Bauchi, Nigeria
046	550-0043	N3285M N6Q VR-CCI N801JP N112SH
047	550-0044	N3286M N3526 N550HM N300TW N308TW
048	550-0048	N3288M N534M N161BH N384DA N10BF N19ER
049	551-0010	N3291M YV-137CP N55AL*
050	550-0046	(N3292M) C-GRHC
051	551-0095	N3296M N1AP N66LB G-HOTL N999WA N49TJ N314CK N200TJ (N127TA) C-GAMW
		N627TA N400PC N402TJ N48DK
052	F550-0050	(N3298M) N102FC N362DJ D-CJJJ N250CF F-ODUT F-GMCI
053	550-0053	(N3300M) N4VF N53VP N53KB TC-NKB N550EC N519AA
054	550-0054	(N3301M) N501AA VH-WGJ VH-OYW
055	550-0055	(N3308M) N55CC N2JZ (N1466K) N10EG
056	550-0047	N3313M (N66VM) OB-M-1171 N66VM N44AS
057	550-0075	N3314M N55BH N58BH C-GSFA N710MT N910MT
058	550-0068	N3319M N558CC N558CB N402ST
059	550-0242	N1955E N551BC
060	550-0051	N1958E C-GJAP C-GBCB N678CA ZS-RKV
061	551-0009	N1959E D-IMTM (N458N) rebuild following accident 26Aug96 Coburg, Germany
062	551-0017	N2052A N1UH (N33FW) N53WF N811VC N811VG
063	550-0069	N2069A F-GBPL 3A-MWA HZ-AAA HZ-ALJ N550CE OE-GIN (N269AJ) N551JF N550AB
		C-FFCL N712PD
064	550-0070	N2072A N564CC N108DB N777FL N550KA N892PB
065	550-0065	N4191G N55SX ZS-RCS N144GA
066	550-0071	N4308G C-GDPD N404BF (N404BV) CS-DCI
067	550-0052	N4620G (OO-LFX) OY-ASV N90MJ N534MW N67TM PH-CTZ
068	F550-0073	N4621G F-GBTL VP-CTJ
069	550-0074	N4754G N48ND (N86JM) LN-AAI N386MA (N551GN) (N10GN) D-CIFA LX-THS

CITATION II

Unit No	C/n	Identities									
070	550-0056	N5342J	N752RT	N444FJ	N89D						
071	550-0058	N5348J	N71CJ	N100HB							
072	550-0072	(N2661H)	N360N	N36QN	(N700EA)	N969MT	N551SR	N770JM	N778JM		
073	550-0057	(N2661N)	VH-WNZ								
074	550-0338	(N2661P)	(D-ICWB)	(N71RL)	N22RJ	HB-VGE	N28968	N550DW	N500GM	N500QM	N900SE
		N900MF									
075	550-0060	N26610	(N550KR)	N75KR	N98BE	N315CK	OE-GIL				
076	550-0370	N26613	YV-213CP								
077	550-0061	(N26614)	N456N	N458N							
078	550-0062	(N26615)	(N77SF)	C-GDLR							
079	551-0117	(N26616)	C-GHYD	N11AB	OO-SKS						
080	550-0064	N26617	YV-36CP	N64TF	(N550TJ)						
081	550-0066	N26619	(N3031)	N3032	N733H	N783H	N10JP	(N410JP)	N19HU		
082	550-0077	(N2662A)	N582CC	N578W	XA-PIJ	XA-AGN					
083	550-0078	(N2662B)	N31KW	N71FM	N78GA	C-GPTR	(N277A)	N533MA			
084	551-0122	(N2662F)	N10LR								
085	550-0090	N2662Z	N4110S	N4110C	N410NA	N290VP					
086	550-0371	(N26621)	N551MC	C-GCJN							
087	550-0079	(N26622)	N930BS	(N26DA)	N789SS	N33RH	N232DM				
088	550-0089	(N26623)	N88MJ	(N44JX)	(N444WJ)	N43RW	N81CC				
089	550-0080	(N26624)	G-BFLY	HB-VGR	N22511	N45ME					
090	550-0081	N26626	I-FBCT	N254AM	I-AROO						
091	550-0082	N26627	G-BMCL	N21DA	N49U						
092	551-0024	N26628	N2CA	w/o 18Dec82 Mountain View, MO							
093	550-0084	N26229	N222LB	N808DM	N156N	N226N	N226L	N521WM	(N467MW)	N391AN	
094	550-0067	N2663B	N81TC	N74TC	N867CW	N267CW					
095	551-0018	N2663F	N455DM	N666AJ	N556CC	LN-AAD	N387MA	D-IEAR			
096	550-0086	N2663G	N414GC	(N93CW)	N43SA	XC-HGZ	N43SA				
097	551-0132	N2663J	(C-FCFP)	C-GTBR	N78GA	SE-DYR					
098	551-0133	N2663N	G-JRCT	N222TG	I-JESA						
099	550-0076	(N2663X)	LN-HOT	VH-LSW	VH-TFY	VH-XDD					
100	550-0085	(N2663Y)	OY-GKC	N57AJ	OE-GBA						
101	550-0094	(N26630)	G-JETA	G-RDBS							
102	550-0095	N26631	N400DT	N100UF	N550CG						
103	550-0096	N26632	N550EW	N30UC	N87SF						
104	550-0097	N26634	N404G	N404E	N202CE						
105	550-0098	(N26635)	N17S	N212H	N211JS						
106	551-0020	N26638	YV-147CP	YV-1478P	(N772AC)	YV-678CP	N477A	(N999LL)			
107	551-0021	N26639	N107BB	N307AJ	N551CF	N55LS					
108	551-0141	N2664F	(N108CT)	N95CC	N210MJ	N888RF	N888HW	N100SC	N388MA	CC-CWZ	
109	550-0099	N2664L	N109JC								
110	551-0143	N2664T	(N801L)	N801G	N2S	C-FKHD	N140DA	C-GLMK			
111	550-0101	(N2664U)	N91MJ	(N42BM)	w/o 31Dec95 Marco Island Airport, FL						
112	550-0102	N2664Y	VH-WNP	VH-JCG	VH-JPG						
113	550-0376	N26640	N313BT	N30FJ	N30EJ	N73ST					
114	F550-0092	(N26643)	N89B	N89Q	F-GFPO	N89Q	F-GNLF	N567CA			
115	551-0026	(N26648)	N551R	N12TV	N25NH	N32PB					
116	550-0105	N26649	N116CC	D-CNCP	I-MTNT	N105BA	N550LH				
117	550-0106	N2665A	Argentina AE-129		LQ-TFM	AE-129	(N83MA)	N37CR	N308CK	N820MC	
118	551-0149	N2665D	N550CB	N225AD	N225FM	N550JS					
119	550-0108	(N2665F)	N4TL	N4EK	(N65SA)	VP-CBE					
120	550-0109	N2665N	N753CC								
121	550-0091	(N2665S)	N527AC	N527AG	N601BC						
122	550-0110	(N2665Y)	N222SG	N122G	N550SF*						
123	550-0111	N26652	N3R	N34WP	(N3184Z)	N123VP					
124	550-0112	(N26656)	(C-GDPE)	C-GDPF	N550PS	N3FA					
125	550-0113	N2666A	N227PC	C-GDMF							
126	550-0114	N2745G	(N89B)	N55HF	N88HF	N83HF	(N900BM)	N991BM			
127	550-0115	N2745L	N127SC	SE-DDY	OY-CCU	SE-DDY					
128	550-0116	N2745M	HZ-AAA	HZ-AA1	PT-LGM	N413CA	N669MA				
129	550-0117	N2745R	N575FM	N150HR	N150HE	N550RB					
130	550-0162	N2745T	VH-UOH	N550KP	N1UA						
131	550-0118	N2745X	LV-PHH	N131ET	N999BL	N162DW	EC-743	EC-FIL	N118EA		
132	551-0163	N27457	N80BS	D-IGRC	ZS-ARG						
133	550-0378	N2746B	YV-299CP	N3999H	OH-CAT	D-CIFA					
134	550-0121	N2746C	N655PC	OB-M-1195	OB-1195	N850BA	N51FT	N896MA			
135	550-0122	N2746E	N135CC	N70GM	C-FCEL	G-OSMC	HB-VKH	N221GA	C-GCUL		
136	550-0123	N2746F	(CC-CGX)	N36CJ	N81TF	SE-DEV	LN-NEA	SE-DEV	LN-NLA	N748DC	
		N948DC*									
137	550-0124	N2746U	LN-VIP	N4557W	N57MK	N57MF	N124CR	N109GA			
138	550-0125	N2746Z	N5500F	N320S	N125RR	5N-NPF					
139	551-0169	(N2747R)	OE-GHP	N26863	N82RP	N82RZ	N50HW	N700YM	N14RM		
140	550-0103	N2747U	XA-JEZ	N90MA							
141	551-0171	N26178	(9V-PUW)	ZS-PMC	5R-MHF						
142	550-0184	N2619M	N80DR	N813DH	N200NC	(N20TV)					
143	550-0127	N2631N	N29TC	(N29TG)	N550TJ	G-GAUL	G-ESTA				
144	551-0174	N2631V	N536M	N220LA	YU-BPU	RC-BPU	9A-BPU	F-WLEF	EI-CIR	N60AR	EI-CIR
145	550-0129	N2632Y	N537M	N129TC	N122MM	N122HM					

CITATION II

Unit No	C/n	Identities								
146	550-0104	N2633N	CC-ECN	Chile E-301						
147	550-0132	N2633Y	G-CJHH	N13627	N500VB	(N330MG)	PT-LLU			
148	550-0133	N2634Y	G-BHBH	C-GRIO	N228CC					
149	551-0179	N2635D	HZ-AAI	HZ-ZTC	N203BE	N127BU				
150	551-0029	N26369	(G-BHGH)	N168CB	N551PL	N500ER	D-ICUR			
151	551-0180	N8520J	(D-CACS)	N852WR	D-ICAB	N166MA	(N729MJ)	N222VV*		
152	551-0181	N2638A	N56GT	N137CF	N29B	N565VV				
153	550-0138	N2646X	XC-SCT							
154	550-0139	N2646Y	ZS-KOO	N222MJ	PT-LJA	N39FA	PT-ORD	(PT-WQG)		
155	550-0140	N2646Z	N55WL	(N45WL)						
156	550-0141	N26461	VH-ING	VH-INX						
157	550-0142	N2648Z	PT-LCR	N387SC						
158	550-0143	N2649D	N100VV	N550TT	PT-LQW	(N660AC)	N150RD			
159	550-0144	N2649E	RP-C689							
160	550-0145	N2653R	N444JJ	VH-TFQ	P2-MBN	P2-TAA				
161	550-0146	N26610	N580AV	(N611RR)	N501LC					
162	551-0036	N162CC	N160D	N317SM	N3170B					
163	551-0191	N222AG	N550CP	(N771R)	N107SB	D-IVOB	N127KR	N386AM		
164	550-0149	N116K								
165	550-0150	N2668A	N1SV							
166	550-0279	(N88838)	N566CC							
167	550-0152	N88840	(N107)	RP-C581	N88840	N550CA				
168	550-0153	(N88842)	N27BA	N278A	N50HS	N50HE	N27MH	N37MH		
169	550-0130	(N88845)	N77RC	N778C*						
170	550-0381	(N88848)	N170CC	N155PT	N155BT	(N49VP)	N391BC			
171	550-0154	(N8777N)	G-DJBE	G-EJET	G-JETJ					
172	551-0032	(N98715)	YV-300CP	N551TT	N852SP					
173	550-0383	(N98718)	N551AB	N561AS						
174	551-0031	(N98749)	N6565C	YV-301CP	N75TG	N5T	N5TQ			
175	550-0155	N6566C	(YV-209CP)	YV-298CP	N65TF	N31RC	N155TJ	N168AM	N215CW	
176	550-0156	N98784	N6567C	(N31F)	N205SG	N205SC				
177	551-0201	N177CJ	C-GGSP	N550JB	N550GB					
178	550-0175	N10JK	C-FWWW	C-GHWW						
179	550-0165	N98871	3D-ACQ	ZS-LHU	N976GA					
180	550-0166	N88731	PH-MBX	N166CF	N166VP	N367JC				
181	551-0205	N88732	N999AU	XA-KIQ	N3951Z	N342DA	HB-VIO			
182	550-0167	N88737	N100CJ							
183	550-0158	N88738	(N662AA)	N423D	N550AJ	N2JW	N49HS			
184	550-0168	N88740	(VH-ICT)	VH-TNP	VH-LJK	N785CA	VH-LJK	N68GA	ZS-NII	
185	550-0169	(N88743)	N185CC	N6001L	XC-HHA	N6001L				
186	550-0170	N88791	N550TP	N550TR	N37BM	N500CV	N508CV	N550DA		
187	550-0172	N88795	(N28MM)	N72MM	N88JJ	N78CS	N412P			
188	550-0171	(N88797)	(C-GDPE)	N43D	N934H	(N984H)	N333CG	EI-BYN	(N171VP)	N19AJ
189	550-0234	N88798	N511WC	C-FLPD						
190	551-0214	N8881N	N107T	N163DA	N178HH	N9SS				
191	551-0215	N88822	(N36NW)	N286G	N169JM	(N169DA)	N550HP	(N151PR)	N500PX	N551CL
192	550-0179	N88824	N60MM	N673LP	N673LR					
193	550-0180	N88825	N320V	N77WD	N77WU	N3030C	(N303GC)	(N89TA)	N3030T	
194	550-0181	N88826	RP-C653	N550GP	N50US					
195	550-0182	N88830	(F-BKFB)	F-GCSZ	N78TF	F-GEFB	N30XX	N165MC		
196	551-0050	N98403	N1823B	N196HA	N196HR	N228AK				
197	550-0186	N98418	N80AW	YV-187CP	N80AW					
198	550-0187	N98432	N303X	N143DA	N6WU	N57CE	N57CK	C-GHOM	N598CA	
199	550-0218	N98436	N45EP	PT-LPP						
200	551-0223	N98468	(N200MR)	N550LP	LN-AFG	5B-CIS	LN-AAC	N754AA	YV-2567P	N28GZ^
201	550-0174	(N98510)	N201CC	N666WW	N87PT					
202	550-0151	(N98528)	N35HC	N495CM						
203	550-0176	N98563	N552TF	N900TF	(N900TE)	N900TJ	N83SF	N83SE	(N24TR)	N61MA
204	551-0023	N98599	N155TA	N34DL	PT-LME					
205	550-0189	N98601	D-CAAT	HB-VGP	D-CCCF					
206	550-0183	N98630	(XC-DUF)	HB-VGS						
207	550-0188	N98675	VH-SWL	HB-VIZ	N38NA	N280PM				
208	550-0147	N98682	N155JK	N80GM						
209	550-0190	N98715	F-BTEL							
210	550-0083	N98718	N54CC	N200VT						
211	550-0164	N164CC	N7YP	(N24PT)	N916RC	N721DR				
212	551-0033	N88692	D-IJHM	w/o 19May82 Kassel, Germany						
213	550-0191	N88707	C-GWCR	C-GWCJ	N550PA					
214	550-0192	N88716	N44ZP	YV-900CP						
215	550-0249	N88718	N829JM	(N401U)	N201U	PT-LZO	(N48NA)	N39GA	N456AB	
216	550-0159	(N88721)	N45ZP	N188SF	C-GAPT	N444GB				
217	550-0194	N88723	N91B							
218	550-0205	(N88727)	N30JD							
219	550-0196	N6798Y	N68DS	N1212H	N800EC	N88ML	N400DK	HB-VLS	N196JS	
220	550-0197	N6798Z	(N30F)	N44FC	HB-VIT					
221	550-0198	(N67980)	XC-DOK	XA-SQV						
222	550-0199	N67983	N586RE							
223	550-0260	N67986	N32JJ	N82JJ	N8CF	N6HF				

CITATION II

Unit No	C/n	Identities									
224	551-0245	N67988	N224CC	LN-AAE	w/o 15Nov89 Mt Langfjelltind, nr Bardufoss, Norway						
225	550-0200	N67989	(G-BHVA)	N34SS	N28S	N287	N28S	N284	N810MC		
226	550-0206	N6799C	XC-DUF	XA-SQW	N280TA						
227	550-0201	N6799E	N334AM	N566TX	N1GH						
228	550-0185	N6799L	N815GK	N600EZ	N370AC	N511DR	N511DL	N317HC			
229	550-0157	N6799T	N550K	N101BX	N257CW						
230	550-0202	N6799Y	N590RB	N10CF	(N5GA)	N175VB					
231	550-0203	N67990	N12JA	N62HA	N766AE	(N766AF)	N857BT*				
232	550-0209	N67997	N121C	N101KK	(N877GB)						
233	550-0238	N67999	N97S								
234	550-0207	N6800C	(N95CC)	N163CB	N60BB	N1823C	HB-VJH	N207BA	N196RJ		
235	550-0135	N6800J	VH-KDI	N39142	ZS-LLO	N555BC	TF-JET	N555BC	N550BP	YV-888CP	
236	550-0214	N6800S	N13BJ	N44WF	N75Z	N75ZA					
237	550-0222	N6800Z	N17RG	PT-LNC							
238	550-0215	N68003	N500WP	(N400MT)	N40MT						
239	550-0204	(N6801H)	N820	N200JR	(N300PR)	N815CE					
240	550-0216	N6801L	N240AR	(N911NJ)	N550PG						
241	550-0208	N6801P	N54RC	N222WL	cx Mar91; scrapped for spares						
242	550-0223	N6801Q	N900BA	N901RM	N701RM	N400PC	N81TJ	N239CD			
243	550-0284	N6801R	I-ARIB	OY-JEV							
244	550-0211	N6801T	XA-LOT	N611CF	N77PH	N77PR					
245	550-0212	(N6801V)	N245CC								
246	551-0038	N6801Z	D-IBPF	N550DA	N103M						
247	550-0210	N68018	N762PF	(N177CM)	N3PC	N37WP	(N3184V)	N19VP	XA-SDN	XA-KMX	
248	550-0220	N6802S	N95CC	N275CC	N288CC	HI-500	HI-500SP	HI-500CT	N80513	(N962HA)	N4CS
		N4ZS									
249	550-0193	N6802T	(N47RP)	XC-FOO	XC-ROO	N2160N	N492ST	N72FL	N260J		
250	550-0213	N6802X	N420P	N421TX	N550HB						
251	550-0224	N6802Y	YV-O-MTC	YV-O-MTC-20		Venezuela 2222					
252	550-0228	N6802Z	(N702BC)	5N-AWJ	N96CS	VH-EXM					
253	550-0221	N68026	N253W	N95AX							
254	550-0227	N68027	N254CC	(N71CG)	PT-LND						
255	550-0229	N6803E	N550JM	OY-GRC	N50FC	C-FGAT	N229MC				
256	550-0239	N6803L	8P-BAR	N4720T	N66MC						
257	550-0235	(N6803T)	N67SG	I-PNCA							
258	550-0225	(N6803Y)	(N34SS)	N258CC	PT-LTJ						
259	550-0195	N68032	N60JD	(N41CK)	N61CK						
260	550-0236	N68033	N611ER	N611CR	N711VR	LN-AAD	N823NA				
261	550-0248	N6804C	N550SA								
262	550-0226	N6804F	N29WS	N300JK	N550RG	N772HP					
263	550-0217	N6804L	N88DD	N66DD	N66DN	N340DA	I-CIGA	N217SA			
264	550-0237	N6804M	3D-ACT	ZS-NHO							
265	550-0230	(N6804N)	(G-OTKI)	N3254G	N270RA	N141DA	N550EK	N550WB			
266	551-0285	N6804S	(N550RL)	N551SR	ZS-MLN	N551HK	Venda VDF-030		ZS-MLN		
267	551-0046	N6804Y	C-GDDC	N34YL	N81GD						
268	550-0241	N6804Z	N10FN	N268J	(N32TJ)	XC-BCS	N241FT	XA-...			
269	550-0390	N6805T	N58GG	(N500EE)	N500AE	N135BC	N136BC	VT-VPS			
270	550-0250	N68599	N9LR	N33GK	N250VP						
271	550-0231	N6860A	N28RF	(N221BW)	N671B	N88TB	N140DR	N148DR	N41SM		
272	551-0289	N6860C	N98GC	N666JT	N551BW	PT-LJF					
273	550-0243	N6860L	TI-APZ	VR-BHG	N1333Z	XA-POR	XA-REN				
274	550-0307	N6860R	N37BM	N550VW							
275	550-0254	N6860S	N171CB	XA-TEL	(N828SH)	N112SA	N888RT				
276	550-0247	N6860T	(N18DD)	N928DS	PT-LJJ	N85NA*					
277	551-0035	N6860U	N277HM	N277JM							
278	551-0039	N6860Y	ECT-023	EC-DOH	N71LP	N550TA					
279	550-0245	N68607	N505GP	N388SB							
280	550-0257	N68609	XC-HEQ	XA-SQQ	N187TA						
281	550-0303	N6861D	(N281AM)	N160VE	N40FJ	N4JS	N450CC	XB-GLZ			
282	551-0296	N6861E	N72TC	N78TC	N69ME	(N396DA)	N68ME	N35BP	N551TK		
283	550-0255	N6861L	I-DEAF	N28GA	I-JESO						
284	550-0232	N6861P	N929DS	N797CW							
285	550-0258	N6861S	N172CB	(N550DD)	N550CM	N463C	N550FB	N258JS	N550PR		
286	550-0256	N6861X	N3300L	N550SM	N550BM	N75HS	N75TP				
287	550-0251	N68615	PK-WSO	PK-TRV	N550HF						
288	550-0261	N68616	N40GS	C-FLDM	N41JP	C-FLDM	(N261VP)	N261SS	N50AZ		
289	550-0259	N68617	VH-KDP	N810JT	OY-BZT						
290	551-0304	N6862C	G-DJHH	G-TIFF	N7028U	N702KH	N304KT				
291	550-0393	N6862D	N12GK	I-FLYD							
292	550-0264	N6862L	N550KC	N777WY							
293	550-0265	N6862Q	(N314MC)	(N265QS)							
294	550-0252	N6862R	N507GP	N6JL							
295	550-0253	N68621	N23ND	N18ND	N31DA	N75EC	N202TS	N953FT			
296	550-0266	N68622	N296CC	N296PH	N296CF	OE-GEC	N15NA				
297	550-0267	N68624	N932LM	N15Y	(N194JM)	N502BG	XA-OAC	N910RB			
298	551-0311	N68625	N298CJ	N500EX	N500FX	N38TT					
299	550-0289	N68629	D-CBAT	OE-GST	N550MD	N820FJ	N820SA	N22HP	C-FTIL		
300	551-0313	N6863B	OE-GLS	N270CF	YV-2426P						

CITATION II

Unit No	C/n	Identities
301	551-0051	N6863C (D-IHAT) D-ICTA
302	550-0269	N6863G N74MG N760 N28RC N1MM N28RC N1MM
303	550-0271	N6863J (N303EC) N555EW N655EW N550CA N303J PT-ORO N167MA N729MJ N1NL
304	550-0290	N6863L VH-JBH OE-GCH N290BA N217LG N312NC
305	550-0285	N6863T N20CN N20CF (N17PL) N40PL N989TW N989TV
306	550-0286	N68631 N306SC SE-DLY N78BA N2GG
307	550-0272	N68633 9M-WAN VH-JPK HB-VKX VR-BVV VP-BVV SE-DVV Sweden 103001 (Swedish AF type designation Tp-103) has code 031
308	550-0273	N68637 N217FS
309	550-0277	N6864B N44LF (N550MT) N550WJ
310	550-0274	N6864C ZS-LDK N14GA HB-VKT VP-CCM
311	551-0323	N6864L (N990Y) N819Y N555RT
312	551-0056	N6864X (N312CC) I-GAMB N214AM I-NIAR
313	550-0280	N6864Y N280MH N864D N300TC N7SN
314	550-0281	N6864Z N31RK N33EK
315	550-0282	N68644 G-JETC G-JCFR
316	550-0283	(N68646) N316CC N316H N316CF N316CC TC-BAY N124GA N225J
317	550-0287	N68648 N444MM N65LC N67LC N920E YV-909CP N550RL N771AA (N221JS) N527DS*
318	550-0276	N68649 C-GGFW N53FT
319	550-0288	N6865C G-JETB N4564P G-JETB G-MAMA G-JETB (G-OXEH) w/o 26May93 Eastleigh, Southampton, UK
320	550-0291	N6887T ZP-PNB ZP-TNB N550CD N41C N1AF
321	550-0292	N6887X N114EL (N63FS) C-FTOM
322	550-0293	N6887Y w/o 19Dec92 Billings, MT; cx May93
323	550-0294	N68872 PH-HET N323CJ PT-LPN
324	551-0335	N68873 N74KV N431DS D-ILCC
325	550-0295	N68876 N483G N800LA N345JR
326	550-0296	N6888C G-BJIR
327	550-0304	N6888D N208TC N369DA (N70PH) N42PH
328	550-0299	N6888L N538M HB-VIR N511AB
329	550-0302	N6888T N329CC N441T N133BC N33BC N792MA
330	550-0306	N6888X N303EC N550MT N341CW
331	551-0065	N6888Z N8AD N99DE N99CN
332	550-0300	N68881 YV-162CP
333	550-0310	N68887 N130TC (N779DD) (N730TC) N779DD N779BD N530P
334	550-0397	N68888 N114DS
335	550-0312	N6889E N58H N61HA N61CF
336	550-0313	N6889K (N393HC) N393RC N246NW N960CP N32TM
337	550-0311	N6889L N43TC N43TE N44TC N121CP N2RC N211SP
338	550-0398	N6889T VH-BRX N101DD I-KESO (N550SC) N398S PH-CTX
339	550-0318	N6889Y N642BB PT-LJT PT-WJZ
340	550-0315	N6889Z N90JD N618DB N59GU
341	550-0308	N68891 3D-AVH N30SA (F-GIRS) N15XM
342	551-0053	(N6890C) N66MS
343	550-0320	(N6890D) N343CC N300GM N800SB N800EL N800VJ
344	550-0322	(N6890E) N7FD N612CC N27U N322CS N5TR
345	550-0319	N6890G N8BX N26SC N26CT N76CK N78CK
346	550-0316	N5428G N828B N143RW N42KC N129TS
347	550-0321	N5430G N321SE TC-COY N321GN VP-CCO
348	551-0355	N5451G N551AS I-ALPG
349	550-0327	N5474G N74JA N74JN PT-LLT
350	550-0400	N5492G N350CC N888EB N53CC w/o 02Oct89 Roxboro, NC; cx Jul90
351	550-0323	(N5703C) OE-GCP TC-FAL TC-FMB TC-YZB N323AM^
352	550-0324	N5873C N171LE I-JESJ N23W HB-VLQ
353	551-0359	N67983 (N551SE)
354	551-0360	N67988 G-BJIL N550MD C-GSCR N24CJ N551EA
355	551-0361	N6799C LV-PNB LV-APL
356	550-0275	N6799L N550JR N550CP N555DS
357	550-0301	N6799T China 091 B-4103
358	550-0333	N67990 PT-LCW N313CE N123GM
359	550-0305	N67999 China 090 B-4105
360	550-0329	N6800C (N49N) N491N
361	550-0334	N6800S N92LT N404KS
362	550-0297	N68003 China 092 B-4104
363	551-0369	N696A N999GP N998GP N68BK
364	551-0066	N6825X N242WT
365	550-0335	N6829Y N1847B N1847P N51PS N667CG N204AB N235TS N187JN*
366	550-0402	N6830X N700LB N717PC N57SF
367	550-0336	N6830Z N90Z
368	550-0337	N6802S N727C N75F (N78BA) N54HJ (N54HC) N406SS
369	550-0326	N6802T N12FC PT-OAF (N983AJ) N390AJ (N390JP)
370	550-0339	N6802Y VH-KTK VH-SCD
371	550-0403	N68027 N101RL N637EH N362CP
372	550-0332	N6803L N372CC N1880F N12CQ N120Q
373	550-0341	N68032 C-GJAP N182U C-FDYL N141JC (N367EA)
374	550-0340	N6804F N374FC N219SC N219CS N219SC N235DB ZP-TWN N38DD
375	551-0378	N6804L G-BJVP N4581Y (N43D) N115VH N6EL (F-OGUO) (F-OGVA) N322MA
376	550-0345	N6804Y N312DC N3GT N30CZ N267TG N267TC (N782NA) (N50NA) N982NA

CITATION II

Unit No	C/n	Identities							
377	551-0060	N6805T	N465D	N46SD	N458HW	(N458H)	(N60HW)	N59GB	
378	550-0344	(N6806Y)	N6806X	N532M	PT-LKR	N550GM			
379	550-0357	N6808C	N632SC	N29G	HB-VJA	N29FA	PT-OAG		
380	550-0347	N6826U	ZS-LEE	VH-ZLE					
381	550-0348	N381CC	I-VIKI	N550CA	C-GSCX				
382	550-0346	N550CF	N106SP						
383	550-0349	N8FD	N870PT	(N221LC)					
384	550-0350	N86SG							
385	550-0405	YV-276CP	YV-604P	YV-778CP					
386	550-0351	N99KW	I-ALKA	(N167WE)					
387	551-0388	N711WM	w/o 06Nov86; no details known; cx Nov87						
388	550-0354	N121CG	N121C	VR-CJR	VP-CJR				
389	550-0358	N6801Q	Myanmar 4400						
390	550-0356	N6801Z	PT-OER	N133WA					
391	550-0343	(N1214D)	G-MINE	N721US	N20GT	N56FB	A6-SMS	G-ORCE	N789TT
392	551-0393	N1214H	(N18CC)	N122SP					
393	550-0352	(N1214J)	(N140DV)	N140V	(N72B)	I-ALKB	N352AM	VT-EUN	
394	550-0363	N1214S	(N777NJ)	N444CC	HK-3400X	N363SP	N741T		
395	551-0396	(N1214Z)	N395CC	N39K	N39KY	N45GA	LV-WXD		
396	550-0362	N12142	N396M						
397	550-0353	(N12149)	G-GAIL	N3251H	N922RA	N922RT	LN-AAB	N922RT	N477KM
398	550-0406	(N1215A)	N398CC	C-GHKY	N551CE	C-FTAM	N781SC	LV-ZPD	
399	550-0366	N1215G	N200E	N2008	N773LP	N55FM	(N614GA)		
400	551-0400	(N67983)	N550WR	N95CT	N280JS	D-IMME			
401	550-0407	(N1215S)	N600CR	(N767TR)	N758S	(N950FC)			
402	550-0368	(N12155)	N94ME	N94MF	N718CK				
403	550-0364	N12157	N100AC	N550AV	C-GLTG	N180FW			
404	550-0365	(N12159)	N712J	N100AG	N100AY	N129DV			
405	550-0367	(N1216A)	N95CC	N17LK	N17LV	N3MB	N45ML		
406	550-0408	N1216H	N400TX	N110WA					
407	550-0409	N1216J	N22T	HI-496	(N22TZ)	HI-496SP	N7153X	VR-CIT	N102HB
408	550-0410	N1216K	(N258P)	N46MK	N46MF	C-GNWM			
409	550-0411	N1216N	N200YM	C-FMPP	N550KW*				
410	550-0412	N1216Q	N410CC	N830VL	N223J				
411	550-0355	(N1216Z)	N122CG	N125CJ	N440TX	N500BR	N355DF		
412	551-0412	N12160	G-OMCL	N413VP	OY-PDN				
413	550-0414	N12162	N342CC	(N414VP)					
414	550-0415	N12164	D-CNCI	OH-CUT	N1949B	N1949M	F-GJYD		
415	550-0416	N12167	N416CC						
416	550-0417	N1217D	ZS-LHW	N17DM					
417	550-0418	N1217H	N550J	N418CG					
418	550-0419	N1217N	G-JETD	VH-JVS	G-WYLX	G-DCFR	G-FJET		
419	551-0419	N1217P	N200RT	N200RN	(N10PX)	I-AGSM	N555KT		
420	550-0421	N1217S	N67HW	N510GP					
421	551-0422	N1217V	N421CJ	OO-RJE	SE-DEF	OE-GES	N550RD	D-IAWA	
422	550-0423	N12171	N45MC	C-GUUU	C-FCCC				
423	550-0424	(N12173)	N18CC	N46A	(N469)	N24AJ	N555DH	N271CG	N551BP
424	550-0425	N1218A	(LN-FOX)	Spain U20-1/01-405					
425	550-0426	N1218F	N404SB	N434SB					
426	550-0427	N1218K	N923RL	PT-LHY	N527EA	N840MC			
427	550-0428	(N1218P)	N7004	N7864J	N107WV	N97BG			
428	551-0428	N1218S	(N70HC)	(N147RP)	w/o 22Dec99 Crisp County/Cordele GA				
429	550-0430	N1218T	N264A	N1278	HB-VLY	N567S	N56FT		
430	551-0431	N1218V	N21EH	N218H	N900TN	N59CC	(N431JC)	N4MM	N4NM
431	550-0369	N1218Y	(N342CC)	N324CC	N431CB	N55MT	N725BA	N725BF	N725FL
432	550-0433	N1219D	I-KIWI	N131GA	N7ZU				
433	550-0434	(N1219G)	N1109	N1178	(N515M)	N152JC	(N152JQ)	(D-CVAU)	N53FP
434	550-0435	(N1219N)	N434CC	N20CL	N390DA	N674G			
435	550-0436	N1219P	N711Z	N717DM					
436	551-0436	N1219Z	N235KK	N437CF	N11SS				
437	550-0438	N12190	(N555TD)	N437CC	N643TD				
438	550-0432	(N12191)	N432CC	I-ASAZ	N76AS				
439	550-0439	N1220A	ZS-LHT	N550RS	HK-3191X	N550RS	N511WS		
440	550-0440	(N1220D)	N31F	N31FT	N120TC	OY-CYV			
441	550-0441	N1220J	N50LM	N56PC	VR-CCE	HB-VKS	N221GA	G-RVHT	
442	550-0442	(N1220N)	N32F	N53M	N943LL	N442MR	N442ME		
443	550-0443	N1220S	N777FE	N777FB	OY-CYT	D-CGAS			
444	550-0444	(N1248G)	N67MP	(N67ME)	N47SW				
445	551-0445	N1248K	(N666WW)	N453S					
446	550-0446	N1248N	Spain U20-2/01-406						
447	550-0447	"N1248K"	N12482	(N447CJ)	HB-VIS				
448	550-0448	N1249B	N964JC	N964J	N309AT	N82GA	N93DW	(N39HD)	N938W
449	550-0449	N1249H	(YV-1107)	YV-2338P	Venezuela 1107		YV-2338P		
450	550-0450	N1249K	N15EA						
451	550-0451	N1249P							
452	550-0452	(N1249T)	N452CJ	N150DM	N707WF	N707PE	N707PF		
453	550-0453	N1249V	N962JC	N962J					
454	550-0454	N1216K	(N258P)	N12490	N93BD	N938D			

CITATION II

Unit No	C/n	Identities							
455	550-0455	N1250B	(YV-04CP)	N90SF	PT-MMO				
456	550-0456	N1250C	(N456CM)	N549CC	N24RF	N20RF	C-GMPQ	N283DF	
457	550-0457	N1250L	N220CC	N457CF	N63TM	OY-TMA			
458	550-0458	N1250P	N458CC	(N458DS)	XA-SET	N25MK	N664SS		
459	550-0459	N12500	N15TW	N15TV	N315ES				
460	550-0460	N12505	N818TP	N818TB	(PT-)	N6523A	PT-OKP		
461	550-0461	N12507	N22FM						
462	550-0462	N12508	N509TC	N67JW	XA-LTH	XB-LTH	N501DK	N550AL	
463	551-0463	N1251B	N121JW	(N131EL)	YV-05C	YV-713CP			
464	550-0464	N1251D	XC-HEP	XA-SQR	N117TA				
465	550-0465	N1251H	N206TC	N68JW	HB-VIU	N784A	N387HA	N551WJ	
466	550-0466	N1251K	HI-420	(N1251K)	HI-420	N1251K	I-TNTR	N412MA	N10LY
467	550-0467	N1251N	N1883	N64PM	N64CM	YV-810CP			
468	550-0468	(N1251P)	N468CJ	D-CBEL	N123FH	N120JP			
469	550-0469	N1251V	G-BKSR	VR-BIZ	HB-VIP	N123SR	N50N		
470	550-0470	N1251Z	N10RU	F-GFJL	N10RU				
471	550-0471	N12510	N797WC	N787WC	N92B				
472	550-0472	N12511	HZ-AFP						
473	550-0473	N12513	HZ-AFQ						
474	550-0474	N12514	ZS-LIG						
475	550-0475	N1252B	N870MH	N475WA					
476	550-0476	N1252D							
477	550-0477	N1252J	N1515P	N151JC	N648WW	N649WW	N47TW	(N477JR)	N269JR N269JD
478	550-0478	N1252N	N4FE	N57BC	N214RW				
479	550-0479	N1252P	N999RC	PT-OOM	N45NS				
480	550-0480	(N12522)	N72K	N72U	YU-BPL	SL-BAC	S5-BAC	N335CC	N380MS ZS-OIE
481	551-0481	N1253D	N550MW	D-IADD	N531A	CC-LLM			
482	550-0482	N1253G	N62GC	N62WG	N594G				
483	550-0483	(N1253K)	N141AB	N483AS	N83AG	N147PS	N483SC		
484	550-0484	N1253N	N84EA						
485	550-0485	N1253P	N474SP	N74SP	N485A	PT-WBV	N727C		
486	550-0486	N1253Y	A40-SC	N410CS	N35PN*				
487	550-0487	N12532	(N487CC)	N444BL	N550DW				
488	550-0488	N12536	N84EB						
489	550-0489	N12539	N63CC	N15RL	N801TA*				
490	550-0490	N1254C	N490CC	N490CD*					
491	550-0491	(N1254D)	I-AVRM						
492	550-0492	(N1254G)	I-AVGM						
493	550-0493	N1254P	(N258P)	N84AW	N84GC				
494	550-0494	N1254X	(XC-JBR?)	N1254X					
495	550-0495	(N1254Y)	N495CC	JA8495	N505GL	PT-LLQ	(N400MC)	N10TC	
496	551-0496	(N12543)	N232CC	N8008F	N999GH	LX-PRS			
497	550-0497	(N12549)	N1257B	(XC-JBQ?)	N1257B				
498	550-0498	(N1255D)	N550CJ	N1823B	N78FK				
499	550-0499	(N1255G)	N550PT	PT-LIV					
500	551-0500	N1255J	N90RC	N501MC					
501	550-0501	N12549							
502	550-0502	N1255D	Turkey 12-001						
503	550-0503	N1255G	Turkey 12-002						
504	550-0504	(N1255J)	N979C	N979G	N72SL	XA-TQA			
505	550-0505	N1255K	(XC-JAY?)	N1255K					

Unit numbers 506 to 549 not used (506 to 531 built as S550s c/n 0001 to 0026 - qv)

Unit No	C/n	Identities							
550	550-0550	N1299N	PT-LOC	N550FM	HK-4128W	N550FM			
551	550-0551	N487LD	N600AT						
552	551-0552	OE-FPA							
553	550-0553	N553CC	N46MT	XA-ODC	(N555SL)	N5XR			
554	550-0554	N1297Y	ZS-NAT	N2140L	N40FC	(N40WE)	N40YC	N700JR	
555	551-0555	N1297Z	(EI-BUN)	EI-BUY	D-IRKE	N93BA	N560CB		
556	551-0556	(N12979)	N200GF						
557	551-0557	N1298C	N711NV						
558	550-0558	(N1298G)	N209G	N558VP	N558AG	LV-WJN			
559	551-0559	(N1298H)	G-BNSC	VR-CHB	D-ICHE	OO-MMP			
560	550-0560	N1298J	ZS-LNP	N560AJ					
561	550-0561	N1298K	I-SALV	N916WJ	PT-OYP	(N234RA)	C-GYCJ		
562	550-0562	(N1298N)	D-CBAT	N562CD	PT-OJT	N813A	N54RM		
563	550-0563	N1298P	G-THCL						
564	550-0564	N1298X	PH-MCX	(N87683)	N564VP	C-GBCF	N674CA	D-CASH	w/o 19Feb96 nr Freilassing, Salzburg, Austria
565	550-0565	N1298Y	N565CJ	N88BM	N565JS	N565NC			
566	550-0566	(N1299B)	N15SP	N15SN	N900PB				
567	550-0567	(N1299H)	N321F	N41BH	N926RM				
568	550-0568	N1299K	N988RS	N83KE					
569	550-0569	N1299P	G-JFRS	G-OSNB	5Y-TWE				
570	550-0570	(N1299T)	N2KH	N570VP	N570WD				
571	550-0571	N12990	N90JJ	(N278S)					
572	550-0572	N12992	N193SS						

CITATION II

Unit No	C/n	Identities						
573	550-0573	(N12993)	C-FJOE	N944AF	PT-OKM	N155AC		
574	551-0574	N12998	N60GL	N60GF	OE-FBS			
575	550-0575	N12999	N910G	N46BA	N337RE	N387RE		
576	550-0576	(N1300G)	N576CC	N438SP				
577	550-0577	(N1300J)	N577CC	N100CX	N120HC	N827JB		
578	550-0578	N1300N	PT-LQJ	N54NS				
579	550-0579	(N13001)	N579L					
580	550-0580	(N13006)	N912BD					
581	550-0581	(N13007)	N905LC					
582	550-0582	(N1301A)	Colombia FAC-1211					
583	550-0583	N1301B	N62WA	(N583VP)	N12L			
584	551-0584	N1301D	N550WW	N550WV	N25QT			
585	550-0585	N1301K	C-GTCI	N94AF	N79SE			
586	550-0586	N1301N	F-GGGA					
587	550-0587	N1301S	ZS-MBX	N550SM	N1301S	N18HJ		
588	550-0588	N1301V	N255CC	N92BD				
589	550-0589	N1301Z	N679BC					
590	550-0590	C-GBCA	N673CA	N88NM*				
591	551-0591	C-GBCE	N672CA	N1AT				
592	550-0592	N1302N	Spain U20-3/01-407					
593	550-0593	N1302V	N26621	(XC-JBT?)	N26621			
594	550-0594	N1302X	N2531K					
595	550-0595	N2734K						
596	550-0596	N96TD	D-CAWA	EC-HGI				
597	550-0597	N13027	G-SSOZ	G-MRTC	N24EP	N400LX	N400EX	N213JS
598	550-0598	N13028	(PT-)	XC-ROO	N7WY			
599	550-0599	G-SYKS	N599FW	VR-BPF	VR-BYE	N571BC		
600	550-0600	N1303H	PT-LSR	(N675DM)	N415AJ			
601	550-0601	(N1303M)	G-ELOT	G-OCDB				
602	550-0602	N2663Y	(XC-JAZ?)	N2663Y				
603	550-0603	N603CJ	C-GMSM					
604	550-0604	N821G	N30WE	LV-WIT	N64VP	N827JB	N887SA	
605	550-0605	N26494						
606	550-0606	N770BB	N602AT					
607	550-0607	N26496						
608	550-0608	N12419	PT-LTL	N608VP	N608AM	N990M		
609	550-0609	(N1242A)	N609TC	D-CHOP	N344A	F-GLTK		
610	550-0610	N1242B	"M-JMF"	9M-JMF	(9M-UEM)	9M-NSA		
611	550-0611	(N1242K)	F-GGGT					
612	550-0612	N1244V	N300AK	N380AK	(N534M)	N578M		
613	550-0613	N1250P	PT-OAC					
614	551-0614	(either N1251P or N1251V)			D-ILAN			
615	550-0615	N12522	N88HF	N87CF	CS-AYS	N615EA	N577VM	
616	550-0616	(N1253K)	N55LS	(D-IAFA)	PT-OVV			
617	551-0617	(N1253Y)	N617CM	D-ILTC	N450GM	N747JB*		
618	550-0618	N1254C	PT-LXG	PP-ESC				
619	550-0619	(N1254D)	N170TC	(N619BA)	N550BD			
620	550-0620	N1254G	PT-LYA	N250GM	N508DW			
621	550-0621	N12543	ZS-MLS	N502SU	OY-RDD	N102PA	N99TK	
622	550-0622	(N1255J)	N326EW	N826EW	HB-VKP			
623	550-0623	(N1255L)	N89LS					
624	550-0624	N1255Y	PT-LYS					
625	550-0625	(N12554)	PT-LYN	N625EA	N6846T			
626	550-0626	(N1256G)	N117GS	N626VP	LV-PLR	LV-WOZ	N466SS	
627	550-0627	(N1256N)	N17FL	N650WC				
628	550-0628	(N1256P)	N183AJ	N183AB	Ecuador IGM-628			
629	550-0629	N1256T	D-CHVB	w/o 25Jan95 Allendorf, Germany; cx Mar95				
630	550-0630	N1257K	PH-CSA	N220AB	N198DF	N198ND		
631	550-0631	(N1257M)	N631CC	XA-RUD	XA-ICP	N631EA		
632	550-0632	N12570	5N-AYA					
633	550-0633	N12576	PT-OSK	N388FA	N7AB	N550AB		
634	550-0634	(N1258B)	PH-MDX	N550SB	SE-DVT			
635	550-0635	N1258H	PT-OAA	N550NS	(N622EX)	N622VH		
636	550-0636	N1258M	N4EW	N50NF				
637	550-0637	(N1258U)	YV-376CP					
638	550-0638	(N12582)	N500RR	N1717L	N255TC			
639	550-0639	(N1259B)	N22RG	N62RG	N100DS			
640	550-0640	(N1259K)	N1308V	PT-ODL				
641	550-0641	(N1259N)	N1309A	PT-OOA	N1309A	PT-WON		
642	550-0642	(N1259R)	N1309K	XA-JRF	XA-SEX			
643	550-0643	(N1259S)	N13091	PT-ODW	N643MC	N747CR		
644	550-0644	(N1259Y)	(either N13092 or N1310B)			XC-PGM		
645	550-0645	(N1259Z)	N1310C	PT-ODZ				
646	550-0646	(N12593)	(N1310G)	N9VF				
647	550-0647	(N12596)	N647CC	N205BE				
648	550-0648	N1260G	(N1310Q)	XC-PGP				
649	550-0649	(N1310Z)	I-ATSE	N4320P	N44LC	N44LQ	HB-VMH	

CITATION II

Unit No	C/n	Identities						
650	550-0650	(N1311A)	PK-WSG+	N28RC	N824CT			
		+marks carried but was not officially regd						
651	550-0651	(N1131K)	N24E					
652	550-0652	(N1311P)	N3262M					
653	550-0653	N36854	N30RL					
654	550-0654	N36886	XA-RZB	XB-BON				
655	550-0655	N37201						
656	550-0656	(N)	N30GR					
657	550-0657	N3986G	CC-DGA					
658	550-0658	(N)	N550MZ	RP-C1180				
659	550-0659	N4614N	(XC-HGZ?)	N4614N				
660	550-0660	N5233J	D-CMJS	5B-CIQ	N550JF	D-CILL	N160SP	N827DP
661	550-0661	N5252C	N550RA	N847HS	N3444B			
662	550-0662	N5294C	N911CB					
663	550-0663	N5314J						
664	550-0664	N5315J	N67LH	XA-RYR	N70PC			
665	550-0665	N5348J	N665MC	N998BC				
666	550-0666	(N5703C)	N5408G	(XC-JBS?)	N5408G			
667	550-0667	(N)	EC-621	EC-FDL	N668EA	VR-CWM	VP-CWM	N167EA
668	550-0668	(N)	N668CM	N1879W				
669	550-0669	N6170C	N98TJ	N6170C	N846HS			
670	550-0670	N6637G						
671	550-0671	(N6761L)	9M-TAA	N671EA	G-BWOM			
672	550-0672	N6763C	PT-OMB	N550PF	G-OTIS	N550PF	G-OTIS	
673	550-0673	N6763L	(XC-HHA?)	N6763L				
674	550-0674	(N6770S)	(N550FB)	N1883M	N1888M	N45TP		
675	550-0675	N6773P	PT-OJK	N275BD	PT-WKQ			
676	550-0676	N67741	PT-OJG					
677	550-0677	N6775C						
678	550-0678	N6775U	EC-777	EC-FES				
679	550-0679	(N6776P)	I-FJTO	N250GM				
680	550-0680	N6776T						
681	550-0681	(N6776Y)	N1200N					
682	550-0682	(N)	N682CM	YV-662CP	N682CJ	N90BL		
683	550-0683	(N)	YV-701CP					
684	550-0684	N6778L	C-FJXN					
685	550-0685	(N)	C-FJWZ					
686	550-0686	(N)	C-FKCE					
687	550-0687	(N)	N6778Y	C-FKDX				
688	550-0688	(N)	C-FKEB					
689	550-0689	(N)	N12001	XA-JPA	XA-JYO			
690	550-0690	N6780C	OE-GLZ					
691	550-0691	(N)	N910H	C-GAPD	C-GAPV			
692	550-0692	(N)	N692TT	N75RJ				
693	550-0693	(N)	VR-BTR	VP-BTR	N594WP			
694	550-0694	(N)	N694CM	N550KE				
695	550-0695	N6782T	N695VP	N870WC	N7851M			
696	550-0696	(N)	N29PF	N67PC				
697	550-0697	N6851C	ZS-NFL	N697EA	HB-VMP			
698	550-0698	N12003	YV-911CP	N550RM				
699	550-0699	(N)	C-FKLB					
700	550-0700	(N)	C-FJCZ					
701	550-0701	(N)	C-FLZA					
702	550-0702	(N)	C-FMFM					
703	550-0703	(N)	N308A					
704	550-0704	(N)	N704CD	(N197GH)	N197HF			
705	550-0705	(N)	N521TM					
706	550-0706	(N)	7Q-YLF					
707	550-0707	N1202T	RP-C4654	N707EA	(SE-DYY)	OE-GDM		
708	550-0708	N12022	N720WC					
709	550-0709	N1203D	N709CC	N12RN	N18RN	N85KC	N709VP	N709RS*
710	550-0710	N1203N	ZP-TCA	N510VP	N90BJ			
711	550-0711	N1203S	N711CN	N58LC				
712	550-0712	(N12030)	PH-LAB					
713	550-0713	N12033	N293PC	N95HE				
714	550-0714	N12035	N593EM	G-SPUR				
715	550-0715	N1204A	PT-OTN	N715AB	LV-PNL	LV-YHC		
716	550-0716	N1205A	N4VR	(N800KC)	VR-CTE	VP-CTE	VP-CTF	
717	550-0717	(N1205M)	XA-TCM	N600GH	TC-SES			
718	550-0718	N12060	XA-FIR					
719	550-0719	N12068	(N550BG)					
720	550-0720	(N1207A)	N720CC	XA-SMV	N72WE	N848HS		
721	550-0721	N1207B	N721CC					
722	550-0722	N1207C	XA-SMT	N1886G				
723	550-0723	N1207D	N5NE	(N888NA)				
724	550-0724	N1207F	LV-PGU	LV-WEJ				
725	550-0725	N1207Z	N222FA	N725CC				
726	550-0726	N1209T	XT-AOK	N918GA	VP-CMD			

CITATION II

Unit No	C/n	Identities						
727	550-0727	(N1209X)	N727CM	N521BH	LV-ZNR			
728	550-0728	(N1210N)	N728CC	LV-PHN	LV-WJO			
729	550-0729	N1210V	VR-CBM	VP-CBM				
730	550-0730	N1211M	N730BR	(N730VP)	N2NT	N773VP	(N650JP)	N501JP
731	550-0731	N12117	N550BP	XA-SST				
732	550-0732	N1213S	N101AF					
733	550-0733	N1213Z	C-GFCI	N4347F	N550VR	N550TR		
734	550-0734	first Bravo model		(N1214J)	N550BB			

Production continues as Citation Bravo

CITATION BRAVO

C/n	Identities			
550-0801	N5135K	N801BB		
550-0802	N5135R	N802CB	N550HH	
550-0803	N52113	N550FB		
550-0804	N5214J	N804CB	N550BC	
550-0805	N5214K	N108RF		
550-0806	N52141	N300PY		
550-0807	N52144	C-FANS		
550-0808	N5216A	N1299B	SE-DVZ	
550-0809	N800AK	N300AK		
550-0810	N5218T	VH-MGC		
550-0811	N5221Y	PT-MMV		
550-0812	N5223P	C-FJBO		
550-0813	N5096S	N813CB	N100KU	
550-0814	N5093L	PT-WNH		
550-0815	N51038	N126TF		
550-0816	N5225K	C-FMCI		
550-0817	N5076J	N817CB	(YV-)	N123GF
550-0818	N5097H	LV-PMV	LV-WYH	N818AJ
550-0819	N5092D	N1259B	N15CV	
550-0820	N5117U	N820CB		
550-0821	N5093Y	N77797		
550-0822	N5214L	N550TG	N822CB	N52MW
550-0823	N50715	(N823CB)	N25FS	
550-0824	N5121N	N824CB		
550-0825	N5060P	N25HV		
550-0826	N51072	N595PC		
550-0827	N51042	D-CCAB		
550-0828	N5058J	N6FR		
550-0829	N5096S	N829CB		
550-0830	N5076J	(N550KE)	N830KE	
550-0831	N5145P	N331PR		
550-0832	N5148B	PT-WSO	N832UJ	
550-0833	N5145P	PT-WVC		
550-0834	N834CB	D-CALL		
550-0835	N835CB	N198SL		
550-0836	N51872	N122NC		
550-0837	N5185J	OE-GPS		
550-0838	N49FW			
550-0839	N839DW			
550-0840	N5086W	N442SW	N773CA	
550-0841	N5086W	N841WS		
550-0842	N86AJ	N842CB		
550-0843	N5079V	N627L		
550-0844	N550KL			
550-0845	N51817	N550WS		
550-0846	N5101J	N517AF		
550-0847	N5076K	N133AV		
550-0848	N997HT			
550-0849	(N849CB)	N51143	N541JG	
550-0850	N5073G	N551G		
550-0851	N7NN			
550-0852	N5076J	VH-FGK		
550-0853	N5086W	N398LS		
550-0854	N5188A	N550KH	N550KJ	
550-0855	N132LF			
550-0856	N820JM	N300GF		
550-0857	N51246	VP-CNM	VP-CCP	
550-0858	N1273Q	N100WT		
550-0859	N551KH	(N550KH)	I-BENN	
550-0860	N860JH			

CITATION BRAVO

C/n	Identities			
550-0861	N861BB	N26CB		
550-0862	N442SW	N1962J		
550-0863	N704JW			
550-0864	N864CB	OE-GTZ		
550-0865	N505X			
550-0866	N866CB	D-CHZF		
550-0867	N161TM			
550-0868	N5117U	N627BC		
550-0869	N98RX	N499WM		
550-0870	N50612	VP-CED		
550-0871	N5108G	N871CB	I-GIWW	
550-0872	N5093L	OE-GKK		
550-0873	N5109R	PT-XCX		
550-0874	N5194B	D-CHAN		
550-0875	N51055	TG-BAC		
550-0876	N5135A	N876CB	5Y-MNG	
550-0877	N5085J	N21SL		
550-0878	N5135K	VH-ZLT		
550-0879	N5000R	N4M		
550-0880	N5112K	N7YA		
550-0881	N5105F	N546MT	N312RD*	
550-0882	N5068R	N488A	N12MA*	
550-0883	N469DE			
550-0884	N5090Y	N602BW	N1318Y	N361DB*
550-0885	N5109W	N820JM	N88AJ	
550-0886	N550KH			
550-0887	N887BB			
550-0888	N550BF	N162TJ*		
550-0889	N619JM			
550-0890	N1961S			
550-0891	N82MA			
550-0892	N22GR			
550-0893	N5073G	N333EB		
550-0894	N51160	N550TE		
550-0895	N199BB			
550-0896	N121L			
550-0897	N5079V	EI-GHP		
550-0898	N550GH			
550-0899	N5076K	N899DC		
550-0900	N327LJ			
550-0901	N5058J	N857AA		
550-0902	N5095N	N770JM		
550-0903	N51055	N14HB		
550-0904	N5093Y	N904BB		
550-0905	N5101J	N505AG		
550-0906	N5166T	C-GLCE		
550-0907	N5155G	N316MA	D-	
550-0908	N5264M	N242SW		
550-0909	N5076J	N706CP	(N909CA)	C-GDSH
550-0910	N5207V	N574M		
550-0911	N52655	N575M		
550-0912	N5117U	N588AC		
550-0913	N5096S	N232BC		
550-0914	N897MC			
550-0915	N51143	N915BB		
550-0916	N5265N	N555BK		
550-0917	N5100J	EI-DAB		
550-0918	N5109R	N45VM		
550-0919	N52601	N100Y		
550-0920	N5109W	N63LB		
550-0921	N5073G	N40MF		
550-0922	N51896			
550-0923	N51160	N676BB		
550-0924	N5090Y	XT-		
550-0925	N5090V			
550-0926	N5154J	N72PB		
550-0927	N5061P			
550-0928				
550-0929				
550-0930				
550-0931	N233DW			
550-0932	N	G-MIRO^		
550-0933	N417KW			
550-0934	N200AS			
550-0935	N	EI-PAL^		
550-0936	N550TM			
550-0937	N440CE			
550-0938				

CITATION BRAVO

C/n	Identities
550-0939	N939BB^
550-0940	
550-0941	
550-0942	
550-0943	
550-0944	
550-0945	
550-0946	
550-0947	N947CB
550-0948	
550-0949	N550KG
550-0950	N555HM
550-0951	
550-0952	
550-0953	
550-0954	
550-0955	
550-0956	
550-0957	
550-0958	
550-0959	
550-0960	
550-0961	
550-0962	
550-0963	
550-0964	
550-0965	
550-0966	
550-0967	
550-0968	
550-0969	
550-0970	
550-0971	
550-0972	
550-0973	
550-0974	
550-0975	
550-0976	
550-0977	
550-0978	
550-0979	
550-0980	
550-0981	
550-0982	
550-0983	
550-0984	
550-0985	
550-0986	
550-0987	
550-0988	
550-0989	
550-0990	
550-0991	
550-0992	
550-0993	
550-0994	
550-0995	
550-0996	
550-0997	
550-0998	
550-0999	
550-1000	
550-1001	
550-1002	
550-1003	
550-1004	
550-1005	
550-1006	
550-1007	
550-1008	
550-1009	
550-1010	
550-1011	
550-1012	
550-1013	
550-1014	
550-1015	
550-1016	

CITATION 550 UNIT NUMBER CROSS REFERENCE

C/n	Unit	C/n	Unit	C/n	Unit	C/n	Unit	C/n	Unit	C/n	Unit
550-0001	001	550-0082	091	550-0169	185	550-0245	279	550-0326	369	550-0428	427
550-0004	004	550-0083	210	550-0170	186	550-0247	276	550-0327	349	550-0430	429
550-0005	005	550-0084	093	550-0171	188	550-0248	261	550-0329	360	550-0432	438
550-0006	006	550-0085	100	550-0172	187	550-0249	215	550-0332	372	550-0433	432
550-0007	007	550-0086	096	550-0174	201	550-0250	270	550-0333	358	550-0434	433
550-0008	008	550-0089	088	550-0175	178	550-0251	287	550-0334	361	550-0435	434
550-0009	009	550-0090	085	550-0176	203	550-0252	294	550-0335	365	550-0436	435
550-0010	010	550-0091	121	550-0179	192	550-0253	295	550-0336	367	550-0438	437
550-0011	012	550-0092	114	550-0180	193	550-0254	275	550-0337	368	550-0439	439
550-0012	013	550-0094	101	550-0181	194	550-0255	283	550-0338	074	550-0440	440
550-0013	016	550-0095	102	550-0182	195	550-0256	286	550-0339	370	550-0441	441
550-0014	015	550-0096	103	550-0183	206	550-0257	280	550-0340	374	550-0442	442
550-0016	017	550-0097	104	550-0184	142	550-0258	285	550-0341	373	550-0443	443
550-0017	021	550-0098	105	550-0185	228	550-0259	289	550-0343	391	550-0444	444
550-0018	019	550-0099	109	550-0186	197	550-0260	223	550-0344	378	550-0446	446
550-0019	022	550-0101	111	550-0187	198	550-0261	288	550-0345	376	550-0447	447
550-0021	011	550-0102	112	550-0188	207	550-0264	292	550-0346	382	550-0448	448
550-0024	041	550-0103	140	550-0189	205	550-0265	293	550-0347	380	550-0449	449
550-0025	025	550-0104	146	550-0190	209	550-0266	296	550-0348	381	550-0450	450
550-0026	026	550-0105	116	550-0191	213	550-0267	297	550-0349	383	550-0451	451
550-0027	027	550-0106	117	550-0192	214	550-0269	302	550-0350	384	550-0452	452
550-0028	028	550-0108	119	550-0193	249	550-0271	303	550-0351	386	550-0453	453
550-0029	029	550-0109	120	550-0194	217	550-0272	307	550-0352	393	550-0454	454
550-0031	031	550-0110	122	550-0195	259	550-0273	308	550-0353	397	550-0455	455
550-0032	032	550-0111	123	550-0196	219	550-0274	310	550-0354	388	550-0456	456
550-0033	033	550-0112	124	550-0197	220	550-0275	356	550-0355	411	550-0457	457
550-0034	034	550-0113	125	550-0198	221	550-0276	318	550-0356	390	550-0458	458
550-0035	042	550-0114	126	550-0199	222	550-0277	309	550-0357	379	550-0459	459
550-0036	036	550-0115	127	550-0200	225	550-0279	166	550-0358	389	550-0460	460
550-0037	037	550-0116	128	550-0201	227	550-0280	313	550-0362	396	550-0461	461
550-0038	038	550-0117	129	550-0202	230	550-0281	314	550-0363	394	550-0462	462
550-0040	040	550-0118	131	550-0203	231	550-0282	315	550-0364	403	550-0464	464
550-0041	043	550-0121	134	550-0204	239	550-0283	316	550-0365	404	550-0465	465
550-0042	044	550-0122	135	550-0205	218	550-0284	243	550-0366	399	550-0466	466
550-0043	046	550-0123	136	550-0206	226	550-0285	305	550-0367	405	550-0467	467
550-0044	047	550-0124	137	550-0207	234	550-0286	306	550-0368	402	550-0468	468
550-0045	045	550-0125	138	550-0208	241	550-0287	317	550-0369	431	550-0469	469
550-0046	050	550-0127	143	550-0209	232	550-0288	319	550-0370	076	550-0470	470
550-0047	056	550-0129	145	550-0210	247	550-0289	299	550-0371	086	550-0471	471
550-0048	048	550-0130	169	550-0211	244	550-0290	304	550-0376	113	550-0472	472
550-0050	052	550-0132	147	550-0212	245	550-0291	320	550-0378	133	550-0473	473
550-0051	060	550-0133	148	550-0213	250	550-0292	321	550-0381	170	550-0474	474
550-0052	067	550-0135	235	550-0214	236	550-0293	322	550-0383	173	550-0475	475
550-0053	053	550-0138	153	550-0215	238	550-0294	323	550-0390	269	550-0476	476
550-0054	054	550-0139	154	550-0216	240	550-0295	325	550-0393	291	550-0477	477
550-0055	055	550-0140	155	550-0217	263	550-0296	326	550-0397	334	550-0478	478
550-0056	070	550-0141	156	550-0218	199	550-0297	362	550-0398	338	550-0479	479
550-0057	073	550-0142	157	550-0219	035	550-0299	328	550-0400	350	550-0480	480
550-0058	071	550-0143	158	550-0220	248	550-0300	332	550-0402	366	550-0482	482
550-0060	075	550-0144	159	550-0221	253	550-0301	357	550-0403	371	550-0483	483
550-0061	077	550-0145	160	550-0222	237	550-0302	329	550-0405	385	550-0484	484
550-0062	078	550-0146	161	550-0223	242	550-0303	281	550-0406	398	550-0485	485
550-0064	080	550-0147	208	550-0224	251	550-0304	327	550-0407	401	550-0486	486
550-0065	065	550-0149	164	550-0225	258	550-0305	359	550-0408	406	550-0487	487
550-0066	081	550-0150	165	550-0226	262	550-0306	330	550-0409	407	550-0488	488
550-0067	094	550-0151	202	550-0227	254	550-0307	274	550-0410	408	550-0489	489
550-0068	058	550-0152	167	550-0228	252	550-0308	341	550-0411	409	550-0490	490
550-0069	063	550-0153	168	550-0229	255	550-0310	333	550-0412	410	550-0491	491
550-0070	064	550-0154	171	550-0230	265	550-0311	337	550-0414	413	550-0492	492
550-0071	066	550-0155	175	550-0231	271	550-0312	335	550-0415	414	550-0493	493
550-0072	072	550-0156	176	550-0232	284	550-0313	336	550-0416	415	550-0494	494
550-0073	068	550-0157	229	550-0234	189	550-0315	340	550-0417	416	550-0495	495
550-0074	069	550-0158	183	550-0235	257	550-0316	346	550-0418	417	550-0497	497
550-0075	057	550-0159	216	550-0236	260	550-0318	339	550-0419	418	550-0498	498
550-0076	099	550-0162	130	550-0237	264	550-0319	345	550-0421	420	550-0499	499
550-0077	082	550-0164	211	550-0238	233	550-0320	343	550-0423	422	550-0501	501
550-0078	083	550-0165	179	550-0239	256	550-0321	347	550-0424	423	550-0502	502
550-0079	087	550-0166	180	550-0241	268	550-0322	344	550-0425	424	550-0503	503
550-0080	089	550-0167	182	550-0242	059	550-0323	351	550-0426	425	550-0504	504
550-0081	090	550-0168	184	550-0243	273	550-0324	352	550-0427	426	550-0505	505

Note: From c/n 550-0550 onwards, unit number and c/n correspond

CITATION 551 UNIT NUMBER CROSS REFERENCE

C/n	Unit	C/n	Unit	C/n	Unit	C/n	Unit
551-0001	-	551-0038	246	551-0169	139	551-0359	353
551-0002	014	551-0039	278	551-0171	141	551-0360	354
551-0003	024	551-0046	267	551-0174	144	551-0361	355
551-0004	003	551-0050	196	551-0179	149	551-0369	363
551-0006	020	551-0051	301	551-0180	151	551-0378	375
551-0007	018	551-0053	342	551-0181	152	551-0388	387
551-0009	061	551-0056	312	551-0191	163	551-0393	392
551-0010	049	551-0060	377	551-0201	177	551-0396	395
551-0017	062	551-0065	331	551-0205	181	551-0400	400
551-0018	095	551-0066	364	551-0214	190	551-0412	412
551-0020	106	551-0071	023	551-0215	191	551-0419	419
551-0021	107	551-0077	030	551-0223	200	551-0422	421
551-0023	204	551-0084	039	551-0245	224	551-0428	428
551-0024	092	551-0095	051	551-0285	266	551-0431	430
551-0026	115	551-0117	079	551-0289	272	551-0436	436
551-0027	002	551-0122	084	551-0296	282	551-0445	445
551-0029	150	551-0132	097	551-0304	290	551-0463	463
551-0031	174	551-0133	098	551-0311	298	551-0481	481
551-0032	172	551-0141	108	551-0313	300	551-0496	496
551-0033	212	551-0143	110	551-0323	311		
551-0035	277	551-0149	118	551-0335	324		
551-0036	162	551-0163	132	551-0355	348		

Note: From c/n 551-0550 onwards, unit number and c/n correspond

CITATION CONVERSIONS

The following Citations have been converted from 550 to 551 or 551 to 550:

550-0002 to 551-0027
550-0020 to 551-0071
550-0030 to 551-0077
550-0040 to 551-0085 to 550-0040
550-0044 to 551-0092 to 550-0044
550-0049 to 551-0095
550-0059 to 551-0122
550-0063 to 551-0117
550-0074 to 551-0109 to 550-0074
550-0084 to 551-0129 to 550-0084
550-0087 to 551-0132
550-0088 to 551-0133
550-0092 to 551-0146
550-0093 to 551-0141
550-0098 to 551-0140 to 550-0098
550-0100 to 551-0143
550-0107 to 551-0149
550-0118 to 551-0162 to 550-0118
550-0126 to 551-0169
550-0128 to 551-0174
550-0131 to 551-0201
550-0134 to 551-0179
550-0136 to 551-0180
550-0137 to 551-0181
550-0139 to 551-0184
550-0148 to 551-0191
550-0160 to 551-0171
550-0161 to 551-0205
550-0163 to 551-0214
550-0177 to 551-0223 to 550-0177 to 551-0223
550-0178 to 551-0245
550-0240 to 551-0285
550-0244 to 551-0289
550-0246 to 551-0296
550-0249 to 551-0236 to 550-0249
550-0253 to 551-0308 to 550-0253
550-0262 to 551-0304
550-0266 to 551-0309 to 550-0266
550-0268 to 551-0311
550-0270 to 551-0313
550-0278 to 551-0323
550-0298 to 551-0335
550-0299 to 551-0339 to 550-0299
550-0306 to 551-0341
550-0313 to 551-0345 to 550-0313
550-0314 to 551-0396
550-0317 to 551-0355
550-0328 to 551-0360
550-0331 to 551-0369
550-0342 to 551-0378
550-0353 to 551-0398 to 550-0353
550-0359 to 551-0400
550-0373 to 551-0018

550-0413 to 551-0413
550-0420 to 551-0419
550-0422 to 551-0422
550-0429 to 551-0428
550-0435 to 551-0434
550-0437 to 551-0436
550-0450 to 551-0450
550-0452 to 551-0452
550-0459 to 551-0459
550-0460 to 551-0460 to 550-0460
550-0463 to 551-0463
550-0475 to 551-0475 to 550-0475
550-0476 to 551-0476 to 550-0476
550-0481 to 551-0481
550-0485 to 551-0485 to 550-0485
550-0487 to 551-0487 to 550-0487
550-0490 to 551-0491 to 550-0490
550-0496 to 551-0496
550-0559 to 551-0559
550-0574 to 551-0575
550-0584 to 551-0584
550-0591 to 551-0591
550-0604 to 551-0604 to 550-0604
550-0617 to 551-0617
551-0005 to 550-0013
551-0008 to 550-0219
551-0014 to 550-0068
551-0012 to 550-0242
551-0016 to 550-0338 to 551-0016 to 550-0338
551-0018 to 550-0373
551-0019 to 550-0371
551-0022 to 550-0376
551-0025 to 550-0378
551-0026 to 550-0377 to 551-0026
551-0029 to 550-0379 to 551-0029
551-0030 to 550-0383
551-0047 to 550-0390
551-0048 to 550-0307
551-0049 to 550-0381
551-0050 to 550-0385 to 551-0050
551-0052 to 550-0228
551-0055 to 550-0400
551-0057 to 550-0402
551-0058 to 550-0403
551-0059 to 550-0397
551-0062 to 550-0406
551-0109 to 550-0074
551-0341 to 550-0306
551-0345 to 550-0313
551-0351 to 550-0322
551-0496 to 550-0496 to 551-0496
551-0551 to 550-0551
551-0567 to 550-0567

CESSNA S550 CITATION II

C/n	Unit No	Identities								
0001	(0506)	(N1255L)	N95CC	(N969MC)	(N36H)	N969MC	N969MQ	N151DD	N86BA	
0002	(0507)	(N1255Y)	(N507CC)	N507CJ	N111VP	N211VP	CC-CWW			
0003	(0508)	(N12554)	(N21AG)	N847G	N847C					
0004	(0509)	N1256B	N830CB	N554CA	N72AM					
0005	(0510)	(N1256G)	N666LN							
0006	(0511)	(N1256N)	N101EC	N71FM	N71EM	N27MH	(N66EA)	N29EA	N65DT	N181G
0007	(0512)	(N1256P)	N51JH	N573CC	TC-SAM	N30CX	CS-DCE			
0008	(0513)	(N1256T)	N40PL	SE-DKI	N204A	(N40KM)				
0009	(0514)	N1256Z	N550A							
0010	(0515)	(N1257K)	N651CC	N49MJ	N47MJ	XA-INF	XA-INK	N747RL		
0011	(0516)	(N1257M)	N68SK	N211QS						
0012	(0517)	(N12570)	N550TB	N550RV						
0013	(0518)	(N12576)	(N518AS)	N277AL	N389L					
0014	(0519)	(N12583)	N32JJ	N32TJ	N214QS					
0015	(0520)	(N1258U)	C-GMTV	N600EA						
0016	(0521)	(N1259B)	(N99VC)	N85MP						
0017	(0522)	(N1259G)	(N47LP)	N1259G	N88G	(N1259G)	(N188G)	N88GD	N86PC	
0018	(0523)	(N1259K)	N501NB	N814CC	N1AF	N145DF				
0019	(0524)	(N1259M)	N15TT	N519CJ	N29AU	N119EA	(N600VE)	N550TB		
0020	(0525)	(N1259R)	N550AS							
0021	(0526)	(N1259S)	N593M	N693M	N320DG					
0022	(0527)	(N1259Y)	N258P	N360M						
0023	(0528)	(N1259Z)	N420CC	N94RT						
0024	(0529)	(N12593)	PT-LGI	N34NS						
0025	(0530)	(N12596)	PT-LGJ	w/o 06Sep88 Rio-Santos Dumont, Brazil						
0026	(0531)	(N1260G)	N19AF	(N126LP)	N24PH	N24PF	N32TX*			
0027		N1260K	D-CBUS	N27EA	N27FP					
0028		(N1260L)	HB-VHH	S5-BAX						
0029		(N1260N)	N185SF	N608LB	HB-VMJ					
0030		(N1260V)	N7007V	N7007Q	(N999GL)	N999HC				
0031		(N12605)	N531CC	N50DS	N54WJ	N50BK				
0032		(N1261A)	N532CC	N532CF	N232QS	CS-DNA				
0033		(N1261K)	(G-BLSG)	G-BLXN	N550ST	N531CM				
0034		(N1261M)	OE-GAP	N34CJ	N59EC					
0035		(N1261P)	N712S	N711JG	N711JN	XA-THO				
0036		(N12615)	N95CC	N36H	N36HR	N27B	N63JG	N63JU*		
0037		(N12616)	C-GERC	N72WC	N573BB					
0038		N3D	N1982U	N100KP						
0039		N22UL								
0040		(N1269D)	C-FEMA							
0041		(N1269E)	N772M	N592M	N692M	N74BJ	N74LM			
0042		(N1269J)	N250AL							
0043		(N1269N)	N101EG	(N727NA)	(N727AL)	N727NA				
0044		(N1269P)	N92ME							
0045		N1269Y	YU-BOE	BH-BIH	T9-BIH					
0046		(N12690)	N553CC	N760NB	N103VF					
0047		N12695	I-CEFI	N16RP						
0048		N1270D	N797TJ	N999TJ	N705SP					
0049		N1270K	B-4101							
0050		N1270S	B-4102							
0051		N1270Y	N251QS	CS-DNB						
0052		N12703	N4TL	N4TU	(N552CF)	N27SD	N27GD	N57BJ		
0053		N12705	N75BL	N253QS	N1223N	N393E				
0054		N12709	N717LS	N57MB	N999CB					
0055		N1271A	N374GS	N374GC	N87FL					
0056		(N1271B)	C-GERL	N550F	substantially damaged 02Feb98 Miami, FL					
0057		N1271D	N1UL	N1UH	N1UL	N57CJ				
0058		N1271E	N633EE							
0059		(N1271N)	PT-LHD	N36NS	N829JC					
0060		(N1271T)	N85AB	N588CT	N314G	N260QS				
0061		(N12712)	N540JB	N46A	(N464)	N53JM	N200LX			
0062		N12715	I-AVVM							
0063		(N12717)	VH-EMO							
0064		(N1272G)	N2000X	N200CX	(N990HP)	N45H	N200CX	N200CV		
0065		(N1272N)	N7118A	N612ST	(N900RG)	(N909RG)	N995DC			
0066		N1272P	N711MD							
0067		(N1272V)	N550FS	C-GMAV	N70AF	N789MA	(N67VP)	(EW94228)+ HC-BTY	N550HA	N900DM
		+was painted on a/c								
0068		N1272Z	N404G	N4049	N7070A					
0069		(N12720)	N43VS							
0070		(N12722)	N570CC	N570RC						
0071		(N12727)	N571CC	N1865M						
0072		(N1273A)	(N572CC)	N1273A	N186MT	N686MC	TC-NMC	N62NS		
0073		(N1273E)	N1958N							
0074		N1273J	N550LC	N22EH	N274QS					
0075		(N1273N)	N554CC	N882KB	N882RB	(N275VP)				
0076		(N1273Q)	N95CC	C-GQMH	N89TD	N52CK*				

S550 CITATION II

C/n	Identities							
0077	(N1273R)	N747CP	(N747GP)	N277QS	CS-DNC			
0078	N1273X	ZS-CAR						
0079	(N1273Z)	N1000W	N100QW	N97AJ	N97LB	(N27TB)		
0080	N12730	C-GTDO	N581EA	(N269MT)	XA-TMI			
0081	(N1274B)	N168HC	N550KM					
0082	N1274D	N97TJ	N9KH	N282QS	N27TB			
0083	N1274K	N511BB	N511BR	OE-GNS	N511BR	N883PF		
0084	N1274N	PT-LJL						
0085	N1274P	N683MB	N683CF	N54AM	(N285CF)	N220CA	N8BG	N143BP
0086	(N1274X)	N586CC	N900RB	N86QS	4X-COO			
0087	N1274Z	N21EG						
0088	(N12744)	N825HL	N288QS					
0089	N12745	(N289CC)	N134GB	VT-RHM	VT-ETG	to be confirmed		
0090	N12746	N777GF	N320S	N76FC	(N4BP)	N97BP		
0091	(N12747)	N595CC	N595CM	N241LA				
0092	(N1275A)	N92QS	N923S					
0093	N1275B	N593CC	N33DS	N93QS				
0094	(N1275D)	N594CC	(N347CP)	(F-O)	N594CC	F-OHAH	N560AJ	N6LL
0095	N1275H	N200NK	N200NV	N345CC				
0096	(N1275N)	N95CC	N29X	N29XA	w/o 05Mar89 Poughskeepie, NY			
0097	N1290B	N97QS	N828WB	N551BE				
0098	N1290E	N98QS						
0099	N1290G	N44GT	N299QS	N777FD				
0100	(N1290N)	N3000W	(N616GB)	N300QW				
0101	(N1290Y)	N101QS						
0102	N1290Z	N287MC	N285MC					
0103	N12900	N103QS	N22HP					
0104	N12903	N224KC						
0105	(N12907)	N105BG						
0106	(N12909)	N106QS	N666TR					
0107	N1291E	N474L	N713DH	N550HT				
0108	(N1291K)	N108QS	N316MH*					
0109	N1291P	N509CC	N1GC	N7QC	N38EC	N61TL*		
0110	N1291V	N45GP						
0111	(N1291Y)	N111QS	N777HN*					
0112	(N12910)	N112QS	A2-MCB					
0113	(N12911)	N553CC	PT-LJQ					
0114	N1292A	PT-LKS						
0115	(N1292B)	N505CC	N520RP	C-FDDD	C-GWBF	N92JT	N92JC	
0116	N1292K	N125CG	N550HC					
0117	N1292N	PT-LKT	w/o 01Dec92 Sao Paulo-Congonhas, Brazil					
0118	N12920	N600TF	N820FJ	N820F	VH-IWU			
0119	(N12922)	N261WR	N261WD	N700SW	N700SV	(N500LH)	N11TS	
0120	N12924	N1283M	N716DB					
0121	(N12925)	D-CLOU	N23NM	N20NM^				
0122	N12929	I-TALG	N122WS					
0123	N1293A	N121CG						
0124	(N1293E)	N1867W	N52CK	N550JC				
0125	N1293G	N122CG	N97CT	N552SM*				
0126	N1293K	N126QS						
0127	N1293N	N14UM	(N127CF)	PT-OSL	N14UM	N674JM		
0128	N1293V	N911BB	N370M					
0129	N1293X	N87TH	N480CC					
0130	(N1293Z)	N130CC	N302PC	N550PL				
0131	N12934	D-CHJH	N87BA					
0132	(N1294D)	N533CC	N91ME	N91ML				
0133	(N1294K)	G-VKRS	N7047K	I-ZAMP	N133VP	N431WM		
0134	N1294M	N134QS	D-CFAI	SE-DYO				
0135	(N1294N)	OE-GPD	D-CIAO	N2235	VT-KMB			
0136	(N1294P)	converted on line to prototype Citation V c/n 560-0001						
0137	(N12945)	D-CNCA	HB-VKA	N100TB	PT-WIB			
0138	(N1295A)	N538CC	N305PC	N138QS	N713HH	(N501BE)	N552BE	
0139	(N1295B)	N906SB	N706SB	N39TF				
0140	(N1295G)	C-GLCR	N575EW					
0141	(N1295J)	N907SB	N707SB	N26JJ	N550AJ			
0142	(N1295M)	N542CC	C-FALI					
0143	(N1295N)	N143QS	N1VA					
0144	(N1295P)	D-CNCB	N6516V	N543SC				
0145	(N1295Y)	(PH-HMC)	(PH-HMA)	PH-RMA				
0146	(N1296B)	(G-JBCA)	N1296B	N81SH	N815H			
0147	N1296N	OO-OSA						
0148	N1296Z	ZS-IDC	N170RD	D-CSFD				
0149	N149QS	C-GMGB	N816V	N810V	N43RC			
0150	(N1297B)	N150CJ	N107RC					
0151	(N2634E)	N151QS	N151Q	N550SP				
0152	N26369	N848G	N843G	N987CJ				
0153	(N2637R)	N153QS	N242LA					
0154	N26379	PT-LQI	N910DS	N660AJ				

S550 CITATION II

C/n	Identities					
0155	(N2638A)	N155QS	N155GB			
0156	(N2638U)	N156QS	N766NB	(N400AJ)	N901PV	N63JT
0157	N2639N	N157QS				
0158	(N2639Y)	N158QS	N301QS	N158QS	N66EH	
0159	(N2646X)	N50GT	N289CC	N9GT		
0160	N2642Z	N550GT	PT-OSM			

Production complete

CESSNA 552 CITATION (T-47A)

C/n	Identities			
0001	N552CC	N12855	162755	w/o 20Jly93 in hangar fire Forbes Field, Topeka, KS
0002	N12756	162756	w/o 20Jly93 in hangar fire Forbes Field, Topeka, KS	
0003	N12557	162757	w/o 20Jly93 in hangar fire Forbes Field, Topeka, KS	
0004	N12058	162758	w/o 20Jly93 in hangar fire Forbes Field, Topeka, KS; cx Sep93	
0005	N12859	162759	w/o 20Jly93 in hangar fire Forbes Field, Topeka, KS; cx Sep93	
0006	N12660	162760	w/o 20Jly93 in hangar fire Forbes Field, Topeka, KS; cx Sep93	
0007	N12761	162761	w/o 20Jly93 in hangar fire Forbes Field, Topeka, KS; cx Sep93	
0008	N12762	162762	w/o 20Jly93 in hangar fire Forbes Field, Topeka, KS; cx Sep93	
0009	N12763	162763	w/o 20Jly93 in hangar fire Forbes Field, Topeka, KS; cx Sep93	
0010	N12564	162764	w/o 20Jly93 in hangar fire Forbes Field, Topeka, KS; cx Sep93	
0011	N12065	162765	w/o 20Jly93 in hangar fire Forbes Field, Topeka, KS; cx Sep93	
0012	N12566	162766	in compound outside Columbus State Community College hangar at Columbus Bolton Field OH as N12566	
0013	N12967	162767	w/o 20Jly93 in hangar fire Forbes Field, Topeka, KS; cx Sep93	
0014	N12568	162768		
0015	N12269	162769	w/o 20Jly93 in hangar fire Forbes Field, Topeka, KS; cx Sep93	

Production complete

CESSNA 560 CITATION V/ULTRA/ENCORE

C/n	Identities								
707	N5079V	N560VU	Citation Ultra Encore prototype (possibly c/n 0424 reworked)						
550-0001	N560CC	Model 550 a/c cvtd to 560 standard							
560-0001	(N1294P)	N560CV	N1217V	cvtd on production line from c/n S550-0136					
0002	N1209T	N562CV	N90PG	N101HB					
0003	(either N1209X or N1216A)			N563CV	SY-AAP	Seychelles SY-001		S7-AAP	Seychelles SY-001
	N560BA	N560ER							
0004	(either N1210N or N1216J)			N189H					
0005	(either N1210V or N1216K)			N953F					
0006	(either N1211M or N1216N)			N962JC	N566VP	N570MH	N269TA		
0007	(either N12117 or N1216Q)			N964JC	(N57VP)	N717MB			
0008	(either N1213S or N1216Z)			N561B					
0009	(either N1213Z or N12160)			N456FB	VH-HEY	N77HN			
0010	(either N1214J or N12162)			N205PC	N205BC	N643RT			
0011	(either N1214Z or N1217H)			N700TF					
0012	N1217N	N560ME							
0013	(N1217P)	N560WH							
0014	N1217S	N1MC	N88TJ	N12ST					
0015	N12171	N800DL	N560MR						
0016	N12173	N68HC	N68HQ	N462B					
0017	(either N1218P or N1223A)			N89BM	N560H				
0018	(either N1218Y or N12249)			N164DW	N114CP				
0019	(either N1219D or N1226X)			N99WR	OE-GRW	N61TW			
0020	(either N1219G or N1228N)			N520CV	N560HC				
0021	N1228V	N682D	C-FDLT	N560DC					
0022	(N1228Y)	N211MA							
0023	(N12283)	OE-GDP	VR-CTL	N560JM	N31RC				
0024	(N12284)	N501QS	N4CS						
0025	(N12285)	CNA-NV							
0026	(N12286)	N560LC	N49MJ	N350RD	N380RD				
0027	(N12289)	N560JR							
0028	(N1229A)	N6FE	N6FZ	N757CK					
0029	(N1229C)	N590A							
0030	(N1229D)	N560W	XB-MTS	N570BJ					
0031	N1229F	D-CHDE							
0032	N1229M	G-DBII	N96MT						
0033	N1229N	I-ATSB	N4333W	C-GAPC					
0034	(N1229Q)	N895LD							
0035	N1229Z	N36H	N561EJ						
0036	(either N12295 or N2663B)			(N107CF)	(N107CR)	HZ-ZTC	N532MA	(N560EJ)	
0037	(either N12297 or N2663X)			N17LK					
0038	(either N12298 or N2663Y)			N301QS	N2296S				
0039	(either N1230A or N26630)			CNA-NW					
0040	(either N1230G or N2664U)			N12403	N71NK	N91NK	N91NL	N560CF	
0041	N26643	VH-NTH	N400KS						
0042	(N26648)	N42CV	D-CAWU						
0043	(N2665F)	N991PC	w/o 30Dec95 Eagle River Airport, WI; cx May96 - remains to White Inds at Bates City, MO						
0044	N2665S	N111VP							
0045	N2665Y	PT-LZQ							
0046	(N26656)	G-CZAR							
0047	N2666A	N500FK							
0048	N2667X	N4TL	N74TL	N57CE	N57CN	N870AJ			
0049	(N2672X)	N560EL							
0050	(N26771)	(N208BC)	N208PC	N208BC	N501CW				
0051	N2680A	N599SC	N599SG	N314RW					
0052	N2680D	N500LE	N500UB						
0053	(N2680X)	N53CV	I-NYCE	N111CF	C-GCUW	C-FACO			
0054	(N26804)	N531F	N100SC	N100SY					
0055	N2681F	HB-VJZ	N282RH	(N21JJ)	(N560CP)	N200CP			
0056	N2682F	N78AM							
0057	(N2683L)	N560BL	N561BC						
0058	(N2686Y)	F-GKGL							
0059	(N2687L)	F-GKHL							
0060	(N2689B)	N2697Y	N90MF	damaged on landing 30Aug97 Manitowish Waters, WI; status?					
0061	(N2697X)	N2701J	D-CNCI						
0062	N2716G	ZS-MVV	N560EA	EC-411	EC-GLM	N500UJ			
0063	(N2701J)	N7FE	(N7FZ)	N68CK					
0064	N2717X	(ZS-MYN)	ZS-MVZ						
0065	N2721F	N77711	N560JV	N608CT					
0066	(N27216)	N60S							
0067	N2722F	N45BA	JA119N						
0068	N2722H	(N40PL)	N711GF	N712GF	N246NW				
0069	(N2724R)	D-CNCP	N65229	N70TG	N357WC				
0070	(N2725A)	F-GJXX							
0071	(N2725X)	N271CA							
0071A	N2728N	N45RC							

CITATION V

C/n	Identities					
0072	N2726J	(N72FE)	(N91FA)	N572CV	N72CT	
0073	(N2726X)	N100WP				
0074	N2727F	N27WW	N174JS	N593MD		
0075	(N2745L)	N75CV				
0076	(N2745M)	N777FE	N777FH			
0077	N2745R	G-BSVL	C-GNND	N42NA	HB-VLV	
0078	N2748B	SE-DLI	OY-CKT			
0079	(N2746C)	N560GL				
0080	N2746E	JA8576				
0081	(N2746F)	OE-GID	N560HP	N318CT		
0082	(N2746U)	N950WA				
0083	(N2747R)	N22LP				
0084	(N2747U)	N16NM	C-GHEC			
0085	(N2748F)	N591M	N891M			
0086	(N2748V)	SE-DPG	N560CX			
0087	N2749B	5N-IMR	N167WE	N600BW		
0088	(N6783X)	OE-GSW				
0089	N67830	ZS-MPT	N54DD			
0090	(N67839)	N30PC				
0091	N6784P	(N18SK)	N56GT	N3GT		
0092	N6784X	XA-RTT	XB-RTT			
0092A	N6784Y	N906SB	N592VP	(N713HH)		
0093	(N6785C)	F-GKJL				
0094	N6785D	N1823S	(N594VP)	N340DR	N1827S	
0095	N6788P	N707CV	N404G			
0096	N67890	(N96JJ)	N10TD			
0097	(N6790L)	N898CB				
0098	(N6790P)	(N18SK)	N59DF			
0099	(N67905)	OE-GPA	D-CDUW			
0100	(N6792A)	PH-PBM	N560WE	N560AF		
0101	(N67980)	N101CV	N560EC	N560DM	N560EP*	
0102	(N67988)	VR-BUL	VP-BUL	N560BA		
0103	(N67989)	N98E				
0104	(N6799L)	(N560CT)	N400CT	(N416H)	N815CM	
0105	(N6800C)	N105CV	LN-AAA	N147VC	N149VG	N560MH
0106	N6801H	(HB-V)	(N560PT)	N60SH	N525RD	
0107	(N6801L)	N78NP	N560RJ	N365EA		
0108	(N6801P)	N8HJ	VH-NHJ	N777KY	N73ME	
0109	(N6801Q)	N6801V	N2	N27	N109VP	
0109A	(N68018)	N907SB	N560RS	(N22YP)	N4MM*	
0110	(N6802S)	N560LC	N832CB	N832QB		
0111	(N6802T)	(N91AN)	OE-GAA			
0112	(N68027)	N4110S				
0113	N6803L	N26	N4			
0114	(N6803T)	OE-GPS	D-CZAR			
0115	N6803Y	I-NEWY	N91YC			
0116	N68032	N901RM				
0117	(N6804F)	D-CMEI				
0118	N6804L	XA-RXO	XA-SKX	N118DF	N626SL	
0119	(N6804N)	F-GLIM				
0120	(N6804Y or N6806X)		N120CV	N1824S		
0121	N6808C	PT-MTG	N898GF			
0122	(N6808Z)	N261WR	N510MT			
0123	(N6809G)	N611ST				
0124	(N6809T)	D-CBIG	N124VP	OB-1626		
0125	N6809V	OE-GCC				
0126	N68097	LV-PFN	LV-RED			
0127	(N6810L)	N64HA	N127VP			
0128	(N6810N)	N19MK	N19ME	N85KC	N504BW	
0129	(N6811F)	N22AF				
0130	(N6811T)	N130CV	N14VF	(N19VF)		
0131	(N6811X)	N131CV	PT-ORE	N223JV		
0132	N6811Z	HZ-SFA	N226JV			
0133	(N68118)	N77HF	N88HF	N93DW		
0134	N6812D	YV-811CP				
0135	(N6812L or N6871L)		N560BB	N560RL		
0136	(N6812Z or N6872T)		(N136CV)	N501T	N772AA	N999AD
0137	(N560RB)	N6874Z	N7338	N733H	N193G	
0138	(N68746)	(OY-JET)	OY-FFV	N511WV		
0139	(N68753)	N561A	N75F			
0140	(N6876Q)	N562E	N75G			
0141	N6876S	N141AQ				
0142	N6876Z	PT-OLV	N722OL	PT-WPC	N560FA	N560GT
0143	N6877C	N65HA	N543VP*			
0144	N6877G	N2000X	N500VC			
0145	(N6877L)	N57MK	N57ML	D-CFLY		
0146	(N6877Q)	N2000M				
0147	(N6877R)	N27SD	XA-RKX	N125RH	N410J	N147RJ

CITATION V

C/n	Identities							
0148	N68770	N92HW	N560FB	N115K				
0149	(N68786)	N565JW						
0150	(N6879L)	D-CTAN	(N560ED)	N191VF				
0151	N6881Q	ZS-NDU	V5-CDM					
0152	N6882R	ZS-NDX						
0153	N6804Y	N502T	N502F	(N153VP)	N1SN	SE-DYZ		
0154	N6805T	N503T	(N503F)	N154VP	(N154SV)			
0155	N6872T	N40WP						
0156	(F-GLIM)	N6885L	XA-RKH	N560L	N75B			
0157	N6885V	N5734	N5704	N502TS				
0158	(N6885Y)	N601AB	N801AB	N560RP				
0159	(N68854)	N68MA	D-CLEO					
0160	N6886X	ZS-NDT						
0161	N68860	Spain TR.20-01/403-11						
0162	N68864	(painted as N6864 for a short while end 1991)					XA-SDT	
0163	N68869	N529X	N953C					
0164	(N6887T)	N164CV	N392BS					
0165	(N6887X)	N910V	C-GAPD	N24HX				
0166	N68872	ZS-NDW	N166JV					
0167	(N68873)	N20CN	(N167WE)	N211DG	N311DG			
0168	(N68876)	N168CV						
0169	N6888C	N80AB						
0170	N6888L	N170CV	N814CM	N417H*				
0171	(N6888T)	N5735	N573F	N567F				
0172	(N6888X)	N172CV						
0173	N68881							
0174	N6889E	N563C						
0175	(N564D)	N1279Z	N49LD					
0176	N12798	PT-OOR	N176VP	PT-WOM				
0177	N12799	VR-CNS	D-CHHS	N242AC				
0178	N1280A	N531CC	N500PX^					
0179	(N179CJ)	N1280D	N865M					
0180	N1280K	N550WW						
0181	N1280R	N181SG						
0182	(N1280S)	N560RA	N920PM					
0183	N12807	N83RR	N83RE					
0184	N1281A	N873DB	N410DM					
0185	N1281K	N29WE	N29WF	N989TW				
0186	N1281N	N583M	(N586CC)	N583N	N586CC			
0187	N12812	N60GL	N80GE					
0188	N12813	(N188CJ)	N64PM	N395R				
0189	N12815	N189CV	N62HA					
0190	N12816	LV-PGC	LV-VFY	N555WF	N303CB			
0191	N12817	PT-ORT	N2JW	N45KB				
0192	(N1282D)	D-CEWR	N713HH	N238JC				
0193	N1282K	Spain TR.20-02/403-12						
0194	(N1282M)	N194CV	N352WC					
0195	N1282N	PT-ORC						
0196	N12824	N196CV	XA-SEJ	N560JS	N4JS	(N560JS)	N357AZ	N560RW
0197	N12826	N197CV	(EI-DUN)	XA-SJC				
0198	N1283F	N135BC	N560RG					
0199	(N1283K)	N63HA	N7895Q*					
0200	N1283M	OE-GDA						
0201	N1283N	ZS-NGM	N98GA	SU-EWA				
0202	N1283V	(N202CV)	ZS-NGL					
0203	N1283X	(N203CV)	ZS-NHC	N7700L	N9700T			
0204	N1283Y	N1000W						
0205	N12838	F-GLYC						
0206	N1284A	N560TX						
0207	(N1284B)	N207CV	N52SN	N780BF				
0208	(N1284D)	N208CV	N892SB	N88G				
0209	(N1284F)	N209CV						
0210	N1284N	N20MK	N420DM	N277RC				
0211	(N1284P)	N250SP						
0212	N1284X	TC-LAA						
0213	N12845	PT-OTS						
0214	(N1285D)	OE-GCP						
0215	(N1285G)	PT-OTT	N23NS	N315EJ^				
0216	N1285N	TC-LAB						
0217	N1285P	N602AB	N802AB					
0218	N1285V	XA-SIT	N218BR	N218DF	N5T	N5GE		
0219	N12850	N318MM						
0220	N12852	N23UD	N23UB	N73KH				
0221	(N1286A)	N24UD	N24UB	N701DK				
0222	N1286C							
0223	N1286N	N575PC	N93AG	N500MG*				
0224	N1287B	N224CV	N523KW	N528KW	(N47TW)			
0225	N1287C	(N1865S)	N1823S					

CITATION V

C/n	Identities					
0226	N1287D	N893CM				
0227	N1287F	(N227CV)	LV-PGR	LV-WDR		
0228	N1287G	N228CV	XA-SLA			
0229	N1287K	XA-SNX				
0230	N1287N	YV-169CP				
0231	N1287Y	N501E	N12CQ			
0232	(N12879)	N502E				
0233	N1288A	Pakistan 0233				
0234	N1288B	N234AQ				
0235	N1288D	N22RG	N52RG	N129PJ	N560MM	N335EJ*
0236	N1288N	N506E				
0237	N1288P	N593M	N893M			
0238	N238CV	N1288T	N46WB	(N95HW)	N194SA	
0239	N1288Y	N239CV	N1GC	N93CV		
0240	N1289G	N91ME	N966JM			
0241	N1289N	N241CV	ZS-NGS			
0242	N1289Y	N242CV	N605AT	N826AC		
0243	N12890	N39N				
0244	(N12895)	(N244CV)	N60RD			
0245	N12896	N615AT				
0246	N1290N	N5060P	LV-PHD	LV-WGY		
0247	N12907	N94TX				
0248	N12909	N248CV	N226N	N229N*		
0249	N1291K	N10CN	N733M			
0250	(N1291K)	(N250CV)	N1291Y	N205CM		
0251	N12910	LV-PGZ	LV-WGO			
0252	N12911	N252CV	N44GT			
0253	N1292B	N253CV	N46MT			
0254	N12921	N560GB	(N561GB)	N568GB	N710MT	
0255	N12922	N255CV	ZS-NHD			
0256	N12929	N22KW	N52KW	N356EJ*		
0257	N1293E	N155PT				
0258	N1293Y	PT-OZB	N60NS			
0259	N1293Z	N37WP				

CITATION ULTRA

C/n	Identities					
0260	N1294B	N260CV	C-GPAW			
0261	N1294K	N261CV	XB-PYC	N261UH		
0262	N1294N	N262CV	N444GG			
0263	N12945	N979C	N560GS*			
0264	N1295A	N5250K	N264CV	N264U		
0265	N1295P	N5270K	LV-PHJ	LV-WIJ	N86CE	
0266	N1295G	N456JW	N458JW	N269JR*		
0267	N1295J	N96NB	N197JH			
0268	N1295M	N5270M+	(XA-)	N12012	N269CM	N750FL
	+ marks painted on aircraft circa Sep94					
0269	N1295N	N331EC	N357EC			
0270	N1295Y	N68HC				
0271	N1296N	PH-VLG				
0272	N5094B	N220JT				
0273	N5095N	N910PC	N61JB	N861CE*		
0274	N5096S	N751CF	N511DR			
0275	N1297V	(N5097H)+	D-CVHA			
0276	N5100J	N183AJ	N376QS			
0277	(N5101J)+	D-CFOX				
0278	N5103J	N2HJ	VH-FHJ			
0279	(N51038)+	(N331EC)	N361EC			
0280	(N51042)+	PH-MDC				
0281	(N5105F)+	N511ST				
0282	N51055	D-CBEN				
0283	(N51072)+	N560JC	N1CH			
0284	N5108G	N966SW	(N369TC)			
0285	(N5109R)+	N285CV	N147VC	N285CC		
0286	(N5109W)+	N286CV	N57MB			
0287	(N5112K)+	N287CV	N117CC	N117MR		
0288	N5141F	N522JA				
0289	N51444	LV-PHY	LV-WLS			
0290	N5145P	N97BH				
0291	N5148B	N744R				
0292	N5148N	N1295N	HL7501			
0293	N51575	N293QS				
0294	N5161J	N1295Y	HL7502			
0295	(N5162W)+	N295CV	N61HA	N80LP*		
0296	(N5163C)+	N560LC				
0297	N5165T	N1296N	HL7503			

CITATION ULTRA

C/n	Identities						
0298	N5166U	N200CK					
0299	N5168F	(N550TM)	VT-EUX				
0300	N51743	N1297V	HL7504				
0301	N5180K	(HB-)	VR-BQB	N560AG			
0302	(N5223Y)	N560CE	I-NYSE	N560CE	N580CE*		
0303	N5225K	(N560BD)	(D-CAFB)	N560BJ	N190JH		
0304	N5226B	N47VC					
0305	N5228Z	LV-PLE	LV-WMT				
0306	N5231S	N49MJ					
0307	N5233J	N307QS					
0308	N5235G	PT-WFD					
0309	N52352	N212BD					
0310	N5241Z	N410CV	N868JT				
0311	(N5244F)	N311QS					
0312	(N52457)	N312QS					
0313	N5246Z	N313CV					
0314	N5250E	N314CV	C-FYMM				
0315	(N5250K)	N315QS					
0316	(N5251Y)	N12RN					
0317	(N52526)	N317QS					
0318	N5261R	N1273R	N877RF				
0319	N52613	N1319D	N52613	LV-WOE	N2RC		
0320	N5262B	N46WB	(N28ET)	VR-CCV	VP-CCV	N320VP	VH-SMF
0321	N5262W	N320QS					
0322	N5262X	ZS-NNV"	ZS-NVV	N850BA	N300QS		
	" painted in error						
0323	(N5097H)	N323QS					
0324	N5100J	N55LC					
0325	(N5101J)	N96AT					
0326	N5103J	N583M	N711Z^				
0327	(N51038)	N327QS					
0328	(N5104Z)	N554R					
0329	N5105F	N330QS					
0330	(N51055)	N351WC					
0331	N51072	N331QS					
0332	(N5108G)	N332LC					
0333	(N5109R)	N333QS					
0334	N5109W	N4TL					
0335	N335QS						
0336	N5265B	N336QS					
0337	N5265N	N108LJ					
0338	N52645	N592M					
0339	N339QS						
0340	N5267T	N21CV					
0341	N341QS						
0342	N5267T	(N14VF)	XA-RDM	N86CW	(N82CW)		
0343	N5268A	N343CV	N60AE	N303QS			
0344	N5268M	N344QS					
0345	N5268E	N345CV	N75Z				
0346	N5269A	N346CC	C-GFCL				
0347	N5268V	N72FC					
0348	N52682	N348QS					
0349	N5151S	N1127P	JA001A				
0350	N51522	N645M	N250JH	N991L			
0351	N5153K	N699CC					
0352	N5153X	N352QS					
0353	N51564	N353CV	N1873				
0354	N5157E	N4200K					
0355	N51575	N355CV	N67GW				
0356	N5153Z	N354QS					
0357	N5148N	N81SH					
0358	N5163C	N358CV	N12TV				
0359	N5166U	ZS-SMB					
0360	N5168F	N6780A	N62WA				
0361	N5156B	N361QS					
0362	N5183U	OE-GMI					
0363	N5180K	N59KG					
0364	N5260Y	N991PC					
0365	N5235G	N7547P	N375CM	N712L			
0366	N52352	SX-DCI					
0367	N5161J	N367QS					
0368	N5194J	N343CC					
0369	N52113	N5200	N520G	N5200			
0370	N5262B	N607RJ					
0371	N5262X	N371CV	N315CS				
0372	N52601	N372CV	N76CK	N372QS*			
0373	N373QS						
0374	N5214L	N7728T	N166KB	N163L			

CITATION ULTRA

C/n	Identities				
0375	N375QS				
0376	N5097H	VR-BCY	N1217H	N713DH	N600LF
0377	N5264A	N377RA	N450RA	N377QS	
0378	N5090A	N350WC			
0379	N5101J	C-GWCR			
0380	N5103J	N380CV	N190KL		
0381	N2762J	N857BL	N214L		
0382	N382QS				
0383	N51038	N57ST	N63TM		
0384	N5231S	N196SA			
0385	N5109R	N333WM			
0386	N7274A	N720SJ	N615L		
0387	N5108G	US Army 95-0123		(UC-35A)	
0388	N5269A	N92SS			
0389	N5092B	PT-WRR	N389JV		
0390	N5093L	N390CV	C-GMGB		
0391	N5092D	N391CV			
0392	N5124F	US Army 95-0124		(UC-35A)	
0393	N5156V	N393QS			
0394	N5093Y	N394QS			
0395	N5093Y	(N395QS)	N19MK	N19MU*	
0396	N50938	N396QS			
0397	N50715	PT-WKS	N397AF	N560RC*	
0398	N5061W	ZS-NUZ			
0399	N51881	N97NB			
0400	N51942	N916CS			
0401	N5197A	N401CV	VP-CSN		
0402	N5200U	N302QS			
0403	N5201J	N1202D	JA01TM		
0404	N5201M	US Army 96-0107		(UC-35A)	
0405	N5202D	PT-WMQ			
0406	N5203S	PT-WMZ			
0407	N5204D	N1218Y	F-OHRU		
0408	N5207A	PT-WOA	N560NS	N304QS	
0409	N52081	PT-WVH			
0410	N5211A	US Army 96-0108		(UC-35A)	
0411	N5226B	PT-WNE	N38NS		
0412	N5228Z	PT-WNF			
0413	N5233J	N413CV	VP-CKM	N8041R	
0414	N5235G	ZS-CDS			
0415	N52457	US Army 96-0109		(UC-35A)	
0416	N5109R	N19PV	N713DH*		
0417	N5090A	N1248B	RP-C8818	N560TJ	VH-XTT
0418	N5112K	N318QS			
0419	N5233J	EC-GOV			
0420	N51942	US Army 96-0110		(UC-35A)	
0421	N322QS				
0422	N20SB	N5XP			
0423	N5073G	N324QS			
0424	(N324QS)	N424CV	cx Sep97 converted to prototype Citation Ultra Encore with c/n 707 N5079V and then re-reg'd N560VU qv		
0425	N325QS				
0426	N5101J	US Army 96-0111		(UC-35A)	
0427	N5105F	N11LC	N11LQ		
0428	N328QS				
0429	N392QS				
0430	N433CV	C-GLIM			
0431	N5076K	PT-WZW	N431JV	N560JP	
0432	N51143	N356WC			
0433	N5231S	N33LX			
0434	N334QS				
0435	N52352	N410NA			
0436	N5086W	N36LX			
0437	N337QS				
0438	N5207A	(PT-WQE)	N438MC		
0439	N50612	(N39LX)	VP-CSC		
0440	N5076K	PT-WSN			
0441	N314QS				
0442	N5226B	N23UD			
0443	N5228Z	N24UD			
0444	N343QS				
0445	N5000R	N345QS			
0446	N51038	HB-VLZ			
0447	N5108G	N51246	N261WR		
0448	N5100J	C-GSUN			
0449	N5120U	N560BP			
0450	N51246	PT-XCF			
0451	N5124F	N351QS			

CITATION ULTRA

C/n	Identities			
0452	N5130J	US Army 97-0101	(UC-35A)	
0453	N5132T	N453CV		
0454	N5135K	TC-ROT	N1216Z	TC-ROT
0455	N51396	N358QS		
0456	N51444	US Army 97-0102	(UC-35A)	
0457	N51564	N59HA		
0458	N5161J	LV-PNR	LV-YMA	
0459	N5162W	N79PM		
0460	N5157E	N360QS		
0461	N5185V	XA-ICO		
0462	N5183U	US Army 97-0103	(UC-35A)	
0463	N50612	N56K	N58KJ	N48LC
0464	N420DM			
0465	N5086W	N465CV	N848G	
0466	N366QS			
0467	N5096S	ZS-OFM		
0468	N51042	US Army 97-0104	(UC-35A)	
0469	N5183V	N701CR		
0470	N44FG			
0471	N5188A	N371QS		
0472	N5097H	US Army 97-0105	(UC-35A)	
0473	N5093D	N9LR		
0474	N51160	N474CV	XA-TKZ	
0475	N374QS			
0476	N150S			
0477	N5085E	N50GP		
0478	N5095N	N70BR		
0479	N5125J	N379QS		
0480	N51246	N71JJ	N560VR	
0481	N5153K	C-GXCO		
0482	N5156D	N44LC		
0483	N383QS			
0484	N5125J	C-GYMM		
0485	N998SA			
0486	N386QS			
0487	N50820	N46MW		
0488	N12688	N555WF	N555WL	
0489	N66U			
0490	N390QS			
0491	N51564	N404MM		
0492	N5152X	N492CV	C-GDSH	N41VP
0493	N391QS			
0494	N5166T	N80GR		
0495	N	US Army 98-0006	(UC-35A)	
0496	N395QS			
0497	N5161J	TC-MET		
0498	(N24QT)	N26QT		
0499	N556BG			
0500	N500CU			
0501	N51896	US Army 98-0007	(UC-35A)	
0502	N1298X	D2-EBA		
0503	N52059	(ZS-FCB)	VP-BDB	
0504	N504CC			
0505	N52229	US Army 98-0008	(UC-35A)	
0506	N50820	G-RIBV		
0507	N5095N	N1129L		
0508	N5085E	US Army 98-0009	(UC-35A)	
0509	N309QS			
0510	N399QS			
0511	N200NK			
0512	N29WE			
0513	N5061W	US Army 98-0010	(UC-35A)	
0514	N340QS			
0515	N51042	VH-PSU		
0516	N316QS			
0517	N5145V	G-OTGT		
0518	N51817	N1295B	JA02AA	
0519	N319QS			
0520	N51072	N620AT		
0521	N5086W	N521CV	N22LC	
0522	N398QS			
0523	N332QS			
0524	N5091J	US Marines 165740	(UC-35A?)	
0525	N5093Y	N593M		
0526	N326QS			
0527	N51396	N627AT		
0528	N52WF			
0529	N5097H	US Marines 165741	(UC-35B?)	

CITATION ULTRA/ENCORE

C/n	Identities		
0530	N353QS		
0531	N397QS		
0532	N5268V	US Army 99-0100	(UC-35A)
0533	N591M		
0534	N5112K	US Army 99-0101	(UC-35A)
0535	N5267D	N1247V	N57MK
0536	N363QS		
0537	N5181U	G-TTFN	
0538	N51143	US Army 99-0102	(UC-35A)
0539	N5108G	N539CE	(first production Encore)
0540	N540CV		
0541	N541CV		
0542			
0543	N543LE		
0544			
0545		US Army 99-0103*	(UC-35B)
0546			
0547			
0548		US Army 99-0104*	(UC-35B)
0549			
0550			
0551			
0552			
0553			
0554			
0555			
0556			
0557			
0558			
0559			
0560			
0561			
0562			
0563			
0564			
0565			
0566			
0567			
0568			
0569			
0570			
0571			
0572			
0573			
0574			
0575			
0576			
0577			
0578			
0579			
0580			
0581			
0582			
0583			
0584			
0585			
0586			
0587			
0588			
0589			
0590			
0591			
0592			
0593			
0594			
0595			
0596			
0597			
0598			
0599			
0600			

+ indicates test marks not fully confirmed

CESSNA 560XL CITATION EXCEL

Note: Aircraft has truncated Citation X cabin with wings and empennage of 560 Ultra.

C/n	Identities				
706	N560XL	ff 29Feb96			
5001	N561XL				
5002	N5060K	N562XL			
5003	N5165T	N563XL	(PT-WZO)	PT-FPP	
5004	N5148N	OE-GAP			
5005	N51575	N208PC			
5006	N5141F	N8005			
5007	N5200R	N83RR			
5008	N5204D	N207PC			
5009	N52113	N398RS			
5010	N52178	N27XL			
5011	N52141	N560L			
5012	N52144	N561DA	I-JETS		
5013	N5216A	N1243C	N1PB		
5014	N5221Y	N60GL	(N58KJ)	N56K	N1SN
5015	N5223D	N523KW			
5016	N615RG				
5017	N517XL	N157AE			
5018	N5250E	ZS-FCB			
5019	N980DK	N990DK			
5020	N5246Z	PT-XCL	(N61850)		
5021	N5244F	D-CMIC			
5022	N522XL	HZ-FYZ			
5023	N51933	N822MJ			
5024	N654EL				
5025	N534CC				
5026	N5201M	N17UC	N17UG*		
5027	N5202D	N560GB			
5028	N5203J	N528XL			
5029	N5203S	(PT-)	SE-DYX		
5030	N52038	N1228N	N899BC		
5031	N531BJ	N560BT			
5032	N165JB	N108EK			
5033	N5211Q	N456JW			
5034	N52113	PT-RAA			
5035	N5213S	N35XL	N4JS		
5036	N52136	N884BB	N36XL	N884BB*	
5037	N5214J	D-CIII			
5038	N5214K	N404BT			
5039	N39JV	N88WU			
5040	N5214L	N54HA			
5041	N52141	N1XL			
5042	N52178	N42XL			
5043	N5218R	PT-XIB			
5044	N5218T	N544XL			
5045	N5221Y	PP-JFM			
5046	N5223D	N966MT			
5047	N5223P	C-FCEL			
5048	N868JB	N548XL	VP-CAI		
5049	N5223Y	N24PH			
5050	N5225K	N184G			
5051	N5226B	N1324B	SX-DCM		
5052	N5228Z	N990MF			
5053	N5231S	I-BENT			
5054	N5233J	N1306V	N80X		
5055	N488CP				
5056	N51993	D-CVHB			
5057	N52457	N350RD			
5058	N5235G	N555WF			
5059	N55HA				
5060	N5201J	PT-WYU			
5061	N5200R	HB-VMO			
5062	N5197A	N22KW			
5063	N5200U	N56HA			
5064	N5194J	N2JW			
5065	N5204D	N100SC			
5066	N134SW				
5067	N42PA	HB-VMZ			
5068	N57HA				
5069	N5201M	N404SB			
5070	N5207A	VP-CNM			
5071	N51881	N671QS			
5072	N52178	N565AB			
5073	N5214K	D-CDBW			

CITATION EXCEL

C/n	Identities	
5074	N636GS	N466LM
5075	N558R	
5076	N521RA	
5077	N51575	N221LC
5078	N5203J	C-FPWC
5079	N5218T	ZS-OHZ
5080	N52141	N90CF
5081	N4000K	
5082	N145SM	
5083	N52144	N520G*
5084	N5211A	N684QS
5085	N52113	N85XL
5086	N51817	N62GB
5087	N5165T	
5088	N52081	
5089	N51942	N868JB
5090	N51246	N690QS
5091	N5183V	N560CH
5092	N5125J	N692QS
5093	N5203S	
5094	N1094L	
5095	N5135A	N95XL
5096		
5097	N5226B	
5098	N5244F	N200PF
5099	N58XL	N58HA
5100	N51444	
5101	N5216A	
5102	N5153K	
5103	N5218R	
5104	N5223D	F-HACD*
5105	N5185V	
5106	N5221Y	
5107		
5108	N562DB	
5109	N324LX	N324LE*
5110		
5111		
5112		
5113		
5114	N20SB	
5115		
5116		
5117		
5118		
5119		
5120		
5121		
5122		
5123		
5124	N24NG	
5125		
5126	N626QS	
5127	N560KT	
5128		
5129		
5130	N630QS	
5131	N631QS	
5132	N632QS	
5133	N23NG	
5134		
5135		
5136		
5137	N637QS	
5138		
5139	N639QS	
5140		
5141		
5142		
5143		
5144		
5145		
5146		
5147		
5148		
5149	N627XL	
5150		
5151		

CITATION EXCEL

C/n	Identities
5152	
5153	
5154	
5155	
5156	
5157	
5158	
5159	
5160	
5161	
5162	
5163	N63LX
5164	N64LX
5165	
5166	
5167	
5168	
5169	
5170	
5171	
5172	
5173	
5174	
5175	
5176	
5177	
5178	
5179	
5180	
5181	
5182	
5183	
5184	
5185	
5186	
5187	
5188	
5189	
5190	
5191	
5192	
5193	
5194	
5195	
5196	
5197	
5198	
5199	
5200	

CESSNA 650 CITATION III

C/n	Identities									
696	N650CC	ff 30May79 cx Nov89; wfu								
697	N650	converted to Citation VII standards 1991; fitted with GMA3007 turbofan in connection with Citation X programme 1992								
0001	N651CC	N1AP	(N651AP)	N654CC	N651CC	N651CG*				
0002	N652CC	N5000C	(N650BG)							
0003	N653CC	HZ-AAA	N187CP	N92LA	OY-CCG					
0004	(N654AR)	N654GC	N650GT							
0005	N137S	N439H	N693BA*							
0006	N656CC	N44HS	(N306QS)	N58RW	N1TS	N650TS	N39RE	N27TS		
0007	(N13047)	(N3Q)	N657CC	N929DS	C-FLTL					
0008	(N13049)	N618CC	N10TC	N84TJ	N84WU	N926CB				
0009	(N1305C)	N933DB	N933SH							
0010	(N1305N)	N2UP	N2EP	(N610VP)	OK-NKN	N650LW				
0011	N1305U	(C-GWPA)	(N90LA)	N91LA	N17TE	N17TN				
0012	N1305V	N15VF	OE-GCO							
0013	(N13052)	N119EL	(N13QS)	N313QS	N377JE*					
0014	(N1306B)	(N664RB)	N650CJ	C-GHOO	OE-GCN	(N855DH)				
0015	(N1306F)	N83CT	N369G	N15QS	N766MH					
0016	N1306V	N720ML	N720ME	N555DH	(N45US)	N32MG				
0017	N1307A	C-GHLM	N900CM							
0018	(N1307C)	N715BC	N275WN	N650SB						
0019	(N1307D)	(N44BH)	N30CJ	N333RL	N833RL	XA-TBA	N650JL			
0020	N1307G	XA-VIT	N488JT	N10PN	N650WB					
0021	N2624M	N2604	N650SS	N460CP						
0022	N650J									
0023	N889G	C-GHKY	N658MA	VR-CCC	N38DD	N650CG				
0024	N1UP	N1UH	N624VP	N643CR	N95SR	N650SL	N422BC^			
0025	N10PX	N200RT	(N376HW)	(N277HG)	N700RR	N650VP	N625VP	N16FE	(N522GS)	N16SU
0026	(N656CC)	damaged on factory production line early 1984 and not completed; fuselage used as test frame								
0027	N375SC	N875SC	N650NY							
0028	N148C	N328QS	LN-NLC							
0029	(N30CJ)	N600GH	N70TT	N81TT*						
0030	N650SC	SE-DHL	N650SC							
0031	N631CC	N1ZC								
0032	N54WC	N38WP	N3184Z							
0033	(N1309A)	CC-ECE	Chile E-302		w/o 09Jly92 4km fr runway 20 Concepcion, Chile					
0034	N80CC	N34QS	N777LF	(N45US)	N650GH					
0035	N650MD	N400JD	N408JD							
0036	N700CS	(N700RD)	N20RD	N36CD	N43TC	(N143RC)	XA-TGA			
0037	N411BB	N37CD	VH-OZI	N37VP	I-GASD					
0038	N366G	N366GE	N373DJ							
0039	N81TC	N39WP	N171L							
0040	N82TC	VR-BJY	HB-VIY	N650WE						
0041	N55BH									
0042	N142AB	N342QS	N342AS	C-GPOP						
0043	(N1310B)	OY-GKL								
0044	(N234HM)	N650M	(D-CRRR)	N129PJ						
0045	N84G	N67SF	N67SE	N669W						
0046	N658CC	N57TT	N650TT							
0047	N1102	(N1109)	N650CN	N33BC	N33BQ					
0048	N98BD	N98DD	N986M	N650MM						
0049	(N1311A)	C-FJOE	PJ-MAR	PT-LSN	N30AF	N650AN*				
0050	(N1311K)	N44M								
0051	(N1311P)	N910F	N651BH							
0052	N20MW	XA-SDU								
0053	N367G	N306PA								
0054	(N1312D)	N1103	N1183	(N26RG)	N17AN	N47AN				
0055	N173LP	N173LR	N515VC	N16AS						
0056	N273LP	(N273LB)	N760EW	N397CS						
0057	N368G	N101YC	(N101PC)	N400PC						
0058	N88DD	N70DJ	(N282PC)	(N292PC)						
0059	N1313G	PT-LHA	N660AA							
0060	(N1313J)	HB-VHW	N848US	TC-CAO	N660TJ	N220TW				
0061	(N1313T)	N137M	(N129TC)	N137X	N650TP	N650TC				
0062	N626CC	C-GHGK	N388DA	N19FR	N342HM	N650CN	N475M			
0063	N13138	N41ST	N72LE							
0064	(N1314H)	N801CC	N650TC	N444CW						
0065	(N1314T)	N500E	C-FIMO							
0066	(N1314V)	N138M	N138V	N650CD						
0067	(N1314X)	N210F								
0068	(N1314X)	N273W	N985M	N9KL	N650AJ	XA-TMZ				
0069	(N13142)	N910M	XA-							
0070	(N1315A)	N149C	N370QS	N370TG	LN-NLD					
0071	(N1315B)	N334H								
0072	(N1315C)	N277W	N651CN	N72ST						
0073	(N1315D)	N650JA	N673JS	N85DA	XA-					
0074	(N1315G)	(N555EW)	N234YP	N194DC						

CITATION III

C/n	Identities									
0075	N1315T	N16AJ								
0076	N1315V	N376SC	N876SC	HB-VJT	N731GA	XA-SEP	N424LB			
0077	(N1315Y)	N677CC	N701AG	VR-BGB	(N42NA)	TC-EES	TC-SIS			
0078	(N13150)	N652CC	PK-TRJ	PK-WSE	N650WJ	N50DS	(XA-)	N50DS	N650WL	N650KB
0079	(N1316A)	N66ME	N290SC	N288CC	N59CD	N217RR	N211RR	N69VC		
0080	N1316E	N69LD								
0081	(N1316N)	PT-LGT	(N881BA)	N910DP						
0082	(N13162)	N651AP	N1AP	N81AP	N82VP	N4VF				
0083	N13166	N944H	N944CA	TC-TOP						
0084	(N13168)	N85AW	N431CB							
0085	N1317G	JA8249	N650DA	I-CIST						
0086	(N1317X)	PT-LHC								
0087	(N1317Y)	N988H	N988HL	N687VP	C-FQCY	N680BC	N37VP			
0088	(N13170)	PT-LGZ	N290AS	N590AS	N650TA					
0089	(N13175)	N653CC	N650JC	N86WP	N86VP*					
0090	(N1318A)	N694CC	N1823S	N651TC	N850MC					
0091	N1318E	N68HC	N58HC	PT-LUE						
0092	(N1318L)	N692CC	N692BE							
0093	(N1318M)	(N693CC)	N773M	N93VP	N222GT	CS-DND	N196SG	N196SD		
0094	(N1318P)	N5114	N6114	N94VP	N94TJ	5B-CSM	N650SP	N651RS	N650SP	N926HC
0095	(N1318Q)	N5115	N6115	(N95VP)	N882KB					
0096	(N1318X)	N5116	N96VP	N700SW						
0097	(N1318Y)	N697MC	N725WH	N697MC*						
0098	(N13189)	N399W	N389W	N54HC						
0099	N1319B	(N555EW)	N26SD	N403CB*						
0100	(N1319D)	N200LH	N200LL	N202JK						
0101	N1319M	N847G	C-GPEA	N330TJ	N650HR	XB-GXV	XA-LTH			
0102	(N1319X)	(N406M)	N406MM	N406LM	N24237					
0103	(N13194)	(N407M)	N407MM	N407LM	N2411A					
0104	N13195	I-BETV	N650CF	C-FLMJ						
0105	(N1320B)	N655CC	N15TT	N48TT						
0106	(N1320K)	N106CC	N650CE							
0107	(N1320P)	N8000U	N650MP	N650JG						
0108	(N1320U)	N650Z								
0109	(N1320V)	(N650AT)	N20AT	N134M	(N134MJ)	(N649AF)	N109ST	N106ST		
0110	(N1320X)	N76D	N303PC							
0111	(N13204)	N500CM								
0112	N1321A	N60BE	N93DK	N598C						
0113	N1321C	N10ST	N872EC	(N650AF)	N652JM					
0114	(N1321J)	N7000G	N651AF							
0115	N1321K	PT-LJC	N1419J	N541S						
0116	(N1321L)	N78D	(N78DL)	N788BA	C-FJJC					
0117	N1321N	F-GGAL								
0118	(N13210)	N6000J	N118CD	N770MP	N770MR					
0119	(N13217)	VR-BJS	HB-VIN	N100WH	EC-EQX	N96AF	8P-KAM	N770AF	N147PS	
0120	N13218	N143AB	(N818TP)	(N650AF)	I-SALG	N650AF	N1223N	N30NM		
0121	(N1322D)	D-CATP	N1322D	N121AG	N24VB					
0122	(N1322K)	EC-EAS	N650TT	(N650MT)	N65WL					
0123	(N1322X)	N624CC	N434H							
0124	(N1322Y)	N95CC	N7HV	N650HC						
0125	(N13222)	EC-EAP	N650AF	N170HL						
0126	(N1323A)	N55HF	N65HF	XA-RZQ	N65HF	N311MA	N101PG			
0127	N1323D	N723BH	N92TX	(N18PV)						
0128	(N1323K)	N628CC	N125Q							
0129	(N1323N)	N61BE	(N309TA)	PT-LUO	N125N					
0130	(N1323Q)	N227LA	N227BA	N543SC	N159M	N159MR	N130TS	(N130RK)		
0131	(N1323R)	CC-ECL	Chile E-303							
0132	N1323V	N24KT								
0133	N1323X	N633CC	N133LE	N133LH	ZK-NLJ	N133LE	N250CM			
0134	(N1323Y)	N75RD	N75RN	N27SD	N123SL	N1239L	D-			
0135	(N1324B)	N5109	N135AF							
0136	(N1324D)	N841G	N60AF	N779AZ	N779AF					
0137	(N1324G)	N874G								
0138	(N1324R)	N828G	N650JV							
0139	(N13242)	N4EG	N96CP							
0140	(N1325D)	N95CC	N290SC	N220CC	N90CN	(N650SS)	N4FC			
0141	N1325E	N110TM	TC-CMY							
0142	(N1325L)	N142CC	N20RD	D-CRHR						
0143	N1325X	N143WR	N11NZ	N28S	N312CF	N40FC				
0144	N1325Y	N644CC	VH-KTI	N644CC	N650KM	N2605	PK-TSM			
0145	N1325Z	C-GCFP	N650AF	N29AU						
0146	N13256	N646CC	XA-PIP	N650FC						
0147	N13259	OE-GNK	N148N	N141M	N456AF	N94BJ	N151DR*			
0148	N1326A	N55SC	N55SQ	N50PH						
0149	N1326B	N649CC	N139M	N139N	(CS-DNE)	D-CBPL				
0150	N1326D	N150F								
0151	N1326G	G-MLEE	N91D	PK-KIG	N660AF	N321AR				
0152	(N1326H)	(N4EG)	N650AE	(N152VP)	N627R					

CITATION III

C/n	Identities								
0153	N1326K	N95CC	N653CC	N47CM					
0154	(N1326P)	N154CC	N696HC	N650CH					
0155	N13264	N788NB	N97AL						
0156	N13267	N68SK	N38SK	XA-ARS	N209A	N74VF			
0157	N1327A	N657CC	N516SM	N10JP					
0158	N1327B	N658CJ	N121AT	N135HC					
0159	N13113	N683MB	N267TG						
0160	N1312D	N95CC	N24UM	N831CB	N830CB	(N830GB)	N33UL		
0161	(N1312K)	N161CC	I-ATSA	N500AE	N510SD				
0162	N1312Q	N202RB	N275GC						
0163	N1312T	N137M	(N137MR)	N163AF	N749CP				
0164	N1312V	N138M	N138MR	N164AF					
0165	N1312X	XA-FCP	XC-PGN	N650GJ*					
0166	N1313J	PT-LTB							
0167	N667CC	N532CC							
0168	N1314H	N175J							
0169	N169CC	N88JJ	N749DC						
0170	N1314V	N95CC	N170CC	N32JJ					
0171	N1354G	PT-LVF							
0172	(N1772E)	N672CC	N934H						
0173	(N1779E)	N843G	N173VP						
0174	(N1782E)	N674CC	D-CLUE						
0175	(N175J)	N1820E	N235KK						
0176	N176L	N1874E	N1526L	N2TF	N48TF	N176AF			
0177	N1930E	JA8367	N707HJ	N834H					
0178	N1958E	N95CC	N178CC	JA8378	N178CC	N603AT	TC-RAM	N650BA	N57CE
0179	N1959E	N679CC	XA-RMY						
0180	N2098A	N768NB	N498CS						
0181	N2131A	(N181CC)	PT-OBX	N743CC					
0182	N26105	N682CC	N491JB						
0183	N2614Y	EI-SNN	N820FJ						
0184	N2615D	N95CC	N1128B	N11288					
0185	N2615L	N708CT	N708CF	N185VP	VR-BMG	N650HS	N533CC		
0186	N2616L	PT-OAK	N186VP						
0187	N2617K	N187CM	N500RP	(N55PC)	N70PT	(N78PT)	D-CAYK	N39VP	LN-AAA
0188	N2617P	N587S	N650FP						
0189	N26174	XA-RGS							
0190	(N2621U)	N142B	N190JJ	N350CD					
0191	(N2621Z)	N191CM	N59B	TC-KLS	N650TJ	N650SG			
0192	N2622C	N15TT	N15TZ*						
0193	N2622Z	N95CC	N95CM	N55HF	N55HD	N650CC			
0194	N26228	N111VW	N2606						
0195	N26233	N411BB	N411BP	C-GAPT					
0196	(N2625C)	N196CM	N896EC	N534H					
0197	N2625Y	N95CC	N197CC	(N197VP)	N797T	N800R			
0198	N2624L	(N650GA)	N198CM	N553AC	(N650BW)	XA-INF			
0199	(N2626X)	(N900JD)	N65KB	N890MC*					
0200	Built as Citation VI (qv)								
0201	Built as Citation VI (qv)								
0202	Built as Citation VI (qv)								
0203	N26271	N95CC	(N203CD)	N4612	(N4612S)	N4612Z			
0204	N2630B	XA-RZK	(N691DE)	N811JT	N108WV				
0205	N2630N	PT-OMU							
0206	N2630U	PT-OKV	N39H						

Production complete

CESSNA 650 CITATION VI

Note: The Citation VI was to have used model number 660 but in the end used 650 in common with the Citation III and VII

C/n	Identities				
0200	(N2626Z)	N650CM	PT-OMV	w/o 23Mar94 25 miles NW Bogota, Colombia	
0201	(N26264)	N40PH			
0202	N2627A	(N202CV)	PT-OJO	N202TJ	N65BP
0203	Built as Citation III (qv)				
0204	Built as Citation III (qv)				
0205	Built as Citation III (qv)				
0206	Built as Citation III (qv)				
0207	(N2632Y or N6812D)	N207CC	N334WC	N107CG	
0208	N6812L	N91TG	I-TALW	N500FR	
0209	(N6812Z)	N650L	N198DF		
0210	(N6868P)	N610CM	VR-CVP	N7059U	N733H
0211	N6820T	N335WC	N333WC	(N59CC)	N211CC
0212	(N6820Y)	N805GT			
0213	(N6823L)	N900JD			
0214	N68231	N95CC	N95CM	TC-CEY	N771JB	N7777B
0215	(N900JD)	(N6824G)	N215CM	N650KC	
0216	N68269	I-BLUB			
0217	(N6828S)	N217CM	PH-MEX		
0218	N6829X	XA-GAN	N218CC		
0219	N6829Z	N219CC	G-HNRY		
0220	N6830T	B-4106			
0221	N1301A	B-4107			
0222	N222CD	N733K			
0223	N1301D	N111Y			
0224	N224CD	N1UP			
0225	N1301Z	(N225CV)	N606AT		
0226	N1302A				
0227	N1302C	(N227CV)	N2UP		
0228	N1302V	N228CM	XA-SLB		
0229	N1302X	TC-ANT			
0230	N1305N	N616AT			
0231	N13052	LV-WHY	N67SF		
0232	N1303A	F-GKJS	N517MT	N512MT*	
0233	N1303H	CC-DAC			
0234	N1306V+	N334CM	TC-SBH	N733AU	N733A
0235	(N1307A)	N1303V	N235CM	N235SV	
0236	(N1307C)	N1303M	N600JD		
0237	(N1307D)	N1306B	N650MC		
0238	N1304B	(N9UC)	N19UC	N19QC*	
0239	N1304G	N17UC	N17QC	N68ED	
0240	N51143	PH-MFX			
0241	N5202D	(N651JM)	N666JM	N651JM	N651EJ

Production complete

CESSNA 650 CITATION VII

Note: The Citation VII was to have used model number 670 but in the end used 650 in common with the Citation III and VI

7001	N1259B	N701CD	N111RF	N404JF	N701HA	
7002	N1259K	N702CM	N95CC	N19SV		
7003	N1259N	N1AP	N17AP	N888TX	N650RJ*	
7004	N1259R	N708CT	N913SQ			
7005	N1259S	N200LH				
7006	(N1259Y)	N966H	N966K	(N706VP)	TC-KOC	
7007	N1259Z	N944H	N944L	N28TX		
7008	N12593	(N708CM)	N95CC	N901SB	N902SB	
7009	N12596	(N709CM)	N93TX			
7010	N1260G	N1S	(N1902)	N317MZ	N150JP	
7011	N1260N	N5111	(N6111)	N700VP	SE-DVY	
7012	N1260V	N712CM	N5112	N5144	N317MB	
7013	N12605	N5113	N5118	(N713VP)	N2NT	
7014	N1261A	N864EC				
7015	N1261K	N5115	N5119	(N715VP)	(N317MX)	N317MQ
7016	N1261M	N18SK	N68SK			
7017	(N1261M)	N775M				
7018	(N1261P)	N5114	N5174	N718VP	N119RM	N623PM
7019	N12616	XA-TCZ				
7020	N1262A	N95CC	N700RR	N832CB		
7021	N1262B	PT-MGS				
7022	N1262E	N722CM	2000th Citation		N902RM	

CITATION VII

C/n	Identities				
7023	N1262G	N6110			
7024	N1262Z	Turkey 93-7024		code ETI-024	
7025	N1263B	N442WT	N442WJ	N68BC	
7026	N1263G	Turkey 93-7026		code ETI-026	
7027	N1263P	N500	N657ER		
7028	(N1263V)	N728CM	XA-SPQ		
7029	(N1263Y)	N95CM	XA-SOK	N650RL	
7030	N12632	N1263Z	N8JC	(N703VP)	N95CC
7031	N12636	N40N			
7032	N12637	XA-XIS			
7033	N1264B	PT-OVU			
7034	N1264E	XA-SWM	N4360S	VP-CDW	damaged by fire late 1999 at Chester UK
7035	N1264M	VR-CIM	N3273H	PT-WLC	N95RX
7036	N1264P	N95CC	N95HF	N77HF	
7037	(N1264V)	N737CC	N95TX		
7038	N12642	N399W			
7039	N12643	D-CACM	OY-GGG		
7040	N1265B	N504T			
7041	N1265C	N430SA	(N449SA)		
7042	N1265K	N657T			
7043	N1265P	N78D	N78DL	TC-ATC	
7044	N1265U	N7005			
7045	N12652	N95CM	CC-PGL		
7046	N51160	N746CM	N746BR		
7047	N5117U+	N647CM	N1828S		
7048	N51176	N18GB			
7049	N5120U	N749CM	N900FL		
7050	N5121N	N6150B	N33GK		
7051	N51817	(N95CC)	N965JC	N77LX*	
7052	N5183U+	N752CM	N24NB		
7053	(N5183V)	N344AS	N650AS	N650AB	N123SL
7054	N5185J	(N754CM)	PT-WFC	N7243U	LV-WTN
7055	N5185V	N755CM	N317M	N317MZ	
7056	N52144	N6781C	N60PL		
7057	N5216A	N157CM	N653EJ		
7058	N52178	N625CC			
7059	N5218R	(N95CC)	N4EG		
7060	N5218T	N55SC			
7061	N5221Y	N903SB			
7062	N5262Z	N876G			
7063	N52623	N95CC	N877G		
7064	N52626	HB-VLP	N5117		
7065	N52627	(N765W)	N650W		
7066	N5263D	N766CG			
7067	(N5263S)	N51143	N502T		
7068	N51160	N111HZ	N111BZ	N7AB	
7069	N5117U	(N769CM)	XA-TMX		
7070	N51176	N95CM	N22RG	N322RG	(N770VP) N654EJ
7071	N5120U	HS-DCG	N1130N	HS-DCG	
7072	N5141F	(N8494C)	N35HS		
7073	N51444	N1867M			
7074	N5183V	PT-WLY			
7075	N52613	N12295	N711GF		
7076	N5213S	N286MC			
7077	N5203J	N877CM	N532JF	(N582JF)	VP-CGE
7078	N5079V	N78BR			
7079	N779QS				
7080	N780QS	CS-DNF			
7081	N781QS	CS-DNG			
7082	N5086W	N782QS			
7083	N50820	PT-WQH			
7084	N5094D	TC-KON	N1127G	TC-KON	
7085	N5112K	N785QS			
7086	N51342	N860W			
7087	N5163C	N787QS			
7088	N5073G	N449SA			
7089	N5117U	N789QS			
7090	N790QS				
7091	N791QS				
7092	N792QS				
7093	N793QS	CS-DNE			
7094	N794QS				
7095	N795QS				
7096	N5162W	N796QS	N287MC		
7097	N797QS				
7098	N5212M	N798QS	N601AB		
7099	N5141F	PT-XFG			
7100	N710QS				

CITATION VII

C/n	Identities		
7101	N5157E	N602AB	
7102	N5223X	D-CNCJ	
7103	N713QS		
7104	N5148B	VH-ING	
7105	N715QS		
7106	N5188A	N716QS	N71NK
7107	N559AM		
7108	N202AV		
7109	N5269A	N709QS	reported w/o Dec99 in ground accident Wichita A/P KS
7110	N52235		
7111	N5172M	N256W	
7112	N5174W	N257W	
7113	N5192E		
7114	N68BR		
7115	N314SL		
7116			
7117			
7118			
7119			

Production is reported to terminate with c/n 7119

+ indicates test marks not fully confirmed

CESSNA 680 CITATION SOVEREIGN

Cessna launched a new 10-seat, midsize Citation development at the 1998 NBAA Convention in Las Vegas, announcing that it held 80 orders for the new type - incluuding 50 for Executive Jet International's NetJets fleet (together with 50 options). Certification is targeted for mid-2002.

CESSNA 750 CITATION X

C/n	Identities				
703	N750CX	ff 21Dec93			
0001	N751CX	ff 27Sep94 TC-ATV			
0002	N752CX	N902QS			
0003	N5223D	N1AP			
0004	N5223P	N754CX	(N96UD)	N597U	
0005	N5263S	N99BB			
0006	N5263U	N76D	N484T		
0007	N52655	N750EC			
0008	N5266F	N1014X	N353WC		
0009	N5223Y	N96TX	N909QS		
0010	N5225K	N5112			
0011	N5122X	N944H			
0012	N52136	N966H			
0013	N5241Z	N5113			
0014	N5244F	N757T			
0015	N5085E	N715CX	N326SU		
0016	N5263U	N206PC			
0017	N51072	N5114			
0018	N5091J	N95CC	N5115		
0019	N5109W	N5116			
0020	N5125J	N95CM	N8JC		
0021	N5131M	(N164M)	N138A	N630M	
0022	N51313	(N5116)	N52639	(N722CX)	N10JM OH-CXO
0023	N5000R	N923QS			
0024	N52682	N164M	N5125J	N924EJ	N504SU
0025	N50612	N750RL		2500th Citation built	
0026	N5066U	N926QS			
0027	N5068R	N354WC			
0028	N5058J	N728CX	N100FF		
0029	N5090V	N500RP			
0030	N5095N	N355WC			
0031	N5061W	N22RG			
0032	N932QS				
0033	N5093D	N710AW			
0034	N934QS				
0035	N5071M	N97DK			
0036	N5085E	N936QS			
0037	N51160	N75HS			
0038	N51176	(N938QS)	N739CX		
0039	N51055	N98TX	N750LM	N22NG	
0040	N52136	N68LP			
0041	N5066U	(N95CC)	(N22NG)	N98TX	C-GIWD
0042	N5090A	N95CM	N915RB		
0043	N5090Y	N943QS			
0044	N5103J	N96RX			
0045	N5109R	N45BR			
0046	N5109W	N746CX	N946EJ	N749DX	
0047	N5091J	N947QS			
0048	N5135A	N84PJ			
0049	N5153K	N949QS			
0050	N5156D	N950QS			
0051	N5058J	N750J	(N1419J)	N119RM	
0052	N5000R	N712JC			
0053	N5061P	N795HG			
0054	N45ST				
0055	N5068R	N955QS			
0056	N5105F	PP-JQM			
0057	N505MA				
0058	N5120U	N758CX			
0059	N5108G	N751BH			
0060	N5090Y	N95CM	N98CX		
0061	N5109R	N961QS			
0062	N724CC				
0063	N51038	N750JB			
0064	N964QS	N964EJ			
0065	N5163C	(N965QS)	N750JJ		
0066	N750GM				
0067	N967QS				
0068	N5100J	N377SF			
0069	N51055	N100FR			
0070	N970QS				
0071	N971QS				
0072	N	XA-VER			
0073	(N532JF)	N999CX			
0074	N774CZ	N2418Y	N2418N*		
0075	N5196U	G-HERS	SE-DZX*		

CITATION X

C/n	Identities			
0076	N5197M	N400RB		
0077	N977QS			
0078	N51160	N199NP		
0079	N979QS			
0080	N5165T	ZS-SAB		
0081	N810X			
0082	N82BG			
0083	N983QS			
0084	N984QS			
0085	(N985QS)	N5103J	D-BTEN	
0086	N5124F	N888CN		
0087	N987QS			
0088	N5130J	N88EJ		
0089	N989QS			
0090	N5132T	N1932P		
0091	N5061P	N991EJ		
0092	N5066U	PT-WUM		
0093	N993QS			
0094	N51038	N750XX		
0095	N415FW			
0096	N585M			
0097	N5060K	(N81SN)	VP-CYK	
0098	N5090V	N998EJ		
0099	N5090A	N442WT		
0100	N5100J	N104CT		
0101	N901QS	N881G		
0102	N51995	N901QS		
0103	N5260Y	N96TX	N750HS	
0104	N5147B	N5T		
0105	N905QS			
0106	N52642	N106CX		
0107	N5086W	N107CX	(N332CM)	N520CM
0108	N51744	N908QS		
0109	N900EJ			
0110	N910QS			
0111	N5264A	N750BP		
0112	N51072	N1107Z		
0113	N913QS			
0114	N50820	N114CX		
0115	N5085E	OH-PPI*		
0116	N916QS			
0117	N50612	N426CM		
0118	N5266F	N753BD		
0119	N5223X	XA-SAR*		
0120	N920QS			
0121				
0122	N800W			
0123	N900QS			
0124	N924QS			
0125				
0126	N962QS			
0127				
0128	N67CX			
0129	N929QS			
0130	N930QS			
0131				
0132				
0133	N933QS			
0134				
0135	N935QS			
0136				
0137	N937QS			
0138				
0139				
0140				
0141	N941QS			
0142				
0143				
0144	N944QS			
0145				
0146				
0147				
0148				
0149	N948QS			
0150				
0151	N951QS			
0152				
0153	N953QS			

CITATION X

C/n	Identities
0154	
0155	
0156	N956QS
0157	
0158	N958QS
0159	
0160	N960QS
0161	
0162	N903QS
0163	
0164	N964QS
0165	
0166	N966QS
0167	
0168	
0169	
0170	
0171	
0172	
0173	
0174	
0175	
0176	
0177	
0178	
0179	
0180	
0181	
0182	
0183	
0184	
0185	
0186	
0187	
0188	
0189	
0190	
0191	
0192	
0193	
0194	
0195	
0196	
0197	
0198	
0199	
0200	
0201	
0202	
0203	
0204	
0205	
0206	
0207	
0208	
0209	
0210	
0211	
0212	
0213	
0214	
0215	
0216	
0217	
0218	
0219	
0220	
0221	
0222	
0223	
0224	
0225	
0226	
0227	
0228	
0229	

+ indicates test marks not fully confirmed

DASSAULT FALCON 10/100

C/n	Series	Identities
01	10	F-WFAL ff 01Dec70 w/o 31Oct72 Romorantin, France
02	10	F-WTAL ff 15Oct71 F-ZJTA France 02/F-ZACB wfu preserved training school at Toulouse-Montaudran
03	10	F-WSQN ff 14Oct72 F-BSQN CofA expired Apr81, wfu, cx 1988
1	10	F-WSQU ff 30Apr73 F-BSQU PH-ILT F-WJLH F-BJLH N333FJ
2	10	F-WJMM N10FJ N103JM C-GRIS
3	10	F-WJMJ N100FJ N731FJ N661GL (N10PN) N52TJ
4	10	F-WJMK N101FJ XB-SII EC-353 EC-FTV XA-SYY
5	100	F-WLCT F-BVPR F-V10F F-WVPR F-BVPR
6	10	F-WJML N102FJ N600BT (N110FJ) N10AG N139DD C-GRDT N54H N999MH N32BL N32VC N59CC
7	10	F-WJMN VR-BFF F-BXAG HB-VDE I-LUBE HB-VKE D-CASH HB-VKE
8	10	F-WJMN N104FJ N21ES N21ET N21EK N88ME N108KC
9	10	F-WJMM N103FJ N10TX N149TJ N510CL
10	10	F-WJMJ N105FJ N253K w/o 30Jan80 Chicago, IL; remains to White Inds, Bates City, MO
11	10	F-WJMK N106FJ N23ES N23ET (N23ED) N942C N452DP (N190DB) N211TJ (N11WC) N419WC
12	10	F-WJML N107FJ N3100X N10F (N76TJ)
13	10	F-WLCS N108FJ N734S N210FJ N72EU N10JZ N777SN N15TX b/u for spares 1992; cx Feb93
14	10	F-WJMK SE-DEL N59TJ (N50B)
15	10	F-WJMM N109FJ N60MB w/o 03Apr77 Denver, CO
16	10	F-WLCT N110FJ N48TT F-GELA N416AS N416HC
17	10	F-WLCS OH-FFB VH-FFB N29966 N27DA N33HL F-GHDZ EC-949 F-GNDZ
18	10	F-WJMJ N111FJ N78MD N48MS (N74TJ) N1TJ N80CC N1TJ
19	10	F-WLCU N112FJ N30JM (N30JH) (N36KA) N36JM N937J F-GJFZ 3A-MGT (while regd and painted as 3A-MGT used call sign C-GORI at 1995 NBAA) LX-TRG
20	10	F-WLCV N113FJ N42G
21	10	F-WJMK (HB-VDT) 3D-ACB N40WJ
22	10	F-WLCX N114FJ N44JC N48JC F-GJLL
23	10	F-WLCY N115FJ N73B N310FJ N91MH N20WP
24	10	F-WJML N116FJ N1924V F-GBTI N301JJ N991RV
25	10	F-WJMJ N117FJ N40N N83RG N22EH N83RG N60FC N600GM N719AL N177BC
26	10	F-WJMK N118FJ N592DC N707AM N720DF
27	10	F-WLCX SE-DDF OK-EEH N38DA
28	10	F-WJML N119FJ N130B N813AV N500DS N42EH (N655DB)
29	10	F-WJMM N120FJ N234U N66MF N332J N999F N404JW
30	10	F-WLCT N121FJ N294W N30FJ N156X N3WZ N191MC N171MC Accident 24Jan96 Romulus, MI as N191MC; to White Inds probably for parted out
31	10	F-WLCU N122FJ N2MP N27C N50TC N81P (N952TC) (N29AA) N27AJ
32	MER	France 32
33	10	F-WJMJ N123FJ N881P (N246N) N900UC F-GHFO N54WJ (N18BG) TC-ORM N20373 C-FBVF
34	10	F-WLCS N124FJ N110M N220M
35	10	F-WLCV N125FJ N54V N777JJ
36	10	F-WJMJ HB-VDD N10UN N224CC N894CA N676PC N76AF XA-MMM
37	10	F-WJML C-GFCS N39515 N123VV N123TG N347K N48JC N72GW N945MC
38	10	F-WJMM N127FJ N20ES N20ET N20EE F-GBRF
39	MER	F-WPUX France 39 w/o 30Jan80 Toul-Rosieres, France
40	10	F-WJMN N128FJ N10XX N15SJ XA-LIO
41	10	F-WLCS N129FJ N1HM N50DM N53DB F-GKLV N61TJ N116DD
42	10	F-WLCU N126FJ N18X (N9147F) N100UB N282T
43	10	F-WJMN N135FJ N1515P N510CP (F-GHFI) F-GIQP N17TJ
44	10	F-WJMJ N130FJ N205X N62TJ N277SF N244TJ N90AB^
45	10	F-WJML N131FJ N120HC N110CG C-FTEN
46	10	F-WLCT N134FJ N911RF N815LC (N908SB) N908RF N401JW
47	10	F-WLCY N132FJ YV-07CP PJ-AYA YV-221CP YV-101CP N3914L N101GZ N91LA N90LA N79PB (N190MD) F-GJGB w/o 30Sep93 Besancon, France
48	10	F-WJMM N133FJ N720ML N720ME N333SR F-WGTF F-GHRV LX-EPA N20LW
49	10	F-WLCV N136FJ (N490A) N49AS N449A N26EN N700TT PT-LMO N67LC
50	10	F-WLCS VH-MEI (ZK-WNL) N133FJ PT-OHM N411SC N299DB
51	10	F-WJML N137FJ N51BP
52	10	F-WLCX N138FJ N342G N52TJ N8100E N860E N711TF
53	10	F-WLCS N139FJ N8100E N810US N125EM (N890E) N891CQ I-LCJG N53WA
54	10	F-WPUU N140FJ (XA-SAR) N464AC N4875 N53SN N54FJ VR-BFW VP-BFW N561D N110LA
55	10	F-WPUV N141FJ N55FJ N702NC N702NG N700AL N700PD*
56	10	F-WPUY HB-VDX OY-FRM N56WJ N16DD N56WJ
57	10	F-WJMJ N142FJ N142V N50TB (N50YJ) N10YJ (N6366W) w/o 30Jun97 White Plains, NY; to White Inds, MO for spares
58	10	F-WJMM N143FJ N76FJ N58AS N458A N500FF (F-GHJL) N170CS
59	10	F-WJMN N144FJ N300GN N300A N302A N633WW
60	10	F-WJML N145FJ N77GT N810E SE-DKD N69WJ
61	10	F-WPUV D-CBMB F-WZGD (F-BIPF) F-BFDG 3D-ART w/o 03Oct86 Magoebaskloof, Transvaal, S Africa
62	10	F-WJMM N146FJ N12LB N6VG
63	10	F-WLCX N147FJ PT-KTO N70TS N876MA

FALCON 10/100

C/n	Series	Identities
64	10	F-WLCT N148FJ N100BG N721DP N500DE N718CA N444WJ
65	10	F-WJMJ N149FJ XB-BAK N21DB (F-GJMA) N66CF
66	10	F-WJMN N150FJ N50RL YV-70CP N63TS
67	10	F-WLCU N151FJ D-COME N427CJ
68	10	F-WLCV N152FJ N7NP (N7NL) N11DH N91DH N80MP F-GFPF
69	10	F-WJML N153FJ N43CC N3RC F-GELE N7TJ N711JC
70	10	F-WJMM HB-VEG F-WQCO VR-BCH VP-BCH N349JC
71	10	F-WJMM D-CMAN N229JB (N728SA) (N203PV) N190H
72	10	F-WLCX N154FJ N10TB N31SJ N50TY
73	10	F-WNGL N155FJ N88AT C-GDCO N130FJ YV-601CP N130FJ VR-BNT N378C
74	10	F-WJMJ N156FJ N30TH N34TH N518S N108MR N5JY
75	10	F-WNGM N157FJ N12U N937D (N75MH) N97TJ N796SF
76	10	F-WPUU F-BYCC N727TS
77	10	F-WNGN N158FJ N82MD N301HC N53TS N107TB
78	10	F-WLCT N159FJ N83MD (N83MF) N784CE N178TJ
79	10	F-WPXB F-BPXB N160FJ N73B
80	10	F-WPXD N161FJ N48R F-GMJS N1080Q N39RE (N320GP) N577RT N4RT (N803RA) N567RA
81	10	F-WPXF N162FJ N700BD N81TX
82	10	F-WPXE N168FJ N97MC N602NC
83	10	F-WPXG N163FJ N5GD XA-FIU N83EA N67TJ N76MB
84	10	F-WPXH N164FJ N8447A JA8447 N8447A N526D N6PA N192MC (N100TW) N106TW
85	10	F-WPXI N165FJ N85JM (N95DW) OE- N85JM w/o 17Feb93 Aurillac, France; scrapped for spares 1993 at White Inds, Bates City, MO
86	10	F-WPXJ N166FJ N410WW N411WW N50TE scrapped for spares after accident by White Inds, Bates City, MO
87	10	F-WPXK N167FJ (N200AF) N662D N682D C-FBSS N80TS N99BL N549AS C-FNND
88	10	F-WPXL N169FJ N3600X (F-GKCD) F-GHER N71M
89	10	F-WPXM D-CADB F-WZGF I-CAIC 3X-GCI HB-VIG I-EJIC HB-VKF D-CENT TC-AND (N888WJ)
90	10	F-WNGD N170FJ N14U N12TX
91	10	F-WJMJ D-CBAG N790US N23VP
92	10	F-WNGM N172FJ (N61BP) N1PB (N58B) F-GHLT N95TJ N724DS
93	10	F-WNGN F-BYCV N40180 (N98TW) wfu to White Inds, Bates City, MO, for spares; still current
94	10	F-WNGO N171FJ N54RS N13BK
95	10	F-WPXD N173FJ PT-ASJ w/o 17Feb89 nr Rio-Santos Dumont, Brazil
96	10	F-WNGD N174FJ XA-SAR OE-GLG I-LCJT N174FJ N96TJ N115TD
97	10	F-WPXF N175FJ
98	10	F-WPXG D-CBUR w/o 08Aug96 near Offenburg, Germany
99	10	F-WPXH N176FJ N10TJ (N65HS) N656PC N500GM N67JW F-GKBC
100	10	F-WPXI N177FJ N10FJ YV-17CP (N217CP) N100FJ
101	MER	F-WPXJ France 101
102	10	F-WPXK N178FJ N61BP
103	10	F-WPXL F-GBMH N103TJ N339TG N103TJ N9TE
104	10	F-WPUU N179FJ N90DM VR-BHJ N4557P N913V N913VL N800SB
105	10	F-WPUV N180FJ N942B N71TJ N711MT N16DD N16WJ N804JJ
106	10	F-WPUX N181FJ N1JN N10FJ N730PV (N918PC) N902PC N913VS N103MM N20CF
107	10	F-WPUY N182FJ XB-ZRB XB-CAM XB-FWX XC-ZRB N160TJ N100T
108	10	F-WPUZ (HZ-KAI) HZ-AKI F-WZGF F-BIPC N246FJ N11DH N91DH N88LD (F-GFJK) F-GJHK w/o 26Mar92 Brest, France; scrapped Mar93
109	10	F-WNGD N183FJ N77NR C6-BEN N69EC N89EC
110	10	F-WNGO N184FJ N90MH N901MH I-SHIP N712US N104DD N43US
111	10	F-WNGO N185FJ N8200E N820CE N10HE N983MC^
112	10	F-WPXD N186FJ N12XX N12MB N598JC
113	10	F-WPXE (I-SHOP) I-CHOC HB-VIW (F-GFHG) F-GFHH LX-DPA
114	10	F-WPXF N187FJ N200YM N100YM N807F N15TM N555DH N108TG N982MC
115	10	F-WPXH N188FJ N511S N211SR N420JD F-GGAR I-ITPR N115WA N636SC
116	10	F-WNGL N189FJ N4DS (N927DS) N925DS N525RC F-GJMA damaged 27Sep96 Madrid-Barjas, Spain
117	10	F-WPXG N190FJ N23DS N923DS N18MX
118	10	F-WPXI HZ-AMA HZ-NOT HZ-A02 N848MP I-DNOR F-GJJL HB-VJN F-GIJG N41TJ (N97RJ) N118AD
119	10	F-WPXK N191FJ N257W N257V
120	10	F-WPXM N192FJ N20ES N359V N369V N100WG N402JW
121	10	F-WPUU (HB-VFS) HB-VFT F-GDLR
122	10	F-WPUV N193FJ N22ES N312A N312AT OE-GSC
123	10	F-WPUX N194FJ N23ES N312AT N312AM N312AN N50TK N25FF SE-DKC N23WJ N110TP
124	10	F-WPUY F-GBTC w/o 15Jan86 nr Chalon-Vatry, France
125	10	F-WNGD N195FJ N400SP N100CK XA-SAR
126	10	F-WNGM (N196FJ) I-CHIC F-WZGS I-CHIC HB-VIX (F-GFHH) F-GFHG N26WJ
127	10	F-WZGG F-GCTT I-CALC N8GA
128	10	F-WNGO N197FJ N1871R N79HA N79PB N99MC N99BC N175BC
129	MER	F-WZGA France 129
130	10	F-WZGB I-SFRA (N777ND) N921GS N432EZ N454DP*
131	10	F-WZGC N196FJ N654PC (D-CAJC) HB-VME N133EP
132	10	F-WZGD N198FJ N500GS N580GS SE-DKB N250MA TC-ATI dbr Nov94 Le Bourget A/P, Paris, France; cx Mar95; to N9258U; fuselage with White Inds, Bates City, MO by Apr96

FALCON 10/100

C/n	Series	Identities									
133	MER	F-WZGE	F-ZGTI	France 133							
134	10	F-WZGF	N202FJ	N900T	N509TC	VH-MCX					
135	10	F-WZGG	N199FJ	N835F	N969F	N707CX	N245SP				
136	10	F-WZGH	I-MUDE	F-WZGS	F-GFMD						
137	10	F-WZGI	N200FJ	N837F	C-GTVO						
138	10	F-WZGJ	N203FJ	N30TH	N100BG	(N942M)	F-GGVR	N236DJ			
139	10	F-WZGK	N204FJ	N10AH	(N810J)	(N610J)	(N110J)	(N803SR)	N110J		
140	10	F-WZGL	N205FJ	N70WC	N88WL	F-GHDX					
141	10	F-WZGM	N206FJ	(N10AH)	N900D	N77SF					
142	10	F-WZGN	N207FJ	N10HK	N11DH	N5LP	N174B				
143	MER	F-WZGO	France 143								
144	10	F-WZGP	N208FJ	N1TC	(N79FJ)	N101TF	(N144HE)	N502BG			
145	10	F-WZGQ	N209FJ	N244A							
146	10	F-WZGR	N211FJ	F-GHVK	(N17ZU)	N461AS					
147	10	F-WZGS	N212FJ	N12TX	F-GHPL	N125GA	N212FJ				
148	10	F-WZGT	N213FJ	N103PJ	N79TJ						
149	10	F-WZGU	N214FJ	N711FJ	(N830SR)						
150	10	F-WZGV	N215FJ	N212N	N212NC	(HB-V)	N99WA				
151	10	F-WZGX	N217FJ	N26CP	OE-GAG	N4581R	N27AC	N256W	N256V		
152	10	F-WZGY	N216FJ	N8463	JA8463	N8463	F-GDRN	SE-DPK	N152WJ	N999LL	
153	10	F-WZGZ	N218FJ	N344A	N81P						
154	10	F-WZGA	N219FJ	PT-LCO	N777FJ	N149HP	reported to White Ind, MO Oct97 for spares				
155	10	F-WZGC	(N220FJ)	D-CIEL	N725PA	F-GTOD					
156	10	F-WZGE	N221FJ	N618S	SE-DEK	ZS-SEA					
157	10	F-WZGF	N222FJ	(N900AR)	N101EF	N80GP	F-GFBG	N157EA	N64AM	N703JS	(N157JA)
		(N814AA)	N450CT*								
158	10	F-WZGI	N223FJ	N81LB	N220SC	N790FH	N700FH				
159	10	F-WZGJ	N224FJ	N224RP	N224BP	(N88TB)	N10WE	N707DC	N707AM		
160	10	F-WZGK	N225FJ	N223HS	N31TM	F-GFFP	LX-JCG				
161	10	F-WZGM	N230FJ	N30CN	N50SL	I-CREM					
162	10	F-WZGN	N226FJ	N664JB	N796MA	N47RK	(N162TJ)	N713G*			
163	10	F-WZGP	N227FJ	N151WC	N163F	F-GJRN	(N2CH)	N163CH	N163AV	N73TJ*	
164	10	F-WZGQ	N228FJ	N222MU							
165	10	F-WZGR	N229FJ	N111WW	N56LP						
166	10	F-WZGS	N232FJ	N94MC	(F-GIPH)	F-GJFB	N94MG	N747AC	N21CL	(N166SS)	N211EC
167	10	F-WZGT	N233FJ	N39K	5V-TAE	5V-MBG	5V-TAE	N167AC	N516SM	N82CG	
168	10	F-WZGU	N234FJ	N175BL	N43EC						
169	10	F-WZGV	N235FJ	VH-DJT	N725P	F-GHFB	(N107AF)	PT-WSF			
170	10	F-WZGX	N236FJ	N821LG	w/o 22Feb86 Westchester, PA						
171	10	F-WZGY	N237FJ	N30TB	N26ES	PT-OIC	N42US				
172	10	F-WZGZ	N238FJ	YV-99CP	N172CP	N10NC					
173	10	F-WZGA	N239FJ	N72BB	N441DM	N211CN	N555SR	N554SR	9A-CRL	N8LT	
174	10	F-WZGE	N240FJ	N5ES	N402ES	RP-C1911					
175	10	F-WZGF	N241FJ	XA-LOK	N12EP						
176	10	F-WZGI	N242FJ	HK-2968X	HK-2968	N179AG	N66HH	N231JH			
177	10	F-WZGJ	N243FJ	N533CS	F-GFGB	N101VJ					
178	10	F-WZGK	N244FJ	N10QD	N79BP	N87TH					
179	10	F-WZGL	I-DJMA	(F-GGRA)	F-GERO	N100RR					
180	10	F-WZGM	N245FJ	N593DC							
181	10	F-WZGC	N247FJ	N87GT	N151GS	(N151DC)	F-GJHG	N138DM			
182	10	F-WZGN	N248FJ	N111MU	N809F						
183	100	F-WZGO	N249FJ	N82CR	N183SR	SE-DLB					
184	10	F-WZGP	N250FJ	N346P	N4AC	(C-)	N725DM				
185	MER	F-WZGQ	France 185								
186	10	F-WZGB	N251FJ	N2426	N2426G	N63TJ	N420PC	N186TJ	N555DH*		
187	10	F-WZGR	N252FJ	N2427F	N2427N+	N81TJ	N303PL	N555DH	N1DH		
		+ although worn these marks were not entered onto USCAR									
188	10	F-WZGS	N253FJ	N188DH	N64F	D-CLLL	HB-VJM	I-TFLY	N84TJ		
189	10	F-WZGT	N254FJ	N605T	N60SL	N600PB	N812KC	N189JM			
190	10	F-WZGU	N255FJ	N1887S	N36BG	N190L					
191	10	F-WZGV	N256FJ	N700DK	w/o 23Sep85 Palwaukee, IL						
192	100	F-WZGX	N258FJ	N100FJ	N121FJ	w/o 15Oct87 Sacramento, CA					
193	100	F-WZGY	N259FJ	N3BY	OH-AMB						
194	100	F-WZGZ	N260FJ	N100FJ	N61FC	F-GIPH					
195	100	F-WZGA	N261FJ	N561NC	N5736	N10NL	(N10NV)	N95WJ	TS-IAM		
196	100	F-WZGB	N262FJ	N581NC	N5734	N573J	N125CA				
197	100	F-WZGC	F-GEDB	F-WEDB	F-GEDB	N888G	N52N				
198	100	F-WZGF	N263FJ	N551NC	N5738	N100RB	N1PB	N91PB			
199	100	F-WZGG	N264FJ	N330MC	(N1CN)	N39TH	PT-OXB	N886MJ	N486MJ	N96VR	
200	100	F-WZGG	N265FJ	N662D	(N682D)	N80BL					
201	100	F-WZGH	N266FJ	N8494	JA8494	N30TH	(F-GKPZ)	F-GKCC	N100NW	N844F	
202	100	F-WZGD	F-GDSA	3D-ADR	N80WJ	N202DN					
203	100	F-WZGJ	N267FJ	VR-CLA	N100CT	XA-TBL	N45JB				
204	100	F-WZGK	N268FJ	N101EU	F-WGTG	XA-TAB					
205	100	F-WZGL	N269FJ	N700DW	N606AM						
206	100	F-WZGM	N270FJ	N100FJ	N367F	N46MK					
207	100	F-WZGN	N271FJ	N711MT	F-GKPB	(N107US)	N207US	N456CM	N55DG	N456CM	N55DG
208	100	F-WZGO	F-GELS	I-OANN	N71M	F-WQBJ	F-GSLZ				

FALCON 10/100

C/n	Series	Identities						
209	100	F-WZGP	N272FJ	N312AT	(N312AR)	HB-VKR	OY-PHN	
210	100	F-WZGR	N273FJ	N312AM	N812AM	N85WN	N35WN	N110PP
211	100	F-WZGT	F-GELT					
212	100	F-WZGU	CN-TNA					
213	100	F-WZGV	N274FJ	ZK-MAZ	F-GKAE	F-WKAE	N711HF	
214	100	F-WZGX	N275FJ	N147G				
215	100	F-WZGY	F-GHPB					
216	100	F-WZGZ	N276FJ	N100H	VH-JDW	9M-ATM	N999WJ	SE-DYB
217	100	F-WZGA	N277FJ	N100FJ	N100WG	F-GIFL	N68GT	
218	100	F-WZGB	F-GHSK	TC-ARK	N218BA	N130DS		
219	100	F-WZGC	N123FJ	N2649	PT-ORS	N219JW		
220	100	F-WZGD	N124FJ	N368F	N326EW	N326LW	N702NC	
221	100	F-WZGH	OE-GHA	F-GPFD				
222	100	F-WZGF	N125FJ	N100CK	N98VR			
223	100	F-WZGG	N126FJ	PT-LVD				
224	100	F-WZGH	N128FJ	(PT-)	C-FREE	N135FJ	SE-DVP	
225	100	F-WZGI	N127FJ	PT-LXJ	N225CC	(N814PJ)		
226	100	F-WZGJ	N130FJ	XA-RLX	N121AT			

Production complete

DASSAULT FALCON 20/200

Notes: "European Line Numbers" are quoted alongside the c/n where appropriate. These were numbers allocated by Dassault for administrative purposes but do from time to time get quoted as the c/n on its own, or jointly with the actual c/n.

Aircraft converted as part of the TFE-731 re-engining programme are known as 20-5s; known conversions are shown in the series column. Aircraft with TFE-731-5A engines (the earlier conversion) retain the series number in the designation, eg 20C-5 (c/n 24), while later conversions which use the TFE-731-5B engines (as also used in the Falcon 900B) do not retain the series letter; we have however retained this so that readers can be aware of the original model type.

C/n	Series	Identities
01	20	F-WLKB ff 04May63 F-BLKB F-WLKB last flt 06Feb76; mock-up for Guardian; in Musee de l'Air, le Bourget, Paris
1/401	20C	F-WMSH ff 01Jan65 F-BMSH F-WMSH France 1/F-ZACV wfu 31Dec81; TT 6,248 hrs, TL 13,329; to Bordeaux-Merignac Museum as F-WMSH
2/402	20C	F-WMSS F-BMSS
3/403	20C	F-WMKG F-BMSX VR-BCG HB-VAV N92MH N301R
4	20C	F-WMKF N801F N116JD N121GW w/o 18May78 Memphis, TN
5	20C	F-WMKI N804F N747W F-GJPR N295TW
6	20C	F-WMKH F-BMKH N805F N20JM N21JM (N21DT) C-GOQG N65311 N497 N750SS EC-EDC
7	20C	F-WMKK N807F N607S N740L CF-GWI N777FA N20GH N12GH N110CE N93CP N600JC
8	20C	F-WMKJ N806F N1500 N150CG N1500 N190BD N612GA
9	20C	F-WMKI N809F N366G N3668 C-GSKA LV-PLC LV-WMF
10	20C	F-WMKK N810F N111M b/u for spares; cx Aug87; remains at Av-Mats' facility at Paynesville, MO
11	20C	F-WMKH N808F CF-SRZ N2200M N220CM N30CC N30CQ N4351M N4351N N409PC OO-DDD N983AJ N216CA
12	20C	F-WMKI N803F N221B N51SF LN-AAB cx Mar89; to USA, no marks allocated; b/u for spares Jul89 Memphis, TN
13	20C	F-WMKH F-BOEF TR-LOL F-BOEF D-CILL F-BTCY N977TW
14	20C	F-WMKJ N804F CF-DML N22DL N22HC N91JF N41MH
15	20C	F-WMKK N806F N622R N1502 N151CG N1501
16	20DC	F-WNGL N807F N354H N10FE N122CA N120AF N216TW N216SA
17	20C	F-WMKF N802F N545C N5450 N5C N5CE N55TH N234CA*
18	20C	F-WNGM N840F N803LC D-COLO N777JF N9DM N210RS wfu 1996 for spares
19	20C	F-WNGN N841F N500PC N500PX N41PC (N41PD) C-GKHA
20	20DC	F-WMKJ N842F N367G N367GA N5FE (N146FE) (N25FR) N903FR G-FRAJ
21	20C	F-WMKI N843F N3444G N370 (N500NU) N500EW N91TS XA-SWC N20LT C-FTUT
22/404	20C	F-WMKK F-BMKK France 22/F-ZACS
23	20C	F-WNGL F-BNKX N844F N424JX N15CC N256EN N256MA (N582G) Venezuela 5761 stored
24	20C-5	F-WNGM N845F N297AR N30JM (N13FE) N2255Q N738RH N60SM N60SN N703SC N20YA N25TX N204JP N1M N240TJ N794SB*
25/405	20C	F-WNGN F-BOON HB-VCO F-BSYF N813AA TG-GGA N813AA reported wfu
26	20C	F-WNGO N846F N802F N11827 N819AA
27	20C-5	F-WMKJ N847F N677SW N33TP N174GA
28	20C	F-WMKG N848F N367EJ N10WA N573EJ YV-78CP N50CA (N280RC) (N126JM) N50CA C-GEAQ N333AV at Montreal - Saint Hubert Aeronautical College
29	20C	F-WMKI N849F N368G N368L C-GSKC LV-PLD? LV-WMM
30	20CF	F-WMKF N804F N368EJ YV-126CP N368EJ N407PC CS-ATD F-GPIM N514SA
31	20C	F-WNGM N806F N34C N814AA N828AA N131MV
32	20C	F-WNGL N805F N418S N218S 5B-CGB TL-AJK F-GIVT N232TW
33	20C	F-WNGO N807F N369EJ N888AR w/o 07Aug76 Acapulco, Mexico
34	20C	F-WMKJ N808F N369G N3690 C-GSKS LV-PHV LV-WLH w/o 07Feb97 into mountains near Salta, Argentina
35	20C	F-WMKG N809F (N1777R) N809P 9M-BCR
36	20C	F-WMKI N810F N900P N711BC N644X N85N OE-GUS N818AA
37/406	20C	F-WMKF (HB-VWW) HB-VAP (N7922) (N11WA) w/o 01Oct77 Goose Bay, Canada; parts used in rebuild of c/n 28
38	20C	F-WMKF N842F N1107M N957TH wfu 1987; wfu Spirit of St Louis May88; cx Jan93; remains to Elberry, MO
39	20C	F-WNGM N843F N5555U N6565A N50MM N910U XA-LOB XB-EDU XA-RMA
40	20C	F-WNGL N870F CF-BFM N19BC N354H N354WC N854WC N65LC N65LE C-GSKQ N240TW
41/407	20C/ECM	F-WNGL (S Africa 431) F-BOED LN-FOI Norway 041
42	20C	F-WNGO N871F N1503 N7824M w/o 16Jan74 Fort Worth, TX
43	20C	F-WMKJ N872F N990L w/o 03Mar75 Dallas, TX
44	20C	F-WNGN N873F N355WB N355WC N355WG N692G N76TS N377BT N773HS*
45	20C	F-WMKI N876F N147X N159FC N90JF N202KH N175GA substantially damaged 04Apr00 Opa Locka A/P FL
46	20DC	F-WMKG CF-ESO N23555 N7FE (N144FE) N46VG EC-EHC
47	20C	F-WNGM N875F N1846 w/o 13Mar68 Parkersburg, WV
48	20C-5	F-WMKG N878F N910Y N91CV (N23NQ) N23ND
49/408	20C	F-WNGN France 49/F-RAFJ F-TEOA France 49/F-RHFA (120-FA)
50	20DC	F-WMGO N879F N804F N565A N6FE (N145FE) N56VG EC-EDO N699TW

FALCON 20/200

C/n	Series	Identities
51	20C	F-WMKJ N880F N880P N218US N425JF N425JA scrapped for spares Aug91; cx Oct94
52	20C	F-WNGN N881F N72ET N85DB N825TC D-CLBR
53/417	20C/ECM	F-WNGO F-BNRE LN-FOD Norway 053
54	20C-5	F-WMKI N886F N200P N2005 N10726 N54SN N100HG (N205TS) (N103RA) N380RA N405JW
55/410	20C	F-WNGO VR-BCJ HB-VBS EC-EHD N550AL CCCP-01100 UR-EFA
56	20C	F-WNGM N882F N671SR N100SR N185S N932S (OO-PPP) OO-OOO N388AJ (N560RA)
57	20C	F-WNGO N883F N499MJ N678BM N677BM N3JJ N76RY N711KG N812AA
58	20C	F-WNGL N884F N600KC F-BTQZ HB-VDG N2954T scrapped for spares spring 1987 Van Nuys, CA
59	20DC	F-WNGO N971F N263MW N710MW N710MR N710MT N227GC N227CC N202TA N72BB N771LD
60	20C	F-WMKJ N885F N805F w/o 05Jly71 Boca Raton, FL
61	20C	F-WMKI N887F N299NW N20NY
62/409	20C	F-WMKJ F-BOLX LN-FOE w/o 12Dec73 Norwich, UK (N17401) used by Federal Express for spares
63/411	20C	F-WMKI PH-LPS D-CBNA
64	20C	F-WMKG N889F N806F N200JW N916AN N513AN N513AG
65	20C	F-WNGN N890F N383RF (N393RF) N393F N777WJ N777WL N1U N5052U C-GSKN N165TW
66	20C	F-WNGL N891F N401AB N581SS N109RK N181RB
67/414	20C	F-WJMN F-BOOA F-BTML N821AA N826AA
68	20C-5	F-WMKJ N892F N577S N458SW
69	20C	F-WMKF N893F N176NP N176BN N31LT
70	20C	F-WMKH N966F N647JP (N647SA) N78JR (N400NL) wfu 20Mar89; b/u for spares Mojave, CA (TT 4,326 hrs) remains to Aviation Warehouse film prop yard at El Mirage CA
71	20C	F-WNGM N967F N807F N807PA N33SC N818SH N818CP (N293GT) N195AS
72/413	20C	F-WNGO HB-VAW N1270F N99KT VH-DWA N725P F-GJCC
73/419	20C	F-WJML VH-BIZ (F-BRHB) F-WMKG 9Q-CKZ (OO-RJX) (OO-ADA) LX-AAA LN-AAA cx Dec89; scrapped for spares May89 Memphis, TN
74	20C-5	F-WMKG N968F N1851T N1MB N57HH N800MC N800PA N800DC N702DM
75	20C	F-WNGL N969F N100V N256MA N2568 N800DC N77QM UR-EFB
76	20C	F-WMKF N970F N937GC N776DS F-GGFO F-GJDB
77/429	20C-5	F-WNGO I-RIED (F-GJBR) F-GHDN F-WGTF F-GHSG N613GA
78/412	20C	F-WNGM Australia A11-078 VH-JSX N6555C
79/415	20C	F-WMKH F-BNRH France 79/F-ZACT
80	20C	F-WMKI N972F N115K N356WB N356WC N356JB N76MB N24TW
81	20C	F-WNGN N973F N799G N661JB N661J N747T N93RS N810RA
82/418	CC117	F-WJMM Canada 20501 Canada 117501 G-FRAS
83	20C	F-WJMJ N974F N805CC N80506 N22JW N12WP N1TC N55ME N68JK N20PL N82SR*
84	20C	F-WJMK N975F N530L N1FE (N150FE) N9FE exhibited outside Federal Express HQ, Memphis, TN
85/425	20C	F-WMKH Australia A11-085 VH-JSY N6555L
86	20C	F-WMKI N976F N808F N622R (G-BBEK) F-BUYI G-BBEK (HB-VDW) F-WRGQ France 86/F-ZACG
87/424	CC117	F-WJMJ Canada 20502 Canada 117502 G-FRAT
88	20C	F-WNGN N977F N130B N665P N665B N41CD N617GA substantially damaged Monroe, MI 12May98
89	20C	F-WMKG N978F N345BM N71CP N505AJ
90/426	20C	F-WNGL Australia A11-090 VH-JSZ VH-CIR PK-
91	20C-5	F-WMKJ N979F N115TW N25DB N8WN (N91MH) N777DC N20UA
92/421	CC117	F-WJMM Canada 20503 Canada 117503 C-GWPB in use as instructional airframe/preserved
93/435	20C	F-WMKF F-RAFN F-RBQA France 93/F-RAFN France 93/F-RAEC France 93/F-RAED code 65-ED
94/428	20C	F-WNGO I-ATMO F-ODSK CS-ATE F-GLNL N614GA
95	20C	F-WNGO N980F N802F N664P (OO-EEF) N664B N950RA
96	20C	F-WNGM N981F N511S N5RT N89SC F-GERT France 96/F-ZACB
97/422	CC117	F-WJMJ Canada 20504 Canada 117504 G-FRAU
98/434	20C	F-WNGN TU-VAD OY-AZT N408PC OO-RRR N781AJ N980R
99	20C	F-WJMK N982F N921ML
100	20C	F-WJMN N983F N605RP N200FT I-VEPA N179GA
101	20C	F-WMKJ N984F N342K N342F N97WJ
102	20C	F-WMKI N985F N223B N53SF N710EC (N710EG) N710WB N403JW
103/423	CC117/ECM	F-WMKH Canada 20505 Canada 117505 G-FRAV F-GPAA
104/454	20C	F-WJMK (OT-JFA) F-BOXV France 104/F-ZACW
105	20C	F-WNGL N986F N243K N77GR N97FJ N460MC wfu and b/u for spares Jly87 Memphis, TN; cx Mar89; remains to Clarkesville, MO
106	20C	F-WJMM N987F F-GBPG N9300M N31V EC-EKK
107	20C	F-WMKJ N988F N965BC N155NK N330PC N213LS
108/430	20DC	F-WNGO (D-CDAS) D-CBAT N5CA N4FE (N147FE) N26VG N101ZE N108R
109/427	CC117/ECM	F-WNGM Canada 20506 Canada 117506 C-FIGD
110	20C	F-WMKG N989F CF-WRA C-FWRA VH-FWO wfu and b/u for spares Oct88 Memphis, TN; cx Feb89
111	20C	F-WMKI N990F N111AC N111AM N111BP (XC-HIX)
112	20C	F-WJMJ N991F N2989 N830MF N200CX (HB-V) CS-ATF UR-CCD UR-NIK

FALCON 20/200

C/n	Series	Identities
113	20C-5	F-WNGL N993F PP-FOH PT-FOH (N713PE) N100WK N333WF N315PA N500HK (N731RG) F-WTFF N731F N129JE N129JF N400PC N400PG
114/420	CC117/ECM	F-WJMM Canada 20507 Canada 117507 G-FRAW
115/432	SNA	F-WJML France 115/F-UGWL France F-UKJG code 339-JG
116	20C-5	F-WMKJ N994F HB-VJD OO-JBB F-WGTH (F-GPNG) F-GLMM F-WLMM F-GLMM N770FG
117	20C-5	F-WMKH N995F N171PF N421ZC TS-IRS HB-VKC EC-855 EC-FJP F-GLMD
118	20C	F-WMKG N996F N512T F-GGKE N820AA
119/431	20C	F-WJMK I-SNAV F-GHFP N20FJ
120	20C-5	F-WMKI N4340F N410US N205FJ (F-GKAF) F-GICF N20AF N647JP
121	20C	F-WJMJ N4341F N242LB N813PA N813P N1199M N25CP N500BG N121DJ
122	20C	F-WNGL N4342F N779P N335WR N335WJ N32PB N900LC N33QS N302TT*
123	20C	F-WNGM N4343F N513T N45MR N223TW
124/433	20C	F-WJMJ France 124/F-ZACC
125	ECM	F-WJMN N4344F N6810J N812PA LN-FOE Norway 0125
126/438	20C	F-WMKH HB-VBL PH-BAG N1047T N10VG N102ZE N126R
127	20C	F-WNGN N4345F N50AD XB-EPB XA-REY XB-GCR XB-HRA
128/436	20C	F-WMKJ 5A-DAF YN-BZH C-GNAA EC-551 EC-FAM N228CK N70CK
129	20C	F-WJMM N4346F N1823F N1823A N666DA N68TS PT-WUV
130	20C	F-WMKJ N4347F N514T XA-SCL N130MV
131/437	20C	F-WJMK France 131/F-ZACD
132	20DC	F-WMKG N4348F N560L N2FE (N149FE) (N23FR) N902FR G-FFRA
133	20C	F-WNGO N4349F N894F VR-BKR F-GJLA N133FJ N200JE
134	20C	F-WMKH N4350F N895F N897DM N897D I-NLAE w/o 25Sep91 Kiel-Holtenhau, Germany
135	20C-5	F-WMKI N4351F N6820J N40XY N9999E N194MC
136/439	20C	F-WJMJ HB-VBM 9K-ACQ F-GCGU HB-VBM SP-FCP LX-IAL
137	20C	F-WLLK F-BLLK F-WLLK N4352F N8999A N777PV N200GT
138/440	20C	F-WLCS D-CALL D-CGJH (G-BAOA) F-BUIC France 138/F-ZACR
139	20C	F-WNGM N4353F N334JR N926LR N1868M N1868N N23PL N900WB N235CA
140	20C/PW305	F-WNGN N4354F N4350M N3350M N160WC N314AE N165WC Volpar PW305 conversion; ff 05Feb91; wfu 1994 at Willow Run, Detroit, MI, and used for spares by Active Aero
141/441	20C-5	F-WMKF F-BPIO F-BIHY (UR-BCA) UR-CCB
142	20C-5	F-WJMM N4355F N100S N1BF N298W N777WJ N511T N511TA N43SM N220RT (N205FJ) XA-RNB N300BA
143/442	20C	F-WMKH 5A-DAG
144	20C	F-WJMJ N4356F N888L N888JR N800LS (N200WF) N800KR N911RG
145/443	20C	F-WNGN F-BPJB OO-PJB F-GCGY France 145/F-ZACU
146	20CF	F-WJMN N4357F N946M N777EG N11TC C-FCDS N182GA
147/444	20CF	F-WLCH PH-ILF (D-CORT) (D-CCNA) N41154 N183GA
148	20C	F-WMKG N4358F N120HC N126HC N657MC N888WS N148WC N148TW
149	20C	F-WNGO N4359F N1818S (N4359F) N568Q EC-263 EC-EQP
150/445	20C	F-WMKH HB-VBO (N95591) N8227V N777XX N679RE N123RE (VR-C) TG-RBW HC-BSS
151	20DC	F-WMKI N4360F N810F N810PA N3FE (N148FE) (N24FR) N904FR G-FRAL
152/446	20DC	F-WJMJ CN-MBG CN-ANN
153	20C	F-WLCT N4361F N70MD N207CA
154/447	20C	F-WLCV France 154/F-RAFK w/o 22Jan76 nr Villacoublay, France
155	20C	F-WJMK N4362F N500Y N205SC N212C (N205SE) N404R N68BC N68BP
156/448	20C	F-WMKI 7T-VRE w/o 30May81 Bamako, Mali
157	20C	F-WJMM N4363F N166RS Canada 117508 C-GRSD-X C-GRSD
158/449	20C	F-WMKJ D-CMAX N450MA N158TW
159	20C	F-WMKJ N4364F N5RC N411CC N96WC N96RT
160/450	20C	F-WMKG I-DKET F-GHBT N48BT N100UF N301TT
161	20C	F-WMKF N4365F N93CD N19BD N93FH N21NC N10PP N10RZ
162/451	20C	F-WNGO OO-WTB D-CBBT HB-VED F-ODOK OO-DOK (F-GFLL) F-GFUN N162CT N911DG
163	20D	F-WNGM N4366F (N500HD) N500FE N500LD N178GA
164	20C	F-WJMN N4367F N654E N164NW
165/452	ECM	F-WJMJ CN-MBH CNA-NM
166	20C-5	F-WLCS N4368F N33D
167/453	20C	F-WMKG France 167/F-RAFL France 167/F-RAEB code 65-EB wears full "regn" on tail
168	20C-5	F-WLCX N4369F N100KW N108NC N300FJ N731RG N112CT N514JJ*
169	20C	F-WNGN N4370F XC-SEY
170/455	20C	F-WPUV I-EKET F-GHPA
171	20D-5	F-WMKG N4371F N570L N900JL (F-GHRE) F-GICB N217AJ
172/456	20C	F-WNGM F-BRHB I-LIAB
173	20D	F-WLCU F-BLCU N70PA N729S PK-TRI
174/457	20C	F-WNGL TL-AAY TL-KAZ (HB-VER) F-WSHT HZ-KA3 HZ-NES
175	20D-5	F-WMKF N4373F N866MM F-BUFG D-COFG F-ODHA F-GBMS I-CAIB N4246R N688MC N116BK HB-VJW (SU-OAE) HB-VJW SU-OAE
176/458	20C-5	F-WMKG I-SNAM F-WGTM F-GHDT
177	20D	F-WMKI N4374F N6701 N14FG N41BP
178/459	20C	F-WPXF OH-FFA G-FRBA
179	20D	F-WNGO N4375F N10LB N12LB N12MF N17JT
180/460	20C-5	F-WMKF OY-BDS I-GOBJ
181	20D	F-WNGL N4376F N836UC N966L N200GH N200GL N817JS
182/461	20C	F-WNGN HB-VCB F-WTDJ I-ROBM F-WVFV F-BVFV France 182/F-ZJTA France 182/F-UKJA
183	20D	F-WLCY N4377F N2979 EC-EFR RA-09003

FALCON 20/200

C/n	Series	Identities
184/462	20D	F-WRQQ F-BTMF D-COMF F-GAPC OE-GCJ EC-HCX
185/467	20D-5	F-WMKF I-IRIF N3WN N147X
186/463	SNA	F-WPXL France 463/F-UGWM code 339-WM; then code 339-JE 463/F-UKJE code 339-JE
187	20D	F-WLCV N4379F N40AC N750R N811AA
188/464	20C	F-WJMK F-BRPK 188/F-ZACX
189	20D	F-WPUU N4380F N950L N47JF N47JE N444BF EC-EFI w/o 11Oct87 off Keflavik, Iceland
190/465	SNA	F-WNGN Libya 002 5A-DCO
191	20D-5	F-WPUX N4381F N910L N200DE N200CG N800CF OE-GCR N20HF
192	20DF	F-WPUY N4382F N920L N57JF N910W N192R
193	20D	F-WMKG N4383F N930L N37JF N400DB 9Q-CTT N219CA
194	20DF	F-WPUZ N4384F N100M N555RA N297W N287W w/o 11Feb88 Akron, OH; b/u Jun89; cx Jun92; remains at Av-Mats' facility at Paynesville, MO
195	20D	F-WPXD N4385F N200SR N186S N191C N500GM N43JK N195MP N822AA
196	20D	F-WPXE N4386F N811PA N701MG N369WR N216BG N79AE N255RK N196TS
197	20D	F-WPXF N4387F N399SW C-GTAK
198/466	20D	F-WNGO VR-BDK (N14FE) N74196 (XC-GAM) XC-BIN XA-SQS N520TJ N339TG
199	20DC	F-WMKH N4388F N8FE wfu Aug83; stored National Air & Space (Smithsonian) Museum, Washington DC, Paul E Garber repair facility, Maryland, MA
200	20D	F-WMKJ N4389F N550MC N44CC N48CC N38CC YV-200C HC-BUP
201/469	20D	F-WLCY D-CELL "D-CEUU" D-CELL I-DRIB
202	20D-5	F-WNGM N4391F N814PA N33L
203	20D	F-WPXH N4378F N1857B N20BE N911WT OE-GDR N36P N821AA
204	20DC	F-WMKI N4392F N26FE N120FS EC-113 EC-EGM N204TW
205	20D	F-WPXF N4393F N21W N82A N4LH (N426CC) N815AA
206	20D	F-WLCS N4394F N815AC N632PB N801SC
207	20DC	F-WMKF N4395F N27FE N908FR G-FRAP
208/468	20D	F-WPXD HB-VCA VH-BRR N300JJ N125CA w/o 29Jun89 Cartersville, GA
209	20DC	F-WLCX N4396F N28FE N909FR G-FRAR
210	20DC	F-WNGL N4397F N29FE N66VG EC-ECB w/o 30Sep87 Las Palmas, Canaries, Spain
211	20DC	F-WJMK N4398F N30FE Portugal 8101 Portugal 17101 N618GA
212	20DC	F-WPXG N4399F N31FE N212R
213	20DC	F-WJMM N4390F N32FE N905FR G-FRAK (N213FC)
214	20DC	F-WNGO N4400F N33FE N906FR G-FRAO
215	20DC	F-WLCS N4401F N34FE Portugal 8102 Portugal 17102 N619GA
216	20DC	F-WLCT N4402F N9FE Venezuela 5840 stored
217	20DC	F-WLCY N4403F N35FE Portugal 8103 Portugal 17103
218	20DC	F-WMKJ N4372F N36FE N86VG OO-STE N86VG EC-EEU N218CA
219/470	20D	F-WPXH EC-BVV Spain TM11-3/401-04 Spain TM11-3/45-04
220	20DC	F-WPUU N4404F N24FE N36VG OO-STF EC-EDL EC-EDC+ N220CA + believed painted as EC-EDC for at least one flight (to Luton, UK) during 1987
221	20DC	F-WPUV N4406F N25FE N300NL EC-165 EC-EIV N221TW
222/471	20D	F-WNGL EC-BXV Spain TM11-2/401-03 Spain TM11-2/45-03
223	20DC	F-WPUX N4407F N22FE (N904FR) N900FR G-60-01 G-FRAH
224	20DC	F-WPUY N4408F N23FE N907FR G-FRAM
225/472	20D	F-WPXD TR-KHA TR-LRU F-BOFH OH-FFJ N125MJ N37WT N332FE N338DB (N30AD) N102AD C-FONX
226	20DC	F-WPXI F-WSQK N4409F N21FE N226R
227	20DC	F-WMKG N4410F N14FE N24EV N227R
228/473	20D	F-WNGL ZS-LAL ZS-LLG 3D-LLG C-GWSA HB-VEZ 5N-AYM OE-GRU N823AA
229	20DC	F-WJMJ N4411F N15FE N25EV N229R
230	20DC	F-WJML N4412F N16FE N26EV N230RA
231/474	20D	F-WPXE HB-VCG w/o 20Feb72 nr St Moritz, Switzerland
232	20DC	F-WJMN N4413F N17FE N27EV N232RA w/o 15Feb89 Bingham, NY; cx Mar91
233	20DC	F-WLCV N4414F N18FE N76VG I-TIAG N817AA
234/475	20D	F-WLCU (D-CIBM) D-COLL I-LIAC
235	20DC	F-WPXJ N4415F N20FE Venezuela 0442 stored
236	20D	F-WPXK (N4416F) CF-JES C-FJES N375PK N375BK YR-DSA N128AP N618GH
237/476	20D-5	F-WPXF (D-CHCH) (D-CALM) D-CITY N4227Y VR-CBT VR-BKH HB-VJV
238/477	20C	F-WRQP France 238/F-RAFM France 238/F-RAED France 238/F-RAEE France 238/F-RAFM France 238/F-RAEE code 65-EE
239	20F	F-WPXM N4417F N10MT C-GBFL N134CJ I-AGEC PH-OMC
240/478	20E	F-WLCX I-SNAG N240AT HB-VMN
241/479	20E	F-WRQP SE-DCO N48AD HZ-HE4 HZ-PL7 I-FLYK N241JC
242	20F	F-WPUZ N4418F N800CF (N320FJ) N2622M N911TR N66WB YR-DSB N129AP (N711RT) N4RT+ painted as such but never on USCAR (N242RJ) N513AC
243/480	20F	F-WMKH OH-FFW w/o 01Mar72 nr Montreal, Canada; remains to Sunstream Avn, Chicago-DuPage County A/P, MI, gone by Jun95
244	20F	F-WMKI N4420F N20FJ N11LB N226G N61LL VR-BJB w/o 15Jan88 Lugano, Switzerland; remains to Dodson Avn, Ottawa, KS
245/481	20E	F-WLCS SX-ABA F-BUIX HB-VDP HB-VDY EL-VDY to spares by Dodson Int'l Parts, Rantoul, KS circa Oct98
246/482	20F	F-WJMK F-BSTR (F-GLMT) N970GA
247	20E	F-WPXE N4419F N730S VH-FAX N730S N67JR N95JR N70PL
248/483	20F	F-WRQV OH-FFV N37JJ XB-AQU XB-OEM XB-VRM XC-HIX
249	20F	F-WJMM N4421F N11AK N777JF N451DP
250	20F	F-WMKF N4422F N111AM XA-HEW N223BG
251/484	20E	F-WRQR EP-VAP EP-FIE

FALCON 20/200

C/n	Series	Identities
252/485	20E	F-WRQP I-GIAZ France 252/F-ZACA
253/486	20E	F-WRQS EC-BZV Spain T11-1/401-02 Spain T11-1/45-02
254	20F	F-WNGO N4423F CF-YPB C-FYPB G-FRAC F-GPAB
255/487	20E	F-WRQP Jordan 122 HB-VDZ N2724K VH-HIF VH-MIQ N721J F-GHLN w/o 20Jan95 Paris-Le Bourget A/P, France
256	20F	F-WNGL N4416F N3RC C-GNTZ F-GKME UR-CCA N368DS
257	20F-5	F-WMKH N4425F N781W N300CC C-GNTL (F-GJPI) F-GKDD HB-VKO
258	20F	F-WNGM N4426F N20JM N544X N20AE N300SF
259	20F	F-WLCT N4418F N212H N45WH N45WN SE-DHK F-GIFP N569BW N569DW
260/488	20E	F-WMKJ France 260/F-RAEA code 65-EA
261	20F-5	F-WLCU N4368F N200WK
262	20F	F-WJMK N4427F N720ML N750ME VH-WLH N501AS C-GTLU F-GHVR (N) D2-ESV
263/489	20E	F-WMKJ HB-VCR (PH-LEN) F-BSBU France 263/F-ZACY
264	20F	F-WJMN N4428F N373KC N777V N773V (N86BL) F-GJJS CS-ATG
265	20F	F-WLCX N4429F N606RP N265MP
266/490	20EF	F-WRQR PH-ILX N4115B N184GA
267/491	20E	F-WRQZ I-REAL N731G
268/492	20E	F-WNGN France 268/F-RAEB France 268/F-RAFK France 268/F-RAEF code 65-EF
269	20F	F-WPUX N4430F N1902W N501F XA-NAY XA-DUC
270	20DC	F-WPUZ N4435F N37FE (N907FR) N901FR G-FRAI
271/493	20E	F-WNGN 7T-VRP (F-GHPO) F-GKDB
272	20E	F-WMKF N4431F N20FJ N732S N888RF N913MK N813MK (N803MM) XA-TAN (N272FA) N272JP N885BH
273	20F	F-WPUU N4432F N212T N212TC N212TG 5N-EPN F-WQBK N596DA
274	20F-5	F-WJMM N4433F N370WT N121WT N256M N26LA (D-CHEF) N260MB N100AS
275	20E	F-WMKH N4434F N661JB N9FB VR-BRJ SX-DKI N999EQ (N999BG)
276/494	20E	F-WNGL Belgium CM-01
277/501	20E	F-WPXD Pakistan J-753
278/495	20E	F-WNGM Belgium CM-02
279/502	20E	F-WMKJ I-FKET F-GHFQ N279AL F-GROC N854GA
280/503	20E	F-WPXK I-EDIS N910FR G-FRAE
281/498	20F	F-WRQR D-CORF N20CG LN-AAC N70830 N347K N281JJ N341K
282	20E	F-WMKG N4436F N131JA N282JJ N282C XC-DIP
283/497	20E	F-WRQX EP-AGX w/o 21Nov74 Kermanshah, Iran
284	20E	F-WPXM N4437F N132JA N284JJ N98RH N444FJ N441FA XA-BCC N441FA N284CE N501MD
285/504	20EF	F-WRQT A40-AA A40-GA PH-WMS VR-CCF PH-WMS N285AP N285TW
286/498	20E	F-WRQU EP-AGY
287	20E	F-WMKF N4438F YV-T-AVA YV-38CP XB-ALO XA-SAG
288/499	20E	F-WRQZ F-BUYE France 288/F-ZACV
289	20F	F-WMKG N4439F N20FJ N54J N54JJ N1HF N40994 N211HF N105TW
290	20E	F-WMKH N4440F N133JA I-TIAL N816AA
291/505	20E	F-WRQT France 291/F-RAEC France 291/F-RCAP France 291/F-RAEG code 65-EG
292	20F-5B	F-WMKI N4441F N733S
293	20E-5	F-WMKJ N4442F N2615 N2613 HZ-PL1 HB-VJX OY-CKY F-WQBN F-GOBZ I-GOBZ
294/506	20E-5B	F-WRQT F-BVPM SU-AXN
295/500	20E	F-WRQQ I-EDIM N911FR G-FRAF
296/507	20F-5	F-WRQP HB-VDB D2-EBB J5-GAS N4960S N214JP N297CK N19TX N20TX
297	20E	F-WMKF N4443F (N370EU) N121EU PK-TIR N297AG+ CS-DCK + believed marks never painted on the aircraft
298	20E	F-WMKG N4444F N86W N98LB OE-GNN N827AA
299	20F	F-WMKI (N734S) N21FJ N456SR N90CN N585UC F-GJSF TC-EZE (N669AC) N299JC
300/508	20E	F-WRQP I-EDIF (F-GIBT) (F-GEJX) F-GGMM N300FJ (N953DC) N600WD
301/509	20E	F-WNGL EP-AKC
302/510	20E	F-WRQP D-COMM OE-GDP N84V F-WQBM F-GOPM
303	20F	F-WMKH N4445F N27R w/o 12Nov76 Naples, FL
304/511	20E	F-WRQP G-BCYF G-FRAD
305	20F	F-WMKJ N4446F N16R N56SL VR-CDB N282U N34CW N715WS*
306/512	20E	F-WRQS (HB-VDY) (HB-VDO) D-CGSO VH-HFJ (N725P) N76662 N205WM
307/513	20E	F-WRQT HB-VDV I-GCAL OE-GLL F-GKIS
308	20F	F-WMKF N4447F N668P N668S N37RM SE-DKA N81AJ N453SB
309/514	20SNA	F-WRQT TR-LUW France 309/F-RAFU France 309/F-UGWP code 339-WP, named L'Etoile du Berger w/o 02Dec91 Villacoublay, France
310	20F	F-WMKH N4450F (N370ME) N121AM N831HG
311/515	20F-5	F-WRQS F-BVPN
312	20F	F-WMKH N4448F N2605 N619MW N1971R N132AP
313	20F-5B	F-WMKJ N4449F N220FJ N744CC N56CC N560R I-PERF F-GHCR N212PB N183TS
314/516	20E	F-WNGL D-COTT F-GDLU N314TW
315/517	20E-5	F-WRQP F-BVPQ OO-VPQ F-GDLO F-SEBI F-GSXF
316	20F-5	F-WMKF N4451F N734S N242CT
317	20F	F-WMKG N4452F N31CM N99E N92K N88FE HB-VEV N939CK
318/518	20E	F-WRQT (EP-VAS) EP-VSP EP-FIG Iran 15-2533
319	20F-5	F-WMKF N4453F N730V N44NT C-GNTM N70LG N77LA N205K
320/519	20E	F-WRQS EP-AHV EP-FIF
321	20F-5	F-WJMJ N4454F N2525 N702SC N244CA N20FM (PH-BPS) N104SB PH-BPS
322	20F	F-WMKH N4455F N1971R N999DC N94GW N464M N300CV
323/520	20E	F-WRQS HB-VEB I-FCIM OE-GLF XU-008

FALCON 20/200

C/n	Series	Identities
324	20F	F-WMKF N4456F N444SC N324TC N312K
325	20F	F-WMKG N4457F N100GN N400GN (N400GX) (N700GN) VH-RRC N7WG N599RR N555TF
326/521	20E	F-WRQQ PH-ILY TC-CEN N555TF
327	20F	F-WMKI N4458F N3H N2H N96L VH-NMN N900DB N25WG XA-HHF
328/522	20F	F-WMKJ (N4459F) YK-ASA
329/523	20E	F-WRQV D-CMET
330	20F	F-WNGM N4460F N300AL C-GNTY N770MC
331/524	20F	F-WRQS YK-ASB
332/525	20E	F-WRQP EC-CTV Spain TM11-4/401-05 Spain TM11-4/45-01
333/526	20E	F-WNGL Iran 5-2801 Iran 15-2235
334/527	20E	F-WRQU EP-FIC
335	20F	F-WMKF N4459F N901TC N903SB D-CFAI N335AJ N707JC (N707JZ) (N301FC)
336/528	20E	F-WRQP Iran 5-2802
337/529	20F	F-WRQR YI-AHH status following Gulf War?
338/530	20E	F-WMKG EP-FID
339	20F-5	F-WMKH N4461F N200GN N100GN N200GN (N200GX) N131DB (N402NC) N22FS N19MX SE-DSA N38TJ
340/531	20E	F-WRQX Iran 5-2803
341	20F	F-WMKF N4462F N20FJ N66GA N511WP N511WR N78BC N311JS VR-CDT F-OHCJ F-GYSL
342/532	20F	F-WRQP YI-AHI J2-KAC France 342/F-RAEC France 342/F-RAEG France 342/F-RAEC code 65-EC
343/533	20F	F-WRQR YI-AHJ status following Gulf War?
344/534	20F-5	F-WRQP A6-HEM A6-EXA N344FJ (N731F) N731AS (N731AE) N227WE
345	20F	F-WMKI N4463F N678BM F-GHMD N133AP OH-FPC
346/535	20E	F-WRQP Iran 5-2804
347	20F	F-WMKF N4464F N744CC N298CK N347HS N20VF
348/536	20E	F-WRQR Iran 5-4039 Iran 5-3020 w/o 03Mar97 Ardabil, Iran
349	20F	F-WMKG N4465F N273K N66NT N767AC N767AG
350/537	20E	F-WRQS Iran 5-4040 Iran 5-3021
351/538	20F	F-WMKJ Iran 5-9001
352	20F-5	F-WMKF N4466F N920G
353/539	20F	F-WRQP Iran 5-9002
354/540	20F	F-WRQR Iran 5-9003
355	20F	F-WMKF N4467F N20FJ N27AC N344G N550M N63PM N61PM N200MK N712ME
356	20F	F-WMKG N4468F N27R N27RX G-FRAB F-GPAE N111F N11UF
357	20F-5	F-WMKI N4469F N435T N435TP N342K
358/541	20F-5B	F-WRQS SU-AZJ F-WRQY SU-AZJ
359/542	20F	F-WRQR (N64769) HZ-TAG HZ-A01 N64769 N647JP N35RZ N50SL (N508L) N369CA N369CE OH-WIP
360	20F	F-WMKJ N1010F N901YP N905SB N911SB F-GJEA N165PA N865VP
361/543	20F-5	F-WMKF SU-AYD
362	20G	(F-WZAS) F-WATF F-WDFJ F-GDFJ F-WDFJ
363/544	20F-5	F-WRQV HZ-DC2 N363FJ N3VF
364	20F	F-WMKI N1013F N235U N285U OE-GCS N285U XA-FLM
365	20F	F-WMKJ N1018F N777TX N50BH
366	20F	F-WMKG N1020F N83V N300CT N100AC
367/545	20F	F-WRQR EP-SEA
368	20F-5	F-WMKI N1036F N800CF N200DE N800CF VH-NCF N83D I-FIPE N110TJ F-GHTK N110TJ N65TS N107LW N23A N15H
369	20F	F-WRQP N1037F N20SR (N414JC) N415JW N509WP N420J N138FJ
370	20F	F-WMKG N1038F HL7234 N370HF N269SR N20WN
371	HU25C	F-WMKJ N1039F USCG 2141
372/546	20F	F-WRQV ST-PRS
373	20F-5	F-WMKI N1041F N53DS N922DS N91Y (N620CC) N610CC N620CC N399FG
374	HU25A	F-WRQP N1045F USCG 2101
375/547	20F	F-WRQR F-GBMD France 375/F-ZACZ
376	20F-5B	F-WRQS N103F N2624M N2614 N2616H N1892S N1897S
377/548	20F-5	F-WRQP D-CCMB N30FT
378	20F-5	F-WRQT N107F (N662PP) N662P (N6621) N305AR N500JD
379	20F-5	F-WMKF N130F (N37AH) (N33AJ) N33AH F-GGBL N62570 N892SB
380	20F	F-WMKI N136F N8BX N1BX N9654N N922ML (N288MM) N289MM N3848U
381/548	20F-5	F-WRQS (I-LAFA) D-CCDB N20TZ N20T
382	20F	F-WMKG N138F HP-1A N138F N138E N382E
383/550	20F-5	F-WRQR D-CONU 5N-AYO HB-VJS N900CH N908CH
384/551	20F-5	F-WRQU OO-PSD N384JK N120CG N120TF
385	20F-5	F-WJMJ N139F N118R G-FRAA N120WH
386	HU25A	F-WJMK N149F USCG 2102 stored AMARC Davis-Monthan, AZ circa Aug95
387	20F	F-WJML N162F N56CC N676DW N387CE N676DW N384K
388	20F-5	F-WJMM N169F N90GS N920CF F-WTFE N731RG N756
389/552	20F	F-WRQV I-CMUT
390	HU25C	F-WJMN N173F USCG 2104
391	20F	F-WLCS N175F N376SC N876SC VH-HPF N503F N995PT N990PT N550PT N420DP N420CL
392/553	20F	F-WRQT D-CALL N328EW N326EW N326LW (N392FJ) N713MC
393	20F	F-WLCT N176F N21NL N76TA N809F XA-REY XA-PUE XB-FVH XC-FVH
394	HU25A	F-WMKF N178F USCG 2103

FALCON 20/200

C/n	Series	Identities
395/554	20F	F-WRQX (HZ-AKI) OD-PAL (N395BB) unmarked at the White Inds facility at Bates City, MO circa Oct98
396	20F-5	F-WMKG N179F N881J N711GL
397/555	20F	F-WRQP F-GBTM F-WBTM F-GBTM
398	HU25A	F-WMKF N183F USCG 2105 stored AMARC Davis-Monthan, AZ circa Aug95
399	20F-5	F-WMKI N184F N881G N70NE N70NF N70U
400/556	20F	F-WRQR RP-C1980 w/o 24Apr96 at Davao City, Philippines; spares use at White Industries, MO
401	200	F-WZAH F-GATF (F-WDHA) N200FJ N207FJ F-GATF VR-BJJ F-GATF VR-BJJ F-GEXF Chile 301 "VP-1" N699GA N501KC*
402	HU25A	F-WJMJ N187F USCG 2106 stored AMARC Davis-Monthan, AZ circa Aug95; park code 41-007
403	20F	F-WJMK N189F N15AT N108BG N960TX
404	20F	F-WJMK N404F N28C
405	HU25A	F-WMKI N405F USCG 2108 stored AMARC Davis-Monthan, AZ; park code 41-015
406/557	20F	F-WMKF G-BGOP N800FF
407	HU25A	F-WJMJ N406F USCG 2109 stored AMARC Davis-Monthan, AZ
408	20F	F-WRQS (PK-CAJ) PK-CAG (N508TC) N408PA
409	HU25A	F-WMKJ N407F USCG 2107
410	20F-5B	F-WRQT N200CP N200J
411	HU25A	F-WMKG N408F USCG 2110
412	20F-5	F-WMKI N409F N85V N85VE N2FU N12FU N620A
413	HU25A	F-WJMK N410F USCG 2111
414	20F	F-WJML N412F N1881Q
415	HU25A	F-WLCV N413F USCG 2112
416	20F	F-WLCT N415F N416F N88NT N9VG N416F
417	HU25A	F-WJMM N416F N416FJ USCG 2113 stored AMARC Davis-Monthan, AZ circa Aug95
418	HU25A	F-WJMN N417F USCG 2114 stored AMARC Davis-Monthan, AZ circa Aug95
419	HU25A	F-WMKJ N419F USCG 2115
420	HU25A	F-WMKG N420F USCG 2116 stored AMARC Davis-Monthan, AZ; park code 41-005
421	HU25A	F-WMKI N422F USCG 2117
422	20F	F-WRQU (N422F) F-ZJTJ France 422/F-RCAL France 422/F-RAEH code 65-EH
423	HU25B	F-WJMJ N423F USCG 2118
424	HU25A	F-WMKF N424F USCG 2119 stored AMARC Davis-Monthan, AZ, with parts missing; was damaged in storms Nov93 Mobile, AL; has park code 41-002
425	HU25A	F-WMKG N425F USCG 2120
426	20F	F-WJMK N427F N123WH N555PT N416RM I-BAEL
427	20F	F-WRQV 5N-AYN I-ACTL N42WJ
428	20F-5B	F-WMKI N426F N98R I-FLYF N98R N148MC
429	20F-5B	F-WMKF VR-BHL HB-VHY N4286A N149MC
430	20F-5	F-WMKG N428F N660P
431	HU25A	F-WMKJ N429F USCG 2121
432	20F-5B	F-WJMK N430F N667P N237PT
433	HU25B	F-WJML N432F USCG 2122
434	20F	F-WRQP Peru 300/OB-1433
435	HU25A	F-WJMM N433F USCG 2123 stored AMARC Davis-Monthan, AZ, with parts missing; was damaged in storms Nov93 Mobile, AL; has park code 41003
436	20F-5	F-WJMN N434F N181CB N436MP N8000U
437	HU25A	F-WMKG N435F USCG 2124
438	20F-5	F-WMKI N442F N263K N256A N258A
439	HU25B	F-WMKJ N443F USCG 2125
440	20F	F-WRQQ N452F N5152 N768J (N768V) VR-CAR N32TC N32TE N7000G
441	HU25A	F-WJMK N445F USCG 2126
442	20F-5	F-WJML N446F VH-FJZ N203TA I-SREG N747CX
443	HU25A	F-WMKG N447F USCG 2127 stored AMARC Davis-Monthan, AZ; has park code 41-001; parked in Celebrity Row circa Oct95
444	20F-5	F-WJMJ N453F N665P
445	HU25A	F-WJMM N449F USCG 2128 stored AMARC Davis-Monthan, AZ; has park code 41-013
446	20F	F-WJMN N454F N31WT N901SB N904SB N270RA N446D
447	HU25A	F-WLCS N455F USCG 2129
448	20G	F-WJMK France 48/F-ZWVF
449	20F	F-WLCT N457F
450	HU25A	F-WMKG N458F USCG 2130 stored AMARC Davis-Monthan, AZ; has park code 41-004
451	20F	F-WRQR F-ZJTS France 339/F-UGWN/F-UKJC code 339-WN, then code 339-JC named "Fil d'Ariane"
452	HU25A	F-WMKI N459F USCG 2131
453	20F	F-WJMK N460F N25S N189MM N520AW
454	HU25A	F-WJML N461F USCG 2132
455	20F-5	F-WRQS F-GKAL N555SR
456	HU25A	F-WJMJ N462F USCG 2133
457	20F-5	F-WJMM N463F N4351M N4362M N47LP
458	HU25B	F-WJMN N465F USCG 2134
459	HU25A	F-WMKJ N466F USCG 2135
460	HU25B	F-WJML N467F USCG 2136
461	20F	F-WMKG N469F N747V N353CP
462	HU25A	F-WMKI N470F USCG 2137 stored AMARC Davis-Monthan, AZ
463	20F	F-WJMJ N471F N134JA N132EP
464	HU25A	F-WJMK N472F USCG 2138 stored AMARC Davis-Monthan, AZ; has park code 41-009
465	20G	France F-ZJTS/65
466	HU25C	F-WJML N473F USCG 2139
467	HU25A	F-WJMM N474F USCG 2140

FALCON 20/200

C/n	Series	Identities									
468	20F	F-WMKG	Pakistan J-468								
469	20F	F-WMKI	Pakistan J-469								
470	20F	F-WJMJ	N477F	N607RP	N470G						
471	20F	F-WJMK	N478F	N44JC							
472	20G	France F-Z /72									
473	20F	F-WRQT	F-GEJR	3A-MGR							
474	20F-5	F-WMKF	F-GFFS	I-ACCG	F-WGTG	N211HF	N1HF				
475	20F	F-WJML	Spain T.11-5/45-05								
476	20F	F-WJMM	France F-ZJTD		Venezuela 1650						
477	20G	France F-Z /77									
478	20F-5	F-WJMN	N161WT	N181WT							
479	200	F-WPUU	N200FJ	(N200FX)	N200WD	(N200FJ)	N200LS	N400WT	(N60DD)	(N200SA)	N349MG
480	20G	France F-ZJSA/80									
481	20F	F-WLCS	N502F	N250RA	OH-WIN						
482	200	F-WPUZ	F-WDSB	F-GDSB	SE-DDZ	F-WGDZ	VR-CCL	VP-CCL	(N94TJ)		
483	20F	F-WRQQ	France 483/F-UKJI code 339-JI								
484	200	F-WPUV	N202FJ	N28U	N357CL	N422MU	N24JG*				
485	20F-5	F-WLCT	N161EU	N997TT	N23SJ*						
486	20F-5	F-WLCV	F-GEFS	N6VF							
487	200	F-WZZB	(N206FJ)	F-GDSD	"I-WDSD"	I-SOBE	N137TA				
488	200	F-WZZF	HB-VHS	N682JB	N123CC	N2HW	C-GTNT	N146CF			
489	200	F-WPUX	N203FJ	(N109FC)	N109NC	N109NQ	N200RT	(TC-)	N7654F	TC-DEM	N489TK
490	200	F-WPUY	N204FJ	N14EN	N806F	N2TF	N95JT	N200RT	(N208RT)	HC-BVH	N917JC
491	200	F-WZZA	N205FJ	N200FJ	N120FJ	VH-PDJ	VH-HPJ	N491MB	N343MG	N843MG	N500RR
492	200	F-WPUV	VR-BHZ	N805C	N803F	N412AB					
493	200	F-WZZC	N208FJ	N901SB	N1847B	VH-ECG					
494	200	F-WZZD	N209FJ	N85LB	LV-PFM	LV-BAI	N49US	N204DD	EC-HEG		
495	200	F-WZZE	N210FJ	(N290BC)	VH-BGL	N522C	N48FU	N48HU	N800HM	C-GSCL	C-GSCR
496	200	F-WZZC	VR-BHY	F-GFAY	I-LXOT	(F-GGAR)	F-OGSR	F-WGSR	Chile 302	CC-PES	N496RT
		N227TA	N256JC								
497	200	F-WZZA	N212FJ	N720HC	N20CL						
498	200	F-WPUV	N215FJ	N200ET	N422D	N422L	N69EC				
499	200	F-WZZJ	N213FJ	N565A	N14CJ						
500	200	F-WPUU	N214FJ	N595DC							
501	200	F-WZZD	I-MAFU	F-WWGP	F-GOJT	N200TJ	N57TT				
502	200	F-WPUU	N216FJ	N5732	N573E	N232F	N64YP	N64YR^			
503	200	F-WPUY	N218FJ	N300HA	N50MW	N50MX*					
504	200	F-WPUX	N217FJ	N902SB	N702SB	VH-CPE					
505	200	F-WZZA	N221FJ	ZK-MAY	VH-NGF	XA-SKO	w/o 26Aug94 Lake Pontchartrain, New Orleans-				
		Lakefront A/P, LA		N221FJ	to spares Dodson Int'l Parts Inc, Ratoul, KS circa Oct98						
506	200	F-WPUZ	I-CNEF	N147TA	XA-MAM						
507	200	F-WPUV	N220FJ	N200FJ	(N122FJ)	C-FCEH	N79MB	N50MG	N50LG*		
508	200	F-WPUU	N219FJ	N1851T	XA-RKE	N777FC					
509	200	F-WPUX	N222FJ	(N8495B)	JA8270	N70TH	N200WY				
510	200	F-WPUY	N223FJ	N79PM	N515DB	N510LF					
511	200	F-WWGR	F-OGSI	F-WGTF	F-OLET	(F-GNMF)	VT-TTA				
512	200	F-WPUU	N224FJ	N45WH	N999TH						
513	200	F-WPUV	N225FJ	XB-ECR	XA-ECR	N881JT	(N200UP)	(N10UU)	N5UU	N5UQ*	
514	200	F-WWGP	(F-GJIS)	F-OHES	PT-OQG	N531WB	(N81AG)	N87AG	N322RR		
515	200	F-WWGO	VR-CCQ	VR-CHC	F-GOBE	XA-PFM	N181RK				

Production complete

Notes: The French AF (CEV) marks in the F-R.../F-Z... series are not normally painted on the aircraft
One of the two Iraqi Airways Falcon 20F's, either YI-AHH c/n 337 or YI-AHJ c/n 343 is reported to have crashed at Basra on 16Mar00

DASSAULT FALCON 50

* Denotes Falcon 50EX

C/n	Identities
1	F-WAMD ff 07Nov76 F-WNDB F-BNDB F-WNDB F-BNDB F-WNDB wfu fuselage to Conservatoire de l'Air et de l'Espace d'Aquitaine, Merignac circa Oct99
2	F-WINR F-BINR France 2/F-RAFJ F-BINR F-GSER
3	F-WFJC F-GBIZ N50FJ N50EJ N880F N8805 N728LW
4	F-WZHA N110FJ N50FJ YV-452CP
5	(F-WZHB) (F-GBRF) France 5/F-RAFI
6	F-WZHB N50FB N1871R N815CA 9XR-NN w/o 06Apr94 Kigali, Rwanda
7	F-WZHA HZ-AKI HZ-A03 N8516Z N26LB N5DL N50HE F-WQBN
8	F-WZHC N50FE N50PG N409ER (N408ER) (N119HB) (N119HT) N119PH N508EJ
9	F-WZHD I-SAFP XA-LOH (HB-IED) VR-CBR "N100WJ"+ F-GGCP +These marks not officially allocated
10	F-WZHD N50FG N65B
11	F-WZHE N50FH N501NC N5739 F-GGVB
12	F-WZHC CN-ANO
13	F-WZHF N50FK N150BG (N150NW) N150TX
14	F-WZHG N50FL N233U N283U N9X N955E
15	F-WZHM PH-ILR N350JS
16	F-WZHH (N50FM) D-BIRD D-BFAR
17	F-WZHI 5A-DGI TY-BBM HB-IEB N4679T N3456F N349K N349KS N727S
18	F-WZHJ N50FN N187S N720M N1102A N82RP N82LP N518EJ
19	F-WZHB N50FM N63A N253L N519CW*
20	F-WZHK N50FR C6-BER N63537
21	F-WZHN (9K-ACQ) 9K-AEE N299W (F-GJKT) F-GHGT N70AF N77CE N770E N56LT
22	F-WZHF N50FS N203BT N866FP XA-SFP XA-AVE
23	F-WZHG (D-BBAD) D-BBWK PH-ILD N725PA N821BS N523CW*
24	F-WZHL N51FJ N817M N200RT
25	F-WZHI Yugoslavia 72101/YU-BPZ (now carries both marks) status following 1999 war, is unknown
26	F-WZHA N52FJ N190MC
27	F-WZHN HB-IEU F-WGTG France 27/F-RAFK
28	F-WZHE N53FJ N131WT PH-LEM N47UF
29	F-WZHB I-SAFR F-WGTH CS-TMF N534MA N290TJ N529CW*
30	F-WZHD I-SNAC (YV-553CP) I-SNAC F-WQFZ (for French Navy)
31	F-WZHC (N54FJ) I-KIDO N211CN N145W N145WF N105EJ XA-AAS N931CC (N931EJ) N890FH
32	F-WZHJ VR-BTT N80TR
33	F-WZHA N56FJ N8100E N8300E
34	F-WZHH HB-IEV F-WEFS France 34/F-RAFL
35	F-WZHF N57FJ N800BD N907M N350AF XA-FVK
36	F-WZHJ N54FJ N345PA N450AF N59GS F-WWHZ F-ZWTA F-ZJTL (Centre d'Essais en Vol) France 36 (Aeronavale)
37	F-WZHM (I-CAIK) I-SAME
38	F-WZHK N58FJ N993
39	F-WZHL N59FJ N754S N326FB
40	F-WZHG 9K-AEF N90005 N50GF N1PR N695ST N150JT
41	F-WZHI N60FJ N546EX (N760DL) N76FD (N76FB) N352JS
42	F-WZHE N61FJ N82MP D-BDWO OE-HCS OO-LFT
43	F-WZHO Yugoslavia 72102 YU-BNA
44	F-WZHA N62FJ N150JP N50LT N44MK N285CP
45	F-WZHF N63FJ N731F N9BX N569BW
46	F-WZHK N64FJ N908EF N911RF N725LB N728LB N347K
47	F-WZHP N65FJ N150WC N23AC N23AQ N1BX (N81CH) N601CH*
48	F-WZHK HB-IET I-ERDN N134AP N247EM N2478*
49	F-WZHL N66FJ N43ES N43BE N978W
50	F-WZHQ N67FJ N747 N747Y XA-GCH
51	F-WZHR N70FJ N52DC N52DQ F-GMGA N113WA^
52	F-WZHV F-BMER F-WZHV JY-HAH N18G N86AK N163WW
53	F-WZHS N150JT (N77SW) N45SJ (N50SJ) N22T N22TZ N90AM N53FJ N22YP
54	F-WZHT N71FJ N450X (N50EF) N204DD N202DD N392U N130A (OY-GDA) LX-GED N589KM N100DV
55	F-WZHU N73FJ N839F (N30N) N1CN N332MC N332MQ N625CR N300CR N96UH N200UP
56	F-WZHR F-WDFE F-GDFE N112FJ N84HP
57	F-WZHC HB-IER N57B N138F N138E N505TC
58	F-WZHA N72FJ N744X
59	F-WZHB N75FJ N31DM N31V N900JB
60	F-WZHD JY-HZH N900W N50RG*
61	F-WZHI HB-IES
62	F-WZHE N77FJ N292BC N50FH N562EJ
63	F-WZHF N78FJ N841F HB-IAL VR-CGP N48GP C-FKCI
64	F-WZHH N79FJ N418S N300A
65	F-WZHT N50FJ N90FJ N65HS D-BFFB N50LV N1EV F-GPPF
66	F-WZHP (PH-SDL) F-WZHP N500BL N50BL N4413N (VR-B) 9U-BTB
67	F-WZHG N76FJ HB-IEP Switzerland T-783
68	F-WZHQ 5A-DCM
69	F-WZHJ N80FJ N650X
70	F-WZHL N81FJ N230S N130K (N651SB) N699SC N300ES N306ES
71	F-WZHF YI-ALB J2-KBA

FALCON 50

C/n	Identities										
72	F-WZHM	N82FJ	N1181G	w/o 12May85 Lake Geneva, WI; remains to Clarkesville, MO							
73	F-WPXE	HZ-SAB	F-WGTG	VR-CCQ	N48TW	N15TW	(N15TA)	N573CW			
74	F-WZHA	N83FJ									
75	F-WZHH	N95FJ	N45ES	N45BE	N850CA	N78LT					
76	F-WZHB	N84FJ	N85MD	N410WW	N411WW	N450CL					
77	F-WZHC	N85FJ	N366F	N992							
78	F-WPXF	F-ODEO	TR-LAI	F-GEOY	No78/F-RAFJ						
79	F-WZHE	N86FJ	N60CN								
80	F-WZHN	N87FJ	XB-OEM	XA-FTC	N4154G	XA-GFC	N80WE	N50SJ			
81	F-WZHA	N89FJ	N718DW								
82	F-WZHG	N88FJ	N293BC	RP-C754	(N767W)	(N40F)	N511GG	N450KP	N150BP		
83	F-WZHJ	N88U	N881M								
84	F-WZHK	N2711B	F-WZHK	Spain T16-1/401-09		Spain T16-1/45-20					
85	F-WZHO	N90FJ	N50FJ	N40TH	N254DV						
86	F-WPXD	N94FJ	N238U	F-GKDR	HB-IAT	N150UC					
87	F-WZHS	N91FJ	N283K	N55NT							
88	F-WZHU	N92FJ	XA-OVR	N188FJ	F-WQCP	VR-CRT	VP-CRT	N588FJ	F-WQBK	F-GYOL	LZ-010
	F-GYOL										
89	F-WZHV	N93FJ	N212K	N212KM	N890GA	N400PC	(N400LC)	N120TJ	N97BZ		
90	F-WZHX	N290W	N298W	N600AS	(N650AS)	N4351M					
91	F-WZHY	(ZS-BFB)	ZS-BMB	ZS-CAS							
92	F-WZHZ	N97FJ	N85A	N40CN							
93	F-WZHB	N98FJ	N844X								
94	F-WZHC	N99FJ	N82NC	N212JP	XA-MVR						
95	F-WPXD	VR-CBL	N3950N	N331MC	C-GSSS	TC-KAM	F-WQBJ	N29YY	N70FL		
96	F-WPXE	N4AC	C-FMFL								
97	F-WZHL	(N101FJ)	C-FSCL	N33GG	N33GQ	LZ-011					
98	F-WPXF	VR-CBO	N39461	N50MK	(N50ML)	N600WG					
99	F-WZHM	(N96FJ)	C-FMYB	N816M							
100	F-WZHN	N102FJ	N14CG								
101	F-WPXH	YI-ALC	Iran as either 9011, 9012 or 9013 (also reported as 5-9...)								
102	F-WZHO	N103FJ	N50BX	(N50WB)	N350WB						
103	F-WZHQ	N104FJ	N83MP	N370KP							
104	F-WZHR	N105FJ	N90AE	F-GFGQ	F-WWHK	N50VG	SE-DVG	N351JS	LX-UAE		
105	F-WZHS	N106FJ	N80CN								
106	F-WZHT	N96FJ	N50BF	N9300C							
107	F-WPXK	(ZS-LJM)	LX-RVR	VR-BUC	VP-BUC	F-WQBM	F-GIQZ	VP-BCZ			
108	F-WZHM	N101FJ	N350X	N150K							
109	F-WZHV	N109FJ	N280BC	N280BG							
110	F-WPXG	5N-ARE	VR-BJA	N77TE							
111	F-WZHZ	N297W	F-GKTV	VR-CDF	N50AH	F-GMOT					
112	F-WZHA	N107FJ	N144AD								
113	F-WZHB	N108FJ	N186S	N394U	N35RZ						
114	F-WPXM	ST-PSR									
115	F-WZHC	N111FJ	N777MJ	N50TC	N522GS	(N369CA)	N569CA	N569CC	N502JB		
116	F-WZHD	N112FJ	N781B	N69R	F-GIDC	N70AF	XA-SOL	XB-SOL			
117	F-WPXI	HB-ITH	N50TG	N124HM	N50J						
118	F-WZHF	N113FJ	N784B	(N183B)	N784B	w/o 10Nov85 on approach to Teterboro A/P, NJ					
119	F-WZHN	N114FJ	N83FC	N57DC							
120	F-WPXJ	YI-ALD	Iran as either 9011, 9012 or 9013 (also reported as 5-9...)								
121	F-WZHO	N115FJ	N9311	N824R							
122	F-WZHG	YI-ALE	Iran as either 9011, 9012 or 9013 (also reported as 5-9...)								
123	F-WZHH	(F-GDSC)	VH-SFJ	N211EF	F-GPSA						
124	F-WZHA	N116FJ	N711TU	N6666R	N500RE	N600JM	N25JM*				
125	F-WZHB	N118FJ	N711KT	I-DENR							
126	F-WZHI	N119FJ	(YV-269CP)	N9312	N931G	N52DC					
127	F-WZHD	N121FJ	N1896T	N1896F	N129JE						
128	F-WZHF	N122FJ	N9313	N733E	N223DD						
129	F-WZHQ	N123FJ	N1903W	N4903W	N99JD						
130	F-WZHR	N124FJ	N9314	N630L	N988T						
131	F-WPXD	HZ-BB2	I-ADAG	(F-GPLH)	(F-GOAL)	F-WGTF	F-GOAL				
132	F-WPXF	I-EDIK									
133	F-WPXH	HB-IEA	HZ-AKI	HB-IEA	ZS-CAQ						
134	F-WPXK	HB-IEC	VR-CLD	VP-CLD	F-GOGL	VP-BCD	F-GUDP	F-WQBN	N134FJ		
135	F-WZHA	N125FJ	N293BC								
136	F-WZHB	N126FJ	N204HC	(N500HC)	N50HC	VR-BLL	N6550W	YV-455CP			
137	F-WZHC	N127FJ	N50FJ	(N119FJ)	C-GTPL	N119FJ	N117SF				
138	F-WPXD	N75G	N941CC	I-CAFB	N138NW	VR-CEZ	VP-CEZ	N380TJ	N138AV		
139	F-WZHD	N128FJ	N96CE	N1S							
140	F-WPXH	VR-BHX	(F-GJTR)	F-WGTF	I-MMEA	N303JW					
141	F-WZHE	N129FJ	N16R	(N222MC)	N86MC	N96NX					
142	F-WZHK	N132FJ	N4350M								
143	F-WZHI	N130FJ	N77CP	N444PE							
144	F-WZHL	N133FJ	N70FL	VR-BZE	VP-BZE	N544RA	LX-FTJ+				
	+ marks taped over										
145	F-WPXE	F-GEXE	A6-ZKM	I-CAFC	N50KD						
146	F-WZHA	N131FJ	N747	N7228K							
147	F-WPXG	HB-IED	F-WPXG	VR-BKG	VP-BKG	N526CC					

FALCON 50

C/n	Identities								
148	F-WZHB	N134FJ	N81R	N81U	YR-FNA	N28KB	N254NA	N50LQ	
149	F-WZHJ	N135FJ	N1904W	F-GHAQ	N149MD	N1971R	N198M	N198MR	
150	F-WZHC	N136FJ	HB-IAE	N8200E	N8400E				
151	F-WPXD	Italy (MM151)		Italy MM62020					
152	F-WZHD	N137FJ	N1841F	N75W	N75WE				
153	F-WZHE	N138FJ	N50FJ	N16CP	N50HM				
154	F-WZHA	N139FJ	N320K	N920K	N404R	N404E	N154PA		
155	F-WPXH	Italy MM62021							
156	F-WZHF	N140FJ	N5733	N4MB					
157	F-WPXG	N141FJ	N312A	N341M	N911HB				
158	F-WZHH	N142FJ	N54YR						
159	F-WZHC	LX-NUR	I-LXAG	VR-CWI	VP-CWI				
160	F-WZHI	N143FJ	N48R	N487F					
161	F-WZHA	N144FJ	N863BD	N800BD	TC-EYE	N301JJ	N770MP		
162	F-WZHB	N145FJ	N90R	C-GYPJ	N244AD				
163	F-WZHA	N146FJ	N50FJ	(N165FJ)	N185FJ	N5VF	N5VH	N85HP	
164	F-WZHD	N164FJ	HB-IAM	N164MA	N164GB				
165	F-WZHF	HZ-SM3	LX-FMR						
166	F-WZHE	N165FJ	N500AF	(N3115U)	N500AE	N316PA	N5VF		
167	F-WZHG	N166FJ	N186HG	N2T					
168	F-WZHH	N167FJ	N711SC	N48GL	XA-RXZ	N48GL	VR-CQZ	N48GL	N420JP*
169	F-WPXD	I-SNAB							
170	F-WZHI	N169FJ	N293K	N500AF					
171	F-WZHJ	N170FJ	N171FJ	N40AS	(N650AS)	N750H			
172	F-WZHK	N170FJ	N98R	N9000F	N256A				
173	F-WZHL	N172FJ	(JA)	PT-LJI					
174	F-WPXE	HB-IAG	N79PF	N565A					
175	F-WZHM	N177FJ	N50FJ	N334MC	N330MC	N200RT	VR-B	N530AR	
176	F-WZHN	N178FJ	VH-PDJ	N157SP	N95GC	I-DEGF	VR-CFI	C-FNNC	
177	F-WPXF	9Q-CGK	9Q-CPK						
178	F-WZHO	N179FJ	N239R	N59PM	N634H				
179	F-WZHP	N180FJ	HL7386	N222MC	N212Q				
180	F-WWHC	I-POLE	N45FG	N2254S	N50SF				
181	F-WWHA	N181FJ	N345AP	N367TP	N93AX	N600CH			
182	F-WWHB	N182FJ	N250AS						
183	F-WWHF	I-CAFD							
184	F-WWHD	N183FJ	N50FJ	N89FC	N25MB				
185	F-WWHE	N184FJ	C-GDCO	N23SY	N238Y	F-GKBZ			
186	F-WWHH	N278FJ	N450K						
187	F-WWHG	N279FJ	N4CP	N4QP	VH-PPF				
188	F-WWHA	N280FJ	N50FJ	PT-WAN	LV-WXV				
189	F-WWHB	N281FJ	N50WG	N55SN	N51V				
190	F-WWHG	I-CAFE	CS-TMJ						
191	F-WWHD	N282FJ	N950F						
192	F-WWHE	N283FJ	N212T	N96LT	N96UT				
193	F-WWHH	Italy MM62026							
194	F-WWHM	N284FJ	N10AT	N10LT	N95PH				
195	F-WWHK	Portugal 7401		Portugal 17401					
196	F-WWHD	N285FJ	N8575J	JA8575	N71TH	D-BNTH	VP-BSA		
197	F-WWHA	N286FJ	N50FJ	N500KJ	N404JF				
198	F-WWHC	Portugal 7402		Portugal 17402					
199	F-WWHB	N287FJ	N291BC						
200	F-WWHE	N288FJ	N664P						
201	F-WWHA	N289FJ	N41TH	N54DA	N553M				
202	F-WWHB	N290FJ	N212N	N97LT	N97UT	N202CP			
203	F-WWHA	I-CSGA	C-GNCA	N203NC					
204	F-WWHD	F-GKAR	VR-CGP	VP-CGP	EC-GPN	EC-HHS			
205	F-WWHD	N291FJ	N57EL	N59EL	N52JJ				
206	F-WWHB	VR-BMF	VP-BMF						
207	F-WWHC	N292FJ	N55BP	N50CS	N396EG				
208	F-WWHP	I-CSGB	VR-CCQ	C-GWEI	N50AE	N50HC			
209	F-WWHE	N293FJ	N59CF	N59CH	EC-168	EC-FPG	N1902W	N96DS	VP-BSL
210	F-WWHL	F-GICN							
211	F-WWHR	Italy MM62029							
212	F-WWHH	N294FJ	N50FJ	N30TH	N40TH	N85WN			
213	F-WWHW	N295FJ	XA-RVV						
214	F-WWHX	N296FJ	N55AS						
215	F-WWHT	N297FJ	XA-SIM	D-BOOK					
216	F-WWHZ	N298FJ	N180AR	N56SN					
217	F-WWHV	N122FJ	N5732	N573AC					
218	F-WWHA	N50NK	N218WA	D-BERT					
219	F-WWHS	N129FJ	YV-450CP						
220	F-WWHG	N131FJ	N75RD	N100RR	N528JR				
221	F-WWHL	Portugal 7403		Portugal 17403					
222	F-WWHM	D-BELL	OE-HIT						
223	F-WWHN	N132FJ	N633L	N840FJ					
224	F-WWHO	N133FJ	VR-CNV	XA-SDK	XA-BEG	N800BD			
225	F-WWHP	N134FJ	N50FJ	N32TC					

FALCON 50

C/n	Identities								
226	F-WWHC	N119AM							
227	F-WWHE	N226FJ	N50FJ	(N227FJ)	N1848U	N630SR	N37LC	(N37LQ)	C-GGFP
228	F-WWHR	(F-GNFS)	F-GNFF	VR-BJJ	F-GJEK	F-WWHR	N313GH	VR-CAE	C-GAZU
229	F-WWHH	N114FJ	C-GMII	C-GMID	N550WM				
230	F-WWHD	F-GNGL	HB-IAV	3B-NSY	OY-LIN				
231	F-WWHA	N228FJ	(VR-B)	XA-SIF	N10PQ	N10PP			
232	F-WWHT	F-WNLR	F-GNLR	N244FJ	N45NC				
233	F-WWHB	(N233FJ)	N232FJ	N48HB					
234	F-WWHC	N233FJ	PT-AAF						
235	F-WWHM	F-GKRU	(UR-ACA)	UR-CCC					
236	F-WWHD	N234FJ	N50FJ	N70FJ	XA-HGF	N195SV	N196SV*		
237	F-WWHE	N237FJ	N2425	(N5425)	N94BJ	N74BJ	N89BM		
238	F-WWHF	N238FJ	N50FJ	XA-LRA	N796A	N238DL	SE-DVL		
239	F-WWHG	N239FJ	N200SG						
240	F-WWHH	F-GNMO	(N40SK)	N780F	N33TY	N34TY			
241	F-WWHF	F-OKSI	N233BC						
242	F-WWHA	N241FJ	XA-SPM	N599SC	N900OF				
243	F-WWHM	N243FJ	N742R						
244	F-WWHK	N243FJ	N50FJ	N95HC					
245	F-WWHL	N240FJ	N720ML						
246	F-WWHF	N246FJ	TC-YSR						
247	F-WWHP	N247FJ	N740R						
248	F-WWHB	N249FJ	N25UD	N25UB	N67PW				
249	F-WWHN	N248FJ	(XA-DMS)	N663MN	SE-DVK				
250	F-WWHR	N250FJ	N696HC						
251*	F-WOND	ff 10Apr96		(F-GOND)	VR-CLN	VP-CLN	(F-GIVD)	N870	
252*	F-WWHE	(N313GH)	N93GH	N50FJ	XA-TDD				
253*	F-WWHA	N253EX	PT-WSC	N85F					
254*	F-WWHB	N50FJ	N50AE	N345AP					
255*	F-WWHC	N255CM							
256*	F-WWHD	VP-CBT	N600N						
257*	F-WWHE	F-OKSY							
258*	F-WWHF	F-WQHU	VP-BST						
259*	F-WWHG	VP-CHG							
260*	F-WWHK	N586CS							
261*	F-WWHL	N140RT	(N97FJ)	N73GH					
262*	F-WWHM	N262EX	N1896T						
263*	F-WWHN	N8550A							
264*	F-WWHO	F-GVDN	C6-BHD	N900CH					
265*	F-WWHP	N9550A							
266*	F-WWHQ	VP-BPA	N50NM						
267*	F-WWHR	(D-BETI)	F-OHFO						
268*	F-WWHS	EC-GTR							
269*	F-WWHT	F-GPBG	F-GJBZ						
270*	F-WWHU	N270EX	N148M						
271*	F-WWHV	TC-BHO							
272*	F-WWHW	N272EX	N50FJ	C-GMII					
273*	F-WWHX	N158M							
274*	F-WWHY	N138M							
275*	F-WWHA	F-GODP	N56LC						
276*	F-WWHB	N159M							
277*	F-WWHC	N368M	N198M						
278*	F-WWHD	VP-CFI							
279*	F-WWHE	N181MC							
280*	F-WWHF	N50FJ	N1829S*						
281*	F-WWHG	N17AN							
282*	F-WWHH	N191MC							
283*	F-WWHK	VP-CEF							
284*	F-WWHL	N904SB							
285*	F-WWHM	N901TF							
286*	F-WWHN	(F-GKIN)	VP-BMI						
287*	F-WWHO	ZS-ONG							
288*	F-WWHP	N288EX	N33TY						
289*	F-WWHQ	N214DV							
290*	F-WWHR?	N44SK	N42SK						
291*	F-WWHS	N294EX							
292*	F-WWHT	N292EX	N38WP						
293*	F-WWHU?	N293EX	N195SV^						
294*	F-WWHV	N39WP							
295*	F-WWHW								
296*	F-WWHX?	N296EX							
297*	F-WWHY								
298*	F-WWHZ	N615SR							
299*	F-W	N299EX							
300*	F-W	N344CM							
301*									
302*									
303*									

FALCON 50

C/n	Identities
304*	
305*	
306*	
307*	
308*	
309*	
310*	
311*	
312*	
313*	
314*	
315*	

DASSAULT FALCON 900

C/n	Series	Identities							
1	B	F-WIDE	ff 21Sep84	F-GIDE	converted to prototype 900B				
2		F-WFJC	F-GFJC	France 2/F-RAFP					
3		F-WWFA	N403FJ	N327K	N991RF				
4		F-WWFC	(HB-)	VR-BJX	F-WWFA	France 4/F-RAFQ			
5		F-WWFB	N404FJ	VH-BGF	F-GGRH	N905TS	PT-WQM	N905FJ	
6		F-WWFD	N405FJ	N80F					
7		F-WWFG	TR-LCJ	3B-XLA					
8		F-WWFE	N406FJ	N5731					
9		F-WWFJ	(PH-ILC)	HB-IAB	C6-BHN	N900TR	N193TR		
10		F-WWFF	N407FJ	N900FJ	(N910FJ)	N26LB	N96LB	N5MC	N349K
11		F-WWFK	LX-AER	F-WEFX	UN-09002	F-GLGY			
12		F-WWFH	N408FJ	N991AS	N77CE				
13		F-WWFI	N409FJ	N328K	(N75V)	(N75W)	N75V		
14		F-WWFL	N410FJ	N900SB	N906SB	N324SR	VP-BLP		
15		F-WWFM	HB-IAK	XA-RGB					
16		F-WWFN	N412FJ	(N187HG)	N187H	VR-CTA	N619BD	VP-CBD	
17		F-WWFO	N411FJ	N944AD					
18		F-WWFA	N413FJ	N72PS					
19		F-WWFB	N414FJ	N900SJ					
20		F-WWFC	N415FJ	(N711T)	N999PM	N70FJ	N911RF	N256DV	
21		F-WWFJ	(HZ-R4A)	HZ-AFT					
22		F-WWFD	N416FJ	N54DC					
23		F-WWFK	I-BEAU						
24		F-WWFE	N417FJ	N901B	N67WB	N93GR	N93CR		
25		F-WWFF	N418FJ	N70EW	N75EW				
26		F-WWFM	HB-IAC	SX-ECH					
27		F-WWFH	N419FJ	N90EW					
28		F-WWFK	N420FJ	N85D					
29		F-WWFA	N421FJ	C-GTCP					
30		F-WWFL	HB-IAF	F-WGTH	(F-GIRZ)	I-DIES			
31		F-WWFB	N422FJ	N900FJ	N910JW				
32		F-WWFG	N423FJ	VH-BGV	F-GJBT	N800BL	N500BL	N10MZ	
33		F-WWFC	N424FJ	N298W	F-GHEA	N9138Y	N901SB		
34		F-WWFD	N425FJ	N8100E	N8200E				
35		F-WWFC	HB-IAD	F-GLMU					
36		F-WWFE	N426FJ	N96PM	N91MK	N922JW			
37		F-WWFN	N427FJ	N45SJ	N41SJ	VH-FCP	VH-ACE		
38		F-WWFE	Spain T.18-1/45-40						
39		F-WWFF	N428FJ	(N900BF)	N1818S	N181BS	N5733		
40		F-WWFH	N429FJ	N904M	N145W	N369BG			
41		F-WWFI	N430FJ	N404F	N404FF	N76FD*			
42		F-WWFJ	N431FJ	N900FJ	N42FJ	N117TF	N901BB*		
43		F-WWFC	I-M[illegible]DE	N288Z					
44		F-WWFA	N432FJ	N914J	N914JL	HB-IBY	N100UP		
45		F-WWFB	N433FJ	N64BE	N298W				
46		F-WWFD	N434FJ	N329K	N779SG				
47		F-WWFA	A6-ZKM						
48		F-WWFM	N435FJ	N900MJ	N233KC^				
49		F-WWFD	VR-BLB	VP-BLB					
50		F-WWFH	N436FJ	N330K	N900TA				
51		F-WWFG	N437FJ	N59LB	N26LB	N50RG*			
52		F-WWFC	5N-FGO						
53		F-WWFN	N438FJ	JA8570					
54		F-WWFC	(LX-IMN)	I-FICV					
55		F-WWFO	N439FJ	C-FJES	N495GA	N404R			
56		F-WWFB	N440FJ	JA8571					
57		F-WWFK	N441FJ	N900WK					
58		F-WWFE	OE-ILS						
59		F-WWFD	N442FJ	N32B					
60		F-WWFG	N443FJ	N900FJ	N91TH				
61		F-WWFB	VR-CSA	HZ-AB2	HZ-AFZ				
62		F-WWFJ	F-GIVR	N62FJ	F-WQBL	F-GSCN			
63		F-WWFF	N445FJ	N90TH	N127EM	N75W			
64		F-WWFH	N446FJ	Malaysia M37-01					
65		F-WWFM	N447FJ	N216FP	N216FB	N990MC			
66		F-WWFE	F-GJPM	CS-TMK					
67		F-WWFD	N448FJ	N900MA					
68		F-WWFL	N449FJ	N900HC					
69		F-WWFD	I-SNAX						
70		F-WWFN	N450FJ	Australia A26-070					
71		F-WWFB	N451FJ	(N900BF)	PK-TRP	N280BC			
72		F-WWFF	VR-BLM	VP-BLM					
73		F-WWFA	N452FJ	Australia A26-073					
74		F-WWFF	N453FJ	Australia A26-074					
75		F-WWFC	N458FJ	C-FWSC	HB-IAI	N60RE			
76		F-WWFE	N454FJ	Australia A26-076					
77		F-WWFG	N455FJ	Australia A26-077					

FALCON 900

C/n	Series	Identities								
78		F-WWFH	N456FJ	N332MC	C-GSSS	N522KM	LX-GES			
79	B	F-WWFM	N457FJ	N900FJ	N901FJ	N6BX				
80		F-WWFA	N459FJ	N914BD						
81		F-WWFL	7T-VPA							
82		F-WWFM	7T-VPB							
83		F-WWFG	N460FJ	N900WG	N900NE					
84		F-WWFD	A6-AUH							
85		F-WWFC	N461FJ	N74FS						
86		F-WWFE	A6-UAE							
87		F-WWFA	N462FJ	N33GG						
88		F-WWFH	VR-BLT	F-GNDA						
89		F-WWFB	I-NUMI							
90		F-WWFG	Spain T.18-2/45-41							
91		F-WWFH	A7-AAD							
92		F-WWFL	N463FJ	PT-OEX						
93		F-WWFM	EC-617	EC-FEN	N900Q					
94		F-WWFC	A7-AAE							
95		F-WWFO	N464FJ	N478A	N343MG					
96		F-WWFF	F-GHTD	F-WWFF	5N-OIL	5N-FGE				
97		F-WWFA	EC-765	EC-FFO	XA-SJX	(N900DU)	N902NC			
98		F-WWFM	N465FJ	N900FJ	(N903FJ)	N59CF				
99		F-WWFE	ZS-NAN							
100		F-WWFN	YK-ASC							
101		F-WWFO	N466FJ	D-ALME						
102		F-WWFK	N467FJ	N906WK						
103	B	F-WWFL	F-GHYB	F-WWFJ	V5-NAM					
104	B	F-WWFA	N468FJ	N104FJ	N881G	N900CS				
105	B	F-WWFD	N469FJ	N8572	JA8572	N71TH	F-GTGJ	F-WQBJ	F-GTGJ	CN-TFU
106	B	F-WWFL	F-GKDI	9M-BAN	F-GJRH	N332EC	N333EC			
107	B	F-WWFJ	N470FJ	XA-GTR						
108	B	F-WWFN	N471FJ	N334MC	N511WM					
109	B	F-WWFB	G-BTIB	Belgium CD-01						
110	B	F-WWFH	OY-CKK							
111	B	F-WWFH	N472FJ	N8BX						
112	B	F-WWFM	N473FJ	N246AG						
113	B	F-WWFB	HZ-SAB2							
114	B	F-WWFC	N474FJ	XA-SIM						
115	B	F-WWFL	EC-235	EC-FPI						
116	B	F-WWFO	N475FJ	N900FJ	N5VF	N5VN	N82RP			
117	B	F-WWFA	N476FJ	N70TH						
118	B	F-WWFB	F-GNFI	RA-09000						
119	B	F-WWFD	N477FJ	N22T						
120	B	F-WWFN	VR-BNJ	VP-BNJ						
121	B	F-WWFE	N478FJ	9M-BAB						
122	B	F-WWFF	N479FJ	XA-SGW	N612BH					
123	B	F-WWFL	RA-09001							
124	B	F-WWFG	N480FJ	VR-BWS	VP-BWS	N14NA				
125	B	F-WWFL	F-GPAX	F-WWFL	VR-BSK	VP-BSK				
126	B	F-WWFM	N481FJ	N900FJ	N733A	N733HL	N910CS			
127	B	F-WWFC	N482FJ	N654CN	N390F					
128	B	F-WWFM	N128FJ	N999PM	N999PN*					
129	B	F-WWFD	N483FJ	XA-VTO						
130	B	F-WWFC	F-GOAB	F-WWFB	VR-CID	VP-CID				
131	B	F-WWFH	N131FJ	N900FJ	N158JA	XA-TJG				
132	B	F-WWFI	N132FJ	N707WB						
133	B	F-WWFH	F-GODE	HZ-OFC3	N395L					
134	B	F-WWFA	N134FJ	N88YF	N322CP					
135	B	F-WWFJ	VR-BPW	VP-BPW						
136	B	F-WWFE	N137FJ	N1818S						
137	B	F-WWFF	N139FJ	XA-GAE	N99DQ					
138	B	F-W	VR-BHJ	VP-BHJ						
139	B	F-WWFG	N140FJ	N523AC						
140	B	F-WWFL	VR-CES	N70HS						
141	B	F-WWFK	N141FJ	XA-OVR						
142	B	F-WWFN	N142FJ	N10AT	F-WSMF	F-GSMF	TC-CAG	F-HAAP		
143	B	F-WWFH	F-GNMR	ZS-ZBB	VP-B					
144	B	F-WWFO	N144FJ	N453JS						
145	B	F-WWFK	VR-CGB	VP-CGB						
146	B	F-WWFF	N146FJ	N216FP	N881P					
147	B	F-WWFG	N147FJ	N900FJ	(N901FJ)	OE-IMI				
148	B	F-WWFD	N148FJ	N522AC						
149	B	F-WWFH	VR-BPI	VP-BPI						
150	B	F-WWFC	N150FJ	N335MC	HB-IUW					
151	B	F-WWFK	G-OPWH	EC-HHK						
152	B	F-WWFJ	N337MC	N660EG						
153	B	F-WWFK	N153FJ	N57EL						
154	B	F-WWFL	VR-BJA	VP-BJA	F-WQBJ	VP-BGF				
155	B	F-WWFM	N2056	N730SA	N814M	substantially damaged 17Mar00 Hyannis MA				

FALCON 900

C/n	Series	Identities				
156	B	F-WWFA	N202FJ	HL7301	N910Q	
157	B	F-WWFB	N157FJ	N1868M		
158	B	F-WWFC	N158FJ	N900FJ	N404VL	
159	B	F-WWFD	P4-NAN	N263PW	LX-NAN	F-WQBL	LX-NAN
160	B	F-WWFE	N176CF			
161	B	F-WWFF	F-GSAB	VP-CTT	G-GSEB	PH-ILC
162	B	F-WWFJ	N162FJ	N611JW		
163	B	F-WWFM	N163FJ	F-WWFM	(PH-EFA)	(F-GSAD)	VP-BEH
164	B	F-WWFC	G-MLTI			
165	B	F-WWFD	G-EVES			
166	B	F-WWFG	N166FJ	N900FJ	F-GLHI	N995SK
167	B	F-WWFO	F-GUEQ			
168	B	F-WWFA	N167FJ	XA-TEL		
169	C	F-WWFP	F-GRDP	VP-BGC		
170	B	F-WWFR	VP-BKA	N900DA		
171	B	F-WWFW	TC-AKK			
172	B	F-WWFD	N177FJ	N352AF		
173	B	F-WWFI	PH-LBA			
174	B	F-WWFK	N138FA	N138F		
175	B	F-WWFN	CS-TMQ			
176	B	F-WWFW	N900SM	N909PM		
177	B	F-WWFY	N886DC			
178	B	F-WWFF	N179FJ	XA-APE		
179	C	F-WWFQ	N900FJ	N900DW		
180	C	F-WWFX	N90TH			
181	C	F-WWFZ	HB-IUY			
182	C	F-W	N168HT			
183	C	F-WWFK	N900CC			
184	C					
185	C					
186	C					
187	C					
188	C					
189	C					
190	C					

DASSAULT FALCON 900EX

C/n	Identities					
1	F-WREX	ff 01Jun95 F-GREX	PH-ERP	N900HG		
2	F-WWFA	N200L				
3	F-WWFG	N903FJ	JA50TH			
4	F-WWJC	N204FJ	N8100E			
5	F-WWFJ	N205FJ	9M-JJS	N905EX	N500VM	
6	F-WWFK	F-OIBL	EC-GMO			
7	F-WWFN	N907FJ	N45SJ			
8	F-WWFB	N30LB				
9	F-WWFE	N909FJ	N70LF			
10	F-WWFG	N910FJ	N22CS			
11	F-WWFI	F-GOYA				
12	F-WWFJ	N913FJ	N900EX	(N900SB)	N912EX	F-WQBL	F-HAXA
13	F-WWFK	VP-BRO				
14	F-WWFN	N72WS				
15	F-WWFO	N915EX	N914J			
16	F-WWFA	N916EX	N67WB			
17	F-WWFB	N600AS	N990H			
18	F-WWFE	N918EX	N18RF	N166FB		
19	F-WWFJ	N919EX	N7301	N96DS		
20	F-WWFN	N920EX	N158JA			
21	F-WWFH	N330MC	N331MC^			
22	F-WWFQ	N331MC	(N332MC)	N21HJ*		
23	F-WWFS	SE-DVE				
24	F-WWFU	TR-LEX				
25	F-WWFV	N925EX	N55TY			
26	F-WWFX	N900SB				
27	F-WWFY	N927EX	N900EX	N626CC		
28	F-WWFZ	HB-IAH				
29	F-WWFA	N25UD				
30	F-WWFB	N662P				
31	F-WWFC	F-GSAI	HZ-OFC4			
32	F-WWFE	N2425				
33	F-WWFF	N933EX	(N810M)	XA-TMH	XA-BEG	
34	F-W	VP-CLB				
35	F-WWFJ	N2BD	HB-IAQ			
36	F-WWFM	N326K				
37	F-WWFV	N327K				
38	F-WWFX	N328K				
39	F-WWFA	N939EX	VP-BID			
40	F-W	N940EX	N900EX	N606DR*		
41	F-WWFC	N5737				
42	F-WWFD	N942EX	VP-BMS			
43	F-WWFE	F-GSDP				
44	F-WWFG	G-JCBG	N900PL	N947LF		
45	F-WWFJ	Italy MM62171				
46	F-WWFM	N946EX	XA-FEX			
47	F-WWFO	N58CG				
48	F-WWFP	G-GPWH				
49	F-WWFR	N949EX	N404F			
50	F-WWFS	F-GPNJ				
51	F-WWFU	F-GVDP				
52	F-WWFV	Italy MM62172				
53	F-WWFW	N953EX	PT-WQS*			
54	F-WWFY	HB-IUX				
55	F-WWFA	N498A				
56	F-WWFC	N956EX	N404A			
57	F-W	N900MT				
58	F-WWFF	N958EX				
59	F-W	N959EX	N694JP			
60	F-WWFI	N960EX	PT-			
61	F-W	N961EX				
62	F-WWFM					
63	F-WWFO	N963EX				
64	F-W	N900VM				
65	F-W	N965EX	N965M*			
66	F-WWFA	N377SC				
67	F-W	N967EX				
68	F-WWFC	N390DE				
69	F-WWFD	N969EX				
70	F-W	N970EX				
71	F-W	N111NG				
72	F-W	N2BD				
73						
74						
75						
76						
77						

FALCON 900EX

C/n	Series	Identities
78		
79		
80		

DASSAULT FALCON 2000

C/n	Identities				
1	(F-WNEW)	F-WNAV	rolled out 10Feb93; ff 04Mar93 for 75 mins		
2	rolled out Dec93; ff 11Jly94	F-WNEW	ZS-NNF	F-GJHJ	
3	F-WWFA	N2000A	N15AS		
4	F-WWMA	N925AJ			
5	F-WWMB	N27R			
6	F-WWMD	F-GPAM	F-WQBL	N93GH	
7	F-WWME	N28R			
8	F-WWMF	N610AS			
9	F-WWMG	N435T			
10	F-WWMH	N652PC	N131EP		
11	F-WWMK	N101NS	(N787RA)	N721BS	N248JF
12	F-WWMM	I-SNAW	F-GLHJ*		
13	F-WWML	N2004	N722JB		
14	F-WWMN	N2034	N70KS		
15	F-WWMO	N790L			
16	F-WWMB	HB-IAW			
17	F-WWMA	N2035	N77A	N88TY*	
18	F-WWMG	F-GMPR	EI-LJR	VP-CJA	
19	F-WWMC	N790M			
20	F-WWME	N389GS			
21	F-WWMA	N390GS			
22	F-WWMF	N200NE			
23	F-WWMH	N2036	N375SC		
24	F-WWMK	N2039	N376SC		
25	F-WW	N2042	N96FG		
26	F-WWMN	N2046	N2000A	F-WQFL	TC-CIN
27	F-WWMM	G-JCBI			
28	F-WWMO	N596A			
29	F-WWMA	N2028	XA-TDU		
30	F-WWMB	HB-IAZ			
31	F-WWMC	N2032	N790Z		
32	F-WWMD	N65SD			
33	F-WWME	HB-IAX			
34	F-WWMF	HB-IAY			
35	F-WWMG	N27WP			
36	F-WWMA	F-GSAA			
37	F-WWMH	EC-GNK			
38	F-WWMI	N3BM			
39	F-WWMJ	N2061	N151AE		
40	F-WW	N1C			
41	F-WWMD	N2073	N48CG		
42	F-WWMG	HB-IBH			
43	F-WWMK	(N2077)	PT-MML	N101BE	
44	F-WWML	N2074	N2000A	N49MW	
45	F-WWMM	N45SC			
46	F-WWMN	N2080	(N220JM)	F-WWMN	F-GMCK	CS-DCM
47	F-WWMB	N220JM	N800BL		
48	F-WWMC	N2089	N701WC		
49	F-WWMD	(PH-EFB)	VP-BEF	G-GEDI	
50	F-WWME	D-BEST			
51	F-WWMF	N82AT	N2AT		
52	F-WWMI	N212T			
53	F-WWMJ	N981	N149VB		
54	F-WWML	D-BIRD			
55	F-WWMM	HB-IVM			
56	F-WWMO	TC-CYL	N784BX		
57	F-WWMA	N2132	N18CG		
58	F-WWMB	N2133	N326EW		
59	F-WWMC	N2146	PT-WYC		
60	F-WWMD	N2147	XA-GNI		
61	F-WWME	HB-IVN			
62	F-WWMF	HB-IVO			
63	F-WWMG	N2155	N2000A	N804JH	
64	F-WWMH	N996AG			
65	F-WWMI	F-GODO	(F-OIBA)	VT-TAT	
66	F-WWMJ	N30TH			
67	F-WWMK	N150BC			
68	F-WWMN	N200GN			
69	F-WWMA	N220JN	(N220JM)	N220EJ	(N220MR)	N220DF
70	F-WWMB	N2168	N207QS		
71	F-WWMC	N92LT			
72	F-WWMD	N2169	N96LT		
73	F-WWMG	N2176	(N97LT)	N273JC	
74	F-WWMH	HB-IUZ			
75	F-WWMK	N275QS			
76	F-WWML	OY-CKN			
77	F-WWMM	N278QS			

FALCON 2000

C/n	Identities			
78	F-WWMJ	G-PYCO		
79	F-WWMN	N929HG		
80	F-WWMO	N2CW		
81	F-WWVA	N281QS		
82	F-WWVB	N752S		
83	F-WWVC	N1128B		
84	F-WWVD	N1929Y		
85	F-WWVE	N220JM	N221EJ	
86	F-WWVF	N111HZ		
87	F-WWVG	N287QS		
88	F-WWVH	N753S		
89	F-WWVI	N2189	N2000A	N800GH*
90	F-WWVJ	F-GKIP		
91	F-WWVK	N46HA		
92	F-WWVL	N2191	N2000L	
93	F-WWVM	N292QS		
94	F-WWVN	N48HA		
95	F-WWVO	N628CC		
96	F-WWVP	N88DD		
97	F-WWVQ	N620AS	N922H	
98	F-WWVR	N298QS		
99	F-WWVS	(N2099)	N111VU	N111VW
100	F-WWVT	VP-CGA		
101	F-W	N2093	N399FA	OO-GFD
102	F-W	N515TK	N440AS	
103	F-WWVX	I-FLYP		
104	F-WWVY	N204QS		
105	F-W	N220EJ		
106	F-WWVA	N635E		
107	F-WWVB			
108	F-WWVC	I-FLYV		
109	F-WWVD	CS-DNP	F-WWVD	N2218
110	F-W	N2194		
111	F-W			
112	F-W	N2197		
113	F-W	N213QS		
114	F-W			
115	F-W			
116	F-WWVL	N2216		
117	F-W	N2217		
118	F-W	N218QS		
119	F-W			
120				
121				
122				
123				
124				
125				
126				
127				
128				
129				
130				
131				
132				
133				
134				
135				
136				
137				
138				
139				
140				

G1159 GULFSTREAM II

Notes: G1159B Gulfstream IIB conversion programme numbers have been included alongside the c/n (see also at the end of the production list)

TT indicates aircraft with tip tanks (some 2Bs were built as "TT" models)

SP indicates a specialist conversion by Aviation Partners with winglets, known as Gulfstream IISPs; these are not 2B aircraft

C/n	Series	Identities								
1	SP	N801GA	ff 02Oct66 N55RG							
2	SP	N802GA	N801GA	N369CS	N869CS	N721SW	N434JW			
3		N831GA	N214GP	N311JJ	N555RS	N300GP	N417RD*			
4/8	2B	N832GA	N680RW	N680RZ	9K-ACY	VR-CAS	HZ-MPM	N849OP	N36RR	
5		N100P	N100PJ	N65ST	N655TJ					
6		N834GA	N430R	N122DJ	N122DU					
7	SP	CF-HOG	N930O	N93QQ	N118NP	N701JA				
8	SP	N833GA	N18N	N400SJ	N400SA	HB-IMV	N400SA	N777GG	PJ-ARI	N504TF
		N5UD	N225CC	N11UF	N22CX	S9-CRH	S9-GOT	ZS-TGG	N267PS	
9/33	2B	CF-SBR	N320FE	(N115RS)	N209GA	N343K	N48EC			
10	SP	N343K	N343N	N888CF	XA-ROI	N555LG	N51TJ	N667CX*		
11		N835GA	N902	N902GA	N611TJ	N463HK				
12	SP	N500R	N11UM	N154X	N115MR	N121EA	N160WC	N212TJ	(prototype SP)	
13		N678RW	N678RZ	N98AM	5N-AMN	N2GP	N373LP	N373LB	VR-BOS	N269MH
		N269HM								
14	SP	N663P	N663B	N217JD	N369AP	N500JW	XA-RBS			
15		N375PK	N77SW	N416SH	N125JJ	N571BJ				
16/13	2B	N890A	N697A	N711MT	N38GL	N24YS				
17	SP	N119K	N819GA	N456AS	N91AE	N305AF	N917R	N217GA	N1PR	(N121PR)
		N422DV	N143G	N143V						
18		N838GA	N205M	N43R	(N48RA)	XA-SDE	XA-LZZ	XC-AA70		
19	SP	N839GA	N1929Y	N19NW	N590CH					
20		N2PG	N755S	N4SP	N331P					
21		N4PG	N3PG	N7ZX	N8PG	N8PQ	cx Jan93; to CIS; unable to obtain CofA			
		N8PQ	N244DM							
22	SP	N862GA	N5152	N145ST	N22FS	N683FM	N206MD	(N800TE)	(N655JH)	N217RR
23	VC-11A	N863GA	USCG 01	N7TJ						
24		N536CS	N4S	(N98G)	N26WP	(N224TS)	N800XL	N800XC*		
25		N327K	N527K	N711RL						
26	SP	N328K	N202GA	PK-PJZ	N975GA	(N711RT)	N4RT			
27	SP	N1807Z	N121JJ	N430BC	N227TS	(N227TJ)				
28		N695ST	N700ST	N7004T	C-GCFB	N120EA	N85EQ	N68DM		
29		N869GA	N930BS	N919G	N41RC	N71TJ	N941CW	N188JS		
30/4	2B	N870GA	N788S	N2601	N2607	N333AX	N338AX	N47HR	XA-FHR	
31		N1621	N685TA	N789FF	N200CC	N105TB	special a/c with nose probe and underwing pods			
32/2	2B	N7602	(N7601)	N976B	N971EC					
33	SP	N1624	N1324	N217TL	(N217TE)	N327TL	N327TC			
34		N230E	N130A	N11SX	VR-CBM	N500JR	N204RC	w/o 17Jun91 Caracas-Oscar Machada,		
		Venezuela; cx Oct91								
35		N1004T	N830TL	N30PR						
36/3	2B	N26L	N26LA	N5400G	(N211GA)	N901K	N901KB	N74A		
37		N179AR	N179AP	N994JD	N397RD					
38		N80A	N880A	Quiet Spey development a/c with BAC1-11 thrust reverser on starboard engine;						
		stored Aug94 Detroit-Willow Run, MI; cx Jun95; wfu for spares								
39		N80Q	N8000	N401HR	(N124BN)	N425A	(N12BN)	N1TJ	N87HB	N87TD
40		N1040	(N5040)	N1039	VR-BLJ	w/o 20Jun96 Jos, 465m NE of Lagos, Nigeria				
41	SP	N38N	(N417GA)	N401GA	N416K					
42/12	2B	N8000J	N937M	N880GM	VR-BMQ	N1164A	N36PN			
43		N17583	F-BRUY	N84X	N33ME	N691RC	(N243TS)	N270TS	N899GA	
44		N814GA	N830G	N585A	N830G					
45	SP	N815GA	N711R	PK-PJG	N152RG	N215RL	VR-BHA	N115GA	N40CE	US Army 89-0266
		N51741	US Army 89-0266		N245GA	N250MS				
46	TT	N806CC	N40CC	N111RF	C-GSLK	N9272K	N721CP	N9BF	N505JT	N565KC
47	SP	N803GA	N35JM	N553MD	N809GA	N809LS	N800FL	N800RT		
48/29	2B	N109G	N4411	N711MC	N61WH					
49		N871GA	N747G	N74JK	N830TL	N830TE	N830TL	(N830TE)	N830BH	N511PA
50		N39N	N39NX	N767FL	N800FL	N220FL	N220JR			
51	SP	N2013M	VR-BNE	N7C	N20H	N20HE*				
52		CF-FNM	C-FFNM	N69SF	N38KM	N5SJ	(N52NE)	(N52TJ)+	N711MT	N211MT
		N52NW								
		+marks painted on a/c at 1994 NBAA Show but not on official Register								
53	SP	N107A	N167A	N102AB						
54/36	2B	N123H	CF-NOR	C-FNOR	N955CC					
55		N875GA	N225SF	N225SE	N125DC					
56	SP	N10XY	N20XY	N105Y	N805Y	N610CC				
57	SP	N876GA	N770AC	N300DK	N300DL	N333ST*				
58		N878GA	N720Q	w/o 24Jun74 Kline, SC, USA						
59	SP	N879GA	N1823D							
60		N892GA	N500J	w/o 26Sep76 Hot Springs, VA, USA						

GULFSTREAM II

C/n	Series	Identities								
61	SP	N18N	N711MM	N497TJ	N800MC	N57BG	N61LH	N41AV		
62		N834GA	N372CM	N372GM	N1PG	N3ZQ	N7PG	N7PQ		
		Russia 62 (Black or Dark Blue)			(N777TX)	N20LW	N262PA			
63		N835GA	N238U	N239P	N149JW	N17ND	(N20GP)	N12GP		
64/27	2B	N836GA	N940BS	N950BS	N341NS	N95SV	N620K	N82CK	N43RJ	
65		N837GA	N720E	N1JG	N500PC	N58JF	(N300FN)			
66		N838GA	N720F	N165W	N165U	N718JS				
67	SP	N839GA	N711S	EL-WRT	N10HR	N400JD	N67PR			
68		N308EL	N308EE							
69	SP	N69NG	N25JM	N33CR	N45JM	N45Y	N45YP	VH-HKR	N21066	N123CC
		N440DR	N701S							
70/1	2B	N711SC	N711SB	VR-BML	N165A	N451CS	N451GS	N908EJ		
71		N4CP	N4CQ	N711SW	N907SW	N48JK	N47A	N200AB		
72		N397F	w/o 22Feb76 Burlington, VT, USA							
73/9	2B	N116K	N555CS	N920DS	N436JW					
74	SP	N845GA	N111AC	N311AC	(3X-GBD)	N204GA	N92SV	N74TJ	N74HH	
75/7	2B	N823GA	N1000	N100AC	N100CC	N600CS	N760U	N94TJ	N211SJ	
76	SP	N711LS	N227G	N227GL	N227GX	N227G	N227GA			
77		N824GA	N100WK	N40CH	N140CH	N34MZ	N84MZ	N777JS	N385M	N7TJ
		N707SH	N7TJ	N700JP	N125WM	N994GC				
78	SP	N17585	PH-FJP	CF-IOT	C-FIOT	N90HH	HP-1A			
79	SP	N826GA	N719GA	N204A	XA-SFB	XA-STO	XA-ARA			
80	SP	N827GA	N85V	N85VT	N500RH					
81	SP	N828GA?	N777SW	N44MD	N281GA	N283MM	N688MC	N681AR	XB-PGR+	N681AR
		(N281NW)	N151SD			+ was not canx from USCAR at this time				
82	SP	N711DP	N10LB	N9040	N600B	N600BT	N728T	N492JT		
83		N404M	N409M	N409MA	(N48MS)	w/o 03May95 Quito, Ecuador				
84		N5101	N5101T	N27SL						
85	SP	N5102	Denmark F-085		N5102	N510G	N86SK	N931CW	N93AT	N524MM
86/16	2B	N880GA	N179T	N179DE*						
87/775/6	2B	N804GA	N13GW	N723J	N6PC					
88/21	2B	N881GA	N2600	N2637M	HB-IMZ	N901AS	N80WD			
89	SP	N882GA	N100A	N203A	N36MW	was conv to prototype "Paragon" before SP				
90		N883GA	N7789	N20GP						
91	SP	N17586	G-AYMI	VH-ASM	N219GA	G-OVIP	VR-BRM	N291GA	N99ST	N183SC
		N81FC*								
92	SP	N884GA	N300L	N300U	N114HC	N994JD	N430SA	N722TP	N589HM	N691HM
93	SP	N885GA	N8785R	TJ-AAK	N215GA	N62K	N484TL			
94		N886GA	N200A	N202A	N623MW	N420JM	N420JT*			
95/39	2B	N887GA	VH-ASG	N427AC	N836MF	N836ME	N113CS			
96		N888GA	N100KS	N100WC	N75WC	N75SR	XC-MEX	XB-EBI		
97	SP	N889GA	I-SMEG	N66TF	N11AL	N930SD	N397J	(N397L)	N55HY	
98/38	2B	N850GA	N93M	N955H	N988H	N988DS	N925DS	N17MX	XA-CHR	XA-PSD
		N198AV	N812RS							
99	SP	N851GA	N99GA	N822CA	N900VL	N900MP				
100	SP	N852GA	N4000X	N400CX	N234DB	N911DB	XB-FVL	N400D		
101		N853GA	N1159K	(N237LM)	N240CX	N623CX				
102/32	2B	N854GA	N88AE	N210GA	N119CC	N400CC	N102CX			
103		N855GA	N801GA	G-BDMF	N833GA	P2-PNF	P2-PNG	N833GA	HZ-MS4	N103WJ
104/10	2B/2	N856GA	N856W	N858W	(cvtd back to G2 standards 1989; wings to G3 c/n 303)					
		C-FHPM								
105		N807GA	N23M	N5997K	N405GA	N6060	N711TE			
106		N808GA	N33M	(N519TW)	N397LE	N226GA				
107		N809GA	N5113H	N10123						
108	SP	N810GA	N11UC	N60GG	N600MB	N700FS	N801GA	N200GH	(N200GL)	
109	SP	N811GA	N679RW	N882W	N86CE	N862CE	N73AW			
110	SP	N814GA	N5000G	N200GN	N200PB	N21AM	N21AX			
111		N815GA	N10LB	N13LB	N765A	N900BR	N900DH			
112	SP	N816GA	N102ML	N102HS	VR-BJG	N36JK	N909L	N108DB	N87AG	
113	SP	N817GA	N30RP	N34RP	N60CT	N203GA	N2S	N32HC	N2S	N216HE
		(N216MF)	N1BL	N211BL	N217JS	N74RT				
114		N818GA	N100PM	N25BF	XA-TDK					
115	SP	N819GA	N677S	N457SW	N47JK	N200BP	N700BH	N40AG		
116		N821GA	9M-ARR	N20XY	N23W	(N410LR)	N716TE			
117		N822GA	N580RA	N888SW	N75CC					
118		N823GA	N399CB	(N301FP)	N399FP	N650PF/NASA650 (for Prop Fan Experiments)				(N651NA)
		N945NA								
119/22	2B	N824GA	TU-VAF	N825GA	C-FHBX	N2991Q	N60HJ	(N875E)	N720G	N73LP
		N928GF	(N103EL)							
120	SP	N825GA	N901BM	N777V	N677V	N20FX	N393BD	N392BD*		
121	SP	N200P	N90EA	N507JC	N721RL	N721PL*				
122		N832GA	N429JX	N4290X	N61SM	N84A	N500RL			
123/25	2B	N805CC	N345CP	N345AA	N344AA					
124		N834GA	HB-IEW	(VR-BGL)	VR-BGO	N203GA	Venezuela 0004			
125/26	2B	N870GA	N367G	N364G	N3643	N92LA	N92NA			
126		N43M	N581WD	(HB-I)	N578DF	N416K	N901WG			
127	TT	N17581	TR-KHB	w/o 06Feb80 Ngaoundere, Cameroun						
128		N73M	N367EG	N128TS						

GULFSTREAM II

C/n	Series	Identities								
129	SP	N871GA	N1H	N711DS	N83TE	N626TC	N711EV			
130	SP	N872GA	N127V	N518GS	N512SD					
131/23	2B	N17582	9M-ATT	N759A	N2JR					
132		N873GA	N400M							
133	TT	N88906	N17583	5X-UPF	N44UP	N444QG				
134		N806CC	C-FROC	N555HD	N555KH					
135		N83M	N113EV	(N518FE)	N518JT	N515JT	N552JT			
136	SP	N874GA	N65M	ZS-JIS	3D-AAC	N207GA	6V-AFL	6V-AGQ	N26WB	XA-ABA
137	SP	N875GA	N1875P	N2711M	VR-BJT	N23AH	N115MC	N485GM*		
138		N6JW								
139/11	2B	N880GA	N18N	HZ-PET	HB-ITV	N2UJ	(N763PD)	N663PD		
140/40	2B	N881GA	C-GTWO	N2667M	(N101AR)	N104AR	N212GA	VR-BJQ	N189TC	N730TK
		N159NB								
141		N17584	JA8431	(Mitsubishi special test aircraft)						
142		N882GA	N60CC	N5RD						
143		N883GA	N334	N204C	w/o 04Sep91 Kota Kinabalu, Borneo; cx Nov93					
144		N17585	HB-ITR	N944NA						
145		N894GA	N871D	N871E	N339H					
146		N897GA	N946NA							
147		N898GA	N947NA							
148/5	2B	N710MR	N710MP	N2615	N2815	N180AR				
149		N896GA	N17586	5V-TAA	w/o 26Dec74 Lome, Togo					
150	SP	N803GA	N966H	N988H	N636MF	N638MF	(N631CK)	N613CK	N319GP	N60GU
151/24	2B	N804GA	N979RA	N979GA	N908JE	N988JE*				
152		N17587	XA-FOU	N202GA	N62WB	N559LC				
153		N881GA	N23A	(N602CM)	N111VW	N110VW				
154/28	2B	N1625	N1JN	N18JN	N836MF	N110GD				
155/14	2B	N308A	XA-GAC	N477GG						
156/31	2B	N806GA	N400SJ	N7000G	N16NK	N18NK	N525JT			
157		N805GA	N914BS	N940BS	N74JK	N658PC	N683EC			
158	SP	N76CS	N76QS	N401M	N2S	N889JC				
159		N345UP	N800DM	N800DJ	N880RJ					
160		N80J	N801	N214GA	N900TP	N919TG	N1123G			
161		N17589	XA-ABC	XC-FEZ	XC-CFE	Mexico TP-04/XC-UJK		XB-GSN	XA-RUS	XA-AHM
		(also on Mexican register as XB-GSN)								
162		(C-GANE)	N530SW	N74RV	C-GTCB	N74RV	N666JT			
163	SP	N17581	(YV-60CP)	PJ-ABA	N117JJ	N117JA	N117JJ			
164	SP	N17582	9K-ACX	A6-HHZ	N93LA	N80AG				
165/37	2B	N810GA	N7000C	N788C	VR-BHR	N26L	N965CC			
166/15	2B	N811GA	N515KA	N66AL	(N84AL)	N826GA	N826AG	XA-SWP	N776MA	
167	SP	N17583	5V-TAC	VR-CBC	N204GA	N900SF	N430DP	N681FM	N82204	N682FM
		N683FM	N120GS	N368AG						
168	SP	N812GA	N10LB	N26LB	N193CK	N635AV	N168JW	N317AF	(N370SP)	N318SP
169	SP	N17584	HB-IEX	N39JK	N31SY	N710JL	N7155P	N169P	N169EA	
170		N991GA	N14PC	N502PC	(N318GD)	N111GD				
171		N17585	HZ-AFH							
172		N804GA	N903G	N903GA	N903AG					
173	TT	N801GA	XC-PET	XA-SQU	N98FT	N173EL				
174	SP	N805GA	N401M	N144ST	N7766Z	N900ES	N540EA			
175	SP	N17586	HZ-AFG	5T-UPR	N770PA	XA-FNY				
176		N806GA	N176P	N176SB	N15UC	N15UG				
177		N17587	5N-AGV							
178	SP	N819GA	N390F	N104ME	(N128AD)	N42LC	N720JW			
179		N17588	HZ-CAD	HZ-PCA						
180		N859GA	N329K	N359K	N37WH	(N47WH)	N702JA			
181		N860GA	N24DS	N924DS	N48CC					
182	TT	N17589	CN-ANL							
183	SP	N17581	A40-AA	N23AZ	(N10NW)	N801WC	(conv from TT Series)			
184		N861GA	N80E	N220GA	N254CR					
185	SP	N862GA	N372CM	N372GM	N3E	N3EU	N511WP	XA-BRE	N297GB	
186		N17582	(D-ACVG)	D-AFKG	5N-AML	(D-AAMD)	VR-BJV	VP-BJV		
187		N17583	N804GA	HZ-ADC	N202GA	N802CC				
188		N823GA	N862G	N662G	N555MW	N555MU	N188DC			
189/42	2B	N333AR	N512VB	(N515JT)	N555XL	N404AC				
190	SP	N130K	N159B	N169B	N900WJ	N1WP	N7WQ	N59CD	N59JR	N914DZ
191	SP	N810GA	N680RW	N679RW	N677RW	N675RW	N951RK			
192	SP	N811GA	N678RW	N677RW	HB-ITW	N273LP				
193		N808GA	N26L	N26LT	N54J					
194		N17584	HB-IMW	C6-BEJ	C6-BFE	VR-BRM	N194WA	N57HJ		
195		N212K	N71TP	XA-ILV						
196		N400J	N200BE	N610MC						
197		N800GA	N5117H	N217AH*						
198/35	2B	N825GA	N365G	N3652	N91LA	N91NA				
199/19	2B	N829GA	N75WC	N75RP	N74RP	N71RP	VR-BND	VP-BND	N900TJ	
200	SP	N826GA	N1806P	N135CP	N99VA	XA-AVR	N17GG	N281RB		
201	TT	N17585	HZ-AFI							
202	TT	N17586	A9C-BG							
203	TT	N17587	HZ-AFJ							

GULFSTREAM II

C/n	Series	Identities							
204	SP	N17588	G-CXMF	N806CC	N937US	N659PC	N659WL	VR-CPA	VP-CPA
205		N25UG	N1000						
206	SP	N2PK	N900BF						
207/34	2B	N700PM	(N780PM)	N111UB	VR-CUB	VP-CUB			
208		N808GA	N62CB	C-FNCG					
209	SP	N806GA	N277T						
210		HB-IEY	G-IIRR	(HK-)	8P-LAD	N30FW			
211		N17581	VR-BGT	VP-BGT					
212	TT	N807GA	N551MD	N807CC					
213	SP	N1707Z	N96JA	(N96BK)					
214		N17585	G-BSAL	A40-HA	Oman 601	N11NZ			
215		N816GA	N748MN						
216	TT	HB-IEZ	N63SD	N200RG	HZ-ND1	HZ-HA1			
217		N88GA	N81728	N880WD					
218		TU-VAC	N218GA	N187PH	(N187PA)	N188MR			
219/20	2B	N84V	VR-BJD	N307AF	N923ML	N505RX	N575E		
220		N805GA	N404M	N307M	N405MM	N315TS	N117GL		
221	SP	N575SF	N575SE	N2HF	N600CD	N827K			
222		N817GA	N5253A	N948NA					
223	SP	N510US	N257H	N510US					
224	TT	N17584	N810GA	N631SC	N90CP				
225	SP	N17585	G-BGLT	N55922	N289K	N225TR			
226	SP	N1902P	N1902L	N5DL					
227	SP	N818GA	N1841D	N1841L	N1BX	N18XX	N200LS	N264CL	
228	SP	N819GA	(N700CQ)	(N30B)	N157LH	N189WS			
229		N821GA	N702H	N117FJ	Substantially damaged La Guardia, NY, 25May97				
230		N17586	7T-VHB	w/o 03May82 over NW Iranian border					
231		N808GA	N1102	VR-CAG	VR-BHD	N18RN	N205K	N47EC	
232		N806GA	C-GDPB	N71WS	N508T	N10RQ			
233	TT	N807GA	N320TR	N233RS					
234	TT	N808GA	N910S	N910R	N480GA	N222PV	(N220GA)	N500JW	
235	TT	N17581	G-HADI	N5519C	N16FG	N256M	N430RG		
236	TT	N812GA	N2998	N630PM	N50PM	N54BM	N211DH		
237/43	2B	N816GA	N25BH	XA-MIX	XA-BAL	XA-SDM	EC-363	EC-FRV	
238	TT	N831GA	N335H						
239	TT	N17582	HZ-AFK						
240		5A-DDR	TT-AAI	(N240EA)					
241	SP	N830GA	(N60TA)	(N801GA)	N90MD	N902MP			
242		5A-DDS							
243		N119R	N119RC	N46TE	w/o 19Jan90 Little Rock, AR				
244		N17584	9K-AEB	N500T	N509T	N509TT	N811DF		
245/30	2B	N829GA	N141GS	N871D	N99WJ	N222NB			
246	TT	N17587	HB-IEZ	N14LT	N81RR				
247	SP	N828GA	N888MC	C-GTEP	N73MG	N75MG	N530GA		
248	SP	N17589	9K-AEC	N501T	N510T	N510TL	N248TH		
249		Gulfstream 3 airframe							
250	TT	N821GA	N309EL						
251		N944H	N9PG	N9PY	N567A	N36GS	N251JS		
252		Gulfstream 3 airframe							
253	SP	N15TG	N154C						
254/41	2B	N254AR	N706TS						
255/18	2B	N442A	N4NR						
256		N17581	HZ-MSD	N135WJ					
257/17	2B	N822GA	N872E	N411WW	N911WW	N56D			
258		N823GA	N301EC	N929GV	N437H				
775		see c/n 87							

Production complete

GULFSTREAM G1159B CONVERSION PROGRAMME

No	C/n	Completion date
1	70	17Sep81
2	32	02Apr82
3	36	13Aug82
4	30	06Aug82
5	148	18Aug82
6	775	19Sep82
7	75	16Nov82
8	4	29Nov82
9	73	15Dec82
10	104	09Feb83
11	139	15Mar83
12	42	05May83
13	16	09May83
14	155	22Jun83
15	166	14Jly83
16	86	09Aug83
17	257	17Oct83
18	255	09Nov83
19	199	04Jan84
20	219	17Feb84
21	88	18Feb84
22	119	27Mar84
23	131	25Apr84
24	151	04Jun84
25	123	11Jun84
26	125	11Jly84
27	64	28Sep84
29	48	02Nov84
30	245	10Jan85
31	156	19Feb85
32	102	07Mar85
33	9	30Apr85
34	207	02May85
35	198	07May85
36	54	05Jly85

PLUS

No	C/n	Completion date	
37	165	Dec85	
38	98	Jan86	
39	95	Mar86	
40	140	Jun86	
41	254	Sep86	(rolled out as G1159B 06Oct86)
42	189	Jly87	
43	237	Oct87	

The following aircraft were built as Gulfstream 2TT aircraft those marked * have been converted to SP

46, 127, 133, 173, 182, 183*, 201, 202, 203, 212, 216, 228*, 234, 235, 236, 238, 239, 246

G1159A GULFSTREAM III

C/n	Series	Identities								
249		N300GA	ff 02Dec79	N901GA	Denmark F-249					
252		(N777SL)	N17582	(N301GA)	XA-MEY					
300		N300GA	N700VA	N71TJ	N918BG*					
301		N100P	N21NY	(N100P)	N110BR	N444GA				
302		N302GA	N62GG	N2610	N56L	N56LA	(XA-TOT)	(N561ST)	VP-BCT	N49US
303		N300GA	N303GA	TU-VAF	rebuilt with wings fr G2B c/n 104/10				N1761W	N303GA
304		N17583	HZ-NR2	N600YY	N768J	N763J	(N18SL)	VR-BSL	N304TS	
305		N305GA	N235U	N305MD	N682FM	PK-OCN	N552JT	N553JT		
306		N306GA	N777SW	N72RK	N72PK	N862CE	N863CE	(N868CE)	N104BK	
307		N17584	C-GSBR	C-GGPM						
308		N717A	N606PT	VR-BNO	N308GA	N308HG				
309		N18LB	N1NA							
310		N719A	C-FYAG	N6513X	(N373LP)	(N173LP)				
311		N17585	HZ-AFL	N311GA	N721RB	N711SW*				
312		N304GA	N100GN	N200GN	N200JJ	N800JH				
313		Denmark F-313								
314		N1040	N1540	N1640	N93CX					
315		N315GA	N2600	N2600Z	N315GS	N710EC				
316		N316GA	N2601	N26018	PK-CAP	PK-BND	N316FA			
317		C-GKRL	N344GA	A6-CKZ	N83D	HZ-DG2				
318		N308GA	N300L	(N300LF)	(XA-)	N70050	N150GX	N150QX	N150RK	N500WW
319		N319Z	N200SK							
320		N873E	N69FF	VR-BNX	N320WE	N624BP				
321		N30RP	N94GC	N321GA	N100GX	N100QX	N313RG	N310RG	N9KL	
322		N130A	N110LE	(N110EE)	N322GA	N555NT	N600ES	N606ES	N706JA	
323		XA-MIC								
324		N17587	HZ-AFM	N44200	N67JR					
325		N890A	N89QA	N393U	N155MM					
326		N17582	TR-KHC	N333GA	(N326DD)	N420JC				
327		N70PS	(N72PS)	N57BJ	N777RY	N711LT				
328		N309GA	N75RP	N78RP	N98RP	N97AG				
329		N301GA	N862G	N1JN						
330		Denmark F-330		w/o 03Aug96 nr Vagar, Faroe Islands						
331		N307GA	N17LB	HZ-RC3						
332		N310GA	N77TG	N300BE	N65BE	N121JM				
333		N600PM	N50PM	N901FH						
334		N1PG	(N1PU)	N41PG	N700SB					
335		HB-IMX	N117MS							
336		N3PG	N3PY	(N523TX)	(N523PT)	N102PT*				
337		N456SW								
338		N862GA	N372CM	N372GM	N87HP	(N338RJ)	N750SW			
339		N302GA	N522SB	N339A	N684AT					
340		F-WDHK	F-GDHK	N99WJ	N90WJ	N340GA	N4PC	N2LY	N57NP	
341		N263C	N1PR							
342		N441A	N91LJ	N82A	N82AE	N1AQ	N1JK			
343		N305GA	N664P	N664S	N400AL	N221CM				
344		N306GA	N7000C	5N-IMR	N344DD					
345		N17585	G-BSAN	VR-CCN	G-GIII	5X-UOI	N76TJ			
346		N17581	HZ-RH2	HZ-HR2						
347		N17583	VR-BJE	N545JT						
348		N756S	N357PR							
349		N89AE	N89AB	N1KE	N6453	N6458	N711EG*			
350		N317GA	N1454H							
351		N888MC	N308AF	N836MF	N18TM	N623MS				
352		N17586	HB-ITM	Mexico TP-06 c/s XC-UJN						
353		N26619	HZ-BSA	HZ-108						
354		3D-AAC	3D-AAI	N16NK	N420RC					
355		N318GA	N676RW	(N103HS)	N876RW	8P-GAC	(N105HS)	N355TS		
356		N17608	A6-HEH	N356TJ	N356BR					
357		N303GA	N340	N802GA	N891MG					
358		N1761B	HZ-DA1	N9711N	N200DE	(N1149E)	N475DJ			
359		N800J	N305TC							
360		N341GA	N90LC	(N405LM)	N705JA					
361		(N875E)	N874RA	N361RA*						
362		N408M	N800AR							
363		N83AL	N77FK	N77EK						
364		N1761D	HZ-AFN							
365		N1761J	HZ-AFO	CN-ANU						
366		N2SP	N90SF	N222KC	N333KC	(N333KD)	N555KC	N333LX		
367		(N910A)	N17588	HB-ITN	(N6164Z)	N367GA	N700FS			
368		N17589	7T-VRB	N368GA	(N368TJ)	C-GBBB				
369		N910A	N740SS							
370		N319GA	N100A	N200A	N400K	N697BJ				
371		HZ-NR3	N680FM	N8220F	N681FM	N353VA				
372		N320GA	N200A	N500E	N500EX	N724DB				
373		N340GA	N232HC	VR-BAB	VP-BAB	N162JC				

GULFSTREAM III

C/n	Series	Identities									
374		N339GA	N122DJ	VR-CMF	N24GA	N270MC					
375		N955CP	VR-BOB	N375GA	N375NM	N375NW					
376		N17582	A6-HHS	N70AG	(N5HG)	N60AG					
377		N342GA	N40CH	N707RX							
378		N343GA	N955H	N378HC	N803CC	N960DC					
379		N17586	HZ-MAL	N379RH	N282Q	N28QQ	N900LA				
380		N345GA	N159B	N30WR							
381		N304GA	N277NS	(N46ES)	N747G	N1871R	N621S				
382	C20A	N305GA	83-0500								
383	C20A	N308GA	83-0501								
384		N1982C	N399WW	N399BH	N369CS						
385		N1761K	HZ-MS3								
386		N316GA	N902K	N902KB	Mexico TP-07 c/s XC-UJO						
387		N26L	N621JH	N621JA	N620JH						
388		N309GA	N902C	N1C	N748T	N561ST	N8JL				
389	C20A	N310GA	83-0502								
390		N200SF	VR-BKS	VR-BLO	VR-BOK	VP-BOK	N67TJ	N1M			
391		N349GA	N29S	N1S	N194	(N222AP)	N94BN	N14SY			
392		N30AH	N6BX	N6BZ	N60GN	N1GN	N9WN	N800WC			
393		N17587	A9C-BB	HZ-MWD	N33GZ						
394		N1761P	N311GA	N379XX							
395		N1761Q	PK-PJA								
396		N1761S	7T-VRC	N437GA	N800MK	N175BG					
397		N351GA	N59HA	N978FL	N692TV						
398		N315GA	N88AE	N827GA	N827G*						
399		N17581	7T-VRD	N188TJ	N528AP						
400		N17585	Venezuela 0005								
401		N352GA	N717	N400LH	(N80AG)	Denmark F-400		N97AG	N370FL		
402		N301GA	N303HB	N3338	VR-BLN	VP-BLN	w/o 06Feb98 Lac du Bourget, Chambery, France				
403		N347GA	N39NA	N39N	XA-TCO	(N333KC)	N403NW	XB-HIZ			
404		N355GA	N404M	N404MM	N403LM	(N402LM)	N8115N	N24TJ*			
405		N348GA	N40NB	N40N	N91CH	N91CR	N990WC	N991WC	(N9718P)	N789TP	N789TR*
406		N356GA	N80L								
407		N17603	G-XMAF	N407GA	N913MK						
408		N17608	9K-AEG	YI-AKI	reported w/o 1991 Baghdad Airport, Iraq during Operation Desert Storm; wreckage advertised for sale Jly92 by Kuwait Airways						
409		(N353GA)	N300BK	N320GA	N1526M	N1526R	N457ST	N457SF	N828MG		
410		N350GA	HZ-AFR								
411		N314GA	N966H	N461GT							
412		N354GA	N20XY	N50XY	N610CC	N105Y					
413		N357GA	N77SW	N778W	N1	N8226M	Ireland 249		N166WC	N766WC	
414		N358GA	N165ST	N165G							
415		N17582	(HZ-SOG)	HZ-HR4	HZ-NR2						
416		N312GA	N500AL	N883A	N4500X						
417		N317GA	N111AC	N1119C	N300M	N431JT					
418		N17583	JY-ABL	JY-AMN	N717TR	PT-ALK	N103CD				
419		9K-AEH	YI-AKJ	reported w/o 1991 Baghdad Airport, Iraq during Operation Desert Storm; wreckage advertised for sale Jly92 by Kuwait Airways							
420		N333GA	"40420"	N47449	India K2980/VT-ENR	(in 1997 did not carry marks K2980, inside or outside)					
421		N318GA	N99GA	N421GM	N721FF						
422		N319GA	N750AC	(N128AG)	N407CA						
423		N1761D	HZ-MIC	(VR-CMC)	N7134E	N225SF					
424		N320GA	N60AC	N228G	N94FL						
425		N344GA	N425SP	N492A							
426		N321GA	N151MZ	N751MZ	VR-CNJ	VP-CNJ	N703JA				
427		N327GA	N44MD	N42MD	N87AC	N300WY					
428		N322GA	N760A	N760G							
429		N323GA	N429SA	N423SA	N100HG						
430		N324GA	N760C	N23A	N600BG						
431		N25SB	(N259B)	PK-CTP	N99WJ						
432		N333GA	N713KM	N995BC	N997CM	(N997HM)	N704JA				
433		N325GA	N399CB	N579TG							
434		N326GA	N811JK	N311JK	N226G	N226GC	XA-SNG	XB-FXD	N23ET	(N23SK)	
435		N17581	HB-ITS	N435U	N888PM	N32KA					
436		N346GA	V8-HB3	V8-A11	V8-007	V8-009	N436GA	N10EH			
437		N380TT									
438		N302GA	N1841D	N911KT							
439		N17586	SU-BGU								
440		N304GA	N5103	(N3PY)	N222BW	N265A					
441		N306GA	N80J								
442		N17587	SU-BGV								
443		N315GA	N5104	N21AM							
444		N328GA	N110MT	N555HD							
445		N316GA	(N5103)	N5105							
446		N309GA	N446U								
447		N186DS	N186DC	N144PK	N707JA						
448		N339GA	N117JJ	N255SB	I-MADU	N123AP*					

GULFSTREAM III

C/n	Series	Identities									
449		N310GA	XA-FOU	N7C	N85V	N85VT					
450		N329GA	HZ-AFS	N329GA	PT-AAC	VR-CTG	N888VS				
451		(N370GA)	N330GA	Italy MM62022							
452		N331GA	N27R	N633P	VR-BNZ	VP-BNZ					
453		N332GA	HZ-109	Saudi Arabia 103		HZ-103					
454		N334GA	N60CT	N1GT	N273G	N111G					
455		N335GA	N1SF	(N103GA)	N103GC	N123CC	N123MR				
456	C20C	N336GA	US Army 85-0049								
457		N337GA	N457H	N972G							
458	C20C	N338GA	US Army 85-0050								
459		N321GA	N600B	N586C	N566C						
460		N322GA	N500LS	N500VS	N500MM	N500MN	I-FCHI	N2TQ	N2TF	N317ML	
461		N323GA	N104AR	N108AR							
462		N324GA	N303GA	TU-VAF							
463		N327GA	N80AT	N808T	VR-BMY	VP-BMY					
464		N340GA	N535CS								
465	C20B	N17586	86-0200	N465GA	Chile 911						
466		N17583	N325GA	N37HE							
467		N341GA	JY-HAH	N551AC							
468	C20B	N342GA	86-0202								
469		N343GA	JY-HZH	N1956M							
470	C20B	N344GA	86-0201								
471		N347GA	N888WL	N583D							
472		N348GA	N800CC	N806CC	N800CC	N806CC	N357H	N780RH			
473	C20C	N326GA	US Army 86-0403								
474		N311GA	D2-ECB								
475	C20B	N312GA	86-0203								
476	C20B	N314GA	86-0204								
477	C20B	N317GA	86-0205	US Coast Guard 01							
478	C20B	N318GA	86-0206								
479		N319GA	Italy MM62025								
480	C20D	N302GA	USN 163691								
481	C20D	N304GA	USN 163692								
482		N306GA	N333HK	N600BL	N164RJ						
483		N309GA	N66DD	N766DD							
484		N310GA	N4UP	N856W	N506T	VP-BOR					
485		N315GA	N721CW	N777MW							
486		N316GA	TJ-AAW								
487		N324GA	(TJ-)	TC-GAP	N377GA	N90005	N488SB	N618KM	N416WM		
488		N325GA	N700CN	(N100BG)	N800BG	N446GA	N401RJ	N401PJ	N399SC	(N45PG)	N500GF
489		N328GA	N272JS	N888CW							
490		N332GA	N28R	N388MM							
491		N337GA	N73RP	N998JB	N531JF	(N531JC)	N101PT				
492		N339GA	N212AT	N212AD	PT-WRC	N492DD	N188TC				
493		N322GA	N400J	N40QJ	Ghana G540						
494		N370GA	India K2961) order not confirmed								
495		N371GA	India K2962)								
496		N372GA	N310SL	N21NY	N89AE	N89AB	N99SC	(N99SU)	N843HS	VP-CNP	
497	C20E	N373GA	US Army 87-0139		N7096G	US Army 87-0139					
498	C20E	N374GA	US Army 87-0140		N7096E	US Army 87-0140					
875		N333GA	N333GU	N210GK	N290GA	N728CP	N845FW	N298TB			

Production complete

Notes: C/ns 494 and 495 only have three windows each side instead of the normal five, and both have a cargo door

GULFSTREAM IV

We have been advised by Gulfstream Aerospace that the Gulfstream IV does not have a type number. For many years we and other publications have referred to it as a G1159C therefore this nomenclature should be deleted.

C/n	Series	Identities							
1000		N404GA	ff 19Sep85		N234DB				
1001		N17581	N441GA	N400GA	VR-BSS	VP-BSS	N31001	N981SW	
1002		N440GA	N168WC						
1003		N403GA	N986AH	N685TA					
1004		N424GA							
1005		N17582	VR-BJZ	N823GA					
1006		N99GM	N3338						
1007		N420GA	N100GN	N100GJ	N59JR				
1008		N26LB	N10LQ	N10LB	VR-BLH	N412GA	N119R		
1009		N423GA	N500LS	N500VS	N700LS	N780LS	VR-BOY	Netherlands V-11	
1010		N426GA	N444TJ	N824CA					
1011		N17581	A6-HHH						
1012		N445GA	N636MF	N838MF					
1013		N446GA	N130B	N321PT	N321RT	N1625	(N16251)	N97FT	
1014		N447GA	N777SW	N779SW	Sweden 102001 code "021" (type Tp-102)				
1015		N17583	VR-BRF	VP-BRF					
1016		N427GA	N95AE	N29GY	N880GC				
1017		N405GA	N678RW	(C-FNCG)	VR-BHG	VP-BHG			
1018		N407GA	N300L	N43KS					
1019		N17584	TU-VAD						
1020		N408GA	N600CS	N9300	N93AT^				
1021		N412GA	N3M	N3NU	EC-HGH				
1022		"N63M" (painted on a/c but not officially regd)					N23M	N23MU	
1023		N415GA	N77SW	N778W	N85M				
1024		(N130B)	N412GA	N96AE					
1025		N419GA	N5BK	N420SZ	N420SL	N421SZ			
1026		N17584	N151A	N277RP	N277AG*				
1027		N416GA	TC-GAP						
1028		N428GA	N712CW	N712CC					
1029		N429GA	VR-BKI	VP-BKI	VP-BKH				
1030		N430GA	N811JK	N1WP					
1031		N434GA	HZ-AFU						
1032		N17585	C-FSBR	N315MA	N315MC	N888UE	N432QS	N254GA	
1033		(HB-IMY)	N69GP	N173LP	N1KE	N6453			
1034		N413GA	N800BG						
1035		N435GA	HZ-AFV						
1036		N152A							
1037		N17588	VR-BKE	HZ-ADC					
1038		N17603	N438GA	HZ-AFW					
1039		(N431GA)	N1901M						
1040		N432GA	N74RP	N620DS					
1041		N433GA	N366F						
1042		N17608	N400GA	N22	N220GA	N71TJ	N68SL		
1043		N1761B	TC-ANA	TC-ATA					
1044		N423GA	N1040	N1540	N154G				
1045		N420GA	N227G	N227GH					
1046		N1761D	(HB-ITT)	VR-BKU	(HB-ITE)	VR-BKU	HB-ITP	N119K	N400CC
1047		N1761J	N461GA	N23AC	w/o 30Oct96 Pal-Waukee, IL; canx Apr97				
1048		N1761K	N448GA	(VR-BKL)	SU-BGM				
1049		N402GA	N372CM						
1050		N153RA	N195WS						
1051		N403GA	N399CC						
1052		N419GA	N800CC	N940DC					
1053		N47SL	N26SL	N91AE	N165ST				
1054		N426GA	N400UP	N480UP	N745UP	N745UR	N789DK		
1055		N1761P	VR-BKV	XB-EXJ	XB-OEM	N255GA			
1056		N436GA	N33M	N33MX					
1057		N437GA	N43M	N43MU	N222AD				
1058		N458GA	N70PS	VP-BSF					
1059		N17581	V8-RB1	V8-AL1	V8-SR1	V8-007	N415GA	N701QS	N799WW
1060		N427GA	N1SF						
1061		N17582	N457GA	F-GPAK					
1062		N17583	N462GA	N688H	VR-CMF	VP-CMF			
1063		N17584	N54SB	N333AX					
1064		N439GA	HB-ITT	N7RP					
1065		N442GA	N584D	N511C					
1066		N443GA	N118R						
1067		N446GA	N145ST	N200LC					
1068		N17585	N95AE	N90AE	N82A				
1069		N459GA	N765A						
1070		N407GA	N107A						
1071		N410GA	N1						
1072		N17586	N100A	N500E					
1073		N75RP	N75PP	N177BB					
1074		N17587	(HB-I)	VR-BKT	VP-BKT				

GULFSTREAM IV

C/n	Series	Identities					
1075		N412GA	N901K	N121JJ			
1076		N17586	HZ-MNC	N338MM			
1077		N445GA	N119R	N119RC	PK-NSP	N477TS	N457DS
1078		N17589	(G-BPJM)	G-DNVT			
1079		N17603	XA-PUV	(N100WJ)	(N15WJ)	N479TS	N691RC
1080		N447GA	N20XY	N205X			
1081		N955H	(N955HC)	N777SA			
1082		N1082A	(N82BR)				
1083		N1761Q	HB-ITZ	VH-CCC			
1084		(N448GA)	N1761S	HB-IMY			
1085		N449GA	N88GA	N864CE			
1086		N460GA	N888MC	N23SY	N1086		
1087		N463GA	(N94SL)	N310SL	N1TM	N110TM	
1088		N464GA	N4UP	N2600			
1089		N465GA	N53M	N53MU			
1090		N466GA	VR-CYM	VP-CYM			
1091		N467GA	N364G				
1092		N468GA	N937US	N3H	N3HX	N661R	N18RF
1093		VR-BLC	HB-ITX				
1094		N2610					
1095		N469GA	N311EL				
1096		N17582	(G-)	VR-CBW	VP-CBW		
1097		N402GA	N900AL				
1098		N403GA	N404CC	XA-AIS	N282CD	N7800	
1099		N489H	N299FB	(N499QS)	N199QS	N999LX	
1100		N100AR	N100GX				
1101		N404GA	N365G				
1102		N405GA	N910B				
1103		N433GA	N90005	N103BC	VP-BIV		
1104		N600ML	N700GD				
1105		N408GA	N312EL				
1106		N17608	9M-ISJ				
1107		N17581	(JA8366)	N101MU	N11FX	VH-CCO	N74TJ	N844GS
1108		N17584	N410GA	N114AN	(N11AN)	N522AC	VH-NCP
1109		N1761D	V8-AL1	V8-SR1	V8-007	N101GA	
1110		N415GA	N404M	N404MY			
1111		N416GA	N111JL	N111ZT			
1112		N417GA	N12UT	N12U			
1113		N423GA	N902K	N168TR			
1114		N428GA	N444LT	N555WL	XA-BAL	XA-TOO	N314GA
1115		N430GA	N410M	N410MY			
1116		N431GA	N971L				
1117		N1761J	G-HARF				
1118		N439GA	N1526M	N2WL			
1119		N407GA	N614HF	N768J			
1120		N410GA	VR-BOB	N400SA	N70AG		
1121		N412GA	N7776	N411WW			
1122		N40N	N226G	N317M			
1123		N457GA	I-LUBI				
1124		N420GA	N1900W				
1125		N432GA	N415SH	N700WB	N888LK	N888LG	N56AG
1126		N426GA	5N-FGP				
1127		N427GA	VR-BLR	VR-BUS	VP-BUS		
1128		N429GA	HZ-MFL				
1129		N17585	EI-CAH	ZS-NMO			
1130		N436GA	N401MM	N404LM			
1131		N437GA	N679RW				
1132		N442GA	A6-ALI	N60NY	N604M		
1133		N443GA	N700CN				
1134		N445GA	VR-BJD	VP-BJD			
1135		N435GA	N500MM	N100ES			
1136		N401GA	N27CD				
1137		N402GA	N299DB	N21CZ	N7RX*		
1138		N403GA	N200A				
1139		N404GA	N99WJ	N21KR	N21KP*		
1140		N405GA	N811JK	(N827JK)			
1141		N407GA	N767FL	N767EL			
1142		N408GA	I-LADA	N142NW	N222		
1143		N410GA	HZ-AFX				
1144		N415GA	N100PM	N250J			
1145		N416GA	N102MU	N797CD			
1146		N417GA	N77SW	(N778W)	N777UE	N776US	
1147		N419GA	N200PM				
1148		N427GA	(JA8380)	N427GA	HB-IEJ		
1149		N430GA	N777SW	N149GU	N152KB	N108DB	
1150		N433GA	V8-AL1	V8-009	V8-SR1	N151G	VP-BIS
1151		N375GA	N80AT				
1152		N446GA	N63M	N63MU*			

GULFSTREAM IV

C/n	Series	Identities				
1153		N448GA	N110LE	N589HM	N590HM	
1154		N1761D	N150PG	N150GX	N151GX	N186DS
1155		N1761B	N910S			
1156		N1761K	N987AC	N987AR	VH-TGG	
1157		N17581	9K-AJA	N457GA		
1158		N17582	N917W			
1159		N17583	9K-AJB	N458FA		
1160		N17584	Ireland 251			
1161		N17585	9K-AJC	N459FA		
1162	C20F	N457GA	US Army 91-0108		N7096B	US Army 91-0108
1163		N458GA	Turkey 12-003			
1164		N459GA	N300GX	N420CC		
1165		N460GA	N780E			
1166		N461GA	HZ-SAR	HZ-AFY		
1167		N17586	N1SL			
1168		N462GA	A40-AB			
1169		N463GA	N500DG	N600DW		
1170		N464GA	N711SW	(N811SW)	N997BC	
1171		N465GA	N72RK	N686CG		
1172		N466GA	XA-SEC	N472TS	N85V	
1173		N17587	Botswana OK1			
1174		N467GA	N174LM	HB-IEQ	N174SJ	N4PC N6VB
1175		N17588	HB-ITJ	(N1175B)	VH-CCA	N18WF
1176		N468GA	V8-008	N176G	VP-CRY	
1177		N469GA	N677RW			
1178		N470GA	N900LS			
1179		N471GA	N41CP	N41QR	N265ST	
1180		N472GA	N700LS			
1181	C20?	N473GA	USAF 90-0300			
1182		N475GA	N200LS			
1183	SP	N476GA	ff as G1159C 23Dec91; converted to SP prototype and ff as such 24Jun92		VR-BDC	HB-IBX
1184		N477GA	N111NL			
1185	SP	N478GA	N485GA	N635AV		
1186		N479GA	8P-MAK	N345AA		
1187	C20G	N481GA	US Navy 165093 (cargo door)			
1188		N482GA	HL7222			
1189	C20G	N402GA	US Navy 165094; code JR (cargo door)			
1190		N403GA	JA001G			
1191	SP	N404GA	N979RA			
1192	SP	N407GA	N212K			
1193	SP	N412GA	(N980ML)	N163M	N620K	
1194	SP	N415GA	N77CP	N77QR	N473CW*	
1195	SP	N419GA	XA-CHR	N47HR	N867CE	N888PM
1196		N420GA	A40-AC			
1197		N423GA	N150GX	XA-CAG	N969SG	
1198		N425GA	N99GA			
1199	C20G	N428GA	US Navy 165151; code RG			
1200	C20G	N430GA	US Marines 165153			
1201	C20G	N431GA	US Navy 165152			
1202		N432GA	V8-MSB	V8-009	JY-RAY	
1203	SP	N434GA	N410WW			
1204		N435GA	N212AT			
1205	SP	N439GA	VH-ASQ	N8203K		
1206		N437GA	N1040			
1207		N441GA	C-FDCS	C-FJES	N77SW	
1208	SP	N443GA	VR-BNY	VP-BNY		
1209		N445GA	N157H			
1210		N448GA	(N909SP)	N9PC	N410QS	N144PK
1211		N447GA	N2107Z			
1212	SP	N413GA	VR-BOT	VP-BOT	N88HP	
1213		N416GA	N56L			
1214		N405GA	N414BM	N2615		
1215	SP	N426GA	Sweden 102002 (type Tp-102B)			
1216	SP	N440GA	Sweden 102003 (type Tp-102B)			
1217	SP	N417GA	N981HC	N711MC	N711HE*	
1218	SP	N418SP	N5MC			
1219	SP	N446GA	PK-NZK	N50HE	N87HP	
1220	SP	N449GA	N79RP			
1221	SP	N451GA				
1222	SP	N452GA	N71RP	N171JC*		
1223	SP	N453GA	N935SH	N257H		
1224	SP	N454GA	N18TM			
1225	SP	N459GA	N316GS			
1226	SP	N460GA	N41PR			
1227	SP	N463GA	(XA-VAD)	XA-DPS	N626TG	N626TC
1228	SP	N464GA	N18AN			
1229	SP	N465GA	N830EC	N270SC		
1230	SP	N467GA	9M-TRI	N101CV		

GULFSTREAM IV

C/n	Series	Identities					
1231	SP	N470GA	N250VC				
1232	SP	N471GA	N232K				
1233	SP	N472GA	N575SF				
1234	SP	N475GA	N924ML	I-LXGR			
1235	SP	N477GA	N100A				
1236	SP	N478GA	N100GN				
1237	SP	N480GA	N1904W				
1238	SP	N483GA	N499SC	(N71LA)	N92LA		
1239	SP	N484GA	N1JN	N909RX			
1240	SP	N486GA	N333PV				
1241	SP	N487GA	N169CA				
1242	SP	N490GA	N982HC				
1243	SP	N491GA	N404SP	VR-CBL	N39WH	N37WH	N39WH*
1244	SP	N404GA	JA002G				
1245	SP	N405GA	N101HC	(N7602)	N7601		
1246	SP	N407GA	N49RF				
1247	SP	N408GA	(N990UH)	N14UH	N477RP		
1248	SP	N422GA	N62MS				
1249	SP	N423GA	N63HS				
1250	SP	N425GA	VR-CBB	VP-CBB			
1251	SP	N429GA	(N321PT)	N60PT	N60PE		
1252	SP	N433GA	N252C				
1253	SP	N435GA	N676RW				
1254	SP	N436GA	N801CC	N930DC			
1255	SP	N437GA	N600PM				
1256	C20H	N438GA	USAF 92-0375				
1257	SP	N448GA	N4CP				
1258	SP	N416GA	N400UP	N585D			
1259	SP	N495GA	N1PG				
1260	SP	N461GA	N3PG				
1261	SP	N469GA	N399CB				
1262	SP	N496GA	N462QS				
1263	SP	N497GA	N830CB	N263S			
1264	SP	N499GA	N464QS				
1265	SP	N465GA	N540W				
1266	SP	N412GA	N300K	N61LA	N91LA		
1267	SP	N417GA	N301K	N624GJ			
1268	SP	N427GA	N990WC				
1269	SP	N434GA	N677SW				
1270	U4	N442GA	Japan 75-3251				
1271	U4	N452GA	Japan 75-3252				
1272	SP	N454GA	N621JH				
1273	SP	N457GA	N372BC	N372BG			
1274	SP	N458GA	LV-WOW (painted in error)			LV-WOM	
1275	SP	N459GA	N475QS				
1276	SP	N460GA	N1955M				
1277	SP	N462GA	N5GF				
1278	SP	N464GA	VR-CTA	N98LT			
1279	SP	N466GA	N2002P				
1280	SP	N468GA	N531MD				
1281	SP	N470GA	N481QS				
1282	SP	N471GA	(N96FL)	VR-CFL	VP-CFL		
1283	SP	N472GA	N401JL				
1284	SP	N475GA	N1GN	N21GN	N150CM	(N577SW)	N90AM
1285	SP	N477GA	N874A				
1286	SP	N480GA	(N486GA)	N286GA	N464SP		
1287	SP	N484GA	N487QS				
1288	SP	N403GA	7T-VPR				
1289	SP	N405GA	N844HS	N802WC			
1290	SP	N408GA	N6NB	N730BA			
1291	SP	N412GA	7T-VPS				
1292	SP	N413GA	N1GT				
1293	SP	N415GA	N493QS				
1294	SP	N416GA	HZ-MAL	N416GA	HZ-KAA		
1295	SP	N417GA	N495QS				
1296	SP	N419GA	N725LB				
1297	SP	N420GA	LV-WSS				
1298	SP	N422GA	N501PC				
1299	SP	N423GA	N499QS				
1300	SP	N432GA	N1BN				
1301	SP	N433GA	N92AE				
1302	SP	N434GA	(N98AE)	N93AE			
1303	U4	N435GA	Japan 85-3253				
1304	SP	N436GA	N404QS				
1305	SP	N439GA	(N913SC)	N888SQ			
1306	SP	N441GA	N540CH				
1307	SP	N443GA	N94AE				
1308	SP	N446GA	N408QS				

GULFSTREAM IV

C/n	Series	Identities		
1309	SP	N447GA	N309GA	
1310	SP	N448GA	(N2425)	N902
1311	SP	N449GA	N411QS	
1312	SP	N453GA	9M-ABC	
1313	SP	N455GA	N94LT	
1314	SP	N461GA	N429SA	
1315	SP	N413GA	N315GA	
1316	SP	N427GA	N416QS	
1317	SP	N417GA	N929WT	
1318	SP	N418GA	N1624	
1319	SP	N429GA	N878SM	
1320	SP	N437GA	N420QS	
1321	SP	N444GA	(N600CC)	N500CD
1322	SP	N445GA	N422QS	
1323	SP	N454GA	N503PC	
1324	SP	N457GA	N424QS	
1325	SP	N459GA	N102FM	
1326	U4	N325GA	Japan 95-3254	
1327	SP	N327GA	TR-KHD	TR-KSP
1328	SP	N328GA	N428QS	
1329	SP	N329GA	SU-BNC	
1330	SP	N324GA	N400J	
1331	SP	N331GA	N878G	
1332	SP	N332GA	SU-BND	
1333	SP	N333GA	N800J	
1334	SP	N334GA	N434QS	
1335	SP	N335GA	N720BA	
1336	SP	N636GA	N41CP	
1337	SP	N637GA	N52MK	
1338	SP	N638GA	N401WT	
1339	SP	N339GA	N327TL	
1340	SP	N340GA	N1TF	N800AL
1341	SP	N341GA	N441QS	
1342	SP	N342GA	N555KC	
1343	SP	N343GA	N99SC	
1344	SP	N344GA	N18AC	
1345	SP	N345GA	(JY-ONE)	N457ST
1346	SP	N346GA	N104AR	
1347	SP	N347GA	N988H	
1348	SP	N348GA	N80A	
1349	SP	N349GA	HZ-KS1	
1350	SP	N330GA	N396U	
1351	SP	N351GA	N451QS	
1352	SP	N352GA	N452QS	
1353	SP	N353GA	A9C-BAH	
1354	SP	N354GA	N397J	N397JJ
1355	SP	N355GA	N66DD	
1356	SP	N319GA	(JY-TWO)	N600DR
1357	SP	N357GA	N77FK	
1358	SP	N358GA	N1625	
1359	SP	N359GA	Japan 05-3255	
1360	SP	N360GA	N460QS	
1361	SP	N361GA	N545CS	
1362	SP	N362GA	N888LK	
1363	SP	N363GA	N463QS	
1364	SP	N364GA	N143KS	
1365	SP	N365GA	HZ-MS04	
1366	SP	N320GA	N404M	
1367	SP	N367GA	HZ-KS2	
1368	SP	N322GA	N1967M	
1369	SP	N323GA	N469QS	
1370	SP	N370GA	N240CX	
1371	SP	N371GA	VP-CIP	
1372	SP	N372GA	N472QS	
1373	SP	N373GA	N373KM	N106KA
1374	SP	N374GA	N7PG*	N1PG^
1375	SP	N375GA		
1376	SP	N376GA	N12NZ	
1377	SP	N377GA	N477QS	
1378	SP	N378GA	N2PG	
1379	SP	N379GA	N60PT	
1380	SP	N380GA	N480QS	
1381	SP	N381GA	VP-BZA	
1382	SP	N382GA	N1TF	
1383	SP	N383GA	N955H	
1384	SP	N384GA	HZ-KS3	
1385	SP	N485GA	N577SW*	
1386	SP	N486GA	N486QS	

GULFSTREAM IV

C/n	Series	Identities		
1387	SP	N487GA	N254SD	
1388	SP	N477GA	N38BG*	
1389	SP	N389GA	N489QS	
1390	SP	N490GA		
1391	SP	N391GA		
1392	SP	N392GA	N492QS*	
1393	SP	N393GA	N297MC*	
1394	SP	N394GA	N721RL*	
1395	SP	N395GA		
1396	SP	N396GA	N890A*	
1397	SP	N397GA	N669BJ*	
1398	SP	N398GA	N498QS*	
1399	SP	N499GA		
1400	SP	N478GA		
1401	SP	N401GA		
1402	SP	N479GA	N602PM	
1403	SP	N403GA	N403QS*	
1404	SP	N404GA	N404HS*	
1405	SP	N310GA		
1406	SP	N311GA		
1407	SP	N312GA		
1408	SP	N316GA	(N448QS)	N401QS
1409	SP	N317GA		
1410	SP	N318GA		
1411	SP	N411GA		
1412	SP	N412GA		
1413	SP	N413GA		
1414	SP	N323GA		
1415	SP	N415GA		
1416	SP	N416GA		
1417	SP	N417GA	N417QS*	
1418	SP	N418GA		
1419	SP	N419GA		
1420	SP	N420GA		
1421	SP	N324GA		
1422	SP	N422GA		
1423	SP	N423GA		
1424	SP	N328GA		
1425	SP	N425GA		
1426	SP	N426GA		
1427	SP	N427GA		
1428	SP	N330GA		
1429	SP	N429GA		
1430	SP	N331GA		
1431	SP	N334GA		
1432	SP	N335GA		
1433	SP			
1434	SP			
1435	SP			
1436	SP			
1437	SP			
1438	SP			
1439	SP			
1440	SP			
1441	SP			
1442	SP			
1443	SP			
1444	SP			
1445	SP			
1446	SP			
1447	SP			
1448	SP			
1449	SP			
1450	SP			
1451	SP			
1452	SP			
1453	SP			
1454	SP			
1455	SP			
1456	SP			
1457	SP			
1458	SP			
1459	SP			
1460	SP			
1461	SP			
1462	SP			
1463	SP			
1464	SP			

GULFSTREAM IV

C/n	Series	Identities
1465	SP	
1466	SP	
1467	SP	
1468	SP	
1469	SP	
1470	SP	
1471	SP	
1472	SP	
1473	SP	
1474	SP	
1475	SP	
1476	SP	
1477	SP	
1478	SP	
1479	SP	
1480	SP	
1481	SP	
1482	SP	
1483	SP	
1484	SP	
1485	SP	
1486	SP	
1487	SP	
1488	SP	
1489	SP	
1490	SP	
1491	SP	
1492	SP	
1493	SP	
1494	SP	
1495	SP	
1496	SP	
1497	SP	
1498	SP	
1499	SP	
1500	SP	

GULFSTREAM V

We have been advised by Gulfstream Aerospace that the Gulfstream V does not have a type number and is therefore not the G1159D as has been quoted elsewhere.

C/n	Series	Identities						
501		N501GV	rolled out 22Sep95; ff 28Nov95 N22					
502		N502GV	N502KA					
503		N503GV	N767FL					
504		N504GV	N313RG					
505		N505GV	EI-WGV					
506		N506GV	N158AF					
507		N507GA	N300L					
508		N508GA	N777GV	N899GM				
509		N509GA	V8-009	V8-001	V8-009	N509GA	N61GV+	N5GA
		+ (for display purposes at the NBAA 1999 convention)						
510		N598GA	N513MW					
511		N511GA	VP-CBX					
512		N512GV	N636MF					
513		N513GA	HB-IVL					
514		N514GA	N777SW	N304K				
515		N599GA	V8-007	V8-001				
516		N516GA	N555CS	N740BA				
517		N517GA	HB-IMJ					
518		N518GA	HZ-MIC	N555GN	(N36GA)	N1GN	N555GN	N555GV
519		N597GA	VP-CMG					
520		N596GA	N17GV					
521	C-37A	N521GA	USAF 97-0400					
522		N595GA	(N158RA)	N39PY	N20H^			
523		N523GA	N711SW	N790MC				
524		N524GA	N400JD					
525		N594GA	N252JS					
526		N526GA	N675RW					
527		N527GA	N5SA					
528		N528GA	N80RP	N75RP				
529		N529GA	N73RP					
530		N530GA	N780F					
531		N531GA	(N8CA)	N531AF				
532		N532GA	N282Q					
533		N533GA	XA-CPQ					
534		N534GA	(N158JJ)	N920DC				
535		N593GA	N775US					
536		N536GA	N5UH					
537		N537GA	8P-MAK					
538		N538GA	N601MD					
539		N539GA	N1GC					
540		N640GA	XA-OEM					
541		N641GA	N405LM					
542	C-37A	N642GA	USAF 97-0401					
543		N643GA	N91CW					
544		N644GA	N910DC					
545		N645GA	N1HC					
546		N646GA	XA-BAL					
547		N647GA	N73M					
548		N648GA	N245TT					
549		N649GA	N317JD	(N718MC)				
550		N650GA	N5101					
551		N651GA	N5102					
552		N652GA	N9SC					
553		N653GA	N516GH					
554		N654GA	N589HM					
555		N655GA	VP-BSM					
556		N656GA	N556AR					
557		N657GA	N83M					
558		N658GA	N750BA					
559		N659GA	N559GV					
560		N660GA	9K-AJD					
561		N661GA						
562		N662GA	N95AE					
563		N463GA	N8CA					
564		N664GA	(JY-)	N18VS+	N664GA	N54PR		
		+ (for display purposes at the NBAA 1999 convention)						
565		N460GA	N77CP					
566	C-37?	N466GA	US Army 97-0049					
567		N467GA	N93M					
568		N461GA	N845HS					
569		N469GA	9K-AJE					
570		N470GA	N451CS					
571	C-37A	N671GA	USAF 99-0402					
572		N472GA						

GULFSTREAM V

C/n	Series	Identities		
573		N673GA	9K-AJF	
574		N674GA	N1KE	
575		N475GA	N410M	
576		N476GA	N991LF	
577		N577GA	HB-IVZ	
578		N578GA	N1GN	
579		N579GA	N23M	
580		N580GA	N1540	
581		N581GA	N379P	
582		N582GA	N271JG	
583		N583GA		
584		N584GA	N84GV	
585		N585GA	N18NK	N16NK*
586		N586GA		
587		N587GA	N300K*	
588		N588GA		
589		N589GA	N15UC*	
590		N590GA		
591		N591GA	N301K*	
592		N592GA		
593		N593GA		
594		N594GA		
595		N595GA		
596		N596GA		
597		N495GA	N302K*	
598		N598GA		
599		N496GA		
600		N650GA		
601		N536GA		
602		N538GA		
603		N539GA		
604		N551GA		
605		N554GA		
606		N558GA		
607		N559GA		
608		N561GA		
609		N566GA		
610		N567GA		
611		N568GA		
612		N569GA		
613		N570GA		
614		N571GA		
615		N572GA		
616		N574GA		
617		N575GA		
618		N585GA		
619		N608GA		
620		N535GA		
621		N621GA		
622		N622GA		
623		N623GA		
624		N624GA		
625				
626				
627				
628				
629				
630				
631				
632				
633				
634				
635				
636				
637				
638				
639				
640				
641				
642				
643				
644				
645				
646				
647				
648				
649				
650				

GULFSTREAM V

C/n	Series	Identities
651		
652		
653		
654		
655		
656		
657		
658		
659		
660		

IAI 1125 ASTRA

Note: The SPX has model number 1125A

C/n	Series	Identities						
001		4X-WIN	ff 19Mar84; wfu Aug86					
002		4X-WIA						
003		non-flying test airframe						
004		4X-CUA	N96PC	N425TS+	N96PC	N425TS	OB-1703	
		+ marks painted on aircraft but not officially regd						
005		)						
006		)						
007		) aircraft not built as the owner of the first aircraft to be delivered specified that he did not want						
008		) one of the first ten aircraft being built!						
009		)						
010		)						
011		4X-CUK	N450PM	N450BM	N705MA			
012		4X-CUL	N1125A	N25AG	N312W	N27BH	N610HC	
013		4X-CUM	(N413SC)	N713SC	N112PR			
014		4X-CUN	N400J	N400JF	N8484P	N116JC		
015		4X-CUP	N887PC	N46UF	N46UP	N14SR		
016		4X-CUK	N716W	N36FD	N221DT	N221PA		
017		4X-CUD	N717WW	VR-BES	N996JP	N711JG	N711JQ*	
018		4X-CUR	N1188A	N500M	N500MQ	N72FL		
019		4X-CUE	N30AJ	N49MW	(N499MW)	N49MN		
020		4X-CUS	N279DP					
021		4X-CUR	N1125A	N1125S				
022		4X-CUT	PT-MBZ					
023		4X-CUG	N125GB	N23TJ	N345GC			
024		4X-CUT	N300JJ	N999BL				
025		4X-CUH	N387PA					
026		4X-CUI	N120BJ	N120WH	N120WS	N9VL	N24PR	
027		4X-CUJ	N199GH	N199HF				
028		N10MZ	N11MZ	N816HB				
029		N79AD	N15TW	N94TW	N154DD	N131DA		
030		4X-CUI	N50AJ	N90U	N90UG			
031		N40AJ	N125AJ	N987GK				
032		4X-CUN	N1125A	N232S	N125MG			
033		4X-CUP	N980ML	N922RA	N52KS	N441BC		
034		4X-CUJ	N53SF	VR-CMG	N511WA			
035		N1125K						
036		I-FLYL	N82RT	N195FC				
037		N3PC	N589TB	N100SR				
038		N803JW	N930SC*					
039		N359V	N359VP	N359VS	N402TS	N885CA*		
040		N279DS						
041	SP	N96AR	VR-BME	N45MS				
042	SP	N60AJ	N575ET	N575EW	EC-339	EC-GIA	N588R	N528RR
043	SP	N56AG	(N34CE)	N90CE				
044	SP	N50AJ	N676TC					
045	SP	N91FD	VH-FIS	D-CFIS	VH-FIS			
046	SP	N140DR	N630S					
047	SP	N30AJ	(N134RV)	N166RM				
048	SP	N1125V	N88MF					
049	SP	N1125Y	JA8379	N4420E	N145AS	N323P		
050	SP	N4EM	XA-TJF					
051	SP	N1125A						
052	SP	N90AJ						
053	SP	N227N	N227NL	(N315S)				
054	SP	N70AJ	N198HF					
055	SP	4X-CUI	N1125Z	N1MC	N828C			
056	SP	4X-CUG	N3175T	N790FH				
057	SP	4X-CUH	N3175S	YV-2199P	YV-785CP	YV-2564P		
058	SP	N1125E	C-FDAX					
059	SP	N4341S	D-CCAT					
060	SP	N227AN	YV-757CP	VR-BON	VP-BON			
061	SP	4X-CUG	N60AJ	N550M				
062	SP	4X-CUJ	N1125	N999GP	N9990P	N100AK		
063	SP	4X-CUI	Eritrea 901		call sign	ER-J901	N74TJ	N331SK
064	SP	N650GE						
065	SP	N75TT	N50TG	N50TQ				
066	SP	N101NS	N419MK					
067	SP	N20FE	N28NP	(N28NR)	N28NF			
068	SP	N1125Z						
069	SP	N804JW						
070	SP	N300AJ	N805JW					
071	SP	4X-CUW	N60AJ					
072	SP	N1125L	N314AD					
073	SPX	4X-WIX	N173W	first model SPX; has winglets and model number 1125A				
074	SP	N500AJ						

ASTRA

C/n	Series	Identities					
075	SP	4X-CUW	ZS-BCT	N75GZ			
076	SP	4X-CUV	N1125	4X-CUV	N1125	N1125G	
077	SP	N220AJ	N771CP	YV-771CP			
078	SP	N1125J					
079	SPX	4X-CUX	C-FCFP				
080	SPX	4X-CUY	(D-CCBT)	N333AJ	N333CZ	VP-CUT	C-GSSS
081	SPX	N800AJ					
082	SPX	N121GV					
083	SPX	N383SF					
084	SPX	N795HP	N795HB				
085	SPX	N796HP	N796HR				
086	SPX	N793A	PT-WBC				
087	SPX	4X-CUU	C-FRJZ				
088	SPX	N398AG	USAF 94-1569		(C-38A)		
089	SPX	N918MK					
090	SPX	N399AG	USAF 94-1570		(C-38A)		
091	SPX	N297GA	N500MZ	N500M			
092	SPX	N789A	VP-BMA	N92UJ	N8MC*		
093	SPX	N65TD					
094	SPX	N294S					
095	SPX	N98AD					
096	SPX	N66KG	VP-CKG				
097	SPX	N273RA					
098	SPX	N275RA					
099	SPX	N987A	5B-CJG				
100	SPX	N807JW					
101	SPX	N202GA	N297GA	N711WK			
102	SPX	N525M	N359V				
103	SPX	N755A					
104	SPX	N957P					
105	SPX	N217PT	HB-VMG				
106	SPX	N122GV					
107	SPX	N997GA	D-CRIS				
108	SPX	N998GA	N999GP				
109	SPX	N96FL					
110	SPX	N97FL					
111	SPX	N848GA	N297GA	HB-			
112	SPX	N633GA	N1MC				
113	SPX	N113GA	HB-VMK	N35GX	N297GA*		
114	SPX	N114GA	N114SN				
115	SPX	N526GA					
116	SPX	N527GA	N456PR				
117	SPX	N528GA					
118	SPX	N529GA					
119	SPX		for Taiwan				
120	SPX	N635GA					
121	SPX	N843GA					
122	SPX	N69GX					
123	SPX	N36GX					
124	SPX	N42GX					
125	SPX	N44GX					
126							
127							
128							
129							
130							
131							
132							
133							
134							
135							

IAI 1126 GALAXY

C/n	Series	Identities				
001		reportedly non-flying test airframe				
002		reportedly non-flying test airframe				
003		4X-IGA	rolled out 04Sep97; ff 25Dec97			
004		4X-IGO	4X-CVF (not confirmed)		(N7AU)	N844GA
005		4X-IGB	N505GA			
006		N7AU				
007		N847GA	(C-GRJZ)	HB-IUT		
008		N998G				
009		N849GA				
010		N808JW				
011		N634GA	HB-IUU			
012		N845GA				
013		N13GX				
014		N37GX				
015		N38GX				
016		N40GX				
017		N48GX				
018						
019						
020						
021						
022						
023						
024						
025						
026						
027						
028						
029						
030						
031						
032						
033						
034						
035						
036						
037						
038						
039						
040						

JET COMMANDER/WESTWIND

C/n	Series	Identities
1	1121	N610JC ff 27Jan63 N112AC N172AC dismantled 1975
2	1121	N611JC test aircraft for static fatigue
3	1121	N612J N316 N316E N400WT N409WT
4	1121	N77F N77TC N72TC N72TQ
5	1121	N364G N334RK N18CA C-GKFT N18CA cx Oct86; b/u Miami, FL mid 1986; remains to Dodson Avn, Ottawa, KS
6	1121	N5418 CF-ULG N420P N42QB wfu; cx Dec91; b/u 1982 by White Inds, Bates City, MO
7	1121	N112JC N1173Z N22CH N30RJ (N711VK) N77KT N77NT b/u for spares 1989; cx Nov91
8	1121	N157JF N31CF N749MC N749MP N101LB wfu 1998 Tucson, AZ
9	1121	N450JD N459JD CF-WUL N9BY N66EW N89MR (N98KK) wfu cx Jan94 remains to Aviation Warehouse prop facility at El Mirage CA
10	1121	N31S N31SB N600CD N5BP N9023W wfu Jul87 Bardufoss Videregarude Skole, Norway; TT 5322 hrs
11	1121	N1172Z N1172L N111TD
12	1121	N8300 N613J N777V N37BB N711GW N302AT N344DA LV-RDD w/o (details unknown); wreckage noted 14May92 Moran, Argentina
13	1121	N450RA N50VF N12CJ N1JU (N404PC) XA-SFS wfu; b/u 1983 by White Inds, Bates City, MO
14	1121	N350M N121BN N87DC N87DG scrapped remains with White Inds, Bates City, MO; cx Jly94
15	1121	N365G HB-VAX N125K N320W wfu; b/u 1983 by White Inds, Bates City, MO; cx Apr91
16	1121	N96B N217PM N177A YV-123CP wfu Mar93 Caracas, Venezuela; derelict Feb97
17	1121	(HB-VAL) CF-SUA C-FSUA N91669 wfu - still current remains to Aviation Warehouse prop facility at El Mirage CA
18	1121	N1166Z N121HM wfu Dec79 Skolen for Luftfahrtsuddannel, Copenhagen-Kastrup, Denmark
19	1121	N95B sold May88 in Norway as technical airframe
20	1121	N334LP N1121E
21	1121	N252R CF-WOA N2579E wfu; b/u 1983 by White Inds, Bates City, MO; last allocated US marks not worn; cx Mar91
22	1121	N148E w/o 13Sep68 Burbank, CA
23	1121	N2100X N349M b/u 1983 by White Inds, Bates City, MO
24	1121	N94B N360M N360MC N7GW N360MC N560MC wfu 1993
25	1121	N555DM to spares 1992 with Dodson Avn, Ottawa, KS; cx Aug92
26	1121	N614J N614JC N10MC N77FV cx Oct88; to spares Aug88 Wiley Post, OK
27	1121	N93B N93BE b/u for spares 1989 by White Inds, Bates City, MO; cx Apr91
28	1121	N1190Z N77NR N234G
29	1121	N615J 4X-COJ w/o 21Jan70 Tel Aviv, Israel
30	1121	N401V N400CP w/o 21Jan71 Burlington, VT
31	1121	N399D N99GS wfu 1994
32	1121B	N92B N92BT N32JC N101BU N98SC
33	1121	N1180Z N151CR N104CJ VT-ERO wfu and b/u in India, rear fuselage and some other parts to Hollister CA
34	1121	N1210 N1210G N102SV N102SY N329HN N777MH N130RC N111XL N500MF TG-OMF N500MF wfu; remains with White Inds, Bates City, MO
35	1121	N6504V N22AC N100TH N101GS N189G N7HL N710JW cx Nov92 as "destroyed/scrapped"
36	1121	N1121M N730PV N780PV sold May88 in Norway as technical airframe
37	1121	N967L N123JB N723JB N445 noted derelict 11May88 Wiley Post, OK; still regd
38	1121	N901JL N217PM N217AL N1776F (N200WN) N106CJ N37SJ
39	1121	N6505V N550NM N666JD N66TS N80TF N1BC N16FP N10EA wfu May82 Skolen for Luftfahrtsuddannel, Copenhagen-Kastrup, Denmark; cx Apr91
40	1121	N913HB N40JC N40AJ N40UA wfu; remains with White Inds, Bates City, MO
41	1121	N6510V N187G N41FL ZP- N40593 N499TR
42	1121	N6511V N599KC N3DL N6361C N111Y (N359C) N111YL noted derelict 12Mar86 Wiley Post, OK; cx Jly94 wfu
43	1121	N6518V N271E N186G N121CS (N385G) N386G wfu; b/u for parts 1989; cx Oct90
44	1121	N200M N700C N700CB N273LP N273LF N69GT N60CD
45	1121	N920R N340DR N340ER N121PG N910MH wfu; at aeronautical college, nr.La Guardia A/P, NY
46	1121	N1500C N200BP N200RM N200GT N220ST N99W wfu for spares at Tamiami, FL
47	1121	N6513V HB-VBX N33GL N222GL N222HM N200LF cx Sep87; b/u for parts by White Inds, Bates City, MO
48	1121	N541SG N541M N400LR N444WL N8LC N486G N85MA N929GV N502U N301AJ w/o 13Aug90 Cozumel, Mexico; cx Oct92
49	1121	N430C N5JR wfu; remains with White Inds, Bates City, MO
50	1121	N612JC N133ME in scrapyard 12Oct88 Wiley Post, OK; still regd
51	1121	N618JC SE-DCK N303LA N69WW N21BC N93JR N18JL N1EC b/u Dodson Avn, Ottawa, KS; cx Sep94
52	1121	N701AP N1121G N696GW N159YC N159MP N159DP wfu; displayed Darwin Aviation Museum, Australia; some parts to Dodson Avn, Ottawa, KS
53	1121	N1230 N1230D N10MF N103F N925HB N27BD wfu; remains with White Inds, Bates City, MO
54	1121	N6534V N848C cx Aug88; b/u for spares 1989
55	1121B	(D-CHAS) D-CEAS 4X-CON N11MC N747LB
56	1121	N6550V (N53AA) N382AA
57	1121	N6544V N770WL N121AJ wfu May82; b/u for spares
58	1121	N90B N721AS N120GH N660W N957RC CP-2263
59	1121	N6538V N59JC N21AK b/u for spares; still regd
60	1121	N6545V N100RC w/o 14Nov70 Lexington, KY

JET COMMANDER/WESTWIND

C/n	Series	Identities
61	1121	N1196Z N666DC N51CH N100NR N999FB N29LP N29LB w/o 19Dec80 Many Airport, LA
62	1121	N5415 N1777T C-GKFS N1777T wfu circa 1995 at Tucson, AZ
63	1121	N6546V N7784 N15G N9DM N8GA N8GE wfu to spares White Inds, Bates City, MO
64	1121	N6512V N500GJ N124JB N124VS wfu Manila, Philippines circa 1999
65	1121	N500JR w/o 26Sep66 North Platte, SD
66	1121	N1966J wfu; remains with White Inds, Bates City, MO
67	1121	N650M N1121G wfu; used for spares by Dodson Avn, Ottawa, KS
68	1121	N196KC w/o 01Jly68 Fayetteville, AR
69	1121	N6527V N89B N10SN N50JP wfu; remains with Dodson Avn, Ottawa, KS
70	1121	N1194Z N129K wfu; remains with White Inds, Bates City, MO
71	1121	N1500M N150CM N150CT N150HR N721GB 4X-COA preserved Israeli Air Force Museum at Hatzerim with Mig-21 nose
72	1121	N757AL N777WJ N7KR I-LECO N2WU VR-CAU N2WU w/o 02Dec90 Laguna del Saule, Uruguay
73	1121	N98SA N98S N100W N100WM parted out at Sarasota, FL
74	1121	N6610V N535D N47DM N300DH N93RM N74GM
75	1121	N6611V N1121R N212CW wfu with White Inds, Bates City, MO
76	1121	N6612V N1121C CF-VVX N100DG N100DR N100TR wfu with OK Aircraft, Gilroy, CA; still regd - fuselage reported at Hollister, CA, Sep95
77	1121	N1121X N523AC N442WT N11BK N21JW N121JC N177JC
78	1121	N6613V N1121E N866DH N102CJ used as spares at Opa Locka, FL, circa Dec95
79	1121	N454SR N100LL N36PT reportedly scrapped; cx Jan97
80	1121	N87B N900JL N173AR N925R wfu 1994
81	1121	N6617V CF-KBI C-FEYG w/o 26May78 Winnipeg, Canada
82	1121	N9932 N4NK N82JC N927S C-GPDH N103BW N240AA
83	1121A	N4550E N23FF N83AL C-GHPR N503U w/o 19Dec95 Guatemala City, Guatemala
84	1121	N312S N600TD N600TP N600ER N16MK
85	1121	N4554E N201S XC-HAD b/u 1990 Mexico City, Mexico
86	1121	N1100M N2JW N13TV N116MC XA-RIW XA-SHA wfu Houston-Hobby, TX, to Dodson Int'l Parts, KS
87	1121	N920G N920GP N400PC N430PC N430DC N116KX wfu to spares at Hollister CA
88	1121	N963WM N70CS N751CR b/u May87; still regd remains to Aviation Warehouse prop facility at El Mirage CA
89	1121	N6B N1195N N10BK N163DC
90	1121	N188WP N1121E N93SC
91	1121	N365RJ N1972W N73535 N711JT w/o 13Mar75 Tullahoma, TN
92	1121	N5420 N524X N33PS N401DE b/u; remains at Wiley Post, OK 12May88; cx Mar89
93	1121	N619JC N221CF N50LB (N999RA) N1PT wfu; cx Oct94 "destroyed/scrapped" - used for spares
94	1121	N1424 N1424Z (N144JC) N1424 N94WA N64AH
95	1121B	N5412 N6412 N7090 N709Q N210FE N100CA N200MP (N3031) N200MZ N95JK N614MH CP-2259 N85JW
96	1121	N56S N56WH N59CT N7EC N1QL N1QH N10JP N10JV (N2ES) YV-2454P
97	1121	N4644E N96B N3032 N3082B N34SW being parted out at Hollister CA early 2000
98	1121	N1121N C-FWRN N6DB N101DE N482G N301L N333BG dismantled for spares use
99	1121B	N4661E N922CR N922CP N22RT N22RD N63357
100	1121	N4663E N605V N16GR N11WP N305AJ wfu; still regd; remains to Aviation Warehouse prop facility at El Mirage CA
101	1121	N899S N100KY N45JF N5JC N16A N16MA N16SK sold May88 in Norway as technical airframe
102	1121	N27MD wfu 1986 for spares; remains with White Inds, Bates City, MO; still regd
103	1121	N1121S N136K N487G N10HV N13AD N77HH N998RD
104	1121	N4674E N87B N8RA
105	1121	N618JC F-BPIB N230RC C-GWPV N5094B wfu with White Inds, Bates City, MO
106	1121B	N4690E N3711H N40AB N88AD N114HH (N114HE) N180TJ N814K (N814T)
107	1123	N4691E 4X-COL (4X-COK) Israel 4X-JYG/064 N2120Q Ciskei CA-01 N2120Q b/u 1988 Oklahoma City, OK; cx Dec90
108	1121B	N1121Z N1WP N12JA N12JX N77ST LV-WHZ
109	1121	N350X N9DC N379TH N1MW TG-VWA XA-THF
110	1121B	N4716E 4X-CPA N101SV N181SV N16GH N1121N wfu to spares at Hollister CA
111	1121	N344PS N999CA C-GDJW N1121M cx Aug92; wfu for spares by OK Aircraft, Gilroy, CA; remains to scrapyard Long Beach, CA
112	1121B	N4730E N91B N91WG N4WG N44WG N773WB N372Q
113	1121	N4732E 4X-CPB N8534
114	1121	N4734E 4X-CPC N442WT N448WT N111ST N10GR N85MR N333SV to spares at Hollister, CA, circa 1995
115	1121	C-FWEC N3252J N500VF XB-FJI b/u Monterrey, Mexico
116	1121	N4743E N236JP w/o 31Oct69 Marion, VA
117	1121	N237JF N200BP N400HC N220KP N54WC N34NW being parted out Sep97 White Industries, Bates City, MO
118	1121	N312S N438 N117GM (N712GM) N716BB N381DA N696RV
119	1121	C-FFBC N119AC LV- still wearing N119AC Apr95
120	1121	N200M N203M scrapped during 1984; cx Jan85
121	1121A	N1121X N840AR N250JP N1121R N250UA (N121JC) w/o 27Apr78 Flatwood, LA
122	1121B	N4940E N801NM N122JC N666BP N122HL N122ST (XA-SCV)
123	1121A	N5410 N155VW N1121A N580WE
124	1121B	N1300M N300M XA-REO XA-RQT N8070U (for spares) cx Jan99
125	1121A	N1121N N30LS N1121R

JET COMMANDER/WESTWIND

C/n	Series	Identities
126	1121B	4X-COM N4983E N315SA N113MR N87DC N87DL LV-WEN w/o 28Sep94 Cordoba, Argentina
127	1121A	N6B N27X N34HD N209RR N20GB N100SR N550K N277MG
128	1121A	N660RW N74XL N74XE N1121U N386MC (N386JM) N404WC
129	1121A	N5032E N525AW N110ST (N1121B) N102CE N121PA
130	1121A	N5038E 4X-CPD N84 N44 w/o 02Nov88 en route Westmoreland County A/P, Latrobe, LA
131	1121A	N5039E 4X-CPE N83 N43 N7028F at Fairmont State College, WV; canx as possibly scrapped Aug96
132	1121	N200M N403M w/o 16Dec79 Salt Lake City, UT
133	1121B	N5041E N1172Z N56AG N56AZ N133JC N666JM N22976 N161X N122JB XA-LYM XB-GBZ N132LA
134	1121B	N111E 4X-FVN UAF1 5X-AAB 4X-COP N7638S N134N
135	1121B	N5043E N700HB N2DB N1KT N721GB N1121N XC-COL
136	1121	N5044E SE-DCY w/o 04Dec69 Stockholm, Sweden
137	1121B	N5045E SE-DCZ N50VF N3VF N873 N500LS N300LS N5BP N700BF (N700GA) N707TE XB-FKV
138	1121B	N5046E 4X-COB N5BA N972TF
139	1121B	N5047E 4X-CPF N8535 I-ARNT N188G N481DH
140	1121	N9040N 4X-CPG N200RC w/o 25Sep73 Tampa, FL
141	1121B	N9041N 4X-CPH N100CJ N160WC N177PC N177HB N163WC N163WS 5N-EZE N163WS
142	1121C	N9042N 4X-CPI N82 N42 N50138 N51038 N1944P at Pittsburgh Inst of Aeronautics
143	1121C	N9043N 4X-CPJ N81 N41 N30AD scrapped at Boeing Field, WA circa May98
144	1121C	N9044N 4X-CPK N80 N45 N20K wfu with White Industries, KS N920KP*
145	1121B	N9045N HB-VCC (N17DW) F-BTDA N349DA N145BW N145AJ (N805SA) N805SM
146	1121B	N9046N N99CV N99CK N923JA N926JM N444TJ b/u for spares at Atlanta Air Salvage, Griffin GA circa 1999
147	1121B	N9047N N720ML N728MC N147JK N912DA (N888MP)
148	1121B	N9048N 4X-CPL N8536 N200DE N200DF N101NK N600K (N22LL) cx Jun99 - being parted out at Hollister CA mid 99
149	1121B	N9049N 4X-CPM N100MC N100PC N45SL N489G N78MN N700R N1121E (N9LP) (N149BP) N606JM N666JM (N129ME) N343DA N303AJ (N308AJ) (N803AU) N149SF
150	1121B	N9050N 4X-CPN N1884Z N173MC N121FM N1121F w/o 20May97 San Louis Potosi, Mexico
151	1123	4X-CJD N1123E N88WP ZP-AGD stored Fort Lauderdale Executive, FL
152	1124N	4X-CJC Israel 4X-JYF/029 4X-CJC Israel 4X-JYR/035 Israel 4X-JYR/929
153	1123	4X-CJB N773EJ N200WC N223WW XA-PUF
154	1124	4X-CJA (D-CBBE) N919JH D-CBBE N722AW
155	1123	4X-CJE N23Y N707TE N707TF
156	1123	4X-CJF N1123H N40AS N40BG (N666MP) N566MP N35D
157	1123	4X-CJG N1123Q N10MB (N820RT) wfu; b/u c 1989-90; cx Aug92; remains with OK Aircraft, Gilroy, CA
158	1123	4X-CJH N1123G N123DR
159	1123	4X-CJI N1123E N722W N1123Z (N12FH) N344CK N96TS wfu to spares at Hollister CA
160	1123	4X-CJJ N1123R USCG 160 4X-CJJ N1123W N221MJ N221RJ XA-AVE XA-MUI XA-RIZ
161	1123	4X-CJK D-CGLS (N653J) N185G N33WD XA-POJ wfu after accident (no details known); remains with Dodson Avn, Ottawa, KS
162	1123	4X-CJL N1123S N78LB N234RC N9VC N9VQ XA-SDW (N163W) N13GW HK- cx from USCAR early 1995 but still marked N13GW circa Feb97 at Bogota-El Dorado, Colombia
163	1123	4X-CJM N1123T N4444U N47DC N163DL canx Oct97, status?
164	1123	4X-CJN D-CAAS N9114S N32WE b/u by White Inds, Bates City, MO; still regd
165	1123	4X-CJO N1123R C-GWSH N102BW N22RD
166	1123	4X-CJP C-GDOC N360HK b/u during 1989; still regd
167	1123	4X-CJQ N873EJ N1123H being parted out by White Industries 1998
168	1123	4X-CJR N973EJ N66SM N111NF b/u Dallas-Love Field circa 1998
169	1123	4X-CJS N1123U N1500C N1100D N44PR
170	1123	4X-CJT N1123W N112RC N150HR N90HM wfu; cx May94
171	1123	4X-CJU C-GJLL N223PA N89XL (ZS-ODP) parted out at Lanseria, South Africa
172	1123	4X-CJV N1123H XB-AER N19EE YV-58CP YV-2482P
173	1123	4X-CJW N1123Q N680K N30JM N30AN wfu with OK Aircraft, Gilroy, CA; still regd
174	1124	4X-CJX N1123X N112MR N124VF N74TS N760C*
175	1123	4X-CJY N1123R N500M N500ML N51TV N523RB (N571MC)
176	1123	4X-CJZ N1123T C-GJCD N661MP C-FNRW N661MP N27AT
177	1123	4X-CKA N1123U N11WC N777CJ N118AF (N114ED) cx 1991 wfu
178	1123	4X-CKB N1123Z N999U N123CV
179	1123	4X-CKC N1123Y LV-WJU
180	1123	4X-CKD HP-1A N1019K (N180JS) N72LT N72ET (N190LH) N192LH N3VL
181	1124	4X-CKE HK-2150X HK-2150 N107CF N325AJ N325LJ N345BS
182	1123	4X-CKF N1123Q N200HR N700EC N13KH N18BL N78BL N10122 LV-WYL
183	1123	4X-CKG Honduras 318 HR-001 XB-DNY N51990 LV-WLR
184	1123	4X-CKH N1123T N666JM N866JM YV-119P (N) CC-CRK N481MC
185	1124N	4X-CKI N1123U Israel 4X-JYJ/027 Israel 4X-JYJ/927
186	1123N	4X-CKJ N1123R Israel 4X-JYO/031 Israel 4X-JYO/931
187	1124	4X-CKK N1124N N18GW (N943CL) (N715GW) (N416NL) N516AC (N789DD) N1M N280DB (N1TS) (N187TS) N241RH N187TJ
188	1124	4X-CKL N1124G C-GRDP
189	1124	4X-CKM N26DS N926DS N200DL N42CM
190	1124	4X-CKN N50AL N890WW N190WW
191	1124	4X-CKO N3VF N13VF N711MR YV-777CP (N771AC) N326AJ N900FS
192	1124	4X-CKP N71M (N736US) N319BG N819RC

JET COMMANDER/WESTWIND

C/n	Series	Identities									
193	1124	4X-CKQ	N60AL	(YV-37CP)	N101HS	N420J	N420JM	N428JM	N515LG		
194	1124	4X-CKR	N222SR	N343AP	N124FM	N40TA					
195	1124	4X-CKS	N887PL	N880WW	(N24TE)	TC-ASF	(N195ML)	N951DB			
196	1124	4X-CKT	N1124E	N250JP	N505U	N500WK	(N615DM)	N863AB			
197	1124	4X-CKU	N214CC	N29GH	N29CL	SE-DLK	w/o 21Sep92 Umea, Sweden; cx Jan93				
198	1124	4X-CKV	N800Y	N744JR	N600TJ	N98TS	N51MN				
199	1124	4X-CKW	N1124P	N111AG	N999MS	D-CHDL					
200	1124	4X-CKX	N1124X	N4WG							
201	1124	4X-CKY	N1124Q	N1124N	N56AG	N58WW	N85EQ	(N85EA)	N95CP	N300TE	(N29UF)
		C-FOIL									
202	1124	4X-CKZ	D-CBAY	N49968	N54MC	(N254MC)	N202DD	(N37WC)	N141LB	N168DB	YV-297CP
		N274HM									
203	1124	4X-CLA	N1124G	N124WW	N880Z						
204	1124	4X-CLB	N221MJ	N156CW	N26TJ	N10UJ					
205	1124	4X-CLC	N96BA	N967A	N124NY	N125AC	SE-DLL	N205AJ	N775JC*		
206	1124	4X-CLD	N215G	N215C	N215M	N943LL	N943JL	N100ME	N148H		
207	1124	4X-CLE	N1124P	N6053C	N330PC	N519ME	N666K	D-CHAL			
208	1124	4X-CLF	N961JC	(N961JD)	N961JE	N208MD	N208ST	N324AJ	N311DB		
209	1124	4X-CLG	N661JB	N663JB	N662JB	N938WH	N988WH	N222LH			
210	1124	4X-CLH	N662JB	N69HM	N661CP	N662JB	N23AC	N38WW	N444MM	N59KC	N337RE
		N425JF	N428JF*								
211	1124	4X-CLI	YV-160CP	w/o 19Feb97 near Guatemala City/La Aurora, Guatemala							
212	1124	4X-CLJ	N212WW	N900CS	N700MD						
213	1124	4X-CLK	N213WW	N555J	N530GV	N580GV	N30YM	(4X-NOY)	4X-CLK		
214	1124	4X-CLL	N1124N	N214WW	N24RH	(N248H)	N46BK				
215	1124	4X-CLM	N215DH	N500WH	N946GM						
216	1124	4X-CLN	N216SC	N1124G	(N65BK)	N290CA					
217	1124	4X-CLO	N8QP	N8QR	N217SC	N217SQ	N217WC	N163WC			
218	1124	4X-CLP	N218WW	N100AK	C-GFAN	N218DJ	N74GR	N218PM	N425RJ		
219	1124	4X-CLQ	YV-190CP								
220	1124	4X-CLR	N1124G	C-GHBQ	N9134Q	N106BC	N9RD				
221	1124	4X-CLS	N108GM	N969PW	N969KC	(N969EG)	VH-AJS	w/o 27Apr95 Alice Springs, Australia			
222	1124	4X-CLT	N294W	N294B	N36EF	N86EF	N700R	N3RC	N598JM		
223	1124	4X-CLU	N1124P	N124TY	N303PC	N20KH					
224	1124	4X-CLV	N898SR	XA-KUG	N2756T	N349MC					
225	1124	4X-CLW	N1124U	N30MR							
226	1124	4X-CLX	N500LS	N300LS	N100BC	(N10BY)	N124MB	N120S	D-CHBL		
227	1124	4X-CLY	N250PM	N64FG	N624KM						
228	1124	4X-CLZ	N305BB								
229	1124	4X-CMA	N1212G	N1625	N162E	N40GG					
230	1124	4X-CMB	N4995N	XC-HCP	XC-HDA	N102U	N1KT				
231	1124	4X-CMC	HB-VFP	N8514Y	N777CF	N70CA	(N27TA)	N331CW	N331GW		
232	1124	4X-CMD	N1124Q	N19UC	N190M	N773AW	N4MH				
233	1124	4X-CME	N1124X	N650GE	N650G	N67DF					
234	1124	4X-CMF	(N1124Z)	HC-BGL	N1124Z	N161X					
235	1124	4X-CMG	N1124E	(N24PP)	N65A	N30AB					
236	1124	4X-CMH	N35LH	N236W	N22LZ						
237	1124	4X-CMI	N39GW	N723M	N28TJ	N24KL					
238	1124	4X-CMJ	VH-AJP								
239	1124A	4X-CMK	(conv to 1124A prototype)			HK-2485	HK-2485W				
240	1124	4X-CML	N240WW	(N400Q)	N400SJ	N400NE	N72787				
241	1124	4X-CMM	N789TE	N300TC							
242	1124	4X-CMN	N340DR	N140DR							
243	1124	4X-CMO	N1124G	N59WK	N215SC	4X-AIP	w/o 23Jly96 Rosh-Pina/Mahanaim-I-Ben-Yaakov, Israel				
244	1124	4X-CMP	N124PA	N911SP	N124PA	N911SP					
245	1124	4X-CMQ	N1124P	N404CB	N270LC						
246	1124	4X-CMR	N101SV	N911CU							
247	1124	4X-CMS	N1125G	N280LM	N280AZ						
248	1124	4X-CMT	N25RE	VH-AJJ							
249	1124	4X-CMU	N1JS	reported stolen/cr 1985 Mexico							
250	1124	4X-CMV	N250WW	C-GFAO	N29995	N60RV					
251	1124	4X-CMW	N6MJ	CX-CMJ	PT-LDY						
252	1124	4X-CMX	N1WS	(N9WW)							
253	1124	4X-CMY	N511CC	N511CQ	N800WW	N800WS	N253MD	VH-LLW	b/u Jandakot, W.A. by 06Apr98		
254	1124	4X-CMZ	N600TD	N888R	N112AB	N72HB	N60AV				
255	1124	4X-CNA	N222MW								
256	1124	4X-CNB	VH-AJK								
257	1124	4X-CNC	N573P	N317M	N317MB	N755CM	N942FA	N124UF			
258	1124	4X-CND	N10MR	N1857W	N29AP	N24DS	YV-770CP	N258AV	(N258CF)	N572M	
259	1124	4X-CNE	N1124N	C-GSWS	N19AP	N315JM	VH-LLX	b/u Jandakot, W.A. by 06Apr98			
260	1124	4X-CNF	N401BP	N525ML	C-GAGP	N49TA	(N503RH)	N80FD			
261	1124	4X-CNG	N167C	N249E	N87GS	N39JN	N11LN				
262	1124	4X-CNH	N262WW	N40DG	YV-393CP	N262WC	N79KF*				
263	1124	4X-CNI	N29PC								
264	1124	4X-CNJ	N351C	XA-MAR	N351C	(N125NY)	N88PV	N351C			
265	1124	4X-CNK	N167J	N7DJ							
266	1124	4X-CNL	N24KT	N24KE	N50DR	N7HM					
267	1124	4X-CNM	N297W	N297A	N100SR	N241CT					

JET COMMANDER/WESTWIND

C/n	Series	Identities										
268	1124	4X-CNN	(N13HH)	N821H	N606AB	N21CX	N200HR	N41WH	N56BP			
269	1124	4X-CNO	N3031	N50SL								
270	1124	4X-CNP	(N270WW)	N270A	(N27SJ)	(N270DT)	N501DT					
271	1124	4X-CNQ	N368S	N102KJ	N218SC	C-GWKF						
272	1124	4X-CNR	N26GW	N723R	VH-LLY	b/u Jandakot, W.A. by 06Apr98						
273	1124	4X-CNS	N104RS	(N566PG)								
274	1124	4X-CNT	N701Z	N701W	N274K							
275	1124	4X-CNU	N1141G	N1621	N36PT	N6TM						
276	1124	4X-CNV	VR-CAD	XA-BQA	N269AJ	N800XL	N300XL					
277	1124	4X-CNW	N288WW	(N2AJ)	N504JC	D-CHCL						
278	1124	4X-CNX	N505BC	C-GJLK	N10S							
279	1124	4X-CNY	N1126G	N885DR	N230TL	N230JK	N952HF	N400TF				
280	1124	4X-CNZ	N290W	(N5BP)	(N5S)	N29LP	N250RA	N500R	N508R	N949CC		
281	1124	4X-CQA	VH-AJQ	N4251H	N1124F	N200XJ*						
282	1124	4X-CQB	N711MB	N186G	VH-AJV							
283	1124	4X-CQC	N483A	N666JM	(N70WW)	N17UC	N95JK					
284	1124	4X-CQD	N99WH	N296NW	N217BL	N727AT						
285	1124	4X-CQE	VR-CAC	XA-LIJ	VR-CBK	XA-LIJ						
286	1124	4X-CQF	N1124U	C-GMBH	N4447T	N92FE						
287	1124	4X-CQG	N146BF	N530DL								
288	1124	4X-CQH	N1124Q	C-GMTT	N116AT	N94AT	N48AH	N711KE				
289	1124	4X-CQI	N711CJ	N45SJ	N23SJ	VR-CIL	N900VP					
290	1124	4X-CQJ	N800JJ	N719CC								
291	1124	4X-CQK	N124WK	N917BE								
292	1124	4X-CQL	N292JC	N741C								
293	1124	4X-CQM	N26TV	N26T	N26TZ							
294	1124	4X-CQN	D-CBBA	N24DB	(N73GB)	HK-3884X	N147A					
295	1124A	4X-CQO	N295WW	N100AK	N100AQ	N555CW	N730CA					
296	1124	4X-CQP	D-CBBB	N64KT	N770JJ	N92WW	N89TJ	N710SA				
297	1124	4X-CQQ	D-CBBC	N76TG	N51PD	N801SM						
298	1124	4X-CQR	N610JA	C-GESO	C-GRGE	N298CM	N809JC					
299	1124A	4X-CQS	N922CR	N922CK	N74JM	N600TC	(N288SJ)	N67TJ				
300	1124A	4X-CQT	N500M	N500MD	(N20NW)	N10MV						
301	1124A	4X-CQU	N500GK	N815RC	N815BC	XB-GRN	N230JS	N301KF				
302	1124A	4X-CQV	N600J	N60QJ	N100AK	N422BC	w/o 26Dec99 Milwaukee, WI					
303	1124A	4X-CQW	N500J	N50QJ	N211ST							
304	1124A	4X-CQX	N304WW	N369BG	N389BG	N10NL						
305	1124A	4X-CQY	N464EC	N717LA								
306	1124A	4X-CQZ	YV-387CP	N555BY	(N9WW)	(N722W)	HK-3971X					
307	1124A	4X-CRA	YV-388CP	N1124K	N300HC	(N301HC)	N825JL	N925Z	N97SM	N494BP		
308	1124A	4X-CRB	YV-210CP	YV-O-CVG-1	N308JS	N308TS	N628KM*					
309	1124A	4X-CRC	(N200LH)	N240S	N50SK	w/o 04Apr86 nr Rosewater, TX						
310	1124	4X-CRD	D-CBBD	N78GJ								
311	1124	4X-CRE	N700MM	N50XX	N700MM	N788MA						
312	1124	4X-CRF	N200LH	N300LH	N97HW							
313	1124	4X-CRG	N146J	C-FAWW	N711WU	N711WV						
314	1124	4X-CRH	VH-IWW	N2454M	N84PH	N2HZ						
315	1124A	4X-CRI	N371H	N400YM	VH-BCL	VH-NJW	N315TR	N89TJ^				
316	1124	4X-CRJ	VH-ASR	N93KE								
317	1124	4X-CRK	VH-AYI	P2-BCM	VH-JPW	(VH-NIJ)	VH-UUZ					
318	1124	4X-CRL	N298W	N298A	N10FG	N38AE						
319	1124A	4X-CRM	XA-LOR	N560SH	N700WM	(N50XX)	N200KC	N225N				
320	1124	4X-CRN	N60JP	N204TM								
321	1124	4X-CRO	N900WW	N1124N	N83CT	N93WW	N666K					
322	1124A	4X-CRP	N2AV	N990S								
323	1124	4X-CRQ	N816H	VH-KNS								
324	1124A	4X-CRR	N3VF	N90CL	C-FCEJ							
325	1124	4X-CRS	VH-WWY	N504U	N124HL	SE-DPT	N525AJ	N467MW				
326	1124	4X-CRT	(N88JE)	N66JE	w/o 21Feb95 Denver-Stapleton Airport, CO							
327	1124	4X-CRU	N50M									
328	1124A	4X-CRV	N816JA	N819JA	C-GPFC	N328PC						
329	1124	4X-CRW	N30NS	N711SE								
330	1124A	4X-CRX	N52GW	N723K	YV-332CP							
331	1124	4X-CRY	N556N	N228N	N228L	LV-WOV	N228L	N811VC				
332	1124A	4X-CRZ	N24SR	N332DF	N43RP*							
333	1124	4X-CTA	HR-002	HR-CEF								
334	1124A	4X-CTB	(N45MP)	N40MP	N325LW							
335	1124A	4X-CTC	N300HR	N359JS	N501BW	EC-254	EC-GIB	N21HR				
336	1124	4X-CTD	N245S	C-FOIL	N336SV	N255RB	N525XX					
337	1124A	4X-CTE	N14BN	N639J	N900NW	4X-CTE	N2518M					
338	1124A	4X-CTF	N338W	N350PM	N850WW	N114WL	N50PL	w/o 12Dec99, Gouldsboro PA				
339	1124A	4X-CTG	(XC-HDA)	N333CG	N782PC	N74AG	N90KC					
340	1124A	4X-CTH	4X-CUA	(XC-BDA)	N1124L	N212CP	PT-OLN	N340PM	N118MP	N3RC		
341	1124A	4X-CTI	4X-CUB	N1124P	N23AC	N23AQ	N80RE	N555HD	N556HD	N728LW	N728LM	N868CP
342	1124A	4X-CTJ	XA-MAK	N342AJ	N39RE	N342TS	N204AB					
343	1124A	4X-CTK	YV-451CP	YV-O-CVG-3								
344	1124A	4X-CTL	N334	N311BR	N849HS							

JET COMMANDER/WESTWIND

C/n	Series	Identities
345	1124A	4X-CTM N1424 (N533) N534 N534R N345TR
346	1124A	4X-CTN N100AG N1124N N610HC N610SE
347	1124	4X-CTO N347WW N30PD N21GG YV-666CP N666CP N178HH N347GA
348	1124A	4X-CTP N348WW N348SJ N960FA
349	1124A	4X-CTQ N78WW N65GW N723L N728L N123RC
350	1124A	4X-CTR VR-CBB XA-MAK N3838J N777LU N309CK w/o 15Dec93 Orange County A/P, CA; cx Oct95
351	1124A	4X-CTS N106WT N351TC N722AZ
352	1124A	4X-CTT N15BN N117JW N117AH
353	1124A	4X-CTU N379JR N90CH N86UR N89UH C-GRGE EC-GSL
354	1124	4X-CTV N443A N512CC N506U N124LS N894TW
355	1124A	4X-CUI N355WW N355JK
356	1124A	4X-CUJ N356WW N8GA N533 N530GV N929GV N43ZZ N861GS N767AC N38TJ N993DS
357	1124	4X-CUK (N357W) C-GDUC N357EA N66FG N357BC N914DM*
358	1124A	4X-CUL N358CT N13UR N800MA N830MA N787RP
359	1124A	4X-CUM N8JL N86RR N500RR N500AX C-GRGE
360	1124	4X-CUN N816S N816ST N816S N500KE
361	1124A	4X-CUO N6053C N610HC N3AV
362	1124	4X-CUP N445A
363	1124	4X-CUQ N3320G N1629 N54PT N723JM*
364	1124A	4X-CUR N60DG N199GH N198GH N198HF N198HE RP-C2480 N944M
365	1124A	4X-CUS N793JR (N185BR) N185MB N2BG N73CL
366	1124	4X-CUT VH-SQH VH-LOF N388GA N707BC
367	1124	4X-CUD N446A N511CC N455S N367WW
368	1124A	4X-CUE N28WW N368MD N83SG
369	1124A	4X-CUF N24SB (N54BC) N300JK N85WC N76ER
370	1124	4X-CUG N641FG N471TM N875HS
371	1124	4X-CUH VH-IWJ w/o 10Oct85 nr Sydney, Australia
372	1124	4X-CUB N372WW N988NA N810MT (N800MT) N810ME (N5TH) N921DT N502BG N444MW
373	1124A	4X-CUK N373CM N900LM N555DH N794TK
374	1124A	4X-CUL N18SF N56AG N248H N33MK
375	1124A	4X-CUF N79AD N79AP N66LX
376	1124A	4X-CUH 4X-CJP N1124P N110SF N376WA N376BE
377	1124A	4X-CUJ N301PC
378	1124	4X-CUI N84LA N481NS
379	1124	4X-CUJ N52FC N62ND
380	1124A	4X-CUM N50DW N380DA C-FMWW w/o 27Jan94 Meadow Lake, Saskatchewan, Canada; cx Jly94
381	1124	4X-CUO VH-KNJ N501U N929GV N928GV N928G N92EB N381W N50FD
382	1124A	4X-CUP N900BF N410NA (N445BL) N999BL N445BL w/o 01May92 Waterbury, Oxford, CT; cx Mar93
383	1124	4X-CUQ (N301PC) N82HH N20DH N84WU N84VV*
384	1124A	4X-CUB N48WW N61RS (N50MF)
385	1124A	4X-CUC N96AL YV-962CP N962MV N317JS
386	1124	4X-CUE N68WW (VH-JPL)
387	1124A	4X-CUJ N97AL VH-NGA
388	1124	4X-CUH N1124K N900H
389	1124A	4X-CUF N49WW N812M (N612M) N812G N100WP N812G N89AM
390	1124A	4X-CUB N57WW N3RL (N303E) N290RA ZS-MZM (HB-) N59SM N122MP
391	1124	4X-CUG N24WW N24VH C-GMPF N155ME
392	1124A	4X-CUA N92WW N95WC N793BG
393	1124	4X-CUK N53WW
394	1124A	4X-CUM N94WW N314AD N352TC N516CC
395	1124A	4X-CUC N95WW VH-SGY VH-APU N395SR N395TJ
396	1124	4X-CUR 8P-BAR N1124N N37BE
397	1124A	4X-CUN N52SM N11CS N777HD
398	1124	4X-CUO N98WW N59AP N41C*
399	1124A	4X-CUF N78WW N48SD
400	1124A	4X-CUP N200LS N300LS N900PA
401	1124	4X-CUQ N84WW
402	1124A	4X-CUS N87WW N999LC N51TV
403	1124	4X-CUH N403W (N825EC)
404	1124A	4X-CUG 4X-CJR N404W N29CL
405	1124A	4X-CUJ N1124L N211DB N420TJ
406	1124	4X-CUA N406W N651E (N651ES) N100CH
407	1124A	4X-CUK N407W
408	1124	4X-CUB N408W N408MJ
409	1124A	4X-CUM VH-JJA 4X-CUM? 4X-CUO Chile 130 N7051J N409WW XA-RET N4426Z N217RM N217BM N26KL
410	1124A	4X-CUO N1124Z (N410EL) N22BG N26VF N26VB N777DC
411	1124	4X-CUC N96WW N47LP N47LR HC-BVX
412	1124A	4X-CUP N412W N412SC N50XX N50HS
413	1124	4X-CJS 4X-CUD N413WW N35LH
414	1124A	4X-CPO 4X-CUC N86MF (N66MF) N980AW N24MN N524RH*
415	1124A	4X-CUS N415EL N105BE N415EL
416	1124	4X-CUD N416W N303TS
417	1124A	4X-CUE N417EL (N417GW) N700WE N115BP

JET COMMANDER/WESTWIND

C/n	Series	Identities							
418	1124	4X-CUB	PT-LIP	N124PA	N662K	N317MX	(N317MV)	N420MP	N26T
419	1124A	4X-CUF	N419W	N551TP					
420	1124A	4X-CUH	N420W	N91SA					
421	1124	4X-CUJ	N111HN	N801MS	N317MQ	N520MP			
422	1124A	4X-COC	4X-CUI	N422AW	N251SP	N87GS			
423	1124	4X-CUC	N223WA						
424	1124A	4X-CUJ	N424W	N790JR					
425	1124A	4X-CUK	N425WA	N600LE	N365CX				
426	1124	4X-CUF	N426WW	N75BC					
427	1124A	4X-CUN	N427WW	N256N	N229N	N229D			
428	1124A	4X-CUO	N428W	(N92BE)	N327SA				
429	1124	4X-CUK	(N429W)	C-FROY					
430	1124	4X-CUM	N430W	N821LG	N430A	N430BJ			
431	1124	4X-CUN	N431AM	C-FGGH					
432	1124	4X-CUH	N87NS	N317M	N62276	N317MB	(N317MT)	N320MP	N432HS
433	1124A	4X-CUH	N433WW	N433WR	N433GM				
434	1124A	4X-CUC	N330MG	(N346CP)	N222KC	N601DR	N187EC	N919BT	
435	1124	4X-CUG	(N435W)	N501CB	(N501CP)	(N669SB)	N297JS	N140VJ	
436	1124A	4X-CUE	N436WW	N50XX	N436WW	N110AF	N1904G	N100AK	N444EP
437	1124A	4X-CUF	N437WW	N437SJ					
438	1124	4X-CUJ	(N438W)	N438AM	N100BC				
439	1124A	4X-CUG	N439WW						
440	1124A	4X-CUJ	N440WW	N127SA					
441	1124	4X-CUP	PT-LPV	HK-3893X	C-FZEI				
442	1124A	4X-CUO	N406W	N830	N71WF				

Production complete

LEARJET MODELS 23 & 24

C/n	Model	Identities
001	23	N801L ff 07Oct63 w/o 04Jun64 Wichita, KS
002	23	N802L ff 05May64; last flight 17Jun66; to Smithsonian Institute, Washington, DC
003	23	N803L N200Y N2008 (N10MC) N3BL
004	23	N804LJ became c/n 23-015A
005	23	N232R N570FT N994SA N721HW N721GB N15BE N500JW b/u for spares around Mar87; cx Aug87 - remains to Bounty Avn Scrapyard, Detroit-Willow Run, MI
006	23	N505PF N578LJ N23CH N111JD N505PF donated Oct93 to Kansas Aviation Museum
007	23	N826L D-IHAQ w/o 12Dec65 Zurich
008	23	N825LJ N1203 N20S N20BD N20EP wfu c Mar93; exhibited outside White Inds, Bates City, MO
009	23	N425EJ N5BL N13SN N49CK
010	23	N805LJ N292BC N2920C N333BF N29BF N400BF N500BF b/u for spares Oct88 Detroit-Willow Run, MI - remains to Bounty Avn Scrapyard, Detroit-Willow Run, MI
011	24A	N806LJ N233VW N1966K N150WL N50JF N711PJ N711TJ N225LJ N24LG (N40TV)
012	24	N1965L N1967L N1969L N1965L
013	23	N613W N201BA N888DS N37BL N28ST w/o 31Jul87 10km east of Guatemala City/La Aurora A/P, Guatemala; cx Dec89
014	23	N814L N426EJ JY-AEG (HB-VEL) F-BXPT
015	24	N88B donated 28Feb92 to Pima County Air Museum, AZ; cx Mar92
015A	23	N804LJ w/o 21Oct65 nr Jackson, MI
016	23	N500K N7CF N7GF N96CK
017	23	N233R N658L N32SD N30BP F-GBTA F-GDAV w/o 30Jan89 Lisbon, Portugal; cx Nov92
018	23	N807LJ N661FS D-IKAA N652J N866DB N866JS w/o 06May80 Richmond, VA; remains with White Inds, Bates City, MO
019	24	N4641J HB-VAI N889JF N654DN N100EA N747SC (N954SC)
020	23	N388R N338KK N2GP N210GP N310KR (N144WC) N388R N820L
021	23	N427EJ N427NJ N133W w/o Burbank, CA; cx Jul81, parted out
022	23	N428EJ N400CS N103TC N88TC N456SC N114GB b/u; cx Feb93; remains to White Inds, Bates City, MO
023	23	N429EJ JY-AEH HB-VEL F-GAMA dbf on ground 05Jun81 Le Bourget, France and stored; cx 10Feb92
024	23	N202Y N21U N488J N803JA (N702RK) N3ZA b/u for spares 1982; cx Apr91; remains to White Inds, Bates City, MO
025	23	N600G N60QG N5DM N3JL N37DM N50DM N508M N24SA b/u for spares after accident 21Jun85; cx May89
026	23	N706L HB-VBA F-BSTP N26008 N404AJ N222GH N404DB N540CL being parted out at Hollister, CA circa early 2000
027	23	N430EJ JY-AEI HB-VES F-GAPY (N108TW) b/u for spares 1983 Kansas City, KS; remains to White Inds, Bates City, MO; rear fuselage & tail unit used as engineering testbed for Avcom Intl ventral fin retrofit programme
028	23	N818LJ N5DM (N56PR) (N500YY) N5QY N37CP b/u for spares 1994 Kansas City, KS; remains to White Inds, Bates City, MO
028A	23	N803LJ N432EJ w/o 25Oct67 Muskegon, MI
029	23	N7000K N715BC N1BU N66AS N61TS wfu Sep88; b/u for spares Detroit-Willow Run, MI; cx Jan96
030	23	N431EJ N431CA ZS-JWC N431CA ZS-JWC
031	24A	N175FS N477BL N777TF N777TE N202BA N175FS
032	23	N235R w/o 23Apr66 Clarendon, TX
033	23	N158MJ N453LJ N453JT XA-LGM XA-GAM N60DH N23TJ wfu Sep87; remains at Broward Community College, FL; cx Feb93
034	23	N242WT N241BN N24FF N154AG
035	23	N100X (N10QX) N992TD
036	23	N477K N210PC N111WM N38DM YV-278CP N123MJ
037	23	N266JP N988SA N51AJ N65LJ N41AJ N13LJ N10LJ N50AJ XA-ESS XC-UJP XC-AA28
038	23	N812LJ VR-BCF LN-NPE N1002B 9Q-CGM 9Q-CHB N433J N433JB N100TA N100JZ N300TA N175BA PT-LKQ wfu Detroit-Willow Run, MI; to a Detroit tech school as instructional airframe
039	23	N43B N800JA N15SC N30SC N9JJ (N43CT) N121CK
040	23	N433EJ N673WM YV-01CP N98386 N12HJ b/u for spares 1989
041	23	N205RJ N666MP C-GDDB N77VJ
042	23	N293BC N2932C N1ZA N701RZ N69KB b/u for spares 1982 by White Inds, Bates City, MO; cx Dec91; remains still present Nov94
043	24	N368MJ N39T N24MW N50BA (N43AC) sold for spares during 1987; cx Sep89
044	23	N22B HB-VAM w/o 28Aug72 Innsbruck, Austria
045	23	N242F N711MR N100TA w/o 06May82 Savannah, GA
045A	23	N803LJ HB-VBB F-BSUX N959SC w/o 23Jly91 Detroit City, MI
046	23	N434EJ w/o 09May70 Pellston, MI
047	23	N2503L N347J YV-E-GPA YV-15CP N9260A N444WC N2503L being parted out at Rantoul, KS. circa early 2000
048	23	N805LJ N1GW N48MW N140RC
049	23	NASA701 N701NA N933NA (N933N)
050	24	N828MW N828M N823M N650CA N24ET
050A	23	N808LJ N808JA w/o 23May(?) 1982 in ground fire; probably at Sarasota-Bradenton, FL, where burnt fuselage was noted 25Jun82; remains to Taylorville, IL
051	24	N1500B N1500G N100MJ (N69LL) N990TM N70JC N24VM b/u for spares 1987 by White Inds, Bates City, MO

LEARJET 23/24

C/n	Model	Identities
052	23	N360EJ HB-VBD N360EJ N856JB
053	23	N361EJ HB-VBC F-BTQK N23AJ b/u for spares by Dodson Avn 1988; cx Sep92
054	23	CF-TEL N351WB N351WC N351NR N351N
055	24	N809LJ N2366Y N511WH N711CW
056	23	N362EJ N332PC w/o 06Jan77 Flint, MI; remains with White Inds, Bates City, MO
057	23	N448GC N448GG b/u for spares; remains with Dodson Avn, Ottawa, KS
058	23	N363EJ N66MP N7FJ N153AG
059	23	N364EJ N31DP N331DP b/u for spares Jun87 Detroit-Willow Run, MI - remains to Bounty Avn Scrapyard
060	24	N889WF N90J
061	23	N316M w/o 19Mar66 Lake Michigan, MI
062	23	N670MF N20TA
063	23	N234F w/o 14Nov65 Palm Springs, FL
064	23	N365EJ N200G N400RB N401RB N73JT N66AM ZS-MBR 3D-AFJ ZS-MBR wfu Oct93 Lanseria, S Africa; to Atlanta Air Salvage, Griffin, GA, Jan95 for spares for possible re-build N259DB
065	24	N2000M N200DM N7500K (N750QK) N750WJ N957SC N707SC
065A	23	N388Q N28BP (N28BR) N1GZ N122M (N156AG)
066	23	N216RG N72MK N66MW XA-RVB XA-SDP N211TS
067	23	N815LJ N2ZA N703DC N720UA N331DP w/o 18Jan90 nr Dayton, OH; cx Oct90
068	23	N460F N902AR N902AB N575HW N9RA N400PG N152AG XA-ARG XB-GRR N73CE
069	23	N814LJ N9AJ N6GJ N37BL (N34TR) (converted at some time to Model 24 standards) substantially damaged 04Mar98 Oakland, CA, remains to White Ind's, Bates City, MO circa Oct98
070	23	CF-ARE N1976L N197GL N111CT N101DB XA-RZM XA-TII
071	23	N1001A N71LJ XA-RZC N6262T with Dodson Avn, Rantoul, KS, for parts Jly95, still marked as XA-RZC
072	23	N331WR N331JR N4VS N31S N2SN RP-C848 b/u for spares by White Industries 1998
073	23	N806LJ
074	23	5A-DAC D-IATD N23TC N74MW N23AN N68WM N150AG XA-LAR XB-GRQ N83CE
075	23	5A-DAD w/o 05Jun67 Damascus, Syria
076	23	N1966W N801JA N12GP N50PJ N83LJ
077	23	N812LJ N740J N868J N500P N90658 N88EA (N611CA) N745F w/o 30Jul88 March AFB, Riverside, CA; cx Mar90
078	23	N690LJ w/o 30Nov67 Orlando, FL
079	23	N240AG N240AQ N31CK
080	23	N822LJ w/o 09Dec67 Detroit, MI
081	23	N369EJ N437LJ XC-JOA N418LJ (N81LJ) ZS-MDN
082	23	N280C N805JA N7GP (N700NP) (N216SA) wfu Hampton - Tara Field, Atlanta GA
082A	23	N823LJ N255ES N744CF N100TA N613BR N618BR (N118LS)
083	23	N824LJ donated to the Kalamazoo Air Zoo, FL for public static display
084	23	N788DR N101JR N119BA
085	23	N825LJ N385J N101PP w/o 04Jun84 Windsor Locks, CT
086	23	N1021B w/o 06Nov69 Racine, WI
087	24	N407V CF-UYT N7VS D-IKAB C-GEEN N998RL N24YA N24YE*
088	23	N816LJ N616PS N11JK N804JA N48AS N500FM (N500LH) w/o 02Jul91 Columbia, TN; noted dumped Oct91 Bounty Avn Scrapyard, Detroit-Willow Run, MI; cx Jun99
089	23	N869B N969B N1968W
090	23	PP-FMX w/o 30Aug69 Rio de Janeiro, Brazil
091	23	N430JA N430J N110M N11QM cx Dec89; b/u for spares 1989
092	23	N415LJ N422JR N105BJ N344WC N415LJ
093	23	N416LJ N3350 N416LJ N12TA N38JD N486G N101AR N101AD N97MJ XA-SHN N80775 N7GF
094	23	N417LJ N20M w/o 15Dec72 Detroit, MI
095	23	N366EJ N974D N5D N9RA
096	24A	N1967W N421L N527ER N33BK N1972L N1973L N1972L N464CL
097	23	N425SC N79LS N1968A N1963A to spares 1995 remains at Hampton - Tara Field, Atlanta GA
098	23	N112T N11111 N2DD N711 N711AE N99TC b/u for spares May87 Cincinnati-Lunken Field, OH but still regd; remains to Brandis Avn, Taylorville, IL
099	23	N7200K
100	24A	N427LJ CF-BCJ N144X N989SA N424NJ N361AA N24BA N616SC N427LJ N224SC w/o 26Sep99 Gainsville GA; remains to Atlanta Air Salvage, Griffin GA
101	24	N316M N316MF N15PL N473EJ N473 N68DM (N68FN) N24GJ XA-SGU N24WX noted in wfu condition at Corona Municipal A/p, CA 1997 - current status?
102	24A	N436LJ N365EJ N705NA N805NA
103	24	N430LJ N714X ZS-LTK N72442 ZS-LTK N90532 ZS-LTK N90532 ZS-LTK N90532 ZS-LTK N105EC
104	24	N433LJ N924ED N45ED
105	24	N425NJ N111EK N111EJ TR-LYB F-GDAE
106	24	N888NS N969J N100GP N70RL N103RB N888MC
107	24A	N48L
108	24	N1966L N745W N661CP N661BS N661SS C-GSIV N45811 N29LA N900JA N315AJ
109	24	HB-VAS OY-RYA SE-DCW (F-GBBV(2)) N900DL XA-NLK
110	24A	N388R N1969H N362AA N35JF N88JF b/u Oct86 possibly following accident at Detriot, MI in Oct86; cx Jul89; remains with Brandis Avn, Taylorville, IL
111	24A	N900Y N500FM N44WD N900NA
112	24	N447LJ CF-ECB N2200T N10CP (OB-) N112DJ N104GA XA-
113	24	N438LJ (N402Y) N204Y N100SQ to spares 1989 by Brandis Avn, Taylorville, IL
114	24	N443LJ N999M N99DM PT-LNE

LEARJET 23/24

C/n	Model	Identities
115	24	N449LJ N458LJ N591D N591DL N86CC b/u for spares during 1989 Denver, CO; remains with Brandis Avn, Taylorville, IL
116	24A	N461F N52EN N77GH N8FM N400EP N40BP N51B N105GA (N12MB) N1420*
117	24XR	N288VW F-BRAL N16MJ HZ-SMB N90DH N92DF N140EX
118	24	N452LJ N100GS N1008S N1919W N31SK w/o 27Mar87 on approach to Eagle County A/P, Vail, CO
119	24	N453LJ N453SA N605GA N994SA N110W N500PP N500P (N500PJ) N61CK N63CK
120	24	N457LJ N633J N633NJ N44AJ N44NJ PT-LMF
121	24	N454LJ N454GL N454RN w/o 26Feb73 Atlanta, GA
122	24	N461LJ PT-CXK w/o 04May73 Rio Galeon, Brazil
123	24	N262HA N700C (N700ET) XA-JSC XA-JSO N35EC
124	24	N462LJ OY-EGE SE-DCU (N252DL) XA-RTV N991TD
125	24A	N651LJ
126	24	N653LJ N352WR N332FP (N345SF) N16HC
127	24	N654LJ N654JC N654LD N111LJ N127LJ N37CB (N6462) N124JL
128	24	N655LJ HB-VBK N914BA N333X N383X N4CR HB-VBK N37594 N802W (D-CJAD) N128BJ N911KB XA-TDP (N128WD) to spares by Dodson Int'l parts, Rantoul, KS circa 1999
129	24	N656LJ D-IFUM N44GA C-GSAX N44GA w/o 30Jan84 Santa Catalina, CA; cx Nov86
130	24	N657LJ N420WR N1871R N1871P N130J N33CJ N330J N234MR b/u for spares Dec87
131	24	N659LJ N232R N282R N11FH N241JA
132	24	N658LJ N233R N238R N32CA
133	24	N660LJ N40JF N40JE N555PV N46WB N16WJ N133DF N133BL
134	24	N231R N281R N282R N215J N200GP (N202GP) N200TC N270TC N7GN N911TR N26BA being parted out at Rantoul KS circa early 2000
135	24	N85W N77LB LV-WMR w/o 28Aug95 Pasadas, Argentina; fuselage at Buenos Aires-Aeroparque, for spares
136	24	N664LJ N222RB N954S N24LW XA-JLV wfu following flood damage; to spares Oct94 Spirit of St Louis A/P
137	24	N907CS N73HG N77RY N72FP N151AG
138	24	N37P N808DP N808D N575G N106CA N45JF (N106CA) N400RS N94JJ N130RS
139	24	N590GA N52JH N42AJ N481EZ N96AA
140	24	N663LJ N663L N663LJ N593KR N252M N100VC N100VQ
141	24	N348VL N348BJ N43AJ N141PJ XB-FJW XB-GHO
142	24	N591GA N200NR N777MR
143	24	N592GA N145JN N778GA N49AJ N900BD N2YY (N727LG) N724LG N24WF wfu at Uvalde TX still painted as N724LG
144	24	N593GA N397L N397BC N9KC N700C N303AF b/u for spares 1986 by White Inds, Bates City, MO; remains still present Nov94
145	24	N690J N57ND (N57NB) N282AC
146	24	N672LJ N235Z N44CJ w/o 02Oct81 Felt, OK
147	24	N673LJ N595GA N16CP N444KW N33NJ N825AA (N67CK)
148	24	N406L N80CB N133TW HB-VDH N8482B N426PS (N47NR) N41MP
149	24	N294BC N2945C N300HH N300LB N64HB N995TD
150	24XR	N3807G N596GA N596HF N211HJ N211BL N24XR XA-RQB
151	24	N153H N111HJ N664CL N664GL N50JF N24AJ N53GH N6177Y
152	24	N3807G N597GA N21U N98DK N9LM N48BA wfu 1993 Kissimmee, FL; cx Aug93; to Dodson Avn at Rantoul
153	24	N524SC N1TK N159J (N53DE) N878DE (N555DH) N153BR N120RA
154	24	N123VW N12315 N424RD N7HA N11AK N123RE w/o 17Oct78 Lancaster, CA
155	24	N598GA N422U N462B N462BA N833GA N210FP N660A b/u for spares during 1987; remains with OK Aircraft, Gilroy, CA
156	24	N599GA N468DM N111RF N111RP N712R
157	24	N640GA N1919W N1919G N191DA N94HC N124WL N43ZP N659AT (N157BP) XA-SNZ (N650AT) N659AT N157TW
158	24	N642GA N392T N855GA N500MH PT-LPX N500MH N220PM PT-WEW
159	24	N647GA N855W N661JB N66MR N710TV (N269AL)
160	24	N645G N111WJ C-GTJT N4791C N989TL
161	24	N649G N224KT N24KT N24KF N222TW
162	24	N841G N338DS N91MK N919K N835AC N835AG N55NJ w/o 07May86 Hollywood, FL; remains with Dodson Avn, Ottawa, KS
163	24	N701AP N1AP N65339 N77AE (N777JA) N65WM N68LU wfu and donated to mechanics school, Lewis Univ, IL Jul86
164	24	N711L N464J N924BW N831RA XA-RYN N831RA XA-TKC+ N831RA + remained current on USCAR
165	24	N844GA N469J ZS-KJY V5-KJY ZS-KJY V5-KJY ZS-KJY
166	24	N993KL N500SB N124PJ N124HF N993TD
167	24	N847GA N841LC N888B N664CL
168	24	N109JR N109JB N51CH C-GBWB N155BT N333TW
169	24	D-ICAR N9033X (N127DN) N127DM N927AA N93BP
170	24	N200DH N151WW
171	24	N737FN N417WW
172	24	N234WR N48AJ wfu; remains with White Inds, Bates City, MO; still regd
173	24	N852GA N872JR N110SQ N33ST N102GP N3GL N623RC YV-824CP
174	24	N854GA N661CP N661JG N999JR N321GL N77WD N77GJ XA-LNK
175	24	N859GM N859L N288K N28BK N881FC w/o 02Feb92 New Tamiami, FL; cx Mar93
176	24	PT-CXJ
177	24	N321Q N104MB N555LB N555LA N555LB (N524DW)

LEARJET 23/24

C/n	Model	Identities
178	24	N674LJ N55KS N55KX N56LB N56LS N24AJ N41BJ N723JW N11AQ
179	24	N920FF N300CC N111RA N111RE N410PD N410PB N412PD N717DB XC-GII XA-RQP N994TD
180	24	N566RB N802JA N100RA XA-SBR XA-NLA
181	24B	N234Q N1QC N651J N44PA (N144PA) N87CF N254JT N426TA
182	24B	N945GA N171L N500ZA N500ZH N155J
183	24B	N676LJ OY-AGZ F-BRNL w/o 18Dec85 Toulouse, France
184	24B	N950GA D-IMWZ N84J N36RS N78BH N28DL N58DM N58FN
185	24B	N754M N44CP N144CP being parted out at Rantoul KS circa early 2000
186	24B	N266P N100AJ N1SS N18G (N7300G) N7300K N73PS N196CF
187	24B	ZS-SGH F-GAJD N5WJ N129DM b/u for spares Feb90
188	24B	N230R N280R
189	24B	D-CJET D-IKAF D-CONA N14MJ N711DS N711DX N915US
190	24B	N4291G N9HM N50TC HZ-GP4 F-GBLA N190SC (N190DB) N190BP
191	24B	N855W N44LJ (N44TL) N80DH b/u 1984 after accident; cx Mar89; remains to Dodson Avn, Ottawa, KS
192	24B	N1919W N12MK w/o 06Jan77 Palm Springs, CA
193	24B	D-IOGI N31TC N500RP N500RE N33RE N140CA N83H N83HC (N488BL) N193JF
194	24B	N952GA N77LS N851BA N62DM (N62FN)
195	24B	N202BT N272GL F-BUUV N803L N555LJ
196	24B	N99SC N1125E N99ES N99E N173LP N573LP N573LR N88RD N196AF N196TB
197	24B	N953GA CF-CSS C-FCSS N52GH N87AC C-FCSS N711CN N711 N711UR N710TJ XB-SUD XA-RXA
198	24B	N66RP N111GW N21XL N21XB N39KM
199	24B	N333CR N855W N444HC N70TJ
200	24B	(N24NP) N721J N721JA N246CM N119MA being parted out at Bates City MO circa early 2000
201	24B	N3871J N273GL D-IDDD D-CDDD C-GTFA N100DL substantially damaged 23May98, Orlando Executive A/p, FL being parted out at Bates City MO circa early 2000
202	24B	N3816G N77JN F-BUFN N26MJ N999MF N123SV N814HH N814JR N333RY*
203	24B	N515WC N3GW (N43TL) N55LJ N55MJ N203CK N203JL
204	24B	N957GA N957E N176CP N510ND N510MS
205	24B	N974JD N64CF N64CE (N721J)
206	24B	HB-VBY F-BTYV N116RM N24YA^
207	24XR	N851JH N878W N457JA ZS-MGJ
208	24B	D-ILDE N72335 N42HC N444AG N32MJ N444AG N444AQ N14PT XA-AAA
209	24B	N970GA N16MT N14BC ZS-LWU
210	24B	ZS-LLG F-BSRL w/o 10Jun85 over Provins nr Paris, France
211	24B	N388P N30EH N222AP N31LB N413WF N680CJ
212	24B	N291BC N328TL N328JK
213	24B	N555MH N986WC N886WC N999RA N43KC N103TC N95AB
214	24B	N192MH N192MB N666CC N668MC N214MJ N42NF N234CM w/o 16Dec88 nr Monclova, Mexico; cx Apr91
215	24B	N971GA N201WL N10EC N29CA (N57JR) N29CA (N57JR) N400EP
216	24B	N212LF N723LL N711DB N411SP (N821LL) N777LB N900GG
217	24B	N777MC N777MQ C-GPDB N8536Y C-GDKS N45824 N217AT C-FZHT N876MC
218	24B	N682LJ N101VS
219	24B	N658AT N711CE N100KK F-GECI N977GA ZS-TOY
220	24B	N292BC N248J N17FN wfu for spares by Dodson Avn, Ottawa, KS
221	24B	N977GA N570P (N570JG) N59JG N233TW
222	24B	N692LJ N740E N740F N740EJ
223	24B	D-IOGA D-COGA D-IFVG D-CFVG N7074X wfu for spares by Feb94
224	24B	D-IOGE N99606 N30DH C-GPCL N102PA (N722DM) N61DM (N61FN) (N51GJ) XA-TCA
225	24B	N618R D-IHLZ w/o 18Jun73 Marlensel, W Germany
226	24B	N454LJ N335JW (N335JR) N335RY
227	24B	XA-TIP N90797 N10CB N43W N4576T N28AT N27BJ
228	24B	N245GL N4292G N7DL (D-IIDD) D-IIPD N777SA N150AB PT-OBD
229	24B	N293BC N298H N551AS N864CL w/o 08Oct84 San Francisco, CA
230	24D	N252GL N329HN N93C N93CB N433J N433JA N18SD N477JB N482CP N819GF N67JR N7121K XA-VVI N32287 XA-SSU
231	24D	HB-VBU I-CART N693LJ N37DH (N93BR) wfu; remains with Brandis Avn, Taylorville, IL; still regd
232	24D	N123CB w/o 17Apr71 Butte, MT
233	24R	N253GL D-IGSO N78AF N23SG N23SQ N500RW N124TS (N56GH)
234	24D	LV-PRA LV-JTZ
235	24XR	N51VL N701SC
236	24D	N26VM N48JW N25ZW N55DD N3TJ N25LJ N236TS N236WJ N93DD N990PT
237	24D	N902AR N111TT N25TA N112J N32AA N353J N889WF XA- N25RJ N825DM N237TW
238	24D	N262GL N472EJ N49DM N48FN
239	24D	D-ILVW D-ILHM F-GBLZ N83MJ PT-LAU w/o 10Sep94 Brasilia A/P, Brazil
240	24D	LV-PRB LV-JXA
241	24D	HB-VCT N120J N363BC (N61TJ) N63GA
242	24D	N1972G N45CP N1972G N999WA
243	24XR	HB-VCI N2909W (N85DH) N83RG N56WS N57FL N37HT
244	24D	PT-DZU w/o 23Aug71 Sao Paulo, Brazil
245	24D	N275LE N275E JA8446 N275E (N44KB)
246	24D	N215Z N21NA N5SJ N35SJ N50SJ (N69SF) N61BA N184AL N600JC N444SC (N444HE) N24TE N99JB N6JM N500MS

LEARJET 23/24

C/n	Model	Identities
247	24D	HB-VCN D-ICAP N23AM N42PG N247DB N997TD*
248	24D	OO-LFA 9Q-CBC w/o 18Jan94 Kinshasa, Zaire
249	24D	9J-ADF N27MJ N999M N998M XA-POS XC-AA63 N249RA N440KT
250	24D	N112C D-IMAR N122CG N2U N1U N85CA N85CD Venezuela 0006
251	24D	N333X N338X N251TJ N95DD XA-SBZ XA-RIC N46JA N69XW N39EL
252	24D	N711L N711LD N972 N157AG (N252TJ) (C6-BGF)
253	24D	N123VW N999U N30FL N711DB (N30FL) N97DM N417JD N97DM w/o 05Mar86 over Pacific Ocean nr San Clemente Is (collided with Learjet 35-040 N39DM, qv)
254	24D	D-ICAY D-CCAT N13606 PT-LCV
255	24D	XC-SAG XA-BBE XA-SMU
256	24D	HB-VCW N703J C-GWFG
257	24D	N427JX C-GHDP N888FA
258	24D	N75KV N25VZ N25GW N19TJ N24CK (N24DZ) (N77RS) N424RS
259	24D	N200JR N22MH (N24EA) (N22ML) I-EJIA N22MH XA-RRC to White Inds, Bates City, MO, for spares
260	24D	N60GL C-GFJB XA-ROX XA-GBA
261	24D	D-IDAT D-COOL C-GBWA b/u for spares 1993 by Global Inds; cx Jun94; remains to Bounty Avn Scrapyard, Detroit-Willow Run, MI
262	24D	N2GR OH-GLB N38788 N110PS OH-GLB
263	24D	N3812G XB-JOY w/o 29Jun76 Mexico City, Mexico
264	24XR	PI-C1747 RP-C1747
265	24D	N2WL N32WL N456JA w/o 24Oct85 Juneau, AK
266	24D	N266BS VH-BSJ N266BS N266TW
267	24XR	HB-VCY N46032 N78AE N124GA VR-BHC HB-VCY N95DA VR-BMN N267MP ZS-OEA
268	24D	N53GL N111WW N123CC N92TC (N66FN) N58BL N98WJ
269	24D	XA-DIJ
270	24D	XB-NAG XA-BUY N3979P PT-LEM w/o 07Apr99 Ribeirao Preto, Brazil
271	24D	N3818G HB-VDK F-BVEC N4305U XA-SCE
272	24D	N51GL N117K
273	24D	OH-GLA N118J 5Y-GEO N51AJ XC-DOP XB-DZR
274	24D	N3871J N1U N48CT
275	24D	XB-NUR N24TC N216HB PT-LPH
276	24D	PT-JGU N25CV N56PT
277	24D	N131CA N181CA (N163ME) (N181RW) N106MC N57BC N277TW
278	24D	PT-JKR N5695H N202JS
279	24D	VH-SBC N849GL N3DU N3DZ I-FREU N75CJ N101AR
280	24XR	D-ICHS N79RS ZS-NGG
281	24D	SE-DFB OY-BIZ N23MJ N281FP
282	24D	D-INKA N300JA w/o 02Dec79 Dutch Harbor, AK
283	24D	SE-DFA D-IEGO N51JT N20GT N31WT N47WT (N711SC) N24XR
284	24D	PT-JKQ
285	24D	XC-AZU XA-REK XB-GBC N995DR (N995RD) N430JW
286	24XR	N59GL N86GC N56RD N57DB N77JL
287	24D	HB-VDN EC-CJA HB-VDN I-MABU N92565 PT-LCN w/o 04Apr84 Florianapolis, Brazil
288	24D	N288DF
289	24D	(HB-VDO) F-BRGF N131MA XA-RUJ N131MA N289SA N289G N98CG
290	24D	N462B N23JC N934H N87AP N627ER N24TK XA-RMF
291	24D	ZS-GLD N45862 N148J N24PJ PT-LYL N114WC (N919MA) N488DM N483DM
292	24D	N426NA N600PC N426NA N800PC N888TW
293	24D	XA-TIP N917BF N293MC
294	24D	N4F PT-LNK PP-EIW PT-WKL
295	24D	N717HB N717HE N49TJ (N160GC) N590CH N295NW
296	24D	XA-FIW N222BN N500RK N500DJ PT-LMS
297	24D	N297EJ XA-ACC N716US (N317MR) HK-3265 N8094U N24S
298	24D	N298EJ XA-ADD N98AC N151AG N470TR N169US
299	24D	N299EJ XA-ABB XC-JCN XB-GJS N299TW
300	24D	N300EJ N455JA w/o 20Aug85 Gulkana, AK
301	24D	N137JL N111TT (N87MJ) N31BG N249HP
302	24D	N302EJ N39DM N302EJ w/o 14Apr83 Puerta Vallarta, Mexico
303	24D	N303EJ PT-LOJ
304	24D	N304EJ N304LP N500CG N588CG
305	24D	N305EJ N98DK N305EJ (N725DM) N43DM (N43FN) N510PA N666MW
306	24D	N306EJ N55CD N98AA N132MA XA-SAV XA-SAA+ N306JA N243RK* + noted as such in Oct97
307	24D	N307EJ N307BJ XA-RRK w/o 02Jan98 Tampico, Mexico to spares by Dodson Int'l Parts, Rantoul, KS
308	24D	N308EJ N99AA N39TT (N308LJ)
309	24D	N310LJ N45FC N45AJ (N4445J) N789AA N80CK
310	24D	HB-VDU I-AMME w/o 06Feb76 Bari, Italy
311	24D	N66LW N5TR N5TD N19HM N19FM N50DR N56DR N748GM N10WJ (N76PW)
312	24D	Ecuador IGM-401 N312NA N80AP
313	24D	Mexico MTX-01 Mexico MTX-02 reported w/o 20Nov98 Mexico City, Mexico - being parted out at Bates City MO circa early 2000
314	24D	N501MH N13MJ w/o 06Nov82 Elizabeth City, NC; cx Sep92
315	24D	PT-KPE engineless and parts missing at Sao Paulo - Congonhas, Brazil circa Sep99
316	24D	LV-LRC Argentina T-03 LV-LRC
317	24D	N133GL ZS-JJO N45AJ XA-JIQ
318	24D	N114JT N611DB
319	24XR	XC-SUP XA-SUP XC-SUP N174RD

LEARJET 23/24

C/n	Model	Identities						
320	24D	N3802G	YU-BIH	SL-BAB	S5-BAB	N996TD		
321	24D	N10WF	N122RW	N224JB	C-FRNR	N33TP		
322	24D	XA-DAT	N105GL	N972H	N7RL	N322TJ^		
323	24D	N61AW	N744JC	N104MC	N453			
324	24D	N107GL	(possibly XA-SUY)		XA-SCY (marks not confirmed)		N324TW	
325	24D	N76RV	N416G	N500SW				
326	24D	N326EJ	(N400XB)	N326KE	N322AU			
327	24D	N327EJ	F-GGPG	N327GJ	N711PC			
328	24D	D-IMMM	D-CMMM					
329	24E	N102GL	N21AG	N22MJ	XA-RAQ	XA-PFA	N329TJ	N24FW
330	24E	N511AT	N330TW					
331	24E	N12MJ	XA-REA	N32DD				
332	24F	N13KL	N56MM					
333	24E	N76TR	N32WT	N75GP	N75GR	PT-LQK		
334	24E	N6KM	N66MJ	N944KM				
335	24E	N721GL	N87JL	N2DD	N8AE			
336	24F	N3818G	I-DDAE	N162J	N9LD			
337	24F	XA-GEO	XA-DET					
338	24E	N729GL	N30LM	N30EM	b/u for spares 1989; cx Dec89; remains with Brandis Avn, Taylorville, IL			
339	24E	N15MJ	N851CC	N690	N60FN	N1TJ	N52DD	
340	24E	N10FU	C-FHFP	N54JC	(N95CP)	N106TJ	N457GM	
341	24E	N22BM	N22NM	N3PW	(N103JW)	N14DM		
342	24F	N40144	YV-178CP	N824GA	N123DG			
343	24E	N102B	N102C	N1DK				
344	24F	N81MC	w/o 10Nov84 St Thomas, Virgin Islands					
345	24E	N500RP	N500RR	D-CFPD	N435AS			
346	24E	N61SF	N41TC	N117AJ	N117AE			
347	24E	N724GL	N124EZ	N500LL	N500TS	N500SR		
348	24F	N725GL	N4RT	N4RU	(N106M)	N8BG	N444TW	
349	24F	VH-FLJ	N349BS	XA-CAP	XB-DZD			
350	24F	N741GL	N500ZA					
351	24E	N19MJ	N31WT	N81WT	N77MR	(N94BD)		
352	24F	N101US	(N449JS)	N352MD				
353	24F	N740GL	N711PD	N411MM	N63BW	PT-LMA	w/o 24Feb88 Macre, Brazil	
354	24F	N678SP	PT-LYE	ZS-FUN				
355	24E	N7AB	N7ZB	N500NH	N165CM			
356	24F	N3283M	N677SW	N113JS	PT-LKD			
357	24F	N288J	N129ME					

Production complete

LEARJET MODEL 25

C/n	Series	Identities
001		N463LJ used in construction of 25-002
002		N661LJ wfu Jul72 AiResearch engine tests
003		N594GA N11JC N4PN N97DM N97FN
004		N641GA N1121 N1121C N7GJ N47MJ N251AF
005		N646GA N1969W N777RA N707TR (N707TP) (N24FN) N28FN N711SQ XA-SDQ N39CK
006		N6804L N256P N90MH N88CJ (N88GJ) N522SC N852SC N188FC (N25JX) (N857SC) N252SC N44CP
007		N551MD N551MB N7TJ N25NM N500JA N52JA (N58JA) N726WR*
008		N648GA N744W VP-BDM N744W N1976S N645L N88NJ N800GG
009		N843GA N670LJ 9Q-CHC N40LB w/o 25Sep73 Omaha, NB
010		N846GA N846HC N671WM N102PS (N10BF) (N82UH) (N121GL) N121EL
011		N167J N49BA C-GHMH N108GA N525TW
012		N853GA N853DS N191DA N846YT N846YC N102AR
013		N856G N515VW w/o 17Apr69 Delemont, Switzerland
014		N857GA N914SB N204A N316M N127AJ N8CL N14LJ N754DB
015		N858GM CF-HMV N713US N708TR N25FN N25GJ N125U
016		N145JN CF-KAX N424RD N711EV N83TH N8FF N976BS (N35WE)
017		N720AS N101WR N16JP N666WL N55WJ N128DM N123JS N53FL
018		N861GA N323WA N77SA N32PC N99ES N117CH N15MJ (N23FN) N29FN wfu; with Brandis Avn, Taylorville, IL; still regd
019		N591KR N88EP N88FP N100MK w/o 21Oct78 Sandusky, OH
020		N941GA N215Z N30TT (N90TC) N113AK N900JD N900CJ N500JS
021		N942GA N111LL N1JR N1LL N40SW N40SN N6NF wfu; cx Apr95; displayed Ozark Municipal A/p, AL
022	XR	N943GA N925WP N1ZC N99CQ (N93JH) N131MS N24BS N111WB N111WR ZS-SSM
023		N577LJ N72CD N13CR (N861L) N47AJ (N820RT) (N12RA) N850SC N767SC N147TW
024		N425RD N125ST N137BC N20HJ N20RZ
025		N920S N928S N920S N92V N49BB N242AG N225DS (N111LM)
026		N4005S N7ZA C-GMAP N283R N281R N25EC
027		N7000G N423RD N35WB N835WB (N835GM) EC-EBM N500DL N900AJ
028		N592KR N263GL N277LE N33PF
029	XR	N280LC N28LA N107HF ran off runway at Orlando, FL 19May98
030		N951GA N999M N999MK N745W N30PS N48HM N380LC N45DM N51CA w/o 30Mar83 Newark, NJ
031		N294NW (N294M)
032		N373W N711DB N712DC N357HC XA-ZYZ XA-RQI on display in terminal Mexico City A/P, Mexico
033		HB-VBP N143J N786MS YV-88CP N77NJ
034		N954GA N954FA N242WT N6GC N3UC N17AR N19FN N309AJ N309LJ
035		N683LJ N33GF N33TR N616NA
036	TF	N956GA N956J N741E N741ED N15CC N15M (also carried "N25TF") N45BK
037		N737EF N18JF N28AA N155AG
038		HB-VBR EC-CKD HB-VBR N738GL N36MW N444WS N83GG N400AJ N813JW
039		N959GA N959RE N17JF N66NJ N308AJ (N25VJ)
040		N687LJ HB-VBI F-BSUR (N2273G) C-GOSL N41AJ N9CZ (N98RH) N23FN N238CA
041		N960GA N205SC N205SA N31AA (N25RE)
042		N958GA N958DM (N429TJ) N50DT N800JA N797SC (N25LG) N125WD*
043		N30LJ N808DP N300PP N234ND N473TC
044		N962GA N658TC w/o 18Jan72 Victoria, TX
045		N963GA CF-DWW N815J N33CJ N123EL N24FN N28CK
046		N964GA N55KC N55KQ N33PT N345MC
047		N222B (N68CK)
048		N965GA N200G XA-TCY N48GR
049		N966GA N900P N900Q HP-1141P N900Q N70HJ N70SK
050		N44EL N44EE D-CONE N27MJ N55FN N999MF
051		N973GA N70MP PT-LPT N12WW N76UM
052		N232MD N8280 N828QA N250CC (N132MA) N133MA N692FC N692FG (N69LJ)
053		N974GA N974M N37MB N37GB N153TW
054		OY-AKL N12373 N500JW N509G N25MD
055		N1500B N65RC N511AJ
056	XR	N780A PT-LBW
057		CF-TXT C-FTXT N920EA (N225EA)
058		N2366Y N273LP N273LR
059		N425JX N211MB w/o 03Mar80 Port au Prince, Haiti
060		N695LJ N564CL
061	C	N251GL PT-DUO N9CN YV-203CP
062		OY-AKZ N4981 N105BJ N303JJ HZ-GP4 N86MJ N27FN N25ME
063		N919S C-GPDZ N184J N680J N68PJ N5DM N24LT N25FM
064		N266GL rebuilt to Model 28 standard to act as prototype; reverted to Model 25 standards N566NA wfu 1998; on display at the John C.Stennis Space Center, MS
065		airframe not built
066		airframe not built
067		airframe not built
068		airframe not built
069		airframe not built
070	C	N255GL CF-ROX C-FROX N32SM C-FZHU N911LM
071	C	N257GL YV-T-DTT YV-130P YV-132CP N97AM

LEARJET 25

C/n	Series	Identities
072	C	N256GL PT-IBR w/o 26Sep76 Sao Paulo, Brazil
073	XR	HB-VCM I-TAKY N3JL N3JX HZ-SMB N63SB N85FJ N888DB N45CP
074	B	N251GL SX-ASO w/o 18Feb72 Antibes, France
075	B	N241AG N241AQ N417PJ N138JB VR-CGD VR-CHT VP-CHT VP-CJF N82025
076	B	HB-VCL D-CCWK N160J N711CA N831WM N222MC N222MQ N77KW XA-SJS
077	B	PT-DVL w/o 12Nov76 Sao Paulo, Brazil
078	B	N258GL N64MP N64MR N276LE N188BC N778JC
079	B	D-CCAT OE-GLA N50DH N36CC (N85HR)
080	B	N1976L N1978L (N90DH) N30AP XA-POG
081	B	N111GL N110GL HZ-MOA HZ-AZP HZ-BB1 N66TJ N524DW
082	B	HB-VCK N30P N427RD N15AK N11AK N654 N700FC
083	C	N31CS N200Y N200MH N54FN
084	C	N2000M (C-GWUZ) N200QM N200SF F-BYAL N777TX
085	B	N8MA N8MQ b/u for spares
086	B	N123DM N28BP N23DB N65WH
087	C	N723LF N777LF N99XZ N25TE
088	B	N88GC N88GQ N123SF N176G N42FE N125JL N5UJ
089	C	PT-IIQ N890K*
090	B	N265GL N112CT N112CH N112ME C-GBOT
091	B	N500CA N500CD N500MJ D-CBPD N96MJ C-FDAC N2138T (N816JA) VR-CCH N91PN
092	B	N1ED N9671A N258G N18AK N113ES N60DK
093	B	N33HM N33NM PT-LEN
094	C	SX-CBM VR-BFV N97J N77RS w/o 14Dec78 Anchorage, AK; remains to White Inds, Bates City, MO
095	B	N200BC N303SC N303SQ C-GRCO N2094L
096	B	N742E N742Z N48FN N405RS C-GCJD N235JW N20NW
097	C	HB-VCS (OY-ASK) I-SFER N22NJ
098	C	N7JN VR-BEM N139J VR-BGF YV-26CP N96MJ N502MH ZS-NYG
099	C	PT-IKR PT-FAF PT-LHU w/o 28Jly92 Icuape, Brazil
100	B	N262JE N262E N741E N741F N59AC N25TK N829AA
101	B	N268GL N575GD N269AS N30AP N156CB N600HT N600HD N74JL N821AW N47MR
102	B	N267GL N999M N999ML N311CC N52AJ N962 N52AJ N64WH N254SC
103	B	N428JX b/u for parts 1989 by Brandis Avn, Taylorville, IL
104	B	N1JR N101JR N392T XA-JAX XA-RIN
105	B	N1BR N1RA N711WE N713Q N234RB N905WJ N7AT N55PD XA-SXD N55PD
106	XR	N10NP N10FL N974JD N458JA N458J w/o 01Jly91 Columbus, OH; cx Aug91
107	B	N225CC N57DM N25NP N25NB N252BK
108	C	PT-CMY w/o 06Apr90 Juiz de Fora, Brazil
109	B	N888DH N333HP C-GSAS N860MX
110	B	N50GL N63ET N75CA N110HA N52SD N343RK
111	B	N30TP N55ES PT-LXS N825A
112	B	OY-BFC N173J N279LE
113	C	PT-ISN w/o 04Nov89 Belo Horizonte-Pampulha, Brazil
114	B	N47HC (C-GLRE) N45HB N77PK N25JD N114HC
115	C	PT-ISO
116	C	CF-CXY N600PC N819GY (N818GY) N666TW
117	B	N40AS N170GT N170RL N4402 N4405 C-FMGM N731CW
118	B	OO-LFZ (D-CITO) N601J N118SE (N800JA) N124MA (N79AX) VP-CMB
119	B	N3810G PT-JBQ w/o 04Sep82 Rio Branco, Brazil
120	B	N111AF N744MC N278LE N10BD N10BU VH-OVS (N100FU) N101FU N120SL
121	B	N7GA HZ-MRP N39JJ N500PP N1036N may have been XA-SAL XA-SIO N8005Y (N821MS)
122	B	N23TA N332LS N122BS N122WC N751CA
123	B	N360AA N973JD (N914RA) N906SU N688GS
124	B	N44MJ N39JE N59BP N15CC N15CU N54H N54HU (N400DB) (N95TW) N33TW
125	B	N4MR N9AT (N85AT) N89AT N94AT N97AC (N11MC) N10VG
126	C	N12WK N114CC (N162AC) N14FN
127	B	N93C N93CE N83JM (N42BJ) N450 N450SC N222AK N425JL
128	B	N67PC N1MX N40BC w/o 06Jly79 Pueblo, CO; remains to White Inds, Bates City, MO
129	C	N551WC N71DM (N193DR) N25MR
130	B	N111BL N25PL N26AT
131	C	N3803G PT-JDX w/o 26Dec78 Sao Paulo-Congonhas, Brazil; front of fuselage in use at Belo Horizonte-Pampulha, Brazil as a link trainer
132	B	N202BT N132GL N54MC N54MQ N715JF N715MH
133	B	N10RE N10RZ N51MJ N58CP XA-RZY N233CA
134	B	N52GL N15BH N712JA N26FN N65A
135	B	G-BBEE N3803G N1103R G-BBEE N7600K (N1RW) N50RW
136	B	N920CC N920US N180YA N221TC N71CE (N48WA) N753CA N48WA
137	B	N400 N37BJ N500WW N752CA N752EA
138	B	N11BU N100EP N36204 N777PD N711PD N811PD (N2HE) N73LJ
139	XR	N618R N225AC N12MH (N14PT) N605NE N111MP
140	B	N42G N42GX N68TJ N401AC N403AC N140CA
141	XR	N52L N424JR N424JP N94RS N25HA ZS-BXR
142	B	N515WH N42HC (N142HC) N70CE (N70WA) N49WA
143	B	N96VF (N33VF) N111RF N113RF N143CK
144	B	N10NT N44PA w/o Dec91 (no further details known); b/u Jun92
145	B	N131GL C-GRDR N2127E N145SH
146	C	N146LJ N9HM N9HN C-GRQX N9HN N6KJ I-BMFE
147	B	N55KC N25KC N150WW N911JG N147BP XA-GGG

LEARJET 25

C/n	Series	Identities
148	XR	N58GL N336WR N98RS (N98JA)
149	B	HB-VDI EC-CIM N149J N239CA
150	B	N714K N714KP N888RB (N25LP) N251JA
151	B	N366AA w/o 31Aug74 Briggsdale, CO
152	XR	N50L N515SC N452ET XA-POI XA-JSC N105BA
153	B	N501PS w/o 26May77 Detroit, MI; remains to Dodson Avn, Ottawa, KS
154	B	N100K N30DK N47DK N82TS N210NC N82TS
155	B	N24TA PT-LEA
156	C	PT-KAP N613SZ
157	B	N2427F N157CA N57CK N50CK
158	B	N158GL HZ-GP3 N85MJ N334LS N71RB N924BW
159	B	Peru FAP 522/OB-1429 N24RZ
160	B	ZS-MTD VP-WKY Z-WKY ZS-MTD 3D-AEZ ZS-MTD
161	B	N4VC N61EW N236CA
162	XR	N62ZS N661MP N663JB N97RS N97JJ N150RS
163	B	SE-DFC N70606 N173LP N173LR C-FBEA N333AW N59SG N25RE (N65RC) N911AJ
164	B	Peru FAP 523/OB-1430 N23RZ
165	C	PT-KBC w/o 04Jun96 Riberao Preto, Brazil; cx Aug97
166	B	PT-KBD N918TD
167	B	C-GBFP
168	B	N72TP N88BT N88BY
169	B	N471MM N743E N743F N893WA N59FL
170	B	N131G N711DS N170EV (N170EP) N98796 N627WS w/o 13Jan98 Houston Intercontinental A/p, TX; cx Oct98
171	B	I-ELEN N1DD OY-ASP N1DD N55MF N55PT N42DG N888LR N401AJ
172	C	PT-KKV w/o 11Jan91 nr Belo Horizonte, Brazil
173	XR	N780AC N780AQ N777NJ N104BW
174	B	N74G N410SP N412SP N16KK
175	XR	N462B N462BA N96RS (N96JJ) N307AJ N75SJ
176	C	N55VL N50PE N25KV N28KV PT-LLN
177	B	N11PH N745W D-CDPD w/o 18May83 in Atlantic approx 320 km S of Reykjavik, Iceland
178	B	N75B N999M N999MV N999HG w/o 08Sep77 Sanford, NC
179	B	N659HX C-GBQC C-GSKL
180	B	VH-BLJ N95BS C-FEWB N95BS VH-LJB N266BS N102VS
181	C	VH-TNN N94PK N73TW
182	B	C-GLBT N4300L F-GFMZ N225JL N99MC
183	B	N66JD N5LL N83CK
184	B	EC-CKR w/o 13Aug96 RAF Northolt, UK; to spares by White Industries 1998
185	B	N666LP N55V N988DB N988AA N988AC
186	B	YU-BJH w/o 18Jan77 Sarajevo, Yugoslavia
187	B	YU-BJG status following 1999 war is unknown
188	B	G-BCSE A40-AJ N1JR w/o 28Jly84 Waterville, ME and used for spares; remains to White Inds, Bates City, MO
189	B	N111SF N111SZ N352SC N888DF N67HB
190	B	XA-DAK
191	B	N1DD N78BT N38DJ w/o 12Jun92 Sheboygan, WI; cx Dec94; remains to Hampton - Tara Field, Atlanta GA
192	B	Bolivia 008
193	B	HB-VEF I-KISS HB-VIE I-SIMD N80GR N350DH N125RM N125TN
194	B	XA-COC XB-EGP XA-SXG XC-NSP
195	B	OB-M-1004 N108PA b/u for spares 1984; still current
196	B	N711WD N25TA w/o 11Apr80 New Mexico
197	B	N104GL N240AG N197WC N197CF
198	B	N20DK N29TS N198JA
199	XR	HB-VEI HZ-RI1 HZ-GP5 w/o 11Jan82 Narssarssuaq, Greenland
200	B	N2022R N680BC N350JH
201	B	N227RW N777SA N111AD N11TK N713B
202	B	N3807G Yugoslavia 10401 Yugoslavia 70401 YU-BRA status following 1999 war is unknown
203	B	N3811G Yugoslavia 10402 Yugoslavia 70402 YU-BRB
204	B	N376SC N373SC N472J PT-KZY w/o 16May82 Uberaba, Brazil
205	B	N1468B YU-BKJ Z3-BAA
206	D	N206EC N206EQ ZS-LXH
207	D	N3513F (I-GIAN) I-LEAR (N3513F) N207JC parted out by White Industries, Bates City MO circa 99
208	D	N54YR N54YP C-GZIM "N500PP" N54YP N500PP N500MP N300SC
209	D	N36SC N770AC (N770PA) N770AQ N18NM N30LJ
210	D	N133MR XA-JIN XA-RPV N97FT N75TJ
211	D	N3514F Bolivia 010
212	D	N1450B N911MG N212NE b/u for spares during 1989
213	D	N551DP HZ-SS2 VR-CDH N803PF N925DW
214	D	N30W N3UW N90BR I-AVJD N61826 N214ME N214LJ N245BS
215	D	N44FE N325JL N25UJ
216	D	N3556F N2426 (N345FJ) N80RE N80RP (N87MW) XA-PRO N216SA N767SA
217	D	N41H
218	D	N18MJ N155AU XA-RAX N14NA N251DS
219	XR	N55SL
220	XR	N220HS (N419BL) (N25WL) N220NJ N99NJ
221	D	N3819G YU-BKR

LEARJET 25

C/n	Series	Identities
222	XR	N1476B N726GL N4MR XA-KEY XA-MHA N4MR N225TJ
223	D	N23AM XC-DAD XA-BBA w/o 18Jun94 Washington-Dulles A/P, VA
224	D	N50B (N32TJ) N711NM N80AX
225	D	9J-AED N222AP N808DS N140GC
226	D	N333SG N234SV
227	D	N44BB N444PB N882SB XA-ROO (N25RE) N227EW N25RE
228	D	N228SW
229	D	N39415 LV-MBP CX-ECO
230	D	N16GT N16LJ N161AC N7RL N207HF
231	D	(OO-LFW) (OO-HFW) N999M N999ME N60DK N31MJ N225HW N531CW
232	D	N744LC N500EW N500LW
233	D	N55LJ N75LM N947TC
234	D	N3815G (N27GW) N234KK (N234EJ) (N28CC) XA-ESQ N234KK (N11SQ) N300JE N39BL N88DJ (N432AS) N18BL
235	XR	N400PC N400JS N400VC (N25XR)
236	D	N1466B XC-RPP
237	D	(N28BP) N137GL w/o 19Jan79 Detroit, MI (had marks N55MF reserved when w/o)
238	D	N39416 N40SW N45ZP N238MP N500TL
239	D	N192MH N45H N499EH
240	D	N78GL N83EA N33PT N339BA*
241	D	N432SL N25TA N25TB N711WD N712BW N713RR N713LJ N213CA
242	D	N749GL N363HA N102RA N242GM (N242AF) N242GS
243	D	N711JT PT-LSD w/o 02Mar96 Serra de Cantareira, near Sao Paulo, Brazil
244	D	N7LA XA-LET N24EP N831LH
245	D	N39398 LV-PAF LV-MST N245DK N60DK N606GB
246	XR	N40162 N51DB w/o 21Oct86 nr Jeddah, Saudi Arabia
247	D	N300PL scrapped for spares 1989
248	D	N80BT N80BE N500PP N900WA N95CK
249	D	N20PY N249SC N211JB (N500EF) N249LJ XA-FMU N800L XA-FMU N34TN
250	D	N30LM N438DM (N60DK) N112JM*
251	D	N752GL N78SD N290 N25FA TG-VOC N85TW
252	D	N1468B N44FH N444MK
253	D	N253EJ N97DK (N202DR) N253J N253M N253SC N8MF
254	D	N973 I-AVJE N76AX
255	D	N1433B N1ED N91ED N91MT N25GJ N717EP
256	D	N6LL N75CK
257	D	N700BJ N377C N377Q N988AS
258	D	N144FC (N54888) N54TA N888GC N333CD N258MD PT-LLL w/o 18Mar91 Brasilia, Brazil
259	D	LV-PAW LV-MMV w/o 23Sep89 in Marana River, nr Posadas, Argentina
260	D	N39413 (D-CHBM) D-CHEF N43783 N74RD
261	D	N3802G N180MC N24JK N261WC
262	D	N23HM N440F N333CG
263	D	N40162 N14VC N20DL N825D
264	D	N716NC N133JF N502JC N547JG
265	D	N1462B N265EJ N279TG N265LJ N31WT (N61WT) N69GF N265TW
266	D	N3807G PT-KYR reported w/o circa Aug89; no further details; cx during 1990
267	D	N15ER
268	D	N268WC XA-SPL N268WC
269	D	N109SJ N269MD N51BL LV-PLL LV-WOC
270	D	N842GL (N123CG) N842GL N123CG (N45KB) N75AX
271	D	N183AP N125NE w/o 21May80 Gulf of Mexico; cx Nov82
272	D	N272EJ N272JM N747AN N717AN
273	D	N321AS N73DJ
274	D	N600CD D-CEPD N3131G N602NC N602N N110FP N274LJ XA-MAL XA-RZE XA-FMR
275	D	N211CD N254CL
276	D	N188TC N188TQ N188TA
277	D	N20MJ N34CW N283U N321GL N81MW
278	D	N70JF
279	D	N41ZP N81AX
280	D	N280LA N18TA N18RA N225AC N95EC (N510L) N280C
281	D	(N245KK) N45KK N45KB N555PG N800RF
282	D	N711WD
283	D	N40144 XC-DAA N45826 N312GK N444WW
284	D	XC-CFM N284TJ
285	D	N6666R (N28RW) N6666K N666KK N422G I-COTO w/o Feb86 Paris-Le Bourget and dismantled
286	D	N28MJ XA-ROZ N6596R XA-RVI XC-AA83+ XA-TAQ N850MX + report of these marks possibly incorrect
287	D	N39416 RP-C4121 N63KH N287MF XA-ZYZ N20AD XA-ZZZ
288	D	N31WT N61WT N40BC N100WN (N40BC)
289	D	N1087T RP-C6610 RP-C400 N389GA N321GL
290	D	N221AP XA-ELR N221EL N321RB N600GM
291	D	N1088D N666RB N952 N600JT N530DC (N477MM)
292	D	N1088C N92MJ N92CS N711VT N711VK N604AS
293	D	N999TH N97JP XA-PIU
294	D	N27K N419GL N125TJ N161RB N88NJ
295	D	N229AP N137K ZS-LUD OE-GHL N295DJ (N298GS) N45ES XC-AGR N25HF
296	D	N712RW N712SJ N55DD N55MJ PT-OHD

LEARJET 25

C/n	Series	Identities									
297	D	N297EJ	N36NW	N297EJ	N24KW	N389AT					
298	D	N923GL	N711TG	N711TQ	(N712CB)	XA-ABH	N298DR				
299	D	N222LW	I-KIOV	(N8217W)	N299MW	(N5B)					
300	D	(N46BA)	N659HX								
301	D	N416RM	N610LM	(N888JA)	N25CZ	N82AX*					
302	D	N521JP	N28BP	N740K	N700DA						
303	D	XA-JOC									
304	D	N25NY									
305	D	N88JA	N53TC	N188R							
306	D	XA-DUB	XC-GUB								
307	D	LV-PEU	LV-OEL								
308	D	N23AM	XA-RMF	N2721U	XB-GDR	XA-SXY	N102RR	N727LM			
309	D	XA-GRB	XB-DKS	XA-DAZ	XA-PAZ						
310	D	N1088C	N211PD	N211JC							
311	D	N39391	N199BT	ZS-NJF	N199BT						
312	D	N94MJ	XC-HIS								
313	D	N31MJ	N31GS	N37RR	N727AW	N727CS	N631CW	N727CS			
314	D	N1466B	I-DEAN	HB-VHM	N38328	N30AD	N40AD	XA-LUZ	XA-REE	N42825	N95BP
315	D	N10873	N3798A	N83TC	N273KH	N273M					
316	D	N3793X	N1AH	(N782JR)	N17AH						
317	D	N821LM	N660TC	N969SS	(N96DC)						
318	D	N522JP	N522TA	N999BH	w/o 05Sep93 Rowe Mera, 30m from Santa Fe Municipal A/P, NM; cx May94						
319	D	N319EJ	N911EM	N680JC							
320	D	N320EJ	OO-LFR	N690JC							
321	D	N25AM									
322	D	5N-AOC									
323	D	N323EJ	N70SE	N6YY	PT-LMM						
324	D	N711BF	XA-POP	N970WJ							
325	D	N123NC	N523SA	N1411S	XA-RXB	N1411S	N2U	XA-TBV	N325JB	XB-HGE	
326	D	N771CB	N25NB								
327	D	N54GP	N52DA	(N54JC)	(N327BC)	N444TG					
328	D	N7LC	(N12FS)	OB-R-1313	OB-1313	N58DJ	N200NR	N725DM	N328JW	N518JG	
329	D	N3799B	XC-GNL	XA-GNL	N613GL	N83TE	N401DP				
330	D	(N523JP)	N521JP	XA-RZT	XA-RCG	XC-AA84	N330LJ				
331	D	N462B	N422B	N462B	N482CP						
332	D	XC-FIF	XB-DZQ								
333	D	N34MJ	N555SD								
334	D	N20RD	N57DL	N334MD	XA-RYH						
335	D	N27KG	PT-LUZ								
336	D	XA-LAP	N6354N	XA-VYA							
337	G	N3810G	N937GL	N337GL	LV-P	LV-WBP					
338	D	XA-LOF	N4447P								
339	D	N3798D	HK-2624X	HK-2624P	N21HR	Mexico MTX-03					
340	D	N980A	N625AU								
341	D	N341FW	N101DL	XA-TAM	(N)	XA-SAE	N58HC	damaged 02Feb98 Opa Locka, FL			
342	D	N820M	N984JD	(N187DY)	I-RJVA	N707CA	XA-RXQ	N342AA	N342GG	N25PW	
343	D	N3797L	N456CG	(N458CG)							
344	D	N3798L	N37943	5N-ASQ	w/o 22Jly83 Lagos, Nigeria						
345	D	N345EJ	N345KB	N711SC	LV-PHU	LV-WLG					
346	D	N39412	N3798V	N300WG	N41TC	N72AX*					
347	D	N39415	N347EJ	D-CHIC	N25NM	N347MD	N347AC	N202JW	N347AC	(N347JW)	N347JV
348	D	N37949	N440DM	N522GS	N522JS	N988AA					
349	D	N40146	N349EJ	N20GT	XA-NOG	w/o 02Sep93 Tijuana, Mexico					
350	D	N350AG	(N428CH)								
351	D	N878ME	XA-POQ	N837CS	N302PC	N402DP	N425RH				
352	D	N3794P	RP-C1261	N7035C	XA-MMO	(N352XR)	N25FN				
353	D	N353EJ	N800DR	(N50MT)	XA-RKP	XA-RLI	N510TP	N71AX			
354	D	N3795U	N515TC								
355	D	(N830WM)	N202WM	N7801L	N713DJ	XA-SNO	XA-EAS	N355AM	LV-WRE		
356	D	N78DT	N100NR	N108NR	N25PT	N251MD					
357	D	N40149	N3797U	N148JW	N812MM	XA-ROC	N250LB	N27KG	LV-WXY		
358	D	N1461B	N37971								
359	D	N6307H	N37973	N359SK	N666RE	N666PE	N116JR	XA-LRJ			
360	D	N6340T	N8563B	N618R	N618P	N360JG					
361	D	N4291K	N218NB	N218NR	N804PH						
362	D	N39398	N25GL	N52CT	N717CW	(N107MS)	N107RM				
363	D	N39416	N85654	N91MT	N2PW	XA-RSU	N197LS				
364	D	N10873	N8565Y	N25TZ	XA-TIE						
365	D	N1473B	N7260C	N218R	N365CM	XA-SJN					
366	D	N1088D	N7261B	(ZS-LRI)	XA-SWX	N366LJ	ZS-CAT				
367	D	N7262A	N51DT	VT-SWP	N4488W						
368	D	N1088A	N8567J	XA-PIM	N8567J						
369	D	N10872	N8566Z	N369MJ	N2213T						
370	D	N39399	N72600	N610JR	N610JB	N220TG	N223TG	C-GSWS	XA-SJO	N370LJ	N252HS
		N972H									
371	D	N1468B	N72603	N125DB	N44SK	N1WT	N1U	(N102U)	N4ZB		
372	D	N40149	N72606	N5NC	damaged 13Oct97 Newport News, VA; struck a deer on take off						
373	D	N3819G	N29EW	EC-EGY							

Production complete

LEARJET MODEL 28

C/n	Identities					
001	N9RS	N9KH	N128MA	N3AS		
002	N39404	N511DB	XC-VSA			
003	N157CB	N42ZP	N555JK	N44QG	N14QG	N28LR	N25GW
004	N39394	N125NE	HB-VGB	XA-KAJ	N225MS	XA-KAJ	N28AY
005	(N31WT)	N8LL	N500LG				

Production complete

LEARJET MODEL 29

C/n	Identities			
001	HB-VFY	N929GL	XC-IST	
002	N723LL	N920GL	XC-DFS	XC-HIE
003	N289CA	VT-EHS		
004	N39412	N294CA	VT-EIH	

Production complete

LEARJET MODEL 31

C/n	Series	Identities					
001		N311DF	N984JD	w/o 23Feb90 Taiyuan, China; cx Mar90; to spares by Dodson Avn, Ottawa, KS			
002		N7262Y	PT-LVO	N102NW	N350DS		
003		N10873	N31CG	N331CC	N888CP		
004		N1088D	XA-ZTH				
005		N39415	XA-GMD	XA-RFS	N942BY	(N963Y)	N431BC
006		N6331V	N26LC				
007		N3819G	PT-LXX				
008		N71JC	dbf 02Sep97 Aberdeen, MS; to Atlanta Air Salvage, GA Nov97 for spares				
009		OO-JBA	N173PS				
010		N31LJ	N446	PT-LLK	N311TS	N89HB	
011		N3803G	HB-VJI				
012		N917MC	XA-RUU				
013		PT-LVR	N213PA	PT-XTA			
014		N1468B	N5VG	PT-OFJ	N5VG		
015		N111TT	N260LF				
016		N4291K	N666RE	N92LJ	N1DE		
017		N4289U	N17VG	PT-OFK	Crashed 26Feb93 Santos Dumont, rebuilt with new wingset	N17VG	
		N600AW					
018		N40144	HB-VIM	N19TJ	N20LL		
019		(N19LT)	PT-OFL	N19LT			
020		N42905	N31LJ	N337FP			
021		N3802G	XA-RNK				
022		N331N					
023		N111VV					
024		N30LJ	LV-PFK	LV-RBV	N90PB	N92EC	
025		N39399	I-AIRW				
026		N91164	XA-HRM	XA-HGF	XA-DIN	N39TJ	N45HG
027		N91201	N30LJ	N2FU			
028		N90WA					
029		N9173L	(XB-ZRB)	XB-FKT			
030		N525AC	N255DV				
031		N5000E	N9132Z	N31HA	ZS-OFW		
032		N5010U	XA-AAP				
033		N5012H	9V-ATA	N603LJ	N632PB		
033A		N2603S	9V-ATC	N311LJ	N156JS		
033B		N2600S	9V-ATD	w/o 21Jly97 30m S of Ranong, Thailand			
033C		N5013L	9V-ATE	N310LJ	N158JS		
033D		N5023D	9V-ATF	N312LJ	N157JS		
034		N5015U	9V-ATB	N604LJ	N45PK		
035	A	N50111	N618R	N618RF	N3VJ		
036	A	N31LJ	N88MM	D-CVGP	N316LJ	N127V	
037	A	N31TF	PT-OVZ				
038	A	N5016V	N4	N131NA	N500WR		
039	A	N90LJ	N10ST				
040	A	VR-CHJ	N9HJ	VR-CHJ	VR-CGS	N340LJ	N314MK
041	A	N131TA	N9CH				
042	A	D-CGGG					
043	A	N5009V	C-GLRJ	N43LJ			
044	A	N50163	XA-MJG	XA-HRM			
045	A	N50159	N67SB				
046	A	D-CCKV	N131PT	N352EF			
047	A	N31UK	N39TW				
048	A	N43SF	N43SE				
049	A	D-CDEN					
050	A	N92UG					
051	A	N9152R	N1905H	N351AC			
052	A	N50LJ	N301AS	N75MC	N899CS		
053	A	N9173Q	N44QG				
054	A	N2603G	N92FD	N82KK			
055	A	N9143F	N666RE	N425M			
056	A	N25685	N303WB	N56LF			
057	A	N9147Q	D-CSAP				
058	A	N5017J	N26018	N770CC	ZS-OJO+	N258SC*	
		+marks ntu but were painted on a/c					
059	A	N25999	(N31LJ)	N31TK	(N67MP)		
060	A	N2600Z	N156SC	N156EC			
061	A	N51057	(N740E)	N9152X	N740E	N740F	N261SC
062	A	N25997	AP-BEK				
063	A	(N27)	N2				
064	A	N142GT	N444HC				
065	A	N50153	N26005	N44SF	N44SU		
066	A	N5009V	N26006	PK-CAH			
067	A	N9173M	TG-AIR				
068	A	N2603X	N743E	N743F	N500CG		
069	A	N9173V	N744E	N744N	N169SC*		
070	A	N2602Y	N741E	N741F	(N270SC)	N370SC	
071	A	N9173N	N742E	N742F	N271SC		

LEARJET 31

C/n	Series	Identities					
072	A	N31LJ	N45UF				
073	A	N46UF					
074	A	N999AU	(VP-B)	N999AU	N128GB		
075	A	N418R	N418RT	N631SF			
076	A	N40339	XA-SPR	XA-PIC			
077	A	N26002	PK-CAJ				
078	A	N40280	N31LJ	XA-SNM	N112CM		
079	A	N40349	N41DP	N91DP			
080	A	N2601K	N80LJ	N986MA			
081	A	(N31LJ)	N81LJ	N83WM	N83WN	LV-YMB	
082	A	N5014F	N4022X	PT-MVI	N727BT		
083	A	N5012Z	N40363	N789SR			
084	A	N4034H	N196HA	N840SW			
085	A	N5013Y	N4005G	XA-PEN	N531AT		
086	A	N2603Q	N867JS	N105FX	OY-LJB		
087	A	N9173T	N868JS	N106FX	OY-LJC		
088	A	N50088	N31LJ	N500JE			
089	A	N5009L	N77PH	N77PY			
090	A	N9173X	N78PH	N78PR			
091	A	N5019Y	V5-NAG				
092	A	N50302	N711FG				
093	A	N4031K	(N917BD)	N916BD			
094	A	N4027K	N31AX	(N916BD)	N917BD		
095	A	N50459	N163JD	OK-AJD	N395LJ		
096	A	N5009V	N4006G	N30LX	N30TK	(N31TK)	N37BM
097	A	N50207					
098	A	N5012H	N50378	N148C			
099	A	N5049J	N1932P	N1932K			
100	A	N5001X	N31LR	PT-MCB			
101	A	N5010J	N293SA				
102	A	N5002D	N107FX				
103	A	N5003F	(N31AZ)	PT-TOF			
104	A	N4010N	N108FX				
105	A	N51054	N5005K	N109FX			
106	A	N29RE	N531RA	N581RA*			
107	A	N5012H	N31HY	C-GHCY			
108	A	N110FX					
109	A	N5029F	N261PC	N261PQ			
110	A	N40130	PT-WIV				
111	A	N50114	C-GRVJ				
112	A	N5082S	LX-PCT				
113	A	N31LJ	N331SJ				
114	A	N524HC					
115	A	(N5005M)	N112FX	N31NR	ZS-NYV		
116	A	N113FX	N112FX				
117	A	N317LJ					
118	A	N318LJ	N815A	N815E			
119	A	N114FX					
120	A	N5020Y	I-TYKE				
121	A	N121LJ					
122	A	(N112FX)	N122LJ	PT-WLO			
123	A	N323LJ					
124	A	N124LJ	N931FD				
125	A	N125LJ	N527JG				
126	A	N8066P	N22SF				
127	A	N80727	HB-VLR				
128	A	N8082J	N400				
129	A	N8079Q	N115FX				
130	A	N5013N	N31PV				
131	A	N80631	N31LR	N319SC			
132	A	N116FX					
133	A	N8073Y	N117FX				
134	A	N5014E	N118FX				
135	A	N80645	PT-WSB				
136	A	N119FX					
137	A	N120FX					
138	A	N138LJ	V5-NPC				
139	A	N139LJ	N131AR				
140	A	N140LJ	N96LF	VP-BML	N314AC		
141	A	N121FX					
142	A	N142LJ	ZS-EAG				
143	A	N122FX					
144	A	N144LJ	JA01CP				
145	A	N124FX	N145LJ	N29RE			
146	A	N30046	N218NB	(ZS-DCT)	ZS-AGT		
147	A	N198KF	N202LC				
148	A	N148LJ	(PT-XIT)	PT-XPP			
149	A	N1904S					

LEARJET 31

C/n	Series	Identities				
150	A	N31NR	N6666R	N6666A	N316RS	N316AS
151	A	N3019S	N583PS			
152	A	N517GP				
153	A	N6666R	N30111	RP-C6153		
154	A	N337RB				
155	A	N525GP				
156	A	N124FX	(N29RE)			
157	A	N125FX				
158	A	N126FX				
159	A	N127FX				
160	A	N31LR	VP-BMX			
161	A	N3016X	N177JB			
162	A	N525GP	N162LJ	N125GP		
163	A	N128FX				
164	A	N131GM	N164SB			
165	A	N31TD	N885TW			
166	A	N166DT	N811PS*			
167	A	N167LJ	I-ERJB			
168	A	N168LJ	N811CP	N31CV	YV-952CP	
169	A	N197PH				
170	A	N31NR	(ZS-DHL)	ZS-OML*		
171	A	N50157	N129FX			
172	A	N197PH	N130FX			
173	A	N173LC				
174	A	N9VL	Mexico MTX-02			
175	A	N131FX				
176	A	N176WS				
177	A	N132FX				
178	A	N50145	RP-C6178			
179	A	N133FX				
180	A	N1926S				
181	A	N134FX	N526GP			
182	A	N136FX	N527GP			
183	A	N183DT	N183ML			
184	A	N931RS				
185	A	N31LR				
186	A	N137FX				
187	A	N932FD				
188	A	N70AE				
189	A	N138FX	N316RS			
190	A	N316AC				
191	A	N631AT				
192	A	N50088				
193	A	N44SF				
194	A	N29SM				
195	A	N134FX				
196	A	N136FX				
197	A	N20XP				
198	A	N500MP				
199	A	N900P				
200	A					
201	A					
202	A	N	ZS-PNP*			
203	A	N63SE				
204						
205						
206						
207						
208						
209						
210						
211						
212						
213						
214						
215						
216						
217						
218						
219						
220						

LEARJET MODEL 35

An Asterisk (*) after the series letter indicates the aircraft has been fitted with Avcom delta fins.

C/n	Series	Identities									
001		N731GA	ff 22Aug73	N351GL							
002		N352GL	N35SC	C-GVVA							
003		N731GA	N931BA	N263GL	N370EC	N4RT	N960AA	N700WL	N703MA	N111WB	
004		N74MP	N74MB	N74MJ	C-GIRE						
005		EC-CLS	TR-LXP	EC-CLS	N175J	N178CP					
006		N356P	N39DM	N39FN							
007		D-CONI	N75DH	N47JR	(N65FN)	N35UJ					
008		N673M	PT-LFS	PP-ERR							
009		N44EL	N14EL	N275J	N263GL	PT-LGR					
010		N888DH	N888DE	N35AJ							
011		N3816G	N400RB	N408RB	N531AJ						
012		N711	N71LA	C-GVCB	N2242P	N95SC	N975AA	N975AD	N97TJ	XA-SVX	
013	*	N1DA	N7TJ	N304AF	N35JN	N35BN	N535TA				
014		N71TP	N73TP	(N72TB)	N98VA	N69PS	N77LJ	N190GC			
015		N291BC	N57FF	N58FF	N58CW	N335JL	(N335SS)	N354PM			
016		N136GL	N5867	N9CN	N1SC	N18CV					
017		N119GS	N551CC	N456MS	N600DT						
018		D-CORA	F-GBMB	N696SC	N435JL	N696SC	N435JL	(N435EC)			
019		N959AT	PT-LGF	N19NW	N71LG						
020		XA-BUX	N95TC	w/o 20Dec84 Waco Airport, TX; remains to White Inds, Bates City, MO							
021	A	N101GP	N91CH	N33TS	N442JT	N4415S					
022		OY-BLG	N90WR								
023		N986WC	N886WC	N886CS	N443RK						
024		N316	N24GA	N528JD	N528EA	N241RT					
025		9K-ACT	N40TF	N135TX	N510LJ	N185BA	(N188JA)				
026		D-CDHS	D-CBRK	N54754	N89TC						
027		N31WS									
028		N135GL	N20BG	XC-IPP (carries dual marks XC-IPP/TP104)							
029		N711AF	w/o Katab, Egypt 11Aug79 en route Athens-Jeddah								
030		N816M	N16FN	N542PA code "TX"	N30TK*						
031		N77FC	N77U	N77TE	N160AT	N233CC					
032		N711CH	(N711QH)	N711MA	N235JW	N711MA	N710GS				
033		N7KA	HZ-KA1	N2297B	N31FN	N524PA					
034		N37TA									
035		N711R	(N711RQ)	N7125	N350TS	N92TS					
036		N134GL	N76GL	N76GP	N90AH						
037		N1462B	N100GL	N58M	N35GQ	N600WT	N520PA code "OR"	N45TK			
038		(VH-UDC)	VH-ELJ	C-FBFP							
039		N1HP	N382TC*								
040		C-GGYV	N39DM	w/o 05Mar86 over Pacific Ocean nr San Clemente Island; collided with Learjet 24D-253 N97DM (qv)							
041		N202BT	N202BD	N711BH	N41PJ	(N433JW)					
042		N221UE	N73TJ	N270CS							
043		C-GVCA									
044		N38TA	N44MW	N44VW	N130F						
045		N1461B	HB-VEN	N35HB	N99786	N999M	XA-HOS	N45MJ	N117CH	N304TZ	N304AT
		N1140A	(N40AN)								
046		VH-SLJ	VH-FSX	VH-LJL	N58EM						
047	A	XA-ALE	N13MJ	N701AS							
048		N233R	N64MH	F-GHMP	N8040A						
049		JY-AEV	N3759C	C-GBWL	N235JL	N899WA					
050		CC-ECO	Chile FAC 351								
051		SE-DEA	N2BA	(N123MJ)							
052		JY-AEW	w/o 28Apr77 Riyadh, Saudi Arabia								
053		N1976L	N53FN	N541PA							
054		VR-BFX	N53650	N54PR	N109MC	N435MS					
055		D-CONO	N70WW	I-NIKJ	N255RG	N255JH	C-GCJD	N354LQ			
056		(JY-AEX)	N106GL	N645G							
057		N551MD	N57GL	C-GHOO	N57GL	N35MR	C-GTDE				
058		C-GPUN	w/o 11Jan95 Massett, Queen Charlotte Is, BC, Canada								
059		N221Z	N51FN	w/o 02Apr90 Carlsbad, CA; remains to White Inds, Bates City, MO							
060		N64MP	N64MR	N47BA	(N590CH)	w/o 25Oct99 near Mina SD					
061		N424DN	N4246N	N238RC	N235EA						
062		N217CS	ZS-LII	TL-ABD	N701US	N310BA	N31DP				
063		N828M	N663CA	N80PG							
064		N290BC	N291BC	N100GP	(N257DP)	N257SD					
065		N425DN	N4358N								
066		CC-ECP	Chile 352								
067	A	N118K	N888DJ	(N66FN)	N32FN	(N52FL)	N135FA				
068	A	HB-VEM	Switzerland T-781								
069	A	N103GL	N591D	N1CA	N10AQ	N35NW	N48GP*				
070	A	D-CITA	N3GL	N503RP	N50FN	N543PA	N50FN				
071	A	JY-AFD	F-WDCP	F-GDCP	N82GA	N199CJ					
072	A	N2015M	N4415M								
073	A	N108GL	N163A	(N64FN)	N352TX						

LEARJET 35

C/n	Series	Identities
074	A	N5000B N530J N666JR N100T N198T
075	A	N3503F HB-VEV JY-AFE N3503F (N117DA) N48RW N30FN SE-DHP
076	A	N959SA
077	A	N814M N819JE (N707BJ) N46TJ (XA-) ZS-NRZ N98LC
078	A	N95BA N95BH N711SW N711SD N440JB N112EL N45AW N145AM
079	A	N6000J N660CJ N560KC N7777B N500DS N68QB*
080	A	N109GL N23HB N10AZ
081	A	N3523F JY-AFF N3523F N118DA
082	A	N235HR N285HR N700GB N700SJ
083	A	(N600CC) N400CC (N400MJ) (N45SL) N500CD N121CL YV-100CP
084	A	N111GL N56HF N135WB N184TS (N696JH)
085	A	N15WH
086	A	N435M N26DA N98MD N86CS N860S
087	A	N720GL N835GA N862PD (N862BD) N18AX
088	A	N3545F HB-VEW N35GE OE-GBR N72JF
089	A	N3547F D-CCHB
090	A	HB-VEY I-FIMI N88BG
091	A	VH-TLJ C-GBLF N8GA D-CIRS N37FA N900JV*
092	A	N722GL N424JR C-GPFC N46931 N92NE N92EJ N39WA*
093	A	N804CC C-GFRK N5474G N44PT PT-LOT
094	A	N506C N935BD N200EC N92EC N94GP (N65PF) (N35PF) N94AF
095	A	N971H N971F N68UW
096	A	N214LS (N11JV) N87AT (D-CHRC) N96FA N94RL
097	A	N135J N108RB
098	A	N20CR N21GL N44UC (N998DJ) (N998M) N72DA
099	A	N40146 HB-VFC I-MCSA w/o 22Feb78 Palermo, Sicily
100	A	N550E N558E C-GRFO
101	A	N40149 N109JR N109JU N721AS
102	A	N1451B N232R PT-OEF w/o 02May92 Morelia, Mexico
103	A	N96RE N50MJ PT-LCD
104	A	N87W N873LP w/o 22Sep85 Auburn, AL
105	A	(N720GH) N102GH N102GP N612KC N18FN
106	A	N101BG N15TW w/o 08Dec85 Minneapolis, MN; remains to Brandis Avn, Taylorville, IL
107	A	N723GL w/o 12Dec85 Esterwood, TX
108	A	D-COCO F-GCLE N86PC (N86PQ) D-CJPG
109	A	N506GP N911AE
110	A	(N12EP) N4J
111	A	N3815G (HB-VFE) (I-SIDU) OE-GMA I-LIAD
112	A	N3810G D-CCAY N247TA
113	A	N763GL N35CL N35RN N14M N684LA N684HA N113AN*
114	A	N3807G D-CONA N18G N851L D-CATY w/o 14Dec94 Moscow-Sheremetyevo A/P, Russia; to Dodson Avn for spares use; restored as N851L
115	A	Argentine T-21
116	A	I-MMAE N116AM N58CW
117	A	N3155B N78MC struck deer on take off Atlantic City 18Oct97
118	A	N39391 HB-VFK N115MA N50MT N88JA N118FN
119	A	HB-VFG D-CHER N93MJ OY-ASO N93MJ N36FN (N64DH) N549PA code "GA"
120	A	N400JE (N400RV) (Avcom Inds - ventral delta fin retrofit aircraft)
121	A	N43EL (D-CFVG) N43TJ
122	A	D-CCHS OE-GMP N27TT
123	A	N3802G N900JE N900BJ
124	A	N1500E N35WG N8LA C-GTJL
125	A	N3803G N777MC N777NQ N111MZ N125GA N351EF
126	A	N744GL N15EH
127	A	N727GL N351TX
128	A	N231R N257AL
129	A	N22BX N229X XA-ZAP
130	A	N230R (N44KW) N757AL
131	A	N3812G N26GB N26GD N155AM
132	A	N431M N420PC N37TJ N135AG
133	A	N728GL N35NB N58RW I-ALPM N133GJ N133EJ
134	A	N1473B N88EP N235DH N238JA*
135	A	(OO-LFX) N22MJ D-CDAX N719US N11AK I-ZOOM
136	A	Argentine T-22
137	A	N3819G HB-VFL EC-DEB N41FN N35TJ
138	A	N7735A N31FB N3RA N83TJ N35WH N100MS
139	A *	N15SC D-CGFD
140	A	N742GL N888BL N72TP N40BD
141	A	N743GL N66WM N553M N553V
142	A	N815A N815L
143	A	N3811G N301SC OE-GER N20DK
144	A	N39398 D-CCAP N705US N35KC OY-CCT N118MA N135JW (N118MA) N56HF N56EM
145	A	N39394 HB-VFB Switzerland T-782 N145GJ (N166AG) VH-SLD
146	A	N55AS N351AS
147	A	N717W HZ-KTC N499G N717W N55F
148	A	N103GH N103GP N333RP N500RW w/o 24May88 Teterboro, NJ
149	A	OO-KJG HB-VGN N85351 N273MC N273MG N600LE N600AE N600AW N800AW (N40AN)
150	A	N100EP w/o 12May87 West Mifflin, PA; cx Apr90

LEARJET 35

C/n	Series	Identities
151	A	N39399 N711L N813M a/c stolen 13Apr85; fate unknown
152	A	N101HB N964CL confiscated in Bolivia and donated post 12Jun90 to Bolivian AF as FAB-009 N964CL
153	A	C-GZVV N573LP N573LR
154	A	N650NL N117RB
155	A	N760LP N760DL N110KG N1001L+ N110AE +Res marks only, but were applied to aircraft
156	A	N170L N190EB N190DA
157	A	N746GL YV-01CP N57FF N57FP N157DJ ZS-MWW N26GP
158	A	N835AC N158MJ N158NE N800GP
159	A	N93C N93CK (N135CK) D-CAPO
160	A	D-CCCA
161	A	N39415 YV-65CP N433DD
162	A	N751GL (HB-VFO) N711HH N1978L N222SL XA-CZG
163	A	YV-173CP N27BL
164	A	N1473B N248HM N50MJ
165	A	N40144 A40-CA VH-HOF N16BJ N72CK
166	A	N831CJ N831J N719JB
167	A *	N725P N813AS
168	A	N22SF N22SY N36TJ N75RJ N68TJ C-GPDO C-FZQP
169	A	N135ST
170	A	N100K N354RZ C-GPDQ C-GFEH N335NA
171	A *	N747GL C-GNSA N823J N1968A N1968T N196DT N455RM (N48DK) N40DK N171WH
172	A	N748GL SE-DDG N72TJ N32JA SX-BFJ (N32JA) N50AK
173	A	N750GL HZ-MIB N750GL (HZ-NCI) N100GU N116EL (N83DM) YU-BPY N326DD
174	A	TR-LYC N65DH D-CAVI (F-GGRG) N130TA D-CAMB N82283 N38AM
175	A	D-CDWN
176	A	N317MR XA-ACC N176JE (N67GA) XA-BUX
177	A	N1461B N77CP N77CQ N174CP D-CITY
178	A	N40146 N22CP N22CQ N35GG N900JC (N104AA)
179	A	N39412 D-CCAR D-CAPD N718SW (N696SC) C-FHLO N801PF D-CGFA
180	A	N3819G N222BE N222BK N35CX N44HG N701DA
181	A	N35LJ N35PR N35PD N5114G PT-LSJ
182	A	N1450B N33HB N3HB N3HA N221SG
183	A	N3802G N720M N72JM N106XX N51TJ N137RS (N137TS) N183FD
184	A	N1462B HB-VFO w/o 06Dec82 Paris-Le Bourget, France N7092C (for rebuild?)
185	A	N99ME N99VA N10BF N99VA N900EM TC-GEM OE-GAV ZS-SES
186	A	N753GL N590 N96DM (N317JD) N96FN
187	A	N755GL N32HM (N888DT)
188	A	VH-AJS N39293 N20RT (N38FN) N3MJ N343MG N135AC N35TK N88TJ N999JF N924AM
189	A	N3811G VH-AJV N39292 (N189TC) N32TC N32FN N35KC N18NM N727JP I-AVJG w/o 24Oct99 on approach to Genoa A/P Italy
190	A	N32BA N202VS N202WR
191	A	N3810G (YV-15CP) HB-VFX N75TF N35NP N35SE N535AF
192	A	N4995A N225CC N225QC N49PE N49BE
193	A	N1465B (YV-131CP) VH-SBJ N620J VH-SBJ N2743T N9EE N359EF*
194	A	N91W N86BL N86BE w/o 5Apr00 Marianna Municipal A/P FL
195	A	N1471B D-CONY N555JE SE-DHO
196	A	HB-VFU EC-DFA w/o 13Aug80 Palma, Spain
197	A	N754GL
198	A	N25FS I-ALPT N198GJ
199	A	N40144 N9HM (N9HV) N30DH N34TC N444HC N235JS
200	A	N3818G D-CCAR OO-LFY N200LJ
201	A	N39415 N79MJ N35RT N35RF XA-PIN N35AZ
202	A	VH-MIQ N499G D-CGPD
203	A	N744E N744P VR-CUC N203RW
204	A	N1466B D-COSY N87MJ N99ME N7PE (N277AM) D-CFTG
205	A	N39418 N80SM N59DM N59FN N568PA
206	A	N760GL (N66HM) HB-VGH N189TC N123CC N38PS (N46KB)
207	A	N40146 N711 N3PW N620JM
208	A	N40149 N40TA (N691NS) N39DK (N39DJ) N67PA
209	A	N399W N339W N711DS N22MS
210	A	N840GL (N35HM) N42HM N721CM XB-FNF N210WL
211	A	N1461B D-CATY N15MJ N600LC N500KK N500GM N998JP N44TT
212	A	N3803G N180MC N291A N989AL
213	A	N800RD (N935NA) XC-CUZ
214	A	N279DM
215	A	VH-UPB N2951P N80CD N80GD N35ED
216	A	N3819G D-CATE N24MJ N39MB N142LG N335RD
217	A	N39412 N111RF N122JW
218	A	N256TW N481FM (N601WT) N83TE*
219	A	N39416 VH-BJQ N502G N350JF shot down & w/o 29Aug99 Ethiopian/Eritrea Border
220	A	N79BH N333RB N220GH N873LP N873LR (N373LP)
221	A	N1462B N845GL VH-WFE VH-FSY N221TR
222	A	N1468B HB-VFZ I-EJID N90AL HB-VFZ N789KW
223	A	N215JW D-CGRC
224	A *	N96AC N56PB N40RW N28MJ
225	A	N225MC TG-JAY N34TJ

LEARJET 35

C/n	Series	Identities
226	A	N1127M N30HJ
227	A	N211BY N25RF N88NE N85GW (N227MJ) N902JC
228	A	N101PG N4GB SX-BNT N100NW
229	A	N1476B N8MA N717JB N718EA N41WT N31WT (N214LS) N415LS N4415W
230	A	N39418 N714K PT-WAR N81458 N356AC N37HJ*
231	A	(N10AB) (N712DM) N911DB N62DK VH-JCR
232	A	N8281
233	A	N35SL N35AW (N442HC) N23A
234	A	N35WR
235	A	N841GL N600CN N256MA (N256MB) N166HL N166HE LV-
236	A	G-ZOOM N8537B N90LP N4XL N900EC N600GP (N415RD) EC-HLB
237	A	N843GL N78MN I-KUSS (N37DJ) N72LE N237TJ (N36BP) N300TW N300TE
238	A	N844GL N80HK ZS-INS 3D-ACZ ZS-INS N248DA N500CG N500HG N500HZ
239	A	N1473B N847GL (HB-VGC) VH-KTI VH-LEQ N239GJ N521PA code "OR" w/o 14Dec94 Fresno, CA; cx Jun95
240	A	N240B N249B
241	A	N42FE N500GP N500FD N240JS N500EX N500ED
242	A	N846GL VH-WFJ VH-FSZ N242DR
243	A	N3812G HZ-ABM N81863 I-AGEB N2217Q XA-HYS N152TJ XA-THD
244	A	N1451B RP-57 RP-C57 N244TS N244LJ
245	A	N2WL N1526L N30PA
246	A	N50PH N50PL N555GB N1DC N628DB
247	A	YV-265CP N110JD N38FN N523PA code "NY" N544PA
248	A	N3811G C-GBFA N128CA
249	A	N107JM I-KALI N249DJ N300DA C-FICU
250	A	N3250 (N87RS) N63LE N63LF N947GS
251	A	N27NB N27HF N251CT N387HA*
252	A	N28CR PT-KZR
253	A	N40144 N211DH N611CM N611SH
254	A	N666CC N34FN N522PA N54TK*
255	A	N44EL N44ET N610HC N616HC XB-LHS XB-FNW
256	A	N712L N6GG N50DD N911ML
257	A	F-GCMS N257DJ N417BA
258	A	(N1700) N28BG N35MH N583PS N583BS
259	A	N39413 HB-VGC N9113F N259HA (N259JC) HK-3983X
260	A	N40PK
261	A	N900RD XA-ELU N35SJ N35FN N63DH N58MM
262	A	N237GA N237AF
263	A	D-CCAD N4577Q N37FN EC-GXX N8228P EC-GXX
264	A	XA-ATA N35GX N40DK N3056R VR-CDI N64CP
265	A	N1462B (G-ZEST) G-LEAR
266	A	N3904 SE-DDI N922GL N35GC
267	A	N39418 XA-LAN w/o 08Jan93 nr Hermosillo, Mexico
268	A	N10870 YV-286CP N3857N (N286CP) N510SG N2U D-CGFB
269	A	N881W N225F N211WH N886R
270	A	N10871 (YV-15CP) YV-O-MRI-1 Venezuela FAV0013
271	A	N1088A LV-PET LV-OAS N40AN
272	A	N39398 N272HS N500EF N321AN
273	A	N1465B N35FH N103C N103CL
274	A	N1087Y N274JS N274JH N83CP N711BE (N35WG) N274FD N274JS
275	A	N10872 G-ZEAL (N43PE) N43FE (N65WH) N235SC N72LL
276	A	N44LJ N613RR N69BH
277	A	N925GL N723LL N70CN N127HC XA-PUI N350MD (N9876S) N27TJ N42B (N6362D) (N489) N2WQ
278	A	N1476B HB-VGL ECT-028 EC-DJC N300ES N17GL N12RP
279	A	N19LH w/o 15Jly97 Avon Park, FL
280	A (C21A?)	N80MJ HP-912 YN-BVO US Army 87-0026 N35AX
281	A	N80WG N425M N425AS
282	A	N504Y N80CD N80GD N9CH N444CM N62MB
283	A	N920C N205EL N205FL N386CM
284	A	(D-CEFL) D-CCAX OO-GBL
285	A	N777RA N75KV N34TB VH-MZL
286	A	N333X (N333XX) N200SX PT-LSW N286WL
287	A	N17EM N71HS
288	A	N1476B HB-VGM N43DD N288NE N288JE N288JP
289	A	N3JL N802CC N289MJ N289NE N289LJ N36TJ N217TA
290	A	N2022L XA-RAV
291	A	N7US N535PC w/o 14Feb91 2 miles N of Aspen Airport, CO; cx Jly91
292	A	N634H N292ME
293	A	N182K
294	A	N745E N745F N35VP N440HM w/o 27Feb97 Greenville, SC; remains to White Inds, Bates City, MO
295	A	PT-LAA
296	A	N296BS XA-LML N51JA N66NJ
297	A	N746E N746F N38US N777DM
298	A	I-FLYC N298NW
299	A	N244FC PT-LGS N148X
300	A	N365N

LEARJET 35

C/n	Series	Identities									
301	A	N301TP	N999RB	N102ST	N102BT	N190VE	N98AC	N945W*			
302	A	N717DS	N780A	N78QA	N41ST	N631CW	N51LC				
303	A	N771A	PT-LLS								
304	A	N464HA	N112PG	N534H	N534A	N53GH	N53GL	(N97QA)			
305	A	N3VG	N33NJ								
306	A	N926GL	N66LM	N601MC	N77LN	N111US	N111OS	N71E	(N63602)	(N485)	N9ZD
307	A	N120MB	(N119HB)	N677CT							
308	A	N99MJ	N747GM	(N7LA)	(N747RL)						
309	A	(YV-328CP)	HB-VGT	OE-GAR	N8216Z	N100MN	D-CHPD				
310	A	N97JL	N13HB	(N13HQ)	N8280	(N310ME)					
311	A	D-CDHS	N723US	N35BG	OE-GPN	N311BP	HC-BSZ	N121JT			
312	A	LV-PHX	LV-OFV	N369BA							
313	A	N39413	(F-GCLT)	TR-LZI	N31WR						
314	A	N35AK	(N118GM)								
315	A	N927GL	N662AA	D-CCAA	(N121JT)						
316	A	N39398	N1503	N1507	N35AH	N18ST					
317	A	N10871	SE-DEM	N98TE	N317TT						
318	A	N444WB	N103CF	N318NW							
319	A	Argentine T-23									
320	A	N905LC	N905LD	N35FS	N320M	N30GJ	N393JP				
321	A	N14TX	(N19LM)	N77LP	XA-RVB	XC-AA60	(N321WJ)				
322	A	N305SC	PT-WGF								
323	A	N735A									
324	A	G-JJSG	G-JETN	G-JETG							
325	A	D-CARO	I-FFLY	N325NW							
326	A	PT-LAS	N155WL	N255JC	N612DG	N35SA*					
327	A	N3797N	N135UT	N327F	N32PF	N32PE					
328	A	N3807G	N1502	N35NY	N35NX	N392JP					
329	A	N39412	N53DM	N261PC	N261PG						
330	A	N930GL	partially destroyed Dec89 during US invasion of Panama; b/u for spares; cx Jly91								
331	A	N10870	HB-VGU	I-EJIB	N700NW	N435JW	D-CGFC				
332	A	N600LN	N332FG	(N598WW)	N543WW						
333	A	Argentine T-24		w/o 07Jun82 S Atlantic							
334	A	N2815	N350RB	N334SP	(N334AB)	N235MC					
335	A	N25MJ	N155TD	N8YY	N15Y	N335DJ	N335NE	N335EE	N800CD	N800CH	
336	A	HB-VGW	N590J	N166RM	N782JR	XA-PYC	(N336EA)	XA-BNO			
337	A	N80ED	N337WC	N710AT							
338	A	N1473B	RP-C7272	N610GE	RP-C610						
339	A	N24JK	N24CK	N15CC	N1500	PT-LZP					
340	A	N11AM	N11YM	N504F							
341	A	N3802G	D-CARE	XA-HOS							
342	A	N1088D	N37931	VH-SDN	VH-LGH	N678S	YV-15CP	N56JA			
343	A	N135MB	N80BT	N21NA	N21NG						
344	A	N40149	YV-327CP	N344MC							
345	A	N3818G	N10RE	VH-EMP	N345LJ	N30DK					
346	A	N3803G	C-GMGA	N35AJ	I-DLON						
347	A	OE-GNP	N85SV								
348	A	(N17ND)	N3798B	N600BE	N500MJ	N35TL	N35DL	(N8JA)			
349	A	N272T	XA-TCI								
350	A	N88NE	N35WB								
351	A	N500RP	N500DD	N500ND							
352	A	YV-326CP	N30GD	N600G	N71A	(N999JA)	N35CZ	N800GJ			
353	A	N3819G	C-GDJH								
354	A	N1450B	D-CART	N212GA	N405GJ						
355	A	N1468B	LV-PJZ	LV-ONN	N64RV	N345	N351WB				
356	A	N54YR	N54YP	N800WJ	(VR-C)	PT-LUG					
357	A	N3797S	N1001L	(N289GA)	ZS-MGK	(N100L)					
358	A	N524HC	N358PG								
359	A	(N127RM)	HB-VHB	N136JP							
360	A	N185FP	N1129M	(N360GL)	N360LJ	(N901MS)	N987DK*				
361	A	N924GL	PT-LBS	PT-FAT	PT-OCZ						
362	A	N3794M	N888MV	N399KL	N773LP	N633DS					
363	A	N52MJ	N183JC	N19RP							
364	A	N3794Z	(N65TA)	N981TH	N950CS	N490BC	N353EF				
365	A	G-ZONE	(N4564S)	G-ZIPS	G-SEBE	G-CJET	G-GJET				
366	A	N411LC	N49AT	(N94AA)	N119CP	N350DA					
367	A	N714S	(N67TJ)	N97RJ	N232CC						
368	A	N35FM	SE-DHE	N368BG	N99KW	N450MC					
369	A	Argentina VR-17		report to T-25							
370	A	HB-VGY	N11MY	N1MY	(N56PR)	VR-BKB	N8216Q	XA-RKY			
371	A	LV-PLX	LV-ALF	N399BA							
372	A	HB-VGX	N372AS	PT-LJK	w/o 26Oct96 Sao Paulo-Congonhas, Brasil						
373	A	SE-DER	XA-BRE	XA-RUY	N97AN						
374	A	HZ-106	probably w/o 07Jan98 Dubai, UAE								
375	A	(YV-270CP)	HZ-107								
376	A	N458JA	N77FK	N33WB	XA-SBF	N979RF					
377	A	(N711EV)	N933GL	N10WF	N18WE						
378	A	CX-BOI/FAU 500		(N900DG)	N354ME						

LEARJET 35

C/n	Series	Identities
379	A	N23VG N18LH
380	A	N82JL N291BX N291BC N281BC XA-SBA N11SQ XA-SGK XA-MSH N903WJ C-GAJS
381	A	D-CORA N65DH (N40TM) N300CM N335K
382	A	N382BL N382BP OE-GAF N60WL
383	A	N66FE N364CL
384	A	N37984 N811DF N811DD
385	A	N535MC N350EF
386	A	N13VG N999FA
387	A	D-CARL
388	A	N1929S N388PD N388LS w/o 24Dec96 Smarts Mountain on approach to Lebanon-Municipal, NH; cx May98
389	A	N59MJ N377C N31WT N31WE VR-BLU N436DM
390	A	N500PP N508P N831CW
391	A	N3793D N444BF N813RR N89AT I-RYVA N888PT XA-SWF w/o 23Jun95 Tepico, Mexico
392	A	N931GL N1ED
393	A	N923GL N666RB N700WJ PT-LOE
394	A	N1466K N816JA N94MJ N60DK N626JS
395	A	HB-VHD N3261L N30GL N246CM
396	A	N2000M N938GL N5139W VR-CBU N5FF N74JL PT-OPJ
397	A	N33PT D-CLAN N200TW
398	A	N3797A N1AH w/o 16May97 Great Falls, MT; cx Nov97; to spares by White Industries 1998
399	A	N37965 N540HP (N399DJ) N399AZ PT-OVC
400	A	VH-CPH (VH-CPQ) VH-TPR VH-JIG
401	A	N66LJ N177SB*
402	A	N3402 N610JR N7AB N35BG
403	A	N37966 N312CT N312CF N312CE N100NR N101HW N100HW
404	A	N500JS N404BB N404KA N404DP
405	A	N41MJ (N181GL) N35AS N35FS N442DM
406	A	N764G N35Q I-KELM
407	A	N3793P N234DT N221MC N407MR C-GIWD C-GIWO
408	A	(N33VG) N3798P LV-POG LV-AIT
409	A	N50PD N858TM N123LC N888BS N35FE N351AM
410	A	N12109 N1210M C-FHDM N441CW (N21WS) N820RP
411	A	PT-LBY N94GP
412	A	N37980 N6666R N412GL (N31LM) N314C
413	A	HB-VHE N2637Z F-GHAE N413MA N27KG D-CFCF
414	A	(N135AB) N39MW PT-SMO N414TJ N196SD N196SP N815DD*
415	A	N125AX N19GL N415DJ D-COSY SE-DZZ*
416	A	N306M N35MV N40GG N841TT
417	A	N934GL N117FJ (N117RJ) D-CONO N97D N90RK HC-BTN (N37HR) N281CD LX-ONE
418	A	XA-KCM
419	A	N935GL N25EL N53JM N35SM
420	A	N35RT N35PT N100KK N100KZ
421	A	N44MJ N85CA N85QA (N88AH) N3AH N413JP I-VULC
422	A	YV-434CP N86BL N45AE
423	A	N369XL N200TC (N335GA) D-CAVE
424	A	N2844 N508GP
425	A	N111KK N111KZ
426	A	D-CARD N43W N43H ZS-NID N1128J RP-C1426
427	A	N1087Z VH-FOX N42LL N358AC
428	A	N1465B VH-ELC N17LH VH-SLE
429	A	G-ZING G-GAYL G-ZENO
430	A	N10870 Finland LJ-1
431	A	N1088A YV-433CP N34FD N431CW N431AS
432	A	F-GDCN N4445Y N330BC VR-CAD G-HUGG
433	A	N39416 D-CARG HB-VCZ N26583 N95AC (N93RC) PT-LIH w/o 15Mar91 Uberlandia, Brazil
434	A	N4401
435	A	N435N XC-HHJ
436	A	N37988 PT-LDN N436BL N100AT
437	A	N3803G YV-432CP
438	A	N17ND N600LL N12GJ N300R
439	A	N439ME HK-3121X HK-3121 N55RZ N35LW (N35FT)
440	A	N101HK N101PK N903HC N908HC (N354EM)
441	A	N1471B N551WC TC-MEK N441PC N441PG N74SP N404JS RP-C1404 N699ST
442	A	N40149 N3799C N35BK N442NE w/o 26Jul88 Morristown, NJ; remains to White Inds, Bates City, MO
443	A	N135RJ N258G
444	A	N3818G D-CARH N44695 N444MJ N144WB N1U N44SK N615HP
445	A	N3802G HB-VHG I-MOCO
446	A	N37962 N80AS N96CP N96CR N794GC
447	A	N127K N300FN D-COKE
448	A	N48MJ N222BG
449	A	N37947 N777LF N449QS XA-GDO
450	A	N450KK N950SP
451	A	N1462B Finland LJ-2
452	A	N25MJ N279SP
453	A	N124MC N802JW (N802EC)
454	A	N3794W (N379BW) N80AR (N80KR)

LEARJET 35

C/n	Series	Identities									
455	A	N3794U	N455NE	N988QC							
456	A	N711CD	N456CL								
457	A	N1451B	N900P	N974JD	(N113LB)	N874JD	N113LB	N49WL			
458	A	N276JS	YV-997CP	N86RX							
459	A	VH-MIE	N306SP	N80BL	N969MT	N829CA					
460	A	XC-PGR	XA-MPS								
461	A	N64CF									
462	A	N3811G	N8562W	N147K	N801K	N7117					
463	A	N1088D	VH-ULT	VH-FSW	VH-FSU	N68LL	N32HJ				
464	A	(N75PK)	N1DC	PT-LHX	N464WL	VP-BJS					
465	A	N465NW									
466	A	VH-WFP	N39SA	(N700WJ)	N600WJ	D-COCO	w/o 08Jun93 Cologne-Bonn, Germany; remains to Dodson Avn, Ottawa, KS				
467	A	N3796Q	HZ-MS1								
468	A *	VH-ANI	N468LM	OY-CCJ							
469	A	N39416	N3202A	N660SA	N444TG	N71MH					
470	A	N3810G	Finland LJ-3								
471	A	VH-BQR	N95AP	N110FT							
472	A	N1468B	N448GC	N448WC	N448WG	PT-ONK	(N472AS)	N54HF	N35TN		
473	A	N3796P	PT-LFT	N3UJ	N44AB	N35TH					
474	A	N39413	N37975	PT-LEB							
475	A	N10873	N3797K	3D-ADC	ZS-TOW						
476	A	N3818G	N476VC	N777LB							
477	A	N40162	N3797B	N82GL	N80CD	N95EC	N477WB	(N477MS)	N24JG	N235UJ	
478	A	N3815G	LV-TDF	w/o 15May84 Ushuaia, Argentina							
479	A	N3816G	N8565J	N31WT	N30SA	PT-LHT					
480	A *	N3819G	(VH-ALH)	N8563A	N35CK	(N484)	(N35FH)	N39DK			
481	A	N1466B	N6666K	N666KK	N728MP	N729HS	HK-3122X	HK-3122	N729HS	N27NR	OO-LFV
482	A	N482U	w/o at 2130 13Feb83 en route Kuala Lumpur-Colombo; restored May94 N2286D; purpose unknown								
483	A	N40144	N8562Y	N202BT	(N203AL)						
484	A	N4289U	Argentina VR-18		report to T-26						
485	A	N4290C	N485S	XA-RZZ	N710WL	N485AC					
486	A	N4291G	N821PC	N117EL	N810CC	N925DM					
487	A	N4289Y	N206FC	N206EC	N400MC	N391JP					
488	A	N8563G	N848GL	N30W	N30WY	N900R					
489	A	N1473B	N222BE								
490	A	N1087Z	N64MP								
491	A	N1087Y	N8563N	N491HS	N241AG	N485	I-AGEN	N135PG			
492	A	N39399	N8566B	N35NP	N37SV						
493	A	N3811G	N8564M	N482SG	I-FFRI	N493NW	N493CH				
494	A	N1476B	PT-LDM								
495	A	N1088D	N440MC								
496	A	N3803G	N8564K	N856RR	N496SW	N39TH	N496SW	(N496LJ)	N825LJ		
497	A	N1450B	N8565N	N50PH	N21DA	N15RH					
498	A	N3815G	N8564P	I-FLYH	N498JR						
499	A	N3818G	N85645	N84AD	PT-LII	HK-3921	N38AL	N499WJ	N1TS	N911DX	
500	A	N1465B	N8566X	N66LN	N101US	N81CH					
501	A	N3816G	HB-VHR	N711PR	N35HW	N326HG					
502	A	N1476B	N8565X	N747CP							
503	A	N1087Z	N8567A	HB-VII	HK-3646X	N8567A	N77NR				
504	A	N10871	N8568B	G-RAFF							
505	A	N1471B	N7259J	N505EE							
506	A	N3819G	N317BG	N10BD							
507	A	N3802G	N35GJ	N35HP	N42HP	N42HN					
508	A	N40144	N741E	N741F	N7777B	N881CA					
509	C21A	N6317V	N7263C	84-0063	N35AL	N826RD					
510	C21A	N6331V	N7263D	84-0064							
511	C21A	N4289X	N7263E	84-0065							
512	C21A	N4290J	N7263F	84-0066							
513	C21A	N4291G	N7263H	84-0067	N35AQ	N117PK					
514	C21A	N4289Z	N7263K	84-0068							
515	C21A	N4290K	N7263L	84-0069 code KS							
516	C21A	N4291K	N7263N	84-0070 code KS							
517	C21A	N6340T	N7263R	84-0071 code KS							
518	C21A	N4289Y	N7263X	84-0072 code KS							
519	C21A	N6307H	N400AD	84-0073							
520	C21A	N42905	N400AK	84-0074							
521	C21A	N4291N	N400AN	84-0075							
522	C21A	N4290Y	N400AP	84-0076							
523	C21A	N4289U	N400AQ	84-0077							
524	C21A	N6317V	N400AS	84-0078							
525	C21A	N6331V	N400AT	84-0079							
526	C21A	N4289X	N400AU	84-0080							
527	C21A	N4290J	N400AX	84-0081							
528	C21A	N4289Z	N400AY	84-0082							
529	C21A	N4291G	N400AZ	84-0083							
530	C21A	N4290K	N400BA	84-0084							
531	C21A	N4291K	N400FY	84-0085							

LEARJET 35

C/n	Series	Identities					
532	C21A	N6340T	N400BN	84-0086			
533	C21A	N4289Y	N400BQ	84-0087 code OF			
534	C21A	N6307H	N400BU	84-0088 code OF			
535	C21A	N4290C	N400BY	84-0089 code OF	N61905*		
536	C21A	N42905	N400BZ	84-0090 code OF			
537	C21A	N4290Y	N400CD	84-0091 code OF			
538	C21A	N400CG	84-0092 code FF				
539	C21A	N400CJ	84-0093 code OF				
540	C21A	N400CK	84-0094 code OF				
541	C21A	N400CQ	84-0095 code OF				
542	C21A	N400CR	84-0096				
543	C21A	N400CU	84-0097				
544	C21A	N400CV	84-0098				
545	C21A	N400CX	84-0099				
546	C21A	N400CY	84-0100				
547	C21A	N400CZ	84-0101				
548	C21A	N400DD	84-0102				
549	C21A	N400DJ	84-0103 code CS				
550	C21A	N400DL	84-0104 code CS				
551	C21A	N400DN	84-0105 code CS				
552	C21A	N400DQ	84-0106 code CS				
553	C21A	N400DR	84-0107 code CS				
554	C21A	N400DU	84-0108				
555	C21A	N400DV	84-0109				
556	C21A	N400DX	84-0110				
557	C21A	N400DY	84-0111				
558	C21A	N400DZ	84-0112				
559	C21A	N400EC	84-0113 code FF				
560	C21A	N400EE	84-0114 code FF				
561	C21A	N400EF	84-0115 code FF				
562	C21A	N400EG	84-0116 code FF				
563	C21A	N400EJ	84-0117 code FF				
564	C21A	N400EK	84-0118				
565	C21A	N400EL	84-0119				
566	C21A	N400EM	84-0120				
567	C21A	N400EN	84-0121	w/o 15Jan87 Alabama, LA			
568	C21A	N400EQ	84-0122 code AU				
569	C21A	N400ER	84-0123 code AU				
570	C21A	N400ES	84-0124 code AU				
571	C21A	N400ET	84-0125 code AU				
572	C21A	N400EU	84-0126 code RA				
573	C21A	N400EV	84-0127				
574	C21A	N400EX	84-0138 code RA				
575	C21A	N400EY	84-0128				
576	C21A	N400EZ	84-0129				
577	C21A	N400FE	84-0130				
578	C21A	N400FG	84-0131				
579	C21A	N400FH	84-0132				
580	C21A	N400FK	84-0133				
581	C21A	N400FM	84-0134 code RA				
582	C21A	N400FN	84-0135 code RA				
583	C21A	N400FP	84-0136 code RA	w/o 17Apr95 Alexandra City, AL			
584	C21A	N400FQ	84-0141 code RA				
585	C21A	N400FR	84-0137 code CS				
586	C21A	N400FT	84-0142				
587	C21A	N400FU	84-0139				
588	C21A	N400FV	84-0140				
589	A	N1087T	N8567K	PT-GAP			
590	A	N1451B	N35GA	N35KT	N969MC	N827CA	
591	A	N3803G	N8567Z	N72626	N500EX	N822CA	
592	A	N3810G	N952GL	N45KK	N93LE		
593	A	N40146	N32B	I-FLYG	N593LR		
594	A	N1088C	N72596	N7007V	(ZS-PTL)	(ZS-EFD)	OY-LJA
595	A	N3815G	N85PM	N414KL			
596	A	N1473B	N72612	N62WM	YV-850CP	N850MM	N826CA
597	A	N39394	N8567R	N54GL	N597BL	N597JT	N355CA
598	A	N39415	N8567T	PT-LGW			
599	A	N40144	N58GL				
600	A	N823CA					
601	A	N3818G	China HY986				
602	A	N10873	China HY987				
603	A	N1471B	China HY988				
604	A	N1462B	N59GL	N604BL	N73LP		
605	A	N1088D	N185HA	N35AS	N825CA		
606	A	N3803G	N1735J	N35PD	N3WP	N96GS	
607	A	N39399	N72614	PT-LIJ	N68MJ		
608	A	N40162	N8567Z	N111SF	N14T	N96AX	
609	A	N4290J	N36NW	N788QC	XA-JRH		

LEARJET 35

C/n	Series	Identities
610	A	N1473B N101AR N161MA N610LJ
611	A	N39413 N622WG N611TW
612	A	N3812G N8568D N2FU N501TW N551TW N551HM
613	A/R35A	N4289X Brazil 35A-6000 (prefix 35A- not confirmed)
614	A	N3815G G-PJET HB-VJC G-SOVN G-VIPS G-OCFR
615	A/R35A	N1466B N7260E Brazil 35A-6001 (prefix 35A- not confirmed)
616	A	N3807G N8568Q PT-LQF N616LJ N876CS
617	A/R35A	N4289Z Brazil 35A-6002 (prefix 35A- not confirmed)
618	A	N10871 YU-BOL SL-BAA S5-BAA
619	A	N4290K N8568V PT-POK
620	A	N1451B I-KODM VR-BNI N232FX
621	A	N1468B N999TH N999TN PT-OFW N242MT
622	A	N4290C N7260H N610R N81MR
623	A	N40149 N7260Q Thailand 60504
624	C21A	N39404 86-0374
625	C21A	N4289Y 86-0375 N625BL
626	A	N39398 N7261R N35AJ N711NF C-GNPT
627	A	N4289U N7260T PT-LMY
628	C21A	N3810G 86-0376 N628BL N628WJ
629	C21A	N40144 86-0377
630	A	N42905 N72630 N742E N742P N388PD
631	A/VU35A	N3818G Brazil 35A-2710
632	A/VU35A	N1461B Brazil 35A-2711
633	A/VU35A	N39416 Brazil 35A-2712
634	A	N1462B I-EAMM N626BM
635	A	N1471B Thailand 60505
636	A/VU35A	N1476B Brazil 35A-2713
637		airframe not built
638	A/VU35A	N39412 Brazil 35A-2714
639	A/VU35A	N6317V Brazil 35A-2715
640	A/VU35A	N3816G N8568Y Brazil 35A-2716
641	A/VU35A	N1087Y N7261H Brazil 35A-2717
642	A/VU35A	N1465B N7262X Brazil 35A-2718
643	A	N39418 G-LJET (N35NK)
644	A	N1088C N1043B PT-LLF (N54SB) C-GMMY
645	A	N43TR
646	A	N3812G XA-UMA N646EA N717JB N712JB G-MURI w/o 2May00 Lyon-Satolas A/P, France
647	A	N410RD N915RB N815RB (N647TJ) ZS-DJB N335PR
648	A	N1045J N974JD XB-LHS N648JW RP-C648 N648J N97LE
649	A	N10870 HB-VJJ
650	A	N1022G PT-LYF N135MW N650LR
651	A	HB-VJK
652	A	N6307H N99FN D-CURE N652SA N49AZ
653	A	HB-VJL
654	A	N4290K N633WW N600LF (N95EC) (B-98183) ZS-NSB B-98183
655	A	N1088A N16FG PT-MFR N785JM C-GMMA
656	A	N3810G G-JETL N335SB N356JW
657	A	N1473B N1CA N10AH
658	A	N39404 N573LP
659	A	N4290Y N873LP
660	A	N1087Z C-GLJQ N660L C-GLJQ
661	A	(N8888D) N1268G VH-PFA operated by Singapore AF as a target towing aircraft
662	A	G-NEVL G-BUSX N35UK
663	A	N91480 D-CCCB
664	A	N9130F N117RJ C-GRMJ
665	A	N5009T N291K
666		airframe not built, as this number is considered unlucky in the USA
667	A	N5018G N91566 N135DE
668	A	N5011L N9168Q N441PC
669	A	N5014F N91452 OO-JBS N7XJ (N487LP) A6-FAJ N669LJ N393CF
670	A	N5012K N35UK N599SC OY-CCO (HP-) HK-3949X (N670WJ) OY-CCO N787LP
671	A	N9141N (ZS-NEX) (ZS-NFS) ZS-NFK N671BA LV-PLV LV-WPZ
672	A	N9140Y N672DK N45KK
673	A	N5014F N9173G C-FBDH C-GPDO
674	A	N5.... N2601G N22SF N22SN N900JE
675	A	N5.... N2602M B-98181 w/o 17Sep94; shot down in error while target towing off east coast of Taiwan
676	A	N5012Z N35LJ N235AC

Production complete

LEARJET MODEL 36

An Asterisk (*) after the series letter indicates the aircraft has been fitted with Avcom delta fins.

C/n	Series	Identities
001		N26GL ff 09Jan73 C-GBRW cx Apr97 as wfu to Montral - St Hubert Aeronautical College
002		N362GL D-CMAR YV-T-ASG YV-161P YV-89CP N18AT D-CELA N3239A N84DM N84FN
003		N363GL N36TA N55CJ
004		N1918W (D-CCAC) D-CCPD N50DT N180GC
005*		LV-LOG N9108Z
006		(I-CRYS) HB-VEA D-CAFO D-CDFA w/o 25Mar80 Libya
007		N138GL N173JA N226CC SX-AHF VR-BHB N83DM N83FN
008		N20JA VR-BJD VR-BJO N84MJ N101AR (N701AR) N101AJ (N43A) (survey aircraft)
009		N2000M N704J N44GL N25CL N15CC N505RA N505HG
010		N50SF N45FG
011		PT-KQT N26MJ N26FN*
012		N139GL N215RL VR-BFR N2267Z C-GBWD N666TB N36CW N222AW N55GH N712JE N547PA code "AK"
013		N352WC (N852WC) SE-DDH N3280E N3PC N13JE D-CBRD N71PG
014		N900Y N200Y VH-SLJ
015		N14CF N10FN
016*		HB-VEE JY-AET F-GBGD N616DJ N12FN
017		N1010A N17LJ (N32JA)
018*	A	PT-KTU N418CA PT-ACC
019	A	N300CC N89MJ C-GLMK N718US N300DK N300DL C-GLAL N719JE N540PA N527PA
020	A	JY-AFC w/o 21Sep77 Amman
021	A	N3524F I-AIFA w/o 10Dec79 Forli, Italy
022	A	N761A N38WC N36PD N44EV
023	A	N1871R N1871P N187MZ (N64FN) N767RA N6YY N56PA
024	A	N38D N978E
025	A	N774AB N730GL OE-GLP C-GVVB N500MJ (N98A) N800BL N32PA
026	A	(N762L) N762GL N23G C-GGPF N6617B N8U (N888TN) (N8UB)
027	A	N836GA N484HB N27MJ
028	A	N731GA N75TD N545PA code "HI"
029	A	(N79JS) HB-VFD N116MA
030	A	N71TP N74TP N360LS N36PJ (N36AX) N160GC
031	A	N20UC N20UG D-CFOX N20UG N62PG
032	A	N40146 N745GL N22BM N36BP HB-VLK N950G
033	A	N762L N14TX w/o 06Dec96 Stephenville, Newfoundland, Canada; cx Aug98
034	A	N763R China HY985
035	A	N3807G VH-BIB N266BS VH-BIB N71CK
036	A	N1462B N610GE N36MJ
037	A	RP-C5128 N555WH
038	A	N304E N15FN N548PA N700GG
039	A	N217CS C-GSRN N4998Z N25PK N99RS
040	A	HB-VFV N902WJ N110PA N70UT N70UP (N444SC) (N442SC) N500SV
041	A	N79SF w/o 08Jan88 Monroe, LA
042	A	N39391 HB-VFS w/o 23Sep95 Zarzaitine, Algeria
043	A	N1010G N43LJ N53JA (N143JW) N432JW
044	A	N1010H N44LJ N54JA (N77JW)
045	A	(N700MD) N900MD N13FN N546PA
046	A	F-BKFB N4448Y N146MJ N17A
047	A	G-ZEIZ N2972Q N14CN N36SK OE-GMD
048	A	HB-VHF N3999B (N14FU) N2FU N24PT N3NP PT-WGM N32AJ
049	A	N661AA N136ST VH-SLF
050	A	N3456L XA-RIA Mexico TP-105 callsign XC-UJR; also carries XC-AA24
051	A	N4290J Peru 524/OB-1431
052	A	N1087T Peru 525/OB-1432
053	A	N39418 China HY984
054	A/U36A	(N54GL) N1087Z Japan 9201
055	A	N10871 OE-GNL N365AS PP-JAA
056	A/U36A	N3802G Japan 9202
057	A	N39394 HB-VIF
058	A/U36A	N4290J Japan 9203 w/o 28Feb91 Shikoku Island, Japan
059	A/U36A	N1087Z Japan 9204
060	A/U36A	N1088A Japan 9205
061	A/U36A	N50154 N2601B Japan 9206
062	A	N4291N D-CGFE
063	A	N6340T N1048X D-CGFF
064	A	believed for Japan as a U36A

Production complete

LEARJET MODEL 45

C/n	Series	Identities			
001		N45XL	ff 07Oct95		
002		N45LJ	N452LJ		
003		N453LJ	N789H*		
004		N454LJ	w/o 27Oct98 Wallops Island, VA		
005		N455LJ			
006		N456LJ	ZS-OIZ		
007		N457LJ	(ZS-JBR)	(ZS-BAR)	
008		N745E			
009		N984GC	N459LJ		
010		(D-CWER)	N41DP	N903HC	
011		N741E			
012		N5009V	N412LJ	(OE-)	D-COMM
013		N5010U	N413LJ	D-CEWR	
014		N708SP			
015		N31V			
016		N743E			
017		(D-CWER)	N417LJ	D-CESH	
018		N418LJ	OO-LFS		
019		N56WD	N45LJ	C-GCMP	N
020		N5000E	HB-VMA		
021		N5009T	HB-VMB		
022		N5012G	PT-TJB		
023		N740E			
024		N145ST	C-FBCL		
025		N742E			
026		N405FX			
027		N156PH			
028		N5014E			
029		N5013Y	9V-ATG		
030		N5012H	N157PH		
031		N5016V	9V-ATH		
032		N4FE			
033		N50162	9V-ATI		
034		N45FE			
035		N5013U	9V-ATJ		
036		N345WB			
037		N50145	OE-GDI		
038		N454AS			
039		N456AS			
040		(N145MC)	N68PC		
041		N541LJ	C-GPDQ		
042		N10R			
043		D-CRAN	N45VB		
044		D-CLUB	N888CX		
045		N4545			
046		ZS-PTL	ZS-OLJ	ZS-BAR	
047		N158PH	(2000th Learjet built)		
048		N	PT-XLR		
049		N711R			
050		N16PC			
051		N145KC			
052		N5011L	ZS-DCT		
053		N685RC			
054		N345MA			
055		N63MJ	N45LR		
056		N196PH			
057		N75TE			
058		N50111			
059		N50153	VP-CVL		
060		N1MG			
061		N111KK			
062		N512RB			
063		N10J			
064		N800MA			
065		N100KK			
066		N94CK			
067		N5087B			
068		N	I-ERJD		
069		N50157	SU-MSG		
070					
071		N145K			
072		N5016Z			
073		N65U	N66SG		
074		N815A			
075		N450BC			
076		N245K			
077		N5018G			

LEARJET 45

C/n	Series	Identities	
078		N5016Z	N116AS
079		N5FE	
080		N42HP	
081		N76TE	
082		N40082	N1HP^
083		N5013Y	
084		N5009V	
085		N454CG	
086			
087		N645HJ	
088		N454MK	
089		N406FX	
090		N407FX	
091		N408FX	
092			
093			
094		N300JE	
095		N409FX	
096			
097			
098			
099		N545RS	
100			
101		N410FX	
102		N411FX	
103		N412FX	
104			
105		N105LJ	
106		N145XL	
107			
108			
109			
110			
111			
112			
113			
114			
115			
116			
117			
118			
119			
120			
121		N316SR	
122		N945FD	
123			
124			
125			
126			
127			
128			
129			
130			
131			
132			
133			
134			
135			
136			
137			
138			
139			
140			
141			
142			
143			
144			
145			
146			
147			
148			
149			
150			
151			
152			
153			
154			
155			

LEARJET 45

C/n	Series	Identities
156		
157		
158		
159		
160		
161		
162		
163		
164		
165		
166		
167		
168		
169		
170		
171		
172		
173		
174		
175		
176		
177		
178		
179		
180		
181		
182		
183		
184		N45VP
185		
186		
187		
188		N21BD

LEARJET MODEL 55

C/n Series Identities

001 60 N551GL model 55 prototype converted to 55C prototype N551DF has been stretched and used as Model 60 prototype N60XL cx Sep96; wfu
002 N552GL given new c/n 55-139A on conversion to 55C standards (qv) cx Apr91
003 N553GP N162GA N553DJ N553GJ*
004 N90E N50L N24JK N24CK D-CLIP (N500FA) N155DD
005 N40ES N128VM N550CS (N94TJ) N440DM
006 N113EL N212JP N126EL N355DB
007 N41ES I-KILO w/o 04Apr94 San Pablo Airport, Seville, Spain; remains to Atlanta Air Salvage, Griffin, GA
008 N551SC
009 N42ES N55SJ HB-VIB N955FD N955MD N955LS
010 N57TA w/o 13Nov81 Waterkloof AFB, S Africa
011 N37951 (N57TA) N411GL N574W D-CREW N200BA ES-PVV
012 N55GH N23G N104BS N48HC
013 N10872 (D-CCHS) OE-GNK N3238K PT-LEL N82679 (N519AC) (N155AJ) (D-CEWR) D-CUTE N82679 D-CUTE N155SB
014 N40144 N90BS N55KC XA-PIL N550RH N155MP (N554EM) N455EM
015 (YV-41CP) N39413 HB-VGV N515DJ N550LJ D-CION N27DD
016 N646G
017 N760AC N760AQ D-CCGN
018 N39E N599EC N797CS
019 YV-41CP N141SM C-GSWP
020 N720M N20DL N57B N8GT N123LC N35PF N55NY
021 N3794B N700TG EI-BSA I-LOOK
022 N64WM VR-BOL VP-BOL N155GM
023 N3796B N7784 N110ET
024 HB-VGZ N224DJ HB-VGZ N900FA (N54NW)
025 N236R N57PM N57FM N92MG
026 N8565H N55HD N21VB D-CILY (N96AF) N421QL (N321GL) N318JH
027 N3796X OE-GKN N3796X N123LC B-3980 N227A B-3980 N59HJ
028 N3794C PT-LDR N3794C PT-LOF N7244W (N53HJ) N556GA N556HJ*
029 N4CP D-CLIP N29DJ N10CP PT-OHU N10CP N82JA N100VA N29NW
030 N986WC N959WC N117WC N55LJ (N155CD)
031 YV-12CP
032 N75TP (N72TP) N71TP N81CH N11TS N83SD
033 N96CE N960E N917S N414RF N155CS (VR-CJA) VR-CML PT-OOW N38JA (N377JW) (N77JW) N971EC N398AC
034 N3795Y D-CARX N84DJ D-CLUB N77JW N37JA (N234LC) (N334JW) N123LC N550TC
035 N115EL (N100GU) N1968A N127EL D-CVIP N97AF C-GPCS
036 N3803G N555GL N81CH N76AW N81CH N236JW N155HM N723CC
037 N41CP N86AJ PT-OBR N53HJ
038 N551HB N50AF
039 N39418 N770JM N97J VR-BQF N339BC
040 N3802G HZ-AM11 HZ-AM2 N426EM N55HK N554CL
041 N401JE N155PJ N41EA N550RH (HP-) HK-4016X
042 N1462B N3796U N160TL D-CMTM N575GH
043 N5543G N785B (N500JC) N500JW N30AF N430HM (N455EC) N83WM
044 N3797C PT-LHR
045 N1451B HB-VHK EC-DSI VR-BHV EC-DSI (N90583) N49PE (N49PD) I-AGER N550AK (N123LC)
046 N23HB (N13HB) N3HB N55HL
047 N600C
048 (N734) N3796Z VH-LGH N73TP N67RW PT-OBS N558AC N558HJ
049 N6317V N3796C D-CCHS N150MS
050 N4289X D-CARP (HB-) (N122JD) OY-FLK N220JC N552BA*
051 N734 N22G N22GH N55KS N55KD D-CATL
052 N4289Z YV-292CP N55GF N551DB D-COOL
053 N4290Z N85653 YV-347CP (N1450B) N500RP N501RP N205EL (N205EF) N253S
054 N42905 N54GL HB-VHL N54NW
055 (N155JC) N155LP N970H N970F N825MG
056 N8563E (N854GA) N946FP N59GS N272TB N270AS OH-IPP N156JC
057 N4290Y N10CR N733EY N733E
058 (N55BE) N500BE N200PC N129SP N58SR
059 (N211BY) D-CAEP N50AF N59LJ OE-GRR
060 N6331V N60MJ N53JL N86AJ N8YY N60LT PT-OUG N6364U N255TS
061 N117EL N222MC N132EL D-CFUX
062 N62GL N24G N316 N292RC N855DB
063 N40146 N8563P N1744P N74RY
064 N255ST
065 N1088C N8565K N555GL N1125M
066 N237R (N550DD) N50DD N717HB
067 N39412 N120EL N127GT
068 N1088A N38D
069 N551UT N102ST
070 N1471B F-GDHR w/o 05Feb87 over Cameroons nr Nigerian border
071 N3807G (N155UT) N155JC
072 N58AS N55AS N55AQ PT-MSM N72ET SX-BNS
073 N1087Z HB-VHN I-VIKY D-CARE N355DH N73WE N357PR N857PR
074 N5574 N74GL N151PJ N701DB

LEARJET 55

C/n	Series	Identities
075		N39415 N8563Z N675M N55GM N55GH N90NE
076		(N155JC) N2855 N30GL C-GKTM
077		N3812G N8563M N58M N85NC N245MS
078		N39391 (N55GJ) N55GV N56TG (N120GR) I-ALPR
079		N39404 (N2855) N1983Y
080		N1465B N85632 PT-LET
081		N1468B N85631 N777MC N777MQ
082		N39394 N1075X N33GL N68LP N817AM
083		N40149 N55GZ N6789 (N6780) N551AS (N500HG) N550HG
084		N39413 N85643 N740AC I-FLYJ
085		N238R N58PM N58FM N55NM
086		N40162 D-CACP N8227P PT-LUK
087	ER	N1451B N8564Z N103C N520SC
088		N1461B N55GJ N155GS N900JB N901JC
089		N4289U N8564X N170VE N555CJ N789PF*
090		N40146 N723H D-CGIN N181EF
091		N3810G N8566F N91CH N991CH N91PR (N69B) N700JE
092		N1462B N724J N400JT D-CLUB N500FA N40DK
093		N725K N32KJ
094		N1088C N235HR N236HR*
095		N39398 N8565Z N55RT
096		N1087T N1045X N8010X N126KD
097		N4290C N8566Q N40CR N20CR
098	ER	N726L D-CCON
099		(N5599) N2992 N17GL N95WK
100		N3807G N552UT N552SQ N500NH
101	ER	N39415 N101HK N101PK N101HK N211EF N501TW N251VG (C-FNRG) N251NG C-FNRG N1129M
102	ER	N1087Y N55DG I-OSUA N44GA PT-WSS
103	ER	N10870 N921FP w/o 06Aug86 Rutland, VT
104		N39404 N18CG N18CQ (N95TJ) N277AL
105		N39391 N55GK N22G N274 C-GQBR
106		N3812G N60E N90AM N318JH N824MG
107	ER	N1466B N760G N155JT N304AT D-CWAY
108		(N888FK) N77FK N78FK N222MC N220VE (N551AM) N517AM
109		N348HM D-CVIP
110		N39412 N55GY (N24RH) N455RH
111		N1461B N7260G PT-LIG w/o 09Nov94 Guanabara Bay, Rio de Janeiro, Brazil - remains to Dodson Avn, Ottawa, KS
112		N3802G (YV-325CP) N325CP LN-VIP N7AU EC-HAI
113		N1450B N7262M N713M N236HR N57MH
114		N39398 N72608 N34GB
115		N1476B N6666R N6666K N633AC N155BC
116		N1087Y N85GL N116DA N51V N51VL
117		N3807G N8567X N255MB N155RB
118		N39416 C-FCLJ
119		N3816G N72613 N273MC N273MG
120		N39418 N72629 N55LK (N486) N1127M
121		N3811G N8568J N65Y N155SC N747AN
122		N10870 N8568P N18ZD N99KW N99KV C-FHJB OE-GRO
123		N6331V N44EL N121US N150NE
124		N39391 N58CG N58CQ SX-BTV
125	ER	N6307H N610JR
126		N4291G N7260J YV-125CP N7260J N16LJ
127	B	N6340T HZ-AM2 N73GP
128	B	N1087T N255BL N7US N7UA N10BF N717JB
129	B	N4290Y N75GP
130	B	N4291N N55VC
131	B	N1088A N7260K N52CT
132	B	N4291K N67WM N133WB (N333GJ) (N133SU) N122SU
133	B	N155PL N155LJ N55LF N700R
134	B	N39399 N7261D PT-LDR
135	C	N1055C PT-LXO
136	C	N3811G N767AZ N767NY N155PS OE-GCF
137	C	N39413 N95SC N155SP
138	C	N4291G TC-MEK TC-FBS VR-CDK N9LR N338FP
139	C	N39391 N1039L PT-LZS PT-GMN
139A	C	converted from 55-002 (qv) N4289X N994JD N984JD N55GM (N55ZT)
140	C	N72616 PT-OCA Brazil FAB6100
141	C	N155DB
142	C	N555MX
143	C	N10871 D-CMAD
144	C	N144LT PT-OJH N40CR
145	C	N66WM N10CR
146	C	N9125M PT-ORA
147	C	N55UK N499SC N111US N160NE

Production complete

LEARJET MODEL 60

C/n	Identities							
55-001	N60XL	converted to Model 60 standards						
001	N601LJ	rolled out 05May92; ff 15Jun92						
002	N602LJ	C-GLRS	C-GLRL	N602LJ	N190AS	N1940		
003	N60LJ	N961MR						
004	N60UK	N194AL						
005	N5011L	N610TM	N869JS	N205FX	OY-LJD			
006	N60VE							
007	N448HM	(N212FX)	N219FX	N204FX				
008	N608LJ	PT-OVI	N608LJ	N222FX				
009	N26029	N54						
010	N5012H	N477DM	N477BM	HB-VLU	N525CF	N928CD	N928GD	C-FBDR
011	N5013U	N60T	OY-LJE	N61YC				
012	N5014H	N123CC	N147CC	N626KM				
013	(N960H)	N26011	N55					
014	N7US							
015	N960H	N960HL*						
016	N50153	TC-MEK						
017	N50157	N9173R	N760AC	N660AH				
018	N5009T	N4016G	N24G					
019	N50153	N40366	HB-VKI					
020	N600L							
021	N600LC							
022	N2602Z	N22G						
023	N40323	N60SB						
024	N2601V	LV-PGX	LV-WFM					
025	N9155Z	N299SC	N299SG					
026	N4026Z	N60LJ	N700GS	N60LJ	N347GS	N14T		
027	N4027S	XA-ICA	N4230S	N12FU				
028	N50298	N870JS	N206FX					
029	N4029P	N55KS	C-FBLU					
030	N4030W	N164PA	TC-ELL					
031	N4031L	N228N						
032	N5013D	OE-GNL						
033	N4031A	N56						
034	N5034Z	9M-CAL						
035	N50353	VR-BST	N116AS	N1DC				
036	N5014E	N60LR	N44EL					
037	N5017J	N4037A	N637LJ	N101HW				
038	N4007J	N638LJ						
039	N50154	N5003X	N57	N8071J	N57			
040	N399SC	N899SC	N660AS					
041	N5004Y	N699SC	N166HL					
042	N4010K	N90AG	N90AQ					
043	N5043D	C-GHKY	N43NR					
044	N5044N	N618R	(N618P)	N1618R*				
045	N5045S	N60WM	N711VT					
046	N50157	N5006G	(PT-WGB)	N214FX				
047	N5007P	N418R	N50DS					
048	N5008Z	N648LJ						
049	N50298	N227N	N247N	N126CX				
050	N50450	N207FX						
051	N5051X	N63BL						
052	N5022C	ZS-NTV						
053	N5012Z	N5053Y	B-3981					
054	N65BL	VP-BMM						
055	N5014E	N5055F	N1CA					
056	N5013Y	N60LR	N117RJ	N700CH				
057	(N5010U)	N50050	N58					
058	N5016V	N92BL	XA-BRE					
059	N5059J	N208FX						
060	N50602	N209FX						
061	N50162	N98BL						
062	N5012H	N5006T	(N510SG)	N707SG	N707SQ	C-GLRS		
063	N5015U	N5003U	N8270					
064	N210FX							
065	N5006V	N30W						
066	N5006K	N8271						
067	N799SC	N118HC						
068	(N96ZC)	N95ZC	N823TR					
069	N50324	N60CE						
070	N5035R	N21AC						
071	N60LJ	N940P						
072	N5072L	9M-FCL						
073	N50761	N256M	N860PD					
074	N8074W	N620JF						
075	N675LJ	N9CU						

LEARJET 60

C/n	Identities				
076	N211FX				
077	N212FX	N677LJ	C-GLRS	N227FX	
078	N5068F	N188TC	N188TG		
079	N319LJ	N95AG			
080	N8080W	N59			
081	N681LJ	N60LJ	N180CP		
082	N682LJ	N600LN			
083	N683LJ	N383MB			
084	N684LJ	N59FD	N100R		
085	N685LJ	N99KW			
086	(N213FX)	N686LJ	(N777CB)	N797CB	
087	N687LJ	N411ST	N410ST*		
088	N688LJ	XA-TZF			
089	N8089Y	XA-MDM			
090	N8090P	PT-WMO	N460BG		
091	N8071L	N896R	N91LE		
092	N5092R	C-FBLJ			
093	N80683	RP-C648	N109JE	N109JR	
094	N60LR	A6-SMS	(N511CL)	N93BA	TC-ARC
095	N5005X	N602SC			
096	N8086L	N603SC			
097	N8067Y	N897R	N60TX*		
098	N50758	N218FX			
099	N212FX				
100	N6100	N60MN			
101	N215FX				
102	N8082B	LV-WXN	N102LJ		
103	N216FX				
104	N104LJ	N83WM	N903AM		
105	N217FX				
106	N106LJ	N140JC			
107	N107LJ	D-CFFB			
108	N220FX				
109	N109LJ	N707SG			
110	N60LJ	N928CD			
111	N221FX				
112	N299SC				
113	N599SC	N60LH			
114	N3014R	N199SC	N114PJ		
115	N3015F	N500	N500ZH	N600GG	
116	N116LJ	XA-VIG			
117	N889DW				
118	N3018C	N11AM			
119	N119LJ	N626LJ			
120	N120LJ	D-CSIX			
121	N621LJ	PT-XFS			
122	N622LJ	N61DP			
123	N356WA				
124	N223FX				
125	N60LR	VP-CRB			
126	N224FX				
127	N225FX				
128	N226FX				
129	N629LJ	D-CBAD			
130	N630LJ	N90MC			
131	N631LJ	XA-JJS			
132	N228FX				
133	N133LJ	C-FIDO			
134	N134LJ	XA-ZTA			
135	N135LJ	N98JV			
136	N136LJ	N60RL			
137	N229FX				
138	N230FX				
139	N233FX	N139XX			
140	N98JV	N140LJ	Argentina T-10		
141	N234FX	N141LJ	OY-JKH		
142	(N642LJ)	N426JN			
143	N235FX	N6666R			
144	N60144	D-CKKK			
145	N145LJ	LX-PRA			
146	N50776	N261PC			
147	N138SP				
148	N80701	D-CETV			
149	N149LJ	(ZS-JRM)	SU-BNL		
150	N80667	A6-SMS			
151	N234FX				
152	N50126	Mexico MTX-01			
153	N235FX				

LEARJET 60

C/n	Identities	
154	N233FX	
155	N88V	
156	N76SF	
157	N236FX	
158	N237FX	
159	N43SF	
160	N	D-CDNY
161	N	D-CDNZ
162	N99ZC	
163	N238FX	
164	N60LJ	
165	N929GW	
166	N239FX	
167	N240FX	
168	N706CJ	
169	N5014F	OE-GII
170	N50154	D-COWS
171	N422CP	
172	N241FX	
173	N	OY-LJF
174	N242FX	
175	N243FX	
176	N176MB	
177	N60LR	
178	N244FX	
179		
180	N777MC	
181	N273MC	
182	N245FX	
183	N246FX	
184		
185	N464TF	
186	N186ST	N58ST*
187	N247FX	
188	N248FX	
189		
190		
191		
192		
193		
194		
195		
196		
197		
198		
199		
200		
201		
202		
203		
204		
205		
206		
207		
208	N235HR^	
209		
210		
211		
212		
213		
214		
215		
216		
217		
218		
219		
220		
221	N255BD	

LOCKHEED JETSTAR

Aircraft which were converted to -731s by Garrett AiResearch were given a sequential conversion number by that company; these numbers appear alongside the c/n in the production list.

C/n	Series	Identities
1001		N329J ff 04Sep57, last flight 16Aug82; donated to Pacific Vocational Inst, Vancouver, Canada
1002		N329K N711Z displayed Andrews AFB in USAF colours, code 89001
5001/53	731	N9201R ff 21Oct60 N1 N21 N1 N11 N7145V wfu; donated to Pratt Community College, KS; to spares by White Industries 1998
5002	6	N9202R EP-VRP N106GM N69TP N81JJ N148PE b/u for spares Mar85 Minneapolis, MN
5003	6	N9203R NASA14 N814NA cx Dec89; stored NASA ramp at Edwards AFB, CA
5004	6	N9204R N13304 N524AC N777EP N69HM N777EP displayed Graceland Estate, Memphis, TN
5005	6	N161LM N176LG N12121 N716RD N712RD N70TP XA-SIN XB-DLV (N22265) wfu as XB-DLV Van Nuys, CA; only fuselage remains
5006/40	731	N9280R N12R N227K N731JS N222Y N6NE (VR-CCC) wfu Southampton, UK, after landing accident
5007/45	731	N9205R N110G N72CT N971AS impounded 1992 Atlanta-Peachtree GA; b/u for spares 1993
5008	6	N500Z N400M w/o 27Dec72 Saranac Lake, NY
5009	6	N9206R N540G N767Z N717X N717 (HB-VET) N717JM cx Sep84; b/u for spares
5010	6/C140A	59-5958 displayed Travis AFB Museum, CA in camouflage c/s
5011/1	731	N9282R Indonesia T17845 PK-PJS 9V-BEE PK-PJH N731A C-GKRS N10461 N159B N88JM b/u for spares late 1985; fuselage at Lincoln, NE 1988
5012	6	N9283R D-BABE N10123 N1012B N500SJ N501AL wfu Opa Locka, FL; cx Jan94; derelict Mar94
5013	8	N9284R N322K N523AC N11JC HZ-MAC N11JC N8AD N158DP (N5AX) b/u for spares Mar88 by White Inds, Bates City, MO
5014	6	N58CG N9MD N54BW N95GS b/u for spares 1989 Miami, FL
5015	6	NASA4 N172L N103KC N505T N9046F N66MP wfu at South Seattle Community College, WA; still current
5016	6	N9210R N2222R (N222R) N20TF HZ-AFS HZ-SH2 N4258P N712GW N440RM open storage Roswell, NM circa Oct97
5017	6/VC140B	N9286R 61-2488 AMARC park code CL006; preserved Warner-Robins AFB, GA
5018	6	N9287R (CF-DTX) C-FDTX preserved National Aviation Museum, Rockcliffe, Canada
5019	6	N9288R N105GM N105GN (N70TP) N5UD N50UD b/u 1986; fuselage at Fort Lauderdale Executive, FL; tail section at North Perry, FL 1989; fuselage converted into mobile home!
5020	6	N9207R N371H N300CR N308WC cx Sep88; b/u for spares
5021	6	CF-ETN C-FETN N564MG b/u for spares Memphis, TN
5022	6/VC140B	61-2489 AMARC park code CL006; preserved Pima County Museum, Tucson, AZ
5023	6	N9221R I-SNAL N711Z N1107Z N767Z N979RA N879RA N723ST N20PY N2ES (N6ES) b/u for spares Mar88 by White Inds, Bates City, MO
5024	6/VC140B	61-2490 stored AMARC Davis-Monthan AFB, AZ with park code CL004; to Western Air Parts
5025	6	(62-12166) W Germany CA101 W Germany 1101 SU-DAF
5026	6/C140A	59-5959 noted 29Sep92 Scott AFB
5027	6/VC140B	61-2491 displayed Rhein-Main AFB, Germany
5028	6/C140A	59-5960 wfu; open storage Greenville, TX
5029/38	731	N3E N3EK N340 N39BL N1BL N166AC N112TJ (N25TX) N1406^
5030	6/C140A	59-5961 w/o 07Nov62 Warner-Robins AFB, GA
5031	6/VC140B	61-2492 preserved USAF Museum, Wright Patterson AFB, OH
5032	6/C140A	59-5962 at Edwards AFB, CA, for Museum
5033/56	731	N1620 N16200 N33EA N100CC N100AC N200CC N200CG XB-FIS N25WA N50EC (N890MC) N500MA
5034	6/VC140B	61-2493 stored AMARC Davis-Monthan AFB, AZ with park code CL003; to Western Air Parts
5035	6	(62-12167) W Germany CA102 w/o 16Jan68 Bremen, W Germany; reported stored Bremen
5036/42	731	N1622 N1622D N41TC N776JM N444JH N90KR N900CR
5037/24	731	N9211R N2600 (damaged in pressurisation tests; rebuilt as c/n 5128, but still known as c/n 5037) N519L N3060 N60CN N60CH N11UF (N71UF) N90TC N10DR N6JL N552JH N770JR
5038	6	N9212R N341NS N341N N22CH N11UF N11UE (N44KF) b/u; cx Dec92; remains to Aviation Warehouse film prop yard at El Mirage CA
5039	6	N600J N60QJ N81MR N86HM N200CK cx Sep90; was stored Spirit of St Louis A/P, MO; presumed since scrapped
5040	6	N505C N518L N7SZ N888RW cx May88; spares May88; remains blown up Fort Lauderdale, FL for film
5041	6/C140B	62-4197 stored AMARC Davis-Monthan AFB, AZ with park code CL007; to Western Air Parts
5042	6/C140B	62-4198 to Battle Damage Repair Unit, Mildenhall AFB, UK; b/u by 22Jan92 Mildenhall
5043	6/C140B	62-4199 stored AMARC Davis-Monthan AFB, AZ with park code CL002; to Western Air Parts
5044	6/C140B	62-4200 stored AMARC Davis-Monthan AFB, AZ with park code CL005; to Western Air Parts
5045	6/C140B	62-4201 stored AMARC Davis-Monthan AFB, AZ with park code CL008; preserved Hill AFB, UT
5046	6	N9282R PK-IJS Indonesia T9446 Indonesia A9446 wfu and stored Jakarta-Halim AFB, Indonesia
5047	6	N9214R N409M N409MA N555PB cx Oct90; scrapped
5048	6	N9215R N40N N40NC N98KR N98MD N500WN N500WZ N428DA (N130LW)
5049	6	N9216R N1230R N96B N96BB wfu at South Seattle Community College, WA
5050/34	731	N207L N208L N141TC HZ-THZ N434AN b/u Apr94 by Atlanta Air Salvage, Griffin, GA
5051	6	N9217R N400KC N44MF N31S N310AD N555BS N488JS N488GR

JETSTAR

C/n	Series	Identities
5052	6	N9218R N300P N66CR CF-DTM C-FDTM N9739B b/u for spares early 1989 Bi-States Park, St Louis, MO; cx Jun92
5053/2	731	N9219R N12R N121CN N69CN N14WJ XA-POU XC-JCC
5054/59	731	N9220R N7600J N7600 N20AP N354CA N721PA
5055/21	731	N9222R N296AR N303H N90ZP N85BP (N43JK) (N86BP) (N79MB) N304CK N707EZ N99FT wfu at Chino, CA, circa Sep95; cx Mar96
5056	6	N9223R N105G N105GH N300AG HZ-FNA scrapped Spirit of St Louis A/P, MO
5057	6	N1007 N90U N90ME cx Mar87; b/u Memphis, TN during 1988
5058/4	731	N100A N100AL N1500M N50AS N600TT (N600DT) N600TP N381AA N131EL N200DW
5059	6	Indonesia T1645 Indonesia A1645 preserved in museum Yogjakarta-Adisutjipto, Indonesia
5060	6	N9225R N31F N55NC cx May88; b/u Jun88 Fort Lauderdale International, FL
5061/48	731	N9226R N506T N506D N47BA N67GT N152GS N161GS N123GA (N888WW) N488MR N488EC N333EC N338EC
5062/12	731	N679RW N2200M RP-57 N111G VR-BHF EC-697 EC-FGX
5063	6	N9228R N420L N420A N420G N499PB
5064/51	731	N184GP N3QS N3QL being parted out Rantoul KS circa early 2000
5065	6	N9229R N1966G S9-NAD wfu 1989; used as spares for c/n 5085
5066/46	731	N9230R N228Y N7782 XA-HRM XA-JHR XA-SAE XA-MIK reported w/o 16Nov95, no other details
5067	6	N871D N711Z N207L (N267AD) N267L w/o 29Mar81 Luton, UK
5068/27	731	N9231R N96GS w/o 06Jan90 Miami A/P, FL; used as spares; cx Jan91
5069/20	731	N910M N918MM XA-PGO N197JS reported for spares; cx Feb99
5070/52	731	N992 N9921 C-GAZU N9921 N177NC N731AG N114CL N888CF N888WT N712TE N731WL
5071	6	(62-12845) W Germany CA103 1103 SU-DAH
5072/23	731	N9233R N500Z N74AG scrapped cx Dec99
5073	6	N7775 fuselage used as interior mock-up by KC Avn, Dallas, TX
5074/22	731	N9234R N67B N267P N267GF N168DB N777SG N171JL
5075/19	731	N397B N540G N2345M N1DB N500ES
5076/17	731	N9235R N100C N3E N3EK N69ME N76HG
5077	6	N9236R N1924V N1EM w/o 25Mar76 Chicago, IL
5078/3	731	N711Z N7105 N472SP N52TJ N916RC (N916RG) N515AJ N124RM
5079/33	731	N9238R XA-RGB XA-MAZ N58TS
5080	6	N914X N914P N77HW wfu
5081	8	N200A N200AL N4SP N4SX cx Sep87; b/u for spares during 1987
5082/36	731	N320S N917J N82SR TC-OMR
5083/49	731	N208L N141LM N161LM N257H N257HA C-GAZU N27FW N817BD
5084/8	731	N9240R N83M N732M N910E N520S w/o 11Feb81 Westchester, NY
5085	6	N9241R N586 N5861 S9-NAE VR-CCY to Abu Dhabi Higher College of Technology, marked as "HCT"
5086/44	731	N9242R N27R N27RL N600J N60UJ HZ-FBT N711AG N27RC (N65JW)
5087/55	731	N9243R N41N N800J N31LJ N31WG N75MG N33SJ
5088	6	N9244R CF-DTF C-FDTF cx late 1986; preserved Halifax, Canada
5089	8	N9245R N324K N120AR (N85DL) (XA-) N120AR used for spares Jan94 by TAESA Mexico City, Mexico
5090	8	N9246R N106G N10MJ N55CJ N555SG wfu 1989 Fort Lauderdale Executive, FL (qv c/n 5094)
5091	6	N9247R N107G N107GH N118B N118BA wfu; remains to White Inds, Bates City, MO; cx May93
5092/58	731	N9248R N372H N901H N110AN N110DD VR-CSM VP-CSM
5093	6	N9249R N711Z N5000C N5000B N76EB N22RB cx Oct90; b/u for spares circa Sep90
5094	6	N9250R N3030 N3080 rebuilt with tail section fr c/n 5090 wfu Opa Locka, FL; derelict there Feb94
5095/30	731	N9251R N78MP N780RH N731L
5096/10	731	N9252R N530G
5097/60	731	N9253R N300L N306L N77D N81366 N1BL
5098/28	731	N9254R N1967G N5098G (N98MD) N417PJ N199LA N792AA N942Y
5099/5	731	N9255R N533EJ N594KR N277NS N323P N62K N62KK N18BH
5100/41	731	N9256R N207L XA-FIU N35JJ XA-GZA N510TS
5101/15	731	N9208R N7008 N7008J N760DL N760DE XA-JJS N26MJ N800AF N511TS
5102	8	N9235R N326K N500ZB N75CC N7500 N85CC N601JJ wfu Oct94 Spirit of St Louis A/P, MO & scrapped cx Feb00
5103	8	N23M N672M N176BN N176AN N101AW XA-TAZ (N101AW) XA-TAV
5104/6	731	N902K N902KB N155AV
5105	8	N277T N2277T N7005 N17005 HZ-MA1
5106/9	731	N238U N288U CF-GWI N8SC N1329K YV-03CP
5107	8	N118K N337US N7788 YV-187CP N7788 N69MT parted out Jun93 Hollister, CA
5108	8	N7953S N1207Z N24UG N68CT N680TT XA-SWD N104CE
5109/13	731	N7954S N968GN N968BN N678BC b/u for spares 1992 Chandler Municipal A/P, AZ; fuselage noted Apr94 on fire dump Phoenix-Skyharbor A/P, AZ; gone by Oct98
5110/47	731	N7955S N2600 N2601 N788S N49UC b/u for spares during 1990; cx Dec93
5111	8	N7956S N5111H N11SX N115MR N115DX b/u circa Aug91 Addison, TX; wings to Spirit of St Louis A/P, MO
5112/7	731	N7957S N910G N99MR N499PC N728PX
5113/25	731	N7958S N505C N124RP N303LE (N1967J) (N65JW) N1962J N77BT
5114/18	731	N7959S N930MT N930M N94K N111GU N26GL 5B-CHE
5115/39	731	N933LC N933CY N26TR N40XY N8300E N1151K dismantled at Willard A/P, Champaign, IL Aug95

JETSTAR

C/n	Series	Identities
5116	8	N7961S N222QA N3HB N60BC wfu 29Sep92 Spirit of St Louis A/P, MO; fuselage still present circa Apr96
5117/35	731	N7962S N210EK N310CK VR-BSH VP-BSH (N858SH) VP-BLD
5118	8	N7963S N333QA N333KN N222KN b/u 1987 Memphis, TN
5119/29	731	N7964S N11HM N508T N508TA N500AG N1DB
5120/26	731	N7965S N40DC HZ-TNA
5121	8	N7966S W Germany 1102 SU-DAG wfu 1994 Cairo, Egypt
5122	8	N7967S N1107Z N1107M N213AP cx Mar89; b/u during 1989
5123/14	731	N7968S N1844S N559GP N441A N47UC N123GN N57NP N57NR
5124	8	N7969S N46F N7SZ XA-SBQ XA-SKI report to XC-SKI
5125/31	731	N7970S N47UC N48UC N31BP
5126	8	N7971S N955H N955HL N20S N39E N39Q b/u for spares Aug83
5127	8	N7972S N42G N42GB N3GR N636C (N636MC) N636 N171CC derelict 1991 Van Nuys, CA; cx Jun92 remains to Aviation Warehouse film prop yard at El Mirage CA
5128/16	731	N7973S N26S 5B-CGP N128BP
5128S		see c/n 5037/24
5129	8	N7974S Saudi Arabia 101 XA-TJW XA-TZW
5130	8	N7975S Saudi Arabia 103 Saudi Arabia 102 XA-TJV XA-TZV
5131	8/Fanstar	N7976S N30RP N31RP N64C N212JW N380AA derelict 1991 Van Nuys, CA; cx Mar92
5132/57	731	N7977S N1620 N1620N N100GL N801 N1JN N989JN XA-PSD XA-BEB
5133	8	N7978S N329K N322K C-GPGD VR-CAW HZ-WBT HZ-WT1 HZ-FK1 XA-ROF XA-ROK wfu Jan95 Mexico City A/P, Mexico, used as ticket office in car park of Wal-Mart store in eastern Mexico City
5134/50	731	N7979S N295AR N500S N50PS N72HT N136MA XA-JMN XA-TPD
5135	8	N7980S N636 N900H N500WN N500FG at Spirit of St.Louis circa Sep97 still marked N500WN and reported will now be used for spares
5136	8	N5500L Libya 001 5A-DAJ
5137	8	N5501L EP-VRP Iran 1004 (it is now known that c/n 5203 is 1003, therefore we assume this must be 1004, not 1003 as previously recorded)
5138	8	N5502L N1301P N333RW N31DK N801 (N700MJ)
5139/54	731	N5503L N991 N991F N10DR XA-RVG N1189A to Atlanta Air Salvage yard at Griffin, GA, Apr97 still marked as XA-RVG; US marks cx Apr97
5140	8	N5504L XB-VIW XA-JCG XA-EMO
5141	8	N5505L N711Z N7967S N12241 N244 N4436S HZ-SH1 N4493S XB-CXO N3982A N747GB derelict at Lagos, Nigeria, circa Jan98
5142	8	N5506L N5113H N1UP N20SH HZ-SH3 N90658 N86TP N91LJ N91UJ N86TP N39LG N23FE XA-SOY
5143	8	N5507L N100UA N31UT N5070L N5878D C-GATU N620JB N326CB b/u; cx Jan00
5144	8	N5508L Mexico JS10201 Mexico FAM DN-01 Mexico JS10201
5145	8	N5509L N46K XB-DBJ XA-JFE N511TD
5146	8	N5510L N80GM C-GWSA N4990D N499AS N545BF b/u for spares Jan87
5147	8	N5511L N744UT N718R N212AP wfu for spares Jan93 Greenwood, LA
5148	8	N5512L N964M N21SH HZ-SH4 N900SA XA-ROK XA-ROF XA-OLI
5149/11	731	N5513L N711Z N157JF N157QP N524AC N110MN N110MT N100MZ VR-BJI b/u for spares Feb91
5150/37	731	N5514L N516WC N200CC N200CG N42C N312CK N100TM (N345CK) (N710JA) N721CR N911CR
5151	8	N5515L N711Z N46KJ N45K XA-PUL wfu Jan94 for spares by TAESA Mexico City, Mexico, used as ticket office in car park of Wal-Mart store in southern Mexico City
5152	8	N5516L N500JD N113KH XA-SOC
5153/61	731	N5517L N711JS N500PG N430MB
5154	8	N5518L N3031 N756 N766 XC-SRH N43AR
5155/32	731	N5519L N711Z XA-FES N4248Z N55NE N10PN N79AE N59CD N1DB (VR-BQG) (N120RL) VR-BRL VP-BRL N84GA
5156	8	N5520L 9K-ACO N70TP XB-DBT N16AZ wfu for spares
5157	8	N5521L N9WP N29WP XB-DUH displayed at entrance to Dodson Avn at Rantoul, KS painted as "N001DT"
5158	8	N5522L N516DM C-GTCP N1DT XA-POO XA-FHR XA-TDG
5159	8	N5523L N520M XB-DBS wfu
5160	8	N5524L C-FRBC (N60EE) b/u late 1988 Memphis, TN
5161/43	731	N5525L N22ES N60SM N119SE N1329L N200PB N99VR LY-AMB N5161R
5162	8	N5526L N10CX N10JJ XA-HNY
5201	2	N5527L N711Z N711DZ (N93JD) N93JM N745DM N777AY
5202	2	N5528L N717 N717X N333KN N20GB EC-232 EC-FQX
5203	2	N5529L EP-VLP Iran 1003 w/o 05Jan95 Isfahan, Iran (to be confirmed)
5204	2	N5530L N19ES N59AC N500PR N167R N25WZ (N220ES) N202ES
5205	2	N5531L N5000C N500QC N718R N713R YV-826CP N16BL N454JB N72GW
5206	2	N5532L N107GM XA-STG XA-JML N329JS
5207	2	N5533L N176BN N34WR
5208	2	N5534L N322CS N123CC (N29TC) N38BG N95BD
5209	2	N5535L N500S
5210	2	N5536L N400KC N707WB N787WB reportedly being scrapped for spares
5211	2	N5537L N500T (N500YY) N56PR N821MD N118B
5212	2	N5538L N3030 N5030 N167G XA-ACC N167G (N95SR)
5213	2	N5539L N501T N501J N60JM (N600JT) N65JT
5214	2	N5540L N530M N601CM N760DL N760DE (N9366Q) N106JL N848AB

JETSTAR

C/n	Series	Identities									
5215	2	N5541L	(N215HZ)	VR-BJH	N329MD	N777WJ	XA-FHS	N215DL	N215TS	(N1X)	N1TS
5216	2	N5542L	N95BA	N99E	N797WC						
5217	2	N5543L	N106G	N814CE	N500EX	N504EX	N1MJ				
5218	2	N5544L	N716RD	N816RD	N901C						
5219	2	N5545L	N107G	N21VB	C-GBDX	N219MF	N104BK	N770DR			
5220	2	N5546L	N32KR	A6-KAH							
5221	2	N5547L	5A-DAR	w/o 16Jan83 en route Libya-Algeria							
5222	2	N5548L	N509T	(N509TF)	N509J	C-GAZU	VP-BCP	A6-CPC			
5223	2	N5549L	N105G	N341K	N1DB	N644JW					
5224	2	N4016M	N1924G	N285LM	N3QS	N6QZ					
5225	2	N4021M	N746UT	N990CH	N42KR	TC-IHS					
5226	2	N4026M	N2MK	N815RC	N308SG						
5227	2	N4033M	N211PA	N23SB	N30Y	(N811)	N110AN	N171SG			
5228	2	N4034M	N372H	XA-RMD	N400MP						
5229	2	N4038M	N7NP	N351WC	N851WC	(N50NM)	N500NM	VR-CNM	N222MF		
5230	2	N4042M	N257H	N901FH	N901EH	N701JH					
5231	2	N4043M	N196KC	(N788JS)	N988MW	N112MC	XA-FHR	XA-TPJ			
5232	2	N4046M	N90CP	N90QP	N77C						
5233	2	N4048M	YI-AKA	7T-VHP							
5234	2	N4049M	N357H	N920DY	N920DG	N234TS+	XA-EKT				
		+ painted on aircraft and displayed in 1997 NBAA static park as such, but never regd as such									
5235	2	N4055M	YI-AKB	status following Gulf War?							
5236	2	N4056M	N531M	N2JR	N34TR	N741AM					
5237	2	N4058M	YI-AKC	status following Gulf War?							
5238	2	N4062M	YI-AKD	status following Gulf War?							
5239	2	N4063M	YI-AKE	status following Gulf War?							
5240	2	N4065M	YI-AKF	status following Gulf War?							

Production complete

Note: AMARC = Aerospace Maintenance & Regeneration Center, Davis Monthan, AZ

MBB HFB 320 HANSA JET

C/n	Series	Identities
V1/1001		D-CHFB ff 21Apr64 w/o 12May65 Torrejon, Spain
V2/1002		D-CLOU (D-CASE) wfu 24Sep70; preserved Deutsches Museum, Munich, W Germany
1021		D-CARA wfu Braunschweig 25May84; on static display at Finkenwerder, Germany
1022		D-CARE CofA exp 28Apr72; in Finow Museum, Germany
1023		D-CARI N320J N1320U N320AF N103F b/u for spares, date?
1024		D-CARO W Germany (YA111) W Germany (CA111) W Germany D9536 W Germany 1607 F-WZIH preserved Museé de l'Air, Paris, France
1025		D-CARU W Germany (YA112) W Germany (CA112) W Germany D9537 W Germany 1608 to instructional airframe
1026		D-CARY N890HJ N71CW (N1026) N71DL TC-FNS cx 1991; wfu Hannover, Germany circa Sep88; to Museum Hannover Laatzen marked "D-CARY"
1027		D-CASO I-TALC (D-CASO) D-CITO N905MW N127MW w/o 05Oct84 Aberdeen, SD
1028		D-CASU 5N-AMF w/o 25Jly77 Abidjan, Ivory Coast
1029		D-CASY w/o 29Jun72 Blackpool, UK
1030		D-CATE N247GW N111DC reported wfu 1995, noted dismantled at Monroe, MI Aug95
1031		D-CERA N300SB N750SB cx Dec90; wfu Fort Lauderdale Executive, FL; hulk stored Opa Locka, FL for spares
1032		D-CERE PH-HFA N130MW N132MW wfu; b/u
1033		D-CERI PH-HFB N132MW N130MW b/u 1989
1034		D-CERO N320J N320MC w/o 09Mar73 Phoenix, AZ and b/u; cx Oct90
1035		D-CERU PH-HFC N128SD wfu for spares use Monroe, MI circa Aug97
1036		D-CESA N891HJ N380EX N2MK N136MW (N92047)
1037		D-CESE N892HJ N5ZA N6MK N6ML N555JM YV-999P N604GA
1038		D-CESI N110WS N5627 (N18RA) N192AT N301AT N605GA
1039		D-CESO N118RA N893HJ CF-WDU N666LC N666LQ N205MM N208MM N171GA
1040		D-CESU I-ITAL N7158Q b/u for spares Mojave, CA
1041		D-CIRA W Germany 1601 (D-CIRA) N92045 (N62452) N602GA wfu Toledo OH noted Mar00 devoid of marks
1042		D-CIRE W Germany 1602 TC-LEY TC-SEN TC-GSB (N7684X) N106TF (N603GA) b/u circa 2000 - remains being used by Fire Department at Louisville KY
1043		D-CIRI W Germany 1603 TC-KHE TC-LEY
1044		D-CIRO w/o 18Dec70 Texel Is, Netherlands
1045		D-CIRU N5602 N894HJ N4ZA N7ES wfu Fort Lauderdale Executive, FL, for spares; remains to Opa Locka, FL
1046		D-CISA W Germany 1604 TC-NSU cx 1991; wfu
1047		D-CISE W Germany 1605 TC-OMR cx 1991; wfu
1048		D-CISI W Germany 1606 preserved GAF Museum, Gatow, Berlin
1049		D-CISO XC-DGA XC-TIJ b/u 1991; possibly following accident at San Diego, CA on 11Jun84; remains to Mojave, CA
1050		D-CISU LV-POP LQ-JRH (N1184L) N2675W N777PV N777PS N777PZ N777PQ wfu for spares use Monroe, MI circa Aug97
1051		D-CORE N895HJ N6ZA N888DL b/u Jly 90 for spares - remains to Aviation Warehouse film prop yard at El Mirage CA
1052		D-CORI PT-IDW N173GA wfu Louisville, KY, circa May99
1053		D-CORO PT-IOB N176GA
1054		D-CORU N896HJ N480LR cx Feb87; to spares use Monroe, MI circa Aug97
1055		D-CORY N897HJ N11NT N87950 N30AV (N21SU) TC-GSA (N7685T) N105TF
1056		D-COSA reported preserved in museum, Germany
1057		D-CLMA D-COSE (N107TW) VR-CYR YV-388CP
1058	ECM	D-COSI Germany 1621 N322AF b/u at Hollister, CA circa Jly98
1059	ECM	D-COSO W Germany 9825 W Germany 1622 w/o 27Nov76 Schwabmuenchen, W Germany
1060	ECM	D-COSU W Germany 9826 Germany 1623 (D-CCCH) N321AF b/u at Hollister, CA circa Jly98
1061	ECM	(D-CUNA) D-CANI Germany 1624 (D-CEDL) N320AF
1062	ECM	(D-CURE) D-CANO Germany 1625 N323AF b/u at Hollister, CA circa Jly98
1063	ECM	(D-CURI) D-CANU Germany 1626 preserved GAF Museum, Gatow, Berlin
1064	ECM	(D-CURO) D-CAMA Germany 1627 N324AF b/u at Hollister, CA circa Jly98
1065	ECM	(D-CURU) D-CAME Germany 1628 N325AF b/u at Hollister, CA circa Jly98
1066		(D-CURY) (D-CAMO)
1067		(D-CUSA) (D-CAMU)
1068		(D-CUSE) (D-CALA)
1069		(D-CUSI) (D-CALE)
1070		(D-CUSO) (D-CALI)
1071		(D-CUSU) (D-CALO)
1072		(D-CUSY) (D-CALU)
1073		(D-CADA)
1074		(D-CADE)
1075		(D-CADI)
1076		(D-CADO)
1077		(D-CADU)
1078		(D-CATI)
1079		(D-CANA)
1080		(D-CANE) (D-CINA) (D-CCVW) (D-CDVW)

Notes: 1021 to 1065 above also have a secondary c/n (S1 to S45)
1066 to 1080 not completed; used for spares

Production complete

MS760 PARIS

C/n	Series	Identities
01		F-WGVO ff 29Jly54 F-BGVO w/o 01May58 Lisbon, Portugal
02		used as static test airframe and b/u
03		F-BHOK France 03 F-SDIA (F-Z) F-SDIA w/o 24Dec64 Mont de Marsan, France
001		F-WIET France 1 F-ZADS F-SDIB F-ZADS F-SDIB 330-DB/F-SDDB
002		EP-HIM F-BOJO N760MM N1EP N207MJ
003		Argentina A-01/E201 wfu 1994 and stored with IV Brigada Aerea, Mendoza
004	2	Argentina A-02/E202
005	1A	F-WJAA N760H N2NC N2TE XB-FJO N2TE (N760LB) w/o 30Nov96 Santa Ana/Orange County, CA; cx Mar97
006		F-WJAB N84J N760J b/u 05Apr81; cx May81
007		Argentina A-03/E203 w/o 27Jan61 Mendoza, Argentina
008		F-WJAC G-36-2 G-APRU N60GT
009		F-WJAD N300ND N722Q
010		Argentina A-04/E204 wfu 1998 and stored with IV Brigada Aerea, Mendoza
011		Argentina A-05/E205
012		France 12/F-YDJ? w/o 13Apr59 Hyeres, France
013		Argentina A-06/E206 w/o 11Mar88 Mendoza, Argentina
014		France 14 France 312-DF/F-RHDF dismantled at Long Beach circa Dec97 for possible spares use
015		Argentina A-07/E207
016		Argentina A-08/E208
017		Argentina A-09/E209 wfu 1995 and stored with IV Brigada Aerea, Mendoza
018		Argentina A-10/E210 w/o 09Nov59 Cordoba, Argentina
019		France 19 France 41-AR/F-SCAR stored Chateaudun, France Apr97
020		France 20 F-SDIC 20-Q/F-RABQ w/o 26Oct62 Bernay en Brie, France
021		Argentina A-11/E211 w/o 06Oct89 Mendoza, Argentina
022		Argentina A-12/E212
023		France 23 330-DO/F-SDDO stored Chateaudun, France Apr97
024		France 24 65-KW/F-FBLW stored Chateaudun, France circa Sep99
025		France 25 42-AP/F-SCAP
026		F-WJAA France 26 -LN/F-RBLN stored Chateaudun, France circa Sep99
027		France 27 -DE/F-RHDE
028		F-WJAE I-SNAI N760X
029		France 29 65-LC/F-RBLC stored Chateaudun, France Apr97
030		France 30 65-LI/F-RBLW
031		France 31/F-YCB. wfu 23Jly72; instructional airframe Rochefort, France
032		32 Aeronavale/Marine
033		33 Aeronavale/Marine
034		France 34 43-BB/F-SCBB 113-CG
035		France 35 43-BL/F-SCBC
036		France 36 44-CC/F-SCCC 316-DH stored Chateaudun, France circa Sep99
037		France 37 34-Z/F-RABZ w/o 07Dec67 Les Loges, France
038		France 38 41-A/F-SCAS 115-ME stored Chateaudun, France circa Sep99
039	1A	F-WJAA F-BJET stored Reims-Prunay, France circa Jly99
040		40 Aeronavale/Marine
041		41 Aeronavale/Marine N41NY
042		42 Aeronavale/Marine
043		(N888JK) (N776JK) N776K N760C N760S
044		France 44 4D-L/F-RBLD stored Chateaudun, France circa Sep99
045		France 45 43-B./F-SCB. 316-DI stored Chateaudun, France circa Sep99
046		46 Aeronavale/Marine
047		47 Aeronavale/Marine wfu
048		France 48 Aeronavale/Marine w/o 04Jan68
049		N760M w/o 03May69 Evadale, TX
050	2	CN-MAJ CF-MAJ N6068 N111ER N42BL N23ST w/o 11Sep90 Albuquerque, NM; cx Jun91
051		Brazil C41-2912 France 51 330-DC/F-SDDC N751PJ
052		Brazil C41-2911 wfu
053		Brazil C41-2910 France 53 OD/F-RHDD N53PJ
054		Brazil C41-2913 France 54 41-A./F-SCA.
055		Brazil C41-2914 wfu
056		Brazil C41-2915 France 56 65-LG/F-RBLG 133-CM stored Chateaudun, France circa Sep99
057		Brazil C41-2918 France 57 41-AC/F-SCAC
058		Brazil C41-2920 France 58 65-LB/F-RBLB 312-DG stored Chateaudun, France circa Sep99
059		Brazil C41-2916 France 59 41-A./F-SCA. 133-CF
060		Brazil C41-2917 France 60 41-AT/F-SCAT N7601R
061		Brazil C41-2919 France 61 -LY/F-RBLY
062		Brazil C41-2921 France 62 65-LV/F-RBLV 314-DO
063		Brazil C41-2923 wfu
064		Brazil C41-2922 stored Santa Cruz, Brazil
065		Brazil C41-2924 France 65 65-LF/F-RBLF 330-DP
066		Brazil C41-2925 wfu
067		Brazil C41-2926 w/o 29Oct62 Nova Lima, Brazil
068		Brazil C41-2927 France 68 NB/F-ZJNB
069		HB-PAA Switzerland J-4117 HB-PAA cx Jun84; on display Musee Europeen de L'Aviation de Chasse Montelimar, Ancone
070		Brazil C41-2928 France 70 65-LF/F-RBLF
071		Brazil C41-2929 France 71 65-LE/F-RBLE
072	1A	F-BJLV N760FR

PARIS

C/n	Series	Identities
073		France 73
074		Brazil C41-2930 France 74 w/o 02Dec80 Natal, Brazil
075		Brazil C41-2931 France 75 65-LZ/F-RBLZ stored Chateaudun, France circa Sep98
076		Brazil C41-2932 preserved Brazilian AF Museum, Camp de Abonsas, nr Rio de Janeiro, Brazil
077		Brazil C41-2933 France 77 65-LP/F-RBLP stored Chateaudun, France circa Jun95
078		Brazil C41-2934 France 78 65-LY/F-RBLY 115-ME stored Chateaudun, France Apr97
079		Brazil C41-2935 France 79 wfu 15Apr79; to SOPEMEA Villacoublay, France 31Jan89 for stress tests
080		Brazil C41-2936 France 80 314-D/F-RHD. GE-316 80/DE wfu Chateaudun, France - on dump by 20Jun98
081		Brazil C41-2937 France 81 41-A./F-RBLL ELA61 N81PJ
082		Brazil C41-2938 France 82 65-L./F-RBL.
083		Brazil C41-2939 France 83 NC/F-ZJNC
084		84 Aeronavale/Marine w/o 23Dec70 Le Bourget, Paris, France
085		85 Aeronavale/Marine
086	1A	F-BJLX N9035Y
087		87 Aeronavale/Marine N87NY
088		88 Aeronavale/Marine N88NY
089	2	F-BJLY N999PJ
090		D-INGE N334RK N454HC N69X
091		France 91 65-LU/F-RBLU
092		France 92 118-DA/F-RHDA 316-DL stored Chateaudun, France circa Sep99
093		France 93 65-LD/F-RBLD
094		France 94 65-L./F-RBL.
095		France 95 /F-RBL. w/o 03Aug67 Melun, France
096		France 96 65-LU/F-RBLU w/o 29May82 Villacoublay, France
097		France 97 65-LH/F-RBLH reported as G1-330 "330 DC" N97PJ
098	2	D-INGA F-BOHN HB-VEP 3A-MPP F-GKPP w/o Oct91 Calvi, Corsica; used for spares for C6-BEV c/n 111 Nice, France Jul96
099		I-SNAP w/o 27Oct62 Milan, Italy
100		F-ZJNJ France 100
101	2	France 101 F-BNRG (N7038Z) N760PJ N444ET (N760PJ) N520DB
102	2B	F-BJZQ PH-MSR N760E HB-VEU N99HB N20DA
103	2B	F-BJZR PH-MSS N760N YV-163CP N760N N760T wfu Oct94 Mojave, CA
104	2B	F-BJZS PH-MST N760P N760R stored Santa Maria CA
105	2B	F-BJZT PH-MSU N760Q F-BXQL stored Reims-Prunay, France circa Jly99
106	2B	F-BJZU PH-MSV N5878 being used as a source of spare parts for c/n 008 N60GT
107	2B	F-BJZV PH-MSW N5879
108	2B	F-BJZX PH-MSX N760AR
109		airframe never built; marks F-BJZY were reserved; RLS, The Netherlands, options cx
110		airframe never built; marks F-BJZZ were reserved; RLS, The Netherlands, options cx
111	2	I-FINR C6-BEV
112		F-EXAA HB-PAC F-BOJY N65218 N7277X N710K noted dismantled 26Feb91 Mojave, CA
113		France 113 F-ZJNI
114		France 114 F-ZJNJ
115		France 115 F-ZJOV
116		France 116 F-ZJON
117		France 117 F-ZJAZ
118		France 118 F-ZJNQ
119		France 119 F-ZLNL
01	3	F-WLKL F-BLKL stored Reims-Prunay, France circa Jly99

Production complete

Production by FMA in Argentina

A-1	Argentina E-213	w/o 29Mar73; collided with E-217 c/n A-5 Santa Luis, Argentina
A-2	Argentina E-214	w/o 30Dec74 Cordoba, Argentina
A-3	Argentina E-215	wfu and stored with IV Brigada Aerea, Mendoza, Argentina
A-4	Argentina E-216	w/o 26Apr62 Moran, Argentina
A-5	Argentina E-217	w/o 29Mar73; collided with E-213 c/n A-1 Santa Luis, Argentina
A-6	Argentina E-218	w/o 11Feb81 Mendoza, Argentina
A-7	Argentina E-219	wfu 1998 and stored with IV Brigada Aerea, Mendoza, Argentina
A-8	Argentina E-220	
A-9	Argentina E-221	wfu 1994 and stored with IV Brigada Aerea, Mendoza, Argentina
A-10	Argentina E-222	wfu 1994 and stored by Lockheed Martin Aircraft Argentina, Sociedad Anonima
A-11	Argentina E-223 coded 23	wfu 1994 and stored by Escuela de Suboficiales de la Fuerza Aerea (ESFA)
A-12	Argentina E-224	wfu 1998 and stored with IV Brigada Aerea, Mendoza, Argentina
A-13	Argentina E-225	wfu 1994 and stored with Area Material Quilmes (AMQ), Argentina
A-14	Argentina E-226	wfu 1994 and stored with IV Brigada Aerea, Mendoza, Argentina
A-15	Argentina E-227	
A-16	Argentina E-228 coded 28	w/o 16Aug65 Formosa, Argentina

PARIS

C/n	Series	Identities	
A-17		Argentina E-229 coded 29	wfu 1994 and stored by Lockheed Martin Aircraft Argentina, Sociedad Anonima
A-18		Argentina E-230	wfu 1994 and stored Escuela Nacional Education Tecnica, Mendoza, Argentina
A-19		Argentina E-231	w/o 09Dec64 "EAM"?
A-20		Argentina E-232	
A-21		Argentina E-233	wfu 1995 and stored with IV Brigada Aerea, Mendoza, Argentina
A-22		Argentina E-234	w/o 1990 Mendoza, Argentina
A-23		Argentina E-235	wfu 1998 and stored with IV Brigada Aerea, Mendoza, Argentina
A-24		Argentina E-236	wfu 1998 and stored with IV Brigada Aerea, Mendoza, Argentina
A-25		Argentina E-237	w/o 04Nov83 San Luis, Argentina
A-26		Argentina E-238	w/o 30Dec78 Mendoza, Argentina
A-27		Argentina E-239	w/o 13Jun78 Mendoza, Argentina
A-28		Argentina E-240	w/o 20Mar85 San Juan, Argentina
A-29		Argentina E-241	
A-30		Argentina E-242	
A-31		Argentina E-243	wfu 1998 and stored with IV Brigada Aerea, Mendoza, Argentina
A-32		Argentina E-244	wfu 1998 and stored with IV Brigada Aerea, Mendoza, Argentina
A-33		Argentina E-245	wfu 1998 and stored with IV Brigada Aerea, Mendoza, Argentina
A-34		Argentina E-246	w/o 09Feb77 Cordoba, Argentina
A-35		Argentina E-247	wfu 1993 to Museo Nactional de Aeronautica, Aeroparque Aeroporto, Buenos Aires, Argentina
A-36		Argentina E-248	w/o 08Nov77 Cordoba, Argentina

Production complete

MU300 DIAMOND

C/n	Series	Identities								
001SA	2	JQ8001	N181MA	to Beech Field, Wichita, KS fire department for fire training						
002	1	JQ8002	N81DM	JQ8003	JA8248					
A003SA	1A	N300DM	N300TS	(N300TJ)						
A004SA	1A	JQ8004	N302DM	(N40BK)	N59TJ	N102WR	(N88TJ)	N541CW		
A005SA	1A	JQ8005	N304DM	N450TJ	N15AR	N40GC	N700LP	N30HD	N110DS	
A006SA	1	N325DM	C-FPAW	N400TJ	N777JJ	N750TJ	N200LP			
A007SA	1A	N301DM	N707CW	N507CW						
A008SA	1A	N303DM	(N56SK)	N399DM						
A009SA	1A	N305DM	N909GA	N306P	N318RS					
A010SA	1A	N306DM	N69PC	(N9FC)	N300DH	N703JH				
A011SA	1A	N307DM	(N77GA)	N114DM	N211GA					
A012SA	1A	N308DM	N82CT	N7RC	N107T	I-GIRL	N112GA			
A013SA	1	N81HH	I-VIGI	w/o 15Oct99 Parma, Italy						
A014SA	1	N15TW	N339DM	OH-KNE						
A015SA	1A	N315DM	N415RC	N271MB	N870P	N789DD	N789DJ			
A016SA	1A	N133RC	N100DE	N208F	N530RD	N10NM	N706JH			
A017SA	1A	N14DM	N75BL	(N33MM)	N399MM					
A018SA	1A	N900LH	C-GRDS	N138DM	N118GA	N83BG	(N831TJ)			
A019SA	1	N311DM	N9LP	N6PA	N319DM	N400GK				
A020SA	1A	N399RP								
A021SA	1	N222Q	N4LK							
A022SA	1A	N313DM	N18KE	(N816S)	N322MD	N322BE	N800TJ	N811DJ	(N397SL)	
A023SA	1A	N314DM	OY-BPC	SE-DDW	OY-BPC	N79GA	N17TJ	N22BN		
A024SA	1A	N316DM	N320CH	N95TJ	N450PC	N674AC				
A025SA	1	N317DM	N63GH	N1843S	N1843A	N400HH				
A026SA	1	N5UE	N55JM	N900DW	N140AK	N526CW	N326CW			
A027SA	1	N319DM	N237CC	N800RD	N27TJ	N7PW				
A028SA	1A	N320DM	N331DC	N900WJ						
A029SA	1A	N321DM	N1UT	N10TE	N89TJ	N100RS	N22CX*			
A030SA	1A	N322DM	N191GS	N41UT	N58TJ	N301P	N83SA			
A031SA	1A	N174B	N2220G	N956PP						
A032SA	1A	N323DM	N132GA	N320T	N929WG	N83CG	N996DR*			
A033SA	1A	N312DM	N520TT	N223S	N5EJ	N717CF				
A034SA	1A	N318DM	N303P	N334KC						
A035SA	1A	N300HH	HB-VHX	N135GA	N702JH					
A036SA	1	N326DM	N18BA	N997MX						
A037SA	1A	N327DM	OY-CCB	LN-SJA	N109TW	N134RG				
A038SA	1	N338DM	N147DA	N147WC	N42SR	(N212PA)				
A039SA	1A	N328DM	C-GRDX	N139DM	N399MJ	PT-OXT				
A040SA	1A	(N329DM)	N82CS	N188ST	N40GA					
A041SA	1A	N330DM	(N444SL)	N45GL	N83AE	N300AA				
A042SA	1A	N331DM	N420TJ	N8LE						
A043SA	1A	N332DM	N19R							
A044SA	1A	N334DM	N309DM	N110DK	N146GA	N606JM	N600GW			
A045SA	1A	N335DM	N334DM	N99FF	N154GA	N60B	N61GA	N777DC	N545TP	
A046SA	1A	N346DM	(YV-274CP)	(N146GA)	N151SP	N272BC	N272BG	N900BT	N109PW	
A047SA	1	N347DM	N138RC	N76LE	N47TJ	N45NP	N47PB	N333TS	N2WC	
A048SA	1A	N335DM	(OO-EBA)	VH-JEP	N335DM	PT-LNN				
A049SA	1A	N336DM	N300LA	YV-309P	YV-29CP	N40MF	XA-SOD	N411SP		
A050SA	1A	N350DM	N257CB							
A051SA	1A	(N357DM)	N351DM	N550HS	(N35P)	D-CGFV	TC-YIB	DBR in ground accident; to Dodson Avn,		
		Rantoul, KS, for spares			(N550HS)					
A052SA	1	N352DM	HB-VHT	I-FRAB	N70XX					
A053SA	1	N353DM	D-CDRB	JA30DA						
A054SA	1A	N354DM	N850TJ	N141H						
A055SA	1A	N877S	N877T	N89EM	N600MS	N600CG				
A056SA	1A	N341DM	N101AD	N156GA	I-FRTT	N255DG				
A057SA	1A	N342DM	N119MH	N334WM						
A058SA	1A	N343DM	N384DM	VR-BKA	N7050V					
A059SA	1A	N345DM	N344DM	I-DOCA	N126GA					
A060SA	1A	N345DM	(N300SJ)	N585TC						
A061SA	1A	N348DM	N18T	N500PP						
A062SA	1A	N349DM	G-JMSO	N362MD	3D-AFH	N426DA	TG-LAR	N64EZ	N616MM	N817GR*
A063SA	1A	N363DM	N54BE	N51B	N51BE					
A064SA	1A	N364DM	N246GA	I-SELM	N800LE	HI-646SP	N2225J	N400ML*		
A065SA	1A	N361DM	N65JN	N165GA	OY-CDK	I-GENC	N54RM	N16MF		
A066SA	1A	N366DM	N1TX	(N185GA)	N66FG+	N88MF	N88ME			
		+Marks carried during Oct87 but ntu								
A067SA	1A	N367DM	N123VJ	I-ALGU	N184SC	N65SA	N63DR	N617BG		
A068SA	1A	N368DM	N368PU	N103HC						
A069SA	1A	N355DM	N56MC	N250GP	(N197SL)					
A070SA	1A	N370DM	D-CNEX	OY-BPI	N84GA	N60EF				
A071SA	1A	N371DM	(N106GA)	N70GA	N71GH					
A072SA	1A	N372DM	PT-LGD	N174SA	N777DC	N779DC				
A073SA	1A	N356DM	N717VL	N1715G	N94LH					
A074SA	1A	N374DM	N22WJ	JA8298	N19GA	N32HP				
A075SA	1A	N375DM	N11WF	N824DW						

DIAMOND 1

C/n	Series	Identities						
A076SA	1A	N376DM	N76LE	C-GLIG	w/o 01Mar95 Jasper-Hinton A/P, Alberta, Canada			N8221M
		for spare parts with White Industries, Bates City MO						
A077SA	1A	N377DM	N68PL	N66PL	N975GR			
A078SA	1A	N378DM	N710MB	w/o 15Dec93 nr Goodland, KS				
A079SA	1A	N379DM	(N574U)	N574CF				
A080SA	1A	N380DM	N380CM	N770PC	N925WC	N275HS		
A081SA	1A	N381DM	N381MG	N81TJ	N317CC	N317GC	N750TJ	N50EF
A082SA	1A	N382DM	N105HS	N555FA	N62CH			
A083SA	1A	N383DM	N12WF	N83TK	N417KT			
A084SA	1A	N484DM	(N484VS)	(N84DT)	N840TJ	N160S	N160H	
A085SA	1A	N485DM	I-TORA	N485DM	N777MJ	(N911JJ)	N70VT	
A086SA	1A	N486DM	N515KK					
A087SA	1A	N487DM	HB-VIA	PH-JSL*				
A088SA	1A	N482DM						
A089SA	1A	N483DM	N100EA	N89SC	N88CR	N20PA		
A090SA	1A	N312DM	G-TOMY	N300LG	(N64EZ)	C-GLIG		
A091SA	1A	N357DM	(N357MD)	PT-OVM	(N485DM)	N611AG	N400HG	N400NF
A092SA	1A	JA8246	w/o 23Jly86 Sado Island, Japan					

Production complete

Note: Diamond 2s are included under Beechjet 400s.

NORTH AMERICAN/ROCKWELL SABRE MODELS

T-39 SERIES

C/n Series Identities

265-1 CT-39A 59-2868 N2259V displayed Kirtland AFB, NM as 59-2868
265-2 CT-39A 59-2869 N4999G 59-2869 AMARC park code TG033 stored wfu Sep93 Memphis Airport, TN
265-3 NT-39A 59-2870 operational Edwards AFB, CA
265-4 T-39A 59-2871 w/o 13Nov69 Eglin AFB, FL
265-5 CT-39A 59-2872 N2296C 59-2872 AMARC park code TG015
265-6 T-39A 60-3478 operational Edwards AFB, CA
265-7 CT-39A 60-3479 AMARC park code TG082
265-8 CT-39A 60-3480 AMARC park code TG013
265-9 CT-39A 60-3481 AMARC park code TG085 to Lane Community College, Eugene, OR
265-10 CT-39A 60-3482 AMARC park code TG016 N510TA XA-TFD w/o 4Feb00 Merida, Mexico
265-11 T-39A 60-3483 displayed Travis AFB, CA
265-12 CT-39A 60-3484 AMARC park code TG024 N7043U XB-GDU XA-TFC w/o 16May97 20km S of Monterrey-Del Norte, Mexico
265-13 CT-39A 60-3485 AMARC park code TG003 West Intl Aviation, Tucson, AZ
265-14 CT-39A 60-3486 AMARC park code TG008 XA-TIY
265-15 CT-39A 60-3487 AMARC park code TG021 N510TD cx Sep98 still in Davis Monthan wearing 60-3486
265-16 CT-39A 60-3488 N431NA to Des Moines Educational Resource Center, IA
265-17 CT-39A 60-3489 AMARC park code TG058 to Houston Community College, TX
265-18 CT-39A 60-3490 AMARC park code TG062 to South Seattle Community College, WA
265-19 CT-39A 60-3491 AMARC park code TG009
265-20 CT-39A 60-3492 AMARC park code TG007 to Thief River Falls Tech College, MN
265-21 CT-39A 60-3493 AMARC park code TG057
265-22 CT-39A 60-3494 AMARC park code TG094
265-23 CT-39A 60-3495 displayed Scott AFB, IL
265-24 CT-39A 60-3496 AMARC park code TG072 to Cochise College, Douglas, AZ
265-25 CT-39A 60-3497 AMARC park code TG066
265-26 CT-39A 60-3498 AMARC park code TG077 at Chandler Williams Gateway, AZ, Apr94
265-27 CT-39A 60-3499 AMARC park code TG037
265-28 CT-39A 60-3500 AMARC park code TG030 to Letourneau College, Longview, TX
265-29 CT-39A 60-3501 AMARC park code TG093
265-30 CT-39A 60-3502 AMARC park code TG095 to Dr Robert Smirnow, E North Port, NY
265-31 GCT-39A 60-3503 preserved Air Classics Museum, Aurora, IL
265-32 CT-39A 60-3504 donated to Bi-States College, St Louis, MO
265-33 T-39A 60-3505 displayed Edwards Flight Test Museum, CA
265-34 T-39A 60-3506 w/o 09Feb74 Colorado, CO
265-35 CT-39A 60-3507 AMARC park code TG061 West LA College, Los Angeles, CA marked as "0350" - painted as N3507W (these marks are current on a PA-32)
265-36 CT-39A 60-3508 AMARC park code TG042 believed b/u
265-37 CT-39A 61-0634 displayed Dyess AFB, TX
265-38 CT-39A 61-0635 AMARC park code TG054 to Lafayette Regional A/P, LA
265-39 CT-39A 61-0636 AMARC park code TG089
265-40 CT-39A 61-0637 AMARC park code TG035
265-41 CT-39A 61-0638 AMARC park code TG096 to ground trainer Keesler AFB, MS
265-42 CT-39A 61-0639 AMARC park code TG086 N21092 donated to Blackhawk Technical College, Janesville, WI
265-43 T-39A 61-0640 w/o 16Apr70 Halifax County A/P, NC (midair collision with a TA-4F)
265-44 CT-39A 61-0641 AMARC park code TG036 to Rock Valley College, Rockford, IL
265-45 CT-39A 61-0642 AMARC park code TG045
265-46 CT-39A 61-0643 AMARC park code TG022
265-47 T-39A 61-0644 w/o 07May63 Andrews AFB, VA
265-48 CT-39A 61-0645 AMARC park code TG091 N6CF XA-TFL
265-49 T-39A 61-0646 w/o 14May75 10 miles north of Richmond, VA
265-50 CT-39A 61-0647 AMARC park code TG078 to Coast Community College, Costa Mesa, GA
265-51 CT-39A 61-0648 AMARC park code TG017 to Davis Monthan, AZ, scrapyard 1993; to West Intl Aviation, Tucson, AZ
265-52 T-39A 61-0649 N1064 61-0649 at Portland A/P Museum, OR, ex storage AMARC park code TG047; regd N1064 to USAF
265-53 CT-39A 61-0650 AMARC park code TG043 to Everett Community College, WA
265-54 CT-39A 61-0651 AMARC park code TG040 to F.D Tech Florence Community College, SC
265-55 CT-39A 61-0652 N4999H 61-0652 AMARC park code TG087
265-56 CT-39A 61-0653 AMARC park code TG071 to Community College of San Francisco, CA
265-57 CT-39A 61-0654 AMARC park code TG044 at Embry Riddle Aeronautical School, Daytona Beach, FL, marked "N1ERAU"
265-58 CT-39A 61-0655 at scrapyard Davis Monthan, AZ Jan91; sold 1992 to Avmats, St Louis, MO; ex storage AMARC park code TG005
265-59 CT-39A 61-0656 AMARC park code TG010
265-60 CT-39A 61-0657 AMARC park code TG023 to Rice Aviation, Houston-Hobby, TX
265-61 CT-39A 61-0658 AMARC park code TG034 to Frederick Community College, Frederick, MD
265-62 CT-39A 61-0659 AMARC park code TG026 XA-
265-63 T-39A 61-0660 displayed McClellan AFB, CA
265-64 T-39A 61-0661 w/o 29Jul62 Paine Field-Seattle, WA
265-65 CT-39A 61-0662 AMARC park code TG032 wfu 02Jul90 Spirit of St Louis, MO; all marks painted out; remains to Clarkesville, MO, by 1993
265-66 CT-39A 61-0663 AMARC park code TG067 believed b/u
265-67 T-39A 61-0664 AMARC park code TG063 to Deuel Vo-Tech Inst, Tracy, CA

SABRE T-39 SERIES

C/n Series Identities

265-68 CT-39A 61-0665 AMARC park code TG028
265-69 CT-39A 61-0666 AMARC park code TG014
265-70 CT-39A 61-0667 AMARC park code TG088 N7143N to Essam Alredi of Saudi Arabia, at Santa Monica, CA
265-71 CT-39A 61-0668 AMARC park code TG051 believed b/u
265-72 CT-39A 61-0669 AMARC park code TG075 to Metro Tech Aviation Career Center, Oklahoma City, OK
265-73 CT-39A 61-0670 operational Maxwell AFB, AL
265-74 CT-39A 61-0671 AMARC park code TG090 to ground trainer Keesler AFB, MS
265-75 T-39A 61-0672 w/o 13Mar79 S Korea
265-76 CT-39A 61-0673 AMARC park code TG038N4313V XA-TJZ
265-77 CT-39A 61-0674 displayed Hill AFB, UT
265-78 CT-39A 61-0675 displayed Yokota AFB, Japan; reported b/u circa 1998
265-79 CT-39A 61-0676 AMARC park code TG049
265-80 T-39A 61-0677 N9166Y at N Dakota University, Helena, ND
265-81 CT-39A 61-0678 AMARC park code TG012
265-82 T-39A 61-0679 AMARC park code TG069 N6581E at Spokane Community College, WA
265-83 CT-39A 61-0680 AMARC park code TG039 N32010 Central Missouri State University, MO; at Warrensburg, MO marked "1068"
265-84 CT-39A 61-0681 preserved Willow Run AF Museum, Detroit, MI
265-85 CT-39A 61-0682 AMARC park code TG031 to Southwest Michigan College, Dowagiac, MI
265-86 CT-39A 61-0683 AMARC park code TG025 N510TB XB-GDW XA-GDW (still current on USCAR as N510TB as well as being current on the Mexican Register)
265-87 T-39A 61-0684 scrapyard Davis Monthan, AZ/"Bob's Air Park" believed b/u
265-88 T-39A 61-0685 preserved US Army Aviation Museum, Fort Rucker, AL

270-1 T-39B 59-2873 Wright-Patterson AFB, OH
270-2 T-39B 59-2874 AMARC park code TG103
270-3 T-39B 60-3474 operational Edwards AFB, CA
270-4 T-39B 60-3475 AMARC park code TG098
270-5 T-39B 60-3476 AMARC park code TG102
270-6 T-39B 60-3477 AMARC park code TG101

276-1 T-39A 62-4448 w/o 28Jan64 Erfurt, W Germany
276-2 CT-39A 62-4449 AMARC park code TG092 preserved Pima County Museum, Tucson, AZ
276-3 CT-39A 62-4450 at scrapyard Davis Monthan, AZ, Jan91 AMARC park code TG006
276-4 CT-39A 62-4451 AMARC park code TG060 N31403 XA-
276-5 T-39A 62-4452 displayed Travis AFB, CA
276-6 T-39A 62-4453 N6552R XA-TGO
276-7 CT-39A 62-4454 AMARC park code TG018
276-8 CT-39A 62-4455 AMARC park code TG065 N4314B XA-TJU
276-9 CT-39A 62-4456 at Northrop University, Los Angeles, CA ex AMARC park code TG056
276-10 CT-39A 62-4457 AMARC park code TG002
276-11 T-39A 62-4458 w/o 25Mar65 Clark AFB, Philippines
276-12 CT-39A 62-4459 AMARC park code TG041 to Clover Park Vo-Tech, Tacoma, WA
276-13 T-39A 62-4460 w/o 28Feb70 Torrejon AFB, Spain
276-14 T-39A 62-4461 displayed Warner-Robins AFB, GA
276-15 CT-39A 62-4462 AMARC park code TG046
276-16 CT-39A 62-4463 AMARC park code TG100
276-17 CT-39A 62-4464 AMARC park code TG004 to Utah State University, Salt Lake City, UT
276-18 T-39A 62-4465 preserved March AFB, CA
276-19 CT-39A 62-4466 AMARC park code TG019 to Detroit School District, Detroit, MI
276-20 CT-39A 62-4467 at GTCC Aviation Center, Greensboro, NC; in use as instructional airframe with AMARC park code TG-083
276-21 CT-39A 62-4468 AMARC park code TG020 N63611 XA-TIX
276-22 CT-39A 62-4469 AMARC park code TG064 to East Coast Technical School, Lexington, MA
276-23 CT-39A 62-4470 displayed Maxwell AFB, AL
276-24 CT-39A 62-4471 displayed Ramstein AFB, W Germany
276-25 CT-39A 62-4472 AMARC park code TG011 N39RG XA-
276-26 CT-39A 62-4473 AMARC park code TG029 to Dr Robert Smirnow, E Northport, NY
276-27 CT-39A 62-4474 AMARC park code TG027 XB-GDV N510TC XA-TDX
276-28 CT-39A 62-4475 noted flying during 1991 ex storage at AMARC (had AMARC park code TG084); at Technical College, Milwaukee, WI, 14Sep92
276-29 T-39A 62-4476 AMARC park code TG099
276-30 CT-39A 62-4477 AMARC park code TG048 to Milwaukee Technical College, WI
276-31 T-39A 62-4478 preserved USAF Museum Wright-Patterson AFB, OH
276-32 CT-39A 62-4479 AMARC park code TG052 N988MT to Metro-Tech Aviation Center, Oklahoma, OK
276-33 CT-39A 62-4480 AMARC park code TG068 N24480 N39FS
276-34 CT-39A 62-4481 N33UT to University of Tennessee, Tullahoma, TN
276-35 CT-39A 62-4482 displayed Kelly AFB, TX
276-36 CT-39A 62-4483 AMARC park code TG055 to Indian Hills Community College, IA
276-37 T-39A 62-4484 displayed Kadena AFB, Japan
276-38 CT-39A 62-4485 displayed Yokota AFB, Japan
276-39 CT-39A 62-4486 AMARC park code TG050 N265WB XA-TJY
276-40 CT-39A 62-4487 displayed SAC Museum site midway between Lincoln & Omaha NB
276-41 CT-39A 62-4488 operational Andrews AFB, MD
276-42 CT-39A 62-4489 AMARC park code TG074 N65618 to Colorado Northwestern Community College, Rangely, CO; cx Sep95; status?
276-43 CT-39A 62-4490 AMARC park code TG079 stored at Lawrenceville/Gwinnet County GA

SABRE T-39 SERIES

C/n	Series	Identities
276-44	CT-39A	62-4491 AMARC park code TG081 N63811 XA-TIW
276-45	CT-39A	62-4492 painted as N1SJ with San Jose University's Avn Dept, San Jose Airport, CA (the real N1SJ is Cessna 310 (U3) s/n 57-5856)
276-46	CT-39A	62-4493 AMARC park code TG076 believed b/u
276-47	CT-39A	62-4494 displayed Chanute ALB, IL
276-48	CT-39A	62-4495 AMARC park code TG059 N6612S N1929P to college in Yunlin, Taiwan
276-49	CT-39A	62-4496 w/o 20Apr85 Scranton/Wilkes Barre, PA
276-50	CT-39A	62-4497 AMARC park code TG053 believed b/u
276-51	CT-39A	62-4498 AMARC park code TG080 to Salt Lake City Community College, UT
276-52	CT-39A	62-4499 w/o 24Jun69 McCook, NB
276-53	CT-39A	62-4500 AMARC park code TG070 to Linn Technical College, Linn, MO
276-54	CT-39A	62-4501 AMARC park code TG073 to O'Fallon Technical College, St Louis, MO
276-55	T-39A	62-4502 w/o 31Dec68 Langley AFB, VA
277-1	T-39D	150542 stored China Lake NWC, CA
277-2	T-39D	150543 AMARC park code 7T-027
277-3	T-39D	150544 AMARC park code 7T-006
277-4	T-39D	150545 wfu and b/u
277-5	T-39D	150546 coded 201 AMARC park code 7T-014
277-6	T-39D	150547 AMARC park code 7T-021
277-7	T-39D	150548 coded 10 AMARC park code 7T-008
277-8	T-39D	150549 coded 11 AMARC park code 7T-011 believed b/u
277-9	T-39D	150550 at Pensacola NAS, FL
277-10	T-39D	150551 AMARC park code 7T-002 believed b/u
285-1	T-39D	150969 AMARC park code 7T-026
285-2	T-39D	150970 N431NA cx Dec91; wfu and b/u
285-3	T-39D	150971 AMARC park code 7T-001 believed b/u
285-4	T-39D	150972 at Pensacola NAS, FL
285-5	T-39D	150973 AMARC park code 7T-013
285-6	T-39D	150974 AMARC park code 7T-015
285-7	T-39D	150975 AMARC park code 7T-007 believed b/u
285-8	T-39D	150976 AMARC park code 7T-016
285-9	T-39D	150977 at Pensacola NAS, FL
285-10	T-39D	150978 AMARC park code 7T-009
285-11	T-39D	150979 AMARC park code 7T-017
285-12	T-39D	150980 AMARC park code 7T-004 believed b/u
285-13	T-39D	150981 AMARC park code 7T-012 believed b/u
285-14	T-39D	150982 AMARC park code 7T-022 believed b/u
285-15	T-39D	150983 AMARC park code 7T-023 believed b/u
285-16	T-39D	150984 AMARC park code 7T-010
285-17	T-39D	150985 N32508 preserved National Museum of Naval Aviation, Pensacola, FL, as 150985
285-18	T-39D	150986 displayed Warner-Robins AFB, GA
285-19	T-39D	150987 preserved NAS Patuxent River, MD
285-20	T-39D	150988 AMARC park code 7T-005
285-21	T-39D	150989 stored China Lake NWC, CA
285-22	T-39D	150990 coded 213 AMARC park code 7T-024
285-23	T-39D	150991 coded 77 AMARC park code 7T-003
285-24	T-39D	150992 active at China Lake NWC, CA circa May97
285-25	T-39D	151336 coded 214 AMARC park code 7T-025
285-26	T-39D	151337 at Pensacola NAS, FL
285-27	T-39D	151338 preserved USS Lexington Museum, Corpus Christi, TX noted "parked" at Patterson/Williams Memorial LA 18Mar99
285-28	T-39D	151339 preserved US Naval Aviation Museum, NAS Pensacola, FL
285-29	T-39D	151340 coded 216 AMARC park code 7T-018 believed b/u
285-30	T-39D	151341 AMARC park code 7T-019
285-31	T-39D	151342 AMARC park code TG-097
285-32	T-39D	151343 dumped NAS Pensacola, FL believed b/u

AMARC indicates aircraft at Aerospace Maintenance and Regeneration Center, Davis Monthan, AZ

As at Apr94 only the following aircraft were reported to be still intact at the AMARC or at Bob's Scrapyard when marked *. It is assumed that the remaining aircraft must have been broken up, although some may have moved to technical colleges. Reported sightings at these colleges would be most welcome.

USAF aircraft

59-2872, 60-3475, 60-3479, 60-3480, 60-3485*, 60-3486*, 60-3491, 60-3493, 60-3495, 60-3499, 60-3501, 61-0636, 61-0637, 61-0642, 61-0643, 61-0648*, 61-0652, 61-0655*, 61-0656, 61-0659*, 61-0665, 61-0666, 61-0673*, 61-0676, 61-0678, 61-0683, 62-4450*, 62-4454, 62-4455*, 62-4457, 62-4462*, 62-4468, 62-4474*

US Navy aircraft

150543, 150544, 150546, 150547, 150548, 150549, 150969, 150973, 150974, 150975, 150969, 150976, 150978, 150979, 150980, 150981, 150982, 150983, 150984, 150988, 150990, 150991, 151336, 151340, 151341, 151342

SABRE 40

C/n	Series	Identities
282-1	R	N7820C N177A N766R XC-OAH XC-JCK (N351JM) N116SC
282-2	T-39N	N577R N577PM N100WF N108W N108U N57GS N67WW N16TA N304NT US Navy 165512
282-3		N570R (N57QR) N467H
282-4		N6358C N14M N75JD N111MS N408TR
282-5		N30W w/o 21Dec67 Perryville, MO
282-6		N6360C N600R XB-HHF XA-SBS XA-GYR
282-7		N6361C N360J N576R N1102D N43NR N101US N43NR N122RP XA-SEN XB-EZV XA-STU N706A wfu; b/u Opa Locka, FL
282-8		N6362C N520S N366N N369N N140MM wfu Sep93 and parted out; cx Nov96
282-9	T-39N	N6363C N620M N620K N327JB (N327RH) N329SS N301NT US Navy 165509
282-10		N6364C N525N N9503Z w/o 07Mar73 Blaine, MN
282-11		N6365C N167H N167G N73PC N10SL wfu for spares Fort Lauderdale Executive, FL
282-12		N6366C N905M N888PM N368DA N107CJ wfu Opa Locka, FL; cx Mar97
282-13		N6367C N899TG N408S N408CS N408CC XA-SMP N502RR XA-TKW
282-14		N6368C N2009 N31BC N31BQ N30BE (N30PN) b/u during 1986; remains at Clarkesville, MO
282-15		N6369C N106G N1062 N32BC N32BQ (N19MS) N40SE N21PF N43W
282-16		N6370C N227SW N227S N40GP N41GS b/u for spares Miami A/P, FL during 1989
282-17		N6371C N911Q N382RF N392F N900CS XA-HOK wfu; remains at Clarkesville, MO
282-18		N6372C N107G N1072 N113SC N15TS N131BH
282-19	R/T-39N	N6373C N881MC N881MD N100CE N100OE (N40R) N311NT US Navy 165519
282-20	T-39N	N6374C N265R N3298D N40YA (N282AM) N315NT/US Navy 165523 wears dual marks
282-21		N6375C N168H N168D N87CM wfu Clarkesville, MO; still regd; to spares 1992
282-22		N6376C N747 N747E w/o 21Dec94 Buenos Aires-Aeroparque, Argentina; to spares at Buenos Aires-Don Don-Torcuato
282-23		N6377C N282NA N8400B N800M N80QM N301HA N50TX (N265AC) N123CD (N55ME)
282-24		N6378C N720J N360Q N40DW N8AF
282-25		N6379C HB-VAK I-SNAK N40SJ I-NICK wfu; to White Inds, Bates City, MO for spares Oct98
282-26		N6380C N60Y N6087 N737E N153G N300CH XA-RED reported to XA-DAN
282-27		N6381C N720R N129GP N129GB N111EA N61RH wfu Oct93 to College of Technology, Tulsa Int'l A/P OK
282-28	T-39N	N6382C N6565A N6565K N524AC N524AG N27DA N197DA N40CD N482HC N314NT US Navy 165522
282-29	T-39N	N6383C N910E N170JL N170AL N170DD N303NT US Navy 165511
282-30	T-39N	N6384C N526N N7090 N709Q N801MS N306NT US Navy 165514
282-31		N23G N236Y N800Y N700R N577VM N34AM wfu; to spares 1993 Spirit of St Louis, MO; remains with Fire Service at Springfield Airport, IL
282-32	T-39N	N100Y N100HC N711UC N40SL N40WP N8GA N456JP N312NT US Navy 165520
282-33		N737R N903K N903KB N168W
282-34		N6389C N575R N5PC N5PQ N400CS N940CC reported wfu
282-35		N6390C N341AP N341AR N567DW b/u circa 1985; remains to Clarkesville, MO; still regd
282-36		N6391C N1903W N1908W N22BN N59PK N59K N59KQ N63A N88JM N200MP N40LB
282-37		N6392C N265W N77AP w/o 07Nov77 New Orleans, LA
282-38		N6393C N2997 N299LR N100FS (N68AA) N999VT N921JG*
282-39	R	N6394C N442A N947R N333B XA-BAF (N4492V) XA-RGC XA-RTM N
282-40		N6395C N738R N715MR N40BP wfu Oct93; to spares Clarkesville, MO
282-41		N6396C N661P N300RC N300RG N707JM N57RM (N300TK) (N116AC) N240AC
282-42		N6397C N727R N904K N904KB (N61FC) N40EL N500RK N50CD w/o 03May90 (place unknown); cx Oct91; remains to Spirit of St Louis A/P 1995
282-43	R	N6398C N730R XA-JUD N4469F Ecuador 043
282-44		N6399C N4567 N1DC N1QC N44NP N600JS N64MA
282-45		N6552C N747UP N344UP N255GM N333GM N333NM
282-46	CT-39E	N6553C N339NA 157352 w/o 21Dec75 Alameda AFB, CA
282-47		N740R N34W w/o 04Jan74 Midland, TX
282-48	R	N6555C N747R N90GM (N153G) XA-JUE N4469M XA-CPQ N4469M XA-RGC N47VL
282-49		N6556C N757R N905K N905KB Sweden 86001
282-50		N6557C N757E N956 N956CC XA-SMQ N282CA wfu Spirit of St Louis circa early 2000 still wearing previous identity XA-SMQ
282-51		N733R N108G N108X N227LS N225LS (N51MN) noted 31Aug91 wfu Spirit of St Louis A/P, MO; remains at Elsberry, MO
282-52	R	N7502V N200A N2000 N2004 N40R N77MR (N77MK) N303A N282MC N64DH
282-53		N7503V N999BS N123MS N101T N62K N62Q (ZS-GSB) ZS-PTJ N67201 N600BP N555PT cx Jan91; b/u 1989; remains at Elsbury, MO
282-54		N7504V N255CT N256CT XA-EEU w/o 1980 ground accident in Mexico
282-55		N7505V N2007 N353WB N353WC N68HC N68HQ N221PH (N221PX) b/u during 1986; cx Feb91; remains at Elsbury, MO
282-56		N7506V N322CS N10CC N722ST N722FD (N722ED) N204TM N85DA XA-RPS reported wfu
282-57		N7507V N27C N545C N1909R N1909D to spares at Spirit of St Louis A/P, MO circa May97
282-58		N7508V N1101G N110FS wfu; to spares by Executive Aircraft Corp, KS, but still regd
282-59		N7509V N48WS N48WP (N2SN) N17LT XA-ESR N465S N40SE N43CF wfu for spares Oct94 Perryville, MO; cx Aug95

SABRE 40

C/n	Series	Identities
282-60	T-39N	N7510V N903G N66TP N22TP N256MA N256EN N256EA N555AE N555AB N141H N316NT US Navy 165524
282-61	T-39N	N550L N550LL N231A XA-RGC XA-EGC N2568S (N60WL) N33TW N309NT US Navy 165517
282-62		N1863T cx Sep87; wfu
282-63		N325K
282-64		N7514V N9000V N9000S N800CS b/u 1986; cx Feb90
282-65		N2232B N145G cx Nov99 - status?
282-66	T-39N	N2233B N355MJ N4943A N737R N40NR N40HC N48TC N54CF N98CF N305NT US Navy 165513
282-67	A	N2234B N711T N140RF
282-68	R	N2235B N788R N801NC N22MY N22MV N60RB XA-LEL N4469N Ecuador 068 w/o 03Jun88 Quito A/P, Ecuador
282-69		N2236B N125N N256MA N125NL N1MN N43NR N777V N777VZ N49RJ
282-70		N2236C N377P N874AJ N111AB N654E N22CH N70SL N17LT N34LP N3280G impounded for many years in Commander Mexicana hangar, Mexico City, Mexico; still complete Jan94 but with a few parts missing
282-71		N2239B N957 N957CC XA-SMR (not confirmed)
282-72	T-39N	N744R (N880HL) (N69CG) N78GP N986JB N307NT US Navy 165515
282-73		N630M N630N cx Jun85; b/u for spares; remains to Clarkesville, MO
282-74		N2241B N572R N707TG N707FH
282-75		N2241C N48CG b/u 1983; marks N48CE reserved Jan88 but ntu; remains to Clarkesville, MO
282-76		N2242B N474VW D-CAVW N787R N124H N415CS N415GS N350E N58025 N8345K N265CM N257TM
282-77	T-39N	N2244B N608S N608AR N189AR N96CM N27KG N310NT US Navy 165518
282-78		N739R w/o 16May67 Ventura, CA
282-79		N2248C N797R N701NC N35CC N111AC
282-80		N2249B N36050 N360E N40JF N40WH XA-FTN
282-81	T-39N	N2250B N36065 N360N N99CR N416CS N1GY N302NT US Marines 165510
282-82		N574R N736R N713MR (N777ST) N19MS N366DA XB-EQR N39RG
282-83		N726R N642LR N232T N160TC N82ML wfu for spares c Oct94 Clarkesville, MO; cx Mar95
282-84	CT-39E	N2254B 157353 code 353RW; stored Davis Monthan, AZ AMARC park code 7T-028
282-85	CT-39E	N2255B 157354
282-86		N86 cx Sep92; wfu; stored in bare metal Oklahoma City, OK, no marks visible
282-87		N87 N36P N399P at Pittsburgh Inst of Aeronautics, PA
282-88		N88 cx Dec93; at Hampton University/Hughes Training Inc Aero Science Center at Newport News, VA
282-89		N89 cx Oct91; b/u for spares
282-90	T-39N	N2569B N928R CF-NCG C-FNCG N3831C N155GM N362DA N308NT US Navy 165516
282-91		N9500B N5511A N5511Z N66ES N40NR Sweden 86002
282-92	CT-39E	N2676B 158382 N825SB
282-93	CT-39E	N4701N 158381 w/o during 1991 nr Spratley Islands, S China Sea
282-94	T-39N	N4703N N16R N216R N6TE N147CF N40TA N313NT US Navy 165521
282-95	CT-39E	N4704N 158380 N425NA reportedly returned to 158380
282-96	CT-39E	N4705N 158383 reported wfu
282-97		N4706N N85 w/o 14Jan76 Recife, Brazil
282-98	A	N4707N N40SC N516WP N516LW
282-99	A	N7594N N78TC N22CH N400GM N100FG N12BW
282-100	A/T-39N	N19HF N82CF XA-LEG N71325 (N302NT) N317NT US Navy 165525
282-101	A	N7596N N1BX N111XB N101RR N160W
282-102	A	N7597N N2WR N800DC N74MG N74MJ (N157AT) XA-PIH
282-103	A	N7598N N44P N9MS N217A N217TE N217E N730CA N730CP
282-104	A	N40CH N78BC N99XR N100KS N26SC N26SE N925BL XA-SEU N104SL
282-105	A	N2HW N2QW N22BJ N312K N921JG XA-SCN XC-AA73
282-106	A	N7595N XB-DUS XA-RKG (N22NB) N333GM
282-107	A	N7584N N40NR CF-BRL w/o 27Feb74 Frobisher Bay, Canada
282-108	A	N7596N N442WT N442WP N306CW N85CC
282-109	A	N4NP N700CF N93AC N77AT Ecuador 047
282-110	A	N7597N N477X N477A N250EC
282-111	A	N7662N N9NR XA-SAG N32654 N213BM (N200CK) (N431DA) (N246GS) N7KG
282-112	A	N7667N N6789 N6789D N301PC N306PC N55MT N164DA N74MB N164DA N164DN N40ZA
282-113	A	N8311N N40SC N40BT N30AF N430MB N430MP
282-114	A	N64MC N64MG XA-ATC XC-SUB XA-ATC (N7SL) XB-RGS XB-RGO
282-115	A	N8333N N376D N376DD N376RP XA-MNA XA-GCH XA-LML
282-116	A	N4PH XB-BBL
282-117	A	N8338N (HB-VCZ) I-MORA N1WZ Mexico TP108 callsign XC-UJH N3159U N265SC (N298AS)
282-118	A	N8339N PT-JNJ N19BG wfu Aug93 still as PT-JNJ; to spares c Oct94 Clarkesville, MO; cx Aug95
282-119	A	N8341N N5565 w/o 15Jan74 Oklahoma City, OK
282-120	A	N73HP N73DR
282-121	A	N8349N PP-SED fuselage to Spirit of St.Louis circa Sep97
282-122	A	N40JW N188PS
282-123	A	N8350N XA-APD XB-ESS
282-124	A	N193AT N200E N2006 N40JE N20ES
282-125	A	N8356N XB-NIB XA-SQA

SABRE 40

C/n	Series	Identities							
282-126	A	N40NS	XA-SNI	N40GT					
282-127	A	N110PM	N183AR	N63SL	OB-T-1319	OB-1319	w/o 03Sep93 Buenos Aires, Argentina; remains to Opa Locka, FL		
282-128	A	N99AP	XA-LIX	N99114					
282-129	A	N75W	N75WA	N75MD	(N99FF)	XA-RLH			
282-130	A	N33LB	N44NR	XC-SRA	Mexico TP107		Mexico TP105 callsign XC-UJG		XC-HEY
		Mexico TP105 callsign XC-UJI			XC-PGE	XA-REG	XC-AA51		
282-131	A	N9251N	N3BM	N3QM	N82R	LV-WND			
282-132	A	N9252N	N28TP	N70BC	N240CF				
282-133	A	N65740	N41NR	I-RELT					
282-134	A	N40NR	N60RC	(YV-64CP)	N66CD	XB-MVG			
282-135	A	N4GV	N777SL	N7778L	N55PP	N820JR	N200E	N2006	(N67BK)
282-136	A	N44PH	N211SF	N112ML	CP-2317				
282-137	A	N65763	N5511A	N5512A	N53WC	N9NR	N87CR	N870R	N881DM

Production complete

Note: T-39N aircraft "converted" by Sabreliner Corp for use in US Navy training contract have the following serials applied as shown, however are all still current on the USCAR

282-2, 282-9, 282-19, 282-20, 282-28, 282-29, 282-30, 282-32, 282-60, 282-61, 282-66, 282-72, 282-77, 282-81, 282-90, 282-94 and 282-100

SABRE 60

C/n	Series	Identities
306-1		N306NA N978R N521N N571NC XA-REC N359WJ
306-2		N307NA N968R N22MA N277CT N2710T N666BR XA-PUR N27RZ^
306-3		N177A N1001G N925Z N61MD N424R N160CF LV-WPO w/o 16Jly98 Cordobo, Argentina
306-4		N4709N N178W N1210 N121JE
306-5	A	N365N N302H N7090 OO-IBS N7090 (N477JM) N161CM
306-6	A	N4712N N662P N662F N311RM XA-HHR XA-ADC XA-SMF
306-7		N4715N N523N N63NC N531NC N30PY N60GH N60EX N60CR N64AM XA-SND XB-HDL
306-8		N4716N N73G N73GR N361DA N84LP N613BR N813BR
306-9		N4717N N47MN N998R N958R N1298 N32UT N5071L N4LG
306-10		N4720N N30W N9000V N9001V N19CM N125MC N946JR being parted out from Paynesville MO circa early 2000
306-11		N4721N N723R N743R w/o 13Apr73 Montrose, CO
306-12		N4722R N90N N9QN N18N N900P XA-ACF XA-CCB XC-HHL XC-AA26 to spares following flood damage reportedly in 1994; fuselage at Festus, MO, circa Apr96
306-13		N4723N N60Y N555SL N33BC N33BQ (N256MT) N60EL N306CF
306-14		N4724N N24G N24GB (N60AG) N24GB N1JN N43GB N60JN wfu; fuselage at Festus, MO, circa Apr96
306-15		N4725N N101L N60BK N360CH N221PH N221PF XA-RUQ N604MK N600SJ (rebuilt with spares from c/n 306-16)
306-16	A	N4726N N787R N5415 (N542S) N7090 N967R N100PW N160RW N105UA N33UT N38UT N5075L b/u for spares Sep92 Spirit of St Louis A/P, MO; remains to Clarkesville, MO; canx May95
306-17		N4727N (D-COUP) N988R N2UP N2UR N13SL N401MS
306-18		N4728N N908R N339GW N18HH N36HH (N60RL) N11AQ N12PB
306-19		N4729N N918R N8000U N50DG to spares Perryville, MO; cx Jan99
306-20		N4730N N938R N330U N22JW N44SB N78JP N55BP N155EC XA-PEI N155EC XA-REI XA-TLL
306-21		N4731N N948R N442A N60HC XB-LRD XB-QND
306-22		N4732N N746UP N743UP (N450CE) XA-CHP
306-23		N4733N N908R CF-BLT C-FBLT N15RF N77AT N68MA N85HS
306-24	A	N4734N N958R N5419 N300TB N58JM N990AC (N995RD) N600GL
306-25		N4735N N210F N212F N47MM (N613E) N60DL N60DE OB-1550 N60DE LV-WOF
306-26		N4736N N644X N323R N71CD N31CJ (N377EM) XA-CEN
306-27		N4737N N978R I-SNAD N11AL N888WL N105DM (N777CR) (N55ME) (N105SS) N103TA*
306-28		N741R N741RL N353CA
306-29		N4741N N3000 N3008 N995 N3008 N771WW cx Jan95 as destroyed reportedly on 10Jan95 - cabin fire at Lexington-Blue Grass Airport, KY; to White Inds, Bates City, MO N771WB (for spares use) cx Aug98
306-30		N4742N N905R N905BG N2440G N2440C N1116A N104SS wfu Fort Lauderdale, FL; for spares; to White Inds, Bates City, MO
306-31		N307D N274CA
306-32		N4743N N3278 being parted out at Spirit of St Louis circa early 2000
306-33		N4745N N600B XB-APD XA-APD N3FC N30TC N711TW N60JF (N660BW) N78RR N500RR N399SR HC-BQT CC-CGT N633SL
306-34		N4746N N3533 N747RC XA-VIO Mexico MTX-02 Mexico MTX-01 XC-DDA
306-35		N4748N N3456B XB-JMR
306-36		N4749N N918R N18N N90R N436CC XA-RIR
306-37		N4750N N4S N4SE (N60EX) N562R
306-38		N4751N N253MZ N251MA N229LS N230A XA-PEK XA-DCO XC-HGY
306-39		N4752N N10PF N888MC N507TF N747UP N745UP XA-RTH XA-SLH N82197 (N39SL) to spares Sep97 at Spirit of St.Louis, still as XA-SLH
306-40		N4753N N907R N711WK N1UP N1UT N997ME XA-SBX N306SA
306-41		N4754N N925N N173A N1909R (N8909R) N614MM LV-WLX (N62DW) N856MA
306-42		N4755N N915R N80L N58CG N60EL N120JC N128JC XA-VEL
306-43		N4757N N5420 N6NR N6NP N6NE N60AH N10UM N115CR
306-44		N4760N D-CEVW N111VW N45RS N86Y N60RS (N83RH) N129KH HC-BQU N562MS
306-45		N4763N N742R N742K N169RF w/o 07Nov92 Phoenix-Sky Harbor A/P, AZ; cx Jan95
306-46		N4764N N3600X N100FL N100FN N642RP
306-47	A	N4765N N927R XB-ZUM XA-ZUM XA-ZOM XB-ESX
306-48		N7519N N938R N234U N284U N60AG N75HP N86HP N4228A N4NT
306-49		N7522N N29S N29SX N645CC XA-POR XA-RNR reported wfu 1991
306-50		N7529N N948R N100Y XA-VIT XA-MUL XB-FSZ N601GL
306-51		N7531N N928R C-GDCC N141JA N60JC
306-52	CT-39G	N7571N N955R 158843 AMARC with park code 7T031 - to Mojave, CA by Oct98
306-53		N7573N N957R N99AA N963WL N963WA N624FA N48MG N68TA N999KG (N999LG) N699RD
306-54		N7574N N370VS N1020P N38JM N100EU N38JM N33TR N97SC N610RA
306-55	CT-39G	N7575N N908R N5419 158844 to AMARC with park code 7T034
306-56		N7576N N935R N14M N19M N19U XA-CMN XA-RXP XA-DSC
306-57		N7577N N937R N7NR N53G N22EH N122EH N701FW N465JH XA-RLS
306-58		N7578N N80E N80ER N1MN N1PN N529SC N529SQ N529CF
306-59		N945R N20G N20GX N10LX
306-60		N947R N115L N31BC N555RR N15H N15HF
306-61		N965R N961R (N1VC) N76GT N1JN N1JX
306-62		N967R N66NR N7090 N905R N905P N32BC N62CF N162JB
306-63		N978R XB-BIP XA-CIS XA-ABC XA-LRA XB-FST XB-FUZ XA-FNP XB-ZNP
306-64		N8357N N21BM N370L N1024G (N500RK) N96CP N74BS

SABRE 60

C/n Series Identities

306-65 CT-39G N8364N 159361 reported wfu Sigonella, Italy 1992
306-66 CT-39G N8365N 159362 AMARC with park code 7T032
306-67 CT-39G 159363 wfu; dumped Jan97 Edwards AFB, CA circa 1996
306-68 N8000 N2HW N2HX N265DP Ecuador 049
306-69 CT-39G 159364 to AMARC with park code 7T030
306-70 CT-39G 159365
306-71 A N31BM N370M N1028Y N71CC
306-72 N231CA N231A N550SL N6TM N60TM XA-RYD N97SC XA-GIH
306-73 N65745 N7NR N601MG N90EC XC-OAH XA-TNW N442RM
306-74 N920G w/o 27Dec74 Lancaster, PA
306-75 N110G N666WL N709AB N509AB N11LX
306-76 N65750 N67NR N333PC N333NC N82MW N86CP (N760SA)
306-77 N65751 N180AR N787R wfu; to spares 1994 Spirit of St Louis A/P, MO; cx Apr95
306-78 N65752 C-GRRS N140JA N477X
306-79 N4NR N4NE N768DV (N7682V) N43JG N539PG
306-80 N65756 PT-KOT N61FB
306-81 A N6NR N6ND N30CC wfu; to spares c Oct94; remains to Av-Mats' facility at Clarkville,
MO; cx Jan96
306-82 N65759 N60SL N59K
306-83 N14CG N14CQ N411MD N300YM N99FF XA-RLL
306-84 N65762 PT-KOU N8025X N383TS N55ZM N265GM
306-85 N65764 N217A N500RK N355CD N855CD N211BR
306-86 N65765 N60SL N60TG XA-ICK
306-87 N65767 N100CE N60RS N100MA N400CE N200CE XA-RFB
306-88 N65769 N992 N22CG XA-RAP
306-89 N65770 N23DS N86RM XA-ECM N86RM XA-STI
306-90 N65772 N181AR N13SL N148JP N123FG N265MK
306-91 N65774 N204R N204G N60BP N660RM (N45MM) LV-WXX
306-92 N65775 N711S N328JS N74AB N33JW
306-93 N65777 N366N N182AR N200CX N507U XA-JCE
306-94 N65778 HZ-MA1 HZ-NCB N75JT N217RM N217RN
306-95 N65783 N999DC N124DC
306-96 N65784? N54784 N68HC N48HC (N1318E) N315JM XB-ETV
306-97 N65785 I-FBCA N3WQ N344K N85DB N707DB N98LB XA-RWY XA-SVH N90TT
N97NL N15DJ
306-98 N65786 N6MK N169AC N531AB
306-99 N65789 N905R N16PN N66GE
306-100 N65790 N881MC N81HP N5379W N60SE XA-RLR XB-LAW XA-TMF
306-101 A N65791 N68NR N376D N60FS N376D
306-102 N65792 N108G N555AE N444MA N265TJ N70HL
306-103 N65794 N11UL N40TL N234DC
306-104 CT-39G N65795 160053 returned to service circa 1999
306-105 CT-39G N65796 160054 to Mojave by Oct98
306-106 CT-39G N65797 160055
306-107 CT-39G N65798 160056 AMARC park code 7T-029
306-108 CT-39G N65799 160057 w/o 03Mar91 approx 1.5 miles from Glenview NAS, IL
306-109 A N2101J N522N N64NC N521NC N602KB XA-SBV
306-110 N2103J N60RS HZ-MA1 N13SL XA-RTP N75GM XB-HJS
306-111 N2106J N300RC XA-SKB
306-112 N2107J N740R N740RC CC-CTC
306-113 N2108J N712MR N2626M N113T
306-114 65 N2109J N65R N60TF N65R
306-115 N2118J (XA-LEI) Bolivia FAB-001
306-116 A N2119J N605RG N44WD N39CB
306-117 N2120J N22MY Ecuador FAE-001A reported wfu
306-118 N2122J N65NR N711MR N2635M N607SR N607CF
306-119 A N2123J N167H N110MH XA-JMD N109MC
306-120 N2124J N265C N265SR N1GM^
306-121 N2130J N880KC (N15CK) N880CK XA-SYS N789SG
306-122 A N2131J N168H N56RN
306-123 N2132J N710MR N2627M N128VM (N213BE) N28VM XA-PAX N97SC XA-ATE
306-124 A N2133J N65NR N60RS N48WS
306-125 N2134J N32PC XA-RGC N265RW N261T XA-SLJ N28HH
306-126 N2141J N60SL N7NR N7NF N1CH N85HP N4227N HC-BUN N111F
306-127 N2142J N5NE N60DD XA-CUR
306-128 N2143J N80CR N100CE N117JL N24TK+ N117JL XA-
+ painted as such but marks only reserved
306-129 N2144J N711ST N749UP N95RC N60ML
306-130 N2145J XA-OVR XA-JIK XB-JMM
306-131 N2149J N5DL N35DL N61DF N131JR (N131SE)
306-132 N2150J N60RS N108W (N994W) N60AG N265U
306-133 N2151J N6NE N9NP N700WS I-PATY N360CF N400JH
306-134 N2152J N323EC N282WW
306-135 N2535E N9NR N9NT N64CM N59JM N60AM N921MB
306-136 65 N2501E N465S N65RS redesignated c/n 465-1 1981 as first Sabre 65 (qv)
306-137 N2506E N60SL N650C N18X XA-SAH
306-138 N2508E N22BX N800RM N700JR N702JR XA-RVT
306-139 Mexico TP105 Mexico TP103 callsign XC-UJE

SABRE 60

C/n	Series	Identities						
306-140		N636	N636MC	N60AF	N26SC	N26SQ		
306-141		N8NR	(N89N)	(N8NF)	N141SL			
306-142		N60RS	N80CR	N742R	N742RC	N190MD	N40KJ	(N70LW) N700MH
306-143		N800M	N80QM	N741R	N741RC	XA-SIM	XA-SUN	XA-TPU
306-144		N2519E	Mexico TP106		Mexico TP104 callsign XC-UJF			
306-145		N60SL	N730CA	XA-LOQ	XC-JDC			
306-146		N301MC	N301MG	N360CH	XA-ARE	(N146BJ)	N31CR	

Production complete

SABRE 75

C/n	Series	Identities
370-1		N7572N used as parts for other test aircraft
370-2		N7585N N75NR N8NR N80K N10M
370-3		N7586N N70NR N125N N125NX
370-4		N7587N N75U N75UA N37GF N370BH N400DB
370-5		N7588N N75NR N23G N55KS N55KZ N58KS N250BC N265SR XA-RYJ
370-6		N7589N N2TE XA-SGR N29019 (N30EV) wfu; cx Sep91; remains to Clarkesville, MO
370-7	A	N7590N N75NR N60PM N60PT N75DE XB-ERU N670C (N26TJ)
370-8		N7591N N3TE N70HC b/u for spares Sep90 Little Rock, AR; canx Jun96; remains to Paynesville, MO
370-9		N7592N N8NR N8NB N55CR XA-RZW XB-GJO N370SL being parted out at Spirit of St Louis, CIRCA EARLY 2000 still wearing its previous identity XB-GJO

Production complete

SABRE 75A

C/n	Series	Identities
380-1		N7593N N6K N87Y N30GB N100EJ
380-2		N8445N N2440G N2440C N19PC N380SR N9GN N642TS N406PW*
380-3		N8467N Argentina T-10 Argentina T-11
380-4	80A	N65733 N5105 N510AA N75SE XA-RLP N11887 (LV-) N11887
380-5		N51 N125MS N223LP N71460
380-6	80A	N65741 N5106 N50GG N75TJ N711GL N711GD N184PC
380-7		N65744 N67KM w/o 14Jun75 Watertown, SD
380-8		N65749 N5107 N500NL wfu; parted out Feb93 - possibly following an accident on 23Feb75 at Oakland-Pontiac
380-9	80A	N5108 N510BB N6SP N383CF N995RD
380-10		N52 cx Sep95 assumed wfu
380-11	80A	N5109 N5109T N265SR N151TB
380-12		N65758 (N335K) HB-VEC D-CLAN N75SL D-CLAN N120YB (N4WJ) N75BS
380-13		N65761 Argentina AE-175
380-14		N53 N72028 being parted out at Rantoul KS circa early 2000
380-15		N65766 (N338K) N80NR N1841D N1841F N15PN N18TF N18TZ XA-LEG N22JW N424R
380-16		N54 N126MS N12659
380-17	80A	N65768 (N339K) N80RS 5N-AMM N70TF N15RF N111Y N1115 N380BC
380-18		N55 N127MS wfu; for spares Perryville, MO; cx Jly95
380-19		N65771 D-CLUB N500TF N100RS XB-EPM XA-EPM N54HH N80HG
380-20		N56 N773W
380-21	80A	N65773 N711A N75A N22NT N25AT N577SW N111AG N840MA N647JP N82AF
380-22		N57 N132MS N131MS wfu; for spares Perryville, MO; cx Jly95
380-23		N65776 N68KM N102RD N800CD
380-24	80	N58 N219TT
380-25		N50PM N90AM N16LF N13NH N400RS
380-26		N59 N128MS N2200A
380-27		N65787 N8NR N8NB N10CN N6NR N6NG N90GM N90GW N85DW
380-28		N60 cx Jun96; presumed wfu
380-29		N61 N131MS N58966 N132MS N71543 used for fire training by University of Illinois and destroyed as a result
380-30		N65793 N69KM N265CH N265DP N818DW N818LD
380-31		N62 N75CN being parted out at Rantoul KS circa early 2000
380-32	80A	N2100J N75RS N64MP N64MQ N66ES N66ED (N86SH) N380DJ N198GB
380-33		N63 N129MS N7148J
380-34		N2104J N6LG (N112KH) N382MC Ecuador FAE-034 Ecuador AEE-403 N97SC XA-
380-35		N64 w/o 29Sep86 where?; cx Aug88
380-36		N2105J N75A JY-AFM N75HL (N835MA) XB-MCB N377HS
380-37		N65 N774W
380-38		N2102J D-CAVW N85031 N3RN HZ-AMN N95TJ N75AK N316EC
380-39		N2110J N7NR N102MJ N88JM N38JM (N60WP) N40WP XA-PON N2093P XA-SXK XC-ONA N354SH (N805HD) (N55HD) N105HD
380-40		N2112J N4NR N4NB N75NL N920DY N820DY N14TN
380-41		N2113J N33NT N400N N400NR
380-42		N2114J N75RS D-CHIC N75AG XA-MVT
380-43		N2115J N6NR N2265Z wfu prior Sep90 Clarkesville, MO
380-44	80A	N2116J N2440G N380GK*
380-45		N2117J D-CCVW N218US (N218UB) N753TW Ecuador FAE-045 believed to Ecuador AEE-402, which was w/o 10Dec92 nr Quito A/P, Ecuador
380-46		N2125J (N50K) N90C XA-RIH XC-HFY XC-AA89 (not confirmed)
380-47		N2126J N25BH N25BX
380-48	80A	N2127J N8NR N8NG N805RG N6PG N27TS N132DB N100BP
380-49	80A	N2128J N4PG (N41B) N4PQ N4PG N673SH N673FH N221PH N265KC

SABRE 75A

C/n	Series	Identities									
380-50	80A	N2129J	N5PG	N5EQ	N5PG	N179S	XA-ROD	XA-RLR	XA-TDQ		
380-51		N2135J	N43R	N4343	N711BY	(N12GP)	N808EB	N80LX	N180NA	N382LS	
380-52		N2136J	N75A	N177NC	N177NQ	N70KM	N84NG				
380-53		N2137J	N75NR	JY-AFN	HZ-THZ	N8526A	N75HZ	XC-FIA	XB-DVP	N380SR	N827SL
380-54		N2138J	N6NR	N62NR	N10CN	N350MT	N81GD	N999M	N176DC	N380CF	N910BH
380-55		N2139J	N33KA	HZ-CA1	N120KC	XA-OAF	XB-RDB	XB-GSP			
380-56		N2146J	JY-AFL	N14JD	(N914JC)	N22NB					
380-57		N2147J	N80RS	N75A	HZ-RBH	JY-AFH					
380-58		N2148J	N75RS	N380T	XA-CHA	XA-SEB	XA-GHR				
380-59		N80AB	(N935PC)	N83AB	N911CR	N27LT					
380-60		N2521E	D-CBVW	N4260K	N100TM	XB-RSG	XB-SHA	XA-RDY			
380-61		N2522E	JY-AFO	9L-LAW	N727US	to spares at Spirit of St.Louis circa 1996 cx Jan00					
380-62		JY-AFP									
380-63		N75RS	N448W								
380-64		N75NR	N75Y	N942CC							
380-65		YU-BLY	RC-BLY	9A-BLY	N88JJ	N69JN					
380-66		N2536E	N6PG	N6VL	N6PG	N75L	N943CC	N819GY			
380-67		N2528E	Mexico TP 103		Mexico TP 101 callsign XC-UJC			w/o 26Oct89 Saltillo, Mexico; remains to Elsberry, MO			
380-68		N2538E	Mexico TP 104		Mexico TP 102 callsign XC-UJD						
380-69		N2542E	N111VW	(N111VS)	N111VX	N547JL	w/o 18Jly98 near Marion, KS				
380-70		(N13ME)	(N15ME)	N101ME	N1NR	(N380RS)	N110AJ				
380-71		HZ-NR1									
380-72		HZ-SOG	N380N	N90N	N555JR	N933JC					

Production complete

SABRE 65

C/n	Identities								
465-1	N2501E	N465S	N65RS	N77A	N65KJ	N117MB	(N117MN)	N65HH	
	originally Sabre 60 c/n 306-136								
465-2	N465T	N251JE	N45H						
465-3	N65RS	N6K	N170JL	N170CC	N1CF				
465-4	N1058X	N14M	N141PB	N800TW	N804PA				
465-5	N24G	N55KS	N52GG	N60CE	N241H				
465-6	N65NC	N511NC	N65SR	N1CC					
465-7	N10580	N2000	N2800	N2000					
465-8	N10581	XA-GAP							
465-9	N6NP	N769KC	(N769EG)	N6GV					
465-10	N65SL	N77TC	N336RJ						
465-11	N3000	N3030	N25UG	N5739	N57MQ				
465-12	XA-OVR	XA-PVR	XB-GMD	N112PR	N112PV	N529SC			
465-13	N7HF	N13MF	N945CC						
465-14	N651S	N301MC	N67SC	N71RB	N740R	N25SR	XA-SPM		
465-15	N2513E	XA-ZUM	N465TS						
465-16	N31BC	N7000G	N700QG	N65SR	N112CF	N920CC			
465-17	N2537E	N905K	N4MB	N32290	(N322TW)	N74VC			
465-18	N4M	N696US							
465-19	N65RC	N91BZ							
465-20	N2544E	N173A							
465-21	N2586E	(N65HM)	N465LC	(N265CA)	N701FW				
465-22	N996W	N678AM	9H-ABO	VR-CEE	N927AA	N883RA			
465-23	N904K	(N904KB)	N223LB						
465-24	N65NR	N2545E	N8000U	N800CU	N65JR	N265PC	N741R	N777SK	N271MB
465-25	N9000F	N25MF	N125BP	N324ZR	N821WN				
465-26	N465SL	N2548E	N65DD	N31SJ	N488DM				
465-27	XA-ARE	XA-AVR	XA-FVK	N351AF	N111AD	N39TR			
465-28	N2549E	N333PC	N742R	N24RF	N129BA*				
465-29	N6NR								
465-30	N25ZC	(N25ZG)	N89MM	N65TC					
465-31	N2550E	N65FC	N265M						
465-32	N97RE	N303A	HB-VCN						
465-33	N994	N869KC	(N869EG)	(N271MB)	N465SR	N265C			
465-34	(N50DG)	N112KM	N80FH	N65TS	N47SE				
465-35	N2590E	N65AK							
465-36	N651GL	N652MK	N424JM	N65MC					
465-37	N750CS	N750CC							
465-38	N850CS	N850CC							
465-39	N2551E	N5511A	N551FA	N203JK					
465-40	N341AP	N465RM	N465PM	N801SS					
465-41	N2556E	N800M							
465-42	N2561E	N415CS	N41TC	N15CC	N150HN	N15CC	N64SL	N45NP	
465-43	N950CS	N228LS	N83TF	N955PR					
465-44	N7NR								
465-45	N442WT	N448WT	N65TJ	N265DR*					
465-46	N20UC	N79CD	N65FF	N65CC					
465-47	N265A	N33TR							
465-48	N2539E	XA-MLG	N500WD	N265SP					
465-49	N455SF	N455LB	N500RR	N82CR					
465-50	N2570E	N129GP	N959C	N920DY					
465-51	N3BM	N3QM	N114LG						
465-52	N500E	N96RE							
465-53	N76NX	N80R							
465-54	N2579E	N6000J	N600QJ	N1909R	N65SR				
465-55	N2574E	XA-LUC	XA-RYO	XB-RYO	XA-TOM				
465-56	N544PH	N265JS	N65TL	N499NH					
465-57	N903K	N355CD							
465-58	N65AM	N670AS							
465-59	N65AN	HB-VJF	N59SR	N61DF	N8500	N35CC			
465-60	N2580E	N88BF							
465-61	N23BX	N117JW							
465-62	N56NW	N65AF							
465-63	N2N	N605Y	N2N	N2NL					
465-64	N99S	w/o 11Jan83 Toronto, Canada; cx Aug91							
465-65	N29S	N29SZ	N65AD	(N925WL)	N963WL	XA-SCR			
465-66	N964C								
465-67	N65AR	N921CC							
465-68	N65AH	OO-IBC	N68LX	N165NA	N930RA				
465-69	N33BC	(N31BC)	N400KV	N25KL	N65ML*				
465-70	N15AK	N15EN	N58CM	N58HT					
465-71	N728C	N75G	N75GL	N75VC					
465-72	N857W	(OO-RSA)	(OO-RSB)	OO-RSE	N465SP				
465-73	N64MC	N64MQ	N651MK						
465-74	N700JC								
465-75	N2581E	N570R							
465-76	N65L								

Production complete

PIAGGIO PD808

C/n	Series	Identities	
501	TA	MM577	wfu by 1996, on dump at Practica di Mare by Mar98
502	TA	MM578	
503	VIP	I-PIAI	w/o 18Jun68 San Sebastian, Spain
504	VIP	I-PIAL	wfu 1998
505	GE1	MM61958	wfu at Practica di Mare by Nov97
506	VIP	MM61948	
507	VIP	MM61949	wfu mid-1990's to Ditellandia Air Park, Castel Volturno by Sep99
508	VIP	MM61950	
509	VIP	MM61951	wfu at Practica di Mare by Mar98
510	TP	MM61952	converted to PD808 GE2
511	TP	MM61953	w/o 15Sep93 Venice, Italy
512	TP	MM61954	
513	TP	MM61955	converted to PD808 GE2
514	TP	MM61956	wfu to dump at Practica di Mare by Mar98
515	TP	MM61957	wfu at Practica di Mare by Mar98
516	GE1	MM61959	wfu at Practica di Mare by Mar98
517	GE1	MM61960	
518	GE1	MM61961	
519	GE1	MM61962	
520	GE1	MM61963	wfu before Jun93 Pisa, Italy; dismantled at Practica di Mare by Nov97 remains to Ditellandia Air Park, Castel Volturno by Nov99
521	RM	MM62014	wfu at Practica di Mare by Jly99
522	RM	I-PIAY	MM62015 wfu at Practica di Mare by Mar98
523	RM	MM62016	wfu at Practica di Mare by Nov97
524	RM	MM62017	wfu by Feb98, on dump at Practica di Mare by Mar98

Production complete

RAYTHEON 390 PREMIER I

The Premier I has a composite carbonfibre/honeycomb fuselage structure and is powered by two Williams-Rolls FJ44-2A engines. Reported IFR range is 2775 kilometres at a maximum cruising speed of 461 knots and operating altitude of 41000 feet.

C/n	Identities	
RB-1	N390RA	rolled out 19Aug98; ff 23Dec98 for 62 minutes
RB-2	N704T	
RB-3	N390TC	
RB-4	N842PM	
RB-5		
RB-6	N390R	
RB-7		
RB-8		
RB-9	N390EM	
RB-10		
RB-11		
RB-12	N390TA	N390P
RB-13		
RB-14	N969RE	
RB-15		
RB-16	N151KD	
RB-17		
RB-18		
RB-19	N65TB	
RB-20		
RB-21		
RB-22	N45NB	
RB-23		
RB-24		
RB-25		
RB-26		
RB-27		
RB-28	N128RM	
RB-29	N747BK	
RB-30		
RB-31		
RB-32		
RB-33		
RB-34		
RB-35	N435K	
RB-36		
RB-37		
RB-38	N972PF	
RB-39	N39KT	
RB-40		
RB-41		
RB-42		
RB-43		
RB-44		
RB-45		
RB-46		
RB-47		
RB-48		
RB-49		
RB-50		
RB-51		
RB-52		
RB-53		
RB-54		
RB-55	N390PL	
RB-56		
RB-57	N457K	
RB-58		
RB-59		
RB-60		
RB-61		
RB-62		
RB-63		
RB-64		
RB-65		
RB-66		
RB-67		
RB-68		
RB-69		
RB-70		
RB-71		
RB-72		
RB-73		
RB-74		

RAYTHEON 390 PREMIER I

C/n	Identities
RB-75	
RB-76	
RB-77	
RB-78	N390JW*
RB-79	
RB-80	
RB-81	
RB-82	
RB-83	
RB-84	
RB-85	
RB-86	N390TA
RB-87	
RB-88	
RB-89	
RB-90	
RB-91	
RB-92	
RB-93	
RB-94	
RB-95	
RB-96	
RB-97	
RB-98	
RB-99	
RB-100	
RB-101	
RB-102	
RB-103	
RB-104	
RB-105	
RB-106	
RB-107	
RB-108	
RB-109	
RB-110	
RB-111	
RB-112	
RB-113	
RB-114	
RB-115	
RB-116	
RB-117	
RB-118	
RB-119	
RB-120	
RB-121	N390GM*

SN601 CORVETTE

C/n	Identities
01	F-WRSN ff 16Jly70 w/o 23Mar71 Marseille, France (model SN600)
1	F-WUAS ff 20Dec72 F-BUAS F-WUAS F-BUAS France (CEV) 1/F-ZVMV coded MV
2	F-WRNZ F-BRNZ France (CEV) 2/F-ZVMW coded MW
3	F-WUQN F-BUQN F-WUQN F-BUQN
4	F-WUQP F-BUQP
5	F-BVPA F-ODJX F-BVPA CN-TDE
6	F-WUQR F-BVPB F-OGJL F-BVPB
7	F-OBZR N611AC F-BVPK
8	F-WPTT 6V-AEA F-GJAS
9	F-WRQK F-BRQK N612AC F-BTTR F-OCRN TN-ADI reported wfu South of France
10	F-BVPO N600AN F-GFEJ France (CEV) 10/F-ZVMX coded MX
11	(F-WIFU) N613AC F-BTTS TR-LWY F-ODKS F-BTTV EI-BNY F-WFPD (F-GFPD) F-GKGA
12	F-BVPC TR-LYM TJ-AHR
13	F-BVPD N601AN F-GFDH
14	F-BVPS SP-FOA F-GIRH*
15	F-WIFA SE-DEN OO-MRA OO-MRE F-GDUB SE-DEN N17AJ F-GEQF D6-ECB F-GNAF EC-HHZ
16	F-BVPT 5R-MVN cx 2000 reason not known
17	F-WNGQ N614AC F-BTTM F-ODTM YV-572CP w/o? 21Jun91 Las Delicias A/P, Santa Barbara del Zulia, Venezuela
18	F-WNGR N615AC F-BTTO N604AN cx Dec90; sold to Drenair, Spain, for spares use
19	F-BVPL F-OCJL F-BVPL TZ-PBF (F-GDRC) F-SEBH F-GEPQ EC-HIA
20	F-WNGS N616AC F-BTTN TR-LZT F-GKJB wfu 31Mar93 for spares at Toulouse, France; wings used in rebuild of c/n 28; forward fuselage to cabin trainer use
21	F-BVPE OY-SBS w/o 03Sep79 Nice, France
22	F-WNGT N617AC F-BTTU F-ODFE TN-ADB w/o 30Mar79 Nkayi, Congo Republic
23	F-BVPF OY-SBR
24	F-BVPI EC-DQC sold in USA for scrap/spares but b/u Mar92 Toulouse, France
25	F-WNGU F-BVPG F-OBZV F-BVPG
26	F-WNGV N618AC F-ODFQ PH-JSB F-GDAY EC-DQE cx 1997, status?
27	F-BVPH reported to N26674 but not confirmed EC-DQG
28	F-WNGX F-BTTL (OO-TTL) F-GPLA
29	F-WNGY F-BVPJ F-OBZP F-BVPJ F-OBZP TY-BBK w/o 16Nov81 Lagos, Nigeria
30	F-WNGQ F-BTTP OO-MRC TR-LAH OO-MRC EC-DUE (F-GKGB) F-GLEC
31	F-WNGZ F-BTTK N602AN F-WZSB EC-DYE F-GJAP
32	F-WNGR F-BTTQ OY-ARA SE-DED OY-ARA EC-DUF F-GILM
33	F-BTTT OY-SBT
34	F-WNGS F-BYCR OY-ARB SE-DEE OY-ARB SE-DEE F-GKGD CN-TCS
35	PH-JSC F-GDAZ YV-589CP YV-01CP F-ODSR 5R-MVD F-ODSR
36	F-BTTS PH-JSD F-OCDE XB-CYA XB-EWF XA-BCC N601RC N600RA
37	F-BTTU w/o 31Jul90 St Yan, France; cx 12Feb91 as "reformed" 04Dec90
38	F-ODIF 5A-DCK
39	F-WNGY F-OBYG TL-SMI TL-RCA F-GJLB
40	F-WNGZ F-ODJS XB-CYI N601CV N200MT

Production complete

EXPERIMENTAL & NON-PRODUCTION TYPES

CHICHESTER-MILES LEOPARD

C/n	Identities
001	G-BKRL first flight late 1988; currently under test
002	G-BRNM

DASSAULT 30

C/n	Identities
01	F-WAMD wfu Bordeaux, France; never entered production; fuselage at Vitrolles Engineering University, nr Marseilles, France, 1990

GULFSTREAM 550 PEREGRINE

C/n	Identities
551	N9881S N550GA N84GP wfu Mar92; to Oklahoma Air & Space Museum

HONDA MH02

C/n	Identities
001	N3097N ff 05Mar93 - undertook 170 hours of test flying which ended in Aug96

McDONNELL MD220

C/n	Identities
1	N11917 N220N N4AZ never entered production; ferried Albuquerque, NM, to El Paso, TX 21Dec85 - where it is wfu

NORTH AMERICAN UTX

C/n	Identities
246-1	N4060K b/u circa 1967

SABRE 50

C/n	Identities
287-1	N287NA N50CR still flying; never entered production

SCALED COMPOSITES 143 TRIUMPH

C/n	Identities
001	N143SC ff 12Jly88; further development abandoned; wfu Sep92 Mojave, CA; placed on poles and on display outside Scaled Composites premises at Mojave CA

SINO-SWEARINGEN SJ-30

C/n	Identities
001	N30SJ ff 13Feb91 Stinson Field, TX. Stretched to become SJ-30-2 prototype and ff 8Nov96 cx Oct99 wfu Airframe stored minus engines at Martinsburg WV

Note: Was originally to be known as the SA-30 Fanjet.

VISIONAIRE VANTAGE

C/n	Identities
001	N247VA

NOTES : Visionaire announced at the 1997 NBAA Convention that it held 90 firm orders for the Vantage from 9 different countries. Production aircraft will be built in Ames in Iowa and Arad in Israel.

WILLIAMS V-JET II

C/n	Identities
001	N222FJ

NOTES : Officially registered as a Scale Composites 271. The V-Jet II is a small, all-composite 6-seat jet powered by a single Williams FJX-2 engine. It was built primarily as a test bed for the FJX-2 engine rather than for series production.

MASTER INDEX

Civil-registered bizjets are arranged in order of country registration prefix, registration relating to each country being listed in alphabetical or numerical order as appropriate. For each registration, a two- or three-letter character abbreviation for the type of aircraft is given (see decode below), followed by the c/n (except for Citation I and II models, where the unit number is quoted where this is known).

All civil registered aircraft which are in current use are indicated by bold typeface; reserved marks are given in the normal typeface.

Bizjets in military use are arranged in alphabetical order of country name.

MASTER INDEX DE-CODE

Code	Type	Code	Type
AST	IAI 1125 Astra	25(letter)	Learjet 25 (letter indicates sub-type)
CVT	SN601 Corvette	28	Learjet 28
D1A	MU300 Diamond	29	Learjet 29
EC	Falcon 20 ECM	30	Dassault 30
G2	G1159 Gulfstream II	31(letter)	Learjet 31 (letter indicates sub-type)
G3	G1159A Gulfstream III	35(letter)	Learjet 35 (letter indicates sub-type)
G4	Gulfstream IV	36(letter)	Learjet 36 (letter indicates sub-type)
G5	Gulfstream V	45	Learjet 45
HFB	MBB HFB320 Hansa	50	Dassault Falcon 50
LEO	Chichester-Miles Leopard	55(letter)	Learjet 55 (letter indicates sub-type)
MON	Honda MH02	60	Learjet 60
MSP	MS760 Paris	100	Dassault Falcon 100
M20	McDonnell MD220	125	BAe 125 Series
PER	Gulfstream 550 Peregrine	200	Dassault Falcon 200
PRM	Raytheon 390 Premier I	2xx	Dassault Falcon 2000
SJ3	Swearingen SJ30	400	Beechjet 400
STR	Lockheed Jetstar	500	Cessna 500/501 Citation I
S40	Sabre 40	525	Cessna 525 Citation
S50	Sabre 50	550	Cessna 550/551 Citation II
S55	Cessna S550 Citation II		Cessna Citation Bravo
S60	Sabre 60	552	Cessna 552 Citation (T-49A)
S65	Sabre 65	560	Cessna 560 Citation V
S75	Sabre 75		Cessna 560XL Citation Excel
S80	Sabre 80	600	CL600 Challenger
T1A	Jayhawk (Beech 400)	601	CL601 Challenger
TRI	Scaled Composites 143 Triumph	604	CL604 Challenger
T39	T39 Sabre Series	650	Cessna 650 Citation III
UTX	North American UTX	660	Cessna 650 Citation VI
VAN	Visionaire Vantage	670	Cessna 650 Citation VII
VII	Williams V-Jet II	700	BD700 Global Express
WWD	Jet Commander/Westwind	750	Cessna 750 Citation X
10	Dassault Falcon 10	808	Piaggio PD808
20	Dassault Falcon 20	900	Dassault Falcon 900
23	Learjet 23	90X	Dassault Falcon 900EX
24(letter)	Learjet 24 (letter indicates sub-type)		

Civil Index

Nicaragua
(see also YN-)

AN-BPR	125	256037

Pakistan

AP-BEK	**31A**	**062**
AP-BEX	**400A**	**RK-80**

Botswana

A2-AGM	**501**	**652**
A2-MCB	**S550**	**0112**

Oman

A40-AA	20	285/504
A40-AA	G2	183
A40-AB	**G4**	**1168**
A40-AC	**G4**	**1196**
A40-AJ	25B	188
A40-CA	35A	165
A40-GA	20	285/504
A40-HA	G2	214
A40-SC	550	486

United Arab Emirates

A6-ALI	G4	1132
A6-AUH	**900**	**84**
A6-CKZ	G3	317
A6-CPC	**STR**	**5222**
A6-EXA	20	344/534
A6-FAJ	35A	669
A6-HEH	G3	356
A6-HEM	20	344/534
A6-HHH	**G4**	**1011**
A6-HHS	G3	376
A6-HHZ	G2	164
(A6-HMK)	125	258093
A6-KAH	**STR**	**5220**
A6-RAK	125	256063
A6-RKH	500	268
A6-SMH	500	402
A6-SMS	550	391
A6-SMS	60	094
A6-SMS	**60**	**150**
A6-UAE	**900**	**86**
A6-ZKM	50	145
A6-ZKM	**900**	**47**

Qatar

A7-AAD	**900**	**91**
A7-AAE	**900**	**94**

Bahrain

A9C-BAH	**G4**	**1353**
A9C-BB	G3	393
A9C-BG	**G2**	**202**

China & Taiwan

B-3980	55	027
B-3981	**60**	**053**
B-3989	**400A**	**RK-203**
B-3990	**125**	**258408**
B-4005	601	3046
B-4006	601	3047
B-4007	601	3052
B-4010	601	5024
B-4011	601	5025
B-4101	**S550**	**0049**
B-4102	**S550**	**0050**
B-4103	**550**	**357**
B-4104	**550**	**362**
B-4105	**550**	**359**
B-4106	**650**	**0220**
B-4107	**650**	**0221**
B-4108	**525**	**0204**
B-98181	35A	675
B-98183	**35A**	**654**

Hong Kong

B-HSS	**125**	**257169**

Bosnia
(see also T9-)

BH-BIH	S550	0045

Canada
(see also CF-)

(C-)	10	184
(C-)	125	259024
C-	**560**	**5078**
C-	601	5170
C-	601	5185
C-	601	5186
C-	604	5447
C-	604	5448
C-	604	5449
C-FAAL	601	3005
C-FAAU	125	258099
C-FACO	**560**	**0053**
C-FADL	500	067
C-FALC	125	25087
C-FALI	**S550**	**0142**
C-FANL	125	25042
C-FANS	**550**	**0807**
C-FAOS	125	25278
C-FAWW	WWD	313
C-FBAX	500	020
C-FBCL	**45**	**024**
C-FBCL	500	042
C-FBCM	500	071
C-FBDH	35A	673
C-FBDR	**60**	**010**
C-FBEA	25B	163
C-FBEL	**601**	**3028**
C-FBFP	**35**	**038**
C-FBGX	700	9001
C-FBHX	601	5018
C-FBKR	601	5020
C-FBLJ	**60**	**092**
C-FBLT	S60	306-23
C-FBLU	**60**	**029**
C-FBMG	**125**	**257066**
C-FBNK	125	25221
C-FBNS	**604**	**5364**
C-FBOM	**601**	**5124**
C-FBSS	10	87
C-FBVF	**10**	**33**
C-FCCC	**550**	**422**
C-FCCP	604	5310
C-FCDF	601	5024
C-FCDS	20	146
C-FCEH	200	507
C-FCEJ	**WWD**	**324**
C-FCEL	550	135
C-FCEL	**560**	**5047**
C-FCFL	125	25213
C-FCFP	500	125
(C-FCFP)	551	097
C-FCFP	**AST**	**079**
C-FCGS	601	5025
C-FCHJ	500	091
C-FCLJ	**55**	**118**
C-FCPW	500	002
C-FCSS	24B	197
C-FDAC	25B	091
C-FDAT	601	5029
C-FDAX	**AST**	**058**
C-FDCS	G4	1207
C-FDDD	**125**	**258038**
C-FDDD	S550	0115
C-FDJQ	500	018
C-FDLT	560	0021
C-FDOM	125	25018
C-FDRS	604	5432
C-FDTF	STR	5088
C-FDTM	STR	5052
C-FDTX	STR	5018
C-FDYL	550	373
C-FEAQ	600	1035
C-FEMA	**S550**	**0040**
C-FENJ	500	122
C-FETN	STR	5021
C-FETZ	601	5041
C-FEUV	601	5042
C-FEWB	25B	180
C-FEXB	125	257152
C-FEYG	WWD	81
C-FFAB	125	257030
C-FFBC	WWD	119
C-FFBY	601	5044
C-FFCL	550	063
C-FFNM	G2	52
C-FFSO	601	5045
C-FFTM	125	258161
C-FGAT	**500**	**199**
C-FGAT	550	255
C-FGGH	**WWD**	**431**
C-FGGX	700	9014
C-FGLF	125	258141
C-FHBX	G2	119/22
C-FHDM	35A	410
C-FHFP	24E	340
C-FHGX	**700**	**9002**
C-FHHD	601	5061
C-FHJB	55	122
C-FHLL	125	25034
C-FHLO	35A	179
C-FHPM	**G2**	**104/10**
C-FHSS	125	256003
C-FICU	**35A**	**249**
C-FIDO	**60**	**133**
C-FIGD	**20**	**109/427**
C-FIGR	601	5069
C-FIMA	**525**	**0191**
C-FIMO	**650**	**0065**
C-FIOB	601	5064
C-FIOT	G2	78
C-FIPE	**125**	**258319**
C-FIPG	125	257132
C-FIPJ	125	25053
C-FJBO	**550**	**0812**
C-FJCZ	**550**	**700**
C-FJDF	601	5079
C-FJES	20	236
C-FJES	900	55
C-FJES	G4	1207
C-FJGR	601	5080
C-FJGX	**700**	**9003**
C-FJJC	**650**	**0116**
C-FJOE	550	573
C-FJOE	650	0049
C-FJPI	601	5085
C-FJWZ	**550**	**685**
C-FJXN	**550**	**684**
C-FKCE	**550**	**686**
C-FKCI	125	25137
C-FKCI	**50**	**63**
C-FKDX	**550**	**687**
C-FKEB	**550**	**688**
C-FKGX	**700**	**9004**
C-FKHD	551	110
C-FKIY	601	5092
C-FKLB	**550**	**699**
C-FKMC	**500**	**073**
C-FKNN	601	5094
C-FKTD	601	5096
C-FKVW	601	5097
C-FLDM	550	288
C-FLDO	550	038
C-FLMT	**650**	**0104**
C-FLPC	601	5006
C-FLPC	**604**	**5392**
C-FLPD	**550**	**189**
C-FLTL	**650**	**0007**
C-FLUT	601	5087
C-FLYJ	601	5102
C-FLZA	**550**	**701**
C-FMAN	500	086
C-FMCI	**550**	**0816**
C-FMDB	125	25075
C-FMFL	**50**	**96**
C-FMFM	**550**	**702**
C-FMGM	25B	117
C-FMKF	125	25170
C-FMPP	550	409
C-FMTC	125	25104
C-FMVQ	601	5105
C-FMWW	WWD	380
C-FMYB	50	99
C-FNCG	**G2**	**208**
(C-FNCG)	G4	1017
C-FNCG	S40	282-90
C-FNER	125	25176
C-FNNC	**50**	**176**
C-FNND	**10**	**87**
C-FNNT	**601**	**5068**
C-FNOC	500	182
C-FNOR	G2	54/36
C-FNRG	55ER	101
C-FNRW	WWD	176
C-FOIL	**WWD**	**201**
C-FOIL	WWD	336
C-FONX	**20**	**225/472**
C-FOPC	125	25016
C-FOPC	400A	RK-70
C-FOSK	601	5114
C-FOSM	**500**	**343**
C-FPAW	D1A	A006SA
C-FPCP	**125**	**258095**
C-FPEL	**550**	**044**
C-FPIY	601	5125
C-FPOX	601	5128
C-FPPN	125	25280
C-FPQG	125	25036
C-FQCY	650	0087
C-FQNS	125	25152
C-FQYT	601	3049
C-FRBC	STR	5160
C-FREE	100	224
C-FRGV	601	5142
C-FRHL	500	343
C-FRJX	601	5147
C-FRJZ	**AST**	**087**
C-FRNR	24D	321
C-FROC	G2	134
C-FROX	25C	070
C-FROY	**WWD**	**429**
C-FRPP	125	258121
C-FRQA	601	5146
(C-FRST)	600	1059
C-FRVE	525	0062
C-FSBR	G4	1032
C-FSCI	**125**	**258105**
C-FSCL	50	97
C-FSDH	125	25192
C-FSEN	125	25027
C-FSIM	125	25039
C-FSIP	600	1048
C-FSJR	**604**	**5413**
C-FSKC	**500**	**018**
C-FSUA	WWD	17
C-FSUN	500	292
C-FSXG	600	1043
C-FSXH	601	5156

C-FSYK	601	5158
C-FTAM	125	25108
C-FTAM	550	398
C-FTBZ	**604**	**5991**
C-FTEC	125	25232
C-FTEN	**10**	**45**
C-FTIE	601	5041
C-FTIL	**550**	**299**
C-FTLA	125	258015
C-FTNE	601	5162
C-FTNN	601	5159
C-FTOH	601	5165
C-FTOM	**550**	**321**
C-FTUT	**20**	**21**
C-FTXT	25	057
C-FUND	**601**	**5172**
C-FURG	**601**	**3063**
C-FVUC	604	5301
C-FVZC	601	5182
C-FWCE	125	257206
C-FWCE	**125**	**258163**
C-FWEC	WWD	115
C-FWGE	601	5178
C-FWOS	125	25159
C-FWRA	20	110
C-FWRN	WWD	98
C-FWSC	900	75
C-FWWW	550	178
C-FXCK	601	5189
C-FXHE	604	5304
C-FXIP	601	5194
C-FXKE	604	5303
C-FXUQ	604	5307
C-FXZS	604	5309
C-FYAG	G3	310
C-FYMM	**560**	**0314**
C-FYPB	20	254
C-FYXC	604	5317
C-FYYH	604	5318
C-FZDY	604	5321
C-FZEI	**WWD**	**441**
C-FZHT	24B	217
C-FZHU	25C	070
C-FZQP	**35A**	**168**
C-FZRR	604	5332
C-FZVN	604	5335
C-GAAA	**125**	**257179**
C-GAAA	501	549
C-GAAA	501	677
C-GABX	**125**	**257047**
C-GAGP	WWD	260
C-GAGU	**125**	**258181**
C-GAJS	**35A**	**380**
C-GAMW	551	051
(C-GANE)	G2	162
C-GAPC	**560**	**0033**
C-GAPD	550	691
C-GAPD	560	0165
C-GAPT	550	216
C-GAPT	**650**	**0195**
C-GAPV	**550**	**691**
C-GATU	STR	5143
C-GAUK	604	5343
C-GAWH	**125**	**258087**
C-GAZU	**50**	**228**
C-GAZU	STR	5070/52
C-GAZU	STR	5083/49
C-GAZU	STR	5222
C-GBBB	**G3**	**368**
C-GBCA	550	590
C-GBCB	550	060
C-GBCC	600	1005
C-GBCE	551	591
C-GBCF	550	564
C-GBCK	500	204
C-GBDH	600	1005
C-GBDK	604	5347
C-GBDX	STR	5219
C-GBEY	600	1008
C-GBFA	35A	248
C-GBFL	20	239
C-GBFP	**25B**	**167**
C-GBFY	600	1009
C-GBHS	600	1011
C-GBHZ	600	1013
C-GBJA	601	5038
C-GBJA	601	5082
C-GBJA	601	5111
C-GBJA	601	5151
C-GBJA	604	5302
C-GBJA	604	5339
C-GBJA	**604**	**5341**
C-GBKB	**600**	**1045**
C-GBKC	600	1007
C-GBKE	600	1012
C-GBKE	604	5352
C-GBLF	35A	091
C-GBLL	600	1014
C-GBLL-X	600	1014
C-GBLN	600	1015
C-GBLX	601	3010
C-GBNE	**500**	**461**
(C-GBNS)	125	256047
C-GBNS	125	256051
C-GBOQ	600	1036
C-GBOT	**25B**	**090**
C-GBPX	600	1017
C-GBQC	25B	179
C-GBRM	125	257093
C-GBRQ	604	5358
C-GBRW	36	001
C-GBSZ	600	1047
C-GBTB	501	525
C-GBTK	600	1057
C-GBTT	600	1062
C-GBUB	600	1064
C-GBUU-X	601	3001
C-GBVE	600	1065
C-GBWA	24D	261
C-GBWB	24	168
C-GBWD	36	012
C-GBWL	35	049
C-GBXH	601	3002
C-GBXW	601	3018
C-GBYC	601	3011
C-GBZE	600	1067
C-GBZK	600	1077
C-GBZQ	601	3047
C-GCCZ	604	5367
C-GCEO	125	25285
C-GCFB	G2	28
C-GCFG	**601**	**3022**
C-GCFI	**601**	**3020**
C-GCFP	650	0145
C-GCGR-X	600	1001
C-GCGS	**125**	**258123**
C-GCGS-X	600	1002
C-GCGT	**600**	**1003/3991**
C-GCGT-X	600	1003/3991
C-GCGY	700	9006
C-GCGY	**700**	**9056**
C-GCIB	**125**	**258048**
C-GCIB	600	1010
C-GCJD	25B	096
C-GCJD	35	055
C-GCJN	**550**	**086**
C-GCLQ	**500**	**348**
C-GCMP	45	019
C-GCQB	604	5369
C-GCRP	125	258124
C-GCRW	700	9007
C-GCSN	600	1006
C-GCTB	601	3031
C-GCTD	500	056
C-GCUL	**550**	**135**
C-GCUN	601	3035
C-GCUP	601	3036
C-GCUR	601	3037
C-GCUT	601	3038
C-GCUW	560	0053
C-GCVQ	600	1009
C-GCVZ	604	5373
C-GCZU	600	1030
C-GDAO	125	257099
C-GDBG	700	9008
C-GDBX	601	3046
C-GDBZ	604	5378
C-GDCC	S60	306-51
C-GDCO	10	73
C-GDCO	50	185
C-GDCQ	601	3052
C-GDDB	23	041
C-GDDC	551	267
C-GDDM	501	468
C-GDDP	601	5001
C-GDDR	**600**	**1048**
C-GDEQ	601	5002
C-GDFA	604	5380
C-GDGO	700	9009
C-GDGQ	700	9010
C-GDGW	700	9011
C-GDGY	700	9012
C-GDHP	601	5003
C-GDHW	125	256028
C-GDJH	**35A**	**353**
C-GDJW	WWD	111
C-GDKO	601	5004
C-GDKS	24B	217
C-GDLH	604	5384
C-GDLR	**550**	**078**
C-GDMF	**550**	**125**
C-GDOC	WWD	166
C-GDPB	G2	232
C-GDPD	550	066
(C-GDPE)	550	124
(C-GDPE)	550	188
C-GDPF	550	124
C-GDPF	**601**	**5145**
C-GDSH	**550**	**0909**
C-GDSH	560	0492
C-GDUC	WWD	357
C-GDUP	125	256020
C-GDVM	604	5388
C-GDWN	500	029
C-GDWS	500	303
C-GDXU	700	9013
C-GDXV	700	9014
C-GDXX	700	9015
C-GDZE	604	5392
C-GEAQ	20	28
C-GEEN	24	087
C-GEGM	604	5380
C-GEGX	700	9005
C-GEIM	700	9016
C-GEIR	700	9017
C-GENA	601	5006
C-GENJ	500	196
C-GEPF	**125**	**257149**
C-GERC	S550	0037
C-GERL	S550	0056
C-GESO	WWD	298
C-GESR	**601**	**3003**
C-GESZ	500	022
C-GETU	604	5409
C-GEVF	501	460
C-GEVO	**700**	**9018**
C-GEVU	700	9019
C-GEVV	700	9020
C-GEWV	**700**	**9026**
C-GEYY	700	9021
C-GEYZ	700	9022
C-GEZD	700	9023
C-GEZF	700	9024
C-GEZJ	**700**	**9025**
C-GEZX	**700**	**9027**
C-GEZY	**700**	**9028**
C-GEZZ	**700**	**9029**
C-GFAD	**700**	**9030**
C-GFAE	700	9031
C-GFAK	700	9032
C-GFAN	**700**	**9033**
C-GFAN	WWD	218
C-GFAO	WWD	250
C-GFAP	700	9034
C-GFAQ	700	9035
C-GFAT	700	9036
C-GFCD	125	25234
(C-GFCD)	600	1059
C-GFCI	550	733
C-GFCL	125	25107
C-GFCL	**560**	**0346**
C-GFCS	10	37
C-GFEE	**501**	**566**
C-GFEH	35A	170
C-GFJB	24D	260
C-GFJQ	700	9037
C-GFJR	**700**	**9038**
C-GFJS	700	9039
C-GFJT	700	9040
C-GFKT	700	9041
C-GFKV	700	9042
C-GFKW	700	9043
C-GFKX	700	9044
C-GFKY	**700**	**9045**
C-GFLS	700	9046
C-GFLU	**700**	**9047**
C-GFLW	700	9048
C-GFLX	700	9049
C-GFLZ	**700**	**9050**
C-GFOE	604	5430
C-GFRK	35A	093
C-GFWI	**700**	**9051**
C-GFWP	**700**	**9052**
C-GFWX	**700**	**9053**
C-GFWY	**700**	**9054**
C-GFWZ	**700**	**9055**
C-GGFP	**50**	**227**
C-GGFW	550	318
C-GGIR	**700**	**9057**
C-GGJA	**700**	**9058**
C-GGJF	**700**	**9059**
C-GGJH	**700**	**9060**
C-GGJJ	**700**	**9061**
C-GGJR	**700**	**9062**
C-GGJS	**700**	**9063**
C-GGJU	**700**	**9064**
C-GGKA	**700**	**9065**
C-GGKC	**700**	**9066**
C-GGPF	36A	026
C-GGPM	**G3**	**307**
C-GGSP	551	177
C-GGYV	35	040
C-GHBQ	WWD	220
C-GHCY	**31A**	**107**
C-GHDP	24D	257
C-GHEC	500	161
C-GHEC	**560**	**0084**
C-GHGK	650	0062
C-GHKY	550	398
C-GHKY	60	043
C-GHKY	**604**	**5343**
C-GHKY	650	0023
C-GHLM	650	0017
C-GHMH	25	011
C-GHOL	550	013
C-GHOM	550	198
C-GHOO	35	057
C-GHOO	650	0014
C-GHOS	501	375
C-GHPP	**525**	**0220**
C-GHPR	WWD	83
C-GHRX	501	432
C-GHWW	**550**	**178**
C-GHYD	551	079
C-GIAC	500	076
C-GIAD	500	185
C-GINT	**525**	**0062**
C-GIOH	**601**	**5034**
C-GIRE	**35**	**004**
C-GIWD	35A	407
C-GIWD	**750**	**0041**
C-GIWO	**35A**	**407**
C-GJAP	500	080
C-GJAP	550	060
C-GJAP	550	373
C-GJBJ	**125**	**257198**
C-GJCD	WWD	176
C-GJCM	125	256040
C-GJEM	500	011
C-GJLK	WWD	278
C-GJLL	WWD	171
C-GJLQ	500	058
C-GJPG	600	1043
C-GJPG	**601**	**3017**
C-GJTX	500	254
C-GKCC	125	256044

C-GKCI	125	257066
C-GKCO	125	25170
C-GKFS	WWD	62
C-GKFT	WWD	5
C-GKHA	**20**	**19**
C-GKHR	**125**	**256021**
C-GKLB	125	258105
C-GKPM	**125**	**257049**
C-GKRL	125	25111
C-GKRL	125	258007
C-GKRL	G3	317
C-GKRS	125	257087
C-GKRS	STR	5011/1
C-GKTM	**55**	**076**
C-GLAL	36A	019
C-GLBD	125	256032
C-GLBT	25B	182
C-GLCE	**550**	**0906**
C-GLCR	S550	0140
C-GLEO	125	25080
C-GLFI	125	25028
C-GLIG	D1A	A076SA
C-GLIG	**D1A**	**A090SA**
C-GLIM	**560**	**0430**
C-GLJQ	**35A**	**660**
C-GLMK	36A	019
C-GLMK	**551**	**110**
(C-GLRE)	25B	114
C-GLRJ	31A	043
C-GLRL	60	002
C-GLRS	60	002
C-GLRS	**60**	**062**
C-GLRS	60	077
C-GLTG	550	403
C-GLWR	600	1018
C-GLWR	601	3051
C-GLWR	601	5005
C-GLWR	601	5025
C-GLWR	601	5057
C-GLWR	601	5078
C-GLWR	601	5102
C-GLWR	601	5123
C-GLWR	601	5135
C-GLWR	601	5147
C-GLWR	601	5159
C-GLWR	601	5183
C-GLWR	604	5311
C-GLWR	604	5333
C-GLWR	604	5348
C-GLWR	604	5359
C-GLWR	604	5372
C-GLWR	604	5396
C-GLWR	604	5407
C-GLWR	604	5420
C-GLWR	604	5431
C-GLWR	604	5442
C-GLWT	600	1019
C-GLWT	601	3052
C-GLWT	601	5006
C-GLWT	601	5019
C-GLWT	601	5026
C-GLWT	601	5041
C-GLWT	601	5071
C-GLWT	601	5084
C-GLWT	601	5094
C-GLWT	601	5120
C-GLWT	601	5142
C-GLWT	601	5166
C-GLWT	601	5190
C-GLWT	604	5319
C-GLWT	604	5343
C-GLWT	604	5391
C-GLWT	604	5415
C-GLWT	604	5443
C-GLWV	600	1020
C-GLWV	600	1042
C-GLWV	600	1062
C-GLWV	600	1079
C-GLWV	601	3010
C-GLWV	601	3016
C-GLWV	601	3025
C-GLWV	601	3041
C-GLWV	601	3053
C-GLWV	601	5007
C-GLWV	601	5018
C-GLWV	601	5027
C-GLWV	601	5040
C-GLWV	601	5059
C-GLWV	601	5079
C-GLWV	601	5103
C-GLWV	601	5131
C-GLWV	601	5155
C-GLWV	601	5179
C-GLWV	604	5329
C-GLWV	604	5355
C-GLWV	604	5379
C-GLWV	604	5403
C-GLWV	604	5427
C-GLWV	604	5444
C-GLWX	600	1021
C-GLWX	600	1043
C-GLWX	600	1063
C-GLWX	600	1080
C-GLWX	601	3011
C-GLWX	601	3017
C-GLWX	601	3026
C-GLWX	601	3042
C-GLWX	601	3054
C-GLWX	601	5008
C-GLWX	601	5017
C-GLWX	601	5028
C-GLWX	601	5039
C-GLWX	601	5062
C-GLWX	601	5082
C-GLWX	601	5106
C-GLWX	601	5128
C-GLWX	601	5152
C-GLWX	601	5176
C-GLWX	604	5306
C-GLWX	604	5325
C-GLWX	604	5352
C-GLWX	604	5400
C-GLWX	604	5424
C-GLWX	604	5445
C-GLWZ	600	1022
C-GLWZ	600	1044
C-GLWZ	600	1064
C-GLWZ	600	1081
C-GLWZ	601	3018
C-GLWZ	601	3027
C-GLWZ	601	3043
C-GLWZ	601	3055
C-GLWZ	601	5009
C-GLWZ	601	5029
C-GLWZ	601	5058
C-GLWZ	601	5107
C-GLWZ	601	5125
C-GLWZ	601	5137
C-GLWZ	601	5161
C-GLWZ	604	5314
C-GLWZ	604	5338
C-GLWZ	604	5362
C-GLWZ	604	5386
C-GLWZ	604	5410
C-GLWZ	604	5435
C-GLWZ	604	5446
C-GLXB	600	1023
C-GLXB	600	1045
C-GLXB	600	1065
C-GLXB	600	1082
C-GLXB	601	3012
C-GLXB	601	3019
C-GLXB	601	3028
C-GLXB	601	3037
C-GLXB	601	3056
C-GLXB	601	5010
C-GLXB	601	5030
C-GLXB	601	5054
C-GLXB	601	5076
C-GLXB	601	5100
C-GLXB	601	5127
C-GLXB	601	5151
C-GLXB	601	5175
C-GLXB	604	5305
C-GLXB	604	5324
C-GLXB	604	5335
C-GLXB	604	5351
C-GLXB	604	5375
C-GLXB	604	5399
C-GLXB	604	5423
C-GLXB	604	5441
C-GLXD	600	1024
C-GLXD	600	1046
C-GLXD	600	1066
C-GLXD	600	1083
C-GLXD	601	3013
C-GLXD	601	3029
C-GLXD	601	3044
C-GLXD	601	3057
C-GLXD	601	5011
C-GLXD	601	5031
C-GLXD	601	5047
C-GLXD	601	5065
C-GLXD	601	5085
C-GLXD	601	5108
C-GLXD	601	5124
C-GLXD	601	5148
C-GLXD	601	5172
C-GLXD	604	5302
C-GLXD	604	5313
C-GLXD	604	5337
C-GLXD	604	5361
C-GLXD	604	5385
C-GLXD	604	5433
C-GLXF	600	1025
C-GLXF	601	5032
C-GLXF	601	5049
C-GLXF	601	5067
C-GLXF	601	5090
C-GLXF	601	5112
C-GLXF	601	5138
C-GLXF	601	5162
C-GLXF	604	5315
C-GLXF	604	5339
C-GLXF	604	5363
C-GLXF	604	5387
C-GLXF	604	5411
C-GLXF	604	5436
C-GLXH	600	1026
C-GLXH	600	1047
C-GLXH	600	1067
C-GLXH	600	1084
C-GLXH	601	3014
C-GLXH	601	3030
C-GLXH	601	3045
C-GLXH	601	5015
C-GLXH	601	5033
C-GLXH	601	5055
C-GLXH	601	5074
C-GLXH	601	5088
C-GLXH	601	5098
C-GLXH	601	5111
C-GLXH	601	5129
C-GLXH	601	5153
C-GLXH	601	5177
C-GLXH	604	5307
C-GLXH	604	5328
C-GLXH	604	5353
C-GLXH	604	5377
C-GLXH	604	5401
C-GLXH	604	5425
C-GLXH	604	5450
C-GLXK	600	1027
C-GLXK	600	1048
C-GLXK	600	1068
C-GLXK	600	1076
C-GLXK	601	3004
C-GLXK	601	3031
C-GLXK	601	3046
C-GLXK	601	5034
C-GLXK	601	5050
C-GLXK	601	5068
C-GLXK	601	5097
C-GLXK	601	5118
C-GLXK	601	5139
C-GLXK	601	5163
C-GLXK	601	5187
C-GLXK	604	5316
C-GLXK	604	5340
C-GLXK	604	5364
C-GLXK	604	5388
C-GLXK	604	5412
C-GLXK	604	5437
C-GLXK	604	5451
C-GLXM	600	1028
C-GLXM	600	1049
C-GLXM	600	1069
C-GLXM	600	1077
C-GLXM	601	3015
C-GLXM	601	3032
C-GLXM	601	3047
C-GLXM	601	5051
C-GLXM	601	5069
C-GLXM	601	5091
C-GLXM	601	5113
C-GLXM	601	5140
C-GLXM	601	5164
C-GLXM	601	5188
C-GLXM	604	5341
C-GLXM	604	5365
C-GLXM	604	5389
C-GLXM	604	5413
C-GLXM	604	5432
C-GLXM	604	5438
C-GLXM	604	5452
C-GLXO	600	1029
C-GLXO	600	1050
C-GLXO	600	1070
C-GLXO	600	1075
C-GLXO	601	3020
C-GLXO	601	3048
C-GLXO	601	5052
C-GLXO	601	5070
C-GLXO	601	5119
C-GLXO	601	5141
C-GLXO	601	5165
C-GLXO	604	5318
C-GLXO	604	5342
C-GLXO	604	5366
C-GLXO	604	5390
C-GLXO	604	5414
C-GLXO	604	5453
C-GLXQ	600	1030
C-GLXQ	600	1051
C-GLXQ	600	1071
C-GLXQ	600	1085
C-GLXQ	601	3021
C-GLXQ	601	3033
C-GLXQ	601	3049
C-GLXQ	601	3066
C-GLXQ	601	5016
C-GLXQ	601	5038
C-GLXQ	601	5056
C-GLXQ	601	5077
C-GLXQ	601	5092
C-GLXQ	601	5101
C-GLXQ	601	5130
C-GLXQ	601	5154
C-GLXQ	601	5178
C-GLXQ	604	5320
C-GLXQ	604	5344
C-GLXQ	604	5368
C-GLXQ	604	5392
C-GLXQ	604	5416
C-GLXQ	604	5439
C-GLXS	600	1031
C-GLXS	600	1052
C-GLXS	600	1086
C-GLXS	601	3022
C-GLXS	601	3050
C-GLXS	601	5045
C-GLXS	601	5063
C-GLXS	601	5086
C-GLXS	601	5109
C-GLXS	601	5122
C-GLXS	601	5134
C-GLXS	601	5158
C-GLXS	604	5310
C-GLXS	604	5332
C-GLXS	604	5346
C-GLXS	604	5358
C-GLXS	604	5370
C-GLXS	604	5382
C-GLXS	604	5394
C-GLXS	604	5406
C-GLXS	604	5418

C-GLXS	604	5430
C-GLXU	600	1032
C-GLXU	600	1057
C-GLXU	601	3003
C-GLXU	601	3034
C-GLXU	601	3058
C-GLXU	601	5012
C-GLXU	601	5035
C-GLXU	601	5053
C-GLXU	601	5075
C-GLXU	601	5099
C-GLXU	601	5110
C-GLXU	601	5126
C-GLXU	601	5150
C-GLXU	601	5174
C-GLXU	604	5304
C-GLXU	604	5323
C-GLXU	604	5334
C-GLXU	604	5350
C-GLXU	604	5374
C-GLXU	604	5398
C-GLXU	604	5422
C-GLXU	604	5440
C-GLXW	600	1033
C-GLXW	600	1058
C-GLXW	600	1072
C-GLXW	601	3035
C-GLXW	601	3059
C-GLXW	601	5013
C-GLXW	601	5036
C-GLXW	601	5046
C-GLXW	601	5064
C-GLXW	601	5087
C-GLXW	601	5116
C-GLXW	601	5136
C-GLXW	601	5146
C-GLXW	601	5160
C-GLXW	601	5171
C-GLXW	601	5184
C-GLXW	604	5312
C-GLXW	604	5336
C-GLXW	604	5347
C-GLXW	604	5360
C-GLXW	604	5376
C-GLXW	604	5384
C-GLXW	604	5408
C-GLXY	600	1034
C-GLXY	600	1059
C-GLXY	600	1073
C-GLXY	601	3006
C-GLXY	601	3023
C-GLXY	601	3036
C-GLXY	601	3060
C-GLXY	601	5014
C-GLXY	601	5037
C-GLXY	601	5048
C-GLXY	601	5066
C-GLXY	601	5089
C-GLXY	601	5117
C-GLXY	601	5149
C-GLXY	601	5173
C-GLXY	604	5303
C-GLXY	604	5322
C-GLXY	604	5349
C-GLXY	604	5397
C-GLXY	604	5421
C-GLXY	604	5434
C-GLYA	600	1035
C-GLYA	600	1053
C-GLYA	601	3024
C-GLYA	601	3038
C-GLYA	601	3065
C-GLYA	601	5020
C-GLYA	601	5042
C-GLYA	601	5083
C-GLYA	601	5093
C-GLYA	601	5114
C-GLYA	601	5143
C-GLYA	601	5167
C-GLYA	601	5191
C-GLYA	604	5321
C-GLYA	604	5345
C-GLYA	604	5393
C-GLYA	604	5417
C-GLYA	604	5991
C-GLYC	600	1036
C-GLYC	600	1054
C-GLYC	601	3064
C-GLYC	601	5021
C-GLYC	601	5043
C-GLYC	601	5072
C-GLYC	601	5095
C-GLYC	601	5115
C-GLYC	601	5144
C-GLYC	601	5168
C-GLYC	601	5192
C-GLYC	604	5326
C-GLYC	604	5354
C-GLYC	604	5378
C-GLYC	604	5402
C-GLYC	604	5426
C-GLYE	600	1037
C-GLYE	600	1055
C-GLYE	601	3007
C-GLYH	600	1038
C-GLYH	600	1056
C-GLYH	601	3039
C-GLYH	601	3063
C-GLYH	601	5024
C-GLYH	601	5061
C-GLYH	601	5081
C-GLYH	601	5105
C-GLYH	601	5133
C-GLYH	601	5157
C-GLYH	601	5181
C-GLYH	604	5309
C-GLYH	604	5331
C-GLYH	604	5357
C-GLYH	604	5381
C-GLYH	604	5405
C-GLYH	604	5429
C-GLYK	600	1039
C-GLYK	600	1060
C-GLYK	600	1074
C-GLYK	601	3008
C-GLYK	601	3040
C-GLYK	601	3062
C-GLYK	601	5022
C-GLYK	601	5044
C-GLYK	601	5073
C-GLYK	601	5096
C-GLYK	601	5121
C-GLYK	601	5145
C-GLYK	601	5169
C-GLYK	601	5193
C-GLYK	604	5327
C-GLYK	604	5371
C-GLYK	604	5383
C-GLYK	604	5395
C-GLYK	604	5419
C-GLYM	600	1040
C-GLYO	600	1041
C-GLYO	600	1061
C-GLYO	600	1078
C-GLYO	601	3009
C-GLYO	601	3061
C-GLYO	601	5023
C-GLYO	601	5060
C-GLYO	601	5080
C-GLYO	601	5104
C-GLYO	601	5132
C-GLYO	601	5156
C-GLYO	601	5180
C-GLYO	604	5308
C-GLYO	604	5330
C-GLYO	604	5356
C-GLYO	604	5380
C-GLYO	604	5404
C-GLYO	604	5428
C-GMAJ	**500**	**247**
C-GMAP	25	026
C-GMAT	500	231
C-GMAV	S550	0067
C-GMBA	125	257206
C-GMBH	WWD	286
C-GMEA	125	25137
C-GMGA	35A	346
C-GMGB	**560**	**0390**
C-GMGB	S550	0149
C-GMID	50	229
C-GMII	50	229
C-GMII	**50**	**272**
C-GMII	601	3012
C-GMLC	500	305
C-GMLR	**125**	**258025**
C-GMMA	**35A**	**655**
C-GMMO	500	227
C-GMMY	**35A**	**644**
C-GMOL	125	258163
C-GMPF	WWD	391
C-GMPQ	550	456
C-GMSM	**550**	**603**
C-GMTR	**125**	**258157**
C-GMTT	WWD	288
C-GMTV	S550	0015
C-GNAA	20	128/436
C-GNAZ	**125**	**257030**
C-GNCA	50	203
C-GNND	**125**	**257118**
C-GNND	560	0077
C-GNPT	**35A**	**626**
C-GNSA	35A	171
C-GNSA	**500**	**160**
C-GNTL	20	257
C-GNTM	20	319
C-GNTY	20	330
C-GNTZ	20	256
C-GNWM	**550**	**408**
C-GOCM	500	154
C-GOGM	**125**	**257143**
C-GOGO	600	1022
C-GOIL	500	361
C-GOQG	20	6
"C-GORI"	10	19
C-GOSL	25	040
C-GPAW	550	004
C-GPAW	**560**	**0260**
C-GPCC	125	257057
C-GPCC	601	3039
C-GPCL	24B	224
C-GPCO	500	317
C-GPCS	**55**	**035**
C-GPDB	24B	217
C-GPDH	WWD	82
C-GPDO	35A	168
C-GPDO	**35A**	**673**
C-GPDQ	35A	170
C-GPDQ	**45**	**041**
C-GPDZ	25	063
C-GPEA	650	0101
C-GPFC	35A	092
C-GPFC	**604**	**5310**
C-GPFC	WWD	328
C-GPGD	601	3039
C-GPGD	601	5145
C-GPGD	604	5310
C-GPGD	**604**	**5432**
C-GPGD	STR	5133
C-GPJW	500	104
C-GPLN	**500**	**016**
C-GPOP	**650**	**0042**
C-GPOT	**601**	**5088**
C-GPPS	125	257027
C-GPTC	501	429
C-GPTR	550	083
C-GPUN	35	058
C-GQBQ	**601**	**5051**
C-GQBR	**55**	**105**
C-GQCC	**500**	**066**
C-GQMH	S550	0076
C-GQPA	**604**	**5379**
C-GRBC	601	3041
C-GRCO	25B	095
C-GRDP	**WWD**	**188**
C-GRDR	25B	145
C-GRDS	D1A	A018SA
C-GRDT	10	6
C-GRDX	D1A	A039SA
C-GRFO	**35A**	**100**
C-GRGE	125	258124
C-GRGE	WWD	298
C-GRGE	WWD	353
C-GRGE	**WWD**	**359**
C-GRHC	**550**	**050**
C-GRIO	550	148
C-GRIO	**604**	**5353**
C-GRIS	**10**	**2**
C-GRJC	500	112
C-GRJQ	500	250
(C-GRJZ)	GXY	007
C-GRMJ	**35A**	**664**
C-GRPF	**601**	**5168**
C-GRQA	500	455
C-GRQX	25C	146
C-GRRS	S60	306-78
C-GRSD	**20**	**157**
C-GRSD-X	20	157
C-GRVJ	**31A**	**111**
C-GSAP	**601**	**3034**
C-GSAS	25B	109
C-GSAX	24	129
C-GSBR	G3	307
C-GSCL	125	257030
C-GSCL	200	495
C-GSCR	**200**	**495**
C-GSCR	551	354
C-GSCX	**550**	**381**
C-GSFA	550	057
C-GSIV	24	108
C-GSKA	20	9
C-GSKC	20	29
C-GSKL	**25B**	**179**
C-GSKN	20	65
C-GSKQ	20	40
C-GSKS	20	34
C-GSKV	125	25141
C-GSLK	G2	46
C-GSLL	501	390
C-GSQI	**601**	**5096**
C-GSRN	36A	039
C-GSSS	50	95
C-GSSS	900	78
C-GSSS	**AST**	**080**
C-GSTR	501	647
C-GSTT	125	256021
C-GSUM	501	485
C-GSUN	501	485
C-GSUN	**560**	**0448**
C-GSWP	**55**	**019**
C-GSWS	25D	370
C-GSWS	WWD	259
C-GTAK	**20**	**197**
C-GTBR	551	097
C-GTCB	G2	162
C-GTCI	550	585
C-GTCP	**900**	**29**
C-GTCP	STR	5158
C-GTDE	**35**	**057**
C-GTDN	125	257148
C-GTDO	S550	0080
(C-GTEL)	500	161
C-GTEP	G2	247
C-GTFA	24B	201
C-GTJL	**35A**	**124**
C-GTJT	24	160
C-GTLG	125	257174
C-GTLU	20	262
C-GTNT	125	258038
C-GTNT	200	488
C-GTOR	**125**	**257029**
C-GTPC	125	256025
C-GTPL	50	137
C-GTTS	**125**	**25108**
C-GTVO	**10**	**137**
C-GTWO	G2	140/40
C-GTXV	600	1046
C-GUUU	550	422
C-GVCA	**35**	**043**
C-GVCB	35	012
C-GVER	**500**	**454**
C-GVKL	**500**	**341**
C-GVQR	125	25232
C-GVVA	**35**	**002**
C-GVVB	36A	025
C-GVVT	501	474
C-GWBF	S550	0115

C-GWCJ	550	213
C-GWCR	550	213
C-GWCR	**560**	**0379**
C-GWEI	50	208
C-GWFG	**24D**	**256**
C-GWFM	**125**	**258015**
C-GWKF	**WWD**	**271**
(C-GWPA)	650	0011
C-GWPB	20	92/421
C-GWPV	WWD	105
C-GWRT	600	1016
C-GWSA	20	228/473
C-GWSA	STR	5146
C-GWSH	WWD	165
(C-GWUZ)	25C	084
C-GWVC	500	107
C-GXCO	**560**	**0481**
C-GXFZ	500	032
C-GXKQ	600	1004
C-GXPT	125	25018
C-GXPT	500	096
C-GXYN	125	257114
C-GYCJ	**550**	**561**
C-GYMM	**560**	**0484**
C-GYPH	125	257155
C-GYPH	**125**	**258007**
C-GYPJ	50	162
C-GYYZ	125	257008
C-GZIM	25D	208
C-GZVV	35A	153
C-GZXA	500	252
C-GZZX	125	257161

Chile

CC-CGT	S60	306-33
(CC-CGX)	550	136
CC-CRK	WWD	184
CC-CTC	**S60**	**306-112**
CC-CTE	501	426
CC-CWW	501	558
CC-CWW	**S550**	**0002**
CC-CWZ	**551**	**108**
CC-DAC	**650**	**0233**
CC-DGA	**550**	**657**
CC-ECE	650	0033
CC-ECL	650	0131
CC-ECN	550	146
CC-ECO	35	050
CC-ECP	35	066
CC-LLM	**551**	**481**
CC-PES	200	496
CC-PGL	**650**	**7045**
CC-PVJ	**525**	**0243**
CC-PZM	**500**	**203**

Russia

CCCP-01100	20	55/410

Canada
(see also C-)

CF-AAG	125	25137
CF-ALC	125	25087
CF-ANL	125	25042
CF-AOS	125	25278
CF-ARE	23	070
CF-BAX	500	020
CF-BCJ	24A	100
CF-BCL	500	042
CF-BCM	500	071
CF-BFM	20	40
CF-BLT	S60	306-23
CF-BNK	125	25221
CF-BRL	S40	282-107
CF-CFL	125	25193
CF-CFL	125	25213
CF-CFP	500	125
CF-CPW	500	002
CF-CSS	24B	197
CF-CXY	25C	116
CF-DML	20	14
CF-DOM	125	25018
CF-DSC	125	25086
CF-DTF	STR	5088
CF-DTM	STR	5052
(CF-DTX)	STR	5018
CF-DWW	25	045
CF-ECB	24	112
CF-ENJ	500	122
CF-ESO	20	46
CF-ETN	STR	5021
CF-FNM	G2	52
CF-GWI	20	7
CF-GWI	STR	5106/9
CF-HLL	125	25034
CF-HMV	25	015
CF-HOG	G2	7
CF-HSS	125	256003
CF-IOT	G2	78
CF-IPG	125	25053
CF-IPJ	125	25053
CF-JES	20	236
CF-KAX	25	016
CF-KBI	WWD	81
CF-KCI	125	25137
CF-MAJ	MSP	050
CF-MDB	125	25075
CF-NCG	S40	282-90
CF-NOR	G2	54/36
CF-OPC	125	25016
CF-PQG	125	25036
CF-QNS	125	25152
CF-ROX	25C	070
CF-RWA	125	25016
CF-SBR	G2	9/33
CF-SDA	125	25022
CF-SDH	125	25192
CF-SEN	125	25027
CF-SHZ	125	25095
CF-SIM	125	25039
CF-SRZ	20	11
CF-SUA	WWD	17
CF-TEC	125	25232
CF-TEL	23	054
CF-TXT	25	057
CF-ULG	WWD	6
CF-UYT	24	087
CF-VVX	WWD	76
CF-WDU	HFB	1039
CF-WOA	WWD	21
CF-WOS	125	25159
CF-WRA	20	110
CF-WUL	WWD	9
CF-YPB	20	254

Morocco

CN-ANL	**G2**	**182**
CNA-NM	**EC**	**165/452**
CN-ANN	**20**	**152/446**
CN-ANO	**50**	**12**
CN-ANU	**G3**	**365**
CNA-NV	**560**	**0025**
CNA-NW	**560**	**0039**
CN-MAJ	MSP	050
CN-MBG	20	152/446
CN-MBH	EC	165/452
CN-TCS	**CVT**	**34**
CN-TDE	**CVT**	**5**
CN-TFU	**900**	**105**
CN-TNA	**100**	**212**

Bolivia

CP-2105	501	541
CP-2131	500	083
CP-2259	WWD	95
CP-2263	**WWD**	**58**
CP-2317	**S40**	**282-136**

Portugal

CS-ATD	20	30
CS-ATE	20	94/428
CS-ATF	20	112
CS-ATG	**20**	**264**
CS-AYS	550	615
CS-AYY	**501**	**567**
CS-DBM	**500**	**200**
CS-DCA	500	157
CS-DCE	**S550**	**0007**
CS-DCI	**550**	**066**
CS-DCK	20	297
CS-DCM	**2xx**	**46**
CS-DNA	**S550**	**0032**
CS-DNB	**S550**	**0051**
CS-DNC	**S550**	**0077**
CS-DND	650	0093
(CS-DNE)	650	0149
CS-DNE	**650**	**7093**
CS-DNF	**650**	**7080**
CS-DNG	**650**	**7081**
CS-DNH	**125**	**258193**
CS-DNI	**125**	**258183**
CS-DNJ	**125**	**258399**
CS-DNK	**125**	**258430**
CS-DNL	**125**	**258439**
CS-DNM	**125**	**258422**
CS-DNN	**125**	**258435**
CS-DNP	2xx	109
CS-MAC	**601**	**5178**
(CS-MAI)	125	258366
CS-TMF	50	29
CS-TMJ	**50**	**190**
CS-TMK	**900**	**66**
CS-TMQ	**900**	**175**

Uruguay

CX-BOI	35A	378
CX-CMJ	WWD	251
CX-ECO	**25D**	**229**

Bahamas
(see also VP-B)

C6-BDH	125	256028
C6-BEJ	G2	194
C6-BEN	10	109
C6-BER	50	20
C6-BET	125	257054
C6-BEV	**MSP**	**111**
C6-BEY	125	25051
C6-BFE	G2	194
(C6-BGF)	24D	252
C6-BHD	50	264
C6-BHN	900	9
C6-BPC	125	25016
C6-MED	**125**	**25140**

Mozambique

C9-TAC	125	257175
(C9-TTA)	125	257175

Germany

D-	**550**	**0907**
D-	**650**	**0134**
(D-AAFX)	601	5070
(D-AAMD)	G2	186
D-ACTU	**601**	**5085**
(D-ACVG)	G2	186
D-ADND	**604**	**5403**
D-ADNE	**604**	**5422**
D-AETV	**604**	**5417**
D-AFKG	G2	186
(D-AFLW)	700	9035
D-AGKG	601	5049
D-AJAB	**604**	**5327**
D-ALME	**900**	**101**
D-AMIM	**604**	**5317**
(D-AMTM)	601	5018
D-AOHP	601	5068
(D-ASTS)	604	5375
D-ASTS	**604**	**5378**
D-AUKE	**604**	**5389**
(D-AZPP)	604	5369
D-BABE	STR	5012
(D-BBAD)	50	23
(D-BBAD)	600	1008
D-BBWK	50	23
D-BDWO	50	42
D-BELL	50	222
D-BERT	**50**	**218**
D-BEST	**2xx**	**50**
(D-BETI)	50	267
D-BFAR	**50**	**16**
D-BFFB	50	65
D-BIRD	**2xx**	**54**
D-BIRD	50	16
(D-BJET)	125	259016
D-BJET	600	1005
D-BMTM	600	1029
D-BNTH	50	196
D-BOOK	**50**	**215**
D-BSNA	**600**	**1066**
D-BTEN	**750**	**0085**
D-BUSY	**600**	**1070**
(D-C)	125	258201
D-CAAS	WWD	164
D-CAAT	550	205
D-CACM	650	7039
D-CACP	55	086
(D-CACS)	551	151
D-CADA	125	257007
(D-CADA)	HFB	1073
D-CADB	10	89
(D-CADE)	HFB	1074
(D-CADI)	HFB	1075
(D-CADO)	HFB	1076
(D-CADU)	HFB	1077
D-CAEP	55	059
(D-CAFB)	560	0303
D-CAFI	125	25037
D-CAFO	36	006
(D-CAJC)	10	131
(D-CALA)	HFB	1068
(D-CALE)	HFB	1069
(D-CALI)	HFB	1070
D-CALL	20	138/440
D-CALL	20	392/553
D-CALL	**550**	**0834**
(D-CALM)	20	237/476
(D-CALO)	HFB	1071
(D-CALU)	HFB	1072
D-CAMA	HFB	1064
D-CAMB	125	25157
D-CAMB	35A	174
D-CAME	HFB	1065
(D-CAMO)	HFB	1066
(D-CAMU)	HFB	1067
(D-CANA)	HFB	1079
(D-CANE)	HFB	1080
D-CANI	HFB	1061
D-CANO	HFB	1062
D-CANU	HFB	1063
D-CAPD	35A	179
D-CAPO	**35A**	**159**
D-CARA	HFB	1021
D-CARD	35A	426
D-CARE	35A	341
D-CARE	55	073
D-CARE	HFB	1022
D-CARG	35A	433
D-CARH	35A	444
D-CARI	HFB	1023
D-CARL	**35A**	**387**
D-CARO	35A	325
D-CARO	HFB	1024
D-CARP	55	050
D-CART	35A	354
D-CARU	HFB	1025
D-CARX	55	034
D-CARY	HFB	1026

(D-CASE)	HFB	V2/1002
D-CASH	10	7
D-CASH	550	564
D-CASO	HFB	1027
D-CASU	HFB	1028
D-CASY	HFB	1029
D-CATE	35A	216
D-CATE	HFB	1030
(D-CATI)	HFB	1078
D-CATL	**55**	**051**
D-CATP	650	0121
D-CATY	35A	114
D-CATY	35A	211
D-CAVE	**35A**	**423**
D-CAVI	35A	174
D-CAVW	125	258233
D-CAVW	75A	380-38
D-CAVW	S40	282-76
D-CAWA	550	596
D-CAWU	**560**	**0042**
D-CAYK	650	0187
(D-CAZH)	125	258043
D-CBAD	**60**	**129**
D-CBAE	125	257031
D-CBAG	10	91
D-CBAT	20	108/430
D-CBAT	550	299
D-CBAT	550	562
D-CBAY	WWD	202
D-CBBA	WWD	294
D-CBBB	WWD	296
D-CBBC	WWD	297
D-CBBD	WWD	310
D-CBBE	WWD	154
D-CBBT	20	162/451
D-CBEL	550	468
D-CBEN	**560**	**0282**
D-CBIG	560	0124
D-CBMB	10	61
D-CBMV	125	258345
D-CBMW	125	258155
D-CBMW	**125**	**258345**
D-CBNA	**20**	**63/411**
D-CBPD	25B	091
D-CBPL	**650**	**0149**
D-CBRD	36	013
D-CBRK	35	026
D-CBUR	10	98
D-CBUS	S550	0027
D-CBVW	125	25231
D-CBVW	125	258235
D-CBVW	75A	380-60
D-CBWW	**125**	**259028**
D-CCAA	**35A**	**315**
D-CCAB	**550**	**0827**
(D-CCAC)	36	004
D-CCAD	35A	263
D-CCAP	35A	144
D-CCAR	35A	179
D-CCAR	35A	200
D-CCAT	24D	254
D-CCAT	25B	079
D-CCAT	**AST**	**059**
D-CCAX	35A	284
D-CCAY	35A	112
(D-CCBT)	AST	080
D-CCCA	**35A**	**160**
D-CCCB	**35A**	**663**
D-CCCF	**550**	**205**
(D-CCCH)	HFB	1060
D-CCDB	20	381/548
(D-CCEX)	125	256015
D-CCGN	**55**	**017**
D-CCHB	**35A**	**089**
D-CCHS	35A	122
(D-CCHS)	55	013
D-CCHS	55	049
D-CCKV	31A	046
D-CCMB	20	377/548
(D-CCNA)	20	147/444
D-CCON	**55ER**	**098**
D-CCPD	36	004
D-CCVW	125	258237
D-CCVW	75A	380-45
(D-CCVW)	HFB	1080
D-CCWK	25B	076
(D-CDAS)	20	108/430
D-CDAX	35A	135
D-CDBW	**560**	**5073**
D-CDDD	24B	201
D-CDEN	**31A**	**049**
D-CDFA	36	006
D-CDHS	35	026
D-CDHS	35A	311
D-CDNY	**60**	**160**
D-CDNZ	**60**	**161**
D-CDPD	25B	177
D-CDRB	D1A	A053SA
D-CDUW	**560**	**0099**
(D-CDVW)	HFB	1080
D-CDWN	**35A**	**175**
D-CEAS	WWD	55
(D-CEDL)	HFB	1061
(D-CEFL)	35A	284
D-CEIS	**400A**	**RK-10**
D-CELA	36	002
D-CELL	20	201/469
D-CENT	10	89
D-CEPD	25D	274
D-CERA	HFB	1031
D-CERE	HFB	1032
D-CERI	HFB	1033
D-CERO	HFB	1034
D-CERU	HFB	1035
D-CESA	HFB	1036
D-CESE	HFB	1037
D-CESH	**45**	**017**
D-CESI	HFB	1038
D-CESO	HFB	1039
D-CESU	HFB	1040
D-CETV	**60**	**148**
"D-CEUU"	20	201/469
D-CEVW	125	258067
D-CEVW	S60	306-44
D-CEWR	**45**	**013**
(D-CEWR)	55	013
D-CEWR	560	0192
D-CFAI	20	335
D-CFAI	S550	0134
D-CFAN	**125**	**258094**
D-CFCF	125	25248
D-CFCF	**35A**	**413**
D-CFFB	**60**	**107**
D-CFIS	AST	045
(D-CFKG)	125	25005
D-CFLY	**560**	**0145**
D-CFOX	36A	031
D-CFOX	**560**	**0277**
D-CFPD	24E	345
D-CFRC	125	258036
D-CFSK	125	256053
D-CFTG	**35A**	**204**
D-CFUX	**55**	**061**
D-CFVG	24B	223
(D-CFVG)	35A	121
D-CFVW	125	258073
D-CGAS	**550**	**443**
D-CGFA	**35A**	**179**
D-CGFB	**35A**	**268**
D-CGFC	**35A**	**331**
D-CGFD	**35A**	**139**
D-CGFE	**36A**	**062**
D-CGFF	**36A**	**063**
D-CGFV	D1A	A051SA
D-CGGG	**31A**	**042**
D-CGIN	55	090
D-CGJH	20	138/440
D-CGLS	WWD	161
D-CGPD	**35A**	**202**
D-CGRC	**35A**	**223**
D-CGSO	20	306/512
D-CGVW	125	258076
D-CHAL	**WWD**	**207**
D-CHAN	**550**	**0874**
(D-CHAS)	WWD	55
D-CHBL	**WWD**	**226**
(D-CHBM)	25D	260
(D-CHCH)	20	237/476
D-CHCL	**WWD**	**277**
D-CHDE	**560**	**0031**
D-CHDL	**WWD**	**199**
D-CHEF	125	258038
(D-CHEF)	20	274
D-CHEF	25D	260
D-CHER	35A	119
D-CHFB	HFB	V1/1001
D-CHHS	560	0177
D-CHIC	25D	347
D-CHIC	75A	380-42
D-CHJH	S550	0131
D-CHOP	550	609
D-CHPD	**35A**	**309**
(D-CHRC)	35A	096
D-CHSW	**400A**	**RK-84**
D-CHTH	125	25143
D-CHVB	550	629
D-CHZF	**550**	**0866**
D-CIAO	S550	0135
(D-CIBM)	20	234/475
D-CIEL	10	155
D-CIFA	550	069
D-CIFA	**550**	**133**
D-CIGM	400A	RK-103
D-CIII	**560**	**5037**
D-CILL	20	13
D-CILL	550	660
D-CILY	55	026
(D-CINA)	HFB	1080
D-CION	55	015
D-CIRA	HFB	1041
D-CIRE	HFB	1042
D-CIRI	HFB	1043
D-CIRO	HFB	1044
D-CIRS	35A	091
D-CIRU	HFB	1045
D-CISA	HFB	1046
D-CISE	HFB	1047
D-CISI	HFB	1048
D-CISO	HFB	1049
D-CISU	HFB	1050
D-CITA	35A	070
(D-CITO)	25B	118
D-CITO	HFB	1027
D-CITY	20	237/476
D-CITY	**35A**	**177**
(D-CJAD)	24	128
D-CJET	125	256027
D-CJET	24B	189
D-CJJJ	550	052
D-CJPG	**35A**	**108**
D-CKCF	125	25105
D-CKIM	125	257094
D-CKKK	**60**	**144**
(D-CKOW)	125	25105
D-CLAN	35A	397
D-CLAN	75A	380-12
D-CLBA	**400A**	**RK-25**
D-CLBR	**20**	**52**
D-CLEO	**560**	**0159**
D-CLIP	55	004
D-CLIP	55	029
D-CLLL	10	188
D-CLMA	HFB	1057
D-CLOU	HFB	V2/1002
D-CLOU	S550	0121
(D-CLSG)	400A	RK-10
(D-CLUB)	125	257112
D-CLUB	45	044
D-CLUB	55	034
D-CLUB	55	092
D-CLUB	75A	380-19
D-CLUE	**650**	**0174**
D-CLVW	125	257100
D-CMAD	**55C**	**143**
D-CMAN	10	71
D-CMAR	36	002
D-CMAX	20	158/449
D-CMEI	**560**	**0117**
D-CMET	**20**	**329/523**
D-CMIC	**560**	**5021**
D-CMIR	125	258110
D-CMJS	550	660
D-CMMM	**24D**	**328**
D-CMTM	55	042
D-CMVW	125	257112
D-CNCA	S550	0137
D-CNCB	S550	0144
D-CNCI	550	414
D-CNCI	**560**	**0061**
D-CNCJ	**650**	**7102**
D-CNCP	550	116
D-CNCP	560	0069
D-CNEX	D1A	A070SA
D-COCO	35A	108
D-COCO	35A	466
D-COFG	20	175
D-COGA	24B	223
D-COKE	**35A**	**447**
D-COLL	20	234/475
D-COLO	20	18
D-COMA	125	25005
D-COME	10	67
D-COME	125	25025
D-COMF	20	184/462
D-COMI	125	25058
D-COMM	20	302/510
D-COMM	**45**	**012**
D-CONA	24B	189
D-CONA	35A	114
D-CONE	25	050
D-CONI	35	007
D-CONO	35	055
D-CONO	35A	417
D-CONU	20	383/550
D-CONY	35A	195
D-COOL	24D	261
D-COOL	**55**	**052**
D-CORA	35	018
D-CORA	35A	381
D-CORE	HFB	1051
D-CORF	20	281/498
D-CORI	HFB	1052
D-CORO	HFB	1053
(D-CORT)	20	147/444
D-CORU	HFB	1054
D-CORY	HFB	1055
D-COSA	HFB	1056
D-COSE	HFB	1057
D-COSI	HFB	1058
D-COSO	HFB	1059
D-COSU	HFB	1060
D-COSY	35A	204
D-COSY	35A	415
D-COTT	20	314/516
(D-COUP)	S60	306-17
D-COWS	**60**	**170**
D-CPAS	**125**	**258130**
D-CRAN	45	043
D-CREW	55	011
D-CRHR	**650**	**0142**
D-CRIS	**AST**	**107**
(D-CRRR)	650	0044
D-CSAP	**31A**	**057**
D-CSFD	**S550**	**0148**
D-CSIX	**60**	**120**
D-CSRB	125	258226
D-CSRI	125	258212
D-CTAN	**125**	**258450**
D-CTAN	560	0150
(D-CUNA)	HFB	1061
D-CURE	35A	652
(D-CURE)	HFB	1062
(D-CURI)	HFB	1063
(D-CURO)	HFB	1064
(D-CURU)	HFB	1065
(D-CURY)	HFB	1066
(D-CUSA)	HFB	1067
(D-CUSE)	HFB	1068
(D-CUSI)	HFB	1069
(D-CUSO)	HFB	1070
(D-CUSU)	HFB	1071
(D-CUSY)	HFB	1072
D-CUTE	55	013
(D-CVAU)	550	433
D-CVGP	31A	036
D-CVHA	**560**	**0275**

D-CVHB 560 5056
D-CVIP 55 035
D-CVIP 55 109
D-CWAY 55ER 107
D-CWBW 125 258213
(D-CWER) 45 010
(D-CWER) 45 017
D-CWOL 125 258235
D-CZAR 560 0114
D-IAAS 525 0321
D-IABC 500 182
D-IADD 551 481
D-IAEC 501 609
D-IAEV 501 365
(D-IAFA) 550 616
(D-IAFD) 525 0105
D-IAJJ 500 245
D-IALL 525 0143
D-IAME 525 0315
D-IAMM 525 0041
D-IANE 500 121
D-IANE 501 501
D-IANO 501 523
D-IATC 500 116
D-IATD 23 074
D-IAVB 525 0172
D-IAWA 551 421
D-IBIT 525 0393
D-IBMS 525 0309
D-IBPF 551 246
D-IBWB 501 421
D-IBWG 501 566
D-ICAB 551 151
D-ICAP 24D 247
D-ICAR 24 169
D-ICAY 24D 254
D-ICCA 500 317
D-ICCC 500 269
D-ICEE 525 0096
D-ICEY 525 0286
D-ICFA 500 290
D-ICGT 525 0164
D-ICHE 551 559
D-ICHS 24X 280
D-ICOL 525 0353
D-ICPW 500 100
D-ICSS 525 0121
D-ICTA 551 301
D-ICUR 551 150
D-ICUW 500 319
D-ICWB 525 0349
(D-ICWB) 550 074
D-IDAG 525 0144
D-IDAT 24D 261
D-IDAU 500 131
D-IDBW 525 0044
D-IDDD 24B 201
D-IDFD 500 225
D-IDPD 501 382
D-IDWH 500 126
D-IDWN 500 288
D-IEAR 551 095
D-IEGO 24D 283
D-IEIR 501 674
D-IEWS 525 0217
D-IEXC 500 036
D-IFAI 500 100
D-IFAN 525 0214
(D-IFGP) 501 673
D-IFUM 24 129
D-IFUP 525 0126
D-IFVG 24B 223
D-IGAS 525 0223
D-IGGK 501 535
D-IGLU 501 537
D-IGMB 501 442
D-IGME 525 0279
D-IGRC 551 132
D-IGSO 24R 233
D-IGZA 525 0260
D-IHAQ 23 007
(D-IHAT) 551 301
D-IHEB 525 0064
(D-IHEB) 525 0073
D-IHEY 501 432
D-IHGW 525 0126
D-IHHS 525 0082
D-IHLZ 24B 225
D-IHOL 525 0229
D-IHSV 500 164
(D-IIDD) 24B 228
D-IIJS 525 0310
D-IIPD 24B 228
(D-IIRR) 525 0315
D-IJHM 551 212
D-IJON 500 346
D-IJYP 525 0165
D-IKAA 23 018
D-IKAB 24 087
D-IKAF 24B 189
D-IKAN 500 040
D-IKFJ 500 178
(D-IKHV) 525 0264
D-IKOP 525 0016
D-IKPW 500 361
(D-IKUC) 500 269
D-ILAN 551 614
D-ILAT 525 0209
D-ILCB 525 0193
D-ILCC 551 324
D-ILDE 24B 208
D-ILHM 24D 239
D-ILLL 501 659
D-ILTC 551 617
D-ILVW 24D 239
D-IMAN 500 025
D-IMAR 24D 250
D-IMEN 500 279
D-IMLN 500 129
D-IMMD 525 0211
D-IMME 551 400
D-IMMI 525 0303
D-IMMM 24D 328
D-IMRX 501 688
D-IMSM 500 194
D-IMTM 551 061
D-IMWZ 24B 184
D-INCC 500 128
D-INCI 500 255
D-INGA MSP 098
D-INGE MSP 090
D-INHH 500 079
D-INKA 24D 282
D-IOBO 525 0025
D-IOGA 24B 223
D-IOGE 24B 224
D-IOGI 24B 193
D-IOMP 525 0143
D-IRKE 525 0123
D-IRKE 551 555
D-IRMA 525 0366
D-IRON 525 0168
D-IRWR 525 0118
D-ISCH 525 0040
D-ISGW 525 0070
D-ISHW 525 0289
D-ISIS 501 583
D-ISSS 500 489
D-ISWA 525 0236
D-ITSV 525 0084
D-IURH 525 0196
D-IURS 525 0343
D-IVBG 525 0310
D-IVHA 525 0103
(D-IVID) 525 0188
D-IVIN 525 0188
D-IVOB 551 163
D-IWHL 525 0029
D-IWIL 525 0221

Angola

D2-EBA 560 0502
D2-EBB 20 296/507
D2-ECB G3 474
D2-EDC 500 071
D2-EFM 125 25260
D2-ESV 20 262
D2-EXR 125 25215

Comores Islands

D6-ECB CVT 15

Spain

(EC-) 125 25058
(EC-) 525 0096
EC-113 20 204
EC-115 125 256034
EC-121 125 256023
EC-165 20 221
EC-168 50 209
EC-183 125 256039
EC-193 125 258022
EC-232 STR 5202
EC-235 900 115
EC-254 WWD 335
EC-261 525 0133
EC-263 20 149
EC-272 125 256012
EC-319 125 256062
EC-339 AST 042
EC-349 125 256063
EC-353 10 4
EC-363 G2 237/43
EC-375 125 257040
EC-411 560 0062
EC-500 500 331
EC-551 20 128/436
EC-617 900 93
EC-621 550 667
EC-697 STR 5062/12
EC-704 525 0065
EC-743 550 131
EC-765 900 97
EC-777 550 678
EC-855 20 117
EC-949 10 17

EC-BVV 20 219/470
EC-BXV 20 222/471
EC-BZV 20 253/486
EC-CCY 500 082
EC-CGG 500 108
EC-CIM 25B 149
EC-CJA 24D 287
EC-CJH 500 116
EC-CKD 25 038
EC-CKR 25B 184
EC-CLS 35 005
EC-CMU 125 25271
EC-CQT 125 256045
EC-CTV 20 332/525
EC-DEB 35A 137
EC-DFA 35A 196
EC-DJC 35A 278
EC-DOH 551 278
EC-DQC CVT 24
EC-DQE CVT 26
EC-DQG CVT 27
EC-DSI 55 045
EC-DUE CVT 30
EC-DUF CVT 32
EC-DYE CVT 31
EC-EAC 125 256005
EC-EAO 125 256039
EC-EAP 650 0125
EC-EAS 650 0122
EC-EAV 125 256032
EC-EBM 25 027
EC-EBR 500 089
EC-ECB 20 210
EC-EDC 20 220
EC-EDC 20 6
EC-EDL 20 220
EC-EDN 501 370
EC-EDO 20 50
EC-EEU 20 218
EC-EFI 20 189
EC-EFR 20 183
EC-EGL 125 256023
EC-EGM 20 204
EC-EGS 125 256034
EC-EGT 125 25080
EC-EGY 25D 373
EC-EHC 20 46
EC-EHD 20 55/410
EC-EHF 125 256011
EC-EIV 20 221
EC-EKK 20 106
EC-ELK 125 258022
EC-EOQ 125 256012
EC-EQP 20 149
EC-EQX 650 0119
EC-ERJ 125 256063
EC-ERX 125 256062
EC-ETI 125 257040
EC-FAM 20 128/436
EC-FDL 550 667
EC-FEN 900 93
EC-FES 550 678
EC-FFO 900 97
EC-FGX STR 5062/12
EC-FIL 550 131
EC-FJP 20 117
EC-FPG 50 209
EC-FPI 900 115
EC-FQX STR 5202
EC-FRV G2 237/43
EC-FTV 10 4
EC-FUM 500 331
EC-FZP 525 0065
EC-GIA AST 042
EC-GIB WWD 335
EC-GIE 525 0133
EC-GJF 501 482
EC-GLM 560 0062
EC-GMO 90X 6
EC-GNK 2xx 37
EC-GOV 560 0419
EC-GPN 50 204
EC-GSL WWD 353
EC-GTR 50 268
EC-GTS 500 037
EC-GXX 35A 263
EC-HAI 55 112
EC-HBC 525 0264
EC-HBX 525 0304
EC-HCX 20 184/462
EC-HEG 200 494
EC-HFY 500 157
EC-HGH G4 1021
EC-HGI 550 596
EC-HHK 900 151
EC-HHS 50 204
EC-HHZ CVT 15
EC-HIA CVT 19
EC-HIN 525 0197
EC-HJL 125 258444
EC-HLB 35A 236
ECT-023 551 278
ECT-028 35A 278

Ireland

EI-BGW 125 25080
EI-BJL 551 039
EI-BJN 501 555
EI-BNY CVT 11
EI-BRG 125 25281
EI-BSA 55 021
(EI-BUN) 551 555
EI-BUY 551 555
(EI-BXN) 600 1048
(EI-BYD) 600 1035
EI-BYM 500 179
EI-BYN 550 188
EI-CAH G4 1129
EI-CIR 551 144
EI-COV 125 257178
EI-DAB 550 0917

(EI-DUN) 560 0197
EI-GHP 550 0897
EI-GPA 600 1016
EI-LJG 601 5023
EI-LJR 2xx 18
EI-MAS 601 5194
EI-PAL 550 0935
EI-RRR 125 257170
EI-SNN 650 0183
EI-SXT 601 5159
(EI-TAM) 601 3006
EI-TAM 604 5367
EI-WDC 125 25132
EI-WGV G5 505

Turkmenistan
(see also EZ-)

EK-B021 125 259029

Liberia

EL-VDY 20 245/481
EL-WRT G2 67

Iran

EP-AGX 20 283/497
EP-AGY 20 286/498
EP-AHK 125 25154
EP-AHV 20 320/519
EP-AKC 20 301/509
EP-FIC 20 334/527
EP-FID 20 338/530
EP-FIE 20 251/484
EP-FIF 20 320/519
EP-FIG 20 318/518
EP-HIM MSP 002
EP-KIA 500 295
EP-KIC 550 025
(EP-KID) 550 025
EP-PAO 500 295
EP-PAP 500 301
(EP-PAQ) 500 377
EP-PBC 501 370
EP-SEA 20 367/545
EP-VAP 20 251/484
(EP-VAS) 20 318/518
EP-VLP STR 5203
EP-VRP STR 5002
EP-VRP STR 5137
EP-VSP 20 318/518

Estonia

ES-PVV 55 011

Byelorussia

(EW94228) S550 0067

Turkmenistan
(see also EK-)

EZ-B021 125 259029

France

F-BFDG 10 61
F-BGVO MSP 01
F-BHOK MSP 03
F-BIHY 20 141/441
F-BINR 50 2
F-BIPC 10 108
(F-BIPF) 10 61
F-BJET MSP 039
F-BJLH 10 1
F-BJLV MSP 072
F-BJLX MSP 086
F-BJLY MSP 089
F-BJZQ MSP 102
F-BJZR MSP 103
F-BJZS MSP 104
F-BJZT MSP 105
F-BJZU MSP 106
F-BJZV MSP 107
F-BJZX MSP 108
F-BKFB 36A 046
(F-BKFB) 550 195
F-BKMC 125 256035
F-BKMF 125 25007
F-BLCU 20 173
F-BLKB 20 01
F-BLKL MSP 01
F-BLLK 20 137
F-BMER 50 52
F-BMKH 20 6
F-BMKK 20 22/404
F-BMSH 20 1/401
F-BMSS 20 2/402
F-BMSX 20 3/403
F-BNDB 50 1
F-BNKX 20 23
F-BNRE 20 53/417
F-BNRG MSP 101
F-BNRH 20 79/415
F-BOED 20 41/407
F-BOEF 20 13
F-BOFH 20 225/472
F-BOHN MSP 098
F-BOHU 125 25025
F-BOJO MSP 002
F-BOJY MSP 112
F-BOLX 20 62/409
F-BOOA 20 67/414
F-BOON 20 25/405
F-BOXV 20 104/454
F-BPIB WWD 105
F-BPIO 20 141/441
F-BPJB 20 145/443
F-BPMC 125 25131
F-BPXB 10 79
F-BRAL 24X 117
F-BRGF 24D 289
F-BRHB 20 172/456
(F-BRHB) 20 73/419
F-BRNL 24B 183
F-BRNZ CVT 2
F-BRPK 20 188/464
F-BRQK CVT 9
F-BRUY G2 43
F-BSBU 20 263/489
F-BSIM 125 25130
F-BSQN 10 03
F-BSQU 10 1
F-BSRL 24B 210
F-BSSL 125 25223
F-BSTP 23 026
F-BSTR 20 246/482
F-BSUR 25 040
F-BSUX 23 045A
F-BSYF 20 25/405
F-BTCY 20 13
F-BTDA WWD 145
F-BTEL 550 209
F-BTMF 20 184/462
F-BTML 20 67/414
F-BTQK 23 053
F-BTQZ 20 58
F-BTTK CVT 31
F-BTTL CVT 28
F-BTTM CVT 17
F-BTTN CVT 20
F-BTTO CVT 18
F-BTTP CVT 30
F-BTTQ CVT 32
F-BTTR CVT 9
F-BTTS CVT 11
F-BTTS CVT 36
F-BTTT CVT 33
F-BTTU CVT 22
F-BTTU CVT 37
F-BTTV CVT 11
F-BTYV 24B 206
F-BUAS CVT 1
F-BUFG 20 175
F-BUFN 24B 202
F-BUIC 20 138/440
F-BUIX 20 245/481
F-BUQN CVT 3
F-BUQP CVT 4
F-BUUL 500 136
F-BUUV 24B 195
F-BUYE 20 288/499
F-BUYI 20 86
F-BUYL 500 133
F-BUYP 125 256033
F-BVEC 24D 271
F-BVFV 20 182/461
F-BVPA CVT 5
F-BVPB CVT 6
F-BVPC CVT 12
F-BVPD CVT 13
F-BVPE CVT 21
F-BVPF CVT 23
F-BVPG CVT 25
F-BVPH CVT 27
F-BVPI CVT 24
F-BVPJ CVT 29
F-BVPK CVT 7
F-BVPL CVT 19
F-BVPM 20 294/506
F-BVPN 20 311/515
F-BVPO CVT 10
F-BVPQ 20 315/517
F-BVPR 100 5
F-BVPS CVT 14
F-BVPT CVT 16
F-BXAG 10 7
F-BXPT 23 014
F-BXQL MSP 105
F-BYAL 25C 084
F-BYCC 10 76
F-BYCR CVT 34
F-BYCV 10 93
F-BYFB 125 257166
F-EXAA MSP 112
F-GAJD 24B 187
F-GAMA 23 023
F-GAPC 20 184/462
F-GAPY 23 027
F-GASL 125 257022
F-GATF 20 401
(F-GBBV) 24 109
F-GBGD 36 016
F-GBIZ 50 3
F-GBLA 24B 190
F-GBLZ 24D 239
F-GBMB 35 018
F-GBMD 20 375/547
F-GBMH 10 103
F-GBMS 20 175
F-GBPG 20 106
F-GBPL 550 063
F-GBRF 10 38
(F-GBRF) 50 5
F-GBTA 23 017
F-GBTC 10 124
F-GBTI 10 24
F-GBTL 550 068
F-GBTM 20 397/555
F-GCGU 20 136/439
F-GCGY 20 145/443
F-GCLE 35A 108
(F-GCLT) 35A 313
F-GCMS 35A 257
F-GCSZ 550 195
F-GCTT 10 127
F-GDAE 24 105
F-GDAV 23 017
F-GDAY CVT 26
F-GDAZ CVT 35
F-GDCN 35A 432
F-GDCP 35A 071
F-GDFE 50 56
F-GDFJ 20 362
F-GDHK G3 340
F-GDHR 55 070
F-GDLO 20 315/517
F-GDLR 10 121
F-GDLU 20 314/516
(F-GDRC) CVT 19
F-GDRN 10 152
F-GDSA 100 202
F-GDSB 200 482
(F-GDSC) 50 123
F-GDSD 200 487
F-GDUB CVT 15
F-GECI 24B 219
F-GECR 125 25128
F-GEDB 100 197
F-GEFB 550 195
F-GEFS 20 486
F-GEJR 20 473
(F-GEJX) 20 300/508
F-GELA 10 16
F-GELE 10 69
F-GELS 100 208
F-GELT 100 211
F-GEOY 50 78
F-GEPL 500 164
F-GEPQ CVT 19
F-GEQF CVT 15
F-GERO 10 179
F-GERT 20 96
F-GESL 125 258016
F-GESZ 501 443
F-GEXE 50 145
F-GEXF 20 401
F-GFAY 200 496
F-GFBG 10 157
F-GFDB 125 25131
F-GFDH CVT 13
F-GFEJ CVT 10
F-GFFP 10 160
F-GFFS 20 474
F-GFGB 10 177
F-GFGQ 50 104
(F-GFHG) 10 113
F-GFHG 10 126
F-GFHH 10 113
(F-GFHH) 10 126
F-GFJC 900 2
(F-GFJK) 10 108
F-GFJL 550 470
(F-GFLL) 20 162/451
F-GFMD 10 136
F-GFMP 125 25125
F-GFMZ 25B 182
(F-GFPD) CVT 11
F-GFPF 10 68
F-GFPO 550 114
F-GFUN 20 162/451
F-GGAL 650 0117
F-GGAR 10 115
(F-GGAR) 200 496
F-GGBL 20 379
F-GGCP 50 9
F-GGFO 20 76
F-GGGA 550 586
F-GGGT 550 611
F-GGKE 20 118
F-GGMM 20 300/508
F-GGPG 24D 327
(F-GGRA) 10 179
(F-GGRG) 35A 174
F-GGRH 900 5
F-GGVB 50 11
F-GGVR 10 138
F-GHAE 35A 413
F-GHAQ 50 149
F-GHBT 20 160/450
F-GHCR 20 313
F-GHDN 20 77/429
F-GHDT 20 176/458
F-GHDX 10 140
F-GHDZ 10 17
F-GHEA 900 33
F-GHER 10 88

F-GHFB	10	169
(F-GHFI)	10	43
F-GHFO	10	33
F-GHFP	20	119/431
F-GHFQ	20	279/502
F-GHGT	50	21
F-GHHG	125	257055
(F-GHJL)	10	58
F-GHLN	20	255/487
F-GHLT	10	92
F-GHMD	20	345
F-GHMP	35	048
F-GHPA	**20**	**170/455**
F-GHPB	**100**	**215**
F-GHPL	10	147
(F-GHPO)	20	271/493
(F-GHRE)	20	171
F-GHRV	10	48
F-GHSG	20	77/429
F-GHSK	100	218
F-GHTD	900	96
F-GHTK	20	368
(F-GHUA)	550	028
F-GHVK	10	146
F-GHVR	20	262
F-GHYB	900	103
(F-GIBT)	20	300/508
F-GICB	20	171
F-GICF	20	120
F-GICN	**50**	**210**
F-GIDC	50	116
F-GIDE	900	1
F-GIFL	100	217
F-GIFP	20	259
(F-GIHT)	500	067
(F-GIHU)	500	201
F-GIJG	10	118
F-GILM	**CVT**	**32**
(F-GIPH)	10	166
F-GIPH	**100**	**194**
F-GIQP	10	43
F-GIQZ	50	107
F-GIRH	CVT	14
(F-GIRS)	500	308
(F-GIRS)	550	341
(F-GIRZ)	900	30
(F-GIVD)	50	251
F-GIVR	900	62
F-GIVT	20	32
F-GJAP	**CVT**	**31**
F-GJAS	**CVT**	**8**
(F-GJBR)	20	77/429
F-GJBT	900	32
F-GJBZ	**50**	**269**
F-GJCC	**20**	**72/413**
F-GJDB	**20**	**76**
F-GJDE	125	25131
F-GJDG	**F502**	**312**
F-GJEA	20	360
F-GJEK	50	228
F-GJFB	10	166
F-GJFZ	10	19
F-GJGB	10	47
F-GJHG	10	181
F-GJHJ	**2xx**	**2**
F-GJHK	10	108
(F-GJIS)	200	514
F-GJJL	10	118
F-GJJS	20	264
(F-GJKT)	50	21
F-GJLA	20	133
F-GJLB	**CVT**	**39**
F-GJLL	**10**	**22**
F-GJMA	10	116
(F-GJMA)	10	65
(F-GJPI)	20	257
F-GJPM	900	66
F-GJPR	20	5
F-GJRH	900	106
F-GJRN	10	163
F-GJSF	20	299
(F-GJTR)	50	140
F-GJXX	**560**	**0070**
F-GJYD	**550**	**414**
F-GKAE	100	213
(F-GKAF)	20	120
F-GKAL	20	455
F-GKAR	50	204
F-GKBC	**10**	**99**
F-GKBZ	**50**	**185**
F-GKCC	100	201
(F-GKCD)	10	88
(F-GKCJ)	400A	RK-14
F-GKDB	**20**	**271/493**
F-GKDD	20	257
F-GKDI	900	106
F-GKDR	50	86
F-GKGA	**CVT**	**11**
(F-GKGB)	CVT	30
F-GKGD	CVT	34
F-GKGL	**560**	**0058**
F-GKHL	**560**	**0059**
F-GKID	**500**	**319**
F-GKIL	500	319
(F-GKIN)	50	286
F-GKIP	**2xx**	**90**
F-GKIR	**500**	**361**
F-GKIS	**20**	**307/513**
F-GKJB	CVT	20
F-GKJL	**560**	**0093**
F-GKJS	650	0232
F-GKLV	10	41
F-GKME	20	256
F-GKPB	100	207
F-GKPP	MSP	098
(F-GKPZ)	100	201
F-GKRU	50	235
F-GKTV	50	111
F-GLEC	**CVT**	**30**
F-GLGY	**900**	**11**
F-GLHI	900	166
F-GLHJ	2xx	12
F-GLIM	**560**	**0119**
(F-GLIM)	560	0156
F-GLJA	500	264
F-GLMD	**20**	**117**
F-GLMM	20	116
(F-GLMT)	20	246/482
F-GLMU	**900**	**35**
F-GLNL	20	94/428
(F-GLOR)	400A	RK-37
(F-GLPD)	400A	RK-37
F-GLTK	**550**	**609**
F-GLYC	**560**	**0205**
F-GLYO	400A	RK-14
F-GMCI	**550**	**052**
F-GMCK	2xx	46
F-GMGA	50	51
F-GMJS	10	80
F-GMLH	500	308
F-GMOT	**50**	**111**
F-GMPR	2xx	18
(F-GNAB)	500	337
F-GNAF	CVT	15
F-GNCJ	525	0024
F-GNCP	**550**	**004**
F-GNDA	**900**	**88**
(F-GNDB)	125	257127
F-GNDZ	**10**	**17**
F-GNFF	50	228
F-GNFI	900	118
(F-GNFS)	50	228
F-GNGL	50	230
F-GNLF	550	114
F-GNLR	50	232
(F-GNMF)	200	511
F-GNMO	50	240
F-GNMR	900	143
F-GOAB	900	130
F-GOAL	**50**	**131**
F-GOBE	200	515
F-GOBZ	20	293
F-GODB	125	257127
F-GODE	900	133
F-GODO	2xx	65
F-GODP	50	275
F-GOGL	50	134
F-GOJT	200	501
(F-GOND)	50	251
F-GOPM	**20**	**302/510**
F-GOYA	**90X**	**11**
F-GPAA	**20**	**103/423**
F-GPAB	**20**	**254**
F-GPAE	20	356
F-GPAK	**G4**	**1061**
F-GPAM	2xx	6
F-GPAX	900	125
F-GPBG	50	269
F-GPFC	**525**	**0101**
F-GPFD	**100**	**221**
F-GPIM	20	30
F-GPLA	**CVT**	**28**
F-GPLF	**525**	**0291**
(F-GPLH)	50	131
F-GPLT	550	033
(F-GPNG)	20	116
F-GPNJ	**90X**	**50**
F-GPPF	**50**	**65**
F-GPSA	**50**	**123**
F-GRDP	900	169
F-GREX	90X	1
F-GROC	20	279/502
F-GRON	**125**	**257166**
F-GRRM	**525**	**0166**
F-GSAA	**2xx**	**36**
F-GSAB	900	161
(F-GSAD)	900	163
F-GSAI	90X	31
F-GSCN	**900**	**62**
F-GSDP	**90X**	**43**
F-GSER	**50**	**2**
F-GSLZ	**100**	**208**
F-GSMC	**500**	**308**
F-GSMF	900	142
F-GSXF	**20**	**315/517**
F-GTGJ	900	105
F-GTMD	**525**	**0312**
F-GTOD	**10**	**155**
F-GTRY	**525**	**0359**
F-GUDP	50	134
F-GUEQ	**900**	**167**
F-GVDN	50	264
F-GVDP	**90X**	**51**
F-GYOL	**50**	**88**
F-GYSL	**20**	**341**
F-HAAP	**900**	**142**
F-HACD	560	5104
F-HAXA	**90X**	**12**

France d'Outremer

(F-O)	S550	0094
F-OBYG	CVT	39
F-OBZP	CVT	29
F-OBZR	CVT	7
F-OBZV	CVT	25
F-OCDE	CVT	36
(F-OCGK)	125	25025
F-OCJL	CVT	19
F-OCRN	CVT	9
F-ODEO	50	78
F-ODFE	CVT	22
F-ODFQ	CVT	26
F-ODHA	20	175
F-ODIF	CVT	38
F-ODJS	CVT	40
F-ODJX	CVT	5
F-ODKS	CVT	11
F-ODOK	20	162/451
F-ODSK	20	94/428
F-ODSR	**CVT**	**35**
F-ODTM	CVT	17
F-ODUT	550	052
F-OGJL	CVT	6
F-OGSI	200	511
F-OGSR	200	496
(F-OGUO)	551	375
(F-OGVA)	551	375
F-OHAH	S550	0094
F-OHCJ	20	341
F-OHES	200	514
F-OHFO	**50**	**267**
F-OHRU	**560**	**0407**
(F-OIBA)	2xx	65
F-OIBL	90X	6
F-OKSI	50	241
F-OKSY	**50**	**257**
F-OLET	200	511

France - Test Marks

F-W	2xx	101
F-W	2xx	102
F-W	2xx	105
F-W	2xx	110
F-W	**2xx**	**111**
F-W	2xx	112
F-W	2xx	113
F-W	**2xx**	**114**
F-W	**2xx**	**115**
F-W	2xx	116
F-W	**2xx**	**117**
F-W	2xx	118
F-W	**2xx**	**119**
F-W	50	299
F-W	50	300
F-W	900	138
F-W	900	182
F-W	90X	34
F-W	90X	40
F-W	90X	57
F-W	90X	59
F-W	90X	61
F-W	90X	64
F-W	90X	65
F-W	90X	67
F-W	90X	68
F-W	90X	69
F-W	90X	70
F-W	90X	71
F-W	90X	72
F-WAMD	30	01
F-WAMD	50	1
F-WATF	20	362
F-WBTM	20	397/555
F-WDCP	35A	071
F-WDFE	50	56
F-WDFJ	**20**	**362**
(F-WDHA)	20	401
F-WDHK	G3	340
F-WDSB	200	482
F-WEDB	100	197
F-WEFS	50	34
F-WEFX	900	11
F-WFAL	10	01
F-WFJC	50	3
F-WFJC	900	2
F-WFPD	CVT	11
F-WGDZ	200	482
F-WGSR	200	496
F-WGTF	10	48
F-WGTF	20	77/429
F-WGTF	200	511
F-WGTF	50	131
F-WGTF	50	140
F-WGTG	100	204
F-WGTG	20	474
F-WGTG	50	27
F-WGTG	50	73
F-WGTH	20	116
F-WGTH	50	29
F-WGTH	900	30
F-WGTM	20	176/458
F-WGVO	MSP	01
F-WIDE	900	1
F-WIET	MSP	001
F-WIFA	CVT	15
(F-WIFU)	CVT	11
F-WINR	50	2
F-WJAA	MSP	005
F-WJAA	MSP	026
F-WJAA	MSP	039
F-WJAB	MSP	006
F-WJAC	MSP	008

F-WJAD	MSP	009-
F-WJAE	MSP	028
F-WJLH	10	1
F-WJMJ	10	10
F-WJMJ	10	18
F-WJMJ	10	25
F-WJMJ	10	3
F-WJMJ	10	33
F-WJMJ	10	36
F-WJMJ	10	44
F-WJMJ	10	57
F-WJMJ	10	65
F-WJMJ	10	74
F-WJMJ	10	91
F-WJMJ	20	112
F-WJMJ	20	121
F-WJMJ	20	124/433
F-WJMJ	20	136/439
F-WJMJ	20	144
F-WJMJ	20	152/446
F-WJMJ	20	229
F-WJMJ	20	321
F-WJMJ	20	385
F-WJMJ	20	402
F-WJMJ	20	407
F-WJMJ	20	423
F-WJMJ	20	444
F-WJMJ	20	456
F-WJMJ	20	463
F-WJMJ	20	470
F-WJMJ	20	83
F-WJMJ	20	87/424
F-WJMJ	20	97/422
F-WJMJ	EC	165/452
F-WJMK	10	11
F-WJMK	10	14
F-WJMK	10	21
F-WJMK	10	26
F-WJMK	10	4
F-WJMK	20	104/454
F-WJMK	20	119/431
F-WJMK	20	131/437
F-WJMK	20	155
F-WJMK	20	188/464
F-WJMK	20	211
F-WJMK	20	246/482
F-WJMK	20	262
F-WJMK	20	386
F-WJMK	20	403
F-WJMK	20	404
F-WJMK	20	413
F-WJMK	20	426
F-WJMK	20	432
F-WJMK	20	441
F-WJMK	20	448
F-WJMK	20	453
F-WJMK	20	464
F-WJMK	20	471
F-WJMK	20	84
F-WJMK	20	99
F-WJML	10	12
F-WJML	10	24
F-WJML	10	28
F-WJML	10	37
F-WJML	10	45
F-WJML	10	51
F-WJML	10	6
F-WJML	10	60
F-WJML	10	69
F-WJML	20	115/432
F-WJML	20	230
F-WJML	20	387
F-WJML	20	414
F-WJML	20	433
F-WJML	20	442
F-WJML	20	454
F-WJML	20	460
F-WJML	20	466
F-WJML	20	475
F-WJML	20	73/419
F-WJMM	10	15
F-WJMM	10	2
F-WJMM	10	29
F-WJMM	10	38
F-WJMM	10	48
F-WJMM	10	58
F-WJMM	10	62
F-WJMM	10	70
F-WJMM	10	71
F-WJMM	10	9
F-WJMM	20	106
F-WJMM	20	114/420
F-WJMM	20	129
F-WJMM	20	142
F-WJMM	20	157
F-WJMM	20	213
F-WJMM	20	249
F-WJMM	20	274
F-WJMM	20	388
F-WJMM	20	417
F-WJMM	20	435
F-WJMM	20	445
F-WJMM	20	457
F-WJMM	20	467
F-WJMM	20	476
F-WJMM	20	82/418
F-WJMM	20	92/421
F-WJMN	10	40
F-WJMN	10	43
F-WJMN	10	59
F-WJMN	10	66
F-WJMN	10	7
F-WJMN	10	8
F-WJMN	20	100
F-WJMN	20	146
F-WJMN	20	164
F-WJMN	20	232
F-WJMN	20	264
F-WJMN	20	390
F-WJMN	20	418
F-WJMN	20	436
F-WJMN	20	446
F-WJMN	20	458
F-WJMN	20	478
F-WJMN	20	67/414
F-WJMN	EC	125
F-WKAE	100	213
F-WLCH	20	147/444
F-WLCS	10	13
F-WLCS	10	17
F-WLCS	10	34
F-WLCS	10	41
F-WLCS	10	50
F-WLCS	10	53
F-WLCS	20	138/440
F-WLCS	20	166
F-WLCS	20	206
F-WLCS	20	215
F-WLCS	20	245/481
F-WLCS	20	391
F-WLCS	20	447
F-WLCS	20	481
F-WLCT	10	16
F-WLCT	10	30
F-WLCT	10	46
F-WLCT	10	64
F-WLCT	10	78
F-WLCT	100	5
F-WLCT	20	153
F-WLCT	20	216
F-WLCT	20	259
F-WLCT	20	393
F-WLCT	20	416
F-WLCT	20	449
F-WLCT	20	485
F-WLCU	10	19
F-WLCU	10	31
F-WLCU	10	42
F-WLCU	10	67
F-WLCU	20	173
F-WLCU	20	234/475
F-WLCU	20	261
F-WLCV	10	20
F-WLCV	10	35
F-WLCV	10	49
F-WLCV	10	68
F-WLCV	20	154/447
F-WLCV	20	187
F-WLCV	20	233
F-WLCV	20	415
F-WLCV	20	486
F-WLCX	10	22
F-WLCX	10	27
F-WLCX	10	52
F-WLCX	10	63
F-WLCX	10	72
F-WLCX	20	168
F-WLCX	20	209
F-WLCX	20	240/478
F-WLCX	20	265
F-WLCY	10	23
F-WLCY	10	47
F-WLCY	20	183
F-WLCY	20	201/469
F-WLCY	20	217
F-WLEF	551	144
F-WLKB	20	01
F-WLKL	MSP	01
F-WLLK	20	137
F-WLMM	20	116
F-WMGO	20	50
F-WMKF	20	141/441
F-WMKF	20	161
F-WMKF	20	17
F-WMKF	20	175
F-WMKF	20	180/460
F-WMKF	20	185/467
F-WMKF	20	207
F-WMKF	20	250
F-WMKF	20	272
F-WMKF	20	287
F-WMKF	20	297
F-WMKF	20	30
F-WMKF	20	308
F-WMKF	20	316
F-WMKF	20	319
F-WMKF	20	324
F-WMKF	20	335
F-WMKF	20	341
F-WMKF	20	347
F-WMKF	20	352
F-WMKF	20	355
F-WMKF	20	361/543
F-WMKF	20	37/406
F-WMKF	20	379
F-WMKF	20	38
F-WMKF	20	394
F-WMKF	20	398
F-WMKF	20	4
F-WMKF	20	406/557
F-WMKF	20	424
F-WMKF	20	429
F-WMKF	20	474
F-WMKF	20	69
F-WMKF	20	76
F-WMKF	20	93/435
F-WMKG	20	110
F-WMKG	20	118
F-WMKG	20	132
F-WMKG	20	148
F-WMKG	20	160/450
F-WMKG	20	167/453
F-WMKG	20	171
F-WMKG	20	176/458
F-WMKG	20	193
F-WMKG	20	227
F-WMKG	20	28
F-WMKG	20	282
F-WMKG	20	289
F-WMKG	20	298
F-WMKG	20	3/403
F-WMKG	20	317
F-WMKG	20	325
F-WMKG	20	338/530
F-WMKG	20	349
F-WMKG	20	35
F-WMKG	20	356
F-WMKG	20	366
F-WMKG	20	370
F-WMKG	20	382
F-WMKG	20	396
F-WMKG	20	411
F-WMKG	20	420
F-WMKG	20	425
F-WMKG	20	430
F-WMKG	20	437
F-WMKG	20	443
F-WMKG	20	450
F-WMKG	20	46
F-WMKG	20	461
F-WMKG	20	468
F-WMKG	20	48
F-WMKG	20	64
F-WMKG	20	73/419
F-WMKG	20	74
F-WMKG	20	89
F-WMKH	20	103/423
F-WMKH	20	11
F-WMKH	20	117
F-WMKH	20	126/438
F-WMKH	20	13
F-WMKH	20	134
F-WMKH	20	143/442
F-WMKH	20	150/445
F-WMKH	20	199
F-WMKH	20	243/480
F-WMKH	20	257
F-WMKH	20	275
F-WMKH	20	290
F-WMKH	20	303
F-WMKH	20	310
F-WMKH	20	312
F-WMKH	20	322
F-WMKH	20	339
F-WMKH	20	6
F-WMKH	20	70
F-WMKH	20	79/415
F-WMKH	20	85/425
F-WMKI	20	102
F-WMKI	20	111
F-WMKI	20	12
F-WMKI	20	120
F-WMKI	20	135
F-WMKI	20	151
F-WMKI	20	156/448
F-WMKI	20	177
F-WMKI	20	204
F-WMKI	20	21
F-WMKI	20	244
F-WMKI	20	29
F-WMKI	20	292
F-WMKI	20	299
F-WMKI	20	327
F-WMKI	20	345
F-WMKI	20	357
F-WMKI	20	36
F-WMKI	20	364
F-WMKI	20	368
F-WMKI	20	373
F-WMKI	20	380
F-WMKI	20	399
F-WMKI	20	405
F-WMKI	20	412
F-WMKI	20	421
F-WMKI	20	428
F-WMKI	20	438
F-WMKI	20	45
F-WMKI	20	452
F-WMKI	20	462
F-WMKI	20	469
F-WMKI	20	5
F-WMKI	20	54
F-WMKI	20	61
F-WMKI	20	63/411
F-WMKI	20	80
F-WMKI	20	86
F-WMKI	20	9
F-WMKJ	20	101
F-WMKJ	20	107
F-WMKJ	20	116
F-WMKJ	20	128/436
F-WMKJ	20	130
F-WMKJ	20	14
F-WMKJ	20	158/449
F-WMKJ	20	159
F-WMKJ	20	20

F-WMKJ	20	200
F-WMKJ	20	218
F-WMKJ	20	260/488
F-WMKJ	20	263/489
F-WMKJ	20	27
F-WMKJ	20	279/502
F-WMKJ	20	293
F-WMKJ	20	305
F-WMKJ	20	313
F-WMKJ	20	328/522
F-WMKJ	20	34
F-WMKJ	20	351/538
F-WMKJ	20	360
F-WMKJ	20	365
F-WMKJ	20	371
F-WMKJ	20	409
F-WMKJ	20	419
F-WMKJ	20	43
F-WMKJ	20	431
F-WMKJ	20	439
F-WMKJ	20	459
F-WMKJ	20	51
F-WMKJ	20	60
F-WMKJ	20	62/409
F-WMKJ	20	68
F-WMKJ	20	8
F-WMKJ	20	91
F-WMKK	20	10
F-WMKK	20	15
F-WMKK	20	22/404
F-WMKK	20	7
F-WMSH	20	1/401
F-WMSS	20	2/402
F-WNAV	**2xx**	**1**
F-WNDB	50	1
(F-WNEW)	2xx	1
F-WNEW	2xx	2
F-WNGD	10	109
F-WNGD	10	125
F-WNGD	10	90
F-WNGD	10	96
F-WNGL	10	116
F-WNGL	10	73
F-WNGL	20	105
F-WNGL	20	113
F-WNGL	20	122
F-WNGL	20	16
F-WNGL	20	174/457
F-WNGL	20	181
F-WNGL	20	210
F-WNGL	20	222/471
F-WNGL	20	228/473
F-WNGL	20	23
F-WNGL	20	256
F-WNGL	20	276/494
F-WNGL	20	301/509
F-WNGL	20	314/516
F-WNGL	20	32
F-WNGL	20	333/526
F-WNGL	20	40
F-WNGL	20	41/407
F-WNGL	20	58
F-WNGL	20	66
F-WNGL	20	75
F-WNGL	20	90/426
F-WNGM	10	126
F-WNGM	10	75
F-WNGM	10	92
F-WNGM	20	109/427
F-WNGM	20	123
F-WNGM	20	139
F-WNGM	20	163
F-WNGM	20	172/456
F-WNGM	20	18
F-WNGM	20	202
F-WNGM	20	24
F-WNGM	20	258
F-WNGM	20	278/495
F-WNGM	20	31
F-WNGM	20	330
F-WNGM	20	39
F-WNGM	20	47
F-WNGM	20	56
F-WNGM	20	71
F-WNGM	20	78/412
F-WNGM	20	96
F-WNGN	10	77
F-WNGN	10	93
F-WNGN	20	127
F-WNGN	20	140
F-WNGN	20	145/443
F-WNGN	20	169
F-WNGN	20	182/461
F-WNGN	20	19
F-WNGN	20	25/405
F-WNGN	20	268/492
F-WNGN	20	271/493
F-WNGN	20	44
F-WNGN	20	49/408
F-WNGN	20	52
F-WNGN	20	65
F-WNGN	20	81
F-WNGN	20	88
F-WNGN	20	98/434
F-WNGN	SN	190/465
F-WNGO	10	110
F-WNGO	10	111
F-WNGO	10	128
F-WNGO	10	94
F-WNGO	20	108/430
F-WNGO	20	133
F-WNGO	20	149
F-WNGO	20	162/451
F-WNGO	20	179
F-WNGO	20	198/466
F-WNGO	20	214
F-WNGO	20	254
F-WNGO	20	26
F-WNGO	20	33
F-WNGO	20	42
F-WNGO	20	53/417
F-WNGO	20	55/410
F-WNGO	20	57
F-WNGO	20	59
F-WNGO	20	72/413
F-WNGO	20	77/429
F-WNGO	20	94/428
F-WNGO	20	95
F-WNGQ	CVT	17
F-WNGQ	CVT	30
F-WNGR	CVT	18
F-WNGR	CVT	32
F-WNGS	CVT	20
F-WNGS	CVT	34
F-WNGT	CVT	22
F-WNGU	CVT	25
F-WNGV	CVT	26
F-WNGX	CVT	28
F-WNGY	CVT	29
F-WNGY	CVT	39
F-WNGZ	CVT	31
F-WNGZ	CVT	40
F-WNLR	50	232
F-WOND	50	251
F-WPLT	550	033
F-WPTT	CVT	8
F-WPUU	10	104
F-WPUU	10	121
F-WPUU	10	54
F-WPUU	10	76
F-WPUU	20	189
F-WPUU	20	220
F-WPUU	20	273
F-WPUU	20	479
F-WPUU	200	500
F-WPUU	200	502
F-WPUU	200	508
F-WPUU	200	512
F-WPUV	10	105
F-WPUV	10	122
F-WPUV	10	55
F-WPUV	10	61
F-WPUV	20	170/455
F-WPUV	20	221
F-WPUV	200	484
F-WPUV	200	492
F-WPUV	200	498
F-WPUV	200	507
F-WPUV	200	513
F-WPUX	10	106
F-WPUX	10	123
F-WPUX	10	39
F-WPUX	20	191
F-WPUX	20	223
F-WPUX	20	269
F-WPUX	200	489
F-WPUX	200	504
F-WPUX	200	509
F-WPUY	10	107
F-WPUY	10	124
F-WPUY	10	56
F-WPUY	20	192
F-WPUY	20	224
F-WPUY	200	490
F-WPUY	200	503
F-WPUY	200	510
F-WPUZ	10	108
F-WPUZ	20	194
F-WPUZ	20	242
F-WPUZ	20	270
F-WPUZ	200	482
F-WPUZ	200	506
F-WPXB	10	79
F-WPXD	10	112
F-WPXD	10	80
F-WPXD	10	95
F-WPXD	20	195
F-WPXD	20	208/468
F-WPXD	20	225/472
F-WPXD	20	277/501
F-WPXD	50	131
F-WPXD	50	138
F-WPXD	50	151
F-WPXD	50	169
F-WPXD	50	86
F-WPXD	50	95
F-WPXE	10	113
F-WPXE	10	82
F-WPXE	20	196
F-WPXE	20	231/474
F-WPXE	20	247
F-WPXE	50	145
F-WPXE	50	174
F-WPXE	50	73
F-WPXE	50	96
F-WPXF	10	114
F-WPXF	10	81
F-WPXF	10	97
F-WPXF	20	178/459
F-WPXF	20	197
F-WPXF	20	205
F-WPXF	20	237/476
F-WPXF	50	132
F-WPXF	50	177
F-WPXF	50	78
F-WPXF	50	98
F-WPXG	10	117
F-WPXG	10	83
F-WPXG	10	98
F-WPXG	20	212
F-WPXG	50	110
F-WPXG	50	147
F-WPXG	50	157
F-WPXH	10	115
F-WPXH	10	84
F-WPXH	10	99
F-WPXH	20	203
F-WPXH	20	219/470
F-WPXH	50	101
F-WPXH	50	133
F-WPXH	50	140
F-WPXH	50	155
F-WPXI	10	100
F-WPXI	10	118
F-WPXI	10	85
F-WPXI	20	226
F-WPXI	50	117
F-WPXJ	10	101
F-WPXJ	10	86
F-WPXJ	20	235
F-WPXJ	50	120
F-WPXK	10	102
F-WPXK	10	119
F-WPXK	10	87
F-WPXK	20	236
F-WPXK	20	280/503
F-WPXK	50	107
F-WPXK	50	134
F-WPXL	10	103
F-WPXL	10	88
F-WPXL	SN	186/463
F-WPXM	10	120
F-WPXM	10	89
F-WPXM	20	239
F-WPXM	20	284
F-WPXM	50	114
F-WQAU	125	259032
F-WQBJ	100	208
F-WQBJ	50	95
F-WQBJ	900	105
F-WQBJ	900	154
F-WQBK	20	273
F-WQBK	50	88
F-WQBL	2xx	6
F-WQBL	900	159
F-WQBL	900	62
F-WQBL	90X	12
F-WQBM	20	302/510
F-WQBM	50	107
F-WQBN	20	293
F-WQBN	50	134
F-WQBN	**50**	**7**
F-WQCD	125	258233
F-WQCO	10	70
F-WQCP	50	88
F-WQFL	2xx	26
F-WQFZ	**50**	**30**
F-WQHU	50	258
F-WREX	90X	1
F-WRGQ	20	86
F-WRNZ	CVT	2
F-WRQK	CVT	9
F-WRQP	20	238/477
F-WRQP	20	241/479
F-WRQP	20	252/485
F-WRQP	20	255/487
F-WRQP	20	296/507
F-WRQP	20	300/508
F-WRQP	20	302/510
F-WRQP	20	304/511
F-WRQP	20	315/517
F-WRQP	20	332/525
F-WRQP	20	336/528
F-WRQP	20	342/532
F-WRQP	20	344/534
F-WRQP	20	346/535
F-WRQP	20	353/539
F-WRQP	20	369
F-WRQP	20	374
F-WRQP	20	377/548
F-WRQP	20	397/555
F-WRQP	20	434
F-WRQQ	20	184/462
F-WRQQ	20	295/500
F-WRQQ	20	326/521
F-WRQQ	20	440
F-WRQQ	20	483
F-WRQR	20	251/484
F-WRQR	20	266/490
F-WRQR	20	281/498
F-WRQR	20	337/529
F-WRQR	20	343/533
F-WRQR	20	348/536
F-WRQR	20	354/540
F-WRQR	20	359/542
F-WRQR	20	367/545
F-WRQR	20	375/547
F-WRQR	20	383/550
F-WRQR	20	400/556
F-WRQR	20	451
F-WRQS	20	253/486
F-WRQS	20	306/512
F-WRQS	20	311/515
F-WRQS	20	320/519
F-WRQS	20	323/520
F-WRQS	20	331/524

F-WRQS	20	350/537
F-WRQS	20	358/541
F-WRQS	20	376
F-WRQS	20	381/548
F-WRQS	20	408
F-WRQS	20	455
F-WRQT	20	285/504
F-WRQT	20	291/505
F-WRQT	20	294/506
F-WRQT	20	307/513
F-WRQT	20	309/514
F-WRQT	20	318/518
F-WRQT	20	378
F-WRQT	20	392/553
F-WRQT	20	410
F-WRQT	20	473
F-WRQU	20	286/498
F-WRQU	20	334/527
F-WRQU	20	384/551
F-WRQU	20	422
F-WRQV	20	248/483
F-WRQV	20	329/523
F-WRQV	20	363/544
F-WRQV	20	372/546
F-WRQV	20	389/552
F-WRQV	20	427
F-WRQX	20	283/497
F-WRQX	20	340/531
F-WRQX	20	395/554
F-WRQY	20	358/541
F-WRQZ	20	267/491
F-WRQZ	20	288/499
F-WRSN	CVT	01
F-WSHT	20	174/457
F-WSMF	900	142
F-WSQK	20	226
F-WSQN	10	03
F-WSQU	10	1
F-WTAL	10	02
F-WTDJ	20	182/461
F-WTFE	20	388
F-WTFF	20	113
F-WUAS	CVT	1
F-WUQN	CVT	3
F-WUQP	CVT	4
F-WUQR	CVT	6
F-WVFV	20	182/461
F-WVPR	100	5
F-WW	2xx	25
F-WW	2xx	40
F-WWFA	2xx	3
F-WWFA	900	104
F-WWFA	900	117
F-WWFA	900	134
F-WWFA	900	156
F-WWFA	900	168
F-WWFA	900	18
F-WWFA	900	29
F-WWFA	900	3
F-WWFA	900	4
F-WWFA	900	44
F-WWFA	900	47
F-WWFA	900	73
F-WWFA	900	80
F-WWFA	900	87
F-WWFA	900	97
F-WWFA	90X	16
F-WWFA	90X	2
F-WWFA	90X	29
F-WWFA	90X	39
F-WWFA	90X	55
F-WWFA	90X	66
F-WWFB	900	109
F-WWFB	900	113
F-WWFB	900	118
F-WWFB	900	130
F-WWFB	900	157
F-WWFB	900	19
F-WWFB	900	31
F-WWFB	900	45
F-WWFB	900	5
F-WWFB	900	56
F-WWFB	900	61
F-WWFB	900	71

F-WWFB	900	89
F-WWFB	90X	17
F-WWFB	90X	30
F-WWFB	90X	8
F-WWFC	900	114
F-WWFC	900	127
F-WWFC	900	130
F-WWFC	900	150
F-WWFC	900	158
F-WWFC	900	164
F-WWFC	900	20
F-WWFC	900	33
F-WWFC	900	35
F-WWFC	900	4
F-WWFC	900	43
F-WWFC	900	52
F-WWFC	900	54
F-WWFC	900	75
F-WWFC	900	85
F-WWFC	900	94
F-WWFC	90X	31
F-WWFC	90X	41
F-WWFC	90X	56
F-WWFC	90X	68
F-WWFD	900	105
F-WWFD	900	119
F-WWFD	900	129
F-WWFD	900	148
F-WWFD	900	159
F-WWFD	900	165
F-WWFD	900	172
F-WWFD	900	22
F-WWFD	900	34
F-WWFD	900	46
F-WWFD	900	49
F-WWFD	900	59
F-WWFD	900	6
F-WWFD	900	67
F-WWFD	900	69
F-WWFD	900	84
F-WWFD	90X	42
F-WWFD	90X	69
F-WWFE	900	121
F-WWFE	900	136
F-WWFE	900	160
F-WWFE	900	24
F-WWFE	900	36
F-WWFE	900	38
F-WWFE	900	58
F-WWFE	900	66
F-WWFE	900	76
F-WWFE	900	8
F-WWFE	900	86
F-WWFE	900	99
F-WWFE	90X	18
F-WWFE	90X	32
F-WWFE	90X	43
F-WWFE	90X	9
F-WWFF	900	10
F-WWFF	900	122
F-WWFF	900	137
F-WWFF	900	146
F-WWFF	900	161
F-WWFF	900	178
F-WWFF	900	25
F-WWFF	900	39
F-WWFF	900	63
F-WWFF	900	72
F-WWFF	900	74
F-WWFF	900	96
F-WWFF	90X	33
F-WWFF	90X	58
F-WWFG	900	124
F-WWFG	900	139
F-WWFG	900	147
F-WWFG	900	166
F-WWFG	900	32
F-WWFG	900	51
F-WWFG	900	60
F-WWFG	900	7
F-WWFG	900	77
F-WWFG	900	83
F-WWFG	900	90
F-WWFG	90X	10

F-WWFG	90X	3
F-WWFG	90X	44
F-WWFH	900	110
F-WWFH	900	111
F-WWFH	900	12
F-WWFH	900	131
F-WWFH	900	133
F-WWFH	900	143
F-WWFH	900	149
F-WWFH	900	27
F-WWFH	900	40
F-WWFH	900	50
F-WWFH	900	64
F-WWFH	900	78
F-WWFH	900	88
F-WWFH	900	91
F-WWFH	90X	21
F-WWFI	900	13
F-WWFI	900	132
F-WWFI	900	173
F-WWFI	900	41
F-WWFI	90X	11
F-WWFI	90X	60
F-WWFJ	900	103
F-WWFJ	900	107
F-WWFJ	900	135
F-WWFJ	900	152
F-WWFJ	900	162
F-WWFJ	900	21
F-WWFJ	900	42
F-WWFJ	900	62
F-WWFJ	900	9
F-WWFJ	90X	12
F-WWFJ	90X	19
F-WWFJ	90X	35
F-WWFJ	90X	45
F-WWFJ	90X	5
F-WWFK	900	102
F-WWFK	900	11
F-WWFK	900	141
F-WWFK	900	145
F-WWFK	900	151
F-WWFK	900	153
F-WWFK	900	174
F-WWFK	900	183
F-WWFK	900	23
F-WWFK	900	28
F-WWFK	900	57
F-WWFK	90X	13
F-WWFK	90X	6
F-WWFL	900	103
F-WWFL	900	106
F-WWFL	900	115
F-WWFL	900	123
F-WWFL	900	125
F-WWFL	900	14
F-WWFL	900	140
F-WWFL	900	154
F-WWFL	900	30
F-WWFL	900	68
F-WWFL	900	81
F-WWFL	900	92
F-WWFM	900	112
F-WWFM	900	126
F-WWFM	900	128
F-WWFM	900	15
F-WWFM	900	155
F-WWFM	900	163
F-WWFM	900	26
F-WWFM	900	48
F-WWFM	900	65
F-WWFM	900	79
F-WWFM	900	82
F-WWFM	900	93
F-WWFM	900	98
F-WWFM	90X	36
F-WWFM	90X	46
F-WWFM	**90X**	**62**
F-WWFN	900	100
F-WWFN	900	108
F-WWFN	900	120
F-WWFN	900	142
F-WWFN	900	16
F-WWFN	900	175

F-WWFN	900	37
F-WWFN	900	53
F-WWFN	900	70
F-WWFN	90X	14
F-WWFN	90X	20
F-WWFN	90X	7
F-WWFO	900	101
F-WWFO	900	116
F-WWFO	900	144
F-WWFO	900	167
F-WWFO	900	17
F-WWFO	900	55
F-WWFO	900	95
F-WWFO	90X	15
F-WWFO	90X	47
F-WWFO	90X	63
F-WWFP	900	169
F-WWFP	90X	48
F-WWFQ	900	179
F-WWFQ	90X	22
F-WWFR	900	170
F-WWFR	90X	49
F-WWFS	90X	23
F-WWFS	90X	50
F-WWFU	90X	24
F-WWFU	90X	51
F-WWFV	90X	25
F-WWFV	90X	37
F-WWFV	90X	52
F-WWFW	900	171
F-WWFW	900	176
F-WWFW	90X	53
F-WWFX	900	180
F-WWFX	90X	26
F-WWFX	90X	38
F-WWFY	900	177
F-WWFY	90X	27
F-WWFY	90X	54
F-WWFZ	900	181
F-WWFZ	90X	28
F-WWGO	200	515
F-WWGP	200	501
F-WWGP	200	514
F-WWGR	200	511
F-WWHA	50	181
F-WWHA	50	188
F-WWHA	50	197
F-WWHA	50	201
F-WWHA	50	203
F-WWHA	50	218
F-WWHA	50	231
F-WWHA	50	242
F-WWHA	50	253
F-WWHA	50	275
F-WWHB	50	182
F-WWHB	50	189
F-WWHB	50	199
F-WWHB	50	202
F-WWHB	50	206
F-WWHB	50	233
F-WWHB	50	248
F-WWHB	50	254
F-WWHB	50	276
F-WWHC	50	180
F-WWHC	50	198
F-WWHC	50	207
F-WWHC	50	226
F-WWHC	50	234
F-WWHC	50	255
F-WWHC	50	277
F-WWHD	50	184
F-WWHD	50	191
F-WWHD	50	196
F-WWHD	50	204
F-WWHD	50	205
F-WWHD	50	230
F-WWHD	50	236
F-WWHD	50	256
F-WWHD	50	278
F-WWHE	50	185
F-WWHE	50	192
F-WWHE	50	200
F-WWHE	50	209
F-WWHE	50	227

F-WWHE	50	237
F-WWHE	50	252
F-WWHE	50	257
F-WWHE	50	279
F-WWHF	50	183
F-WWHF	50	238
F-WWHF	50	241
F-WWHF	50	246
F-WWHF	50	258
F-WWHF	50	280
F-WWHG	50	187
F-WWHG	50	190
F-WWHG	50	220
F-WWHG	50	239
F-WWHG	50	259
F-WWHG	50	281
F-WWHH	50	186
F-WWHH	50	193
F-WWHH	50	212
F-WWHH	50	229
F-WWHH	50	240
F-WWHH	50	282
F-WWHK	50	104
F-WWHK	50	195
F-WWHK	50	244
F-WWHK	50	260
F-WWHK	50	283
F-WWHL	50	210
F-WWHL	50	221
F-WWHL	50	245
F-WWHL	50	261
F-WWHL	50	284
F-WWHM	50	194
F-WWHM	50	222
F-WWHM	50	235
F-WWHM	50	243
F-WWHM	50	262
F-WWHM	50	285
F-WWHN	50	223
F-WWHN	50	249
F-WWHN	50	263
F-WWHN	50	286
F-WWHO	50	224
F-WWHO	50	264
F-WWHO	50	287
F-WWHP	50	208
F-WWHP	50	225
F-WWHP	50	247
F-WWHP	50	265
F-WWHP	50	288
F-WWHQ	50	266
F-WWHQ	50	289
F-WWHR	50	211
F-WWHR	50	228
F-WWHR	50	250
F-WWHR	50	267
F-WWHR	50	290
F-WWHS	50	219
F-WWHS	50	268
F-WWHS	**50**	**291**
F-WWHT	50	215
F-WWHT	50	232
F-WWHT	50	269
F-WWHT	50	292
F-WWHU	50	270
F-WWHU	50	293
F-WWHV	50	217
F-WWHV	50	271
F-WWHV	50	294
F-WWHW	50	213
F-WWHW	50	272
F-WWHW	**50**	**295**
F-WWHX	50	214
F-WWHX	50	273
F-WWHX	50	296
F-WWHY	50	274
F-WWHY	**50**	**297**
F-WWHZ	50	216
F-WWHZ	50	298
F-WWHZ	50	36
F-WWJC	90X	4
F-WWMA	2xx	17
F-WWMA	2xx	21
F-WWMA	2xx	29
F-WWMA	2xx	36
F-WWMA	2xx	4
F-WWMA	2xx	57
F-WWMA	2xx	69
F-WWMB	2xx	16
F-WWMB	2xx	30
F-WWMB	2xx	47
F-WWMB	2xx	5
F-WWMB	2xx	58
F-WWMB	2xx	70
F-WWMC	2xx	19
F-WWMC	2xx	31
F-WWMC	2xx	48
F-WWMC	2xx	59
F-WWMC	2xx	71
F-WWMD	2xx	32
F-WWMD	2xx	41
F-WWMD	2xx	49
F-WWMD	2xx	6
F-WWMD	2xx	60
F-WWMD	2xx	72
F-WWME	2xx	20
F-WWME	2xx	33
F-WWME	2xx	50
F-WWME	2xx	61
F-WWME	2xx	7
F-WWMF	2xx	22
F-WWMF	2xx	34
F-WWMF	2xx	51
F-WWMF	2xx	62
F-WWMF	2xx	8
F-WWMG	2xx	18
F-WWMG	2xx	35
F-WWMG	2xx	42
F-WWMG	2xx	63
F-WWMG	2xx	73
F-WWMG	2xx	9
F-WWMH	2xx	10
F-WWMH	2xx	23
F-WWMH	2xx	37
F-WWMH	2xx	64
F-WWMH	2xx	74
F-WWMI	2xx	38
F-WWMI	2xx	52
F-WWMI	2xx	65
F-WWMJ	2xx	39
F-WWMJ	2xx	53
F-WWMJ	2xx	66
F-WWMJ	2xx	78
F-WWMK	2xx	11
F-WWMK	2xx	24
F-WWMK	2xx	43
F-WWMK	2xx	67
F-WWMK	2xx	75
F-WWML	2xx	13
F-WWML	2xx	44
F-WWML	2xx	54
F-WWML	2xx	76
F-WWMM	2xx	12
F-WWMM	2xx	27
F-WWMM	2xx	45
F-WWMM	2xx	55
F-WWMM	2xx	77
F-WWMN	2xx	14
F-WWMN	2xx	26
F-WWMN	2xx	46
F-WWMN	2xx	68
F-WWMN	2xx	79
F-WWMO	2xx	15
F-WWMO	2xx	28
F-WWMO	2xx	56
F-WWMO	2xx	80
F-WWVA	2xx	106
F-WWVA	2xx	81
F-WWVB	**2xx**	**107**
F-WWVB	2xx	82
F-WWVC	2xx	108
F-WWVC	2xx	83
F-WWVD	2xx	109
F-WWVD	2xx	84
F-WWVE	2xx	85
F-WWVF	2xx	86
F-WWVG	2xx	87
F-WWVH	2xx	88
F-WWVI	2xx	89
F-WWVJ	2xx	90
F-WWVK	2xx	91
F-WWVL	2xx	92
F-WWVL	2xx	116
F-WWVM	2xx	93
F-WWVN	2xx	94
F-WWVO	2xx	95
F-WWVP	2xx	96
F-WWVQ	2xx	97
F-WWVR	2xx	98
F-WWVS	2xx	99
F-WWVT	2xx	100
F-WWVX	2xx	103
F-WWVY	2xx	104
F-WZAH	20	401
(F-WZAS)	20	362
F-WZGA	10	129
F-WZGA	10	154
F-WZGA	10	173
F-WZGA	100	195
F-WZGA	100	217
F-WZGB	10	130
F-WZGB	10	186
F-WZGB	100	196
F-WZGB	100	218
F-WZGC	10	131
F-WZGC	10	155
F-WZGC	10	181
F-WZGC	100	197
F-WZGC	100	219
F-WZGD	10	132
F-WZGD	10	61
F-WZGD	100	202
F-WZGD	100	220
F-WZGE	10	133
F-WZGE	10	156
F-WZGE	10	174
F-WZGF	10	108
F-WZGF	10	134
F-WZGF	10	157
F-WZGF	10	175
F-WZGF	10	89
F-WZGF	100	198
F-WZGF	100	222
F-WZGG	10	127
F-WZGG	10	135
F-WZGG	100	199
F-WZGG	100	200
F-WZGG	100	223
F-WZGH	10	136
F-WZGH	100	201
F-WZGH	100	221
F-WZGH	100	224
F-WZGI	10	137
F-WZGI	10	158
F-WZGI	10	176
F-WZGI	100	225
F-WZGJ	10	138
F-WZGJ	10	159
F-WZGJ	10	177
F-WZGJ	100	203
F-WZGJ	100	226
F-WZGK	10	139
F-WZGK	10	160
F-WZGK	10	178
F-WZGK	100	204
F-WZGL	10	140
F-WZGL	10	179
F-WZGL	100	205
F-WZGM	10	141
F-WZGM	10	161
F-WZGM	10	180
F-WZGM	100	206
F-WZGN	10	142
F-WZGN	10	162
F-WZGN	10	182
F-WZGN	100	207
F-WZGO	10	143
F-WZGO	100	183
F-WZGO	100	208
F-WZGP	10	144
F-WZGP	10	163
F-WZGP	10	184
F-WZGP	100	209
F-WZGQ	10	145
F-WZGQ	10	164
F-WZGQ	10	185
F-WZGR	10	146
F-WZGR	10	165
F-WZGR	10	187
F-WZGR	100	210
F-WZGS	10	126
F-WZGS	10	136
F-WZGS	10	147
F-WZGS	10	166
F-WZGS	10	188
F-WZGT	10	148
F-WZGT	10	167
F-WZGT	10	189
F-WZGT	100	211
F-WZGU	10	149
F-WZGU	10	168
F-WZGU	10	190
F-WZGU	100	212
F-WZGV	10	150
F-WZGV	10	169
F-WZGV	10	191
F-WZGV	100	213
F-WZGX	10	151
F-WZGX	10	170
F-WZGX	100	192
F-WZGX	100	214
F-WZGY	10	152
F-WZGY	10	171
F-WZGY	100	193
F-WZGY	100	215
F-WZGZ	10	153
F-WZGZ	10	172
F-WZGZ	100	194
F-WZGZ	100	216
F-WZHA	50	112
F-WZHA	50	124
F-WZHA	50	135
F-WZHA	50	146
F-WZHA	50	154
F-WZHA	50	161
F-WZHA	50	163
F-WZHA	50	26
F-WZHA	50	33
F-WZHA	50	4
F-WZHA	50	44
F-WZHA	50	58
F-WZHA	50	7
F-WZHA	50	74
F-WZHA	50	81
F-WZHB	50	113
F-WZHB	50	125
F-WZHB	50	136
F-WZHB	50	148
F-WZHB	50	162
F-WZHB	50	19
F-WZHB	50	29
(F-WZHB)	50	5
F-WZHB	50	59
F-WZHB	50	6
F-WZHB	50	76
F-WZHB	50	93
F-WZHC	50	115
F-WZHC	50	12
F-WZHC	50	137
F-WZHC	50	150
F-WZHC	50	159
F-WZHC	50	31
F-WZHC	50	57
F-WZHC	50	77
F-WZHC	50	8
F-WZHC	50	94
F-WZHD	50	10
F-WZHD	50	116
F-WZHD	50	127
F-WZHD	50	139
F-WZHD	50	152
F-WZHD	50	164
F-WZHD	50	30
F-WZHD	50	60
F-WZHD	50	9
F-WZHE	50	11

F-WZHE	50	141
F-WZHE	50	153
F-WZHE	50	166
F-WZHE	50	28
F-WZHE	50	42
F-WZHE	50	62
F-WZHE	50	79
F-WZHF	50	118
F-WZHF	50	128
F-WZHF	50	13
F-WZHF	50	156
F-WZHF	50	165
F-WZHF	50	22
F-WZHF	50	35
F-WZHF	50	45
F-WZHF	50	63
F-WZHF	50	71
F-WZHG	50	122
F-WZHG	50	14
F-WZHG	50	167
F-WZHG	50	23
F-WZHG	50	40
F-WZHG	50	67
F-WZHG	50	82
F-WZHH	50	123
F-WZHH	50	158
F-WZHH	50	16
F-WZHH	50	168
F-WZHH	50	34
F-WZHH	50	64
F-WZHH	50	75
F-WZHI	50	126
F-WZHI	50	143
F-WZHI	50	160
F-WZHI	50	17
F-WZHI	50	170
F-WZHI	50	25
F-WZHI	50	41
F-WZHI	50	61
F-WZHJ	50	149
F-WZHJ	50	171
F-WZHJ	50	18
F-WZHJ	50	32
F-WZHJ	50	36
F-WZHJ	50	69
F-WZHJ	50	83
F-WZHK	50	142
F-WZHK	50	172
F-WZHK	50	20
F-WZHK	50	38
F-WZHK	50	46
F-WZHK	50	48
F-WZHK	50	84
F-WZHL	50	144
F-WZHL	50	173
F-WZHL	50	24
F-WZHL	50	39
F-WZHL	50	49
F-WZHL	50	70
F-WZHL	50	97
F-WZHM	50	108
F-WZHM	50	15
F-WZHM	50	175
F-WZHM	50	37
F-WZHM	50	72
F-WZHM	50	99
F-WZHN	50	100
F-WZHN	50	119
F-WZHN	50	176
F-WZHN	50	21
F-WZHN	50	27
F-WZHN	50	80
F-WZHO	50	102
F-WZHO	50	121
F-WZHO	50	178
F-WZHO	50	43
F-WZHO	50	85
F-WZHP	50	179
F-WZHP	50	47
F-WZHP	50	66
F-WZHQ	50	103
F-WZHQ	50	129
F-WZHQ	50	50
F-WZHQ	50	68

F-WZHR	50	104
F-WZHR	50	130
F-WZHR	50	51
F-WZHR	50	56
F-WZHS	50	105
F-WZHS	50	53
F-WZHS	50	87
F-WZHT	50	106
F-WZHT	50	54
F-WZHT	50	65
F-WZHU	50	55
F-WZHU	50	88
F-WZHV	50	109
F-WZHV	50	52
F-WZHV	50	89
F-WZHX	50	90
F-WZHY	50	91
F-WZHZ	50	111
F-WZHZ	50	92
F-WZIG	125	257055
F-WZIH	**HFB**	**1024**
F-WZSB	CVT	31
F-WZZA	200	491
F-WZZA	200	497
F-WZZA	200	505
F-WZZB	200	487
F-WZZC	200	493
F-WZZC	200	496
F-WZZD	200	494
F-WZZD	200	501
F-WZZE	200	495
F-WZZF	200	488
F-WZZJ	200	499

France - Govt Operated

(F-Z)	MSP	03
F-ZADS	MSP	001
F-ZGTI	10	133
F-ZJAZ	**MSP**	**117**
F-ZJNB	**MSP**	**068**
F-ZJNC	**MSP**	**083**
F-ZJNI	**MSP**	**113**
F-ZJNJ	MSP	100
F-ZJNJ	**MSP**	**114**
F-ZJNQ	**MSP**	**118**
F-ZJON	**MSP**	**116**
F-ZJOV	**MSP**	**115**
F-ZJTA	10	02
F-ZJTJ	20	422
F-ZJTL	50	36
F-ZJTS	20	451
F-ZLNL	**MSP**	**119**
F-ZWTA	50	36

United Kingdom

G-5-11	125	25026
G-5-11	125	25101
G-5-11	125	25110
G-5-11	125	25119
G-5-11	125	25126
G-5-11	125	25131
G-5-11	125	25134
G-5-11	125	25137
G-5-11	125	25139
G-5-11	125	25154
G-5-11	125	25197
G-5-11	125	25240
G-5-11	125	25276
G-5-11	125	25277
G-5-11	125	256015
G-5-11	125	256021
G-5-11	125	256045
G-5-11	125	256052
G-5-11	125	256070
G-5-11	125	257008
(G-5-11)	125	257022
G-5-11	125	257039
G-5-11	125	257051
G-5-11	125	257065
G-5-11	125	257093
G-5-11	125	257105
G-5-11	125	257119
G-5-11	125	257131
G-5-11	125	257144
G-5-11	125	257150
G-5-11	125	257164
G-5-11	125	257177
G-5-11	125	257186
G-5-11	125	257196
G-5-11	125	258001
G-5-11	125	258008
G-5-11	125	258032
G-5-11	125	258042
G-5-11	125	258047
G-5-11	125	258053
G-5-12	125	25129
(G-5-12)	125	25138
G-5-12	125	25141
G-5-12	125	25144
G-5-12	125	25219
G-5-12	125	25244
G-5-12	125	25279
G-5-12	125	256028
G-5-12	125	256050
G-5-12	125	256060
G-5-12	125	257009
G-5-12	125	257025
G-5-12	125	257041
G-5-12	125	257073
G-5-12	125	257083
G-5-12	125	257095
G-5-12	125	257103
G-5-12	125	257142
G-5-12	125	257151
G-5-12	125	257163
G-5-12	125	257184
G-5-12	125	257185
G-5-12	125	257197
G-5-12	125	257199
G-5-12	125	257212
(G-5-12)	125	258005
G-5-12	125	258018
G-5-12	125	258019
G-5-12	125	258027
G-5-12	125	258028
G-5-12	125	258034
G-5-12	125	258043
G-5-12	125	258044
G-5-13	125	25113
G-5-13	125	25148
G-5-13	125	25150
(G-5-13)	125	25181
G-5-13	125	25256
G-5-13	125	25270
G-5-13	125	256041
G-5-13	125	256056
G-5-13	125	256063
G-5-13	125	257011
G-5-13	125	257042
G-5-13	125	257056
G-5-13	125	257066
G-5-13	125	257075
G-5-13	125	257106
G-5-13	125	257120
G-5-13	125	257134
G-5-13	125	257146
G-5-14	125	25130
G-5-14	125	25135
G-5-14	125	25147
G-5-14	125	25217
G-5-14	125	25219
G-5-14	125	25243
G-5-14	125	25271
G-5-14	125	256031
G-5-14	125	256061
G-5-14	125	256071
G-5-14	125	257012
G-5-14	125	257032
G-5-14	125	257034
G-5-14	125	257057
G-5-14	125	257068
G-5-14	125	257077
G-5-14	125	257084
G-5-14	125	257096
G-5-14	125	257108
G-5-14	125	257121
G-5-14	125	257133
G-5-14	125	257147
G-5-14	125	257158
G-5-14	125	257165
G-5-14	125	257170
G-5-14	125	257178
G-5-14	125	257187
G-5-14	125	257192
G-5-14	125	257200
G-5-14	125	257203
G-5-14	125	258013
G-5-14	125	258020
G-5-14	125	258025
G-5-14	125	258030
G-5-15	125	25160
G-5-15	125	25223
G-5-15	125	25272
G-5-15	125	256002
G-5-15	125	256006
G-5-15	125	256048
G-5-15	125	256062
G-5-15	125	256066
G-5-15	125	256070
G-5-15	125	257004
G-5-15	125	257058
G-5-15	125	257069
G-5-15	125	257078
G-5-15	125	257085
G-5-15	125	257098
G-5-15	125	257110
G-5-15	125	257122
G-5-15	125	257135
G-5-15	125	257159
G-5-15	125	257167
G-5-15	125	257171
G-5-15	125	257179
G-5-15	125	257188
G-5-15	125	257193
G-5-15	125	257204
G-5-15	125	258004
G-5-15	125	258005
G-5-15	125	258009
G-5-15	125	258014
G-5-15	125	258021
G-5-15	125	258023
G-5-15	125	258031
G-5-15	125	258037
G-5-15	125	258040
G-5-15	125	258054
G-5-16	125	25138
(G-5-16)	125	25140
G-5-16	125	25163
(G-5-16)	125	25246
G-5-16	125	25249
G-5-16	125	25289
G-5-16	125	256026
G-5-16	125	256047
G-5-16	125	256065
G-5-16	125	256068
G-5-16	125	257035
G-5-16	125	257048
G-5-16	125	257055
G-5-16	125	257062
G-5-16	125	257079
G-5-16	125	257087
G-5-16	125	257094
G-5-16	125	257099
G-5-16	125	257111
G-5-16	125	257123
G-5-16	125	257137
G-5-16	125	257180
G-5-16	125	257181
G-5-16	125	257206
G-5-16	125	257213
(G-5-16)	125	258002
G-5-16	125	258017
G-5-16	125	258022
G-5-16	125	258029
G-5-16	125	258045
G-5-16	125	258048
G-5-17	125	25140
G-5-17	125	25169

G-5-17	125	25252
G-5-17	125	256012
G-5-17	125	256054
G-5-17	125	256057
G-5-17	125	256064
G-5-17	125	257014
G-5-17	125	257022
G-5-17	125	257036
G-5-17	125	257044
G-5-17	125	257049
G-5-17	125	257059
G-5-17	125	257071
G-5-17	125	257076
G-5-17	125	257086
G-5-17	125	257101
G-5-17	125	257113
G-5-17	125	257125
G-5-17	125	257138
G-5-17	125	257148
G-5-17	125	257152
G-5-17	125	257156
G-5-17	125	257161
G-5-17	125	257173
G-5-17	125	257182
G-5-17	125	257191
G-5-17	125	257202
G-5-17	125	257214
G-5-17	125	258006
G-5-17	125	258015
G-5-18	125	25143
G-5-18	125	25183
G-5-18	125	25235
G-5-18	125	25253
G-5-18	125	256017
G-5-18	125	256045
G-5-18	125	256058
G-5-18	125	257006
G-5-18	125	257015
G-5-18	125	257037
G-5-18	125	257050
G-5-18	125	257060
G-5-18	125	257072
G-5-18	125	257080
G-5-18	125	257089
G-5-18	125	257102
G-5-18	125	257114
G-5-18	125	257126
G-5-18	125	257139
G-5-18	125	257145
G-5-18	125	257154
G-5-18	125	257162
G-5-18	125	257166
G-5-18	125	257174
G-5-18	125	257195
G-5-18	125	257198
G-5-18	125	257207
G-5-18	125	257210
G-5-18	125	258012
G-5-18	125	258016
G-5-18	125	258024
G-5-18	125	258026
G-5-18	125	258036
G-5-18	125	258041
G-5-18	125	258051
G-5-19	125	25153
G-5-19	125	25159
G-5-19	125	25171
G-5-19	125	25235
G-5-19	125	25239
G-5-19	125	25257
G-5-19	125	256015
G-5-19	125	256055
G-5-19	125	256059
G-5-19	125	257003
G-5-19	125	257017
G-5-19	125	257038
G-5-19	125	257052
G-5-19	125	257061
G-5-19	125	257074
G-5-19	125	257081
G-5-19	125	257090
G-5-19	125	257100
G-5-19	125	257116
G-5-19	125	257128
G-5-19	125	257140
G-5-19	125	257149
G-5-19	125	257155
G-5-19	125	257160
G-5-19	125	257201
G-5-19	125	257205
G-5-19	125	257208
(G-5-19)	125	258005
G-5-19	125	258010
G-5-19	125	258033
G-5-19	125	258039
G-5-19	125	258049
G-5-20	125	25145
G-5-20	125	25189
G-5-20	125	25214
G-5-20	125	25241
G-5-20	125	25242
G-5-20	125	25273
G-5-20	125	25274
G-5-20	125	256068
G-5-20	125	257002
G-5-20	125	257053
G-5-20	125	257063
G-5-20	125	257092
G-5-20	125	257104
G-5-20	125	257117
G-5-20	125	257129
G-5-20	125	257141
G-5-20	125	257143
G-5-20	125	257157
G-5-20	125	257168
G-5-20	125	257176
G-5-20	125	257183
G-5-20	125	257209
G-5-20	125	257215
G-5-20	125	258003
G-5-20	125	258007
G-5-20	125	258011
G-5-20	125	258035
G-5-20	125	258038
G-5-20	125	258046
G-5-20	125	258052
G-5-21	125	257169
G-5-501	125	258037
G-5-502	125	257115
G-5-503	125	258050
G-5-504	125	258055
G-5-505	125	256042
G-5-506	125	258059
G-5-508	125	258057
G-5-509	125	258056
G-5-510	125	258058
G-5-511	125	258060
G-5-514	125	258064
G-5-515	125	258061
G-5-516	125	258062
G-5-518	125	258063
G-5-519	125	257064
G-5-520	125	258065
G-5-521	125	258066
G-5-522	125	258001
G-5-524	125	257076
G-5-525	125	258067
G-5-526	125	258069
G-5-527	125	258070
G-5-528	125	258071
G-5-529	125	258072
G-5-530	125	257178
G-5-531	125	257088
G-5-532	125	258073
G-5-533	125	258075
G-5-534	125	257028
G-5-535	125	258076
G-5-536	125	257112
G-5-538	125	258077
G-5-539	125	258068
G-5-540	125	258080
G-5-541	125	258074
G-5-542	125	258079
G-5-543	125	258081
G-5-544	125	258078
G-5-545	125	257136
G-5-546	125	258083
G-5-547	125	258084
G-5-548	125	258082
G-5-549	125	257100
G-5-550	125	258086
G-5-551	125	258085
G-5-552	125	258087
G-5-553	125	257112
G-5-554	125	258007
G-5-555	125	258089
G-5-556	125	258090
G-5-557	125	258001
G-5-558	125	258092
G-5-559	125	258093
G-5-560	125	258091
G-5-561	125	258095
G-5-562	125	258096
G-5-563	125	258088
G-5-564	125	258098
G-5-565	125	258099
G-5-566	125	258100
G-5-567	125	258097
G-5-568	125	257172
G-5-569	125	258022
G-5-570	125	257178
G-5-571	125	257076
G-5-572	125	258101
G-5-573	125	258102
G-5-574	125	258103
G-5-575	125	258104
G-5-576	125	258094
G-5-577	125	258105
G-5-578	125	258107
G-5-579	125	258108
G-5-580	125	258106
G-5-581	125	258109
G-5-582	125	258111
G-5-583	125	258112
G-5-584	125	258110
G-5-585	125	256027
G-5-586	125	258114
G-5-587	125	258113
G-5-588	125	257130
G-5-589	125	258117
(G-5-590)	125	258118
G-5-591	125	258119
G-5-592	125	258116
G-5-593	125	258121
G-5-594	125	258122
G-5-595	125	258034
G-5-596	125	258124
G-5-597	125	258126
G-5-598	125	257055
G-5-599	125	258115
G-5-600	125	258123
G-5-601	125	258125
G-5-602	125	258127
G-5-603	125	258128
G-5-604	125	257070
G-5-605	125	258118
G-5-606	125	258120
G-5-607	125	258132
G-5-608	125	258135
G-5-609	125	258136
G-5-610	125	258137
G-5-611	125	258131
G-5-612	125	258139
G-5-613	125	258140
G-5-614	125	258138
G-5-615	125	258141
G-5-616	125	258133
G-5-617	125	258142
G-5-618	125	258144
G-5-619	125	258145
G-5-620	125	258130
G-5-621	125	258147
G-5-622	125	258129
G-5-623	125	25127
G-5-624	125	25254
G-5-625	125	258150
G-5-626	125	258152
G-5-627	125	258153
G-5-628	125	258155
G-5-629	125	258146
G-5-630	125	258148
G-5-631	125	257010
G-5-632	125	258157
G-5-633	125	258160
G-5-634	125	258134
G-5-635	125	258149
G-5-636	125	258161
G-5-637	125	258058
G-5-638	125	258162
G-5-639	125	258163
G-5-640	125	258074
G-5-641	125	258166
G-5-642	125	258133
G-5-643	125	258168
G-5-644	125	258169
G-5-645	125	258170
G-5-646	125	258171
G-5-647	125	258172
G-5-648	125	258173
G-5-649	125	258174
G-5-650	125	258175
G-5-651	125	25217
G-5-652	125	258176
G-5-653	125	258068
G-5-654	125	258164
G-5-655	125	258154
G-5-656	125	258143
G-5-657	125	258165
G-5-658	125	258178
G-5-659	125	257212
G-5-660	125	258179
G-5-661	125	258156
G-5-662	125	258167
G-5-663	125	258181
G-5-664	125	258112
G-5-665	125	258115
G-5-666	125	258183
G-5-667	125	258158
G-5-668	125	258177
G-5-669	125	258185
G-5-670	125	258187
G-5-670	125	258208
G-5-671	125	258188
G-5-672	125	25247
G-5-673	125	258189
G-5-674	125	258191
G-5-675	125	258180
G-5-676	125	258182
G-5-677	125	258193
G-5-678	125	258184
G-5-679	125	258195
G-5-680	125	258196
G-5-681	125	258199
G-5-682	125	258200
G-5-683	125	258186
G-5-684	125	258190
G-5-685	125	258202
G-5-686	125	258203
G-5-687	125	258204
G-5-688	125	258206
G-5-689	125	258205
G-5-690	125	258207
G-5-691	125	258192
G-5-692	125	258194
G-5-693	125	257196
G-5-694	125	258198
G-5-695	125	258209
G-5-696	125	258197
G-5-697	125	258040
G-5-698	125	256052
G-5-699	125	258201
G-5-700	125	258208
G-5-701	125	257031
G-5-702	125	259003
G-5-703	125	258146
G-5-704	125	258019
G-5-705	125	258210
G-5-706	125	258214
G-5-707	125	25248
G-5-708	125	257062
G-5-709	125	258213
G-5-710	125	258212
G-5-711	125	259013
G-5-712	125	259014
G-5-713	125	258078
G-5-714	125	258216

G-5-715	125	258217
G-5-716	125	259009
G-5-717	125	259011
G-5-718	125	259015
G-5-719	125	259017
G-5-720	125	259008
G-5-721	125	257007
G-5-722	125	259010
G-5-723	125	259020
G-5-724	125	258211
G-5-725	125	258218
G-5-726	125	259012
G-5-727	125	258215
G-5-728	125	258220
G-5-729	125	259023
G-5-730	125	259019
G-5-731	125	258221
G-5-732	125	259016
G-5-733	125	258223
G-5-734	125	259022
G-5-735	125	259005
G-5-736	125	259021
G-5-737	125	259024
G-5-738	125	258068
G-5-739	125	258225
G-5-740	125	258219
G-5-741	125	259018
G-5-742	125	258025
G-5-743	125	259026
G-5-744	125	258229
G-5-745	125	258222
G-5-746	125	259027
G-5-747	125	257178
G-5-748	125	258230
G-5-749	125	259028
G-5-750	125	258231
G-5-751	125	259029
G-5-752	125	258232
G-5-753	125	259030
G-5-754	125	259031
G-5-755	125	258226
G-5-756	125	259033
G-5-757	125	258234
G-5-758	125	258228
G-5-759	125	259025
G-5-760	125	259032
G-5-761	125	259034
G-5-762	125	259036
G-5-763	125	258224
G-5-764	125	258236
G-5-765	125	257172
G-5-766	125	257196
G-5-767	125	258238
G-5-768	125	258239
G-5-769	125	258227
G-5-770	125	258233
G-5-771	125	259037
G-5-772	125	258240
G-5-773	125	259035
G-5-774	125	258235
G-5-775	125	258237
G-5-776	125	259038
G-5-777	125	258241
G-5-778	125	258243
G-5-779	125	259004
G-5-780	125	258244
G-5-781	125	259039
G-5-782	125	258246
G-5-783	125	259040
G-5-784	125	258248
G-5-785	125	259041
G-5-786	125	258249
G-5-787	125	258251
G-5-788	125	258252
G-5-789	125	259042
G-5-790	125	258253
G-5-791	125	258254
G-5-792	125	258255
G-5-793	125	258242
G-5-794	125	259043
G-5-795	125	258256
G-5-796	125	258257
G-5-797	125	259044
G-5-798	125	258258

G-5-799	125	258259
G-5-800	125	258260
G-5-801	125	259045
G-5-802	125	258261
G-5-803	125	258262
G-5-804	125	258263
G-5-805	125	259046
G-5-806	125	258264
G-5-807	125	258067
G-5-808	125	257107
G-5-809	125	258265
G-5-810	125	257097
G-5-811	125	258266
G-5-812	125	258267
G-5-813	125	258247
G-5-814	125	258269
G-5-815	125	258250
G-5-816	125	258270
G-5-817	125	259047
G-5-818	125	258271
G-5-819	125	258272
G-5-820	125	258273
G-5-821	125	25281
G-5-822	125	258274
G-5-823	125	258275
G-5-824	125	258276
G-5-826	125	259048
G-5-827	125	258282
G-5-828	125	258283
G-5-829	125	258268
G-5-830	125	258284
G-5-831	125	258285
G-5-832	125	258286
G-5-833	125	258287
G-5-834	125	258289
G-5-835	125	258290
G-5-836	125	258291
"G-5-837"	125	258291
G-5-837	125	259049
G-5-838	125	258292
G-5-839	125	258293
G-5-840	125	258294
G-5-841	125	258295
G-5-842	125	258296
G-5-843	125	258298
G-5-844	125	258299
G-5-845	125	258300
G-5-846	125	259050
G-5-847	125	258302
G-5-848	125	258288
G-5-849	125	258303
G-5-850	125	258307
G-5-851	125	258308
G-5-852	125	258310
G-5-853	125	258312
G-5-854	125	258314
G-5-855	125	258316
G-5-856	125	258318
G-5-857	125	258321
G-5-858	125	258323
G-5-859	125	259051
G-5-860	125	258324
G-5-861	125	258327
G-5-862	125	258329
G-5-863	125	259052
G-5-864	125	258305
G-5-865	125	258332
G-5-866	125	258328
G-5-867	125	258335
G-5-868	125	258337
G-5-869	125	258330
G-5-870	125	257194
G-36-2	MSP	008
G-37-65	125	25011
G-60-01	20	223
(G-)	125	257094
(G-)	G4	1096
G-APRU	MSP	008
G-ARYA	125	25001
G-ARYB	125	25002
G-ARYC	125	25003
G-ASEC	125	25004
G-ASNU	125	25005
(G-ASSH)	125	25007

G-ASSH	125	25017
G-ASSI	125	25008
G-ASSJ	125	25013
G-ASSK	125	25014
G-ASSL	125	25016
G-ASSM	125	25010
G-ASTY	125	25007
G-ASYX	125	25019
G-ASZM	125	25020
G-ASZN	125	25021
G-ASZO	125	25022
G-ASZP	125	25023
G-ATAY	125	25026
G-ATAZ	125	25029
G-ATBA	125	25030
G-ATBB	125	25031
G-ATBC	125	25032
G-ATBD	125	25033
G-ATCO	125	25035
G-ATCP	125	25038
G-ATFO	125	25037
G-ATGA	125	25043
G-ATGS	125	25046
G-ATGT	125	25047
G-ATGU	125	25051
G-ATIK	125	25052
G-ATIL	125	25057
G-ATIM	125	25060
G-ATKK	125	25064
G-ATKL	125	25065
G-ATKM	125	25066
G-ATKN	125	25070
G-ATLI	125	25073
G-ATLJ	125	25075
G-ATLK	125	25078
G-ATLL	125	25079
G-ATNM	125	25082
G-ATNN	125	25084
G-ATNO	125	25088
G-ATNP	125	25091
G-ATNR	125	25096
G-ATNS	125	25098
G-ATNT	125	25100
G-ATOV	125	25074
G-ATOW	125	25083
G-ATOX	125	25087
G-ATPB	125	25089
G-ATPC	125	25009
G-ATPD	**125**	**25085**
G-ATPE	125	25092
G-ATSN	125	25093
G-ATSO	125	25095
G-ATSP	125	25097
G-ATUU	125	25102
G-ATUV	125	25103
G-ATUW	125	25104
G-ATUX	125	25107
G-ATUY	125	25108
G-ATUZ	125	25109
G-ATWH	125	25094
G-ATXE	125	25101
G-ATYH	125	25111
G-ATYI	125	25112
G-ATYJ	125	25114
G-ATYK	125	25115
G-ATYL	125	25118
G-ATZE	125	25110
G-ATZN	125	25116
G-AVAD	125	25119
G-AVAE	125	25121
G-AVAF	125	25122
G-AVAG	125	25123
G-AVAH	125	25124
G-AVAI	125	25125
G-AVDL	125	25126
G-AVDM	125	25129
G-AVDX	125	25113
G-AVGW	125	25120
G-AVHA	125	25134
G-AVHB	125	25136
G-AVJD	125	25137
G-AVOI	125	25128
G-AVOJ	125	25139
G-AVOK	125	25141

G-AVOL	125	25142
G-AVPE	125	25127
G-AVRD	125	25130
G-AVRE	125	25131
G-AVRF	125	25133
G-AVRG	125	25144
G-AVRH	125	25146
G-AVRI	125	25148
G-AVRJ	125	25149
G-AVTY	125	25151
G-AVTZ	125	25152
G-AVVA	125	25138
G-AVVB	125	25140
G-AVXK	125	25143
G-AVXL	125	25145
G-AVXM	125	25153
G-AVXN	125	25155
G-AVZJ	125	25156
G-AVZK	125	25158
G-AVZL	125	25159
G-AWKH	125	25160
G-AWKI	125	25161
G-AWMS	125	25150
G-AWMV	125	25163
G-AWMW	125	25170
G-AWMX	125	25173
G-AWMY	125	25174
G-AWPC	125	25175
G-AWPD	125	25176
G-AWPE	125	25179
G-AWPF	125	25180
G-AWUF	125	25106
G-AWWL	125	25169
G-AWXB	125	25183
G-AWXC	125	25187
G-AWXD	125	25188
G-AWXE	125	25185
G-AWXF	125	25186
G-AWXN	125	25177
G-AWXO	125	25178
G-AWYE	125	25090
G-AXDM	**125**	**25194**
G-AXDO	125	25190
G-AXDP	125	25191
G-AXDR	125	25195
G-AXDS	125	25196
G-AXEG	125	25172
(G-AXFY)	125	25189
G-AXJD	125	25198
G-AXJE	125	25200
G-AXJF	125	25201
G-AXJG	125	25202
G-AXLU	125	25181
G-AXLV	125	25182
G-AXLW	125	25184
G-AXLX	125	25199
G-AXOA	125	25203
G-AXOB	125	25204
G-AXOC	125	25205
G-AXOD	125	25207
G-AXOE	125	25208
G-AXOF	125	25210
G-AXPS	125	25135
G-AXPU	125	25171
G-AXPX	125	25206
G-AXTR	125	25211
G-AXTS	125	25212
G-AXTT	125	25213
G-AXTU	125	25214
G-AXTV	125	25216
G-AXTW	125	25218
G-AXYE	125	25220
G-AXYF	125	25222
G-AXYG	125	25224
G-AXYH	125	25225
G-AXYI	125	25226
G-AXYJ	125	25217
G-AYBH	125	25256
G-AYEP	125	25219
G-AYER	125	25238
G-AYFM	125	25227
G-AYIZ	125	25223
G-AYLG	125	25254
G-AYLI	125	25240

G-AYMI	G2	91
G-AYNR	125	25235
(G-AYOI)	125	25243
G-AYOJ	125	25246
G-AYOK	125	25250
G-AYRR	125	25247
(G-AYRR)	125	25258
G-AYRY	125	25105
G-AZAF	125	25249
G-AZCH	125	25154
G-AZEK	125	25259
G-AZEL	125	25260
G-AZEM	125	25269
G-AZHS	125	25258
G-AZUF	125	256001
G-AZVS	125	25132
G-BABL	125	25271
G-BACI	125	25283
(G-BAOA)	20	138/440
G-BARR	125	256019
G-BART	125	256005
G-BATA	125	25257
G-BAXG	125	25063
G-BAXL	125	25069
G-BAYT	125	256012
G-BAZA	125	25272
G-BAZB	125	25252
G-BBAS	125	256017
G-BBCL	125	256015
G-BBEE	25B	135
G-BBEK	20	86
G-BBEP	125	256030
G-BBGU	125	25270
G-BBMD	125	256024
G-BBRO	125	256042
G-BBRT	125	256029
(G-BBRT)	125	256036
G-BCCL	125	256039
G-BCII	500	176
G-BCJU	125	256041
G-BCKM	500	198
G-BCLR	125	25228
G-BCRM	500	227
G-BCSE	25B	188
G-BCUX	125	256043
G-BCXF	125	256054
G-BCXL	125	256049
G-BCYF	20	304/511
G-BDJE	125	256052
G-BDKF	125	25242
G-BDMF	G2	103
G-BDOA	125	256056
G-BDOB	125	256061
G-BDOP	125	256055
G-BDYE	125	25080
G-BDZH	125	256066
G-BDZR	125	256068
G-BEDT	125	256070
G-BEFS	125	256071
G-BEFZ	125	257001
G-BEIN	125	256067
G-BEIO	125	256069
G-BEIZ	500	363
G-BEME	125	25231
G-BERP	125	257003
G-BERV	125	257005
G-BERX	125	257006
G-BETV	125	256035
(G-BEWV)	125	257008
G-BEWW	125	256001
G-BEYC	125	257009
G-BFAJ	125	257011
G-BFAN	125	25258
G-BFAR	500	402
G-BFBI	125	257012
G-BFDW	125	257014
G-BFFH	125	257016
G-BFFL	125	257015
G-BFFU	125	257017
G-BFGU	125	257018
(G-BFGV)	125	257019
G-BFIC	125	256060
G-BFLF	125	257023
G-BFLG	125	257024
(G-BFLY)	550	028
G-BFLY	550	089
G-BFMO	125	257026
G-BFMP	125	257027
G-BFPI	125	257025
G-BFRM	**550**	**027**
G-BFSI	125	257030
G-BFSO	125	257028
G-BFSP	125	257031
(G-BFTP)	125	257020
G-BFUE	125	257032
G-BFVI	125	257037
(G-BFVN)	125	257020
G-BFXT	125	257034
G-BFYH	125	257044
G-BFYV	125	257043
G-BFZI	125	257047
G-BFZJ	125	257045
G-BGBJ	125	257052
G-BGBL	125	257049
G-BGDM	125	257004
G-BGGS	125	257061
G-BGKN	125	256058
G-BGLT	G2	225
G-BGOP	20	406/557
G-BGSR	125	257066
G-BGTD	125	257073
G-BGYR	**125**	**256045**
G-BHBH	550	148
G-BHFT	125	25215
(G-BHGH)	551	150
G-BHIE	125	256048
G-BHIO	125	257085
(G-BHIW)	501	544
(G-BHKF)	125	257075
G-BHLF	125	257091
G-BHMP	125	257093
G-BHSK	125	257099
G-BHSU	125	257103
G-BHSV	125	257107
G-BHSW	125	257109
G-BHTJ	125	257097
G-BHTT	500	560
(G-BHVA)	550	225
(G-BIHZ)	125	257118
G-BIMY	125	257132
G-BIRU	125	257136
G-BIZZ	500	645
G-BJCB	125	256015
G-BJCB	125	256065
G-BJDJ	**125**	**257142**
G-BJHH	551	039
G-BJIL	551	354
G-BJIR	**550**	**326**
G-BJOW	125	257153
G-BJOY	125	256030
(G-BJUT)	125	256005
G-BJVP	551	375
G-BJWB	125	257158
G-BKAA	125	257139
G-BKAJ	125	25235
G-BKBA	125	25270
G-BKBH	125	256052
G-BKBM	125	256039
G-BKBU	125	256042
G-BKCD	125	256056
G-BKFS	125	257172
G-BKHK	125	257189
G-BKJV	125	257046
G-BKRL	LEO	001
G-BKSR	550	469
G-BKTF	125	258001
G-BKUW	125	258003
G-BLEK	125	257213
G-BLGZ	125	258004
G-BLJC	125	258005
(G-BLKS)	125	258010
(G-BLMJ)	125	257208
(G-BLMK)	125	257210
G-BLOI	125	256050
G-BLPC	125	258015
(G-BLSG)	S550	0033
G-BLSM	**125**	**257208**
G-BLTP	**125**	**257210**
G-BLUW	125	256059
G-BLXN	S550	0033
G-BMCL	550	091
G-BMIH	**125**	**257115**
G-BMMO	125	258048
G-BMOS	125	257064
G-BMWW	125	257076
G-BMYX	125	257178
G-BNBO	125	257112
G-BNDX	125	256012
G-BNEH	125	258078
G-BNFW	125	257100
G-BNSC	551	559
(G-BNUB)	125	258099
G-BNVU	125	257130
G-BNVY	500	098
(G-BNZP)	500	114
G-BNZW	125	258105
G-BOCB	125	25106
G-BOGA	500	220
G-BOOA	125	258088
G-BOTX	125	258121
G-BOXI	125	257055
G-BPCP	500	540
(G-BPGR)	125	258115
(G-BPGS)	125	258118
(G-BPJM)	G4	1078
G-BPXW	125	258161
(G-BPYD)	125	258146
(G-BPYE)	125	258148
G-BRBZ	400	RJ-60
G-BRCZ	125	258163
G-BRDI	125	257097
G-BRNM	**LEO**	**002**
G-BROD	125	25253
G-BRXR	125	25217
G-BSAA	125	25117
G-BSAL	G2	214
G-BSAN	G3	345
G-BSHL	125	256024
G-BSPH	125	256063
G-BSUL	125	258186
G-BSVL	560	0077
G-BSZP	400	RJ-56
G-BTAB	**125**	**258088**
G-BTAE	125	258190
G-BTIB	900	109
G-BTMG	125	258197
G-BTSI	125	259007
G-BTTG	125	259006
G-BTTX	125	259005
G-BTUF	125	25248
G-BTYN	125	259009
G-BTYO	125	259011
G-BTYP	125	259013
G-BTYR	125	259014
G-BTYS	125	259015
G-BUCP	125	258212
G-BUCR	125	258050
G-BUID	125	258208
G-BUIM	125	258068
G-BUIX	125	259024
G-BUIY	125	258025
G-BUKW	125	259021
G-BULI	125	259016
G-BUNL	125	257007
G-BUNW	125	259029
G-BUPL	125	259030
G-BURV	125	258213
G-BUSX	35A	662
G-BUUW	125	258227
G-BUUY	125	259031
G-BUWC	125	258240
(G-BUWD)	125	258243
G-BUWX	125	259034
G-BUZX	125	258067
G-BVAS	125	258076
G-BVBH	125	258073
G-BVCM	**525**	**0022**
G-BVCU	125	258226
G-BVDL	125	259025
G-BVFC	125	258130
G-BVFE	125	258242
G-BVHW	125	258079
G-BVJI	125	258258
G-BVJY	125	257054
G-BVLO	125	259027
G-BVRF	125	258247
G-BVRG	125	258250
G-BVRW	125	258266
G-BVTP	125	25255
G-BVTR	125	25264
G-BVTS	125	25266
G-BVTT	125	25268
G-BVYV	125	258268
G-BVYW	125	258277
G-BVZK	125	258278
G-BVZL	125	258279
G-BWCB	125	259032
G-BWCR	125	257070
G-BWDC	125	258280
G-BWDD	125	258281
G-BWDW	125	258282
G-BWFL	500	264
G-BWGB	125	258283
G-BWGC	125	258284
G-BWGD	125	258285
G-BWGE	125	258286
(G-BWJX)	125	257062
G-BWKL	125	257118
G-BWOM	**550**	**671**
G-BWRN	125	258237
G-BWSY	**125**	**258201**
G-BWVA	125	258235
G-BXPU	125	25171
G-BYFO	125	257040
G-BYHM	**125**	**258233**
G-CBBI	125	257013
G-CCAA	125	257130
G-CCCL	500	363
G-CITI	**501**	**463**
G-CJET	35A	365
G-CJHH	550	147
G-CXMF	G2	204
G-CYII	125	256005
G-CZAR	**560**	**0046**
G-DAAC	**604**	**5424**
G-DANI	500	402
G-DBAL	125	25117
G-DBBI	125	257130
G-DBII	560	0032
G-DBOW	125	256032
G-DCCC	125	258002
G-DCCI	125	259030
G-DCFR	550	418
G-DEZC	**125**	**257070**
G-DJAE	**500**	**339**
G-DJBB	501	365
G-DJBE	550	171
G-DJBI	551	030
G-DJHH	551	290
G-DJLW	125	25140
G-DJMJ	125	25106
G-DMAN	125	256033
G-DNVT	**G4**	**1078**
G-EFPT	125	257020
G-EJET	550	171
G-ELOT	550	601
G-ELRA	125	259003
G-ESTA	**550**	**143**
G-ETOM	125	258130
G-EVES	**900**	**165**
G-EXLR	125	258151
G-EXLR	**125**	**259001**
(G-FANN)	125	256019
G-FASL	125	258149
G-FBMB	601	5041
G-FDSL	125	258130
G-FERY	551	030
G-FFLT	125	256057
G-FFRA	**20**	**132**
G-FIVE	125	25004
G-FJET	**550**	**418**
G-FLVU	**501**	**580**
G-FOUR	125	25131
G-FRAA	20	385
G-FRAB	20	356
G-FRAC	20	254

G-FRAD 20 304/511
G-FRAE 20 280/503
G-FRAF 20 295/500
G-FRAH 20 223
G-FRAI 20 270
G-FRAJ 20 20
G-FRAK 20 213
G-FRAL 20 151
G-FRAM 20 224
G-FRAO 20 214
G-FRAP 20 207
G-FRAR 20 209
G-FRAS 20 82/418
G-FRAT 20 87/424
G-FRAU 20 97/422
G-FRAV 20 103/423
G-FRAW 20 114/420
G-FRBA 20 178/459
G-GAEL 125 258007
(G-GAIL) 125 257139
G-GAIL 550 397
G-GAUL 550 143
G-GAYL 35A 429
G-GDEZ 125 259026
G-GEDI 2xx 49
G-GEIL 125 258021
G-GENE 501 573
G-GGAE 125 25157
G-GIII G3 345
G-GJCB 125 258079
G-GJET 35A 365
G-GLXD 604 5409
G-GPWH 90X 48
G-GSAM 125 258133
G-GSEB 900 161
G-HADI G2 235
G-HALK 125 256033
G-HARF G4 1117
G-HCFR 125 258240
G-HERS 750 0075
G-HHOI 125 257097
G-HJCB 125 259031
G-HMMV 525 0358
G-HNRY 650 0219
G-HOLL 500 088
G-HOTL 551 051
G-HUGG 35A 432
G-HYGA 125 258034
G-IBIS 125 25171
G-ICED 501 638
G-ICFR 125 258050
G-IECL 125 257002
G-IFTC 125 25171
G-IFTE 125 257037
G-IIRR G2 210
G-IJET 125 257212
G-ILLS 125 25133
G-IUAN 525 0324
(G-JBCA) S550 0146
G-JCBG 90X 44
G-JCBI 2xx 27
G-JCFR 550 315
G-JEAN 500 339
G-JEEN 550 029
G-JETA 550 101
G-JETB 550 319
G-JETC 550 315
G-JETD 550 418
G-JETE 500 198
G-JETG 125 257070
G-JETG 35A 324
G-JETI 125 258056
G-JETJ 550 171
G-JETK 125 258133
G-JETL 35A 656
G-JETN 35A 324
G-JFCX 125 258215
G-JFRS 550 569
G-JHSX 125 258245
G-JJCB 125 258022
G-JJSG 35A 324
G-JMAX 125 258456
G-JMSO D1A A062SA
G-JRCT 551 098

G-JSAX 125 25157
G-KASS 125 25127
G-LEAR 35A 265
G-LJET 35A 643
G-LOFT 500 331
G-LORI 125 25246
G-LRBJ 125 259004
G-LTEC 125 257103
G-MAMA 550 319
G-MARS 400 RJ-36
G-MFEU 125 256062
G-MHIH 125 257139
G-MINE 550 391
G-MIRO 550 0932
G-MKOA 125 25227
G-MLEE 650 0151
G-MLTI 900 164
G-MRFB 125 25132
G-MRTC 550 597
G-MSFY 125 257200
G-MSLY 551 030
G-MTLE 501 573
G-MURI 35A 646
G-NCFR 125 257054
G-NCMT 500 645
G-NEVL 35A 662
G-OBAE 125 257094
G-OBEL 500 220
G-OBLT 125 258164
G-OBOB 125 25069
(G-OBSM) 125 257189
G-OCAA 125 257091
G-OCBA 125 25132
G-OCCC 125 258013
G-OCCI 125 258201
G-OCDB 550 601
G-OCFR 35A 614
G-OCPI 500 093
G-OCSB 525 0177
G-OEJA 500 264
G-OHEA 125 25144
G-OHLA 501 514
G-OICE 525 0028
G-OJOY 125 257061
G-OJPB 125 25258
G-OKSP 500 392
G-OLDD 125 258106
G-OLFR 125 25217
G-OMCA 125 25106
G-OMCL 551 412
G-OMGA 125 256024
G-OMGB 125 256039
G-OMGC 125 256056
G-OMGD 125 257184
G-OMGE 125 258197
G-OMGG 125 258058
G-OMID 125 257214
G-ONPN 125 25063
G-OOSP 125 25178
G-OPFC 125 258159
G-OPFC 125 259002
G-OPOL 125 25171
G-OPWH 900 151
G-ORCE 550 391
G-ORHE 500 220
G-ORJB 500 392
G-OSAM 125 257189
G-OSCA 500 270
G-OSMC 550 135
G-OSNB 550 569
G-OTGT 560 0517
G-OTIS 550 672
(G-OTKI) 550 265
G-OTMC 400 RJ-50
(G-OVIP) 125 258010
G-OVIP G2 91
G-OWDB 125 257040
G-OWEB 125 257040
G-OXEC 500 093
(G-OXEH) 550 319
G-PBWH 125 258182
G-PJET 35A 614
G-PJWB 125 256033
G-PLGI 125 257034

G-PNNY 500 165
G-POSN 125 258120
G-PRMC 125 257031
G-PYCO 2xx 78
G-RAAR 125 258210
G-RACL 125 257212
G-RAFF 35A 504
G-RAHL 400A RK-61
G-RAVY 500 109
G-RCDI 125 257142
G-RCEJ 125 258021
G-RDBS 550 101
G-RIBV 560 0506
G-RJRI 125 257130
G-RSCJ 525 0298
G-RSRS 400 RJ-36
G-RVHT 550 441
G-SBEC 501 661
G-SCCC 125 259037
G-SEBE 35A 365
G-SHEA 125 258240
G-SHEB 125 258243
G-SHEC 125 259037
G-SHOP 125 25248
G-SOVN 35A 614
G-SPUR 550 714
G-SSOZ 550 597
G-SUFC 125 256035
G-SVLB 125 257112
G-SWET 500 270
G-SYKS 550 599
G-TACE 125 25223
G-TCAP 125 258115
G-TCDI 125 25248
G-TEFH 500 176
G-THCL 550 563
G-TIFF 551 290
G-TJCB 125 257127
G-TJHI 500 363
G-TMAS 125 256062
G-TOMI 125 256030
G-TOMY D1A A090SA
G-TOPF 125 25238
G-TPHK 125 258130
G-TSAM 125 258028
G-TTFN 560 0537
G-UESS 500 326
G-UKCA 125 257214
G-UWWB 125 258001
G-VIPI 125 258222
G-VIPS 35A 614
G-VJAY 125 25254
G-VKRS S550 0133
G-WBPR 125 258085
G-WYLX 550 418
G-XMAF G3 407
G-XRMC 125 258180
G-YUGO 125 25094
G-ZAPI 500 560
G-ZEAL 35A 275
G-ZEIZ 36A 047
G-ZENO 35A 429
(G-ZEST) 35A 265
G-ZING 35A 429
G-ZIPS 35A 365
G-ZIZI 525 0345
G-ZONE 35A 365
G-ZOOM 35A 236

Switzerland

(HB-) 55 050
(HB-) 560 0301
(HB-) 900 4
HB- AST 111
(HB-) WWD 390
(HB-I) G2 126
(HB-I) G4 1074
HB-IAB 900 9
HB-IAC 900 26
HB-IAD 900 35
HB-IAE 50 150
HB-IAF 900 30

HB-IAG 50 174
HB-IAH 90X 28
HB-IAI 900 75
HB-IAK 900 15
HB-IAL 50 63
HB-IAM 50 164
HB-IAQ 90X 35
HB-IAT 50 86
HB-IAV 50 230
HB-IAW 2xx 16
HB-IAX 2xx 33
HB-IAY 2xx 34
HB-IAZ 2xx 30
HB-IBH 2xx 42
HB-IBX G4 1183
HB-IBY 900 44
HB-IEA 50 133
HB-IEB 50 17
HB-IEC 50 134
HB-IED 50 147
(HB-IED) 50 9
HB-IEJ G4 1148
HB-IEP 50 67
HB-IEQ G4 1174
HB-IER 50 57
HB-IES 50 61
HB-IET 50 48
HB-IEU 50 27
HB-IEV 50 34
HB-IEW G2 124
HB-IEX G2 169
HB-IEY G2 210
HB-IEZ G2 216
HB-IEZ G2 246
HB-IKJ 604 5327
HB-IKQ 604 5318
HB-IKS 601 5042
HB-IKT 601 5003
HB-IKU 601 5005
HB-IKV 601 5092
HB-IKW 601 5096
HB-IKX 601 3006
HB-IKY 601 5125
HB-ILH 600 1025
HB-ILK 601 3033
HB-ILL 604 5373
HB-ILM 601 3024
HB-IMJ G5 517
HB-IMV G2 8
HB-IMW G2 194
HB-IMX G3 335
(HB-IMY) G4 1033
HB-IMY G4 1084
HB-IMZ G2 88/21
(HB-ITE) G4 1046
HB-ITH 50 117
HB-ITJ G4 1175
HB-ITM G3 352
HB-ITN G3 367
HB-ITP G4 1046
HB-ITR G2 144
HB-ITS G3 435
(HB-ITT) G4 1046
HB-ITT G4 1064
HB-ITV G2 139/11
HB-ITW G2 192
HB-ITX G4 1093
HB-ITZ G4 1083
HB-IUR 700 9013
HB-IUT GXY 007
HB-IUU GXY 011
HB-IUW 900 150
HB-IUX 90X 54
HB-IUY 900 181
HB-IUZ 2xx 74
HB-IVL G5 513
HB-IVM 2xx 55
HB-IVN 2xx 61
HB-IVO 2xx 62
HB-IVP 604 5369
HB-IVR 604 5318
HB-IVS 601 5166
HB-IVT 604 5394
HB-IVV 604 5384

HB-IVZ	**G5**	**577**
HB-PAA	MSP	069
HB-PAC	MSP	112
(HB-V)	10	150
(HB-V)	20	112
(HB-V)	560	0106
HB-VAG	125	25006
HB-VAH	125	25007
HB-VAI	24	019
HB-VAK	S40	282-25
(HB-VAL)	WWD	17
HB-VAM	23	044
HB-VAN	125	25063
HB-VAP	20	37/406
HB-VAR	125	25025
HB-VAS	24	109
HB-VAT	125	25090
HB-VAU	125	25099
HB-VAV	20	3/403
HB-VAW	20	72/413
HB-VAX	WWD	15
HB-VAY	125	25135
HB-VAZ	125	25130
HB-VBA	23	026
HB-VBB	23	045A
HB-VBC	23	053
HB-VBD	23	052
HB-VBI	25	040
HB-VBK	24	128
HB-VBL	20	126/438
HB-VBM	20	136/439
HB-VBN	125	25138
HB-VBO	20	150/445
HB-VBP	25	033
HB-VBR	25	038
HB-VBS	20	55/410
HB-VBT	125	25171
HB-VBU	24D	231
HB-VBW	125	25199
HB-VBX	WWD	47
HB-VBY	24B	206
HB-VBZ	125	25215
HB-VCA	20	208/468
HB-VCB	20	182/461
HB-VCC	WWD	145
HB-VCE	125	25235
HB-VCG	20	231/474
HB-VCI	24X	243
HB-VCK	25B	082
HB-VCL	25B	076
HB-VCM	25XR	073
HB-VCN	24D	247
HB-VCN	**S65**	**465-32**
HB-VCO	20	25/405
HB-VCR	20	263/489
HB-VCS	25C	097
HB-VCT	24D	241
HB-VCU	500	038
HB-VCW	24D	256
HB-VCX	500	008
HB-VCY	24X	267
HB-VCZ	35A	433
(HB-VCZ)	S40	282-117
HB-VDA	500	081
HB-VDB	20	296/507
HB-VDC	500	100
HB-VDD	10	36
HB-VDE	10	7
HB-VDG	20	58
HB-VDH	24	148
HB-VDI	25B	149
HB-VDK	24D	271
HB-VDL	125	256021
HB-VDM	500	126
HB-VDN	24D	287
(HB-VDO)	20	306/512
(HB-VDO)	24D	289
HB-VDP	20	245/481
(HB-VDR)	500	187
HB-VDS	125	256048
(HB-VDT)	10	21
HB-VDU	24D	310
HB-VDV	20	307/513
(HB-VDW)	20	86
HB-VDX	10	56
HB-VDY	20	245/481
(HB-VDY)	20	306/512
HB-VDZ	20	255/487
HB-VEA	36	006
HB-VEB	20	323/520
HB-VEC	75A	380-12
HB-VED	20	162/451
HB-VEE	36	016
HB-VEF	25B	193
HB-VEG	10	70
HB-VEH	500	230
HB-VEI	25XR	199
HB-VEK	125	257094
(HB-VEL)	23	014
HB-VEL	23	023
HB-VEM	35A	068
HB-VEN	35	045
HB-VEO	500	299
HB-VEP	MSP	098
(HB-VER)	20	174/457
HB-VES	23	027
(HB-VET)	STR	5009
HB-VEU	MSP	102
HB-VEV	20	317
HB-VEV	35A	075
HB-VEW	35A	088
HB-VEX	500	338
HB-VEY	35A	090
HB-VEZ	20	228/473
HB-VFA	125	257007
HB-VFB	35A	145
HB-VFC	35A	099
HB-VFD	36A	029
(HB-VFE)	35A	111
HB-VFF	500	392
HB-VFG	35A	119
HB-VFH	500	180
HB-VFI	501	413
HB-VFK	35A	118
HB-VFL	35A	137
(HB-VFO)	35A	162
HB-VFO	35A	184
HB-VFP	WWD	231
(HB-VFS)	10	121
HB-VFS	36A	042
HB-VFT	10	121
HB-VFU	35A	196
HB-VFV	36A	040
HB-VFW	600	1049
HB-VFX	35A	191
HB-VFY	29	001
HB-VFZ	35A	222
HB-VGA	600	1029
HB-VGB	28	004
(HB-VGC)	35A	239
HB-VGC	35A	259
HB-VGD	500	082
(HB-VGD)	501	478
HB-VGE	550	074
HB-VGF	125	257062
HB-VGG	125	257070
HB-VGH	35A	206
(HB-VGI)	500	251
HB-VGK	550	035
HB-VGL	35A	278
HB-VGM	35A	288
HB-VGN	35A	149
HB-VGO	500	053
HB-VGP	550	205
HB-VGR	550	089
HB-VGS	**550**	**206**
HB-VGT	35A	309
(HB-VGU)	125	25199
HB-VGU	35A	331
HB-VGV	55	015
HB-VGW	35A	336
HB-VGX	35A	372
HB-VGY	35A	370
HB-VGZ	55	024
HB-VHA	501	524
HB-VHB	35A	359
HB-VHC	600	1028
HB-VHD	35A	395
HB-VHE	35A	413
HB-VHF	36A	048
HB-VHG	35A	445
HB-VHH	S550	0028
HB-VHI	500	344
HB-VHK	55	045
HB-VHL	55	054
HB-VHM	25D	314
HB-VHN	55	073
HB-VHO	600	1053
HB-VHR	35A	501
HB-VHS	200	488
HB-VHT	D1A	A052SA
HB-VHU	125	258152
HB-VHV	**125**	**258153**
HB-VHW	650	0060
HB-VHX	D1A	A035SA
HB-VHY	20	429
HB-VIA	D1A	A087SA
HB-VIB	55	009
HB-VIC	501	464
HB-VID	501	523
HB-VIE	25B	193
HB-VIF	**36A**	**057**
HB-VIG	10	89
HB-VII	35A	503
HB-VIK	**125**	**258091**
HB-VIL	**125**	**258097**
HB-VIM	31	018
HB-VIN	650	0119
HB-VIO	**551**	**181**
HB-VIP	550	469
HB-VIR	550	328
HB-VIS	**550**	**447**
HB-VIT	**550**	**220**
HB-VIU	550	465
HB-VIV	500	340
HB-VIW	10	113
HB-VIX	10	126
HB-VIY	650	0040
HB-VIZ	550	207
HB-VJA	550	379
HB-VJB	**501**	**442**
HB-VJC	35A	614
HB-VJD	20	116
HB-VJE	400	RJ-44
HB-VJF	S65	465-59
HB-VJH	550	234
HB-VJI	**31**	**011**
HB-VJJ	**35A**	**649**
HB-VJK	**35A**	**651**
HB-VJL	**35A**	**653**
HB-VJM	10	188
HB-VJN	10	118
(HB-VJP)	500	178
HB-VJQ	525	0041
HB-VJR	500	343
HB-VJS	20	383/550
HB-VJT	650	0076
HB-VJV	**20**	**237/476**
HB-VJW	20	175
HB-VJX	20	293
HB-VJY	125	258176
HB-VJZ	560	0055
HB-VKA	S550	0137
HB-VKB	**525**	**0037**
HB-VKC	20	117
HB-VKD	501	643
HB-VKE	**10**	**7**
HB-VKF	10	89
HB-VKH	550	135
HB-VKI	**60**	**019**
HB-VKJ	125	257067
HB-VKK	**500**	**178**
HB-VKM	125	258035
HB-VKN	125	258036
HB-VKO	**20**	**257**
HB-VKP	**550**	**622**
HB-VKR	100	209
HB-VKS	550	441
HB-VKT	550	310
HB-VKV	125	258228
HB-VKW	**125**	**258246**
HB-VKX	550	307
HB-VKY	501	476
HB-VLA	125	257031
HB-VLB	501	638
HB-VLC	125	257127
HB-VLD	501	589
HB-VLE	**500**	**313**
HB-VLF	**125**	**258264**
HB-VLG	**125**	**258265**
HB-VLH	125	257017
HB-VLI	125	258120
HB-VLJ	125	257030
HB-VLK	36A	032
HB-VLL	125	257105
HB-VLM	**400A**	**RK-66**
HB-VLN	400A	RK-94
HB-VLP	650	7064
HB-VLQ	**550**	**352**
HB-VLR	**31A**	**127**
HB-VLS	550	219
HB-VLT	125	258240
HB-VLU	60	010
HB-VLV	**560**	**0077**
HB-VLW	**400A**	**RK-103**
HB-VLY	550	429
HB-VLZ	**560**	**0446**
HB-VMA	**45**	**020**
HB-VMB	**45**	**021**
HB-VMD	125	257040
HB-VME	10	131
HB-VMF	**125**	**258175**
HB-VMG	**AST**	**105**
HB-VMH	**550**	**649**
HB-VMI	**125**	**258210**
HB-VMJ	**S550**	**0029**
HB-VMK	AST	113
HB-VMN	**20**	**240/478**
HB-VMO	**560**	**5061**
HB-VMP	**550**	**697**
HB-VMT	**525**	**0250**
HB-VMZ	**560**	**5067**
(HB-VWW)	20	37/406

Ecuador

HC-BGL	WWD	234
HC-BQT	S60	306-33
HC-BQU	S60	306-44
HC-BSS	**20**	**150/445**
HC-BSZ	35A	311
HC-BTJ	550	017
HC-BTN	35A	417
HC-BTQ	501	444
HC-BTT	**125**	**25228**
HC-BTY	S550	0067
HC-BUN	S60	306-126
HC-BUP	**20**	**200**
HC-BUR	125	256053
HC-BVH	200	490
HC-BVP	501	481
HC-BVX	**WWD**	**411**

Dominican Republic

HI-420	550	466
HI-493	501	406
HI-496	550	407
HI-496SP	550	407
HI-500	550	248
HI-500CT	550	248
HI-500SP	550	248
HI-527	501	369
HI-527SP	501	369
(HI-530)	550	022
HI-534	550	022
HI-534CA	550	022
HI-581SP	**501**	**599**
HI-646SP	D1A	A064SA

Colombia

(HK-)	G2	210
HK-	WWD	162
HK-2150	WWD	181
HK-2150X	WWD	181
HK-2485	WWD	239
HK-2485W	**WWD**	**239**
HK-2624P	25D	339
HK-2624X	25D	339
HK-2968	10	176
HK-2968X	10	176
HK-3121	35A	439
HK-3121X	35A	439
HK-3122	35A	481
HK-3122X	35A	481
HK-3191X	550	439
HK-3265	24D	297
HK-3400X	550	394
HK-3607X	550	040
HK-3646X	35A	503
HK-3653	125	25216
HK-3653X	125	25216
HK-3884X	WWD	294
HK-3885	500	135
HK-3893X	WWD	441
HK-3921	35A	499
HK-3949X	35A	670
HK-3971X	**WWD**	**306**
HK-3983X	**35A**	**259**
HK-4016X	**55**	**041**
HK-4128W	550	550

Korea

HL	**604**	**5429**
HL7202	601	5081
HL7222	**G4**	**1188**
HL7226	500	294
HL7234	20	370
HL7277	**500**	**327**
HL7301	900	156
HL7386	50	179
HL7501	**560**	**0292**
HL7502	**560**	**0294**
HL7503	**560**	**0297**
HL7504	**560**	**0300**
HL7522	604	5303
HL7576	**700**	**9019**
HL7577	**601**	**5182**

Panama

(HP-)	35A	670
(HP-)	55	041
HP-1A	20	382
HP-1A	**G2**	**78**
HP-1A	WWD	180
HP-125JW	125	25216
HP-912	35A	280
HP-1128P	125	25216
HP-1141P	25	049
HP-1262	125	258133
HP-1410HT	**525**	**0350**

Honduras

HR-001	WWD	183
HR-002	WWD	333
HR-AMD	125	25186
HR-CEF	**WWD**	**333**

Thailand

HS-DCG	**650**	**7071**
HS-JJA	601	5188
(HS-TDL)	601	5102
HS-TVA	601	5102
HS-UCM	400A	RK-95

Saudi Arabia

(HZ-)	125	259010
HZ-103	**G3**	**453**
HZ-106	35A	374
HZ-107	**35A**	**375**
HZ-108	**G3**	**353**
HZ-109	**125**	**258146**
HZ-109	G3	453
HZ-110	125	258148
HZ-A01	20	359/542
HZ-A02	10	118
HZ-A03	50	7
HZ-A04	600	1006
HZ-AA1	125	256019
HZ-AA1	550	128
HZ-AAA	550	063
HZ-AAA	550	128
HZ-AAA	650	0003
HZ-AAI	551	149
HZ-AB2	900	61
HZ-ABM	35A	243
HZ-ADC	G2	187
HZ-ADC	**G4**	**1037**
HZ-AFA2	**604**	**5320**
HZ-AFG	G2	175
HZ-AFH	**G2**	**171**
HZ-AFI	**G2**	**201**
HZ-AFJ	**G2**	**203**
HZ-AFK	**G2**	**239**
HZ-AFL	G3	311
HZ-AFM	G3	324
HZ-AFN	**G3**	**364**
HZ-AFO	G3	365
HZ-AFP	**550**	**472**
HZ-AFQ	**550**	**473**
HZ-AFR	**G3**	**410**
HZ-AFS	G3	450
HZ-AFS	STR	5016
HZ-AFT	**900**	**21**
HZ-AFU	**G4**	**1031**
HZ-AFV	**G4**	**1035**
HZ-AFW	**G4**	**1038**
HZ-AFX	**G4**	**1143**
HZ-AFY	**G4**	**1166**
HZ-AFZ	**900**	**61**
HZ-AK1	601	3032
HZ-AKI	10	108
(HZ-AKI)	20	395/554
HZ-AKI	50	133
HZ-AKI	50	7
HZ-ALJ	550	063
HZ-AM11	55	040
HZ-AM2	55	040
HZ-AM2	55B	127
HZ-AMA	10	118
(HZ-AMA)	601	3017
HZ-AMM	125	256064
HZ-AMN	75A	380-38
HZ-AZP	25B	081
HZ-BB1	25B	081
HZ-BB2	50	131
HZ-BIN	125	25106
HZ-BL2	**125**	**258126**
HZ-BO1	125	25094
HZ-BSA	G3	353
HZ-CA1	75A	380-55
HZ-CAD	G2	179
HZ-DA1	125	257067
HZ-DA1	G3	358
HZ-DA2	125	257088
HZ-DA3	125	257115
HZ-DA4	**125**	**257124**
HZ-DAC	125	256059
HZ-DC2	20	363/544
HZ-DG2	**G3**	**317**
HZ-FBT	STR	5086/44
HZ-FK1	STR	5133
HZ-FMA	125	25105
HZ-FNA	STR	5056
HZ-FYZ	**560**	**5022**
HZ-GP3	25B	158
HZ-GP4	24B	190
HZ-GP4	25	062
HZ-GP5	25XR	199
HZ-HA1	**G2**	**216**
HZ-HE4	20	241/479
HZ-HR2	**G3**	**346**
HZ-HR4	G3	415
HZ-KA1	35	033
HZ-KA2	125	256057
HZ-KA3	20	174/457
HZ-KA5	**125**	**256049**
HZ-KAA	**G4**	**1294**
(HZ-KAI)	10	108
HZ-KS1	**G4**	**1349**
HZ-KS2	**G4**	**1367**
HZ-KS3	**G4**	**1384**
HZ-KSA	125	258022
HZ-KTC	35A	147
HZ-MA1	S60	306-110
HZ-MA1	S60	306-94
HZ-MA1	**STR**	**5105**
HZ-MAC	STR	5013
HZ-MAL	G3	379
HZ-MAL	G4	1294
HZ-MF1	125	256060
HZ-MF1	600	1070
HZ-MFL	**G4**	**1128**
HZ-MIB	35A	173
HZ-MIC	G3	423
HZ-MIC	G5	518
HZ-MMM	125	257010
HZ-MNC	G4	1076
HZ-MOA	25B	081
HZ-MPM	G2	4/8
HZ-MRP	25B	121
HZ-MS04	**G4**	**1365**
HZ-MS1	**35A**	**467**
HZ-MS3	**G3**	**385**
HZ-MS4	G2	103
HZ-MSD	G2	256
HZ-MWD	G3	393
HZ-NAD	125	257064
HZ-NC1	500	319
HZ-NCB	S60	306-94
(HZ-NCI)	35A	173
HZ-ND1	G2	216
HZ-NES	**20**	**174/457**
HZ-NOT	10	118
HZ-NR1	**75A**	**380-71**
HZ-NR2	G3	304
HZ-NR2	**G3**	**415**
HZ-NR3	G3	371
HZ-OFC	125	257064
HZ-OFC	125	258050
HZ-OFC	125	259008
HZ-OFC2	125	259008
HZ-OFC3	900	133
HZ-OFC4	**90X**	**31**
HZ-PCA	**G2**	**179**
HZ-PET	G2	139/11
HZ-PL1	20	293
HZ-PL7	20	241/479
(HZ-R4A)	900	21
HZ-RBH	75A	380-57
HZ-RC1	125	257040
HZ-RC2	125	257055
HZ-RC3	**G3**	**331**
HZ-RFM	**600**	**1074**
HZ-RH2	G3	346
HZ-RI1	25XR	199
HZ-SAA	600	1074
HZ-SAB	50	73
HZ-SAB2	**900**	**113**
HZ-SAR	G4	1166
HZ-SFA	560	0132
HZ-SFS	601	3017
HZ-SH1	STR	5141
HZ-SH2	STR	5016
HZ-SH3	STR	5142
HZ-SH4	STR	5148
HZ-SJP	125	256059
HZ-SJP	125	257214
HZ-SJP	125	258068
HZ-SJP2	125	259012
HZ-SJP3	**604**	**5346**
HZ-SM3	50	165
HZ-SMB	24X	117
HZ-SMB	25XR	073
HZ-SOG	75A	380-72
(HZ-SOG)	G3	415
HZ-SS2	25D	213
HZ-TAG	20	359/542
HZ-TAG	600	1007
HZ-TAG	600	1014
HZ-THZ	75A	380-53
HZ-THZ	STR	5050/34
HZ-TNA	**STR**	**5120/26**
HZ-WBT	STR	5133
HZ-WBT1	600	1074
HZ-WT1	STR	5133
HZ-WT2	600	1074
HZ-YA1	125	256033
HZ-ZTC	551	149
HZ-ZTC	560	0036

Italy

I-ACCG	20	474
I-ACIF	400	RJ-28
I-ACTL	20	427
I-ADAG	50	131
I-AEAL	**500**	**053**
I-AGEB	35A	243
I-AGEC	20	239
I-AGEN	35A	491
I-AGER	55	045
(I-AGIK)	501	539
I-AGSM	551	419
I-AIFA	36A	021
I-AIRV	501	486
I-AIRW	**31**	**025**
I-ALBS	500	023
I-ALGU	D1A	A067SA
I-ALKA	**550**	**386**
I-ALKB	550	393
I-ALPG	**551**	**348**
I-ALPM	35A	133
I-ALPR	**55**	**078**
I-ALPT	35A	198
I-ALSE	400	RJ-10
I-ALSI	400	RJ-31
I-ALSO	400	RJ-34
(I-ALSU)	400	RJ-23
I-ALSU	400A	RK-11
I-AMAW	500	095
I-AMBR	500	180
I-AMCT	500	114
I-AMCU	500	109
I-AMCY	**500**	**192**
I-AMME	24D	310
I-ARIB	550	243
I-ARNT	WWD	139
I-AROO	**550**	**090**
I-ASAZ	550	438
I-ASER	**400A**	**RK-204**
I-ATMO	20	94/428
I-ATSA	650	0161
I-ATSB	560	0033
I-ATSE	550	649
I-AUNY	**501**	**618**
I-AVGM	**550**	**492**
I-AVJD	25D	214
I-AVJE	25D	254
I-AVJG	35A	189
I-AVRM	**550**	**491**
I-AVVM	**S550**	**0062**
I-BAEL	**20**	**426**
I-BEAU	**900**	**23**
I-BENN	**550**	**0859**
I-BENT	**560**	**5053**
I-BETV	650	0104
I-BEWW	**601**	**5020**
I-BLSM	600	1076
I-BLUB	**650**	**0216**
I-BMFE	**25C**	**146**
I-BOGI	125	25138
I-CAFB	50	138
I-CAFC	50	145
I-CAFD	**50**	**183**

I-CAFE	50	190
I-CAIB	20	175
I-CAIC	10	89
(I-CAIK)	50	37
I-CALC	10	127
I-CART	24D	231
I-CASG	125	258033
(I-CCCB)	501	382
I-CEFI	S550	0047
I-CHIC	10	126
I-CHOC	10	113
I-CIGA	550	263
I-CIGB	**501**	**539**
I-CIGH	**125**	**257201**
I-CIPA	501	559
I-CIST	**650**	**0085**
I-CITY	500	053
I-CLAD	**500**	**223**
I-CMUT	**20**	**389/552**
I-CNEF	200	506
I-COKE	500	251
I-COTO	25D	285
I-CREM	**10**	**161**
(I-CRYS)	36	006
I-CSGA	50	203
I-CSGB	50	208
I-CTPT	601	5013
(I-DAEP)	501	414
I-DAGF	**525**	**0347**
I-DDAE	24F	336
I-DDVA	**125**	**258389**
I-DEAF	550	283
I-DEAN	25D	314
I-DECI	501	504
I-DEGF	50	176
I-DENR	**50**	**125**
I-DIDY	501	514
I-DIES	**900**	**30**
I-DJMA	10	179
I-DKET	20	160/450
I-DLON	**35A**	**346**
I-DNOR	10	118
I-DOCA	D1A	A059SA
I-DRIB	**20**	**201/469**
(I-DRVM)	125	257017
I-DUMA	500	263
I-DVAL	501	649
I-DVMR	125	257017
I-EAMM	35A	634
I-EDEM	**525**	**0155**
I-EDIF	20	300/508
I-EDIK	**50**	**132**
I-EDIM	20	295/500
I-EDIS	20	280/503
I-EJIA	24D	259
I-EJIB	35A	331
I-EJIC	10	89
I-EJID	35A	222
I-EKET	20	170/455
I-ELEN	25B	171
I-ERDN	50	48
I-ERJA	**501**	**358**
I-ERJB	**31A**	**167**
I-ERJD	**45**	**068**
I-ESAI	**525**	**0235**
I-FARN	**500**	**565**
I-FBCA	S60	306-97
I-FBCK	500	178
I-FBCT	550	090
I-FCHI	G3	460
I-FCIM	20	323/520
I-FERN	500	152
I-FFLY	35A	325
I-FFRI	35A	493
I-FICV	**900**	**54**
I-FIMI	35A	090
I-FINR	MSP	111
I-FIPE	20	368
I-FIPP	601	5069
I-FJTO	550	679
I-FKET	20	279/502
I-FLYA	**501**	**467**
I-FLYB	500	489
I-FLYC	35A	298
I-FLYD	**550**	**291**
I-FLYF	20	428
I-FLYG	35A	593
I-FLYH	35A	498
I-FLYJ	**55**	**084**
I-FLYK	20	241/479
I-FLYL	AST	036
I-FLYP	**2xx**	**103**
I-FLYV	**2xx**	**108**
I-FOMN	501	498
I-FRAB	D1A	A052SA
I-FREU	24D	279
I-FRTT	D1A	A056SA
I-FSJA	400A	RK-41
I-FTAL	400	RJ-42
I-GAMB	551	312
I-GASD	**650**	**0037**
I-GCAL	20	307/513
I-GCFA	400	RJ-44
I-GENC	D1A	A065SA
I-GERA	501	511
(I-GIAN)	25D	207
I-GIAZ	20	252/485
I-GIRL	D1A	A012SA
I-GIWW	**550**	**0871**
I-GJBO	125	25240
I-GJMA	501	542
I-GOBJ	**20**	**180/460**
I-GOBZ	**20**	**293**
I-IDAG	**525**	**0093**
I-IFPC	400A	RK-71
I-IGNO	125	258040
I-INCZ	400	RJ-22
I-IPFC	400A	RK-6
I-IPIZ	**400A**	**RK-29**
I-IRIF	20	185/467
I-ITAL	HFB	1040
I-ITPR	10	115
I-JESA	**551**	**098**
I-JESE	500	330
I-JESJ	550	352
I-JESO	**550**	**283**
I-JETS	**560**	**5012**
I-JUST	501	621
I-KALI	35A	249
I-KELM	**35A**	**406**
I-KESO	550	338
I-KIDO	50	31
I-KILO	55	007
I-KIOV	25D	299
I-KISS	25B	193
I-KIWI	550	432
I-KODE	501	626
I-KODM	35A	620
I-KUNA	500	053
I-KUSS	35A	237
I-KWYJ	501	412
I-LADA	G4	1142
(I-LAFA)	20	381/548
I-LAWN	501	612
I-LCJG	10	53
I-LCJT	10	96
I-LEAR	25D	207
I-LECO	WWD	72
I-LIAB	**20**	**172/456**
I-LIAC	**20**	**234/475**
I-LIAD	**35A**	**111**
I-LOOK	**55**	**021**
I-LPHZ	600	1069
I-LUBE	10	7
I-LUBI	**G4**	**1123**
I-LXAG	50	159
I-LXGR	**G4**	**1234**
I-LXOT	200	496
I-MABU	24D	287
I-MADU	G3	448
I-MAFU	200	501
I-MCSA	35A	099
I-MESK	**551**	**024**
I-MILK	**604**	**5304**
I-MMAE	35A	116
I-MMEA	50	140
I-MOCO	**35A**	**445**
I-MORA	S40	282-117
I-MPIZ	400	RJ-25
I-MRDV	600	1078
I-MTDE	900	43
I-MTNT	550	116
I-MUDE	10	136
I-NEWY	560	0115
I-NIAR	**551**	**312**
I-NICK	S40	282-25
I-NIKJ	35	055
I-NLAE	**20**	**134**
I-NNUS	601	5044
I-NORT	500	320
I-NUMI	**900**	**89**
I-NYCE	560	0053
I-NYSE	560	0302
I-OANN	100	208
I-OMEP	501	476
I-ONDO	400	RJ-20
I-OSLO	125	258050
I-OSUA	55ER	102
I-OTEL	**501**	**414**
I-OTTY	**400**	**RJ-25**
I-PALP	501	583
I-PAPE	501	659
I-PATY	S60	306-133
I-PEGA	**500**	**081**
I-PERF	20	313
I-PIAI	808	503
I-PIAL	808	504
I-PIAY	808	522
I-PLLL	500	230
I-PNCA	**550**	**257**
I-POLE	50	180
I-PTCT	600	1082
I-RACE	125	25006
I-RASO	125	25131
I-RDSF	400	RJ-36
I-REAL	20	267/491
I-RELT	**S40**	**282-133**
I-RIED	20	77/429
I-RJVA	25D	342
I-ROBM	20	182/461
I-ROST	500	445
I-RYVA	35A	391
I-SAFP	50	9
I-SAFR	50	29
I-SALG	650	0120
I-SALV	550	561
I-SAME	**50**	**37**
I-SAMI	400	RJ-35
I-SATV	501	524
I-SDFG	**125**	**258136**
I-SELM	D1A	A064SA
I-SFER	25C	097
I-SFRA	10	130
I-SHIP	10	110
(I-SHOP)	10	113
(I-SIDU)	35A	111
I-SIMD	25B	193
I-SMEG	G2	97
I-SNAB	**50**	**169**
I-SNAC	50	30
I-SNAD	S60	306-27
I-SNAF	125	25145
I-SNAG	20	240/478
I-SNAI	MSP	028
I-SNAK	S40	282-25
I-SNAL	STR	5023
I-SNAM	20	176/458
I-SNAP	MSP	099
I-SNAV	20	119/431
I-SNAW	2xx	12
I-SNAX	**900**	**69**
I-SOBE	200	487
I-SREG	20	442
I-STAP	400	RJ-18
I-TAKY	25XR	073
I-TALC	HFB	1027
I-TALG	S550	0122
I-TALW	650	0208
I-TFLY	10	188
I-TIAG	20	233
I-TIAL	20	290
I-TNTR	550	466
I-TOIO	**501**	**657**
I-TOPJ	**400**	**RJ-44**
I-TORA	D1A	A085SA
I-TOSC	501	410
I-TYKE	**31A**	**120**
I-UNSA	400A	RK-20
I-UUNY	**500**	**377**
I-VEPA	20	100
I-VIGI	D1A	A013SA
I-VIKI	550	381
I-VIKY	55	073
I-VULC	**35A**	**421**
"I-WDSD"	200	487
I-ZAMP	S550	0133
I-ZOOM	**35A**	**135**

Japan

JA001A	**560**	**0349**
JA001G	**G4**	**1190**
JA002G	**G4**	**1244**
JA01CP	**31A**	**144**
JA01TM	**560**	**0403**
JA02AA	**560**	**0518**
JA30DA	**D1A**	**A053SA**
JA50TH	**90X**	**3**
JA119N	**560**	**0067**
(JA)	50	173
JA8246	D1A	A092SA
JA8247	500	259
JA8248	**D1A**	**002**
JA8249	650	0085
JA8270	200	509
JA8283	601	5011
JA8284	501	631
JA8298	D1A	A074SA
(JA8360)	601	5037
(JA8361)	501	476
JA8361	601	5068
(JA8366)	G4	1107
JA8367	650	0177
JA8378	650	0178
JA8379	AST	049
JA8380	**501**	**350**
(JA8380)	G4	1148
JA8418	500	226
JA8420	**525**	**0056**
JA8421	500	021
JA8422	500	040
JA8431	**G2**	**141**
JA8438	500	321
JA8446	24D	245
JA8447	10	84
JA8463	10	152
JA8474	**500**	**629**
JA8493	**501**	**672**
JA8494	100	201
JA8495	550	495
JA8570	**900**	**53**
JA8571	**900**	**56**
JA8572	900	105
JA8575	50	196
JA8576	**560**	**0080**
JQ8001	D1A	001SA
JQ8002	D1A	002
JQ8003	D1A	002
JQ8004	D1A	A004SA
JQ8005	D1A	A005SA

Jordan

(JY-)	G5	564
JY-ABL	G3	418
JY-AEG	23	014
JY-AEH	23	023
JY-AEI	23	027
JY-AET	36	016
JY-AEV	35	049
JY-AEW	35	052
(JY-AEX)	35	056
JY-AFC	36A	020
JY-AFD	35A	071

JY-AFE	35A	075
JY-AFF	35A	081
JY-AFH	**75A**	**380-57**
JY-AFL	75A	380-56
JY-AFM	75A	380-36
JY-AFN	75A	380-53
JY-AFO	75A	380-61
JY-AFP	**75A**	**380-62**
JY-AMN	G3	418
JY-HAH	50	52
JY-HAH	G3	467
JY-HZH	50	60
JY-HZH	G3	469
JY-ONE	**604**	**5426**
(JY-ONE)	G4	1345
JY-RAY	**G4**	**1202**
(JY-TWO)	G4	1356

Djibouti

J2-KAC	20	342/532
J2-KBA	**50**	**71**

Guinea-Bissau

J5-GAS	20	296/507

Norway

LN-AAA	20	73/419
LN-AAA	560	0105
LN-AAA	**650**	**0187**
LN-AAB	20	12
LN-AAB	550	397
LN-AAC	20	281/498
LN-AAC	551	200
LN-AAD	550	260
LN-AAD	551	095
LN-AAE	551	224
LN-AAF	**500**	**311**
LN-AAI	550	069
LN-AFC	501	397
LN-AFG	551	200
LN-FOD	20	53/417
LN-FOE	20	62/409
LN-FOE	EC	125
LN-FOI	20	41/407
(LN-FOX)	550	424
LN-HOT	550	099
LN-NAT	500	331
LN-NEA	550	136
LN-NLA	550	136
LN-NLC	**650**	**0028**
LN-NLD	**650**	**0070**
LN-NPA	125	25125
LN-NPC	125	25145
LN-NPE	125	25097
LN-NPE	23	038
LN-SJA	D1A	A037SA
LN-VIP	55	112
LN-VIP	550	137

Argentina

LQ-JRH	HFB	1050
LQ-MRM	**500**	**470**
LQ-TFM	550	117
LV-	**35A**	**235**
(LV-)	80A	380-4
LV-	WWD	119
LV-AIT	**35A**	**408**
LV-ALF	35A	371
LV-ALW	125	257133
LV-APL	**551**	**355**
LV-AXZ	**125**	**25251**
LV-BAI	200	494
LV-JTZ	**24D**	**234**
LV-JXA	**24D**	**240**
LV-LOG	36	005
LV-LRC	**24D**	**316**
LV-LZR	500	332
LV-MBP	25D	229
LV-MGB	501	423
LV-MMR	501	459
LV-MMV	25D	259
LV-MST	25D	245
LV-MYN	501	510
LV-MZG	501	506
LV-OAS	35A	271
LV-OEL	**25D**	**307**
LV-OFV	35A	312
LV-ONN	35A	355
LV-P	25G	337
LV-PAF	25D	245
LV-PAM	400	RJ-37
LV-PAT	501	459
LV-PAW	25D	259
LV-PAX	500	470
LV-PDW	501	506
LV-PDZ	501	510
LV-PET	35A	271
LV-PEU	25D	307
LV-PFK	31	024
LV-PFM	200	494
LV-PFN	560	0126
LV-PGC	560	0190
LV-PGR	560	0227
LV-PGU	550	724
LV-PGX	60	024
LV-PGZ	560	0251
LV-PHD	560	0246
LV-PHH	550	131
LV-PHJ	560	0265
LV-PHN	550	728
LV-PHU	25D	345
LV-PHV	20	34
LV-PHX	35A	312
LV-PHY	560	0289
LV-PJZ	35A	355
LV-PLC	20	9
LV-PLD	20	29
LV-PLE	560	0305
LV-PLL	25D	269
LV-PLM	501	478
LV-PLR	550	626
LV-PLT	400A	RK-104
LV-PLV	35A	671
LV-PLX	35A	371
LV-PMH	400A	RK-118
LV-PML	501	580
LV-PMM	125	257133
LV-PMP	500	148
LV-PMV	550	0818
LV-PNB	551	355
LV-PNL	550	715
LV-PNR	560	0458
LV-POG	35A	408
LV-POP	HFB	1050
LV-PRA	24D	234
LV-PRB	24D	240
LV-PUY	500	332
LV-PZI	501	423
LV-RBV	31	024
LV-RCT	400	RJ-37
LV-RDD	WWD	12
LV-RED	**560**	**0126**
LV-TDF	35A	478
LV-VFY	560	0190
LV-WBP	**25G**	**337**
LV-WDR	**560**	**0227**
LV-WEJ	**550**	**724**
LV-WEN	WWD	126
LV-WFM	**60**	**024**
LV-WGO	**560**	**0251**
LV-WGY	**560**	**0246**
LV-WHY	650	0231
LV-WHZ	**WWD**	**108**
LV-WIJ	560	0265
LV-WIT	550	604
LV-WJN	**550**	**558**
LV-WJO	**550**	**728**
LV-WJU	**WWD**	**179**
LV-WLG	**25D**	**345**
LV-WLH	20	34
LV-WLR	**WWD**	**183**
LV-WLS	**560**	**0289**
LV-WLX	S60	306-41
LV-WMF	**20**	**9**
LV-WMM	**20**	**29**
LV-WMR	24	135
LV-WMT	**560**	**0305**
LV-WND	**S40**	**282-131**
LV-WOC	**25D**	**269**
LV-WOE	560	0319
LV-WOF	**S60**	**306-25**
LV-WOI	501	478
LV-WOM	**G4**	**1274**
LV-WOV	WWD	331
LV-WOW	G4	1274
LV-WOZ	550	626
LV-WPE	**400A**	**RK-104**
LV-WPO	S60	306-3
LV-WPZ	**35A**	**671**
LV-WRE	**25D**	**355**
LV-WSS	**G4**	**1297**
LV-WTN	**650**	**7054**
LV-WTP	**400A**	**RK-118**
LV-WXD	**551**	**395**
LV-WXJ	**500**	**148**
LV-WXN	60	102
LV-WXV	**50**	**188**
LV-WXX	**S60**	**306-91**
LV-WXY	**25D**	**357**
LV-WYH	550	0818
LV-WYL	**WWD**	**182**
LV-YGC	**125**	**25046**
LV-YHC	**550**	**715**
LV-YLB	**600**	**1034**
LV-YMA	**560**	**0458**
LV-YMB	**31A**	**081**
LV-YRB	**500**	**191**
LV-ZHY	**125**	**258372**
LV-ZNR	**550**	**727**
LV-ZPD	**550**	**398**
LV-ZPU	**500**	**265**
LV-ZRS	**125**	**257046**

Luxembourg

LX-AAA	20	73/419
LX-AEN	601	3046
LX-AER	900	11
LX-BYG	125	258392
LX-DPA	**10**	**113**
LX-EPA	10	48
LX-FMR	**50**	**165**
LX-FTJ	**50**	**144**
LX-GBY	**125**	**258392**
LX-GDL	**550**	**033**
LX-GED	50	54
LX-GES	**900**	**78**
LX-IAL	**20**	**136/439**
(LX-IMN)	900	54
LX-JCG	**10**	**160**
LX-MJM	125	257010
LX-MMB	**601**	**5146**
LX-NAN	**900**	**159**
LX-NUR	50	159
LX-ONE	**35A**	**417**
LX-PCT	**31A**	**112**
LX-PRA	**60**	**145**
LX-PRS	**551**	**496**
LX-RVR	50	107
LX-THS	**550**	**069**
LX-TRG	**10**	**19**
LX-UAE	**50**	**104**
LX-YKH	**500**	**086**

Lithuania

LY-	**125**	**257212**
LY-AMB	STR	5161/43

Bulgaria

LZ-010	50	88
LZ-011	**50**	**97**

United States of America

(N)	125	256053
(N)	125	258035
(N)	20	262
(N)	25D	341
N	**45**	**019**
N	45	048
N	45	068
N	525	0211
N	525	0236
N	525	0274
N	525	0298
N	525	0315
N	525	0329
N	525	0359
N	525	0393
N	550	0932
N	550	0935
(N)	550	656
(N)	550	658
(N)	550	667
(N)	550	668
(N)	550	682
(N)	550	683
(N)	550	685
(N)	550	686
(N)	550	687
(N)	550	688
(N)	550	689
(N)	550	691
(N)	550	692
(N)	550	693
(N)	550	694
(N)	550	696
(N)	550	699
(N)	550	700
(N)	550	701
(N)	550	702
(N)	550	703
(N)	550	704
(N)	550	705
(N)	550	706
N	560	0495
N	560	5104
N	60	160
N	60	161
N	60	173
N	700	9051
N	700	9056
N	750	0072
N	**S40**	**282-39**
(N)	WWD	184
"N001DT"	STR	5157
N1	G3	413
N1	**G4**	**1071**
N1	STR	5001/53
N1AB	125	259005
N1AB	125	259036
N1AF	S550	0018
N1AF	**550**	**320**
N1AH	25D	316
N1AH	35A	398
N1AP	24	163
N1AP	500	322
N1AP	551	051
N1AP	650	0001
N1AP	650	0082
N1AP	650	7003
N1AP	**750**	**0003**
N1AQ	G3	342
N1AT	501	537
N1AT	**551**	**591**
N1BC	WWD	39
N1BF	20	142
N1BG	125	25281
N1BG	125	258011
N1BL	G2	113
N1BL	STR	5029/38

N1BL STR 5097/60
N1BN G4 1300
N1BR 25B 105
N1BU 23 029
N1BX 20 380
N1BX 50 47
N1BX G2 227
N1BX S40 282-101
N1C 125 25200
N1C 125 257206
N1C 2xx 40
N1C G3 388
N1CA 35A 069
N1CA 35A 657
N1CA 501 387
N1CA 60 055
N1CC S65 465-6
N1CF S65 465-3
N1CG 400 RJ-17
N1CH 560 0283
N1CH S60 306-126
(N1CN) 100 199
N1CN 50 55
N1CR 501 561
N1DA 35 013
N1DA 500 288
N1DB STR 5075/19
N1DB STR 5119/29
N1DB STR 5155/32
N1DB STR 5223
N1DC 35A 246
N1DC 35A 464
N1DC 60 035
N1DC S40 282-44
N1DD 25B 171
N1DD 25B 191
N1DE 31 016
N1DG 604 5386
N1DH 10 187
N1DK 24E 343
N1DK 500 175
N1DT STR 5158
N1EC WWD 51
N1ED 25B 092
N1ED 25D 255
N1ED 35A 392
N1EF 525 0167
N1EM STR 5077
N1EP MSP 002
"N1ERAU" T39 265-57
N1EV 50 65
N1FE 20 84
N1FE 600 1055
N1FE 600 1074
(N1GB) 500 309
N1GC 560 0239
N1GC 604 5329
N1GC G5 539
N1GC S550 0109
N1GH 550 227
N1GM S60 306-120
N1GN G3 392
N1GN G4 1284
N1GN G5 518
N1GN G5 578
N1GT G3 454
N1GT G4 1292
N1GW 23 048
N1GY S40 282-81
N1GZ 23 065A
N1H G2 129
N1HA 501 447
N1HC G5 545
N1HF 20 289
N1HF 20 474
N1HM 10 41
N1HM 500 101
N1HP 35 039
N1HP 45 082
N1HS 400A RK-106
N1JB 501 569
N1JG G2 65
N1JK G3 342
N1JN 10 106
N1JN 500 309
N1JN G2 154/28
N1JN G3 329
N1JN G4 1239
N1JN S60 306-14
N1JN S60 306-61
N1JN STR 5132/57
N1JR 25 021
N1JR 25B 104
N1JR 25B 188
N1JS WWD 249
N1JU WWD 13
N1JX S60 306-61
N1KC 501 459
N1KE G3 349
N1KE G4 1033
N1KE G5 574
N1KT WWD 135
N1KT WWD 230
N1LB 500 212
N1LL 25 021
N1LQ 501 526
N1M 20 24
N1M G3 390
N1M WWD 187
N1MB 20 74
N1MC 560 0014
N1MC AST 055
N1MC AST 112
N1MG 45 060
N1MJ STR 5217
N1MM 550 302
N1MN S40 282-69
N1MN S60 306-58
N1MW WWD 109
N1MX 25B 128
N1MX 501 556
N1MY 125 25082
N1MY 35A 370
N1NA G3 309
N1NL 550 303
N1NR 75A 380-70
N1PB 10 92
N1PB 100 198
N1PB 560 5013
N1PG G2 62
N1PG G3 334
N1PG G4 1259
N1PG G4 1374
N1PN S60 306-58
N1PR 50 40
N1PR G2 17
N1PR G3 341
N1PT WWD 93
(N1PU) G3 334
N1QC 24B 181
N1QC S40 282-44
N1QF 604 5329
N1QH 125 25261
N1QH WWD 96
N1QL WWD 96
N1RA 25B 105
(N1RW) 25B 135
N1S 50 139
N1S 650 7010
N1S G3 391
N1SC 35 016
N1SF G3 455
N1SF G4 1060
"N1SJ" T39 276-45
N1SL G4 1167
N1SN 560 0153
N1SN 560 5014
N1SS 24B 186
N1SV 550 165
N1TC 10 144
N1TC 20 83
N1TF G4 1340
N1TF G4 1382
N1TJ 10 18
N1TJ 24E 339
N1TJ G2 39
N1TK 24 153
N1TK 601 5025
N1TM 700 9006
N1TM G4 1087
N1TS 35A 499
N1TS 650 0006
N1TS STR 5215
(N1TS) WWD 187
N1TX D1A A066SA
N1U 20 65
N1U 24D 250
N1U 24D 274
N1U 25D 371
N1U 35A 444
N1UA 550 130
(N1UB) 501 364
N1UG 500 309
N1UH 551 062
N1UH 650 0024
N1UH S550 0057
N1UL 501 482
N1UL S550 0057
N1UP 650 0024
N1UP 650 0224
N1UP S60 306-40
N1UP STR 5142
N1UT 500 267
N1UT D1A A029SA
N1UT S60 306-40
N1VA S550 0143
N1VC 500 183
(N1VC) S60 306-61
N1VQ 125 257113
N1VU 501 545
N1WP G2 190
N1WP G4 1030
N1WP WWD 108
N1WS WWD 252
N1WT 25D 371
N1WZ S40 282-117
N1X 500 236
(N1X) STR 5215
N1XL 560 5041
N1XT 525 0162
N1YE 125 25065
N1ZA 23 042
N1ZC 25XR 022
N1ZC 650 0031
N2 31A 063
N2 500 084
N2 550 006
N2 560 0109
(N2AJ) WWD 277
N2AT 2xx 51
N2AV WWD 322
N2BA 35 051
N2BD 90X 35
N2BD 90X 72
N2BG 125 258207
N2BG WWD 365
N2BT 501 419
N2CA 551 092
(N2CH) 10 163
N2CJ 525A 708
N2CW 2xx 80
N2DB WWD 135
N2DD 23 098
N2DD 24E 335
(N2DP) 501 531
N2EL 500 038
N2EP 650 0010
N2ES STR 5023
(N2ES) WWD 96
N2FA 500 140
N2FE 20 132
N2FE 600 1075
N2FE 601 5095
N2FU 20 412
N2FU 31 027
N2FU 35A 612
N2FU 36A 048
N2G 125 25139
(N2G) 125 25163
N2G 125 258354
N2GG 550 306
N2GP 23 020
N2GP G2 13
N2GR 24D 262
N2H 20 327
N2HD 500 078
(N2HE) 25B 138
N2HF G2 221
N2HJ 560 0278
N2HP 125 257180
N2HW 200 488
N2HW S40 282-105
N2HW S60 306-68
N2HX S60 306-68
N2HZ WWD 314
N2JR G2 131/23
N2JR STR 5236
N2JW 550 183
N2JW 560 0191
N2JW 560 5064
N2JW WWD 86
N2JZ 550 055
N2KH 550 570
N2KN 125 25020
N2KW 125 25020
N2KW 125 257201
N2LN 501 483
N2LY G3 340
N2MG 125 258092
N2MK HFB 1036
N2MK STR 5226
N2MP 10 31
N2N S65 465-63
N2NC MSP 005
N2NL S65 465-63
N2NT 550 730
N2NT 650 7013
N2PG G2 20
N2PG G4 1378
N2PK G2 206
N2PW 25D 363
N2QL 125 257197
N2QW S40 282-105
N2RC 550 337
N2RC 560 0319
N2S 551 110
N2S G2 113
N2S G2 158
N2SG 125 258090
N2SG 125 259019
N2SN 23 072
(N2SN) S40 282-59
N2SP G3 366
N2T 50 167
N2TE 75 370-6
N2TE MSP 005
N2TF 200 490
N2TF 650 0176
N2TF G3 460
N2TN 500 231
N2TQ G3 460
N2U 24D 250
N2U 25D 325
N2U 35A 268
N2U 500 285
N2UJ G2 139/11
N2UP 650 0010
N2UP 650 0227
N2UP S60 306-17
N2UR S60 306-17
N2WC D1A A047SA
N2WL 24D 265
N2WL 35A 245
N2WL G4 1118
N2WQ 35A 277
N2WR S40 282-102
N2WU WWD 72
N2YG 125 258090
N2YY 24 143
N2ZA 23 067
N2ZC 501 420
N3AH 35A 421
N3AL 125 25169
N3AS 28 001
N3AV WWD 361
N3BL 23 003

N3BM	**2xx**	**38**
N3BM	S40	282-131
N3BM	S65	465-51
N3BY	100	193
N3D	S550	0038
N3DL	WWD	42
N3DU	24D	279
N3DZ	24D	279
N3E	G2	185
N3E	STR	5029/38
N3E	STR	5076/17
N3EK	STR	5029/38
N3EK	STR	5076/17
N3EU	G2	185
N3FA	**550**	**124**
N3FC	S60	306-33
N3FE	20	151
N3FE	501	678
N3FE	**601**	**5054**
N3GL	**125**	**257197**
N3GL	24	173
N3GL	35A	070
N3GN	**501**	**466**
N3GR	STR	5127
N3GT	550	376
N3GT	**560**	**0091**
N3GW	24B	203
N3H	20	327
N3H	G4	1092
N3HA	35A	182
N3HB	35A	182
N3HB	55	046
N3HB	**600**	**1059**
N3HB	STR	5116
N3HX	G4	1092
N3JJ	20	57
N3JJ	500	016
N3JJ	500	299
N3JL	23	025
N3JL	25XR	073
N3JL	35A	289
N3JL	**600**	**1080**
N3JX	25XR	073
N3LG	500	112
N3M	G4	1021
N3MB	550	405
N3MF	125	25093
N3MJ	35A	188
N3NP	36A	048
N3NU	G4	1021
N3PC	36	013
N3PC	500	067
N3PC	550	247
N3PC	**601**	**5066**
N3PC	AST	037
N3PG	G2	21
N3PG	G3	336
N3PG	**G4**	**1260**
N3PW	125	256009
N3PW	24E	341
N3PW	35A	207
N3PY	G3	336
(N3PY)	G3	440
N3Q	500	238
(N3Q)	650	0007
N3QE	500	121
N3QL	STR	5064/51
N3QM	S40	282-131
N3QM	S65	465-51
N3QS	STR	5064/51
N3QS	STR	5224
N3QZ	500	238
N3R	550	123
N3RA	35A	138
N3RC	10	69
N3RC	20	256
N3RC	WWD	222
N3RC	**WWD**	**340**
N3RL	WWD	390
N3RN	75A	380-38
N3TE	75	370-8
N3TJ	24D	236
N3UC	25	034
(N3UG)	501	526
N3UJ	35A	473
N3UW	25D	214
N3VF	**20**	**363/544**
N3VF	WWD	137
N3VF	WWD	191
N3VF	WWD	324
N3VG	35A	305
N3VJ	**31A**	**035**
N3VL	**WWD**	**180**
N3W	500	143
N3WN	20	185/467
N3WP	35A	606
N3WQ	S60	306-97
N3WZ	10	30
N3ZA	23	024
N3ZD	500	224
N3ZQ	G2	62
N4	31A	038
N4	500	084
N4	**560**	**0113**
N4AC	10	184
N4AC	50	96
N4AC	500	218
N4AZ	**M20**	**1**
(N4BP)	S550	0090
N4BR	125	256032
N4CH	500	062
N4CH	550	045
N4CP	50	187
N4CP	55	029
N4CP	G2	71
N4CP	**G4**	**1257**
N4CQ	G2	71
N4CR	**125**	**25109**
N4CR	24	128
N4CR	550	045
N4CS	550	248
N4CS	**560**	**0024**
N4DS	10	116
(N4EF)	525	0167
N4EG	650	0139
(N4EG)	650	0152
N4EG	**650**	**7059**
N4EK	550	119
N4EM	AST	050
N4ES	**125**	**25243**
N4EW	550	636
N4F	24D	294
N4FC	**650**	**0140**
N4FE	20	108/430
N4FE	**45**	**032**
N4FE	550	478
N4FE	600	1062
N4GA	**525**	**0272**
N4GB	35A	228
N4GV	S40	282-135
N4J	**35A**	**110**
N4JS	550	281
N4JS	560	0196
N4JS	**560**	**5035**
N4KH	500	062
N4LG	500	130
N4LG	**S60**	**306-9**
N4LH	20	205
N4LK	500	140
N4LK	**D1A**	**A021SA**
N4M	**550**	**0879**
N4M	S65	465-18
N4MB	**50**	**156**
N4MB	S65	465-17
N4MH	**WWD**	**232**
N4MM	551	430
N4MM	560	0109A
N4MR	25B	125
N4MR	25XR	222
N4NB	75A	380-40
N4NE	S60	306-79
N4NK	WWD	82
N4NM	**551**	**430**
N4NP	S40	282-109
N4NR	75A	380-40
N4NR	**G2**	**255/18**
N4NR	S60	306-79
N4NT	**S60**	**306-48**
N4PC	G3	340
N4PC	G4	1174
N4PG	601	5052
N4PG	80A	380-49
N4PG	G2	21
N4PH	S40	282-116
N4PN	125	25185
N4PN	25	003
N4PQ	80A	380-49
N4QB	**125**	**25255**
N4QP	50	187
N4RH	**525**	**0306**
N4RT	10	80
N4RT	20	242
N4RT	24F	348
N4RT	35	003
N4RT	**G2**	**26**
N4RU	24F	348
N4S	G2	24
N4S	S60	306-37
N4SE	S60	306-37
N4SG	601	5111
N4SP	G2	20
N4SP	STR	5081
N4SX	STR	5081
N4TE	500	149
N4TF	**525**	**0076**
N4TK	500	192
N4TL	500	149
N4TL	550	119
N4TL	560	0048
N4TL	**560**	**0334**
N4TL	S550	0052
N4TS	125	256004
N4TS	551	030
N4TU	S550	0052
N4UP	G3	484
N4UP	G4	1088
N4VC	25B	161
N4VF	500	045
N4VF	550	053
N4VF	**650**	**0082**
N4VR	550	716
N4VS	23	072
N4WC	**125**	**25278**
N4WG	WWD	112
N4WG	**WWD**	**200**
(N4WJ)	75A	380-12
N4XL	35A	236
N4YA	525	0004
N4ZA	HFB	1045
N4ZB	**25D**	**371**
N4ZK	500	140
N4ZS	**550**	**248**
N5AH	**125**	**256004**
(N5AX)	STR	5013
(N5B)	25D	299
N5B	500	021
N5B	500	081
N5B	500	150
N5B	500	225
N5BA	WWD	138
N5BK	G4	1025
N5BL	23	009
N5BP	WWD	10
N5BP	WWD	137
(N5BP)	WWD	280
N5C	125	258083
N5C	20	17
N5CA	20	108/430
N5CE	20	17
N5D	23	095
N5DL	125	256051
N5DL	50	7
N5DL	**G2**	**226**
N5DL	S60	306-131
N5DM	23	025
N5DM	23	028
N5DM	25	063
N5EJ	D1A	A033SA
N5EQ	80A	380-50
N5ES	10	174
N5ES	125	259024
N5FE	20	20
N5FE	**45**	**079**
N5FF	35A	396
N5FG	500	224
N5FW	**500**	**187**
N5G	125	258053
(N5GA)	550	230
N5GA	**G5**	**509**
N5GD	10	83
N5GE	**560**	**0218**
N5GF	**G4**	**1277**
(N5HG)	G3	376
N5JC	WWD	101
N5JR	WWD	49
N5JY	**10**	**74**
N5LG	500	150
N5LL	25B	183
N5LP	10	142
N5MC	900	10
N5MC	**G4**	**1218**
(N5MW)	125	25233
N5NC	**25D**	**372**
N5NE	**550**	**723**
N5NE	S60	306-127
N5NG	125	256020
N5NR	**125**	**256053**
N5PC	S40	282-34
N5PG	601	5053
N5PG	80A	380-50
N5PQ	S40	282-34
N5Q	500	018
N5Q	550	036
N5QY	23	028
N5QZ	500	018
N5RC	20	159
N5RD	**G2**	**142**
N5RL	501	638
N5RT	20	96
(N5S)	WWD	280
N5SA	**G5**	**527**
N5SJ	125	256014
N5SJ	24D	246
N5SJ	G2	52
N5T	551	174
N5T	560	0218
N5T	**750**	**0104**
N5TC	501	424
N5TD	24D	311
(N5TH)	WWD	372
N5TK	500	266
N5TM	**601**	**5076**
N5TQ	**551**	**174**
N5TR	24D	311
N5TR	500	288
N5TR	**550**	**344**
N5UD	G2	8
N5UD	STR	5019
N5UE	D1A	A026SA
N5UH	**G5**	**536**
N5UJ	**25B**	**088**
N5UM	501	550
N5UQ	200	513
N5UU	**200**	**513**
N5V	125	25282
N5VF	50	163
N5VF	**50**	**166**
N5VF	900	116
N5VG	**31**	**014**
N5VH	50	163
N5VN	900	116
N5VP	**501**	**405**
N5WF	**501**	**460**
N5WJ	24B	187
N5XP	**560**	**0422**
N5XR	**550**	**553**
N5YP	501	462
N5ZA	HFB	1037
N5ZZ	500	155
N6	550	006
N6B	WWD	127
N6B	WWD	89
N6BB	**601**	**5082**
N6BX	**900**	**79**
N6BX	G3	392
N6BZ	G3	392

N6CD	500	151
N6CF	T39	265-48
N6DB	WWD	98
N6EL	551	375
(N6ES)	STR	5023
N6FE	20	50
N6FE	560	0028
N6FR	**550**	**0828**
N6FZ	560	0028
N6GC	25	034
N6GG	125	257108
N6GG	125	258030
N6GG	35A	256
N6GJ	23	069
N6GQ	125	257108
N6GV	**S65**	**465-9**
N6HF	**550**	**223**
N6HT	501	362
N6JB	125	257023
N6JB	125	258189
N6JB	**601**	**5131**
N6JL	500	101
N6JL	**550**	**294**
N6JL	STR	5037/24
N6JM	24D	246
N6JU	500	101
N6JW	**G2**	**138**
N6K	75A	380-1
N6K	S65	465-3
N6KJ	25C	146
N6KM	24E	334
N6LG	75A	380-34
N6LL	25D	256
N6LL	**S550**	**0094**
N6MJ	WWD	251
N6MK	HFB	1037
N6MK	S60	306-98
N6ML	HFB	1037
N6NB	G4	1290
N6ND	S60	306-81
N6NE	S60	306-133
N6NE	S60	306-43
N6NE	STR	5006/40
N6NF	25	021
N6NG	75A	380-27
N6NP	S60	306-43
N6NP	S65	465-9
N6NR	75A	380-27
N6NR	75A	380-43
N6NR	75A	380-54
N6NR	S60	306-43
N6NR	S60	306-81
N6NR	**S65**	**465-29**
N6PA	10	84
N6PA	D1A	A019SA
N6PC	**G2**	**87/775/6**
N6PG	75A	380-66
N6PG	80A	380-48
N6Q	550	046
N6QZ	**STR**	**5224**
N6RF	501	460
N6SG	601	5046
N6SP	80A	380-9
N6SS	**125**	**25100**
N6TE	S40	282-94
N6TM	125	258026
N6TM	S60	306-72
N6TM	**WWD**	**275**
N6TU	125	258026
N6UB	125	257023
N6UB	125	258189
N6VB	**G4**	**1174**
N6VC	125	257056
N6VF	**20**	**486**
N6VF	500	045
N6VG	**10**	**62**
N6VL	75A	380-66
N6WU	550	198
N6YY	25D	323
N6YY	36A	023
N6ZA	HFB	1051
N7	500	084
N7AB	24E	355
N7AB	35A	402

N7AB	550	633
N7AB	**650**	**7068**
N7AT	25B	105
N7AU	55	112
(N7AU)	GXY	004
N7AU	**GXY**	**006**
N7C	125	258025
N7C	G2	51
N7C	G3	449
N7CC	**525**	**0004**
N7CC	550	029
N7CF	23	016
N7CJ	501	509
N7CT	125	257131
N7DJ	**WWD**	**265**
N7DL	24B	228
N7EC	WWD	96
N7EN	525	0151
N7ES	HFB	1045
N7FD	550	344
N7FE	20	46
N7FE	560	0063
N7FJ	23	058
(N7FZ)	560	0063
N7GA	25B	121
N7GF	23	016
N7GF	**23**	**093**
N7GJ	25	004
N7GJ	**500**	**021**
N7GN	24	134
N7GP	23	082
N7GW	WWD	24
N7HA	24	154
N7HF	S65	465-13
N7HL	WWD	35
N7HM	**WWD**	**266**
N7HV	125	25282
N7HV	650	0124
N7JN	25C	098
N7KA	35	033
N7KG	**S40**	**282-111**
N7KH	500	045
N7KR	WWD	72
N7LA	25D	244
(N7LA)	35A	308
N7LC	25D	328
N7LG	125	25185
N7MC	501	576
N7NE	501	352
N7NF	S60	306-126
(N7NL)	10	68
N7NN	**550**	**0851**
N7NP	10	68
N7NP	125	25234
N7NP	STR	5229
N7NR	75A	380-39
N7NR	S60	306-126
N7NR	S60	306-57
N7NR	S60	306-73
N7NR	**S65**	**465-44**
N7PE	35A	204
N7PG	G2	62
N7PG	G4	1374
N7PQ	G2	62
N7PW	**D1A**	**A027SA**
N7QC	S550	0109
N7QJ	501	509
N7RC	550	022
N7RC	D1A	A012SA
N7RL	24D	322
N7RL	25D	230
N7RP	**G4**	**1064**
N7RX	G4	1137
N7SJ	**125**	**25250**
(N7SL)	S40	282-114
N7SN	**550**	**313**
N7SP	600	1076
N7SZ	125	25100
N7SZ	STR	5040
N7SZ	STR	5124
N7TJ	10	69
N7TJ	25	007
N7TJ	35	013
N7TJ	**G2**	**23**

N7TJ	G2	77
N7TK	**501**	**509**
N7UA	55B	128
N7UF	**501**	**632**
N7UJ	125	257093
N7US	35A	291
N7US	55B	128
N7US	**60**	**014**
N7VS	24	087
N7WC	125	25273
N7WC	**125**	**257036**
N7WF	501	370
(N7WG)	125	25187
N7WG	125	257131
N7WG	20	325
N7WQ	G2	190
N7WY	**550**	**598**
N7XJ	35A	669
N7YA	**550**	**0880**
N7YP	550	211
N7ZA	25	026
N7ZB	24E	355
N7ZU	**550**	**432**
N7ZX	G2	21
N8AD	551	331
N8AD	STR	5013
N8AE	**24E**	**335**
N8AF	**S40**	**282-24**
N8BG	24F	348
N8BG	S550	0085
N8BX	20	380
N8BX	550	345
N8BX	**900**	**111**
(N8CA)	G5	531
N8CA	**G5**	**563**
N8CF	550	223
N8CL	25	014
N8DE	500	166
N8DX	**500**	**303**
N8EH	501	483
N8FC	500	124
N8FD	550	383
N8FE	20	199
N8FF	25	016
N8FM	24A	116
N8GA	**10**	**127**
N8GA	35A	091
N8GA	S40	282-32
N8GA	WWD	356
N8GA	WWD	63
N8GE	WWD	63
N8GT	55	020
N8HJ	560	0108
(N8JA)	35A	348
N8JC	650	7030
N8JC	**750**	**0020**
N8JG	500	074
N8JL	**G3**	**388**
N8JL	WWD	359
N8KG	125	257189
N8KG	**600**	**1012**
N8KH	**500**	**163**
N8LA	35A	124
N8LC	WWD	48
N8LE	**D1A**	**A042SA**
N8LG	501	477
N8LL	28	005
N8LT	**10**	**173**
N8MA	25B	085
N8MA	35A	229
N8MC	604	5329
N8MC	AST	092
(N8ME)	400A	RK-19
N8MF	**25D**	**253**
N8MQ	25B	085
N8NB	75	370-9
N8NB	75A	380-27
(N8NC)	501	567
(N8NF)	S60	306-141
N8NG	80A	380-48
N8NR	75	370-2
N8NR	75	370-9
N8NR	75A	380-27
N8NR	80A	380-48

N8NR	S60	306-141
N8P	501	369
N8PG	G2	21
N8PJ	501	369
N8PL	125	257058
N8PQ	G2	21
N8QP	WWD	217
N8QR	WWD	217
N8RA	**WWD**	**104**
N8RF	501	293
N8SC	STR	5106/9
N8SP	**125**	**258380**
N8TG	500	253
N8U	**36A**	**026**
(N8UB)	36A	026
N8UP	**125**	**258083**
N8VB	**700**	**9021**
N8WN	20	91
N8YM	**400**	**RJ-4**
N8YY	35A	335
N8YY	55	060
N9AJ	23	069
N9AT	25B	125
(N9AT)	500	241
N9AX	500	016
N9AZ	**125**	**256063**
N9BF	G2	46
N9BX	50	45
N9BY	WWD	9
N9CH	**31A**	**041**
N9CH	35A	282
N9CN	25C	061
N9CN	35	016
N9CU	**60**	**075**
N9CZ	25	040
N9DC	WWD	109
N9DM	20	18
N9DM	WWD	63
N9EE	35A	193
N9FB	20	275
(N9FC)	D1A	A010SA
N9FE	20	216
N9FE	20	84
N9GN	75A	380-2
N9GT	501	438
N9GT	**S550**	**0159**
N9HJ	31A	040
N9HM	24B	190
N9HM	25C	146
N9HM	35A	199
N9HN	25C	146
(N9HV)	35A	199
N9JJ	23	039
N9KC	24	144
N9KH	28	001
N9KH	S550	0082
N9KL	650	0068
N9KL	**G3**	**321**
N9LD	**24F**	**336**
N9LM	24	152
N9LP	D1A	A019SA
(N9LP)	WWD	149
N9LR	125	258050
N9LR	525	0025
N9LR	550	270
N9LR	55C	138
N9LR	**560**	**0473**
N9MD	STR	5014
N9MS	S40	282-103
N9NB	125	258317
N9NE	501	593
N9NP	S60	306-133
N9NR	S40	282-111
N9NR	S40	282-137
N9NR	S60	306-135
N9NT	S60	306-135
N9PC	G4	1210
N9PG	G2	251
N9PW	**400A**	**RK-7**
N9PY	G2	251
N9QN	S60	306-12
N9RA	23	068
N9RA	**23**	**095**
N9RD	**WWD**	**220**

N9RS	28	001
N9SC	**G5**	**552**
N9SS	**551**	**190**
N9TE	**10**	**103**
N9TK	501	437
(N9UC)	650	0238
N9UJ	500	198
N9UP	**125**	**258147**
N9V	500	150
N9VC	WWD	162
N9VF	**550**	**646**
N9VG	20	416
N9VL	31A	174
N9VL	AST	026
N9VQ	WWD	162
N9WN	G3	392
N9WP	STR	5157
(N9WW)	WWD	252
(N9WW)	WWD	306
N9X	50	14
N9ZD	**35A**	**306**
N10	500	084
(N10AA)	125	258023
(N10AB)	35A	231
N10AG	10	6
N10AH	10	139
(N10AH)	10	141
N10AH	**35A**	**657**
N10AQ	35A	069
N10AT	50	194
N10AT	900	142
N10AZ	**35A**	**080**
N10BD	25B	120
N10BD	**35A**	**506**
(N10BF)	25	010
N10BF	35A	185
(N10BF)	500	118
N10BF	550	048
N10BF	55B	128
N10BK	WWD	89
N10BU	25B	120
(N10BY)	WWD	226
N10C	125	25236
N10C	**125**	**257050**
(N10CA)	501	387
N10CB	24B	227
N10CC	S40	282-56
N10CF	550	230
N10CN	**125**	**257155**
N10CN	560	0249
N10CN	75A	380-27
N10CN	75A	380-54
N10CP	24	112
N10CP	55	029
N10CR	55	057
N10CR	**55C**	**145**
N10CX	STR	5162
N10CZ	125	257038
N10D	**125**	**25029**
N10DG	500	028
N10DG	500	120
N10DR	STR	5037/24
N10DR	STR	5139/54
N10EA	WWD	39
N10EC	24B	215
N10EG	**550**	**055**
N10EH	501	350
N10EH	**G3**	**436**
N10F	**10**	**12**
N10FE	20	16
N10FE	600	1074
N10FE	**601**	**5188**
N10FG	**500**	**295**
N10FG	WWD	318
N10FJ	10	100
N10FJ	10	106
N10FJ	10	2
N10FL	25XR	106
N10FL	**400A**	**RK-266**
N10FL	400A	RK-27
N10FM	500	292
N10FN	**36**	**015**
N10FN	550	268
N10FQ	**400A**	**RK-27**
N10FU	24E	340
N10GE	501	385
(N10GN)	550	069
(N10GR)	500	132
N10GR	WWD	114
N10HE	10	111
N10HK	10	142
N10HR	G2	67
N10HV	WWD	103
N10J	400A	RK-31
N10J	**45**	**063**
N10J	501	408
N10JJ	STR	5162
N10JK	550	178
N10JM	750	0022
N10JP	500	080
N10JP	550	081
N10JP	**650**	**0157**
N10JP	WWD	96
N10JV	WWD	96
N10JX	400A	RK-31
N10JZ	10	13
N10LB	20	179
N10LB	G2	111
N10LB	G2	168
N10LB	G2	82
N10LB	G4	1008
N10LJ	23	037
N10LN	125	25156
N10LQ	G4	1008
N10LR	**551**	**084**
N10LT	50	194
N10LX	**S60**	**306-59**
N10LY	**550**	**466**
N10M	**75**	**370-2**
N10MB	WWD	157
(N10MC)	23	003
N10MC	WWD	26
N10MF	WWD	53
N10MJ	STR	5090
N10MR	WWD	258
N10MT	20	239
N10MV	**WWD**	**300**
(N10MZ)	600	1084
N10MZ	**900**	**32**
N10MZ	AST	028
N10NB	125	258331
N10NC	**10**	**172**
N10NL	100	195
N10NL	501	417
N10NL	**WWD**	**304**
N10NM	D1A	A016SA
N10NP	25XR	106
N10NT	25B	144
(N10NV)	100	195
(N10NW)	G2	183
N10PF	S60	306-39
(N10PN)	10	3
N10PN	**600**	**1072**
N10PN	650	0020
N10PN	STR	5155/32
N10PP	20	161
N10PP	**50**	**231**
N10PQ	50	231
N10PS	500	252
N10PW	125	257104
(N10PX)	551	419
N10PX	650	0025
N10QD	10	178
(N10QX)	23	035
N10R	**45**	**042**
N10RE	25B	133
N10RE	35A	345
N10RQ	**G2**	**232**
N10RU	**550**	**470**
N10RZ	**20**	**161**
N10RZ	25B	133
N10S	**WWD**	**278**
N10SL	S40	282-11
N10SN	WWD	69
N10ST	**31A**	**039**
N10ST	650	0113
N10TB	10	72
N10TC	125	258096
N10TC	**550**	**495**
N10TC	650	0008
N10TD	**560**	**0096**
N10TE	D1A	A029SA
N10TJ	10	99
N10TN	**125**	**257085**
N10TX	10	9
N10UC	**125**	**257119**
N10UC	500	083
N10UC	500	283
N10UH	**500**	**304**
N10UJ	**WWD**	**204**
N10UM	S60	306-43
N10UN	10	36
N10UP	500	080
N10UQ	500	083
(N10UU)	200	513
N10VG	20	126/438
N10VG	**25B**	**125**
N10WA	20	28
N10WE	10	159
N10WF	125	258030
N10WF	24D	321
N10WF	35A	377
N10WJ	**24D**	**311**
N10XX	10	40
N10XY	G2	56
N10YJ	10	57
N10YJ	**125**	**258099**
N11	STR	5001/53
N11A	500	111
N11AB	551	079
N11AF	**125**	**256057**
N11AK	20	249
N11AK	24	154
N11AK	25B	082
N11AK	35A	135
N11AL	G2	97
N11AL	S60	306-27
N11AM	35A	340
N11AM	**60**	**118**
(N11AN)	G4	1108
N11AQ	**24**	**178**
N11AQ	500	045
N11AQ	S60	306-18
N11AR	125	25098
N11AZ	600	1032
N11BK	WWD	77
N11BU	25B	138
N11CS	WWD	397
N11DH	10	108
N11DH	10	142
N11DH	10	68
N11DH	500	019
N11DH	500	048
N11DH	501	385
N11DQ	500	019
N11FH	24	131
N11FH	**550**	**013**
N11FX	125	25273
N11FX	G4	1107
N11GE	400A	RK-19
N11HJ	**500**	**034**
N11HM	STR	5119/29
N11JC	25	003
(N11JC)	501	463
N11JC	STR	5013
N11JK	23	088
(N11JV)	35A	096
N11KA	500	119
N11LB	20	244
N11LC	560	0427
N11LN	**WWD**	**261**
N11LQ	**560**	**0427**
N11LX	**S60**	**306-75**
(N11MC)	25B	125
N11MC	WWD	55
N11MN	**500**	**266**
N11MY	35A	370
N11MZ	AST	028
N11NT	HFB	1055
N11NZ	650	0143
N11NZ	**G2**	**214**
N11PH	25B	177
N11QC	500	008
N11QD	125	25108
N11QM	23	091
N11SQ	125	25206
(N11SQ)	25D	234
N11SQ	35A	380
N11SQ	501	477
N11SS	**551**	**436**
N11SX	G2	34
N11SX	STR	5111
N11TC	20	146
N11TC	500	008
N11TK	25B	201
N11TM	**501**	**435**
N11TS	125	257191
N11TS	55	032
N11TS	**S550**	**0119**
N11UC	G2	108
N11UE	STR	5038
N11UF	**20**	**356**
N11UF	G2	8
N11UF	STR	5037/24
N11UF	STR	5038
N11UL	S60	306-103
N11UM	G2	12
(N11WA)	20	37/406
(N11WC)	10	11
(N11WC)	125	258308
N11WC	500	058
N11WC	WWD	177
N11WF	**400A**	**RK-236**
N11WF	D1A	A075SA
N11WP	WWD	100
N11WQ	500	058
N11YM	35A	340
N11YR	**125**	**257206**
N12AC	550	035
N12AE	125	25214
N12AM	**500**	**235**
N12BN	125	25214
(N12BN)	G2	39
N12BW	**S40**	**282-99**
N12CJ	WWD	13
N12CQ	501	458
N12CQ	550	372
N12CQ	**560**	**0231**
N12CV	**501**	**458**
N12DE	501	458
N12EP	**10**	**175**
(N12EP)	35A	110
N12F	**125**	**258182**
N12FC	550	369
(N12FH)	WWD	159
N12FN	**36**	**016**
(N12FS)	25D	328
N12FU	20	412
N12FU	**60**	**027**
N12GH	20	7
N12GJ	35A	438
N12GK	550	291
N12GP	23	076
(N12GP)	75A	380-51
N12GP	**G2**	**63**
N12GS	**525**	**0374**
N12HJ	23	040
N12JA	550	231
N12JA	WWD	108
N12JX	WWD	108
N12KW	125	25097
N12L	**550**	**583**
N12LB	10	62
N12LB	20	179
N12MA	550	0882
N12MB	10	112
(N12MB)	24A	116
N12MB	500	101
N12MB	500	137
N12ME	500	137
N12MF	20	179
N12MH	25XR	139
N12MJ	24E	331
N12MK	24B	192
N12NM	**501**	**660**
N12NZ	**G4**	**1376**

N12PA	**525**	**0012**
N12PB	**S60**	**306-18**
N12R	STR	5006/40
N12R	STR	5053/2
(N12RA)	25	023
N12RN	501	625
N12RN	550	709
N12RN	**560**	**0316**
N12RP	**35A**	**278**
N12ST	**560**	**0014**
N12TA	23	093
N12TV	551	115
N12TV	**560**	**0358**
N12TX	10	147
N12TX	**10**	**90**
N12U	10	75
N12U	**G4**	**1112**
N12UT	G4	1112
N12WF	**400A**	**RK-228**
N12WF	D1A	A083SA
N12WH	**501**	**437**
N12WK	25C	126
N12WP	20	83
N12WW	25	051
N12XX	10	112
N12YS	125	25186
N13AD	WWD	103
N13BJ	550	236
N13BK	**10**	**94**
N13BK	501	644
(N13BN)	501	641
N13BT	501	453
N13CR	25	023
(N13FE)	20	24
N13FH	**525**	**0185**
N13FN	36A	045
N13GW	G2	87/775/6
N13GW	WWD	162
N13GX	**GXY**	**013**
N13HB	35A	310
(N13HB)	55	046
(N13HH)	WWD	268
N13HJ	500	182
(N13HQ)	35A	310
N13JE	36	013
N13KH	WWD	182
N13KL	24F	332
N13LB	G2	111
N13LJ	23	037
(N13ME)	75A	380-70
N13MF	S65	465-13
N13MJ	125	25137
N13MJ	24D	314
N13MJ	35A	047
N13NH	75A	380-25
(N13QS)	650	0013
N13RC	501	431
N13SL	S60	306-110
N13SL	S60	306-17
N13SL	S60	306-90
N13SN	23	009
N13ST	**501**	**439**
N13TV	WWD	86
N13UR	500	011
N13UR	WWD	358
N13US	400A	RK-193
N13VF	WWD	191
N13VG	35A	386
N14BC	24B	209
N14BN	WWD	337
(N14BR)	125	256032
N14CF	36	015
N14CF	501	097
N14CG	**50**	**100**
N14CG	S60	306-83
N14CJ	**200**	**499**
N14CN	36A	047
N14CQ	S60	306-83
N14DM	**24E**	**341**
N14DM	D1A	A017SA
N14EA	501	418
N14EL	35	009
N14EN	200	490
(N14FE)	20	198/466
N14FE	20	227
N14FE	600	1064
N14FG	20	177
N14FN	**25C**	**126**
(N14FU)	36A	048
N14GA	550	310
N14GD	125	25141
N14GD	125	256068
N14GD	125	259011
N14GD	**601**	**5005**
N14GQ	125	25141
N14HB	**550**	**0903**
N14HH	**125**	**25118**
N14JA	125	257051
N14JA	500	195
N14JD	75A	380-56
N14JL	500	015
N14JZ	500	143
N14LJ	25	014
N14LT	G2	246
N14M	35A	113
N14M	S40	282-4
N14M	S60	306-56
N14M	S65	465-4
N14MH	500	174
N14MJ	24B	189
N14NA	25D	218
N14NA	**900**	**124**
N14PC	G2	170
N14PN	601	3014
N14PT	24B	208
(N14PT)	25XR	139
N14QG	28	003
N14R	**604**	**5319**
N14RM	**551**	**139**
N14SR	**AST**	**015**
N14SY	125	257101
N14SY	**G3**	**391**
N14T	35A	608
N14T	500	143
N14T	**60**	**026**
N14TN	**75A**	**380-40**
N14TT	500	237
N14TV	501	499
N14TV	525	0126
N14TX	35A	321
N14TX	36A	033
N14U	10	90
N14UH	G4	1247
N14UM	S550	0127
N14VA	**501**	**521**
N14VC	25D	263
N14VF	**560**	**0130**
(N14VF)	560	0342
(N14WJ)	125	257120
N14WJ	STR	5053/2
N15AG	125	257156
N15AK	25B	082
N15AK	S65	465-70
N15AR	D1A	A005SA
N15AS	**2xx**	**3**
N15AT	20	403
N15AW	**500**	**139**
N15BE	23	005
N15BH	25B	134
N15BN	WWD	352
N15C	**525**	**0377**
N15CC	20	23
N15CC	25B	124
N15CC	25TF	036
N15CC	35A	339
N15CC	36	009
N15CC	500	101
N15CC	S65	465-42
(N15CK)	S60	306-121
N15CQ	**500**	**101**
N15CU	25B	124
N15CV	501	547
N15CV	**550**	**0819**
N15DJ	**S60**	**306-97**
N15EA	**550**	**450**
N15EH	**35A**	**126**
N15EN	S65	465-70
N15ER	**25D**	**267**
N15FE	20	229
N15FN	36A	038
N15FS	500	016
N15G	WWD	63
N15H	**20**	**368**
N15H	S60	306-60
N15HF	**S60**	**306-60**
N15M	25TF	036
(N15ME)	75A	380-70
N15MJ	24E	339
N15MJ	25	018
N15MJ	35A	211
N15NA	**550**	**296**
N15NY	501	496
N15PL	24	101
N15PN	75A	380-15
N15PR	501	452
N15QS	650	0015
N15RF	80A	380-17
N15RF	S60	306-23
N15RH	**35A**	**497**
N15RL	550	489
N15SC	23	039
N15SC	35A	139
N15SJ	10	40
N15SN	550	566
N15SP	550	566
(N15TA)	50	73
N15TG	G2	253
N15TM	10	114
N15TS	S40	282-18
N15TT	650	0105
N15TT	**650**	**0192**
N15TT	S550	0019
N15TV	550	459
N15TW	35A	106
N15TW	50	73
N15TW	550	459
N15TW	AST	029
N15TW	D1A	A014SA
N15TX	10	13
N15TZ	650	0192
(N15UB)	125	25038
N15UC	G2	176
N15UC	G5	589
N15UG	**G2**	**176**
(N15UJ)	501	547
N15VF	650	0012
N15WH	**35A**	**085**
(N15WJ)	G4	1079
N15XM	**550**	**341**
N15Y	35A	335
N15Y	550	297
N16A	WWD	101
N16AJ	**650**	**0075**
N16AS	**650**	**0055**
N16AZ	STR	5156
N16BJ	35A	165
N16BL	STR	5205
N16CP	24	147
N16CP	50	153
N16DD	10	105
N16DD	10	56
N16FE	20	230
N16FE	650	0025
N16FG	35A	655
N16FG	G2	235
N16FN	35	030
N16FP	WWD	39
N16GA	125	256018
N16GH	WWD	110
N16GR	WWD	100
N16GS	125	257186
N16GT	25D	230
N16GX	**700**	**9016**
N16HC	**24**	**126**
N16HL	**501**	**431**
N16JP	25	017
N16KK	**25B**	**174**
N16KW	501	664
N16LF	75A	380-25
N16LG	**500**	**174**
N16LJ	25D	230
N16LJ	**55**	**126**
N16MA	WWD	101
N16MF	**D1A**	**A065SA**
N16MJ	24X	117
N16MK	**WWD**	**84**
N16MT	24B	209
N16NK	G2	156/31
N16NK	G3	354
N16NK	G5	585
N16NL	**501**	**417**
N16NM	560	0084
N16PC	**45**	**050**
N16PJ	125	25078
N16PN	S60	306-99
N16R	20	305
N16R	50	141
N16R	S40	282-94
N16RP	**S550**	**0047**
N16SK	WWD	101
N16SU	**650**	**0025**
N16TA	S40	282-2
N16TS	**551**	**030**
N16TS	600	1016
N16VG	**501**	**553**
(N16VT)	125	256037
N16VT	**125**	**256040**
N16WG	125	25187
N16WJ	10	105
N16WJ	24	133
N17A	**36A**	**046**
N17AH	**25D**	**316**
N17AJ	CVT	15
N17AN	**50**	**281**
N17AN	650	0054
N17AP	650	7003
N17AR	25	034
N17CN	601	3027
N17DD	**125**	**258161**
N17DM	**550**	**416**
(N17DW)	WWD	145
N17EM	35A	287
N17FE	20	232
N17FL	550	627
N17FN	24B	220
N17GG	G2	200
N17GL	35A	278
N17GL	55	099
N17GV	**G5**	**520**
N17HV	125	25282
N17JF	25	039
N17JT	**20**	**179**
N17KD	**500**	**337**
N17LB	G3	331
N17LH	35A	428
N17LJ	**36**	**017**
N17LK	550	405
N17LK	**560**	**0037**
N17LT	S40	282-59
N17LT	S40	282-70
N17LV	550	405
N17MX	G2	98/38
(N17ND)	35A	348
N17ND	35A	438
N17ND	G2	63
(N17PL)	550	305
N17QC	650	0239
N17RG	550	237
N17S	550	105
N17SL	125	25082
N17TE	**601**	**5007**
N17TE	650	0011
N17TJ	**10**	**43**
N17TJ	501	375
N17TJ	D1A	A023SA
N17TN	**650**	**0011**
N17TZ	601	5007
N17UC	560	5026
N17UC	650	0239
N17UC	WWD	283
N17UG	560	5026
N17VB	**525**	**0206**
N17VG	31	017
(N17ZU)	10	146
N18AC	**G4**	**1344**
N18AF	500	283

N18AK	25B	092
N18AN	**G4**	**1228**
N18AT	36	002
N18AX	**35A**	**087**
N18BA	**125**	**257167**
N18BA	D1A	A036SA
(N18BG)	10	33
N18BG	500	292
N18BG	501	378
N18BH	**STR**	**5099/5**
N18BL	**25D**	**234**
N18BL	WWD	182
N18BR	**400A**	**RK-221**
N18CA	WWD	5
N18CC	550	423
(N18CC)	551	392
N18CG	**2xx**	**57**
N18CG	55	104
N18CQ	55	104
N18CV	**35**	**016**
(N18DD)	550	276
N18FE	20	233
N18FM	**500**	**014**
N18FN	**35A**	**105**
N18G	125	257153
N18G	24B	186
N18G	35A	114
N18G	50	52
N18GA	**525**	**0216**
N18GB	**650**	**7048**
N18GW	WWD	187
N18GX	125	25281
N18HC	**501**	**627**
N18HH	S60	306-18
N18HJ	500	036
N18HJ	**550**	**587**
N18JF	25	037
N18JL	WWD	51
N18JN	400	RJ-6
N18JN	G2	154/28
N18KE	D1A	A022SA
N18LB	G3	309
N18LH	**35A**	**379**
N18MJ	25D	218
N18MX	**10**	**117**
N18N	G2	139/11
N18N	G2	61
N18N	G2	8
N18N	S60	306-12
N18N	S60	306-36
N18ND	550	295
N18NK	G2	156/31
N18NK	G5	585
N18NM	25D	209
N18NM	35A	189
(N18PV)	650	0127
N18RA	25D	280
(N18RA)	HFB	1038
N18RF	601	5152
N18RF	90X	18
N18RF	**G4**	**1092**
N18RN	501	625
N18RN	550	709
N18RN	G2	231
N18SD	24D	230
N18SF	WWD	374
N18SH	**125**	**257157**
(N18SK)	560	0091
(N18SK)	560	0098
N18SK	650	7016
(N18SL)	G3	304
N18ST	**35A**	**316**
N18T	D1A	A061SA
N18TA	25D	280
N18TF	75A	380-15
N18TM	G3	351
N18TM	**G4**	**1224**
N18TZ	75A	380-15
N18UR	500	011
N18VS	G5	564
N18WE	**35A**	**377**
N18WF	**G4**	**1175**
N18X	10	42
N18X	S60	306-137
N18XX	G2	227
N18ZD	55	122
N19AF	S550	0026
N19AJ	500	174
N19AJ	**550**	**188**
N19AP	WWD	259
N19BC	20	40
N19BD	20	161
N19BG	S40	282-118
N19CJ	525	0019
N19CM	500	169
N19CM	S60	306-10
N19CP	**551**	**003**
N19EE	WWD	172
N19ER	**550**	**048**
N19ES	STR	5204
N19FM	24D	311
N19FN	25	034
N19FR	650	0062
N19GA	D1A	A074SA
N19GB	501	682
N19GL	35A	415
N19H	**125**	**25261**
N19HE	125	256004
N19HF	600	1081
N19HF	S40	282-100
N19HH	125	256004
N19HM	24D	311
N19HU	**550**	**081**
N19J	501	408
N19J	601	3057
N19LH	35A	279
(N19LM)	35A	321
N19LT	**31**	**019**
N19M	500	165
N19M	500	303
N19M	S60	306-56
N19ME	560	0128
N19MJ	24E	351
N19MK	560	0128
N19MK	**560**	**0395**
N19MQ	500	165
(N19MS)	S40	282-15
N19MS	S40	282-82
N19MU	560	0395
N19MX	20	339
N19NW	35	019
N19NW	G2	19
N19PC	75A	380-2
N19PV	**560**	**0416**
N19QC	650	0238
N19R	**D1A**	**A043SA**
N19RP	**35A**	**363**
N19SV	**650**	**7002**
N19TJ	24D	258
N19TJ	31	018
N19TX	20	296/507
N19U	500	303
N19U	S60	306-56
N19UC	650	0238
N19UC	WWD	232
(N19VF)	560	0130
N19VP	550	247
N20AD	25D	287
N20AE	20	258
N20AF	20	120
N20AP	STR	5054/59
N20AT	650	0109
N20BD	23	008
N20BE	20	203
N20BG	35	028
N20CC	**501**	**397**
N20CF	**10**	**106**
N20CF	550	305
N20CG	20	281/498
N20CL	**200**	**497**
N20CL	550	434
N20CN	550	305
N20CN	560	0167
N20CR	35A	098
N20CR	**55**	**097**
(N20CV)	400	RJ-20
N20CX	600	1051
N20DA	**MSP**	**102**
N20DH	WWD	383
N20DK	25B	198
N20DK	**35A**	**143**
N20DL	25D	263
N20DL	55	020
N20EE	10	38
N20EP	23	008
N20ES	10	120
N20ES	10	38
N20ES	**S40**	**282-124**
N20ET	10	38
N20FE	20	235
N20FE	AST	067
N20FJ	**20**	**119/431**
N20FJ	20	244
N20FJ	20	272
N20FJ	20	289
N20FJ	20	341
N20FJ	20	355
N20FL	**400A**	**RK-247**
N20FL	500	169
N20FL	525	0069
N20FM	**125**	**256055**
N20FM	20	321
N20FM	500	011
N20FM	551	014
N20FX	125	257121
N20FX	G2	120
N20G	600	1085
N20G	**601**	**5136**
N20G	S60	306-59
N20GB	STR	5202
N20GB	WWD	127
N20GH	20	7
(N20GP)	G2	63
N20GP	**G2**	**90**
(N20GT)	125	257009
N20GT	24D	283
N20GT	25D	349
N20GT	501	579
N20GT	550	391
N20GX	600	1085
N20GX	S60	306-59
N20H	G2	51
N20H	G5	522
N20HE	G2	51
N20HF	**20**	**191**
N20HJ	25	024
N20JA	36	008
N20JM	20	258
N20JM	20	6
N20K	WWD	144
N20KH	**WWD**	**223**
(N20KW)	501	557
N20LL	**31**	**018**
N20LT	20	21
N20LW	**10**	**48**
N20LW	G2	62
N20M	23	094
N20MJ	25D	277
N20MK	560	0210
N20MW	650	0052
N20NM	S550	0121
N20NW	**25B**	**096**
(N20NW)	WWD	300
N20NY	**20**	**61**
N20PA	**D1A**	**A089SA**
N20PL	20	83
N20PY	25D	249
N20PY	STR	5023
N20RD	25D	334
N20RD	650	0036
N20RD	650	0142
N20RF	500	033
N20RF	550	456
N20RG	125	25091
N20RG	125	25226
N20RM	**501**	**389**
N20RT	35A	188
N20RT	500	033
N20RZ	**25**	**024**
N20S	125	25250
N20S	125	257059
N20S	125	258042
N20S	23	008
N20S	STR	5126
N20SB	560	0422
N20SB	**560**	**5114**
N20SH	STR	5142
N20SK	125	257059
N20SM	500	001
N20SP	501	398
N20SR	20	369
N20T	**20**	**381/548**
N20TA	**23**	**062**
N20TF	STR	5016
(N20TV)	550	142
N20TX	**20**	**296/507**
N20TZ	20	381/548
N20UA	**20**	**91**
N20UC	36A	031
N20UC	S65	465-46
N20UG	36A	031
N20VF	**20**	**347**
N20VL	**525**	**0069**
N20VP	500	187
N20WN	**20**	**370**
N20WP	**10**	**23**
N20WP	500	392
N20XP	**31A**	**197**
N20XY	G2	116
N20XY	G2	56
N20XY	G3	412
N20XY	G4	1080
N20YA	20	24
N21	STR	5001/53
N21AC	**60**	**070**
N21AG	24E	329
(N21AG)	S550	0003
N21AK	WWD	59
N21AM	G2	110
N21AM	**G3**	**443**
N21AR	125	25146
N21AX	**G2**	**110**
N21BC	WWD	51
N21BD	**45**	**188**
N21BH	125	256007
N21BM	S60	306-64
N21BS	501	389
N21CC	500	099
N21CL	10	166
N21CL	601	5126
N21CV	**560**	**0340**
N21CX	601	5014
N21CX	WWD	268
N21CZ	G4	1137
N21DA	35A	497
N21DA	550	091
N21DB	10	65
(N21DT)	20	6
N21EG	**S550**	**0087**
N21EH	501	576
N21EH	551	430
N21EK	10	8
N21EL	**125**	**258396**
N21EP	**501**	**412**
N21ES	10	8
N21ES	125	25203
N21ET	10	8
N21FE	20	226
N21FJ	20	299
N21GG	WWD	347
N21GL	35A	098
N21GN	125	25115
N21GN	G4	1284
N21HJ	501	444
N21HJ	90X	22
N21HR	25D	339
N21HR	**WWD**	**335**
(N21JJ)	560	0055
N21JM	20	6
N21JW	WWD	77
N21KP	G4	1139
N21KR	**G4**	**1139**
N21MF	125	25097
N21NA	24D	246
N21NA	35A	343
N21NA	500	174

N21NC	20	161
N21NG	**35A**	**343**
N21NL	20	393
N21NT	125	257207
N21NY	125	257207
N21NY	601	5126
N21NY	G3	301
N21NY	G3	496
N21PF	S40	282-15
N21SA	**125**	**256006**
N21SH	STR	5148
N21SL	**550**	**0877**
(N21SU)	HFB	1055
N21SV	550	016
N21SW	550	016
N21TV	500	078
N21U	23	024
N21U	24	152
N21VB	55	026
N21VB	STR	5219
N21VC	**525**	**0106**
N21W	20	205
(N21WS)	35A	410
N21XB	24B	198
N21XL	24B	198
N22	G4	1042
N22	**G5**	**501**
N22AC	WWD	35
N22AF	**560**	**0129**
N22AZ	600	1060
N22B	23	044
N22BG	WWD	410
N22BH	125	256009
N22BH	**700**	**9040**
N22BJ	S40	282-105
N22BM	24E	341
N22BM	36A	032
N22BN	**D1A**	**A023SA**
N22BN	S40	282-36
N22BX	35A	129
N22BX	S60	306-138
(N22CA)	500	004
N22CG	S60	306-88
N22CH	S40	282-70
N22CH	S40	282-99
N22CH	STR	5038
N22CH	WWD	7
N22CP	35A	178
N22CQ	35A	178
N22CS	**90X**	**10**
N22CX	D1A	A029SA
N22CX	G2	8
N22DE	125	25060
N22DH	125	25224
N22DL	125	25060
N22DL	125	256051
N22DL	20	14
N22DN	500	127
N22EH	10	25
N22EH	125	25179
N22EH	125	257043
N22EH	500	185
N22EH	S550	0074
N22EH	S60	306-57
N22ES	10	122
N22ES	STR	5161/43
N22FE	20	223
N22FH	500	185
N22FM	500	229
N22FM	**550**	**461**
N22FS	20	339
N22FS	G2	22
N22G	55	051
N22G	55	105
N22G	**60**	**022**
N22GA	**550**	**031**
N22GE	125	25139
N22GH	55	051
N22GR	**550**	**0892**
N22HC	20	14
N22HP	550	299
N22HP	**S550**	**0103**
N22JG	500	208
N22JW	20	83
N22JW	75A	380-15
N22JW	S60	306-20
N22KH	**125**	**257043**
N22KW	560	0256
N22KW	**560**	**5062**
N22LC	**560**	**0521**
N22LH	500	319
(N22LL)	WWD	148
N22LP	**560**	**0083**
N22LZ	**WWD**	**236**
N22MA	S60	306-2
N22MB	500	337
N22MH	24D	259
N22MJ	24E	329
N22MJ	35A	135
(N22ML)	24D	259
N22MS	**35A**	**209**
N22MV	S40	282-68
N22MY	S40	282-68
N22MY	S60	306-117
N22NB	**75A**	**380-56**
(N22NB)	S40	282-106
N22NG	**750**	**0039**
(N22NG)	750	0041
N22NJ	**25C**	**097**
N22NM	24E	341
N22NT	80A	380-21
N22RB	STR	5093
N22RD	**WWD**	**165**
N22RD	WWD	99
N22RG	550	639
N22RG	560	0235
N22RG	650	7070
N22RG	**750**	**0031**
N22RJ	550	074
N22RT	WWD	99
N22SD	501	578
N22SF	**31A**	**126**
N22SF	35A	168
N22SF	35A	674
N22SN	35A	674
N22SY	35A	168
N22T	50	53
N22T	550	407
N22T	**900**	**119**
N22TP	501	371
N22TP	S40	282-60
N22TS	501	473
N22TY	501	473
N22TZ	50	53
(N22TZ)	550	407
N22UL	**S550**	**0039**
N22UP	125	259040
N22WJ	400	RJ-44
N22WJ	D1A	A074SA
N22YP	**50**	**53**
(N22YP)	560	0109A
N23A	20	368
N23A	**35A**	**233**
N23A	G2	153
N23A	G3	430
N23AC	50	47
N23AC	G4	1047
N23AC	WWD	210
N23AC	WWD	341
N23AH	G2	137
N23AJ	23	053
N23AM	24D	247
N23AM	25D	223
N23AM	25D	308
N23AN	23	074
N23AQ	50	47
N23AQ	WWD	341
N23AZ	G2	183
N23BH	125	256010
N23BJ	125	257199
N23BJ	**601**	**3012**
N23BX	S65	465-61
N23CH	23	006
N23CJ	**125**	**25152**
N23DB	25B	086
N23DS	10	117
N23DS	S60	306-89
(N23ED)	10	11
N23EH	501	576
N23EJ	**125**	**257199**
N23ES	10	11
N23ES	10	123
N23ET	10	11
N23ET	**G3**	**434**
N23FE	20	224
N23FE	STR	5142
N23FF	WWD	83
(N23FN)	25	018
N23FN	25	040
(N23FR)	20	132
N23G	36A	026
N23G	55	012
N23G	75	370-5
N23G	S40	282-31
N23HB	35A	080
N23HB	55	046
N23HM	25D	262
N23JC	24D	290
N23KG	**525**	**0326**
N23KL	125	25080
N23M	G2	105
N23M	G4	1022
N23M	**G5**	**579**
N23M	STR	5103
N23MJ	24D	281
N23MU	**G4**	**1022**
N23ND	**20**	**48**
N23ND	500	345
N23ND	550	295
N23NG	**560**	**5133**
N23NM	S550	0121
(N23NQ)	20	48
N23NS	**560**	**0215**
N23PL	20	139
N23RZ	**25B**	**164**
N23SB	125	257016
N23SB	**601**	**5074**
N23SB	STR	5227
N23SG	24R	233
N23SJ	20	485
N23SJ	WWD	289
N23SK	125	257016
(N23SK)	G3	434
(N23SN)	125	257016
N23SQ	24R	233
N23ST	MSP	050
N23SY	50	185
N23SY	G4	1086
N23TA	25B	122
N23TC	23	074
N23TJ	23	033
N23TJ	AST	023
N23UB	560	0220
N23UD	560	0220
N23UD	**560**	**0442**
N23VG	35A	379
N23VP	**10**	**91**
N23W	550	352
N23W	G2	116
N23WJ	10	123
N23WK	500	191
N23Y	WWD	155
N23YZ	**501**	**473**
N24AJ	24	151
N24AJ	24	178
N24AJ	**500**	**221**
N24AJ	550	423
N24BA	24A	100
N24BA	400	RJ-19
N24BH	125	256011
N24BS	25XR	022
N24CH	125	25198
(N24CH)	501	655
N24CJ	525	0004
N24CJ	551	354
N24CK	24D	258
N24CK	35A	339
N24CK	55	004
N24DB	WWD	294
N24DS	G2	181
N24DS	WWD	258
(N24DZ)	24D	258
N24E	**550**	**651**
(N24EA)	24D	259
N24EP	25D	244
N24EP	550	597
N24ET	**24**	**050**
N24EV	20	227
N24FE	20	220
N24FF	23	034
(N24FN)	25	005
N24FN	25	045
(N24FR)	20	151
N24FW	**24E**	**329**
N24G	55	062
N24G	**60**	**018**
N24G	S60	306-14
N24G	S65	465-5
N24GA	35	024
N24GA	G3	374
N24GB	S60	306-14
N24GJ	24	101
N24HX	**560**	**0165**
N24JG	200	484
N24JG	35A	477
N24JK	25D	261
N24JK	35A	339
N24JK	55	004
N24JK	600	1070
N24JK	**601**	**5118**
N24KE	WWD	266
N24KF	24	161
N24KL	**WWD**	**237**
N24KT	24	161
N24KT	**650**	**0132**
N24KT	WWD	266
N24KW	25D	297
N24LG	**24A**	**011**
N24LT	25	063
N24LW	24	136
N24MJ	35A	216
N24MN	WWD	414
N24MW	24	043
N24NB	**650**	**7052**
N24NG	**560**	**5124**
(N24NP)	24B	200
N24PA	500	236
N24PF	**S550**	**0026**
N24PH	**560**	**5049**
N24PH	S550	0026
N24PJ	24D	291
(N24PP)	WWD	235
N24PR	**AST**	**026**
N24PT	36A	048
(N24PT)	550	211
(N24QT)	560	0498
N24RF	550	456
N24RF	**S65**	**465-28**
(N24RH)	55	110
N24RH	WWD	214
N24RP	125	258033
N24RZ	**25B**	**159**
N24S	125	25250
N24S	**24D**	**297**
N24S	500	230
N24SA	23	025
N24SB	125	258049
N24SB	WWD	369
N24SP	125	258049
N24SR	WWD	332
N24TA	25B	155
N24TC	24D	275
N24TE	24D	246
(N24TE)	WWD	195
N24TJ	G3	404
N24TK	24D	290
N24TK	S60	306-128
(N24TR)	550	203
N24TW	**20**	**80**
N24UB	560	0221
N24UD	560	0221
N24UD	**560**	**0443**
N24UG	STR	5108
N24UM	560	0160
N24VB	**650**	**0121**
N24VH	WWD	391

N24VM	24	051
N24WF	24	143
N24WW	WWD	391
N24WX	24	101
N24XR	**24D**	**283**
N24XR	24X	150
N24YA	24	087
N24YA	24B	206
N24YE	24	087
N24YS	**G2**	**16/13**
N25	500	084
N25AG	AST	012
N25AM	**25D**	**321**
N25AT	80A	380-21
N25AW	125	25095
N25BE	125	256013
N25BF	G2	114
N25BH	125	256013
N25BH	75A	380-47
N25BH	G2	237/43
N25BN	400	RJ-7
N25BR	400	RJ-57
N25BX	**75A**	**380-47**
N25CJ	500	325
N25CJ	501	625
N25CJ	525	0002
N25CK	500	250
N25CL	36	009
N25CP	20	121
N25CS	500	219
N25CV	24D	276
N25CZ	25D	301
N25DB	20	91
N25DD	501	475
N25EC	**25**	**026**
N25EL	35A	419
N25EV	20	229
N25FA	25D	251
N25FE	20	221
N25FF	10	123
N25FM	**25**	**063**
N25FN	25	015
N25FN	**25D**	**352**
(N25FR)	20	20
N25FS	35A	198
N25FS	**550**	**0823**
N25GJ	25	015
N25GJ	25D	255
N25GL	25D	362
N25GT	**501**	**572**
N25GW	24D	258
N25GW	**28**	**003**
N25HA	25XR	141
N25HC	500	034
N25HF	**25D**	**295**
N25HS	**501**	**592**
N25HV	**550**	**0825**
N25JD	25B	114
N25JM	50	124
N25JM	G2	69
N25JT	**125**	**25053**
(N25JX)	25	006
N25KC	25B	147
N25KL	S65	465-69
N25KV	25C	176
N25LA	125	25108
(N25LG)	25	042
N25LJ	24D	236
(N25LP)	25B	150
N25MB	**50**	**184**
N25MD	**25**	**054**
N25ME	**25**	**062**
N25MF	S65	465-25
N25MH	501	404
N25MJ	125	25142
N25MJ	35A	335
N25MJ	35A	452
N25MK	125	257056
N25MK	550	458
N25MR	**25C**	**129**
N25NB	25B	107
N25NB	**25D**	**326**
N25NH	551	115
N25NM	25	007
N25NM	25D	347
N25NP	25B	107
N25NY	**25D**	**304**
N25PA	500	250
N25PK	36A	039
N25PL	25B	130
N25PM	125	25114
N25PT	25D	356
N25PW	**25D**	**342**
N25QT	**551**	**584**
(N25RE)	25	041
N25RE	25B	163
N25RE	**25D**	**227**
N25RE	WWD	248
N25RF	35A	227
N25RJ	24D	237
N25S	20	453
N25SB	**601**	**5115**
N25SB	G3	431
N25SR	600	1075
N25SR	S65	465-14
N25TA	24D	237
N25TA	25B	196
N25TA	25D	241
N25TB	25D	241
N25TE	**25C**	**087**
"N25TF"	25TF	036
N25TK	25B	100
N25TX	20	24
(N25TX)	STR	5029/38
N25TZ	25D	364
N25UB	50	248
N25UD	50	248
N25UD	**90X**	**29**
N25UG	G2	205
N25UG	S65	465-11
N25UJ	**25D**	**215**
(N25VJ)	25	039
N25VZ	24D	258
N25W	**125**	**258221**
N25W	400	RJ-15
N25WA	400	RJ-15
N25WA	STR	5033/56
N25WG	20	327
(N25WL)	25XR	220
N25WX	**125**	**258359**
N25WZ	STR	5204
(N25XR)	25XR	235
N25ZC	S65	465-30
(N25ZG)	S65	465-30
N25ZW	24D	236
N26	560	0113
(N26AA)	501	678
N26AT	**25B**	**130**
N26BA	24	134
N26BH	125	256014
N26CB	525	0117
N26CB	**550**	**0861**
N26CP	10	151
N26CT	550	345
N26DA	35A	086
(N26DA)	550	087
N26DK	**525**	**0257**
N26DS	WWD	189
N26EN	10	49
N26ES	10	171
N26EV	20	230
N26FE	20	204
N26FN	25B	134
N26FN	36	011
N26GB	35A	131
N26GD	35A	131
N26GL	36	001
N26GL	STR	5114/18
N26GP	**35A**	**157**
N26GW	WWD	272
N26H	125	257143
(N26HA)	501	627
N26HC	500	174
N26JJ	S550	0141
N26JP	**400A**	**RK-74**
N26KL	**WWD**	**409**
N26L	G2	165/37
N26L	G2	193
N26L	G2	36/3
N26L	G3	387
N26LA	20	274
N26LA	G2	36/3
N26LB	50	7
N26LB	900	10
N26LB	**900**	**51**
N26LB	G2	168
N26LB	G4	1008
N26LC	**31**	**006**
N26LC	501	654
N26LT	G2	193
N26ME	**125**	**257165**
N26MJ	24B	202
N26MJ	36	011
N26MJ	STR	5101/15
(N26MW)	501	485
N26NS	**500**	**340**
N26PA	500	254
N26QB	**525**	**0117**
N26QT	**560**	**0498**
(N26RG)	650	0054
N26S	STR	5128/16
N26SC	**125**	**257117**
N26SC	550	345
N26SC	S40	282-104
N26SC	S60	306-140
N26SD	650	0099
N26SE	S40	282-104
N26SL	G4	1053
N26SQ	**S60**	**306-140**
N26T	125	25037
N26T	WWD	293
N26T	**WWD**	**418**
(N26TJ)	75A	370-7
N26TJ	WWD	204
N26TL	125	25037
N26TR	STR	5115/39
N26TV	WWD	293
N26TZ	**WWD**	**293**
N26VB	WWD	410
N26VF	WWD	410
N26VG	20	108/430
N26VM	24D	236
N26WB	G2	136
N26WD	500	282
N26WJ	**10**	**126**
(N26WJ)	125	25037
N26WP	G2	24
(N27)	31A	063
N27	560	0109
N27AC	10	151
N27AC	20	355
N27AJ	**10**	**31**
N27AT	**WWD**	**176**
N27B	S550	0036
N27BA	550	168
N27BD	WWD	53
N27BH	125	256016
N27BH	**600**	**1051**
N27BH	AST	012
N27BJ	**24B**	**227**
N27BL	**35A**	**163**
N27C	10	31
N27C	S40	282-57
N27CD	**G4**	**1136**
N27CJ	**525**	**0301**
N27DA	10	17
N27DA	S40	282-28
N27DD	**55**	**015**
N27EA	S550	0027
N27EV	20	232
N27FE	20	207
N27FL	**125**	**258426**
N27FN	25	062
N27FP	**S550**	**0027**
N27FW	STR	5083/49
N27GD	S550	0052
(N27GW)	25D	234
N27HF	35A	251
N27K	25D	294
N27KG	25D	335
N27KG	25D	357
N27KG	35A	413
N27KG	S40	282-77
N27KL	125	257125
N27L	**500**	**038**
N27LT	**75A**	**380-59**
N27MD	WWD	102
N27MH	550	168
N27MH	S550	0006
N27MJ	24D	249
N27MJ	25	050
N27MJ	**36A**	**027**
N27NB	35A	251
N27NR	35A	481
N27PA	500	249
N27R	20	303
N27R	20	356
N27R	**2xx**	**5**
N27R	G3	452
N27R	STR	5086/44
N27RC	125	25038
N27RC	**STR**	**5086/44**
N27RL	STR	5086/44
N27RX	20	356
N27RZ	S60	306-2
N27SD	560	0147
N27SD	650	0134
N27SD	S550	0052
N27SF	**500**	**064**
(N27SJ)	WWD	270
N27SL	**G2**	**84**
(N27TA)	WWD	231
(N27TB)	S550	0079
N27TB	**S550**	**0082**
N27TJ	35A	277
N27TJ	D1A	A027SA
N27TS	501	541
N27TS	**650**	**0006**
N27TS	80A	380-48
N27TT	**35A**	**122**
N27U	550	344
N27WP	**2xx**	**35**
N27WW	**500**	**359**
N27WW	560	0074
N27X	WWD	127
N27XL	**560**	**5010**
N28AA	25	037
N28AT	24B	227
N28AY	**28**	**004**
N28BG	35A	258
N28BH	125	256018
N28BK	24	175
N28BP	23	065A
N28BP	25B	086
(N28BP)	25D	237
N28BP	25D	302
(N28BR)	23	065A
N28C	**20**	**404**
(N28CC)	25D	234
N28CK	**25**	**045**
N28CR	35A	252
N28DL	24B	184
(N28ET)	560	0320
N28FE	20	209
N28FN	25	005
N28GA	**525**	**0215**
N28GA	550	283
N28GC	**501**	**449**
N28GE	125	25267
N28GG	125	257135
N28GP	125	25267
N28GP	**125**	**257135**
N28GZ	551	200
N28HH	**S60**	**306-125**
N28JG	501	591
N28KB	50	148
N28KV	25C	176
N28LA	25XR	029
N28LR	28	003
N28M	125	25038
N28MJ	25D	286
N28MJ	**35A**	**224**
(N28MM)	125	25038
(N28MM)	550	187
N28NF	**AST**	**067**
N28NP	AST	067

(N28NR)	AST	067
N28PA	500	267
N28QQ	G3	379
N28R	**2xx**	**7**
N28R	G3	490
N28RC	550	302
N28RC	550	650
N28RF	550	271
(N28RW)	25D	285
N28S	550	225
N28S	650	0143
N28ST	23	013
N28TJ	WWD	237
N28TP	S40	282-132
N28TS	**125**	**256009**
N28TX	**650**	**7007**
N28U	200	484
(N28U)	500	054
N28VM	S60	306-123
N28WW	WWD	368
(N29AA)	10	31
N29AC	501	635
N29AP	WWD	258
N29AU	**650**	**0145**
N29AU	S550	0019
N29B	551	152
N29BF	23	010
N29BH	125	256020
N29CA	24B	215
N29CA	501	492
N29CL	WWD	197
N29CL	**WWD**	**404**
N29CR	125	25098
N29DJ	55	029
N29EA	S550	0006
N29EW	25D	373
N29FA	550	379
N29FE	20	210
N29FN	25	018
N29G	550	379
N29GD	125	257069
N29GH	WWD	197
N29GP	125	257069
N29GP	**125**	**258344**
N29GY	G4	1016
N29HE	501	604
N29LA	24	108
N29LB	WWD	61
N29LP	WWD	280
N29LP	WWD	61
(N29MW)	500	166
N29NW	**55**	**029**
N29PC	**WWD**	**263**
N29PF	550	696
N29RE	31A	106
N29RE	**31A**	**145**
(N29RE)	31A	156
N29RP	125	257088
N29S	G3	391
N29S	S60	306-49
N29S	S65	465-65
N29SM	**31A**	**194**
N29SX	S60	306-49
N29SZ	S65	465-65
N29TC	550	143
(N29TC)	STR	5208
(N29TG)	550	143
N29TS	25B	198
N29UF	**501**	**640**
(N29UF)	WWD	201
N29WE	560	0185
N29WE	**560**	**0512**
N29WF	560	0185
N29WP	STR	5157
N29WS	550	262
N29X	S550	0096
N29XA	S550	0096
N29YY	50	95
N30AB	**WWD**	**235**
(N30AD)	20	225/472
N30AD	25D	314
N30AD	WWD	143
(N30AF)	501	559
N30AF	55	043
N30AF	650	0049
N30AF	S40	282-113
N30AH	G3	392
N30AJ	AST	019
N30AJ	AST	047
N30AN	WWD	173
N30AP	25B	080
N30AP	25B	101
N30AV	**550**	**026**
N30AV	HFB	1055
(N30B)	G2	228
N30BE	S40	282-14
N30BK	501	666
N30BP	23	017
N30CC	20	11
N30CC	S60	306-81
N30CJ	650	0019
(N30CJ)	650	0029
N30CN	10	161
N30CQ	20	11
N30CX	S550	0007
N30CZ	550	376
N30DH	24B	224
N30DH	35A	199
N30DK	25B	154
N30DK	**35A**	**345**
N30EF	125	25084
N30EH	24B	211
N30EJ	550	113
N30EM	24E	338
(N30EV)	75	370-6
N30F	125	25153
N30F	125	258035
(N30F)	550	220
N30FD	125	25153
N30FE	20	211
N30FJ	10	30
N30FJ	550	113
N30FL	24D	253
N30FN	35A	075
N30FT	**20**	**377/548**
N30FW	**G2**	**210**
N30GB	75A	380-1
N30GD	35A	352
N30GJ	35A	320
N30GL	35A	395
N30GL	55	076
N30GR	**550**	**656**
N30HD	D1A	A005SA
N30HJ	**35A**	**226**
N30JD	**550**	**218**
(N30JH)	10	19
N30JM	10	19
N30JM	20	24
N30JM	WWD	173
N30JN	**500**	**272**
N30LB	**90X**	**8**
N30LJ	25	043
N30LJ	**25D**	**209**
N30LJ	31	024
N30LJ	31	027
N30LM	24E	338
N30LM	25D	250
N30LS	WWD	125
N30LX	31A	096
N30MR	**WWD**	**225**
(N30N)	50	55
N30NM	**650**	**0120**
N30NS	WWD	329
N30P	25B	082
N30PA	**35A**	**245**
N30PC	**560**	**0090**
N30PD	WWD	347
(N30PN)	S40	282-14
N30PP	125	25207
N30PR	125	25207
N30PR	125	257065
N30PR	**G2**	**35**
N30PS	25	030
N30PY	S60	306-7
N30RE	501	491
N30RJ	WWD	7
N30RL	501	491
N30RL	**550**	**653**
N30RP	G2	113
N30RP	G3	321
N30RP	STR	5131
N30SA	35A	479
N30SA	550	341
N30SB	500	272
N30SC	23	039
(N30SF)	400A	RK-79
N30SJ	SJ3	001
N30TB	10	171
N30TC	S60	306-33
N30TH	10	138
N30TH	10	74
N30TH	100	201
N30TH	**2xx**	**66**
N30TH	50	212
N30TK	31A	096
N30TK	35	030
N30TP	25B	111
N30TT	25	020
N30UC	550	103
N30W	25D	214
N30W	35A	488
N30W	**60**	**065**
N30W	S40	282-5
N30W	S60	306-10
N30WE	550	604
N30WR	**G3**	**380**
N30WY	35A	488
N30XX	550	195
N30Y	STR	5227
N30YM	WWD	213
N31AA	**25**	**041**
N31AJ	501	393
N31AS	125	25111
N31AS	125	257135
N31AX	31A	094
(N31AZ)	31A	103
N31B	125	25108
N31BC	S40	282-14
N31BC	S60	306-60
N31BC	S65	465-16
(N31BC)	S65	465-69
N31BG	24D	301
N31BM	S60	306-71
N31BP	**STR**	**5125/31**
N31BQ	S40	282-14
(N31CF)	501	641
N31CF	WWD	8
N31CG	31	003
N31CJ	525	0031
N31CJ	**525**	**0360**
N31CJ	S60	306-26
N31CK	**23**	**079**
N31CM	20	317
N31CR	**S60**	**306-146**
N31CS	25C	083
N31CV	31A	168
N31DA	550	295
(N31DC)	600	1032
N31DK	STR	5138
N31DM	50	59
N31DP	23	059
N31DP	**35**	**062**
N31F	125	258036
(N31F)	550	176
N31F	550	440
N31F	STR	5060
N31FB	35A	138
N31FE	20	212
N31FN	35	033
N31FT	550	440
N31GS	25D	313
N31GT	**125**	**25204**
N31HA	31	031
N31HD	**525**	**0261**
N31HY	31A	107
N31JM	501	411
N31KW	550	083
N31LB	24B	211
N31LG	125	257068
N31LH	500	287
N31LJ	31	010
N31LJ	31	020
N31LJ	31A	036
(N31LJ)	31A	059
N31LJ	31A	072
N31LJ	31A	078
(N31LJ)	31A	081
N31LJ	31A	088
N31LJ	31A	113
N31LJ	STR	5087/55
(N31LM)	35A	412
N31LR	31A	100
N31LR	31A	131
N31LR	31A	160
N31LR	**31A**	**185**
N31LT	**20**	**69**
N31MJ	25D	231
N31MJ	25D	313
N31MT	501	473
N31MW	500	045
N31NR	31A	115
N31NR	31A	150
N31NR	31A	170
N31PV	**31A**	**130**
N31RC	501	465
N31RC	550	175
N31RC	**560**	**0023**
N31RK	550	314
N31RP	STR	5131
N31S	23	072
N31S	STR	5051
N31S	WWD	10
N31SB	WWD	10
N31SG	**525**	**0207**
N31SJ	10	72
N31SJ	S65	465-26
N31SK	24	118
N31ST	500	029
N31SY	G2	169
N31TC	24B	193
N31TD	31A	165
N31TF	31A	037
N31TJ	125	25202
N31TK	**31A**	**059**
(N31TK)	31A	096
N31TM	10	160
N31UK	31A	047
N31UT	STR	5143
N31V	20	106
N31V	**45**	**015**
N31V	50	59
N31VT	125	25195
N31WE	35A	389
N31WG	STR	5087/55
N31WH	601	5014
N31WR	**35A**	**313**
N31WS	**35**	**027**
N31WT	20	446
N31WT	24D	283
N31WT	24E	351
N31WT	25D	265
N31WT	25D	288
(N31WT)	28	005
N31WT	35A	229
N31WT	35A	389
N31WT	35A	479
N31WT	600	1073
N32AA	24D	237
N32AJ	**36A**	**048**
N32B	35A	593
N32B	**900**	**59**
N32BA	35A	190
(N32BC)	125	258299
N32BC	**125**	**258321**
N32BC	600	1053
N32BC	S40	282-15
N32BC	S60	306-62
N32BL	10	6
N32BQ	600	1053
N32BQ	S40	282-15
N32CA	**24**	**132**
N32DA	501	494
N32DD	**24E**	**331**
N32DD	500	043
N32F	125	25155
N32F	550	442

N32FE	20	213
N32FM	**501**	**616**
N32FN	35A	067
N32FN	35A	189
N32GG	601	5033
N32GM	**125**	**25198**
N32HC	G2	113
(N32HE)	125	25033
N32HJ	**35A**	**463**
N32HM	**35A**	**187**
N32HP	**D1A**	**A074SA**
N32JA	35A	172
(N32JA)	36	017
N32JC	WWD	32
N32JJ	501	380
N32JJ	550	223
N32JJ	**650**	**0170**
N32JJ	S550	0014
N32KA	**G3**	**435**
N32KB	**125**	**25280**
N32KJ	**55**	**093**
N32KR	STR	5220
N32MG	**650**	**0016**
N32MJ	24B	208
N32MJ	501	434
N32PA	**36A**	**025**
N32PB	20	122
N32PB	**551**	**115**
N32PC	25	018
N32PC	S60	306-125
N32PE	**35A**	**327**
N32PF	35A	327
N32RP	125	256066
N32SD	23	017
N32SM	25C	070
N32SX	501	477
N32TC	20	440
N32TC	35A	189
N32TC	**50**	**225**
N32TE	20	440
(N32TJ)	25D	224
(N32TJ)	550	268
N32TJ	S550	0014
N32TM	**550**	**336**
N32TX	S550	0026
N32UT	S60	306-9
N32VC	10	6
N32W	500	105
N32WE	WWD	164
N32WL	24D	265
N32WT	24E	333
N33AA	501	388
N33AH	20	379
(N33AJ)	20	379
N33BC	**125**	**258292**
N33BC	550	329
N33BC	650	0047
N33BC	S60	306-13
N33BC	S65	465-69
N33BE	501	476
N33BK	125	25064
N33BK	125	257049
N33BK	24A	096
N33BQ	**650**	**0047**
N33BQ	S60	306-13
N33CJ	24	130
N33CJ	25	045
N33CJ	**525**	**0245**
N33CP	125	25286
N33CP	125	257053
N33CR	G2	69
N33CX	501	456
N33D	**20**	**166**
N33DS	S550	0093
N33DT	**525**	**0080**
N33EA	STR	5033/56
N33EK	**550**	**314**
N33FE	20	214
N33FW	**525**	**0203**
(N33FW)	551	062
N33GF	25	035
N33GG	50	97
N33GG	**900**	**87**
N33GK	550	270
N33GK	**650**	**7050**
N33GL	55	082
N33GL	WWD	47
N33GQ	50	97
N33GZ	**G3**	**393**
N33HB	35A	182
N33HC	**501**	**492**
N33HL	10	17
N33HM	25B	093
N33JW	**S60**	**306-92**
N33KA	75A	380-55
(N33KW)	501	437
N33L	**20**	**202**
N33LB	S40	282-130
N33LX	**560**	**0433**
N33M	G2	106
N33M	G4	1056
N33ME	F502	312
N33ME	G2	43
N33MK	**WWD**	**374**
(N33MM)	D1A	A017SA
N33MQ	F502	312
N33MX	**G4**	**1056**
N33NH	500	206
N33NJ	24	147
N33NJ	**35A**	**305**
N33NM	25B	093
N33NT	75A	380-41
N33PF	**25**	**028**
N33PS	WWD	92
N33PT	25	046
N33PT	25D	240
N33PT	35A	397
N33QS	**20**	**122**
N33RE	24B	193
N33RH	125	257011
N33RH	550	087
N33RP	125	256068
N33SC	20	71
N33SJ	**STR**	**5087/55**
N33ST	24	173
N33TH	500	024
N33TP	20	27
N33TP	**24D**	**321**
N33TR	25	035
N33TR	S60	306-54
N33TR	**S65**	**465-47**
N33TS	35A	021
N33TW	**25B**	**124**
N33TW	S40	282-61
N33TY	50	240
N33TY	**50**	**288**
N33UL	**650**	**0160**
N33UT	S60	306-16
N33UT	T39	276-34
(N33VF)	25B	143
(N33VG)	35A	408
(N33VV)	501	482
N33WB	35A	376
N33WD	WWD	161
N33WW	**501**	**440**
N34AA	501	475
N34AM	S40	282-31
N34BH	125	256022
N34C	20	31
N34CD	601	3030
N34CD	**601**	**5139**
(N34CE)	AST	043
N34CH	125	257021
N34CJ	S550	0034
N34CW	20	305
N34CW	25D	277
N34DL	501	436
N34DL	551	204
N34FD	35A	431
N34FE	20	215
N34FN	35A	254
N34GB	**55**	**114**
N34GG	125	257034
N34HD	WWD	127
N34LP	S40	282-70
N34MJ	25D	333
N34MZ	G2	77
N34NS	**S550**	**0024**
N34NW	WWD	117
N34QS	650	0034
N34RE	125	257022
N34RP	G2	113
N34SS	550	225
(N34SS)	550	258
N34SW	WWD	97
N34TB	35A	285
N34TC	35A	199
N34TC	**525**	**0083**
N34TH	10	74
N34TJ	**35A**	**225**
N34TN	**25D**	**249**
(N34TR)	23	069
N34TR	STR	5236
N34TY	**50**	**240**
N34UT	500	043
N34VP	400A	RK-39
N34W	S40	282-47
N34WP	550	123
N34WR	**STR**	**5207**
N34YL	551	267
N35AA	501	497
N35AH	35A	316
N35AJ	**35**	**010**
N35AJ	35A	346
N35AJ	35A	626
N35AK	**35A**	**314**
N35AL	C21A	509
N35AQ	C21A	513
N35AS	35A	405
N35AS	35A	605
N35AW	35A	233
N35AX	**35A**	**280**
N35AZ	**35A**	**201**
N35BG	35A	311
N35BG	**35A**	**402**
N35BH	125	256023
N35BK	35A	442
N35BN	35	013
N35BP	551	282
N35CC	S40	282-79
N35CC	**S65**	**465-59**
N35CK	35A	480
N35CL	35A	113
N35CX	35A	180
N35CZ	35A	352
N35D	125	257044
N35D	**WWD**	**156**
N35DL	125	256051
N35DL	**35A**	**348**
N35DL	S60	306-131
N35EC	**24**	**123**
N35ED	**35A**	**215**
N35FE	20	217
N35FE	35A	409
N35FH	35A	273
(N35FH)	35A	480
N35FM	35A	368
N35FN	35A	261
N35FP	601	3048
N35FS	35A	320
N35FS	35A	405
(N35FT)	35A	439
N35GA	35A	590
N35GC	**35A**	**266**
N35GE	35A	088
N35GG	35A	178
N35GJ	35A	507
N35GQ	35	037
N35GX	35A	264
N35GX	**AST**	**113**
N35HB	35	045
N35HC	550	202
(N35HM)	35A	210
N35HP	35A	507
N35HS	**650**	**7072**
N35HW	35A	501
N35JF	24A	110
N35JF	501	404
N35JJ	STR	5100/41
N35JM	G2	47
N35JN	35	013
(N35K)	501	404
N35KC	35A	144
N35KC	35A	189
N35KT	35A	590
N35LD	501	494
N35LH	WWD	236
N35LH	**WWD**	**413**
N35LJ	35A	181
N35LJ	35A	676
N35LM	125	257023
N35LT	500	132
N35LW	**35A**	**439**
N35MH	35A	258
N35MR	35	057
N35MV	35A	416
N35NB	35A	133
(N35NK)	35A	643
N35NP	35A	191
N35NP	35A	492
N35NW	35A	069
N35NX	35A	328
N35NY	35A	328
(N35P)	D1A	A051SA
N35PD	35A	181
N35PD	35A	606
(N35PF)	35A	094
N35PF	55	020
N35PN	550	486
N35PR	35A	181
N35PT	35A	420
N35Q	35A	406
N35RF	35A	201
N35RN	35A	113
N35RT	35A	201
N35RT	35A	420
N35RZ	20	359/542
N35RZ	**50**	**113**
N35SA	35A	326
N35SC	35	002
N35SE	35A	191
N35SE	500	035
N35SJ	24D	246
N35SJ	35A	261
N35SL	35A	233
N35SM	**35A**	**419**
N35TH	**35A**	**473**
N35TJ	**35A**	**137**
N35TK	35A	188
N35TL	35A	348
N35TL	501	637
N35TM	501	497
N35TN	**35A**	**472**
N35UJ	**35**	**007**
N35UK	**35A**	**662**
N35UK	35A	670
N35VP	35A	294
N35WB	25	027
N35WB	**35A**	**350**
(N35WE)	25	016
N35WG	35A	124
(N35WG)	35A	274
N35WH	35A	138
N35WN	100	210
N35WP	**125**	**256029**
N35WR	**35A**	**234**
N35XL	560	5035
(N36AX)	36A	030
N36BG	10	190
N36BH	125	256025
(N36BP)	35A	237
N36BP	36A	032
N36CC	**25B**	**079**
N36CC	501	406
N36CD	650	0036
N36CE	550	036
N36CJ	500	306
N36CJ	550	136
N36CW	36	012
N36EF	WWD	222
N36FD	501	614
N36FD	AST	016
N36FE	20	218
N36FN	35A	119
(N36GA)	G5	518
N36GC	501	434

N36GS	125	257095
N36GS	G2	251
N36GX	**AST**	**123**
N36H	**125**	**258332**
N36H	560	0035
(N36H)	S550	0001
N36H	S550	0036
N36HH	S60	306-18
N36HR	S550	0036
N36JG	501	364
N36JK	G2	112
N36JM	10	19
(N36KA)	10	19
N36LB	600	1020
N36LX	**560**	**0436**
N36MC	500	159
N36MJ	**36A**	**036**
N36MK	125	25073
N36MW	25	038
N36MW	G2	89
N36NP	125	257035
N36NS	S550	0059
N36NW	25D	297
N36NW	35A	609
(N36NW)	551	191
N36P	20	203
N36P	S40	282-87
N36PD	36A	022
N36PJ	36A	030
N36PN	**G2**	**42/12**
N36PT	WWD	275
N36PT	WWD	79
N36QN	550	072
N36RR	**G2**	**4/8**
N36RS	24B	184
N36SC	25D	209
N36SJ	500	306
N36SK	36A	047
N36TA	36	003
N36TJ	35A	168
N36TJ	35A	289
N36VG	20	220
(N36WS)	501	420
N36XL	**560**	**5036**
(N37AH)	20	379
N37BB	WWD	12
N37BE	**WWD**	**396**
N37BH	125	256026
N37BJ	25B	137
N37BL	23	013
N37BL	23	069
N37BM	**31A**	**096**
N37BM	550	186
N37BM	550	274
N37CB	24	127
N37CD	650	0037
N37CP	23	028
N37CR	550	117
N37DG	**525**	**0109**
N37DH	24D	231
(N37DJ)	35A	237
N37DM	23	025
N37DW	500	284
N37FA	35A	091
N37FE	20	270
N37FN	35A	263
N37GB	25	053
N37GF	75	370-4
N37GX	**GXY**	**014**
N37HE	**G3**	**466**
N37HG	550	037
N37HJ	35A	230
(N37HR)	35A	417
N37HT	**24X**	**243**
N37HW	501	581
N37JA	55	034
N37JF	20	193
N37JJ	20	248/483
N37LA	501	457
N37LB	600	1015
N37LC	50	227
(N37LQ)	50	227
N37MB	25	053
N37MH	**550**	**168**
N37P	125	257015
N37P	24	138
N37PL	125	257012
N37RM	20	308
N37RR	25D	313
N37SG	125	256021
N37SJ	**WWD**	**38**
N37SV	**35A**	**492**
N37TA	**35**	**034**
N37TJ	35A	132
N37VP	650	0037
N37VP	**650**	**0087**
(N37WC)	WWD	202
N37WH	G2	180
N37WH	G4	1243
N37WP	550	247
N37WP	**560**	**0259**
N37WT	20	225/472
N38AE	**WWD**	**318**
N38AL	35A	499
N38AM	**35A**	**174**
N38BG	G4	1388
N38BG	STR	5208
N38BH	125	256032
N38CC	20	200
N38CJ	500	308
N38D	36A	024
N38D	**55**	**068**
N38DA	**10**	**27**
N38DA	501	375
N38DD	**550**	**374**
N38DD	650	0023
N38DJ	25B	191
(N38DL)	501	375
N38DM	23	036
N38EC	**S550**	**0109**
(N38FN)	35A	188
N38FN	35A	247
N38GL	G2	16/13
N38GX	**GXY**	**015**
N38JA	**55**	**033**
N38JD	23	093
N38JM	75A	380-39
N38JM	S60	306-54
N38KM	G2	52
N38LB	**125**	**25276**
N38MH	500	265
(N38MM)	500	275
N38N	G2	41
N38NA	550	207
N38NS	**560**	**0411**
N38PA	**125**	**257012**
N38PS	**35A**	**206**
N38RT	501	563
N38SA	**500**	**297**
N38SK	650	0156
N38SM	500	001
N38SW	601	3008
N38SW	**604**	**5423**
N38TA	35	044
N38TJ	**20**	**339**
N38TJ	WWD	356
N38TM	501	483
N38TS	**125**	**25190**
(N38TS)	125	25205
N38TT	**551**	**298**
N38US	35A	297
N38UT	S60	306-16
N38WC	36A	022
N38WP	**50**	**292**
N38WP	650	0032
N38WW	WWD	210
N39BE	501	476
N39BH	125	256034
(N39BL)	125	258236
N39BL	25D	234
N39BL	STR	5029/38
N39CB	**S60**	**306-116**
N39CD	**601**	**3030**
N39CJ	**525**	**0039**
N39CK	**25**	**005**
(N39DJ)	35A	208
N39DK	35A	208
N39DK	**35A**	**480**
N39DM	24D	302
N39DM	35	006
N39DM	35	040
N39E	55	018
N39E	STR	5126
N39EL	**24D**	**251**
N39FA	550	154
N39FN	**35**	**006**
N39FS	**T39**	**276-33**
N39GA	550	215
N39GW	WWD	237
N39H	**650**	**0206**
(N39HD)	550	448
N39HF	**400A**	**RK-65**
N39J	500	207
N39JE	25B	124
N39JJ	25B	121
N39JK	G2	169
N39JN	WWD	261
N39JV	560	5039
N39K	10	167
N39K	551	395
N39KM	**24B**	**198**
N39KT	**PRM**	**RB-39**
N39KY	551	395
N39LG	STR	5142
N39LH	**500**	**089**
N39LL	501	568
(N39LX)	560	0439
N39MB	35A	216
N39ML	551	014
N39MW	35A	414
N39N	**560**	**0243**
N39N	G2	50
N39N	G3	403
N39NA	G3	403
N39NX	G2	50
N39PY	G5	522
N39Q	STR	5126
N39RE	10	80
N39RE	500	311
N39RE	**600**	**1049**
N39RE	650	0006
N39RE	WWD	342
N39RG	**S40**	**282-82**
N39RG	T39	276-25
N39SA	35A	466
(N39SL)	S60	306-39
N39T	24	043
N39TF	**S550**	**0139**
N39TH	100	199
N39TH	35A	496
N39TJ	31	026
N39TR	**S65**	**465-27**
N39TT	**24D**	**308**
N39TW	**31A**	**047**
N39VP	650	0187
N39WA	35A	092
N39WH	G4	1243
N39WP	**50**	**294**
N39WP	650	0039
N40AB	WWD	106
N40AC	20	187
N40AC	500	331
(N40AD)	125	25026
N40AD	25D	314
N40AG	**G2**	**115**
N40AJ	**501**	**393**
N40AJ	AST	031
N40AJ	WWD	40
(N40AN)	35	045
(N40AN)	35A	149
N40AN	**35A**	**271**
N40AS	25B	117
N40AS	50	171
N40AS	WWD	156
N40AW	501	584
N40BC	25B	128
N40BC	25D	288
N40BD	**35A**	**140**
N40BG	WWD	156
N40BH	125	256038
(N40BK)	D1A	A004SA
N40BP	24A	116
N40BP	S40	282-40
N40BT	S40	282-113
N40CC	G2	46
N40CD	S40	282-28
N40CE	G2	45
N40CH	G2	77
N40CH	G3	377
N40CH	S40	282-104
N40CN	125	257120
N40CN	**50**	**92**
N40CR	55	097
N40CR	**55C**	**144**
N40DA	500	392
N40DC	125	25078
N40DC	125	25079
N40DC	STR	5120/26
N40DG	WWD	262
N40DK	35A	264
N40DK	35A	171
N40DK	**55**	**092**
N40DW	S40	282-24
N40EL	S40	282-42
N40ES	55	005
(N40F)	50	82
N40FC	550	554
N40FC	**650**	**0143**
N40FJ	501	547
N40FJ	550	281
N40GA	**D1A**	**A040SA**
N40GC	D1A	A005SA
N40GG	35A	416
N40GG	**WWD**	**229**
N40GP	S40	282-16
N40GS	550	288
N40GT	125	257002
N40GT	**S40**	**282-126**
N40GX	**GXY**	**016**
N40HC	S40	282-66
N40HL	500	128
N40HP	500	104
N40JC	WWD	40
N40JE	24	133
N40JE	S40	282-124
N40JF	24	133
N40JF	500	079
N40JF	S40	282-80
N40JW	S40	282-122
N40KJ	S60	306-142
(N40KM)	S550	0008
N40LB	25	009
N40LB	**S40**	**282-36**
N40MF	**550**	**0921**
N40MF	D1A	A049SA
N40MM	500	275
N40MP	WWD	334
N40MT	**550**	**238**
N40N	10	25
N40N	**650**	**7031**
N40N	G3	405
N40N	G4	1122
N40N	STR	5048
N40NB	G3	405
N40NC	STR	5048
N40NR	S40	282-107
N40NR	S40	282-134
N40NR	S40	282-66
N40NR	S40	282-91
N40NS	S40	282-126
N40PC	125	25214
N40PC	125	256010
N40PD	500	059
N40PH	**650**	**0201**
N40PK	**35A**	**260**
N40PL	**125**	**258347**
N40PL	400A	RK-138
N40PL	501	646
N40PL	550	305
(N40PL)	560	0068
N40PL	S550	0008
N40QJ	G3	493
(N40R)	S40	282-19
N40R	S40	282-52
N40RD	500	059
(N40RF)	500	266

N40RW 35A 224
N40RW 500 107
N40SC S40 282-113
N40SC S40 282-98
N40SE S40 282-15
N40SE S40 282-59
N40SJ S40 282-25
N40SK 125 25186
(N40SK) 50 240
N40SL S40 282-32
N40SN 25 021
N40SW 25 021
N40SW 25D 238
N40TA 35A 208
N40TA S40 282-94
N40TA WWD 194
N40TF 35 025
N40TH 50 212
N40TH 50 85
N40TL S60 306-103
(N40TM) 35A 381
(N40TV) 24A 011
N40UA WWD 40
N40WB 125 257002
(N40WE) 550 554
N40WH S40 282-80
N40WJ 10 21
N40WP 560 0155
N40WP 75A 380-39
N40WP S40 282-32
N40XY 20 135
N40XY STR 5115/39
N40Y 125 25234
N40YA S40 282-20
N40YC 550 554
N40ZA S40 282-112
N41 WWD 143
N41AJ 23 037
N41AJ 25 040
(N41AJ) 501 393
N41AV G2 61
(N41B) 80A 380-49
N41BH 125 25220
N41BH 125 256040
N41BH 550 567
N41BJ 24 178
N41BP 20 177
N41C 550 320
N41C WWD 398
(N41CC) 125 257010
N41CD 20 88
(N41CK) 550 259
N41CP 55 037
N41CP G4 1179
N41CP G4 1336
N41DP 31A 079
N41DP 45 010
N41EA 55 041
N41EB 525 0116
N41ES 55 007
N41FL WWD 41
N41FN 35A 137
N41GS S40 282-16
N41GT 501 494
N41H 25D 217
N41HL 500 338
N41JP 501 466
N41JP 550 288
N41ME 400A RK-19
N41MH 20 14
N41MJ 35A 405
N41MP 24 148
N41N STR 5087/55
N41NK 525 0190
N41NK 525 0281
N41NR S40 282-133
N41NY MSP 041
N41PC 20 19
(N41PD) 20 19
N41PG 525 0175
N41PG G3 334
N41PJ 35 041
N41PR G4 1226
N41QR G4 1179
N41RC G2 29
N41SH 500 267
N41SJ 900 37
N41SM 550 271
N41ST 35A 302
N41ST 501 485
N41ST 650 0063
N41TC 24E 346
N41TC 25D 346
N41TC S65 465-42
N41TC STR 5036/42
N41TH 50 201
N41TJ 10 118
(N41TJ) 400 RJ-34
N41UT D1A A030SA
N41VP 560 0492
N41WH WWD 268
N41WT 35A 229
N41ZP 25D 279
N42 WWD 142
N42AJ 24 139
N42AS 125 25150
N42B 35A 277
N42BH 125 25221
N42BH 125 256044
(N42BJ) 25B 127
N42BL 125 25275
N42BL MSP 050
(N42BM) 550 111
N42C STR 5150/37
N42CK 125 25038
N42CM WWD 189
N42CV 560 0042
N42DG 25B 171
N42EH 10 28
N42ES 55 009
N42FD 125 25042
N42FE 25B 088
N42FE 35A 241
N42FJ 900 42
N42G 10 20
N42G 25B 140
N42G STR 5127
N42GB STR 5127
N42GX 25B 140
N42GX AST 124
N42HC 24B 208
N42HC 25B 142
N42HM 35A 210
N42HM 501 452
N42HN 35A 507
N42HP 35A 507
N42HP 45 080
N42KC 550 346
N42KR STR 5225
N42LC G2 178
N42LL 35A 427
N42MD G3 427
N42NA 560 0077
(N42NA) 650 0077
N42NF 24B 214
N42PA 560 5067
N42PG 24D 247
N42PH 550 327
N42QB WWD 6
(N42SE) 125 257036
N42SK 400A RK-111
N42SK 400A RK-28
N42SK 50 290
N42SR 125 257036
N42SR 400 RJ-9
N42SR D1A A038SA
N42TS 125 256003
N42TS 125 256041
N42TS 125 257067
N42US 10 171
(N42US) 125 258152
N42WJ 20 427
N42XL 560 5042
N42ZP 28 003
N43 WWD 131
(N43A) 36 008
(N43AC) 24 043
N43AJ 24 141
N43AR STR 5154
N43B 23 039
N43BE 50 49
N43BG 501 407
N43BH 125 25222
N43BH 125 256046
N43CC 10 69
N43CF S40 282-59
(N43CT) 23 039
N43D 550 188
(N43D) 551 375
N43DD 35A 288
N43DM 24D 305
N43EC 10 168
N43EL 35A 121
N43ES 50 49
N43FE 35A 275
(N43FN) 24D 305
N43GB S60 306-14
N43H 35A 426
N43JG S60 306-79
N43JK 20 195
(N43JK) STR 5055/21
N43KC 24B 213
N43KS G4 1018
N43LJ 31A 043
N43LJ 36A 043
N43M G2 126
N43M G4 1057
N43MU G4 1057
N43NR 60 043
N43NR S40 282-69
N43NR S40 282-7
N43NW 600 1043
(N43PE) 35A 275
N43PR 601 5002
N43R 601 5134
N43R 604 5334
N43R 75A 380-51
N43R G2 18
N43RC S550 0149
N43RJ G2 64/27
N43RK 601 5134
N43RP WWD 332
N43RW 550 088
N43SA 550 096
N43SE 31A 048
N43SF 31A 048
N43SF 60 159
N43SM 20 142
N43SP 501 648
(N43TC) 500 149
N43TC 550 337
N43TC 650 0036
N43TE 550 337
N43TJ 35A 121
(N43TL) 24B 203
N43TR 35A 645
N43US 10 110
N43VS S550 0069
N43W 24B 227
N43W 35A 426
N43W S40 282-15
N43WJ 125 25031
N43ZP 24 157
N43ZZ WWD 356
N44 WWD 130
N44AB 35A 473
N44AJ 24 120
N44AS 550 056
N44BB 125 257105
N44BB 25D 227
N44BH 125 25224
(N44BH) 125 25236
(N44BH) 125 256047
(N44BH) 650 0019
N44BW 500 048
N44CC 20 200
N44CJ 24 146
N44CN 125 25203
N44CP 24B 185
N44CP 25 006
N44EE 25 050
N44EL 25 050
N44EL 35 009
N44EL 35A 255
N44EL 55 123
N44EL 60 036
N44ET 35A 255
N44EV 36A 022
N44FC 550 220
N44FE 25D 215
N44FE 525 0334
N44FG 560 0470
N44FH 25D 252
N44FJ 525 0003
N44FM 501 534
N44GA 24 129
N44GA 55ER 102
N44GL 36 009
N44GT 551 002
N44GT 560 0252
N44GT S550 0099
N44GX AST 125
N44HC 500 295
N44HG 35A 180
N44HH 125 258223
N44HS 650 0006
N44JC 10 22
N44JC 20 471
N44JF 500 262
(N44JX) 550 088
N44K 125 25114
(N44KB) 24D 245
(N44KF) STR 5038
N44KG 125 25114
(N44KW) 35A 130
N44LC 501 577
N44LC 550 649
N44LC 560 0482
N44LF 550 309
N44LJ 24B 191
N44LJ 35A 276
N44LJ 36A 044
N44LQ 550 649
N44M 650 0050
N44MC 501 434
N44MD G2 81
N44MD G3 427
N44MF STR 5051
N44MJ 25B 124
N44MJ 35A 421
N44MK 50 44
N44MW 35 044
N44NJ 24 120
N44NP S40 282-44
N44NR S40 282-130
N44NT 20 319
N44P S40 282-103
N44PA 24B 181
N44PA 25B 144
N44PH S40 282-136
N44PR WWD 169
N44PT 35A 093
N44PW 125 25123
N44QG 28 003
N44QG 31A 053
N44RD 500 334
N44RD 501 464
N44SA 500 109
N44SB S60 306-20
N44SF 31A 065
N44SF 31A 193
N44SK 25D 371
N44SK 35A 444
N44SK 50 290
N44SU 31A 065
N44SW 501 552
N44TC 550 337
N44TG 125 25100
(N44TL) 24B 191
N44TQ 125 25100
N44TT 35A 211
N44UC 35A 098
N44UP G2 133
N44VW 35 044
N44WD 24A 111
N44WD S60 306-116

N44WF	550	236
N44WG	WWD	112
N44ZP	550	214
N45	WWD	144
N45AE	**35A**	**422**
N45AF	125	257128
N45AF	**501**	**433**
N45AJ	24D	309
N45AJ	24D	317
(N45AQ)	501	411
N45AW	35A	078
N45BA	560	0067
N45BE	50	75
N45BH	125	25225
N45BH	125	256051
N45BK	**25TF**	**036**
N45BR	**750**	**0045**
N45CP	24D	242
N45CP	**25XR**	**073**
N45DM	25	030
N45ED	**24**	**104**
N45EP	550	199
N45ES	25D	295
N45ES	50	75
N45FC	24D	309
N45FE	**45**	**034**
N45FG	**36**	**010**
N45FG	50	180
N45GA	551	395
N45GL	D1A	A041SA
N45GP	**S550**	**0110**
N45H	25D	239
N45H	S550	0064
N45H	**S65**	**465-2**
N45HB	25B	114
N45HG	**31**	**026**
N45JB	**100**	**203**
N45JF	24	138
N45JF	WWD	101
N45JM	G2	69
N45K	STR	5151
(N45KB)	25D	270
N45KB	25D	281
N45KB	**560**	**0191**
N45KG	**125**	**257189**
N45KK	125	257158
N45KK	25D	281
N45KK	35A	592
N45KK	**35A**	**672**
N45LC	500	326
N45LJ	45	002
N45LJ	45	019
N45LR	**45**	**055**
N45MC	501	531
N45MC	550	422
N45ME	**550**	**089**
N45MH	**525**	**0386**
N45MJ	35	045
N45MK	**501**	**571**
N45ML	**550**	**405**
N45MM	**501**	**444**
(N45MM)	S60	306-91
(N45MP)	WWD	334
N45MR	20	123
N45MS	**AST**	**041**
N45NB	**PRM**	**RB-22**
N45NC	125	25225
N45NC	**50**	**232**
(N45ND)	125	25225
N45NP	D1A	A047SA
N45NP	**S65**	**465-42**
N45NQ	125	25225
N45NS	**550**	**479**
(N45PG)	G3	488
N45PH	**601**	**3004**
N45PK	**31**	**034**
N45PM	125	25118
N45RC	**560**	**0071A**
N45RK	**400A**	**RK-43**
N45RS	S60	306-44
N45SC	**2xx**	**45**
N45SJ	50	53
N45SJ	900	37
N45SJ	**90X**	**7**
N45SJ	WWD	289
N45SL	125	25098
(N45SL)	35A	083
N45SL	WWD	149
N45ST	**750**	**0054**
N45TK	**35**	**037**
N45TL	**501**	**375**
N45TP	**550**	**674**
N45UF	**31A**	**072**
(N45US)	650	0016
(N45US)	650	0034
N45VB	**45**	**043**
N45VM	**550**	**0918**
N45VP	**45**	**184**
N45WH	20	259
N45WH	200	512
(N45WL)	550	155
N45WN	20	259
N45XL	**45**	**001**
N45Y	125	258009
N45Y	**125**	**258140**
N45Y	G2	69
N45YP	G2	69
N45ZP	25D	238
N45ZP	550	216
N46A	550	423
N46A	S550	0061
N46B	125	25261
N46B	125	256044
(N46BA)	25D	300
N46BA	550	575
(N46BE)	125	256044
N46BH	125	25226
N46BK	**WWD**	**214**
N46DA	550	033
N46ES	600	1079
(N46ES)	G3	381
N46F	**601**	**5055**
N46F	STR	5124
N46FE	400A	RK-16
N46HA	**2xx**	**91**
N46JA	24D	251
(N46JA)	500	168
N46JW	**525**	**0002**
N46K	STR	5145
(N46KB)	35A	206
N46KJ	STR	5151
N46MF	550	408
N46MK	**100**	**206**
N46MK	550	408
N46MT	501	689
N46MT	550	553
N46MT	**560**	**0253**
N46MW	**560**	**0487**
N46PL	125	257055
N46RB	500	058
N46RD	500	244
N46SC	501	521
N46SD	551	377
N46SG	601	5111
N46SR	600	1046
N46SR	**601**	**3046**
N46TE	G2	243
N46TG	125	25123
N46TJ	125	257104
N46TJ	35A	077
N46UF	**31A**	**073**
N46UF	AST	015
N46UP	AST	015
N46VG	20	46
N46WB	24	133
N46WB	560	0238
N46WB	560	0320
N46WC	**125**	**257195**
N47A	G2	71
N47AJ	25	023
N47AN	**650**	**0054**
N47BA	35	060
N47BA	STR	5061/48
N47BH	125	25228
N47CF	501	634
N47CG	125	258169
N47CM	**650**	**0153**
N47DC	WWD	163
N47DK	25B	154
N47DM	WWD	74
N47EC	**G2**	**231**
N47ES	600	1083
N47EX	125	256047
N47FH	**525**	**0047**
N47HC	25B	114
N47HR	**601**	**5174**
N47HR	G2	30/4
N47HR	G4	1195
N47HV	**125**	**256014**
N47HW	125	256014
N47JE	20	189
N47JF	20	189
N47JK	G2	115
N47JR	35	007
N47LP	**20**	**457**
(N47LP)	S550	0017
N47LP	WWD	411
N47LR	WWD	411
N47MJ	25	004
N47MJ	S550	0010
N47MM	S60	306-25
N47MN	S60	306-9
N47MR	**25B**	**101**
(N47NR)	24	148
N47PB	**125**	**257055**
N47PB	D1A	A047SA
N47RK	10	162
(N47RP)	550	249
N47SE	**S65**	**465-34**
N47SL	G4	1053
N47SW	**550**	**444**
N47TH	525	0047
N47TH	**525**	**0119**
N47TJ	125	257036
N47TJ	125	257040
(N47TJ)	125	258139
N47TJ	D1A	A047SA
N47TL	**501**	**605**
N47TW	550	477
(N47TW)	560	0224
N47UC	STR	5123/14
N47UC	STR	5125/31
N47UF	**50**	**28**
N47VC	125	258139
N47VC	**560**	**0304**
N47VL	**S40**	**282-48**
(N47VP)	525	0047
(N47WH)	G2	180
N47WT	24D	283
N47WU	125	256047
N48AD	20	241/479
N48AH	WWD	288
N48AJ	24	172
N48AS	23	088
N48BA	24	152
N48BH	125	25229
N48BT	20	160/450
N48CC	20	200
N48CC	**G2**	**181**
N48CG	**2xx**	**41**
N48CG	S40	282-75
N48CK	**400**	**RJ-22**
N48CT	**24D**	**274**
N48DA	500	297
N48DD	**125**	**25115**
(N48DD)	125	258207
(N48DK)	35A	171
N48DK	**551**	**051**
N48EC	**G2**	**9/33**
N48FB	**125**	**257129**
N48FJ	501	547
N48FN	**24D**	**238**
N48FN	25B	096
N48FU	200	495
N48FU	**601**	**5021**
N48GA	400	RJ-28
N48GL	50	168
N48GP	35A	069
N48GP	50	63
N48GR	**25**	**048**
N48GX	**GXY**	**017**
N48HA	**2xx**	**94**
N48HB	**50**	**233**
N48HC	**55**	**012**
N48HC	S60	306-96
N48HM	25	030
N48HU	200	495
N48JC	10	22
N48JC	10	37
N48JK	G2	71
N48JW	24D	236
N48L	**24A**	**107**
N48LC	**560**	**0463**
N48MF	**400A**	**RK-218**
N48MG	S60	306-53
N48MJ	35A	448
N48MS	10	18
(N48MS)	G2	83
N48MW	23	048
(N48NA)	550	215
N48ND	550	069
N48PL	**400A**	**RK-138**
N48R	10	80
N48R	50	160
(N48RA)	G2	18
N48RW	35A	075
N48SD	**WWD**	**399**
N48SE	**400A**	**RK-48**
N48SR	**400**	**RJ-39**
N48TC	S40	282-66
N48TF	650	0176
N48TT	10	16
N48TT	**650**	**0105**
N48TW	50	73
N48UC	125	25046
N48UC	STR	5125/31
N48US	125	25252
N48WA	**25B**	**136**
N48WP	S40	282-59
N48WS	S40	282-59
N48WS	**S60**	**306-124**
N48WW	WWD	384
N48Y	**125**	**258009**
N49AJ	24	143
N49AS	10	49
N49AT	35A	366
N49AZ	**35A**	**652**
N49BA	25	011
N49BB	25	025
N49BE	**35A**	**192**
N49BH	125	25230
N49BL	501	633
N49CJ	**525**	**0049**
N49CK	**23**	**009**
N49DM	24D	238
N49E	500	017
N49EA	500	017
N49FW	**550**	**0838**
N49HS	**550**	**183**
N49LC	501	577
N49LD	**560**	**0175**
N49MJ	560	0026
N49MJ	**560**	**0306**
N49MJ	S550	0010
N49MN	**AST**	**019**
N49MP	501	519
N49MW	**2xx**	**44**
N49MW	AST	019
(N49N)	550	360
(N49PD)	55	045
N49PE	35A	192
N49PE	55	045
N49R	500	072
N49R	500	281
N49RF	**G4**	**1246**
N49RJ	**S40**	**282-69**
(N49TA)	501	683
N49TA	WWD	260
N49TJ	24D	295
N49TJ	551	051
N49U	**550**	**091**
N49UC	STR	5110/47
N49UR	601	5016
N49US	200	494
N49US	**G3**	**302**
N49VG	125	258139

(N49VP) 550 170
N49WA 25B 142
N49WC 501 490
N49WL 35A 457
N49WW WWD 389
N50AC 500 159
N50AD 20 127
N50AE 50 208
N50AE 50 254
N50AF 55 038
N50AF 55 059
N50AH 50 111
N50AJ 23 037
N50AJ AST 030
N50AJ AST 044
N50AK 35A 172
N50AL WWD 190
N50AM 500 041
N50AS 125 25083
N50AS 500 041
N50AS STR 5058/4
N50AZ 550 288
(N50B) 10 14
N50B 25D 224
N50BA 24 043
N50BF 50 106
N50BH 125 25233
N50BH 20 365
N50BK S550 0031
N50BL 50 66
N50BN 125 258142
N50BX 50 102
N50CA 20 28
N50CC 500 080
N50CD S40 282-42
N50CK 25B 157
N50CR S50 287-1
N50CS 50 207
N50DD 35A 256
N50DD 55 066
N50DG S60 306-19
(N50DG) S65 465-34
N50DH 25B 079
N50DM 10 41
N50DM 23 025
N50DR 24D 311
N50DR WWD 266
N50DS 501 570
N50DS 60 047
N50DS 650 0078
N50DS S550 0031
N50DT 25 042
N50DT 36 004
N50DW WWD 380
N50EB 125 25253
N50EC STR 5033/56
(N50EF) 50 54
N50EF D1A A081SA
N50EJ 50 3
N50ET 525 0251
N50FB 50 6
N50FC 125 25253
N50FC 550 255
N50FD WWD 381
N50FE 50 8
N50FG 50 10
N50FH 50 11
N50FH 50 62
N50FJ 50 137
N50FJ 50 153
N50FJ 50 163
N50FJ 50 175
N50FJ 50 184
N50FJ 50 188
N50FJ 50 197
N50FJ 50 212
N50FJ 50 225
N50FJ 50 227
N50FJ 50 236
N50FJ 50 238
N50FJ 50 244
N50FJ 50 252
N50FJ 50 254
N50FJ 50 272
N50FJ 50 280
N50FJ 50 3
N50FJ 50 4
N50FJ 50 65
N50FJ 50 85
N50FK 50 13
N50FL 50 14
(N50FM) 50 16
N50FM 50 19
N50FN 35A 070
N50FN 50 18
N50FR 50 20
N50FS 50 22
N50FT 500 023
N50GD 125 256024
N50GF 50 40
(N50GG) 550 042
N50GG 80A 380-6
N50GL 25B 110
N50GP 560 0477
N50GT 501 438
N50GT S550 0159
N50HC 50 136
N50HC 50 208
N50HE 50 7
N50HE 550 168
N50HE G4 1219
N50HH 125 25022
N50HM 50 153
N50HS 125 257098
N50HS 550 168
N50HS WWD 412
N50HW 551 139
N50J 50 117
N50JF 24 151
N50JF 24A 011
N50JG 501 579
N50JM 125 257033
N50JP WWD 69
N50JR 125 257159
(N50K) 75A 380-46
N50KD 50 145
N50KH 400A RK-59
N50L 25XR 152
N50L 55 004
N50LB WWD 93
N50LG 200 507
N50LJ 31A 052
N50LM 550 441
N50LQ 50 148
N50LT 50 44
N50LV 50 65
N50M WWD 327
N50MC 501 381
(N50MF) WWD 384
N50MG 200 507
N50MJ 125 25152
N50MJ 35A 103
N50MJ 35A 164
N50MK 50 98
(N50ML) 50 98
N50MM 20 39
N50MM 500 118
N50MM 501 622
(N50MT) 25D 353
N50MT 35A 118
N50MW 200 503
N50MX 200 503
N50N 550 469
(N50NA) 550 376
N50NE 125 25236
N50NF 550 636
N50NK 50 218
N50NM 50 266
(N50NM) STR 5229
N50PA 600 1004
N50PD 35A 409
N50PE 25C 176
N50PG 50 8
N50PH 35A 246
N50PH 35A 497
N50PH 650 0148
N50PJ 23 076
N50PL 35A 246
N50PL WWD 338
N50PM 125 258183
N50PM 75A 380-25
N50PM G2 236
N50PM G3 333
N50PR 500 091
N50PS STR 5134/50
N50QJ WWD 303
N50RD 500 260
N50RG 50 60
N50RG 900 51
N50RL 10 66
N50RW 25B 135
N50SF 36 010
N50SF 50 180
N50SJ 24D 246
(N50SJ) 50 53
N50SJ 50 80
N50SK 500 046
N50SK WWD 309
N50SL 10 161
N50SL 125 25187
N50SL 20 359/542
N50SL 500 046
N50SL WWD 269
N50SS 125 25028
N50TB 10 57
N50TC 10 31
N50TC 24B 190
N50TC 50 115
N50TE 10 86
N50TG 50 117
N50TG 601 3054
N50TG AST 065
N50TK 10 123
N50TN 125 257033
N50TQ AST 065
N50TR 500 325
N50TX S40 282-23
N50TY 10 72
N50UD STR 5019
N50US 501 424
N50US 501 527
N50US 550 032
N50US 550 194
N50VF WWD 13
N50VF WWD 137
N50VG 50 104
(N50WB) 50 102
N50WG 50 189
N50WJ 501 397
N50WM 500 246
(N50WP) 501 512
N50XX 550 042
N50XX WWD 311
(N50XX) WWD 319
N50XX WWD 412
N50XX WWD 436
N50XY G3 412
(N50YJ) 10 57
N51 75A 380-5
N51AJ 23 037
N51AJ 24D 273
N51B 24A 116
N51B 400A RK-261
N51B 500 027
N51B D1A A063SA
N51BE D1A A063SA
N51BH 125 25234
N51BL 25D 269
N51BP 10 51
N51BP 500 051
N51BR 500 051
N51CA 25 030
N51CC 501 457
N51CD 525 0163
N51CG 501 457
N51CH 24 168
N51CH WWD 61
N51CJ 501 351
N51DB 25XR 246
N51DT 25D 367
N51EB 400 RJ-28
N51ET 501 450
N51FJ 50 24
N51FN 35 059
N51FT 550 134
N51GA 500 363
(N51GJ) 24B 224
N51GL 24D 272
N51GY 601 5136
N51JA 35A 296
N51JH S550 0007
N51JT 24D 283
N51LC 35A 302
N51MJ 25B 133
N51ML 400A RK-22
N51MN 125 25190
(N51MN) S40 282-51
N51MN WWD 198
N51MW 500 085
N51NP 400A RK-224
N51PD WWD 297
N51PS 550 365
N51SF 20 12
N51TJ 35A 183
N51TJ 600 1066
N51TJ G2 10
N51TV WWD 175
N51TV WWD 402
N51V 125 25070
N51V 50 189
N51V 55 116
N51VL 24X 235
N51VL 55 116
N51WP 501 528
N52 75A 380-10
N52AJ 25B 102
N52AJ 500 061
N52AN 500 030
N52BH 125 25236
N52CC 501 352
N52CK S550 0124
N52CK S550 0076
N52CT 25D 362
N52CT 55B 131
N52DA 25D 327
N52DC 50 126
N52DC 50 51
N52DD 24E 339
N52DQ 50 51
(N52EB) 400 RJ-52
N52EN 24A 116
N52ET 500 056
N52FC WWD 379
N52FJ 50 26
(N52FL) 35A 067
N52FP 500 052
N52FT 500 056
N52GA 400 RJ-36
N52GG S65 465-5
N52GH 24B 197
N52GL 25B 134
N52GW WWD 330
N52JA 25 007
N52JH 24 139
N52JJ 50 205
N52KS AST 033
N52KW 560 0256
N52L 25XR 141
N52LC 125 257131
N52LT 525 0322
N52MA 500 052
N52MJ 35A 363
N52MK G4 1337
N52MW 550 0822
N52N 100 197
(N52NE) G2 52
N52NW G2 52
N52PK 525 0052
N52PM 500 222
N52RF 550 011
N52RG 560 0235
N52SD 25B 110
N52SM 125 259010
N52SM WWD 397
N52SN 560 0207
N52TC 500 324

N52TJ	**10**	**3**
N52TJ	10	52
(N52TJ)	G2	52
N52TJ	STR	5078/3
N52TL	**501**	**418**
N52WF	**560**	**0528**
(N52WS)	500	110
N53	75A	380-14
(N53AA)	WWD	56
N53AJ	500	243
N53BB	**501**	**545**
N53BH	125	25239
N53CC	550	350
N53CG	**525**	**0233**
N53CJ	525	0053
N53CV	560	0053
N53DB	10	41
(N53DE)	24	153
N53DF	**601**	**5078**
N53DF	601	5133
N53DM	35A	329
N53DS	20	373
N53EB	400	RJ-53
N53EZ	**501**	**497**
N53FB	500	271
N53FJ	50	28
N53FJ	50	53
N53FL	**25**	**017**
N53FN	35	053
N53FP	**550**	**433**
N53FT	500	238
N53FT	**550**	**318**
N53G	S60	306-57
N53GH	**125**	**257164**
N53GH	24	151
N53GH	35A	304
N53GL	24D	268
N53GL	**35A**	**304**
(N53HJ)	55	028
N53HJ	**55**	**037**
N53J	500	152
N53JA	36A	043
N53JL	55	060
N53JM	35A	419
N53JM	S550	0061
N53KB	550	053
N53M	550	442
N53M	G4	1089
N53MJ	500	068
N53MJ	500	317
N53MS	**400A**	**RK-64**
N53MU	**G4**	**1089**
N53PJ	**MSP**	**053**
N53RC	501	497
N53RG	**500**	**402**
N53SF	20	102
N53SF	AST	034
N53SN	10	54
N53SR	600	1078
N53TC	25D	305
N53TS	10	77
N53VP	550	053
N53WA	**10**	**53**
N53WC	S40	282-137
N53WF	551	062
N53WW	**WWD**	**393**
N54	**60**	**009**
N54	75A	380-16
N54AM	S550	0085
(N54BC)	WWD	369
N54BE	D1A	A063SA
N54BH	125	25241
N54BM	G2	236
N54BW	STR	5014
N54CC	550	210
N54CF	S40	282-66
N54CG	**501**	**677**
N54CJ	**525**	**0054**
N54CM	501	293
N54DA	50	201
(N54DA)	550	036
N54DC	**900**	**22**
N54DD	**560**	**0089**
N54DS	501	350
N54FJ	10	54
(N54FJ)	50	31
N54FJ	50	36
N54FN	**25C**	**083**
(N54FT)	500	054
N54FT	**501**	**485**
N54GD	125	256068
N54GL	35A	597
N54GL	55	054
(N54GL)	U36A	054
N54GP	25D	327
N54H	10	6
N54H	25B	124
N54HA	**560**	**5040**
(N54HC)	550	368
N54HC	**650**	**0098**
N54HD	**400A**	**RK-49**
N54HF	35A	472
N54HH	75A	380-19
N54HJ	550	368
N54HP	**400A**	**RK-160**
N54HP	400A	RK-49
N54HU	25B	124
N54J	20	289
N54J	**G2**	**193**
N54JA	**36A**	**044**
N54JC	**125**	**25249**
N54JC	24E	340
(N54JC)	25D	327
N54JJ	20	289
N54MC	25B	132
N54MC	500	154
N54MC	WWD	202
N54MH	501	545
N54MJ	501	612
N54MQ	25B	132
N54NS	**550**	**578**
(N54NW)	55	024
N54NW	**55**	**054**
(N54PA)	600	1081
N54PR	35	054
N54PR	601	3054
N54PR	**G5**	**564**
N54PT	WWD	363
N54RC	550	241
N54RM	**550**	**562**
N54RM	D1A	A065SA
N54RS	10	94
N54SB	125	258258
(N54SB)	35A	644
N54SB	G4	1063
N54SK	500	054
N54SN	20	54
N54TA	25D	258
N54TB	501	482
N54TK	35A	254
N54TS	**501**	**293**
N54V	10	35
N54WC	650	0032
N54WC	WWD	117
N54WJ	10	33
N54WJ	**125**	**257007**
N54WJ	S550	0031
N54YP	25D	208
N54YP	35A	356
N54YR	25D	208
N54YR	35A	356
N54YR	**50**	**158**
N55	**60**	**013**
N55	75A	380-18
N55AK	500	299
N55AL	551	049
N55AQ	55	072
N55AR	600	1044
N55AS	35A	146
N55AS	**50**	**214**
N55AS	55	072
N55B	125	25261
(N55BE)	501	476
(N55BE)	55	058
N55BH	125	25244
N55BH	550	057
N55BH	**650**	**0041**
N55BM	501	606
N55BP	50	207
N55BP	550	032
N55BP	S60	306-20
N55CC	550	055
N55CD	24D	306
N55CJ	**36**	**003**
N55CJ	501	355
N55CJ	STR	5090
N55CR	75	370-9
N55DD	24D	236
N55DD	25D	296
N55DG	**100**	**207**
N55DG	525	0044
N55DG	55ER	102
N55ES	25B	111
N55F	**35A**	**147**
N55FJ	10	55
N55FM	**550**	**399**
N55FN	25	050
N55FT	**500**	**009**
N55G	125	25141
N55G	**125**	**25163**
N55GF	55	052
N55GH	36	012
N55GH	55	012
N55GH	55	075
(N55GJ)	55	078
N55GJ	55	088
N55GK	55	105
N55GM	55	075
N55GM	**55C**	**139A**
N55GR	**500**	**217**
N55GV	55	078
N55GY	55	110
N55GZ	55	083
N55H	501	552
N55HA	**560**	**5059**
N55HD	55	026
N55HD	650	0193
(N55HD)	75A	380-39
N55HF	500	261
N55HF	550	126
N55HF	**601**	**5183**
N55HF	650	0126
N55HF	650	0193
N55HK	55	040
N55HL	501	671
N55HL	**55**	**046**
N55HY	**G2**	**97**
N55JM	D1A	A026SA
N55KC	25	046
N55KC	25B	147
N55KC	55	014
N55KD	55	051
N55KQ	25	046
N55KS	24	178
N55KS	55	051
N55KS	60	029
N55KS	75	370-5
N55KS	S65	465-5
N55KX	24	178
N55KZ	75	370-5
N55LC	**560**	**0324**
N55LF	500	261
N55LF	55B	133
N55LJ	24B	203
N55LJ	25D	233
N55LJ	**55**	**030**
N55LK	55	120
N55LS	550	616
N55LS	**551**	**107**
N55ME	20	83
(N55ME)	S40	282-23
(N55ME)	S60	306-27
N55MF	25B	171
N55MJ	24B	203
N55MJ	25D	296
N55MT	125	257046
N55MT	550	431
N55MT	S40	282-112
N55NC	STR	5060
N55NE	STR	5155/32
N55NJ	24	162
N55NM	**55**	**085**
N55NT	**50**	**87**
N55NY	**55**	**020**
N550PF	550	672
(N55PC)	650	0187
N55PD	**25B**	**105**
N55PG	600	1045
N55PP	S40	282-135
N55PT	25B	171
N55PZ	**525**	**0285**
N55RF	**125**	**25020**
N55RG	**G2**	**1**
N55RT	**55**	**095**
N55RZ	**125**	**25262**
N55RZ	35A	439
N55SC	650	0148
N55SC	**650**	**7060**
N55SH	500	315
N55SJ	55	009
N55SK	500	315
N55SK	**525**	**0063**
N55SL	**25XR**	**219**
N55SN	50	189
N55SQ	650	0148
N55SR	600	1055
N55SX	550	065
N55TH	20	17
N55TK	501	682
N55TS	125	257046
N55TY	**90X**	**25**
N55UK	55C	147
N55V	25B	185
N55VC	**55B**	**130**
N55VL	25C	176
N55WG	501	604
N55WH	501	426
N55WJ	25	017
N55WL	**550**	**155**
N55ZM	S60	306-84
(N55ZT)	55C	139A
N56	**60**	**033**
N56	75A	380-20
N56AG	AST	043
N56AG	**G4**	**1125**
N56AG	WWD	133
N56AG	WWD	201
N56AG	WWD	374
N56AZ	WWD	133
N56BE	**400A**	**RK-13**
N56BH	125	25237
N56BL	125	25201
N56BP	**WWD**	**268**
N56CC	20	313
N56CC	20	387
(N56CJ)	501	495
N56D	**G2**	**257/17**
N56DR	24D	311
N56DV	500	346
N56EM	**35A**	**144**
N56FB	550	391
N56FJ	50	33
N56FT	**550**	**429**
N56GA	400	RJ-50
(N56GH)	24R	233
N56GT	551	152
N56GT	560	0091
N56HA	**560**	**5063**
N56HF	35A	084
N56HF	35A	144
N56JA	**35A**	**342**
N56K	525	0005
N56K	560	0463
N56K	560	5014
N56L	G3	302
N56L	**G4**	**1213**
N56LA	G3	302
N56LB	24	178
N56LC	**50**	**275**
N56LF	**31A**	**056**
N56LP	**10**	**165**
N56LS	24	178
N56LT	**50**	**21**
N56LW	**501**	**620**
N56MC	501	386
N56MC	501	620

N56MC	D1A	A069SA
N56MJ	501	614
N56MK	**501**	**386**
N56MM	**24F**	**332**
N56MT	501	386
N56NW	S65	465-62
N56NZ	525	0056
N56PA	**36A**	**023**
N56PB	35A	224
N56PB	**501**	**625**
N56PC	550	441
(N56PR)	23	028
(N56PR)	35A	370
N56PR	STR	5211
N56PT	**24D**	**276**
N56RD	24X	286
N56RN	**S60**	**306-122**
N56S	WWD	96
(N56SK)	D1A	A008SA
N56SL	20	305
N56SN	**50**	**216**
N56TG	55	078
N56VG	20	50
N56WD	45	019
N56WE	**501**	**426**
N56WH	WWD	96
N56WJ	**10**	**56**
N56WS	24X	243
N57	**60**	**039**
N57	75A	380-22
N57AJ	550	100
N57B	**400A**	**RK-36**
N57B	50	57
N57B	55	020
N57BC	24D	277
N57BC	550	478
N57BG	G2	61
N57BH	125	25245
N57BJ	G3	327
N57BJ	**S550**	**0052**
N57CE	550	198
N57CE	560	0048
N57CE	**650**	**0178**
N57CJ	**S550**	**0057**
N57CK	25B	157
N57CK	550	198
N57CN	560	0048
N57DB	24X	286
N57DC	**50**	**119**
N57DL	25D	334
N57DM	25B	107
N57EL	50	205
N57EL	**900**	**153**
N57FF	125	258033
N57FF	35	015
N57FF	35A	157
N57FJ	50	35
N57FL	24X	243
N57FM	55	025
N57FP	35A	157
N57G	125	25098
N57GL	35	057
N57GS	S40	282-2
N57HA	**560**	**5068**
N57HA	601	5010
N57HC	**525**	**0157**
N57HH	20	74
N57HJ	**G2**	**194**
(N57HK)	601	5010
N57JF	20	192
(N57JR)	24B	215
N57LC	500	309
N57LL	**500**	**025**
N57MB	500	287
N57MB	550	044
N57MB	**560**	**0286**
N57MB	S550	0054
N57MC	**501**	**636**
N57MF	550	137
N57MH	**55**	**113**
N57MJ	501	624
N57MK	550	137
N57MK	560	0145
N57MK	**560**	**0535**
N57ML	560	0145
N57MQ	**S65**	**465-11**
(N57NB)	24	145
N57ND	24	145
N57NP	**G3**	**340**
N57NP	STR	5123/14
N57NR	**STR**	**5123/14**
N57PM	125	258218
N57PM	55	025
(N57QR)	S40	282-3
N57RM	S40	282-41
N57SF	**550**	**366**
N57ST	560	0383
N57TA	55	010
(N57TA)	55	011
(N57TS)	125	25035
N57TT	**200**	**501**
N57TT	650	0046
N57TW	501	624
(N57VP)	560	0007
N57WW	WWD	390
N58	**60**	**057**
N58	80	380-24
(N58AN)	500	018
N58AN	550	036
N58AS	10	58
N58AS	55	072
N58AU	400	RJ-14
N58AU	400	RJ-45
(N58B)	10	92
(N58BD)	501	549
N58BH	125	25261
N58BH	550	057
N58BL	**125**	**258236**
N58BL	24D	268
N58BT	125	25023
(N58BT)	500	100
N58BT	501	375
N58BT	501	625
N58CC	500	015
N58CG	55	124
N58CG	**90X**	**47**
N58CG	S60	306-42
N58CG	STR	5014
N58CM	S65	465-70
N58CP	25B	133
N58CQ	55	124
N58CW	35	015
N58CW	**35A**	**116**
N58DJ	25D	328
N58DM	24B	184
(N58DT)	501	375
N58EM	**35**	**046**
N58FF	35	015
N58FJ	50	38
N58FM	55	085
N58FN	**24B**	**184**
N58GG	550	269
N58GL	25XR	148
N58GL	**35A**	**599**
N58H	550	335
N58HA	**560**	**5099**
N58HC	**25D**	**341**
N58HC	650	0091
N58HT	**S65**	**465-70**
(N58JA)	25	007
N58JF	**G2**	**65**
N58JM	S60	306-24
N58KJ	525	0005
N58KJ	560	0463
(N58KJ)	560	5014
N58KS	75	370-5
N58LC	**550**	**711**
N58M	35	037
N58M	55	077
N58MM	**35A**	**261**
N58PL	500	033
N58PM	**125**	**258220**
N58PM	55	085
N58RW	35A	133
N58RW	650	0006
N58SR	**55**	**058**
N58ST	60	186
(N58T)	501	397
N58TC	**500**	**261**
N58TJ	D1A	A030SA
N58TS	**STR**	**5079/33**
N58WW	WWD	201
N58XL	560	5099
N59	**60**	**080**
N59	75A	380-26
N59AC	25B	100
N59AC	STR	5204
N59AP	**WWD**	**398**
N59B	650	0191
N59BH	125	25262
N59BP	25B	124
N59BP	400A	RK-226
N59BR	**125**	**258425**
N59BR	400A	RK-226
N59CC	**10**	**6**
N59CC	501	488
N59CC	551	430
(N59CC)	650	0211
N59CD	650	0079
N59CD	G2	190
N59CD	STR	5155/32
N59CF	50	209
N59CF	**900**	**98**
N59CH	50	209
N59CL	500	173
N59CT	WWD	96
N59DF	**560**	**0098**
N59DM	35A	205
N59EC	**S550**	**0034**
N59EL	50	205
N59FD	60	084
N59FJ	50	39
N59FL	**25B**	**169**
N59FN	35A	205
N59GB	**551**	**377**
N59GL	24X	286
N59GL	35A	604
N59GS	50	36
N59GS	55	056
N59GU	**550**	**340**
N59HA	**560**	**0457**
N59HA	G3	397
N59HJ	**55**	**027**
N59JC	WWD	59
N59JG	24B	221
N59JM	S60	306-135
N59JR	125	256065
N59JR	G2	190
N59JR	**G4**	**1007**
N59K	S40	282-36
N59K	**S60**	**306-82**
N59KC	WWD	210
N59KG	**560**	**0363**
N59KQ	S40	282-36
N59LB	900	51
N59LJ	55	059
N59MA	**501**	**398**
N59MJ	35A	389
N59MJ	550	033
N59PC	501	418
N59PK	S40	282-36
N59PM	50	178
N59SG	25B	163
N59SM	WWD	390
N59SR	S65	465-59
N59TJ	**10**	**14**
(N59TJ)	125	257073
N59TJ	D1A	A004SA
N59TS	500	160
N59WK	WWD	243
N59WP	501	498
N60	75A	380-28
N60AC	G3	424
N60AE	560	0343
N60AF	650	0136
N60AF	S60	306-140
N60AG	**G3**	**376**
N60AG	S60	306-132
(N60AG)	S60	306-14
N60AG	S60	306-48
N60AH	S60	306-43
N60AJ	AST	042
N60AJ	AST	061
N60AJ	**AST**	**071**
N60AL	WWD	193
(N60AM)	125	25142
N60AM	S60	306-135
N60AR	551	144
N60AV	**WWD**	**254**
N60B	125	25195
N60B	400A	RK-33
N60B	D1A	A045SA
N60BB	550	234
N60BC	STR	5116
N60BD	125	25195
N60BE	650	0112
N60BK	S60	306-15
N60BP	S60	306-91
N60CC	550	034
N60CC	G2	142
N60CD	**WWD**	**44**
N60CE	**60**	**069**
N60CE	S65	465-5
N60CH	STR	5037/24
N60CN	**50**	**79**
N60CN	STR	5037/24
N60CR	S60	306-7
N60CT	604	5325
N60CT	G2	113
N60CT	G3	454
(N60DD)	20	479
N60DD	S60	306-127
N60DE	S60	306-25
N60DG	WWD	364
N60DH	23	033
N60DK	**25B**	**092**
N60DK	25D	231
N60DK	25D	245
N60DK	25D	250
N60DK	35A	394
N60DL	S60	306-25
N60E	55	106
(N60EE)	STR	5160
N60EF	**D1A**	**A070SA**
N60EL	S60	306-13
N60EL	S60	306-42
N60ES	**525**	**0053**
N60EW	**501**	**665**
(N60EX)	S60	306-37
N60EX	S60	306-7
N60FC	10	25
N60FC	601	5062
N60FJ	50	41
N60FJ	**551**	**018**
N60FN	24E	339
N60FS	S60	306-101
N60GF	551	574
N60GG	601	5007
N60GG	G2	108
N60GH	S60	306-7
N60GL	24D	260
N60GL	551	574
N60GL	560	0187
N60GL	560	5014
N60GN	G3	392
N60GT	**MSP**	**008**
N60GU	**G2**	**150**
N60HC	S60	306-21
N60HJ	125	257057
N60HJ	**600**	**1058**
N60HJ	G2	119/22
N60HU	125	25103
(N60HU)	125	257057
(N60HW)	551	377
N60JC	125	25174
N60JC	**S60**	**306-51**
N60JD	550	259
N60JF	S60	306-33
N60JM	125	257036
N60JM	STR	5213
N60JN	S60	306-14
N60JP	WWD	320
N60KR	601	5073
N60LH	**60**	**113**
N60LJ	60	003
N60LJ	60	026

N60LJ	60	071
N60LJ	60	081
N60LJ	60	110
N60LJ	**60**	**164**
N60LR	60	036
N60LR	60	056
N60LR	60	094
N60LR	60	125
N60LR	**60**	**177**
N60LT	55	060
N60MB	10	15
N60MJ	55	060
N60ML	**S60**	**306-129**
N60MM	550	192
N60MN	**60**	**100**
N60MP	500	325
N60MS	125	257014
N60MS	500	170
N60MS	601	3051
N60MU	601	3051
N60NS	**560**	**0258**
N60NY	G4	1132
N60PC	125	25214
N60PE	**G4**	**1251**
N60PL	**650**	**7056**
N60PM	125	258187
N60PM	75A	370-7
N60PR	501	549
N60PT	75A	370-7
N60PT	G4	1251
N60PT	**G4**	**1379**
N60QA	125	25214
N60QG	23	025
N60QJ	STR	5039
N60QJ	WWD	302
N60RB	S40	282-68
N60RC	S40	282-134
N60RD	**560**	**0244**
N60RE	125	25232
N60RE	**900**	**75**
N60RL	**60**	**136**
(N60RL)	S60	306-18
N60RS	S60	306-110
N60RS	S60	306-124
N60RS	S60	306-132
N60RS	S60	306-142
N60RS	S60	306-44
N60RS	S60	306-87
N60RV	**WWD**	**250**
N60S	**560**	**0066**
N60SB	**60**	**023**
N60SE	S60	306-100
N60SH	560	0106
N60SL	10	189
N60SL	S60	306-126
N60SL	S60	306-137
N60SL	S60	306-145
N60SL	S60	306-82
N60SL	S60	306-86
N60SM	20	24
N60SM	STR	5161/43
N60SN	20	24
N60T	60	011
(N60TA)	G2	241
N60TC	**125**	**258179**
N60TF	S60	306-114
N60TG	S60	306-86
N60TM	S60	306-72
N60TN	125	257036
N60TX	60	097
N60UJ	STR	5086/44
N60UK	60	004
N60VE	**60**	**006**
N60WL	**35A**	**382**
(N60WL)	S40	282-61
N60WM	60	045
(N60WP)	75A	380-39
N60XL	55	001
N60XL	**60**	**55-001**
N60Y	S40	282-26
N60Y	S60	306-13
N61	75A	380-29
N61AF	601	3008
N61AW	24D	323

N61BA	24D	246
N61BE	650	0129
N61BL	125	25095
N61BP	**10**	**102**
(N61BP)	10	92
N61BR	500	051
N61CD	501	545
N61CF	**550**	**335**
N61CJ	525	0061
N61CK	24	119
N61CK	**550**	**259**
N61CT	125	258108
N61DF	**125**	**258386**
N61DF	S60	306-131
N61DF	S65	465-59
N61DM	24B	224
N61DP	**60**	**122**
N61DT	**501**	**569**
N61EW	25B	161
N61FB	**S60**	**306-80**
N61FC	100	194
(N61FC)	S40	282-42
N61FJ	50	42
(N61FN)	24B	224
N61GA	D1A	A045SA
N61GV	G5	509
N61HA	550	335
N61HA	560	0295
N61JB	560	0273
N61LA	G4	1266
N61LH	G2	61
N61LL	20	244
N61MA	**550**	**203**
N61MD	S60	306-3
N61MJ	500	180
N61MS	125	25229
N61MS	125	25263
N61MX	125	25229
N61PM	20	355
N61PR	501	639
N61RH	S40	282-27
N61RS	**WWD**	**384**
N61SB	125	256002
N61SF	24E	346
N61SH	**525**	**0095**
N61SM	**400A**	**RK-60**
N61SM	G2	122
N61TF	125	256039
(N61TF)	525	0118
N61TJ	10	41
(N61TJ)	24D	241
N61TL	S550	0109
N61TS	**125**	**256001**
N61TS	23	029
N61TW	**560**	**0019**
N61WH	**G2**	**48/29**
(N61WT)	25D	265
N61WT	25D	288
N61YC	**60**	**011**
N62	75A	380-31
N62BH	125	25263
N62BL	600	1062
N62BR	**500**	**093**
N62CB	G2	208
N62CF	S60	306-62
N62CH	125	25221
N62CH	**D1A**	**A082SA**
N62DK	35A	231
N62DM	**24B**	**194**
(N62DW)	S60	306-41
N62EA	125	257062
N62FJ	50	44
N62FJ	900	62
(N62FN)	24B	194
N62GB	**560**	**5086**
N62GC	550	482
N62GG	G3	302
N62GL	55	062
N62HA	550	231
N62HA	**560**	**0189**
N62HB	500	213
N62K	G2	93
N62K	S40	282-53
N62K	STR	5099/5

N62KK	STR	5099/5
N62KM	400A	RK-53
N62MB	**35A**	**282**
N62MS	125	257017
N62MS	601	3050
N62MS	**G4**	**1248**
N62MU	601	3050
N62ND	**WWD**	**379**
N62NR	75A	380-54
N62NS	**S550**	**0072**
N62PG	**36A**	**031**
N62Q	S40	282-53
N62RG	**501**	**601**
N62RG	550	639
N62TC	125	25261
N62TC	125	258239
N62TF	125	25232
N62TJ	10	44
N62TW	**500**	**281**
N62WA	550	583
N62WA	**560**	**0360**
N62WB	G2	152
N62WG	550	482
N62WH	125	257125
N62WL	125	257125
N62WM	35A	596
N62ZS	25XR	162
N63	75A	380-33
N63A	50	19
N63A	S40	282-36
N63BH	125	25265
N63BL	125	25033
N63BL	**60**	**051**
N63BW	24F	353
N63CC	550	489
N63CF	501	097
N63CG	**501**	**519**
N63CK	**24**	**119**
N63DH	35A	261
N63DR	D1A	A067SA
N63EM	**125**	**25272**
N63ET	25B	110
N63FJ	50	45
(N63FS)	550	321
N63GA	**24D**	**241**
N63GH	D1A	A025SA
N63HA	**560**	**0199**
N63HB	525	0019
N63HJ	**600**	**1021**
N63HS	**G4**	**1249**
N63JG	**S550**	**0036**
N63JT	**S550**	**0156**
N63JU	S550	0036
N63KH	25D	287
N63LB	525	0127
N63LB	**550**	**0920**
N63LE	35A	250
N63LF	35A	250
N63LF	**525**	**0127**
N63LX	**560**	**5163**
"N63M"	G4	1022
N63M	**G4**	**1152**
N63MJ	45	055
N63MU	G4	1152
N63NC	S60	306-7
N63PM	125	257167
N63PM	125	258183
N63PM	20	355
N63SB	25XR	073
N63SD	G2	216
N63SE	**31A**	**203**
N63SL	S40	282-127
N63ST	**601**	**5149**
N63TJ	10	186
N63TM	550	457
N63TM	**560**	**0383**
N63TS	**10**	**66**
N64	75A	380-35
N64AH	**WWD**	**94**
(N64AJ)	500	085
N64AM	10	157
N64AM	S60	306-7
N64BE	900	45
N64BH	125	25267

N64BH	**501**	**673**
N64BH	601	5027
N64C	STR	5131
N64CA	551	030
N64CE	**24B**	**205**
N64CF	24B	205
N64CF	**35A**	**461**
N64CM	550	467
N64CM	S60	306-135
N64CP	**35A**	**264**
(N64DH)	35A	119
N64DH	**S40**	**282-52**
N64EZ	D1A	A062SA
(N64EZ)	D1A	A090SA
N64F	10	188
N64F	601	5021
N64FC	600	1035
N64FG	WWD	227
N64FJ	50	46
(N64FN)	35A	073
(N64FN)	36A	023
N64GG	125	257157
N64GL	600	1064
N64HA	125	257051
N64HA	560	0127
N64HB	24	149
N64KT	WWD	296
N64LF	**525**	**0218**
N64LX	**560**	**5164**
N64MA	**S40**	**282-44**
N64MC	S40	282-114
N64MC	S65	465-73
N64MG	S40	282-114
N64MH	35	048
N64MP	25B	078
N64MP	35	060
N64MP	**35A**	**490**
N64MP	80A	380-32
N64MQ	80A	380-32
N64MQ	S65	465-73
N64MR	25B	078
N64MR	35	060
N64NC	S60	306-109
N64PM	**525**	**0394**
N64PM	550	467
N64PM	560	0188
N64RT	**501**	**585**
N64RV	35A	355
N64SL	S65	465-42
N64TF	**550**	**080**
N64VM	**400**	**RJ-1**
N64VP	550	604
N64WH	25B	102
N64WM	55	022
N64YP	200	502
N64YP	601	5077
N64YR	200	502
N65	75A	380-37
N65A	**25B**	**134**
N65A	WWD	235
N65AD	S65	465-65
N65AF	**S65**	**465-62**
N65AH	S65	465-68
N65AK	**S65**	**465-35**
N65AM	S65	465-58
N65AN	S65	465-59
N65AR	S65	465-67
N65B	**50**	**10**
N65BE	G3	332
N65BH	125	25273
(N65BK)	WWD	216
N65BL	60	054
N65BP	**650**	**0202**
N65CC	**S65**	**465-46**
N65DD	S65	465-26
N65DH	35A	174
N65DH	35A	381
N65DL	125	25287
N65DL	**125**	**257174**
N65DT	S550	0006
N65DW	125	25208
N65EC	125	25208
N65FC	125	25091
N65FC	S65	465-31

N65FF	S65	465-46
N65FJ	50	47
(N65FN)	35	007
(N65GB)	125	256013
N65GW	WWD	349
N65HA	560	0143
N65HF	650	0126
N65HH	**S65**	**465-1**
N65HJ	**600**	**1038**
(N65HM)	S65	465-21
(N65HS)	10	99
N65HS	50	65
N65JN	D1A	A065SA
N65JR	S65	465-24
N65JT	**STR**	**5213**
(N65JW)	STR	5086/44
(N65JW)	STR	5113/25
N65KB	650	0199
N65KJ	S65	465-1
N65L	**S65**	**465-76**
N65LC	125	257202
N65LC	20	40
N65LC	550	317
N65LE	20	40
N65LJ	23	037
N65LT	125	25202
N65M	501	511
N65M	G2	136
N65MA	500	033
N65MC	**S65**	**465-36**
N65MK	125	25032
N65ML	S65	465-69
N65NC	S65	465-6
N65NR	S60	306-118
N65NR	S60	306-124
N65NR	S65	465-24
(N65PF)	35A	094
N65R	**S60**	**306-114**
N65RA	**400**	**RJ-9**
N65RA	501	434
N65RC	25	055
(N65RC)	25B	163
N65RC	S65	465-19
N65RS	**S60**	**306-136**
N65RS	S65	465-1
N65RS	S65	465-3
N65SA	**500**	**114**
(N65SA)	550	119
N65SA	D1A	A067SA
N65SD	**2xx**	**32**
N65SL	S65	465-10
N65SR	S65	465-16
N65SR	**S65**	**465-54**
N65SR	S65	465-6
N65ST	G2	5
(N65T)	501	624
(N65TA)	35A	364
N65TB	**PRM**	**RB-19**
N65TC	**S65**	**465-30**
N65TD	**AST**	**093**
N65TF	550	175
N65TJ	S65	465-45
N65TL	S65	465-56
N65TS	**125**	**25043**
N65TS	20	368
N65TS	S65	465-34
N65U	45	073
N65WH	**25B**	**086**
(N65WH)	35A	275
N65WL	**650**	**0122**
N65WM	24	163
N65WS	**500**	**076**
N65WW	**501**	**591**
N65Y	55	121
N66AG	**501**	**520**
N66AL	G2	166/15
N66AM	125	25087
N66AM	23	064
N66AM	**525**	**0160**
N66AS	23	029
N66AT	501	520
N66AT	550	044
N66BH	125	25275
N66CC	500	066

N66CD	S40	282-134
N66CF	**10**	**65**
N66CR	STR	5052
N66DD	550	263
N66DD	G3	483
N66DD	**G4**	**1355**
N66DN	550	263
(N66EA)	S550	0006
N66ED	80A	380-32
N66EH	**S550**	**0158**
N66ES	500	314
N66ES	525	0053
N66ES	**525**	**0244**
N66ES	550	032
N66ES	80A	380-32
N66ES	S40	282-91
N66EW	WWD	9
N66FE	35A	383
N66FG	D1A	A066SA
N66FG	WWD	357
N66FJ	50	49
(N66FN)	24D	268
(N66FN)	35A	067
N66GA	20	341
N66GE	500	258
N66GE	**S60**	**306-99**
N66HA	125	25126
N66HH	10	176
(N66HM)	35A	206
N66JD	25B	183
N66JE	WWD	326
N66KC	125	25038
N66KG	AST	096
N66LB	551	051
N66LE	**500**	**170**
N66LJ	35A	401
N66LM	35A	306
N66LN	35A	500
N66LW	24D	311
N66LX	**WWD**	**375**
N66MC	**550**	**256**
N66ME	650	0079
N66MF	10	29
N66MF	600	1036
(N66MF)	WWD	414
N66MJ	24E	334
N66MP	23	058
N66MP	STR	5015
N66MR	24	159
N66MS	**551**	**342**
N66MW	23	066
N66NJ	25	039
N66NJ	**35A**	**296**
N66NR	S60	306-62
N66NT	20	349
N66PL	D1A	A077SA
N66RP	24B	198
N66SG	**45**	**073**
N66SM	WWD	168
N66TF	G2	97
N66TJ	25B	081
N66TP	S40	282-60
N66TR	500	299
N66TS	WWD	39
N66U	**560**	**0489**
N66VG	20	210
N66VM	550	056
N66WB	20	242
N66WM	35A	141
N66WM	55C	145
N67B	600	1066
N67B	STR	5074/22
N67BE	500	184
N67BF	**500**	**184**
N67BH	125	25276
(N67BK)	S40	282-135
N67CC	501	367
(N67CK)	24	147
N67CX	**750**	**0128**
N67DF	**WWD**	**233**
N67EC	125	25285
N67FJ	50	50
(N67GA)	35A	176
N67GH	**525**	**0149**

N67GM	501	619
N67GT	STR	5061/48
N67GW	**560**	**0355**
N67HB	**25B**	**189**
N67HW	550	420
N67JR	20	247
N67JR	24D	230
N67JR	500	048
N67JR	**G3**	**324**
N67JW	10	99
N67JW	550	462
N67KM	75A	380-7
N67LC	**10**	**49**
N67LC	550	317
N67LH	550	664
N67MA	500	277
(N67ME)	550	444
(N67MP)	31A	059
N67MP	500	277
N67MP	550	444
N67MR	125	256067
N67MR	601	5029
N67NR	S60	306-76
N67PA	**35A**	**208**
N67PC	25B	128
N67PC	**550**	**696**
N67PR	**G2**	**67**
N67PW	125	257147
N67PW	**50**	**248**
N67RW	55	048
N67SB	**31A**	**045**
N67SC	S65	465-14
N67SE	650	0045
N67SF	500	184
N67SF	650	0045
N67SF	**650**	**0231**
N67SG	550	257
N67TJ	10	83
N67TJ	125	25159
(N67TJ)	35A	367
N67TJ	G3	390
N67TJ	**WWD**	**299**
N67TM	550	067
N67TS	**125**	**25097**
(N67VP)	S550	0067
N67VW	**525**	**0212**
N67WB	900	24
N67WB	**90X**	**16**
N67WM	55B	132
N67WW	S40	282-2
(N68AA)	S40	282-38
N68AG	500	238
N68BC	20	155
N68BC	**650**	**7025**
N68BH	125	25278
N68BK	**551**	**363**
N68BP	**20**	**155**
N68BR	**650**	**7114**
(N68BW)	125	25261
N68CB	125	25263
N68CB	**125**	**258453**
N68CB	500	270
N68CJ	525	0068
N68CJ	**525**	**0169**
(N68CK)	25	047
N68CK	**560**	**0063**
N68CT	STR	5108
N68DA	125	258052
N68DM	24	101
N68DM	**G2**	**28**
N68DS	550	219
N68EA	**501**	**438**
N68ED	**650**	**0239**
(N68FN)	24	101
N68GA	**125**	**256047**
N68GA	550	184
N68GP	125	258068
N68GT	**100**	**217**
N68HC	560	0016
N68HC	**560**	**0270**
N68HC	650	0091
N68HC	S40	282-55
N68HC	S60	306-96
N68HQ	560	0016

N68HQ	S40	282-55
N68HR	**125**	**258068**
N68JK	20	83
N68JW	550	465
N68KM	75A	380-23
N68LL	35A	463
N68LP	55	082
N68LP	**750**	**0040**
N68LU	24	163
N68LX	S65	465-68
N68MA	560	0159
N68MA	S60	306-23
N68ME	551	282
N68MJ	**35A**	**607**
N68NR	S60	306-101
N68PC	**45**	**040**
N68PJ	25	063
N68PL	D1A	A077SA
N68QB	35A	079
N68SD	**600**	**1062**
N68SK	650	0156
N68SK	**650**	**7016**
N68SK	S550	0011
N68SL	**G4**	**1042**
N68TA	S60	306-53
N68TJ	25B	140
N68TJ	35A	168
N68TS	20	129
N68UW	**35A**	**095**
N68WM	23	074
N68WW	**WWD**	**386**
(N69B)	55	091
N69BH	125	25279
N69BH	**35A**	**276**
(N69CG)	S40	282-72
N69CN	STR	5053/2
N69EC	10	109
N69EC	**200**	**498**
N69EP	501	531
N69FF	G3	320
N69GF	25D	265
N69GP	G4	1033
N69GT	WWD	44
N69GX	**AST**	**122**
N69HM	STR	5004
N69HM	WWD	210
N69JN	**75A**	**380-65**
N69KA	125	25273
N69KB	23	042
N69KM	75A	380-30
N69LD	**650**	**0080**
(N69LJ)	25	052
(N69LL)	24	051
N69ME	551	282
N69ME	STR	5076/17
N69MT	STR	5107
N69NG	G2	69
N69PC	D1A	A010SA
N69PS	35	014
N69R	50	116
N69SB	**125**	**257177**
(N69SF)	24D	246
N69SF	G2	52
N69TP	STR	5002
N69VC	**650**	**0079**
N69WJ	**10**	**60**
N69WW	WWD	51
N69X	**MSP**	**090**
N69XW	24D	251
N70AA	501	619
N70AE	**31A**	**188**
N70AF	50	116
N70AF	50	21
N70AF	S550	0067
N70AG	G3	376
N70AG	**G4**	**1120**
N70AJ	AST	054
N70AP	125	25271
N70AR	125	257144
N70BC	S40	282-132
N70BG	**501**	**387**
N70BH	125	25280
N70BJ	**400A**	**RK-39**
N70BR	**560**	**0478**

N70CA	**500**	**234**
N70CA	WWD	231
N70CE	25B	142
N70CG	**501**	**576**
N70CK	**20**	**128/436**
N70CN	35A	277
N70CS	WWD	88
N70DJ	600	1070
N70DJ	**650**	**0058**
N70EW	900	25
N70FC	125	257145
N70FJ	50	236
N70FJ	50	51
N70FJ	900	20
N70FL	50	144
N70FL	**50**	**95**
N70GA	D1A	A071SA
N70GM	550	135
N70HB	125	25043
(N70HC)	551	428
N70HC	75	370-8
N70HF	**125**	**257082**
N70HJ	25	049
N70HL	**S60**	**306-102**
N70HS	**900**	**140**
(N70HW)	525	0070
N70JC	125	25203
N70JC	24	051
N70JF	**25D**	**278**
N70KM	75A	380-52
N70KS	**2xx**	**14**
N70KW	**525**	**0050**
N70LF	**90X**	**9**
N70LG	20	319
(N70LW)	S60	306-142
N70LY	125	25244
N70MD	20	153
N70MG	**500**	**063**
N70MP	25	051
N70NE	**125**	**258107**
N70NE	20	399
N70NF	20	399
N70NR	75	370-3
N70PA	20	173
(N70PB)	500	248
N70PC	**550**	**664**
(N70PH)	550	327
N70PL	**20**	**247**
N70PM	125	257141
N70PM	125	257147
N70PM	125	258238
N70PN	125	257147
N70PS	**700**	**9012**
N70PS	G3	327
N70PS	G4	1058
N70PT	650	0187
N70RL	24	106
N70SE	25D	323
N70SK	125	257098
N70SK	125	258006
N70SK	**25**	**049**
N70SL	S40	282-70
N70TF	**500**	**274**
N70TF	80A	380-17
N70TG	500	308
N70TG	560	0069
N70TH	200	509
N70TH	**900**	**117**
N70TJ	**24B**	**199**
N70TP	STR	5005
(N70TP)	STR	5019
N70TP	STR	5156
N70TR	525	0014
N70TS	10	63
N70TT	650	0029
N70U	**20**	**399**
N70U	500	304
N70UP	36A	040
N70UT	36A	040
N70VP	501	444
N70VT	**D1A**	**A085SA**
(N70WA)	25B	142
(N70WA)	500	192
N70WA	**500**	**320**
N70WC	10	140
N70WP	501	512
N70WW	35	055
(N70WW)	WWD	283
N70X	**125**	**257011**
N70X	550	008
N70XA	**550**	**008**
N70XX	**D1A**	**A052SA**
N71A	35A	352
N71AX	**25D**	**353**
N71BH	125	25281
N71BL	125	25084
N71CC	**S60**	**306-71**
N71CD	S60	306-26
N71CE	25B	136
(N71CG)	550	254
N71CJ	550	071
N71CK	**36A**	**035**
N71CP	20	89
N71CW	HFB	1026
N71DL	HFB	1026
N71DM	25C	129
N71E	35A	306
N71EM	S550	0006
N71FE	400A	RK-16
N71FJ	50	54
N71FM	550	083
N71FM	S550	0006
N71GA	400	RJ-35
N71GH	**D1A**	**A071SA**
N71GW	**525**	**0059**
N71HB	500	275
N71HS	**35A**	**287**
N71JC	31	008
N71JJ	560	0480
N71L	**501**	**646**
N71LA	35	012
(N71LA)	G4	1238
N71LG	**35**	**019**
N71LJ	23	071
N71LP	**501**	**487**
N71LP	551	278
N71M	**10**	**88**
N71M	100	208
N71M	600	1077
N71M	WWD	192
N71MA	**125**	**257107**
N71MH	**35A**	**469**
N71MT	**125**	**258230**
N71NK	560	0040
N71NK	**650**	**7106**
N71NP	125	258041
N71PG	**36**	**013**
N71RB	25B	158
N71RB	S65	465-14
N71RC	500	184
(N71RL)	550	074
N71RP	G2	199/19
N71RP	**G4**	**1222**
N71TH	50	196
N71TH	900	105
N71TJ	10	105
N71TJ	G2	29
N71TJ	G3	300
N71TJ	G4	1042
N71TP	35	014
N71TP	36A	030
N71TP	55	032
N71TP	G2	195
(N71UF)	STR	5037/24
N71WF	**WWD**	**442**
N71WS	G2	232
N72AM	**S550**	**0004**
N72AX	25D	346
(N72B)	550	393
N72BB	10	173
N72BB	20	59
N72BC	500	270
N72BH	125	25282
(N72BJ)	400A	RK-72
N72CD	25	023
N72CK	**35A**	**165**
N72CT	**560**	**0072**
N72CT	STR	5007/45
N72DA	**35A**	**098**
N72DJ	**500**	**072**
N72ET	20	52
N72ET	55	072
N72ET	WWD	180
N72EU	10	13
N72FC	**560**	**0347**
(N72FE)	560	0072
N72FJ	50	58
N72FL	550	249
N72FL	**AST**	**018**
N72FP	24	137
N72GW	10	37
N72GW	**STR**	**5205**
N72HA	125	25249
N72HB	WWD	254
N72HC	125	25287
N72HT	125	25249
N72HT	STR	5134/50
N72JF	**35A**	**088**
N72JM	35A	183
N72K	125	258141
N72K	550	480
N72LE	35A	237
N72LE	**650**	**0063**
N72LL	**35A**	**275**
N72LT	WWD	180
N72MK	23	066
N72MM	550	187
N72NP	125	258044
N72NP	**604**	**5385**
N72PB	**550**	**0926**
N72PK	G3	306
N72PS	**900**	**18**
(N72PS)	G3	327
N72RC	551	024
N72RK	G3	306
N72RK	G4	1171
N72SG	525	0308
N72SL	550	504
N72SR	**600**	**1013**
N72ST	**650**	**0072**
(N72TB)	35	014
N72TC	551	282
N72TC	WWD	4
N72TJ	35A	172
N72TP	25B	168
N72TP	35A	140
(N72TP)	55	032
N72TQ	**WWD**	**4**
N72U	550	480
N72WC	500	281
N72WC	S550	0037
N72WE	550	720
N72WS	**90X**	**14**
N73AW	**G2**	**109**
N73B	10	23
N73B	**10**	**79**
N73BE	**400**	**RJ-15**
N73BH	125	25283
N73BL	400	RJ-15
N73BL	**400A**	**RK-71**
N73CE	**23**	**068**
N73CL	**WWD**	**365**
N73DJ	**25D**	**273**
N73DR	**S40**	**282-120**
N73FJ	50	55
N73FW	501	562
N73G	125	257150
N73G	S60	306-8
(N73GB)	WWD	294
N73GH	**50**	**261**
N73GP	**55B**	**127**
N73GR	S60	306-8
N73HB	500	256
N73HG	24	137
N73HM	**400A**	**RK-70**
N73HP	S40	282-120
N73JA	125	256065
N73JH	125	25203
N73JT	23	064
N73KH	**560**	**0220**
N73LJ	**25B**	**138**
N73LL	500	287
N73LP	**35A**	**604**
N73LP	G2	119/22
N73M	G2	128
N73M	**G5**	**547**
N73ME	**560**	**0108**
N73MG	G2	247
N73MP	**500**	**164**
N73PC	S40	282-11
N73PM	125	257167
N73PM	**525**	**0287**
N73PS	24B	186
N73RP	G3	491
N73RP	**G5**	**529**
N73SK	**501**	**679**
N73ST	**550**	**113**
N73TF	500	256
N73TJ	10	163
N73TJ	35	042
N73TP	35	014
N73TP	55	048
N73TW	**25C**	**181**
N73UP	**125**	**258473**
N73WC	500	213
N73WC	500	338
N73WE	55	073
N73WF	**125**	**258141**
N74A	**G2**	**36/3**
N74AB	S60	306-92
N74AG	STR	5072/23
N74AG	WWD	339
N74B	125	25276
N74B	**125**	**257014**
N74BH	125	25284
N74BJ	50	237
N74BJ	S550	0041
N74BS	**S60**	**306-64**
N74FC	500	196
N74FH	**501**	**525**
N74FS	**900**	**85**
N74G	25B	174
N74G	**550**	**042**
N74GL	55	074
N74GM	**WWD**	**74**
N74GR	**601**	**3001**
N74GR	WWD	218
N74HH	**G2**	**74**
N74JA	125	257079
N74JA	550	349
N74JA	**600**	**1060**
(N74JE)	125	257079
N74JK	G2	157
N74JK	G2	49
N74JL	25B	101
N74JL	35A	396
N74JM	WWD	299
N74JN	550	349
N74KV	551	324
N74LL	**500**	**212**
N74LM	600	1069
N74LM	**S550**	**0041**
N74MB	35	004
N74MB	S40	282-112
N74MG	550	302
N74MG	S40	282-102
N74MJ	35	004
N74MJ	S40	282-102
N74MP	35	004
N74MW	23	074
N74ND	**125**	**258063**
N74NP	**125**	**258168**
N74PC	**125**	**258166**
N74PM	501	499
(N74PN)	501	499
N74RD	**25D**	**260**
N74RP	G2	199/19
N74RP	G4	1040
N74RT	125	25214
N74RT	**G2**	**113**
N74RV	G2	162
N74RY	**55**	**063**
N74SP	35A	441
N74SP	550	485
N74TC	550	094
(N74TJ)	10	18

(N74TJ)	125	256015
(N74TJ)	600	1063
N74TJ	AST	063
N74TJ	G2	74
N74TJ	G4	1107
N74TL	560	0048
N74TP	36A	030
N74TS	WWD	174
N74VC	**S65**	**465-17**
N74VF	400A	RK-34
N74VF	**650**	**0156**
N74WA	500	320
N74WF	125	25221
N74XE	WWD	128
N74XL	WWD	128
N75A	75A	380-36
N75A	75A	380-52
N75A	75A	380-57
N75A	80A	380-21
N75AG	75A	380-42
N75AK	75A	380-38
N75AX	**25D**	**270**
N75B	25B	178
N75B	**560**	**0156**
N75B	600	1064
N75BC	**WWD**	**426**
N75BH	125	25285
N75BL	D1A	A017SA
N75BL	S550	0053
N75BS	**75A**	**380-12**
N75C	125	25141
N75CA	25B	110
N75CC	**G2**	**117**
N75CC	STR	5102
N75CJ	24D	279
N75CK	**25D**	**256**
N75CN	75A	380-31
N75CS	125	25190
N75CS	**125**	**258066**
N75CT	125	25047
N75CV	**560**	**0075**
N75DE	75A	370-7
N75DH	35	007
N75EC	550	295
N75EW	**900**	**25**
N75F	550	368
N75F	**560**	**0139**
N75FJ	50	59
N75FN	500	257
N75G	50	138
N75G	**560**	**0140**
N75G	S65	465-71
N75GF	400A	RK-179
N75GK	**400A**	**RK-179**
N75GL	S65	465-71
N75GM	**500**	**169**
N75GM	S60	306-110
N75GN	125	25161
N75GP	24E	333
N75GP	**55B**	**129**
N75GR	24E	333
N75GW	**500**	**257**
N75GZ	**AST**	**075**
N75HL	75A	380-36
N75HP	S60	306-48
N75HS	550	286
N75HS	**750**	**0037**
N75HZ	75A	380-53
N75JD	S40	282-4
N75JT	S60	306-94
(N75KC)	500	187
N75KR	550	075
N75KV	24D	258
N75KV	35A	285
N75L	75A	380-66
N75LM	25D	233
N75MC	31A	052
N75MD	S40	282-129
N75MG	G2	247
N75MG	STR	5087/55
(N75MH)	10	75
N75MN	500	257
N75MT	**125**	**258231**
N75NL	75A	380-40
N75NP	**125**	**258170**
N75NR	75	370-2
N75NR	75	370-5
N75NR	75A	370-7
N75NR	75A	380-53
N75NR	75A	380-64
(N75PK)	35A	464
N75PP	G4	1073
N75PX	500	248
N75QS	125	25190
N75RD	125	25228
N75RD	50	220
N75RD	650	0134
N75RJ	35A	168
N75RJ	**550**	**692**
N75RN	125	25228
N75RN	650	0134
N75RP	G2	199/19
N75RP	G3	328
N75RP	G4	1073
N75RP	**G5**	**528**
N75RS	75A	380-42
N75RS	75A	380-58
N75RS	75A	380-63
N75RS	80A	380-32
N75SE	80A	380-4
N75SJ	**25XR**	**175**
N75SL	75A	380-12
N75SR	G2	96
N75ST	125	257013
N75TD	36A	028
N75TE	**45**	**057**
N75TF	35A	191
N75TG	551	174
N75TJ	125	25190
N75TJ	**25D**	**210**
N75TJ	501	689
N75TJ	80A	380-6
N75TP	55	032
N75TP	**550**	**286**
N75TT	AST	065
N75U	75	370-4
N75UA	75	370-4
N75V	**900**	**13**
N75VC	**S65**	**465-71**
N75W	50	152
(N75W)	900	13
N75W	**900**	**63**
N75W	S40	282-129
N75WA	S40	282-129
N75WC	G2	199/19
N75WC	G2	96
N75WE	**50**	**152**
N75Y	75A	380-64
N75Z	550	236
N75Z	**560**	**0345**
N75ZA	**550**	**236**
N76AE	**525**	**0139**
N76AF	10	36
(N76AM)	500	258
N76AS	**550**	**438**
N76AW	55	036
N76AX	**25D**	**254**
N76BH	125	25286
N76CK	550	345
N76CK	560	0372
N76CS	**601**	**5103**
N76CS	G2	158
N76D	650	0110
N76D	750	0006
N76EB	STR	5093
N76ER	**WWD**	**369**
(N76FB)	50	41
N76FC	S550	0090
N76FD	50	41
N76FD	900	41
N76FJ	10	58
N76FJ	50	67
N76GL	35	036
N76GP	35	036
N76GT	500	313
N76GT	S60	306-61
N76HG	**STR**	**5076/17**
(N76JY)	501	676
N76LE	D1A	A047SA
N76LE	D1A	A076SA
N76MB	**10**	**83**
N76MB	20	80
N76NX	S65	465-53
(N76PW)	24D	311
N76QS	G2	158
N76RE	500	091
N76RV	24D	325
N76RY	20	57
N76SF	**60**	**156**
N76TA	20	393
N76TE	**45**	**081**
N76TG	WWD	297
(N76TJ)	10	12
N76TJ	**G3**	**345**
N76TR	24E	333
N76TS	20	44
N76UM	**25**	**051**
N76VG	20	233
N77A	2xx	17
N77A	S65	465-1
N77AE	24	163
N77AP	S40	282-37
N77AT	S40	282-109
N77AT	S60	306-23
N77BT	125	25155
N77BT	**STR**	**5113/25**
N77C	125	25123
N77C	125	256038
N77C	**STR**	**5232**
N77CD	125	25123
N77CE	50	21
N77CE	**900**	**12**
N77CP	35A	177
N77CP	50	143
N77CP	500	173
N77CP	G4	1194
N77CP	**G5**	**565**
N77CQ	35A	177
N77CS	**125**	**258065**
N77CU	125	256038
N77D	125	25093
N77D	125	257101
N77D	STR	5097/60
N77EK	**G3**	**363**
N77F	WWD	4
N77FC	35	031
N77FD	**501**	**663**
N77FJ	50	62
N77FK	35A	376
N77FK	55	108
N77FK	G3	363
N77FK	**G4**	**1357**
N77FV	WWD	26
N77GA	**400**	**RJ-5**
(N77GA)	D1A	A011SA
N77GH	24A	116
N77GJ	24	174
N77GJ	501	497
N77GR	20	105
N77GT	10	60
N77HF	560	0133
N77HF	**650**	**7036**
N77HH	WWD	103
N77HN	**560**	**0009**
N77HW	STR	5080
N77JL	**24X**	**286**
N77JN	24B	202
(N77JW)	36A	044
(N77JW)	55	033
N77JW	55	034
N77KT	WWD	7
N77KW	25B	076
N77LA	**125**	**258029**
N77LA	20	319
N77LB	24	135
N77LJ	125	25098
N77LJ	35	014
N77LN	35A	306
N77LP	125	257122
N77LP	35A	321
N77LS	24B	194
N77LX	650	7051
(N77MK)	S40	282-52
N77MR	**24E**	**351**
N77MR	S40	282-52
N77ND	**550**	**005**
N77NJ	**25**	**033**
N77NR	10	109
N77NR	**35A**	**503**
N77NR	WWD	28
N77NT	WWD	7
N77PA	**501**	**639**
N77PH	31A	089
N77PH	550	244
N77PK	25B	114
N77PR	**550**	**244**
N77PY	**31A**	**089**
N77QM	20	75
N77QR	G4	1194
N77RC	500	184
N77RC	550	169
N77RE	500	224
(N77RS)	24D	258
N77RS	25C	094
N77RY	24	137
N77SA	25	018
N77SF	**10**	**141**
(N77SF)	550	078
N77ST	WWD	108
(N77SW)	50	53
N77SW	G2	15
N77SW	G3	413
N77SW	G4	1023
N77SW	G4	1146
N77SW	**G4**	**1207**
N77TC	**125**	**258275**
N77TC	S65	465-10
N77TC	WWD	4
N77TE	35	031
N77TE	**50**	**110**
N77TG	G3	332
N77TW	501	519
N77U	35	031
N77UB	501	644
N77VJ	**23**	**041**
N77VK	125	25051
N77VR	**525**	**0344**
N77W	**125**	**258150**
N77WD	24	174
N77WD	550	193
N77WU	550	193
N78AB	501	444
N78AD	601	5063
N78AE	24X	267
N78AF	24R	233
N78AG	**125**	**25101**
N78AM	**560**	**0056**
N78BA	550	306
(N78BA)	550	368
N78BC	20	341
N78BC	S40	282-104
N78BH	125	25287
N78BH	24B	184
N78BL	WWD	182
N78BR	**650**	**7078**
N78BT	25B	191
(N78BT)	501	478
N78CK	**550**	**345**
N78CS	125	257137
N78CS	550	187
N78D	650	0116
N78D	650	7043
(N78DL)	650	0116
N78DL	650	7043
N78DT	25D	356
N78FA	551	039
N78FJ	50	63
N78FK	55	108
N78FK	**550**	**498**
N78GA	550	083
N78GA	551	097
N78GJ	**WWD**	**310**
N78GL	25D	240
N78GP	S40	282-72
N78JP	S60	306-20
N78JR	20	70

N78LB WWD 162
N78LT 50 75
N78MC 35A 117
(N78MC) 500 150
N78MD 10 18
N78MN 35A 237
N78MN WWD 149
N78MP STR 5095/30
N78NP 560 0107
N78PH 31A 090
N78PH 550 025
N78PP 601 5038
N78PR 31A 090
N78PR 550 025
(N78PT) 650 0187
N78QA 35A 302
(N78QS) 125 257137
N78RP 601 5038
N78RP 604 5338
N78RP G3 328
N78RR S60 306-33
N78RZ 125 25114
N78SD 25D 251
N78SR 600 1057
N78TC 551 282
N78TC S40 282-99
N78TF 550 195
N78WW WWD 349
N78WW WWD 399
N79AD 601 5063
N79AD 601 5140
N79AD AST 029
N79AD WWD 375
N79AE 125 25031
N79AE 20 196
N79AE STR 5155/32
N79AP WWD 375
(N79AX) 25B 118
N79B 125 25228
N79BH 125 256002
N79BH 35A 220
N79BK 501 498
N79BP 10 178
N79CD 551 023
N79CD S65 465-46
N79DD 500 254
N79EL 400A RK-214
(N79FJ) 10 144
N79FJ 50 64
N79GA D1A A023SA
N79HA 10 128
N79HC 125 257063
(N79JS) 36A 029
N79KF WWD 262
N79LS 23 097
N79MB 200 507
(N79MB) STR 5055/21
N79MJ 35A 201
N79PB 10 128
N79PB 10 47
N79PF 50 174
N79PM 200 510
N79PM 560 0459
N79RP G4 1220
N79RS 24X 280
N79RS 500 107
N79SE 550 585
N79SF 36A 041
N79TJ 10 148
N79TJ 125 25079
N79TS 125 25042
N80 WWD 144
N80A G2 38
N80A G4 1348
N80AB 560 0169
N80AB 75A 380-59
N80AG G2 164
(N80AG) G3 401
N80AJ 500 100
N80AP 24D 312
N80AR 35A 454
N80AS 35A 446
N80AT 600 1036
N80AT G3 463
N80AT G4 1151
N80AW 550 197
N80AX 25D 224
N80BE 25D 248
N80BF 125 258012
N80BF 601 5117
N80BH 125 256003
N80BL 100 200
N80BL 35A 459
N80BR 125 258012
N80BS 551 132
N80BT 25D 248
N80BT 35A 343
N80CB 24 148
N80CC 10 18
N80CC 125 25095
(N80CC) 125 258027
N80CC 500 132
N80CC 650 0034
N80CD 35A 215
N80CD 35A 282
N80CD 35A 477
N80CJ 525 0080
N80CK 24D 309
N80CL 125 257170
N80CN 50 105
N80CR S60 306-128
N80CR S60 306-142
N80CS 601 3010
N80DH 24B 191
N80DR 550 142
N80DX 400A RK-26
N80E G2 184
N80E S60 306-58
N80ED 35A 337
N80ER S60 306-58
N80F 900 6
N80FD WWD 260
N80FH S65 465-34
N80FJ 50 69
N80G 125 257131
N80GB 500 094
N80GD 35A 215
N80GD 35A 282
N80GE 560 0187
N80GM 550 208
N80GM STR 5146
N80GP 10 157
N80GR 25B 193
N80GR 560 0494
N80HG 75A 380-19
N80HK 35A 238
N80J G2 160
N80J G3 441
N80K 125 257138
N80K 75 370-2
N80KA 125 257001
N80KM 125 257094
N80KM 400A RK-50
(N80KR) 35A 454
N80L G3 406
N80L S60 306-42
N80LJ 31A 080
N80LP 560 0295
N80LX 75A 380-51
N80MF 501 558
N80MJ 35A 280
N80MP 10 68
N80NR 75A 380-15
N80PG 35 063
N80PM 125 257141
N80PM 125 258236
N80PN 125 257141
N80Q G2 39
N80QM S40 282-23
N80QM S60 306-143
N80R S65 465-53
N80RE 25D 216
N80RE WWD 341
N80RP 25D 216
N80RP 601 3026
N80RP G5 528
N80RS 75A 380-57
N80RS 80A 380-17
N80SF 501 582
N80SL 501 483
N80SM 35A 205
N80TF 525 0076
N80TF 600 1054
N80TF WWD 39
N80TR 50 32
N80TS 10 87
N80TS 125 256013
N80WD G2 88/21
N80WE 50 80
N80WG 35A 281
N80WJ 100 202
N80X 560 5054
N81 WWD 143
N81AB 125 259005
(N81AG) 200 514
N81AJ 20 308
N81AP 650 0082
N81AX 25D 279
N81BA 500 038
N81BH 125 256004
N81CC 501 492
N81CC 550 088
N81CH 125 257212
N81CH 35A 500
(N81CH) 50 47
N81CH 55 032
N81CH 55 036
N81CN 125 257212
N81D 125 256011
N81DM D1A 002
N81EB 501 355
N81FC G2 91
N81FJ 50 70
N81GD 551 267
N81GD 75A 380-54
N81HH 125 257189
N81HH 125 259034
N81HH D1A A013SA
N81HP S60 306-100
N81JJ STR 5002
N81KA 125 257038
N81LB 10 158
(N81LJ) 23 081
N81LJ 31A 081
N81MC 24F 344
N81MJ 500 301
N81MR 35A 622
N81MR STR 5039
N81MW 25D 277
N81P 10 153
N81P 10 31
N81PJ MSP 081
N81QV 125 257058
N81R 50 148
N81RA 525 0194
N81RR 125 25196
N81RR G2 246
N81SH 560 0357
N81SH S550 0146
N81SN 125 258460
(N81SN) 750 0097
N81T 125 25225
N81TC 550 094
N81TC 650 0039
N81TF 550 136
N81TJ 10 187
N81TJ 400A RK-14
N81TJ 550 242
N81TJ D1A A081SA
(N81TT) 400A RK-65
N81TT 650 0029
N81TX 10 81
N81U 50 148
N81WT 24E 351
N82 WWD 142
N82A 20 205
N82A 600 1072
N82A G3 342
N82A G4 1068
N82AE G3 342
N82AF 80A 380-21
N82AJ 501 428
N82AT 2xx 51
N82AT F502 312
N82AX 25D 301
N82BG 750 0082
N82BH 125 256001
(N82BL) 125 258126
(N82BR) G4 1082
(N82CF) 500 330
N82CF S40 282-100
N82CG 10 167
N82CK G2 64/27
N82CN 600 1050
N82CR 100 183
N82CR S65 465-49
N82CS D1A A040SA
N82CT D1A A012SA
(N82CW) 560 0342
N82CW 600 1050
N82CW 604 5395
N82FJ 50 72
N82GA 35A 071
N82GA 550 448
N82GL 35A 477
N82HH WWD 383
N82JA 55 029
N82JC WWD 82
N82JJ 550 223
N82JL 35A 380
N82JT 500 208
N82KK 31A 054
N82LP 50 18
N82LS 501 681
N82MA 550 0891
N82MD 10 77
N82MJ 500 377
N82ML S40 282-83
N82MP 50 42
N82MW S60 306-76
N82NC 50 94
N82P 501 612
N82PP 125 256001
N82R S40 282-131
N82RP 125 256001
N82RP 50 18
N82RP 551 139
N82RP 900 116
N82RT AST 036
N82RZ 551 139
N82SE 500 346
N82SR 20 83
N82SR STR 5082/36
N82TC 650 0040
N82TS 25B 154
(N82UH) 25 010
N82VP 650 0082
N82XP 125 258173
N83 WWD 131
N83AB 75A 380-59
N83AE D1A A041SA
N83AG 550 483
N83AL G3 363
N83AL WWD 83
N83BG D1A A018SA
N83CE 23 074
N83CG D1A A032SA
N83CK 25B 183
N83CP 35A 274
N83CT 650 0015
N83CT WWD 321
N83D 20 368
N83D G3 317
(N83DM) 35A 173
N83DM 36 007
N83DM 501 634
N83EA 10 83
N83EA 25D 240
N83FC 50 119
N83FJ 50 74
N83FN 36 007
N83GG 25 038
N83H 24B 193
N83HC 24B 193
N83HF 550 126
N83JM 25B 127

N83KE	**550**	**568**
N83LC	**601**	**5029**
N83LJ	**23**	**076**
N83M	G2	135
N83M	**G5**	**557**
N83M	STR	5084/8
(N83MA)	550	117
N83MD	10	78
(N83MF)	10	78
N83MJ	24D	239
N83MP	50	103
N83ND	501	580
N83RE	**560**	**0183**
N83RG	10	25
N83RG	24X	243
(N83RH)	S60	306-44
N83RR	560	0183
N83RR	**560**	**5007**
N83SA	**D1A**	**A030SA**
N83SD	**55**	**032**
N83SE	550	203
N83SF	550	203
N83SG	**WWD**	**368**
N83TC	25D	315
N83TE	25D	329
N83TE	35A	218
N83TE	G2	129
N83TF	500	256
N83TF	S65	465-43
N83TH	25	016
N83TJ	125	256070
N83TJ	35A	138
(N83TJ)	501	462
N83TK	D1A	A083SA
N83TR	525	0185
N83V	20	366
N83WM	31A	081
N83WM	**55**	**043**
N83WM	60	104
N83WN	31A	081
N84	WWD	130
N84A	125	258010
N84A	G2	122
N84AD	35A	499
(N84AL)	G2	166/15
N84AW	550	493
N84BA	125	258047
N84BA	**125**	**258313**
N84BJ	400	RJ-17
N84CF	501	460
N84CF	**501**	**658**
N84CP	125	25286
N84CT	**125**	**258239**
N84DJ	55	034
N84DM	36	002
(N84DT)	D1A	A084SA
N84EA	**550**	**484**
N84EB	**550**	**488**
N84FA	125	258047
N84FG	**525**	**0192**
N84FJ	50	76
N84FN	**36**	**002**
N84G	650	0045
N84GA	D1A	A070SA
N84GA	**STR**	**5155/32**
N84GC	**550**	**493**
N84GP	PER	551
N84GV	**G5**	**584**
N84HP	**50**	**56**
N84J	24B	184
N84J	MSP	006
N84LA	WWD	378
N84LP	S60	306-8
N84MJ	36	008
N84MZ	G2	77
N84NG	**75A**	**380-52**
N84PH	WWD	314
N84PJ	**750**	**0048**
N84TF	125	25169
N84TJ	**10**	**188**
N84TJ	650	0008
(N84TV)	501	499
N84UP	**125**	**258484**
N84V	20	302/510
N84V	G2	219/20
N84VV	WWD	383
N84W	125	25070
N84WA	125	259007
N84WU	650	0008
N84WU	WWD	383
N84WW	**WWD**	**401**
N84X	G2	43
N85	**601**	**5138**
N85	S40	282-97
N85A	50	92
N85AB	S550	0060
(N85AT)	25B	125
N85AT	500	087
N85AW	650	0084
N85BN	**400**	**RJ-7**
N85BP	STR	5055/21
N85CA	24D	250
N85CA	35A	421
N85CC	**S40**	**282-108**
N85CC	STR	5102
N85CD	24D	250
N85CR	400A	RK-22
N85D	**900**	**28**
N85DA	650	0073
N85DA	S40	282-56
N85DB	20	52
N85DB	S60	306-97
(N85DH)	24X	243
(N85DL)	STR	5089
N85DW	125	258034
N85DW	**75A**	**380-27**
(N85EA)	WWD	201
N85EQ	G2	28
N85EQ	WWD	201
N85F	**50**	**253**
N85FJ	25XR	073
N85FJ	50	77
N85FS	501	412
N85GL	55	116
N85GW	35A	227
N85HP	**50**	**163**
N85HP	S60	306-126
(N85HR)	25B	079
N85HS	**S60**	**306-23**
N85JM	10	85
N85JW	**WWD**	**95**
N85KC	550	709
N85KC	560	0128
N85LB	200	494
N85M	**G4**	**1023**
N85MA	WWD	48
N85MD	50	76
N85MG	550	041
N85MJ	25B	158
N85MP	**S550**	**0016**
N85MR	WWD	114
N85N	20	36
N85NA	550	276
N85NC	55	077
N85PM	35A	595
N85QA	35A	421
N85RS	501	654
N85SV	**35A**	**347**
N85TT	400	RJ-35
N85TW	**25D**	**251**
N85V	20	412
N85V	G2	80
N85V	G3	449
N85V	**G4**	**1172**
N85VE	20	412
N85VT	G2	80
N85VT	**G3**	**449**
N85W	24	135
N85WC	WWD	369
N85WN	100	210
N85WN	**50**	**212**
N85WP	501	388
N85XL	**560**	**5085**
N86	**601**	**5167**
N86	S40	282-86
N86AJ	55	037
N86AJ	55	060
N86AJ	550	0842
N86AK	50	52
N86BA	**S550**	**0001**
N86BE	35A	194
(N86BL)	20	264
N86BL	35A	194
N86BL	35A	422
(N86BP)	STR	5055/21
N86CC	24	115
N86CE	**560**	**0265**
N86CE	G2	109
N86CP	**S60**	**306-76**
N86CS	35A	086
N86CW	**560**	**0342**
N86EF	WWD	222
N86FJ	50	79
N86GC	24X	286
N86HM	STR	5039
N86HP	S60	306-48
N86JJ	501	356
(N86JM)	550	069
N86MC	50	141
N86MD	125	257093
N86MF	WWD	414
N86MJ	25	062
N86MT	501	473
N86PC	35A	108
N86PC	**S550**	**0017**
(N86PQ)	35A	108
N86QS	S550	0086
N86RE	500	331
N86RM	S60	306-89
N86RR	WWD	359
N86RX	**35A**	**458**
N86SG	**550**	**384**
(N86SH)	80A	380-32
N86SK	G2	85
N86SS	500	285
N86TP	STR	5142
N86UR	WWD	353
N86VG	20	218
N86VP	650	0089
N86W	20	298
N86WC	125	257108
N86WP	**650**	**0089**
N86Y	S60	306-44
N87	**601**	**5190**
N87	S40	282-87
N87AC	24B	197
N87AC	G3	427
N87AG	125	257065
N87AG	200	514
N87AG	**G2**	**112**
N87AP	24D	290
N87AT	35A	096
N87B	WWD	104
N87B	WWD	80
N87BA	**S550**	**0131**
N87CF	24B	181
N87CF	550	615
N87CM	S40	282-21
N87CR	S40	282-137
(N87DC)	125	25214
N87DC	WWD	126
N87DC	WWD	14
N87DG	WWD	14
N87DL	WWD	126
N87EC	125	258052
N87FJ	50	80
N87FL	501	664
N87FL	**S550**	**0055**
N87GS	WWD	261
N87GS	**WWD**	**422**
N87GT	10	181
N87HB	G2	39
N87HP	G3	338
N87HP	**G4**	**1219**
N87JL	24E	335
(N87MJ)	24D	301
N87MJ	35A	204
(N87MW)	25D	216
N87NS	WWD	432
N87NY	**MSP**	**087**
N87PT	**550**	**201**
(N87RS)	35A	250
N87SF	**550**	**103**
N87TD	**G2**	**39**
N87TH	**10**	**178**
N87TH	S550	0129
N87W	35A	104
N87WW	WWD	402
N87Y	75A	380-1
N88	S40	282-88
N88AD	WWD	106
N88AE	G2	102/32
N88AE	G3	398
N88AF	125	25285
N88AF	500	290
(N88AH)	35A	421
N88AJ	**550**	**0885**
N88AT	10	73
N88AT	600	1036
N88B	**24**	**015**
N88BF	**S65**	**465-60**
N88BG	**35A**	**090**
N88BM	501	500
N88BM	550	565
(N88BR)	501	553
N88BT	25B	168
N88BY	**25B**	**168**
N88CF	501	465
N88CF	501	477
N88CJ	25	006
N88CR	D1A	A089SA
N88DD	**2xx**	**96**
N88DD	550	263
N88DD	650	0058
N88DJ	**125**	**25153**
N88DJ	25D	234
N88EA	23	077
N88EJ	**750**	**0088**
N88EP	25	019
N88EP	35A	134
N88FE	20	317
N88FJ	50	82
N88FP	25	019
N88G	**560**	**0208**
N88G	S550	0017
N88GA	125	25276
N88GA	G2	217
N88GA	G4	1085
N88GC	25B	088
N88GD	S550	0017
(N88GJ)	25	006
N88GJ	**500**	**155**
N88GQ	25B	088
N88HA	601	5072
N88HD	**125**	**258429**
N88HF	550	126
N88HF	550	615
N88HF	560	0133
N88HP	**G4**	**1212**
N88JA	25D	305
N88JA	35A	118
(N88JE)	WWD	326
N88JF	24A	110
N88JJ	501	356
N88JJ	550	187
N88JJ	650	0169
N88JJ	75A	380-65
N88JM	75A	380-39
N88JM	S40	282-36
N88JM	STR	5011/1
N88LD	10	108
N88LD	**525**	**0181**
N88ME	10	8
N88ME	**D1A**	**A066SA**
N88MF	**AST**	**048**
N88MF	D1A	A066SA
N88MJ	550	088
N88ML	550	219
N88MM	31A	036
N88MM	**501**	**689**
N88MR	125	25013
(N88MT)	501	689
N88MX	125	257090
N88NE	35A	227
N88NE	35A	350
N88NJ	25	008

N88NJ 25D 294
N88NM 550 590
N88NT 20 416
N88NW 500 309
N88NY MSP 088
N88PV WWD 264
N88RD 24B 196
N88SJ 125 25286
(N88TB) 10 159
N88TB 501 353
N88TB 550 271
N88TC 23 022
N88TJ 35A 188
N88TJ 560 0014
(N88TJ) 600 1063
(N88TJ) D1A A004SA
N88TY 2xx 17
N88U 50 83
N88V 60 155
N88WG 400 RJ-26
N88WG 601 5068
N88WL 10 140
N88WP WWD 151
N88WU 560 5039
N88YF 900 134
N89 S40 282-89
N89AB G3 349
N89AB G3 496
N89AE G3 349
N89AE G3 496
N89AM WWD 389
N89AT 25B 125
N89AT 35A 391
N89B 550 114
(N89B) 550 126
N89B WWD 69
N89BM 50 237
N89BM 560 0017
N89D 550 070
N89EC 10 109
N89EM D1A A055SA
N89FC 50 184
N89FJ 50 81
N89GA 400 RJ-60
N89GN 125 257101
N89HB 125 25097
N89HB 31 010
N89K 125 258102
N89KK 400 RJ-62
N89KM 400 RJ-62
N89KM 400A RK-56
(N89KT) 125 258102
N89LS 550 623
N89MD 125 257134
N89MJ 36A 019
N89MM S65 465-30
N89MR WWD 9
(N89N) S60 306-141
N89NC 125 258102
N89PP 125 257098
N89PP 125 257101
N89Q 550 114
N89QA G3 325
N89SC 20 96
N89SC D1A A089SA
N89SR 125 25285
(N89TA) 550 193
N89TC 35 026
N89TD S550 0076
N89TJ 125 257031
N89TJ D1A A029SA
N89TJ WWD 296
N89TJ WWD 315
N89UH WWD 353
N89XL WWD 171
N90AB 10 44
N90AE 50 104
N90AE G4 1068
N90AG 60 042
N90AG 604 5414
N90AH 35 036
N90AJ AST 052
N90AL 35A 222
N90AM 50 53

N90AM 55 106
N90AM 75A 380-25
N90AM G4 1284
N90AQ 60 042
N90AR 125 257107
N90AR 601 5137
N90B 125 256034
N90B 125 257117
N90B WWD 58
N90BA 500 117
N90BJ 550 710
N90BL 125 256034
N90BL 550 682
(N90BN) 125 257117
N90BR 25D 214
N90BS 55 014
N90C 75A 380-46
N90CC 500 076
N90CE AST 043
N90CF 501 575
N90CF 560 5080
N90CH WWD 353
N90CL WWD 324
N90CN 20 299
N90CN 650 0140
N90CP G2 224
N90CP STR 5232
N90DH 24X 117
(N90DH) 25B 080
N90DM 10 104
N90E 55 004
N90EA G2 121
N90EB 500 361
N90EC S60 306-73
N90EW 900 27
N90FJ 50 65
N90FJ 50 85
N90GM 75A 380-27
N90GM S40 282-48
N90GS 20 388
N90GW 75A 380-27
N90HH G2 78
N90HM WWD 170
N90J 24 060
N90JD 550 340
N90JF 20 45
N90JJ 550 571
N90KC WWD 339
N90KR STR 5036/42
N90LA 10 47
(N90LA) 650 0011
N90LC G3 360
N90LJ 31A 039
N90LP 35A 236
N90MA 550 140
N90MC 60 130
N90MD G2 241
N90ME 125 258082
N90ME STR 5057
N90MF 560 0060
N90MH 10 110
N90MH 25 006
N90MJ 550 067
(N90MT) 501 509
N90N 75A 380-72
N90N S60 306-12
N90NE 55 075
N90PB 31 024
N90PG 560 0002
N90PM 125 258183
N90QP STR 5232
N90R 50 162
N90R S60 306-36
N90RC 551 500
N90RG 125 25091
N90RK 35A 417
N90SF 550 455
N90SF G3 366
(N90SR) 125 25116
N90SR 400 RJ-26
(N90TC) 25 020
N90TC STR 5037/24
N90TH 900 180
N90TH 900 63

N90TT S60 306-97
N90U AST 030
N90U STR 5057
N90UC 600 1023
N90UG AST 030
N90WA 31 028
(N90WA) 500 263
N90WJ 500 053
N90WJ G3 340
N90WP 125 25032
(N90WP) 125 25141
N90WP 125 256068
N90WR 35 022
N90Z 550 367
N90ZP STR 5055/21
N91AE G2 17
N91AE G4 1053
(N91AN) 560 0111
N91AP 501 506
N91B 550 217
N91B WWD 112
N91BA 500 168
(N91BH) 125 25261
(N91BS) 500 244
N91BZ S65 465-19
N91CH 125 258030
N91CH 35A 021
N91CH 55 091
N91CH G3 405
N91CM 125 257092
N91CR G3 405
N91CV 20 48
N91CW G5 543
N91D 500 343
N91D 650 0151
N91DH 10 108
N91DH 10 68
N91DP 31A 079
N91DV 125 258211
N91DZ 500 343
N91ED 25D 255
(N91FA) 560 0072
N91FD AST 045
N91FJ 50 87
N91HR 125 256046
N91JF 20 14
N91KH 125 256003
N91KH 601 5038
N91KP 125 256003
N91LA 10 47
N91LA 650 0011
N91LA G2 198/35
N91LA G4 1266
N91LE 60 091
N91LJ G3 342
N91LJ STR 5142
N91LS 500 244
N91ME 560 0240
N91ME S550 0132
N91MH 10 23
(N91MH) 20 91
N91MJ 550 111
N91MK 24 162
N91MK 900 36
N91ML S550 0132
N91MT 25D 255
N91MT 25D 363
N91MT 400 RJ-26
N91NA G2 198/35
N91NK 560 0040
N91NL 560 0040
N91PB 100 198
N91PN 25B 091
N91PR 55 091
N91SA WWD 420
N91TG 650 0208
N91TH 900 60
N91TS 20 21
N91UC 600 1051
N91UJ STR 5142
N91W 35A 194
N91WG WWD 112
N91WZ 501 527
N91Y 125 257159

N91Y 20 373
N91YC 560 0115
N92AE G4 1301
N92AJ 500 230
N92B 500 212
N92B 550 471
N92B WWD 32
N92BA 500 207
N92BD 550 588
N92BE 501 464
(N92BE) WWD 428
N92BH 125 25267
N92BL 60 058
N92BT WWD 32
N92C 501 391
N92CC 501 391
N92CS 25D 292
N92DF 24X 117
N92EB WWD 381
N92EC 31 024
N92EC 35A 094
N92EJ 35A 092
N92FA 500 068
N92FD 31A 054
N92FE WWD 286
N92FJ 50 88
N92HW 560 0148
N92JC S550 0115
N92JT S550 0115
N92K 20 317
N92LA 500 338
N92LA 650 0003
N92LA G2 125/26
N92LA G4 1238
N92LJ 31 016
N92LT 2xx 71
N92LT 550 361
N92ME S550 0044
N92MG 55 025
N92MH 20 3/403
N92MJ 25D 292
N92NA G2 125/26
N92ND 525 0186
N92NE 35A 092
N92QS S550 0092
N92RP 125 257022
N92RW 400 RJ-4
N92SM 500 124
N92SS 560 0388
N92SV G2 74
N92TC 24D 268
N92TS 35 035
N92TX 650 0127
N92UG 31A 050
N92UJ AST 092
N92V 25 025
N92WW WWD 296
N92WW WWD 392
N93AC S40 282-109
N93AE G4 1302
N93AG 560 0223
N93AT G2 85
N93AT G4 1020
N93AX 50 181
N93B WWD 27
N93BA 551 555
N93BA 60 094
N93BD 550 454
N93BE WWD 27
N93BH 125 25186
N93BP 24 169
(N93BR) 24D 231
N93C 24D 230
N93C 25B 127
N93C 35A 159
N93CB 24D 230
N93CD 20 161
N93CE 25B 127
N93CK 35A 159
N93CP 20 7
N93CR 125 257117
N93CR 601 3024
N93CR 900 24
N93CT 125 258049

N93CV	**560**	**0239**
(N93CW)	550	096
N93CX	**G3**	**314**
N93DD	24D	236
N93DK	650	0112
N93DW	550	448
N93DW	**560**	**0133**
N93FH	20	161
N93FJ	50	89
N93FR	125	257202
N93GC	125	257195
N93GH	**2xx**	**6**
N93GH	50	252
N93GR	125	257117
N93GR	900	24
(N93JD)	STR	5201
(N93JH)	25XR	022
N93JM	501	569
N93JM	STR	5201
N93JR	WWD	51
N93KE	**WWD**	**316**
N93LA	G2	164
N93LE	**35A**	**592**
N93M	G2	98/38
N93M	**G5**	**567**
N93MJ	35A	119
N93QQ	G2	7
N93QS	**S550**	**0093**
(N93RC)	35A	433
N93RM	WWD	74
N93RS	20	81
N93SC	**WWD**	**90**
N93TC	125	25116
N93TC	125	257025
N93TJ	501	358
N93TS	125	25264
N93TS	125	256018
N93TX	**650**	**7009**
N93VP	650	0093
N93WD	500	220
N93WW	WWD	321
N94	**125**	**258129**
(N94AA)	35A	366
N94AE	**G4**	**1307**
N94AF	**35A**	**094**
N94AF	550	585
N94AJ	**500**	**024**
N94AT	25B	125
N94AT	WWD	288
N94B	125	256055
N94B	125	257189
N94B	WWD	24
N94BA	**601**	**5160**
N94BB	125	256004
N94BD	125	256004
N94BD	125	257024
N94BD	125	258004
(N94BD)	24E	351
N94BE	125	257024
N94BF	125	256055
N94BJ	400	RJ-17
N94BJ	50	237
N94BJ	650	0147
N94BN	G3	391
N94CK	**45**	**066**
N94DE	500	094
N94FJ	50	86
N94FL	**G3**	**424**
(N94FS)	550	015
N94GC	G3	321
N94GP	35A	094
N94GP	**35A**	**411**
N94GW	20	322
N94HC	24	157
N94HE	**400A**	**RK-89**
N94HT	400A	RK-48
N94JJ	24	138
N94K	STR	5114/18
N94LH	**D1A**	**A073SA**
N94LT	**G4**	**1313**
N94MA	500	319
N94MC	10	166
N94ME	550	402
N94MF	550	402
N94MG	10	166
N94MJ	25D	312
N94MJ	35A	394
N94MZ	**525**	**0094**
N94NB	125	258241
N94PK	25C	181
N94RL	**35A**	**096**
N94RS	25XR	141
N94RT	**S550**	**0023**
N94SA	125	257144
N94SD	125	258004
N94SL	501	498
(N94SL)	G4	1087
(N94TJ)	200	482
(N94TJ)	55	005
N94TJ	650	0094
N94TJ	G2	75/7
N94TW	AST	029
N94TX	**560**	**0247**
N94VP	650	0094
N94WA	WWD	94
N94WN	125	258014
N94WW	WWD	394
(N94ZG)	500	163
N95	**125**	**258131**
N95AB	**24B**	**213**
N95AC	35A	433
N95AE	125	258173
N95AE	G4	1016
N95AE	G4	1068
N95AE	**G5**	**562**
N95AG	**60**	**079**
N95AP	35A	471
N95AX	**550**	**253**
N95B	WWD	19
N95BA	35A	078
N95BA	STR	5216
N95BD	**STR**	**5208**
N95BH	35A	078
N95BP	**25D**	**314**
N95BS	25B	180
N95BS	**525**	**0283**
(N95CC)	550	234
N95CC	550	248
N95CC	550	405
N95CC	551	108
N95CC	650	0124
N95CC	650	0140
N95CC	650	0153
N95CC	650	0160
N95CC	650	0170
N95CC	650	0178
N95CC	650	0184
N95CC	650	0193
N95CC	650	0197
N95CC	650	0203
N95CC	650	0214
N95CC	650	7002
N95CC	650	7008
N95CC	650	7020
N95CC	**650**	**7030**
N95CC	650	7036
(N95CC)	650	7051
(N95CC)	650	7059
N95CC	650	7063
N95CC	750	0018
(N95CC)	750	0041
N95CC	S550	0001
N95CC	S550	0036
N95CC	S550	0076
N95CC	S550	0096
N95CK	**25D**	**248**
N95CM	650	0193
N95CM	650	0214
N95CM	650	7029
N95CM	650	7045
N95CM	650	7070
N95CM	750	0020
N95CM	750	0042
N95CM	750	0060
(N95CP)	24E	340
N95CP	WWD	201
N95CT	551	400
N95DA	24X	267
N95DD	24D	251
N95DJ	**525**	**0032**
(N95DQ)	600	1041
N95DR	500	203
(N95DW)	10	85
N95EC	25D	280
N95EC	35A	477
(N95EC)	35A	654
N95EW	501	581
N95FA	**400A**	**RK-99**
N95FE	601	5095
N95FJ	50	75
N95GC	50	176
N95GS	STR	5014
N95HC	**50**	**244**
N95HE	**550**	**713**
N95HF	650	7036
(N95HW)	560	0238
N95JK	**WWD**	**283**
N95JK	WWD	95
N95JR	20	247
N95JT	200	490
N95MJ	501	562
N95NB	125	258244
N95PH	**50**	**194**
N95Q	**500**	**119**
N95RC	S60	306-129
N95RE	501	507
N95RE	501	515
N95RX	**650**	**7035**
N95SC	35	012
N95SC	55C	137
N95SR	601	3050
N95SR	601	3051
N95SR	650	0024
(N95SR)	STR	5212
N95SV	G2	64/27
N95TC	35	020
N95TJ	10	92
(N95TJ)	500	187
(N95TJ)	55	104
N95TJ	75A	380-38
N95TJ	D1A	A024SA
N95TS	125	256051
(N95TW)	25B	124
N95TX	**650**	**7037**
(N95VP)	650	0095
N95WC	WWD	392
N95WJ	100	195
N95WK	**55**	**099**
N95WW	WWD	395
N95XL	**560**	**5095**
N95ZC	60	068
N96	**125**	**258134**
N96AA	**24**	**139**
N96AC	35A	224
N96AE	**G4**	**1024**
(N96AF)	55	026
N96AF	650	0119
N96AL	WWD	385
N96AR	AST	041
N96AT	**560**	**0325**
N96AX	**35A**	**608**
N96B	STR	5049
N96B	WWD	16
N96B	WWD	97
N96BA	501	390
N96BA	WWD	205
N96BB	STR	5049
(N96BK)	G2	213
N96CE	50	139
N96CE	55	033
N96CF	501	529
N96CK	**23**	**016**
N96CM	S40	282-77
N96CP	35A	446
N96CP	**650**	**0139**
N96CP	S60	306-64
N96CR	35A	446
N96CS	550	252
(N96DC)	25D	317
N96DM	35A	186
N96DS	50	209
N96DS	501	437
N96DS	**90X**	**19**
N96EA	500	200
N96EJ	500	043
N96FA	35A	096
N96FB	**500**	**094**
N96FG	**2xx**	**25**
N96FJ	50	106
(N96FJ)	50	99
N96FL	**AST**	**109**
(N96FL)	G4	1282
N96FN	**35A**	**186**
N96G	500	200
N96G	501	444
N96G	**525**	**0034**
N96GD	525	0042
N96GM	**525**	**0114**
N96GS	**35A**	**606**
N96GS	STR	5068/27
N96GT	501	444
N96JA	**G2**	**213**
(N96JJ)	25XR	175
(N96JJ)	560	0096
N96L	20	327
N96LB	900	10
N96LC	**501**	**683**
N96LF	31A	140
N96LT	**2xx**	**72**
N96LT	50	192
N96MJ	25B	091
N96MJ	25C	098
N96MT	**560**	**0032**
N96NB	560	0267
N96NX	**50**	**141**
N96PC	AST	004
N96PM	900	36
N96PR	125	257148
N96RE	35A	103
N96RE	500	331
N96RE	**S65**	**465-52**
N96RS	25XR	175
N96RT	**20**	**159**
N96RX	**750**	**0044**
N96SG	125	25060
N96SK	**501**	**500**
N96TC	501	531
N96TD	501	529
N96TD	550	596
N96TJ	10	96
N96TS	WWD	159
N96TX	750	0009
N96TX	750	0103
(N96UD)	750	0004
N96UH	50	55
N96UT	**50**	**192**
N96VF	25B	143
N96VP	650	0096
N96VR	**100**	**199**
N96WC	20	159
N96WW	**400**	**RJ-34**
N96WW	WWD	411
(N96ZC)	60	068
N97	**125**	**258154**
N97AC	25B	125
N97AF	55	035
N97AG	**G3**	**328**
N97AG	G3	401
N97AJ	S550	0079
N97AL	**650**	**0155**
N97AL	WWD	387
N97AM	**25C**	**071**
N97AN	**35A**	**373**
N97BG	**550**	**427**
N97BH	**560**	**0290**
N97BP	**S550**	**0090**
N97BZ	**50**	**89**
(N97CJ)	525	0183
N97CT	S550	0125
N97D	35A	417
N97DD	**500**	**159**
N97DK	25D	253
N97DK	**750**	**0035**
N97DM	24D	253
N97DM	25	003
N97FB	400A	RK-117

N97FB 400A RK-152
N97FD 501 543
N97FF 400A RK-117
N97FJ 20 105
(N97FJ) 50 261
N97FJ 50 92
N97FJ 604 5374
N97FL AST 110
N97FN 25 003
N97FT 25D 210
N97FT G4 1013
N97HW WWD 312
N97J 25C 094
N97J 55 039
N97JJ 25XR 162
N97JL 35A 310
N97JP 25D 293
N97LA 500 338
N97LB S550 0079
N97LE 35A 648
(N97LT) 2xx 73
N97LT 50 202
N97MC 10 82
N97MJ 23 093
N97NB 560 0399
N97NL S60 306-97
N97PJ MSP 097
(N97QA) 35A 304
N97QS S550 0097
N97RE S65 465-32
(N97RJ) 10 118
N97RJ 35A 367
N97RS 25XR 162
N97S 550 233
N97SC 75A 380-34
N97SC S60 306-123
N97SC S60 306-54
N97SC S60 306-72
N97SH 125 258277
N97SK 500 316
N97SM WWD 307
N97TJ 10 75
N97TJ 35 012
N97TJ S550 0082
N97TS 125 257001
(N97TT) 400A RK-65
N97UT 50 202
N97VF 525 0171
(N97VM) 125 25030
N97WJ 20 101
N98 125 258156
(N98A) 36A 025
N98AA 24D 306
N98AC 24D 298
N98AC 35A 301
N98AD AST 095
(N98AE) G4 1302
(N98AF) 125 257082
N98AM G2 13
N98BD 650 0048
N98BE 550 075
N98BL 60 061
N98CF S40 282-66
N98CG 24D 289
N98CR 601 3024
N98CX 750 0060
(N98DD) 125 258004
N98DD 650 0048
N98DK 24 152
N98DK 24D 305
N98DM 500 296
N98E 560 0103
N98FJ 50 93
N98FJ 604 5374
N98FJ 604 5401
N98FT G2 173
(N98G) G2 24
N98GA 560 0201
N98GC 551 272
(N98JA) 25XR 148
N98JV 60 135
N98JV 60 140
(N98KK) WWD 9
N98KR STR 5048
N98LB 20 298
N98LB S60 306-97
N98LC 35A 077
N98LT G4 1278
N98MB 500 054
N98MD 35A 086
N98MD STR 5048
(N98MD) STR 5098/28
N98ME 501 585
N98Q 500 040
N98QS S550 0098
N98R 20 428
N98R 50 172
N98RG 501 614
N98RH 20 284
(N98RH) 25 040
N98RP G3 328
N98RS 25XR 148
N98RX 550 0869
N98S WWD 73
N98SA WWD 73
N98SC WWD 32
N98TE 35A 317
N98TJ 125 25032
N98TJ 550 669
N98TS WWD 198
(N98TW) 10 93
(N98TW) 600 1063
N98TX 750 0039
N98TX 750 0041
N98VA 35 014
N98VR 100 222
N98WJ 24D 268
N98WW WWD 398
N99 125 258158
N99AA 24D 308
N99AA S60 306-53
N99AP S40 282-128
N99BB 750 0005
N99BC 10 128
N99BC 500 187
N99BC 500 190
N99BL 10 87
N99CJ 525 0333
N99CK 125 25186
N99CK 500 216
N99CK 501 548
N99CK WWD 146
N99CN 551 331
N99CQ 25XR 022
N99CR S40 282-81
N99CV WWD 146
N99DE 551 331
N99DM 24 114
N99DQ 900 137
N99E 20 317
N99E 24B 196
N99E STR 5216
N99ES 24B 196
N99ES 25 018
N99FF D1A A045SA
(N99FF) S40 282-129
N99FF S60 306-83
N99FJ 50 94
N99FJ 604 5412
N99FN 35A 652
N99FT STR 5055/21
N99GA G2 99
N99GA G3 421
N99GA G4 1198
N99GC 125 25149
N99GC 501 369
N99GM G4 1006
N99GS WWD 31
N99HB MSP 102
N99JB 24D 246
N99JB 525 0352
N99JD 125 257148
N99JD 50 129
N99KR 125 25149
N99KT 20 72/413
N99KV 55 122
N99KW 35A 368
N99KW 55 122
N99KW 550 386
N99KW 60 085
N99MC 10 128
N99MC 25B 182
N99MC 500 187
N99MC 500 190
N99ME 35A 185
N99ME 35A 204
N99MJ 35A 308
N99MR STR 5112/7
N99NJ 25XR 220
N99RS 36A 039
N99S S65 465-64
N99SC 125 25149
N99SC 125 25169
N99SC 125 256016
N99SC 24B 196
N99SC G3 496
N99SC G4 1343
N99ST 125 25205
N99ST G2 91
(N99SU) G3 496
N99TC 23 098
N99TD 500 231
(N99TD) 501 529
N99TK 550 621
N99UG 601 5126
N99VA 35A 185
N99VA G2 200
(N99VC) S550 0016
N99VR STR 5161/43
N99W WWD 46
N99WA 10 150
(N99WB) 500 346
N99WH WWD 284
N99WJ G2 245/30
N99WJ G3 340
N99WJ G3 431
N99WJ G4 1139
N99WR 560 0019
N99XR S40 282-104
N99XY 501 369
N99XZ 25C 087
N99ZC 60 162
N100A G2 89
N100A G3 370
N100A G4 1072
N100A G4 1235
N100A STR 5058/4
N100AC 20 366
N100AC 500 195
N100AC 550 403
N100AC G2 75/7
N100AC STR 5033/56
N100AD 500 226
N100AG 125 258238
N100AG 400A RK-150
N100AG 550 404
N100AG WWD 346
N100AJ 24B 186
N100AK AST 062
N100AK WWD 218
N100AK WWD 295
N100AK WWD 302
N100AK WWD 436
N100AL STR 5058/4
N100AQ 500 195
N100AQ WWD 295
N100AR G4 1100
N100AS 20 274
N100AT 35A 436
N100AW 400A RK-150
N100AY 550 404
N100BC WWD 226
N100BC WWD 438
N100BG 10 138
N100BG 10 64
(N100BG) G3 488
N100BP 80A 380-48
N100BX 501 439
N100C STR 5076/17
N100CA WWD 95
N100CC G2 75/7
N100CC STR 5033/56
N100CE S40 282-19
N100CE S60 306-128
N100CE S60 306-87
N100CH 501 628
N100CH WWD 406
N100CJ 501 390
N100CJ 550 182
N100CJ WWD 141
N100CK 10 125
N100CK 100 222
N100CM 500 276
N100CT 100 203
N100CX 550 028
N100CX 550 577
N100DE D1A A016SA
N100DG WWD 76
N100DL 24B 201
N100DR WWD 76
N100DS 550 639
N100DV 50 54
N100EA 24 019
N100EA D1A A089SA
N100EJ 75A 380-1
N100EP 25B 138
N100EP 35A 150
N100ES G4 1135
N100EU S60 306-54
(N100FF) 125 257173
(N100FF) 500 149
N100FF 750 0028
N100FG S40 282-99
N100FJ 10 100
N100FJ 10 3
N100FJ 100 192
N100FJ 100 194
N100FJ 100 206
N100FJ 100 217
N100FL S60 306-46
N100FN S60 306-46
N100FR 750 0069
N100FS S40 282-38
(N100FU) 25B 120
N100GB 125 25022
N100GJ G4 1007
N100GL 35 037
N100GL STR 5132/57
N100GN 20 325
N100GN 20 339
N100GN G3 312
N100GN G4 1007
N100GN G4 1236
N100GP 24 106
N100GP 35 064
N100GS 24 118
N100GU 35A 173
(N100GU) 55 035
N100GX 125 258195
N100GX G3 321
N100GX G4 1100
N100H 100 216
N100HB 550 071
N100HC S40 282-32
N100HE 125 25225
N100HF 125 25183
N100HF 125 25225
N100HG 20 54
N100HG 601 3055
N100HG G3 429
N100HP 500 280
N100HW 35A 403
(N100JC) 500 148
N100JJ 500 192
N100JZ 23 038
N100K 25B 154
N100K 35A 170
N100KK 24B 219
N100KK 35A 420
N100KK 45 065
N100KP S550 0038
N100KS G2 96
N100KS S40 282-104
N100KT 601 5004
N100KT 601 5066
N100KU 550 0813

N100KW 20 168
N100KY WWD 101
N100KZ 35A 420
(N100L) 35A 357
N100LL WWD 79
N100LR 125 25203
N100LR 125 257173
N100LR 600 1064
(N100LR) 600 1069
N100LX 501 628
N100M 20 194
N100MA S60 306-87
N100MC WWD 149
N100ME WWD 206
(N100MH) 125 258137
N100MJ 24 051
N100MK 25 019
N100MN 35A 309
N100MS 35A 138
N100MT 125 25234
N100MZ STR 5149/11
N100NR 25D 356
N100NR 35A 403
N100NR WWD 61
N100NW 100 201
N100NW 35A 228
N100P G2 5
N100P G3 301
N100PC WWD 149
N100PJ G2 5
(N100PM) 125 258027
N100PM G2 114
N100PM G4 1144
N100PW S60 306-16
N100QH 501 628
N100QP 125 256055
N100QR 125 256055
N100QR 600 1043
N100QW S550 0079
N100QX G3 321
N100R 60 084
N100RA 24 180
N100RB 100 198
N100RC WWD 60
N100RG 500 149
N100RH 125 25196
N100RR 10 179
N100RR 50 220
N100RS 75A 380-19
N100RS D1A A029SA
N100S 20 142
N100SC 551 108
N100SC 560 0054
N100SC 560 5065
N100SM 525 0278
N100SN 501 594
N100SQ 24 113
N100SR 20 56
N100SR AST 037
N100SR WWD 127
N100SR WWD 267
N100SV 501 448
N100SY 560 0054
N100T 10 107
N100T 125 25191
N100T 35A 074
N100TA 23 038
N100TA 23 045
N100TA 23 082A
N100TB S550 0137
N100TH WWD 35
N100TM 75A 380-60
N100TM STR 5150/37
N100TR WWD 76
(N100TT) 125 25148
(N100TW) 10 84
N100TW 501 468
N100U 125 259006
N100UA STR 5143
N100UB 10 42
N100UF 20 160/450
N100UF 500 213
N100UF 500 314
N100UF 550 102
N100UH 500 213
N100UP 900 44
N100V 20 75
N100VA 55 029
N100VC 24 140
N100VQ 24 140
N100VV 550 158
N100W WWD 73
N100WC 601 3023
N100WC G2 96
N100WF S40 282-2
N100WG 10 120
N100WG 100 217
N100WH 650 0119
"N100WJ" 50 9
N100WJ 501 376
(N100WJ) G4 1079
N100WK 20 113
N100WK G2 77
N100WM WWD 73
N100WN 25D 288
N100WP 560 0073
N100WP WWD 389
N100WT 550 0858
N100X 23 035
N100Y 125 257083
N100Y 550 0919
N100Y S40 282-32
N100Y S60 306-50
N100YM 10 114
N101AD 125 25284
N101AD 23 093
N101AD D1A A056SA
N101AF 550 732
N101AJ 36 008
N101AR 23 093
N101AR 24D 279
N101AR 35A 610
N101AR 36 008
(N101AR) G2 140/40
N101AW STR 5103
N101BE 2xx 43
N101BG 35A 106
N101BU WWD 32
N101BX 550 229
N101CC 400 RJ-19
N101CD 500 101
N101CV 560 0101
N101CV G4 1230
N101DB 23 070
N101DD 550 338
N101DE WWD 98
N101DL 25D 341
N101EC S550 0006
N101EF 10 157
N101EG S550 0043
N101EU 100 204
N101FC 125 257089
N101FJ 10 4
N101FJ 50 108
(N101FJ) 50 97
N101FU 25B 120
N101GA G4 1109
N101GP 35A 021
N101GS WWD 35
N101GZ 10 47
N101HB 35A 152
N101HB 500 203
N101HB 560 0002
(N101HC) 501 400
N101HC G4 1245
N101HF 125 257013
N101HF 500 203
N101HG 500 213
N101HK 35A 440
N101HK 55ER 101
N101HS 125 25201
N101HS WWD 193
N101HW 35A 403
N101HW 60 037
N101JR 23 084
N101JR 25B 104
N101KK 500 219
N101KK 550 232
N101L S60 306-15
N101LB WWD 8
N101LD 501 462
N101ME 75A 380-70
N101MU G4 1107
N101NK WWD 148
N101NS 2xx 11
N101NS AST 066
(N101PC) 650 0057
N101PG 35A 228
N101PG 650 0126
N101PK 35A 440
N101PK 55ER 101
N101PK 601 5005
N101PP 23 085
N101PT G3 491
N101QS S550 0101
N101RL 550 371
N101RR 501 647
N101RR S40 282-101
N101SK 125 257001
N101SK 600 1033
N101SK 601 5058
N101ST 600 1033
N101SV WWD 110
N101SV WWD 246
N101T S40 282-53
N101TF 10 144
N101US 24F 352
N101US 35A 500
N101US S40 282-7
N101VJ 10 177
N101VS 24B 218
N101WR 25 017
N101XS 125 257001
N101YC 650 0057
N101ZE 20 108/430
N102AB G2 53
N102AD 20 225/472
N102AD 500 280
N102AF 525 0122
N102AR 25 012
N102B 24E 343
N102BT 35A 301
N102BW WWD 165
N102C 24E 343
N102CE WWD 129
N102CJ WWD 78
N102CX G2 102/32
N102FC 550 052
N102FJ 10 6
N102FJ 50 100
N102FM G4 1325
N102GH 35A 105
N102GL 24E 329
N102GP 24 173
N102GP 35A 105
N102HB 550 407
N102HF 500 275
N102HS 501 517
N102HS G2 112
N102KJ WWD 271
N102LJ 60 102
N102MC 400 RJ-50
N102MJ 75A 380-39
N102ML 600 1063
N102ML G2 112
N102MU G4 1145
N102NW 31 002
N102PA 24B 224
N102PA 550 621
N102PS 25 010
N102PT G3 336
N102RA 25D 242
N102RD 75A 380-23
N102RR 25D 308
N102ST 35A 301
N102ST 55 069
N102SV WWD 34
N102SY WWD 34
N102TW 125 25090
(N102U) 25D 371
N102U WWD 230
N102VS 25B 180
N102WR D1A A004SA
N102ZE 20 126/438
N103AD 400 RJ-2
N103AJ 500 072
N103BC G4 1103
N103BW WWD 82
N103C 35A 273
N103C 55ER 087
N103CC 500 103
N103CD G3 418
N103CF 35A 318
N103CJ 125 25271
N103CL 35A 273
(N103EL) G2 119/22
N103F 20 376
N103F HFB 1023
N103F WWD 53
N103FJ 10 9
N103FJ 50 102
(N103GA) G3 455
N103GC G3 455
N103GH 35A 148
N103GL 35A 069
N103GP 35A 148
N103HC D1A A068SA
(N103HS) G3 355
N103JA 500 082
N103JM 10 2
(N103JW) 24E 341
N103KC STR 5015
N103M 551 246
N103MM 10 106
N103PC 501 488
N103PJ 10 148
N103QS S550 0103
(N103RA) 125 256004
(N103RA) 20 54
N103RB 24 106
N103RR 125 25221
N103TA S60 306-27
N103TC 23 022
N103TC 24B 213
N103TJ 10 103
N103VF S550 0046
N103WJ G2 103
N103WV 500 028
N104 125 25100
(N104AA) 35A 178
N104AB 500 402
N104AE 125 257005
N104AR G2 140/40
N104AR G3 461
N104AR G4 1346
N104BK G3 306
N104BK STR 5219
N104BS 55 012
N104BW 25XR 173
N104CE STR 5108
N104CF 501 543
N104CJ WWD 33
N104CT 750 0100
N104DD 10 110
N104FJ 10 8
N104FJ 50 103
N104FJ 900 104
N104GA 24 112
N104GL 25B 197
N104JG 125 257059
N104LJ 60 104
N104MB 24 177
N104MC 24D 323
N104ME G2 178
N104RS WWD 273
N104SB 20 321
N104SL S40 282-104
N104SS S60 306-30
N104UA 500 043
N105AS 125 256064
N105BA 25XR 152
N105BA 550 116
N105BE WWD 415
N105BG S550 0105
N105BJ 23 092
N105BJ 25 062

N105BN	**601**	**5101**
N105CC	500	105
N105CF	501	548
N105CV	560	0105
N105DM	S60	306-27
N105EC	**24**	**103**
(N105EJ)	125	25186
N105EJ	50	31
N105FJ	10	10
N105FJ	50	104
N105FX	31A	086
N105G	STR	5056
N105G	STR	5223
N105GA	24A	116
N105GH	STR	5056
N105GL	24D	322
N105GM	STR	5019
N105GN	STR	5019
N105HD	**75A**	**380-39**
N105HS	**125**	**25031**
N105HS	D1A	A082SA
(N105HS)	G3	355
N105JJ	500	105
N105LJ	**45**	**105**
N105P	**525**	**0336**
(N105SS)	S60	306-27
N105TB	**G2**	**31**
N105TF	**HFB**	**1055**
N105TW	**20**	**289**
N105TW	501	602
N105UA	S60	306-16
N105UP	**601**	**3066**
N105Y	G2	56
N105Y	**G3**	**412**
(N106AE)	125	257164
N106BC	WWD	220
N106CA	24	138
N106CC	650	0106
N106CG	**400**	**RJ-12**
N106CJ	**525**	**0006**
N106CJ	WWD	38
N106CX	**750**	**0106**
N106DM	400	RJ-6
N106EA	501	468
N106FJ	10	11
N106FJ	50	105
N106FX	31A	087
N106G	S40	282-15
N106G	STR	5090
N106G	STR	5217
(N106GA)	D1A	A071SA
N106GC	125	258141
N106GL	35	056
N106GM	STR	5002
N106JL	125	258012
N106JL	STR	5214
N106KA	**G4**	**1373**
N106KC	**400A**	**RK-132**
N106LJ	60	106
(N106M)	24F	348
N106MC	24D	277
N106PR	601	5106
N106QS	S550	0106
N106SP	**550**	**382**
N106ST	**650**	**0109**
N106TF	HFB	1042
N106TJ	24E	340
N106TW	**10**	**84**
N106VC	400	RJ-7
N106WT	WWD	351
N106WV	501	471
N106XX	35A	183
(N107)	550	167
N107A	G2	53
N107A	**G4**	**1070**
(N107AF)	10	169
N107AW	125	25249
N107BB	551	107
N107BJ	400A	RK-23
N107BW	125	25107
N107CC	500	107
N107CC	501	482
(N107CF)	125	258106
(N107CF)	560	0036
N107CF	WWD	181
N107CG	**650**	**0207**
N107CJ	S40	282-12
(N107CR)	560	0036
N107CX	750	0107
N107F	20	378
N107FJ	10	12
N107FJ	50	112
N107FX	**31A**	**102**
N107G	S40	282-18
N107G	STR	5091
N107G	STR	5219
N107GH	STR	5091
N107GL	24D	324
N107GM	**501**	**643**
N107GM	STR	5206
N107HF	**25XR**	**029**
N107JM	35A	249
N107LJ	60	107
N107LT	**125**	**257146**
N107LW	20	368
(N107MS)	25D	362
N107RC	**S550**	**0150**
N107RM	**25D**	**362**
N107RP	**125**	**259038**
N107SB	551	163
N107SC	500	107
N107SF	**500**	**207**
N107T	551	190
N107T	D1A	A012SA
N107TB	**10**	**77**
N107TB	601	5012
(N107TW)	HFB	1057
(N107US)	100	207
N107WV	550	427
(N108AJ)	550	008
N108AR	**G3**	**461**
N108BG	20	403
N108CC	500	108
N108CF	125	258100
N108CJ	**525**	**0108**
N108CR	**525**	**0258**
(N108CT)	501	564
(N108CT)	551	108
N108DB	550	064
N108DB	G2	112
N108DB	**G4**	**1149**
N108EK	**560**	**5032**
N108FJ	10	13
N108FJ	50	113
N108FX	**31A**	**104**
N108G	S40	282-51
N108G	S60	306-102
N108GA	25	011
N108GL	35A	073
N108GM	WWD	221
N108JL	501	526
N108KC	**10**	**8**
N108LJ	**560**	**0337**
N108MC	**500**	**322**
N108MR	10	74
N108NC	20	168
N108NR	25D	356
N108PA	25B	195
N108QS	**S550**	**0108**
N108R	**20**	**108/430**
N108RB	**35A**	**097**
N108RF	**550**	**0805**
N108TG	10	114
(N108TW)	23	027
N108U	S40	282-2
N108W	S40	282-2
N108W	S60	306-132
N108WG	550	035
N108WV	**650**	**0204**
N108X	S40	282-51
N109AF	**125**	**257022**
N109AL	500	037
N109AP	500	046
N109BL	500	046
N109DC	**501**	**595**
N109DM	400	RJ-9
(N109FC)	200	489
N109FJ	10	15
N109FJ	50	109
N109FX	**31A**	**105**
N109G	**125**	**257176**
N109G	G2	48/29
N109GA	**550**	**137**
N109GL	35A	080
N109JB	24	168
N109JC	**550**	**109**
N109JE	60	093
N109JM	125	257101
N109JR	24	168
N109JR	35A	101
N109JR	**60**	**093**
N109JU	35A	101
N109LJ	60	109
N109LR	125	25203
N109MC	35	054
N109MC	**S60**	**306-119**
N109NC	200	489
N109NC	**601**	**5112**
N109NQ	200	489
N109PW	**D1A**	**A046SA**
N109RK	20	66
N109SJ	25D	269
N109ST	650	0109
N109TD	**125**	**258307**
N109TW	D1A	A037SA
N109VP	**560**	**0109**
N110AB	**500**	**262**
N110AE	**35A**	**155**
N110AF	500	262
N110AF	WWD	436
N110AJ	**75A**	**380-70**
N110AN	STR	5092/58
N110AN	STR	5227
N110BR	G3	301
N110CE	20	7
N110CG	10	45
N110CK	500	078
N110DD	STR	5092/58
N110DK	D1A	A044SA
N110DS	**D1A**	**A005SA**
(N110EE)	G3	322
N110EJ	**125**	**257104**
N110ET	**55**	**023**
N110FJ	10	16
(N110FJ)	10	6
N110FJ	50	4
N110FP	25D	274
N110FS	S40	282-58
N110FT	**35A**	**471**
N110FX	**31A**	**108**
N110G	S60	306-75
N110G	STR	5007/45
N110GD	**G2**	**154/28**
N110GL	25B	081
N110H	501	385
N110HA	25B	110
N110J	**10**	**139**
N110JD	35A	247
N110KG	35A	155
N110KS	600	1006
N110LA	**10**	**54**
N110LE	G3	322
N110LE	G4	1153
N110M	10	34
N110M	23	091
N110M	600	1052
N110MH	**125**	**258137**
N110MH	S60	306-119
N110MN	STR	5149/11
N110MT	G3	444
N110MT	STR	5149/11
N110PA	36A	040
N110PM	S40	282-127
N110PP	**100**	**210**
N110PS	24D	262
N110SF	WWD	376
N110SQ	24	173
N110ST	WWD	129
N110TD	600	1052
N110TG	400A	RK-123
N110TJ	20	368
N110TM	650	0141
N110TM	**G4**	**1087**
N110TP	**10**	**123**
N110TP	501	564
N110TV	501	564
N110VW	**G2**	**153**
N110W	24	119
N110WA	**550**	**406**
N110WS	HFB	1038
N111AB	S40	282-70
N111AC	20	111
N111AC	G2	74
N111AC	G3	417
N111AC	**S40**	**282-79**
N111AD	125	25033
N111AD	25B	201
N111AD	S65	465-27
N111AF	25B	120
N111AG	125	25033
N111AG	80A	380-21
N111AG	WWD	199
N111AM	20	111
N111AM	20	250
N111AM	500	135
N111AM	**525**	**0113**
N111AT	500	140
(N111AX)	125	25033
N111BA	**400**	**RJ-11**
N111BB	**500**	**248**
N111BL	25B	130
N111BP	**20**	**111**
N111BZ	650	7068
N111CC	500	111
N111CF	560	0053
N111CT	23	070
N111CX	**400A**	**RK-210**
N111DC	HFB	1030
N111DT	125	25115
N111DT	501	614
N111E	WWD	134
N111EA	S40	282-27
N111EJ	24	105
N111EK	24	105
N111ER	MSP	050
N111F	20	356
N111F	**S60**	**306-126**
N111FJ	10	18
N111FJ	50	115
(N111FS)	500	034
N111G	600	1025
N111G	601	3032
N111G	**G3**	**454**
N111G	STR	5062/12
N111GD	**G2**	**170**
N111GL	25B	081
N111GL	35A	084
N111GU	STR	5114/18
N111GW	24B	198
N111GX	601	3032
N111HJ	24	151
N111HN	WWD	421
N111HZ	**2xx**	**86**
N111HZ	650	7068
N111J	600	1025
N111JD	23	006
N111JL	G4	1111
N111KK	35A	425
N111KK	**45**	**061**
N111KR	500	179
N111KZ	**35A**	**425**
N111LJ	24	127
N111LL	25	021
(N111LM)	25	025
N111LR	525	0222
N111M	20	10
N111MB	125	25195
N111ME	**500**	**146**
N111MP	**25XR**	**139**
N111MS	S40	282-4
N111MU	10	182
N111MU	500	262
N111MZ	35A	125
N111NF	WWD	168
N111NG	**90X**	**71**
N111NL	**G4**	**1184**

N111QP	500	019
N111QS	S550	0111
N111RA	24	179
N111RB	125	25205
N111RB	501	561
N111RE	24	179
N111RF	24	156
N111RF	25B	143
N111RF	35A	217
N111RF	650	7001
N111RF	G2	46
N111RP	24	156
N111SF	25B	189
N111SF	35A	608
N111ST	WWD	114
N111SU	500	119
N111SZ	25B	189
N111TD	**WWD**	**11**
N111TH	500	274
N111TT	24D	237
N111TT	24D	301
N111TT	31	015
N111UB	G2	207/34
N111US	35A	306
N111US	55C	147
N111VP	**560**	**0044**
N111VP	S550	0002
(N111VS)	75A	380-69
N111VU	2xx	99
N111VV	**31**	**023**
N111VW	**2xx**	**99**
N111VW	650	0194
N111VW	75A	380-69
N111VW	G2	153
N111VW	S60	306-44
N111VX	75A	380-69
N111WB	25XR	022
N111WB	**35**	**003**
N111WJ	24	160
N111WM	23	036
N111WR	25XR	022
N111WW	10	165
N111WW	24D	268
N111XB	S40	282-101
N111XL	WWD	34
N111Y	**650**	**0223**
N111Y	80A	380-17
N111Y	WWD	42
N111YL	WWD	42
N111ZN	125	257076
N111ZN	**125**	**258327**
N111ZS	**125**	**257076**
N111ZT	**G4**	**1111**
N112AB	WWD	254
N112AC	WWD	1
N112C	24D	250
N112CF	S65	465-16
N112CH	25B	090
N112CM	**31A**	**078**
N112CP	**500**	**183**
N112CT	20	168
N112CT	25B	090
N112DJ	24	112
N112EB	**501**	**499**
N112EL	35A	078
N112FJ	10	19
N112FJ	50	116
N112FJ	50	56
N112FX	31A	115
N112FX	**31A**	**116**
(N112FX)	31A	122
N112GA	**D1A**	**A012SA**
N112J	24D	237
N112JC	WWD	7
N112JM	25D	250
N112JS	550	032
N112K	**125**	**258042**
(N112KH)	75A	380-34
N112KM	S65	465-34
N112M	125	25207
N112MC	501	404
N112MC	STR	5231
N112ME	25B	090
N112ML	S40	282-136
N112MR	WWD	174
N112NC	601	5112
N112NW	125	258112
N112PG	35A	304
N112PR	**AST**	**013**
N112PR	S65	465-12
N112PV	S65	465-12
N112QS	S550	0112
N112RC	WWD	170
N112SA	550	275
N112SH	**550**	**046**
N112T	23	098
N112TJ	STR	5029/38
N112WC	501	478
N113AK	25	020
N113AN	35A	113
N113CC	500	113
N113CS	**G2**	**95/39**
N113EL	55	006
N113ES	25B	092
N113EV	G2	135
N113FJ	10	20
N113FJ	50	118
N113FX	31A	116
N113GA	AST	113
N113JS	24F	356
N113KH	STR	5152
N113LB	35A	457
N113MR	WWD	126
N113RF	25B	143
N113SC	S40	282-18
N113SH	**500**	**285**
N113T	**S60**	**306-113**
N113WA	50	51
N113WA	601	5068
N114AN	G4	1108
N114AP	400	RJ-31
N114B	125	25196
N114CC	25C	126
N114CL	STR	5070/52
N114CP	**560**	**0018**
N114CX	**750**	**0114**
N114DM	400	RJ-11
N114DM	D1A	A011SA
N114DS	**550**	**334**
(N114ED)	WWD	177
N114EL	550	321
N114FG	525	0307
N114FJ	10	22
N114FJ	50	119
N114FJ	50	229
N114FW	**525**	**0307**
N114FX	**31A**	**119**
N114GA	AST	114
N114GB	23	022
N114HC	**25B**	**114**
N114HC	G2	92
(N114HE)	WWD	106
N114HH	WWD	106
N114JT	24D	318
N114LA	500	072
N114LG	**S65**	**465-51**
N114PC	125	25146
N114PJ	**60**	**114**
N114SN	**AST**	**114**
N114WC	24D	291
N114WD	**125**	**25114**
N114WL	WWD	338
N115BP	**WWD**	**417**
N115CJ	525	0015
N115CR	**S60**	**306-43**
N115DX	STR	5111
N115EL	55	035
N115FJ	10	23
N115FJ	50	121
N115FX	**31A**	**129**
N115GA	G2	45
N115K	20	80
N115K	501	433
N115K	**560**	**0148**
N115L	S60	306-60
N115MA	35A	118
N115MC	G2	137
N115MR	G2	12
N115MR	STR	5111
(N115RS)	125	257067
(N115RS)	G2	9/33
N115TD	**10**	**96**
N115TW	20	91
N115VH	551	375
N115WA	10	115
(N116AC)	S40	282-41
N116AM	35A	116
N116AS	**45**	**078**
N116AS	60	035
N116AT	WWD	288
N116BK	20	175
N116CC	500	116
N116CC	550	116
N116DA	55	116
N116DD	**10**	**41**
N116DD	125	256044
N116DK	525	0257
N116EL	35A	173
N116FJ	10	24
N116FJ	50	124
N116FX	**31A**	**132**
N116JC	**AST**	**014**
N116JD	20	4
N116JR	25D	359
N116K	**550**	**164**
N116K	G2	73/9
N116KX	WWD	87
N116LJ	60	116
N116MA	**36A**	**029**
N116MC	WWD	86
N116RA	**600**	**1011**
N116RM	24B	206
N116SC	**S40**	**282-1**
N117AE	**24E**	**346**
N117AH	**WWD**	**352**
N117AJ	24E	346
N117CC	560	0287
N117CH	25	018
N117CH	35	045
(N117DA)	35A	075
N117EL	35A	486
N117EL	55	061
N117EM	125	256046
N117FJ	10	25
N117FJ	35A	417
N117FJ	**G2**	**229**
N117FX	**31A**	**133**
N117GL	**G2**	**220**
N117GM	WWD	118
N117GS	550	626
N117JA	G2	163
N117JJ	**G2**	**163**
N117JJ	G3	448
N117JL	S60	306-128
N117JW	**S65**	**465-61**
N117JW	WWD	352
N117K	**24D**	**272**
N117MB	S65	465-1
(N117MN)	S65	465-1
N117MR	**560**	**0287**
N117MS	**G3**	**335**
N117PK	**C21A**	**513**
N117RB	**35A**	**154**
N117RH	125	25196
(N117RJ)	35A	417
N117RJ	35A	664
N117RJ	60	056
N117SF	**50**	**137**
N117TA	**550**	**464**
N117TF	**900**	**42**
N117TS	125	25134
N117W	**525**	**0292**
N117WC	55	030
N118AD	**10**	**118**
N118AF	WWD	177
(N118AT)	501	548
N118AZ	525	0118
N118B	STR	5091
N118B	**STR**	**5211**
N118BA	STR	5091
N118CD	650	0118
N118DA	**35A**	**081**
N118DF	560	0118
N118EA	**550**	**131**
N118FJ	10	26
N118FJ	50	125
N118FN	**35A**	**118**
N118FX	**31A**	**134**
N118GA	D1A	A018SA
(N118GM)	35A	314
N118HC	**60**	**067**
N118J	24D	273
N118K	**125**	**258218**
N118K	35A	067
N118K	STR	5107
(N118LS)	23	082A
N118MA	35A	144
N118MP	WWD	340
N118NP	G2	7
N118R	20	385
N118R	**G4**	**1066**
N118RA	HFB	1039
N118SE	25B	118
N118TS	125	25018
N119AC	WWD	119
N119AM	**50**	**226**
N119BA	**23**	**084**
N119CC	125	25225
N119CC	G2	102/32
N119CP	35A	366
N119EA	S550	0019
N119EL	650	0013
N119FJ	10	28
N119FJ	50	126
N119FJ	50	137
N119FX	**31A**	**136**
N119GS	35	017
(N119HB)	35A	307
(N119HB)	50	8
(N119HT)	50	8
N119K	G2	17
N119K	G4	1046
N119LJ	60	119
N119MA	24B	200
N119MH	D1A	A057SA
N119PH	50	8
N119PW	**125**	**259007**
N119R	G2	243
N119R	**G4**	**1008**
N119R	G4	1077
N119RC	G2	243
N119RC	G4	1077
N119RM	650	7018
N119RM	**750**	**0051**
N119SE	STR	5161/43
N120AF	20	16
N120AP	**125**	**258120**
N120AR	STR	5089
N120BJ	AST	026
N120CC	500	120
N120CG	20	384/551
N120CV	560	0120
(N120DP)	501	410
N120EA	G2	28
N120EL	55	067
N120ES	501	381
N120FJ	10	29
N120FJ	200	491
N120FS	20	204
N120FX	**31A**	**137**
N120GA	125	25228
N120GA	125	257014
N120GB	125	25228
N120GH	WWD	58
(N120GR)	55	078
N120GS	G2	167
N120HC	10	45
N120HC	20	148
N120HC	550	577
N120J	24D	241
N120JC	**125**	**257065**
N120JC	S60	306-42
N120JP	**550**	**468**
N120KC	75A	380-55
N120LJ	60	120
N120MB	35A	307

N120MH	**125**	**257053**
N120MH	125	257171
N120MP	601	3034
N120Q	**550**	**372**
N120RA	**24**	**153**
N120RD	501	368
(N120RL)	STR	5155/32
N120S	500	279
N120S	WWD	226
N120SL	**25B**	**120**
N120TC	550	440
N120TF	**20**	**384/551**
N120TJ	50	89
N120WH	**20**	**385**
N120WH	AST	026
N120WS	AST	026
N120YB	**125**	**257116**
N120YB	75A	380-12
(N121AC)	125	25099
N121AG	650	0121
N121AJ	WWD	57
N121AM	20	310
N121AT	**100**	**226**
N121AT	650	0158
N121BN	WWD	14
N121C	550	232
N121C	550	388
N121CG	550	388
N121CG	**S550**	**0123**
N121CK	**23**	**039**
N121CL	35A	083
N121CN	STR	5053/2
(N121CP)	525	0083
N121CP	550	337
N121CS	WWD	43
N121DF	600	1071
N121DF	**601**	**5133**
N121DJ	**20**	**121**
N121EA	G2	12
N121EL	**25**	**010**
N121EU	20	297
N121FJ	10	30
N121FJ	100	192
N121FJ	50	127
N121FM	WWD	150
N121FX	**31A**	**141**
(N121GL)	25	010
N121GV	**AST**	**082**
N121GW	20	4
N121HM	WWD	18
(N121JC)	WWD	121
N121JC	WWD	77
N121JE	**S60**	**306-4**
N121JJ	G2	27
N121JJ	**G4**	**1075**
N121JM	**G3**	**332**
N121JT	**35A**	**311**
(N121JT)	35A	315
N121JW	501	358
N121JW	551	463
N121L	**550**	**0896**
N121LJ	**31A**	**121**
N121PA	**WWD**	**129**
N121PG	WWD	45
(N121PR)	G2	17
N121SG	125	256071
N121SJ	501	384
N121US	55	123
N121UW	501	358
N121VA	125	25272
N121VA	600	1012
N121VF	125	25272
N121WT	20	274
N122AP	**500**	**122**
N122AW	125	25169
N122BS	25B	122
N122CA	20	16
N122CC	500	122
N122CG	24D	250
N122CG	550	411
N122CG	S550	0125
N122DJ	G2	6
N122DJ	G3	374
N122DU	**G2**	**6**
N122EH	S60	306-57
N122FJ	10	31
(N122FJ)	200	507
N122FJ	50	128
N122FJ	50	217
N122FX	**31A**	**143**
N122G	**550**	**122**
N122GV	**AST**	**106**
N122HL	WWD	122
N122HM	**550**	**145**
N122JB	WWD	133
N122JC	WWD	122
(N122JD)	55	050
N122JW	**35A**	**217**
(N122LG)	501	424
N122LJ	31A	122
N122LM	500	122
N122M	**23**	**065A**
N122MM	550	145
N122MP	**WWD**	**390**
N122NC	**550**	**0836**
N122RP	S40	282-7
N122RW	24D	321
N122SP	**551**	**392**
N122ST	**WWD**	**122**
N122SU	**55B**	**132**
N122TY	600	1035
N122WC	25B	122
N122WF	600	1035
N122WF	601	5021
N122WS	**S550**	**0122**
N123AC	125	25122
(N123AG)	125	25122
N123AP	G3	448
N123AV	525	0180
N123CB	24D	232
N123CC	200	488
N123CC	24D	268
N123CC	35A	206
N123CC	500	123
N123CC	60	012
N123CC	G2	69
N123CC	G3	455
N123CC	STR	5208
N123CD	**S40**	**282-23**
N123CG	25D	270
N123CV	**WWD**	**178**
N123CX	500	123
N123DG	**24F**	**342**
N123DM	25B	086
N123DR	**WWD**	**158**
N123EB	**501**	**380**
N123EL	25	045
N123FG	501	534
N123FG	S60	306-90
N123FH	550	468
N123FJ	10	33
N123FJ	100	219
N123FJ	50	129
N123GA	STR	5061/48
N123GF	**550**	**0817**
N123GM	**550**	**358**
N123GN	STR	5123/14
N123H	G2	54/36
(N123HP)	501	611
N123JB	125	25017
N123JB	WWD	37
N123JN	**525**	**0046**
N123JS	25	017
(N123KD)	501	595
N123LC	35A	409
N123LC	55	020
N123LC	55	027
N123LC	55	034
(N123LC)	55	045
N123MJ	**23**	**036**
(N123MJ)	35	051
N123MR	**G3**	**455**
N123MS	S40	282-53
N123NC	25D	325
N123RC	**WWD**	**349**
N123RE	20	150/445
N123RE	24	154
N123RZ	125	25152
N123SF	25B	088
N123SF	501	606
N123SL	650	0134
N123SL	**650**	**7053**
N123SR	550	469
N123SV	24B	202
N123TG	10	37
N123VJ	D1A	A067SA
N123VM	125	25030
N123VP	**550**	**123**
N123VV	10	37
N123VW	24	154
N123VW	24D	253
N123WH	20	426
N124AR	125	257075
N124BC	601	3013
N124BM	125	25101
(N124BN)	G2	39
N124CC	500	124
N124CR	550	137
N124DC	**S60**	**306-95**
(N124DH)	500	261
N124EZ	24E	347
N124FJ	10	34
N124FJ	100	220
N124FJ	50	130
N124FM	WWD	194
N124FX	**31A**	**145**
N124FX	31A	156
N124GA	24X	267
N124GA	550	316
N124GS	125	256026
N124H	S40	282-76
N124HF	24	166
N124HL	WWD	325
N124HM	50	117
N124JB	WWD	64
N124JL	**24**	**127**
N124KC	501	665
N124LJ	31A	124
N124LS	WWD	354
N124MA	25B	118
N124MB	WWD	226
N124MC	35A	453
N124NY	WWD	205
N124PA	WWD	244
N124PA	WWD	418
N124PJ	24	166
N124RM	**STR**	**5078/3**
N124RP	STR	5113/25
N124TS	**24R**	**233**
N124TY	WWD	223
N124UF	**WWD**	**257**
N124VF	WWD	174
N124VP	560	0124
N124VS	WWD	64
N124WK	WWD	291
N124WL	24	157
N124WW	WWD	203
N125AC	600	1072
N125AC	WWD	205
N125AD	125	25046
N125AD	125	257113
N125AE	125	257119
N125AF	125	257111
N125AH	125	257083
N125AH	125	257123
N125AJ	125	25206
N125AJ	125	257077
N125AJ	125	257125
N125AJ	AST	031
N125AK	125	257078
N125AK	125	257129
N125AL	125	25033
N125AL	125	257086
N125AM	125	257075
(N125AM)	125	257081
N125AN	125	257114
N125AN	600	1073
N125AP	125	25220
N125AP	125	257116
N125AP	125	257119
N125AR	125	25220
N125AR	125	257119
N125AS	125	257117
N125AS	**125**	**257188**
N125AS	125	258167
N125AT	125	257120
N125AU	125	257121
N125AW	125	25057
N125AX	35A	415
N125BA	125	257105
N125BA	125	257167
(N125BA)	125	258048
N125BA	125	258086
N125BA	125	258139
N125BA	125	258179
N125BA	125	259013
N125BC	125	257128
N125BD	125	257137
N125BE	125	257140
N125BH	**125**	**25027**
N125BH	125	25236
N125BH	125	25237
N125BH	125	25273
N125BH	125	256007
N125BJ	125	257145
N125BM	125	25023
N125BP	S65	465-25
N125BT	125	25021
N125BW	125	25023
N125BW	125	257057
N125CA	**100**	**196**
N125CA	125	25082
N125CA	125	259019
N125CA	20	208/468
(N125CA)	501	583
N125CF	**125**	**25241**
N125CG	125	257125
N125CG	S550	0116
N125CJ	125	258241
N125CJ	125	259010
N125CJ	125	259014
N125CJ	550	411
N125CK	**125**	**25266**
N125CM	125	25267
N125CS	**125**	**257018**
N125CU	125	256020
N125DB	125	25281
N125DB	25D	371
N125DC	**G2**	**55**
N125DH	125	25211
N125DH	**125**	**25245**
N125DP	125	257188
N125DS	**500**	**258**
N125E	125	25110
N125E	125	256018
N125EA	**501**	**531**
N125EC	125	25232
N125EH	125	25222
N125EM	10	53
N125F	**125**	**25151**
N125FD	**125**	**25123**
N125FJ	10	35
N125FJ	100	222
N125FJ	50	135
N125FM	125	25284
N125FX	**31A**	**157**
N125G	125	25014
N125G	125	25033
N125G	125	25038
N125G	125	25186
N125G	125	25250
N125G	125	257044
N125G	125	257138
N125GA	10	147
N125GA	35A	125
(N125GB)	125	257044
N125GB	AST	023
N125GC	125	25111
N125GC	125	25231
N125GC	125	25238
N125GH	125	25228
N125GK	**125**	**25127**
N125GM	125	259038
N125GP	125	257023
N125GP	**31A**	**162**
N125GS	125	256040

N125GS	125	256055
N125HD	125	25051
N125HF	**125**	**256064**
N125HG	125	25250
N125HH	**125**	**258034**
N125HM	125	257020
N125HS	125	25136
N125HS	125	256021
N125HS	125	256061
N125HS	125	257012
N125HS	125	257058
N125HS	125	257080
N125J	125	25013
N125J	125	25043
N125J	125	25100
N125J	125	25124
N125J	125	25173
N125J	125	25205
N125JA	125	256021
N125JB	125	258089
N125JG	125	25064
N125JJ	125	256021
N125JJ	G2	15
N125JL	25B	088
N125JR	**125**	**25052**
N125JW	125	25216
N125JW	125	258058
N125K	WWD	15
N125KC	125	25021
N125KC	125	25249
N125KR	125	256007
N125L	125	257095
N125LC	125	25033
N125LJ	31A	125
N125LK	125	25121
N125LL	125	25033
N125LM	125	25018
N125MC	S60	306-10
N125MD	125	25201
N125MD	125	25265
N125MD	125	25284
N125MG	**AST**	**032**
N125MJ	20	225/472
N125MS	75A	380-5
N125MT	125	25261
N125MT	125	257192
N125N	600	1079
N125N	601	3044
N125N	**650**	**0129**
N125N	75	370-3
N125N	S40	282-69
N125NA	**125**	**256026**
N125NE	25D	271
N125NE	28	004
N125NL	S40	282-69
N125NT	125	25078
N125NW	**125**	**25222**
N125NX	**75**	**370-3**
(N125NY)	WWD	264
N125P	125	25046
N125P	125	257147
N125PA	125	25263
N125PP	125	25275
N125PS	**601**	**3058**
N125PT	125	25018
N125Q	**650**	**0128**
N125RH	560	0147
N125RJ	400	RJ-25
N125RM	25B	193
N125RR	550	138
(N125RT)	125	25204
N125SB	**125**	**258046**
N125SF	**125**	**256065**
(N125SJ)	125	25250
N125SJ	**125**	**257106**
N125ST	25	024
N125TA	125	257105
N125TB	125	25039
N125TB	125	25053
N125TJ	125	25121
(N125TJ)	125	25231
N125TJ	25D	294
N125TN	**25B**	**193**
N125TR	125	257075

N125TR	125	258132
N125TR	125	258196
N125U	125	257122
N125U	**25**	**015**
N125V	125	25097
N125V	125	257106
N125VC	125	25232
(N125WC)	125	25014
N125WD	25	042
N125WJ	125	256053
N125WM	G2	77
N125XX	**125**	**257075**
N125Y	125	25095
N125Y	125	257098
N126AR	125	257128
N126CX	**60**	**049**
N126EL	55	006
N126FJ	10	42
N126FJ	100	223
N126FJ	50	136
N126FX	**31A**	**158**
N126GA	**D1A**	**A059SA**
N126HC	20	148
(N126JM)	20	28
N126KC	**125**	**258276**
N126KD	**55**	**096**
(N126KP)	500	263
N126KR	500	263
(N126LP)	S550	0026
N126MS	75A	380-16
N126QS	**S550**	**0126**
N126R	**20**	**126/438**
N126R	500	232
N126TF	**550**	**0815**
N127AJ	25	014
N127BU	**551**	**149**
(N127CF)	S550	0127
N127CJ	525	0127
N127CM	125	25241
N127DF	600	1071
N127DM	24	169
(N127DN)	24	169
N127EL	55	035
N127EM	900	63
N127FJ	10	38
N127FJ	100	225
N127FJ	50	137
N127FX	**31A**	**159**
N127GT	**55**	**067**
N127HC	35A	277
N127K	35A	447
N127KC	**125**	**258255**
N127KR	551	163
N127LJ	24	127
N127MS	75A	380-18
N127MW	HFB	1027
(N127RM)	35A	359
N127RP	**125**	**259036**
N127SA	**WWD**	**440**
N127SC	550	127
N127SR	**125**	**257209**
(N127TA)	551	051
N127V	**31A**	**036**
N127V	G2	130
N127VP	**560**	**0127**
(N128AD)	G2	178
(N128AG)	G3	422
N128AP	20	236
N128BJ	24	128
N128BP	**STR**	**5128/16**
N128CA	**35A**	**248**
N128CS	125	257083
N128DM	25	017
N128DR	125	25219
N128FJ	10	40
N128FJ	100	224
N128FJ	50	139
N128FJ	900	128
N128FX	**31A**	**163**
N128GB	**31A**	**074**
N128JC	S60	306-42
(N128JJ)	125	256021
N128MA	28	001
N128MH	125	257171

N128MS	75A	380-26
(N128PE)	601	3065
N128RM	**PRM**	**RB-28**
N128RS	125	258182
N128SD	HFB	1035
(N128TJ)	125	25020
N128TS	**G2**	**128**
N128VM	55	005
N128VM	S60	306-123
(N128WD)	24	128
N129AP	20	242
N129BA	125	256058
N129BA	600	1013
N129BA	S65	465-28
N129BT	**400**	**RJ-29**
N129DB	400	RJ-12
N129DM	24B	187
N129DV	**550**	**404**
N129FJ	10	41
N129FJ	50	141
N129FJ	50	219
N129FX	**31A**	**171**
N129GB	S40	282-27
N129GP	S40	282-27
N129GP	S65	465-50
N129JE	20	113
N129JE	**50**	**127**
N129JF	20	113
N129K	WWD	70
N129KH	S60	306-44
N129MC	**400A**	**RK-129**
N129ME	**24F**	**357**
(N129ME)	WWD	149
N129MS	75A	380-33
N129PJ	560	0235
N129PJ	**650**	**0044**
N129RH	601	5129
N129SP	55	058
N129TC	550	145
(N129TC)	650	0061
N129TF	**601**	**5129**
N129TS	**550**	**346**
N130A	50	54
N130A	G2	34
N130A	G3	322
(N130AE)	125	257089
(N130AL)	500	033
N130B	10	28
N130B	20	88
N130B	G4	1013
(N130B)	G4	1024
N130BA	125	257045
N130BB	125	257063
N130BC	125	257065
N130BD	125	257068
N130BE	125	257069
N130BF	125	257071
N130BG	125	257060
N130BH	125	257059
N130BK	125	257084
(N130BL)	125	257087
N130BL	125	257089
N130CC	S550	0130
N130CE	**500**	**130**
N130CV	560	0130
N130DS	**100**	**218**
N130F	20	379
N130F	**35**	**044**
N130FJ	10	44
N130FJ	10	73
N130FJ	100	226
N130FJ	50	143
N130FX	**31A**	**172**
N130G	500	130
N130J	24	130
N130JS	501	606
N130K	50	70
N130K	G2	190
N130LC	**125**	**258228**
(N130LW)	STR	5048
N130MH	125	257053
N130MR	525	0097
N130MV	**20**	**130**
N130MW	HFB	1032

N130MW	HFB	1033
N130RC	WWD	34
(N130RK)	650	0130
N130RS	**24**	**138**
N130TA	35A	174
N130TC	550	333
N130TS	125	257130
N130TS	**650**	**0130**
N130YB	**125**	**257120**
N131AP	**400**	**RJ-10**
N131AR	**31A**	**139**
N131BH	**S40**	**282-18**
N131CA	24D	277
(N131CJ)	525	0031
N131CV	560	0131
N131DA	**AST**	**029**
N131DB	20	339
(N131EL)	551	463
N131EL	STR	5058/4
N131EP	**2xx**	**10**
N131ET	550	131
N131FJ	10	45
N131FJ	50	146
N131FJ	50	220
N131FJ	900	131
N131FX	**31A**	**175**
N131G	25B	170
N131GA	550	432
N131GL	25B	145
N131GM	31A	164
N131JA	20	282
N131JR	**S60**	**306-131**
N131LA	**125**	**25226**
N131MA	24D	289
N131MS	25XR	022
N131MS	75A	380-22
N131MS	75A	380-29
N131MV	**20**	**31**
N131NA	31A	038
N131PT	31A	046
N131RG	**525**	**0159**
N131SB	500	256
N131SE	S60	306-131
N131SY	501	424
N131TA	31A	041
N131WT	50	28
N132AH	**525**	**0132**
N132AP	**20**	**312**
N132BP	500	132
N132CJ	**525A**	**0003**
N132DB	80A	380-48
N132EL	55	061
N132EP	**20**	**463**
N132FJ	10	47
N132FJ	50	142
N132FJ	50	223
N132FJ	900	132
N132FX	**31A**	**177**
N132GA	D1A	A032SA
N132GL	25B	132
N132JA	20	284
N132LA	**WWD**	**133**
N132LF	**550**	**0855**
N132MA	24D	306
(N132MA)	25	052
N132MS	75A	380-22
N132MS	75A	380-29
N132MW	HFB	1032
N132MW	HFB	1033
N132RL	**125**	**25141**
(N132RP)	525	0132
N133AP	20	345
(N133AV)	525	0180
N133AV	**550**	**0847**
N133BC	550	329
N133BL	**24**	**133**
N133BP	**400A**	**RK-133**
N133CC	500	133
N133DF	24	133
N133DM	501	514
N133EJ	**35A**	**133**
N133EP	**10**	**131**
N133FJ	10	48
N133FJ	10	50

N133FJ 20 133
N133FJ 50 144
N133FJ 50 224
N133FX 31A 179
N133GJ 35A 133
N133GL 24D 317
N133JA 20 290
N133JC WWD 133
N133JF 25D 264
N133JM 500 028
N133LE 650 0133
N133LH 650 0133
N133LJ 60 133
N133MA 25 052
N133ME WWD 50
N133MR 25D 210
(N133N) 500 021
N133RC D1A A016SA
(N133SU) 55B 132
N133TW 24 148
N133VP S550 0133
N133W 23 021
N133WA 550 390
N133WB 55B 132
N134AP 50 48
N134BJ 400A RK-134
N134CC 500 134
N134CJ 20 239
N134CM 400A RK-144
N134FJ 10 46
N134FJ 50 134
N134FJ 50 148
N134FJ 50 225
N134FJ 900 134
N134FX 31A 181
N134FX 31A 195
N134GB S550 0089
N134GL 35 036
N134JA 20 463
N134LJ 60 134
N134M 650 0109
(N134MJ) 650 0109
N134N WWD 134
N134QS S550 0134
N134RG D1A A037SA
(N134RV) AST 047
N134SW 560 5066
(N135AB) 35A 414
N135AC 35A 188
N135AF 650 0135
N135AG 35A 132
N135BC 500 135
N135BC 550 269
N135BC 560 0198
N135BC 601 5080
N135BJ 400A RK-135
N135BK 500 168
N135CC 500 135
N135CC 550 135
N135CK 125 25266
(N135CK) 35A 159
N135CP G2 200
N135DE 35A 667
N135FA 35A 067
N135FJ 10 43
N135FJ 100 224
N135FJ 50 149
N135GA D1A A035SA
N135GL 35 028
N135HC 650 0158
N135J 35A 097
N135JW 35A 144
N135JW 500 140
N135LJ 60 135
N135MA 500 168
N135MB 35A 343
N135MM 525 0038
N135MW 35A 650
N135PG 35A 491
N135RJ 35A 443
N135ST 35A 169
N135TX 35 025
N135UT 35A 327
N135WB 35A 084
N135WJ G2 256
N136BC 550 269
(N136CC) 500 136
(N136CV) 560 0136
N136DH 125 25036
N136F 20 380
N136FJ 10 49
N136FJ 50 150
N136FX 31A 182
N136FX 31A 196
N136GL 35 016
N136JP 35A 359
N136K WWD 103
N136LJ 60 136
N136LK 125 25116
N136MA STR 5134/50
N136MW HFB 1036
N136SA 500 136
N136ST 36A 049
N137AL 525 0002
N137BC 25 024
N137CC 500 137
N137CF 551 152
N137CL 601 5137
N137FJ 10 51
N137FJ 50 152
N137FJ 900 136
(N137FP) 600 1072
N137FX 31A 186
N137GK 501 576
N137GL 25D 237
N137JL 24D 301
N137K 25D 295
N137M 650 0061
N137M 650 0163
(N137MR) 650 0163
N137RS 35A 183
N137S 650 0005
N137TA 200 487
(N137TS) 35A 183
N137WC 500 305
N137WR 125 257035
N137X 650 0061
N138A 750 0021
N138AV 50 138
N138CC 601 5138
N138DM 10 181
N138DM D1A A018SA
N138E 20 382
N138E 50 57
N138F 20 382
N138F 50 57
N138F 900 174
N138FA 900 174
N138FJ 10 52
N138FJ 20 369
N138FJ 50 153
N138FX 31A 189
N138GL 36 007
N138JB 25B 075
N138LJ 31A 138
N138M 50 274
N138M 650 0066
N138M 650 0164
N138MR 650 0164
N138NW 50 138
N138QS S550 0138
N138RC D1A A047SA
N138SA 500 138
N138SP 60 147
N138V 650 0066
N139CD 601 5139
N139DD 10 6
N139DM D1A A039SA
N139F 20 385
N139FJ 10 53
N139FJ 50 154
N139FJ 900 137
N139GL 36 012
N139J 25C 098
N139LJ 31A 139
N139M 125 258330
N139M 650 0149
N139N 650 0149
N139XX 60 139
N140AK 125 25104
N140AK D1A A026SA
N140C 125 25185
N140CA 24B 193
N140CA 25B 140
N140CC 500 140
N140CH 601 5047
N140CH G2 77
N140DA 551 110
N140DR 550 271
N140DR AST 046
N140DR WWD 242
(N140DV) 550 393
N140EX 24X 117
N140FJ 10 54
N140FJ 50 156
N140FJ 900 139
N140GB 400A RK-185
N140GC 25D 225
N140H 500 274
N140JA S60 306-78
N140JC 60 106
N140JS 125 25139
N140LJ 31A 140
N140LJ 60 140
N140MM S40 282-8
N140RC 23 048
N140RF S40 282-67
N140RT 50 261
N140V 550 393
N140VJ WWD 435
N140WC 501 498
N141AB 550 483
N141AQ 560 0141
N141CC 500 141
N141DA 550 265
N141DP 500 120
N141DR 400A RK-184
N141DR 500 120
N141FJ 10 55
N141FJ 50 157
N141FJ 900 141
N141GS G2 245/30
N141H D1A A054SA
N141H S40 282-60
N141JA S60 306-51
N141JC 550 373
N141JL 125 25187
N141LB WWD 202
N141LJ 60 141
N141LM STR 5083/49
N141M 650 0147
N141PB S65 465-4
N141PJ 24 141
N141SG 500 330
N141SL S60 306-141
N141SM 55 019
N141TC STR 5050/34
N141TS 600 1041
N142AB 650 0042
(N142AL) 501 671
N142B 125 25101
N142B 601 5062
N142B 650 0190
N142BJ 400A RK-142
N142CC 500 142
N142CC 650 0142
N142CJ 525A 0004
N142DA 501 356
N142FJ 10 57
N142FJ 50 158
N142FJ 900 142
N142GT 31A 064
(N142HC) 25B 142
N142LG 35A 216
N142LJ 31A 142
N142LL 601 5176
N142NW G4 1142
N142V 10 57
N143AB 650 0120
N143BP S550 0085
N143CC 500 143
N143CK 25B 143
N143CP 125 25224
N143DA 550 198
N143EP 501 357
N143FJ 10 58
N143FJ 50 160
N143G G2 17
N143HM 400A RK-205
N143J 25 033
(N143JW) 36A 043
N143KS G4 1364
N143QS S550 0143
(N143RC) 650 0036
N143RW 550 346
N143SC TRI 001
N143V G2 17
N143WR 650 0143
(N144AB) 501 464
N144AD 50 112
N144AR 501 464
N144CP 24B 185
N144DJ 125 257067
N144FC 25D 258
(N144FE) 20 46
N144FJ 10 59
N144FJ 50 161
N144FJ 900 144
N144GA 550 065
(N144HE) 10 144
N144HM 125 258431
(N144JC) WWD 94
N144JP 500 281
N144LJ 31A 144
N144LT 55C 144
N144PA 125 25224
(N144PA) 24B 181
N144PK G3 447
N144PK G4 1210
N144ST G2 174
N144SX 601 3066
N144WB 35A 444
(N144WC) 23 020
N144X 24A 100
N145AJ 501 425
N145AJ WWD 145
N145AM 35A 078
N145AS AST 049
N145BW WWD 145
N145CC 500 145
N145CJ 525 0145
N145CM 500 224
N145DF 501 425
N145DF S550 0018
N145FC 500 145
(N145FE) 20 50
N145FJ 10 60
N145FJ 50 162
N145G S40 282-65
N145GJ 35A 145
N145JN 24 143
N145JN 25 016
N145K 45 071
N145KC 45 051
N145LJ 31A 145
N145LJ 60 145
(N145MC) 45 040
N145SH 25B 145
N145SM 560 5082
N145ST 45 024
N145ST 601 5104
N145ST G2 22
N145ST G4 1067
N145TA 500 145
N145W 50 31
N145W 900 40
N145WF 50 31
N145XL 45 106
(N146BE) 500 160
N146BF 500 160
N146BF WWD 287
(N146BJ) S60 306-146
N146CF 200 488
(N146FE) 20 20
N146FJ 10 62
N146FJ 50 163

N146FJ	900	146
N146GA	D1A	A044SA
(N146GA)	D1A	A046SA
N146J	WWD	313
N146JB	400	RJ-46
N146JC	500	160
N146LJ	25C	146
N146MJ	36A	046
N146TA	400A	RK-146
N147A	**WWD**	**294**
N147BJ	**400A**	**RK-147**
N147BP	25B	147
N147CC	400	RJ-38
N147CC	400A	RK-4
N147CC	60	012
N147CF	S40	282-94
N147CG	400A	RK-4
N147DA	500	009
N147DA	D1A	A038SA
N147DB	500	009
(N147FE)	20	108/430
N147FJ	10	63
N147FJ	900	147
N147G	**100**	**214**
N147JK	WWD	147
N147K	35A	462
N147PS	550	483
N147PS	**650**	**0119**
N147RJ	**560**	**0147**
(N147RP)	551	428
N147SC	**500**	**077**
N147TA	200	506
N147TW	**25**	**023**
N147VC	560	0105
N147VC	560	0285
N147WC	D1A	A038SA
N147WS	500	009
N147X	**20**	**185/467**
N147X	20	45
N148C	**31A**	**098**
N148C	650	0028
N148CJ	**525**	**0148**
N148DR	550	271
N148E	WWD	22
N148EA	501	542
N148ED	**501**	**542**
(N148FE)	20	151
N148FJ	10	64
N148FJ	900	148
N148H	**WWD**	**206**
N148J	24D	291
N148JB	501	517
N148JP	S60	306-90
N148JS	501	517
N148JW	25D	357
N148LJ	31A	148
N148M	**50**	**270**
N148MC	**20**	**428**
N148N	650	0147
N148PE	STR	5002
N148TW	**20**	**148**
N148WC	20	148
N148X	**35A**	**299**
(N149BP)	WWD	149
N149C	650	0070
N149F	20	386
(N149FE)	20	132
N149FJ	10	65
N149GU	G4	1149
N149HP	10	154
N149J	25B	149
N149JW	G2	63
N149LJ	60	149
N149MC	**20**	**429**
N149MD	50	149
N149PJ	500	149
N149QS	S550	0149
N149SF	**WWD**	**149**
N149TA	400A	RK-149
N149TJ	10	9
N149VB	125	258142
N149VB	**2xx**	**53**
N149VG	560	0105
N149VP	125	258142
N150AB	24B	228
N150AG	23	074
N150BC	**2xx**	**67**
N150BG	50	13
N150BP	**50**	**82**
N150BV	**525**	**0320**
N150CA	**125**	**257121**
N150CC	500	150
N150CG	20	8
N150CJ	S550	0150
N150CM	G4	1284
N150CM	WWD	71
N150CT	WWD	71
N150DM	550	452
N150F	**650**	**0150**
(N150FE)	20	84
N150FJ	10	66
N150FJ	900	150
N150GX	G3	318
N150GX	G4	1154
N150GX	G4	1197
N150HE	550	129
N150HN	S65	465-42
N150HR	550	129
N150HR	WWD	170
N150HR	WWD	71
N150JP	50	44
N150JP	**650**	**7010**
N150JT	**50**	**40**
N150JT	50	53
N150K	**50**	**108**
N150MH	**601**	**3021**
N150MS	**55**	**049**
N150NE	**55**	**123**
(N150NW)	50	13
N150PG	G4	1154
N150QX	G3	318
N150RD	**550**	**158**
(N150RH)	125	257083
N150RK	G3	318
N150RM	**501**	**451**
N150RS	**25XR**	**162**
N150S	**560**	**0476**
N150SA	**125**	**25265**
N150TJ	501	422
N150TT	**500**	**176**
N150TX	**50**	**13**
N150UC	**50**	**86**
N150WC	50	47
N150WL	24A	011
N150WW	25B	147
N151A	G4	1026
N151AE	125	257089
N151AE	**2xx**	**39**
N151AG	**24**	**137**
N151AG	24D	298
N151CC	500	151
N151CC	601	5167
N151CG	20	15
N151CR	WWD	33
(N151DC)	10	181
N151DD	S550	0001
N151DR	650	0147
N151FJ	10	67
N151G	G4	1150
N151GS	10	181
N151GX	G4	1154
N151JC	550	477
N151KD	**PRM**	**RB-16**
N151MZ	G3	426
N151PJ	55	074
(N151PR)	551	191
N151Q	S550	0151
N151QS	S550	0151
N151SD	**G2**	**81**
N151SG	**125**	**25035**
N151SP	**501**	**384**
N151SP	D1A	A046SA
(N151SR)	600	1034
N151TB	**80A**	**380-11**
(N151TT)	525	0151
N151WC	10	163
N151WW	**24**	**170**
N152A	**G4**	**1036**
N152AE	125	257164
N152AG	23	068
N152CC	500	152
N152FJ	10	68
N152GA	550	006
N152GS	STR	5061/48
N152JC	550	433
(N152JQ)	550	433
N152KB	G4	1149
N152KC	525	0152
N152KV	**525**	**0152**
N152NS	**125**	**258191**
N152RG	G2	45
N152SM	600	1077
N152TJ	35A	243
(N152VP)	650	0152
N152WJ	10	152
N153AG	**23**	**058**
N153BJ	400A	RK-153
N153BR	24	153
N153FJ	10	69
N153FJ	900	153
N153G	S40	282-26
(N153G)	S40	282-48
N153H	24	151
N153JP	**500**	**153**
N153NS	**601**	**5056**
N153QS	S550	0153
N153RA	G4	1050
N153SR	600	1034
N153TW	**25**	**053**
(N153VP)	560	0153
N153WB	500	153
N154	125	25236
N154AG	**23**	**034**
N154BA	601	5154
N154C	**G2**	**253**
N154CC	501	687
N154CC	650	0154
N154DD	AST	029
N154FJ	10	72
N154G	500	110
N154G	**G4**	**1044**
N154GA	D1A	A045SA
N154JD	125	257032
N154JS	125	257032
N154NS	**601**	**5169**
N154PA	**50**	**154**
N154SC	**501**	**558**
(N154SV)	560	0154
N154TR	125	25084
N154VP	**560**	**0154**
N154X	G2	12
N155AC	**550**	**573**
N155AG	**25**	**037**
(N155AJ)	55	013
N155AM	**35A**	**131**
N155AU	25D	218
N155AV	**STR**	**5104/6**
N155BC	**55**	**115**
N155BT	24	168
N155BT	550	170
N155CA	500	191
(N155CD)	55	030
N155CJ	525	0155
N155CS	55	033
N155DB	**55C**	**141**
N155DD	**55**	**004**
N155EC	S60	306-20
N155FJ	10	73
N155GB	**S550**	**0155**
N155GM	**55**	**022**
N155GM	S40	282-90
N155GS	55	088
N155HM	55	036
N155J	**24B**	**182**
(N155JC)	55	055
N155JC	**55**	**071**
(N155JC)	55	076
N155JK	550	208
N155JT	55ER	107
N155LJ	55B	133
N155LP	55	055
N155ME	**WWD**	**391**
N155MM	**G3**	**325**
N155MP	55	014
N155NK	20	107
N155PJ	55	041
N155PL	55B	133
N155PS	55C	136
N155PT	550	170
N155PT	**560**	**0257**
N155QS	S550	0155
N155RB	**55**	**117**
N155SB	**55**	**013**
N155SC	55	121
N155SP	**55C**	**137**
N155T	125	258149
N155TA	551	204
N155TD	35A	335
N155TJ	550	175
(N155UT)	55	071
N155VW	WWD	123
N155WL	35A	326
(N156AG)	23	065A
N156CB	25B	101
N156CW	WWD	204
N156EC	**31A**	**060**
N156FJ	10	74
N156GA	D1A	A056SA
N156JC	**55**	**056**
N156JS	**31**	**033A**
(N156K)	125	257121
N156ML	**525**	**0156**
N156N	550	093
N156PH	**45**	**027**
N156QS	S550	0156
N156SC	31A	060
N156X	10	30
N157AE	**560**	**5017**
N157AG	**24D**	**252**
(N157AT)	S40	282-102
(N157BP)	24	157
N157CA	25B	157
N157CB	28	003
N157CM	650	7057
N157DJ	35A	157
N157EA	10	157
N157FJ	10	75
N157FJ	900	157
N157H	125	258033
N157H	**G4**	**1209**
(N157JA)	10	157
N157JF	STR	5149/11
N157JF	WWD	8
N157JS	**31**	**033D**
N157LH	G2	228
N157PH	**45**	**030**
N157QP	STR	5149/11
N157QS	**S550**	**0157**
N157SP	50	176
N157TW	**24**	**157**
N158AF	**G5**	**506**
N158AG	**125**	**25155**
N158DP	STR	5013
N158FJ	10	77
N158FJ	900	158
N158GL	25B	158
N158JA	900	131
N158JA	**90X**	**20**
(N158JJ)	G5	534
(N158JS)	125	257032
N158JS	**31**	**033C**
N158M	**50**	**273**
N158MJ	23	033
N158MJ	35A	158
N158NE	35A	158
N158PH	**45**	**047**
N158QS	S550	0158
(N158RA)	G5	522
(N158TJ)	500	158
N158TW	**20**	**158/449**
N159B	G2	190
N159B	G3	380
N159B	STR	5011/1
N159DP	WWD	52
N159FC	20	45
N159FJ	10	78

Registration	Type	No.
N159J	24	153
N159LC	**501**	**488**
N159M	**50**	**276**
N159M	650	0130
N159MP	WWD	52
N159MR	650	0130
N159NB	**G2**	**140/40**
N159RA	125	258155
N159YC	WWD	52
N160AG	**125**	**25160**
N160AT	35	031
N160BA	125	259035
N160CF	S60	306-3
N160D	551	162
N160FJ	10	79
(N160GC)	24D	295
N160GC	**36A**	**030**
N160H	**D1A**	**A084SA**
N160J	25B	076
N160JS	500	250
N160LC	**600**	**1068**
N160NE	**55C**	**147**
N160NW	**125**	**258160**
N160RW	S60	306-16
N160S	D1A	A084SA
N160SP	550	660
N160TC	S40	282-83
N160TJ	10	107
N160TL	55	042
N160VE	550	281
N160W	**S40**	**282-101**
(N160WC)	125	257090
N160WC	**125**	**258069**
N160WC	20	140
N160WC	G2	12
N160WC	WWD	141
N161AC	25D	230
N161BA	125	259036
N161BH	550	048
N161CB	501	595
N161CC	**500**	**161**
N161CC	650	0161
N161CM	**S60**	**306-5**
N161EU	20	485
N161FJ	10	80
N161G	125	257151
N161GS	STR	5061/48
(N161KK)	500	219
N161LM	STR	5005
N161LM	STR	5083/49
N161MA	35A	610
N161MM	125	257151
N161MM	125	258061
N161MM	**604**	**5416**
N161RB	25D	294
N161TM	**550**	**0867**
N161WC	**125**	**257090**
N161WC	500	117
N161WT	20	478
N161X	WWD	133
N161X	**WWD**	**234**
N162A	125	25183
N162A	125	257012
(N162AC)	25C	126
N162BA	125	258236
N162CC	551	162
N162CT	20	162/451
N162D	125	25183
N162DW	550	131
N162E	WWD	229
N162F	20	387
N162FJ	10	81
N162FJ	900	162
N162GA	55	003
N162J	24F	336
N162JB	**S60**	**306-62**
N162JC	**G3**	**373**
N162LJ	31A	162
(N162TJ)	10	162
N162TJ	550	0888
N163A	35A	073
N163AF	650	0163
N163AG	**125**	**25169**
N163AV	10	163
N163BA	125	258238
N163CB	550	234
N163CH	10	163
N163DA	551	190
N163DC	**WWD**	**89**
N163DL	WWD	163
N163F	10	163
N163FJ	10	83
N163FJ	900	163
N163JD	31A	095
N163L	**560**	**0374**
N163M	601	5113
N163M	G4	1193
(N163ME)	24D	277
N163MR	601	5113
(N163W)	WWD	162
N163WC	WWD	141
N163WC	**WWD**	**217**
N163WS	**WWD**	**141**
N163WW	**50**	**52**
N164AF	**650**	**0164**
N164BA	125	258239
N164CB	501	510
N164CB	501	571
N164CC	500	164
N164CC	550	211
N164CV	560	0164
N164DA	S40	282-112
N164DN	S40	282-112
N164DW	560	0018
N164FJ	10	84
N164FJ	50	164
N164GB	**50**	**164**
(N164GJ)	500	164
(N164M)	750	0021
N164M	750	0024
N164MA	50	164
N164NW	**20**	**164**
N164PA	60	030
N164RJ	**G3**	**482**
N164SB	**31A**	**164**
N164WC	**125**	**257144**
N165A	G2	70/1
(N165AG)	125	25043
N165AG	125	25206
(N165AG)	125	25208
N165BA	125	258241
N165BA	500	159
N165CB	501	353
N165CM	**24E**	**355**
N165DL	125	257174
N165F	400	RJ-16
N165FJ	10	85
(N165FJ)	50	163
N165FJ	50	166
N165G	**G3**	**414**
N165GA	D1A	A065SA
N165HB	**400A**	**RK-90**
N165JB	560	5032
N165MC	**550**	**195**
N165NA	501	557
N165NA	S65	465-68
N165PA	20	360
N165ST	G3	414
N165ST	**G4**	**1053**
N165TW	**20**	**65**
N165U	G2	66
N165W	G2	66
N165WC	20	140
N166A	601	5170
N166AC	STR	5029/38
(N166AG)	35A	145
N166BA	125	258244
N166CB	501	532
N166CF	550	180
N166DT	31A	166
N166FA	**501**	**559**
N166FB	**90X**	**18**
N166FJ	10	86
N166FJ	50	167
N166FJ	900	166
N166HE	35A	235
N166HL	35A	235
N166HL	**60**	**041**
N166JV	**560**	**0166**
N166KB	560	0374
N166MA	**551**	**151**
N166RM	35A	336
N166RM	**AST**	**047**
N166RS	20	157
(N166SS)	10	166
N166VP	550	180
N166WC	G3	413
N167A	G2	53
N167AC	10	167
N167BA	125	259038
N167C	WWD	261
N167CB	501	542
N167EA	**550**	**667**
N167FJ	10	87
N167FJ	50	168
N167FJ	900	168
N167G	S40	282-11
N167G	**STR**	**5212**
N167H	S40	282-11
N167H	S60	306-119
N167J	125	25020
N167J	25	011
N167J	WWD	265
N167LJ	31A	167
N167MA	550	303
N167R	STR	5204
(N167WE)	550	386
N167WE	560	0087
(N167WE)	560	0167
N168AM	550	175
N168BA	125	258209
N168BF	**125**	**258373**
N168CB	551	150
N168CV	**560**	**0168**
N168D	S40	282-21
N168DB	STR	5074/22
N168DB	WWD	202
N168EA	501	568
N168FJ	10	82
(N168H)	125	257171
N168H	S40	282-21
N168H	S60	306-122
N168HC	S550	0081
N168HH	**125**	**258398**
N168HT	**900**	**182**
N168JW	G2	168
N168LJ	31A	168
N168RL	500	271
N168TR	**G4**	**1113**
N168W	**S40**	**282-33**
N168WC	**G4**	**1002**
N169AC	S60	306-98
N169B	125	256061
N169B	G2	190
N169BA	125	259039
N169CA	**G4**	**1241**
N169CC	650	0169
N169CJ	525	0069
(N169CP)	551	018
(N169DA)	551	191
N169EA	**G2**	**169**
N169F	20	388
N169FJ	10	88
N169FJ	50	170
N169JM	551	191
N169P	G2	169
N169RF	S60	306-45
N169SC	31A	069
N169TA	125	257114
N169TA	**601**	**3041**
N169US	**24D**	**298**
N170AL	S40	282-29
N170BG	**525**	**0170**
N170CC	550	170
N170CC	650	0170
N170CC	S65	465-3
N170CS	**10**	**58**
N170CV	560	0170
N170DD	S40	282-29
N170EA	501	573
(N170EP)	25B	170
N170EV	25B	170
N170FJ	10	90
N170FJ	50	171
N170FJ	50	172
N170GT	25B	117
N170HL	501	683
N170HL	**650**	**0125**
N170JL	S40	282-29
N170JL	S65	465-3
N170JS	501	570
N170L	35A	156
N170MD	**500**	**088**
N170RD	S550	0148
N170RL	25B	117
N170TC	550	619
N170VE	55	089
(N171AV)	125	25171
(N171CB)	550	011
N171CB	550	275
N171CC	500	171
N171CC	STR	5127
N171FJ	10	94
N171FJ	50	171
N171GA	**HFB**	**1039**
N171JL	**STR**	**5074/22**
N171JC	G4	1222
N171L	24B	182
N171L	**650**	**0039**
N171LE	550	352
N171MC	10	30
N171PF	20	117
N171SG	**STR**	**5227**
N171TS	**125**	**256071**
(N171VP)	550	188
N171WH	**35A**	**171**
N171WJ	**501**	**574**
N172AC	WWD	1
N172CB	550	285
N172CC	500	172
N172CJ	525	0172
N172CP	10	172
N172CV	**560**	**0172**
N172FJ	10	92
N172FJ	50	173
N172L	STR	5015
N172MA	**500**	**110**
N173A	S60	306-41
N173A	**S65**	**465-20**
N173AR	WWD	80
N173EL	**G2**	**173**
N173F	20	390
N173FJ	10	95
N173GA	HFB	1052
N173HH	500	082
N173J	25B	112
N173JA	36	007
N173LC	**31A**	**173**
N173LP	24B	196
N173LP	25B	163
N173LP	650	0055
(N173LP)	G3	310
N173LP	G4	1033
N173LR	25B	163
N173LR	650	0055
N173MC	WWD	150
N173PS	**31**	**009**
N173SK	501	381
N173TR	**125**	**258039**
N173VP	**650**	**0173**
N173W	**AST**	**073**
N174A	125	258174
N174B	**10**	**142**
N174B	D1A	A031SA
N174CB	501	647
(N174CF)	501	579
N174CP	35A	177
N174FJ	10	96
N174GA	**20**	**27**
N174JS	560	0074
N174LM	G4	1174
N174NW	**125**	**258174**
N174RD	**24X**	**319**
N174SA	D1A	A072SA
N174SJ	G4	1174
N175BA	23	038

N175BC	**10**	**128**
N175BG	**G3**	**396**
N175BJ	**400A**	**RK-175**
N175BL	10	168
N175CC	500	175
N175CP	525	0175
N175F	20	391
N175FJ	**10**	**97**
N175FS	**24A**	**031**
N175GA	**20**	**45**
N175J	35	005
N175J	**650**	**0168**
(N175J)	650	0175
N175PS	400A	RK-213
N175PS	525	0087
N175SB	**525**	**0371**
N175ST	600	1084
N175ST	601	5023
N175VB	**550**	**230**
N176AF	**650**	**0176**
N176AN	STR	5103
N176BN	20	69
N176BN	STR	5103
N176BN	STR	5207
N176CF	**900**	**160**
N176CP	24B	204
N176DC	75A	380-54
N176F	20	393
N176FB	**501**	**650**
N176FJ	10	99
N176G	25B	088
N176G	G4	1176
N176GA	**HFB**	**1053**
N176JE	35A	176
N176L	650	0176
N176LG	STR	5005
N176MB	**60**	**176**
N176NP	20	69
N176P	G2	176
N176RS	125	257162
N176SB	G2	176
N176TS	125	25176
N176VP	560	0176
N176WA	125	258176
N176WS	**31A**	**176**
N177A	S40	282-1
N177A	S60	306-3
N177A	WWD	16
N177BB	**G4**	**1073**
N177BC	**10**	**25**
N177CJ	551	177
(N177CM)	550	247
N177FJ	10	100
N177FJ	50	175
N177FJ	900	172
N177GP	125	25111
N177HB	WWD	141
N177HH	550	043
N177JB	**31A**	**161**
N177JB	525	0182
N177JC	**WWD**	**77**
N177JF	**525**	**0182**
N177JW	**125**	**257110**
N177NC	75A	380-52
N177NC	STR	5070/52
N177NQ	75A	380-52
N177PC	WWD	141
N177RE	**525**	**0030**
N177SB	35A	401
N178CC	650	0178
N178CP	**35**	**005**
N178F	20	394
N178FJ	10	102
N178FJ	50	176
N178GA	**20**	**163**
N178HH	500	082
N178HH	551	190
N178HH	WWD	347
N178TJ	**10**	**78**
N178W	S60	306-4
N179AG	10	176
N179AP	G2	37
N179AR	G2	37
N179CJ	525	0079
(N179CJ)	560	0179
N179DE	G2	86/16
N179EA	500	179
N179F	20	396
N179FJ	10	104
N179FJ	50	178
N179FJ	900	178
N179GA	**20**	**100**
N179S	80A	380-50
N179T	G2	86/16
N180AR	50	216
N180AR	**G2**	**148/5**
N180AR	S60	306-77
N180CC	500	180
N180CH	125	257076
N180CH	600	1005
N180CP	**60**	**081**
N180FJ	10	105
N180FJ	50	179
N180FW	**550**	**403**
N180GC	**36**	**004**
(N180JS)	WWD	180
N180KT	601	5004
N180MC	25D	261
N180MC	35A	212
N180ML	125	25115
N180NA	75A	380-51
N180PF	500	047
N180TJ	WWD	106
N180UF	500	314
N180VP	501	593
N180YA	25B	136
N181AR	S60	306-90
N181BS	900	39
N181CA	24D	277
N181CB	20	436
N181CC	500	181
(N181CC)	650	0181
N181CJ	525	0181
N181EF	**55**	**090**
N181FH	**125**	**258098**
N181FJ	10	106
N181FJ	50	181
N181G	**S550**	**0006**
(N181GL)	35A	405
N181JC	**601**	**5173**
N181JT	**525**	**0081**
N181MA	D1A	001SA
N181MC	**50**	**279**
N181RB	**20**	**66**
N181RK	**200**	**515**
(N181RW)	24D	277
N181SG	**560**	**0181**
N181SV	WWD	110
N181WT	**20**	**478**
N182AR	S60	306-93
N182FJ	10	107
N182FJ	50	182
N182GA	**20**	**146**
N182K	**35A**	**293**
N182U	550	373
N183AB	550	628
N183AJ	550	628
N183AJ	560	0276
N183AP	25D	271
N183AR	S40	282-127
(N183B)	50	118
N183CC	500	183
N183DT	31A	183
N183F	20	398
N183FD	**35A**	**183**
N183FJ	10	109
N183FJ	50	184
N183GA	**20**	**147/444**
N183JC	35A	363
N183ML	**31A**	**183**
N183RD	125	256009
(N183RM)	125	256009
N183SC	G2	91
N183SR	100	183
N183TS	**20**	**313**
N184AL	24D	246
N184F	20	399
N184FJ	10	110
N184FJ	50	185
N184G	**560**	**5050**
N184GA	**20**	**266/490**
N184GP	STR	5064/51
N184J	25	063
N184PC	**80A**	**380-6**
(N184SC)	501	677
N184SC	D1A	A067SA
N184TB	**125**	**257084**
N184TS	**35A**	**084**
N185BA	**35**	**025**
(N185BR)	WWD	365
N185CC	550	185
N185FJ	10	111
N185FJ	50	163
N185FP	35A	360
N185G	WWD	161
(N185GA)	D1A	A066SA
N185HA	35A	605
N185MB	WWD	365
N185S	20	56
N185SF	S550	0029
N185VP	650	0185
N186CJ	525	0186
N186DC	G3	447
N186DS	G3	447
N186DS	**G4**	**1154**
N186FJ	10	112
N186G	**125**	**258011**
N186G	WWD	282
N186G	WWD	43
N186HG	50	167
N186MT	S550	0072
N186MW	500	186
N186NM	**125**	**25186**
N186S	20	195
N186S	50	113
N186SC	**500**	**186**
N186ST	**60**	**186**
N186TJ	**10**	**186**
N186VP	**650**	**0186**
(N187AP)	500	096
N187CM	650	0187
N187CP	650	0003
N187DL	525	0316
(N187DY)	25D	342
N187EC	WWD	434
N187F	20	402
N187FJ	10	114
N187G	WWD	41
N187H	900	16
(N187HG)	900	16
N187JN	550	365
N187MW	500	187
N187MZ	36A	023
(N187PA)	G2	218
N187PH	G2	218
N187S	50	18
N187TA	**550**	**280**
N187TJ	**WWD**	**187**
(N187TS)	WWD	187
N188BC	25B	078
N188CJ	525	0088
(N188CJ)	560	0188
N188DC	**G2**	**188**
N188DH	10	188
N188FC	25	006
N188FJ	10	115
N188FJ	50	88
(N188G)	S550	0017
N188G	WWD	139
(N188JA)	35	025
N188JS	**G2**	**29**
N188K	125	25057
N188MR	**G2**	**218**
N188PS	**S40**	**282-122**
N188R	**25D**	**305**
N188SF	550	216
N188ST	D1A	A040SA
N188TA	**25D**	**276**
N188TC	25D	276
N188TC	60	078
N188TC	**G3**	**492**
N188TG	**60**	**078**
N188TJ	G3	399
N188TQ	25D	276
N188WP	WWD	90
N189AR	S40	282-77
N189B	125	25224
N189B	125	256061
N189B	125	258075
N189CC	500	189
N189CJ	525	0089
N189CM	**525**	**0189**
N189CV	560	0189
N189F	20	403
N189FJ	10	116
N189G	WWD	35
N189GE	125	257001
N189H	**560**	**0004**
N189JM	**10**	**189**
N189K	**601**	**5083**
N189MM	20	453
(N189TC)	35A	189
N189TC	35A	206
N189TC	G2	140/40
N189WS	**G2**	**228**
N190AB	500	157
N190AS	60	002
N190BD	20	8
N190BP	**24B**	**190**
N190CC	500	190
N190DA	**35A**	**156**
(N190DB)	10	11
(N190DB)	24B	190
N190EB	35A	156
N190EK	601	5190
N190FJ	10	117
N190GC	**35**	**014**
N190GG	601	5051
N190H	**10**	**71**
N190JH	**560**	**0303**
N190JJ	650	0190
N190K	501	369
N190K	**501**	**590**
N190KL	**560**	**0380**
N190L	**10**	**190**
(N190LH)	WWD	180
N190M	WWD	232
N190MC	**50**	**26**
(N190MD)	10	47
N190MD	S60	306-142
N190SB	601	5051
N190SC	24B	190
N190VE	35A	301
N190WC	**125**	**257182**
N190WW	**WWD**	**190**
N191AB	500	167
N191BA	604	5410
N191BE	601	5191
N191C	20	195
N191CM	650	0191
N191DA	24	157
N191DA	25	012
N191FJ	10	119
N191GS	D1A	A030SA
N191MC	10	30
N191MC	**50**	**282**
N191NC	**400A**	**RK-143**
N191VF	**560**	**0150**
N192AB	500	177
N192AT	HFB	1038
N192FJ	10	120
N192G	500	163
N192LH	WWD	180
N192MB	24B	214
N192MC	10	84
N192MH	24B	214
N192MH	25D	239
N192R	**20**	**192**
N193AT	S40	282-124
N193CJ	525	0193
N193CK	G2	168
N193DQ	600	1041
(N193DR)	25C	129
N193FJ	10	122
N193G	**560**	**0137**
N193JF	**24B**	**193**

N193RC	**125**	**257081**
N193SS	**550**	**572**
N193TA	125	257001
N193TR	125	258039
N193TR	400	RJ-29
N193TR	**900**	**9**
N194	G3	391
N194AL	**60**	**004**
N194AT	500	146
(N194AT)	500	152
N194BJ	400A	RK-194
N194CV	560	0194
N194DC	**650**	**0074**
N194FJ	10	123
(N194JM)	550	297
N194JS	**125**	**258251**
N194MC	**20**	**135**
N194RC	501	545
N194SA	**560**	**0238**
N194WA	G2	194
N194WM	**604**	**5340**
N195AS	**20**	**71**
N195FC	**AST**	**036**
N195FJ	10	125
N195JH	**400**	**RJ-64**
N195KA	400	RJ-53
N195KC	**125**	**258189**
N195KC	400	RJ-53
N195L	**125**	**259008**
N195ME	**525**	**0110**
(N195ML)	WWD	195
N195MP	20	195
N195SV	50	236
N195SV	50	293
N195WM	**700**	**9041**
N195WS	**G4**	**1050**
N195XP	125	257023
N196AF	24B	196
N196CF	**24B**	**186**
N196CM	650	0196
N196CV	560	0196
(N196DR)	525	0256
N196DT	35A	171
(N196FJ)	10	126
N196FJ	10	131
N196HA	31A	084
N196HA	**525**	**0256**
N196HA	551	196
N196HR	551	196
N196JH	**400**	**RJ-52**
N196JS	**550**	**219**
N196KC	125	25180
N196KC	400	RJ-52
N196KC	STR	5231
N196KC	WWD	68
N196KQ	125	25180
(N196KQ)	400	RJ-52
N196MC	125	258081
N196MG	**125**	**258081**
N196PH	**45**	**056**
N196RJ	**550**	**234**
N196SA	**560**	**0384**
N196SD	35A	414
N196SD	**650**	**0093**
N196SG	650	0093
N196SP	35A	414
N196SV	50	236
N196TB	**24B**	**196**
N196TS	**20**	**196**
N197BE	**400A**	**RK-33**
N197CC	650	0197
N197CF	**25B**	**197**
N197CV	560	0197
N197DA	S40	282-28
N197FJ	10	128
(N197GH)	550	704
N197GL	23	070
N197HF	**550**	**704**
N197JH	**560**	**0267**
N197JS	STR	5069/20
N197LS	**25D**	**363**
N197PF	400A	RK-33
N197PH	**31A**	**169**
N197PH	31A	172
N197SD	**400A**	**RK-126**
(N197SL)	D1A	A069SA
(N197VP)	650	0197
N197WC	25B	197
N198AV	G2	98/38
N198CC	600	1018
N198CM	650	0198
N198DF	550	630
N198DF	**650**	**0209**
N198FJ	10	132
N198GB	**80A**	**380-32**
N198GH	WWD	364
N198GJ	**35A**	**198**
N198GT	**125**	**257123**
N198HE	WWD	364
N198HF	**AST**	**054**
N198HF	WWD	364
N198JA	**25B**	**198**
N198JH	**525**	**0265**
N198KF	31A	147
N198M	50	149
N198M	**50**	**277**
N198MR	**50**	**149**
N198ND	**550**	**630**
N198SL	**550**	**0835**
N198T	**35A**	**074**
N198VP	501	602
N199B	125	25224
N199BA	**604**	**5410**
N199BB	**550**	**0895**
N199BT	**25D**	**311**
N199CJ	**35A**	**071**
N199CK	**500**	**216**
N199FJ	10	135
N199GH	AST	027
N199GH	WWD	364
N199HF	**AST**	**027**
N199LA	STR	5098/28
N199NP	**750**	**0078**
N199QS	G4	1099
N199SC	60	114
N199SG	125	256038
N199SP	500	199
N200A	G2	94
N200A	G3	370
N200A	G3	372
N200A	**G4**	**1138**
N200A	S40	282-52
N200A	STR	5081
N200AB	**G2**	**71**
(N200AF)	10	87
N200AL	STR	5081
N200AS	**550**	**0934**
(N200BA)	500	250
N200BA	55	011
N200BC	25B	095
N200BE	G2	196
N200BL	400A	RK-23
N200BP	G2	115
N200BP	WWD	117
N200BP	WWD	46
N200CC	125	25179
N200CC	125	25265
N200CC	G2	31
N200CC	STR	5033/56
N200CC	STR	5150/37
N200CE	S60	306-87
N200CG	20	191
N200CG	**500**	**230**
N200CG	STR	5033/56
N200CG	STR	5150/37
N200CK	**560**	**0298**
(N200CK)	S40	282-111
N200CK	STR	5039
N200CN	600	1032
N200CP	20	410
N200CP	**560**	**0055**
N200CV	**S550**	**0064**
N200CX	20	112
N200CX	S550	0064
N200CX	S60	306-93
N200DE	20	191
N200DE	20	368
N200DE	**601**	**5015**
N200DE	G3	358
N200DE	WWD	148
N200DF	WWD	148
N200DH	24	170
N200DL	WWD	189
N200DM	24	065
N200DW	**STR**	**5058/4**
N200E	550	399
N200E	S40	282-124
N200E	S40	282-135
N200EC	35A	094
N200ES	501	502
N200ET	200	498
N200FJ	10	137
N200FJ	20	401
N200FJ	20	479
N200FJ	200	491
N200FJ	200	507
N200FT	20	100
(N200FX)	20	479
N200G	23	064
N200G	25	048
(N200G)	551	030
N200GF	501	679
N200GF	**551**	**556**
N200GH	20	181
N200GH	**G2**	**108**
N200GL	20	181
(N200GL)	G2	108
N200GM	**500**	**142**
N200GN	20	339
N200GN	**2xx**	**68**
N200GN	G2	110
N200GN	G3	312
N200GP	24	134
N200GP	**400A**	**RK-53**
(N200GP)	550	022
N200GT	**20**	**137**
N200GT	WWD	46
N200GX	125	257033
N200GX	125	258202
(N200GX)	20	339
N200GY	**125**	**257033**
N200HR	WWD	182
N200HR	WWD	268
N200J	**20**	**410**
N200JE	**20**	**133**
N200JJ	G3	312
N200JP	604	5421
N200JR	24D	259
N200JR	550	239
N200JW	20	64
N200KC	125	25249
N200KC	500	104
N200KC	WWD	319
N200KF	125	258039
N200KQ	500	104
N200L	**90X**	**2**
N200LC	**G4**	**1067**
N200LF	WWD	47
N200LH	650	0100
N200LH	**650**	**7005**
(N200LH)	WWD	309
N200LH	WWD	312
N200LJ	**35A**	**200**
N200LL	650	0100
N200LP	**D1A**	**A006SA**
N200LS	125	258095
N200LS	20	479
N200LS	G2	227
N200LS	**G4**	**1182**
N200LS	WWD	400
N200LX	**S550**	**0061**
N200M	WWD	120
N200M	WWD	132
N200M	WWD	44
N200MH	25C	083
N200MK	20	355
N200MP	S40	282-36
N200MP	WWD	95
(N200MR)	551	200
N200MT	**CVT**	**40**
N200MW	500	200
N200MZ	WWD	95
N200NA	400A	RK-200
N200NC	**550**	**142**
N200NE	**2xx**	**22**
N200NK	**560**	**0511**
N200NK	S550	0095
N200NR	24	142
N200NR	25D	328
N200NV	S550	0095
N200P	20	54
N200P	G2	121
N200PB	125	25121
N200PB	G2	110
N200PB	STR	5161/43
N200PC	55	058
N200PF	125	25121
N200PF	**560**	**5098**
N200PM	**G4**	**1147**
N200QM	25C	084
N200RC	WWD	140
N200RG	G2	216
N200RM	WWD	46
N200RN	551	419
N200RT	200	489
N200RT	200	490
N200RT	50	175
N200RT	**50**	**24**
N200RT	551	419
N200RT	650	0025
(N200SA)	20	479
N200SF	25C	084
N200SF	G3	390
N200SG	**50**	**239**
N200SK	**G3**	**319**
N200SR	20	195
N200SX	35A	286
N200TC	24	134
N200TC	35A	423
N200TJ	200	501
N200TJ	551	051
N200TW	**35A**	**397**
N200UL	604	5316
(N200UP)	200	513
N200UP	**50**	**55**
N200VT	125	25249
N200VT	**550**	**210**
N200WC	WWD	153
N200WD	20	479
(N200WF)	20	144
N200WK	**20**	**261**
N200WN	500	252
(N200WN)	WWD	38
N200WY	**200**	**509**
N200XJ	WWD	281
N200XR	125	256058
N200Y	23	003
N200Y	25C	083
N200Y	36	014
N200YM	10	114
N200YM	550	409
N201BA	23	013
N201CC	550	201
N201H	125	25109
N201PM	125	257192
N201S	WWD	85
N201U	550	215
N201WL	24B	215
N202A	G2	94
N202AV	**650**	**7108**
N202BA	24A	031
N202BD	35	041
N202BT	24B	195
N202BT	25B	132
N202BT	35	041
N202BT	**35A**	**483**
N202CE	**550**	**104**
N202CF	**501**	**436**
N202CH	125	257084
N202CJ	525	0102
N202CJ	525	0202
N202CP	**50**	**202**
(N202CV)	560	0202
(N202CV)	650	0202
N202DD	50	54
N202DD	WWD	202

N202DN 100 202
(N202DR) 25D 253
N202ES STR 5204
N202FJ 10 134
N202FJ 200 484
N202FJ 900 156
N202GA AST 101
N202GA G2 152
N202GA G2 187
N202GA G2 26
(N202GP) 24 134
N202JK 650 0100
N202JS 24D 278
N202JW 25D 347
N202KH 20 45
N202LC 31A 147
N202MW 500 202
N202PB 550 029
N202RB 650 0162
N202TA 20 59
N202TJ 650 0202
N202TS 550 295
N202VP 501 607
N202VS 35A 190
N202VS 500 096
N202VV 500 096
N202WM 25D 355
N202WR 35A 190
N202Y 23 024
N203A G2 89
(N203AL) 35A 483
N203BA 400 RJ-3
N203BE 551 149
N203BT 50 22
(N203CD) 650 0203
(N203CJ) 525 0103
N203CK 24B 203
(N203CV) 560 0203
N203FJ 10 138
N203FJ 200 489
N203G 600 1069
N203GA G2 113
N203GA G2 124
N203JK S65 465-39
N203JL 24B 203
N203LH 501 384
N203M WWD 120
N203NC 50 203
(N203PV) 10 71
N203R 125 258119
N203RW 35A 203
N203TA 20 442
N204A 25 014
N204A G2 79
N204A S550 0008
N204AB 550 365
N204AB WWD 342
N204C G2 143
N204CA 501 429
N204DD 200 494
N204DD 50 54
N204FJ 10 139
N204FJ 200 490
N204FJ 90X 4
N204FX 60 007
N204G S60 306-91
N204GA G2 167
N204GA G2 74
N204HC 50 136
N204J 525 0164
N204JC 125 258175
N204JP 20 24
N204MC 550 017
N204N 125 257113
N204QS 2xx 104
N204R 125 257113
N204R 125 259017
N204R S60 306-91
N204RC G2 34
N204SM 125 258135
N204TM S40 282-56
N204TM WWD 320
N204TW 20 204
N204Y 24 113

N204Y 500 204
(N205A) 600 1029
N205AJ WWD 205
N205BC 560 0010
N205BE 550 647
N205BS 125 257048
N205CM 560 0250
N205EE 601 3011
(N205EF) 55 053
N205EL 35A 283
N205EL 55 053
N205EL 600 1067
N205EL 601 3011
N205FH 525 0355
N205FJ 10 140
N205FJ 20 120
(N205FJ) 20 142
N205FJ 200 491
N205FJ 90X 5
N205FL 35A 283
N205FM 500 264
N205FX 60 005
N205K 20 319
N205K G2 231
N205M G2 18
N205MM 600 1044
N205MM HFB 1039
N205PC 560 0010
N205R 400A RK-30
N205RJ 23 041
N205SA 25 041
N205SC 20 155
N205SC 25 041
N205SC 550 176
(N205SE) 20 155
N205SG 550 176
(N205TS) 20 54
N205WM 20 306/512
N205X 10 44
N205X G4 1080
N206EC 25D 206
N206EC 35A 487
N206EQ 25D 206
N206FC 35A 487
N206FJ 10 141
(N206FJ) 200 487
N206FX 60 028
N206MD G2 22
N206PC 125 258038
N206PC 750 0016
N206TC 550 465
N206WC 125 258038
N207BA 400 RJ-7
N207BA 550 234
N207BS 525 0241
N207CA 20 153
N207CC 650 0207
(N207CF) 501 610
N207CV 560 0207
N207FJ 10 142
N207FJ 20 401
N207FX 60 050
N207G 501 647
N207GA G2 136
N207HF 25D 230
N207JC 25D 207
(N207L) 500 038
N207L STR 5050/34
N207L STR 5067
N207L STR 5100/41
N207MJ MSP 002
N207PC 125 257197
N207PC 125 258185
N207PC 560 5008
N207QS 2xx 70
N207RC 125 257197
(N207RC) 125 258185
N207US 100 207
N208BC 560 0050
N208CV 560 0208
N208D 400 RJ-14
N208EA 501 612
N208F D1A A016SA
N208FJ 10 144

N208FJ 200 493
N208FX 60 059
N208H 125 25141
N208H 125 25163
N208JV 525 0208
N208L STR 5050/34
N208L STR 5083/49
N208MD WWD 208
N208MM HFB 1039
N208N 500 021
N208PC 560 0050
N208PC 560 5005
N208R 125 259011
N208R 400 RJ-14
(N208RT) 200 490
N208ST WWD 208
N208TC 550 327
N208W 501 421
N209A 650 0156
N209BA 400 RJ-9
N209CV 560 0209
N209FJ 10 145
N209FJ 200 494
N209FX 60 060
N209G 550 558
N209GA G2 9/33
N209MW 500 209
N209NC 125 25190
N209RR WWD 127
(N209WE) 600 1034
N209WF 600 1034
N210CJ 525 0010
N210CJ 525 0210
N210EK STR 5117/35
N210F 650 0067
N210F S60 306-25
N210FE WWD 95
N210FJ 10 13
N210FJ 200 495
N210FP 24 155
N210FX 60 064
N210GA G2 102/32
N210GK G3 875
N210GP 23 020
N210M 125 25103
N210MJ 551 108
N210MT 500 210
N210NC 25B 154
N210PC 23 036
N210RS 20 18
(N210ST) 125 256009
N210WL 35A 210
N211BL 24X 150
N211BL G2 113
N211BR S60 306-85
N211BY 35A 227
(N211BY) 55 059
N211CC 650 0211
N211CD 25D 275
N211CN 10 173
N211CN 50 31
N211DB 500 174
N211DB WWD 405
N211DG 560 0167
N211DH 35A 253
N211DH G2 236
N211EC 10 166
N211EF 50 123
N211EF 501 434
N211EF 55ER 101
N211FJ 10 146
N211FX 60 076
N211GA D1A A011SA
(N211GA) G2 36/3
N211GM 525 0208
N211HF 20 289
N211HF 20 474
N211HJ 24X 150
N211JB 25D 249
N211JC 25D 310
N211JS 550 105
N211MA 560 0022
N211MB 25 059
N211MT G2 52

N211PA STR 5227
N211PD 25D 310
N211QS S550 0011
N211RR 650 0079
N211SF S40 282-136
N211SJ G2 75/7
N211SP 550 337
N211SR 10 115
N211ST WWD 303
N211TJ 10 11
N211TS 23 066
N211VP S550 0002
N211WH 35A 269
N211WZ 125 257017
N211X 501 434
N212AD G3 492
N212AP STR 5147
N212AT G3 492
N212AT G4 1204
N212BD 560 0309
N212C 20 155
N212CP WWD 340
N212CT 601 5104
N212CW WWD 75
N212F S60 306-25
N212FJ 10 147
N212FJ 200 497
(N212FX) 60 007
N212FX 60 077
N212FX 60 099
N212GA 35A 354
N212GA G2 140/40
N212H 20 259
N212H 550 105
N212JP 50 94
N212JP 55 006
N212JW STR 5131
N212K 50 89
N212K G2 195
N212K G4 1192
N212KM 50 89
N212LF 24B 216
N212LM 601 5037
N212N 10 150
N212N 50 202
N212NC 10 150
N212NE 25D 212
(N212PA) D1A A038SA
N212PB 20 313
N212Q 50 179
N212R 20 212
N212T 20 273
N212T 2xx 52
N212T 50 192
N212TC 20 273
N212TG 20 273
N212TJ G2 12
N212WW WWD 212
N213AP STR 5122
(N213BE) S60 306-123
N213BK 400A RK-216
N213BM S40 282-111
N213C 125 257213
N213CA 25D 241
(N213CE) 500 213
(N213FC) 20 213
N213FJ 10 148
N213FJ 200 499
(N213FX) 60 086
N213H 125 25119
N213JS 550 597
N213LS 20 107
N213MC 601 5171
N213PA 31 013
N213QS 2xx 113
N213WW WWD 213
N214AM 551 312
N214CA 500 214
N214CC 500 214
N214CC WWD 197
N214DV 50 289
N214FJ 10 149
N214FJ 200 500
N214FX 60 046

N214GA	G2	160
N214GP	G2	3
N214JP	20	296/507
N214JR	125	25070
N214JR	125	25146
N214L	**560**	**0381**
N214LJ	25D	214
N214LS	35A	096
(N214LS)	35A	229
N214ME	25D	214
N214MJ	24B	214
N214QS	**S550**	**0014**
N214RW	**550**	**478**
N214TC	125	25146
N214WM	**400A**	**RK-197**
N214WW	WWD	214
N215C	WWD	206
N215CC	500	215
N215CM	650	0215
N215CW	**550**	**175**
N215DH	WWD	215
N215DL	STR	5215
N215FJ	10	150
N215FJ	200	498
N215FX	**60**	**101**
N215G	125	25058
N215G	125	257095
N215G	WWD	206
N215GA	G2	93
(N215HZ)	STR	5215
N215J	24	134
N215JW	35A	223
N215M	WWD	206
N215RL	36	012
N215RL	600	1068
N215RL	G2	45
N215RS	**125**	**257023**
N215SC	WWD	243
N215TS	STR	5215
N215Z	24D	246
N215Z	25	020
N216BG	20	196
N216CA	**20**	**11**
(N216CC)	500	216
N216CJ	525	0016
N216FB	900	65
N216FJ	10	152
N216FJ	200	502
N216FP	900	146
N216FP	900	65
N216FX	**60**	**103**
N216HB	24D	275
N216HE	G2	113
(N216MF)	G2	113
N216R	S40	282-94
N216RG	23	066
N216SA	**20**	**16**
(N216SA)	23	082
N216SA	25D	216
N216SC	WWD	216
N216TW	20	16
(N216VP)	550	017
N217A	**125**	**256030**
N217A	S40	282-103
N217A	S60	306-85
N217AH	G2	197
N217AJ	**20**	**171**
N217AL	**125**	**258177**
N217AL	WWD	38
N217AT	24B	217
N217BL	WWD	284
N217BM	WWD	409
N217CC	500	217
N217CJ	525	0117
N217CM	650	0217
(N217CP)	10	100
N217CS	35	062
N217CS	36A	039
N217E	S40	282-103
N217F	125	25175
N217FJ	10	151
N217FJ	200	504
N217FS	**550**	**308**
N217FX	**60**	**105**
N217GA	G2	17
N217JD	G2	14
N217JS	G2	113
N217LG	550	304
N217MB	**400A**	**RK-217**
N217PM	WWD	16
N217PM	WWD	38
N217PT	AST	105
N217RM	125	258017
N217RM	S60	306-94
N217RM	WWD	409
N217RN	**S60**	**306-94**
N217RR	501	643
N217RR	650	0079
N217RR	**G2**	**22**
N217S	500	217
N217SA	**550**	**263**
N217SC	WWD	217
N217SQ	WWD	217
N217TA	**35A**	**289**
(N217TE)	G2	33
N217TE	S40	282-103
N217TL	G2	33
N217WC	WWD	217
N218AC	125	256013
N218AM	501	626
N218BA	100	218
N218BR	560	0218
N218CA	**20**	**218**
(N218CC)	500	218
N218CC	**650**	**0218**
N218DF	560	0218
N218DJ	WWD	218
N218FJ	10	153
N218FJ	200	503
N218FX	**60**	**098**
N218GA	G2	218
N218H	551	430
N218JG	**501**	**626**
N218NB	25D	361
N218NB	31A	146
N218NR	25D	361
N218PM	WWD	218
N218QS	**2xx**	**118**
N218R	25D	365
N218RG	400	RJ-45
N218S	20	32
N218SC	WWD	271
N218TJ	**125**	**25018**
(N218UB)	75A	380-45
N218US	20	51
N218US	75A	380-45
N218WA	50	218
N218WW	WWD	218
N219CA	**20**	**193**
N219CC	500	219
N219CC	650	0219
N219CJ	**525**	**0219**
N219CS	550	374
N219EC	**125**	**25219**
N219FJ	10	154
N219FJ	200	508
N219FX	60	007
N219GA	G2	91
N219JA	125	257013
(N219JA)	125	258005
N219JW	**100**	**219**
N219MF	STR	5219
N219SC	550	374
N219ST	125	256009
N219TS	**125**	**257026**
N219TT	**80**	**380-24**
N220AB	550	630
N220AJ	AST	077
N220BJ	400A	RK-220
N220CA	**20**	**220**
N220CA	S550	0085
N220CC	500	118
N220CC	550	040
N220CC	550	457
N220CC	650	0140
N220CJ	525	0220
N220CM	20	11
N220DF	**2xx**	**69**
N220EJ	**2xx**	**105**
N220EJ	2xx	69
(N220ES)	STR	5204
(N220FJ)	10	155
N220FJ	20	313
N220FJ	200	507
N220FL	125	257117
N220FL	G2	50
N220FX	**60**	**108**
N220GA	G2	184
(N220GA)	G2	234
N220GA	G4	1042
N220GH	35A	220
N220HS	25XR	220
N220JC	55	050
(N220JM)	2xx	46
N220JM	2xx	47
(N220JM)	2xx	69
N220JM	2xx	85
N220JN	2xx	69
N220JR	**G2**	**50**
N220JT	**560**	**0272**
N220KP	WWD	117
N220LA	551	144
N220LC	**600**	**1071**
(N220LC)	601	5038
N220M	**10**	**34**
(N220MR)	2xx	69
N220MT	**500**	**135**
N220N	M20	1
N220NJ	25XR	220
N220PM	24	158
N220RT	20	142
N220S	500	192
N220SC	10	158
N220ST	WWD	46
N220T	125	25201
N220TG	25D	370
N220TW	**650**	**0060**
N220VE	55	108
N220W	500	025
N221AC	500	392
N221AM	**500**	**109**
N221AP	25D	290
N221B	20	12
N221BJ	400A	RK-221
(N221BW)	550	271
N221CC	500	118
N221CC	500	221
N221CF	WWD	93
N221CM	**G3**	**343**
N221DT	AST	016
N221EB	501	643
N221EJ	**2xx**	**85**
N221EL	25D	290
N221FJ	10	156
N221FJ	200	505
N221FX	**60**	**111**
N221GA	550	135
N221GA	550	441
N221HB	125	258052
(N221JB)	500	392
(N221JS)	550	317
(N221LC)	550	383
N221LC	**560**	**5077**
N221MC	35A	407
N221MJ	WWD	160
N221MJ	WWD	204
N221PA	**AST**	**016**
N221PF	S60	306-15
N221PH	80A	380-49
N221PH	S40	282-55
N221PH	S60	306-15
(N221PX)	S40	282-55
N221RE	125	258119
N221RJ	WWD	160
N221SG	**35A**	**182**
N221TC	25B	136
N221TR	**35A**	**221**
N221TW	**20**	**221**
N221UE	35	042
N221Z	35	059
N222	**G4**	**1142**
N222AD	**G4**	**1057**
N222AG	551	163
N222AK	25B	127
N222AP	24B	211
N222AP	25D	225
(N222AP)	G3	391
N222AW	36	012
N222B	**25**	**047**
N222BE	35A	180
N222BE	**35A**	**489**
N222BG	**35A**	**448**
N222BK	35A	180
N222BN	24D	296
N222BW	G3	440
N222CC	500	222
N222CD	650	0222
N222FA	550	725
N222FJ	10	157
N222FJ	200	509
N222FJ	**VII**	**001**
N222FX	**60**	**008**
N222G	125	25064
N222GH	23	026
N222GL	WWD	47
N222GT	650	0093
N222HL	125	257088
N222HM	WWD	47
N222KC	G3	366
N222KC	WWD	434
N222KN	STR	5118
N222KW	500	080
N222LB	500	212
N222LB	550	093
N222LH	**WWD**	**209**
N222LW	25D	299
N222MC	25B	076
(N222MC)	50	141
N222MC	50	179
N222MC	55	061
N222MC	55	108
N222MF	**STR**	**5229**
N222MJ	550	154
N222MQ	25B	076
N222MS	**125**	**258132**
N222MS	500	018
N222MU	**10**	**164**
N222MW	**WWD**	**255**
N222NB	**G2**	**245/30**
N222NG	**125**	**25016**
N222PV	G2	234
N222Q	D1A	A021SA
N222QA	STR	5116
(N222R)	STR	5016
N222RB	125	25224
N222RB	125	257004
N222RB	24	136
N222RG	125	25224
N222SG	550	122
N222SL	35A	162
N222SL	500	096
N222SR	WWD	194
N222TG	551	098
N222TW	**24**	**161**
N222VV	500	310
N222VV	551	151
N222WA	**501**	**360**
N222WL	550	241
N222Y	STR	5006/40
N223AS	500	212
N223B	20	102
N223BG	**20**	**250**
N223CC	500	223
N223DD	**50**	**128**
(N223DK)	400A	RK-142
N223FJ	10	158
N223FJ	200	510
N223FX	**60**	**124**
N223G	125	25170
N223GC	501	570
N223HS	10	160
N223J	**550**	**410**
N223JV	**560**	**0131**
N223LB	500	212
N223LB	**S65**	**465-23**
N223LC	**501**	**425**

N223LP	75A	380-5
N223MC	500	212
N223P	500	223
N223PA	WWD	171
(N223RE)	501	486
N223S	500	233
N223S	D1A	A033SA
N223TG	25D	370
N223TW	**20**	**123**
N223WA	**WWD**	**423**
N223WW	WWD	153
N224BP	10	159
N224CC	10	36
(N224CC)	500	224
N224CC	551	224
N224CD	650	0224
N224CJ	**525**	**0224**
N224CV	560	0224
N224DJ	55	024
N224EA	**125**	**257088**
N224F	601	3064
N224F	**601**	**5163**
N224FJ	10	159
N224FJ	200	512
N224FX	**60**	**126**
(N224HF)	601	3064
N224JB	24D	321
N224KC	**S550**	**0104**
N224KT	24	161
N224MC	**400A**	**RK-165**
N224N	601	3064
N224N	**601**	**5108**
N224RP	10	159
N224RP	501	632
N224SC	24A	100
(N224TS)	G2	24
N224U	601	3064
N225AC	25D	280
N225AC	25XR	139
N225AD	551	118
N225BC	500	274
N225BJ	**125**	**257044**
N225CC	**100**	**225**
N225CC	25B	107
N225CC	35A	192
N225CC	G2	8
(N225CV)	650	0225
N225DC	500	148
N225DS	**25**	**025**
(N225EA)	25	057
N225F	35A	269
N225FJ	10	160
N225FJ	200	513
N225FM	551	118
N225FX	**60**	**127**
N225HW	25D	231
N225J	**550**	**316**
N225JL	25B	182
N225K	125	25026
N225KJ	125	25026
N225LJ	24A	011
N225LL	125	25026
N225LS	S40	282-51
N225LY	**604**	**5311**
N225MC	35A	225
N225MS	28	004
N225N	601	5036
N225N	**WWD**	**319**
N225QC	35A	192
N225SE	G2	55
N225SF	G2	55
N225SF	**G3**	**423**
N225TJ	**25XR**	**222**
N225TR	**G2**	**225**
N225WT	501	674
N226B	**525**	**0200**
N226CC	36	007
N226FJ	10	162
N226FJ	50	227
N226FX	**60**	**128**
N226G	125	25170
N226G	20	244
N226G	601	3012
N226G	G3	434
N226G	G4	1122
N226GA	**G2**	**106**
N226GC	G3	434
N226GL	601	3012
N226JV	**560**	**0132**
N226L	550	093
N226N	550	093
N226N	560	0248
N226R	**20**	**226**
N226VP	501	635
N227A	55	027
N227AN	AST	060
N227BA	650	0130
N227CC	20	59
(N227CC)	500	227
N227CC	600	1004
(N227CV)	560	0227
(N227CV)	650	0227
N227DH	125	25027
N227EW	25D	227
N227FJ	10	163
(N227FJ)	50	227
N227FX	**60**	**077**
N227G	600	1059
N227G	G2	76
N227G	G4	1045
N227GA	**G2**	**76**
N227GC	20	59
N227GH	**G4**	**1045**
N227GL	600	1059
N227GL	G2	76
N227GX	G2	76
N227H	500	011
N227HF	125	25118
N227HP	**500**	**227**
N227K	STR	5006/40
N227LA	125	25235
N227LA	650	0130
N227LS	S40	282-51
(N227MJ)	35A	227
N227MS	**125**	**25227**
N227N	60	049
N227N	AST	053
N227NL	**AST**	**053**
N227PC	550	125
N227R	**20**	**227**
N227RW	25B	201
N227S	S40	282-16
N227SW	S40	282-16
N227TA	200	496
(N227TJ)	G2	27
N227TS	**G2**	**27**
N227VG	500	246
N227WE	**20**	**344/534**
N228AJ	501	378
N228AK	501	378
N228AK	**551**	**196**
(N228CC)	500	228
N228CC	**550**	**148**
N228CK	20	128/436
N228CM	650	0228
N228CV	560	0228
N228EA	501	631
N228FJ	10	164
N228FJ	50	231
N228FS	**501**	**378**
N228FX	**60**	**132**
N228G	125	25021
N228G	125	25170
N228G	125	258203
N228G	G3	424
N228GC	125	25284
N228GL	125	25021
N228L	WWD	331
N228LS	S65	465-43
N228N	**60**	**031**
N228N	WWD	331
N228S	**500**	**233**
N228SW	**25D**	**228**
N228TM	**125**	**258458**
N228Y	STR	5066/46
N229AP	25D	295
N229CJ	**525**	**0129**
N229D	**WWD**	**427**
N229FJ	10	165
N229FX	**60**	**137**
N229GC	600	1043
N229JB	10	71
N229LS	S60	306-38
N229MC	**550**	**255**
N229N	560	0248
N229N	WWD	427
N229P	125	25115
N229R	**20**	**229**
N229RY	125	258229
N229U	**125**	**259009**
N229X	35A	129
N230A	S60	306-38
N230CC	500	230
N230DP	125	257060
N230E	G2	34
N230FJ	10	161
N230FX	**60**	**138**
N230H	125	25064
N230JK	WWD	279
N230JS	500	107
N230JS	WWD	301
N230R	**125**	**257202**
N230R	24B	188
N230R	35A	130
N230RA	**20**	**230**
N230RC	WWD	105
N230S	50	70
N230TL	WWD	279
N230TS	**125**	**25134**
N231A	S40	282-61
N231A	S60	306-72
N231CA	S60	306-72
N231JH	**10**	**176**
(N231LC)	501	493
N231R	24	134
N231R	35A	128
N232BC	**550**	**0913**
N232BJ	400A	RK-34
N232CC	**35A**	**367**
N232CC	551	496
N232CW	**550**	**032**
N232DM	**550**	**087**
N232F	200	502
N232FJ	10	166
N232FJ	50	233
N232FX	**35A**	**620**
N232HC	G3	373
N232K	**G4**	**1232**
N232MD	25	052
N232QS	S550	0032
N232R	23	005
N232R	24	131
N232R	35A	102
N232RA	20	232
N232S	AST	032
N232T	S40	282-83
N232TW	**20**	**32**
N233BC	**50**	**241**
(N233BJ)	400	RJ-33
N233CA	**25B**	**133**
N233CC	**35**	**031**
N233CC	500	233
N233CJ	525	0233
N233DB	**500**	**158**
N233DW	**550**	**0931**
N233FJ	10	167
(N233FJ)	50	233
N233FJ	50	234
N233FX	60	139
N233FX	**60**	**154**
N233KC	**125**	**258052**
N233KC	900	48
(N233ME)	F502	312
N233MW	**400A**	**RK-233**
N233R	23	017
N233R	24	132
N233R	35	048
N233RS	**G2**	**233**
N233SG	601	5104
N233TW	**24B**	**221**
N233U	50	14
N233VM	500	233
N233VW	24A	011
N234AQ	**560**	**0234**
N234AT	**500**	**240**
N234CA	20	17
N234CJ	525	0134
N234CM	24B	214
N234DB	G2	100
N234DB	**G4**	**1000**
N234DC	**S60**	**306-103**
N234DK	**400A**	**RK-182**
N234DT	35A	407
(N234EJ)	25D	234
N234F	23	063
N234FJ	10	168
N234FJ	50	236
N234FX	60	141
N234FX	**60**	**151**
N234G	**WWD**	**28**
(N234HM)	650	0044
N234JW	**501**	**408**
N234KK	25D	234
(N234LC)	55	034
N234MR	24	130
N234MW	600	1073
N234ND	25	043
N234Q	24B	181
(N234RA)	550	561
N234RB	25B	105
N234RC	WWD	162
N234RG	600	1073
N234SV	**25D**	**226**
N234TS	STR	5234
N234U	10	29
N234U	S60	306-48
N234UM	**500**	**105**
N234WR	24	172
N234WS	525	0097
N234YP	650	0074
N235AC	**35A**	**676**
N235AV	125	25235
N235CA	**20**	**139**
N235CC	500	235
N235CM	650	0235
N235DB	550	374
N235DH	35A	134
N235EA	**35**	**061**
N235FJ	10	169
N235FX	60	143
N235FX	**60**	**153**
N235HR	35A	082
N235HR	55	094
N235HR	60	208
N235JL	35	049
N235JS	**35A**	**199**
N235JW	25B	096
N235JW	35	032
N235KC	125	25096
N235KK	551	436
N235KK	**650**	**0175**
N235MC	**35A**	**334**
N235R	23	032
N235SC	35A	275
N235SV	**650**	**0235**
N235TS	**550**	**365**
N235U	20	364
N235U	G3	305
N235UJ	**35A**	**477**
N235Z	24	146
N236BN	**125**	**257051**
N236CA	**25B**	**161**
N236CC	500	236
N236DJ	**10**	**138**
N236FJ	10	170
N236FX	**60**	**157**
N236HR	55	094
N236HR	55	113
N236JP	WWD	116
N236JW	55	036
N236R	55	025
N236TS	24D	236
N236TS	500	236
N236W	WWD	236
N236WJ	24D	236
N236Y	S40	282-31

N237AF	**35A**	**262**
N237CC	D1A	A027SA
N237CJ	**525**	**0237**
N237CW	**550**	**037**
N237DG	525	0141
N237FJ	10	171
N237FJ	50	237
N237FX	**60**	**158**
(N237G)	604	5400
N237GA	35A	262
N237GA	601	5019
N237GA	**604**	**5400**
N237JF	WWD	117
(N237JP)	500	330
(N237LM)	G2	101
N237PT	**20**	**432**
N237R	55	066
N237RA	**125**	**258237**
N237SC	501	640
N237TJ	35A	237
N237TW	**24D**	**237**
N238AJ	125	258155
N238CA	**25**	**040**
N238CV	560	0238
N238DL	50	238
N238FJ	10	172
N238FJ	50	238
N238FX	**60**	**163**
N238JA	35A	134
N238JC	**560**	**0192**
N238JS	501	649
N238MP	25D	238
N238R	24	132
N238R	55	085
N238RC	35	061
N238SW	604	5423
N238U	50	86
N238U	G2	63
N238U	STR	5106/9
N238Y	50	185
N239CA	**25B**	**149**
N239CC	500	239
N239CD	**550**	**242**
N239CV	560	0239
N239FJ	10	173
N239FJ	50	239
N239FX	**60**	**166**
N239GJ	35A	239
N239P	G2	63
N239R	**125**	**258119**
N239R	50	178
N240AA	500	202
N240AA	**WWD**	**82**
N240AC	**S40**	**282-41**
N240AG	23	079
N240AG	25B	197
N240AK	**600**	**1067**
N240AQ	23	079
N240AR	550	240
N240AT	20	240/478
N240B	**125**	**258358**
N240B	35A	240
N240CC	500	240
N240CF	**S40**	**282-132**
N240CX	G2	101
N240CX	**G4**	**1370**
(N240EA)	G2	240
N240FJ	10	174
N240FJ	50	245
N240FX	**60**	**167**
N240JS	35A	241
N240S	WWD	309
N240TJ	20	24
N240TW	**20**	**40**
N240WW	WWD	240
N241AG	25B	075
N241AG	35A	491
N241AQ	25B	075
N241BJ	**400**	**RJ-41**
N241BN	23	034
N241CT	**WWD**	**267**
N241CV	560	0241
N241FJ	10	175
N241FJ	50	242
N241FT	550	268
N241FX	**60**	**172**
N241H	**S65**	**465-5**
N241JA	**24**	**131**
N241JC	**20**	**241/479**
N241LA	**S550**	**0091**
N241RH	WWD	187
N241RT	**35**	**024**
(N241SM)	125	258135
N241TR	**400**	**RJ-45**
N241WS	525	0241
N242AC	**560**	**0177**
(N242AF)	25D	242
N242AG	25	025
N242CT	**20**	**316**
N242CV	560	0242
N242DR	**35A**	**242**
N242F	23	045
N242FJ	10	176
N242FX	**60**	**174**
N242GM	25D	242
N242GS	**25D**	**242**
N242LA	**S550**	**0153**
N242LB	20	121
N242LJ	**525**	**0242**
N242MT	**35A**	**621**
(N242RJ)	20	242
N242SR	400	RJ-9
N242SW	**550**	**0908**
N242WT	23	034
N242WT	25	034
N242WT	**551**	**364**
(N243AB)	501	685
N243FJ	10	177
N243FJ	50	243
N243FJ	50	244
N243FX	**60**	**175**
N243K	20	105
N243RK	24D	306
N243SH	**500**	**243**
N243TS	125	25243
(N243TS)	G2	43
N244	STR	5141
N244A	**10**	**145**
N244AD	**50**	**162**
N244BH	601	5027
N244CA	20	321
(N244CV)	560	0244
N244DM	**G2**	**21**
N244FC	35A	299
N244FJ	10	178
N244FJ	50	232
N244FX	**60**	**178**
N244JM	**125**	**258138**
N244LJ	**35A**	**244**
N244SL	501	650
N244TJ	10	44
N244TS	35A	244
N244WJ	500	244
N244WJ	500	252
(N245BC)	500	245
(N245BC)	500	296
N245BS	**25D**	**214**
N245CC	**550**	**245**
N245DK	25D	245
N245FJ	10	180
N245FX	**60**	**182**
N245GA	G2	45
N245GL	24B	228
N245K	**45**	**076**
(N245KK)	25D	281
(N245MG)	500	245
N245MS	**55**	**077**
N245S	WWD	336
N245SP	**10**	**135**
N245TL	**601**	**5001**
N245TT	601	5001
N245TT	**G5**	**548**
N246AG	**900**	**112**
N246CM	24B	200
N246CM	**35A**	**395**
N246FJ	10	108
N246FJ	50	246
N246FX	**60**	**183**
N246GA	D1A	A064SA
(N246GS)	S40	282-111
N246JL	**600**	**1046**
(N246N)	10	33
N246N	125	25261
N246NW	550	336
N246NW	**560**	**0068**
N246RR	**500**	**167**
N246V	**125**	**258417**
N246VF	**125**	**257126**
N247DB	24D	247
N247EM	50	48
N247FJ	10	181
N247FJ	50	247
N247FX	**60**	**187**
(N247GA)	601	5019
N247GW	HFB	1030
N247N	60	049
N247TA	**35A**	**112**
N247VA	**VAN**	**001**
N248CJ	**525**	**0248**
N248CV	560	0248
N248DA	35A	238
N248FJ	10	182
N248FJ	50	249
N248FX	**60**	**188**
(N248H)	WWD	214
N248H	WWD	374
N248HM	35A	164
N248J	24B	220
N248JF	**2xx**	**11**
(N248JH)	125	257029
(N248PA)	400	RJ-9
N248TH	**G2**	**248**
N249AS	501	514
N249B	**35A**	**240**
N249BW	125	25115
N249DJ	35A	249
N249E	WWD	261
N249FJ	100	183
N249FJ	50	248
N249HP	**24D**	**301**
N249LJ	25D	249
N249MW	125	25115
N249RA	24D	249
N249SC	25D	249
N250AA	500	200
N250AL	**S550**	**0042**
N250AS	**50**	**182**
N250BC	75	370-5
N250CC	25	052
N250CC	500	250
N250CF	550	052
N250CJ	525	0250
N250CM	**650**	**0133**
(N250CV)	560	0250
N250DH	**125**	**25187**
N250EC	**S40**	**282-110**
N250FJ	10	184
N250FJ	50	250
N250GM	550	620
N250GM	**550**	**679**
N250GP	**D1A**	**A069SA**
N250HP	**400A**	**RK-250**
N250J	**G4**	**1144**
N250JH	560	0350
N250JP	WWD	121
N250JP	WWD	196
N250JT	125	25053
N250LB	25D	357
N250MA	10	132
N250MS	**G2**	**45**
N250PM	WWD	227
N250RA	20	481
N250RA	WWD	280
N250SP	501	588
N250SP	**560**	**0211**
N250SR	501	588
N250UA	WWD	121
N250VC	**G4**	**1231**
N250VP	**550**	**270**
N250WW	WWD	250
N251AB	125	25226
N251AF	**25**	**004**
N251CT	**35A**	**251**
N251DS	**25D**	**218**
N251FJ	10	186
N251GL	25B	074
N251GL	25C	061
N251JA	**25B**	**150**
N251JE	S65	465-2
N251JS	**G2**	**251**
N251LA	125	25101
N251MA	S60	306-38
N251MD	**25D**	**356**
N251NG	55ER	101
N251P	**500**	**250**
N251QS	S550	0051
N251SP	WWD	422
(N251TJ)	125	258020
N251TJ	24D	251
N251VG	55ER	101
N252BK	**25B**	**107**
N252C	**G4**	**1252**
N252CJ	525	0052
N252CV	560	0252
(N252DL)	24	124
N252FJ	10	187
N252GL	24D	230
N252HS	25D	370
N252JS	**G5**	**525**
N252M	24	140
N252R	WWD	21
N252SC	25	006
(N252TJ)	24D	252
N252V	125	25112
N253CV	560	0253
N253EJ	25D	253
N253EX	50	253
N253FJ	10	188
N253GL	24R	233
N253J	25D	253
N253K	10	10
N253L	50	19
N253M	25D	253
N253MD	WWD	253
N253MT	**125**	**25253**
N253MZ	S60	306-38
N253QS	S550	0053
N253S	**55**	**053**
N253SC	25D	253
N253W	550	253
N254AM	550	090
N254AR	G2	254/41
N254CC	550	254
N254CL	**25D**	**275**
N254CR	**G2**	**184**
N254DV	**50**	**85**
N254FJ	10	189
N254GA	**G4**	**1032**
N254JT	125	25053
N254JT	24B	181
(N254MC)	WWD	202
N254NA	50	148
N254SC	**25B**	**102**
N254SD	**G4**	**1387**
N254TW	501	541
N255BD	**60**	**221**
N255BL	55B	128
N255CB	125	25122
N255CC	550	588
N255CC	601	5156
N255CC	**604**	**5302**
N255CM	**50**	**255**
N255CT	125	257011
N255CT	S40	282-54
N255CV	560	0255
N255DG	**D1A**	**A056SA**
N255DV	**31**	**030**
N255ES	23	082A
N255FJ	10	190
N255GA	**G4**	**1055**
N255GL	25C	070
N255GM	S40	282-45
N255JC	35A	326
N255JH	35	055
N255LJ	500	292
N255MB	55	117

(N255QT) 125 257011
N255RB 125 258059
N255RB WWD 336
N255RG 35 055
N255RK 20 196
N255SB G3 448
N255ST 55 064
N255TC 550 638
(N255TS) 125 25255
N255TS 501 375
N255TS 55 060
N255TT 125 257011
N256A 20 438
N256A 50 172
N256BC 125 258256
N256CC 500 256
N256CT S40 282-54
N256DV 900 20
N256EA S40 282-60
N256EN 125 257129
N256EN 20 23
N256EN S40 282-60
N256FC 125 256003
N256FJ 10 191
N256FS 125 258256
N256GL 25C 072
N256JB 525 0284
N256JC 200 496
N256M 20 274
N256M 60 073
N256M G2 235
(N256MA) 125 257129
N256MA 20 23
N256MA 20 75
N256MA 35A 235
N256MA S40 282-60
N256MA S40 282-69
(N256MB) 35A 235
(N256MT) S60 306-13
N256N WWD 427
N256P 25 006
N256P 501 659
N256TW 35A 218
N256V 10 151
N256W 10 151
N256W 550 026
N256W 650 7111
N256WJ 125 256008
N256WN 500 019
N257AJ 125 257001
N257AL 35A 128
N257CB D1A A050SA
N257CW 550 229
N257DJ 35A 257
(N257DP) 35 064
N257GL 25C 071
N257H 125 25104
N257H G2 223
N257H G4 1223
N257H STR 5083/49
N257H STR 5230
N257HA STR 5083/49
N257SD 35 064
N257TH 125 257007
N257TM S40 282-76
N257V 10 119
N257W 10 119
N257W 650 7112
N257WJ 125 257007
N258A 20 438
N258AV WWD 258
N258CC 550 258
(N258CF) WWD 258
N258FJ 100 192
N258G 25B 092
N258G 35A 443
N258GL 25B 078
N258JS 550 285
N258MD 25D 258
(N258P) 550 408
(N258P) 550 454
(N258P) 550 493
N258P S550 0022
N258RA 125 258273
N258SA 125 258235
N258SC 31A 058
N258SR 125 258051
(N259B) G3 431
N259DB 23 064
N259DH 500 259
N259FJ 100 193
N259HA 35A 259
(N259JC) 35A 259
N260CC 500 260
N260CV 560 0260
N260FJ 100 194
N260J 550 249
N260LF 31 015
N260MB 20 274
N260QS S550 0060
N261CC 500 261
N261CV 560 0261
N261FJ 100 195
N261JP 400A RK-76
N261PC 31A 109
N261PC 35A 329
N261PC 60 146
N261PG 35A 329
N261PQ 31A 109
N261SC 31A 061
N261SS 550 288
N261T S60 306-125
N261UH 560 0261
(N261VP) 550 288
(N261WB) 501 674
N261WC 25D 261
N261WD 501 674
N261WD S550 0119
N261WR 501 674
N261WR 560 0122
N261WR 560 0447
N261WR S550 0119
N262BK 525 0262
(N262CT) 125 258239
N262CV 560 0262
N262E 25B 100
N262EX 50 262
N262FJ 100 196
N262GL 24D 238
N262HA 24 123
N262JE 25B 100
N262PA G2 62
N262WC WWD 262
N262WW WWD 262
N263AL 500 263
N263C G3 341
N263CT 525 0263
N263FJ 100 198
N263GL 25 028
N263GL 35 003
N263GL 35 009
N263K 20 438
N263MW 20 59
N263PW 900 159
N263R 125 259024
N263S G4 1263
N264A 550 429
N264CL G2 227
N264CV 560 0264
N264FJ 100 199
N264TS 125 25264
N264U 560 0264
N264WC 125 257090
(N264WD) 125 25264
N265A G3 440
N265A S65 465-47
(N265AC) S40 282-23
N265C S60 306-120
N265C S65 465-33
(N265CA) S65 465-21
N265CH 75A 380-30
N265CM S40 282-76
N265DL 125 25287
N265DP 75A 380-30
N265DP S60 306-68
N265DR S65 465-45
N265EJ 25D 265
N265FJ 100 200
N265GL 25B 090
N265GM S60 306-84
N265JS S65 465-56
N265KC 80A 380-49
N265LJ 25D 265
N265M S65 465-31
N265MK S60 306-90
N265MP 20 265
N265PC S65 465-24
(N265QS) 550 293
N265R S40 282-20
N265RW S60 306-125
N265SC S40 282-117
N265SP S65 465-48
N265SR 75 370-5
N265SR 80A 380-11
N265SR S60 306-120
N265ST G4 1179
N265TJ S60 306-102
N265TW 25D 265
N265U S60 306-132
N265W S40 282-37
N265WB T39 276-39
N266BS 24D 266
N266BS 25B 180
N266BS 36A 035
N266CJ 525 0266
N266FJ 100 201
N266GL 25 064
N266JP 23 037
N266P 24B 186
(N266TS) 125 25266
N266TW 24D 266
(N267AD) STR 5067
N267CW 550 094
N267FJ 100 203
N267GF STR 5074/22
N267GL 25B 102
N267JE 125 257095
N267L STR 5067
N267MP 24X 267
N267P STR 5074/22
N267PS G2 8
N267TC 550 376
N267TG 550 376
N267TG 650 0159
N267TS 125 257067
N268FJ 100 204
N268GL 25B 101
(N268GM) 500 323
N268J 550 268
(N268TS) 125 25268
N268WC 25D 268
(N269AJ) 550 063
N269AJ WWD 276
(N269AL) 24 159
N269AS 25B 101
N269CM 501 546
N269CM 560 0268
N269FJ 100 205
N269HM G2 13
N269JD 550 477
N269JR 550 477
N269JR 560 0266
N269MD 25D 269
N269MD 501 546
N269MH G2 13
(N269MT) S550 0080
N269RC 500 078
N269SR 20 370
N269TA 560 0006
N269X 125 258129
N270A WWD 270
N270AS 55 056
N270AV 125 25270
N270BH 500 330
(N270BJ) 400 RJ-41
N270CF 551 300
N270CS 35 042
(N270DT) WWD 270
N270EX 50 270
N270FJ 100 206
N270HC 125 258020
N270KA 125 257154
N270LC WWD 245
N270MC 125 256067
N270MC 125 257154
N270MC G3 374
N270MH 125 257152
N270MQ 125 256067
N270NF 501 536
N270PM 500 196
N270RA 20 446
N270RA 550 265
N270RA 604 5337
(N270SC) 31A 070
N270SC G4 1229
N270SF 501 536
N270TC 24 134
N270TS G2 43
(N270WW) WWD 270
N270X 125 258131
(N270X) 125 258134
N271AC 500 218
N271CA 560 0071
N271CG 550 423
N271E WWD 43
N271FJ 100 207
N271JG G5 582
N271MB 600 1055
N271MB D1A A015SA
N271MB S65 465-24
(N271MB) S65 465-33
N271SC 31A 071
(N271X) 125 258131
N271X 125 258134
N272B 125 25175
N272BC 400A RK-192
N272BC 400A RK-2
N272BC D1A A046SA
N272BG D1A A046SA
N272BQ 400A RK-2
N272EJ 25D 272
N272EX 50 272
(N272FA) 20 272
N272FJ 100 209
N272GL 24B 195
N272HS 35A 272
N272JM 25D 272
N272JP 20 272
N272JS G3 489
N272T 35A 349
N272TB 55 056
N272X 125 258154
(N273DA) 501 382
N273FJ 100 210
N273G 601 3002
N273G G3 454
N273GL 24B 201
N273JC 2xx 73
N273K 125 256041
N273K 20 349
N273KH 25D 315
(N273LB) 650 0056
N273LF WWD 44
N273LP 25 058
N273LP 650 0056
N273LP G2 192
N273LP WWD 44
N273LR 25 058
N273M 25D 315
N273MC 35A 149
N273MC 55 119
N273MC 60 181
N273MG 35A 149
N273MG 55 119
N273RA AST 097
N273RC 500 273
N273S 604 5396
N273W 650 0068
N273X 125 258156
N274 55 105
N274CA S60 306-31
N274FD 35A 274
N274FJ 100 213
N274HM WWD 202
N274JH 35A 274
N274JS 35A 274

N274K	**WWD**	**274**
N274LJ	25D	274
N274QS	**S550**	**0074**
N274X	125	258158
N275AL	500	333
N275BD	550	675
N275CC	501	508
N275CC	550	248
N275CQ	501	508
N275E	**24D**	**245**
N275FJ	100	214
N275GC	**650**	**0162**
N275GK	**500**	**275**
N275HS	**D1A**	**A080SA**
N275J	35	009
N275LE	24D	245
(N275PC)	400A	RK-75
N275QS	**2xx**	**75**
N275RA	**AST**	**098**
(N275VP)	S550	0075
N275WN	650	0018
N276AL	550	017
N276CC	500	276
N276FJ	100	216
N276GC	**604**	**5431**
N276JS	35A	458
N276LE	25B	078
(N277A)	550	083
N277AG	G4	1026
N277AL	**55**	**104**
N277AL	S550	0013
(N277AM)	35A	204
(N277CB)	125	257182
N277CC	500	277
N277CJ	525	0277
N277CJ	550	040
N277CT	125	257086
N277CT	S60	306-2
N277FJ	100	217
(N277HG)	650	0025
N277HM	551	277
N277JM	**551**	**277**
N277JW	125	257110
N277LE	25	028
N277MG	**WWD**	**127**
N277NS	G3	381
N277NS	STR	5099/5
N277QS	S550	0077
N277RC	**560**	**0210**
N277RP	G4	1026
(N277RW)	501	444
N277SF	10	44
N277T	**G2**	**209**
N277T	STR	5105
N277TW	**24D**	**277**
N277W	650	0072
N278A	550	168
N278CC	500	278
N278FJ	50	186
N278LE	25B	120
N278QS	**2xx**	**77**
(N278S)	550	571
N278SP	500	278
(N278SR)	500	278
N279AL	20	279/502
N279DM	**35A**	**214**
N279DP	**AST**	**020**
N279DS	**AST**	**040**
N279FJ	50	187
N279LE	**25B**	**112**
N279SP	**35A**	**452**
N279TG	25D	265
N280AJ	125	257102
N280AZ	**WWD**	**247**
N280BC	50	109
N280BC	**900**	**71**
N280BG	**50**	**109**
N280C	23	082
N280C	**25D**	**280**
N280CC	500	280
N280DB	WWD	187
N280FJ	50	188
N280JS	551	400
N280LA	25D	280

N280LC	25XR	029
N280LM	WWD	247
N280MH	550	313
N280PM	**550**	**207**
N280R	**24B**	**188**
(N280RC)	20	28
N280TA	**550**	**226**
N280VC	125	257102
(N281AM)	550	281
N281BC	35A	380
N281CD	35A	417
N281FJ	50	189
N281FP	**24D**	**281**
N281GA	G2	81
N281JJ	20	281/498
(N281NW)	G2	81
N281QS	**2xx**	**81**
N281R	24	134
N281R	25	026
N281RB	**G2**	**200**
N281XP	125	258281
N282AC	**24**	**145**
(N282AM)	S40	282-20
N282C	20	282
N282CA	S40	282-50
N282CC	500	282
N282CD	G4	1098
N282FJ	50	191
N282JJ	20	282
N282MC	S40	282-52
N282NA	S40	282-23
(N282PC)	650	0058
N282Q	G3	379
N282Q	**G5**	**532**
N282QS	S550	0082
N282R	24	131
N282R	24	134
N282RH	560	0055
N282T	**10**	**42**
N282U	20	305
N282WW	**S60**	**306-134**
N283DF	**550**	**456**
N283FJ	50	192
N283K	50	87
N283MM	G2	81
N283R	25	026
N283U	25D	277
N283U	50	14
(N283XP)	125	258283
N284	550	225
N284AM	500	028
N284CC	500	284
N284CE	20	284
N284DB	125	25023
N284DB	**125**	**25179**
N284FJ	50	194
N284JJ	20	284
N284PC	501	433
N284RJ	**501**	**357**
N284TJ	**25D**	**284**
N284U	S60	306-48
N285AP	20	285/504
(N285CC)	500	285
N285CC	**560**	**0285**
(N285CF)	S550	0085
N285CP	**50**	**44**
N285CV	560	0285
N285FJ	50	196
N285HR	35A	082
N285LM	STR	5224
N285MC	**S550**	**0102**
N285TW	**20**	**285/504**
N285U	20	364
N285XP	**125**	**258285**
N286CC	500	286
(N286CP)	35A	268
N286CV	560	0286
N286FJ	50	197
N286G	551	191
N286GA	G4	1286
N286MC	**650**	**7076**
N286PC	**501**	**570**
N286WL	**35A**	**286**
N287	550	225

N287AB	**500**	**287**
N287CC	500	287
N287CV	560	0287
N287FJ	50	199
N287MC	**650**	**7096**
N287MC	S550	0102
N287MF	25D	287
N287NA	S50	287-1
N287QS	**2xx**	**87**
N287W	20	194
(N287XP)	125	258287
N288AG	**525**	**0288**
N288CC	500	288
N288CC	550	248
N288CC	650	0079
N288DF	**24D**	**288**
N288EX	50	288
N288FJ	50	200
N288J	24F	357
N288JE	35A	288
N288JP	**35A**	**288**
N288K	24	175
(N288MM)	20	380
N288MW	125	256018
N288NE	35A	288
N288QS	**S550**	**0088**
(N288SJ)	WWD	299
N288SP	**500**	**241**
N288U	STR	5106/9
N288VW	24X	117
N288WW	WWD	277
N288Z	**900**	**43**
N289CA	29	003
(N289CC)	S550	0089
N289CC	S550	0159
N289FJ	50	201
N289G	24D	289
(N289GA)	35A	357
N289K	**601**	**5132**
N289K	G2	225
N289LJ	35A	289
N289MJ	35A	289
N289MM	20	380
N289NE	35A	289
N289SA	24D	289
N290	25D	251
N290AS	650	0088
N290BA	550	304
(N290BC)	200	495
N290BC	35	064
N290CA	**WWD**	**216**
N290CC	500	290
N290EC	**125**	**258172**
N290FJ	50	202
N290GA	G3	875
N290H	125	259034
N290PC	125	257149
N290RA	WWD	390
N290SC	650	0079
N290SC	650	0140
N290TJ	50	29
N290VP	**550**	**085**
N290W	50	90
N290W	WWD	280
N291A	35A	212
N291BC	24B	212
N291BC	35	015
N291BC	35	064
N291BC	35A	380
N291BC	**50**	**199**
N291BX	35A	380
N291DS	500	291
N291FJ	50	205
N291GA	G2	91
N291H	125	259016
N291K	**35A**	**665**
N291SJ	125	258291
N291XP	125	258291
N292BC	23	010
N292BC	24B	220
N292BC	50	62
N292EX	50	292
N292FJ	50	207
N292GA	125	25219

N292GA	**601**	**3014**
N292H	125	259025
N292JC	WWD	292
N292ME	**35A**	**292**
(N292PC)	650	0058
N292QS	**2xx**	**93**
(N292RC)	125	25219
N292RC	55	062
N293BC	23	042
N293BC	24B	229
N293BC	**50**	**135**
N293BC	50	82
N293EX	50	293
N293FJ	50	209
(N293GT)	20	71
(N293H)	125	258266
N293K	50	170
N293MC	**24D**	**293**
N293PC	550	713
N293QS	**560**	**0293**
N293S	500	193
N293SA	**31A**	**101**
N294AT	**525**	**0294**
N294AW	**400A**	**RK-1**
N294B	WWD	222
N294BC	24	149
N294CA	29	004
N294EX	**50**	**291**
N294FA	400A	RK-1
N294FJ	50	212
N294H	125	258267
(N294M)	25	031
N294NW	**25**	**031**
N294S	**AST**	**094**
N294W	10	30
N294W	125	258014
N294W	WWD	222
N295AR	STR	5134/50
N295CM	525	0295
N295CV	560	0295
N295DJ	25D	295
N295DS	**525**	**0091**
N295FA	**400A**	**RK-68**
N295FJ	50	213
N295H	125	258269
N295NW	**24D**	**295**
N295TW	**20**	**5**
N295WW	WWD	295
N296AB	550	011
N296AR	STR	5055/21
N296BF	**500**	**296**
N296BS	35A	296
N296CC	550	296
N296CF	550	296
N296DC	**525**	**0296**
N296EX	**50**	**296**
N296FA	**400A**	**RK-91**
N296FJ	50	214
(N296H)	125	259045
N296H	125	259047
N296NW	WWD	284
N296PH	550	296
N297A	WWD	267
N297AG	20	297
N297AR	20	24
N297CK	20	296/507
N297EJ	24D	297
N297EJ	25D	297
N297FJ	50	215
N297GA	AST	091
N297GA	AST	101
N297GA	AST	111
N297GA	AST	113
N297GB	**G2**	**185**
N297H	125	258270
N297JD	**125**	**25235**
N297JS	WWD	435
N297MC	G4	1393
N297S	**500**	**197**
N297W	20	194
N297W	50	111
N297W	WWD	267
N297XP	125	258297
N298A	WWD	318

N298AG	**125**	**258014**
(N298AS)	S40	282-117
N298CJ	551	298
N298CK	20	347
N298CM	WWD	298
N298DR	**25D**	**298**
N298EJ	24D	298
N298FJ	50	216
(N298GS)	25D	295
N298H	125	258271
N298H	24B	229
N298NM	125	25278
N298NW	**35A**	**298**
N298QS	**2xx**	**98**
N298TB	**G3**	**875**
N298TS	**125**	**257138**
N298W	20	142
N298W	50	90
N298W	900	33
N298W	**900**	**45**
N298W	WWD	318
N298XP	125	258298
N299AW	**400A**	**RK-212**
N299BW	125	256046
N299CT	125	257090
N299D	**501**	**564**
N299DB	**10**	**50**
N299DB	G4	1137
N299DG	125	256046
N299EJ	24D	299
N299EX	**50**	**299**
N299FB	125	257122
N299FB	G4	1099
N299GA	125	256046
N299H	125	258272
N299JC	**20**	**299**
N299LR	S40	282-38
N299MW	**25D**	**299**
N299NW	20	61
N299QS	S550	0099
N299RP	**501**	**448**
N299SC	60	025
N299SC	**60**	**112**
N299SG	**60**	**025**
N299TB	500	230
N299TJ	125	256046
N299TW	**24D**	**299**
N299W	50	21
N299WV	500	320
N299XP	125	258299
N300A	10	59
N300A	**50**	**64**
N300AA	**D1A**	**A041SA**
N300AG	STR	5056
N300AJ	AST	070
N300AK	**550**	**0809**
N300AK	550	612
N300AL	20	330
N300BA	**20**	**142**
N300BE	G3	332
N300BK	G3	409
N300BL	**125**	**258155**
N300BS	**125**	**257056**
N300BW	125	258074
N300CC	125	25250
N300CC	20	257
N300CC	24	179
N300CC	36A	019
N300CF	125	25276
N300CH	S40	282-26
N300CM	35A	381
N300CQ	525	0300
N300CR	50	55
N300CR	**601**	**5092**
N300CR	STR	5020
N300CT	20	366
N300CV	**20**	**322**
N300DA	35A	249
N300DH	D1A	A010SA
N300DH	WWD	74
N300DK	36A	019
N300DK	G2	57
N300DL	36A	019
N300DL	G2	57
N300DM	D1A	A003SA
N300EC	500	339
N300EJ	24D	300
N300ES	35A	278
N300ES	50	70
N300FJ	20	168
N300FJ	20	300/508
N300FN	35A	447
(N300FN)	G2	65
N300GA	G3	249
N300GA	G3	300
N300GA	G3	303
N300GB	125	25074
N300GB	**400A**	**RK-262**
N300GF	**550**	**0856**
N300GM	550	343
N300GN	10	59
N300GN	125	258057
N300GP	G2	3
N300GX	G4	1164
N300HA	200	503
N300HB	125	257173
N300HC	500	124
N300HC	500	348
N300HC	WWD	307
N300HH	24	149
N300HH	D1A	A035SA
N300HQ	500	124
N300HR	WWD	335
N300HW	125	25021
N300JA	24D	282
N300JE	25D	234
N300JE	**45**	**094**
N300JJ	20	208/468
N300JJ	AST	024
N300JK	550	262
N300JK	WWD	369
N300K	G4	1266
N300K	G5	587
N300KC	125	25118
N300KC	601	5051
N300L	G2	92
N300L	G3	318
N300L	G4	1018
N300L	**G5**	**507**
N300L	STR	5097/60
N300LA	D1A	A049SA
N300LB	24	149
N300LD	125	25202
N300LD	125	25265
(N300LD)	125	257043
(N300LF)	G3	318
N300LG	D1A	A090SA
N300LH	WWD	312
N300LS	125	257173
N300LS	125	258098
N300LS	**125**	**259032**
N300LS	WWD	137
N300LS	WWD	226
N300LS	WWD	400
N300M	G3	417
N300M	WWD	124
N300ND	MSP	009
N300NL	20	221
N300P	125	25226
N300P	STR	5052
N300PB	500	323
N300PB	501	400
N300PB	550	007
N300PL	25D	247
N300PM	125	258193
N300PP	25	043
(N300PR)	550	239
N300PX	500	140
N300PY	**550**	**0806**
N300QC	125	25250
N300QS	**560**	**0322**
N300QW	**S550**	**0100**
N300R	125	25043
N300R	**35A**	**438**
N300RB	**125**	**258013**
N300RC	S40	282-41
N300RC	S60	306-111
N300RG	S40	282-41
(N300RN)	501	517
N300S	601	3026
N300SB	HFB	1031
N300SC	**25D**	**208**
N300SF	**20**	**258**
(N300SJ)	D1A	A060SA
N300TA	23	038
(N300TB)	500	230
N300TB	S60	306-24
N300TC	550	313
N300TC	**WWD**	**241**
N300TE	**35A**	**237**
N300TE	WWD	201
(N300TJ)	D1A	A003SA
(N300TK)	S40	282-41
N300TS	**D1A**	**A003SA**
N300TW	**125**	**257192**
N300TW	35A	237
N300TW	550	047
N300U	G2	92
N300WG	25D	346
N300WK	501	374
N300WY	**G3**	**427**
N300XL	**WWD**	**276**
N300YM	S60	306-83
N301AJ	WWD	48
(N301AS)	125	257188
N301AS	31A	052
N301AT	HFB	1038
N301CK	125	25038
N301DM	D1A	A007SA
N301EC	G2	258
N301EL	**501**	**544**
(N301FC)	20	335
(N301FP)	G2	118
(N301GA)	G3	252
N301GA	G3	329
N301GA	G3	402
N301HA	S40	282-23
N301HC	10	77
N301HC	500	348
(N301HC)	WWD	307
N301JJ	10	24
N301JJ	50	161
N301K	G4	1267
N301K	G5	591
N301KF	**WWD**	**301**
N301L	WWD	98
(N301LX)	125	257188
(N301MC)	501	383
N301MC	501	390
N301MC	S60	306-146
N301MC	S65	465-14
N301MG	501	390
N301MG	S60	306-146
N301NT	S40	282-9
N301P	D1A	A030SA
N301PC	S40	282-112
N301PC	**WWD**	**377**
(N301PC)	WWD	383
N301PH	125	257121
N301PH	**125**	**259031**
N301PP	501	518
N301QS	560	0038
N301QS	S550	0158
N301R	**20**	**3/403**
N301SC	35A	143
N301TP	35A	301
N301TT	**20**	**160/450**
N302A	10	59
N302AT	WWD	12
N302CE	500	302
N302CJ	525	0302
N302DM	D1A	A004SA
N302EC	601	5093
N302EJ	24D	302
N302GA	G3	302
N302GA	G3	339
N302GA	G3	438
N302GA	G3	480
N302H	S60	306-5
N302K	G5	597
(N302NT)	S40	282-100
N302NT	S40	282-81
N302PC	**125**	**257125**
N302PC	25D	351
N302PC	S550	0130
N302QS	**560**	**0402**
N302TS	**501**	**382**
N302TT	20	122
N302XP	125	258302
N303A	S40	282-52
N303A	S65	465-32
N303AF	24	144
N303AJ	WWD	149
N303BC	**125**	**258324**
N303CB	501	422
N303CB	**560**	**0190**
N303DM	D1A	A008SA
(N303E)	WWD	390
(N303EC)	550	303
N303EC	550	330
N303EJ	24D	303
N303GA	**G3**	**303**
N303GA	G3	357
N303GA	G3	462
(N303GC)	550	193
N303H	STR	5055/21
N303HB	G3	402
N303J	550	303
N303JJ	25	062
N303JW	**50**	**140**
N303LA	WWD	51
N303LC	525	0068
N303LE	STR	5113/25
N303MW	125	256033
N303NT	S40	282-29
N303P	D1A	A034SA
N303PC	500	124
N303PC	**650**	**0110**
N303PC	WWD	223
N303PL	10	187
N303QS	**560**	**0343**
N303SC	25B	095
N303SQ	25B	095
N303TS	**WWD**	**416**
N303WB	31A	056
N303X	550	198
N303XP	125	258303
N304AF	35	013
N304AT	35	045
N304AT	55ER	107
N304CC	500	304
N304CK	STR	5055/21
N304DM	D1A	A005SA
N304E	36A	038
N304EJ	24D	304
N304FX	**601**	**5063**
N304GA	G3	312
N304GA	G3	381
N304GA	G3	440
N304GA	G3	481
N304K	**G5**	**514**
N304KT	**551**	**290**
N304LP	24D	304
N304NT	S40	282-2
N304P	125	25226
N304QS	**560**	**0408**
N304TS	**G3**	**304**
N304TZ	35	045
N304WW	WWD	304
N305AF	G2	17
N305AJ	WWD	100
N305AR	20	378
N305BB	500	305
N305BB	**WWD**	**228**
N305CJ	**525**	**0105**
N305DM	D1A	A009SA
N305EJ	24D	305
N305FX	601	5070
N305GA	G3	305
N305GA	G3	343
N305GA	G3	382
N305M	501	443
(N305M)	601	5021
N305MD	G3	305
N305NT	S40	282-66
N305PC	S550	0138

N305S	**500**	**301**
N305SC	35A	322
N305TC	**G3**	**359**
N305TH	**125**	**257150**
N305XP	125	258305
N306CF	**S60**	**306-13**
N306CW	S40	282-108
N306DM	D1A	A010SA
N306EJ	24D	306
N306ES	**50**	**70**
N306FX	**601**	**5175**
N306GA	G3	306
N306GA	G3	344
N306GA	G3	441
N306GA	G3	482
N306JA	24D	306
N306L	125	25093
N306L	STR	5097/60
N306M	35A	416
N306MP	125	25017
N306NA	S60	306-1
N306NT	S40	282-30
N306P	D1A	A009SA
N306PA	**650**	**0053**
N306PC	S40	282-112
(N306QS)	650	0006
N306SA	**S60**	**306-40**
N306SC	550	306
N306SP	35A	459
N307AF	G2	219/20
N307AJ	25XR	175
N307AJ	551	107
N307BJ	24D	307
N307D	S60	306-31
N307DM	D1A	A011SA
N307EJ	24D	307
N307EW	**500**	**323**
N307FX	**601**	**5179**
N307G	125	25121
N307GA	G3	331
N307M	G2	220
N307NA	S60	306-2
N307NT	S40	282-72
N307QS	**560**	**0307**
(N307TC)	125	257007
N307XP	125	258307
N308A	**550**	**703**
N308A	G2	155/14
N308AF	G3	351
N308AJ	**25**	**039**
(N308AJ)	WWD	149
N308AT	501	537
N308CC	500	308
N308CK	550	117
N308DD	**125**	**257069**
N308DM	D1A	A012SA
N308EE	**G2**	**68**
N308EJ	24D	308
N308EL	G2	68
N308FX	**601**	**5110**
N308GA	G3	308
N308GA	G3	318
N308GA	G3	383
N308HG	**G3**	**308**
N308JS	WWD	308
(N308LJ)	24D	308
N308NT	S40	282-90
N308SG	**STR**	**5226**
N308TS	WWD	308
N308TW	**550**	**047**
N308WC	STR	5020
N308XP	125	258308
N309AJ	25	034
N309AT	550	448
N309CK	WWD	350
N309DM	D1A	A044SA
N309EL	**G2**	**250**
N309FX	**604**	**5306**
N309G	**125**	**258108**
N309GA	G3	328
N309GA	G3	388
N309GA	G3	446
N309GA	G3	483
N309GA	**G4**	**1309**
N309LJ	**25**	**034**
N309NT	S40	282-61
N309QS	**560**	**0509**
(N309TA)	650	0129
N309WM	**125**	**257156**
N310AD	STR	5051
N310AF	501	524
N310AS	**125**	**258443**
N310AV	**550**	**028**
N310BA	35	062
N310CK	STR	5117/35
N310FJ	10	23
N310FX	**604**	**5336**
N310GA	G3	332
N310GA	G3	389
N310GA	G3	449
N310GA	G3	484
N310GA	**G4**	**1405**
N310KR	23	020
N310LJ	24D	309
N310LJ	31	033C
(N310ME)	35A	310
N310NT	S40	282-77
N310RG	G3	321
N310SL	G3	496
N310SL	G4	1087
N310U	500	194
N310XP	125	258310
N311AC	G2	74
N311BP	35A	311
N311BP	604	5405
N311BR	WWD	344
N311CC	25B	102
N311DB	**WWD**	**208**
N311DF	31	001
N311DG	**560**	**0167**
N311DM	D1A	A019SA
N311EL	**G4**	**1095**
N311FX	**604**	**5342**
N311G	601	5014
N311GA	G3	311
N311GA	G3	394
N311GA	G3	474
N311GA	**G4**	**1406**
N311GX	601	5014
N311JA	**125**	**25176**
N311JD	125	257020
N311JJ	G2	3
N311JK	G3	434
N311JS	20	341
N311LJ	31	033A
N311MA	650	0126
N311NT	S40	282-19
N311NW	125	257159
N311QS	**560**	**0311**
N311RM	S60	306-6
N311TP	**501**	**597**
N311TS	31	010
(N311TT)	501	597
N311VP	**501**	**600**
N312A	10	122
N312A	50	157
N312AM	10	123
N312AM	100	210
N312AM	**604**	**5312**
N312AN	10	123
(N312AR)	100	209
N312AT	10	122
N312AT	10	123
N312AT	100	209
N312AT	601	5141
N312AT	**604**	**5313**
(N312CC)	551	312
N312CE	35A	403
N312CF	35A	403
N312CF	650	0143
N312CK	STR	5150/37
N312CT	35A	403
N312CT	601	5030
N312DC	550	376
N312DM	D1A	A033SA
N312DM	D1A	A090SA
N312EL	**G4**	**1105**
N312FX	**604**	**5349**
N312GA	550	004
N312GA	G3	416
N312GA	G3	475
N312GA	**G4**	**1407**
N312GK	25D	283
N312GK	501	492
N312K	**20**	**324**
N312K	S40	282-105
N312LJ	31	033D
N312NA	24D	312
N312NC	**550**	**304**
N312NT	S40	282-32
N312QS	**560**	**0312**
N312RD	550	0881
N312S	WWD	118
N312S	WWD	84
N312W	AST	012
N312XP	125	258312
N313BA	500	313
N313BT	550	113
N313CC	**125**	**258043**
N313CE	550	358
N313CK	550	041
N313CV	**560**	**0313**
N313DM	D1A	A022SA
N313GH	50	228
(N313GH)	50	252
N313JL	500	166
N313NT	S40	282-94
N313QS	650	0013
N313RG	G3	321
N313RG	**G5**	**504**
N313VR	125	257207
N313XP	125	258313
N314AC	**31A**	**140**
N314AD	**AST**	**072**
N314AD	WWD	394
N314AE	20	140
N314C	**35A**	**412**
(N314CC)	500	314
N314CK	551	051
N314CV	560	0314
N314DM	D1A	A023SA
N314EB	501	615
N314FX	**604**	**5372**
N314G	S550	0060
N314GA	G3	411
N314GA	G3	476
N314GA	**G4**	**1114**
N314GS	501	669
(N314MC)	550	293
N314MK	**31A**	**040**
N314NT	S40	282-28
N314QS	**560**	**0441**
N314RW	**560**	**0051**
N314SL	**650**	**7115**
N314TC	500	216
N314TW	**20**	**314/516**
N314XP	125	258314
N315AJ	**24**	**108**
N315CK	550	075
N315CS	**560**	**0371**
N315DG	604	5386
N315DM	D1A	A015SA
N315EJ	560	0215
N315ES	**550**	**459**
(N315FX)	601	5063
N315FX	**604**	**5377**
N315GA	G3	315
N315GA	G3	398
N315GA	G3	443
N315GA	G3	485
N315GA	**G4**	**1315**
N315GS	G3	315
N315JM	S60	306-96
N315JM	WWD	259
N315MA	G4	1032
N315MC	G4	1032
N315MK	**600**	**1047**
N315MP	501	451
N315MR	501	451
N315MR	**525**	**0198**
N315NT	S40	282-20
(N315P)	501	409
N315PA	20	113
N315QS	**560**	**0315**
N315R	**400A**	**RK-9**
N315S	**501**	**409**
(N315S)	AST	053
N315SA	WWD	126
N315SL	601	3054
N315TR	**WWD**	**315**
N315TS	G2	220
N316	35	024
N316	55	062
N316	WWD	3
N316AC	**31A**	**190**
N316AS	**31A**	**150**
N316CC	550	316
N316CF	550	316
N316DM	D1A	A024SA
N316E	WWD	3
N316EC	**75A**	**380-38**
N316EJ	**525**	**0316**
N316FA	**G3**	**316**
N316FX	**604**	**5387**
N316GA	G3	316
N316GA	G3	386
N316GA	G3	445
N316GA	G3	486
N316GA	G4	1408
N316GS	**G4**	**1225**
N316H	550	316
N316LJ	31A	036
N316M	23	061
N316M	24	101
N316M	25	014
N316MA	550	0907
N316MF	24	101
N316MH	S550	0108
N316MJ	**525**	**0297**
N316NT	S40	282-60
N316PA	50	166
N316QS	**560**	**0516**
N316RS	31A	150
N316RS	**31A**	**189**
N316SR	**45**	**121**
N316XP	125	258316
(N317AB)	500	017
N317AF	G2	168
N317BG	35A	506
N317CC	**125**	**258093**
N317CC	D1A	A081SA
N317CJ	**525**	**0317**
N317DM	D1A	A025SA
N317EM	125	25115
N317FE	600	1074
N317FX	**604**	**5407**
N317GA	G3	350
N317GA	G3	417
N317GA	G3	477
N317GA	**G4**	**1409**
N317GC	D1A	A081SA
N317HC	**550**	**228**
(N317JD)	35A	186
N317JD	**G5**	**549**
N317JS	**WWD**	**385**
N317LJ	**31A**	**117**
N317M	650	7055
N317M	**G4**	**1122**
N317M	WWD	257
N317M	WWD	432
N317MB	**650**	**7012**
N317MB	WWD	257
N317MB	WWD	432
N317ML	**G3**	**460**
N317MQ	**650**	**7015**
N317MQ	WWD	421
(N317MR)	24D	297
N317MR	35A	176
(N317MT)	WWD	432
(N317MV)	WWD	418
(N317MX)	650	7015
N317MX	WWD	418
N317MZ	650	7010
N317MZ	**650**	**7055**
N317NT	S40	282-100
N317QS	**560**	**0317**

N317SM	551	162
N317TC	**125**	**256007**
N317TT	**35A**	**317**
N317VP	**500**	**317**
N318CT	**560**	**0081**
N318DM	D1A	A034SA
N318FX	**604**	**5415**
N318GA	G3	355
N318GA	G3	421
N318GA	G3	478
N318GA	**G4**	**1410**
(N318GD)	G2	170
N318JH	**55**	**026**
N318JH	55	106
N318LJ	31A	118
N318MM	**560**	**0219**
N318NW	**35A**	**318**
N318QS	**560**	**0418**
N318RS	**D1A**	**A009SA**
N318SP	**G2**	**168**
N318XP	125	258318
N319AT	125	258043
N319BG	WWD	192
N319DM	D1A	A019SA
N319DM	D1A	A027SA
N319EJ	25D	319
N319FX	**604**	**5418**
N319GA	G3	370
N319GA	G3	422
N319GA	G3	479
N319GA	G4	1356
N319GP	G2	150
N319LJ	60	079
N319MF	125	256070
N319NW	125	257171
N319QS	**560**	**0519**
N319SC	**31A**	**131**
N319Z	G3	319
N320AF	HFB	1023
N320AF	**HFB**	**1061**
N320CC	500	320
N320CH	D1A	A024SA
N320CL	**604**	**5370**
N320DG	**S550**	**0021**
N320DM	D1A	A028SA
N320EJ	25D	320
N320FE	G2	9/33
(N320FJ)	20	242
N320FX	**604**	**5425**
N320GA	G3	372
N320GA	G3	409
N320GA	G3	424
N320GA	G4	1366
(N320GP)	10	80
N320GP	125	257173
N320J	HFB	1023
N320J	HFB	1034
N320JJ	125	25198
N320K	50	154
N320M	35A	320
N320MC	HFB	1034
N320MP	WWD	432
N320QS	**560**	**0321**
N320S	550	138
N320S	S550	0090
N320S	STR	5082/36
N320T	D1A	A032SA
N320TR	G2	233
N320V	550	193
N320VP	560	0320
N320W	WWD	15
N320WE	G3	320
N321AF	HFB	1060
N321AN	**35A**	**272**
N321AR	**650**	**0151**
N321AS	25D	273
N321DM	D1A	A029SA
N321F	550	567
N321FM	501	687
N321FX	**604**	**5427**
N321GA	G3	321
N321GA	G3	426
N321GA	G3	459
N321GL	24	174
N321GL	25D	277
N321GL	**25D**	**289**
(N321GL)	55	026
N321GN	550	347
N321PT	G4	1013
(N321PT)	G4	1251
N321Q	24	177
N321RB	25D	290
N321RT	G4	1013
N321SE	550	347
N321VP	501	668
(N321WJ)	35A	321
N322AF	HFB	1058
N322AU	**24D**	**326**
N322BE	D1A	A022SA
N322CC	125	256070
N322CP	**900**	**134**
N322CS	550	344
N322CS	S40	282-56
N322CS	STR	5208
N322DM	D1A	A030SA
N322FX	**604**	**5434**
N322GA	G3	322
N322GA	G3	428
N322GA	G3	460
N322GA	G3	493
N322GA	G4	1368
N322K	STR	5013
N322K	STR	5133
N322LA	**125**	**258410**
N322MA	**551**	**375**
N322MD	D1A	A022SA
N322QS	**560**	**0421**
N322RG	650	7070
N322RR	**200**	**514**
N322TJ	24D	322
N322TP	**125**	**25170**
(N322TW)	S65	465-17
N323AF	HFB	1062
N323AM	550	351
N323CB	501	563
N323CJ	550	323
N323DM	D1A	A032SA
N323EC	S60	306-134
N323EJ	25D	323
N323FX	**604**	**5447**
N323GA	G3	429
N323GA	G3	461
N323GA	G4	1369
N323GA	**G4**	**1414**
N323JB	501	468
N323L	125	258212
N323LJ	**31A**	**123**
(N323LM)	525	0204
N323LM	**525**	**0230**
N323P	**AST**	**049**
N323P	STR	5099/5
N323QS	**560**	**0323**
N323R	S60	306-26
N323WA	25	018
N323XP	125	258323
N324AF	HFB	1064
N324AJ	WWD	208
N324B	**601**	**5069**
N324C	500	324
N324CC	550	431
N324GA	G3	430
N324GA	G3	462
N324GA	G3	487
N324GA	G4	1330
N324GA	**G4**	**1421**
N324K	125	257111
N324K	STR	5089
N324L	**501**	**594**
N324LE	560	5109
N324LX	560	5109
N324QS	**560**	**0423**
(N324QS)	560	0424
N324SA	**125**	**258047**
N324SM	**700**	**9023**
N324SR	900	14
N324TC	20	324
N324TW	**24D**	**324**
N324XP	125	258324
N324ZR	S65	465-25
N325AF	HFB	1065
N325AJ	WWD	181
N325BC	501	450
N325CP	55	112
N325DM	D1A	A006SA
N325GA	G3	433
N325GA	G3	466
N325GA	G3	488
N325GA	G4	1326
N325JB	25D	325
N325JL	25D	215
N325K	**S40**	**282-63**
N325LJ	WWD	181
N325LW	**WWD**	**334**
N325NW	**35A**	**325**
(N325PM)	501	450
N325QS	**560**	**0425**
N326AJ	WWD	191
N326B	**525**	**0302**
N326CB	STR	5143
N326CW	**D1A**	**A026SA**
N326DD	**35A**	**173**
(N326DD)	G3	326
N326DM	D1A	A036SA
N326EJ	24D	326
N326EW	100	220
N326EW	20	392/553
N326EW	**2xx**	**58**
N326EW	550	622
N326FB	**50**	**39**
N326GA	G3	434
N326GA	G3	473
N326HG	**35A**	**501**
N326K	125	257119
N326K	**90X**	**36**
N326K	STR	5102
N326KE	24D	326
N326LW	100	220
N326LW	20	392/553
N326MM	600	1024
N326QS	**560**	**0526**
N326SU	125	258249
N326SU	**750**	**0015**
N326XP	125	258326
(N327BC)	25D	327
N327DM	D1A	A037SA
N327EJ	24D	327
N327F	35A	327
N327GA	G3	427
N327GA	G3	463
N327GA	G4	1327
N327GJ	24D	327
N327JB	S40	282-9
N327K	900	3
N327K	**90X**	**37**
N327K	G2	25
N327LJ	**550**	**0900**
N327QS	**560**	**0327**
(N327RH)	S40	282-9
N327SA	**WWD**	**428**
N327TC	**G2**	**33**
N327TL	G2	33
N327TL	**G4**	**1339**
N327XP	125	258327
N328CC	500	328
N328CJ	**525**	**0328**
N328DM	D1A	A039SA
N328EW	20	392/553
N328GA	G3	444
N328GA	G3	489
N328GA	G4	1328
N328GA	**G4**	**1424**
N328JK	**24B**	**212**
N328JS	S60	306-92
N328JW	25D	328
N328K	900	13
N328K	**90X**	**38**
N328K	G2	26
N328NA	**501**	**568**
N328PC	**WWD**	**328**
N328QS	**560**	**0428**
N328QS	650	0028
N328TL	24B	212
N328XP	125	258328
N329CC	550	329
(N329DM)	D1A	A040SA
N329GA	G3	450
N329GA	G4	1329
N329HN	24D	230
N329HN	WWD	34
N329J	STR	1001
N329JS	**STR**	**5206**
N329K	900	46
N329K	G2	180
N329K	STR	1002
N329K	STR	5133
N329MD	STR	5215
N329SS	S40	282-9
N329TJ	24E	329
N329XP	125	258329
N330BC	35A	432
N330CC	500	330
N330CJ	525	0330
N330DE	125	258060
N330DM	D1A	A041SA
N330G	**125**	**25087**
N330G	125	256033
N330GA	G3	451
N330GA	G4	1350
N330GA	**G4**	**1428**
N330J	24	130
N330K	900	50
N330LJ	**25D**	**330**
N330MC	100	199
N330MC	50	175
N330MC	90X	21
(N330MG)	550	147
N330MG	WWD	434
N330PC	20	107
N330PC	WWD	207
N330QS	**560**	**0329**
N330TJ	650	0101
N330TP	**601**	**5142**
N330TW	**24E**	**330**
N330U	S60	306-20
N330X	125	258060
N330XP	125	258330
N331CC	31	003
N331CC	500	331
N331CW	WWD	231
N331DC	125	256061
N331DC	**125**	**258112**
N331DC	D1A	A028SA
N331DM	D1A	A042SA
N331DP	23	059
N331DP	23	067
N331EC	560	0269
(N331EC)	560	0279
N331FP	600	1072
N331GA	G3	452
N331GA	G4	1331
N331GA	**G4**	**1430**
N331GW	**WWD**	**231**
N331JR	23	072
N331MC	50	95
N331MC	90X	21
N331MC	90X	22
N331MS	525	0330
N331N	**31**	**022**
N331P	**G2**	**20**
N331PR	**550**	**0831**
N331QS	**560**	**0331**
N331SC	125	258093
N331SJ	**31A**	**113**
N331SK	**AST**	**063**
N331TH	**604**	**5325**
N331TP	**604**	**5350**
N331WR	23	072
(N331WT)	600	1073
(N332CM)	750	0107
N332DF	**WWD**	**332**
N332DM	D1A	A043SA
N332EC	900	106
N332FE	20	225/472
N332FG	35A	332
N332FP	24	126
N332GA	G3	453

N332GA	G3	490
N332GA	G4	1332
(N332GJ)	500	015
N332H	500	144
N332J	10	29
N332LC	**560**	**0332**
N332LS	25B	122
N332MC	50	55
N332MC	900	78
(N332MC)	90X	22
N332MQ	50	55
N332PC	23	056
N332QS	**560**	**0523**
N332SE	**500**	**332**
N332TA	125	256032
N332WE	**125**	**257186**
N332XP	125	258332
N333AJ	AST	080
N333AR	G2	189/42
N333AV	20	28
N333AW	25B	163
N333AX	G2	30/4
N333AX	**G4**	**1063**
N333B	S40	282-39
N333BF	23	010
(N333BG)	501	482
N333BG	WWD	98
N333CD	25D	258
N333CG	**25D**	**262**
N333CG	550	188
N333CG	WWD	339
N333CJ	125	25155
N333CR	24B	199
N333CZ	AST	080
N333DP	**125**	**25282**
N333EB	**550**	**0893**
N333EC	**900**	**106**
N333EC	STR	5061/48
N333FJ	**10**	**1**
N333GA	G3	326
N333GA	G3	420
N333GA	G3	432
N333GA	G3	875
N333GA	G4	1333
(N333GJ)	55B	132
N333GJ	**601**	**3042**
N333GM	**S40**	**282-106**
N333GM	S40	282-45
N333GU	G3	875
N333GZ	**125**	**25070**
N333HK	G3	482
N333HP	25B	109
N333JH	**500**	**292**
N333KC	G3	366
(N333KC)	G3	403
(N333KD)	G3	366
N333KN	STR	5118
N333KN	STR	5202
N333LX	**G3**	**366**
N333M	125	25017
N333ME	125	25115
N333ME	125	257003
N333MF	125	25115
N333MG	**601**	**5035**
N333MS	501	584
N333NC	S60	306-76
N333NM	**S40**	**282-45**
N333NR	125	257167
N333PC	**125**	**257008**
N333PC	S60	306-76
N333PC	S65	465-28
N333PD	501	382
N333PE	501	382
N333PP	500	050
N333PV	**G4**	**1240**
N333QA	STR	5118
N333QS	**560**	**0333**
N333RB	35A	220
(N333RB)	501	498
N333RL	**125**	**259027**
N333RL	650	0019
N333RP	35A	148
N333RS	400	RJ-62
N333RU	125	259027

N333RW	STR	5138
N333RY	24B	202
N333SG	25D	226
N333SR	10	48
N333ST	G2	57
N333SV	WWD	114
N333TS	D1A	A047SA
N333TW	**24**	**168**
N333WC	650	0211
N333WF	20	113
N333WM	**560**	**0385**
N333X	24	128
N333X	24D	251
N333X	35A	286
N333X	550	042
(N333XX)	35A	286
N334	125	258013
N334	G2	143
N334	WWD	344
(N334AB)	35A	334
N334AM	550	227
N334CM	650	0234
N334DM	D1A	A044SA
N334DM	D1A	A045SA
N334GA	G3	454
N334GA	G4	1334
N334GA	**G4**	**1431**
N334H	**650**	**0071**
N334JC	500	334
N334JR	125	256020
N334JR	20	139
(N334JW)	55	034
N334KC	**D1A**	**A034SA**
N334LP	WWD	20
N334LS	25B	158
N334MC	50	175
N334MC	900	108
N334MD	25D	334
N334PS	**125**	**256032**
N334PS	500	164
N334QS	**560**	**0434**
N334RC	**500**	**062**
N334RK	MSP	090
N334RK	WWD	5
N334SP	35A	334
N334WC	650	0207
N334WM	**D1A**	**A057SA**
N334XP	125	258334
N335AJ	20	335
N335CC	550	480
N335CJ	525	0335
N335CT	**525**	**0335**
N335DJ	35A	335
N335DM	D1A	A045SA
N335DM	D1A	A048SA
N335EE	35A	335
N335EJ	560	0235
(N335GA)	35A	423
N335GA	G3	455
N335GA	G4	1335
N335GA	**G4**	**1432**
N335H	**G2**	**238**
N335JL	35	015
(N335JR)	24B	226
N335JW	24B	226
N335K	**35A**	**381**
(N335K)	75A	380-12
N335MC	900	150
N335NA	**35A**	**170**
N335NE	35A	335
N335PR	**35A**	**647**
N335QS	**560**	**0335**
N335RD	**35A**	**216**
N335RY	**24B**	**226**
N335SB	35A	656
(N335SS)	35	015
N335WC	650	0211
N335WJ	20	122
N335WR	20	122
N335XP	125	258335
N336CC	500	336
N336DM	D1A	A049SA
(N336EA)	35A	336
N336GA	G3	456

N336MB	125	25153
N336QS	**560**	**0336**
N336RJ	**S65**	**465-10**
N336SV	WWD	336
N336WR	25XR	148
N336XP	125	258336
N337FP	**31**	**020**
N337GA	G3	457
N337GA	G3	491
N337GL	25G	337
N337MC	900	152
N337QS	**560**	**0437**
N337RB	**31A**	**154**
N337RE	**125**	**258024**
N337RE	550	575
N337RE	WWD	210
N337TV	500	236
N337US	STR	5107
N337WC	35A	337
N337XP	125	258337
N338	125	25023
N338	125	25134
N338AX	G2	30/4
N338DB	20	225/472
N338DM	D1A	A038SA
N338DS	24	162
N338EC	**STR**	**5061/48**
N338FP	**55C**	**138**
N338GA	G3	458
(N338K)	75A	380-15
N338KK	23	020
N338MM	**G4**	**1076**
(N338RJ)	G3	338
N338W	WWD	338
N338X	24D	251
N339A	G3	339
N339B	**525**	**0339**
N339BA	25D	240
N339BC	**55**	**039**
(N339BW)	125	257010
N339DM	D1A	A014SA
N339GA	G3	374
N339GA	G3	448
N339GA	G3	492
N339GA	G4	1339
N339GW	S60	306-18
N339H	**G2**	**145**
(N339K)	80A	380-17
N339NA	S40	282-46
N339QS	**560**	**0339**
N339TG	10	103
N339TG	**20**	**198/466**
N339W	35A	209
N340	G3	357
N340	STR	5029/38
N340AC	501	621
N340DA	550	263
N340DN	500	340
N340DR	560	0094
N340DR	WWD	242
N340DR	WWD	45
N340ER	WWD	45
N340GA	G3	340
N340GA	G3	373
N340GA	G3	464
N340GA	G4	1340
N340LJ	31A	040
N340PM	WWD	340
N340QS	**560**	**0514**
(N340RL)	500	340
N341AG	550	043
N341AP	125	258204
N341AP	S40	282-35
N341AP	S65	465-40
N341AR	**525**	**0341**
N341AR	S40	282-35
N341CC	500	320
N341CW	**550**	**330**
N341DM	D1A	A056SA
N341FW	25D	341
N341GA	G3	360
N341GA	G3	467
N341GA	G4	1341
N341K	**20**	**281/498**

N341K	STR	5223
N341M	50	157
N341N	STR	5038
N341NS	G2	64/27
N341NS	STR	5038
N341QS	**560**	**0341**
N342AA	25D	342
N342AC	525	0342
N342AJ	WWD	342
N342AP	500	077
N342AS	650	0042
N342CC	**550**	**413**
(N342CC)	550	431
N342DA	551	181
N342DM	D1A	A057SA
N342F	20	101
N342G	10	52
N342GA	G3	377
N342GA	G3	468
N342GA	G4	1342
N342GG	25D	342
N342HM	650	0062
N342K	20	101
N342K	**20**	**357**
N342QS	650	0042
N342TC	**601**	**5155**
N342TS	WWD	342
N343AP	WWD	194
N343CC	550	343
N343CC	**560**	**0368**
N343CV	560	0343
N343DA	WWD	149
N343DM	D1A	A058SA
N343GA	G3	378
N343GA	G3	469
N343GA	G4	1343
N343K	**601**	**5086**
N343K	G2	10
N343K	G2	9/33
N343MG	200	491
N343MG	35A	188
N343MG	**900**	**95**
N343N	G2	10
N343PJ	525	0166
N343QS	**560**	**0444**
N343RK	**25B**	**110**
N344A	10	153
N344A	550	609
N344AA	**G2**	**123/25**
N344AS	650	7053
N344BA	**604**	**5344**
N344CK	WWD	159
N344CM	**50**	**300**
N344DA	WWD	12
N344DD	**G3**	**344**
N344DM	D1A	A059SA
N344FJ	20	344/534
N344G	20	355
N344GA	G3	317
N344GA	G3	425
N344GA	G3	470
N344GA	G4	1344
N344K	S60	306-97
N344MC	**35A**	**344**
N344PS	WWD	111
N344QS	**560**	**0344**
N344UP	S40	282-45
N344WC	23	092
N345	35A	355
N345AA	G2	123/25
N345AA	**G4**	**1186**
N345AP	50	181
N345AP	**50**	**254**
N345BA	**604**	**5345**
N345BM	20	89
N345BR	**125**	**258308**
N345BS	**WWD**	**181**
N345CC	**S550**	**0095**
(N345CK)	STR	5150/37
N345CP	G2	123/25
N345CT	125	25116
N345CV	560	0345
N345DA	125	25116
N345DM	D1A	A059SA

N345DM	D1A	A060SA
N345EJ	25D	345
(N345FJ)	25D	216
N345GA	G3	380
N345GA	G4	1345
N345GC	**AST**	**023**
N345GL	**125**	**25230**
N345JR	**550**	**325**
N345KB	25D	345
N345KC	500	187
N345LJ	35A	345
N345MA	**45**	**054**
N345MC	**25**	**046**
N345N	**501**	**611**
N345PA	50	36
N345QS	**560**	**0445**
(N345SF)	24	126
N345TL	500	345
N345TR	**WWD**	**345**
N345UP	G2	159
N345WB	**45**	**036**
N346BA	**604**	**5361**
N346CC	560	0346
(N346CP)	WWD	434
N346DM	D1A	A046SA
N346GA	G3	436
N346GA	G4	1346
N346P	10	184
N347AC	25D	347
N347BA	601	5144
(N347CP)	S550	0094
(N347DA)	501	420
N347DA	501	457
N347DM	D1A	A047SA
N347EJ	25D	347
N347GA	G3	403
N347GA	G3	471
N347GA	G4	1347
N347GA	**WWD**	**347**
N347GS	60	026
N347HS	20	347
N347J	23	047
N347JV	**25D**	**347**
(N347JW)	25D	347
N347K	10	37
N347K	20	281/498
N347K	**50**	**46**
N347MD	25D	347
N347WW	WWD	347
N348BJ	24	141
N348DM	D1A	A061SA
N348GA	G3	405
N348GA	G3	472
N348GA	G4	1348
N348HM	55	109
N348KH	**525**	**0348**
N348MC	**125**	**258290**
N348QS	**560**	**0348**
N348SJ	WWD	348
N348VL	24	141
N348WW	WWD	348
N349BS	24F	349
(N349CB)	525	0117
N349DA	WWD	145
N349DM	D1A	A062SA
N349EJ	25D	349
N349GA	G3	391
N349GA	G4	1349
N349JC	**10**	**70**
N349K	50	17
N349K	**900**	**10**
N349KS	50	17
N349M	WWD	23
N349MC	**WWD**	**224**
N349MG	**20**	**479**
N350AF	50	35
N350AG	**25D**	**350**
N350CC	501	350
N350CC	550	350
N350CD	**650**	**0190**
N350DA	**35A**	**366**
N350DH	125	257087
N350DH	25B	193
N350DM	D1A	A050SA

N350DS	**31**	**002**
N350E	S40	282-76
N350EF	**35A**	**385**
N350GA	G3	410
N350GM	525	0172
N350JF	35A	219
N350JH	**25B**	**200**
N350JS	**50**	**15**
N350M	501	499
N350M	WWD	14
N350MD	35A	277
N350MH	125	256069
N350MT	75A	380-54
N350NC	125	25160
N350PM	WWD	338
N350RB	35A	334
N350RD	560	0026
N350RD	**560**	**5057**
N350TS	35	035
N350WB	**50**	**102**
N350WC	125	258018
N350WC	**560**	**0378**
N350WG	125	258018
N350X	50	108
N350X	WWD	109
N351AC	**31A**	**051**
N351AF	S65	465-27
N351AM	**35A**	**409**
N351AS	**35A**	**146**
N351C	**WWD**	**264**
N351DM	D1A	A051SA
N351EF	**35A**	**125**
N351GA	G3	397
N351GA	G4	1351
N351GL	**35**	**001**
(N351JM)	S40	282-1
N351JS	50	104
N351N	**23**	**054**
N351NR	23	054
N351QS	**560**	**0451**
N351SP	**125**	**258280**
N351TC	WWD	351
N351TX	**35A**	**127**
N351WB	23	054
N351WB	**35A**	**355**
N351WC	23	054
N351WC	**560**	**0330**
N351WC	STR	5229
N352AE	**601**	**5041**
N352AF	601	5041
N352AF	**900**	**172**
N352AM	550	393
N352DM	D1A	A052SA
N352EF	**31A**	**046**
N352GA	G3	401
N352GA	G4	1352
N352GL	35	002
N352JS	**50**	**41**
N352MD	**24F**	**352**
N352QS	**560**	**0352**
N352SC	25B	189
N352TC	WWD	394
N352TX	**35A**	**073**
N352WC	125	257095
N352WC	36	013
N352WC	500	275
N352WC	**560**	**0194**
N352WG	500	275
N352WR	24	126
(N352XR)	25D	352
N353CA	**S60**	**306-28**
N353CP	**20**	**461**
N353CV	560	0353
N353DM	D1A	A053SA
N353EF	**35A**	**364**
N353EJ	25D	353
(N353GA)	G3	409
N353GA	G4	1353
N353J	24D	237
N353K	601	5086
N353QS	**560**	**0530**
N353TC	601	5037
N353VA	**G3**	**371**
N353WB	500	359

N353WB	S40	282-55
N353WC	125	257032
N353WC	125	258123
N353WC	**750**	**0008**
N353WC	S40	282-55
N353WG	125	258123
N354CA	STR	5054/59
N354DM	D1A	A054SA
(N354EM)	35A	440
N354GA	G3	412
N354GA	G4	1354
N354H	20	16
N354H	20	40
N354LQ	**35**	**055**
N354ME	**35A**	**378**
N354PM	**35**	**015**
N354QS	**560**	**0356**
N354RZ	35A	170
N354SH	75A	380-39
N354TC	**601**	**5192**
N354WC	125	257058
N354WC	125	258160
N354WC	20	40
N354WC	**750**	**0027**
N354WG	125	258160
N355AM	25D	355
N355CA	**35A**	**597**
N355CC	604	5302
N355CC	**604**	**5393**
N355CD	S60	306-85
N355CD	**S65**	**465-57**
N355CV	560	0355
N355DB	**55**	**006**
N355DF	**550**	**411**
N355DH	55	073
N355DM	D1A	A069SA
N355GA	G3	404
N355GA	G4	1355
N355H	500	213
N355JK	**WWD**	**355**
N355MJ	S40	282-66
N355RB	125	258059
N355TS	**G3**	**355**
N355WB	20	44
N355WC	125	258181
N355WC	20	44
N355WC	**750**	**0030**
N355WG	125	258181
N355WG	20	44
N355WW	WWD	355
N356AC	35A	230
N356BR	**G3**	**356**
N356DM	D1A	A073SA
N356EJ	560	0256
N356GA	G3	406
N356JB	20	80
N356JW	**35A**	**656**
N356N	601	3064
N356P	35	006
N356TJ	G3	356
N356WA	**60**	**123**
N356WB	20	80
N356WC	20	80
N356WC	**560**	**0432**
N356WW	WWD	356
N357AZ	560	0196
N357BC	WWD	357
N357CL	200	484
(N357DM)	D1A	A051SA
N357DM	D1A	A091SA
N357EA	WWD	357
N357EC	**560**	**0269**
N357GA	G3	413
N357GA	G4	1357
N357H	G3	472
N357H	STR	5234
N357HC	25	032
N357JV	**525**	**0357**
(N357MD)	D1A	A091SA
N357PR	55	073
N357PR	**G3**	**348**
N357RT	**600**	**1033**
(N357W)	WWD	357
N357WC	**560**	**0069**

N358AC	**35A**	**427**
N358CC	501	358
N358CT	WWD	358
N358CV	560	0358
N358GA	G3	414
N358GA	G4	1358
N358LL	125	258093
N358PG	**35A**	**358**
N358QS	**560**	**0455**
(N359C)	WWD	42
N359EF	35A	193
N359GA	G4	1359
N359JS	WWD	335
N359K	G2	180
N359SK	25D	359
N359V	10	120
N359V	AST	039
N359V	**AST**	**102**
N359VP	AST	039
N359VS	AST	039
N359WJ	**S60**	**306-1**
N360AA	25B	123
N360BA	125	258052
N360CF	S60	306-133
N360CH	S60	306-146
N360CH	S60	306-15
N360DA	500	056
N360DE	125	257042
N360DJ	501	583
N360E	S40	282-80
N360EJ	23	052
N360GA	G4	1360
(N360GL)	35A	360
N360HK	WWD	166
N360J	S40	282-7
N360JG	**25D**	**360**
N360LJ	35A	360
N360LS	36A	030
N360M	**S550**	**0022**
N360M	WWD	24
N360MC	**501**	**406**
N360MC	WWD	24
N360N	125	257067
N360N	550	072
N360N	S40	282-81
N360Q	S40	282-24
N360QS	**560**	**0460**
N360X	125	257042
N361AA	24A	100
N361BA	125	258053
N361DA	S60	306-8
N361DB	501	687
N361DB	**550**	**0884**
N361DE	**501**	**687**
N361DJ	550	037
N361DM	D1A	A065SA
N361EC	**560**	**0279**
N361EJ	23	053
N361GA	G4	1361
N361QS	**560**	**0361**
N361RA	G3	361
N361RB	**525**	**0361**
N362AA	24A	110
N362BA	125	258057
N362CC	501	362
N362CJ	**525**	**0362**
N362CP	**550**	**371**
N362DA	S40	282-90
N362DJ	550	052
N362EJ	23	056
N362GA	G4	1362
N362GL	36	002
N362KM	**400A**	**RK-227**
N362MD	D1A	A062SA
N363BA	125	258059
N363BC	24D	241
N363DM	D1A	A063SA
N363EJ	23	058
N363FJ	20	363/544
N363GA	G4	1363
N363GL	36	003
N363HA	25D	242
N363K	400A	RK-114
N363K	500	110

N363QS	**560**	**0536**
N363SP	550	394
N364BA	125	258060
N364CL	**35A**	**383**
N364DM	D1A	A064SA
N364EJ	23	059
N364G	G2	125/26
N364G	**G4**	**1091**
N364G	WWD	5
N364GA	G4	1364
N364WC	125	258069
N365AS	36A	055
N365AT	**125**	**258449**
N365BA	125	258061
N365CM	25D	365
N365CX	**WWD**	**425**
N365DA	125	25271
N365DJ	125	25020
N365EA	**560**	**0107**
N365EJ	23	064
N365EJ	24A	102
N365G	G2	198/35
N365G	**G4**	**1101**
N365G	WWD	15
N365GA	G4	1365
N365N	**35A**	**300**
N365N	S60	306-5
N365RJ	WWD	91
N365SB	**125**	**256070**
N366AA	25B	151
N366BA	125	258062
N366BR	125	25134
N366DA	S40	282-82
N366DM	D1A	A066SA
N366EJ	23	095
N366F	50	77
N366F	**G4**	**1041**
N366G	20	9
N366G	650	0038
N366GE	650	0038
N366LJ	25D	366
N366MP	125	25134
N366N	S40	282-8
N366N	S60	306-93
N366QS	**560**	**0466**
N367BA	125	258063
N367DM	**125**	**258367**
N367DM	D1A	A067SA
(N367EA)	550	373
N367EG	G2	128
N367EJ	20	28
N367F	100	206
N367G	20	20
N367G	650	0053
N367G	G2	125/26
N367GA	20	20
N367GA	G3	367
N367GA	G4	1367
N367JC	**550**	**180**
N367QS	**560**	**0367**
N367TP	50	181
N367WW	**WWD**	**367**
N368AG	**G2**	**167**
N368BA	125	258065
N368BG	35A	368
N368DA	S40	282-12
N368DM	D1A	A068SA
N368DS	**20**	**256**
N368EJ	20	30
N368F	100	220
N368G	20	29
N368G	604	5368
N368G	650	0057
N368GA	G3	368
N368K	500	110
N368L	20	29
N368M	50	277
N368MD	WWD	368
N368MJ	24	043
N368PU	D1A	A068SA
N368S	WWD	271
(N368TJ)	G3	368
N369AP	G2	14
N369BA	125	258066

N369BA	**35A**	**312**
N369BG	125	258160
N369BG	**900**	**40**
N369BG	WWD	304
N369CA	20	359/542
(N369CA)	50	115
N369CE	20	359/542
N369CS	125	25214
N369CS	G2	2
N369CS	**G3**	**384**
N369DA	550	327
N369EJ	20	33
N369EJ	23	081
N369G	125	257125
N369G	20	34
N369G	650	0015
N369JB	125	25066
N369JH	**125**	**25275**
N369MJ	25D	369
N369N	S40	282-8
(N369TC)	560	0284
N369TS	125	256069
N369V	10	120
N369WR	20	196
N369XL	35A	423
N370	20	21
N370AC	550	228
N370BH	75	370-4
(N370CL)	604	5370
N370DM	D1A	A070SA
N370EC	35	003
(N370EU)	20	297
N370FL	**G3**	**401**
(N370GA)	G3	451
N370GA	G3	494
N370GA	G4	1370
N370HF	20	370
N370KP	**50**	**103**
N370L	S60	306-64
N370LJ	25D	370
N370M	125	257019
N370M	**S550**	**0128**
N370M	S60	306-71
(N370ME)	20	310
N370QS	650	0070
N370RR	**125**	**257019**
N370SC	**31A**	**070**
N370SL	75	370-9
(N370SP)	G2	168
N370TG	650	0070
N370VS	S60	306-54
N370WT	20	274
N371CL	**604**	**5371**
N371CV	560	0371
N371D	125	257134
N371DM	D1A	A071SA
(N371GA)	501	407
N371GA	G3	495
N371GA	G4	1371
N371GP	501	407
N371H	STR	5020
N371H	WWD	315
N371HH	500	214
N371QS	**560**	**0471**
(N371W)	500	214
N372AS	35A	372
N372BC	125	257026
N372BC	601	3034
N372BC	G4	1273
N372BD	125	257026
N372BG	601	3034
N372BG	**G4**	**1273**
N372CC	550	372
N372CM	125	25073
N372CM	G2	185
N372CM	G2	62
N372CM	G3	338
N372CM	**G4**	**1049**
N372CP	**525**	**0372**
N372CV	560	0372
N372DM	D1A	A072SA
N372G	601	3006
N372G	**604**	**5351**
N372GA	G3	496

N372GA	G4	1372
N372GM	125	25073
N372GM	G2	185
N372GM	G2	62
N372GM	G3	338
N372H	STR	5092/58
N372H	STR	5228
N372PG	601	3034
N372Q	**WWD**	**112**
N372QS	560	0372
N372WW	WWD	372
N372XP	125	258372
N373CM	WWD	373
N373DH	**125**	**25066**
N373DJ	**650**	**0038**
N373G	601	3009
N373GA	G3	497
N373GA	G4	1373
N373KC	20	264
N373KM	G4	1373
N373LB	G2	13
(N373LP)	35A	220
N373LP	G2	13
(N373LP)	G3	310
N373QS	**560**	**0373**
N373SC	25B	204
N373W	25	032
N374BC	601	3034
(N374DH)	125	25066
N374DM	D1A	A074SA
N374FC	550	374
N374G	601	3015
N374G	604	5351
N374G	**604**	**5368**
N374GA	G3	498
N374GA	G4	1374
N374GC	S550	0055
N374GS	501	634
N374GS	501	669
N374GS	S550	0055
N374QS	**560**	**0475**
N375BK	20	236
N375CM	560	0365
N375DM	D1A	A075SA
N375G	601	3019
N375GA	G3	375
N375GA	G4	1151
N375GA	**G4**	**1375**
N375KH	**525**	**0375**
N375NM	G3	375
N375NW	**G3**	**375**
N375PK	20	236
N375PK	600	1018
N375PK	601	3054
N375PK	G2	15
N375QS	**560**	**0375**
N375SC	125	258111
N375SC	**2xx**	**23**
N375SC	650	0027
N376BE	**WWD**	**376**
N376D	S40	282-115
N376D	**S60**	**306-101**
N376DD	S40	282-115
N376DM	D1A	A076SA
N376GA	G4	1376
(N376HW)	650	0025
N376QS	**560**	**0276**
N376RP	S40	282-115
N376SC	125	258124
N376SC	20	391
N376SC	25B	204
N376SC	**2xx**	**24**
N376SC	650	0076
N376WA	WWD	376
N377BT	20	44
N377C	25D	257
N377C	35A	389
N377DM	D1A	A077SA
(N377EM)	S60	306-26
N377GA	G3	487
N377GA	G4	1377
N377GS	**525**	**0179**
N377HS	**75A**	**380-36**
N377JE	650	0013

(N377JW)	55	033
N377KC	501	388
N377P	S40	282-70
N377Q	25D	257
N377QS	**560**	**0377**
N377RA	560	0377
N377SC	**90X**	**66**
N377SF	**750**	**0068**
N378C	**10**	**73**
N378CC	501	378
N378DM	D1A	A078SA
N378GA	G4	1378
N378HC	G3	378
(N379BW)	35A	454
N379DM	D1A	A079SA
N379GA	G4	1379
N379JR	WWD	353
N379P	**G5**	**581**
N379QS	**560**	**0479**
N379RH	G3	379
N379TH	WWD	109
N379XX	**G3**	**394**
N380AA	STR	5131
N380AK	550	612
N380BC	**80A**	**380-17**
N380CF	75A	380-54
N380CM	D1A	A080SA
N380CV	560	0380
N380DA	WWD	380
N380DE	125	258269
N380DJ	80A	380-32
N380DM	D1A	A080SA
N380EX	HFB	1036
N380GA	G4	1380
N380GK	80A	380-44
N380LC	25	030
N380MS	550	480
N380N	75A	380-72
N380RA	20	54
N380RD	**560**	**0026**
(N380RS)	75A	380-70
N380SR	75A	380-2
N380SR	75A	380-53
N380T	75A	380-58
N380TJ	50	138
N380TT	**G3**	**437**
N380X	125	25204
N380X	125	258269
N381AA	STR	5058/4
N381BJ	**500**	**445**
N381CC	550	381
N381CJ	**525**	**0380**
N381DA	WWD	118
N381DM	D1A	A081SA
N381GA	G4	1381
N381MG	D1A	A081SA
N381W	WWD	381
N382AA	**WWD**	**56**
N382BL	35A	382
N382BP	35A	382
(N382DA)	125	25218
N382DM	D1A	A082SA
N382E	**20**	**382**
N382GA	G4	1382
N382JP	500	164
N382LS	**75A**	**380-51**
N382MC	75A	380-34
N382QS	**560**	**0382**
N382RF	S40	282-17
N382TC	35	039
N383CF	80A	380-9
N383DM	D1A	A083SA
N383DT	**604**	**5383**
N383GA	G4	1383
N383MB	**60**	**083**
N383QS	**560**	**0483**
N383RF	20	65
N383SF	**AST**	**083**
N383TS	S60	306-84
N383X	24	128
N384DA	550	048
N384DM	D1A	A058SA
N384GA	G4	1384
N384JK	20	384/551

N384K 20 387
N385CC 501 385
(N385G) WWD 43
N385J 23 085
N385M G2 77
N386AM 551 163
N386CM 35A 283
(N386DA) 501 460
N386G WWD 43
(N386JM) WWD 128
N386MA 550 069
N386MC WWD 128
N386QS 560 0486
N387CE 20 387
N387H 125 258246
N387HA 35A 251
N387HA 550 465
N387MA 551 095
N387PA AST 025
N387RE 550 575
N387SC 550 157
N388AJ 20 56
N388CJ 501 388
N388DA 400 RJ-26
N388DA 650 0062
N388FA 550 633
N388GA WWD 366
N388H 125 258248
N388LS 35A 388
N388MA 551 108
N388MM G3 490
N388P 24B 211
N388PD 35A 388
N388PD 35A 630
N388PG 601 5152
N388Q 23 065A
N388R 23 020
N388R 24A 110
N388SB 550 279
N388WM 125 25052
N389AT 25D 297
N389BG 125 258160
N389BG WWD 304
N389CC 501 389
N389CJ 525 0389
(N389DA) 125 25037
N389GA 25D 289
N389GA G4 1389
N389GS 2xx 20
N389JP 501 643
N389JV 560 0389
N389L S550 0013
N389W 650 0098
N390AJ 550 369
N390CV 560 0390
N390DA 550 434
N390DE 90X 68
N390EM PRM RB-9
N390F 900 127
N390F G2 178
N390GM PRM RB-121
N390GS 2xx 21
(N390JP) 550 369
N390JW PRM RB-78
N390P PRM RB-12
N390PL PRM RB-55
N390QS 560 0490
N390R PRM RB-6
N390RA PRM RB-1
(N390S) 500 290
N390TA PRM RB-12
N390TA PRM RB-86
N390TC PRM RB-3
N391AN 550 093
N391BC 550 170
N391CV 560 0391
N391DA 125 25029
N391GA G4 1391
N391JP 35A 487
N391QS 560 0493
N391XP 125 258391
N392BD G2 120
N392BS 560 0164
N392DA 501 541
N392F S40 282-17
(N392FJ) 20 392/553
N392FV 601 3032
N392GA G4 1392
N392JP 35A 328
N392PT 601 5110
N392QS 560 0429
N392RG 525 0340
N392T 24 158
N392T 25B 104
N392U 50 54
N393BD G2 120
N393CF 35A 669
N393DA 501 584
N393E S550 0053
N393F 20 65
N393GA G4 1393
(N393HC) 550 336
N393JP 35A 320
N393QS 560 0393
N393RC 550 336
(N393RF) 20 65
N393U G3 325
N394GA G4 1394
N394QS 560 0394
N394U 50 113
N394XP 125 258394
(N395BB) 20 395/554
N395CC 551 395
N395GA G4 1395
N395L 900 133
N395LJ 31A 095
(N395QS) 560 0395
N395QS 560 0496
N395R 560 0188
N395RD 125 257064
N395SC 501 395
N395SR WWD 395
N395TJ WWD 395
(N396DA) 551 282
N396EG 50 207
N396GA G4 1396
N396M 550 396
N396QS 560 0396
N396U 125 257071
N396U G4 1350
N397AF 560 0397
N397AT 400A RK-157
N397AT 400A RK-256
N397B STR 5075/19
N397BC 24 144
N397BE 600 1053
N397CS 650 0056
N397F G2 72
N397GA G4 1397
N397J 601 5033
N397J G2 97
N397J G4 1354
N397JJ G4 1354
N397L 24 144
(N397L) G2 97
N397LE G2 106
N397QS 560 0531
N397RD G2 37
N397SC 500 019
(N397SL) D1A A022SA
N398AC 55 033
N398AG AST 088
N398CC 550 398
N398EP 525 0327
N398GA G4 1398
N398LS 550 0853
N398QS 560 0522
N398RP 500 316
N398RS 560 5009
N398S 550 338
N399AG AST 090
N399AZ 35A 399
N399BA 35A 371
N399BH G3 384
N399CB G2 118
N399CB G3 433
N399CB G4 1261
N399CC G4 1051
N399CF 601 5084
N399D WWD 31
(N399DJ) 35A 399
N399DM D1A A008SA
N399FA 2xx 101
N399FG 20 373
N399FL 600 1083
N399FP G2 118
N399G 525 0183
N399GA 125 256004
N399JC 125 258334
N399KL 35A 362
N399MJ D1A A039SA
N399MM D1A A017SA
N399P S40 282-87
N399QS 560 0510
N399RP D1A A020SA
N399SC 60 040
N399SC G3 488
N399SR S60 306-33
N399SW 20 197
N399SW 601 5009
N399W 35A 209
N399W 650 0098
N399W 650 7038
N399WW 601 3011
N399WW G3 384
N400 25B 137
N400 31A 128
(N400A) 400A RK-110
N400A 400A RK-3
N400A 400A RK-34
N400A 400A RK-66
N400A 400A RK-98
N400AD C21A 519
N400AG 125 25206
N400AJ 25 038
N400AJ 400A RK-137
(N400AJ) S550 0156
N400AK C21A 520
N400AL 125 258009
N400AL G3 343
N400AN C21A 521
N400AP C21A 522
N400AQ C21A 523
N400AS C21A 524
N400AT C21A 525
N400AU C21A 526
N400AX C21A 527
N400AY C21A 528
N400AZ C21A 529
N400BA C21A 530
N400BE 400A RK-4
N400BF 23 010
N400BH 125 25230
N400BH 500 244
N400BN C21A 532
N400BQ C21A 533
N400BU C21A 534
N400BY C21A 535
N400BZ C21A 536
N400CC 125 25179
N400CC 35A 083
N400CC G2 102/32
N400CC G4 1046
N400CD C21A 537
N400CE S60 306-87
N400CG C21A 538
N400CH 125 257186
N400CJ C21A 539
N400CK C21A 540
N400CP WWD 30
N400CQ C21A 541
N400CR C21A 542
N400CS 23 022
N400CS S40 282-34
N400CT 560 0104
N400CU C21A 543
N400CV C21A 544
N400CX C21A 545
N400CX G2 100
N400CY C21A 546
N400CZ C21A 547
N400D 125 25216
N400D G2 100
N400DB 20 193
(N400DB) 25B 124
N400DB 501 508
N400DB 75 370-4
N400DD C21A 548
N400DJ C21A 549
N400DK 550 219
N400DL C21A 550
N400DN C21A 551
N400DP 125 25271
N400DQ C21A 552
N400DR C21A 553
(N400DT) 400A RK-66
N400DT 550 102
N400DU C21A 554
N400DV C21A 555
N400DX C21A 556
N400DY C21A 557
N400DZ C21A 558
N400EC C21A 559
N400EE C21A 560
N400EF C21A 561
N400EG C21A 562
N400EJ C21A 563
N400EK C21A 564
N400EL C21A 565
N400EM C21A 566
N400EN C21A 567
N400EP 24A 116
N400EP 24B 215
N400EQ C21A 568
N400ER C21A 569
N400ES C21A 570
N400ET C21A 571
N400EU C21A 572
N400EV C21A 573
N400EX 550 597
N400EX C21A 574
N400EY C21A 575
N400EZ C21A 576
N400FE 125 25222
N400FE C21A 577
N400FG C21A 578
N400FH C21A 579
N400FK C21A 580
N400FM C21A 581
N400FN C21A 582
N400FP C21A 583
N400FQ C21A 584
N400FR C21A 585
N400FT 400 RJ-60
N400FT 400A RK-101
N400FT 400A RK-47
N400FT C21A 586
N400FU C21A 587
N400FV C21A 588
N400FY C21A 531
N400GA G4 1001
N400GA G4 1042
N400GB 501 400
N400GJ 400 RJ-23
N400GK D1A A019SA
N400GM S40 282-99
N400GN 125 258059
N400GN 20 325
N400GP 125 25245
N400GP 125 25270
(N400GX) 20 325
N400HC WWD 117
(N400HF) 125 25207
N400HG D1A A091SA
N400HH D1A A025SA
N400J AST 014
N400J G2 196
N400J G3 493
N400J G4 1330
N400JD 650 0035
N400JD G2 67
N400JD G5 524
N400JE 35A 120
N400JF AST 014
N400JH S60 306-133
N400JK 125 25234

(N400JL)	125	25208
N400JS	25XR	235
N400JT	55	092
N400K	500	102
N400K	G3	370
N400KC	125	25198
(N400KC)	601	5073
N400KC	601	5090
N400KC	STR	5051
N400KC	STR	5210
N400KD	**125**	**25208**
N400KP	**400A**	**RK-125**
N400KS	**560**	**0041**
N400KV	S65	465-69
N400LC	**125**	**25216**
(N400LC)	50	89
N400LH	G3	401
N400LR	WWD	48
N400LX	501	661
N400LX	501	666
N400LX	550	597
N400M	**G2**	**132**
N400M	STR	5008
N400MC	35A	487
(N400MC)	550	495
(N400MJ)	35A	083
N400ML	D1A	A064SA
N400MP	**STR**	**5228**
(N400MR)	125	25241
(N400MT)	550	238
N400MV	**400A**	**RK-269**
N400N	75A	380-41
N400NE	125	256047
N400NE	WWD	240
N400NF	**D1A**	**A091SA**
(N400NL)	20	70
N400NR	**75A**	**380-41**
N400NS	**400A**	**RK-28**
N400NU	125	257041
N400NW	125	25074
N400NW	125	256047
N400NW	125	257041
N400NW	125	258012
N400PC	20	113
N400PC	25XR	235
N400PC	50	89
N400PC	501	425
N400PC	550	242
N400PC	551	051
N400PC	**650**	**0057**
N400PC	WWD	87
N400PG	**20**	**113**
N400PG	23	068
N400PG	501	425
(N400PG)	501	434
N400PH	125	25180
N400PL	400	RJ-42
N400PU	**400A**	**RK-156**
N400Q	400A	RK-39
N400Q	**400A**	**RK-55**
(N400Q)	WWD	240
N400QH	125	257186
N400RB	23	064
N400RB	35	011
N400RB	**750**	**0076**
N400RL	**525**	**0151**
N400RS	24	138
N400RS	**75A**	**380-25**
(N400RV)	35A	120
N400SA	500	223
N400SA	G2	8
N400SA	G4	1120
N400SH	**400A**	**RK-100**
N400SJ	G2	156/31
N400SJ	G2	8
N400SJ	WWD	240
N400SP	10	125
N400SR	501	685
N400T	400	RJ-17
N400TB	125	258039
N400TB	**601**	**5120**
N400TE	**400A**	**RK-187**
N400TF	**WWD**	**279**
N400TJ	D1A	A006SA

N400TX	550	406
N400UP	G4	1054
N400UP	G4	1258
N400UW	125	25074
N400VC	**25XR**	**235**
N400VG	**400A**	**RK-113**
N400VG	400A	RK-3
N400VK	**400A**	**RK-3**
N400VP	**400A**	**RK-110**
N400WP	125	257152
N400WT	125	25286
N400WT	20	479
N400WT	WWD	3
(N400XB)	24D	326
N400Y	400A	RK-66
N400YM	WWD	315
N401AB	20	66
N401AB	400A	RK-7
N401AC	25B	140
N401AJ	**25B**	**171**
N401BP	WWD	260
N401CG	**400**	**RJ-43**
N401CV	560	0401
N401CW	**400A**	**RK-1**
N401DE	WWD	92
N401DP	**25D**	**329**
N401EE	400A	RK-6
(N401FF)	400A	RK-6
N401G	**501**	**667**
N401GA	G2	41
N401GA	G4	1136
N401GA	**G4**	**1401**
N401GJ	**400**	**RJ-26**
N401GN	125	257072
(N401HR)	125	256046
N401HR	G2	39
N401JE	55	041
N401JL	**G4**	**1283**
N401JR	125	25191
N401JW	**10**	**46**
N401LG	**525**	**0154**
N401LS	125	259032
N401M	G2	158
N401M	G2	174
N401MM	G4	1130
N401MS	**S60**	**306-17**
(N401NK)	601	3027
N401NK	**604**	**5409**
N401PJ	G3	488
N401QS	G4	1408
N401RB	23	064
N401RD	500	267
N401RJ	G3	488
(N401TC)	400A	RK-21
(N401TJ)	400	RJ-4
(N401U)	550	215
N401V	WWD	30
N401WT	**G4**	**1338**
N402AC	**125**	**25103**
N402CW	**400A**	**RK-2**
N402DP	25D	351
N402ES	10	174
N402FB	**400**	**RJ-2**
N402GA	G4	1049
N402GA	G4	1097
N402GA	G4	1137
N402GA	G4	1189
N402GJ	125	257034
N402GS	**400A**	**RK-71**
N402HR	125	256046
N402JW	**10**	**120**
(N402LM)	G3	404
(N402NC)	20	339
N402ST	**550**	**058**
N402TJ	551	051
N402TS	**AST**	**039**
(N402Y)	24	113
N403AC	25B	140
N403CB	650	0099
N403CC	501	403
N403DP	**125**	**257114**
N403FJ	900	3
N403GA	G4	1003
N403GA	G4	1051

N403GA	G4	1098
N403GA	G4	1138
N403GA	G4	1190
N403GA	G4	1288
N403GA	G4	1403
N403JW	**20**	**102**
N403LM	G3	404
N403M	WWD	132
N403NW	G3	403
N403QS	G4	1403
N403W	**WWD**	**403**
N404A	**90X**	**56**
N404AC	**G2**	**189/42**
N404AJ	23	026
N404BB	35A	404
N404BF	550	066
N404BS	**125**	**258294**
N404BT	**560**	**5038**
(N404BV)	550	066
N404CB	125	257087
N404CB	601	5090
N404CB	WWD	245
N404CC	G4	1098
N404CE	125	257106
N404CE	**125**	**258293**
N404CF	125	257106
N404DB	23	026
N404DP	**35A**	**404**
N404E	50	154
N404E	550	104
N404F	20	404
N404F	900	41
N404F	**90X**	**49**
N404FF	**900**	**41**
N404FJ	900	5
N404G	500	147
N404G	550	104
N404G	**560**	**0095**
N404G	S550	0068
N404GA	G4	1000
N404GA	G4	1101
N404GA	G4	1139
N404GA	G4	1191
N404GA	G4	1244
N404GA	G4	1404
N404HS	G4	1404
N404JC	**125**	**258400**
N404JF	**50**	**197**
N404JF	650	7001
N404JS	35A	441
N404JW	**10**	**29**
(N404JW)	500	338
N404KA	35A	404
N404KS	**550**	**361**
N404LM	**G4**	**1130**
N404M	G2	220
N404M	G2	83
N404M	G3	404
N404M	G4	1110
N404M	**G4**	**1366**
N404MA	**500**	**126**
N404MM	**560**	**0491**
N404MM	G3	404
N404MY	**G4**	**1110**
(N404PC)	WWD	13
N404QS	**G4**	**1304**
N404R	20	155
N404R	50	154
N404R	**900**	**55**
N404SB	550	425
N404SB	**560**	**5069**
N404SK	601	5058
N404SP	G4	1243
N404VL	**900**	**158**
N404VP	400A	RK-44
N404W	WWD	404
N404WC	**WWD**	**128**
N405CC	501	405
N405DP	125	257130
N405F	20	405
N405FJ	900	6
N405FX	**45**	**026**
N405GA	G2	105
N405GA	G4	1017

N405GA	G4	1102
N405GA	G4	1140
N405GA	G4	1214
N405GA	G4	1245
N405GA	G4	1289
N405GJ	**35A**	**354**
N405JW	**20**	**54**
(N405LM)	G3	360
N405LM	**G5**	**541**
N405MM	G2	220
N405PC	**501**	**562**
N405RS	25B	096
N405TP	**125**	**257130**
N405XP	125	258405
N406CJ	501	406
N406CW	**400A**	**RK-6**
N406F	20	407
N406FJ	900	8
N406FX	**45**	**089**
N406L	24	148
N406LM	650	0102
(N406M)	650	0102
N406MM	650	0102
N406PW	75A	380-2
N406SS	**550**	**368**
N406TS	**400**	**RJ-6**
N406W	WWD	406
N406W	WWD	442
N407CA	**G3**	**422**
N407F	20	409
N407FJ	900	10
N407FX	**45**	**090**
N407GA	G3	407
N407GA	G4	1018
N407GA	G4	1070
N407GA	G4	1119
N407GA	G4	1141
N407GA	G4	1192
N407GA	G4	1246
N407LM	650	0103
(N407M)	650	0103
N407MM	650	0103
N407MR	35A	407
N407PC	20	30
N407SC	500	037
N407V	24	087
N407W	**WWD**	**407**
N408AL	125	258009
N408CA	500	219
N408CC	S40	282-13
N408CS	S40	282-13
(N408ER)	50	8
N408F	20	411
N408FJ	900	12
N408FX	**45**	**091**
N408GA	G4	1020
N408GA	G4	1105
N408GA	G4	1142
N408GA	G4	1247
N408GA	G4	1290
N408JD	**650**	**0035**
N408M	G3	362
N408MJ	**WWD**	**408**
N408MM	501	443
N408MW	501	443
N408PA	**20**	**408**
N408PC	20	98/434
N408PC	**400A**	**RK-47**
N408QS	**G4**	**1308**
N408RB	35	011
N408S	S40	282-13
N408TR	**S40**	**282-4**
N408W	WWD	408
N408WT	125	25286
N409AC	501	433
N409CC	600	1063
N409ER	50	8
N409F	20	412
N409FJ	900	13
N409FX	**45**	**095**
N409KC	600	1052
N409KC	**601**	**5075**
N409M	G2	83
N409M	STR	5047

N409MA	G2	83
N409MA	STR	5047
N409PC	20	11
N409WT	**WWD**	**3**
N409WW	WWD	409
N410AW	125	256039
N410BA	400	RJ-10
N410BT	**125**	**258209**
N410CC	550	410
N410CS	550	486
N410CV	560	0310
N410DM	**560**	**0184**
(N410EL)	WWD	410
N410F	20	413
N410FJ	900	14
N410FX	**45**	**101**
N410GA	G4	1071
N410GA	G4	1108
N410GA	G4	1120
N410GA	G4	1143
N410GB	500	148
N410J	560	0147
(N410JP)	550	081
(N410LR)	G2	116
N410M	G4	1115
N410M	**G5**	**575**
N410MY	**G4**	**1115**
N410N	500	345
N410NA	500	345
N410NA	550	085
N410NA	**560**	**0435**
N410NA	WWD	382
N410ND	500	259
N410PA	125	25198
N410PB	24	179
N410PD	24	179
N410QS	G4	1210
N410RD	35A	647
N410SP	25B	174
N410ST	60	087
N410US	125	258090
N410US	125	259005
N410US	20	120
N410WW	10	86
N410WW	50	76
N410WW	**G4**	**1203**
N411BB	604	5316
N411BB	650	0037
N411BB	650	0195
N411BP	650	0195
N411BW	400	A1008SA
N411CC	20	159
(N411CJ)	501	411
N411DR	500	249
N411DS	501	400
N411FB	**125**	**25074**
N411FJ	900	17
N411FX	**45**	**102**
N411GA	**G4**	**1411**
N411GL	55	011
N411LC	35A	366
N411MD	S60	306-83
N411ME	501	400
(N411MF)	125	25155
N411MM	24F	353
N411PA	**125**	**257017**
N411QS	**G4**	**1311**
N411RA	125	258177
(N411RJ)	501	411
N411SC	10	50
N411SK	**400A**	**RK-111**
N411SK	400A	RK-28
N411SP	24B	216
N411SP	**D1A**	**A049SA**
N411SS	125	257104
N411ST	60	087
(N411TC)	125	256070
N411TP	125	256070
N411WC	501	411
N411WW	10	86
N411WW	50	76
N411WW	G2	257/17
N411WW	**G4**	**1121**
N412AB	**200**	**492**
N412DP	**125**	**257162**
N412F	20	414
N412FJ	900	16
N412FX	**45**	**103**
N412GA	G4	1008
N412GA	G4	1021
N412GA	G4	1024
N412GA	G4	1075
N412GA	G4	1121
N412GA	G4	1193
N412GA	G4	1266
N412GA	G4	1291
N412GA	**G4**	**1412**
N412GL	35A	412
N412LJ	45	012
N412MA	550	466
N412P	**550**	**187**
N412PD	24	179
N412SC	WWD	412
N412SE	**501**	**633**
N412SP	25B	174
N412W	WWD	412
N413CA	550	128
N413CK	**550**	**041**
N413CV	560	0413
N413F	20	415
N413FJ	900	18
N413GA	G4	1034
N413GA	G4	1212
N413GA	G4	1292
N413GA	G4	1315
N413GA	**G4**	**1413**
N413GH	125	25030
N413JP	35A	421
(N413KA)	500	250
N413LJ	45	013
N413MA	35A	413
(N413SC)	AST	013
N413VP	551	412
N413WF	24B	211
N413WW	WWD	413
N414BM	G4	1214
(N414CB)	501	576
N414CB	501	589
N414CC	501	414
N414FJ	900	19
N414GC	550	096
(N414JC)	20	369
N414KL	**35A**	**595**
N414RF	**125**	**257060**
N414RF	55	033
(N414RK)	400A	RK-14
N414TJ	35A	414
(N414VP)	550	413
N414XP	**125**	**258266**
N415AJ	**550**	**600**
N415CS	**525**	**0373**
N415CS	S40	282-76
N415CS	S65	465-42
N415DJ	35A	415
N415EL	**WWD**	**415**
N415F	20	416
N415FC	500	145
N415FJ	900	20
N415FW	**750**	**0095**
N415GA	G4	1023
N415GA	G4	1059
N415GA	G4	1110
N415GA	G4	1144
N415GA	G4	1194
N415GA	G4	1293
N415GA	**G4**	**1415**
N415GS	S40	282-76
N415JW	20	369
N415LJ	**23**	**092**
N415LS	35A	229
N415PT	125	258016
N415RC	D1A	A015SA
N415RD	125	257094
(N415RD)	35A	236
N415SH	G4	1125
N416AS	10	16
N416CC	**550**	**415**
N416CS	S40	282-81
N416CW	**400A**	**RK-16**
N416F	**20**	**416**
N416F	20	417
N416FJ	20	417
N416FJ	900	22
N416G	24D	325
N416GA	G4	1027
N416GA	G4	1111
N416GA	G4	1145
N416GA	G4	1213
N416GA	G4	1258
N416GA	G4	1294
N416GA	**G4**	**1416**
(N416H)	560	0104
N416HC	**10**	**16**
N416K	G2	126
N416K	**G2**	**41**
N416KC	**525**	**0130**
N416LJ	23	093
(N416NL)	WWD	187
N416QS	**G4**	**1316**
N416RD	**125**	**257062**
N416RM	20	426
N416RM	25D	301
N416RP	400A	RK-7
N416SH	G2	15
N416W	WWD	416
N416WM	**G3**	**487**
N417BA	**35A**	**257**
N417BJ	400	RJ-17
N417C	**525**	**0174**
N417CL	**601**	**5107**
N417CW	**400A**	**RK-17**
N417EL	WWD	417
N417F	20	418
N417FJ	900	24
(N417GA)	G2	41
N417GA	G4	1112
N417GA	G4	1146
N417GA	G4	1217
N417GA	G4	1267
N417GA	G4	1295
N417GA	G4	1317
N417GA	G4	1417
(N417GW)	WWD	417
N417H	560	0170
N417JD	24D	253
N417KT	**D1A**	**A083SA**
N417KW	**550**	**0933**
N417LJ	23	094
N417LJ	45	017
N417PJ	25B	075
N417PJ	STR	5098/28
N417QS	G4	1417
N417RC	**501**	**606**
N417RD	G2	3
(N417TF)	125	25038
N417WW	**24**	**171**
N418BA	**125**	**257057**
N418CA	36A	018
N418CG	**550**	**417**
N418CW	**400A**	**RK-18**
N418FJ	900	25
N418GA	G4	1318
N418GA	**G4**	**1418**
N418LJ	23	081
N418LJ	45	018
N418MG	**400**	**RJ-54**
N418R	31A	075
N418R	501	650
N418R	60	047
N418RD	**125**	**257015**
N418RT	31A	075
N418S	20	32
N418S	50	64
N418SP	G4	1218
(N419BL)	25XR	220
N419CW	**400A**	**RK-19**
N419F	20	419
N419FJ	900	27
N419GA	G4	1025
N419GA	G4	1052
N419GA	G4	1147
N419GA	G4	1195
N419GA	G4	1296
N419GA	**G4**	**1419**
N419GL	25D	294
N419K	500	080
N419MB	**400A**	**RK-85**
N419MK	**AST**	**066**
N419MS	400A	RK-121
N419MS	400A	RK-85
N419RD	**125**	**257153**
N419W	WWD	419
N419WC	**10**	**11**
N419XP	125	258419
N420A	STR	5063
N420AM	**501**	**410**
N420CC	**G4**	**1164**
N420CC	S550	0023
N420CH	**525**	**0066**
N420CL	**20**	**391**
N420DM	560	0210
N420DM	**560**	**0464**
N420DP	20	391
N420F	20	420
N420FJ	900	28
N420G	STR	5063
N420GA	G4	1007
N420GA	G4	1045
N420GA	G4	1124
N420GA	G4	1196
N420GA	G4	1297
N420GA	**G4**	**1420**
N420J	20	369
N420J	WWD	193
N420JC	125	25115
N420JC	**G3**	**326**
N420JD	10	115
N420JM	G2	94
N420JM	WWD	193
N420JP	50	168
N420JT	G2	94
N420L	600	1027
N420L	STR	5063
N420MP	WWD	418
N420P	550	250
N420P	WWD	6
N420PC	10	186
N420PC	35A	132
N420PC	501	462
N420QS	**G4**	**1320**
N420RC	501	462
N420RC	**G3**	**354**
N420SL	G4	1025
N420SZ	**601**	**5027**
N420SZ	G4	1025
N420TJ	D1A	A042SA
N420TJ	**WWD**	**405**
N420TX	600	1027
N420W	WWD	420
N420WR	24	130
N421CJ	551	421
N421FJ	900	29
N421GM	G3	421
N421L	24A	096
N421QL	55	026
N421SZ	125	257146
N421SZ	601	5027
N421SZ	**G4**	**1025**
N421TX	550	250
N421ZC	20	117
N422AW	WWD	422
N422B	25D	331
N422BC	650	0024
N422BC	WWD	302
N422CC	501	422
N422CP	**60**	**171**
N422CW	**400A**	**RK-22**
N422D	200	498
N422DA	**501**	**422**
N422DV	G2	17
N422F	20	421
(N422F)	20	422
N422FJ	900	31
N422G	25D	285
N422GA	G4	1248
N422GA	G4	1298

N422GA	**G4**	**1422**
N422JR	23	092
N422L	200	498
N422MU	**200**	**484**
N422QS	**G4**	**1322**
N422TK	**125**	**256060**
N422U	24	155
N422X	**125**	**257074**
N423D	550	183
N423F	20	423
N423FJ	900	32
N423GA	G4	1009
N423GA	G4	1044
N423GA	G4	1113
N423GA	G4	1197
N423GA	G4	1249
N423GA	G4	1299
N423GA	**G4**	**1423**
N423RD	25	027
N423RD	500	227
N423SA	G3	429
N424AD	500	266
N424BT	**400**	**RJ-62**
N424CV	560	0424
N424DA	**500**	**029**
N424DN	35	061
N424F	20	424
N424FJ	900	33
N424GA	**G4**	**1004**
(N424JM)	601	3064
N424JM	S65	465-36
N424JP	25XR	141
N424JR	25XR	141
N424JR	35A	092
N424JX	20	23
N424LB	**650**	**0076**
N424NJ	24A	100
N424QS	**G4**	**1324**
N424R	**75A**	**380-15**
N424R	S60	306-3
N424RD	24	154
N424RD	25	016
(N424RD)	500	190
N424RS	**24D**	**258**
N424W	WWD	424
N425A	G2	39
N425AS	**35A**	**281**
N425DC	125	25079
N425DN	35	065
N425EJ	23	009
N425F	20	425
N425FD	125	25079
N425FJ	900	34
N425GA	G4	1198
N425GA	G4	1250
N425GA	**G4**	**1425**
N425JA	20	51
(N425JF)	125	25284
N425JF	20	51
N425JF	**WWD**	**210**
N425JL	**25B**	**127**
N425JX	25	059
N425K	125	25114
N425M	**31A**	**055**
N425M	35A	281
N425NA	S40	282-95
N425NJ	24	105
N425RD	25	024
N425RH	**25D**	**351**
N425RJ	**WWD**	**218**
N425SC	23	097
N425SP	G3	425
N425TS	AST	004
N425WA	WWD	425
N425WN	125	257159
(N426CC)	20	205
(N426CC)	501	426
N426CM	**750**	**0117**
N426DA	D1A	A062SA
N426EJ	23	014
N426EM	55	040
N426F	20	428
N426FJ	900	36
N426GA	G4	1010
N426GA	G4	1054
N426GA	G4	1126
N426GA	G4	1215
N426GA	**G4**	**1426**
N426JN	**60**	**142**
N426MD	400	RJ-26
N426NA	24D	292
N426PS	24	148
N426TA	**24B**	**181**
N426WW	WWD	426
N426XP	125	258426
N427AC	G2	95/39
N427CJ	**10**	**67**
N427CW	400	RJ-27
N427DA	125	25220
N427DM	500	179
N427EJ	23	021
N427F	20	426
N427FJ	900	37
N427GA	G4	1016
N427GA	G4	1060
N427GA	G4	1127
N427GA	G4	1148
N427GA	G4	1268
N427GA	G4	1316
N427GA	**G4**	**1427**
N427JX	24D	257
N427LJ	24A	100
N427MD	125	257095
N427NJ	23	021
N427RD	25B	082
N427WW	WWD	427
N428AS	125	257026
(N428CH)	25D	350
N428CL	601	5108
N428DA	**STR**	**5048**
N428EJ	23	022
N428F	20	430
N428FJ	900	39
N428FS	125	257026
N428GA	G4	1028
N428GA	G4	1114
N428GA	G4	1199
N428HR	400A	RK-244
N428JF	WWD	210
N428JM	WWD	193
N428JX	25B	103
N428PC	**525**	**0314**
(N428PC)	525	0324
N428QS	**G4**	**1328**
N428W	WWD	428
N428WE	**400A**	**RK-72**
N429AC	125	25115
(N429BA)	125	256058
N429DA	**125**	**25090**
N429EJ	23	023
N429F	20	431
N429FJ	900	40
N429GA	G4	1029
N429GA	G4	1128
N429GA	G4	1251
N429GA	G4	1319
N429GA	**G4**	**1429**
N429JX	G2	122
N429RC	500	078
N429SA	G3	429
N429SA	**G4**	**1314**
(N429TJ)	25	042
(N429W)	WWD	429
N430A	WWD	430
N430BC	G2	27
N430BJ	**WWD**	**430**
N430C	WWD	49
N430CW	400A	RK-30
N430DC	WWD	87
N430DP	G2	167
N430EJ	23	027
N430F	20	432
N430FJ	900	41
N430GA	G4	1030
N430GA	G4	1115
N430GA	G4	1149
N430GA	G4	1200
N430HM	55	043
N430J	23	091
N430JA	23	091
N430JW	**24D**	**285**
N430LJ	24	103
N430MB	S40	282-113
N430MB	**STR**	**5153/61**
N430MP	**S40**	**282-113**
N430PC	WWD	87
N430R	G2	6
N430RG	**G2**	**235**
N430SA	**650**	**7041**
N430SA	G2	92
N430W	WWD	430
N431AM	WWD	431
N431AS	**35A**	**431**
N431BC	**31**	**005**
N431CA	23	030
N431CB	550	431
N431CB	**650**	**0084**
N431CC	501	431
N431CW	35A	431
N431CW	**400A**	**RK-31**
(N431DA)	S40	282-111
N431DS	551	324
N431EJ	23	030
N431FJ	900	42
(N431GA)	G4	1039
N431GA	G4	1116
N431GA	G4	1201
(N431JC)	551	430
N431JT	**G3**	**417**
N431JV	560	0431
N431M	35A	132
N431NA	T39	265-16
N431NA	T39	285-2
N431WM	**S550**	**0133**
N432AC	125	258150
(N432AS)	25D	234
N432CC	550	438
N432CW	**400A**	**RK-32**
N432DG	501	403
N432EJ	23	028A
N432EZ	10	130
N432F	20	433
N432FJ	900	44
N432GA	G4	1040
N432GA	G4	1125
N432GA	G4	1202
N432GA	G4	1300
N432HS	**WWD**	**432**
N432JW	**36A**	**043**
N432QS	G4	1032
N432SL	25D	241
N432XP	125	258432
N433CV	560	0430
N433DD	**35A**	**161**
N433EJ	23	040
N433F	20	435
N433FJ	900	45
N433FS	**604**	**5433**
N433GA	G4	1041
N433GA	G4	1103
N433GA	G4	1150
N433GA	G4	1252
N433GA	G4	1301
N433GM	**WWD**	**433**
N433J	23	038
N433J	24D	230
N433JA	24D	230
N433JB	23	038
(N433JW)	35	041
N433LJ	24	104
N433MM	**501**	**575**
N433WR	WWD	433
N433WW	WWD	433
N434AN	STR	5050/34
N434CC	550	434
N434EJ	23	046
N434F	20	436
N434FJ	900	46
N434GA	G4	1031
N434GA	G4	1203
N434GA	G4	1269
N434GA	G4	1302
N434H	**650**	**0123**
N434JW	**G2**	**2**
N434QS	**G4**	**1334**
N434SB	**550**	**425**
N435AS	**24E**	**345**
N435CC	501	435
N435CW	**400A**	**RK-35**
(N435EC)	35	018
N435F	20	437
N435FJ	900	48
N435GA	G4	1035
N435GA	G4	1135
N435GA	G4	1204
N435GA	G4	1253
N435GA	G4	1303
N435JL	**35**	**018**
N435JW	35A	331
N435K	**PRM**	**RB-35**
N435M	35A	086
N435MS	**35**	**054**
N435N	35A	435
N435T	125	25083
N435T	20	357
N435T	**2xx**	**9**
N435TP	20	357
N435U	G3	435
(N435W)	WWD	435
N436BL	35A	436
N436CC	501	436
N436CC	S60	306-36
N436DM	**35A**	**389**
N436FJ	900	50
N436GA	G3	436
N436GA	G4	1056
N436GA	G4	1130
N436GA	G4	1254
N436GA	G4	1304
N436JW	**G2**	**73/9**
N436LJ	24A	102
N436MP	20	436
N436WW	WWD	436
N437CC	550	437
N437CF	551	436
N437FJ	900	51
N437FT	**604**	**5437**
N437GA	G3	396
N437GA	G4	1057
N437GA	G4	1131
N437GA	G4	1206
N437GA	G4	1255
N437GA	G4	1320
N437H	**G2**	**258**
N437LJ	23	081
N437SJ	**WWD**	**437**
N437T	125	25083
N437WW	WWD	437
N438	WWD	118
N438AM	WWD	438
N438CC	501	438
N438DM	25D	250
N438FJ	900	53
N438GA	G4	1038
N438GA	G4	1256
N438LJ	24	113
N438MC	**560**	**0438**
N438PM	**125**	**257098**
N438SP	**550**	**576**
(N438W)	WWD	438
N439CL	601	5109
N439FJ	900	55
N439GA	G4	1064
N439GA	G4	1118
N439GA	G4	1205
N439GA	G4	1305
N439H	650	0005
N439ME	35A	439
N439WW	**WWD**	**439**
N440AS	**2xx**	**102**
N440BC	**125**	**25218**
N440CE	**550**	**0937**
N440CW	**400A**	**RK-40**
N440DC	125	25079
N440DM	25D	348
N440DM	**55**	**005**

N440DR	G2	69
N440DS	**400A**	**RK-8**
N440EZ	500	195
N440F	25D	262
N440FJ	900	56
N440GA	G4	1002
N440GA	G4	1216
N440HM	35A	294
N440JB	35A	078
N440KT	**24D**	**249**
N440MC	**35A**	**495**
N440MP	400	RJ-16
N440RM	STR	5016
N440TX	550	411
N440WW	WWD	440
N441A	G3	342
N441A	STR	5123/14
N441BC	**AST**	**033**
N441CW	35A	410
N441DM	10	173
(N441EE)	400	RJ-41
N441FA	20	284
N441FJ	900	57
N441GA	G4	1001
N441GA	G4	1207
N441GA	G4	1306
N441JT	501	601
N441PC	35A	441
N441PC	**35A**	**668**
N441PG	35A	441
N441QS	**G4**	**1341**
N441T	550	329
N441TC	**500**	**140**
N442A	G2	255/18
N442A	S40	282-39
N442A	S60	306-21
N442CW	**400A**	**RK-42**
N442DM	**35A**	**405**
N442F	20	438
N442FJ	900	59
N442GA	G4	1065
N442GA	G4	1132
N442GA	G4	1270
(N442HC)	35A	233
N442JB	**500**	**117**
N442JT	35A	021
N442ME	**550**	**442**
N442MR	550	442
N442NE	35A	442
N442RM	**S60**	**306-73**
(N442SC)	36A	040
N442SW	550	0840
N442SW	550	0862
N442WJ	650	7025
N442WP	S40	282-108
N442WT	650	7025
N442WT	**750**	**0099**
N442WT	S40	282-108
N442WT	S65	465-45
N442WT	WWD	114
N442WT	WWD	77
N443A	WWD	354
N443F	20	439
N443FJ	900	60
N443GA	G4	1066
N443GA	G4	1133
N443GA	G4	1208
N443GA	G4	1307
N443LJ	24	114
N443RK	**35**	**023**
N444AG	24B	208
N444AG	501	434
N444AQ	24B	208
N444BF	20	189
N444BF	35A	391
N444BL	550	487
N444CC	550	394
N444CM	35A	282
(N444CW)	501	444
N444CW	**650**	**0064**
N444EP	**WWD**	**436**
N444ET	MSP	101
N444FJ	20	284
N444FJ	550	070
N444GA	**G3**	**301**
N444GA	G4	1321
N444GB	**550**	**216**
N444GG	**560**	**0262**
N444HC	24B	199
N444HC	**31A**	**064**
N444HC	35A	199
(N444HE)	24D	246
N444HH	**125**	**25191**
N444J	500	179
N444JH	STR	5036/42
N444JJ	550	160
N444KV	500	223
N444KW	24	147
N444LP	500	223
N444LT	G4	1114
N444MA	S60	306-102
N444MJ	35A	444
N444MK	**25D**	**252**
N444MM	550	317
N444MM	WWD	210
N444MV	**501**	**401**
N444MW	501	401
N444MW	**WWD**	**372**
N444PB	25D	227
N444PD	125	256001
N444PE	125	256001
N444PE	**50**	**143**
N444QG	**G2**	**133**
N444RF	525	0001
N444RH	525	0001
N444RP	500	250
N444SC	20	324
N444SC	24D	246
(N444SC)	36A	040
(N444SL)	D1A	A041SA
N444TG	**25D**	**327**
N444TG	35A	469
N444TJ	G4	1010
N444TJ	WWD	146
N444TW	**24F**	**348**
N444WA	600	1005
N444WB	35A	318
N444WB	**400**	**RJ-42**
N444WC	23	047
N444WJ	**10**	**64**
(N444WJ)	550	088
N444WL	WWD	48
N444WS	25	038
N444WW	**25D**	**283**
N445	WWD	37
N445A	**WWD**	**362**
N445AC	601	3051
N445BL	WWD	382
N445CC	**400A**	**RK-45**
N445CC	500	445
N445E	400A	RK-45
N445F	20	441
N445FJ	900	63
N445GA	G4	1012
N445GA	G4	1077
N445GA	G4	1134
N445GA	G4	1209
N445GA	G4	1322
N446	31	010
N446A	WWD	367
N446D	**20**	**446**
N446F	20	442
N446FJ	900	64
N446GA	G3	488
N446GA	G4	1013
N446GA	G4	1067
N446GA	G4	1152
N446GA	G4	1219
N446GA	G4	1308
N446M	**400A**	**RK-199**
N446U	**G3**	**446**
N447CC	400	RJ-38
(N447CJ)	550	447
N447F	20	443
N447FJ	900	65
(N447FM)	550	007
N447GA	G4	1014
N447GA	G4	1080
N447GA	G4	1211
N447GA	G4	1309
N447LJ	24	112
N448DC	125	25078
N448DC	125	25079
N448EC	500	191
N448FJ	900	67
N448GA	G4	1048
(N448GA)	G4	1084
N448GA	G4	1153
N448GA	G4	1210
N448GA	G4	1257
N448GA	G4	1310
N448GC	23	057
N448GC	35A	472
N448GG	23	057
N448HM	60	007
(N448QS)	G4	1408
N448W	**75A**	**380-63**
N448WC	35A	472
N448WG	35A	472
N448WT	S65	465-45
N448WT	WWD	114
N449A	10	49
N449F	20	445
N449FJ	900	68
N449GA	G4	1085
N449GA	G4	1220
N449GA	G4	1311
(N449JS)	24F	352
N449LJ	24	115
N449ML	**601**	**5022**
N449QS	35A	449
(N449SA)	650	7041
N449SA	**650**	**7088**
N450	25B	127
N450AF	50	36
N450BC	**45**	**075**
N450BM	AST	011
N450CC	550	281
(N450CE)	S60	306-22
N450CL	**50**	**76**
N450CT	10	157
N450DA	125	256041
N450DK	**604**	**5450**
N450FJ	900	70
N450GM	**551**	**617**
N450JD	125	25148
N450JD	WWD	9
N450K	**50**	**186**
N450KK	35A	450
N450KP	50	82
N450MA	20	158/449
N450MC	**35A**	**368**
N450PC	D1A	A024SA
N450PM	AST	011
N450RA	560	0377
N450RA	WWD	13
N450SC	25B	127
N450TJ	D1A	A005SA
N450X	50	54
N451CJ	501	451
N451CS	G2	70/1
N451CS	**G5**	**570**
N451DP	**20**	**249**
N451FJ	900	71
N451GA	**G4**	**1221**
N451GS	G2	70/1
N451QS	**G4**	**1351**
N452CJ	550	452
N452DP	10	11
N452ET	25XR	152
N452F	20	440
N452FJ	900	73
N452GA	G4	1222
N452GA	G4	1271
N452LJ	24	118
N452LJ	**45**	**002**
N452QS	**G4**	**1352**
N452SM	125	258136
N452WU	**604**	**5452**
N453	**24D**	**323**
N453AD	**604**	**5453**
N453CM	125	25084
N453CV	**560**	**0453**
N453DP	**125**	**256044**
N453EP	125	257014
N453F	20	444
N453FJ	900	74
N453GA	G4	1223
N453GA	G4	1312
N453JS	**900**	**144**
N453JT	23	033
N453LJ	23	033
N453LJ	24	119
N453LJ	45	003
N453S	**551**	**445**
N453SA	24	119
N453SB	**20**	**308**
N453TM	**125**	**258203**
N454AC	**501**	**373**
N454AS	**45**	**038**
N454CG	**45**	**085**
N454DP	10	130
N454DP	125	256044
N454DQ	**501**	**579**
N454EP	125	257017
N454F	20	446
N454FJ	900	76
N454GA	G4	1224
N454GA	G4	1272
N454GA	G4	1323
N454GL	24	121
N454HC	MSP	090
N454JB	**125**	**258003**
N454JB	STR	5205
N454LJ	24	121
N454LJ	24B	226
N454LJ	45	004
N454MK	**45**	**088**
N454RN	24	121
N454SR	WWD	79
N455BE	**600**	**1069**
N455DM	551	095
N455DW	**400**	**RJ-20**
(N455EC)	55	043
N455EM	**55**	**014**
N455F	20	447
N455FJ	900	77
N455GA	G4	1313
N455H	501	552
N455JA	24D	300
N455LB	S65	465-49
N455LJ	**45**	**005**
N455NE	35A	455
N455RH	**55**	**110**
N455RM	35A	171
N455S	WWD	367
N455SF	S65	465-49
N455SR	600	1032
N456AB	**550**	**215**
N456AF	650	0147
N456AS	**45**	**039**
N456AS	G2	17
N456CE	501	630
N456CG	**25D**	**343**
(N456CG)	600	1027
N456CL	**35A**	**456**
N456CM	100	207
(N456CM)	550	456
N456CW	**400A**	**RK-56**
N456DK	**600**	**1081**
N456FB	560	0009
N456FJ	900	78
N456GB	500	256
N456JA	24D	265
N456JG	**400A**	**RK-119**
N456JP	S40	282-32
N456JW	560	0266
N456JW	**560**	**5033**
N456LJ	45	006
N456MS	35	017
N456N	550	077
N456PR	**AST**	**116**
N456R	**501**	**472**
N456SC	23	022
N456SR	20	299
N456SW	**G3**	**337**

N456WH	**125**	**25244**
N457CA	500	131
N457CF	550	457
N457CS	**501**	**578**
N457DS	**G4**	**1077**
N457F	**20**	**449**
N457FJ	900	79
N457GA	G4	1061
N457GA	G4	1123
N457GA	**G4**	**1157**
N457GA	G4	1162
N457GA	G4	1273
N457GA	G4	1324
N457GM	**24E**	**340**
N457H	G3	457
N457HL	**600**	**1063**
N457JA	24X	207
N457K	**PRM**	**RB-57**
N457LJ	24	120
N457LJ	**45**	**007**
N457SF	G3	409
N457ST	G3	409
N457ST	**G4**	**1345**
N457SW	G2	115
N458A	10	58
N458CC	550	458
(N458CG)	25D	343
(N458DS)	550	458
N458F	20	450
N458FA	**G4**	**1159**
N458FJ	900	75
N458GA	G4	1058
N458GA	G4	1163
N458GA	G4	1274
(N458H)	551	377
N458HW	551	377
N458J	25XR	106
N458JA	25XR	106
N458JA	35A	376
N458JW	560	0266
N458LJ	24	115
N458N	**550**	**077**
(N458N)	551	061
N458SW	**20**	**68**
N459F	20	452
N459FA	**G4**	**1161**
N459FJ	900	80
N459GA	G4	1069
N459GA	G4	1164
N459GA	G4	1225
N459GA	G4	1275
N459GA	G4	1325
N459JD	WWD	9
N459LJ	**45**	**009**
N460BG	**60**	**090**
N460CC	501	460
N460CP	**650**	**0021**
N460F	20	453
N460F	23	068
N460FJ	900	83
N460GA	G4	1086
N460GA	G4	1165
N460GA	G4	1226
N460GA	G4	1276
N460GA	G5	565
N460MC	**20**	**105**
N460QS	**G4**	**1360**
N461AS	**10**	**146**
N461CW	**400A**	**RK-61**
N461F	20	454
N461F	24A	116
N461FJ	900	85
N461GA	G4	1047
N461GA	G4	1166
N461GA	G4	1260
N461GA	G4	1314
N461GA	G5	568
N461GT	**G3**	**411**
N461LJ	24	122
N461W	**125**	**258200**
N462B	24	155
N462B	24D	290
N462B	25D	331
N462B	25XR	175
N462B	**560**	**0016**
N462BA	24	155
N462BA	25XR	175
N462CC	501	462
N462CW	**400**	**RK-62**
N462F	20	456
N462FJ	900	87
N462GA	G4	1062
N462GA	G4	1168
N462GA	G4	1277
N462LJ	24	124
N462QS	**G4**	**1262**
N463C	550	285
(N463CJ)	501	463
N463F	20	457
N463FJ	900	92
N463GA	G4	1087
N463GA	G4	1169
N463GA	G4	1227
N463GA	G5	563
N463HK	**G2**	**11**
N463LJ	25	001
N463QS	**G4**	**1363**
(N464)	S550	0061
N464AC	10	54
N464C	**525**	**0325**
N464CL	**24A**	**096**
N464EC	WWD	305
N464FJ	900	95
N464GA	G4	1088
N464GA	G4	1170
N464GA	G4	1228
N464GA	G4	1278
N464HA	35A	304
N464J	24	164
N464M	20	322
N464QS	**G4**	**1264**
N464SP	**G4**	**1286**
N464TF	**60**	**185**
N464WL	35A	464
N465CV	560	0465
N465D	551	377
N465F	20	458
N465FJ	900	98
N465GA	G3	465
N465GA	G4	1089
N465GA	G4	1171
N465GA	G4	1229
N465GA	G4	1265
N465JH	S60	306-57
N465LC	S65	465-21
N465NW	**35A**	**465**
N465PM	S65	465-40
N465R	125	257029
N465RM	S65	465-40
N465S	S40	282-59
N465S	S60	306-136
N465S	S65	465-1
N465SL	S65	465-26
N465SP	**S65**	**465-72**
N465SR	S65	465-33
N465T	S65	465-2
N465TS	**S65**	**465-15**
N466CS	**125**	**258206**
N466F	20	459
N466FJ	900	101
N466GA	G4	1090
N466GA	G4	1172
N466GA	G4	1279
N466GA	G5	566
N466LM	**560**	**5074**
N466MP	125	25155
N466SS	**550**	**626**
N467F	20	460
N467FJ	900	102
N467GA	G4	1091
N467GA	G4	1174
N467GA	G4	1230
N467GA	G5	567
N467H	**S40**	**282-3**
(N467MW)	550	093
N467MW	**WWD**	**325**
N468CJ	550	468
N468DM	24	156
N468FJ	900	104
N468GA	G4	1092
N468GA	G4	1176
N468GA	G4	1280
N468KL	**601**	**5036**
N468LM	125	25221
N468LM	35A	468
(N469)	550	423
N469DE	**550**	**0883**
N469F	20	461
N469FJ	900	105
N469GA	G4	1095
N469GA	G4	1177
N469GA	G4	1261
N469GA	G5	569
N469J	24	165
N469JR	125	257174
N469PW	**500**	**302**
N469QS	**G4**	**1369**
N470F	20	462
N470FJ	900	107
N470G	**20**	**470**
N470GA	G4	1178
N470GA	G4	1231
N470GA	G4	1281
N470GA	G5	570
N470R	125	25058
N470TR	24D	298
N470TS	125	25070
N471DG	**700**	**9049**
N471F	20	463
N471FJ	900	108
N471GA	G4	1179
N471GA	G4	1232
N471GA	G4	1282
N471H	501	471
N471HH	500	050
N471MH	500	050
N471MM	25B	169
N471MM	500	050
N471SB	600	1083
N471SP	600	1083
N471SP	601	5157
N471TM	WWD	370
(N472AS)	35A	472
N472EJ	24D	238
N472F	20	464
N472FJ	900	111
N472GA	G4	1180
N472GA	G4	1233
N472GA	G4	1283
N472GA	**G5**	**572**
N472J	25B	204
N472QS	**G4**	**1372**
N472SP	STR	5078/3
N472SW	**525**	**0033**
N472TS	G4	1172
N473	24	101
N473CC	501	473
N473CW	G4	1194
N473EJ	24	101
N473F	20	466
N473FJ	900	112
N473GA	G4	1181
N473JE	**400A**	**RK-121**
N473LP	500	276
N473LR	500	276
N473TC	**25**	**043**
N474CV	560	0474
N474F	20	467
N474FJ	900	114
N474L	500	323
N474L	S550	0107
N474SP	550	485
N474VW	S40	282-76
N475CC	501	475
N475DJ	**G3**	**358**
N475FJ	900	116
N475GA	G4	1182
N475GA	G4	1234
N475GA	G4	1284
N475GA	G5	575
N475HM	**125**	**258451**
N475M	**650**	**0062**
N475QS	**G4**	**1275**
N475WA	**550**	**475**
N476BJ	**400A**	**RK-176**
N476FJ	900	117
N476GA	G4	1183
N476GA	G5	576
N476VC	35A	476
N476X	501	559
N477A	**551**	**106**
N477A	S40	282-110
N477BL	24A	031
N477BM	60	010
N477DM	60	010
N477DM	601	5174
N477DM	**604**	**5398**
N477F	20	470
N477FJ	900	119
N477GA	G4	1184
N477GA	G4	1235
N477GA	G4	1285
N477GA	**G4**	**1388**
N477GG	**G2**	**155/14**
N477JB	24D	230
(N477JM)	S60	306-5
(N477JR)	550	477
N477K	23	036
N477KM	501	607
N477KM	**550**	**397**
(N477MM)	25D	291
(N477MS)	35A	477
N477QS	**G4**	**1377**
N477RP	**G4**	**1247**
(N477RW)	125	257191
N477TS	G4	1077
N477WB	35A	477
N477X	S40	282-110
N477X	**S60**	**306-78**
N478A	900	95
N478F	20	471
N478FJ	900	121
N478GA	G4	1185
N478GA	G4	1236
N478GA	**G4**	**1400**
N479CC	501	479
N479FJ	900	122
N479GA	G4	1186
N479GA	G4	1402
N479JS	501	479
N479TS	G4	1079
(N480CC)	501	480
N480CC	**S550**	**0129**
N480FJ	900	124
N480GA	G2	234
N480GA	G4	1237
N480GA	G4	1286
N480LR	HFB	1054
N480QS	**G4**	**1380**
N480UP	G4	1054
N481DH	**WWD**	**139**
N481EZ	24	139
N481FJ	900	126
N481FM	35A	218
N481GA	G4	1187
N481JT	600	1034
N481MC	**WWD**	**184**
N481NS	**WWD**	**378**
N481QS	**G4**	**1281**
N482CP	24D	230
N482CP	**25D**	**331**
N482DM	**D1A**	**A088SA**
N482FJ	900	127
N482G	WWD	98
N482GA	G4	1188
N482HC	S40	282-28
N482RJ	**500**	**082**
N482SG	35A	493
N482U	35A	482
N483A	WWD	283
N483AS	550	483
N483DM	**24D**	**291**
N483DM	D1A	A089SA
N483FG	**125**	**257094**
N483FJ	900	129
N483G	550	325

N483GA G4 1238
N483SC 550 483
(N484) 35A 480
N484CC 400 RJ-27
(N484CS) 501 548
N484DM D1A A084SA
N484GA G4 1239
N484GA G4 1287
N484HB 36A 027
N484KA 500 484
N484RA 125 258053
N484T 750 0006
N484TL G2 93
(N484VS) D1A A084SA
N484W 125 256063
(N485) 35A 306
N485 35A 491
N485A 550 485
N485AC 35A 485
N485CC 501 485
N485DM D1A A085SA
(N485DM) D1A A091SA
N485GA G4 1185
N485GA G4 1385
N485GM G2 137
N485RP 501 503
N485S 35A 485
(N486) 55 120
N486CC 501 486
N486DM D1A A086SA
N486G 23 093
N486G WWD 48
N486GA G4 1240
(N486GA) G4 1286
N486GA G4 1386
N486MJ 100 199
N486MJ 125 257035
N486MJ 400 RJ-17
N486MJ 400 RJ-30
N486QS G4 1386
(N487CC) 550 487
N487DM D1A A087SA
N487F 50 160
N487G WWD 103
N487GA G4 1241
N487GA G4 1387
N487HR 501 487
N487LD 550 551
(N487LP) 35A 669
N487LS 501 487
N487QS G4 1287
N488A 550 0882
(N488BL) 24B 193
N488CC 501 488
N488CP 560 5055
N488DM 24D 291
N488DM S65 465-26
N488EC STR 5061/48
N488GR STR 5051
N488J 23 024
N488JS STR 5051
N488JT 650 0020
N488MR STR 5061/48
N488SB G3 487
(N489) 35A 277
N489G WWD 149
N489H G4 1099
N489QS G4 1389
N489TK 200 489
(N490A) 10 49
N490BC 35A 364
N490CC 550 490
N490CD 550 490
N490EA 500 061
N490GA G4 1242
N490GA G4 1390
N490MP 125 257135
N490TN 400A RK-45
N490WC 501 518
N491 500 072
N491BT 500 102
N491DB 600 1049
N491GA G4 1243
N491HS 35A 491
N491JB 650 0182
N491MB 200 491
N491N 550 360
N491TS 600 1049
N492A G3 425
N492BJ 400A RK-192
N492CB 125 257056
N492CV 560 0492
N492DD G3 492
N492JT G2 82
N492QS G4 1392
N492ST 550 249
N493CH 35A 493
N493NW 35A 493
N493QS G4 1293
N494AT 125 258103
N494BP WWD 307
N494CW 400A RK-4
N494G 500 147
N494LC 601 5102
N494RG 125 258378
N495CC 550 495
N495CM 550 202
N495G 125 25017
N495GA 900 55
N495GA G4 1259
N495GA G5 597
N495QS G4 1295
N496EE 400A RK-40
N496G 125 25174
N496GA G4 1262
N496GA G5 599
(N496LJ) 35A 496
N496RT 200 496
N496SW 35A 496
N497 20 6
N497DM 604 5359
N497GA G4 1263
N497PT 125 257093
N497TJ G2 61
N498A 90X 55
N498CS 650 0180
N498JR 35A 498
N498QS G4 1398
N498R 125 25225
N498RS 125 25225
N499AS STR 5146
N499BA 500 196
N499DM 400 RJ-10
N499EH 25D 239
N499G 35A 147
N499G 35A 202
N499GA 125 257130
N499GA G4 1264
N499GA G4 1399
N499MJ 20 57
(N499MW) AST 019
N499NH S65 465-56
N499P 400 RJ-31
N499PB STR 5063
N499PC STR 5112/7
(N499QS) G4 1099
N499QS G4 1299
N499SC 125 25236
N499SC 125 258082
N499SC 55C 147
N499SC G4 1238
N499TR WWD 41
N499WJ 35A 499
N499WM 550 0869
N500 125 257111
N500 60 115
N500 604 5419
N500 650 7027
N500AB 500 110
N500AD 500 006
N500AD 500 091
N500AE 50 166
N500AE 550 269
N500AE 650 0161
N500AF 50 166
N500AF 50 170
N500AG 125 25203
N500AG STR 5119/29
(N500AH) 500 006
N500AJ AST 074
N500AL G3 416
N500AX WWD 359
N500AZ 500 185
N500BE 55 058
N500BF 23 010
N500BG 20 121
N500BK 501 646
N500BL 50 66
N500BL 900 32
N500BR 550 411
N500CA 25B 091
N500CC 500 669
N500CD 25B 091
N500CD 35A 083
N500CD G4 1321
N500CG 24D 304
N500CG 31A 068
N500CG 35A 238
N500CM 650 0111
N500CP 500 087
N500CU 560 0500
N500CV 500 076
N500CV 500 082
N500CV 550 186
(N500CX) 500 300
N500DB 500 056
N500DD 35A 351
N500DD 500 334
N500DE 10 64
N500DG G4 1169
N500DJ 24D 296
N500DL 25 027
N500DL 501 542
N500DN 500 034
N500DS 10 28
N500DS 35A 079
N500E 650 0065
N500E G3 372
N500E G4 1072
N500E S65 465-52
N500ED 35A 241
(N500EE) 550 269
N500EF 125 257086
(N500EF) 25D 249
N500EF 35A 272
N500EL 500 173
(N500EN) 500 135
N500ER 551 150
N500ES STR 5075/19
N500ET 500 180
N500EW 20 21
N500EW 25D 232
N500EX 35A 241
N500EX 35A 591
N500EX 551 298
(N500EX) 600 1047
N500EX G3 372
N500EX STR 5217
(N500FA) 55 004
N500FA 55 092
N500FC 125 257011
N500FD 35A 241
N500FE 20 163
N500FF 10 58
N500FG STR 5135
N500FK 560 0047
N500FM 23 088
N500FM 24A 111
N500FR 650 0208
N500FX 551 298
N500GA 500 217
N500GA 501 632
N500GD 125 256018
N500GE 500 004
N500GF G3 488
N500GJ WWD 64
N500GK WWD 301
N500GM 10 99
N500GM 20 195
N500GM 35A 211
N500GM 550 074
N500GP 35A 241
N500GR 500 098
N500GS 10 132
N500GS 125 257162
N500GS 500 004
N500GS 601 5045
(N500HC) 50 136
N500HC 525 0048
(N500HD) 20 163
N500HF 125 258249
N500HG 35A 238
(N500HG) 55 083
N500HH 500 189
N500HK 20 113
N500HK 500 190
N500HY 400A RK-153
N500HZ 35A 238
N500J 125 258216
N500J G2 60
N500J WWD 303
N500JA 25 007
N500JB 500 185
N500JC 501 430
(N500JC) 55 043
N500JD 20 378
N500JD 500 009
N500JD STR 5152
N500JE 31A 088
N500JK 500 202
N500JR G2 34
N500JR WWD 65
N500JS 25 020
N500JS 35A 404
N500JW 23 005
N500JW 25 054
N500JW 55 043
N500JW G2 14
N500JW G2 234
N500K 23 016
N500K 501 500
N500KE WWD 360
N500KJ 50 197
N500KK 35A 211
N500KP 500 095
N500LD 20 163
N500LE 501 602
N500LE 560 0052
N500LF 500 007
N500LG 28 005
(N500LH) 23 088
N500LH 501 602
(N500LH) S550 0119
N500LJ 500 195
(N500LL) 125 258095
N500LL 24E 347
N500LP 500 251
N500LR 601 5012
N500LS 125 257173
N500LS 600 1048
N500LS G3 460
N500LS G4 1009
N500LS WWD 137
N500LS WWD 226
N500LW 25D 232
N500M AST 018
N500M AST 091
N500M WWD 175
N500M WWD 300
N500MA 125 25237
N500MA 125 256064
N500MA STR 5033/56
(N500MD) 501 370
N500MD WWD 300
N500MF WWD 34
N500MG 560 0223
N500MH 24 158
N500MJ 25B 091
N500MJ 35A 348
N500MJ 36A 025
N500ML WWD 175
N500MM G3 460
N500MM G4 1135
N500MN G3 460
N500MP 25D 208
N500MP 31A 198

N500MQ	AST	018
N500MS	**24D**	**246**
N500MX	500	006
N500MZ	AST	091
N500ND	**35A**	**351**
N500NH	24E	355
N500NH	**55**	**100**
N500NJ	**500**	**113**
N500NL	75A	380-8
N500NM	STR	5229
(N500NU)	20	21
N500NW	501	660
N500NX	500	120
N500P	23	077
N500P	24	119
N500PB	500	017
N500PB	500	232
N500PC	20	19
N500PC	601	3003
N500PC	**601**	**5071**
N500PC	G2	65
N500PE	601	3065
N500PE	**604**	**5440**
N500PG	**601**	**3039**
N500PG	STR	5153/61
(N500PJ)	24	119
N500PP	24	119
N500PP	25B	121
N500PP	25D	208
N500PP	25D	248
N500PP	35A	390
N500PP	**D1A**	**A061SA**
N500PR	STR	5204
N500PX	20	19
N500PX	551	191
N500PX	560	0178
N500QC	STR	5205
N500QM	550	074
N500R	125	256068
N500R	500	127
N500R	**600**	**1077**
N500R	G2	12
N500R	WWD	280
N500RE	24B	193
N500RE	50	124
(N500RH)	125	258013
N500RH	600	1069
N500RH	**G2**	**80**
N500RK	24D	296
N500RK	S40	282-42
(N500RK)	S60	306-64
N500RK	S60	306-85
N500RL	**G2**	**122**
N500RP	24B	193
N500RP	24E	345
N500RP	35A	351
N500RP	55	053
N500RP	650	0187
N500RP	**750**	**0029**
N500RR	**200**	**491**
N500RR	24E	345
N500RR	550	638
N500RR	S60	306-33
N500RR	S65	465-49
N500RR	WWD	359
N500RW	24R	233
N500RW	35A	148
N500S	STR	5134/50
N500S	**STR**	**5209**
N500SB	24	166
N500SJ	**500**	**231**
N500SJ	STR	5012
N500SK	**500**	**129**
N500SR	**24E**	**347**
N500SV	**36A**	**040**
N500SW	**24D**	**325**
N500T	G2	244
N500T	STR	5211
N500TB	601	3003
(N500TB)	601	5120
N500TD	500	070
N500TD	601	3003
N500TF	75A	380-19
N500TH	**400A**	**RK-246**
N500TL	**25D**	**238**
N500TM	**500**	**112**
N500TS	24E	347
N500TW	**501**	**623**
N500UB	**560**	**0052**
N500UJ	**560**	**0062**
N500VB	550	147
N500VC	**560**	**0144**
N500VF	WWD	115
N500VK	500	202
N500VM	**90X**	**5**
N500VS	G3	460
N500VS	G4	1009
N500WD	S65	465-48
N500WH	WWD	215
N500WJ	**500**	**202**
N500WK	WWD	196
N500WN	501	404
N500WN	STR	5048
N500WN	STR	5135
N500WP	500	185
N500WP	550	238
N500WR	**31A**	**038**
N500WR	500	166
N500WW	25B	137
N500WW	**G3**	**318**
N500WZ	STR	5048
N500XX	501	509
N500XY	**125**	**25119**
N500XY	500	347
N500Y	20	155
N500Y	500	110
N500YB	125	25170
(N500YY)	23	028
(N500YY)	STR	5211
N500Z	STR	5008
N500Z	STR	5072/23
N500ZA	24B	182
N500ZA	**24F**	**350**
N500ZB	125	257043
N500ZB	STR	5102
N500ZC	501	435
N500ZH	24B	182
N500ZH	60	115
N501AA	550	054
N501AF	**501**	**526**
N501AL	STR	5012
N501AR	500	128
N501AS	20	262
N501AT	500	208
N501BA	501	443
(N501BB)	500	455
N501BB	**501**	**474**
N501BE	**501**	**354**
(N501BE)	S550	0138
(N501BF)	501	354
N501BG	**400A**	**RK-5**
N501BG	501	432
N501BK	501	683
N501BL	550	028
N501BP	**501**	**604**
N501BW	501	625
N501BW	WWD	335
N501CB	501	423
N501CB	WWD	435
N501CC	**500**	**701**
N501CD	**501**	**432**
N501CE	501	525
N501CF	**501**	**522**
N501CG	**501**	**486**
N501CM	501	631
(N501CP)	WWD	435
N501CR	501	614
N501CW	500	282
N501CW	501	477
N501CW	**560**	**0050**
N501CX	501	432
N501D	**501**	**511**
(N501DB)	501	362
N501DD	**501**	**404**
N501DG	501	578
N501DK	550	462
N501DL	501	375
(N501DP)	501	531
N501DR	500	342
N501DT	**WWD**	**270**
N501DY	**501**	**644**
N501E	501	412
N501E	560	0231
N501ED	501	547
N501EF	501	441
N501EG	**501**	**685**
N501EK	**501**	**453**
(N501EM)	501	382
N501EM	**501**	**516**
N501EZ	501	434
(N501EZ)	501	649
(N501F)	125	257167
N501F	**125**	**258286**
N501F	20	269
(N501FB)	501	386
N501FJ	**501**	**563**
N501FM	501	547
N501FP	**501**	**550**
N501FR	501	683
N501FT	501	434
N501G	**501**	**607**
N501GF	501	507
N501GG	**501**	**532**
N501GK	501	507
N501GP	500	026
N501GR	501	378
N501GS	**501**	**369**
(N501GS)	501	468
N501GV	G5	501
N501GW	501	578
N501HC	501	508
N501HK	500	292
N501HM	501	615
N501HP	501	573
N501HS	**501**	**480**
N501J	STR	5213
N501JC	**500**	**252**
N501JE	**501**	**670**
N501JF	501	382
N501JG	500	150
N501JJ	**501**	**368**
N501JM	**501**	**635**
N501JP	501	477
N501JP	**550**	**730**
N501KC	20	401
N501KC	551	030
N501KG	500	001
N501KG	**500**	**279**
N501KK	**501**	**588**
N501KR	**501**	**446**
N501LB	**500**	**165**
N501LC	**550**	**161**
N501LE	**501**	**671**
(N501LG)	500	294
N501LH	**500**	**342**
N501LL	**501**	**561**
N501LM	501	673
N501LS	501	482
N501LW	501	516
N501MB	**501**	**508**
N501MC	**551**	**500**
N501MD	**20**	**284**
N501MD	501	382
(N501MD)	501	508
N501MH	24D	314
N501MM	125	257079
N501MM	501	601
N501MR	501	661
N501MS	501	674
N501MT	**501**	**675**
N501NA	501	459
N501NB	S550	0018
N501NC	50	11
N501NC	501	578
N501NZ	501	459
N501PC	500	005
N501PC	601	3004
N501PC	601	3023
N501PC	**G4**	**1298**
N501PS	25B	153
N501PV	**501**	**394**
N501QS	560	0024
N501R	125	256068
N501RB	500	132
N501RC	**501**	**557**
N501RF	501	671
N501RG	**501**	**666**
N501RL	500	292
N501RL	500	311
N501RM	500	001
N501RM	**501**	**465**
N501RP	55	053
N501RS	**501**	**479**
N501SC	500	314
N501SE	**500**	**249**
N501SE	501	474
(N501SF)	501	426
N501SJ	501	423
N501SJ	501	474
N501SK	501	459
N501SP	**501**	**383**
N501SR	501	446
N501SS	500	282
N501SS	500	455
N501T	560	0136
N501T	G2	248
N501T	STR	5213
N501TB	501	685
N501TJ	**501**	**372**
N501TK	500	210
N501TP	**501**	**684**
N501TW	35A	612
N501TW	55ER	101
N501U	WWD	381
N501VP	**501**	**352**
N501W	125	25136
N501WB	**501**	**556**
N501WJ	501	353
(N501WK)	501	353
N501WW	500	044
N501X	**501**	**478**
N502AL	550	029
(N502BA)	500	288
N502BE	**500**	**195**
N502BG	**10**	**144**
N502BG	550	297
N502BG	WWD	372
N502CC	500	001
N502CC	500	008
N502CC	**501**	**502**
N502CL	**551**	**014**
N502E	**560**	**0232**
N502F	20	481
N502F	560	0153
N502F	**601**	**5111**
N502G	35A	219
N502GP	500	027
N502GV	G5	502
N502JB	**50**	**115**
N502JC	25D	264
N502KA	**G5**	**502**
N502MH	25C	098
N502PC	**601**	**5121**
N502PC	G2	170
(N502R)	125	257159
N502RL	500	043
N502RR	S40	282-13
N502S	125	257206
N502SU	550	621
N502T	560	0153
N502T	**650**	**7067**
N502TS	**560**	**0157**
N502U	WWD	48
N503CC	**500**	**003**
N503EB	400	RJ-29
N503F	20	391
(N503F)	560	0154
N503GP	500	086
N503GV	G5	503
N503PC	601	3021
N503PC	**G4**	**1323**
N503QS	**125**	**259003**
(N503RH)	WWD	260
N503RP	35A	070
N503T	560	0154
N503U	WWD	83

N504BW	**560**	**0128**
N504CC	500	004
N504CC	**560**	**0504**
N504DM	400	RJ-4
N504EX	STR	5217
N504F	**35A**	**340**
N504GP	500	265
N504GV	G5	504
N504JC	WWD	277
N504M	601	5099
N504SU	**750**	**0024**
N504T	**650**	**7040**
N504TF	G2	8
N504TS	**601**	**5004**
N504U	WWD	325
N504Y	35A	282
N505AG	**550**	**0905**
N505AJ	**20**	**89**
N505AM	500	340
N505BB	500	455
N505BC	501	367
N505BC	WWD	278
N505BG	501	430
N505C	STR	5040
N505C	STR	5113/25
N505CC	500	005
N505CC	501	638
N505CC	S550	0115
N505CF	**501**	**517**
N505EB	400A	RK-17
N505EE	**35A**	**505**
N505GA	**GXY**	**005**
N505GL	550	495
N505GP	500	272
N505GP	550	279
N505GV	G5	505
N505HG	**36**	**009**
N505JC	500	341
N505JH	**501**	**505**
N505JT	G2	46
N505K	**500**	**004**
N505M	**601**	**5100**
N505MA	**750**	**0057**
N505PA	125	25022
N505PF	23	006
N505QS	**125**	**259005**
N505RA	36	009
N505RJ	**501**	**367**
N505RX	G2	219/20
N505SP	501	505
N505T	STR	5015
N505TC	**50**	**57**
N505U	WWD	196
N505W	125	25136
N505W	125	256013
N505X	**550**	**0865**
N506C	35A	094
N506CC	500	006
N506D	STR	5061/48
N506E	**560**	**0236**
N506GP	35A	109
N506GV	G5	506
N506MX	500	006
N506N	125	25136
N506SR	500	006
N506T	G3	484
N506T	STR	5061/48
N506TF	500	006
N506TF	**501**	**351**
N506TN	601	5066
N506TS	**601**	**5006**
N506U	WWD	354
N507AB	551	030
N507CC	500	007
N507CC	600	1026
(N507CC)	S550	0002
N507CJ	S550	0002
N507CW	**D1A**	**A007SA**
N507DM	400	RJ-7
N507DS	**501**	**403**
N507GA	G5	507
N507GP	550	294
N507HC	600	1026
N507JC	G2	121

N507TF	S60	306-39
N507U	S60	306-93
N507WY	600	1026
N508BP	**125**	**258419**
N508CC	500	008
(N508CC)	500	208
N508CC	600	1057
N508CV	550	186
N508DM	400	RJ-3
N508DW	**550**	**620**
N508EJ	**50**	**8**
N508GA	G5	508
N508GP	**35A**	**424**
N508HC	600	1057
(N508L)	20	359/542
N508M	23	025
N508P	35A	390
N508PB	500	017
N508R	WWD	280
N508S	500	192
N508T	G2	232
N508T	STR	5119/29
N508TA	STR	5119/29
(N508TC)	20	408
N509	125	257111
N509AB	S60	306-75
N509CC	500	009
N509CC	S550	0109
N509G	25	054
N509GA	G5	509
N509GP	125	258077
N509J	STR	5222
(N509PC)	601	3002
N509PC	601	3004
N509QC	**125**	**257111**
N509T	G2	244
N509T	STR	5222
N509TC	10	134
N509TC	550	462
(N509TF)	STR	5222
N509TT	G2	244
N509W	601	5099
N509WP	20	369
N510	601	5100
N510AA	80A	380-4
N510BA	**125**	**258331**
N510BB	80A	380-9
(N510CC)	500	001
N510CC	500	010
N510CC	500	310
N510CL	**10**	**9**
N510CP	10	43
N510G	G2	85
N510GA	501	625
N510GP	**550**	**420**
N510HS	125	257034
(N510L)	25D	280
N510LF	**200**	**510**
N510LJ	35	025
N510MS	**24B**	**204**
N510MT	**560**	**0122**
N510ND	24B	204
N510PA	24D	305
N510PC	600	1011
N510PS	600	1011
N510RC	**500**	**282**
N510SD	**650**	**0161**
N510SG	35A	268
(N510SG)	60	062
N510T	G2	248
N510TA	T39	265-10
N510TB	T39	265-86
N510TC	T39	276-27
N510TD	T39	265-15
N510TL	G2	248
N510TP	25D	353
N510TS	**STR**	**5100/41**
N510US	**G2**	**223**
N510VP	550	710
N510WS	**400**	**RJ-24**
N510X	125	25126
N511AB	**550**	**328**
N511AC	**525**	**0098**
N511AJ	**25**	**055**

N511AT	24E	330
N511AT	**500**	**166**
N511BB	S550	0083
N511BR	S550	0083
N511BX	125	25150
N511C	**G4**	**1065**
N511CC	500	011
N511CC	WWD	253
N511CC	WWD	367
(N511CL)	60	094
N511CQ	WWD	253
N511DB	28	002
N511DL	550	228
N511DR	550	228
N511DR	**560**	**0274**
N511GA	G5	511
N511GG	50	82
N511GP	125	257052
N511JF	400A	RK-34
N511JP	**400A**	**RK-219**
N511JP	400A	RK-34
N511KA	**125**	**257052**
N511NC	S65	465-6
N511PA	**G2**	**49**
N511S	10	115
N511S	20	96
N511ST	**560**	**0281**
N511T	20	142
N511TA	20	142
N511TC	**525**	**0074**
N511TD	**STR**	**5145**
N511TS	**STR**	**5101/15**
N511WA	**AST**	**034**
N511WC	550	189
N511WD	125	258196
N511WH	24	055
N511WM	125	25159
N511WM	125	258196
N511WM	601	5134
N511WM	**900**	**108**
N511WN	125	25159
N511WN	**601**	**5134**
N511WP	125	25174
N511WP	20	341
N511WP	G2	185
N511WR	20	341
N511WS	**550**	**439**
N511WV	**560**	**0138**
N511YP	125	25191
(N512AC)	600	1073
N512BC	601	5125
N512CC	**500**	**012**
N512CC	500	112
N512CC	WWD	354
N512DG	601	5157
N512GP	125	257182
N512GV	G5	512
N512MT	650	0232
N512QS	**125**	**259012**
N512RB	**45**	**062**
N512SD	**G2**	**130**
N512T	20	118
N512VB	G2	189/42
N512WP	400	RJ-16
N512WS	400	RJ-24
N513AC	**20**	**242**
N513AG	**20**	**64**
N513AN	20	64
N513CC	500	013
N513CC	501	513
N513CC	550	013
N513GA	G5	513
N513GP	125	257072
N513MW	**G5**	**510**
N513QS	**125**	**259013**
N513T	20	123
N514AJ	125	256033
N514B	125	257071
N514CC	500	014
N514DS	**525**	**0255**
N514GA	G5	514
N514JJ	20	168
N514QS	**125**	**259014**
N514RB	601	5015

N514SA	**20**	**30**
N514T	20	130
N514V	125	25134
N514V	125	256023
N514VA	125	25134
N515AA	500	085
N515AJ	STR	5078/3
N515CC	500	015
(N515CC)	501	502
N515DB	200	510
N515DC	500	112
N515DJ	55	015
N515GP	125	258289
N515JT	G2	135
(N515JT)	G2	189/42
N515KA	G2	166/15
N515KK	**D1A**	**A086SA**
N515LG	**WWD**	**193**
(N515M)	550	433
N515QS	**125**	**259015**
N515SC	25XR	152
N515TC	**25D**	**354**
N515TJ	**400A**	**RK-229**
N515TK	2xx	102
N515VC	650	0055
N515VW	25	013
N515WA	**400A**	**RK-215**
N515WC	24B	203
N515WE	**500**	**208**
N515WH	25B	142
N516AB	500	244
N516AC	WWD	187
N516CC	500	016
N516CC	**WWD**	**394**
N516DM	STR	5158
N516GA	G5	516
N516GH	**G5**	**553**
N516GP	**125**	**258316**
N516LW	**S40**	**282-98**
N516SM	10	167
N516SM	601	5089
N516SM	650	0157
N516WC	STR	5150/37
N516WP	S40	282-98
N517A	501	375
N517AF	**550**	**0846**
N517AM	**55**	**108**
N517BA	501	400
N517CC	500	017
N517GA	G5	517
N517GP	**31A**	**152**
N517MT	650	0232
N517XL	560	5017
(N518AS)	S550	0013
N518BA	125	258075
N518CC	500	018
N518CC	500	318
N518CL	**601**	**5180**
N518EJ	**50**	**18**
(N518FE)	G2	135
N518GA	G5	518
N518GS	G2	130
N518JG	**25D**	**328**
N518JT	G2	135
N518L	STR	5040
N518S	10	74
N518S	125	257202
N519AA	**550**	**053**
(N519AC)	55	013
N519BA	125	258069
N519CC	500	019
N519CJ	S550	0019
N519CW	50	19
N519L	STR	5037/24
N519ME	WWD	207
(N519TW)	G2	106
N520AW	**20**	**453**
N520BA	125	258070
N520BA	**125**	**258317**
N520CC	500	020
N520CC	500	200
N520CM	**750**	**0107**
N520CV	560	0020
N520DB	**MSP**	**101**

N520G	560	0369
N520G	560	5083
N520M	125	25070
N520M	125	257131
N520M	STR	5159
N520MP	**WWD**	**421**
N520N	500	205
N520PA	35	037
N520QS	**125**	**259020**
N520RB	500	282
N520RP	501	607
N520RP	S550	0115
N520S	S40	282-8
N520S	STR	5084/8
(N520SC)	500	208
N520SC	**55ER**	**087**
N520TJ	20	198/466
N520TT	D1A	A033SA
N520WS	**400**	**RJ-53**
N521BA	125	258071
N521BH	550	727
N521CC	500	021
N521CV	560	0521
N521GA	G5	521
N521JP	25D	302
N521JP	25D	330
N521M	125	25129
N521N	S60	306-1
N521NC	S60	306-109
N521PA	35A	239
N521PF	**525**	**0005**
N521RA	**560**	**5076**
N521TM	**550**	**705**
N521WM	550	093
N522AC	**900**	**148**
N522AC	G4	1108
N522BA	125	258072
N522BW	125	25043
N522C	125	256067
N522C	200	495
N522CC	500	022
N522CC	501	522
N522CC	**551**	**002**
N522EE	**400A**	**RK-38**
N522GS	25D	348
N522GS	50	115
(N522GS)	650	0025
N522JA	**560**	**0288**
N522JD	500	022
N522JP	25D	318
N522JS	25D	348
N522KM	900	78
N522M	125	25156
N522M	125	257144
N522ME	125	25043
N522N	S60	306-109
N522PA	35A	254
N522SB	G3	339
N522SC	25	006
N522TA	25D	318
N522X	125	256067
N522XL	560	5022
N523AC	**900**	**139**
N523AC	STR	5013
N523AC	WWD	77
N523AS	**525**	**0092**
N523B	600	1071
N523BA	125	258077
N523BT	**525**	**0311**
N523CC	500	023
N523CC	500	123
N523CC	500	323
N523CW	50	23
N523GA	G5	523
N523JD	500	023
N523JM	**601**	**5106**
(N523JP)	25D	330
N523KW	560	0224
N523KW	**560**	**5015**
N523M	125	25245
N523M	125	257188
N523MA	125	256023
N523N	S60	306-7
N523PA	35A	247
(N523PT)	G3	336
N523QS	**125**	**259023**
N523RB	**WWD**	**175**
N523SA	25D	325
(N523TX)	G3	336
N523WC	**125**	**258086**
N524AC	S40	282-28
N524AC	STR	5004
N524AC	STR	5149/11
N524AF	**525**	**0199**
N524AG	S40	282-28
N524BA	125	258080
N524CA	500	024
N524CC	500	024
(N524DW)	24	177
N524DW	**25B**	**081**
N524GA	G5	524
N524HC	**31A**	**114**
N524HC	35A	358
N524M	**125**	**257204**
N524MA	**550**	**029**
N524MM	**G2**	**85**
N524PA	**35**	**033**
N524PC	601	3023
N524RH	WWD	414
N524SC	24	153
N524X	WWD	92
N525AC	31	030
N525AC	500	343
N525AE	**525**	**0017**
N525AJ	WWD	325
N525AL	**525**	**0011**
N525AP	**525**	**0045**
N525AS	525	0092
N525AS	**525**	**0363**
N525AW	WWD	129
N525AZ	**525A**	**0001**
N525BA	125	258081
N525BE	525	0299
(N525BE)	525	0306
N525BF	525	0191
(N525BL)	525	0191
N525BT	**525**	**0161**
N525CC	500	025
N525CC	525	0001
N525CC	525	0100
N525CF	60	010
N525CH	**525**	**0078**
N525CJ	**525**	**702**
N525CK	**525**	**0058**
N525CP	525	0099
N525CP	525	0378
N525DC	**525**	**0195**
N525DG	**525**	**0057**
N525DJ	**525**	**0024**
N525DL	**525**	**0364**
N525DP	**525**	**0318**
N525DR	**525**	**0308**
N525EC	**525**	**0246**
(N525EF)	525	0153
N525FS	**525**	**0026**
N525FT	**525**	**0367**
N525GA	500	182
N525GG	525	0041
N525GM	**525**	**0240**
N525GP	**31A**	**155**
N525GP	31A	162
N525GP	525	0203
N525HC	**525**	**0270**
(N525HC)	525	0273
N525HS	**525**	**0035**
N525HV	**525**	**0201**
N525J	**525**	**0184**
N525JH	525	0124
N525JM	525	0134
N525JT	**G2**	**156/31**
N525JW	**525**	**0162**
N525KA	**525**	**0019**
N525KH	525	0197
N525KL	525	0136
N525KN	**525**	**0007**
N525LF	**525**	**0382**
N525M	**525**	**0334**
N525M	AST	102
N525MB	**525**	**0036**
N525MC	**525**	**0018**
N525MD	525	0367
N525MH	**525**	**0388**
N525ML	**525**	**0402**
N525ML	WWD	260
N525MP	**525**	**0313**
N525MW	**525**	**0370**
N525N	S40	282-10
N525NA	**525**	**0048**
N525PE	**525**	**0125**
N525PF	**525**	**0232**
N525PL	**525**	**0043**
N525PS	**525**	**0061**
N525QS	**125**	**259025**
N525RA	**525**	**0167**
N525RC	10	116
N525RC	**525**	**0178**
N525RD	**560**	**0106**
N525RF	**525**	**0023**
N525RL	**525**	**0338**
N525RM	**525**	**0225**
N525SC	525	0099
(N525SP)	525	0019
(N525ST)	525	0195
N525TA	**525**	**0141**
N525TF	**525**	**0067**
N525TL	525	0134
N525TW	**25**	**011**
N525WB	**525**	**0079**
N525WC	**525**	**0107**
N525WM	**525**	**0213**
N525WW	**525**	**0060**
N525XX	**WWD**	**336**
N526AC	**125**	**258169**
N526AC	550	038
N526AG	550	038
N526BA	125	258083
N526CA	525	0033
N526CC	**50**	**147**
N526CC	500	026
N526CC	501	526
N526CP	525	0099
N526CW	D1A	A026SA
N526D	10	84
N526DM	125	257156
N526GA	**AST**	**115**
N526GA	G5	526
N526GP	**31A**	**181**
N526M	**125**	**258032**
N526N	S40	282-30
N527AC	**125**	**258104**
N527AC	550	121
N527AG	550	121
N527BA	125	258084
N527CC	500	027
N527CC	550	027
N527DS	550	317
N527EA	550	426
N527ER	24A	096
N527EW	**501**	**669**
N527GA	AST	116
N527GA	G5	527
N527GP	**31A**	**182**
N527JA	**601**	**5058**
N527JG	**31A**	**125**
N527K	G2	25
N527M	**125**	**258054**
N527PA	**36A**	**019**
(N527TA)	500	334
N528AC	**125**	**258070**
N528AP	**G3**	**399**
N528BA	125	258086
N528CC	500	028
N528EA	35	024
N528GA	**AST**	**117**
N528GA	G5	528
N528JD	35	024
N528JR	**50**	**220**
N528KW	**560**	**0224**
N528M	**125**	**258055**
N528RR	**AST**	**042**
N528XL	**560**	**5028**
N529BA	125	258087
N529CC	500	029
(N529CC)	525	0009
N529CF	**S60**	**306-58**
N529CW	50	29
N529DM	125	257156
N529DM	**601**	**3025**
N529GA	AST	118
N529GA	G5	529
N529M	**125**	**258446**
N529SC	S60	306-58
N529SC	**S65**	**465-12**
N529SQ	S60	306-58
N529X	560	0163
N530AR	**50**	**175**
N530BA	125	258089
N530BA	**125**	**258244**
N530CC	500	030
N530DC	**25D**	**291**
N530DL	**WWD**	**287**
N530G	**STR**	**5096/10**
N530GA	**G2**	**247**
N530GA	G5	530
N530GV	WWD	213
N530GV	WWD	356
N530J	35A	074
N530L	20	84
N530M	STR	5214
N530P	**550**	**333**
N530QS	**125**	**259030**
N530RD	D1A	A016SA
N530SW	G2	162
(N530TE)	125	257065
N530TL	125	257065
N530TL	500	342
N531A	551	481
N531AB	**S60**	**306-98**
N531AF	**G5**	**531**
N531AJ	**35**	**011**
N531AT	**31A**	**085**
N531BA	125	258090
N531BJ	560	5031
N531CC	500	031
N531CC	560	0178
N531CC	S550	0031
N531CM	**S550**	**0033**
N531CW	**25D**	**231**
N531F	560	0054
N531GA	G5	531
(N531JC)	G3	491
N531JF	G3	491
N531M	STR	5236
N531MD	**G4**	**1280**
N531NC	S60	306-7
N531RA	**31A**	**106**
N531WB	200	514
N532BA	125	258092
N532CC	500	032
N532CC	**650**	**0167**
N532CC	S550	0032
N532CF	S550	0032
N532CJ	525	0032
N532GA	G5	532
N532JF	650	7077
(N532JF)	750	0073
N532M	550	378
N532MA	**560**	**0036**
N532PJ	**125**	**258448**
N533	125	25083
N533	125	25103
N533	125	257114
(N533)	WWD	345
N533	WWD	356
N533BA	125	258093
N533BF	500	033
N533CC	500	033
N533CC	**650**	**0185**
N533CC	S550	0132
N533CS	10	177
N533EJ	STR	5099/5
N533GA	G5	533
N533JF	**525**	**0247**
N533M	550	041
N533MA	**550**	**083**
N533P	125	258075

N533QS	**125**	**259033**
N534	WWD	345
N534A	35A	304
N534BA	125	258095
N534CC	500	034
N534CC	**560**	**5025**
N534GA	G5	534
N534H	35A	304
N534H	**650**	**0196**
N534M	550	048
(N534M)	550	612
N534MA	50	29
N534MW	550	067
N534R	WWD	345
N535AF	**35A**	**191**
N535BA	125	258096
N535CC	500	035
N535CS	**G3**	**464**
N535D	WWD	74
N535GA	501	583
N535GA	**G5**	**620**
N535LR	**525**	**0128**
N535MA	550	037
N535MC	35A	385
N535PC	35A	291
N535QS	**125**	**259035**
N535TA	**35**	**013**
N536BA	125	258098
N536CC	500	036
N536CS	G2	24
N536GA	G5	536
N536GA	**G5**	**601**
N536M	551	144
N536V	500	032
N537BA	125	258099
N537CC	500	037
N537GA	G5	537
N537M	550	145
N538	125	25083
N538BA	125	258100
N538CC	500	038
N538CC	S550	0138
N538GA	G5	538
N538GA	**G5**	**602**
N538M	550	328
N539BA	125	258101
N539CC	500	039
N539CE	**560**	**0539**
N539GA	G5	539
N539GA	**G5**	**603**
N539PG	**S60**	**306-79**
N539QS	**125**	**259039**
N540B	**125**	**257077**
N540BA	125	258102
N540BA	**125**	**258241**
N540CC	500	040
N540CH	**G4**	**1306**
N540CL	23	026
N540CV	**560**	**0540**
N540EA	**G2**	**174**
N540G	STR	5009
N540G	STR	5075/19
N540HP	35A	399
N540JB	S550	0061
N540M	**125**	**258145**
N540PA	36A	019
N540QS	**125**	**259040**
N540W	601	5062
N540W	**G4**	**1265**
N541AG	500	041
N541BA	125	258103
N541CC	500	041
N541CV	**560**	**0541**
N541CW	**D1A**	**A004SA**
N541DE	**604**	**5390**
N541JG	**550**	**0849**
N541LJ	45	041
N541M	WWD	48
N541MM	600	1044
(N541NC)	500	205
N541PA	**35**	**053**
N541QS	**125**	**259041**
N541S	**650**	**0115**
N541SG	WWD	48

N542BA	125	258104
N542CC	500	042
N542CC	S550	0142
N542PA	35	030
N542QS	**125**	**259042**
(N542S)	S60	306-16
N543CC	500	043
N543LE	**560**	**0543**
N543PA	35A	070
(N543QS)	125	259043
N543SC	650	0130
N543SC	**S550**	**0144**
N543VP	560	0143
N543WW	**35A**	**332**
N544CC	500	044
N544PA	**35A**	**247**
N544PH	S65	465-56
N544QS	**125**	**259044**
N544RA	50	144
N544X	20	258
N544XL	**560**	**5044**
N545BF	STR	5146
N545C	20	17
N545C	S40	282-57
N545CC	500	045
N545CC	501	545
N545CS	**G4**	**1361**
(N545G)	501	368
N545GA	501	368
N545GA	**550**	**040**
N545GM	400	RJ-31
N545JT	**G3**	**347**
N545PA	**36A**	**028**
N545QS	**125**	**259045**
N545RS	**45**	**099**
N545S	**125**	**25188**
N545TP	**D1A**	**A045SA**
N546BC	125	257004
N546BZ	**400A**	**RK-41**
N546CC	500	046
N546EX	50	41
N546MT	**550**	**0881**
N546PA	**36A**	**045**
N546QS	**125**	**259046**
N547CC	500	047
N547CC	501	547
N547JG	**25D**	**264**
N547JL	75A	380-69
N547PA	**36**	**012**
N547QS	**125**	**259047**
N548CC	500	048
N548PA	36A	038
N548QS	**125**	**259048**
N548W	601	5062
N548XL	560	5048
N549AS	10	87
N549CC	500	049
N549CC	550	456
N549PA	**35A**	**119**
N549QS	**125**	**259049**
N550A	**S550**	**0009**
N550AB	550	063
N550AB	**550**	**633**
N550AJ	550	183
N550AJ	**S550**	**0141**
N550AK	**55**	**045**
N550AL	20	55/410
N550AL	**550**	**462**
N550AS	**S550**	**0020**
N550AV	550	403
N550BB	**550**	**734**
N550BC	**550**	**0804**
N550BD	**550**	**619**
N550BF	550	0888
(N550BG)	550	719
N550BM	550	286
N550BP	550	235
N550BP	550	731
N550CA	**550**	**167**
N550CA	550	303
N550CA	550	381
N550CB	551	118
N550CC	500	021
N550CC	500	050

N550CC	S550	686
N550CD	550	320
N550CE	550	063
N550CF	550	382
N550CG	**550**	**102**
N550CJ	550	498
N550CM	550	285
N550CP	550	356
N550CP	551	163
N550CS	55	005
N550CW	**600**	**1084**
N550DA	**550**	**186**
N550DA	551	246
(N550DD)	55	066
(N550DD)	550	285
N550DW	550	074
N550DW	**550**	**487**
N550E	35A	100
N550EC	550	053
N550EK	550	265
N550EW	550	103
N550F	**S550**	**0056**
N550FB	**550**	**0803**
N550FB	550	285
(N550FB)	550	674
N550FM	**550**	**550**
N550FS	S550	0067
N550GA	PER	551
N550GB	**551**	**177**
N550GH	**550**	**0898**
N550GM	**550**	**378**
N550GP	550	194
N550GT	S550	0160
N550H	**125**	**258356**
N550HA	S550	0067
N550HB	**550**	**250**
N550HC	**S550**	**0116**
N550HF	**550**	**287**
N550HG	**55**	**083**
N550HH	**550**	**0802**
N550HM	550	047
N550HP	551	191
N550HS	D1A	A051SA
N550HT	**S550**	**0107**
N550J	550	417
N550JB	551	177
N550JC	**S550**	**0124**
N550JF	550	008
N550JF	550	660
N550JM	550	255
N550JR	550	356
N550JS	**551**	**118**
N550K	550	229
N550K	WWD	127
N550KA	550	064
N550KC	550	292
(N550KE)	550	0830
N550KE	**550**	**694**
N550KG	**550**	**0949**
N550KH	550	0854
(N550KH)	550	0859
N550KH	**550**	**0886**
N550KJ	**550**	**0854**
N550KL	**550**	**0844**
N550KM	**S550**	**0081**
N550KP	550	130
(N550KR)	550	075
N550KW	550	409
N550L	501	388
N550L	S40	282-61
N550LC	S550	0074
N550LH	**550**	**116**
N550LJ	55	015
N550LL	S40	282-61
N550LP	551	200
N550M	20	355
N550M	**AST**	**061**
N550MC	20	200
N550MC	**525**	**0205**
N550MD	550	299
N550MD	551	354
N550MH	**501**	**668**
(N550MT)	550	309
N550MT	550	330

N550MW	551	481
N550MZ	550	658
N550NM	WWD	39
N550NS	550	635
N550PA	**550**	**213**
N550PF	550	672
N550PG	**550**	**240**
N550PL	550	010
N550PL	**S550**	**0130**
N550PM	**550**	**035**
N550PR	**550**	**285**
N550PS	550	124
N550PT	20	391
N550PT	550	499
N550QS	**125**	**259050**
N550RA	550	661
N550RB	**550**	**129**
N550RD	551	421
N550RG	550	262
N550RH	125	258038
N550RH	55	014
N550RH	55	041
N550RL	550	317
(N550RL)	551	266
N550RM	**550**	**698**
N550RP	550	035
N550RS	550	439
N550RV	**S550**	**0012**
N550SA	**550**	**261**
N550SB	550	634
N550SC	550	040
(N550SC)	550	338
N550SF	550	122
N550SL	S60	306-72
N550SM	550	286
N550SM	550	587
N550SP	**S550**	**0151**
N550ST	S550	0033
N550T	501	388
N550T	501	413
N550T	**525**	**0013**
N550TA	**551**	**278**
N550TB	S550	0012
N550TB	**S550**	**0019**
N550TC	**55**	**034**
N550TE	**550**	**0894**
N550TG	501	378
N550TG	550	0822
N550TJ	550	029
(N550TJ)	550	080
N550TJ	550	143
N550TM	**550**	**0936**
(N550TM)	560	0299
N550TP	550	186
N550TR	550	186
N550TR	**550**	**733**
N550TT	550	158
(N550TY)	550	007
N550U	**501**	**413**
N550VR	550	733
N550VW	**550**	**274**
N550WB	**550**	**265**
N550WJ	**550**	**309**
N550WM	**50**	**229**
N550WR	551	400
N550WS	**550**	**0845**
N550WV	551	584
N550WW	551	584
N550WW	**560**	**0180**
N551AB	550	173
N551AC	**G3**	**467**
(N551AM)	55	108
N551AS	24B	229
N551AS	55	083
N551AS	551	348
(N551BA)	125	258105
N551BC	**550**	**059**
N551BE	**S550**	**0097**
N551BP	**550**	**423**
N551BW	551	272
N551CC	35	017
N551CC	500	051
(N551CC)	550	001
N551CE	550	398

N551CF	551	107
N551CL	**551**	**191**
N551DB	55	052
N551DF	55	001
N551DP	25D	213
N551DS	551	023
N551EA	**551**	**354**
N551FA	S65	465-39
N551G	525	0153
N551G	**550**	**0850**
(N551GA)	550	040
N551GA	**G5**	**604**
N551GL	55	001
(N551GN)	550	069
N551HB	55	038
N551HH	**551**	**023**
N551HK	551	266
N551HM	**35A**	**612**
N551JF	550	063
N551KH	550	0859
N551MB	25	007
N551MC	550	086
N551MD	25	007
N551MD	35	057
N551MD	G2	212
N551MS	**501**	**541**
(N551NA)	550	037
N551NC	100	198
N551PL	551	150
N551Q	525	0153
N551QS	**125**	**259051**
N551R	551	115
N551SC	**55**	**008**
(N551SE)	551	353
N551SR	550	072
N551SR	551	266
N551TK	**551**	**282**
N551TP	**WWD**	**419**
N551TT	551	172
N551TW	35A	612
N551UT	55	069
N551WC	25C	129
N551WC	35A	441
N551WJ	**550**	**465**
N552BA	125	258107
N552BA	55	050
N552BE	**S550**	**0138**
N552CC	500	052
N552CC	551	002
N552CC	552	0001
(N552CF)	S550	0052
N552CJ	**525A**	**0005**
N552GL	55	002
N552JH	STR	5037/24
N552JT	**G2**	**135**
N552JT	G3	305
N552MD	501	425
N552N	125	25124
N552QS	**125**	**259052**
N552SM	S550	0125
N552SQ	55	100
N552TF	550	203
N552UT	55	100
N553AC	650	0198
N553BA	125	258108
N553CC	500	053
N553CC	550	553
N553CC	S550	0046
N553CC	S550	0113
N553CJ	551	003
N553DJ	55	003
N553GJ	55	003
N553GP	55	003
N553JT	**G3**	**305**
N553M	125	258027
N553M	35A	141
N553M	**50**	**201**
N553MD	G2	47
N553PF	400A	RK-32
(N553US)	125	258027
N553V	**35A**	**141**
(N554BA)	125	258109
N554BA	125	258111
N554BA	550	040
N554CA	S550	0004
N554CC	500	054
N554CC	S550	0075
N554CL	**55**	**040**
(N554M)	55	014
N554GA	**G5**	**605**
N554R	**560**	**0328**
N554SR	10	173
N554T	501	477
N555AB	S40	282-60
N555AE	S40	282-60
N555AE	S60	306-102
N555AJ	500	007
(N555BA)	125	258110
N555BA	125	258113
N555BC	550	235
N555BK	**550**	**0916**
N555BS	STR	5051
N555BY	WWD	306
N555CB	125	25122
N555CB	125	25285
N555CB	125	256011
N555CB	**125**	**257039**
N555CC	500	039
N555CJ	**55**	**089**
N555CS	G2	73/9
N555CS	G5	516
N555CW	WWD	295
N555DH	10	114
N555DH	10	186
N555DH	10	187
(N555DH)	24	153
N555DH	550	423
N555DH	650	0016
N555DH	WWD	373
N555DM	WWD	25
N555DS	**550**	**356**
N555EW	501	456
N555EW	550	303
(N555EW)	650	0074
(N555EW)	650	0099
N555FA	D1A	A082SA
N555GB	125	256011
N555GB	35A	246
N555GL	55	036
N555GL	55	065
N555GN	G5	518
N555GV	**G5**	**518**
N555HD	G2	134
N555HD	**G3**	**444**
N555HD	WWD	341
N555HM	**550**	**0950**
N555HR	501	643
N555J	WWD	213
N555JE	35A	195
N555JK	28	003
N555JM	HFB	1037
N555JR	75A	380-72
N555KC	G3	366
N555KC	**G4**	**1342**
N555KH	**G2**	**134**
N555KK	**400A**	**RK-92**
N555KT	**551**	**419**
N555KW	**501**	**443**
N555LA	24	177
N555LB	**24**	**177**
N555LG	G2	10
N555LJ	**24B**	**195**
N555MH	24B	213
N555MU	G2	188
N555MW	G2	188
N555MX	**55C**	**142**
N555NT	G3	322
N555PB	STR	5047
N555PG	25D	281
N555PT	20	426
N555PT	S40	282-53
N555PV	24	133
N555RA	20	194
N555RB	125	257140
N555RR	S60	306-60
N555RS	G2	3
N555RT	**551**	**311**
N555SD	**25D**	**333**
N555SG	STR	5090
(N555SL)	550	553
N555SL	S60	306-13
N555SR	10	173
N555SR	**20**	**455**
(N555TD)	550	437
N555TF	**20**	**325**
N555TF	**20**	**326/521**
N555WD	600	1047
N555WD	**604**	**5355**
N555WF	560	0190
N555WF	560	0488
N555WF	**560**	**5058**
N555WH	**36A**	**037**
N555WL	**560**	**0488**
N555WL	G4	1114
N555XL	G2	189/42
N556AR	**G5**	**556**
N556AT	500	020
(N556BA)	125	258111
N556BA	125	258114
N556BG	**560**	**0499**
N556CC	500	056
N556CC	551	095
N556GA	**55**	**028**
N556HD	WWD	341
N556HJ	55	028
N556N	WWD	331
N556WD	600	1047
N557BA	125	258117
N557CC	500	057
N557CC	501	557
N558AC	55	048
N558AG	550	558
N558BA	125	258119
N558CB	550	058
N558CC	500	058
N558CC	550	058
N558E	35A	100
N558GA	**G5**	**606**
N558HJ	**55**	**048**
N558M	125	258027
N558R	**560**	**5075**
N558VP	550	558
N559AM	**650**	**7107**
(N559BA)	125	258121
N559BC	500	059
N559CC	500	059
N559GA	**G5**	**607**
N559GP	STR	5123/14
N559GV	**G5**	**559**
N559LC	**G2**	**152**
N560AF	**560**	**0100**
N560AG	**560**	**0301**
N560AJ	**550**	**560**
N560AJ	S550	0094
N560BA	125	258122
N560BA	560	0003
N560BA	**560**	**0102**
N560BB	560	0135
(N560BD)	560	0303
N560BJ	560	0303
N560BL	560	0057
N560BP	**560**	**0449**
N560BT	**560**	**5031**
N560CB	**551**	**555**
N560CC	500	060
N560CC	**550**	**001**
N560CC	**560**	**550-0001**
N560CE	560	0302
N560CF	**560**	**0040**
N560CH	**560**	**5091**
(N560CP)	560	0055
(N560CT)	560	0104
N560CV	560	560-0001
N560CX	**560**	**0086**
N560DC	**560**	**0021**
N560DM	560	0101
N560EA	560	0062
N560EC	560	0101
(N560ED)	560	0150
(N560EJ)	560	0036
N560EL	**560**	**0049**
N560EP	560	0101
N560ER	**560**	**0003**
N560FA	560	0142
N560FB	560	0148
N560GA	500	217
N560GB	560	0254
N560GB	**560**	**5027**
N560GL	**560**	**0079**
N560GS	560	0263
N560GT	**560**	**0142**
N560H	**560**	**0017**
N560HC	**560**	**0020**
N560HP	560	0081
N560JC	560	0283
N560JM	560	0023
N560JP	**560**	**0431**
N560JR	**560**	**0027**
N560JS	560	0196
N560JV	560	0065
N560KC	35A	079
N560KT	**560**	**5127**
N560L	20	132
N560L	560	0156
N560L	**560**	**5011**
N560LC	560	0026
N560LC	560	0110
N560LC	**560**	**0296**
N560MC	WWD	24
N560ME	**560**	**0012**
N560MH	**560**	**0105**
N560MM	**560**	**0235**
N560MR	**560**	**0015**
N560NS	560	0408
(N560PT)	560	0106
N560R	20	313
(N560RA)	20	56
N560RA	560	0182
(N560RB)	560	0137
N560RC	560	0397
N560RG	**560**	**0198**
N560RJ	560	0107
N560RL	**560**	**0135**
N560RP	**560**	**0158**
N560RS	560	0109A
N560RW	**560**	**0196**
N560SB	**125**	**257105**
N560SH	WWD	319
N560TJ	560	0417
N560TX	**560**	**0206**
N560VR	**560**	**0480**
N560VU	**560**	**707**
N560W	560	0030
N560WE	560	0100
N560WH	**560**	**0013**
N560XL	**560**	**706**
N561A	560	0139
N561AS	**550**	**173**
N561B	**560**	**0008**
N561BA	125	258123
N561BC	**560**	**0057**
N561CC	500	061
N561D	10	54
N561DA	560	5012
N561EJ	**560**	**0035**
N561GA	**G5**	**608**
(N561GB)	560	0254
N561NC	100	195
N561RP	125	256001
(N561ST)	G3	302
N561ST	G3	388
N561XL	**560**	**5001**
N562BA	125	258124
N562CC	500	062
N562CD	550	562
N562CV	560	0002
N562DB	**560**	**5108**
N562E	560	0140
N562EJ	**50**	**62**
N562MS	**S60**	**306-44**
N562R	**S60**	**306-37**
N562XL	**560**	**5002**
N563BA	125	258125
N563C	**560**	**0174**
N563CC	500	063
N563CC	501	563

N563CV	560	0003
N563XL	560	5003
N564BA	125	258126
N564BR	**125**	**257122**
N564CC	500	064
N564CC	550	064
N564CL	**25**	**060**
(N564D)	560	0175
N564MG	STR	5021
N564TS	601	5064
N564VP	550	564
N565A	20	50
N565A	200	499
N565A	**50**	**174**
N565AB	**560**	**5072**
N565BA	125	258127
N565CC	**500**	**065**
N565CJ	550	565
N565GW	**500**	**050**
N565JS	550	565
N565JW	**560**	**0149**
N565KC	**G2**	**46**
N565NC	**550**	**565**
N565SS	**500**	**017**
(N565TW)	500	065
N565V	**501**	**365**
N565VV	501	365
N565VV	**551**	**152**
N566BA	125	258128
N566C	**G3**	**459**
N566CC	500	066
N566CC	**550**	**166**
N566GA	**G5**	**609**
N566MP	WWD	156
N566N	601	3064
N566NA	25	064
(N566PG)	WWD	273
N566RB	24	180
N566TX	550	227
N566VP	560	0006
N567A	G2	251
N567BA	125	258132
N567CA	**550**	**114**
N567CC	500	067
N567DW	S40	282-35
N567EA	**500**	**067**
N567F	**560**	**0171**
N567GA	**G5**	**610**
N567L	501	621
N567ML	600	1024
N567RA	**10**	**80**
N567S	550	429
N567WB	**501**	**491**
N568BA	125	258135
N568CC	500	068
N568CM	500	068
N568GA	**G5**	**611**
N568GB	560	0254
N568PA	**35A**	**205**
N568Q	20	149
N569BA	125	258136
N569BW	20	259
N569BW	**50**	**45**
N569CA	50	115
N569CC	50	115
N569CC	500	069
N569CS	125	25214
N569DW	**20**	**259**
N569GA	**G5**	**612**
N570BA	125	258137
N570BJ	**560**	**0030**
N570CC	500	070
N570CC	501	570
N570CC	S550	0070
N570FT	23	005
N570GA	**G5**	**613**
(N570JG)	24B	221
N570L	20	171
N570MH	560	0006
N570P	24B	221
N570R	S40	282-3
N570R	**S65**	**465-75**
N570RC	**S550**	**0070**
N570VP	550	570

N570WD	**550**	**570**
N571BC	**550**	**599**
N571BJ	**G2**	**15**
N571CC	500	071
N571CC	S550	0071
N571CH	125	25284
N571CH	**125**	**257078**
N571DU	125	256071
N571E	125	256071
N571GA	**G5**	**614**
N571GH	125	25284
(N571K)	500	328
(N571MC)	WWD	175
N571NC	S60	306-1
N572CC	500	072
(N572CC)	S550	0072
N572CV	560	0072
N572GA	**G5**	**615**
N572M	**WWD**	**258**
N572R	S40	282-74
N573AC	**50**	**217**
N573BB	**S550**	**0037**
N573CC	500	073
N573CC	S550	0007
N573CW	**50**	**73**
N573E	200	502
N573EJ	20	28
N573F	560	0171
N573J	100	196
N573L	501	435
N573LP	24B	196
N573LP	35A	153
N573LP	**35A**	**658**
N573LR	24B	196
N573LR	**35A**	**153**
N573P	WWD	257
N574CC	500	074
N574CC	501	657
N574CF	**D1A**	**A079SA**
N574GA	**G5**	**616**
N574M	**550**	**0910**
N574R	S40	282-82
(N574U)	D1A	A079SA
N574W	500	074
N574W	55	011
N575	125	25218
N575CC	500	075
N575CC	501	475
N575CF	601	5188
(N575D)	125	25021
N575DU	125	25021
N575DU	125	25218
N575E	**G2**	**219/20**
N575ET	AST	042
N575EW	AST	042
N575EW	**S550**	**0140**
N575FM	550	129
N575G	24	138
N575GA	**G5**	**617**
N575GD	25B	101
N575GH	**55**	**042**
N575HW	23	068
N575M	**550**	**0911**
(N575MA)	601	5061
N575PC	560	0223
N575R	S40	282-34
N575RD	500	075
N575SE	G2	221
N575SF	G2	221
N575SF	**G4**	**1233**
N575SR	501	597
N575W	550	008
N576CC	500	076
N576CC	501	576
N576CC	550	576
N576R	S40	282-7
N577CC	500	077
N577CC	550	577
N577GA	G5	577
N577JT	**501**	**430**
N577LJ	25	023
N577PM	S40	282-2
N577R	S40	282-2
N577RT	10	80

N577S	20	68
(N577SD)	525	0131
N577SV	**525**	**0131**
N577SW	80A	380-21
(N577SW)	G4	1284
N577SW	G4	1385
N577T	**125**	**258149**
N577VM	501	430
N577VM	**550**	**615**
N577VM	S40	282-31
N578CC	500	078
N578DF	G2	126
N578GA	G5	578
N578LJ	23	006
N578M	**550**	**612**
N578W	550	082
(N578WB)	500	095
N579CC	500	079
N579GA	G5	579
N579L	**550**	**579**
N579TG	**G3**	**433**
N580AV	550	161
N580BA	125	258139
N580CC	500	080
N580CE	560	0302
N580GA	G5	580
N580GS	10	132
N580GV	WWD	213
N580MA	125	25237
N580MA	125	256064
N580R	**500**	**127**
N580RA	G2	117
N580WE	**WWD**	**123**
N580WS	125	25047
N581BA	125	258140
N581CC	500	081
N581EA	S550	0080
N581GA	G5	581
N581NC	100	196
N581RA	31A	106
N581SS	20	66
N581WD	G2	126
N582BA	125	258138
N582CC	500	082
N582CC	550	082
(N582G)	20	23
N582GA	G5	582
(N582JF)	650	7077
N583BA	125	258141
N583BS	**35A**	**258**
N583CC	500	083
N583CM	125	25225
N583D	**G3**	**471**
N583GA	**G5**	**583**
N583M	560	0186
N583M	560	0326
N583MP	501	477
N583N	560	0186
N583PS	**31A**	**151**
N583PS	35A	258
(N583VP)	550	583
N584BA	125	258142
N584CC	500	084
N584CC	501	584
N584D	G4	1065
N584DB	**125**	**25023**
N584GA	G5	584
N585A	G2	44
N585BA	125	258144
N585CC	500	085
N585D	**G4**	**1258**
N585G	**400A**	**RK-94**
N585GA	G5	585
N585GA	**G5**	**618**
N585M	**750**	**0096**
N585TC	**D1A**	**A060SA**
N585UC	20	299
N585UC	601	5002
N586	STR	5085
N586BA	125	258145
N586C	G3	459
N586CC	500	086
N586CC	**560**	**0186**
N586CC	S550	0086

N586CS	**50**	**260**
N586GA	**G5**	**586**
N586JR	125	257014
N586RE	**550**	**222**
N587BA	125	258147
N587CC	500	087
N587GA	G5	587
N587S	650	0188
N588AC	**550**	**0912**
N588BA	125	258150
N588CA	501	471
N588CC	500	088
N588CG	**24D**	**304**
N588CT	S550	0060
N588FJ	50	88
N588GA	**G5**	**588**
N588R	AST	042
N588UC	600	1071
N589BA	125	258157
N589CC	500	089
N589CJ	501	589
N589GA	G5	589
N589HM	G2	92
N589HM	G4	1153
N589HM	**G5**	**554**
N589KM	50	54
N589TB	AST	037
N589UC	125	257137
N590	35A	186
N590A	**560**	**0029**
N590AS	650	0088
N590BA	125	258160
N590CC	500	090
N590CH	125	25222
N590CH	24D	295
(N590CH)	35	060
N590CH	**G2**	**19**
N590EA	500	072
N590EA	500	182
N590GA	24	139
N590GA	**G5**	**590**
N590HM	**G4**	**1153**
N590J	35A	336
N590RB	500	090
N590RB	550	230
N591BA	125	258162
N591CC	500	091
N591D	24	115
N591D	35A	069
N591DL	24	115
N591GA	24	142
N591GA	G5	591
N591KR	25	019
N591M	560	0085
N591M	**560**	**0533**
N592BA	125	258166
N592CC	500	092
N592DC	10	26
N592GA	24	143
N592GA	**G5**	**592**
N592KR	25	028
N592M	**560**	**0338**
N592M	S550	0041
N592VP	**560**	**0092A**
N592WP	**500**	**253**
N593BA	125	258168
N593CC	500	093
(N593CC)	501	593
N593CC	S550	0093
N593DC	**10**	**180**
N593DS	501	593
N593EM	550	714
N593GA	24	144
N593GA	G5	535
N593GA	**G5**	**593**
N593KR	24	140
N593LR	**35A**	**593**
N593M	560	0237
N593M	**560**	**0525**
N593M	S550	0021
N593MD	**560**	**0074**
N594BA	125	258170
N594CC	500	094
N594CC	S550	0094

N594G	**550**	**482**
N594GA	25	003
N594GA	G5	525
N594GA	**G5**	**594**
N594JB	525	0067
N594KR	STR	5099/5
(N594VP)	560	0094
N594WP	**550**	**693**
N595BA	125	258171
N595CC	500	095
N595CC	S550	0091
N595CM	S550	0091
N595DC	**200**	**500**
N595GA	24	147
N595GA	G5	522
N595GA	**G5**	**595**
N595PC	**550**	**0826**
N595PT	**400**	**RJ-18**
N596A	**2xx**	**28**
N596BA	125	258172
N596CC	500	096
N596DA	**20**	**273**
N596GA	24X	150
N596GA	G5	520
N596GA	**G5**	**596**
N596HF	24X	150
N596SW	**125**	**258096**
N597BA	125	258174
N597BL	35A	597
N597CC	501	097
N597CS	**501**	**481**
N597DM	604	5398
N597FJ	601	3061
N597GA	24	152
N597GA	G5	519
N597JT	35A	597
(N597JV)	501	597
(N597N)	400	RJ-29
N597U	**750**	**0004**
N598BA	125	258175
N598C	**650**	**0112**
N598CA	**550**	**198**
N598CC	500	098
N598GA	24	155
N598GA	G5	510
N598GA	**G5**	**598**
N598JC	**10**	**112**
N598JL	400	RJ-19
N598JM	**WWD**	**222**
(N598WW)	35A	332
N599BA	125	258173
N599BR	**501**	**664**
N599CC	500	099
N599EC	125	258183
N599EC	55	018
N599FW	550	599
N599GA	24	156
N599GA	G5	515
N599JL	**400**	**RJ-14**
N599KC	WWD	42
N599RR	20	325
N599SC	35A	670
N599SC	50	242
N599SC	560	0051
N599SC	60	113
N599SG	560	0051
N600AE	**125**	**256068**
N600AE	35A	149
N600AG	125	256069
N600AL	125	256051
N600AN	CVT	10
N600AS	50	90
N600AS	90X	17
N600AT	**550**	**551**
N600AV	125	256015
N600AW	125	256018
N600AW	**31**	**017**
N600AW	35A	149
N600B	G2	82
N600B	G3	459
N600B	S60	306-33
N600BE	35A	348
N600BG	**G3**	**430**
N600BL	G3	482
N600BP	600	1004
N600BP	600	1073
N600BP	S40	282-53
N600BT	10	6
N600BT	G2	82
N600BW	**560**	**0087**
N600BZ	600	1028
N600C	**55**	**047**
(N600CC)	35A	083
(N600CC)	400A	RK-45
N600CC	400A	RK-6
N600CC	600	1056
N600CC	700	9019
(N600CC)	G4	1321
N600CD	25D	274
N600CD	G2	221
N600CD	WWD	10
N600CF	600	1078
N600CG	**D1A**	**A055SA**
N600CH	**50**	**181**
N600CL	600	1005
N600CN	35A	235
N600CP	600	1075
N600CR	550	401
N600CS	G2	75/7
N600CS	G4	1020
(N600DH)	501	576
N600DH	601	5176
N600DL	600	1078
(N600DP)	125	25202
N600DR	601	5176
N600DR	**G4**	**1356**
N600DT	**35**	**017**
(N600DT)	STR	5058/4
N600DW	**G4**	**1169**
N600EA	**S550**	**0015**
(N600EC)	600	1073
N600EG	**125**	**25075**
N600ER	WWD	84
N600ES	**604**	**5439**
N600ES	G3	322
N600EZ	550	228
N600FF	600	1019
N600FL	125	256034
N600G	**125**	**256066**
N600G	23	025
N600G	35A	352
N600GG	**60**	**115**
N600GH	550	717
N600GH	650	0029
N600GL	**S60**	**306-24**
N600GM	10	25
N600GM	**25D**	**290**
N600GP	35A	236
N600GW	**D1A**	**A044SA**
N600HC	125	257036
N600HD	25B	101
N600HR	**525**	**0038**
N600HS	**125**	**256033**
N600HS	125	258029
N600HT	25B	101
N600J	**125**	**258217**
N600J	STR	5039
N600J	STR	5086/44
N600J	WWD	302
N600JA	125	25187
N600JC	**20**	**7**
N600JC	24D	246
N600JD	**650**	**0236**
N600JM	50	124
N600JS	S40	282-44
N600JT	25D	291
(N600JT)	STR	5213
N600JW	600	1061
N600K	WWD	148
N600KC	125	258207
N600KC	20	58
N600KC	600	1012
N600L	125	25187
N600L	**60**	**020**
N600LC	35A	211
N600LC	**60**	**021**
N600LE	35A	149
N600LE	WWD	425
N600LF	35A	654
N600LF	**560**	**0376**
N600LG	**600**	**1052**
N600LL	35A	438
N600LN	35A	332
N600LN	**60**	**082**
N600LP	125	25187
N600LS	125	258114
N600LS	**125**	**259019**
N600LS	600	1048
N600MB	125	256044
N600MB	G2	108
N600MG	600	1020
N600MK	600	1050
N600ML	G4	1104
N600MS	601	3041
N600MS	604	5333
N600MS	D1A	A055SA
N600MT	500	070
N600N	**50**	**256**
N600PB	10	189
N600PC	24D	292
N600PC	25C	116
N600PD	**600**	**1020**
N600PM	G3	333
N600PM	**G4**	**1255**
N600QJ	S65	465-54
N600R	S40	282-6
N600RA	**CVT**	**36**
N600RE	600	1079
N600RM	**501**	**424**
N600SB	125	256034
N600SJ	**S60**	**306-15**
N600SN	125	256064
N600SR	500	236
N600SR	500	275
N600SS	501	623
N600ST	600	1028
N600ST	600	1082
N600ST	600	1085
N600SV	**125**	**25159**
N600TC	WWD	299
N600TD	WWD	254
N600TD	WWD	84
N600TE	**600**	**1056**
N600TF	S550	0118
(N600TH)	125	258029
N600TH	125	258030
N600TJ	WWD	198
N600TP	STR	5058/4
N600TP	WWD	84
N600TT	125	256047
(N600TT)	500	075
N600TT	600	1048
N600TT	STR	5058/4
(N600VE)	S550	0019
N600WD	**20**	**300/508**
N600WG	**50**	**98**
N600WJ	**125**	**256017**
N600WJ	35A	466
N600WM	500	040
N600WT	35	037
N600YY	600	1033
N600YY	G3	304
N601A	601	5166
N601AA	**601**	**3061**
N601AB	560	0158
N601AB	**650**	**7098**
N601AE	**601**	**3050**
N601AF	**601**	**5045**
N601AG	601	3001
N601AG	601	3011
N601AN	CVT	13
N601BA	125	256040
N601BA	**125**	**258082**
N601BC	**550**	**121**
N601BD	**601**	**3010**
N601BF	601	5065
N601BH	601	5043
N601BW	**601**	**5150**
N601CB	601	5090
N601CC	500	101
N601CC	601	5008
N601CC	601	5087
N601CC	604	5324
N601CD	601	5088
N601CH	50	47
N601CH	601	5093
N601CJ	601	5023
N601CL	601	3001
N601CL	601	3016
N601CM	STR	5214
(N601CR)	600	1051
N601CV	601	5144
N601CV	CVT	40
N601DB	601	5080
N601DR	125	258299
(N601DR)	601	5018
N601DR	WWD	434
N601DW	**601**	**5099**
(N601EA)	601	5028
N601EB	601	5153
N601EC	**601**	**5064**
N601EG	**601**	**5008**
N601ER	601	5032
N601ER	601	5141
N601FR	601	5175
N601FS	601	5172
N601GB	601	5130
(N601GF)	601	3052
N601GL	601	3026
N601GL	**S60**	**306-50**
(N601GR)	601	5018
N601GR	601	5149
N601GS	601	5018
N601GT	**601**	**3062**
N601HC	601	5055
N601HC	601	5088
N601HF	601	5183
N601HH	601	5018
N601HJ	601	3046
N601HP	601	3062
N601J	25B	118
N601JA	**125**	**256051**
N601JJ	125	25173
N601JJ	125	256051
N601JJ	STR	5102
N601JM	601	3048
N601JP	**601**	**3065**
(N601JR)	125	257087
N601JR	600	1011
N601KF	**601**	**3023**
N601KJ	**601**	**5187**
N601KK	**125**	**25224**
N601KK	551	030
N601KR	601	5015
N601LJ	**60**	**001**
N601LS	600	1048
N601MC	35A	306
N601MD	601	5078
N601MD	**G5**	**538**
N601MG	601	5078
N601MG	S60	306-73
N601NB	**601**	**5024**
N601PR	**601**	**3045**
N601PR	601	3054
(N601PR)	601	5106
N601PS	125	256051
N601R	**601**	**5194**
N601RC	CVT	36
N601RL	**601**	**5028**
N601RP	601	3045
N601RS	**125**	**258018**
N601S	**601**	**3060**
N601SA	600	1013
N601SA	**600**	**1079**
(N601SN)	601	3060
N601SQ	601	3010
N601SR	600	1051
N601SR	601	3002
N601SR	**601**	**5130**
N601ST	**601**	**5081**
N601TG	601	3013
N601TJ	601	3033
N601TJ	601	3046
N601TL	601	5028
N601TM	**601**	**5141**
N601TP	601	3054

N601TP	**601**	**5156**
N601TX	**601**	**3005**
N601UP	**601**	**5123**
N601UT	601	3010
N601UU	125	25103
(N601UU)	125	257041
N601UU	125	258005
N601VF	**601**	**5154**
N601VH	**601**	**5043**
N601WM	**601**	**5026**
(N601WT)	35A	218
N601WT	501	568
N601WW	600	1047
N601WW	**600**	**1076**
N601Z	600	1079
N601Z	601	5075
N601ZT	601	3054
N602AB	560	0217
N602AB	**650**	**7101**
(N602AN)	601	5178
N602AN	CVT	31
N602AS	**600**	**1054**
N602AT	**550**	**606**
N602BC	**500**	**190**
N602BD	**601**	**5019**
N602BW	550	0884
(N602CC)	500	102
(N602CC)	501	602
N602CC	601	3065
N602CC	601	5029
N602CC	601	5150
N602CF	125	256057
N602CL	600	1020
(N602CM)	G2	153
(N602CN)	601	5038
N602CW	601	3002
N602D	**601**	**5181**
N602DP	601	5154
N602GA	HFB	1041
N602HJ	601	3047
N602JB	601	5131
N602JR	**125**	**25229**
N602KB	S60	306-109
N602LJ	60	002
N602MC	601	5177
N602MM	125	256002
N602N	25D	274
N602NC	**10**	**82**
N602NC	25D	274
N602PM	**G4**	**1402**
N602SC	**60**	**095**
N602TJ	601	3047
N602UK	601	5011
N602WA	601	5068
(N603AF)	601	5129
N603AT	650	0178
(N603CC)	500	103
N603CC	601	5011
N603CC	601	5067
N603CC	604	5333
N603CC	604	5420
N603CJ	550	603
N603CL	600	1019
(N603GA)	HFB	1042
N603GJ	601	3012
N603GY	125	257028
N603HJ	601	3052
(N603JC)	525	0053
N603JM	604	5402
N603KS	601	5130
N603LJ	31	033
N603SC	**60**	**096**
(N603TS)	601	3065
N604AC	601	5102
N604AG	604	5414
N604AN	CVT	18
N604AS	**25D**	**292**
N604B	604	5305
N604BA	601	5153
N604BB	604	5316
N604BD	**604**	**5303**
N604BL	35A	604
N604CA	604	5379
N604CB	**604**	**5448**
(N604CC)	500	104
N604CC	601	5016
N604CC	601	5032
N604CC	601	5101
(N604CC)	601	5179
N604CC	604	5301
N604CC	**604**	**5376**
N604CC	604	5991
N604CE	**604**	**5446**
N604CH	604	5394
N604CL	600	1015
N604CL	600	1030
N604CL	601	3053
N604CL	604	5322
N604CR	604	5376
N604CR	604	5424
N604CT	**604**	**5314**
N604CU	**604**	**5339**
N604D	601	5193
N604DC	604	5365
N604DC	604	5403
N604DD	604	5366
N604DE	604	5380
N604DS	**604**	**5323**
N604FS	604	5357
N604GA	**HFB**	**1037**
N604GM	**604**	**5399**
N604GT	**604**	**5449**
N604HD	**604**	**5445**
N604HJ	601	5024
N604HJ	**604**	**5382**
N604HP	604	5375
N604JA	604	5426
N604JE	604	5389
N604JJ	604	5411
N604JP	604	5346
N604JP	**604**	**5421**
N604KC	604	5312
N604KG	604	5390
N604KM	604	5429
N604KR	604	5319
N604KS	604	5308
N604LA	**604**	**5436**
N604LJ	31	034
N604LS	604	5315
N604M	**G4**	**1132**
(N604MA)	604	5430
N604MC	**601**	**5013**
N604MG	604	5416
N604MK	S60	306-15
N604MU	**604**	**5406**
N604PA	604	5391
N604PL	604	5338
N604PM	**604**	**5354**
N604PN	**604**	**5435**
N604PS	**604**	**5442**
N604RC	604	5334
N604S	604	5400
N604SH	604	5396
(N604TS)	601	5104
N604TS	604	5308
N604VF	**604**	**5444**
N604WB	**601**	**5125**
N605AT	560	0242
N605BA	601	5152
N605CC	601	5113
N605CC	601	5174
N605CC	604	5320
N605CL	600	1057
N605CL	601	3054
N605DC	604	5422
N605GA	24	119
N605GA	**HFB**	**1038**
N605HJ	601	5025
N605JA	**604**	**5443**
N605KC	604	5313
N605MP	604	5417
N605NE	25XR	139
N605PA	604	5397
N605PM	**604**	**5356**
N605RG	S60	306-116
N605RP	20	100
N605RP	601	5184
N605T	10	189
N605T	**601**	**5191**
N605TS	600	1005
N605V	WWD	100
N605W	125	25136
N605Y	S65	465-63
N606AB	WWD	268
N606AM	**100**	**205**
N606AT	**650**	**0225**
N606BA	601	3006
N606CC	500	106
N606CC	601	5018
N606CC	601	5035
N606CC	601	5117
N606CC	604	5340
N606CC	604	5395
N606CL	600	1009
N606DR	90X	40
N606ES	G3	322
N606GB	**25D**	**245**
N606JM	D1A	A044SA
N606JM	WWD	149
N606JR	**525**	**0231**
N606KK	**500**	**306**
N606MM	**525**	**0104**
N606PM	**604**	**5360**
N606PT	G3	308
N606RP	20	265
N606TS	125	256006
(N607CC)	500	107
N607CF	**S60**	**306-118**
N607CJ	501	607
N607CL	600	1071
N607CL	601	3031
N607CL	601	5007
(N607CZ)	601	5007
N607DB	**525**	**0269**
N607PM	**604**	**5362**
N607RJ	**560**	**0370**
N607RP	20	470
N607RP	**601**	**5184**
N607S	20	7
N607SR	S60	306-118
N608AM	550	608
N608AR	S40	282-77
N608CC	601	5023
N608CC	601	5037
N608CC	601	5179
N608CC	**604**	**5301**
N608CL	601	3040
N608CT	**560**	**0065**
N608CW	**601**	**3008**
N608GA	**G5**	**619**
N608LB	S550	0029
N608LJ	60	008
N608RP	**601**	**3055**
N608S	S40	282-77
N608VP	550	608
N609CC	601	5068
N609CC	604	5327
N609CC	**604**	**5438**
N609CL	601	3043
N609CL	601	3066
N609K	601	5072
N609TC	550	609
N610AS	**2xx**	**8**
(N610BA)	125	258176
N610BA	125	258179
N610CC	20	373
(N610CC)	500	110
N610CC	**G2**	**56**
N610CC	G3	412
N610CL	601	3049
N610CM	650	0210
N610DB	601	5132
N610GE	35A	338
N610GE	36A	036
(N610HC)	125	25173
N610HC	125	25253
N610HC	35A	255
N610HC	**AST**	**012**
N610HC	WWD	346
N610HC	WWD	361
(N610J)	10	139
N610JA	WWD	298
N610JB	25D	370
N610JC	WWD	1
N610JR	25D	370
N610JR	35A	402
N610JR	**55ER**	**125**
N610LJ	**35A**	**610**
N610LM	25D	301
N610MC	**G2**	**196**
N610MS	601	3041
N610R	35A	622
N610RA	**S60**	**306-54**
N610SE	**WWD**	**346**
N610TM	60 ·	005
(N610TS)	600	1023
N610TT	**501**	**573**
(N610VP)	650	0010
N611AC	CVT	7
N611AG	D1A	A091SA
N611AT	**501**	**490**
N611BA	**125**	**258178**
(N611CA)	23	077
N611CC	601	5185
N611CF	550	244
N611CL	601	3030
N611CL	601	5002
N611CM	35A	253
N611CR	125	258061
N611CR	550	260
N611DB	**24D**	**318**
N611ER	550	260
N611GS	601	5082
N611JC	WWD	2
N611JW	601	5063
N611JW	**900**	**162**
N611MC	**125**	**257080**
N611MH	601	5011
N611MM	125	258061
N611NT	601	5082
N611PA	**400A**	**RK-78**
(N611RR)	550	161
N611SH	**35A**	**253**
N611ST	**560**	**0123**
N611SW	500	093
N611TJ	G2	11
N611TW	**35A**	**611**
N611WM	**400A**	**RK-249**
N612AC	CVT	9
N612BA	125	258181
N612BH	**900**	**122**
(N612CA)	500	216
N612CC	550	344
N612CC	601	5063
N612CC	601	5186
N612CL	601	3056
N612DG	35A	326
N612DS	501	469
N612G	125	25139
N612GA	**20**	**8**
N612J	WWD	3
N612JC	WWD	50
N612KC	35A	105
(N612M)	WWD	389
N612MC	**125**	**257168**
N612ST	S550	0065
N613AC	CVT	11
N613BA	125	258183
N613BR	23	082A
N613BR	S60	306-8
(N613CC)	500	113
N613CK	G2	150
N613CL	601	3042
N613CL	601	5005
(N613E)	S60	306-25
N613GA	**20**	**77/429**
N613GL	25D	329
N613J	WWD	12
N613MC	**125**	**257151**
N613RR	35A	276
N613SZ	**25C**	**156**
N613W	23	013
N614AC	CVT	17
N614BA	125	258185
(N614CC)	500	114
N614CC	601	5056

N614CC	601	5188
N614CL	601	3059
(N614DD)	501	576
N614GA	**20**	**94/428**
(N614GA)	550	399
N614HF	G4	1119
N614J	WWD	26
N614JC	WWD	26
N614MH	WWD	95
N614MM	S60	306-41
N615AC	CVT	18
N615AT	**560**	**0245**
N615BA	125	258187
(N615DM)	WWD	196
N615EA	550	615
N615HP	**35A**	**444**
N615J	WWD	29
N615L	**560**	**0386**
N615RG	**560**	**5016**
N615SR	**50**	**298**
(N615TJ)	125	256015
N616AC	CVT	20
N616AT	**650**	**0230**
N616BA	125	258188
N616CC	601	5045
N616CC	601	5144
N616DJ	36	016
(N616GB)	S550	0100
N616HC	35A	255
N616LJ	35A	616
N616MM	D1A	A062SA
N616NA	**25**	**035**
N616PA	125	256051
N616PS	23	088
N616SC	24A	100
N617AC	CVT	22
N617BA	125	258189
N617BG	**D1A**	**A067SA**
N617CC	500	117
N617CC	501	617
N617CM	551	617
N617GA	**20**	**88**
N617TM	**125**	**258411**
N618AC	CVT	26
N618BA	125	258191
N618BR	**23**	**082A**
(N618CC)	500	118
N618CC	601	5085
N618CC	601	5166
N618CC	650	0008
N618DB	550	340
N618DB	601	5018
N618DC	601	5004
N618DC	**604**	**5365**
N618GA	**20**	**211**
N618GH	**20**	**236**
N618JC	WWD	105
N618JC	WWD	51
N618JL	**125**	**258224**
N618KM	G3	487
N618P	25D	360
(N618P)	60	044
N618R	24B	225
N618R	25D	360
N618R	25XR	139
N618R	31A	035
N618R	60	044
N618RF	31A	035
N618S	10	156
N619BA	125	258193
(N619BA)	550	619
N619BD	900	16
N619CC	500	119
N619CC	601	5081
N619EA	500	220
N619FE	601	5054
N619GA	**20**	**215**
N619JC	WWD	93
N619JM	**550**	**0889**
N619MW	20	312
N620A	**20**	**412**
N620AS	2xx	97
N620AT	**560**	**0520**
(N620CC)	125	257159
N620CC	20	373
(N620CC)	500	120
N620DS	**G4**	**1040**
N620J	35A	193
N620JB	STR	5143
N620JF	**60**	**074**
N620JH	**G3**	**387**
N620JM	**35A**	**207**
N620K	G2	64/27
N620K	**G4**	**1193**
N620K	S40	282-9
N620M	125	257005
N620M	S40	282-9
N620S	**600**	**1031**
N620SB	**600**	**1025**
N620TC	**525**	**0014**
N621BA	125	256040
N621GA	**G5**	**621**
N621JA	125	257099
N621JA	G3	387
N621JH	125	257099
N621JH	G3	387
N621JH	**G4**	**1272**
N621L	125	25205
N621LJ	60	121
N621MT	**125**	**258036**
N621S	125	25205
N621S	125	257178
N621S	**G3**	**381**
N621ST	125	25014
N622AB	125	257012
N622AB	125	258223
N622AB	601	5016
N622AB	700	9022
N622AD	125	257012
N622AD	125	258223
(N622AD)	601	5016
(N622EX)	550	635
N622GA	**G5**	**622**
N622LJ	60	122
N622R	20	15
N622R	20	86
(N622SS)	501	372
N622VH	**550**	**635**
N622WG	35A	611
N623CW	**601**	**5023**
N623CX	**G2**	**101**
N623GA	**G5**	**623**
N623LB	501	465
N623MS	**G3**	**351**
N623MW	G2	94
N623PM	**650**	**7018**
N623RC	24	173
N623RM	501	623
N624BP	**G3**	**320**
N624CC	650	0123
N624FA	S60	306-53
N624GA	**G5**	**624**
N624GJ	**G4**	**1267**
N624KM	**WWD**	**227**
N624VP	650	0024
N625AU	**25D**	**340**
N625BL	**C21A**	**625**
N625CC	**650**	**7058**
N625CH	501	625
N625CR	50	55
N625EA	550	625
N625GA	500	217
N625J	501	625
N625PG	**525**	**0282**
N625VP	650	0025
N626BM	**35A**	**634**
(N626CC)	500	126
N626CC	650	0062
N626CC	**90X**	**27**
N626CG	**125**	**258041**
N626JS	**35A**	**394**
N626KM	**60**	**012**
N626LJ	**60**	**119**
N626P	500	267
N626QS	**560**	**5126**
N626SL	**560**	**0118**
N626TC	G2	129
N626TC	**G4**	**1227**
N626TG	G4	1227
N626VP	550	626
N627AT	**560**	**0527**
N627BC	**550**	**0868**
N627CR	125	25160
N627CW	**601**	**3027**
N627E	**501**	**513**
N627ER	24D	290
N627HS	125	256013
N627L	501	513
N627L	**550**	**0843**
N627R	**650**	**0152**
N627RP	400A	RK-155
N627TA	551	051
N627WS	25B	170
N627XL	**560**	**5149**
N628BL	C21A	628
N628BS	**500**	**045**
N628CC	**2xx**	**95**
N628CC	650	0128
N628CH	501	628
N628DB	**35A**	**246**
(N628FS)	500	045
N628KM	WWD	308
N628VK	601	5049
N628WC	601	3048
N628WJ	**C21A**	**628**
N628ZG	501	444
N629DM	**525**	**0369**
N629LJ	60	129
N629P	125	25179
N629TS	125	256029
N629TS	**601**	**3029**
N630BA	125	258195
N630CE	501	630
N630L	50	130
N630LJ	60	130
N630M	600	1023
N630M	601	5060
N630M	**750**	**0021**
N630M	S40	282-73
N630N	S40	282-73
N630PM	G2	236
N630QS	**560**	**5130**
N630S	**AST**	**046**
N630SR	50	227
N631AT	**31A**	**191**
N631BA	125	258196
N631CC	550	631
N631CC	650	0031
(N631CK)	G2	150
N631CW	25D	313
N631CW	35A	302
N631EA	**550**	**631**
N631LJ	60	131
N631QS	**560**	**5131**
N631RP	**400A**	**RK-155**
N631RP	400A	RK-7
(N631RR)	400A	RK-7
N631SC	125	25065
N631SC	125	256002
N631SC	G2	224
N631SF	**31A**	**075**
N631SQ	125	25065
N631SQ	125	256002
N632BA	125	258199
(N632CC)	500	132
N632PB	125	25058
N632PB	20	206
N632PB	**31**	**033**
N632PE	125	25058
N632QS	**560**	**5132**
N632SC	500	344
N632SC	550	379
N633AC	55	115
N633AT	**500**	**087**
N633BA	125	258200
N633CC	650	0133
N633CW	**601**	**3013**
N633DS	**35A**	**362**
N633EE	**S550**	**0058**
N633GA	AST	112
N633J	24	120
N633L	50	223
N633NJ	24	120
N633P	G3	452
N633SL	**S60**	**306-33**
N633WW	**10**	**59**
N633WW	35A	654
N634BA	125	258202
N634GA	GXY	011
N634H	35A	292
N634H	**50**	**178**
N635AV	G2	168
N635AV	**G4**	**1185**
N635BA	125	258203
N635E	**2xx**	**106**
N635GA	**AST**	**120**
N636	S60	306-140
N636	STR	5127
N636	STR	5135
N636BA	125	258204
N636C	STR	5127
N636CC	501	636
N636GA	G4	1336
N636GS	560	5074
N636MC	S60	306-140
(N636MC)	STR	5127
N636MF	G2	150
N636MF	G4	1012
N636MF	**G5**	**512**
N636N	**501**	**441**
N636SC	**10**	**115**
N636SC	500	222
N637BA	125	258205
N637EH	550	371
N637GA	G4	1337
N637LJ	60	037
N637ML	600	1024
N637QS	**560**	**5137**
N638BA	125	258206
N638GA	G4	1338
N638LJ	**60**	**038**
N638MF	G2	150
N639BA	125	258207
N639CL	601	3039
N639J	WWD	337
N639QS	**560**	**5139**
N640AC	400A	RK-3
N640BS	501	640
N640CH	**604**	**5428**
N640GA	24	157
N640GA	G5	540
N640M	125	25228
N640PM	125	257167
N640TS	600	1004
N641CA	**604**	**5441**
N641CL	601	5041
N641FG	WWD	370
N641GA	25	004
N641GA	G5	541
N642BB	550	339
N642BJ	**501**	**388**
N642CC	**550**	**038**
(N642CT)	500	262
N642GA	24	158
N642GA	G5	542
(N642LJ)	60	142
N642LR	S40	282-83
N642RP	**S60**	**306-46**
N642TS	75A	380-2
N643CR	**600**	**1055**
N643CR	650	0024
N643GA	G5	543
N643JL	125	25208
N643MC	501	643
N643MC	550	643
N643RT	501	639
N643RT	**560**	**0010**
N643TD	**550**	**437**
(N644CC)	500	144
N644CC	650	0144
N644GA	G5	544
N644JL	125	258012
N644JW	**STR**	**5223**
N644X	20	36
N644X	S60	306-26
N645CC	S60	306-49

N645G	24	160
N645G	**35**	**056**
N645GA	G5	545
N645HJ	**45**	**087**
N645L	25	008
N645M	560	0350
N646CC	650	0146
N646EA	35A	646
N646G	**55**	**016**
N646GA	25	005
N646GA	G5	546
N647CC	550	647
N647CM	650	7047
N647GA	24	159
N647GA	G5	547
N647JP	**20**	**120**
N647JP	20	359/542
N647JP	20	70
N647JP	80A	380-21
(N647SA)	20	70
(N647TJ)	35A	647
N648GA	25	008
N648GA	G5	548
N648J	35A	648
N648JW	35A	648
N648LJ	**60**	**048**
N648WW	125	257004
N648WW	550	477
(N649AF)	650	0109
N649CC	650	0149
N649G	24	161
N649GA	G5	549
N649WW	550	477
N650	**650**	**697**
N650AB	650	7053
N650AC	**501**	**364**
N650AE	650	0152
(N650AF)	650	0113
N650AF	650	0120
N650AF	650	0125
N650AF	650	0145
N650AJ	650	0068
N650AN	650	0049
(N650AS)	50	171
(N650AS)	50	90
N650AS	650	7053
(N650AT)	24	157
(N650AT)	650	0109
N650BA	650	0178
(N650BG)	650	0002
(N650BW)	650	0198
N650C	S60	306-137
N650CA	24	050
N650CC	**650**	**0193**
N650CC	650	696
N650CD	**650**	**0066**
N650CE	**650**	**0106**
N650CF	650	0104
N650CG	**650**	**0023**
N650CH	**650**	**0154**
N650CJ	501	650
N650CJ	650	0014
N650CM	650	0200
N650CN	650	0047
N650CN	650	0062
N650DA	650	0085
N650FC	**650**	**0146**
N650FP	**650**	**0188**
N650G	WWD	233
(N650GA)	650	0198
N650GA	G5	550
N650GA	**G5**	**600**
N650GE	**AST**	**064**
N650GE	WWD	233
N650GH	**650**	**0034**
N650GJ	650	0165
N650GT	**650**	**0004**
N650HC	**650**	**0124**
N650HR	650	0101
N650HS	650	0185
N650J	**650**	**0022**
N650JA	650	0073
N650JC	650	0089
N650JG	**650**	**0107**

N650JL	**650**	**0019**
(N650JP)	550	730
N650JV	**650**	**0138**
N650KB	**650**	**0078**
N650KC	**650**	**0215**
N650KM	650	0144
N650L	650	0209
N650LR	**35A**	**650**
N650LW	**650**	**0010**
N650M	650	0044
N650M	WWD	67
N650MC	**650**	**0237**
N650MD	650	0035
N650MM	**650**	**0048**
N650MP	650	0107
(N650MT)	650	0122
N650MW	**501**	**593**
N650NL	35A	154
N650NY	**650**	**0027**
N650PF	G2	118
N650PM	125	258081
N650RJ	650	7003
N650RL	**650**	**7029**
N650SB	**650**	**0018**
N650SC	**650**	**0030**
N650SG	**650**	**0191**
N650SL	650	0024
N650SP	650	0094
N650SS	650	0021
(N650SS)	650	0140
N650TA	**650**	**0088**
N650TC	**650**	**0061**
N650TC	650	0064
N650TF	500	142
N650TJ	650	0191
N650TP	650	0061
N650TS	650	0006
N650TT	**650**	**0046**
N650TT	650	0122
N650VP	650	0025
N650W	**650**	**7065**
N650WB	**650**	**0020**
N650WC	550	007
N650WC	**550**	**627**
N650WE	**650**	**0040**
N650WG	**550**	**007**
N650WJ	650	0078
N650WL	650	0078
N650X	**50**	**69**
N650Z	**650**	**0108**
N651AC	601	3009
N651AF	**650**	**0114**
(N651AP)	650	0001
N651AP	650	0082
N651BH	**650**	**0051**
N651CC	650	0001
N651CC	S550	0010
N651CG	650	0001
N651CJ	**525**	**0365**
N651CN	650	0072
N651CW	**601**	**3051**
N651E	WWD	406
N651EJ	**650**	**0241**
(N651ES)	WWD	406
N651GA	G5	551
N651GL	S65	465-36
N651J	24B	181
N651JM	650	0241
N651LJ	**24A**	**125**
N651MK	**S65**	**465-73**
(N651NA)	G2	118
N651RS	650	0094
N651S	S65	465-14
(N651SB)	50	70
N651TC	650	0090
N652CC	650	0002
N652CC	650	0078
N652CN	601	5040
N652CW	**601**	**5052**
N652GA	G5	552
N652J	23	018
N652JM	**650**	**0113**
N652MK	S65	465-36
N652ND	**500**	**277**

N652PC	2xx	10
N652SA	35A	652
N653CC	650	0003
N653CC	650	0089
N653CC	650	0153
N653CW	601	5053
N653DR	501	561
N653EJ	**650**	**7057**
N653F	501	638
N653GA	G5	553
(N653J)	WWD	161
N653LJ	24	126
N654	25B	082
(N654AR)	650	0004
N654CC	650	0001
N654CN	900	127
N654DN	24	019
N654E	20	164
N654E	S40	282-70
N654EJ	**650**	**7070**
N654EL	**560**	**5024**
N654GA	G5	554
N654GC	650	0004
N654JC	24	127
N654LD	24	127
N654LJ	24	127
N654PC	10	131
(N655CC)	500	155
N655CC	650	0105
N655CN	601	5069
(N655DB)	10	28
N655EW	550	303
N655GA	G5	555
(N655JH)	G2	22
N655LJ	24	128
N655PC	550	134
N655TJ	**G2**	**5**
N656CC	650	0006
(N656CC)	650	0026
N656GA	G5	556
N656LJ	24	129
N656PC	10	99
N656PS	**550**	**009**
N657CC	650	0007
N657CC	650	0157
N657ER	**650**	**7027**
N657GA	G5	557
(N657K)	125	25032
N657LJ	24	130
N657MC	20	148
N657T	**650**	**7042**
N658AT	24B	219
N658CC	650	0046
N658CJ	650	0158
N658GA	G5	558
N658KA	**125**	**256058**
N658L	23	017
N658LJ	24	132
N658MA	650	0023
N658PC	G2	157
N658TC	25	044
N658TS	125	256058
N659AT	24	157
N659GA	G5	559
N659HX	25B	179
N659HX	**25D**	**300**
N659LJ	24	131
N659PC	G2	204
N659WL	G2	204
N660A	24	155
N660AA	501	480
N660AA	**650**	**0059**
(N660AC)	550	158
N660AF	650	0151
N660AH	**60**	**017**
N660AJ	**S550**	**0154**
N660AS	**60**	**040**
(N660BW)	S60	306-33
N660CJ	35A	079
N660EG	**900**	**152**
N660GA	G5	560
N660KC	501	480
N660L	35A	660
N660LJ	24	133

N660P	**20**	**430**
N660RM	S60	306-91
N660RW	WWD	128
N660SA	35A	469
N660TC	125	256060
N660TC	25D	317
N660TJ	650	0060
N660W	WWD	58
N661AA	36A	049
N661AA	501	357
N661AC	500	121
N661BS	24	108
N661CL	**601**	**5061**
N661CP	24	108
N661CP	24	174
N661CP	WWD	210
N661FS	23	018
N661GA	**G5**	**561**
N661GL	10	3
N661J	20	81
N661JB	125	257106
N661JB	20	275
N661JB	20	81
N661JB	24	159
N661JB	600	1073
N661JB	WWD	209
N661JG	24	174
N661LJ	25	002
N661MP	25XR	162
N661MP	WWD	176
N661P	S40	282-41
N661R	G4	1092
N661SS	24	108
N661TV	501	661
N661TW	501	661
N662AA	35A	315
(N662AA)	550	183
N662D	10	87
N662D	100	200
N662F	S60	306-6
N662G	G2	188
N662GA	G5	562
N662JB	125	257018
N662JB	WWD	209
N662JB	WWD	210
N662K	WWD	418
N662P	20	378
N662P	**90X**	**30**
N662P	S60	306-6
(N662PP)	20	378
N663B	G2	14
N663CA	35	063
N663JB	25XR	162
N663JB	WWD	209
N663L	24	140
N663LJ	24	140
N663MN	50	249
N663P	G2	14
N663PD	**G2**	**139/11**
N664B	20	95
N664CC	501	664
N664CL	24	151
N664CL	**24**	**167**
N664CW	**601**	**3064**
N664GA	G5	564
N664GL	24	151
N664J	550	025
N664JB	10	162
N664JB	125	257106
N664JB	550	025
N664LJ	24	136
N664P	20	95
N664P	**50**	**200**
N664P	G3	343
(N664RB)	650	0014
N664S	G3	343
N664SS	**550**	**458**
N665B	20	88
N665JB	501	357
N665MC	550	665
N665P	**20**	**444**
N665P	20	88
N666AE	125	25046
N666AJ	551	095

N666BP	WWD	122
N666BR	S60	306-2
N666BS	500	045
N666CC	24B	214
N666CC	35A	254
N666CP	WWD	347
N666DA	20	129
N666DC	WWD	61
N666ES	500	045
N666JD	WWD	39
N666JJ	501	537
N666JM	650	0241
N666JM	WWD	133
N666JM	WWD	149
N666JM	WWD	184
N666JM	WWD	283
N666JR	35A	074
N666JT	125	25186
N666JT	551	272
N666JT	**G2**	**162**
N666K	WWD	207
N666K	**WWD**	**321**
N666KK	25D	285
N666KK	35A	481
N666LC	125	256064
N666LC	HFB	1039
N666LN	**S550**	**0005**
N666LP	25B	185
N666LQ	HFB	1039
N666M	125	25075
N666MP	23	041
(N666MP)	WWD	156
N666MW	**24D**	**305**
N666PE	25D	359
N666RB	25D	291
N666RB	35A	393
N666RC	550	044
N666RE	25D	359
N666RE	31	016
N666RE	31A	055
N666SA	500	031
N666SC	125	25098
N666TB	36	012
N666TR	**S550**	**0106**
N666TW	**25C**	**116**
N666WL	25	017
N666WL	S60	306-75
N666WW	550	201
(N666WW)	551	445
N667CC	601	5032
N667CC	650	0167
N667CG	550	365
N667CX	G2	10
N667H	125	258276
N667LC	601	5032
N667LC	**604**	**5324**
N667P	20	432
N668CM	550	668
N668EA	550	667
N668H	125	258287
N668JT	125	25186
N668MC	24B	214
N668P	20	308
N668S	20	308
N668S	**500**	**314**
N668VP	**525**	**0228**
(N669AC)	20	299
N669BJ	G4	1397
(N669DM)	501	669
N669H	125	258289
N669LJ	35A	669
N669MA	**550**	**128**
(N669SB)	WWD	435
N669W	**650**	**0045**
N670AS	**S65**	**465-58**
N670BA	125	258209
N670C	**75A**	**370-7**
N670CL	600	1070
N670H	125	258290
N670LJ	25	009
N670MF	23	062
(N670WJ)	35A	670
N671B	550	271
N671BA	125	258216
N671BA	35A	671
N671EA	550	671
N671GA	G5	571
N671QS	**560**	**5071**
N671SR	20	56
N671SR	600	1071
N671WM	25	010
N672AT	400	RJ-14
N672BA	125	258217
N672CA	551	591
N672CC	650	0172
N672DK	35A	672
N672H	125	258291
N672LJ	24	146
N672M	STR	5103
N673BA	125	258218
N673CA	550	590
N673FH	80A	380-49
N673GA	G5	573
N673H	125	258292
N673JS	650	0073
N673LJ	24	147
N673LP	501	503
N673LP	550	192
N673LR	501	503
N673LR	**550**	**192**
N673M	35	008
N673SH	80A	380-49
N673TM	**125**	**258033**
N673TS	**600**	**1073**
N673WM	23	040
N674AC	**D1A**	**A024SA**
N674BA	125	258220
N674CA	550	564
N674CC	650	0174
N674G	**550**	**434**
N674GA	G5	574
N674JM	**S550**	**0127**
N674LJ	24	178
N674SF	**400A**	**RK-232**
N675BA	125	258221
(N675DM)	550	600
N675LJ	60	075
N675M	55	075
N675RW	G2	191
N675RW	**G5**	**526**
N676BA	125	259020
N676BB	**550**	**0923**
N676CC	**501**	**676**
N676CW	500	169
N676DG	**500**	**256**
N676DW	20	387
N676LJ	24B	183
N676PC	10	36
N676PC	125	25153
N676RW	G3	355
N676RW	**G4**	**1253**
N676TC	**AST**	**044**
(N676WE)	500	169
N677BA	125	258223
N677BM	20	57
N677CC	650	0077
N677CT	**35A**	**307**
N677LJ	60	077
N677RW	125	257191
N677RW	G2	191
N677RW	G2	192
N677RW	**G4**	**1177**
N677S	G2	115
N677SW	20	27
N677SW	24F	356
N677SW	**G4**	**1269**
N677V	G2	120
N678AM	S65	465-22
N678BA	125	258230
N678BC	STR	5109/13
N678BM	20	345
N678BM	20	57
N678CA	550	060
N678CF	501	678
N678CG	**600**	**1027**
N678DG	501	625
(N678DG)	501	652
N678JD	**501**	**452**
(N678JG)	501	452
N678ML	600	1011
N678RW	G2	13
N678RW	G2	192
N678RW	G4	1017
N678RZ	G2	13
N678S	35A	342
N678SB	**125**	**259016**
N678SP	24F	354
N678W	125	257147
N679BA	125	259023
N679BC	**550**	**589**
N679CC	501	679
N679CC	650	0179
N679H	125	258293
N679H	125	259049
N679RE	20	150/445
N679RW	G2	109
N679RW	G2	191
N679RW	**G4**	**1131**
N679RW	STR	5062/12
N680BA	125	259014
N680BC	25B	200
N680BC	650	0087
N680CJ	**24B**	**211**
N680FM	G3	371
N680J	25	063
N680JC	**25D**	**319**
N680K	WWD	173
N680M	600	1023
N680RW	G2	191
N680RW	G2	4/8
N680RZ	G2	4/8
N680TT	STR	5108
N681AR	G2	81
N681FM	G2	167
N681FM	G3	371
N681LJ	60	081
(N681TS)	600	1081
N682B	**125**	**258144**
N682BA	125	258225
N682CC	650	0182
N682CJ	550	682
N682CM	550	682
N682D	10	87
(N682D)	100	200
N682D	560	0021
N682DC	501	682
N682FM	G2	167
N682FM	G3	305
N682H	125	258294
N682HC	**501**	**682**
N682JB	200	488
N682LJ	24B	218
N682LJ	60	082
N683BA	125	258229
N683CF	S550	0085
N683E	**125**	**258113**
N683EC	**G2**	**157**
N683FM	G2	167
N683FM	G2	22
N683H	125	258295
N683LJ	25	035
N683LJ	60	083
N683MB	650	0159
N683MB	S550	0085
N684AT	**G3**	**339**
N684BA	125	259033
N684C	125	258063
N684H	500	113
N684HA	35A	113
N684HA	500	113
N684LA	35A	113
N684LJ	60	084
N684QS	**560**	**5084**
N685BA	125	258231
N685EM	125	257026
N685FM	125	257026
N685H	125	258296
N685LJ	60	085
N685RC	**45**	**053**
N685TA	G2	31
N685TA	**G4**	**1003**
N686BA	125	258232
N686CF	125	258060
N686CG	**G4**	**1171**
N686FG	125	257207
N686LJ	60	086
N686MC	S550	0072
N686SG	125	257207
N686TR	**400A**	**RK-127**
N687LJ	25	040
N687LJ	60	087
N687VP	650	0087
N688CC	125	25142
N688CF	**500**	**147**
N688GS	**25B**	**123**
N688H	G4	1062
N688LJ	60	088
N688MC	20	175
N688MC	G2	81
N689CC	501	689
N689H	125	258300
N690	24E	339
N690EA	**500**	**201**
N690J	24	145
N690JC	**25D**	**320**
N690LJ	23	078
N690MC	501	388
N690QS	**560**	**5090**
(N691DE)	650	0204
N691H	125	258321
N691HM	**G2**	**92**
(N691NS)	35A	208
N691RC	G2	43
N691RC	**G4**	**1079**
N692BE	**650**	**0092**
N692CC	650	0092
N692FC	125	25032
N692FC	25	052
N692FG	**25**	**052**
N692G	20	44
N692LJ	24B	222
N692M	S550	0041
N692QS	**560**	**5092**
N692TT	550	692
N692TV	**G3**	**397**
N693BA	650	0005
N693C	125	258209
(N693CC)	650	0093
N693LJ	24D	231
N693M	S550	0021
N693TJ	**125**	**256027**
N694CC	650	0090
N694CM	550	694
N694JC	125	25107
N694JP	**90X**	**59**
N695BK	**400A**	**RK-235**
N695CC	501	593
N695LJ	25	060
N695ST	50	40
N695ST	G2	28
N695VP	550	695
N696A	551	363
N696GW	WWD	52
N696HC	**50**	**250**
N696HC	650	0154
(N696JH)	125	257055
(N696JH)	35A	084
N696RV	**WWD**	**118**
N696SC	35	018
(N696SC)	35A	179
N696ST	**525**	**0187**
N696TR	400A	RK-127
N696US	**S65**	**465-18**
N697A	550	034
N697A	G2	16/13
N697BJ	**G3**	**370**
N697EA	550	697
N697MC	650	0097
N697NP	125	257052
N698PW	**400A**	**RK-114**
N699CC	**560**	**0351**
N699CW	601	5009
N699EC	125	258193
N699GA	**20**	**401**
N699RD	**S60**	**306-53**
N699SC	125	256026

N699SC	50	70
N699SC	60	041
N699ST	**35A**	**441**
N699TW	**20**	**50**
N700AA	125	257149
(N700AB)	125	25033
N700AC	125	257126
N700AH	700	9016
N700AL	10	55
N700AR	125	257053
N700AS	551	014
N700BA	125	257032
N700BA	125	257058
N700BA	125	257131
N700BA	125	257185
N700BA	125	257189
N700BB	125	257041
N700BB	125	257148
N700BD	10	81
N700BF	WWD	137
N700BH	**700**	**9024**
N700BH	G2	115
N700BJ	25D	257
N700BP	**700**	**9044**
N700BU	**700**	**9043**
N700BV	**700**	**9046**
N700BW	125	25263
N700BW	125	257123
N700BY	**700**	**9048**
N700C	24	123
N700C	24	144
N700C	WWD	44
N700CB	WWD	44
N700CC	125	25202
N700CF	S40	282-109
N700CH	**60**	**056**
N700CJ	125	257178
N700CL	**600**	**1035**
N700CN	125	257102
N700CN	G3	488
N700CN	**G4**	**1133**
(N700CQ)	G2	228
N700CS	650	0036
N700CU	125	257081
N700CW	500	205
N700DA	**25D**	**302**
N700DD	125	257152
N700DE	125	257105
N700DK	10	191
N700DW	100	205
(N700E)	125	257101
(N700EA)	550	072
N700EC	WWD	182
N700ER	125	257010
N700ER	501	542
(N700ET)	24	123
N700FA	125	25229
N700FC	**25B**	**082**
N700FE	**125**	**257108**
N700FH	**10**	**158**
N700FR	125	257130
N700FS	125	257012
N700FS	G2	108
N700FS	**G3**	**367**
(N700GA)	WWD	137
N700GB	125	257050
N700GB	35A	082
N700GB	400A	RK-26
N700GD	**G4**	**1104**
N700GG	125	257154
N700GG	**36A**	**038**
N700GK	**700**	**9020**
N700GM	400A	RK-34
(N700GN)	20	325
N700GS	60	026
N700GT	**700**	**9039**
N700GW	**525**	**0275**
N700GX	**700**	**9014**
N700HA	125	257143
N700HA	125	257149
N700HB	125	257146
N700HB	WWD	135
N700HE	**700**	**9032**
N700HF	**700**	**9034**

N700HG	700	9022
N700HH	**125**	**257045**
(N700HM)	400	RJ-19
N700HS	125	257002
N700HS	125	257012
N700HS	125	257072
N700HS	125	257150
N700HW	125	257173
N700HX	**700**	**9005**
N700JA	**501**	**379**
N700JC	**S65**	**465-74**
N700JD	500	009
N700JE	**55**	**091**
N700JP	G2	77
N700JR	501	379
N700JR	**550**	**554**
N700JR	S60	306-138
N700K	125	257102
N700KC	**601**	**5017**
N700KJ	**700**	**9011**
N700KK	125	257155
N700KK	600	1082
N700KS	**700**	**9015**
N700LB	550	366
N700LL	125	257157
N700LP	**125**	**257159**
N700LP	400	RJ-28
N700LP	D1A	A005SA
N700LS	125	257041
N700LS	G4	1009
N700LS	**G4**	**1180**
N700LW	501	400
N700M	125	25123
(N700MD)	36A	045
N700MD	**WWD**	**212**
N700MH	**S60**	**306-142**
(N700MJ)	STR	5138
N700MK	125	257156
N700MK	601	3011
N700MM	WWD	311
N700MP	500	198
N700NB	**125**	**257131**
N700NH	**125**	**257148**
N700NN	125	257162
(N700NP)	23	082
N700NT	125	257056
N700NW	**125**	**257063**
N700NW	35A	331
N700NY	125	257002
N700NY	**125**	**257140**
N700PD	10	55
N700PD	125	257029
(N700PG)	125	25202
N700PL	125	25229
N700PM	125	258081
N700PM	G2	207/34
N700PP	125	257167
N700QG	S65	465-16
N700R	125	256001
N700R	**55B**	**133**
N700R	S40	282-31
N700R	WWD	149
N700R	WWD	222
N700RD	125	25136
(N700RD)	650	0036
N700RG	125	25136
N700RJ	125	257004
N700RR	125	257161
N700RR	650	0025
N700RR	650	7020
N700RY	500	087
N700SA	125	257141
N700SA	**125**	**257145**
N700SB	125	257121
N700SB	**G3**	**334**
N700SF	125	257061
N700SJ	**35A**	**082**
N700SS	125	257061
N700SS	125	257168
N700ST	G2	28
N700SV	125	257001
N700SV	S550	0119
N700SW	**650**	**0096**
N700SW	S550	0119

N700TF	**560**	**0011**
N700TG	55	021
N700TL	125	257028
N700TT	10	49
N700UK	125	257051
N700UR	125	257057
(N700UU)	125	25103
N700VA	G3	300
N700VC	**500**	**011**
N700VN	**700**	**9031**
N700VP	650	7011
N700VT	**125**	**257158**
N700WB	G4	1125
N700WE	WWD	417
N700WH	125	257010
N700WJ	35A	393
(N700WJ)	35A	466
N700WL	35	003
N700WL	**700**	**9042**
N700WM	WWD	319
N700WS	S60	306-133
N700XJ	**125**	**256015**
N700YM	551	139
N701A	125	256022
N701AG	650	0077
N701AP	24	163
N701AP	WWD	52
(N701AR)	36	008
N701AS	**35A**	**047**
N701AS	500	127
N701AT	500	127
N701BR	500	191
N701CD	650	7001
N701CF	125	257057
N701CP	400A	RK-272
N701CR	**560**	**0469**
N701CW	**125**	**257001**
N701DA	**35A**	**180**
N701DB	**55**	**074**
N701DK	**560**	**0221**
N701FW	S60	306-57
N701FW	**S65**	**465-21**
N701GA	600	1066
N701HA	**650**	**7001**
N701JA	**G2**	**7**
N701JH	**STR**	**5230**
N701LP	**400**	**RJ-61**
N701MG	20	196
N701MS	**125**	**256061**
N701NA	23	049
N701NC	S40	282-79
N701NW	**125**	**257009**
N701QS	600	1066
N701QS	G4	1059
N701RM	550	242
N701RZ	23	042
N701S	**G2**	**69**
N701SC	**24X**	**235**
N701TA	**125**	**257073**
N701TF	**525**	**0190**
N701TS	**125**	**257002**
N701US	35	062
N701VF	501	650
N701W	WWD	274
N701WC	**2xx**	**48**
N701WH	**700**	**9010**
N701Z	125	25234
N701Z	125	256022
N701Z	125	256058
N701Z	WWD	274
N702BA	125	257059
(N702BC)	550	252
N702CM	650	7002
N702D	125	25210
N702DM	**20**	**74**
N702E	125	257198
N702GA	125	25158
N702H	G2	229
N702HC	**125**	**256023**
N702JA	**G2**	**180**
N702JH	**D1A**	**A035SA**
N702JR	S60	306-138
N702KH	551	290
N702LP	**400A**	**RK-87**

N702M	125	25241
N702M	125	257195
N702MA	125	25241
N702NC	10	55
N702NC	**100**	**220**
N702NC	501	579
N702NG	10	55
N702NW	125	257098
N702NY	501	579
N702P	125	25212
N702R	550	015
(N702RK)	23	024
N702S	125	25200
N702SB	200	504
N702SC	20	321
N702SS	125	25200
(N702TJ)	125	257144
N702W	125	257199
N703DC	23	067
N703J	24D	256
N703JA	**G3**	**426**
N703JH	**D1A**	**A010SA**
N703JP	125	257140
N703JS	10	157
N703LP	**400A**	**RK-20**
N703MA	35	003
N703SC	20	24
N703TS	**125**	**257031**
(N703VP)	650	7030
N704CD	550	704
N704CW	**125**	**257004**
N704J	36	009
N704JA	**G3**	**432**
N704JW	**550**	**0863**
N704T	**PRM**	**RB-2**
N705CC	125	257027
N705EA	**125**	**25142**
N705JA	**G3**	**360**
N705JH	125	257029
N705LP	**400A**	**RK-251**
N705MA	**AST**	**011**
N705NA	24A	102
N705SP	**S550**	**0048**
N705US	35A	144
N706A	S40	282-7
N706CJ	**60**	**168**
N706CP	550	0909
N706JA	**G3**	**322**
N706JH	**D1A**	**A016SA**
N706L	23	026
N706M	125	25123
N706SB	S550	0139
N706TS	**G2**	**254/41**
(N706VP)	650	7006
N707AM	**10**	**159**
N707AM	10	26
N707BC	**WWD**	**366**
(N707BJ)	35A	077
N707CA	25D	342
N707CV	560	0095
N707CW	D1A	A007SA
N707CX	10	135
N707DB	S60	306-97
N707DC	10	159
N707DS	125	257148
N707EA	550	707
N707EZ	125	25231
N707EZ	STR	5055/21
N707FH	**S40**	**282-74**
N707GG	601	5037
N707HJ	650	0177
N707JA	**G3**	**447**
N707JC	**20**	**335**
N707JM	S40	282-41
(N707JZ)	20	335
N707PE	**125**	**258171**
N707PE	550	452
N707PF	**550**	**452**
N707RX	**G3**	**377**
N707SB	S550	0141
N707SC	**24**	**065**
N707SG	60	062
N707SG	**60**	**109**
N707SH	125	25231

N707SH	G2	77
N707SQ	60	062
N707TA	**125**	**258296**
N707TE	WWD	137
N707TE	WWD	155
N707TF	**WWD**	**155**
N707TG	S40	282-74
(N707TP)	25	005
N707TR	25	005
N707US	500	339
N707W	**501**	**475**
N707WB	125	256061
N707WB	**900**	**132**
N707WB	STR	5210
N707WF	501	661
N707WF	550	452
N708BW	125	25263
N708CF	650	0185
(N708CM)	650	7008
N708CT	650	0185
N708CT	650	7004
N708SP	**45**	**014**
N708TA	**400A**	**RK-178**
N708TR	25	015
N709AB	S60	306-75
N709CC	550	709
(N709CM)	650	7009
N709EA	125	258226
N709EL	**400A**	**RK-52**
(N709EW)	400A	RK-52
N709JB	400A	RK-52
N709JB	400A	RK-72
N709JM	601	5163
N709Q	S40	282-30
N709Q	WWD	95
N709QS	650	7109
N709R	125	256001
N709RS	550	709
N709TA	**400A**	**RK-180**
N709VP	550	709
N710A	**125**	**258110**
N710AG	125	257193
N710AT	**35A**	**337**
N710AW	**750**	**0033**
N710BA	125	257191
N710BC	125	257186
N710BD	125	257183
N710BF	125	257182
N710BG	125	257180
N710BJ	125	257177
N710BL	125	257174
N710BN	125	257173
N710BP	125	257171
N710BQ	125	257210
N710BR	125	257208
N710BS	125	257207
N710BT	125	257206
N710BU	125	257202
N710BV	125	257201
N710BW	125	257199
N710BX	125	257198
N710BY	125	257195
N710BZ	125	257193
N710EC	20	102
N710EC	**G3**	**315**
(N710EG)	20	102
N710GS	**35**	**032**
N710HM	601	5160
(N710JA)	STR	5150/37
N710JL	G2	169
N710JW	WWD	35
N710K	MSP	112
N710MB	D1A	A078SA
N710MP	G2	148/5
N710MR	20	59
N710MR	G2	148/5
N710MR	S60	306-123
N710MT	20	59
N710MT	550	057
N710MT	**560**	**0254**
N710MW	20	59
N710QS	**650**	**7100**
N710SA	**WWD**	**296**
N710TA	**400A**	**RK-183**
N710TJ	24B	197
N710TV	**24**	**159**
N710WB	20	102
N710WL	35A	485
N711	23	098
N711	24B	197
N711	35	012
N711	35A	207
N711A	80A	380-21
N711AE	23	098
(N711AE)	501	477
N711AF	35	029
N711AG	125	256001
N711AG	STR	5086/44
(N711AJ)	600	1063
N711AQ	125	25173
N711BC	20	36
N711BE	35A	274
N711BE	**525**	**0299**
N711BF	25D	324
N711BH	35	041
N711BP	125	25218
N711BP	550	036
N711BT	501	644
N711BY	75A	380-51
N711CA	25B	076
N711CD	35A	456
N711CE	24B	219
N711CH	35	032
N711CJ	WWD	289
N711CN	24B	197
N711CN	550	711
N711CR	500	016
N711CU	125	257081
N711CW	**24**	**055**
N711DB	24B	216
N711DB	24D	253
N711DB	25	032
N711DB	600	1071
N711DP	G2	82
N711DS	24B	189
N711DS	25B	170
N711DS	35A	209
N711DS	G2	129
N711DX	24B	189
N711DZ	STR	5201
N711EC	400	RJ-53
N711EC	**400A**	**RK-167**
(N711EG)	501	662
N711EG	G3	349
N711EV	25	016
(N711EV)	35A	377
N711EV	**G2**	**129**
N711FC	400	RJ-55
N711FG	**31A**	**092**
N711FG	400	RJ-55
N711FJ	**10**	**149**
(N711FW)	500	196
N711GD	80A	380-6
N711GF	560	0068
N711GF	**650**	**7075**
N711GL	**20**	**396**
N711GL	501	519
N711GL	80A	380-6
N711GW	WWD	12
N711HE	G4	1217
N711HF	**100**	**213**
N711HH	35A	162
N711HL	**125**	**25232**
N711HL	501	503
N711JC	**10**	**69**
N711JG	AST	017
N711JG	S550	0035
N711JN	S550	0035
N711JQ	AST	017
N711JS	STR	5153/61
N711JT	25D	243
N711JT	WWD	91
N711KE	**WWD**	**288**
N711KG	20	57
N711KT	50	125
N711L	24	164
N711L	24D	252
N711L	35A	151
N711LD	24D	252
N711LS	G2	76
N711LT	**G3**	**327**
N711MA	35	032
N711MB	WWD	282
N711MC	G2	48/29
N711MC	**G4**	**1217**
N711MD	**S550**	**0066**
N711MM	G2	61
N711MR	23	045
N711MR	S60	306-118
N711MR	WWD	191
N711MT	10	105
N711MT	100	207
N711MT	**500**	**316**
N711MT	G2	16/13
N711MT	G2	52
N711NF	35A	626
N711NM	25D	224
N711NR	501	387
N711NV	**551**	**557**
N711PC	**24D**	**327**
N711PD	24F	353
N711PD	25B	138
N711PD	601	5013
N711PJ	24A	011
N711PR	35A	501
(N711QH)	35	032
N711R	35	035
N711R	**45**	**049**
N711R	G2	45
N711RL	125	257146
N711RL	**G2**	**25**
N711RP	501	639
(N711RQ)	35	035
(N711RT)	20	242
(N711RT)	G2	26
N711S	G2	67
N711S	S60	306-92
N711SB	G2	70/1
(N711SC)	125	25169
(N711SC)	24D	283
N711SC	25D	345
N711SC	50	168
N711SC	G2	70/1
N711SD	125	25233
N711SD	35A	078
N711SE	500	261
N711SE	**WWD**	**329**
N711SF	500	261
N711SJ	601	3021
(N711SP)	601	3021
N711SQ	25	005
N711SR	601	3007
N711ST	601	3024
N711ST	S60	306-129
(N711SW)	125	25146
N711SW	35A	078
N711SW	G2	71
N711SW	G3	311
N711SW	G4	1170
N711SW	G5	523
N711SX	**601**	**3007**
(N711T)	900	20
N711T	S40	282-67
N711TE	500	342
N711TE	**G2**	**105**
N711TF	**10**	**52**
N711TG	125	257177
N711TG	25D	298
N711TJ	24A	011
N711TQ	25D	298
N711TU	50	124
N711TW	S60	306-33
N711UC	S40	282-32
N711UR	24B	197
N711VF	**501**	**642**
(N711VF)	501	650
N711VK	25D	292
(N711VK)	WWD	7
N711VR	550	260
N711VT	125	25249
N711VT	25D	292
N711VT	**60**	**045**
N711WD	25B	196
N711WD	25D	241
N711WD	**25D**	**282**
N711WE	25B	105
N711WJ	125	25021
N711WK	**AST**	**101**
N711WK	S60	306-40
N711WM	125	25020
N711WM	**125**	**257087**
N711WM	551	387
N711WU	WWD	313
N711WV	**WWD**	**313**
N711YP	125	25265
N711YP	125	257048
N711YR	125	25265
N711Z	550	435
N711Z	560	0326
N711Z	STR	1002
N711Z	STR	5023
N711Z	STR	5067
N711Z	STR	5078/3
N711Z	STR	5093
N711Z	STR	5141
N711Z	STR	5149/11
N711Z	STR	5151
N711Z	STR	5155/32
N711Z	STR	5201
N712BW	25D	241
(N712CB)	25D	298
N712CC	**G4**	**1028**
N712CM	650	7012
N712CW	G4	1028
N712DC	25	032
N712DG	604	5328
(N712DM)	35A	231
N712G	500	060
N712GF	560	0068
(N712GM)	WWD	118
N712GW	STR	5016
N712J	500	060
N712J	500	270
N712J	550	404
N712JA	25B	134
N712JB	35A	646
N712JC	**750**	**0052**
N712JE	36	012
N712L	35A	256
N712L	**560**	**0365**
N712ME	**20**	**355**
N712MR	S60	306-113
N712N	500	270
N712PD	**550**	**063**
N712R	**24**	**156**
N712RD	STR	5005
N712RW	25D	296
N712S	S550	0035
N712SJ	25D	296
N712TA	**400A**	**RK-186**
N712TE	STR	5070/52
N712US	10	110
N712US	500	044
N712VS	125	25174
N713AL	501	576
N713B	**25B**	**201**
N713DH	560	0376
N713DH	560	0416
N713DH	S550	0107
N713DJ	25D	355
N713G	10	162
(N713HH)	560	0092A
N713HH	560	0192
N713HH	S550	0138
N713K	125	257094
N713KM	125	257094
N713KM	G3	432
N713LJ	25D	241
N713M	55	113
N713MC	**20**	**392/553**
N713MR	S40	282-82
(N713PE)	20	113
N713Q	25B	105
N713QS	**650**	**7103**
N713R	STR	5205
N713RL	125	257146

N713RR	25D	241
N713SA	**500**	**132**
N713SC	AST	013
N713SS	**125**	**25174**
N713US	25	015
(N713VP)	650	7013
N714K	25B	150
N714K	35A	230
N714KP	25B	150
N714S	35A	367
N714US	500	040
N714X	24	103
N715AB	550	715
N715BC	23	029
N715BC	650	0018
N715BG	601	5164
N715CX	750	0015
(N715DG)	501	400
N715EK	501	367
(N715GW)	WWD	187
N715JF	25B	132
(N715JM)	501	367
N715JS	**500**	**001**
N715MH	**25B**	**132**
N715MR	S40	282-40
N715QS	**650**	**7105**
N715TA	**400A**	**RK-189**
(N715VP)	650	7015
N715WS	20	305
N716BB	WWD	118
N716CB	**500**	**055**
N716DB	**S550**	**0120**
N716GA	500	210
N716HP	**601**	**3026**
N716NC	25D	264
N716QS	650	7106
N716RD	601	5048
N716RD	STR	5005
N716RD	STR	5218
N716TE	**G2**	**116**
N716US	24D	297
N716W	AST	016
N717	G3	401
N717	STR	5009
N717	STR	5202
N717A	G3	308
N717AN	**25D**	**272**
N717CF	**D1A**	**A033SA**
N717CW	25D	362
(N717DA)	525	0087
N717DB	24	179
N717DD	400A	RK-18
N717DD	**400A**	**RK-207**
N717DM	**550**	**435**
N717DS	35A	302
N717DW	400A	RK-18
N717EP	**25D**	**255**
(N717GF)	125	25047
N717HB	24D	295
N717HB	**55**	**066**
N717HE	24D	295
N717JB	35A	229
N717JB	35A	646
N717JB	**55B**	**128**
N717JL	**501**	**527**
N717JM	STR	5009
N717LA	**WWD**	**305**
N717LS	S550	0054
N717MB	**560**	**0007**
N717PC	550	366
N717RB	501	449
N717TR	G3	418
N717VA	400A	RK-21
N717VL	400A	RK-21
N717VL	D1A	A073SA
N717W	35A	147
N717WW	AST	017
N717X	STR	5009
N717X	STR	5202
N718CA	10	64
N718CK	**550**	**402**
N718DW	**50**	**81**
N718EA	35A	229
N718JS	**G2**	**66**
N718MC	G5	549
N718P	601	5127
N718R	**601**	**5127**
N718R	STR	5147
N718R	STR	5205
N718SA	**501**	**589**
N718SW	35A	179
N718TA	**400A**	**RK-195**
N718US	36A	019
N718VA	500	148
N718VA	550	029
N718VP	650	7018
N719A	G3	310
N719AL	10	25
N719CC	**WWD**	**290**
N719GA	G2	79
N719JB	**35A**	**166**
N719JE	36A	019
N719L	**525**	**0075**
N719US	35A	135
N720AS	25	017
N720BA	**G4**	**1335**
N720C	500	073
N720CC	550	720
N720DF	**10**	**26**
N720E	G2	65
N720F	G2	66
N720G	G2	119/22
(N720GH)	35A	105
N720GL	35A	087
N720HC	200	497
N720J	S40	282-24
N720JW	**G2**	**178**
N720M	35A	183
N720M	50	18
N720M	55	020
N720ME	10	48
N720ME	650	0016
N720ML	10	48
N720ML	20	262
N720ML	**50**	**245**
N720ML	650	0016
N720ML	WWD	147
N720PT	**125**	**257032**
N720Q	G2	58
N720R	S40	282-27
N720SJ	560	0386
N720TA	**125**	**258320**
N720UA	23	067
N720WC	**550**	**708**
N721AS	**35A**	**101**
N721AS	WWD	58
N721BS	2xx	11
N721BW	601	5049
(N721CC)	500	183
N721CC	**550**	**721**
N721CM	35A	210
N721CP	G2	46
N721CR	STR	5150/37
N721CW	G3	485
N721DP	10	64
N721DR	**550**	**211**
N721EW	601	5049
N721FF	**G3**	**421**
N721GB	23	005
N721GB	WWD	135
N721GB	WWD	71
N721GL	24E	335
N721HW	23	005
N721J	20	255/487
N721J	24B	200
(N721J)	24B	205
N721JA	24B	200
N721LH	**125**	**256025**
N721MC	**601**	**5031**
N721PA	**STR**	**5054/59**
N721PL	G2	121
N721RB	**G3**	**311**
N721RL	G2	121
N721RL	G4	1394
N721S	**601**	**5109**
N721SS	**400A**	**RK-34**
N721SW	600	1066
N721SW	601	5049
N721SW	G2	2
(N721TB)	500	281
N721US	501	579
N721US	550	391
N722AW	**WWD**	**154**
N722AZ	**WWD**	**351**
N722CC	**125**	**258008**
N722CM	650	7022
(N722CX)	750	0022
(N722DM)	24B	224
(N722ED)	S40	282-56
N722FD	S40	282-56
N722GL	35A	092
N722HP	600	1039
N722JB	**2xx**	**13**
N722Q	**MSP**	**009**
N722SG	**525**	**0088**
N722ST	S40	282-56
N722TA	**125**	**258322**
N722TP	G2	92
N722US	500	253
N722W	WWD	159
(N722W)	WWD	306
N723BH	650	0127
N723CC	**55**	**036**
N723GL	35A	107
N723H	55	090
N723J	G2	87/775/6
N723JB	WWD	37
N723JM	501	563
N723JM	WWD	363
N723JR	**501**	**584**
N723JW	24	178
N723K	WWD	330
N723L	WWD	349
N723LF	25C	087
N723LL	24B	216
N723LL	29	002
N723LL	35A	277
N723M	WWD	237
N723R	S60	306-11
N723R	WWD	272
N723ST	STR	5023
N723TA	125	258349
N723TS	125	25191
N723US	35A	311
N724AA	400	RJ-22
N724B	**125**	**257006**
(N724CC)	500	203
N724CC	**750**	**0062**
N724DB	**G3**	**372**
N724DS	**10**	**92**
N724EA	501	387
N724GL	24E	347
N724J	55	092
N724KW	**400A**	**RK-263**
N724LG	24	143
N724MH	400A	RK-263
N724TS	**125**	**25192**
N725BA	550	431
N725BF	550	431
N725CC	125	257027
N725CC	**550**	**725**
N725DM	**10**	**184**
(N725DM)	24D	305
N725DM	25D	328
(N725DM)	500	131
N725DW	125	25134
N725FL	**550**	**431**
N725GL	24F	348
N725K	55	093
N725L	**525**	**0140**
N725LB	50	46
N725LB	**G4**	**1296**
N725P	10	169
(N725P)	20	306/512
N725P	20	72/413
N725P	35A	167
N725PA	10	155
N725PA	50	23
(N725RH)	501	503
N725RH	**550**	**006**
N725TA	**125**	**258297**
(N725WH)	125	257015
N725WH	**650**	**0097**
(N726BB)	501	517
N726CC	125	25116
N726GL	25XR	222
N726L	55ER	098
N726R	S40	282-83
N726TA	**125**	**258363**
N726WR	25	007
(N727AL)	S550	0043
N727AT	**WWD**	**284**
N727AW	25D	313
N727BT	**31A**	**082**
N727C	550	368
N727C	**550**	**485**
N727CM	550	727
N727CS	**25D**	**313**
N727EE	500	048
N727GL	35A	127
N727JP	35A	189
N727LE	500	048
(N727LG)	24	143
N727LM	**25D**	**308**
N727MC	501	677
N727NA	**S550**	**0043**
N727R	S40	282-42
N727S	**50**	**17**
N727TA	**125**	**257003**
N727TK	**500**	**141**
N727TS	**10**	**76**
N727US	75A	380-61
N728C	S65	465-71
N728CC	550	728
N728CM	650	7028
N728CP	G3	875
N728CX	750	0028
N728GL	35A	133
N728JW	125	257129
N728KA	125	25224
N728L	WWD	349
N728LB	50	46
N728LM	WWD	341
N728LW	**50**	**3**
N728LW	WWD	341
N728MC	**501**	**507**
N728MC	WWD	147
N728MP	35A	481
N728PX	**STR**	**5112/7**
(N728SA)	10	71
N728T	G2	82
N728TA	**125**	**258364**
N728US	500	171
N729AT	**125**	**258402**
N729GL	24E	338
N729HS	35A	481
N729MJ	550	303
(N729MJ)	551	151
N729PX	501	433
N729S	20	173
N729TA	**125**	**258374**
N730BA	**G4**	**1290**
N730BR	550	730
N730CA	S40	282-103
N730CA	S60	306-145
N730CA	**WWD**	**295**
N730CP	**S40**	**282-103**
N730GL	36A	025
N730H	125	257150
N730PV	10	106
N730PV	WWD	36
N730R	S40	282-43
N730S	20	247
N730SA	900	155
N730TA	**125**	**258383**
(N730TC)	550	333
N730TK	G2	140/40
N730TL	600	1084
N730TS	**125**	**25201**
N730V	20	319
(N730VP)	550	730
N731A	STR	5011/1
(N731AE)	20	344/534
N731AG	STR	5070/52
N731AS	20	344/534
N731BW	125	25075

N731CW	**25B**	**117**
N731DL	**125**	**257048**
N731F	20	113
(N731F)	20	344/534
N731F	50	45
N731FJ	10	3
N731G	125	25153
N731G	125	25195
N731G	**20**	**267/491**
(N731GA)	125	257122
N731GA	35	001
N731GA	35	003
N731GA	36A	028
N731GA	650	0076
N731H	125	25278
N731HS	125	25214
N731HS	125	25229
N731HS	125	25253
N731JS	STR	5006/40
N731KC	125	25118
N731L	**STR**	**5095/30**
N731MS	**125**	**25239**
(N731RG)	20	113
N731RG	20	168
N731RG	20	388
N731TA	**400A**	**RK-273**
N731TC	125	256024
(N731WB)	125	25264
N731WL	**STR**	**5070/52**
N731X	125	25244
N732M	STR	5084/8
N732S	20	272
N732TS	**125**	**25203**
N733A	601	3008
N733A	**650**	**0234**
N733A	900	126
N733AU	650	0234
N733CF	600	1041
N733CF	**601**	**5057**
N733E	50	128
N733E	**55**	**057**
N733EY	55	057
N733EY	**601**	**5113**
N733H	125	257018
N733H	550	081
N733H	560	0137
N733H	**650**	**0210**
N733HL	900	126
N733K	125	25285
N733K	125	258137
N733K	600	1041
N733K	**650**	**0222**
N733M	125	257092
N733M	**560**	**0249**
N733MK	**400A**	**RK-107**
N733R	S40	282-51
N733S	**20**	**292**
N733TA	**125**	**258337**
(N734)	55	048
N734	55	051
N734AK	125	25014
N734S	10	13
(N734S)	20	299
N734S	20	316
N735A	**35A**	**323**
N735GA	400	RJ-42
N735TA	**400A**	**RK-274**
N736R	S40	282-82
(N736US)	WWD	192
N737CC	650	7037
N737E	S40	282-26
N737EF	25	037
N737FN	24	171
N737MM	**400**	**RJ-35**
N737R	S40	282-33
N737R	S40	282-66
N737RJ	**501**	**649**
N737X	125	257052
N738GL	25	038
N738R	S40	282-40
N738RH	20	24
N739CX	**750**	**0038**
N739R	S40	282-78
N739TA	400A	RK-199
N739TA	**400A**	**RK-257**
N740AC	55	084
N740BA	**G5**	**516**
N740E	24B	222
N740E	31A	061
N740E	**45**	**023**
N740EJ	**24B**	**222**
N740F	24B	222
N740F	31A	061
N740GL	24F	353
N740J	23	077
(N740JB)	525	0182
N740JV	525	0252
N740K	25D	302
N740L	20	7
N740R	**50**	**247**
N740R	S40	282-47
N740R	S60	306-112
N740R	S65	465-14
N740RC	S60	306-112
N740SS	**G3**	**369**
N740TA	**400A**	**RK-123**
N741AM	**STR**	**5236**
N741C	**WWD**	**292**
N741CC	**525**	**0227**
N741E	25B	100
N741E	25TF	036
N741E	31A	070
N741E	35A	508
N741E	**45**	**011**
N741ED	25TF	036
N741F	25B	100
N741F	31A	070
N741F	35A	508
N741GL	24F	350
N741JB	500	213
N741R	S60	306-143
N741R	S60	306-28
N741R	S65	465-24
N741RC	S60	306-143
N741RL	S60	306-28
N741T	**550**	**394**
N741TA	**400A**	**RK-201**
N742E	25B	096
N742E	31A	071
N742E	35A	630
N742E	**45**	**025**
N742F	31A	071
N742GL	35A	140
N742K	**500**	**236**
N742K	S60	306-45
N742P	35A	630
N742R	**50**	**243**
N742R	S60	306-142
N742R	S60	306-45
N742R	S65	465-28
N742RC	S60	306-142
N742TA	**400A**	**RK-202**
N742Z	25B	096
N743CC	**650**	**0181**
N743E	25B	169
N743E	31A	068
N743E	**45**	**016**
N743F	25B	169
N743F	31A	068
N743GL	35A	141
N743R	S60	306-11
N743TA	**400A**	**RK-271**
(N743UP)	125	258069
N743UP	S60	306-22
N743UT	125	25118
N744CC	125	25142
N744CC	20	313
N744CC	20	347
N744CF	23	082A
N744DC	125	257146
N744DC	550	009
N744E	31A	069
N744E	35A	203
N744GL	35A	126
N744JC	24D	323
N744JR	WWD	198
N744LC	25D	232
N744MC	25B	120
N744N	31A	069
N744P	35A	203
N744R	**560**	**0291**
N744R	S40	282-72
N744SW	550	009
N744TA	**400A**	**RK-245**
N744UT	STR	5147
N744W	25	008
N744X	**50**	**58**
N745DM	500	131
N745DM	STR	5201
N745E	35A	294
N745E	**45**	**008**
N745F	23	077
N745F	35A	294
N745GL	36A	032
(N745HG)	125	25084
N745TA	**400A**	**RK-145**
N745TH	125	257095
N745TS	**125**	**25220**
(N745UP)	125	258072
N745UP	**125**	**258336**
N745UP	G4	1054
N745UP	S60	306-39
N745UR	G4	1054
N745US	500	025
N745W	24	108
N745W	25	030
N745W	25B	177
(N745WG)	125	25236
N746BC	125	257004
N746BR	**650**	**7046**
N746CM	650	7046
N746CX	750	0046
N746E	35A	297
N746F	35A	297
N746GL	35A	157
N746TA	**400A**	**RK-146**
N746TS	125	257046
N746UP	125	258069
N746UP	S60	306-22
N746UT	STR	5225
N747	50	146
N747	50	50
N747	**604**	**5305**
N747	S40	282-22
N747AC	10	166
N747AC	**525**	**0202**
N747AN	25D	272
N747AN	**55**	**121**
N747BK	**PRM**	**RB-29**
N747CP	**35A**	**502**
N747CP	S550	0077
N747CR	**550**	**643**
N747CX	**20**	**442**
N747E	S40	282-22
N747G	G2	49
N747G	G3	381
N747GB	STR	5141
N747GL	35A	171
N747GM	**35A**	**308**
(N747GP)	S550	0077
N747JB	551	617
(N747KL)	500	345
N747LB	**WWD**	**55**
N747NG	125	258417
N747R	S40	282-48
N747RC	S60	306-34
(N747RL)	35A	308
N747RL	500	345
N747RL	**S550**	**0010**
N747RR	**400A**	**RK-95**
N747SC	**24**	**019**
N747T	20	81
N747TS	**604**	**5347**
N747UP	**125**	**258072**
N747UP	S40	282-45
N747UP	S60	306-39
N747V	20	461
N747W	20	5
N747WA	500	301
N747Y	50	50
N748DC	550	136
N748FB	125	257129
N748GL	35A	172
N748GM	24D	311
N748MN	**G2**	**215**
N748T	G3	388
N748TA	**400A**	**RK-222**
N748TS	125	25224
N748VA	500	148
N749CM	650	7049
N749CP	525	0158
N749CP	**650**	**0163**
N749DC	**650**	**0169**
N749DX	**750**	**0046**
N749GL	25D	242
N749MC	WWD	8
N749MP	WWD	8
N749TA	**400A**	**RK-149**
N749UP	S60	306-129
N750AB	**400A**	**RK-50**
N750AC	G3	422
N750BA	**G5**	**558**
N750BM	600	1012
N750BP	**750**	**0111**
N750CC	**S65**	**465-37**
N750CS	S65	465-37
N750CX	**750**	**703**
N750EC	**750**	**0007**
N750FL	**560**	**0268**
N750GL	35A	173
N750GM	125	25075
N750GM	125	257058
N750GM	**750**	**0066**
N750GT	601	3002
N750H	**50**	**171**
N750HS	**750**	**0103**
N750J	750	0051
N750JB	**750**	**0063**
N750JJ	**750**	**0065**
N750LA	501	398
N750LA	501	570
N750LM	750	0039
N750ME	20	262
N750PM	600	1012
N750PP	**501**	**686**
(N750QK)	24	065
N750R	20	187
N750RL	**750**	**0025**
N750RV	**125**	**258187**
N750SB	HFB	1031
N750SS	20	6
N750SW	**G3**	**338**
N750T	400A	RK-70
N750TA	400A	RK-226
N750TJ	D1A	A006SA
N750TJ	D1A	A081SA
(N750WC)	125	25115
N750WJ	24	065
N750XX	**750**	**0094**
N751BH	**750**	**0059**
N751CA	**25B**	**122**
N751CC	500	266
N751CF	560	0274
N751CR	WWD	88
N751CX	750	0001
N751DB	**600**	**1075**
N751GL	35A	162
N751MZ	G3	426
N751PJ	**MSP**	**051**
N751TA	**400A**	**RK-225**
N752CA	25B	137
N752CC	**550**	**019**
N752CM	650	7052
N752CX	750	0002
N752EA	**25B**	**137**
N752GL	25D	251
N752RT	550	070
N752S	**2xx**	**82**
N752TA	**125**	**258397**
N753BD	**750**	**0118**
N753CA	25B	136
N753CC	**550**	**120**
N753G	125	258162
N753GL	35A	186
N753S	**2xx**	**88**
N753TA	**400A**	**RK-230**

N753TW	75A	380-45
N754AA	551	200
(N754CM)	650	7054
N754CX	750	0004
N754DB	**25**	**014**
N754G	125	258171
N754GL	**35A**	**197**
N754M	24B	185
N754S	50	39
N754TA	**125**	**258406**
N755A	**AST**	**103**
N755CM	550	033
N755CM	650	7055
N755CM	WWD	257
N755GL	35A	187
N755GW	125	25233
N755S	G2	20
N755TA	125	258410
(N755TS)	125	257055
N755WJ	**125**	**25233**
N756	125	25102
N756	**20**	**388**
N756	STR	5154
N756M	125	25102
N756N	125	25161
N756N	125	257182
N756S	G3	348
N757AL	**35A**	**130**
N757AL	WWD	72
N757C	125	257017
N757CK	**560**	**0028**
N757E	S40	282-50
N757M	125	256022
N757M	125	257017
N757M	**125**	**258101**
N757MC	600	1016
N757MC	**601**	**5177**
N757P	125	256022
N757R	S40	282-49
N757T	**750**	**0014**
N757WS	**400A**	**RK-169**
N758CX	**750**	**0058**
N758S	**550**	**401**
N759A	G2	131/23
N760	550	302
N760A	G3	428
N760AC	55	017
N760AC	60	017
N760AQ	55	017
N760AR	**MSP**	**108**
N760C	G3	430
N760C	MSP	043
N760C	WWD	174
N760DE	STR	5101/15
N760DE	STR	5214
N760DL	35A	155
(N760DL)	50	41
N760DL	STR	5101/15
N760DL	STR	5214
N760E	MSP	102
N760EW	650	0056
N760FR	**MSP**	**072**
N760G	55ER	107
N760G	**G3**	**428**
N760GL	35A	206
N760H	MSP	005
N760J	MSP	006
(N760LB)	MSP	005
N760LP	35A	155
N760M	MSP	049
N760MM	MSP	002
N760N	MSP	103
N760NB	S550	0046
N760P	MSP	104
N760PJ	MSP	101
N760Q	MSP	105
N760R	MSP	104
N760S	**MSP**	**043**
(N760SA)	S60	306-76
N760T	MSP	103
N760TA	**125**	**258413**
N760U	G2	75/7
N760X	**MSP**	**028**
N761A	36A	022
N761TA	**400A**	**RK-161**
N762GL	36A	026
(N762L)	36A	026
N762L	36A	033
N762PF	550	247
N763GL	35A	113
N763J	G3	304
(N763PD)	G2	139/11
N763R	36A	034
N764G	35A	406
N765A	G2	111
N765A	**G4**	**1069**
N765CT	525A	0002
N765TS	**125**	**25263**
(N765W)	650	7065
N765WT	**601**	**5039**
N766	STR	5154
N766AE	550	231
(N766AF)	550	231
N766CG	**650**	**7066**
N766DD	**G3**	**483**
N766FT	500	014
N766MH	**650**	**0015**
N766NB	S550	0156
N766R	S40	282-1
N766WC	**G3**	**413**
N767AC	20	349
N767AC	WWD	356
N767AG	**20**	**349**
N767AZ	55C	136
N767EL	**G4**	**1141**
N767FL	G2	50
N767FL	G4	1141
N767FL	**G5**	**503**
N767NY	55C	136
N767PC	500	080
N767RA	36A	023
N767SA	**25D**	**216**
N767SC	25	023
(N767TR)	550	401
(N767W)	50	82
N767Z	STR	5009
N767Z	STR	5023
N768DV	S60	306-79
N768J	20	440
N768J	G3	304
N768J	**G4**	**1119**
N768NB	650	0180
N768TA	**400A**	**RK-168**
(N768V)	20	440
(N769CM)	650	7069
(N769EG)	S65	465-9
(N769EW)	501	669
N769K	500	228
N769KC	S65	465-9
N770AC	25D	209
N770AC	G2	57
N770AF	650	0119
N770AQ	25D	209
N770BB	550	606
(N770BC)	125	25078
N770CA	600	1042
N770CC	31A	058
N770DA	125	25142
N770DR	**STR**	**5219**
N770E	50	21
N770FG	**20**	**116**
N770HS	**125**	**257191**
N770JC	**600**	**1061**
N770JJ	WWD	296
N770JM	55	039
N770JM	550	072
N770JM	**550**	**0902**
N770JR	**STR**	**5037/24**
N770MC	**20**	**330**
N770MH	501	364
N770MP	**50**	**161**
N770MP	650	0118
N770MR	**650**	**0118**
(N770PA)	25D	209
N770PA	G2	175
N770PC	D1A	A080SA
(N770TB)	400	RJ-14
N770TJ	125	257175
(N770VP)	650	7070
N770WL	WWD	57
N771A	35A	303
N771A	550	034
N771AA	550	317
(N771AC)	WWD	191
N771CB	25D	326
N771CP	AST	077
N771EL	400A	RK-4
N771HR	**500**	**206**
N771JB	650	0214
N771LD	**20**	**59**
(N771R)	551	163
N771ST	**550**	**021**
N771WB	**S60**	**306-29**
N771WW	**600**	**1018**
N771WW	S60	306-29
N772AA	560	0136
(N772AC)	551	106
N772C	500	180
N772HP	**550**	**262**
N772M	S550	0041
N772TA	**125**	**258428**
N773A	601	5169
N773AA	**125**	**25175**
N773AW	WWD	232
N773CA	**550**	**0840**
N773EJ	WWD	153
N773FR	501	410
N773HS	20	44
N773LP	35A	362
N773LP	501	450
N773LP	550	399
N773LR	501	450
N773M	650	0093
N773TA	**400A**	**RK-279**
N773V	20	264
N773VP	550	730
N773W	**75A**	**380-20**
N773WB	WWD	112
N774AB	36A	025
N774CA	525	0141
N774CZ	750	0074
N774EC	125	25281
N774GF	125	257207
N774TS	**125**	**25281**
N774W	**75A**	**380-37**
N775JC	WWD	205
N775M	**650**	**7017**
N775TA	**400A**	**RK-276**
N775US	**G5**	**535**
N776DF	**525**	**0111**
N776DS	20	76
(N776JK)	MSP	043
N776JM	STR	5036/42
N776K	MSP	043
N776MA	**G2**	**166/15**
(N776TS)	125	257076
N776US	**G4**	**1146**
N777AJ	501	495
N777AN	500	027
N777AY	**STR**	**5201**
(N777CB)	60	086
N777CF	WWD	231
N777CJ	WWD	177
(N777CR)	S60	306-27
N777DC	20	91
N777DC	D1A	A045SA
N777DC	D1A	A072SA
N777DC	**WWD**	**410**
N777DM	**35A**	**297**
N777EG	20	146
N777EH	**125**	**257020**
N777EP	STR	5004
N777FA	20	7
N777FB	550	443
N777FC	**200**	**508**
N777FC	500	038
N777FD	**S550**	**0099**
N777FE	**400**	**RJ-30**
N777FE	501	498
N777FE	550	443
N777FE	560	0076
N777FH	**560**	**0076**
N777FJ	10	154
N777FL	**400A**	**RK-223**
N777FL	400A	RK-4
N777FL	550	064
N777GA	125	25146
N777GC	**400A**	**RK-86**
N777GF	S550	0090
N777GG	**501**	**495**
N777GG	G2	8
N777GV	G5	508
N777GX	**700**	**9036**
N777HD	**WWD**	**397**
N777HN	S550	0111
(N777JA)	24	163
N777JF	20	18
N777JF	20	249
N777JJ	**10**	**35**
N777JJ	D1A	A006SA
N777JM	500	056
N777JS	G2	77
N777KK	**600**	**1082**
N777KY	560	0108
N777LB	24B	216
N777LB	**35A**	**476**
N777LF	25C	087
N777LF	35A	449
N777LF	650	0034
N777LU	WWD	350
N777MC	24B	217
N777MC	35A	125
N777MC	55	081
N777MC	**60**	**180**
N777MH	WWD	34
N777MJ	50	115
N777MJ	D1A	A085SA
N777MQ	24B	217
N777MQ	**55**	**081**
N777MR	**24**	**142**
N777MW	**G3**	**485**
(N777ND)	10	130
N777ND	400A	RK-71
N777NJ	25XR	173
(N777NJ)	550	394
N777NQ	35A	125
N777PD	25B	138
N777PQ	HFB	1050
N777PS	HFB	1050
N777PV	20	137
N777PV	HFB	1050
N777PZ	HFB	1050
(N777QE)	500	302
N777RA	25	005
N777RA	35A	285
N777RY	G3	327
N777SA	125	25224
N777SA	125	256015
N777SA	125	256055
N777SA	24B	228
N777SA	25B	201
N777SA	**G4**	**1081**
(N777SC)	500	140
N777SG	STR	5074/22
N777SK	S65	465-24
N777SL	**500**	**307**
(N777SL)	G3	252
N777SL	S40	282-135
N777SN	10	13
(N777ST)	S40	282-82
N777SW	**700**	**9037**
N777SW	G2	81
N777SW	G3	306
N777SW	G4	1014
N777SW	G4	1149
N777SW	G5	514
N777TE	24A	031
N777TF	24A	031
N777TK	125	256015
N777TX	20	365
N777TX	**25C**	**084**
(N777TX)	G2	62
N777UE	G4	1146
N777V	20	264
N777V	G2	120
N777V	S40	282-69

N777V	WWD	12
N777VZ	S40	282-69
N777WJ	20	142
N777WJ	20	65
N777WJ	STR	5215
N777WJ	WWD	72
N777WL	20	65
N777WY	**550**	**292**
N777XX	20	150/445
N777XX	600	1017
N777XX	601	5104
N777XX	601	5152
N778C	550	169
N778GA	24	143
N778JA	**125**	**25285**
N778JC	**25B**	**078**
N778JM	**550**	**072**
N778S	125	25179
N778SM	125	25047
N778W	G3	413
N778W	G4	1023
(N778W)	G4	1146
(N778XX)	600	1077
N778XX	601	3017
N778XX	601	5003
N778YY	601	3017
N778YY	601	3023
N779AF	**650**	**0136**
N779AZ	**601**	**5176**
N779AZ	650	0136
N779DC	**D1A**	**A072SA**
N779DD	550	333
N779P	20	122
N779QS	**650**	**7079**
N779SG	**900**	**46**
N779SW	G4	1014
N779XX	601	3018
N779YY	601	3032
N779YY	601	5043
N780A	125	258084
N780A	25XR	056
N780A	35A	302
N780AC	25XR	173
N780AQ	25XR	173
N780BF	**560**	**0207**
N780CF	**550**	**015**
N780E	**G4**	**1165**
N780F	50	240
N780F	**G5**	**530**
N780GT	**400**	**RJ-55**
N780GT	550	015
N780HC	601	5070
N780LS	G4	1009
(N780PM)	G2	207/34
N780PV	WWD	36
N780QS	650	7080
N780RH	**G3**	**472**
N780RH	STR	5095/30
(N780SC)	125	256018
N780TA	**125**	**258437**
N780TP	**400A**	**RK-136**
N781AJ	20	98/434
N781B	50	116
N781L	501	355
N781QS	650	7081
N781SC	550	398
N781TA	**125**	**258281**
N781TP	**400A**	**RK-231**
N781W	20	257
(N782JR)	25D	316
N782JR	35A	336
(N782NA)	550	376
N782PC	WWD	339
N782QS	**650**	**7082**
N782TA	**125**	**258282**
N782TP	**400A**	**RK-243**
N783A	601	3008
N783H	550	081
N783M	125	257092
N783TA	**400A**	**RK-234**
N784A	550	465
N784AE	125	25084
N784B	**50**	**118**
N784BX	**2xx**	**56**
N784CE	10	78
N784TA	**400A**	**RK-237**
N785B	55	043
N785CA	125	258001
N785CA	550	184
N785JM	35A	655
N785QS	**650**	**7085**
N785TA	**400A**	**RK-239**
N786MS	25	033
N786TA	**400A**	**RK-248**
N787BA	500	143
N787LP	**35A**	**670**
N787QS	**650**	**7087**
N787R	S40	282-76
N787R	S60	306-16
N787R	S60	306-77
(N787RA)	2xx	11
N787RP	**WWD**	**358**
N787TA	**400A**	**RK-260**
N787WB	STR	5210
N787WC	550	471
N787X	125	25037
N788BA	650	0116
N788C	G2	165/37
N788DR	23	084
(N788JS)	STR	5231
N788MA	**WWD**	**311**
N788NB	650	0155
N788QC	35A	609
N788R	S40	282-68
N788S	G2	30/4
N788S	STR	5110/47
N788SS	501	433
N788WG	125	257026
N788WG	600	1069
N789A	AST	092
N789AA	24D	309
(N789AA)	500	445
N789BR	**550**	**036**
(N789DD)	500	249
N789DD	**500**	**560**
N789DD	D1A	A015SA
(N789DD)	WWD	187
N789DJ	**D1A**	**A015SA**
N789DK	**G4**	**1054**
N789DR	601	3001
N789FF	G2	31
N789H	45	003
N789KW	**35A**	**222**
N789LB	**125**	**258248**
N789LT	**125**	**258071**
N789MA	S550	0067
N789PF	55	089
N789QS	**650**	**7089**
(N789RR)	550	036
N789SG	**S60**	**306-121**
N789SR	**31A**	**083**
N789SS	550	087
N789TA	**400A**	**RK-268**
N789TE	WWD	241
N789TP	G3	405
N789TR	G3	405
N789TT	**550**	**391**
N790D	551	023
N790EA	500	251
N790FH	10	158
N790FH	**AST**	**056**
N790JR	**WWD**	**424**
N790L	**2xx**	**15**
N790M	**2xx**	**19**
N790MC	**G5**	**523**
N790QS	**650**	**7090**
N790TA	**400A**	**RK-252**
N790US	10	91
N790Z	125	257197
N790Z	**2xx**	**31**
N791MA	500	309
N791QS	**650**	**7091**
N791TA	**125**	**258291**
N792A	125	25248
N792AA	STR	5098/28
N792H	125	259019
N792MA	**550**	**329**
N792QS	**650**	**7092**
N792TA	**400A**	**RK-264**
N793A	AST	086
N793AA	**501**	**501**
N793BG	**WWD**	**392**
N793CJ	**525**	**0021**
N793CT	**601**	**5148**
N793JR	WWD	365
N793QS	650	7093
N793TA	**400A**	**RK-244**
N794EZ	501	397
N794GC	**35A**	**446**
N794QS	**650**	**7094**
N794SB	20	24
(N794SM)	400A	RK-60
N794TK	**WWD**	**373**
(N794WB)	501	621
N795A	**125**	**257127**
N795HB	**AST**	**084**
N795HE	125	257149
N795HG	**750**	**0053**
(N795HL)	125	257149
N795HP	AST	084
N795J	125	25121
N795MA	501	615
N795PH	**125**	**258139**
N795QS	**650**	**7095**
N796A	50	238
N796HP	AST	085
N796HR	**AST**	**085**
N796MA	10	162
N796QS	650	7096
N796SF	**10**	**75**
N797CB	**60**	**086**
N797CD	**G4**	**1145**
N797CS	**55**	**018**
N797CW	**550**	**284**
(N797EM)	125	257193
N797FA	**125**	**257193**
N797QS	**650**	**7097**
N797R	S40	282-79
N797SC	25	042
N797T	650	0197
N797TA	**400A**	**RK-265**
N797TJ	S550	0048
N797WC	550	471
N797WC	**STR**	**5216**
N798QS	650	7098
N798TA	**400A**	**RK-198**
(N799FL)	125	257111
N799G	20	81
N799S	**125**	**258019**
N799SC	125	257068
N799SC	125	258019
N799SC	60	067
N799SM	**400A**	**RK-220**
N799TA	**400A**	**RK-209**
N799WW	**G4**	**1059**
N800AB	500	130
N800AB	600	1067
N800AF	**125**	**25207**
N800AF	STR	5101/15
N800AJ	**AST**	**081**
N800AK	550	0809
N800AL	**G4**	**1340**
N800AR	**G3**	**362**
N800AV	**500**	**209**
N800AW	**35A**	**149**
"N800BA"	125	258001
N800BA	125	258003
N800BA	125	258046
N800BA	125	258124
N800BA	125	258157
N800BA	125	258195
N800BA	125	258223
N800BA	125	258225
N800BD	50	161
N800BD	**50**	**224**
N800BD	50	35
N800BF	**501**	**457**
N800BG	G3	488
N800BG	**G4**	**1034**
N800BH	501	403
(N800BJ)	125	258206
N800BL	**2xx**	**47**
N800BL	36A	025
N800BL	900	32
N800BM	125	258155
N800BP	125	258080
N800BS	125	258014
N800BT	**600**	**1044**
N800CB	125	25179
N800CB	125	257016
N800CC	600	1080
N800CC	G3	472
N800CC	G4	1052
N800CD	35A	335
N800CD	**75A**	**380-23**
N800CF	20	191
N800CF	20	242
N800CF	20	368
N800CH	**35A**	**335**
N800CJ	125	258225
N800CJ	125	258244
N800CS	S40	282-64
N800CU	S65	465-24
N800DA	**125**	**25047**
N800DC	20	74
N800DC	20	75
N800DC	501	403
N800DC	S40	282-102
N800DJ	G2	159
N800DL	560	0015
N800DM	G2	159
N800DP	125	258024
N800DR	**125**	**258202**
N800DR	25D	353
N800DT	**501**	**602**
N800DW	**125**	**258394**
N800DW	501	564
N800EC	**125**	**258114**
N800EC	550	219
N800EE	125	258004
N800EL	550	343
N800EM	125	258456
N800EX	125	258049
N800FD	**125**	**258390**
N800FF	**20**	**406/557**
N800FJ	**125**	**258090**
N800FK	125	258133
N800FL	**125**	**258005**
N800FL	G2	47
N800FL	G2	50
N800FT	400	RJ-9
N800GA	G2	197
N800GE	**125**	**25206**
N800GG	125	258005
N800GG	**25**	**008**
N800GH	2xx	89
N800GJ	**35A**	**352**
N800GN	**125**	**258057**
N800GP	**35A**	**158**
(N800GT)	125	258266
N800GW	**525**	**0276**
N800GX	125	258195
N800HM	200	495
N800HM	400	RJ-19
N800HS	125	258026
(N800HS)	125	258083
N800HS	525	0051
N800HS	525	0100
N800J	G3	359
N800J	**G4**	**1333**
N800J	STR	5087/55
N800JA	23	039
N800JA	25	042
(N800JA)	25B	118
N800JC	125	25201
N800JD	500	022
N800JH	**G3**	**312**
N800JJ	WWD	290
N800JP	125	256066
N800JT	125	25272
N800KC	500	083
(N800KC)	550	716
N800KC	**601**	**5157**
N800KR	20	144
N800L	25D	249
N800LA	550	325

N800LE	D1A	A064SA
N800LL	125	258017
N800LL	**125**	**258079**
N800LS	20	144
(N800M)	501	404
N800M	S40	282-23
N800M	S60	306-143
N800M	**S65**	**465-41**
N800MA	**45**	**064**
N800MA	WWD	358
N800MC	20	74
N800MC	G2	61
N800MD	125	258074
N800MJ	**125**	**258226**
N800MK	G3	396
N800MM	125	258014
N800MN	125	258074
N800MP	**125**	**257152**
(N800MT)	WWD	372
N800N	125	258003
N800NJ	**125**	**258314**
(N800NW)	125	258019
N800PA	**125**	**258162**
N800PA	20	74
N800PC	**125**	**258369**
N800PC	24D	292
N800PE	**125**	**258441**
N800PL	500	102
N800PM	125	258027
N800PP	125	258018
N800QB	125	25179
N800R	**650**	**0197**
N800RD	**125**	**258311**
N800RD	35A	213
N800RD	D1A	A027SA
N800RF	**25D**	**281**
N800RL	**525**	**0158**
N800RM	S60	306-138
N800RT	**G2**	**47**
N800RY	125	258002
N800S	125	258006
N800S	125	258093
N800SB	**10**	**104**
N800SB	550	343
(N800SG)	125	258390
(N800TE)	G2	22
N800TF	125	258045
N800TJ	125	258236
N800TJ	D1A	A022SA
N800TR	125	258038
N800TR	125	258087
N800TR	125	258111
N800TT	125	258012
N800TW	S65	465-4
N800UP	125	258096
N800VA	125	258425
N800VC	**125**	**258122**
N800VF	**125**	**258300**
N800VJ	**550**	**343**
N800VT	**525**	**0001**
N800VV	125	258011
N800W	500	014
N800W	**750**	**0122**
N800WA	**125**	**258121**
N800WC	**G3**	**392**
N800WG	**125**	**258152**
N800WH	**125**	**258080**
N800WJ	35A	356
N800WS	WWD	253
N800WW	125	258006
N800WW	WWD	253
N800XC	G2	24
N800XL	G2	24
N800XL	WWD	276
N800XP	125	258266
(N800XP)	125	258285
N800XP	**125**	**258414**
N800Y	S40	282-31
N800Y	WWD	198
N800ZZ	125	258020
N801	G2	160
N801	STR	5132/57
N801	**STR**	**5138**
N801AB	125	258135
N801AB	560	0158
N801BB	**550**	**0801**
N801BC	125	256032
N801CC	650	0064
N801CC	G4	1254
N801CE	**125**	**258253**
N801CR	**125**	**258001**
N801CW	**125**	**258012**
N801F	20	4
N801FL	601	5063
N801G	125	258017
N801G	551	110
N801GA	G2	1
N801GA	G2	103
N801GA	G2	108
N801GA	G2	173
N801GA	G2	2
(N801GA)	G2	241
N801GC	601	3052
N801JA	23	076
N801JP	550	046
N801JT	125	258296
N801K	35A	462
N801K	500	236
N801L	23	001
N801L	500	236
N801L	501	606
(N801L)	551	110
N801MB	125	258067
N801MB	**125**	**258440**
N801MM	**125**	**258067**
N801MS	S40	282-30
N801MS	WWD	421
N801NC	S40	282-68
N801NM	WWD	122
N801NW	125	258124
N801P	125	258017
N801P	601	5099
N801P	**604**	**5335**
N801PF	35A	179
(N801R)	125	258017
N801R	601	5099
N801RJ	125	258135
N801SC	**20**	**206**
N801SC	500	076
N801SG	500	076
N801SM	**WWD**	**297**
N801SS	**S65**	**465-40**
N801TA	550	489
N801WB	**125**	**258287**
N801WC	**G2**	**183**
N802AB	**560**	**0217**
N802CB	550	0802
N802CC	35A	289
N802CC	**G2**	**187**
N802CE	**125**	**258270**
(N802CW)	125	258002
N802D	125	258024
N802DC	125	258024
N802DC	**125**	**258257**
(N802EC)	35A	453
N802F	20	17
N802F	20	26
N802F	20	95
N802GA	G2	2
N802GA	G3	357
N802H	125	259048
N802JA	24	180
N802JH	**525**	**0376**
N802JT	125	258304
N802JW	**35A**	**453**
N802L	23	002
N802MM	125	258073
N802Q	**600**	**1010**
N802TA	125	258453
N802W	24	128
N802WC	**G4**	**1289**
N802X	**125**	**258125**
(N803AU)	WWD	149
N803CC	G3	378
N803CE	**125**	**258271**
N803E	400	RJ-16
N803F	20	12
N803F	200	492
N803GA	G2	150
N803GA	G2	47
N803H	125	258273
N803JA	23	024
N803JT	125	258309
N803JW	**AST**	**038**
N803L	23	003
N803L	24B	195
N803LC	20	18
N803LJ	23	028A
N803LJ	23	045A
(N803MM)	20	272
N803PF	25D	213
(N803RA)	10	80
(N803SR)	10	139
N803TA	**125**	**258455**
N803X	**125**	**258127**
N804AC	**125**	**258368**
N804CB	550	0804
N804CC	35A	093
N804F	20	14
N804F	20	30
N804F	20	5
N804F	20	50
N804GA	G2	151/24
N804GA	G2	172
N804GA	G2	187
N804GA	G2	87/775/6
N804H	125	258274
N804JA	23	088
N804JH	**2xx**	**63**
N804JJ	**10**	**105**
N804JT	125	258311
N804JW	**AST**	**069**
N804LJ	23	004
N804LJ	23	015A
N804PA	**S65**	**465-4**
N804PH	**25D**	**361**
N804TA	**125**	**258461**
N804X	**125**	**258128**
N805BB	500	305
N805C	200	492
N805C	600	1037
N805CC	20	83
N805CC	G2	123/25
N805F	20	32
N805F	20	6
N805F	20	60
N805GA	G2	157
N805GA	G2	174
N805GA	G2	220
N805GT	**650**	**0212**
N805H	125	258264
(N805HD)	75A	380-39
N805JA	23	082
N805JW	**AST**	**070**
N805LJ	23	010
N805LJ	23	048
N805M	125	257129
N805NA	**24A**	**102**
N805RG	80A	380-48
(N805SA)	WWD	145
N805SM	**WWD**	**145**
N805TA	**125**	**258466**
N805X	**125**	**258205**
N805Y	G2	56
N806C	550	010
N806CC	G2	134
N806CC	G2	204
N806CC	G2	46
N806CC	G3	472
N806F	20	15
N806F	20	31
N806F	20	64
N806F	20	8
N806F	200	490
N806GA	G2	156/31
N806GA	G2	176
N806GA	G2	209
N806GA	G2	232
N806H	125	258265
N806LJ	**23**	**073**
N806LJ	24A	011
N806XM	**125**	**258418**
N807CC	**G2**	**212**
N807F	10	114
N807F	20	16
N807F	20	33
N807F	20	7
N807F	20	71
N807G	125	25121
N807GA	G2	105
N807GA	G2	212
N807GA	G2	233
N807H	125	258286
N807JW	**AST**	**100**
N807LJ	23	018
N807PA	20	71
N807Z	**601**	**5040**
N808BC	501	403
N808CC	**125**	**25286**
N808D	24	138
N808DM	550	093
N808DP	24	138
N808DP	25	043
N808DS	25D	225
N808EB	75A	380-51
N808F	20	11
N808F	20	34
N808F	20	86
N808G	**601**	**5098**
N808GA	G2	106
N808GA	G2	193
N808GA	G2	208
N808GA	G2	231
N808GA	G2	234
N808H	125	258285
N808HS	**525**	**0051**
(N808HS)	525	0100
N808JA	23	050A
N808JW	**GXY**	**010**
N808LJ	23	050A
N808RP	**125**	**256041**
N808T	G3	463
N808V	125	25238
N808WA	**525**	**0290**
N809F	**10**	**182**
N809F	20	35
N809F	20	393
N809F	20	9
N809GA	G2	107
N809GA	G2	47
N809H	125	258268
N809JC	**WWD**	**298**
N809LJ	24	055
N809LS	G2	47
N809M	125	257081
N809P	20	35
N810AA	125	258023
N810BG	**125**	**258010**
N810CC	35A	486
N810CR	125	25241
N810CR	**125**	**257071**
N810D	601	5075
N810D	**604**	**5331**
N810E	10	60
N810F	20	10
N810F	20	151
N810F	20	36
N810GA	G2	108
N810GA	G2	165/37
N810GA	G2	191
N810GA	G2	224
N810GS	**125**	**257061**
N810HS	**125**	**25271**
(N810J)	10	139
N810JT	550	289
N810M	125	257102
(N810M)	90X	33
N810MC	125	25201
N810MC	**550**	**225**
N810ME	WWD	372
N810MT	600	1024
N810MT	WWD	372
N810NE	125	258100
N810PA	20	151
N810RA	**20**	**81**
N810SC	125	257179

N810SC	550	032
N810SG	550	032
N810SS	**525**	**0137**
N810US	10	53
N810V	125	257058
N810V	S550	0149
N810X	**750**	**0081**
(N811)	STR	5227
N811AA	125	258024
N811AA	**20**	**187**
N811BB	601	5039
N811BB	604	5333
N811BP	601	5039
N811BP	**604**	**5405**
N811BR	601	5039
N811CC	125	258267
N811CP	31A	168
N811DD	**35A**	**384**
N811DF	35A	384
N811DF	**G2**	**244**
N811DJ	**D1A**	**A022SA**
N811GA	G2	109
N811GA	G2	166/15
N811GA	G2	192
N811HL	**501**	**503**
N811JK	G3	434
N811JK	G4	1030
N811JK	**G4**	**1140**
N811JT	650	0204
N811JW	601	5063
N811MT	**600**	**1024**
N811PA	20	196
N811PD	25B	138
N811PS	31A	166
(N811SW)	G4	1170
N811VC	551	062
N811VC	**WWD**	**331**
N811VG	**551**	**062**
N812AA	125	258027
N812AA	**20**	**57**
N812AM	100	210
N812G	**604**	**5330**
N812G	WWD	389
N812GA	G2	168
N812GA	G2	236
N812GS	601	5098
N812KC	10	189
N812LJ	23	038
N812LJ	23	077
N812M	125	25052
N812M	125	257081
N812M	WWD	389
N812MM	25D	357
N812N	125	25052
N812PA	EC	125
N812RS	**G2**	**98/38**
N812TT	125	25046
N813A	550	562
N813AA	125	258029
N813AA	**20**	**25/405**
N813AS	**35A**	**167**
N813AV	10	28
N813BR	**S60**	**306-8**
N813CB	550	0813
N813DH	550	142
N813H	125	257009
N813JW	**25**	**038**
N813M	35A	151
N813MK	20	272
N813P	20	121
N813PA	20	121
N813PR	**125**	**25137**
N813RR	35A	391
(N814AA)	10	157
N814AA	20	31
N814CC	S550	0018
N814CE	STR	5217
N814CM	560	0170
N814D	**125**	**25237**
N814GA	G2	110
N814GA	G2	44
N814HH	24B	202
N814JR	**24B**	**202**
N814K	**WWD**	**106**
N814L	23	014
N814LJ	23	069
N814M	125	25196
N814M	35A	077
N814M	**900**	**155**
N814NA	STR	5003
N814P	**125**	**25148**
N814PA	20	202
(N814PJ)	100	225
(N814T)	WWD	106
N815A	31A	118
N815A	35A	142
N815A	**45**	**074**
N815AA	125	258032
N815AA	**20**	**205**
N815AC	20	206
N815BC	WWD	301
(N815BS)	400	RJ-30
N815CA	50	6
N815CC	125	258100
N815CE	**550**	**239**
N815CM	**560**	**0104**
N815DD	35A	414
N815E	**31A**	**118**
N815GA	G2	111
N815GA	G2	45
N815GK	550	228
N815H	**S550**	**0146**
N815HC	500	005
N815J	25	045
N815L	**35A**	**142**
N815LC	10	46
N815LJ	23	067
N815MC	**525**	**0142**
N815RB	35A	647
N815RC	STR	5226
N815RC	WWD	301
N816AA	125	258035
N816AA	**20**	**290**
N816CC	**604**	**5451**
N816CW	**125**	**258016**
N816GA	G2	112
N816GA	G2	215
N816GA	G2	237/43
N816H	125	258288
N816H	WWD	323
N816HB	**AST**	**028**
(N816JA)	25B	091
N816JA	35A	394
N816JA	WWD	328
N816LJ	23	088
N816LL	501	411
N816M	125	25052
N816M	35	030
N816M	**50**	**99**
N816MC	125	25052
N816PD	600	1069
N816QS	**125**	**258416**
N816RD	STR	5218
(N816S)	D1A	A022SA
N816S	WWD	360
N816SP	**601**	**5030**
N816SQ	601	5030
N816SQ	**700**	**9009**
N816SR	700	9009
N816ST	WWD	360
N816V	S550	0149
N817AA	125	258036
N817AA	**20**	**233**
N817AM	**55**	**082**
N817BD	**STR**	**5083/49**
N817CB	550	0817
N817CJ	525	0174
N817GA	G2	113
N817GA	G2	222
N817GR	D1A	A062SA
(N817H)	125	258279
N817JS	**20**	**181**
N817LS	**700**	**9035**
N817M	50	24
N818	125	257020
N818AA	125	258039
N818AA	**20**	**36**
N818AJ	**550**	**0818**
(N818CD)	500	297
N818CD	500	311
N818CP	20	71
N818DW	75A	380-30
(N818E)	600	1069
N818GA	G2	114
N818GA	G2	227
(N818GY)	25C	116
N818LD	**75A**	**380-30**
N818LJ	23	028
N818LS	600	1047
N818LS	601	5090
N818LS	**604**	**5315**
N818R	500	170
N818SH	20	71
N818SL	604	5391
N818TB	550	460
N818TG	125	258018
N818TH	600	1069
N818TH	**601**	**5046**
N818TH	601	5090
N818TP	125	256026
N818TP	550	460
(N818TP)	650	0120
N819AA	125	258041
N819AA	**20**	**26**
N819GA	G2	115
N819GA	G2	17
N819GA	G2	178
N819GA	G2	228
N819GF	24D	230
N819GY	25C	116
N819GY	**75A**	**380-66**
N819H	500	263
N819JA	WWD	328
N819JE	35A	077
N819M	125	257170
N819RC	**WWD**	**192**
N819Y	551	311
N820	500	310
N820	550	239
N820AA	125	258042
N820AA	**20**	**118**
N820CB	**550**	**0820**
N820CE	10	111
N820CE	**525**	**0368**
N820DY	75A	380-40
N820F	S550	0118
N820FJ	500	310
N820FJ	550	299
N820FJ	**650**	**0183**
N820FJ	S550	0118
N820JM	550	0856
N820JM	550	0885
N820JR	S40	282-135
N820L	**23**	**020**
N820M	25D	342
N820MC	125	25211
N820MC	**550**	**117**
N820MG	**125**	**25211**
N820RP	**35A**	**410**
(N820RT)	25	023
(N820RT)	WWD	157
N820SA	550	299
N821AA	125	258044
N821AA	**20**	**203**
N821AA	20	67/414
N821AW	25B	101
N821BS	50	23
N821G	550	604
N821GA	G2	116
N821GA	G2	229
N821GA	G2	250
N821H	WWD	268
N821LG	10	170
N821LG	WWD	430
(N821LL)	24B	216
N821LM	25D	317
N821MD	STR	5211
(N821MS)	25B	121
N821P	**525**	**0354**
N821PC	35A	486
N821WN	**S65**	**465-25**
N822AA	125	258045
N822AA	**20**	**195**
N822BL	**125**	**256067**
N822CA	**35A**	**591**
N822CA	G2	99
N822CB	550	0822
N822CC	125	25142
N822GA	G2	117
N822GA	G2	257/17
N822LJ	23	080
N822MJ	**560**	**5023**
N822QS	125	258422
N823AA	125	258046
N823AA	**20**	**228/473**
N823CA	**35A**	**600**
(N823CB)	550	0823
N823GA	G2	118
N823GA	G2	188
N823GA	G2	258
N823GA	G2	75/7
N823GA	**G4**	**1005**
N823J	35A	171
N823LJ	23	082A
N823M	24	050
N823NA	**550**	**260**
N823TR	**60**	**068**
N824AA	125	258047
N824CA	**G4**	**1010**
N824CB	**550**	**0824**
N824CT	**550**	**650**
N824CW	**125**	**258124**
N824DW	**D1A**	**A075SA**
N824GA	24F	342
N824GA	G2	119/22
N824GA	G2	77
N824JK	601	5118
N824K	125	257111
N824LJ	23	083
N824MG	**55**	**106**
N824R	**50**	**121**
N824TJ	125	25179
N825A	**25B**	**111**
N825AA	**125**	**258049**
N825AA	24	147
N825CA	**35A**	**605**
N825CT	**125**	**257041**
N825D	**25D**	**263**
N825DM	24D	237
(N825EC)	WWD	403
N825GA	525	0027
N825GA	G2	119/22
N825GA	G2	120
N825GA	G2	198/35
N825HL	501	657
N825HL	S550	0088
N825JL	WWD	307
N825LJ	23	008
N825LJ	23	085
N825LJ	**35A**	**496**
N825MG	**55**	**055**
N825PS	125	258117
N825PS	**501**	**630**
N825SB	**S40**	**282-92**
N825TC	20	52
N825XP	125	258425
N826AA	125	258051
N826AA	**20**	**67/414**
N826AC	**560**	**0242**
N826AG	G2	166/15
N826CA	**35A**	**596**
N826CT	**125**	**258117**
N826CW	**125**	**258026**
N826EW	550	622
N826GA	**125**	**258263**
N826GA	G2	166/15
N826GA	G2	200
N826GA	G2	79
N826HS	**525**	**0305**
N826JP	601	5050
N826K	125	257119
N826L	23	007
N826RD	500	290
N826RD	**C21A**	**509**
(N826SU)	125	258249
N827AA	**20**	**298**

N827CA	**35A**	**590**
N827DP	**550**	**660**
N827G	G3	398
N827GA	G2	80
N827GA	**G3**	**398**
N827JB	**550**	**577**
N827JB	550	604
(N827JK)	G4	1140
N827K	**G2**	**221**
N827RH	125	258224
N827SL	**75A**	**380-53**
N828AA	20	31
N828B	550	346
N828C	**AST**	**055**
N828G	650	0138
N828GA	G2	247
N828GA	G2	81
N828M	24	050
N828M	35	063
N828MG	**G3**	**409**
N828MW	24	050
N828QA	25	052
(N828SH)	550	275
N828WB	S550	0097
N829AA	**25B**	**100**
N829CA	**35A**	**459**
N829CB	**550**	**0829**
N829GA	G2	199/19
N829GA	G2	245/30
N829JC	**S550**	**0059**
N829JM	550	215
N829NL	550	037
N830	WWD	442
N830BH	G2	49
N830CB	601	5057
N830CB	650	0160
N830CB	G4	1263
N830CB	S550	0004
N830CD	601	5057
N830EC	G4	1229
N830G	**G2**	**44**
N830GA	G2	241
(N830GB)	650	0160
N830KE	**550**	**0830**
N830MA	WWD	358
N830MF	20	112
(N830SR)	10	149
N830TE	G2	49
N830TL	G2	35
N830TL	G2	49
N830VL	550	410
(N830WM)	25D	355
N831CB	501	640
N831CB	650	0160
(N831CJ)	125	257074
N831CJ	35A	166
N831CJ	**601**	**5050**
N831CW	**35A**	**390**
N831CW	500	159
N831GA	G2	238
N831GA	G2	3
N831HG	**20**	**310**
N831J	35A	166
N831LC	125	25095
N831LH	**25D**	**244**
N831NW	**125**	**25231**
N831RA	**24**	**164**
N831S	**525**	**0031**
(N831TJ)	D1A	A018SA
N831WM	25B	076
N832CB	560	0110
N832CB	**650**	**7020**
N832GA	G2	122
N832GA	G2	4/8
(N832MB)	125	25231
N832MJ	125	258040
N832MR	125	25231
N832MR	**125**	**258040**
N832QB	**560**	**0110**
N832UJ	**550**	**0832**
N833	501	416
N833GA	24	155
N833GA	G2	103
N833GA	G2	8
N833JL	**501**	**416**
N833JP	**125**	**258044**
N833QS	**125**	**258433**
N833RL	650	0019
N834CB	550	0834
N834GA	G2	124
N834GA	G2	6
N834GA	G2	62
N834H	**650**	**0177**
N835AC	24	162
N835AC	35A	158
N835AG	24	162
N835CB	550	0835
N835CW	**125**	**258035**
N835F	10	135
N835GA	35A	087
N835GA	G2	11
N835GA	G2	63
(N835GM)	25	027
(N835MA)	75A	380-36
N835QS	125	258435
N835TS	125	258035
N835WB	25	027
N836GA	36A	027
N836GA	G2	64/27
N836ME	G2	95/39
N836MF	G2	154/28
N836MF	G2	95/39
N836MF	G3	351
N836QS	**125**	**258436**
N836UC	20	181
N837CS	25D	351
N837F	10	137
N837GA	G2	65
N837MA	**500**	**096**
N838GA	G2	18
N838GA	G2	66
N838MF	**G4**	**1012**
N838QS	**125**	**258338**
N839DW	**550**	**0839**
N839F	50	55
N839GA	G2	19
N839GA	G2	67
N840AR	WWD	121
N840F	20	18
N840FJ	**50**	**223**
N840GL	35A	210
N840H	125	25230
N840MA	80A	380-21
(N840MC)	501	448
N840MC	**550**	**426**
N840QS	**125**	**258340**
N840SW	**31A**	**084**
N840TJ	D1A	A084SA
N841F	20	19
N841F	50	63
N841G	24	162
N841G	650	0136
N841GL	35A	235
N841LC	24	167
N841MA	501	532
N841PC	601	5116
N841TT	**35A**	**416**
N841WS	**550**	**0841**
N842CB	**550**	**0842**
(N842CC)	550	038
N842F	20	20
N842F	20	38
N842GL	25D	270
N842PM	**PRM**	**RB-4**
N843B	**125**	**25214**
N843F	20	21
N843F	20	39
N843G	650	0173
N843G	S550	0152
N843GA	25	009
N843GA	**AST**	**121**
N843GL	35A	237
N843HS	G3	496
N843MG	200	491
N844F	**100**	**201**
N844F	20	23
N844GA	24	165
N844GA	**GXY**	**004**
N844GL	35A	238
N844GS	**G4**	**1107**
N844HS	G4	1289
N844X	**50**	**93**
N849CW	125	258045
N845F	20	24
N845FW	G3	875
N845GA	G2	74
N845GA	**GXY**	**012**
N845GL	35A	221
N845HS	**G5**	**568**
N846F	20	26
N846GA	25	010
N846GL	35A	242
N846HC	25	010
N846HS	**550**	**669**
N846YC	25	012
N846YT	25	012
N847C	**S550**	**0003**
N847F	20	27
N847G	650	0101
N847G	S550	0003
N847GA	24	167
N847GA	GXY	007
N847GL	35A	239
N847HS	550	661
N847RH	125	258224
N848AB	**STR**	**5214**
N848C	**400**	**RJ-63**
N848C	WWD	54
N848D	**551**	**039**
N848F	20	28
N848G	**560**	**0465**
N848G	S550	0152
N848GA	AST	111
N848GL	35A	488
N848HS	**550**	**720**
N848MP	10	118
N848N	**125**	**258371**
N848US	650	0060
N848W	125	256044
(N849CB)	550	0849
N849F	20	29
N849GA	**GXY**	**009**
N849GL	24D	279
N849HS	**WWD**	**344**
N850BA	550	134
N850BA	560	0322
N850BL	125	259033
N850BM	125	258142
N850CA	50	75
N850CC	**S65**	**465-38**
N850CS	S65	465-38
N850DG	**525**	**0268**
N850FB	**601**	**5162**
N850FL	601	5162
N850GA	G2	98/38
N850MA	501	481
N850MC	**650**	**0090**
N850MM	35A	596
N850MX	**25D**	**286**
N850SC	25	023
N850SM	**125**	**258074**
N850TJ	D1A	A054SA
N850WW	WWD	338
N851BA	24B	194
N851BC	501	514
N851CC	24E	339
N851CW	**125**	**258051**
N851GA	G2	99
N851JH	24X	207
N851L	35A	114
N851WC	STR	5229
N852GA	24	173
N852GA	G2	100
N852QS	**125**	**258452**
N852SC	25	006
N852SP	**551**	**172**
N852WC	125	257095
(N852WC)	36	013
N852WR	551	151
N853DS	25	012
N853GA	25	012
N853GA	G2	101
N853KB	501	637
N853WC	125	257032
N854GA	**20**	**279/502**
N854GA	24	174
(N854GA)	55	056
N854GA	G2	102/32
N854WC	125	257058
N854WC	20	40
N855CD	S60	306-85
N855DB	**55**	**062**
(N855DH)	650	0014
N855GA	24	158
N855GA	G2	103
N855QS	**125**	**258355**
N855W	24	159
N855W	24B	191
N855W	24B	199
N856BB	**525**	**0381**
N856G	25	013
N856GA	G2	104/10
N856JB	**23**	**052**
N856MA	**S60**	**306-41**
N856RR	35A	496
N856W	G2	104/10
N856W	G3	484
N857AA	**550**	**0901**
N857BL	560	0381
N857BT	550	231
N857GA	25	014
N857PR	**55**	**073**
(N857SC)	25	006
N857W	S65	465-72
N858GM	25	015
N858JR	**125**	**257100**
(N858SH)	STR	5117/35
N858TM	35A	409
N858W	G2	104/10
N859GA	G2	180
N859GM	24	175
N859L	24	175
N860DD	**525**	**0271**
N860E	10	52
N860GA	G2	181
N860JH	**550**	**0860**
N860MX	**25B**	**109**
N860PD	**60**	**073**
N860S	**35A**	**086**
N860W	**650**	**7086**
N861BB	550	0861
N861CE	125	258006
N861CE	560	0273
N861GA	25	018
N861GA	G2	184
N861GS	WWD	356
(N861L)	25	023
N861PD	**525**	**0027**
N861QS	**125**	**258361**
(N862BD)	35A	087
N862CE	**125**	**258089**
N862CE	G2	109
N862CE	G3	306
N862G	G2	188
N862G	G3	329
N862GA	G2	185
N862GA	G2	22
N862GA	G3	338
N862PD	35A	087
N862QS	**125**	**258362**
N863AB	**WWD**	**196**
N863BD	50	161
N863CE	**125**	**258289**
N863CE	G3	306
N863GA	G2	23
N863QS	**125**	**258463**
N864CB	550	0864
N864CE	**G4**	**1085**
N864CL	24B	229
N864D	550	313
N864EC	**650**	**7014**
(N864TT)	501	477
N865M	**560**	**0179**
N865SM	**125**	**258365**
N865VP	**20**	**360**
N866BB	**400A**	**RK-98**

N866CB	550	0866
N866DB	23	018
N866DH	WWD	78
N866FP	50	22
N866JM	WWD	184
N866JS	23	018
N866MM	20	175
N866RR	**125**	**258405**
N867CE	G4	1195
N867CW	550	094
N867JS	31A	086
N868CE	**601**	**5016**
(N868CE)	G3	306
N868CP	**WWD**	**341**
(N868D)	500	338
N868J	23	077
N868JB	560	5048
N868JB	**560**	**5089**
N868JS	31A	087
N868JT	**560**	**0310**
N869B	23	089
N869CS	G2	2
(N869EG)	S65	465-33
N869GA	G2	29
N869JS	60	005
N869K	500	077
N869KC	S65	465-33
N869KM	125	257165
N870	**50**	**251**
N870AJ	**560**	**0048**
N870F	20	40
N870GA	G2	125/26
N870GA	G2	30/4
N870JS	60	028
N870MH	550	475
N870P	400A	RK-20
N870P	D1A	A015SA
N870PT	**550**	**383**
N870R	S40	282-137
N870WC	550	695
N871CB	550	0871
N871D	125	257134
N871D	G2	145
N871D	G2	245/30
N871D	STR	5067
N871E	G2	145
N871F	20	42
N871GA	G2	129
N871GA	G2	49
N872AT	**125**	**258278**
N872D	125	25275
N872E	G2	257/17
N872EC	650	0113
N872F	20	43
N872GA	G2	130
N872JR	24	173
N873	WWD	137
N873D	125	25160
N873D	500	337
N873DB	560	0184
N873E	G3	320
N873EJ	WWD	167
N873F	20	44
N873G	125	25160
N873G	601	3009
N873GA	G2	132
N873LP	35A	104
N873LP	35A	220
N873LP	**35A**	**659**
N873LR	**35A**	**220**
N874A	**G4**	**1285**
N874AJ	S40	282-70
N874G	**650**	**0137**
N874GA	G2	136
N874JD	35A	457
N874QS	**125**	**258474**
N874RA	**G3**	**361**
(N875E)	G2	119/22
(N875E)	G3	361
N875F	20	47
N875G	**601**	**3019**
N875GA	G2	137
N875GA	G2	55
N875H	**601**	**5093**

N875HS	**WWD**	**370**
N875PK	600	1018
N875QS	**125**	**258375**
N875SC	125	258111
N875SC	650	0027
N876CB	550	0876
N876CS	**35A**	**616**
N876F	20	45
N876G	**650**	**7062**
N876GA	G2	57
N876H	**125**	**258303**
N876JC	125	257055
N876MA	**10**	**63**
N876MC	**24B**	**217**
N876RW	G3	355
N876SC	125	258124
N876SC	20	391
N876SC	650	0076
N876WB	**500**	**347**
N877BP	500	255
N877C	501	376
N877CM	650	7077
N877CW	125	258077
N877DM	601	5174
N877G	**650**	**7063**
(N877GB)	550	232
N877J	**400A**	**RK-69**
N877RF	**560**	**0318**
N877RP	**125**	**258084**
N877S	**125**	**258323**
N877S	400	RJ-17
N877S	400A	RK-17
N877S	400A	RK-69
N877S	D1A	A055SA
N877T	D1A	A055SA
N877Z	400A	RK-17
N878DE	24	153
N878F	20	48
N878G	**G4**	**1331**
N878GA	G2	58
N878ME	25D	351
N878SM	**G4**	**1319**
N878W	24X	207
N879F	20	50
N879GA	G2	59
N879QS	**125**	**258379**
N879RA	STR	5023
N880A	G2	38
N880CK	S60	306-121
N880CM	501	398
(N880CR)	125	257177
N880F	20	51
N880F	50	3
N880GA	G2	139/11
N880GA	G2	86/16
N880GC	**G4**	**1016**
N880GM	G2	42/12
(N880HL)	S40	282-72
N880HM	400	RJ-19
N880KC	S60	306-121
N880M	**125**	**258027**
N880M	501	524
N880P	20	51
N880RJ	**G2**	**159**
N880SC	125	256018
N880SP	**125**	**258298**
N880WD	**G2**	**217**
N880WW	WWD	195
N880Z	**WWD**	**203**
(N881BA)	650	0081
N881CA	**35A**	**508**
N881CA	500	132
N88CJ	601	5050
N881DM	**S40**	**282-137**
N881F	20	52
N881FC	24	175
N881G	20	399
N881G	**750**	**0101**
N881G	900	104
N881GA	G2	140/40
N881GA	G2	153
N881GA	G2	88/21
N881J	20	396
(N881JT)	125	259043

N881JT	200	513
N881JT	500	159
N881KS	**525**	**0300**
N881M	**50**	**83**
(N881M)	500	073
N881MC	S40	282-19
N881MC	S60	306-100
N881MD	S40	282-19
N881P	10	33
N881P	**900**	**146**
N881TW	**604**	**5348**
N881W	35A	269
N882C	**601**	**5065**
N882CA	500	296
N882CW	**125**	**258002**
N882F	20	56
N882GA	G2	142
N882GA	G2	89
N882KB	**650**	**0095**
N882KB	S550	0075
N882RB	**S550**	**0075**
N882SB	25D	227
N882W	G2	109
N883A	G3	416
N883F	20	57
N883GA	G2	143
N883GA	G2	90
N883PF	**S550**	**0083**
N883RA	**S65**	**465-22**
N883XL	500	177
N884BB	560	5036
N884F	20	58
N884GA	G2	92
N885BH	**20**	**272**
N885CA	500	255
N885CA	AST	039
N885DR	WWD	279
N885F	20	60
N885GA	G2	93
N885TW	**31A**	**165**
N886CA	500	258
N886CS	35	023
N886CW	**125**	**258006**
N886DC	**900**	**177**
N886F	20	54
N886GA	G2	94
N886GB	125	257002
N886MJ	100	199
N886QS	**125**	**258486**
N886R	**35A**	**269**
N886S	**125**	**257025**
N886WC	24B	213
N886WC	35	023
N887BB	**550**	**0887**
(N887DM)	501	476
N887F	20	61
N887GA	G2	95/39
N887PC	AST	015
N887PL	WWD	195
N887QS	**125**	**258387**
N887SA	**550**	**604**
N888AC	500	349
N888AR	20	33
N888AZ	**601**	**3024**
N888B	24	167
N888BH	501	526
N888BL	35A	140
N888BS	35A	409
N888CF	G2	10
N888CF	STR	5070/52
N888CJ	**125**	**25084**
N888CN	**750**	**0086**
N888CP	**31**	**003**
N888CR	125	25180
N888CW	**G3**	**489**
N888CX	**45**	**044**
N888DB	25XR	073
N888DE	35	010
N888DF	25B	189
N888DH	125	258051
N888DH	25B	109
N888DH	35	010
N888DH	**601**	**5014**
N888DJ	35A	067

N888DL	HFB	1051
N888DS	23	013
N888DS	501	449
(N888DT)	35A	187
N888EB	550	350
N888FA	**24D**	**257**
(N888FK)	55	108
N888FL	**501**	**371**
N888FW	600	1079
N888G	100	197
N888GA	500	132
N888GA	G2	96
N888GC	25D	258
N888GZ	500	349
N888HW	551	108
(N888JA)	25D	301
N888JA	**601**	**5049**
N888JD	500	132
(N888JK)	MSP	043
N888JR	20	144
N888KS	600	1073
N888KU	**525**	**0068**
N888L	20	144
N888LG	G4	1125
N888LK	G4	1125
N888LK	**G4**	**1362**
N888LR	25B	171
N888LW	600	1025
N888MC	**24**	**106**
N888MC	G2	247
N888MC	G3	351
N888MC	G4	1086
N888MC	S60	306-39
N888MJ	**501**	**097**
(N888MP)	WWD	147
N888MV	35A	362
N888MW	550	028
(N888NA)	550	723
N888NS	24	106
N888PM	125	256041
N888PM	G3	435
N888PM	**G4**	**1195**
N888PM	S40	282-12
N888PT	35A	391
N888R	WWD	254
N888RA	**525**	**0135**
N888RB	25B	150
N888RF	20	272
N888RF	551	108
N888RK	**525**	**0331**
N888RT	**550**	**275**
N888RW	STR	5040
N888SQ	**G4**	**1305**
N888SS	125	258106
N888SW	125	257134
N888SW	G2	117
(N888TN)	36A	026
N888TW	**24D**	**292**
N888TX	650	7003
N888UE	G4	1032
N888VS	**G3**	**450**
(N888WJ)	10	89
N888WK	125	25141
N888WL	G3	471
N888WL	S60	306-27
N888WS	20	148
N888WS	**601**	**5170**
N888WT	STR	5070/52
(N888WW)	STR	5061/48
N888XL	**500**	**177**
N888ZZ	**125**	**258017**
N889DH	125	258051
N889DW	**60**	**117**
N889F	20	64
N889G	650	0023
N889GA	G2	97
N889JC	**G2**	**158**
N889JF	24	019
N889WF	24	060
N889WF	24D	237
N890A	125	258071
N890A	G2	16/13
N890A	G3	325
N890A	G4	1396

N890BH	**400A**	**RK-208**
(N890E)	10	53
N890F	20	65
N890FH	**50**	**31**
N890GA	50	89
N890HJ	HFB	1026
N890K	25C	089
N890MC	650	0199
(N890MC)	STR	5033/56
N890RC	125	25084
N890WW	WWD	190
N891CA	**500**	**168**
N891CQ	10	53
N891F	20	66
N891HJ	HFB	1036
N891M	**560**	**0085**
N891MG	**G3**	**357**
N892CA	500	044
N892F	20	68
N892GA	G2	60
N892HJ	HFB	1037
N892PB	**550**	**064**
N892SB	**20**	**379**
N892SB	560	0208
N893AC	**601**	**5018**
N893CA	**501**	**374**
N893CM	**560**	**0226**
N893F	20	69
N893HJ	HFB	1039
N893M	**560**	**0237**
N893QS	**125**	**258393**
N893WA	25B	169
N894CA	10	36
N894CA	**125**	**258366**
N894F	20	133
N894GA	G2	145
N894HJ	HFB	1045
N894TW	**WWD**	**354**
N895CC	**125**	**257072**
N895F	20	134
N895HJ	HFB	1051
N895LD	**560**	**0034**
N896EC	650	0196
N896GA	G2	149
N896HJ	HFB	1054
N896MA	500	290
N896MA	**550**	**134**
N896MB	**500**	**290**
N896R	60	091
N897AT	400A	RK-157
N897CW	125	258077
N897D	20	134
N897DM	20	134
N897GA	G2	146
N897HJ	HFB	1055
N897MC	**550**	**0914**
N897R	**60**	**097**
N898CB	**560**	**0097**
N898GA	G2	147
N898GF	**560**	**0121**
N898R	**604**	**5408**
N898SR	WWD	224
N899BC	**560**	**5030**
N899CS	**31A**	**052**
N899DC	**550**	**0899**
N899DM	**125**	**257028**
N899GA	**G2**	**43**
N899GM	**G5**	**508**
N899N	500	114
N899QS	125	258399
N899S	WWD	101
(N899SA)	125	25146
N899SC	60	040
N899TG	S40	282-13
N899WA	**35**	**049**
N899WW	601	3011
N900AF	550	022
N900AJ	**25**	**027**
N900AL	**G4**	**1097**
(N900AR)	10	157
N900BA	550	242
N900BD	24	143
(N900BF)	900	39
(N900BF)	900	71

N900BF	**G2**	**206**
N900BF	WWD	382
N900BJ	**35A**	**123**
N900BL	125	257185
(N900BM)	550	126
N900BR	G2	111
N900BT	D1A	A046SA
N900CC	125	257043
N900CC	601	3042
N900CC	**900**	**183**
N900CD	125	25111
N900CH	20	383/550
N900CH	**50**	**264**
N900CJ	25	020
N900CL	601	5031
N900CL	**601**	**5122**
N900CM	**650**	**0017**
N900CR	**STR**	**5036/42**
N900CS	**900**	**104**
N900CS	S40	282-17
N900CS	WWD	212
N900D	10	141
N900DA	**900**	**170**
N900DB	20	327
(N900DG)	35A	378
N900DH	501	576
N900DH	**G2**	**111**
N900DL	24	109
N900DL	501	576
N900DM	501	421
N900DM	**S550**	**0067**
N900DP	**600**	**1036**
N900DS	125	25187
(N900DU)	900	97
N900DW	**900**	**179**
N900DW	D1A	A026SA
N900EC	35A	236
N900EJ	**750**	**0109**
N900EL	125	25222
N900EM	35A	185
N900ES	**604**	**5381**
N900ES	G2	174
N900EX	90X	12
N900EX	90X	27
N900EX	90X	40
N900FA	**55**	**024**
N900FC	600	1045
N900FJ	900	10
N900FJ	900	116
N900FJ	900	126
N900FJ	900	131
N900FJ	900	147
N900FJ	900	158
N900FJ	900	166
N900FJ	900	179
N900FJ	900	31
N900FJ	900	42
N900FJ	900	60
N900FJ	900	79
N900FJ	900	98
N900FL	**650**	**7049**
N900FR	20	223
N900FS	**WWD**	**191**
N900G	**500**	**268**
N900GC	**500**	**298**
N900GG	**24B**	**216**
N900GW	**525**	**0323**
N900H	STR	5135
N900H	**WWD**	**388**
N900HC	**900**	**68**
N900HG	**90X**	**1**
N900JA	24	108
N900JB	**50**	**59**
N900JB	55	088
N900JC	**35A**	**178**
N900JD	25	020
N900JD	500	023
(N900JD)	650	0199
N900JD	**650**	**0213**
(N900JD)	650	0215
N900JE	35A	123
N900JE	**35A**	**674**
N900JL	20	171
N900JL	WWD	80

N900JT	**125**	**257147**
N900JV	35A	091
(N900KC)	125	25038
N900KC	125	25191
N900KC	125	257021
N900KC	125	258232
N900KC	500	055
N900LA	**G3**	**379**
N900LC	20	122
N900LC	550	040
N900LH	D1A	A018SA
N900LJ	550	011
(N900LL)	501	499
N900LM	WWD	373
N900LS	**G4**	**1178**
N900MA	**900**	**67**
N900MC	**501**	**427**
N900MD	125	258019
N900MD	36A	045
N900MF	**550**	**074**
N900MJ	900	48
N900MM	501	522
N900MP	500	055
N900MP	**G2**	**99**
N900MR	125	257072
N900MT	**90X**	**57**
N900NA	**24A**	**111**
N900NE	**900**	**83**
N900NM	601	5057
N900NW	WWD	337
N900P	20	36
N900P	25	049
N900P	**31A**	**199**
N900P	35A	457
N900P	525	0234
N900P	S60	306-12
N900PA	**WWD**	**400**
N900PB	**550**	**566**
N900PL	90X	44
N900PS	**501**	**362**
N900Q	25	049
N900Q	**900**	**93**
N900QS	**750**	**0123**
N900R	**35A**	**488**
N900RB	501	664
N900RB	S550	0086
N900RD	35A	261
N900RD	501	664
(N900RG)	S550	0065
N900SA	STR	5148
N900SB	900	14
(N900SB)	90X	12
N900SB	**90X**	**26**
N900SE	550	074
N900SF	G2	167
N900SJ	**900**	**19**
N900SM	900	176
N900T	10	134
N900T	500	135
N900TA	**900**	**50**
(N900TE)	550	203
N900TF	550	203
N900TJ	550	203
N900TJ	**G2**	**199/19**
N900TN	551	430
N900TP	G2	160
N900TR	900	9
N900TW	501	563
N900UC	10	33
N900VL	G2	99
N900VM	**90X**	**64**
N900VP	**WWD**	**289**
N900W	50	60
N900W	500	014
N900WA	25D	248
N900WB	20	139
N900WG	**125**	**25236**
N900WG	900	83
N900WJ	**D1A**	**A028SA**
N900WJ	G2	190
N900WK	**900**	**57**
N900WW	WWD	321
N900Y	24A	111
N900Y	36	014

N901AS	G2	88/21
N901B	900	24
N901BB	900	42
N901BM	601	5044
N901BM	G2	120
N901C	**STR**	**5218**
N901EH	STR	5230
N901FH	**G3**	**333**
N901FH	STR	5230
(N901FJ)	900	147
N901FJ	900	79
N901FR	20	270
N901GA	G3	249
N901H	STR	5092/58
N901JC	**55**	**088**
N901JL	WWD	38
N901K	**125**	**258329**
N901K	G2	36/3
N901K	G4	1075
N901KB	G2	36/3
N901MH	10	110
(N901MS)	35A	360
N901NB	**501**	**661**
N901P	400	RJ-20
N901PV	S550	0156
N901QS	750	0101
N901QS	**750**	**0102**
N901RM	550	242
N901RM	**560**	**0116**
N901SB	20	446
N901SB	200	493
N901SB	650	7008
N901SB	**900**	**33**
N901TC	125	25108
N901TC	20	335
N901TF	**50**	**285**
N901TG	125	25108
N901WG	**G2**	**126**
N901YP	20	360
N902	G2	11
N902	**G4**	**1310**
N902AB	23	068
N902AR	23	068
N902AR	24D	237
N902C	G3	388
N902FR	20	132
N902GA	G2	11
N902JC	**35A**	**227**
N902K	G3	386
N902K	G4	1113
N902K	STR	5104/6
N902KB	G3	386
N902KB	STR	5104/6
N902MP	**G2**	**241**
N902NC	**900**	**97**
N902PC	10	106
(N902PC)	400A	RK-28
N902PM	125	257036
N902QS	**750**	**0002**
N902RM	125	257036
N902RM	**650**	**7022**
N902SB	200	504
N902SB	**650**	**7008**
N902T	500	135
N902WJ	36A	040
N903AG	**G2**	**172**
N903AM	**60**	**104**
(N903FJ)	900	98
N903FJ	90X	3
N903FR	20	20
N903G	G2	172
N903G	S40	282-60
N903GA	G2	172
N903HC	35A	440
N903HC	**45**	**010**
N903K	S40	282-33
N903K	S65	465-57
N903KB	S40	282-33
N903QS	**750**	**0162**
N903SB	20	335
N903SB	**650**	**7061**
N903WJ	35A	380
N904BB	**550**	**0904**
N904FR	20	151

(N904FR)	20	223
N904H	125	258239
N904K	S40	282-42
N904K	S65	465-23
N904KB	S40	282-42
(N904KB)	S65	465-23
N904M	900	40
N904SB	125	258016
N904SB	20	446
N904SB	**50**	**284**
N905BG	S60	306-30
N905EM	550	032
N905EX	90X	5
N905FJ	**900**	**5**
N905FR	20	213
N905H	125	258275
N905K	S40	282-49
N905K	S65	465-17
N905KB	S40	282-49
N905LC	35A	320
N905LC	**550**	**581**
N905LD	35A	320
N905M	S40	282-12
N905MW	HFB	1027
N905P	S60	306-62
N905QS	**750**	**0105**
N905R	S60	306-30
N905R	S60	306-62
N905R	S60	306-99
N905SB	20	360
N905TS	900	5
N905WJ	25B	105
(N905Y)	125	25199
N906FR	20	214
N906SB	125	258016
N906SB	560	0092A
N906SB	900	14
N906SB	S550	0139
N906SU	25B	123
N906WK	**900**	**102**
N907CS	24	137
N907FJ	90X	7
N907FR	20	224
(N907FR)	20	270
N907KH	501	599
N907M	50	35
N907R	S60	306-40
N907SB	560	0109A
N907SB	S550	0141
N907SW	G2	71
N907WS	**601**	**5048**
N908CH	**20**	**383/550**
N908CL	601	5031
N908CL	601	5122
N908EF	50	46
N908EJ	**G2**	**70/1**
N908FR	20	207
N908G	604	5326
N908HC	**35A**	**440**
N908JE	125	257087
N908JE	G2	151/24
N908QS	**750**	**0108**
N908R	**400A**	**RK-44**
N908R	S60	306-18
N908R	S60	306-23
N908R	S60	306-55
N908RF	10	46
(N908SB)	10	46
N909B	125	25082
(N909CA)	550	0909
N909FJ	90X	9
N909FR	20	209
N909GA	D1A	A009SA
N909L	G2	112
N909M	**525**	**0249**
N909MG	600	1010
N909PM	**900**	**176**
N909QS	**750**	**0009**
(N909RG)	S550	0065
N909RX	**G4**	**1239**
(N909SP)	G4	1210
N909ST	**400A**	**RK-194**
(N910A)	G3	367
N910A	G3	369
N910B	**G4**	**1102**
N910BH	**75A**	**380-54**
N910CS	**900**	**126**
N910DC	**G5**	**544**
N910DP	**650**	**0081**
N910DS	S550	0154
N910E	S40	282-29
N910E	STR	5084/8
N910F	650	0051
(N910FJ)	900	10
N910FJ	90X	10
N910FR	20	280/503
N910G	550	575
N910G	STR	5112/7
N910H	550	691
N910JD	125	258258
N910JD	**125**	**258420**
N910JN	**125**	**258258**
N910JW	**900**	**31**
N910L	20	191
N910M	650	0069
N910M	STR	5069/20
N910MH	WWD	45
N910MT	**550**	**057**
N910N	500	158
N910PC	560	0273
N910Q	**900**	**156**
N910QS	**750**	**0110**
N910R	G2	234
N910RB	**550**	**297**
N910S	G2	234
N910S	**G4**	**1155**
N910SH	400A	RK-72
N910U	20	39
N910V	560	0165
N910W	20	192
N910Y	20	48
N910Y	500	158
(N911A)	500	087
N911AE	**35A**	**109**
N911AJ	**25B**	**163**
N911AS	125	25039
N911BB	S550	0128
N911CB	**550**	**662**
(N911CJ)	500	087
N911CR	75A	380-59
N911CR	**STR**	**5150/37**
N911CU	**WWD**	**246**
N911DB	35A	231
N911DB	G2	100
N911DG	**20**	**162/451**
N911DX	**35A**	**499**
N911EM	25D	319
N911FR	20	295/500
N911GM	**500**	**048**
N911HB	**50**	**157**
N911JD	500	082
N911JG	25B	147
(N911JJ)	D1A	A085SA
N911KB	24	128
N911KT	**G3**	**438**
N911LM	**25C**	**070**
N911MG	25D	212
N911ML	**35A**	**256**
N911MM	**501**	**390**
(N911MU)	501	390
(N911NJ)	550	240
N911NP	**525**	**0273**
N911Q	S40	282-17
N911RF	10	46
N911RF	50	46
N911RF	900	20
N911RG	**20**	**144**
N911SB	20	360
N911SP	**WWD**	**244**
N911TR	20	242
N911TR	24	134
N911WT	20	203
N911WW	G2	257/17
N912AS	**125**	**25124**
N912BD	**550**	**580**
N912DA	**WWD**	**147**
N912EX	90X	12
N912SH	**400A**	**RK-128**
N913FJ	90X	12
N913HB	WWD	40
N913JB	604	5338
N913MK	20	272
N913MK	**G3**	**407**
N913QS	**750**	**0113**
N913RC	**500**	**059**
(N913SC)	G4	1305
N913SQ	**650**	**7004**
N913V	10	104
N913V	**125**	**257207**
N913VL	10	104
N913VS	10	106
N914BA	24	128
N914BB	601	3045
N914BD	125	25229
N914BD	601	3045
N914BD	**900**	**80**
N914BS	G2	157
N914CD	**500**	**150**
N914DM	WWD	357
N914DZ	**G2**	**190**
N914H	125	258281
N914J	900	44
N914J	**90X**	**15**
(N914JC)	75A	380-56
N914JL	900	44
N914P	STR	5080
(N914RA)	25B	123
N914SB	25	014
N914SH	**400A**	**RK-193**
N914X	600	1021
N914X	**601**	**5185**
N914X	STR	5080
N914XA	600	1021
N915BB	**550**	**0915**
N915BB	601	5019
N915BD	601	5019
N915BD	**601**	**5091**
N915EX	90X	15
N915JT	125	256002
N915R	S60	306-42
N915RB	35A	647
N915RB	**750**	**0042**
N915US	**24B**	**189**
N916AN	20	64
N916BD	**31A**	**093**
(N916BD)	31A	094
N916CS	**560**	**0400**
N916EX	90X	16
N916H	125	258282
N916PT	125	258103
N916QS	**750**	**0116**
N916RC	**500**	**061**
N916RC	550	211
N916RC	STR	5078/3
(N916RG)	STR	5078/3
N916WJ	550	561
(N917BD)	31A	093
N917BD	**31A**	**094**
N917BE	**WWD**	**291**
N917BF	24D	293
N917J	STR	5082/36
N917JC	**200**	**490**
N917K	125	256015
N917MC	31	012
N917R	G2	17
N917S	55	033
N917W	**G4**	**1158**
N918A	500	168
N918BG	G3	300
N918EX	90X	18
N918GA	550	726
N918H	125	258283
N918MK	**AST**	**089**
N918MM	STR	5069/20
(N918PC)	10	106
N918R	S60	306-19
N918R	S60	306-36
N918TD	**25B**	**166**
(N919AT)	500	209
N919BT	**WWD**	**434**
N919EX	90X	19
N919G	G2	29
N919H	125	258284
N919JH	WWD	154
N919K	24	162
(N919MA)	24D	291
N919P	125	258147
N919S	25	063
N919TG	G2	160
N920C	35A	283
N920CC	25B	136
N920CC	**S65**	**465-16**
N920CF	20	388
N920DC	**G5**	**534**
N920DG	STR	5234
N920DS	**600**	**1023**
N920DS	G2	73/9
N920DY	75A	380-40
N920DY	**S65**	**465-50**
N920DY	STR	5234
N920E	550	317
N920EA	**25**	**057**
N920EX	90X	20
N920FF	24	179
N920G	**20**	**352**
N920G	S60	306-74
N920G	WWD	87
N920GL	29	002
N920GP	WWD	87
N920K	50	154
N920L	20	192
N920MS	**525**	**0089**
N920PM	**560**	**0182**
N920QS	**750**	**0120**
N920R	WWD	45
N920RV	**600**	**1016**
N920S	25	025
N920SA	400A	RK-41
N920US	25B	136
N920W	500	155
N921CC	**S65**	**465-67**
N921DT	WWD	372
N921FP	55ER	103
N921GS	10	130
N921JG	S40	282-38
N921JG	S40	282-105
N921K	601	3044
N921MB	**S60**	**306-135**
N921ML	**20**	**99**
N921RD	125	256032
N921RD	125	257199
N922BA	500	137
N922CK	WWD	299
N922CP	WWD	99
N922CR	125	256014
N922CR	WWD	299
N922CR	WWD	99
N922DS	20	373
N922GL	35A	266
N922GR	125	256014
N922H	**2xx**	**97**
N922JW	**900**	**36**
N922ML	20	380
N922RA	550	397
N922RA	AST	033
N922RR	**125**	**25195**
N922RT	550	397
N922SL	**550**	**034**
N923AR	**525**	**0055**
N923DS	10	117
N923GL	25D	298
N923GL	35A	393
N923JA	WWD	146
N923ML	G2	219/20
N923QS	**750**	**0023**
N923RL	550	426
N923S	**S550**	**0092**
N924AM	**35A**	**188**
N924AS	500	294
N924BW	24	164
N924BW	**25B**	**158**
N924DS	G2	181
N924ED	24	104
N924EJ	750	0024
N924GL	35A	361
N924ML	G4	1234

N924QS	**750**	**0124**
N925AJ	**2xx**	**4**
N925BH	125	256002
N925BL	S40	282-104
N925CT	125	25066
N925DM	**35A**	**486**
N925DP	**125**	**257132**
N925DS	10	116
N925DS	G2	98/38
N925DW	**25D**	**213**
N925EX	90X	25
N925GL	35A	277
N925HB	WWD	53
N925JF	**125**	**258423**
N925N	S60	306-41
N925R	WWD	80
N925WC	125	257132
N925WC	D1A	A080SA
N925WG	125	257132
(N925WL)	S65	465-65
N925WP	25XR	022
N925Z	S60	306-3
N925Z	WWD	307
N926CB	**650**	**0008**
N926CH	**525**	**0087**
N926DS	WWD	189
N926G	125	25038
N926GL	35A	306
N926HC	**650**	**0094**
N926JM	WWD	146
N926LR	125	25098
N926LR	20	139
N926QS	**750**	**0026**
N926RM	**550**	**567**
N926TC	**125**	**257021**
N926ZT	125	257021
N927A	601	3026
N927AA	24	169
N927AA	S65	465-22
(N927DS)	10	116
N927EX	90X	27
N927GL	35A	315
N927R	S60	306-47
N927S	WWD	82
N928CD	60	010
N928CD	**60**	**110**
N928DS	550	276
N928G	WWD	381
N928GD	60	010
N928GF	**G2**	**119/22**
N928GV	WWD	381
N928R	S40	282-90
N928R	S60	306-51
N928RD	**500**	**204**
N928S	25	025
N929A	500	207
N929CA	500	046
N929DS	550	284
N929DS	650	0007
N929GL	29	001
N929GV	G2	258
N929GV	WWD	356
N929GV	WWD	381
N929GV	WWD	48
N929GW	**60**	**165**
N929HG	**2xx**	**79**
N929QS	**750**	**0129**
N929RW	500	046
N929WG	**125**	**258196**
N929WG	D1A	A032SA
N929WT	**G4**	**1317**
N930BS	550	087
N930BS	G2	29
N930DC	**G4**	**1254**
N930GL	35A	330
N930L	20	193
N930M	STR	5114/18
N930MT	STR	5114/18
N930QS	**750**	**0130**
N930RA	**S65**	**465-68**
N930SC	AST	038
N930SD	G2	97
N931BA	35	003
N931CA	500	174

N931CC	50	31
N931CW	G2	85
(N931EJ)	50	31
N931FD	**31A**	**124**
N931G	50	126
N931GL	35A	392
N931RS	**31A**	**184**
N932FD	**31A**	**187**
N932HA	500	220
N932LM	550	297
N932QS	**750**	**0032**
N932S	20	56
N933	125	25186
N933CY	STR	5115/39
N933DB	650	0009
N933EX	90X	33
N933GL	35A	377
N933H	125	258249
N933JC	**75A**	**380-72**
N933LC	STR	5115/39
(N933N)	23	049
N933NA	**23**	**049**
(N933PG)	601	5152
N933QS	**750**	**0133**
N933SH	**650**	**0009**
N934GL	35A	417
N934H	24D	290
N934H	550	188
N934H	**650**	**0172**
N934QS	**750**	**0034**
N935BD	35A	094
N935GA	500	084
N935GL	35A	419
N935H	**125**	**258225**
(N935NA)	35A	213
(N935PC)	75A	380-59
N935QS	**750**	**0135**
N935R	S60	306-56
N935SH	G4	1223
N936H	125	259041
N936QS	**750**	**0036**
N937D	10	75
N937GC	20	76
N937GL	25G	337
N937H	125	258251
(N937H)	125	259041
N937J	10	19
N937M	G2	42/12
N937QS	**750**	**0137**
N937R	S60	306-57
N937US	G2	204
N937US	G4	1092
N938D	**550**	**454**
N938GL	35A	396
N938H	**125**	**258252**
(N938QS)	750	0038
N938R	S60	306-20
N938R	S60	306-48
N938W	**550**	**448**
N938WH	600	1068
N938WH	WWD	209
N939BB	550	0939
N939CK	**20**	**317**
N939EX	90X	39
N939KS	500	289
N939LE	**125**	**258459**
N939SR	500	121
N940BS	G2	157
N940BS	G2	64/27
N940CC	S40	282-34
N940DC	**G4**	**1052**
N940EX	90X	40
N940GA	400	RJ-18
N940HC	125	258195
N940P	**60**	**071**
N940SW	**525**	**0071**
N941CC	50	138
N941CE	**125**	**257083**
N941CW	G2	29
N941GA	25	020
N941H	125	259042
N941HC	**125**	**258195**
N941JC	**500**	**310**
N941QS	**750**	**0141**

N942B	10	105
N942B	500	044
N942BY	31	005
N942C	10	11
N942CC	**75A**	**380-64**
N942DS	**125**	**25032**
N942EX	90X	42
N942FA	WWD	257
N942GA	25	021
N942H	125	258253
(N942M)	10	138
N942WN	**125**	**25079**
N942Y	125	25079
N942Y	**STR**	**5098/28**
N943CC	75A	380-66
N943CE	**125**	**257141**
(N943CL)	WWD	187
N943GA	25XR	022
N943H	125	258254
N943JL	WWD	206
N943LL	**501**	**615**
N943LL	550	442
N943LL	WWD	206
N943QS	**750**	**0043**
N944AD	**900**	**17**
N944AF	550	573
N944B	500	318
N944CA	650	0083
N944H	650	0083
N944H	650	7007
N944H	**750**	**0011**
N944H	G2	251
N944JD	501	424
N944KM	**24E**	**334**
N944L	650	7007
N944M	**WWD**	**364**
N944NA	**G2**	**144**
N944QS	**750**	**0144**
N944TG	501	365
N945AA	501	432
N945BC	501	666
N945CC	**S65**	**465-13**
N945CE	**125**	**257137**
N945FD	**45**	**122**
N945GA	24B	182
N945MC	**10**	**37**
N945NA	**G2**	**118**
N945R	S60	306-59
N945W	35A	301
N946CC	500	206
N946EJ	750	0046
N946EX	90X	46
N946FP	55	056
N946FS	125	25134
N946GM	**WWD**	**215**
N946H	125	258255
N946JR	S60	306-10
N946M	20	146
N946NA	**G2**	**146**
N947CB	**550**	**0947**
N947CC	500	123
N947CE	**125**	**257128**
N947GS	**35A**	**250**
N947H	125	258256
N947LF	**90X**	**44**
N947NA	**G2**	**147**
N947QS	**750**	**0047**
N947R	S40	282-39
N947R	S60	306-60
N947TC	**25D**	**233**
N948DC	550	136
N948H	125	259043
N948N	501	354
N948NA	**G2**	**222**
N948QS	**750**	**0149**
N948R	S60	306-21
N948R	S60	306-50
N949CC	**WWD**	**280**
N949CE	125	257204
N949CV	125	25195
N949CW	125	25195
N949EX	90X	49
N949QS	**750**	**0049**
N950AM	**500**	**095**

N950BS	G2	64/27
N950CS	35A	364
N950CS	S65	465-43
N950F	**50**	**191**
(N950FC)	550	401
N950G	**36A**	**032**
N950GA	24B	184
N950L	20	189
N950P	**525**	**0234**
N950QS	**750**	**0050**
N950RA	**20**	**95**
N950SP	**35A**	**450**
N950SW	**601**	**5032**
N950WA	**560**	**0082**
N951DB	**WWD**	**195**
N951GA	25	030
N951H	125	258257
N951QS	**750**	**0151**
N951RK	**G2**	**191**
N952	25D	291
N952B	125	25100
N952GA	24B	194
N952GL	35A	592
N952HF	WWD	279
(N952TC)	10	31
N953C	**560**	**0163**
(N953DC)	20	300/508
N953EX	90X	53
N953F	**560**	**0005**
N953FT	**550**	**295**
N953GA	24B	197
(N953H)	125	258258
N953QS	**750**	**0153**
N954FA	25	034
N954GA	25	034
N954H	**125**	**258259**
N954S	24	136
(N954SC)	24	019
N955CC	**G2**	**54/36**
N955CP	G3	375
N955DB	**601**	**3044**
N955E	**50**	**14**
N955FD	55	009
N955H	G2	98/38
N955H	G3	378
N955H	G4	1081
N955H	**G4**	**1383**
N955H	STR	5126
(N955HC)	G4	1081
N955HL	STR	5126
N955LS	**55**	**009**
N955MD	55	009
N955PR	**S65**	**465-43**
N955QS	**750**	**0055**
N955R	S60	306-52
(N955WP)	501	528
N956	S40	282-50
N956CC	S40	282-50
N956EX	90X	56
N956GA	25TF	036
N956H	125	259044
N956J	25TF	036
N956PP	**D1A**	**A031SA**
N956QS	**750**	**0156**
N956S	500	056
N957	S40	282-71
N957CC	S40	282-71
N957E	24B	204
N957GA	24B	204
N957H	**125**	**258260**
N957P	**AST**	**104**
N957R	S60	306-53
N957RC	WWD	58
N957SC	24	065
N957TH	20	38
N958DM	25	042
N958EX	**90X**	**58**
N958GA	25	042
N958H	125	258261
N958QS	**750**	**0158**
N958R	S60	306-24
N958R	S60	306-9
N959AT	35	019
N959C	S65	465-50

N959EX	90X	59
N959GA	25	039
N959H	**125**	**258262**
N959KW	125	25020
N959RE	25	039
N959SA	**35A**	**076**
N959SC	23	045A
N959WC	55	030
N960AA	35	003
N960AJ	400A	RK-23
N960CP	550	336
N960DC	**G3**	**378**
N960E	55	033
N960EX	**90X**	**60**
N960FA	**WWD**	**348**
N960GA	25	041
(N960H)	60	013
N960H	60	015
N960HL	60	015
N960JA	**400A**	**RK-191**
N960JJ	400A	RK-191
N960JJ	**400A**	**RK-255**
N960QS	**750**	**0160**
N960TX	**20**	**403**
N961EX	**90X**	**61**
N961H	125	258263
N961JC	**125**	**258062**
N961JC	WWD	208
(N961JD)	WWD	208
N961JE	WWD	208
N961MR	**60**	**003**
N961QS	**750**	**0061**
N961R	S60	306-61
N962	25B	102
N962GA	25	044
N962H	125	259046
(N962HA)	550	248
N962J	**550**	**453**
N962JC	550	453
N962JC	560	0006
N962MV	WWD	385
N962QS	**750**	**0126**
N963EX	**90X**	**63**
N963GA	25	045
N963H	125	259017
N963WA	S60	306-53
N963WL	S60	306-53
N963WL	S65	465-65
N963WM	WWD	88
(N963Y)	31	005
N964C	**S65**	**465-66**
N964CL	**35A**	**152**
N964EJ	**750**	**0064**
N964GA	25	046
N964H	**604**	**5363**
N964J	550	448
N964JC	550	448
N964JC	560	0007
N964M	STR	5148
N964QS	750	0064
N964QS	**750**	**0164**
N965BC	20	107
N965CC	**G2**	**165/37**
N965EX	**90X**	**65**
N965GA	25	048
N965JC	125	257084
N965JC	650	7051
N965M	90X	65
(N965QS)	750	0065
N965R	S60	306-61
N966F	20	70
N966GA	25	049
N966H	650	7006
N966H	**750**	**0012**
N966H	G2	150
N966H	G3	411
N966JM	**560**	**0240**
N966K	650	7006
(N966L)	125	258259
N966L	20	181
N966L	601	3021
N966MT	**560**	**5046**
N966QS	**750**	**0166**
N966SW	**560**	**0284**
N967A	WWD	205
N967EX	**90X**	**67**
N967F	20	71
N967L	125	258273
N967L	601	3004
N967L	601	3021
N967L	601	3023
N967L	WWD	37
N967QS	**750**	**0067**
N967R	S60	306-16
N967R	S60	306-62
N968BN	STR	5109/13
N968DM	501	610
N968F	20	74
N968GN	STR	5109/13
N968L	601	5089
N968R	S60	306-2
N969B	23	089
(N969EG)	WWD	221
N969EX	**90X**	**69**
N969F	10	135
N969F	20	75
N969J	24	106
N969KC	WWD	221
N969MC	35A	590
N969MC	S550	0001
N969MQ	S550	0001
N969MT	35A	459
N969MT	550	072
N969PW	WWD	221
N969RE	**PRM**	**RB-14**
N969SE	**500**	**069**
N969SG	**G4**	**1197**
N969SS	**25D**	**317**
(N969ZS)	500	196
N970EX	**90X**	**70**
N970F	20	76
N970F	55	055
N970GA	**20**	**246/482**
N970GA	24B	209
N970H	55	055
N970QS	**750**	**0070**
N970SU	**525**	**0173**
N970WJ	**25D**	**324**
N971AS	STR	5007/45
N971EC	55	033
N971EC	**G2**	**32/2**
N971F	20	59
N971F	35A	095
N971GA	24B	215
N971H	35A	095
N971L	**G4**	**1116**
N971QS	**750**	**0071**
N972	24D	252
N972D	125	25275
N972F	20	80
N972G	**G3**	**457**
N972GW	500	118
N972H	24D	322
N972H	**25D**	**370**
N972JD	500	118
N972LM	125	257098
N972PF	**PRM**	**RB-38**
N972TF	**WWD**	**138**
N973	25D	254
N973EJ	WWD	168
N973F	20	81
N973GA	25	051
N973JD	25B	123
N974D	23	095
N974F	20	83
N974GA	25	053
N974JD	24B	205
N974JD	25XR	106
N974JD	35A	457
N974JD	35A	648
N974JD	**400A**	**RK-141**
N974M	25	053
N975AA	35	012
N975AD	35	012
N975CM	**400A**	**RK-166**
N975EE	500	135
N975F	20	84
N975GA	G2	26
N975GR	**D1A**	**A077SA**
N976B	G2	32/2
N976BS	**25**	**016**
N976EE	500	025
N976F	20	86
N976GA	**550**	**179**
N977CC	**125**	**257010**
N977EE	500	140
N977F	20	88
N977GA	24B	219
N977GA	24B	221
N977QS	**750**	**0077**
N977TW	**20**	**13**
N978E	**36A**	**024**
N978EE	500	018
N978F	20	89
N978FL	G3	397
N978R	S60	306-1
N978R	S60	306-27
N978R	S60	306-63
N978W	**50**	**49**
N979C	550	504
N979C	560	0263
N979EE	500	015
N979F	20	91
N979G	550	504
N979GA	G2	151/24
N979QS	**750**	**0079**
N979RA	G2	151/24
N979RA	**G4**	**1191**
N979RA	STR	5023
N979RF	**35A**	**376**
N980A	25D	340
N980AW	WWD	414
N980DC	**125**	**258267**
N980DK	560	5019
N980DM	**501**	**421**
N980EE	500	034
N980F	20	95
N980HC	601	5070
N980HC	601	5163
N980ML	AST	033
(N980ML)	G4	1193
N980R	**20**	**98/434**
N981	2xx	53
N981EE	500	005
N981F	20	96
N981HC	G4	1217
N981SW	**G4**	**1001**
N981TH	35A	364
N982AR	**400A**	**RK-206**
N982F	20	99
N982HC	**G4**	**1242**
N982J	**604**	**5308**
N982MC	**10**	**114**
N982NA	**550**	**376**
N983AJ	20	11
(N983AJ)	550	369
(N983CE)	601	5102
N983F	20	100
N983GT	**125**	**257086**
N983MC	10	111
N983QS	**750**	**0083**
N984F	20	101
N984GC	**125**	**258377**
N984GC	45	009
(N984H)	550	188
(N984HF)	125	25183
N984JD	25D	342
N984JD	31	001
N984JD	55C	139A
N984QS	**750**	**0084**
N985BA	550	043
N985F	20	102
N985M	650	0068
(N985QS)	750	0085
N986AH	G4	1003
N986F	20	105
N986H	125	257009
N986JB	S40	282-72
N986M	650	0048
N986MA	**31A**	**080**
N986WC	24B	213
N986WC	35	023
N986WC	55	030
N987A	AST	099
N987AC	G4	1156
N987AR	G4	1156
N987CJ	**S550**	**0152**
N987DK	35A	360
N987F	20	106
N987GK	**AST**	**031**
N987QS	**750**	**0087**
N988AA	25B	185
N988AA	**25D**	**348**
N988AC	**25B**	**185**
(N988AC)	500	349
N988AS	**25D**	**257**
N988DB	25B	185
N988DS	G2	98/38
N988F	20	107
(N988GA)	125	257057
N988H	650	0087
N988H	G2	150
N988H	G2	98/38
N988H	**G4**	**1347**
N988HL	650	0087
N988JE	125	257087
N988JE	G2	151/24
N988JG	400A	RK-255
N988MT	T39	276-32
N988MW	STR	5231
N988NA	WWD	372
N988QC	**35A**	**455**
N988R	S60	306-17
N988RS	550	568
N988SA	23	037
N988T	**50**	**130**
N988WH	WWD	209
N989AL	**35A**	**212**
N989F	20	110
N989JN	STR	5132/57
N989QS	**750**	**0089**
N989SA	24A	100
N989TL	**24**	**160**
N989TV	**550**	**305**
N989TW	550	305
N989TW	**560**	**0185**
N990AC	S60	306-24
N990AK	**604**	**5337**
N990AL	**500**	**033**
N990CB	500	211
N990CH	STR	5225
N990DK	**560**	**5019**
N990F	20	111
N990H	**90X**	**17**
N990HC	**125**	**258412**
(N990HP)	S550	0064
N990L	20	43
N990M	**550**	**608**
N990MC	**900**	**65**
N990MF	**560**	**5052**
N990PT	20	391
N990PT	**24D**	**236**
N990S	**WWD**	**322**
N990TM	24	051
(N990UH)	G4	1247
N990WC	G3	405
N990WC	**G4**	**1268**
(N990Y)	551	311
N991	STR	5139/54
N991AS	900	12
N991BM	**550**	**126**
N991CH	55	091
N991EJ	**750**	**0091**
N991F	20	112
N991F	STR	5139/54
N991GA	G2	170
N991L	**560**	**0350**
N991LF	**G5**	**576**
N991PC	560	0043
N991PC	**560**	**0364**
N991RF	**900**	**3**
N991RV	**10**	**24**
N991TD	**24**	**124**
N991TW	**604**	**5333**
N991WC	G3	405
N992	**50**	**77**

N992 S60 306-88
N992 STR 5070/52
N992GA 400 RJ-22
(N992NW) 501 660
N992SF 125 256044
N992TD 23 035
N993 50 38
N993DS WWD 356
N993F 20 113
N993H 400A RK-241
N993KL 24 166
N993QS 750 0093
N993TD 24 166
N994 S65 465-33
N994CT 601 5161
N994F 20 116
N994GC G2 77
N994JD 55C 139A
N994JD G2 37
N994JD G2 92
N994SA 23 005
N994SA 24 119
N994TA 600 1077
N994TD 24 179
(N994W) S60 306-132
N995 S60 306-29
(N995AU) 501 385
N995BC G3 432
N995DC S550 0065
N995DR 24D 285
N995F 20 117
N995PA 501 649
N995PT 20 391
(N995RD) 24D 285
N995RD 80A 380-9
(N995RD) S60 306-24
N995SA 125 257035
N995SK 125 257035
N995SK 900 166
(N995SL) 125 257035
N995TD 24 149
N996AG 2xx 64
N996DR D1A A032SA
N996F 20 118
N996JP AST 017
N996JR 525 0147
N996TD 24D 320
N996W S65 465-22
N997BC G4 1170
N997CA 500 198
N997CM G3 432
N997GA AST 107
(N997HM) G3 432
N997HT 550 0848
N997ME S60 306-40
N997MX D1A A036SA
(N997S) 500 179
N997TD 24D 247
N997TT 20 485
N998AA 500 310
N998BC 550 665
(N998DJ) 35A 098
N998EJ 750 0098
N998G GXY 008
N998GA AST 108
N998GP 400A RK-32
N998GP 551 363
N998JB G3 491
N998JP 35A 211
N998JR 601 3045
N998M 24D 249
(N998M) 35A 098
N998R S60 306-9
N998RD WWD 103
N998RL 24 087
N998SA 560 0485
N999AD 560 0136
N999AM 500 232
N999AU 31A 074
N999AU 551 181
(N999BG) 20 275
N999BH 25D 318
N999BL 550 131
N999BL AST 024

N999BL WWD 382
N999BS S40 282-53
N999CA WWD 111
N999CB 500 211
(N999CB) 501 631
N999CB S550 0054
N999CM 500 158
N999CV 500 211
N999CX 750 0073
N999DC 20 322
N999DC S60 306-95
N999EB 525 0210
N999EQ 20 275
N999F 10 29
N999FA 35A 386
N999FB WWD 61
N999GH 551 496
(N999GL) S550 0030
N999GP 400A RK-32
N999GP 551 363
N999GP AST 062
N999GP AST 108
N999HC S550 0030
N999HG 25B 178
(N999JA) 35A 352
N999JB 500 114
N999JF 125 257016
N999JF 35A 188
N999JR 24 174
N999JR 601 3061
N999KG S60 306-53
N999LC WWD 402
N999LF 125 25155
(N999LG) S60 306-53
N999LL 10 152
(N999LL) 551 106
N999LX G4 1099
N999M 24 114
N999M 24D 249
N999M 25 030
N999M 25B 102
N999M 25B 178
N999M 25D 231
N999M 35 045
N999M 75A 380-54
N999ME 25D 231
N999MF 24B 202
N999MF 25 050
N999MH 10 6
N999MK 25 030
N999ML 25B 102
N999MS 501 638
N999MS WWD 199
N999MV 25B 178
(N999NM) 125 25186
N999PJ MSP 089
N999PM 900 128
N999PM 900 20
N999PN 900 128
N999PW 501 549
N999RA 24B 213
(N999RA) WWD 93
N999RB 35A 301
N999RB 501 369
(N999RB) 501 578
N999RC 550 479
N999RW 125 25236
N999SA 125 25146
N999SF 500 055
N999SR 600 1042
(N999SW) 601 3008
N999TC 500 120
N999TF 600 1042
N999TH 200 512
N999TH 25D 293
N999TH 35A 621
N999TJ S550 0048
N999TN 35A 621
N999U 24D 253
N999U WWD 178
N999VT S40 282-38
N999WA 24D 242
N999WA 551 051
N999WJ 100 216

N999WS 501 581
N1000 G2 205
N1000 G2 75/7
N1000E 125 259015
N1000E 525 0077
N1000E S40 282-19
"N1000U" 125 259006
N1000W 560 0204
N1000W S550 0079
N1001A 23 071
N1001G S60 306-3
N1001L 35A 155
N1001L 35A 357
N1002B 23 038
N1004T G2 35
N1006F 525 0112
N1007 STR 5057
N1008S 24 118
N1010A 36 017
N1010F 20 360
N1010G 36A 043
N1010H 36A 044
N1012B STR 5012
N1013F 20 364
N1014X 750 0008
N1015B 525 0151
N1018F 20 365
N1019K WWD 180
N1020F 20 366
N1020P S60 306-54
N1021B 23 086
N1021T 501 413
N1022G 35A 650
N1024G S60 306-64
N1025C 125 25108
(N1026) HFB 1026
N1027S 400A RK-141
N1028Y S60 306-71
N1036F 20 368
N1036N 25B 121
N1037F 20 369
N1038F 20 370
N1039 G2 40
N1039F 20 371
N1039L 55C 139
N1040 G2 40
N1040 G3 314
N1040 G4 1044
N1040 G4 1206
N1041B 125 25111
N1041F 20 373
N1043B 35A 644
N1045F 20 374
N1045J 35A 648
N1045T 500 131
N1045X 55 096
N1045X 600 1038
N1047T 20 126/438
N1048X 36A 063
N1055C 55C 135
N1058X S65 465-4
N1061D 601 5140
N1062 S40 282-15
N1064 T39 265-52
N1069L T1A TX-9
N1072 S40 282-18
N1075X 55 082
N1080Q 10 80
N1082A G4 1082
N1083Z 400A RK-131
N1084D 400A RK-114
N1086 G4 1086
N1087T 25D 289
N1087T 35A 589
N1087T 36A 052
N1087T 55 096
N1087T 55B 128
N1087Y 35A 274
N1087Y 35A 491
N1087Y 55 116
N1087Y 55ER 102
N1087Y VU35 641
N1087Z 35A 427
N1087Z 35A 490

N1087Z 35A 503
N1087Z 35A 660
N1087Z 400A RK-132
N1087Z 55 073
N1087Z U36A 054
N1087Z U36A 059
N1088A 25D 368
N1088A 35A 271
N1088A 35A 431
N1088A 35A 655
N1088A 55 068
N1088A 55B 131
N1088A U36A 060
N1088C 25D 292
N1088C 25D 310
N1088C 35A 594
N1088C 35A 644
N1088C 55 065
N1088C 55 094
N1088D 25D 291
N1088D 25D 366
N1088D 31 004
N1088D 35A 342
N1088D 35A 463
N1088D 35A 495
N1088D 35A 605
N1090X 400A RK-110
N1094D 400A RK-134
N1094L 560 5094
N1094N 400A RK-140
N1099S 400A RK-139
N1100D WWD 169
N1100M WWD 86
N1101G S40 282-58
N1102 650 0047
N1102 G2 231
N1102A 50 18
N1102B 400A RK-122
N1102D S40 282-7
N1102U 125 258343
N1103 125 257060
N1103 650 0054
N1103R 25B 135
N1103U 125 258306
N1105U 400A RK-125
N1105Z 125 258301
N1107M 20 38
N1107M STR 5122
N1107Z 601 3016
N1107Z 750 0112
N1107Z STR 5023
N1107Z STR 5122
N1108T 400A RK-148
N1108Y 400A RK-128
N1109 550 433
(N1109) 650 0047
N1110S 35A 306
N1112N 125 258325
N1115 80A 380-17
N1115G 125 258347
N1115V 525 0157
N1116A S60 306-30
N1116R 400A RK-116
N1117S 400A RK-117
N1117Z 400A RK-137
N1118Y 400A RK-118
N1119C 400A RK-119
N1119C G3 417
N1121 25 004
N1121A WWD 123
(N1121B) WWD 129
N1121C 25 004
N1121C WWD 76
N1121E WWD 149
N1121E WWD 20
N1121E WWD 78
N1121E WWD 90
N1121F WWD 150
N1121G WWD 52
N1121G WWD 67
N1121M WWD 111
N1121M WWD 36
N1121N WWD 110
N1121N WWD 125

N1121N	WWD	135
N1121N	WWD	98
N1121R	WWD	121
N1121R	**WWD**	**125**
N1121R	WWD	75
N1121S	WWD	103
N1121U	WWD	128
N1121X	WWD	121
N1121X	WWD	77
N1121Z	400A	RK-121
N1121Z	WWD	108
N1123E	WWD	151
N1123E	WWD	159
N1123G	**G2**	**160**
N1123G	WWD	158
N1123H	WWD	156
N1123H	WWD	167
N1123H	WWD	172
N1123Q	WWD	157
N1123Q	WWD	173
N1123Q	WWD	182
N1123R	WWD	160
N1123R	WWD	165
N1123R	WWD	175
N1123R	WWD	186
N1123S	WWD	162
N1123T	WWD	163
N1123T	WWD	176
N1123T	WWD	184
N1123U	WWD	169
N1123U	WWD	177
N1123U	WWD	185
N1123W	WWD	160
N1123W	WWD	170
N1123X	WWD	174
N1123Y	WWD	179
N1123Z	400A	RK-123
N1123Z	WWD	159
N1123Z	WWD	178
N1124E	WWD	196
N1124E	WWD	235
N1124F	**WWD**	**281**
N1124G	WWD	188
N1124G	WWD	203
N1124G	WWD	216
N1124G	WWD	220
N1124G	WWD	243
N1124K	WWD	307
N1124K	WWD	388
N1124L	WWD	340
N1124L	WWD	405
N1124N	WWD	187
N1124N	WWD	201
N1124N	WWD	214
N1124N	WWD	259
N1124N	WWD	321
N1124N	WWD	346
N1124N	WWD	396
N1124P	WWD	199
N1124P	WWD	207
N1124P	WWD	223
N1124P	WWD	245
N1124P	WWD	341
N1124P	WWD	376
N1124Q	WWD	201
N1124Q	WWD	232
N1124Q	WWD	288
N1124U	WWD	225
N1124U	WWD	286
N1124X	WWD	200
N1124X	WWD	233
N1124Z	400A	RK-124
N1124Z	WWD	234
N1124Z	WWD	410
N1125	125	25023
N1125	125	258101
N1125	AST	062
N1125	AST	076
N1125A	AST	012
N1125A	AST	021
N1125A	AST	032
N1125A	**AST**	**051**
N1125E	125	25149
N1125E	24B	196
N1125E	AST	058
N1125G	125	25019
N1125G	125	25033
N1125G	125	25084
N1125G	**AST**	**076**
N1125G	WWD	247
N1125J	**AST**	**078**
N1125K	**AST**	**035**
N1125L	AST	072
N1125M	**55**	**065**
N1125S	**AST**	**021**
N1125V	AST	048
N1125Y	AST	049
N1125Z	AST	055
N1125Z	**AST**	**068**
N1126G	WWD	279
N1126V	400A	RK-151
N1127G	650	7084
N1127K	525	0278
N1127K	**525**	**0293**
N1127M	35A	226
N1127M	**55**	**120**
N1127P	560	0349
N1127U	400A	RK-127
N1128B	**2xx**	**83**
N1128B	650	0184
N1128G	525	0304
N1128J	35A	426
N1129L	**560**	**0507**
N1129M	35A	360
N1129M	**55ER**	**101**
N1129X	400A	RK-129
N1130B	400A	RK-130
N1130N	650	7071
(N1131K)	550	651
N1133G	525	0347
N1133N	125	258366
N1133T	400A	RK-133
N1135A	125	258345
N1135K	125	25019
N1135U	400A	RK-150
N1136Q	400A	RK-136
N1140A	**35**	**045**
N1141G	WWD	275
(N1149E)	G3	358
N1151K	STR	5115/39
N1159K	G2	101
N1164A	G2	42/12
N1166Z	WWD	18
(N1169D)	125	258002
N1172L	WWD	11
N1172Z	WWD	11
N1172Z	WWD	133
N1173Z	WWD	7
(N1175B)	G4	1175
N1178	550	433
N1180Z	WWD	33
N1181G	50	72
N1183	125	257060
N1183	650	0054
(N1184L)	HFB	1050
N1188A	AST	018
N1189A	STR	5139/54
N1190Z	WWD	28
N1194Z	WWD	70
N1195N	WWD	89
N1196Z	WWD	61
N1199G	125	25174
N1199M	125	25174
N1199M	20	121
N1200N	**550**	**681**
N1202D	560	0403
N1202T	550	707
N1203	23	008
N1203D	550	709
N1203N	550	710
N1203S	550	711
N1204A	550	715
N1205A	550	716
(N1205M)	550	717
(N1207A)	550	720
N1207B	550	721
N1207C	550	722
N1207D	550	723
N1207F	550	724
N1207Z	550	725
N1207Z	STR	5108
N1209T	550	726
N1209T	560	0002
(N1209X)	550	727
N1209X	560	0003
N1210	S60	306-4
N1210	WWD	34
N1210G	WWD	34
N1210M	35A	410
(N1210N)	550	728
N1210N	560	0004
N1210V	550	729
N1210V	560	0005
N1211M	550	730
N1211M	560	0006
N1212G	WWD	229
N1212H	550	219
N1213S	550	732
N1213S	560	0008
N1213Z	550	733
N1213Z	560	0009
(N1214D)	550	391
N1214H	551	392
(N1214J)	550	393
(N1214J)	550	734
N1214J	560	0010
N1214S	550	394
(N1214Z)	551	395
N1214Z	560	0011
(N1215A)	550	398
N1215G	550	399
(N1215S)	550	401
(N1216A)	550	405
N1216A	560	0003
N1216H	550	406
N1216J	550	407
N1216J	560	0004
N1216K	525	0199
N1216K	550	408
N1216K	550	454
N1216K	560	0005
N1216N	525	0226
N1216N	550	409
N1216N	560	0006
N1216Q	550	410
N1216Q	560	0007
(N1216Z)	550	411
N1216Z	560	0008
N1216Z	560	0454
N1217D	550	416
N1217H	550	417
N1217H	560	0011
N1217H	560	0376
N1217N	550	418
N1217N	560	0012
N1217P	551	419
(N1217P)	560	0013
N1217S	550	420
N1217S	560	0014
N1217V	551	421
N1217V	**560**	**560-0001**
N1218A	550	424
N1218F	550	425
N1218K	550	426
(N1218P)	550	427
N1218P	560	0017
N1218S	551	428
N1218T	550	429
N1218V	551	430
N1218Y	550	431
N1218Y	560	0018
N1218Y	560	0407
N1219D	550	432
N1219D	560	0019
(N1219G)	550	433
N1219G	560	0020
(N1219N)	550	434
N1219P	550	435
N1219Z	551	436
N1220A	550	439
(N1220D)	550	440
N1220J	550	441
(N1220N)	550	442
N1220S	550	443
N1223A	560	0017
N1223N	650	0120
N1223N	S550	0053
N1226X	560	0019
N1228N	560	0020
N1228N	560	5030
N1228V	560	0021
(N1228Y)	560	0022
(N1229A)	560	0028
(N1229C)	560	0029
(N1229D)	560	0030
N1229F	560	0031
N1229M	560	0032
N1229N	560	0033
(N1229Q)	560	0034
N1229Z	560	0035
N1230	WWD	53
N1230A	125	257026
N1230A	560	0039
N1230B	125	25088
N1230D	WWD	53
N1230G	125	25091
N1230G	560	0040
N1230R	STR	5049
N1230V	125	25043
(N1234F)	501	501
N1234X	501	394
(N1236P)	501	358
N1239L	650	0134
N1241N	525	0185
(N1242A)	550	609
N1242B	550	610
(N1242K)	550	611
N1243C	560	5013
N1244V	550	612
N1247V	560	0535
N1248B	560	0417
(N1248G)	550	444
"N1248K"	550	447
N1248K	551	445
N1248N	550	446
N1249B	550	448
N1249H	550	449
N1249K	550	450
N1249P	**550**	**451**
(N1249T)	550	452
N1249V	550	453
N1250B	550	455
N1250C	550	456
N1250L	550	457
N1250P	550	458
N1250P	550	613
N1251B	551	463
N1251D	550	464
N1251H	550	465
N1251K	125	258372
N1251K	125	258377
N1251K	550	466
N1251N	550	467
(N1251P)	550	468
N1251P	551	614
N1251V	550	469
N1251V	551	614
N1251Z	550	470
N1252B	550	475
N1252D	**550**	**476**
N1252J	550	477
N1252N	550	478
N1252P	550	479
N1253D	551	481
N1253G	550	482
(N1253K)	550	483
(N1253K)	550	616
N1253N	550	484
N1253P	550	485
N1253Y	550	486
(N1253Y)	551	617
N1254C	550	490
N1254C	550	618
(N1254D)	550	491
(N1254D)	550	619
(N1254G)	550	492

N1254G	550	620
N1254P	550	493
N1254X	**550**	**494**
(N1254Y)	550	495
(N1255D)	550	498
N1255D	550	502
(N1255G)	550	499
N1255G	550	503
(N1255J)	550	504
(N1255J)	550	622
N1255J	551	500
N1255K	**550**	**505**
(N1255L)	550	623
(N1255L)	S550	0001
N1255Y	550	624
(N1255Y)	S550	0002
N1256B	S550	0004
(N1256G)	550	626
(N1256G)	S550	0005
(N1256N)	550	627
(N1256N)	S550	0006
(N1256P)	550	628
(N1256P)	S550	0007
N1256T	550	629
(N1256T)	S550	0008
N1256Z	S550	0009
N1257B	**550**	**497**
N1257K	550	630
(N1257K)	S550	0010
(N1257M)	550	631
(N1257M)	S550	0011
(N1258B)	550	634
N1258H	550	635
N1258M	550	636
(N1258U)	550	637
(N1258U)	S550	0015
N1259B	550	0819
(N1259B)	550	639
N1259B	650	7001
(N1259B)	S550	0016
N1259G	S550	0017
N1259K	125	25170
(N1259K)	550	640
N1259K	650	7002
(N1259K)	S550	0018
(N1259M)	S550	0019
(N1259N)	550	641
N1259N	650	7003
(N1259R)	550	642
N1259R	650	7004
(N1259R)	S550	0020
(N1259S)	550	643
N1259S	650	7005
(N1259S)	S550	0021
(N1259Y)	550	644
(N1259Y)	650	7006
(N1259Y)	S550	0022
(N1259Z)	550	645
N1259Z	650	7007
(N1259Z)	S550	0023
N1260G	550	648
N1260G	650	7010
(N1260G)	S550	0026
N1260K	S550	0027
(N1260L)	S550	0028
N1260N	650	7011
(N1260N)	S550	0029
N1260V	650	7012
(N1260V)	S550	0030
N1261A	650	7014
(N1261A)	S550	0032
N1261K	650	7015
(N1261K)	S550	0033
N1261M	650	7016
(N1261M)	650	7017
(N1261M)	S550	0034
(N1261P)	650	7018
(N1261P)	S550	0035
N1262A	650	7020
N1262B	650	7021
N1262E	650	7022
N1262G	650	7023
N1262Z	650	7024
N1263B	650	7025
N1263G	650	7026
N1263P	650	7027
(N1263V)	650	7028
(N1263Y)	650	7029
N1263Z	650	7030
N1264B	650	7033
N1264E	650	7034
N1264M	650	7035
N1264P	650	7036
N1264V	525	0126
(N1264V)	650	7037
N1265B	650	7040
N1265C	650	7041
N1265K	650	7042
N1265P	650	7043
N1265U	650	7044
N1268G	35A	661
(N1269D)	S550	0040
(N1269E)	S550	0041
(N1269J)	S550	0042
(N1269N)	S550	0043
(N1269P)	S550	0044
N1269Y	S550	0045
N1270D	S550	0048
N1270F	20	72/413
N1270K	500	133
N1270K	S550	0049
N1270S	S550	0050
N1270Y	S550	0051
N1271A	601	5038
N1271A	S550	0055
(N1271B)	S550	0056
N1271D	S550	0057
N1271E	S550	0058
(N1271N)	S550	0059
(N1271T)	S550	0060
(N1272G)	S550	0064
(N1272N)	S550	0065
N1272P	S550	0066
(N1272V)	S550	0067
N1272Z	S550	0068
N1273A	S550	0072
(N1273E)	S550	0073
N1273J	S550	0074
(N1273N)	S550	0075
N1273Q	550	0858
(N1273Q)	S550	0076
N1273R	560	0318
(N1273R)	S550	0077
N1273X	S550	0078
(N1273Z)	S550	0079
(N1274B)	S550	0081
N1274D	S550	0082
N1274K	S550	0083
N1274N	S550	0084
N1274P	S550	0085
(N1274X)	S550	0086
N1274Z	S550	0087
(N1275A)	S550	0092
N1275B	S550	0093
(N1275D)	S550	0094
N1275H	S550	0095
(N1275N)	S550	0096
N1276J	525	0200
N1278	550	429
N1279Z	560	0175
N1280A	525	0177
N1280A	560	0178
N1280D	560	0179
N1280K	560	0180
N1280R	560	0181
N1280S	525	0281
(N1280S)	560	0182
N1281A	560	0184
N1281K	560	0185
N1281N	560	0186
(N1282D)	560	0192
N1282K	560	0193
(N1282M)	560	0194
N1282N	560	0195
N1283F	560	0198
(N1283K)	560	0199
N1283M	560	0200
N1283M	S550	0120
N1283N	560	0201
N1283V	560	0202
N1283X	560	0203
N1283Y	560	0204
N1284A	560	0206
(N1284B)	560	0207
(N1284D)	560	0208
(N1284F)	560	0209
N1284N	560	0210
(N1284P)	560	0211
N1284X	560	0212
(N1285D)	560	0214
(N1285G)	560	0215
N1285N	560	0216
N1285P	560	0217
N1285V	560	0218
(N1286A)	560	0221
N1286C	**560**	**0222**
N1286N	560	0223
N1287B	560	0224
N1287C	560	0225
N1287D	560	0226
N1287F	560	0227
N1287G	560	0228
N1287K	560	0229
N1287N	560	0230
N1287Y	560	0231
N1288A	560	0233
N1288B	560	0234
N1288D	560	0235
N1288N	560	0236
N1288P	560	0237
N1288T	560	0238
N1288Y	560	0239
N1289G	560	0240
N1289N	560	0241
N1289Y	560	0242
N1290B	S550	0097
N1290E	S550	0098
N1290G	S550	0099
N1290N	560	0246
(N1290N)	S550	0100
(N1290Y)	S550	0101
N1290Z	S550	0102
N1291E	S550	0107
N1291K	560	0249
(N1291K)	560	0250
(N1291K)	S550	0108
N1291P	S550	0109
N1291V	S550	0110
N1291Y	560	0250
(N1291Y)	S550	0111
N1292A	S550	0114
N1292B	560	0253
(N1292B)	S550	0115
N1292K	S550	0116
N1292N	S550	0117
N1293A	S550	0123
N1293E	560	0257
(N1293E)	S550	0124
N1293G	525	0204
N1293G	S550	0125
N1293K	S550	0126
N1293N	S550	0127
N1293V	S550	0128
N1293X	S550	0129
N1293Y	560	0258
N1293Z	560	0259
(N1293Z)	S550	0130
N1294B	560	0260
(N1294D)	S550	0132
N1294K	560	0261
(N1294K)	S550	0133
N1294M	S550	0134
N1294N	560	0262
(N1294N)	S550	0135
(N1294P)	560	560-0001
(N1294P)	S550	0136
N1295A	560	0264
(N1295A)	S550	0138
N1295B	560	0518
(N1295B)	S550	0139
N1295G	560	0266
(N1295G)	S550	0140
N1295J	560	0267
(N1295J)	S550	0141
N1295M	560	0268
(N1295M)	S550	0142
N1295N	560	0269
N1295N	560	0292
(N1295N)	S550	0143
N1295P	560	0265
(N1295P)	S550	0144
N1295Y	560	0270
N1295Y	560	0294
(N1295Y)	S550	0145
N1296B	S550	0146
N1296N	560	0271
N1296N	560	0297
N1296N	S550	0147
N1296Z	S550	0148
(N1297B)	S550	0150
N1297V	560	0275
N1297V	560	0300
N1297Y	550	554
N1297Z	551	555
N1298	S60	306-9
N1298C	551	557
(N1298G)	550	558
(N1298H)	551	559
N1298J	550	560
N1298K	550	561
(N1298N)	550	562
N1298P	550	563
N1298X	550	564
N1298X	560	0502
N1298Y	550	565
N1299B	550	0808
(N1299B)	550	566
(N1299H)	550	567
N1299K	550	568
N1299N	550	550
N1299P	550	569
(N1299T)	550	570
(N1300G)	550	576
(N1300J)	550	577
N1300M	WWD	124
N1300N	550	578
(N1301A)	550	582
N1301A	650	0221
N1301B	550	583
N1301D	551	584
N1301D	650	0223
N1301K	550	585
N1301N	550	586
N1301P	STR	5138
N1301S	550	587
N1301V	550	588
N1301Z	550	589
N1301Z	650	0225
N1302A	**650**	**0226**
N1302C	650	0227
N1302N	550	592
N1302V	550	593
N1302V	650	0228
N1302X	550	594
N1302X	650	0229
N1303A	650	0232
N1303H	550	600
N1303H	650	0233
(N1303M)	550	601
N1303M	650	0236
N1303V	650	0235
N1304B	650	0238
N1304G	650	0239
(N1305C)	650	0009
(N1305N)	650	0010
N1305N	650	0230
N1305U	650	0011
N1305V	650	0012
(N1306B)	650	0014
N1306B	650	0237
(N1306F)	650	0015
N1306V	560	5054
N1306V	650	0016
N1306V	650	0234
N1307A	650	0017
(N1307A)	650	0235

(N1307C)	650	0018
(N1307C)	650	0236
(N1307D)	650	0019
(N1307D)	650	0237
N1307G	650	0020
N1308V	550	640
N1309A	550	641
(N1309A)	650	0033
N1309K	550	642
N1310B	550	644
(N1310B)	650	0043
N1310C	550	645
(N1310G)	550	646
(N1310Q)	550	648
(N1310Z)	550	649
(N1311A)	550	650
(N1311A)	650	0049
(N1311K)	650	0050
(N1311P)	550	652
(N1311P)	650	0051
(N1312D)	650	0054
N1312D	650	0160
(N1312K)	650	0161
N1312Q	650	0162
N1312T	650	0163
N1312V	650	0164
N1312X	650	0165
N1313G	650	0059
(N1313J)	650	0060
N1313J	650	0166
(N1313T)	650	0061
(N1314H)	650	0064
N1314H	650	0168
(N1314T)	650	0065
(N1314V)	650	0066
N1314V	650	0170
(N1314X)	650	0067
(N1314X)	650	0068
(N1315A)	650	0070
(N1315B)	650	0071
(N1315C)	650	0072
(N1315D)	650	0073
(N1315G)	650	0074
N1315T	650	0075
N1315V	650	0076
(N1315Y)	650	0077
(N1316A)	650	0079
N1316E	650	0080
(N1316N)	650	0081
N1317G	650	0085
(N1317X)	650	0086
(N1317Y)	650	0087
(N1318A)	650	0090
N1318E	650	0091
(N1318E)	S60	306-96
(N1318L)	650	0092
(N1318M)	650	0093
(N1318P)	650	0094
(N1318Q)	650	0095
(N1318X)	650	0096
N1318Y	**550**	**0884**
(N1318Y)	650	0097
N1319B	650	0099
N1319D	560	0319
(N1319D)	650	0100
N1319M	650	0101
(N1319X)	650	0102
(N1320B)	650	0105
(N1320K)	650	0106
(N1320P)	650	0107
(N1320U)	650	0108
N1320U	HFB	1023
(N1320V)	650	0109
(N1320X)	650	0110
N1321A	650	0112
N1321C	650	0113
(N1321J)	650	0114
N1321K	650	0115
(N1321L)	650	0116
N1321N	650	0117
N1322D	650	0121
(N1322K)	650	0122
(N1322X)	650	0123
(N1322Y)	650	0124
(N1323A)	650	0126
N1323D	650	0127
(N1323K)	650	0128
(N1323N)	650	0129
(N1323Q)	650	0130
(N1323R)	650	0131
N1323V	650	0132
N1323X	650	0133
(N1323Y)	650	0134
N1324	G2	33
N1324B	560	5051
(N1324B)	650	0135
(N1324D)	650	0136
(N1324G)	650	0137
(N1324R)	650	0138
(N1325D)	650	0140
N1325E	650	0141
(N1325L)	650	0142
N1325X	650	0143
N1325Y	650	0144
N1325Z	650	0145
N1326A	650	0148
N1326B	525	0002
N1326B	650	0149
N1326D	525	0003
(N1326D)	525	0005
N1326D	650	0150
N1326G	525	0004
N1326G	650	0151
N1326H	525	0005
(N1326H)	650	0152
N1326K	650	0153
N1326P	525	0006
(N1326P)	650	0154
N1327A	650	0157
N1327B	650	0158
(N1327E)	525	0007
N1327G	**525**	**0008**
N1327J	**525**	**0009**
(N1327K)	525	0010
(N1327N)	525	0011
(N1327Z)	525	0012
N1328A	525	0013
N1328D	525	0014
(N1328K)	525	0015
N1328M	525	0016
(N1328Q)	525	0017
(N1328X)	525	0018
(N1328Y)	525	0019
N1329D	**525**	**0020**
(N1329G)	525	0021
N1329G	**525**	**0146**
N1329K	STR	5106/9
N1329L	STR	5161/43
N1329N	525	0022
(N1329T)	525	0023
(N1330D)	525	0025
(N1330G)	525	0026
N1330N	525	0027
N1330S	525	0028
N1331X	525	0030
N1333Z	550	273
N1354G	501	539
N1354G	501	622
N1354G	525	0033
N1354G	650	0171
N1382C	500	309
N1393	125	25190
N1401L	501	436
N1406	STR	5029/38
N1411S	25D	325
N1419J	650	0115
(N1419J)	750	0051
N1420	24A	116
N1424	WWD	345
N1424	WWD	94
N1424Z	WWD	94
N1433B	25D	255
N1450B	25D	212
N1450B	35A	182
N1450B	35A	354
N1450B	35A	497
(N1450B)	55	053
N1450B	55	113
N1451B	35A	102
N1451B	35A	244
N1451B	35A	457
N1451B	35A	590
N1451B	35A	620
N1451B	55	045
N1451B	55ER	087
N1454H	**G3**	**350**
N1461B	25D	358
N1461B	35	045
N1461B	35A	177
N1461B	35A	211
N1461B	55	088
N1461B	55	111
N1461B	VU35	632
N1462B	25D	265
N1462B	35	037
N1462B	35A	184
N1462B	35A	221
N1462B	35A	265
N1462B	35A	451
N1462B	35A	604
N1462B	35A	634
N1462B	36A	036
N1462B	55	042
N1462B	55	092
N1465B	35A	193
N1465B	35A	273
N1465B	35A	428
N1465B	35A	500
N1465B	55	080
N1465B	VU35	642
N1466B	25D	236
N1466B	25D	314
N1466B	35A	204
N1466B	35A	481
N1466B	35A	615
N1466B	55ER	107
N1466K	35A	394
(N1466K)	550	055
N1468B	25B	205
N1468B	25D	252
N1468B	25D	371
N1468B	31	014
N1468B	35A	222
N1468B	35A	355
N1468B	35A	472
N1468B	35A	621
N1468B	55	081
N1471B	35A	195
N1471B	35A	441
N1471B	35A	505
N1471B	35A	603
N1471B	35A	635
N1471B	55	070
N1473B	25D	365
N1473B	35A	134
N1473B	35A	164
N1473B	35A	239
N1473B	35A	338
N1473B	35A	489
N1473B	35A	596
N1473B	35A	610
N1473B	35A	657
N1476B	25XR	222
N1476B	35A	229
N1476B	35A	278
N1476B	35A	288
N1476B	35A	494
N1476B	35A	502
N1476B	55	115
N1476B	VU35	636
N1500	20	8
N1500	35A	339
N1500	**600**	**1078**
N1500B	24	051
N1500B	25	055
N1500C	WWD	169
N1500C	WWD	46
N1500E	35A	124
N1500G	24	051
N1500M	STR	5058/4
N1500M	WWD	71
N1501	**20**	**15**
N1502	20	15
N1502	35A	328
N1503	20	42
N1503	35A	316
N1507	35A	316
N1515E	125	25035
N1515P	10	43
N1515P	125	25035
N1515P	125	256022
N1515P	550	477
N1526L	35A	245
N1526L	650	0176
N1526M	G3	409
N1526M	G4	1118
N1526R	G3	409
N1540	G3	314
N1540	G4	1044
N1540	**G5**	**580**
N1545N	400A	RK-91
N1546T	400	RJ-46
N1547B	**400**	**RJ-47**
N1548D	400	RJ-48
N1549J	**400**	**RJ-49**
N1549W	**400A**	**RK-88**
N1550Y	400	RJ-50
N1551B	400	RJ-51
N1551B	400A	RK-1
N1554R	400	RJ-54
N1555P	400	RJ-55
N1556W	400	RJ-56
N1557D	400	RJ-57
N1558F	400	RJ-58
N1559U	400	RJ-59
N1560G	400A	RK-89
N1560T	400	RJ-60
N1561B	400	RJ-61
N1563V	400A	RK-86
N1564B	400	RJ-64
N1565B	**400**	**RJ-65**
N1567L	400A	RK-87
N1570B	400A	RK-100
N1570L	400A	RK-90
N1618R	60	044
N1620	125	257155
N1620	601	3025
N1620	STR	5033/56
N1620	STR	5132/57
N1620N	STR	5132/57
N1621	G2	31
N1621	WWD	275
N1622	600	1030
N1622	601	5077
N1622	STR	5036/42
N1622D	STR	5036/42
N1623	601	3065
N1624	G2	33
N1624	**G4**	**1318**
N1625	G2	154/28
N1625	G4	1013
N1625	**G4**	**1358**
N1625	WWD	229
N1629	WWD	363
N1640	**125**	**258376**
N1640	G3	314
N1650	**125**	**258432**
(N1700)	35A	258
N1707Z	G2	213
N1710E	500	540
N1710E	501	623
N1710E	501	673
N1715G	D1A	A073SA
N1717L	550	638
N1728E	501	541
N1735J	35A	606
N1744P	55	063
N1758E	501	542
N1758E	501	624
N1758E	501	674
N1761B	G3	358
N1761B	G4	1043
N1761B	G4	1155
N1761D	G3	364
N1761D	G3	423
N1761D	G4	1046

N1761D	G4	1109
N1761D	G4	1154
N1761J	G3	365
N1761J	G4	1047
N1761J	G4	1117
N1761K	G3	385
N1761K	G4	1048
N1761K	G4	1156
N1761P	G3	394
N1761P	G4	1055
N1761Q	G3	395
N1761Q	G4	1083
N1761S	G3	396
N1761S	G4	1084
N1761W	G3	303
(N1772E)	501	543
N1772E	501	625
N1772E	525	0034
(N1772E)	650	0172
N1776F	WWD	38
(N1777R)	20	35
N1777T	WWD	62
(N1779E)	501	544
N1779E	525	0035
(N1779E)	650	0173
(N1782E)	501	545
N1782E	525	0036
(N1782E)	650	0174
N1806P	G2	200
N1807Z	G2	27
N1812C	600	1018
N1812C	**601**	**5010**
N1818S	20	149
N1818S	**900**	**136**
N1818S	900	39
(N1820E)	501	546
N1820E	525	0037
N1820E	650	0175
N1823A	20	129
N1823B	501	373
N1823B	550	498
N1823B	551	196
N1823C	550	234
N1823D	**G2**	**59**
N1823F	20	129
N1823S	560	0094
N1823S	**560**	**0225**
N1823S	650	0090
N1824S	**560**	**0120**
N1824T	125	257182
N1824T	601	3029
N1827S	**560**	**0094**
N1828S	**650**	**7047**
N1829S	50	280
N1841D	75A	380-15
N1841D	G2	227
N1841D	G3	438
N1841F	50	152
N1841F	75A	380-15
N1841L	G2	227
N1843A	D1A	A025SA
N1843S	125	257155
N1843S	D1A	A025SA
N1844S	STR	5123/14
N1846	20	47
N1847B	200	493
N1847B	550	365
N1847P	550	365
N1848U	50	227
N1848U	604	5316
N1851D	550	022
N1851N	500	310
N1851T	20	74
N1851T	200	508
N1851T	500	310
N1851T	550	022
N1857B	20	203
N1857W	WWD	258
N1863T	S40	282-62
N1865M	**S550**	**0071**
(N1865S)	560	0225
N1867M	**650**	**7073**
N1867W	S550	0124
N1868M	125	257021

N1868M	20	139
N1868M	600	1039
N1868M	601	5012
N1868M	**900**	**157**
N1868N	20	139
N1868S	125	257021
N1868S	600	1039
N1871P	24	130
N1871P	36A	023
N1871R	10	128
N1871R	24	130
N1871R	36A	023
N1871R	50	6
N1871R	G3	381
N1873	**560**	**0353**
(N1874E)	501	547
N1874E	525	0038
N1874E	650	0176
N1875P	G2	137
N1878C	400A	RK-33
N1879W	**550**	**668**
N1880F	550	372
N1880S	500	183
N1881Q	**20**	**414**
N1881W	400A	RK-21
N1883	550	467
N1883M	550	674
N1884	125	256067
N1884	**600**	**1032**
N1884Z	WWD	150
N1886G	**550**	**722**
N1887S	10	190
N1888M	550	674
N1892S	20	376
N1896F	125	257162
N1896F	50	127
N1896T	125	257162
N1896T	50	127
N1896T	**50**	**262**
N1897A	**125**	**258326**
N1897S	**20**	**376**
(N1899)	500	091
N1899K	**125**	**258424**
N1900W	**G4**	**1124**
N1901M	**G4**	**1039**
N1901W	400A	RK-19
(N1902)	650	7010
N1902J	601	5135
N1902L	G2	226
N1902P	**601**	**5135**
N1902P	G2	226
N1902W	20	269
N1902W	400A	RK-2
N1902W	50	209
N1903G	601	5051
N1903G	**604**	**5326**
N1903P	125	258142
N1903W	50	129
N1903W	S40	282-36
N1904G	WWD	436
N1904P	**601**	**5116**
N1904S	**31A**	**149**
N1904W	400A	RK-21
N1904W	50	149
N1904W	**G4**	**1237**
N1905H	31A	051
N1908W	S40	282-36
N1909D	S40	282-57
N1909R	S40	282-57
N1909R	S60	306-41
N1909R	S65	465-54
N1910A	**125**	**258188**
N1910H	125	258023
N1910H	**125**	**258318**
N1910J	**125**	**258023**
N1918W	36	004
N1919G	24	157
N1919W	24	118
N1919W	24	157
N1919W	24B	192
N1920	**400A**	**RK-21**
N1923G	125	25095
N1923M	125	25031
N1924G	STR	5224

N1924L	125	25237
N1924V	10	24
N1924V	STR	5077
N1926S	**31A**	**180**
N1929P	T39	276-48
N1929S	35A	388
N1929Y	**2xx**	**84**
N1929Y	G2	19
(N1930E)	501	548
N1930E	650	0177
N1932K	**31A**	**099**
N1932P	31A	099
N1932P	**750**	**0090**
N1940	**60**	**002**
N1944P	WWD	142
N1949B	550	414
N1949M	550	414
N1951E	500	160
N1951E	501	549
N1955E	501	550
N1955E	550	059
N1955M	**G4**	**1276**
N1956M	**G3**	**469**
(N1958E)	500	551
N1958E	501	626
N1958E	501	676
(N1958E)	501	677
N1958E	525	0039
N1958E	550	060
N1958E	650	0178
N1958N	**S550**	**0073**
N1959E	501	552
N1959E	501	627
N1959E	525	0040
N1959E	551	061
N1959E	650	0179
N1961S	**550**	**0890**
N1962J	**550**	**0862**
N1962J	STR	5113/25
N1963A	23	097
N1965L	**24**	**012**
N1966G	STR	5065
N1966J	WWD	66
N1966K	24A	011
N1966L	24	108
N1966W	23	076
N1967G	STR	5098/28
(N1967J)	STR	5113/25
N1967L	24	012
N1967M	**G4**	**1368**
N1967W	24A	096
N1968A	23	097
N1968A	35A	171
N1968A	55	035
N1968T	35A	171
N1968W	**23**	**089**
N1969H	24A	110
N1969L	24	012
N1969W	25	005
N1971R	20	312
N1971R	20	322
N1971R	50	149
N1972G	24D	242
N1972L	24A	096
N1972W	WWD	91
N1973L	24A	096
N1976L	23	070
N1976L	25B	080
N1976L	35	053
N1976S	25	008
N1978L	25B	080
N1978L	35A	162
N1982C	G3	384
N1982G	125	257116
N1982U	S550	0038
N1983Y	**55**	**079**
(N1996E)	125	257177
N1996F	125	257177
N2000	S40	282-52
N2000	**S65**	**465-7**
N2000A	2xx	26
N2000A	2xx	3
N2000A	2xx	44
N2000A	2xx	63

N2000A	2xx	89
N2000L	**2xx**	**92**
N2000M	24	065
N2000M	25C	084
N2000M	35A	396
N2000M	36	009
N2000M	**560**	**0146**
N2000T	125	257177
N2000X	560	0144
N2000X	S550	0064
N2002P	**G4**	**1279**
N2004	2xx	13
N2004	S40	282-52
N2004G	601	5048
N2005	20	54
N2006	S40	282-124
N2006	**S40**	**282-135**
N2007	S40	282-55
N2008	23	003
N2008	550	399
N2009	S40	282-14
N2013M	G2	51
N2015M	125	257192
N2015M	**125**	**258254**
N2015M	35A	072
N2019V	500	245
N2020	125	25203
N2022L	35A	290
N2022R	25B	200
N2028	2xx	29
N2032	2xx	31
N2034	2xx	14
N2035	2xx	17
N2036	2xx	23
N2039	2xx	24
N2042	2xx	25
N2046	2xx	26
N2052A	501	553
N2052A	501	628
N2052A	501	678
N2052A	551	062
N2056	900	155
N2056E	400A	RK-156
N2061	2xx	39
N2069A	500	554
N2069A	550	063
N2070K	500	133
N2072A	500	629
N2072A	501	555
N2072A	550	064
N2073	2xx	41
N2074	2xx	44
(N2077)	2xx	43
N2079A	501	431
N2080	2xx	46
N2089	2xx	48
N2093	2xx	101
N2093P	75A	380-39
N2094L	**25B**	**095**
N2098A	501	432
N2098A	525	0041
N2098A	650	0180
(N2099)	2xx	99
N2100J	80A	380-32
N2100X	WWD	23
N2101J	S60	306-109
N2102J	75A	380-38
N2103J	S60	306-110
N2104J	75A	380-34
N2105J	75A	380-36
N2106J	S60	306-111
N2107J	S60	306-112
N2107Z	**G4**	**1211**
N2108J	S60	306-113
N2109J	S60	306-114
N2110J	75A	380-39
N2112J	75A	380-40
N2113J	75A	380-41
N2114E	125	256022
N2114J	75A	380-42
N2115J	75A	380-43
N2116J	80A	380-44
N2117J	75A	380-45
N2118J	S60	306-115

N2119J	S60	306-116
N2120J	S60	306-117
N2120Q	WWD	107
N2122J	S60	306-118
N2123J	S60	306-119
N2124J	S60	306-120
N2125	125	25082
N2125J	75A	380-46
N2126J	75A	380-47
N2127E	25B	145
N2127J	80A	380-48
N2128J	80A	380-49
N2129J	80A	380-50
N2130J	S60	306-121
N2131A	501	433
N2131A	650	0181
N2131J	S60	306-122
N2132	2xx	57
N2132J	S60	306-123
N2133	2xx	58
N2133J	S60	306-124
N2134J	S60	306-125
N2135J	75A	380-51
N2136J	75A	380-52
N2137J	75A	380-53
N2138J	75A	380-54
N2138T	25B	091
N2139J	75A	380-55
N2140L	550	554
N2141J	S60	306-126
N2142J	S60	306-127
N2143J	S60	306-128
N2144J	S60	306-129
N2145J	S60	306-130
N2146	2xx	59
N2146J	75A	380-56
N2147	2xx	60
N2147J	75A	380-57
N2148J	75A	380-58
N2148R	125	25070
N2149J	S60	306-131
N2150J	S60	306-132
N2151J	S60	306-133
N2152J	S60	306-134
N2155	2xx	63
N2155P	125	25273
N2158U	**501**	**476**
N2159P	400A	RK-159
N2159X	125	258313
N2160N	550	249
N2164Z	400A	RK-164
N2168	2xx	70
N2168G	400A	RK-168
N2169	2xx	72
N2169X	125	258315
N2170J	500	040
N2173X	125	258317
N2175W	125	258348
N2176	2xx	73
N2189	2xx	89
N2191	2xx	92
N2194	**2xx**	**110**
N2197	**2xx**	**112**
N2200A	**75A**	**380-26**
N2200M	20	11
N2200M	STR	5062/12
N2200R	500	095
N2200T	24	112
N2201J	400A	RK-171
N2201U	500	217
N2204J	**400A**	**RK-174**
N2213T	**25D**	**369**
N2216	**2xx**	**116**
N2217	**2xx**	**117**
N2217Q	35A	243
N2218	**2xx**	**109**
N2220G	D1A	A031SA
N2222R	STR	5016
N2225J	D1A	A064SA
N2225Y	400A	RK-165
(N2231B)	550	026
N2232B	S40	282-65
N2233B	S40	282-66
N2234B	S40	282-67
N2235	S550	0135
N2235B	S40	282-68
N2235V	**400A**	**RK-181**
N2236B	S40	282-69
N2236C	S40	282-70
N2239B	S40	282-71
N2241B	S40	282-74
N2241C	S40	282-75
N2242B	S40	282-76
N2242P	35	012
N2243	**501**	**619**
N2244B	S40	282-77
(N2246)	125	25099
N2248C	S40	282-79
N2249B	S40	282-80
N2250B	S40	282-81
N2252Q	400A	RK-152
N2254B	S40	282-84
N2254S	50	180
N2255B	S40	282-85
N2255Q	20	24
N2259V	T39	265-1
N2265Z	75A	380-43
N2267B	400A	RK-167
N2267Z	36	012
N2272K	**400A**	**RK-172**
(N2273G)	25	040
N2273Z	**400A**	**RK-173**
N2274B	500	295
N2277G	**400A**	**RK-177**
N2277T	STR	5105
N2279K	400A	RK-179
N2283T	400A	RK-196
N2286U	125	258336
N2289B	400A	RK-170
N2290F	400A	RK-190
N2291T	400A	RK-191
N2291X	125	258319
N2293V	400A	RK-233
N2293V	400A	RK-250
N2296C	T39	265-5
N2296S	501	621
N2296S	**560**	**0038**
N2297B	35	033
N2298L	400A	RK-185
N2298S	400A	RK-187
N2298S	501	621
N2298W	400A	RK-188
N2299T	400A	RK-166
N2314F	400A	RK-184
N2320J	125	258342
N2321S	125	258352
N2321V	**125**	**258353**
N2321Z	125	258357
N2322B	400A	RK-182
N2322B	**400A**	**RK-242**
N2322X	125	258320
N2329N	400A	RK-169
N2345M	STR	5075/19
N2349V	400A	RK-236
"N2351M"	125	258341
N2354B	400A	RK-154
N2355N	400A	RK-232
N2355T	400A	RK-155
N2357K	400A	RK-204
N2358X	400A	RK-158
N2359W	400A	RK-203
N2360F	400A	RK-160
N2362G	400A	RK-162
N2363A	400A	RK-163
N2366Y	24	055
N2366Y	25	058
N2409W	**604**	**5391**
N2411A	**650**	**0103**
N2418N	750	0074
N2418Y	750	0074
N2425	50	237
N2425	**90X**	**32**
(N2425)	G4	1310
N2426	10	186
N2426	125	25013
N2426	125	25107
N2426	**125**	**258272**
N2426	25D	216
N2426G	10	186
N2427F	10	187
N2427F	25B	157
N2427N	10	187
N2428	**125**	**258274**
N2428	600	1013
N2440C	75A	380-2
N2440C	S60	306-30
N2440G	75A	380-2
N2440G	80A	380-44
N2440G	S60	306-30
N2454M	WWD	314
N2478	50	48
N2500W	125	25208
N2501E	S60	306-136
N2501E	S65	465-1
N2503L	23	047
N2504	125	25021
N2506E	S60	306-137
N2508E	S60	306-138
N2513E	S65	465-15
N2518M	**WWD**	**337**
N2519E	S60	306-144
N2521E	75A	380-60
N2522E	75A	380-61
N2525	125	25112
N2525	20	321
N2528E	75A	380-67
N2531K	**550**	**594**
N2535E	S60	306-135
N2536E	75A	380-66
N2537E	S65	465-17
N2538E	75A	380-68
N2539E	S65	465-48
N2542E	75A	380-69
N2544E	S65	465-20
N2545E	S65	465-24
N2548E	S65	465-26
N2549E	S65	465-28
N2550E	S65	465-31
N2551E	S65	465-39
N2556E	S65	465-41
N2561E	S65	465-42
N2568	20	75
N2568S	S40	282-61
N2569B	S40	282-90
N2570E	S65	465-50
N2574E	S65	465-55
N2579E	S65	465-54
N2579E	WWD	21
N2580E	S65	465-60
N2581E	S65	465-75
N2586E	S65	465-21
N2590E	S65	465-35
N2600	G2	88/21
N2600	G3	315
N2600	**G4**	**1088**
N2600	STR	5037/24
N2600	STR	5110/47
N2600S	31	033B
N2600Z	31A	060
N2600Z	G3	315
N2601	125	25060
N2601	G2	30/4
N2601	G3	316
N2601	STR	5110/47
N2601B	U36A	061
N2601G	35A	674
N2601K	31A	080
N2601V	60	024
N2602M	35A	675
N2602Y	31A	070
N2602Z	60	022
N2603G	31A	054
N2603Q	31A	086
N2603S	31	033A
N2603X	31A	068
N2604	650	0021
N2605	20	312
N2605	650	0144
N2606	**650**	**0194**
N2607	500	307
N2607	G2	30/4
(N2610)	500	340
N2610	G3	302
N2610	**G4**	**1094**
N2611Y	501	556
N2611Y	501	630
N2611Y	501	679
N2612N	501	557
N2612N	501	631
N2613	20	293
N2613	500	307
N2613C	501	558
N2613C	501	632
N2614	20	376
N2614C	501	559
N2614C	501	633
N2614C	501	680
N2614H	500	560
N2614H	501	634
N2614K	501	561
(N2614Y)	501	634
N2614Y	650	0183
N2615	20	293
N2615	G2	148/5
N2615	**G4**	**1214**
(N2615D)	501	635
N2615D	650	0184
(N2615L)	501	636
N2615L	650	0185
N2616C	501	637
N2616G	501	562
(N2616G)	501	637
N2616G	501	638
N2616G	501	681
N2616H	20	376
(N2616L)	501	563
N2616L	525	0043
N2616L	650	0186
N2617B	501	564
(N2617B)	501	638
N2617B	501	639
N2617B	501	682
N2617K	500	565
(N2617K)	501	640
N2617K	525	0044
N2617K	650	0187
N2617P	525	0045
N2617P	650	0188
N2617U	501	566
N2617U	**501**	**641**
N2619M	550	142
N2621U	525	0047
(N2621U)	650	0190
N2621Z	525	0048
(N2621Z)	650	0191
N2622C	650	0192
N2622M	20	242
N2622Z	650	0193
N2623B	501	646
(N2624L)	501	647
N2624L	650	0198
N2624M	20	376
N2624M	650	0021
N2624Z	501	648
(N2625C)	650	0196
N2625Y	650	0197
N2626A	501	649
N2626J	501	650
N2626M	S60	306-113
(N2626X)	650	0199
N2626Z	501	651
(N2626Z)	650	0200
N2627A	501	434
N2627A	650	0202
N2627M	S60	306-123
N2627N	501	654
N2627U	501	655
N2628B	500	656
N2628Z	501	657
N2629Z	501	658
N2630	125	257161
N2630	500	340
N2630B	650	0204
N2630N	650	0205
N2630U	650	0206
N2631N	501	659

N2631N	550	143
N2631V	501	660
N2631V	551	144
N2632Y	550	145
N2632Y	650	0207
N2633N	501	662
N2633N	550	146
N2633Y	525	0049
N2633Y	550	147
(N2634B)	125	257020
N2634E	525	0050
(N2634E)	S550	0151
N2634Y	550	148
N2634Y	600	1034
N2635D	551	149
N2635M	S60	306-118
N2636N	600	1025
N2637M	G2	88/21
N2637R	525	0051
(N2637R)	S550	0153
N2637Z	35A	413
N2638A	525	0053
N2638A	551	152
(N2638A)	S550	0155
N2638U	525	0054
(N2638U)	S550	0156
N2639N	S550	0157
N2639Y	525	0055
(N2639Y)	S550	0158
N2640	125	257157
N2642F	600	1033
N2642Z	S550	0160
(N2646X)	501	486
N2646X	525	0056
N2646X	550	153
(N2646X)	S550	0159
N2646Y	501	487
N2646Y	550	154
(N2646Z)	501	488
N2646Z	550	155
(N2647U)	501	490
(N2647Y)	501	491
N2647Y	525	0058
(N2647Z)	501	492
N2647Z	525	0059
N2648X	**501**	**493**
(N2648Y)	501	494
N2648Y	525	0060
(N2648Z)	501	495
N2648Z	550	157
N2649	100	219
N2649D	501	498
N2649D	501	667
N2649D	550	158
N2649E	501	499
N2649E	550	159
N2649H	501	500
(N2649J)	501	501
N2649J	525	0063
(N2649S)	501	502
N2649S	525	0064
N2649Y	501	503
N2649Y	525	0065
N2649Z	501	504
N2650	500	341
N2650C	501	513
N2650M	501	514
N2650N	501	515
N2650S	501	516
(N2650V)	501	517
N2650V	525	0068
N2650X	501	518
N2650Y	501	519
N2650Y	501	670
N2651	500	565
N2651B	501	526
N2651B	501	671
N2651G	501	527
N2651J	501	528
N2651J	501	672
(N2651R)	501	529
N2651R	525	0072
N2651S	500	530
(N2651Y)	501	531

N2652U	501	536
N2652Y	501	537
N2652Z	501	538
N2653R	550	160
N2656G	525	0073
(N2661H)	550	072
(N2661N)	550	073
(N2661P)	550	074
(N2662A)	550	082
(N2662B)	550	083
(N2662F)	551	084
N2662Z	550	085
N2663B	550	094
N2663B	560	0036
N2663F	551	095
N2663G	550	096
N2663J	501	669
N2663J	551	097
N2663N	551	098
(N2663X)	550	099
N2663X	560	0037
(N2663Y)	550	100
N2663Y	**550**	**602**
N2663Y	560	0038
N2664F	551	108
N2664L	550	109
N2664T	551	110
(N2664U)	550	111
N2664U	560	0040
N2664Y	550	112
N2665A	550	117
N2665D	551	118
(N2665F)	550	119
(N2665F)	560	0043
N2665N	550	120
(N2665S)	550	121
N2665S	560	0044
(N2665Y)	550	122
N2665Y	560	0045
N2666A	550	125
N2666A	560	0047
N2667M	G2	140/40
N2667X	560	0048
N2668A	550	165
(N2672X)	560	0049
N2675W	HFB	1050
N2676B	S40	282-92
N2677S	600	1004
N2680A	560	0051
N2680D	560	0052
(N2680X)	560	0053
N2681F	560	0055
N2682F	560	0056
(N2683L)	560	0057
(N2686Y)	560	0058
(N2687L)	560	0059
(N2689B)	560	0060
N2690M	**501**	**546**
N2694C	125	25285
(N2697X)	560	0061
N2697Y	560	0060
N2701J	560	0061
(N2701J)	560	0063
N2707T	600	1055
N2710T	S60	306-2
N2711B	50	84
N2711M	G2	137
N2716G	560	0062
N2717X	560	0064
N2720B	600	1049
N2721F	560	0065
N2721U	25D	308
N2722F	560	0067
N2722H	560	0068
N2724K	20	255/487
(N2724R)	560	0069
(N2725A)	560	0070
(N2725X)	560	0071
N2726J	560	0072
(N2726X)	560	0073
N2727F	560	0074
N2728	125	25060
N2728N	560	0071A
N2734K	**550**	**595**

N2741A	501	435
N2741Q	600	1047
N2743T	35A	193
N2745G	550	126
N2745L	550	127
(N2745L)	560	0075
N2745M	550	128
(N2745M)	560	0076
N2745R	550	129
N2745R	560	0077
N2745T	550	130
N2745X	550	131
N2746B	550	133
N2746C	550	134
(N2746C)	560	0079
N2746E	550	135
N2746E	560	0080
N2746F	550	136
(N2746F)	560	0081
N2746U	550	137
(N2746U)	560	0082
N2746Z	550	138
(N2747R)	551	139
(N2747R)	560	0083
N2747U	550	140
(N2747U)	560	0084
N2748B	560	0078
(N2748F)	560	0085
(N2748V)	560	0086
N2749B	560	0087
N2756T	WWD	224
N2757A	501	436
N2762J	560	0381
N2768A	501	437
N2782D	500	152
N2792B	400A	RK-63
N28..B	400A	RK-14
N2800	S65	465-7
N2801L	500	236
N2815	35A	334
N2815	G2	148/5
N2830	125	257161
N2830B	**T1A**	**TT-82**
N2841A	501	438
N2842B	400A	RK-10
N2843B	400A	RK-11
N2844	35A	424
N2855	55	076
(N2855)	55	079
N2868B	T1A	TT-8
N2872B	T1A	TT-6
N2876B	T1A	TT-5
N2886B	T1A	TT-1
N2887A	501	439
N2887B	T1A	TT-2
N2888A	501	440
N2892B	T1A	TT-3
N2896B	T1A	TT-7
N2906A	501	441
N2909W	24X	243
N2920C	23	010
N2932C	23	042
N2937L	500	335
N2945C	24	149
N2951P	35A	215
N2954T	20	58
N2959A	501	442
N2972Q	36A	047
N2979	20	183
N2989	125	257167
N2989	20	112
N2991A	501	443
N2991Q	G2	119/22
N2992	55	099
N2997	S40	282-38
N2998	G2	236
N3000	S60	306-29
N3000	S65	465-11
N3000W	S550	0100
N3007	125	25043
N3007	125	256007
N3007	125	258092
N3008	125	258092
N3008	S60	306-29

N3014R	400A	RK-206
N3014R	60	114
N3015F	400A	RK-207
N3015F	60	115
N3016X	31A	161
N3018C	60	118
N3019S	31A	151
N3025T	400	RJ-25
N3026U	400	RJ-26
N3028U	400A	RK-211
N3029F	400A	RK-212
N3030	S65	465-11
N3030	STR	5094
N3030	STR	5212
N3030C	**500**	**104**
N3030C	550	193
N3030D	400A	RK-205
N3030T	**550**	**193**
(N3031)	550	081
N3031	STR	5154
N3031	WWD	269
(N3031)	WWD	95
N3032	550	081
N3032	WWD	97
N3033A	**400A**	**RK-213**
N3035T	400	RJ-35
N3038V	**400A**	**RK-93**
N3038W	400A	RK-215
N3045	601	3045
N3050P	400A	RK-216
N3051S	400A	RK-94
N3056R	35A	264
N3056R	500	138
N3059H	400A	RK-219
N3060	125	25017
N3060	STR	5037/24
N3060F	125	25017
N3062A	501	444
N3068M	400A	RK-218
N3079S	400A	RK-256
N3080	STR	5094
N3082B	WWD	97
N3097N	MON	001
N3100X	10	12
N3101B	400A	RK-208
N3104M	500	445
N3105M	501	446
N3106Y	400A	RK-251
N3110M	501	447
N3112B	400	RJ-12
N3112K	400	RJ-12
N3113B	**400**	**RJ-13**
N3114B	400	RJ-14
N3114X	400A	RK-95
N3115B	400	RJ-15
(N3115U)	50	166
N3117M	501	448
N3118M	125	25199
N3118M	501	449
N3119H	400A	RK-6
N3119W	400	RJ-19
N3120M	501	450
N3120Y	400	RJ-20
N3121B	**400**	**RJ-21**
N3122B	400	RJ-22
N3122M	501	451
N3123T	400	RJ-23
N3124M	400	RJ-24
(N3124M)	501	452
N3125B	125	25110
(N3127M)	501	453
N3127R	400	RJ-27
N3129E	400	RJ-29
N3129X	400A	RK-229
N3130T	400	RJ-30
N3131G	25D	274
N3132M	500	454
N3134N	400	RJ-34
N3141G	400	RJ-41
N3141M	500	455
N3142E	400	RJ-42
N3143T	400	RJ-43
N3144A	400	RJ-44
N3144M	501	456

N3145F	400	RJ-45
N3145M	501	457
N3146M	501	458
N3147M	501	459
N3150M	501	460
N3155B	35A	117
N3156M	500	461
N3158M	501	462
N3159U	S40	282-117
N3160M	501	463
N3161M	501	464
N3163M	501	465
N3165M	501	466
N3166Q	400A	RK-266
N3170A	501	467
N3170B	**551**	**162**
N3170M	501	468
N3172M	501	469
N3173M	500	470
(N3175M)	501	471
N3175S	AST	057
N3175T	AST	056
N3180M	501	472
N3180T	400	RJ-18
(N3181A)	501	473
(N3183M)	501	474
(N3184V)	550	247
(N3184Z)	550	123
N3184Z	**650**	**0032**
N3189H	125	258360
N3189M	501	475
N3194M	501	476
N3195K	T1A	TX-4
N3195M	501	477
N3195Q	T1A	TX-5
N3195X	T1A	TX-6
N3196N	**400A**	**RK-96**
N3197A	400A	RK-197
N3197K	400A	RK-227
N3197M	501	478
N3197Q	**400A**	**RK-97**
N3198M	501	479
N3199Q	400A	RK-99
N3199Z	400A	RK-245
N3202A	35A	469
N3202A	501	480
N3202M	501	481
N3204M	501	482
N3205M	501	483
N3206M	500	484
(N3207M)	501	485
N3208M	550	013
N3210M	551	014
N3210X	400A	RK-98
N3212M	550	015
N3216M	550	016
N3218L	**400A**	**RK-108**
N3221M	550	017
N3221T	400A	RK-101
N3221Z	T1A	TX-10
N3223M	551	018
N3223R	400A	RK-223
N3224N	400A	RK-224
N3224X	400A	RK-104
(N3225M)	550	019
N3226B	400A	RK-126
N3226Q	400A	RK-226
N3227A	551	020
N3227X	400A	RK-107
N3228M	T1A	TX-7
N3228V	400A	RK-228
N3228V	T1A	TX-8
N3230M	550	021
N3231H	**400A**	**RK-270**
N3232M	550	022
N3232U	**400A**	**RK-102**
N3234S	125	257087
N3235U	**400A**	**RK-105**
N3236M	551	023
N3236Q	400	RJ-36
N3237H	**400A**	**RK-272**
N3237M	551	024
N3237S	600	1070
N3238K	400	RJ-38
N3238K	55	013
N3239A	36	002
N3239K	400	RJ-39
N3239M	550	025
N3240J	**400A**	**RK-240**
N3240J	400A	RK-92
N3240M	**400**	**RJ-40**
N3240M	550	026
N3241Q	400A	RK-241
N3245M	550	027
N3246H	400A	RK-106
(N3246M)	550	028
(N3247M)	550	029
(N3249M)	551	030
N3250	35A	250
N3250M	550	031
N3251H	550	397
N3251M	**125**	**258341**
N3251M	550	032
N3252J	WWD	115
(N3252M)	550	033
N3254G	550	265
N3254P	400A	RK-254
N3255B	400A	RK-255
N3258M	550	034
N3259Z	**400A**	**RK-259**
N3261A	400A	RK-261
N3261L	35A	395
(N3261M)	550	035
N3261Y	125	258333
N3261Y	400A	RK-120
(N3262M)	550	036
N3262M	**550**	**652**
N3263E	125	258367
N3263N	400A	RK-113
N3265A	**400A**	**RK-115**
(N3268M)	550	037
N3269A	**400A**	**RK-109**
N3270X	125	258373
(N3271M)	550	038
N3272L	**400A**	**RK-112**
N3273H	650	7035
(N3273M)	551	039
(N3274M)	550	040
N3274Q	125	25102
N3276M	550	041
N3278	S60	306-32
N3278M	550	042
N3279M	550	043
N3280E	36	013
N3280G	S40	282-70
N3283M	24F	356
N3283M	550	044
N3284M	550	045
N3285M	550	046
N3286M	550	047
N3288M	550	048
N3291M	551	049
(N3292M)	550	050
N3296M	551	051
N3298D	S40	282-20
(N3298M)	550	052
N3300L	550	286
N3300M	500	338
(N3300M)	550	053
(N3301M)	550	054
(N3308M)	550	055
N3312T	501	621
N3313M	550	056
N3314M	550	057
N3319M	550	058
N3320G	WWD	363
N3330L	600	1052
N3330M	600	1052
N3337J	**400A**	**RK-159**
N3338	125	25253
N3338	G3	402
N3338	**G4**	**1006**
N3350	23	093
N3350M	20	140
N3399P	125	257010
N3402	35A	402
N3444B	**550**	**661**
N3444G	20	21
N3444H	125	257122
N3456B	S60	306-35
N3456F	50	17
N3456L	36A	050
N3490L	**500**	**128**
N3503F	35A	075
"N3507W"	T39	265-35
N3513F	25D	207
N3514F	25D	211
N3523F	35A	081
N3524F	36A	021
N3526	550	047
N3533	S60	306-34
N3545F	35A	088
N3547F	35A	089
N3556F	25D	216
N3600X	10	88
N3600X	S60	306-46
N3643	G2	125/26
N3652	G2	198/35
N3668	20	9
N3683G	501	684
N3690	20	34
N3699T	125	25086
N3711H	WWD	106
N3711L	125	25173
(N3728)	601	3006
N3759C	35	049
N3771U	500	139
N3793D	35A	391
N3793P	35A	407
N3793X	25D	316
N3794B	55	021
N3794C	55	028
N3794M	35A	362
N3794P	25D	352
N3794U	35A	455
N3794W	35A	454
N3794Z	35A	364
N3795U	25D	354
N3795Y	55	034
N3796B	55	023
N3796C	55	049
N3796P	35A	473
N3796Q	35A	467
N3796U	55	042
N3796X	55	027
N3796Z	55	048
N3797A	35A	398
N3797B	35A	477
N3797C	55	044
N3797K	35A	475
N3797L	25D	343
N3797N	35A	327
N3797S	35A	357
N3797U	25D	357
N3798A	25D	315
N3798B	35A	348
N3798D	25D	339
N3798L	25D	344
N3798P	35A	408
N3798V	25D	346
N3799B	25D	329
N3799C	35A	442
N3802G	24D	320
N3802G	25D	261
N3802G	31	021
N3802G	35A	123
N3802G	35A	183
N3802G	35A	341
N3802G	35A	445
N3802G	35A	507
N3802G	55	040
N3802G	55	112
N3802G	U36A	056
N3803G	25B	135
N3803G	25C	131
N3803G	31	011
N3803G	35A	125
N3803G	35A	212
N3803G	35A	346
N3803G	35A	437
N3803G	35A	496
N3803G	35A	591
N3803G	35A	606
N3803G	55	036
N3807G	24	152
N3807G	24X	150
N3807G	25B	202
N3807G	25D	266
N3807G	35A	114
N3807G	35A	328
N3807G	35A	616
N3807G	36A	035
N3807G	55	071
N3807G	55	100
N3807G	55	117
N3810G	25B	119
N3810G	25G	337
N3810G	35A	112
N3810G	35A	191
N3810G	35A	470
N3810G	35A	592
N3810G	35A	656
N3810G	55	091
N3810G	C21A	628
N3811G	25B	203
N3811G	35A	143
N3811G	35A	189
N3811G	35A	248
N3811G	35A	462
N3811G	35A	493
N3811G	55	121
N3811G	55C	136
N3812G	24D	263
N3812G	35A	131
N3812G	35A	243
N3812G	35A	612
N3812G	35A	646
N3812G	55	077
N3812G	55	106
N3815G	25D	234
N3815G	35A	111
N3815G	35A	478
N3815G	35A	498
N3815G	35A	595
N3815G	35A	614
N3816G	24B	202
N3816G	35	011
N3816G	35A	479
N3816G	35A	501
N3816G	55	119
N3816G	VU35	640
N3818G	24D	271
N3818G	24F	336
N3818G	35A	200
N3818G	35A	345
N3818G	35A	444
N3818G	35A	476
N3818G	35A	499
N3818G	35A	601
N3818G	VU35	631
N3819G	25D	221
N3819G	25D	373
N3819G	31	007
N3819G	35A	137
N3819G	35A	180
N3819G	35A	216
N3819G	35A	353
N3819G	35A	506
N3819G	35A	480
N3831C	S40	282-90
N3838J	WWD	350
N3848U	**20**	**380**
N3854B	600	1082
N3857N	35A	268
N3871J	24B	201
N3871J	24D	274
N3904	35A	266
N3914L	10	47
N3933A	125	25226
N3950N	50	95
N3951	501	682
N3951Z	551	181
N3952B	550	016
N3979P	24D	270
N3982A	STR	5141
N3986G	550	657

N3999B	36A	048
N3999H	550	133
N4000K	**560**	**5081**
N4000X	600	1058
N4000X	G2	100
N4005G	31A	085
N4005S	25	026
N4006G	31A	096
N4007J	60	038
N4010K	60	042
N4010N	31A	104
N4016G	60	018
N4016M	STR	5224
N4021M	STR	5225
N4022X	31A	082
N4026M	STR	5226
N4026Z	60	026
N4027K	31A	094
N4027S	60	027
N4029P	60	029
N4030W	60	030
N4031A	60	033
N4031K	31A	093
N4031L	60	031
N4033M	STR	5227
N4034H	31A	084
N4034M	STR	5228
N4037A	60	037
N4038M	STR	5229
N4042M	STR	5230
N4043M	STR	5231
N4046M	STR	5232
N4048M	STR	5233
N4049	S550	0068
N4049M	STR	5234
N4053T	**400A**	**RK-253**
N4055M	STR	5235
N4056M	STR	5236
N4058M	STR	5237
N4060K	UTX	246-1
N4062M	STR	5238
N4063M	STR	5239
N4065M	STR	5240
(N4090P)	500	267
N4110C	550	085
N4110S	500	247
N4110S	550	085
N4110S	**560**	**0112**
N4115B	20	266/490
N4154G	50	80
N4191G	550	065
N4196T	501	369
N4200K	**560**	**0354**
"N4203S"	125	256047
N4203Y	125	256047
N4209K	500	164
N4224Y	125	256040
N4227N	S60	306-126
N4227Y	20	237/476
N4228A	S60	306-48
N4230S	60	027
N4234K	500	346
N4238X	500	270
N4246A	501	580
N4246N	35	061
N4246R	20	175
N4246Y	500	290
N4247C	600	1017
N4248Z	STR	5155/32
N4249K	400A	RK-249
N4251H	WWD	281
N4253A	125	256005
N4258P	STR	5016
N4260K	75A	380-60
N4263X	501	514
N4275K	**400A**	**RK-275**
N4286A	20	429
N4289U	31	017
N4289U	35A	484
N4289U	35A	627
N4289U	55	089
N4289U	C21A	523
N4289X	35A	613
N4289X	55	050
N4289X	55C	139A
N4289X	C21A	511
N4289X	C21A	526
N4289Y	35A	487
N4289Y	C21A	518
N4289Y	C21A	533
N4289Y	C21A	625
N4289Z	35A	617
N4289Z	55	052
N4289Z	C21A	514
N4289Z	C21A	528
N4290C	35A	485
N4290C	35A	622
N4290C	55	097
N4290C	C21A	535
N4290J	35A	609
N4290J	36A	051
N4290J	C21A	512
N4290J	C21A	527
N4290J	U36A	058
N4290K	35A	619
N4290K	35A	654
N4290K	C21A	515
N4290K	C21A	530
N4290X	G2	122
N4290Y	35A	659
N4290Y	55	057
N4290Y	55B	129
N4290Y	C21A	522
N4290Y	C21A	537
N4290Z	55	053
N4291G	24B	190
N4291G	35A	486
N4291G	55	126
N4291G	55C	138
N4291G	C21A	513
N4291G	C21A	529
N4291K	25D	361
N4291K	31	016
N4291K	55B	132
N4291K	C21A	516
N4291K	C21A	531
N4291N	36A	062
N4291N	55B	130
N4291N	C21A	521
N4292G	24B	228
N4294A	500	095
N4300L	25B	182
N4305U	24D	271
N4308G	550	066
N4313V	T39	265-76
N4314B	T39	276-8
N4320P	550	649
N4333W	560	0033
N4340F	20	120
N4341F	20	121
N4341S	AST	059
N4342F	20	122
N4343	75A	380-51
N4343F	20	123
N4344F	EC	125
N4345F	20	127
N4346F	20	129
N4347F	20	130
N4347F	550	733
N4348F	20	132
N4349F	20	133
N4350F	20	134
N4350M	20	140
N4350M	**50**	**142**
N4351F	20	135
N4351M	20	11
N4351M	20	457
N4351M	**50**	**90**
N4351N	20	11
N4352F	20	137
N4353F	20	139
N4354F	20	140
N4355F	20	142
N4356F	20	144
N4357F	20	146
N4358F	20	148
N4358N	**35**	**065**
N4359F	20	149
N4360F	20	151
N4360S	650	7034
N4361F	20	153
N4361Q	125	258121
N4362F	20	155
N4362M	20	457
N4363F	20	157
N4364F	20	159
N4365F	20	161
N4366F	20	163
N4367F	20	164
N4368F	20	166
N4368F	20	261
N4369F	20	168
N4370F	20	169
N4371F	20	171
N4372F	20	218
N4373F	20	175
N4374F	20	177
N4375F	20	179
N4376F	20	181
N4377F	20	183
N4378F	20	203
N4378P	**400A**	**RK-278**
N4379F	20	187
N4380F	20	189
N4381F	20	191
N4382F	20	192
N4383F	20	193
N4384F	20	194
N4385F	20	195
N4386F	20	196
N4387F	20	197
N4388F	20	199
N4389F	20	200
N4390F	20	213
N4391F	20	202
N4392F	20	204
N4393F	20	205
N4394F	20	206
N4395F	20	207
N4396F	20	209
N4397F	20	210
N4398F	20	211
N4399F	20	212
N4400E	125	25026
N4400F	20	214
N4401	**35A**	**434**
N4401F	20	215
N4402	**125**	**258199**
N4402	25B	117
N4402F	20	216
N4403	**125**	**258480**
N4403	500	271
N4403F	20	217
N4404F	20	220
N4405	25B	117
N4406F	20	221
N4407F	20	223
N4408F	20	224
N4409F	20	226
N4410F	20	227
N4411	G2	48/29
N4411F	20	229
N4412F	20	230
N4413F	20	232
N4413N	50	66
N4414F	20	233
N4415D	601	3051
N4415F	20	235
N4415M	**35A**	**072**
N4415S	**35A**	**021**
N4415W	**35A**	**229**
(N4416F)	20	236
N4416F	20	256
N4417F	20	239
N4418F	20	242
N4418F	20	259
N4419F	20	247
N4420E	AST	049
N4420F	20	244
N4421F	20	249
N4422F	20	250
N4423F	20	254
N4424P	600	1053
N4425F	20	257
N4426F	20	258
N4426Z	WWD	409
N4427F	20	262
N4428F	20	264
N4429F	20	265
N4430F	20	269
N4431F	20	272
N4432F	20	273
N4433F	20	274
N4434F	20	275
N4434W	500	082
N4435F	20	270
N4436F	20	282
N4436S	STR	5141
N4437F	20	284
N4438F	20	287
N4439F	20	289
N4440F	20	290
N4441F	20	292
N4442F	20	293
N4443F	20	297
N4444F	20	298
N4444J	125	258171
N4444U	WWD	163
N4445F	20	303
(N4445J)	24D	309
N4445N	551	024
N4445Y	35A	432
N4446F	20	305
N4446P	501	373
N4447F	20	308
N4447P	**25D**	**338**
N4447T	WWD	286
N4448F	20	312
N4448Y	36A	046
N4449F	20	313
N4449F	601	3002
N4450F	20	310
N4451F	20	316
N4452F	20	317
N4453F	20	319
N4454F	20	321
N4455F	20	322
N4456F	20	324
N4457A	550	035
N4457F	20	325
N4458F	20	327
(N4459F)	20	328/522
N4459F	20	335
N4460F	20	330
N4461F	20	339
N4462F	20	341
N4463F	20	345
N4464F	20	347
N4465F	20	349
N4465N	125	25053
N4466F	20	352
N4467F	20	355
N4467X	**400A**	**RK-267**
N4468F	20	356
N4469F	20	357
N4469F	S40	282-43
N4469M	S40	282-48
N4469N	S40	282-68
N4488W	**25D**	**367**
(N4492V)	S40	282-39
N4493S	STR	5141
N4500X	**G3**	**416**
N4545	**45**	**045**
N4550E	WWD	83
N4554E	WWD	85
N4555E	125	257001
N4557P	10	104
N4557W	550	137
N4562Q	601	3016
N4564P	550	319
(N4564S)	35A	365
N4567	S40	282-44
N4576T	24B	227
N4577Q	35A	263
N4578F	551	023
N4581R	10	151

N4581Y	551	375
N4612	650	0203
(N4612S)	650	0203
N4612Z	**650**	**0203**
N4614N	**550**	**659**
N4620G	550	067
N4621G	550	068
N4641J	24	019
N4644E	WWD	97
N4646S	125	25013
N4646S	500	051
N4661E	WWD	99
N4663E	WWD	100
N4674E	WWD	104
N4679T	50	17
N4690E	WWD	106
N4691E	WWD	107
N4701N	S40	282-93
N4703N	S40	282-94
N4704N	S40	282-95
N4705N	S40	282-96
N4706N	S40	282-97
N4707N	S40	282-98
N4709N	S60	306-4
N4712N	S60	306-6
N4715N	S60	306-7
N4716E	WWD	110
N4716N	S60	306-8
N4717N	S60	306-9
N4720N	S60	306-10
N4720T	550	256
N4721N	S60	306-11
N4722R	S60	306-12
N4723N	S60	306-13
N4724N	S60	306-14
N4725N	S60	306-15
N4726N	S60	306-16
N4727N	S60	306-17
N4728N	S60	306-18
N4729N	S60	306-19
N4730E	WWD	112
N4730N	S60	306-20
N4731N	S60	306-21
N4732E	WWD	113
N4732N	S60	306-22
N4733N	S60	306-23
N4734E	WWD	114
N4734N	S60	306-24
N4735N	S60	306-25
N4736N	S60	306-26
N4737N	S60	306-27
N4741N	S60	306-29
N4742N	S60	306-30
N4743E	WWD	116
N4743N	S60	306-32
N4745N	S60	306-33
N4746N	S60	306-34
N4748N	S60	306-35
N4749N	S60	306-36
N4750N	S60	306-37
N4751N	S60	306-38
N4752N	S60	306-39
N4753N	S60	306-40
N4754G	550	069
N4754N	S60	306-41
N4755N	S60	306-42
N4757N	S60	306-43
N4759D	125	25272
N4760N	S60	306-44
N4763N	S60	306-45
N4764N	S60	306-46
N4765N	S60	306-47
N4767M	125	25159
N4791C	24	160
N4875	10	54
N4886	125	25046
N4903W	50	129
N4940E	WWD	122
N4943A	S40	282-66
N4960S	20	296/507
N4981	25	062
N4983E	WWD	126
N4990D	STR	5146
N4995A	35A	192
N4995N	WWD	230
N4997E	125	25016
N4998Z	36A	039
N4999G	T39	265-2
N4999H	500	329
N4999H	T39	265-55
N5	35A	674
N5	35A	675
N5000B	35A	074
N5000B	STR	5093
N5000C	**650**	**0002**
N5000C	STR	5093
N5000C	STR	5205
N5000E	31	031
N5000E	45	020
N5000G	G2	110
N5000R	550	0879
N5000R	560	0445
N5000R	750	0023
N5000R	750	0052
N5001G	125	25095
N5001X	31A	100
N5002D	31A	102
N5003F	31A	103
N5003U	60	063
N5003X	60	039
N5004Y	60	041
N5005	500	004
N5005K	31A	105
(N5005M)	31A	115
N5005X	60	095
N5006G	60	046
N5006K	60	066
N5006T	60	062
N5006V	60	065
N5007P	60	047
N5008Z	60	048
N5009L	31A	089
N5009T	35A	665
N5009T	45	021
N5009T	60	018
N5009V	31A	043
N5009V	31A	066
N5009V	31A	096
N5009V	45	012
N5009V	**45**	**084**
N5010J	31A	101
N5010U	31	032
N5010U	45	013
(N5010U)	60	057
N5011L	35A	668
N5011L	45	052
N5011L	60	005
N5012G	45	022
N5012H	31	033
N5012H	31A	098
N5012H	31A	107
N5012H	45	030
N5012H	60	010
N5012H	60	062
N5012K	35A	670
N5012P	125	25095
N5012Z	31A	083
N5012Z	35A	676
N5012Z	60	053
N5013D	60	032
N5013L	31	033C
N5013N	31A	130
N5013U	45	035
N5013U	60	011
N5013Y	31A	085
N5013Y	45	029
N5013Y	**45**	**083**
N5013Y	60	056
N5014E	31A	134
N5014E	**45**	**028**
N5014E	60	036
N5014E	60	055
N5014F	31A	082
N5014F	35A	669
N5014F	35A	673
N5014F	60	169
N5014H	60	012
N5015U	31	034
N5015U	60	063
N5016P	501	358
N5016V	31A	038
N5016V	45	031
N5016V	60	058
N5016Z	**45**	**072**
N5016Z	45	078
N5017J	31A	058
N5017J	60	037
N5018G	35A	667
N5018G	**45**	**077**
N5019Y	31A	091
N5020Y	31A	120
N5022C	60	052
N5023D	31	033D
N5029F	31A	109
N5030	STR	5212
N5032E	WWD	129
N5034Z	60	034
N5035R	60	070
N5038E	WWD	130
N5039E	WWD	131
(N5040)	G2	40
N5041E	WWD	133
N5043D	60	043
N5043E	WWD	135
N5044E	WWD	136
N5044N	60	044
N5045E	WWD	137
N5045S	60	045
N5046E	WWD	138
N5047E	WWD	139
N5049J	31A	099
N5050J	550	001
N5051X	60	051
N5052U	20	65
N5053Y	60	053
N5055F	60	055
N5058J	550	0828
N5058J	550	0901
N5058J	750	0028
N5058J	750	0051
N5059J	60	059
N5060H	601	5060
N5060K	560	5002
N5060K	750	0097
N5060P	550	0825
N5060P	560	0246
N5061P	**550**	**0927**
N5061P	750	0053
N5061P	750	0091
N5061W	560	0398
N5061W	560	0513
N5061W	750	0031
N5066U	750	0026
N5066U	750	0041
N5066U	750	0092
N5068F	60	078
N5068R	525	0142
N5068R	550	0882
N5068R	750	0027
N5068R	750	0055
N5069P	601	3021
N5070L	STR	5143
N5071L	S60	306-9
N5071M	750	0035
N5072E	500	043
N5072L	500	043
N5072L	501	379
N5072L	60	072
N5073	**601**	**5073**
N5073G	550	0850
N5073G	550	0893
N5073G	550	0921
N5073G	560	0423
N5073G	650	7088
N5075L	S60	306-16
N5076J	525	0160
N5076J	550	0817
N5076J	550	0830
N5076J	550	0852
N5076J	550	0909
N5076K	525	0075
N5076K	525	0161
N5076K	550	0847
N5076K	550	0899
N5076K	560	0431
N5076K	560	0440
N5079V	525	0076
N5079V	550	0843
N5079V	550	0897
N5079V	560	707
N5079V	650	7078
N5082S	31A	112
N5085E	525	0078
N5085E	560	0477
N5085E	560	0508
N5085E	750	0015
N5085E	750	0036
N5085E	750	0115
N5085J	550	0877
N5086W	525	0079
N5086W	525	0151
N5086W	550	0840
N5086W	550	0841
N5086W	550	0853
N5086W	560	0436
N5086W	560	0465
N5086W	560	0521
N5086W	650	7082
N5086W	750	0107
N5087B	**45**	**067**
N5090A	525	0080
N5090A	525	0124
N5090A	560	0378
N5090A	560	0417
N5090A	750	0042
N5090A	750	0099
N5090V	525	0081
N5090V	525	0125
N5090V	525	0150
N5090V	525	0153
N5090V	550	0925
N5090V	750	0029
N5090V	750	0098
N5090Y	525	0082
N5090Y	525	0126
N5090Y	550	0884
N5090Y	550	0924
N5090Y	750	0043
N5090Y	750	0060
N5091J	525	0083
N5091J	525	0127
N5091J	560	0524
N5091J	750	0018
N5091J	750	0047
N5092B	560	0389
(N5092D)	525	0084
N5092D	525	0128
N5092D	550	0819
N5092D	560	0391
N5092R	60	092
N5093D	525	0085
N5093D	525	0129
N5093D	525	0158
N5093D	560	0473
N5093D	750	0033
(N5093L)	525	0086
N5093L	525	0130
N5093L	550	0814
N5093L	550	0872
N5093L	560	0390
(N5093Y)	525	0087
N5093Y	525	0131
N5093Y	550	0821
N5093Y	550	0904
N5093Y	560	0394
N5093Y	560	0395
N5093Y	560	0525
N5094B	560	0272
N5094B	WWD	105
N5094D	650	7084
N5095N	550	0902
N5095N	560	0273
N5095N	560	0478
N5095N	560	0507
N5095N	750	0030
N5096S	550	0813

N5096S	550	0829
N5096S	550	0913
N5096S	560	0274
N5096S	560	0467
N5097H	550	0818
(N5097H)	560	0275
(N5097H)	560	0323
N5097H	560	0376
N5097H	560	0472
N5097H	560	0529
N5098G	STR	5098/28
N5100J	525	0146
N5100J	550	0917
N5100J	560	0276
N5100J	560	0324
N5100J	560	0448
N5100J	750	0068
N5100J	750	0100
N5101	G2	84
N5101	**G5**	**550**
N5101J	550	0846
N5101J	550	0905
(N5101J)	560	0277
(N5101J)	560	0325
N5101J	560	0379
N5101J	560	0426
N5101T	G2	84
N5102	G2	85
N5102	**G5**	**551**
N5103	G3	440
(N5103)	G3	445
N5103J	560	0278
N5103J	560	0326
N5103J	560	0380
N5103J	750	0044
N5103J	750	0085
N5104	G3	443
(N5104Z)	560	0328
N5105	80A	380-4
N5105	**G3**	**445**
N5105F	550	0881
(N5105F)	560	0281
N5105F	560	0329
N5105F	560	0427
N5105F	750	0056
N5106	80A	380-6
N5107	75A	380-8
N5108	80A	380-9
N5108G	550	0871
N5108G	560	0284
(N5108G)	560	0332
N5108G	560	0387
N5108G	560	0447
N5108G	560	0539
N5108G	750	0059
N5109	650	0135
N5109	80A	380-11
N5109R	550	0873
N5109R	550	0918
(N5109R)	560	0285
(N5109R)	560	0333
N5109R	560	0385
N5109R	560	0416
N5109R	750	0045
N5109R	750	0061
N5109T	80A	380-11
N5109W	550	0885
N5109W	550	0920
(N5109W)	560	0286
N5109W	560	0334
N5109W	750	0019
N5109W	750	0046
N5111	650	7011
N5111H	STR	5111
N5112	650	7012
N5112	**750**	**0010**
N5112K	525	0152
N5112K	550	0880
(N5112K)	560	0287
N5112K	560	0418
N5112K	560	0534
N5112K	650	7085
N5113	650	7013
N5113	**750**	**0013**
N5113H	G2	107
N5113H	STR	5142
N5114	650	0094
N5114	650	7018
N5114	**750**	**0017**
N5114G	35A	181
N5115	650	0095
N5115	650	7015
N5115	**750**	**0018**
N5116	650	0096
N5116	**750**	**0019**
(N5116)	750	0022
N5117	**650**	**7064**
N5117H	G2	197
N5117U	550	0820
N5117U	550	0868
N5117U	550	0912
N5117U	650	7047
N5117U	650	7069
N5117U	650	7089
N5118	650	7013
N5119	650	7015
N5120U	525	0202
N5120U	560	0449
N5120U	650	7049
N5120U	650	7071
N5120U	750	0058
N5121N	550	0824
N5121N	650	7050
N5122X	525	0162
N5122X	525	0203
N5122X	750	0011
N5124F	560	0392
N5124F	560	0451
N5124F	750	0086
N5125J	560	0479
N5125J	560	0484
N5125J	560	5092
N5125J	750	0020
N5125J	750	0024
N5130J	525	0187
N5130J	560	0452
N5130J	750	0088
N5131M	750	0021
N5132T	525	0155
N5132T	525	0193
N5132T	560	0453
N5132T	750	0090
N5133E	525	0204
N5133K	500	299
N5135A	525	0196
N5135A	550	0876
N5135A	560	5095
N5135A	750	0048
N5135K	525	0089
N5135K	550	0801
N5135K	550	0878
N5135K	560	0454
N5135R	550	0802
N5136J	525	0090
N5136J	525	0206
N5136J	525	0316
N5136J	525	0346
N5138F	525	0091
N5138F	525	0163
N5138F	525	0195
N5139W	35A	396
N5141F	560	0288
N5141F	560	5006
N5141F	650	7072
N5141F	650	7099
N5144	650	7012
N5145P	525	0191
N5145P	525	0318
N5145P	525	0347
N5145P	525	0370
N5145P	550	0831
N5145P	550	0833
N5145P	560	0290
N5145V	525	0278
N5145V	560	0517
N5147B	750	0104
N5148B	525	0165
N5148B	525	0194
N5148B	550	0832
N5148B	560	0291
N5148B	650	7104
N5148N	525	0166
N5148N	525	0319
N5148N	525A	0003
N5148N	560	0292
N5148N	560	0357
N5148N	560	5004
N5151D	525	0280
N5151S	525	0093
N5151S	525	0167
N5151S	525	0197
N5151S	560	0349
N5152	20	440
N5152	G2	22
N5152X	560	0492
N5153J	525	0346
N5153K	525	0095
N5153K	525	0169
N5153K	525	0199
N5153K	525	0330
N5153K	560	0351
N5153K	560	0481
N5153K	750	0049
N5153X	525	0096
N5153X	525	0170
N5153X	525	0208
N5153X	560	0352
(N5153Z)	525	0097
N5153Z	525	0171
N5153Z	525	0200
N5153Z	560	0356
N5154J	525	0281
N5154J	525	0314
N5154J	550	0926
N5155G	550	0907
N5156B	525	0172
N5156B	560	0361
N5156D	525	0098
N5156D	525	0201
N5156D	525	0335
N5156D	525	0360
N5156D	560	0482
N5156D	750	0050
N5156V	525	0099
N5156V	525	0205
N5156V	560	0393
(N5157E)	525	0101
N5157E	525	0174
N5157E	525	0210
N5157E	560	0354
N5157E	560	0460
N5157E	650	7101
N5161J	525	0176
N5161J	525	0332
N5161J	525	0363
N5161J	560	0294
N5161J	560	0367
N5161J	560	0458
N5161J	560	0497
N5161R	**STR**	**5161/43**
N5162W	525	0209
(N5162W)	560	0295
N5162W	560	0459
N5162W	650	7096
N5163C	525	0177
N5163C	525	0324
(N5163C)	560	0296
N5163C	560	0358
N5163C	650	7087
N5163C	750	0065
N5165T	525	0340
N5165T	525	0371
N5165T	560	0297
N5165T	560	5003
N5165T	**560**	**5087**
N5165T	750	0080
N5166T	550	0906
N5166T	560	0494
N5166U	525	0179
N5166U	525	0215
N5166U	560	0298
N5166U	560	0359
N5168F	525	0180
N5168F	525	0213
N5168F	560	0299
N5168F	560	0360
N5172M	650	7111
N5174	650	7018
N5174W	650	7112
N5180K	525	0181
N5180K	560	0301
N5180K	560	0363
N5181U	560	0537
N5183U	525	0182
N5183U	525	0326
N5183U	525	0361
N5183U	560	0362
N5183U	560	0462
N5183U	650	7052
N5183V	525	0216
N5183V	525	0254
N5183V	560	0469
N5183V	560	5091
(N5183V)	650	7053
N5183V	650	7074
N5185J	525	0183
N5185J	525	0333
N5185J	550	0837
N5185J	650	7054
N5185V	525	0184
N5185V	525	0345
N5185V	525	0352
N5185V	560	0461
N5185V	650	7055
N5187B	525	0185
N5188A	550	0854
N5188A	560	0471
N5188A	650	7106
N5188N	525	0239
N5192E	**650**	**7113**
N5194B	550	0874
N5194J	525	0270
N5194J	560	0368
N5194J	560	5064
N5196U	750	0075
N5197A	525	0219
N5197A	525	0260
N5197A	560	0401
N5197A	560	5062
N5197M	750	0076
N5200	**560**	**0369**
N5200R	525	0144
N5200R	560	5007
N5200R	560	5061
N5200U	525	0369
N5200U	560	0402
N5200U	560	5063
N5201J	525	0267
N5201J	560	0403
N5201J	560	5060
N5201M	525	0116
N5201M	560	0404
N5201M	560	5026
N5201M	560	5069
N5202D	525	0217
N5202D	560	0405
N5202D	560	5027
N5202D	650	0241
N5203J	525	0117
N5203J	525	0258
N5203J	560	5028
N5203J	560	5078
N5203J	650	7077
N5203S	525	0118
N5203S	525	0221
N5203S	525	0238
N5203S	560	0406
N5203S	560	5029
N5203S	**560**	**5093**
N5204B	525	0134
N5204D	525	0103
N5204D	560	0407
N5204D	560	5008
N5204D	560	5065
N5207A	525	0104
N5207A	525	0135

N5207A	560	0408
N5207A	560	0438
N5207A	560	5070
N5207V	550	0910
N5209E	525	0295
N5211A	525	0106
N5211A	525	0137
N5211A	560	0410
N5211A	560	5084
N5211F	525	0107
N5211F	525	0138
N5211F	525	0225
N5211F	525	0364
N5211Q	525	0108
N5211Q	525	0223
N5211Q	525	0353
N5211Q	560	5033
N5212M	650	7098
N5213S	525	0110
N5213S	525	0356
N5213S	560	5035
N5213S	650	7076
N5214J	525	0112
N5214J	525	0226
N5214J	525	0245
N5214J	525	0357
N5214J	550	0804
N5214J	560	5037
N5214K	525	0113
N5214K	525	0227
N5214K	550	0805
N5214K	560	5038
N5214K	560	5073
N5214L	525	0114
N5214L	525	0249
N5214L	525	0362
N5214L	550	0822
N5214L	560	0374
N5214L	560	5040
N5216A	525	0228
N5216A	525	0342
N5216A	550	0808
N5216A	560	5013
N5216A	650	7057
N5218R	525	0149
N5218R	525	0229
N5218R	560	5043
N5218R	650	7059
N5218T	525	0230
N5218T	550	0810
N5218T	560	5044
N5218T	560	5079
N5218T	650	7060
N5219T	525	0269
N5220J	500	220
N5221Y	550	0811
N5221Y	560	5014
N5221Y	560	5045
N5221Y	650	7061
N5223D	525	0231
N5223D	560	5015
N5223D	560	5046
N5223D	750	0003
N5223J	500	188
N5223P	525	0123
(N5223P)	525	0252
N5223P	525	0253
N5223P	550	0812
N5223P	560	5047
N5223P	750	0004
N5223X	650	7102
N5223X	750	0119
N5223Y	525	0232
N5223Y	525	0366
(N5223Y)	560	0302
N5223Y	560	5049
N5223Y	750	0009
N5225J	500	225
N5225K	525	0339
N5225K	525	0354
N5225K	525	0375
N5225K	550	0816
N5225K	560	0303
N5225K	560	5050
N5225K	750	0010
N5226B	560	0304
N5226B	560	0411
N5226B	560	0442
N5226B	560	5051
N5226B	**560**	**5097**
N5226J	500	226
N5228Z	560	0305
N5228Z	560	0412
N5228Z	560	0443
N5228Z	560	5052
N5230J	500	230
(N5231J)	500	231
N5231S	560	0306
N5231S	560	0384
N5231S	560	0433
N5231S	560	5053
N5232J	500	232
N5233J	500	233
N5233J	550	660
N5233J	560	0307
N5233J	560	0413
N5233J	560	0419
N5233J	560	5054
(N5234J)	500	234
N5235G	525	0233
N5235G	525	0259
N5235G	525A	0005
N5235G	560	0308
N5235G	560	0365
N5235G	560	0414
N5235G	560	5058
N5235J	500	235
N5236J	500	236
(N5237J)	500	237
(N5238J)	500	238
(N5239J)	500	239
N5240J	500	240
N5241J	500	241
N5241Z	525	0337
N5241Z	525	0377
N5241Z	560	0310
N5241Z	750	0013
N5242J	500	242
N5243J	500	243
N5244F	525	0343
(N5244F)	560	0311
N5244F	560	5021
N5244F	560	5098
N5244F	750	0014
(N5244J)	500	244
N5245J	500	245
(N5246J)	500	246
N5246Z	525	0140
N5246Z	525	0235
N5246Z	525	0351
N5246Z	560	0313
N5246Z	560	5020
(N5247J)	500	247
(N5248J)	500	248
N5249J	500	249
N5250E	525	0141
N5250E	560	0314
N5250E	560	5018
(N5250J)	500	250
N5250K	560	0264
(N5250K)	560	0315
N5251J	500	251
(N5251Y)	560	0316
N5252	525A	0002
N5252C	550	661
N5252J	500	252
N5253A	125	256061
N5253A	500	304
N5253A	G2	222
N5253E	500	304
N5253J	500	253
N5254J	500	254
N5255J	500	255
N5257J	500	257
(N5258J)	500	258
N5259J	500	259
N5259Y	525	0065
(N5260J)	500	260
N5260Y	560	0364
N5260Y	750	0103
N5261J	500	261
N5261R	560	0318
N5262B	560	0320
N5262B	560	0370
N5262J	500	262
N5262W	560	0321
N5262X	560	0322
N5262X	560	0371
N5262Z	650	7062
N5263D	650	7066
(N5263S)	650	7067
N5263S	750	0005
N5263U	750	0006
N5263U	750	0016
N5264A	560	0377
N5264A	750	0111
(N5264E)	525	0119
N5264J	500	264
N5264M	525	0120
N5264M	550	0908
N5264S	525	0121
N5264U	525	0122
N5265B	560	0336
N5265J	500	265
N5265N	550	0916
N5265N	560	0337
N5266F	750	0008
N5266F	750	0118
N5266J	500	266
N5267D	560	0535
N5267J	500	267
N5267T	560	0340
N5267T	560	0342
N5268A	560	0343
N5268E	560	0345
N5268J	500	268
N5268M	560	0344
N5268V	560	0347
N5268V	560	0532
N5269A	560	0346
N5269A	560	0388
N5269A	650	7109
N5269J	500	269
N5270J	500	270
N5270K	560	0265
N5270M	560	0268
N5271J	500	271
N5272J	500	272
N5273J	500	273
(N5274J)	500	274
N5274U	125	25068
(N5275J)	500	275
(N5276J)	500	276
(N5277J)	500	277
(N5278J)	500	278
(N5279J)	500	279
(N5280J)	500	280
N5281J	500	281
(N5282J)	500	282
N5283J	500	283
(N5284J)	500	284
N5285J	500	285
N5286J	500	286
(N5287J)	500	287
(N5288J)	500	288
N5289J	500	289
(N5290J)	500	290
N5291J	500	291
N5292J	500	292
(N5293J)	501	293
N5294C	550	662
N5294J	500	294
N5295J	500	295
(N5296J)	500	296
N5297J	500	297
N5298J	500	298
N5299J	500	299
(N5300J)	500	300
N5301J	500	067
N5301J	500	301
N5302J	500	302
(N5303J)	500	303
N5304J	500	304
(N5305J)	500	305
N5306J	500	306
N5307J	500	307
(N5308J)	500	308
N5309J	500	309
(N5310J)	500	310
N5311J	500	311
N5312J	F502	312
(N5313J)	500	313
N5314J	500	314
N5314J	**550**	**663**
N5315J	500	315
N5315J	550	664
N5316J	500	316
N5318J	500	318
N5319J	500	319
(N5320J)	500	320
N5321J	500	321
N5322J	500	322
N5323J	500	323
(N5324J)	500	324
(N5325J)	500	325
N5326J	500	326
N5327J	500	327
(N5328J)	500	328
N5329J	500	329
(N5330J)	500	330
(N5331J)	500	331
N5332J	500	332
(N5333J)	500	333
N5334J	500	334
N5335J	500	335
(N5336J)	500	336
N5337J	500	337
N5338J	500	338
(N5339J)	500	339
(N5340J)	500	340
(N5341J)	500	341
(N5342J)	500	342
N5342J	550	070
(N5343J)	500	343
(N5344J)	500	344
(N5345J)	500	345
N5346C	501	685
N5346J	500	346
(N5347J)	500	347
(N5348J)	500	348
N5348J	550	071
N5348J	550	665
(N5349J)	500	349
N5350J	501	350
N5351J	501	351
N5352J	501	352
(N5353J)	500	139
N5353J	501	353
N5354J	501	354
N5355J	501	355
N5356J	501	356
N5357J	501	357
(N5358J)	501	358
(N5359J)	500	359
N5360J	501	360
N5361J	500	361
N5362J	501	362
(N5363J)	500	363
(N5364U)	500	032
N5366J	500	366
N5368J	501	368
N5373U	601	3026
N5379W	S60	306-100
N5400G	G2	36/3
N5402X	601	3027
N5408G	**550**	**666**
N5410	WWD	123
N5412	WWD	95
N5415	S60	306-16
N5415	WWD	62
N5418	WWD	6
N5419	S60	306-24
N5419	S60	306-55
N5420	S60	306-43
N5420	WWD	92
(N5425)	50	237

N5428G	550	346
N5430G	550	347
N5450	20	17
N5450M	400	RJ-31
N5451G	551	348
N5474G	35A	093
N5474G	550	349
N5491V	601	3029
N5492G	550	350
N5500F	550	138
N5500L	STR	5136
N5500S	500	048
N5501L	STR	5137
N5502L	STR	5138
N5503L	STR	5139/54
N5504L	STR	5140
N5505L	STR	5141
N5506L	STR	5142
N5507L	STR	5143
N5508L	STR	5144
N5509L	STR	5145
N5510L	STR	5146
N5511A	125	257113
N5511A	S40	282-137
N5511A	S40	282-91
N5511A	S65	465-39
N5511L	STR	5147
N5511Z	S40	282-91
N5512A	S40	282-137
N5512L	STR	5148
N5513L	STR	5149/11
N5514L	STR	5150/37
N5515L	STR	5151
N5516L	STR	5152
N5517L	STR	5153/61
N5518L	STR	5154
N5519C	G2	235
N5519L	STR	5155/32
N5520L	STR	5156
N5521L	STR	5157
N5522L	STR	5158
N5523L	STR	5159
N5524L	STR	5160
N5525L	STR	5161/43
N5526L	STR	5162
N5527L	STR	5201
N5528L	STR	5202
N5529L	STR	5203
N5530L	STR	5204
N5531L	STR	5205
N5532L	STR	5206
N5533L	STR	5207
N5534L	STR	5208
N5535L	STR	5209
N5536L	STR	5210
N5537L	STR	5211
N5538L	STR	5212
N5539L	STR	5213
N5540L	STR	5214
N5541L	STR	5215
N5542L	STR	5216
N5543G	55	043
N5543L	STR	5217
N5544L	STR	5218
N5545L	STR	5219
N5546L	STR	5220
N5547L	STR	5221
N5548L	STR	5222
N5549L	STR	5223
N5555U	20	39
N5565	S40	282-119
N5574	55	074
N5591A	500	289
N5594U	125	25219
N5598Q	400A	RK-18
(N5599)	55	099
N5600M	500	191
N5602	HFB	1045
N5627	HFB	1038
N5680Z	400A	RK-11
N5685X	400A	RK-38
N5695H	24D	278
(N5703C)	550	351
(N5703C)	550	666
N5704	560	0157
N5731	**900**	**8**
N5732	**125**	**258467**
N5732	200	502
N5732	50	217
N5733	50	156
N5733	**900**	**39**
N5734	100	196
N5734	**125**	**258304**
N5734	560	0157
N5735	125	257044
N5735	**125**	**258309**
N5735	560	0171
N5736	100	195
N5737	501	435
N5737	**90X**	**41**
N5738	100	198
N5739	50	11
N5739	S65	465-11
N5794J	125	259021
N5861	STR	5085
N5867	35	016
N5867	500	015
N5873C	550	352
N5878	MSP	106
N5878D	STR	5143
N5879	**MSP**	**107**
N5997K	G2	105
N6000J	35A	079
N6000J	650	0118
N6000J	S65	465-54
N6001H	125	256011
N6001L	**550**	**185**
N6033	125	256033
N6034F	500	239
N6053C	WWD	207
N6053C	WWD	361
N6060	G2	105
N6068	MSP	050
N6087	S40	282-26
N6100	60	100
N6110	**650**	**7023**
(N6111)	650	7011
N6114	650	0094
N6115	650	0095
N6145Q	500	058
N6150B	650	7050
(N6164Z)	G3	367
N6165C	601	3012
N6170C	550	669
N6177Y	**24**	**151**
N6218	125	25205
N6262T	23	071
N6307H	25D	359
N6307H	35A	652
N6307H	55ER	125
N6307H	C21A	519
N6307H	C21A	534
N6317V	55	049
N6317V	C21A	509
N6317V	C21A	524
N6317V	VU35	639
N6331V	31	006
N6331V	55	060
N6331V	55	123
N6331V	C21A	510
N6331V	C21A	525
N6340T	25D	360
N6340T	36A	063
N6340T	55B	127
N6340T	C21A	517
N6340T	C21A	532
N6354N	25D	336
N6358C	S40	282-4
N6360C	S40	282-6
N6361C	S40	282-7
N6361C	WWD	42
N6362C	S40	282-8
(N6362D)	35A	277
N6363C	S40	282-9
N6364C	S40	282-10
N6364U	55	060
N6365C	500	228
N6365C	S40	282-11
N6366C	S40	282-12
(N6366W)	10	57
N6367C	S40	282-13
N6368C	S40	282-14
N6369C	S40	282-15
N6370C	S40	282-16
N6371C	S40	282-17
N6372C	S40	282-18
N6373C	S40	282-19
N6374C	S40	282-20
N6375C	S40	282-21
N6376C	S40	282-22
N6377C	S40	282-23
N6378C	S40	282-24
N6379C	S40	282-25
N6380C	S40	282-26
N6381C	S40	282-27
N6382C	S40	282-28
N6383C	S40	282-29
N6384C	S40	282-30
N6389C	S40	282-34
N6390C	S40	282-35
N6391C	S40	282-36
N6392C	S40	282-37
N6393C	S40	282-38
N6394C	S40	282-39
N6395C	S40	282-40
N6396C	S40	282-41
N6397C	S40	282-42
N6398C	S40	282-43
N6399C	S40	282-44
N6412	WWD	95
N6453	G3	349
N6453	**G4**	**1033**
N6458	**G3**	**349**
(N6462)	24	127
N6504V	WWD	35
N6505V	WWD	39
N6510V	WWD	41
N6511V	WWD	42
N6512V	WWD	64
N6513V	WWD	47
N6513X	**G3**	**310**
N6516V	S550	0144
N6518V	WWD	43
N6523A	550	460
N6525J	500	308
N6527V	WWD	69
N6534V	WWD	54
N6538V	WWD	59
N6544V	WWD	57
N6545V	WWD	60
N6546V	WWD	63
N6550V	WWD	56
N6550W	50	136
N6552C	S40	282-45
N6552R	T39	276-6
N6553C	S40	282-46
N6555C	**20**	**78/412**
N6555C	S40	282-48
N6555L	**20**	**85/425**
N6556C	S40	282-49
N6557C	S40	282-50
N6563C	500	012
N6563C	500	014
N6563C	500	551
N6565A	20	39
N6565A	S40	282-28
N6565C	551	174
N6565K	S40	282-28
N6566C	550	175
N6567C	550	176
N6567G	125	256048
N6581E	T39	265-82
N6596R	25D	286
N6610V	WWD	74
N6611V	WWD	75
N6612S	T39	276-48
N6612V	WWD	76
N6613V	WWD	78
N6617B	36A	026
N6617V	WWD	81
(N6621)	20	378
N6637G	**550**	**670**
N6666A	31A	150
N6666K	25D	285
N6666K	35A	481
N6666K	55	115
N6666R	25D	285
N6666R	31A	150
N6666R	31A	153
N6666R	35A	412
N6666R	50	124
N6666R	55	115
N6666R	**60**	**143**
N6701	20	177
N6702	125	25241
N6709	125	25239
(N6761L)	550	671
N6763C	550	672
N6763L	**550**	**673**
N6763M	501	686
(N6770S)	550	674
N6773P	550	675
N6775C	**550**	**677**
N6775U	550	678
(N6776P)	550	679
N6776T	**550**	**680**
(N6776Y)	550	681
N6777V	501	567
(N6777X)	501	568
N6778C	501	569
(N6778L)	501	570
N6778L	550	684
N6778T	501	571
(N6778V)	501	572
(N6778Y)	501	573
N6778Y	550	687
N6779D	501	576
N6779L	501	577
N6779P	501	578
N6779Y	501	579
(N6780)	55	083
(N6780A)	501	581
N6780A	560	0360
N6780C	501	582
N6780C	550	690
N6780J	501	583
(N6780M)	501	584
N6780Y	501	585
N6780Z	500	586
N6781C	501	588
N6781C	650	7056
(N6781D)	501	589
(N6781G)	501	590
N6781L	501	591
N6781R	501	592
(N6781T)	501	593
N6781Z	501	594
N6782B	501	597
N6782F	500	598
(N6782P)	501	599
(N6782T)	501	600
N6782T	550	695
N6782X	501	601
N6783C	501	604
N6783L	501	605
N6783U	501	606
N6783V	501	607
N6783X	500	608
(N6783X)	560	0088
N6784L	501	611
N6784P	501	612
N6784P	560	0091
N6784T	501	613
N6784X	501	614
N6784X	560	0092
N6784Y	500	645
N6784Y	501	615
N6784Y	560	0092A
N6785C	501	617
(N6785C)	560	0093
N6785D	501	618
N6785D	560	0094
N6785L	501	619
N6788P	560	0095
N6789	55	083
N6789	S40	282-112

N6789D	S40	282-112
(N6790L)	560	0097
(N6790P)	560	0098
(N6792A)	560	0100
N6798Y	550	219
N6798Z	550	220
N6799C	550	226
N6799C	551	355
N6799E	550	227
N6799L	550	228
N6799L	550	356
(N6799L)	560	0104
N6799T	550	229
N6799T	550	357
N6799Y	550	230
N6800C	550	234
N6800C	550	360
(N6800C)	560	0105
N6800J	550	235
N6800S	550	236
N6800S	550	361
N6800Z	550	237
(N6801H)	550	239
N6801H	560	0106
N6801L	550	240
(N6801L)	560	0107
N6801P	550	241
(N6801P)	560	0108
N6801Q	550	242
N6801Q	550	389
(N6801Q)	560	0109
N6801R	550	243
N6801T	550	244
(N6801V)	550	245
N6801V	560	0109
N6801Z	550	390
N6801Z	551	246
N6802S	550	248
N6802S	550	368
(N6802S)	560	0110
N6802T	550	249
N6802T	550	369
(N6802T)	560	0111
N6802X	550	250
N6802Y	550	251
N6802Y	550	370
N6802Z	550	252
N6803E	550	255
N6803L	550	256
N6803L	550	372
N6803L	560	0113
(N6803T)	550	257
(N6803T)	560	0114
(N6803Y)	550	258
N6803Y	560	0115
N6804C	550	261
N6804F	550	262
N6804F	550	374
(N6804F)	560	0117
N6804L	25	006
N6804L	550	263
N6804L	551	375
N6804L	560	0118
N6804M	550	264
(N6804N)	550	265
(N6804N)	560	0119
N6804S	551	266
N6804Y	550	376
N6804Y	551	267
N6804Y	560	0120
N6804Y	560	0153
N6804Z	550	268
N6805T	550	269
N6805T	551	377
N6805T	560	0154
N6806X	550	378
N6806X	560	0120
(N6806Y)	550	378
N6808C	550	379
N6808C	560	0121
(N6808Z)	560	0122
(N6809G)	560	0123
(N6809T)	560	0124
N6809V	560	0125
N6810J	EC	125
(N6810L)	560	0127
(N6810N)	560	0128
(N6811F)	560	0129
(N6811T)	560	0130
(N6811X)	560	0131
N6811Z	560	0132
N6812D	560	0134
N6812D	650	0207
N6812L	560	0135
N6812L	650	0208
N6812Z	560	0136
(N6812Z)	650	0209
N6820J	20	135
N6820T	650	0211
(N6820Y)	650	0212
(N6823L)	650	0213
(N6824G)	650	0215
N6825X	551	364
N6826U	550	380
(N6828S)	650	0217
N6829X	650	0218
N6829Y	550	365
N6829Z	650	0219
N6830T	650	0220
N6830X	550	366
N6830Z	550	367
N6846T	**550**	**625**
N6851C	550	697
N6860A	550	271
N6860C	551	272
N6860L	550	273
N6860R	550	274
N6860S	550	275
N6860T	550	276
N6860U	551	277
N6860Y	551	278
N6861D	550	281
N6861E	551	282
N6861L	550	283
N6861P	550	284
N6861S	550	285
N6861X	550	286
N6862C	551	290
N6862D	550	291
N6862L	550	292
N6862Q	**550**	**293**
N6862R	550	294
N6863B	551	300
N6863C	551	301
N6863G	550	302
N6863J	550	303
N6863L	550	304
N6863T	550	305
"N6864"	560	0162
N6864B	550	309
N6864C	550	310
N6864L	551	311
N6864X	551	312
N6864Y	550	313
N6864Z	550	314
N6865C	550	319
(N6868P)	650	0210
N6871L	560	0135
N6872T	560	0136
N6872T	560	0155
N6874Z	560	0137
(N6876Q)	560	0140
N6876S	560	0141
N6876Z	560	0142
N6877C	560	0143
N6877G	560	0144
(N6877L)	560	0145
(N6877Q)	560	0146
(N6877R)	560	0147
(N6879L)	560	0150
N6881Q	560	0151
N6882R	560	0152
N6885L	560	0156
N6885V	560	0157
(N6885Y)	560	0158
N6886X	560	0160
N6887M	501	620
N6887R	501	621
N6887T	550	320
(N6887T)	560	0164
N6887X	550	321
(N6887X)	560	0165
N6887Y	550	322
N6888C	550	326
N6888C	560	0169
N6888D	550	327
N6888L	550	328
N6888L	560	0170
N6888T	550	329
(N6888T)	560	0171
N6888X	550	330
(N6888X)	560	0172
N6888Z	551	331
N6889E	550	335
N6889E	560	0174
N6889K	550	336
N6889L	550	337
N6889T	550	338
N6889Y	550	339
N6889Z	550	340
(N6890C)	551	342
(N6890D)	550	343
(N6890E)	550	344
N6890G	550	345
(N6960)	125	257024
N7000C	G2	165/37
N7000C	G3	344
N7000G	**20**	**440**
N7000G	25	027
N7000G	650	0114
N7000G	G2	156/31
N7000G	S65	465-16
N7000K	23	029
N7004	550	427
N7004T	G2	28
N7005	125	257024
N7005	**650**	**7044**
N7005	STR	5105
N7006	**125**	**257024**
N7007Q	S550	0030
N7007V	35A	594
N7007V	S550	0030
N7007X	125	257034
N7008	600	1054
N7008	**601**	**5164**
N7008	STR	5101/15
N7008J	STR	5101/15
N7011H	601	3032
N7028F	WWD	131
N7028U	551	290
N7035C	25D	352
(N7038Z)	MSP	101
N7043U	T39	265-12
N7046J	601	5122
N7047K	S550	0133
N7050V	**D1A**	**A058SA**
N7051J	WWD	409
N7055	125	25142
N7059U	650	0210
N7062B	125	257062
N7070A	**S550**	**0068**
N7074X	24B	223
N7090	S40	282-30
N7090	S60	306-16
N7090	S60	306-5
N7090	S60	306-62
N7090	WWD	95
N7096B	G4	1162
N7096E	G3	498
N7096G	G3	497
N7105	STR	5078/3
N7110K	500	016
N7111H	501	595
N7117	**35A**	**462**
N7118A	S550	0065
N7121K	24D	230
N7125	35	035
N7125J	125	25013
N7125J	125	25107
N7134E	G3	423
N7143N	T39	265-70
N7145V	STR	5001/53
N7148J	**75A**	**380-33**
N7153X	550	407
N7155P	G2	169
N7158Q	HFB	1040
N7170J	125	25276
N7171	125	25264
N7200K	**23**	**099**
N7220L	560	0142
N7228K	**50**	**146**
N7243U	650	7054
N7244W	55	028
N7259J	35A	505
N7260C	25D	365
N7260E	35A	615
N7260G	55	111
N7260H	35A	622
N7260J	55	126
N7260K	55B	131
N7260Q	35A	623
N7260T	35A	627
N7261B	25D	366
N7261D	55B	134
N7261H	VU35	641
N7261R	35A	626
N7262A	25D	367
N7262M	55	113
N7262X	VU35	642
N7262Y	31	002
N7263C	C21A	509
N7263D	C21A	510
N7263E	C21A	511
N7263F	C21A	512
N7263H	C21A	513
N7263K	C21A	514
N7263L	C21A	515
N7263N	C21A	516
N7263R	C21A	517
N7263X	C21A	518
N7274A	560	0386
N7277X	MSP	112
N7281Z	**500**	**047**
(N7300G)	24B	186
N7300K	24B	186
N7301	90X	19
N7338	560	0137
N7440C	125	25142
N7465T	125	257046
N7490A	**125**	**257173**
N7500	STR	5102
N7500K	24	065
N7502V	S40	282-52
N7503V	S40	282-53
N7504V	S40	282-54
N7505V	S40	282-55
N7506V	S40	282-56
N7507V	S40	282-57
N7508V	S40	282-58
N7509V	S40	282-59
N7510V	S40	282-60
N7514V	S40	282-64
N7519N	S60	306-48
N7522N	S60	306-49
N7529N	S60	306-50
N7531N	S60	306-51
N7543H	500	266
N7547P	560	0365
N7571N	S60	306-52
N7572N	75	370-1
N7573N	S60	306-53
N7574N	S60	306-54
N7575N	S60	306-55
N7576N	S60	306-56
N7577N	S60	306-57
N7578N	S60	306-58
N7584N	S40	282-107
N7585N	75	370-2
N7586N	75	370-3
N7587N	75	370-4
N7588N	75	370-5
N7589N	75	370-6
N7590N	75A	370-7
N7591N	75	370-8
N7592N	75	370-9
N7593N	75A	380-1

N7594N	S40	282-99
N7595N	S40	282-106
N7596N	S40	282-101
N7596N	S40	282-108
N7597N	S40	282-102
N7597N	S40	282-110
N7598N	S40	282-103
N7600	STR	5054/59
N7600J	STR	5054/59
N7600K	25B	135
(N7601)	G2	32/2
N7601	**G4**	**1245**
N7601R	**MSP**	**060**
N7602	G2	32/2
(N7602)	G4	1245
N7638S	WWD	134
N7654F	200	489
N7662N	S40	282-111
N7667N	S40	282-112
(N7682V)	S60	306-79
(N7684X)	HFB	1042
(N7685T)	HFB	1055
N7700L	560	0203
N7700T	**501**	**662**
N7728	125	257028
N7728T	560	0374
N7735A	35A	138
N7766Z	G2	174
N7775	STR	5073
N7776	G4	1121
N7777B	125	25174
N7777B	35A	079
N7777B	35A	508
N7777B	**650**	**0214**
N7778L	S40	282-135
N7782	125	257025
N7782	STR	5066/46
N7784	55	023
N7784	WWD	63
N7788	125	257073
N7788	601	3011
N7788	STR	5107
N7789	G2	90
N7798D	550	333
N7800	**G4**	**1098**
N7801L	25D	355
N7820C	S40	282-1
N7824M	20	42
N7851M	**550**	**695**
N7864J	550	427
N7895Q	560	0199
(N7922)	20	37/406
N7953S	STR	5108
N7954S	STR	5109/13
N7955S	STR	5110/47
N7956S	STR	5111
N7957S	STR	5112/7
N7958S	STR	5113/25
N7959S	STR	5114/18
N7961S	STR	5116
N7962S	STR	5117/35
N7963S	STR	5118
N7964S	STR	5119/29
N7965S	STR	5120/26
N7966S	STR	5121
N7967S	STR	5122
N7967S	STR	5141
N7968S	STR	5123/14
N7969S	STR	5124
N7970S	STR	5125/31
N7971S	STR	5126
N7972S	STR	5127
N7973S	STR	5128/16
N7974S	STR	5129
N7975S	STR	5130
N7976S	STR	5131
N7977S	STR	5132/57
N7978S	STR	5133
N7979S	STR	5134/50
N7980S	STR	5135
N8000	600	1076
N8000	G2	39
N8000	S60	306-68
N8000J	G2	42/12
N8000U	**20**	**436**
N8000U	650	0107
N8000U	S60	306-19
N8000U	S65	465-24
N8000Z	125	256012
N8005	**560**	**5006**
N8005Y	**25B**	**121**
N8008F	551	496
N8010X	55	096
N8010X	600	1038
N8014Q	400A	RK-37
N8025X	S60	306-84
N8040A	**35**	**048**
N8041R	**560**	**0413**
(N8051H)	400A	RK-45
N8053V	400A	RK-47
N8060V	400A	RK-48
N8060Y	400A	RK-49
N8066P	31A	126
N8067Y	60	097
N8070Q	400A	RK-73
N8070U	WWD	124
N8071J	60	039
N8071L	60	091
N8073R	**400A**	**RK-24**
N8073Y	31A	133
N8074W	60	074
N8079Q	31A	129
N8080W	60	080
N8082B	60	102
N8082J	31A	128
N8083N	400A	RK-62
N8085T	**400A**	**RK-51**
N8086L	60	096
N8089Y	60	089
N8090	125	258090
N8090P	60	090
N8094U	24D	297
N8097V	400A	RK-26
N8100E	10	52
N8100E	10	53
N8100E	50	33
N8100E	900	34
N8100E	**90X**	**4**
N8114G	500	129
N8115N	G3	404
N8125J	125	25148
N8138M	400A	RK-84
N8146J	400A	RK-74
N8152H	400A	RK-9
N8157H	400A	RK-57
N8163G	400A	RK-16
N8164M	400A	RK-64
N8166A	400A	RK-76
N8167G	400A	RK-81
N8167Y	**400A**	**RK-67**
N8169Q	400A	RK-69
N8180Q	400A	RK-80
N8186	**125**	**258186**
N8189J	**501**	**537**
N8200E	10	111
N8200E	50	150
N8200E	**900**	**34**
N8202Q	500	002
N8203K	**G4**	**1205**
N8206S	604	5335
N8210W	400A	RK-72
N8216Q	35A	370
N8216Z	35A	309
(N8217W)	25D	299
N8220F	G3	371
N8221M	**D1A**	**A076SA**
N8226M	G3	413
N8227P	55	086
N8227V	20	150/445
N8228P	35A	263
N8239E	**400A**	**RK-46**
N8249Y	400A	RK-44
(N8252J)	400A	RK-105
N8252J	400A	RK-40
N8253A	125	256061
N8253Y	400A	RK-42
N8260D	**600**	**1063**
N8260L	400A	RK-60
N8265Y	400A	RK-41
N8270	**60**	**063**
N8271	**60**	**066**
N8277Y	400A	RK-77
N8278Z	400A	RK-78
N8279G	**400A**	**RK-79**
N8280	25	052
N8280	**35A**	**310**
N8280J	400A	RK-68
N8281	**35A**	**232**
N8282E	400A	RK-82
N8283C	400A	RK-83
N8288R	**525**	**0090**
N8299Y	400A	RK-85
N8300	WWD	12
N8300E	**50**	**33**
N8300E	STR	5115/39
N8311N	S40	282-113
N8333N	S40	282-115
N8338N	S40	282-117
N8339N	S40	282-118
N8341N	S40	282-119
N8345K	S40	282-76
N8349N	S40	282-121
N8350N	S40	282-123
N8356N	S40	282-125
N8357N	S60	306-64
N8364N	S60	306-65
N8365N	S60	306-66
N8400B	S40	282-23
N8400E	125	257202
N8400E	**50**	**150**
N8417B	550	042
N8418B	550	043
N8445N	75A	380-2
N8447A	10	84
N8463	10	152
N8467N	75A	380-3
N8482B	24	148
N8484P	AST	014
N8490P	G2	4/8
N8494	100	201
(N8494C)	650	7072
(N8495B)	200	509
N8499B	500	338
N8500	S65	465-59
N8508Z	500	284
N8514Y	WWD	231
N8516Z	50	7
N8520J	551	151
N8526A	75A	380-53
N8534	**WWD**	**113**
N8535	WWD	139
N8536	WWD	148
N8536Y	24B	217
N8537B	35A	236
N8550A	**50**	**263**
N8562W	35A	462
N8562Y	35A	483
N8563A	35A	480
N8563B	25D	360
N8563E	55	056
N8563G	35A	488
N8563M	55	077
N8563N	35A	491
N8563P	55	063
N8563Z	55	075
N8564K	35A	496
N8564M	35A	493
N8564P	35A	498
N8564X	55	089
N8564Z	55ER	087
N8565H	55	026
N8565J	35A	479
N8565K	55	065
N8565N	35A	497
N8565X	35A	502
N8565Y	25D	364
N8565Z	55	095
N8566B	35A	492
N8566F	55	091
N8566Q	55	097
N8566X	35A	500
N8566Z	25D	369
N8567A	35A	503
N8567J	**25D**	**368**
N8567K	35A	589
N8567R	35A	597
N8567T	35A	598
N8567X	55	117
N8567Z	35A	591
N8567Z	35A	608
N8568B	35A	504
N8568D	35A	612
N8568J	55	121
N8568P	55	122
N8568Q	35A	616
N8568V	35A	619
N8568Y	VU35	640
N8572	900	105
N8575J	50	196
(N8777N)	550	171
N8785R	G2	93
N8805	50	3
N8881N	551	190
(N8888D)	35A	661
N8900M	501	675
(N8909R)	S60	306-41
N8940	**525**	**0253**
N8999A	20	137
N9000F	50	172
N9000F	**50**	**242**
N9000F	S65	465-25
N9000S	S40	282-64
N9000V	S40	282-64
N9000V	S60	306-10
N9001V	S60	306-10
N9003	525	0257
N9008	600	1054
N9008	**700**	**9008**
N9011R	500	210
N9013S	500	288
N9014S	550	025
N9023W	WWD	10
N9026	125	259026
N9033X	24	169
N9035Y	**MSP**	**086**
N9040	125	25142
N9040	G2	82
N9040N	WWD	140
N9041N	WWD	141
N9042N	WWD	142
N9043N	WWD	143
N9043U	125	256058
N9044N	WWD	144
N9045N	WWD	145
N9046F	STR	5015
N9046N	WWD	146
N9047N	WWD	147
N9048N	WWD	148
N9049N	WWD	149
N9050N	WWD	150
N9060Y	500	241
N9065J	500	247
N9071M	600	1019
N9108Z	**36**	**005**
N9113F	35A	259
N9113J	125	257067
N9114S	WWD	164
N9124N	125	25075
N9125M	55C	146
N9130F	35A	664
N9132Z	31	031
N9134Q	WWD	220
N9138	125	25216
N9138Y	900	33
N9140Y	35A	672
N9141N	35A	671
N9143F	31A	055
(N9147F)	10	42
N9147Q	31A	057
N9149	125	25161
N9152R	31A	051
N9152X	31A	061
N9155Z	60	025
N9166Y	T39	265-80
N9168Q	35A	668
N9173G	35A	673

N9173L	31	029
N9173M	31A	067
N9173N	31A	071
N9173Q	31A	053
N9173R	60	017
N9173T	31A	087
N9173V	31A	069
N9173X	31A	090
N9180K	**525**	**0342**
N9201R	STR	5001/53
N9202R	STR	5002
N9203R	STR	5003
N9204R	STR	5004
N9205R	STR	5007/45
N9206R	STR	5009
N9207R	STR	5020
N9208R	STR	5101/15
N9210R	STR	5016
N9211R	STR	5037/24
N9212R	STR	5038
N9214R	STR	5047
N9215R	STR	5048
N9216R	STR	5049
N9217R	STR	5051
N9218R	STR	5052
N9219R	STR	5053/2
N9220R	STR	5054/59
N9221R	STR	5023
N9222R	STR	5055/21
N9223R	STR	5056
N9225R	STR	5060
N9226R	STR	5061/48
N9228R	STR	5063
N9229R	STR	5065
N9230R	STR	5066/46
N9231R	STR	5068/27
N9233R	STR	5072/23
N9234R	STR	5074/22
N9235R	STR	5076/17
N9235R	STR	5102
N9236R	STR	5077
N9238R	STR	5079/33
N9240R	STR	5084/8
N9241R	STR	5085
N9242R	STR	5086/44
N9243R	STR	5087/55
N9244R	STR	5088
N9245R	STR	5089
N9246R	STR	5090
N9247R	STR	5091
N9248R	STR	5092/58
N9249R	STR	5093
N9250R	STR	5094
N9251N	S40	282-131
N9251R	STR	5095/30
N9252N	S40	282-132
N9252R	STR	5096/10
N9253R	STR	5097/60
N9254R	STR	5098/28
N9255R	STR	5099/5
N9256R	STR	5100/41
N9260A	23	047
N9272K	G2	46
N9280R	STR	5006/40
N9282R	STR	5011/1
N9282R	STR	5046
N9282Y	125	256044
N9283R	STR	5012
N9284R	STR	5013
N9286R	STR	5017
N9287R	STR	5018
N9288R	STR	5019
N9292X	**125**	**258315**
N9300	125	25051
N9300	G2	7
N9300	G4	1020
N9300C	125	25051
N9300C	125	25169
N9300C	**50**	**106**
N9300M	20	106
(N9300P)	125	25169
N9308Y	125	25058
N9311	50	121
N9312	50	126

N9313	50	128
N9314	50	130
(N9366Q)	STR	5214
N9500B	S40	282-91
N9503Z	S40	282-10
N9550A	**50**	**265**
N9654N	20	380
N9671A	25B	092
(N9680N)	601	3050
N9680Z	601	3050
N9700T	**560**	**0203**
N9700X	**601**	**5186**
N9708N	601	3061
N9711N	G3	358
N9712T	501	397
(N9718P)	G3	405
N9739B	STR	5052
N9871R	500	121
(N9876S)	35A	277
N9881S	PER	551
N9921	STR	5070/52
N9932	WWD	82
N9990P	AST	062
N9999E	20	135
N10108	500	035
N10121	125	25098
N10122	125	25029
N10122	WWD	182
N10123	**G2**	**107**
N10123	STR	5012
N10461	STR	5011/1
N10580	S65	465-7
N10581	S65	465-8
N10726	20	54
N10855	**125**	**258159**
N10855	**125**	**259002**
N10857	**125**	**258213**
N10870	35A	268
N10870	35A	331
N10870	35A	430
N10870	35A	649
N10870	55	122
N10870	55ER	103
N10871	35A	270
N10871	35A	317
N10871	35A	504
N10871	35A	618
N10871	36A	055
N10871	55C	143
N10872	25D	369
N10872	35A	275
N10872	55	013
N10873	25D	315
N10873	25D	364
N10873	31	003
N10873	35A	475
N10873	35A	602
N11111	23	098
N11288	**650**	**0184**
N11827	20	26
N11887	**80A**	**380-4**
N11917	M20	1
N12001	550	689
N12003	550	698
N12012	560	0268
N12022	550	708
(N12030)	550	712
N12033	550	713
N12035	550	714
N12058	552	0004
N12060	550	718
N12065	552	0011
N12068	**550**	**719**
N12109	35A	410
N12117	550	731
N12117	560	0007
N12121	STR	5005
N12142	550	396
(N12149)	550	397
(N12155)	550	402
N12157	550	403
(N12159)	550	404
N12160	551	412
N12160	560	0009

N12162	550	413
N12162	560	0010
N12164	550	414
N12167	550	415
N12171	550	422
N12171	560	0015
(N12173)	550	423
N12173	560	0016
N12190	550	437
(N12191)	550	438
N12225	125	25122
N12241	STR	5141
N12249	560	0018
N12269	552	0015
(N12283)	560	0023
(N12284)	560	0024
(N12285)	560	0025
(N12286)	560	0026
(N12289)	560	0027
N12295	560	0036
N12295	650	7075
N12297	560	0037
N12298	560	0038
N12315	24	154
N12373	25	054
N12403	560	0040
N12419	550	608
N12482	550	447
N12490	550	454
N12500	550	459
N12505	550	460
N12507	550	461
N12508	550	462
N12510	550	471
N12511	550	472
N12513	550	473
N12514	550	474
(N12522)	550	480
N12522	550	615
N12532	550	487
N12536	550	488
N12539	550	489
N12543	550	621
(N12543)	551	496
(N12549)	550	497
N12549	**550**	**501**
(N12554)	550	625
(N12554)	S550	0003
N12557	552	0003
N12564	552	0010
N12566	552	0012
N12568	552	0014
N12570	550	632
(N12570)	S550	0012
N12576	550	633
(N12576)	S550	0013
(N12582)	550	638
(N12583)	S550	0014
(N12593)	550	646
N12593	650	7008
(N12593)	S550	0024
(N12596)	550	647
N12596	650	7009
(N12596)	S550	0025
N12605	650	7013
(N12605)	S550	0031
(N12615)	S550	0036
N12616	650	7019
(N12616)	S550	0037
N12632	650	7030
N12636	650	7031
N12637	650	7032
N12642	650	7038
N12643	650	7039
N12652	650	7045
N12659	**75A**	**380-16**
N12660	552	0006
N12688	560	0488
(N12690)	S550	0046
N12695	S550	0047
N12703	S550	0052
N12705	S550	0053
N12709	S550	0054
(N12712)	S550	0061

N12715	S550	0062
(N12717)	S550	0063
(N12720)	S550	0069
(N12722)	S550	0070
(N12727)	S550	0071
N12730	S550	0080
(N12744)	S550	0088
N12745	S550	0089
N12746	S550	0090
(N12747)	S550	0091
N12756	552	0002
N12761	552	0007
N12762	552	0008
N12763	552	0009
N12798	560	0176
N12799	560	0177
N12807	560	0183
N12812	560	0187
N12813	560	0188
N12815	560	0189
N12816	560	0190
N12817	560	0191
N12824	560	0196
N12826	560	0197
N12838	560	0205
N12845	560	0213
N12850	560	0219
N12852	560	0220
N12855	552	0001
N12859	552	0005
(N12879)	560	0232
N12890	560	0243
(N12895)	560	0244
N12896	560	0245
N12900	S550	0103
N12903	S550	0104
N12907	560	0247
(N12907)	S550	0105
N12909	560	0248
(N12909)	S550	0106
N12910	560	0251
(N12910)	S550	0112
N12911	560	0252
(N12911)	S550	0113
N12920	S550	0118
N12921	560	0254
N12922	560	0255
(N12922)	S550	0119
N12924	S550	0120
(N12925)	S550	0121
N12929	560	0256
N12929	S550	0122
N12934	S550	0131
N12945	560	0263
(N12945)	S550	0137
N12967	552	0013
(N12979)	551	556
N12990	550	571
N12992	550	572
(N12993)	550	573
N12998	551	574
N12999	550	575
(N13001)	550	579
(N13006)	550	580
(N13007)	550	581
N13027	550	597
N13028	550	598
(N13047)	650	0007
(N13049)	650	0008
(N13052)	650	0013
N13052	650	0231
N13091	550	643
N13092	550	644
N13113	650	0159
N13138	650	0063
(N13142)	650	0069
(N13150)	650	0078
(N13162)	650	0082
N13166	650	0083
(N13168)	650	0084
(N13170)	650	0088
(N13175)	650	0089
(N13189)	650	0098
(N13194)	650	0103

N13195	650	0104
(N13204)	650	0111
(N13210)	650	0118
(N13217)	650	0119
N13218	650	0120
(N13222)	650	0125
(N13242)	650	0139
N13256	650	0146
N13259	650	0147
N13264	650	0155
N13267	650	0156
N13291	525	0024
N13304	STR	5004
N13308	525	0029
(N13312)	525	0031
(N13313)	525	0032
N13606	24D	254
N13627	550	147
N15693	400A	RK-29
N16200	STR	5033/56
(N16251)	G4	1013
N16777	125	25083
N17005	STR	5105
(N17401)	20	62/409
N17581	G2	127
N17581	G2	163
N17581	G2	183
N17581	G2	211
N17581	G2	235
N17581	G2	256
N17581	G3	346
N17581	G3	399
N17581	G3	435
N17581	G4	1001
N17581	G4	1011
N17581	G4	1059
N17581	G4	1107
N17581	G4	1157
N17582	G2	131/23
N17582	G2	164
N17582	G2	186
N17582	G2	239
N17582	G3	252
N17582	G3	326
N17582	G3	376
N17582	G3	415
N17582	G4	1005
N17582	G4	1061
N17582	G4	1096
N17582	G4	1158
N17583	G2	133
N17583	G2	167
N17583	G2	187
N17583	G2	43
N17583	G3	304
N17583	G3	347
N17583	G3	418
N17583	G3	466
N17583	G4	1015
N17583	G4	1062
N17583	G4	1159
N17584	G2	141
N17584	G2	169
N17584	G2	194
N17584	G2	224
N17584	G2	244
N17584	G3	307
N17584	G4	1019
N17584	G4	1026
N17584	G4	1063
N17584	G4	1108
N17584	G4	1160
N17585	G2	144
N17585	G2	171
N17585	G2	201
N17585	G2	214
N17585	G2	225
N17585	G2	78
N17585	G3	311
N17585	G3	345
N17585	G3	400
N17585	G4	1032
N17585	G4	1068
N17585	G4	1129

N17585	G4	1161
N17586	G2	149
N17586	G2	175
N17586	G2	202
N17586	G2	230
N17586	G2	91
N17586	G3	352
N17586	G3	379
N17586	G3	439
N17586	G3	465
N17586	G4	1072
N17586	G4	1076
N17586	G4	1167
N17587	G2	152
N17587	G2	177
N17587	G2	203
N17587	G2	246
N17587	G3	324
N17587	G3	393
N17587	G3	442
N17587	G4	1074
N17587	G4	1173
N17588	G2	179
N17588	G2	204
N17588	G3	367
N17588	G4	1037
N17588	G4	1175
N17589	G2	161
N17589	G2	182
N17589	G2	248
N17589	G3	368
N17589	G4	1078
N17603	G3	407
N17603	G4	1038
N17603	G4	1079
N17608	G3	356
N17608	G3	408
N17608	G4	1042
N17608	G4	1106
N18243	125	257182
N18328	501	373
N20373	10	33
N21066	G2	69
N21092	T39	265-42
(N22265)	STR	5005
(N22508)	501	474
N22511	550	089
N22976	WWD	133
N23204	**125**	**258346**
N23207	**125**	**258350**
N23208	125	258351
N23395	125	258339
N23451	125	258382
N23455	125	258384
N23466	125	258385
N23479	125	258386
N23488	125	258388
N23493	125	258389
N23509	125	258390
N23525	**400A**	**RK-238**
N23550	125	258403
N23555	20	46
N23556	125	258370
N23566	**125**	**258381**
N23569	125	258392
N23577	125	258395
N23585	125	258396
N23592	**125**	**258401**
N24237	**650**	**0102**
N24480	T39	276-33
N25685	31A	056
N25997	31A	062
N25999	31A	059
N26002	31A	077
N26005	31A	065
N26006	31A	066
N26008	23	026
N26011	125	25060
N26011	60	013
N26018	31A	058
N26018	G3	316
N26029	60	009
N26105	525	0042
N26105	650	0182

N26174	525	0046
N26174	650	0189
N26178	551	141
N26227	501	642
(N26228)	501	643
N26228	650	0194
N26229	550	093
N26232	501	644
N26233	650	0195
N26263	501	652
N26264	501	653
(N26264)	650	0201
N26271	650	0203
N26369	551	150
N26369	S550	0152
N26379	525	0052
N26379	S550	0154
N26461	500	489
N26461	550	156
(N26481)	501	496
N26481	525	0061
(N26486)	501	497
N26486	525	0062
N26492	501	505
N26493	501	506
N26494	501	507
N26494	**550**	**605**
(N26495)	501	508
N26495	525	0066
(N26496)	501	509
N26496	**550**	**607**
N26497	501	510
N26498	501	511
(N26499)	501	512
N26499	525	0067
(N26502)	501	520
N26502	525	0069
N26503	501	521
(N26504)	501	522
N26504	525	0070
N26506	501	523
N26507	501	524
(N26509)	501	525
N26509	525	0071
N26510	501	532
N26514	500	533
N26517	501	534
N26523	501	535
(N26540)	501	507
N26581	525	0074
N26583	35A	433
N26610	550	075
N26610	550	161
N26613	550	076
(N26614)	550	077
(N26615)	550	078
(N26616)	551	079
N26617	550	080
N26619	550	081
N26619	G3	353
(N26621)	550	086
N26621	**550**	**593**
(N26622)	550	087
(N26623)	550	088
(N26624)	550	089
N26626	550	090
N26627	550	091
N26628	551	092
(N26630)	550	101
N26630	560	0039
N26631	550	102
N26632	550	103
N26634	550	104
(N26635)	550	105
N26638	551	106
N26639	551	107
N26640	550	113
N26640	600	1039
(N26643)	550	114
N26643	560	0041
(N26648)	551	115
(N26648)	560	0042
N26649	550	116
N26652	550	123

(N26656)	550	124
(N26656)	560	0046
N26674	CVT	27
(N26771)	560	0050
(N26804)	560	0054
N26863	551	139
N26895	600	1056
(N27216)	560	0066
N27341	600	1051
N27457	551	132
N28686	125	25152
N28968	550	074
N29019	75	370-6
N29687	600	1048
N29858	500	112
N29966	10	17
N29977	125	25028
N29984	600	1060
N29991	500	254
N29995	WWD	250
N30046	31A	146
N30046	400A	RK-206
N30111	31A	153
N30289	125	258404
N30319	125	258408
N30337	125	258409
N30562	**125**	**258407**
N30682	125	258412
N30742	125	258414
N31001	G4	1001
N31016	125	258415
N31046	125	258418
N31079	500	180
N31088	500	079
N31240	600	1063
N31340	125	258420
N31403	T39	276-4
N31428	400	RJ-28
N31432	400	RJ-32
N31437	**400**	**RJ-37**
N31542	400	RJ-42
N31590	125	258430
N31596	125	258439
N31733	400	RJ-33
N31820	**125**	**258421**
N31833	**125**	**258427**
N32010	T39	265-83
N32212	T1A	TX-10
N32287	24D	230
N32290	S65	465-17
N32508	T39	285-17
N32654	S40	282-111
N36050	S40	282-80
N36065	S40	282-81
N36204	25B	138
N36842	501	364
N36846	501	365
N36848	500	366
N36850	501	367
N36854	501	368
N36854	550	653
N36858	501	369
N36859	501	370
N36860	501	371
N36861	501	372
N36862	501	373
N36863	501	374
N36864	501	375
N36869	501	376
N36870	500	377
N36871	501	378
N36872	501	379
N36873	501	380
N36880	501	381
N36881	501	382
N36882	501	383
N36883	501	384
N36884	501	385
N36885	501	386
N36886	501	387
N36886	550	654
N36887	501	388
N36888	501	389
N36890	501	390

N36891	501	391
N36892	500	392
N36893	501	393
N36895	501	394
N36896	501	395
N36897	500	396
N36898	501	397
N36901	501	398
N36906	500	399
N36908	501	400
N36911	501	401
N36912	500	402
N36914	501	403
N36915	501	404
N36916	501	405
N36918	501	406
N36919	501	407
N36922	501	408
N36923	501	409
N36943	501	423
N36949	501	428
N37201	**550**	**655**
N37489	500	317
N37516	125	25271
N37594	24	128
N37643	500	255
N37931	35A	342
N37943	25D	344
N37947	35A	449
N37949	25D	348
N37951	55	011
N37962	35A	446
N37965	35A	399
N37966	35A	403
N37971	**25D**	**358**
N37973	25D	359
N37975	125	257004
N37975	35A	474
N37980	35A	412
N37984	35A	384
N37988	35A	436
N38328	25D	314
N38788	24D	262
N39142	550	235
N39292	35A	189
N39293	35A	188
N39300	501	571
N39301	501	353
N39391	25D	311
N39391	35A	118
N39391	36A	042
N39391	55	078
N39391	55	105
N39391	55	124
N39391	55C	139
N39394	28	004
N39394	35A	145
N39394	35A	597
N39394	36A	057
N39394	55	082
N39398	25D	245
N39398	25D	362
N39398	35A	144
N39398	35A	272
N39398	35A	316
N39398	35A	626
N39398	55	095
N39398	55	114
N39399	25D	370
N39399	31	025
N39399	35A	151
N39399	35A	492
N39399	35A	607
N39399	55B	134
N39404	28	002
N39404	35A	658
N39404	55	079
N39404	55	104
N39404	C21A	624
N39412	25D	346
N39412	29	004
N39412	35A	179
N39412	35A	217
N39412	35A	329
N39412	55	067
N39412	55	110
N39412	VU35	638
N39413	25D	260
N39413	35A	259
N39413	35A	313
N39413	35A	474
N39413	35A	611
N39413	55	015
N39413	55	084
N39413	55C	137
N39415	25D	229
N39415	25D	347
N39415	31	005
N39415	35A	161
N39415	35A	201
N39415	35A	598
N39415	55	075
N39415	55ER	101
N39416	25D	238
N39416	25D	287
N39416	25D	363
N39416	35A	219
N39416	35A	433
N39416	35A	469
N39416	55	118
N39416	VU35	633
N39418	35A	205
N39418	35A	230
N39418	35A	267
N39418	35A	643
N39418	36A	053
N39418	55	039
N39418	55	120
N39461	50	98
N39515	10	37
N40027	**125**	**258434**
N40082	45	082
N40113	125	258438
N40130	31A	110
N40144	24F	342
N40144	25D	283
N40144	31	018
N40144	35A	165
N40144	35A	199
N40144	35A	253
N40144	35A	483
N40144	35A	508
N40144	35A	599
N40144	55	014
N40144	C21A	629
N40146	25D	349
N40146	35A	099
N40146	35A	178
N40146	35A	207
N40146	35A	593
N40146	36A	032
N40146	55	063
N40146	55	090
N40149	25D	357
N40149	25D	372
N40149	35A	101
N40149	35A	208
N40149	35A	344
N40149	35A	442
N40149	35A	623
N40149	55	083
N40162	25D	263
N40162	25XR	246
N40162	35A	477
N40162	35A	608
N40162	55	086
N40180	10	93
N40202	125	258442
N40215	**400A**	**RK-258**
N40252	400A	RK-247
N40280	31A	078
N40310	**125**	**258447**
N40323	60	023
N40339	31A	076
N40349	31A	079
N40363	31A	083
N40366	60	019
N40488	125	258440
N40489	125	258444
N40593	WWD	41
N40708	**125**	**258445**
N40994	20	289
N41093	**125**	**258454**
N41154	20	147/444
N41280	125	258448
N41283	400A	RK-266
N41431	125	258449
N41441	125	258450
N41534	125	258451
N41762	125	258456
N41953	125	25268
N41964	**125**	**258464**
N41984	**125**	**258457**
N42137	600	1011
N42622	125	256011
N42685	**125**	**258458**
N42825	25D	314
N42830	**125**	**258470**
N42905	31	020
N42905	35A	630
N42905	55	054
N42905	C21A	520
N42905	C21A	536
N43079	**125**	**258469**
N43182	**125**	**258482**
N43230	**125**	**258462**
N43259	125	258459
N43265	**125**	**258465**
N43436	**125**	**258468**
N43642	**125**	**258471**
N43675	**125**	**258475**
N43783	25D	260
N43926	**125**	**258481**
N44200	G3	324
N44515	**125**	**258485**
N44648	**125**	**258478**
N44676	**125**	**258476**
N44695	35A	444
N44722	**125**	**258472**
N44767	**125**	**258477**
N44779	**125**	**258479**
N44883	**125**	**258483**
N45500	125	257108
N45793	125	25152
N45811	24	108
N45824	24B	217
N45826	25D	283
N45862	24D	291
N46032	24X	267
N46106	501	382
N46901	125	257014
N46931	35A	092
N47449	G3	420
N48172	125	25028
N49566	125	257094
N49968	WWD	202
N50050	60	057
N50088	31A	088
N50088	**31A**	**192**
N50111	31A	035
N50111	**45**	**058**
N50114	31A	111
N50126	60	152
N50138	WWD	142
N50145	31A	178
N50145	45	037
N50153	31A	065
N50153	45	059
N50153	60	016
N50153	60	019
N50154	60	039
N50154	60	170
N50154	U36A	061
N50157	31A	171
N50157	45	069
N50157	60	017
N50157	60	046
N50159	31A	045
N50162	45	033
N50162	60	061
N50163	31A	044
N50207	**31A**	**097**
N50298	60	028
N50298	60	049
N50302	31A	092
N50324	60	069
N50353	60	035
N50378	31A	098
N50450	60	050
N50459	31A	095
N50602	500	083
N50602	60	060
N50612	550	0870
N50612	560	0439
N50612	560	0463
N50612	750	0025
N50612	750	0117
N50715	550	0823
N50715	560	0397
N50758	60	098
N50761	60	073
N50776	60	146
N50820	525	0077
N50820	560	0487
N50820	560	0506
N50820	650	7083
N50820	750	0114
N50928	600	1067
(N50938)	525	0088
N50938	525	0132
N50938	560	0396
N51038	550	0815
(N51038)	560	0279
(N51038)	560	0327
N51038	560	0383
N51038	560	0446
N51038	750	0063
N51038	750	0094
N51038	WWD	142
N51042	550	0827
(N51042)	560	0280
N51042	560	0468
N51042	560	0515
N51054	31A	105
N51055	550	0875
N51055	550	0903
N51055	560	0282
(N51055)	560	0330
N51055	750	0039
N51055	750	0069
N51057	31A	061
N51072	550	0826
(N51072)	560	0283
N51072	560	0331
N51072	560	0520
N51072	750	0017
N51072	750	0112
N51143	550	0849
N51143	550	0915
N51143	560	0432
N51143	560	0538
N51143	650	0240
N51143	650	7067
N51160	550	0894
N51160	550	0923
N51160	560	0474
N51160	650	7046
N51160	650	7068
N51160	750	0037
N51160	750	0078
N51176	525	0185
N51176	525	0212
N51176	650	7048
N51176	650	7070
N51176	750	0038
N51246	525	0154
N51246	525	0186
N51246	550	0857
N51246	560	0447
N51246	560	0450
N51246	560	0480
N51246	560	5090
N51313	750	0022
N51342	525	0188
N51342	650	7086
N51396	525	0092

N51396	525	0190
N51396	525	0355
N51396	560	0455
N51396	560	0527
N51444	525	0164
N51444	525	0192
N51444	525	0317
N51444	525	0350
N51444	560	0289
N51444	560	0456
N51444	650	7073
(N51522)	525	0094
N51522	525	0168
N51522	525	0198
N51522	560	0350
N51564	525	0100
N51564	525	0173
N51564	525	0336
N51564	525	0358
N51564	560	0353
N51564	560	0457
N51564	560	0491
N51575	525	0338
N51575	560	0293
N51575	560	0355
N51575	560	5005
N51575	560	5077
N51612	525	0303
N51666	525	0286
N51741	G2	45
N51743	525	0214
N51743	560	0300
N51744	525	0291
N51744	750	0108
N51817	525	0157
N51817	550	0845
N51817	560	0518
N51817	560	5086
N51817	650	7051
N51872	525	0159
N51872	525	0207
N51872	525	0334
N51872	550	0836
N51881	525	0218
N51881	560	0399
N51881	560	5071
N51896	**550**	**0922**
N51896	560	0501
N51933	560	5023
N51942	560	0400
N51942	560	0420
N51942	560	5089
N51990	WWD	183
N51993	125	25249
N51993	525	0143
N51993	560	5056
N51995	750	0102
N52038	525	0102
N52038	525	0133
N52038	525	0222
N52038	525	0224
N52038	560	5030
N52059	560	0503
N52081	525	0105
N52081	525	0136
N52081	525	0241
N52081	525	0266
N52081	560	0409
N52081	**560**	**5088**
N52113	525	0109
N52113	550	0803
N52113	560	0369
N52113	560	5009
N52113	560	5034
N52113	560	5085
N52136	525	0111
N52136	525A	0004
N52136	560	5036
N52136	750	0012
N52136	750	0040
N52141	525	0115
N52141	525	0145
N52141	550	0806
N52141	560	5011
N52141	560	5041
N52141	560	5080
N52144	525	0148
N52144	550	0807
N52144	560	5012
N52144	560	5083
N52144	650	7056
N52178	525	0118
N52178	525	0147
N52178	560	5010
N52178	560	5042
N52178	560	5072
N52178	650	7058
N52229	560	0505
N52235	**650**	**7110**
N52352	525	0376
N52352	560	0309
N52352	560	0366
N52352	560	0435
N52457	525	0139
N52457	525	0262
(N52457)	560	0312
N52457	560	0415
N52457	560	5057
(N52526)	560	0317
N52601	550	0919
N52601	560	0372
N52613	560	0319
N52613	650	7075
N52623	650	7063
N52626	650	7064
N52627	650	7065
N52639	750	0022
(N52642)	525	0123
N52642	525	0129
N52642	750	0106
N52645	560	0338
N52655	550	0911
N52655	750	0007
N52682	560	0348
N52682	750	0024
N53584	500	128
N53650	35	054
N54531	500	078
N54555	125	257023
N54754	35	026
N54784	S60	306-96
(N54888)	25D	258
N55922	G2	225
N56327	400A	RK-36
N56356	400A	RK-58
N56400	400A	RK-43
N56423	400A	RK-45
N56576	400A	RK-6
N56616	400A	RK-22
N58025	S40	282-76
N58966	75A	380-29
N59019	500	080
N60144	60	144
(N60181)	500	047
N61572	**501**	**504**
N61826	25D	214
(N61850)	560	5020
N61905	C21A	535
N62276	WWD	432
(N62452)	HFB	1041
N62570	20	379
N62864	501	644
N63357	**WWD**	**99**
N63537	**50**	**20**
(N63602)	35A	306
N63611	T39	276-21
N63810	**125**	**256037**
N63811	T39	276-44
N64688	125	257003
N64769	20	359/542
(N64792)	500	087
N65218	MSP	112
N65229	560	0069
N65311	20	6
N65339	24	163
N65357	601	5075
N65618	T39	276-42
N65733	80A	380-4
N65740	S40	282-133
N65741	80A	380-6
N65744	75A	380-7
N65745	S60	306-73
N65749	75A	380-8
N65750	S60	306-76
N65751	S60	306-77
N65752	S60	306-78
N65756	S60	306-80
N65758	75A	380-12
N65759	S60	306-82
N65761	75A	380-13
N65762	S60	306-84
N65763	S40	282-137
N65764	S60	306-85
N65765	S60	306-86
N65766	75A	380-15
N65767	S60	306-87
N65768	80A	380-17
N65769	S60	306-88
N65770	S60	306-89
N65771	75A	380-19
N65772	S60	306-90
N65773	80A	380-21
N65774	S60	306-91
N65775	S60	306-92
N65776	75A	380-23
N65777	S60	306-93
N65778	S60	306-94
N65783	S60	306-95
N65784	S60	306-96
N65785	S60	306-97
N65786	S60	306-98
N65787	75A	380-27
N65789	S60	306-99
N65790	S60	306-100
N65791	S60	306-101
N65792	S60	306-102
N65793	75A	380-30
N65794	S60	306-103
N65795	S60	306-104
N65796	S60	306-105
N65797	S60	306-106
N65798	S60	306-107
N65799	S60	306-108
N67201	S40	282-53
N67741	550	676
N67780	501	574
N67786	501	575
N67799	501	580
N67805	500	587
N67814	501	595
N67815	500	596
N67822	501	602
N67829	500	603
N67830	501	609
N67830	560	0089
N67839	501	610
(N67839)	560	0090
N67848	501	616
N67890	560	0096
(N67905)	560	0099
(N67980)	550	221
(N67980)	560	0101
N67983	550	222
N67983	**551**	**353**
(N67983)	551	400
N67986	550	223
N67988	551	224
N67988	551	354
(N67988)	560	0102
N67989	550	225
(N67989)	560	0103
N67990	550	231
N67990	550	358
N67997	550	232
N67999	550	233
N67999	550	359
N68003	550	238
N68003	550	362
N68018	550	247
(N68018)	560	0109A
N68026	550	253
N68027	550	254
N68027	550	371
(N68027)	560	0112
N68032	550	259
N68032	550	373
N68032	560	0116
N68033	550	260
N68097	560	0126
(N68118)	560	0133
N68231	650	0214
N68269	650	0216
N68599	550	270
N68607	550	279
N68609	550	280
N68615	550	287
N68616	550	288
N68617	550	289
N68621	550	295
N68622	550	296
N68624	550	297
N68625	551	298
N68629	550	299
N68631	550	306
N68633	550	307
N68637	550	308
N68644	550	315
(N68646)	550	316
N68648	550	317
N68649	550	318
(N68746)	560	0138
(N68753)	560	0139
N68770	560	0148
(N68786)	560	0149
(N68854)	560	0159
N68860	560	0161
N68864	560	0162
N68869	560	0163
N68872	550	323
N68872	560	0166
N68873	551	324
(N68873)	560	0167
N68876	550	325
(N68876)	560	0168
N68881	550	332
N68881	**560**	**0173**
N68887	550	333
N68888	550	334
N68891	550	341
N69566	500	100
N70050	G3	318
N70338	125	25281
N70451	500	063
N70454	500	279
N70467	501	667
N70606	25B	163
N70703	500	025
N70704	500	267
N70830	20	281/498
N70841	500	018
N71325	S40	282-100
N71460	**75A**	**380-5**
N71543	75A	380-29
N72028	75A	380-14
N72335	24B	208
N72442	24	103
N72505	125	257016
N72596	35A	594
N72600	25D	370
N72603	25D	371
N72606	25D	372
N72608	55	114
N72612	35A	596
N72613	55	119
N72614	35A	607
N72616	55C	140
N72626	35A	591
N72629	55	120
N72630	35A	630
N72787	501	561
N72787	**WWD**	**240**
N73535	WWD	91
N74196	20	198/466
(N75471)	501	482
N76662	20	306/512
(N77111)	501	674

N77167	125	25146
N77711	560	0065
N77794	**525**	**0073**
N77797	**550**	**0821**
(N78499)	600	1012
N80364	500	299
N80506	20	83
N80513	550	248
N80544	400A	RK-59
N80631	31A	131
N80639	500	258
N80645	31A	135
N80667	60	150
N80683	60	093
N80701	60	148
N80727	31A	127
N80775	23	093
N80938	400A	RK-54
N81366	STR	5097/60
N81458	35A	230
N81661	400A	RK-35
N81709	400A	RK-14
N81728	G2	217
N81863	35A	243
N81883	500	031
N81918	400A	RK-25
N82025	**25B**	**075**
N82197	S60	306-39
N82204	G2	167
N82283	35A	174
N82378	400A	RK-61
N82400	**400A**	**RK-75**
N82412	400A	RK-63
N82497	400A	RK-71
N82628	400A	RK-20
N82679	55	013
N82884	T1A	TX-1
N82885	T1A	TX-2
N82886	T1A	TX-3
N85031	75A	380-38
N85351	35A	149
N85631	55	081
N85632	55	080
N85643	55	084
N85645	35A	499
N85653	55	053
N85654	25D	363
N87185	501	410
N87253	501	411
N87258	501	412
N87496	501	413
N87510	501	414
(N87683)	550	564
N87950	HFB	1055
N88692	551	212
N88707	550	213
N88716	550	214
N88718	550	215
(N88721)	550	216
N88723	550	217
(N88727)	550	218
N88731	550	180
N88732	551	181
N88737	550	182
N88738	550	183
N88740	550	184
(N88743)	550	185
N88791	550	186
N88795	550	187
(N88797)	550	188
N88798	550	189
N88822	551	191
N88824	550	192
N88825	550	193
N88826	550	194
N88830	550	195
(N88838)	550	166
N88840	550	167
(N88842)	550	168
(N88845)	550	169
(N88848)	550	170
N88906	G2	133
N90005	50	40
(N90005)	700	9008
N90005	G3	487
N90005	G4	1103
N90237	500	170
N90532	24	103
(N90583)	55	045
N90658	23	077
N90658	STR	5142
N90797	24B	227
N91164	31	026
N91201	31	027
N91452	35A	669
N91480	35A	663
N91566	35A	667
N91669	WWD	17
N91884	125	256071
N92045	HFB	1041
(N92047)	HFB	1036
N92565	24D	287
(N95591)	20	150/445
N97941	600	1014
N98386	23	040
N98403	551	196
N98418	550	197
N98432	550	198
N98436	550	199
N98449	500	415
N98468	501	416
N98468	551	200
N98510	501	417
(N98510)	550	201
N98528	501	418
(N98528)	550	202
N98563	501	419
N98563	550	203
N98586	501	420
N98599	501	421
N98599	551	204
N98601	501	422
N98601	550	205
N98630	550	206
N98675	501	424
N98675	550	207
N98682	501	425
N98682	550	208
N98688	501	426
N98715	501	427
N98715	550	209
(N98715)	551	172
(N98718)	501	428
(N98718)	550	173
N98718	550	210
N98749	501	429
(N98749)	551	174
N98751	501	430
(N98751)	550	001
N98753	551	002
N98784	550	176
N98784	551	003
N98786	550	004
N98796	25B	170
N98817	550	005
N98820	550	006
N98830	550	007
N98840	550	008
N98853	550	009
N98858	550	010
N98871	550	011
N98871	550	179
N99114	**S40**	**282-128**
N99606	24B	224
N99786	35	045
(N99876)	550	012

NASA

NASA14	STR	5003
NASA4	STR	5015
NASA650	G2	118
NASA701	23	049

Peru

(OB-)	24	112
OB-1195	550	134
OB-1280	500	019
OB-1313	25D	328
OB-1319	S40	282-127
OB-1429	25B	159
OB-1430	25B	164
OB-1431	**36A**	**051**
OB-1432	**36A**	**052**
OB-1550	S60	306-25
OB-1626	**560**	**0124**
OB-1703	**AST**	**004**
OB-M-1004	25B	195
OB-M-1171	550	056
OB-M-1195	550	134
OB-R-1313	25D	328
OB-S-1280	500	019
OB-T-1319	S40	282-127

Lebanon

OD-PAL	20	395/554

Austria

OE-	10	85
(OE-)	45	012
OE-FAN	**500**	**289**
OE-FAP	500	300
OE-FAU	500	150
OE-FBA	501	615
OE-FBS	**551**	**574**
OE-FDM	**501**	**529**
OE-FDP	500	139
OE-FFK	501	515
(OE-FGG)	525	0146
OE-FGI	**525**	**0254**
OE-FGN	**500**	**291**
OE-FGP	500	006
OE-FHH	**501**	**654**
OE-FHP	501	668
OE-FHW	**501**	**523**
OE-FIW	501	511
OE-FJU	**525**	**0295**
OE-FLG	**525**	**0103**
OE-FLY	501	660
OE-FMS	**501**	**510**
OE-FNG	500	301
OE-FNL	500	100
OE-FNP	500	100
OE-FPA	**551**	**552**
OE-FPH	501	572
OE-FPO	501	353
OE-FYC	501	610
OE-FYF	501	501
OE-GAA	**560**	**0111**
OE-GAF	35A	382
OE-GAG	10	151
OE-GAP	**560**	**5004**
OE-GAP	S550	0034
OE-GAR	35A	309
OE-GAU	550	028
OE-GAV	35A	185
OE-GBA	**550**	**100**
OE-GBR	35A	088
OE-GCC	**560**	**0125**
OE-GCF	**55C**	**136**
OE-GCH	550	304
OE-GCI	**550**	**043**
OE-GCJ	20	184/462
OE-GCN	**650**	**0014**
OE-GCO	**650**	**0012**
OE-GCP	550	351
OE-GCP	**560**	**0214**
OE-GCR	20	191
OE-GCS	20	364
OE-GDA	**560**	**0200**
OE-GDI	**45**	**037**
OE-GDM	**550**	**707**
OE-GDP	20	302/510
OE-GDP	560	0023
OE-GDR	20	203
OE-GEC	550	296
OE-GEP	550	010
OE-GER	35A	143
OE-GES	551	421
OE-GHA	100	221
OE-GHL	25D	295
OE-GHP	551	139
OE-GHS	**125**	**258078**
OE-GIA	125	256027
OE-GID	560	0081
OE-GII	**60**	**169**
OE-GIL	**550**	**075**
OE-GIN	550	063
OE-GIW	550	008
OE-GKK	**550**	**0872**
OE-GKN	55	027
OE-GKP	550	005
OE-GLA	25B	079
OE-GLF	20	323/520
OE-GLG	10	96
OE-GLL	20	307/513
OE-GLP	36A	025
OE-GLS	551	300
OE-GLZ	**550**	**690**
OE-GMA	35A	111
OE-GMD	**36A**	**047**
OE-GMI	**560**	**0362**
OE-GMP	35A	122
OE-GNK	55	013
OE-GNK	650	0147
OE-GNL	36A	055
OE-GNL	**60**	**032**
OE-GNN	20	298
OE-GNP	35A	347
OE-GNS	S550	0083
OE-GPA	560	0099
OE-GPD	S550	0135
OE-GPN	35A	311
OE-GPS	**550**	**0837**
OE-GPS	560	0114
OE-GRO	**55**	**122**
OE-GRR	**55**	**059**
OE-GRU	20	228/473
OE-GRW	560	0019
OE-GSC	**10**	**122**
OE-GST	550	299
OE-GSW	**560**	**0088**
OE-GTZ	**550**	**0864**
OE-GUS	20	36
OE-HCL	601	3045
OE-HCS	50	42
OE-HET	**600**	**1085**
OE-HIT	**50**	**222**
OE-HLE	**601**	**3047**
OE-ILS	**900**	**58**
OE-IMI	**900**	**147**

Finland

OH-AMB	**100**	**193**
OH-BAP	125	257212
OH-CAR	500	144
OH-CAT	550	133
OH-CIT	500	551
OH-COC	500	223
OH-COL	500	311
OH-CUT	550	414
OH-CXO	**750**	**0022**
OH-FFA	20	178/459
OH-FFB	10	17
OH-FFJ	20	225/472
OH-FFV	20	248/483
OH-FFW	20	243/480
OH-FPC	**20**	**345**
OH-GLA	24D	273
OH-GLB	**24D**	**262**
OH-IPP	55	056
OH-JET	**125**	**257136**
OH-JOT	125	258001
OH-KNE	**D1A**	**A014SA**
OH-PPI	750	0115

OH-RIF	400A	RK-79
OH-WIH	**600**	**1029**
OH-WIN	**20**	**481**
OH-WIP	**20**	**359/542**

Czech Republic

OK-AJD	31A	095
OK-BYA	601	5105
OK-EEH	10	27
OK-FKA	500	260
OK-NKN	650	0010
OK-UZI	**400**	**RJ-56**

Slovakia

OM-SKY	125	258314

Belgium

(OO-ADA)	20	73/419
OO-ATS	500	044
OO-DCM	**500**	**182**
OO-DDD	20	11
OO-DOK	20	162/451
(OO-EBA)	D1A	A048SA
(OO-ECT)	501	542
(OO-EEF)	20	95
(OO-FAY)	500	088
OO-FBY	500	093
OO-FNL	**525**	**0332**
OO-GBL	**35A**	**284**
OO-GFD	**2xx**	**101**
OO-GPN	500	225
(OO-HFW)	25D	231
OO-IBC	S65	465-68
OO-IBI	500	238
OO-IBS	S60	306-5
OO-JBA	31	009
OO-JBB	20	116
OO-JBS	35A	669
OO-KJG	35A	149
OO-LCM	**500**	**036**
OO-LFA	24D	248
OO-LFR	25D	320
OO-LFS	**45**	**018**
OO-LFT	**50**	**42**
(OO-LFU)	525	0020
OO-LFV	**35A**	**481**
(OO-LFW)	25D	231
(OO-LFX)	35A	135
(OO-LFX)	550	067
OO-LFY	35A	200
OO-LFZ	25B	118
OO-MMP	**551**	**559**
OO-MRA	CVT	15
OO-MRC	CVT	30
OO-MRE	CVT	15
OO-OOO	20	56
OO-OSA	**S550**	**0147**
OO-PHI	**525**	**0115**
OO-PJB	20	145/443
(OO-PPP)	20	56
OO-PSD	20	384/551
OO-RJE	551	421
OO-RJT	551	023
(OO-RJX)	20	73/419
OO-RRR	20	98/434
(OO-RSA)	S65	465-72
(OO-RSB)	S65	465-72
OO-RSE	S65	465-72
OO-RST	500	063
OO-SEL	500	133
OO-SKJ	125	25089
OO-SKS	**551**	**079**
OO-STE	20	218
OO-STF	20	220
(OO-TTL)	CVT	28
OO-VPQ	20	315/517
OO-WTB	20	162/451

Denmark

OY-AGZ	24B	183
OY-AJV	500	279
OY-AKL	25	054
OY-AKZ	25	062
OY-APM	125	25253
OY-APM	**601**	**5153**
OY-ARA	CVT	32
OY-ARB	CVT	34
OY-ARP	500	040
OY-ARW	500	130
OY-ASD	500	288
(OY-ASK)	25C	097
OY-ASO	35A	119
OY-ASP	25B	171
OY-ASR	500	194
OY-ASV	550	067
OY-AZT	20	98/434
OY-BDS	20	180/460
OY-BFC	25B	112
OY-BIZ	24D	281
OY-BLG	35	022
OY-BPC	D1A	A023SA
OY-BPI	D1A	A070SA
OY-BZT	**550**	**289**
OY-CCB	D1A	A037SA
OY-CCG	**650**	**0003**
OY-CCJ	**35A**	**468**
OY-CCO	35A	670
OY-CCT	35A	144
OY-CCU	550	127
OY-CDK	D1A	A065SA
OY-CEV	**500**	**329**
OY-CGO	500	287
OY-CKK	**900**	**110**
OY-CKN	**2xx**	**76**
OY-CKT	**560**	**0078**
OY-CKY	20	293
OY-CLD	**601**	**5070**
OY-CPK	500	267
OY-CPW	501	487
OY-CYD	501	550
OY-CYT	550	443
OY-CYV	**550**	**440**
OY-DKP	125	25132
OY-DVL	500	036
(OY-EBD)	500	299
OY-EGE	24	124
OY-FFB	**500**	**603**
OY-FFC	500	551
OY-FFV	560	0138
OY-FLK	55	050
OY-FRM	10	56
(OY-GDA)	50	54
OY-GGG	**650**	**7039**
OY-GKC	550	100
OY-GKL	**650**	**0043**
OY-GRC	550	255
OY-INI	501	559
OY-JAI	**500**	**193**
OY-JAT	400	RJ-22
OY-JET	501	644
(OY-JET)	560	0138
OY-JEV	**550**	**243**
OY-JEY	501	600
OY-JKH	**60**	**141**
OY-JMC	**525**	**0277**
OY-JPJ	125	257015
OY-LIN	**50**	**230**
OY-LJA	**35A**	**594**
OY-LJB	**31A**	**086**
OY-LJC	**31A**	**087**
OY-LJD	**60**	**005**
OY-LJE	60	011
OY-LJF	**60**	**173**
OY-MCL	125	258099
OY-MMM	**604**	**5430**
OY-MPA	125	257127
OY-ONE	**501**	**535**
OY-PDN	**551**	**412**
OY-PHN	**100**	**209**
OY-RAA	125	258235
OY-RAC	**125**	**258335**
OY-RDD	550	621
OY-RYA	24	109
OY-SBR	**CVT**	**23**
OY-SBS	CVT	21
OY-SBT	**CVT**	**33**
OY-SUJ	500	121
OY-SVL	**501**	**420**
OY-TAM	500	158
OY-TKI	**500**	**299**
OY-TMA	**550**	**457**
(OY-VIP)	500	311

Netherlands

PH-BAG	20	126/438
PH-BPS	**20**	**321**
PH-CSA	550	630
PH-CTA	500	088
PH-CTB	500	093
PH-CTC	500	098
PH-CTD	500	157
PH-CTE	500	167
PH-CTF	500	177
PH-CTG	500	234
PH-CTW	500	269
PH-CTX	**550**	**338**
PH-CTY	**500**	**044**
PH-CTZ	**550**	**067**
PH-ECI	**525**	**0321**
(PH-EFA)	900	163
(PH-EFB)	2xx	49
PH-ERP	90X	1
PH-FJP	G2	78
PH-HES	551	023
PH-HET	550	323
PH-HFA	HFB	1032
PH-HFB	HFB	1033
PH-HFC	HFB	1035
(PH-HMA)	S550	0145
(PH-HMC)	S550	0145
PH-ILC	**900**	**161**
(PH-ILC)	900	9
PH-ILD	50	23
PH-ILF	20	147/444
PH-ILR	50	15
PH-ILT	10	1
PH-ILX	20	266/490
PH-ILY	20	326/521
(PH-JOB)	501	511
PH-JSB	CVT	26
PH-JSC	CVT	35
PH-JSD	CVT	36
PH-JSL	D1A	A087SA
PH-LAB	**550**	**712**
PH-LBA	**900**	**173**
PH-LEM	50	28
(PH-LEN)	20	263/489
PH-LPS	20	63/411
PH-MBX	550	180
PH-MCX	550	564
PH-MDC	**560**	**0280**
PH-MDX	550	634
PH-MEX	**650**	**0217**
PH-MFX	**650**	**0240**
PH-MGT	**525**	**0042**
PH-MSR	MSP	102
PH-MSS	MSP	103
PH-MST	MSP	104
PH-MSU	MSP	105
PH-MSV	MSP	106
PH-MSW	MSP	107
PH-MSX	MSP	108
PH-OMC	**20**	**239**
PH-PBM	560	0100
PH-RMA	**S550**	**0145**
PH-SAW	500	225
(PH-SDL)	50	66
PH-VLG	**560**	**0271**
PH-WMS	20	285/504
PH-WOL	125	258235

Philippines
(see also RP-)

PI-C1747	24X	264
(PI-C7777)	500	123

Netherlands Antilles

PJ-ABA	G2	163
PJ-ARI	G2	8
PJ-AYA	10	47
PJ-MAR	650	0049
PJ-SLB	125	25223
PJ-SOL	400	RJ-19

Indonesia

PK-	**20**	**90/426**
PK-BND	G3	316
PK-CAG	20	408
PK-CAH	**31A**	**066**
(PK-CAJ)	20	408
PK-CAJ	**31A**	**077**
PK-CAP	G3	316
PK-CTA	125	257153
PK-CTC	**125**	**257099**
PK-CTP	G3	431
PK-DJW	125	25147
PK-ERA	400	RJ-40
PK-HMG	125	256029
PK-HMK	601	5073
PK-IJS	STR	5046
PK-KIG	650	0151
PK-NSP	G4	1077
PK-NZK	G4	1219
PK-OCN	G3	305
PK-PJA	**G3**	**395**
PK-PJD	125	256017
PK-PJE	125	256029
PK-PJG	G2	45
PK-PJH	STR	5011/1
PK-PJR	125	25147
PK-PJS	STR	5011/1
PK-PJZ	G2	26
PK-RGM	125	258106
PK-TIR	20	297
PK-TRI	**20**	**173**
PK-TRJ	650	0078
PK-TRP	900	71
PK-TRV	550	287
PK-TSM	**650**	**0144**
PK-WSE	650	0078
PK-WSG	550	650
PK-WSJ	125	258106
PK-WSO	550	287

Brazil

PP-CRS	**525**	**0346**
PP-EEM	125	25197
PP-EIF	**501**	**680**
PP-EIW	24D	294
PP-ERR	**35**	**008**
PP-ESC	**550**	**618**
PP-FMX	23	090
PP-FOH	20	113
PP-FXB	500	049
PP-JAA	**36A**	**055**
PP-JFM	**560**	**5045**
PP-JQM	**750**	**0056**
PP-LEM	**500**	**171**
PP-OSA	**604**	**5411**
PP-SED	S40	282-121
PP-YOF	**525**	**0356**
(PT-)	100	224
(PT-)	125	258208
(PT-)	400A	RK-58
(PT-)	550	460
(PT-)	550	598
(PT-)	560	5029
PT-	90X	60

PT-AAC	G3	450
PT-AAF	**50**	**234**
PT-ACC	**36A**	**018**
PT-ALK	G3	418
PT-ASJ	10	95
PT-CMY	25C	108
PT-CXJ	**24**	**176**
PT-CXK	24	122
PT-DTY	125	25243
PT-DUO	25C	061
PT-DVL	25B	077
PT-DZU	24D	244
PT-FAF	25C	099
PT-FAT	35A	361
PT-FJA	**525**	**0337**
PT-FNP	**525**	**0319**
PT-FOH	20	113
PT-FPP	**560**	**5003**
PT-FXB	500	049
PT-GAF	**125**	**258261**
PT-GAP	**35A**	**589**
PT-GMN	**55C**	**139**
PT-IBR	25C	072
PT-IDW	HFB	1052
PT-IIQ	25C	089
PT-IKR	25C	099
PT-ILJ	500	057
PT-IOB	HFB	1053
PT-IQL	500	069
PT-ISN	25C	113
PT-ISO	**25C**	**115**
PT-JAA	**125**	**258190**
PT-JBQ	25B	119
PT-JDX	25C	131
PT-JGU	24D	276
PT-JKQ	**24D**	**284**
PT-JKR	24D	278
PT-JMJ	**500**	**134**
PT-JNJ	S40	282-118
PT-JQM	**400A**	**RK-63**
PT-JXS	500	162
PT-KAP	25C	156
PT-KBC	25C	165
PT-KBD	25B	166
PT-KBR	**500**	**156**
PT-KIR	**500**	**103**
PT-KIU	500	172
PT-KKV	25C	172
PT-KOT	S60	306-80
PT-KOU	S60	306-84
PT-KPA	**500**	**181**
PT-KPB	**500**	**188**
PT-KPE	24D	315
PT-KQT	36	011
PT-KTO	10	63
PT-KTU	36A	018
PT-KXZ	500	043
PT-KYR	25D	266
PT-KZR	**35A**	**252**
PT-KZY	25B	204
PT-LAA	**35A**	**295**
PT-LAS	35A	326
PT-LAU	24D	239
(PT-LAW)	500	091
PT-LAX	**500**	**194**
PT-LAY	500	068
PT-LAZ	500	180
PT-LBN	**500**	**079**
PT-LBS	35A	361
PT-LBW	**25XR**	**056**
PT-LBY	35A	411
(PT-LBZ)	500	608
PT-LCC	**500**	**608**
PT-LCD	**35A**	**103**
PT-LCN	24D	287
PT-LCO	10	154
PT-LCR	550	157
PT-LCV	**24D**	**254**
PT-LCW	550	358
PT-LDH	**500**	**049**
PT-LDI	**500**	**335**
PT-LDM	**35A**	**494**
PT-LDN	35A	436
PT-LDR	55	028
PT-LDR	**55B**	**134**
PT-LDY	**WWD**	**251**
PT-LEA	**25B**	**155**
PT-LEB	**35A**	**474**
PT-LEL	55	013
PT-LEM	24D	270
PT-LEN	**25B**	**093**
PT-LET	**55**	**080**
PT-LFR	501	680
PT-LFS	35	008
PT-LFT	35A	473
PT-LGD	D1A	A072SA
PT-LGF	35	019
PT-LGI	S550	0024
PT-LGJ	S550	0025
PT-LGM	550	128
PT-LGR	**35**	**009**
PT-LGS	35A	299
PT-LGT	650	0081
PT-LGW	**35A**	**598**
PT-LGZ	650	0088
PT-LHA	650	0059
PT-LHB	**125**	**258031**
PT-LHC	**650**	**0086**
PT-LHD	S550	0059
PT-LHK	**125**	**25197**
PT-LHR	**55**	**044**
PT-LHT	**35A**	**479**
PT-LHU	25C	099
PT-LHX	35A	464
PT-LHY	550	426
PT-LIG	55	111
PT-LIH	35A	433
PT-LII	35A	499
PT-LIJ	35A	607
PT-LIP	WWD	418
PT-LIV	**550**	**499**
PT-LIX	500	171
PT-LIY	**500**	**219**
PT-LIZ	501	639
PT-LJA	550	154
PT-LJC	650	0115
PT-LJF	**551**	**272**
PT-LJI	**50**	**173**
PT-LJJ	550	276
PT-LJK	35A	372
PT-LJL	**S550**	**0084**
PT-LJQ	**S550**	**0113**
PT-LJT	550	339
PT-LKD	**24F**	**356**
PT-LKQ	23	038
PT-LKR	550	378
PT-LKS	**S550**	**0114**
PT-LKT	S550	0117
PT-LLF	35A	644
PT-LLK	31	010
PT-LLL	25D	258
PT-LLN	**25C**	**176**
PT-LLQ	550	495
PT-LLS	**35A**	**303**
PT-LLT	**550**	**349**
PT-LLU	**550**	**147**
PT-LMA	24F	353
PT-LME	**551**	**204**
PT-LMF	**24**	**120**
PT-LML	550	016
PT-LMM	**25D**	**323**
PT-LMO	10	49
PT-LMS	**24D**	**296**
PT-LMY	**35A**	**627**
PT-LNC	**550**	**237**
PT-LND	**550**	**254**
PT-LNE	**24**	**114**
PT-LNK	24D	294
PT-LNN	**D1A**	**A048SA**
PT-LNV	501	568
PT-LOC	550	550
PT-LOE	**35A**	**393**
PT-LOF	55	028
PT-LOG	**500**	**284**
PT-LOJ	**24D**	**303**
PT-LOS	**500**	**239**
PT-LOT	**35A**	**093**
PT-LPF	500	249
PT-LPH	**24D**	**275**
PT-LPK	**550**	**010**
PT-LPN	**550**	**323**
PT-LPP	**550**	**199**
PT-LPT	25	051
PT-LPV	WWD	441
PT-LPX	24	158
PT-LPZ	**500**	**015**
PT-LQF	35A	616
PT-LQG	500	271
PT-LQI	S550	0154
PT-LQJ	550	578
PT-LQK	**24E**	**333**
PT-LQP	**125**	**258116**
PT-LQQ	**501**	**512**
PT-LQR	**500**	**246**
PT-LQW	550	158
PT-LSD	25D	243
PT-LSF	**500**	**328**
PT-LSJ	**35A**	**181**
PT-LSN	650	0049
PT-LSR	550	600
PT-LSW	35A	286
PT-LTB	**650**	**0166**
PT-LTI	**500**	**226**
PT-LTJ	**550**	**258**
PT-LTL	550	608
PT-LUA	**500**	**346**
PT-LUE	**650**	**0091**
PT-LUG	**35A**	**356**
PT-LUK	**55**	**086**
PT-LUO	650	0129
PT-LUZ	**25D**	**335**
PT-LVB	**501**	**613**
PT-LVD	**100**	**223**
PT-LVF	**650**	**0171**
PT-LVO	31	002
PT-LVR	31	013
PT-LXG	550	618
PT-LXH	**500**	**133**
PT-LXJ	100	225
PT-LXO	**55C**	**135**
PT-LXS	25B	111
PT-LXW	600	1063
PT-LXX	**31**	**007**
PT-LYA	550	620
PT-LYE	24F	354
PT-LYF	35A	650
PT-LYL	24D	291
PT-LYN	550	625
PT-LYS	**550**	**624**
PT-LZO	550	215
PT-LZP	**35A**	**339**
PT-LZQ	**560**	**0045**
PT-LZS	55C	139
PT-MAC	**400A**	**RK-151**
PT-MBZ	**AST**	**022**
PT-MCB	**31A**	**100**
PT-MFR	35A	655
PT-MGS	**650**	**7021**
PT-MIL	**525**	**0086**
PT-MJC	**525**	**0085**
PT-MKO	604	5347
PT-MML	2xx	43
PT-MMO	**550**	**455**
PT-MMV	**550**	**0811**
PT-MPE	**525**	**0015**
(PT-MPE)	525	0030
PT-MPL	**400A**	**RK-158**
PT-MSM	55	072
PT-MSP	**525**	**0259**
PT-MTG	560	0121
PT-MVI	31A	082
PT-OAA	550	635
PT-OAC	**550**	**613**
PT-OAF	550	369
PT-OAG	**550**	**379**
PT-OAK	650	0186
PT-OBD	**24B**	**228**
PT-OBR	55	037
PT-OBS	55	048
PT-OBT	125	258112
PT-OBX	650	0181
PT-OCA	55C	140
PT-OCZ	**35A**	**361**
PT-ODC	**501**	**678**
PT-ODL	**550**	**640**
PT-ODW	550	643
PT-ODZ	**550**	**645**
PT-OEF	35A	102
PT-OER	550	390
PT-OEX	**900**	**92**
PT-OFJ	31	014
PT-OFK	31	017
PT-OFL	31	019
PT-OFW	35A	621
PT-OHB	125	258190
PT-OHD	**25D**	**296**
PT-OHM	10	50
PT-OHU	55	029
PT-OIC	10	171
PT-OIG	**500**	**005**
PT-OJC	125	258177
PT-OJF	**500**	**131**
PT-OJG	**550**	**676**
PT-OJH	55C	144
PT-OJK	550	675
PT-OJO	650	0202
PT-OJT	550	562
PT-OKM	550	573
PT-OKP	**550**	**460**
PT-OKV	650	0206
PT-OLN	WWD	340
PT-OLV	560	0142
PT-OMB	550	672
PT-OMC	125	258206
PT-OMS	**500**	**251**
PT-OMT	**500**	**179**
PT-OMU	**650**	**0205**
PT-OMV	650	0200
PT-ONK	35A	472
PT-OOA	550	641
PT-OOF	**500**	**074**
PT-OOI	**125**	**258214**
PT-OOK	**500**	**039**
PT-OOL	**500**	**060**
PT-OOM	550	479
PT-OOR	560	0176
PT-OOW	55	033
PT-OPJ	**35A**	**396**
PT-OQD	**500**	**244**
PT-OQG	200	514
PT-ORA	**55C**	**146**
PT-ORC	**560**	**0195**
PT-ORD	**550**	**154**
PT-ORE	560	0131
PT-ORH	125	258035
PT-ORJ	125	257145
PT-ORO	550	303
PT-ORS	100	219
PT-ORT	560	0191
PT-OSA	601	5075
PT-OSB	125	258211
PT-OSD	**500**	**325**
PT-OSK	550	633
PT-OSL	S550	0127
PT-OSM	**S550**	**0160**
PT-OSW	**125**	**258184**
PT-OTC	**125**	**258194**
PT-OTH	125	258229
PT-OTN	550	715
PT-OTQ	**500**	**046**
PT-OTS	**560**	**0213**
PT-OTT	560	0215
PT-OUG	55	060
PT-OVC	**35A**	**399**
PT-OVI	60	008
PT-OVK	**500**	**027**
PT-OVM	D1A	A091SA
PT-OVU	**650**	**7033**
PT-OVV	**550**	**616**
PT-OVZ	**31A**	**037**
PT-OXB	100	199
PT-OXT	**D1A**	**A039SA**
PT-OYA	500	072
PT-OYP	550	561
PT-OZB	560	0258
PT-OZT	500	256

PT-OZX	500	299
PT-POK	**35A**	**619**
PT-RAA	**560**	**5034**
PT-SMO	35A	414
PT-TJB	**45**	**022**
PT-TOF	**31A**	**103**
PT-WAB	500	047
PT-WAL	**125**	**258198**
PT-WAN	50	188
PT-WAR	35A	230
PT-WAU	**125**	**258133**
(PT-WAW)	125	258184
PT-WBC	**AST**	**086**
PT-WBV	550	485
PT-WBY	**500**	**008**
PT-WEW	**24**	**158**
PT-WFC	650	7054
PT-WFD	**560**	**0308**
PT-WFT	**500**	**154**
(PT-WGB)	60	046
PT-WGD	**525**	**0120**
PT-WGF	**35A**	**322**
PT-WGM	36A	048
PT-WHB	**400A**	**RK-73**
PT-WHC	**400A**	**RK-58**
PT-WHD	**400A**	**RK-77**
PT-WHE	**400A**	**RK-81**
PT-WHF	**400A**	**RK-82**
PT-WHG	**400A**	**RK-54**
PT-WHH	125	258282
PT-WHZ	500	287
PT-WIA	125	258035
PT-WIB	**S550**	**0137**
PT-WIV	**31A**	**110**
PT-WJS	**400A**	**RK-122**
PT-WJZ	**550**	**339**
PT-WKL	**24D**	**294**
PT-WKQ	**550**	**675**
PT-WKS	560	0397
PT-WLC	650	7035
PT-WLM	400A	RK-28
PT-WLO	**31A**	**122**
PT-WLX	**525**	**0176**
PT-WLY	**650**	**7074**
PT-WLZ	**601**	**5189**
PT-WMA	**125**	**258301**
PT-WMD	**125**	**258312**
PT-WMG	**125**	**258310**
PT-WMO	60	090
PT-WMQ	**560**	**0405**
PT-WMZ	**560**	**0406**
PT-WNE	560	0411
PT-WNF	**560**	**0412**
PT-WNH	**550**	**0814**
PT-WNO	**125**	**258284**
PT-WOA	560	0408
PT-WOD	500	340
PT-WOM	**560**	**0176**
PT-WON	**550**	**641**
PT-WPC	560	0142
PT-WPF	**125**	**258409**
(PT-WQE)	560	0438
(PT-WQG)	550	154
PT-WQH	**650**	**7083**
PT-WQI	**525**	**0238**
(PT-WQJ)	525	0239
PT-WQM	900	5
PT-WQS	90X	53
PT-WRC	G3	492
PT-WRR	560	0389
PT-WSB	**31A**	**135**
PT-WSC	50	253
PT-WSF	**10**	**169**
PT-WSN	**560**	**0440**
PT-WSO	550	0832
PT-WSS	**55ER**	**102**
PT-WUF	400A	RK-171
PT-WUM	**750**	**0092**
PT-WUV	**20**	**129**
PT-WVC	**550**	**0833**
PT-WVG	**125**	**258395**
PT-WVH	**560**	**0409**
PT-WXL	**604**	**5321**
PT-WYC	**2xx**	**59**
PT-WYU	**560**	**5060**
(PT-WZO)	560	5003
PT-WZW	560	0431
PT-XAC	**525**	**0280**
PT-XCF	**560**	**0450**
PT-XCL	**560**	**5020**
PT-XCX	**550**	**0873**
PT-XDB	**525**	**0274**
PT-XDY	**125**	**258442**
PT-XFG	**650**	**7099**
PT-XFS	**60**	**121**
PT-XIB	**560**	**5043**
(PT-XIT)	31A	148
PT-XJS	**525**	**0239**
PT-XLR	**45**	**048**
PT-XMM	**525**	**0267**
PT-XPP	**31A**	**148**
PT-XTA	**31**	**013**
PT-ZAA	125	258031

Papua New Guinea

P2-BCM	WWD	317
P2-MBN	550	160
P2-PNF	G2	103
P2-PNG	G2	103
P2-RDZ	550	021
P2-TAA	**550**	**160**

Aruba

P4-AMB	**125**	**25252**
P4-CMP	**125**	**257214**
P4-NAN	900	159
P4-TAM	601	3006

Russia
(see also CCCP-)

RA-02800	125	257007
RA-02801	**125**	**257097**
RA-02802	125	257054
RA-02803	**125**	**257139**
RA-02804	125	25281
RA-02805	125	25219
RA-02806	125	257017
RA-02807	**125**	**258076**
RA-02809	125	257062
RA-02850	**125**	**257112**
RA-09000	**900**	**118**
RA-09001	**900**	**123**
RA-09003	**20**	**183**

Croatia
(see also 9A-)

RC-BLY	75A	380-65
RC-BPU	551	144

Philippines
(see also PI-)

RP-57	35A	244
RP-57	STR	5062/12
RP-C57	35A	244
RP-C102	500	123
RP-C111	125	25256
RP-C125	**125**	**25033**
RP-C235	125	257130
RP-C237	501	514
RP-C296	550	031
RP-C400	25D	289
RP-C550	550	031
RP-C581	550	167
RP-C610	**35A**	**338**
RP-C648	35A	648
RP-C648	60	093
RP-C653	550	194
RP-C689	**550**	**159**
(RP-C717)	525	0177
RP-C754	50	82
RP-C848	23	072
RP-C1180	**550**	**658**
RP-C1261	25D	352
RP-C1299	500	259
RP-C1404	35A	441
RP-C1426	**35A**	**426**
RP-C1500	500	225
RP-C1600	125	256037
RP-C1714	125	257085
RP-C1747	**24X**	**264**
RP-C1911	**10**	**174**
RP-C1926	125	258226
RP-C1964	**500**	**242**
RP-C1980	20	400/556
RP-C2480	WWD	364
RP-C4121	25D	287
RP-C4654	550	707
RP-C5128	36A	037
RP-C5610	**604**	**5402**
RP-C6153	**31A**	**153**
RP-C6178	**31A**	**178**
RP-C6610	25D	289
RP-C7272	35A	338
RP-C7777	500	123
RP-C8008	125	258212
(RP-C8288)	525	0185
RP-C8818	560	0417

Sweden

SE-DCK	WWD	51
SE-DCO	20	241/479
SE-DCU	24	124
SE-DCW	24	109
SE-DCY	WWD	136
SE-DCZ	WWD	137
SE-DDE	500	063
SE-DDF	10	27
SE-DDG	35A	172
SE-DDH	36	013
SE-DDI	35A	266
SE-DDM	500	244
SE-DDN	500	256
SE-DDO	500	180
SE-DDW	D1A	A023SA
SE-DDX	500	292
SE-DDY	**550**	**127**
SE-DDZ	200	482
SE-DEA	35	051
SE-DED	CVT	32
SE-DEE	CVT	34
SE-DEF	551	421
SE-DEG	**500**	**276**
SE-DEK	10	156
SE-DEL	10	14
SE-DEM	35A	317
SE-DEN	CVT	15
SE-DEO	501	442
SE-DEP	500	377
SE-DER	35A	373
SE-DES	501	600
SE-DET	500	603
SE-DEU	500	036
SE-DEV	550	136
SE-DEX	500	279
SE-DEY	**500**	**396**
SE-DEZ	**501**	**407**
SE-DFA	24D	283
SE-DFB	24D	281
SE-DFC	25B	163
SE-DHE	35A	368
SE-DHH	125	25160
SE-DHK	20	259
SE-DHL	650	0030
SE-DHO	**35A**	**195**
SE-DHP	**35A**	**075**
SE-DKA	20	308
SE-DKB	10	132
SE-DKC	10	123
SE-DKD	10	60
SE-DKF	125	256038
SE-DKI	S550	0008
SE-DKM	500	309
SE-DLB	**100**	**183**
SE-DLI	560	0078
SE-DLK	WWD	197
SE-DLL	WWD	205
SE-DLY	550	306
SE-DLZ	**500**	**645**
(SE-DMM)	500	244
SE-DPG	560	0086
SE-DPK	10	152
SE-DPL	500	037
SE-DPT	WWD	325
SE-DPY	125	257035
SE-DPZ	125	257015
SE-DRS	**400A**	**RK-37**
SE-DRT	500	311
SE-DRV	125	258079
SE-DRZ	**500**	**315**
SE-DSA	20	339
SE-DUZ	**500**	**143**
SE-DVA	**500**	**551**
SE-DVB	**500**	**294**
SE-DVD	**125**	**258339**
SE-DVE	**90X**	**23**
SE-DVG	50	104
SE-DVK	**50**	**249**
SE-DVL	**50**	**238**
SE-DVP	**100**	**224**
SE-DVS	125	25225
SE-DVT	**550**	**634**
SE-DVV	550	307
SE-DVY	**650**	**7011**
SE-DVZ	**550**	**0808**
SE-DYB	**100**	**216**
SE-DYE	**125**	**258382**
SE-DYO	**S550**	**0134**
SE-DYR	**551**	**097**
SE-DYV	**125**	**258385**
SE-DYX	**560**	**5029**
(SE-DYY)	550	707
SE-DYZ	**560**	**0153**
SE-DZX	750	0075
SE-DZZ	35A	415

Slovenia
(see also S5-)

SL-BAA	35A	618
SL-BAB	24D	320
SL-BAC	550	480

Poland

SP-FCP	20	136/439
SP-FOA	CVT	14

Sudan

ST-PRS	**20**	**372/546**
ST-PSR	**50**	**114**

Egypt

SU-AXN	**20**	**294/506**
SU-AYD	**20**	**361/543**
SU-AZJ	**20**	**358/541**
SU-BGM	**G4**	**1048**
SU-BGU	**G3**	**439**
SU-BGV	**G3**	**442**
SU-BNC	**G4**	**1329**
SU-BND	**G4**	**1332**
SU-BNL	**60**	**149**
SU-DAF	**STR**	**5025**
SU-DAG	STR	5121
SU-DAH	**STR**	**5071**
SU-EWA	**560**	**0201**
SU-MSG	**45**	**069**
SU-OAE	**20**	**175**

Greece

SX-ABA 20 245/481
SX-AHF 36 007
SX-ASO 25B 074
SX-BFJ 35A 172
SX-BNS 55 072
SX-BNT 35A 228
SX-BSS 125 25116
SX-BTV 55 124
SX-CBM 25C 094
SX-DCI 560 0366
SX-DCM 560 5051
SX-DKI 20 275
SX-ECH 900 26

Seychelles
(see also S7-)

SY-AAP 560 0003

Slovenia
(see also SL-)

S5-BAA 35A 618
S5-BAB 24D 320
S5-BAC 550 480
S5-BAX S550 0028

Seychelles
(see also SY-)

S7-AAP 560 0003

Sao Tome

S9-CRH G2 8
S9-GOT G2 8
S9-NAD STR 5065
S9-NAE STR 5085

Turkey

(TC-) 200 489
TC-AKH 125 259043
TC-AKK 900 171
TC-ANA G4 1043
TC-ANC 125 258208
TC-AND 10 89
TC-ANT 650 0229
TC-ARC 60 094
TC-ARK 100 218
TC-ASF WWD 195
TC-ATA G4 1043
TC-ATC 650 7043
TC-ATI 10 132
TC-ATV 750 0001
TC-BAY 550 316
TC-BHD 125 258415
TC-BHO 50 271
TC-BYD 400A RK-254
TC-CAG 900 142
TC-CAO 650 0060
TC-CEN 20 326/521
TC-CEY 650 0214
TC-CIN 2xx 26
TC-CMY 650 0141
TC-COS 125 256048
TC-COY 550 347
TC-CRO 525 0102
TC-CYL 2xx 56
TC-DEM 200 489
TC-DHB 601 5094
(TC-DHE) 604 5318
TC-DHE 604 5358
TC-EES 650 0077
TC-ELL 60 030
TC-EMA 525 0121
TC-EYE 50 161
TC-EZE 20 299
TC-FAL 550 351
TC-FBS 55C 138
TC-FMB 550 351
TC-FNS HFB 1026
TC-GAP G3 487
TC-GAP G4 1027
TC-GEM 35A 185
TC-GSA HFB 1055
TC-GSB HFB 1042
TC-IHS STR 5225
TC-KAM 50 95
TC-KHE HFB 1043
TC-KLS 650 0191
TC-KOC 650 7006
TC-KON 650 7084
TC-LAA 560 0212
TC-LAB 560 0216
TC-LEY HFB 1042
TC-LEY HFB 1043
TC-LIM 525 0226
TC-MCX 400A RK-170
TC-MDB 400A RK-164
TC-MDC 125 258384
TC-MDJ 400A RK-120
TC-MEK 35A 441
TC-MEK 55C 138
TC-MEK 60 016
TC-MET 560 0497
TC-MSA 400A RK-124
TC-MSB 400A RK-170
TC-NEO 400A RK-130
TC-NKB 550 053
TC-NMC S550 0072
TC-NNK 400A RK-211
TC-NSU HFB 1046
TC-OKN 125 258388
TC-OMR HFB 1047
TC-OMR STR 5082/36
TC-ORM 10 33
TC-OVA 601 5094
TC-RAM 650 0178
TC-ROT 560 0454
TC-SAM S550 0007
TC-SBH 650 0234
TC-SEN HFB 1042
TC-SES 550 717
TC-SIS 650 0077
TC-SMB 400A RK-148
TC-STR 125 258415
TC-TEK 125 258229
TC-TOP 650 0083
TC-VIN 400A RK-188
TC-YIB D1A A051SA
TC-YRT 400A RK-190
TC-YSR 50 246
TC-YZB 550 351

Iceland

TF-JET 550 235

Guatemala

TG-AIR 31A 067
TG-BAC 550 0875
(TG-FIL) 525 0072
TG-GGA 20 25/405
TG-JAY 35A 225
TG-KIT 501 633
TG-LAR D1A A062SA
TG-MIL 501 633
TG-OMF WWD 34
TG-OZO 500 204
TG-RBW 20 150/445
TG-RIE 501 624
TG-RIF 501 624
TG-RIF 525 0072
TG-VOC 25D 251
TG-VWA WWD 109

Costa Rica

(TI-ACB) 500 187
TI-AFB 500 258
(TI-AHE) 500 245
TI-AHH 500 245
TI-APZ 550 273

Cameroon

(TJ-) G3 487
TJ-AAK G2 93
TJ-AAW G3 486
TJ-AHR CVT 12

Central African Republic

TL-AAW 500 078
TL-AAY 20 174/457
TL-ABD 35 062
TL-AJK 20 32
TL-KAZ 20 174/457
TL-RCA CVT 39
TL-SMI CVT 39

Congo

TN-ADB CVT 22
TN-ADI CVT 9

Gabon

TR-KHA 20 225/472
TR-KHB G2 127
TR-KHC G3 326
TR-KHD G4 1327
TR-KSP G4 1327
TR-LAH CVT 30
TR-LAI 50 78
TR-LAU 125 256052
TR-LCJ 900 7
TR-LDB 125 258192
TR-LEX 90X 24
TR-LFB 125 25130
TR-LOL 20 13
TR-LQU 125 25250
TR-LRU 20 225/472
TR-LTI 500 210
TR-LUW 20 309/514
TR-LWY CVT 11
TR-LXO 125 25130
TR-LXP 35 005
TR-LYB 24 105
TR-LYC 35A 174
TR-LYE 550 033
TR-LYM CVT 12
TR-LZI 35A 313
TR-LZT CVT 20

Tunisia

TS-IAM 100 195
TS-IRS 20 117

Tchad

TT-AAI G2 240

Ivory Coast

TU-VAC G2 218
TU-VAD 20 98/434
TU-VAD G4 1019
TU-VAF G2 119/22
TU-VAF G3 303
TU-VAF G3 462

Benin

TY-BBK CVT 29
TY-BBM 50 17

Mali

TZ-PBF CVT 19

Bosnia
(see also BH-)

T9-BIH S550 0045

Kazakhstan

UN-09002 900 11

Ukraine

(UR-ACA) 50 235
(UR-BCA) 20 141/441
UR-CCA 20 256
UR-CCB 20 141/441
UR-CCC 50 235
UR-CCD 20 112
UR-EFA 20 55/410
UR-EFB 20 75
UR-NIK 20 112

Australia

(VH-) 125 259023
(VH-) 400 RJ-55
VH-ACE 900 37
VH-AJJ WWD 248
VH-AJK WWD 256
VH-AJP WWD 238
VH-AJQ WWD 281
VH-AJS 35A 188
VH-AJS WWD 221
VH-AJV 35A 189
VH-AJV WWD 282
(VH-ALH) 35A 480
VH-ANI 35A 468
VH-ANQ 500 283
VH-APU WWD 395
VH-AQR 500 263
VH-AQS 500 263
(VH-ARJ) 125 256037
VH-ASG G2 95/39
VH-ASM 601 5033
VH-ASM G2 91
VH-ASQ G4 1205
VH-ASR WWD 316
VH-AYI WWD 317
VH-BBJ 125 25169
VH-BBJ 400A RK-26
VH-BCL WWD 315
VH-BGF 900 5
VH-BGL 200 495
VH-BGV 900 32
VH-BIB 36A 035
VH-BIZ 20 73/419
VH-BJC 400A RK-154
VH-BJD 400A RK-35
VH-BJQ 35A 219
VH-BLJ 25B 180
VH-BNK 501 574
VH-BQR 35A 471
VH-BRG 601 5064
VH-BRR 20 208/468
VH-BRX 550 338
VH-BSJ 24D 266
VH-CAO 125 25015
VH-CCA G4 1175
(VH-CCC) 125 258002
VH-CCC G4 1083
VH-CCO G4 1107

VH-CIR 20 90/426
VH-CIT 525 0100
VH-CPE 200 504
VH-CPH 35A 400
(VH-CPQ) 35A 400
VH-CRM 500 130
VH-DJT 10 169
VH-DRM 500 112
VH-DWA 20 72/413
VH-ECD 500 123
VH-ECE 125 25062
VH-ECF 125 25069
VH-ECG 200 493
VH-ELC 35A 428
VH-ELJ 125 258281
VH-ELJ 35 038
VH-EMM 500 051
VH-EMO S550 0063
VH-EMP 35A 345
VH-EXM 550 252
VH-FAX 20 247
VH-FCP 900 37
VH-FFB 10 17
VH-FGK 550 0852
VH-FHJ 560 0278
VH-FIS AST 045
VH-FJZ 20 442
VH-FLJ 24F 349
VH-FOX 35A 427
(VH-FRM) 500 183
VH-FSA 500 237
VH-FSQ 500 225
VH-FSU 35A 463
VH-FSW 35A 463
VH-FSX 35 046
VH-FSY 35A 221
VH-FSZ 35A 242
VH-FWO 20 110
VH-HEY 560 0009
VH-HFJ 20 306/512
VH-HIF 20 255/487
VH-HKR G2 69
VH-HKX 500 050
VH-HOF 35A 165
VH-HPF 20 391
VH-HPJ 200 491
VH-HSP 125 257215
VH-HSS 125 257169
VH-HVM 500 349
VH-ICN 500 024
(VH-ICT) 550 184
VH-ICX 500 051
VH-III 125 258002
VH-IMP 400A RK-26
VH-ING 550 156
VH-ING 650 7104
VH-INX 550 156
VH-IWJ WWD 371
VH-IWU S550 0118
VH-IWW WWD 314
VH-IXL 125 258040
VH-JBH 550 304
VH-JCC 125 257046
VH-JCG 550 112
VH-JCR 35A 231
VH-JDW 100 216
VH-JEP D1A A048SA
VH-JFT 125 257064
VH-JIG 35A 400
VH-JJA WWD 409
VH-JPG 550 112
VH-JPK 550 307
(VH-JPL) WWD 386
VH-JPW WWD 317
VH-JSX 20 78/412
VH-JSY 20 85/425
VH-JSZ 20 90/426
VH-JVS 550 418
VH-KDI 550 235
VH-KDP 550 289
VH-KNJ WWD 381
VH-KNS WWD 323
VH-KTI 35A 239
VH-KTI 650 0144
VH-KTK 550 370
VH-LAW 125 258295
VH-LAW 400A RK-35
VH-LCL 501 538
VH-LEQ 35A 239
VH-LGH 35A 342
VH-LGH 55 048
VH-LGL 500 206
VH-LJB 25B 180
VH-LJG 501 471
VH-LJK 550 184
VH-LJL 35 046
VH-LJL 500 123
VH-LKV 125 258019
VH-LLW WWD 253
VH-LLX WWD 259
VH-LLY WWD 272
VH-LMP 125 257178
VH-LMP 125 259022
VH-LOF WWD 366
VH-LRH 125 257046
VH-LSW 550 099
VH-LYG 125 257001
VH-MAY 550 021
VH-MCG 600 1061
VH-MCX 10 134
VH-MEI 10 50
VH-MGC 550 0810
VH-MIE 35A 459
VH-MIQ 20 255/487
VH-MIQ 35A 202
VH-MOJ 525 0138
VH-MXX 600 1061
VH-MZL 35A 285
VH-MZL 601 3054
VH-NCF 20 368
VH-NCP G4 1108
VH-NEW 500 268
VH-NGA WWD 387
VH-NGF 200 505
VH-NHJ 560 0108
(VH-NIJ) WWD 317
VH-NJA 125 256037
VH-NJM 125 258002
VH-NJW WWD 315
VH-NKS 600 1073
VH-NMN 20 327
VH-NMR 125 258058
VH-NMW 500 279
VH-NTH 560 0041
VH-OIL 500 225
VH-ORE 550 035
VH-OVS 25B 120
VH-OYW 550 054
VH-OZI 650 0037
(VH-OZZ) 600 1057
VH-PAB 125 25265
VH-PDJ 200 491
VH-PDJ 50 176
VH-PFA 35A 661
VH-PNL 400A RK-139
VH-POZ 501 370
VH-PPF 50 187
VH-PSU 560 0515
VH-RRC 20 325
VH-SBC 24D 279
VH-SBJ 35A 193
VH-SCD 550 370
VH-SDN 35A 342
VH-SFJ 50 123
VH-SGY 125 258019
VH-SGY 125 258328
VH-SGY WWD 395
VH-SLD 35A 145
VH-SLE 35A 428
VH-SLF 36A 049
VH-SLJ 35 046
VH-SLJ 36 014
VH-SMF 560 0320
(VH-SOA) 125 257169
VH-SOU 500 333
VH-SQH WWD 366
VH-SWC 501 494
VH-SWL 550 207
VH-TFQ 550 160
VH-TFY 550 099
VH-TGG G4 1156
VH-TLJ 35A 091
VH-TNN 25C 181
VH-TNP 550 184
VH-TOM 125 25242
VH-TPR 35A 400
VH-UCC 500 142
(VH-UDC) 35 038
VH-ULT 35A 463
VH-UOH 550 130
VH-UPB 35A 215
VH-UUZ WWD 317
VH-WFE 35A 221
VH-WFJ 35A 242
VH-WFP 35A 466
VH-WGJ 550 054
VH-WLH 20 262
VH-WNP 550 112
VH-WNZ 550 073
VH-WRM 500 150
VH-WWY WWD 325
VH-XDD 550 099
VH-XMO 125 258243
VH-XTT 560 0417
VH-ZLE 550 380
VH-ZLT 550 0878
VH-ZMD 500 263

Bahamas
(see also C6-)

VP-BDH 125 25206
VP-BDH 125 256028
VP-BDM 25 008

Bermuda
(see also VR-B)

(VP-B) 31A 074
VP-B 900 143
VP-BAB G3 373
VP-BAC 604 5309
VP-BAW 125 258237
VP-BBH 125 257118
VP-BBW 125 256037
VP-BCA 604 5391
VP-BCB 604 5397
VP-BCC 601 5162
VP-BCD 50 134
VP-BCF 125 257214
VP-BCH 10 70
VP-BCI 601 5193
VP-BCM 125 258404
VP-BCN 125 256035
VP-BCO 604 5420
VP-BCP STR 5222
VP-BCT G3 302
VP-BCZ 50 107
VP-BDB 560 0503
VP-BDD 700 9017
VP-BDS 525 0180
VP-BEF 2xx 49
VP-BEH 900 163
VP-BFW 10 54
VP-BGC 900 169
VP-BGF 900 154
VP-BGO 604 5404
VP-BGT G2 211
VP-BHA 604 5307
VP-BHG G4 1017
VP-BHI 501 664
VP-BHJ 900 138
VP-BHL 125 258349
VP-BHO 501 610
VP-BHW 125 257209
VP-BHZ 125 258438
VP-BID 90X 39
VP-BIE 601 3016
VP-BIS G4 1150
VP-BIV G4 1103
VP-BJA 900 154
VP-BJD G4 1134
VP-BJS 35A 464
VP-BJV G2 186
VP-BKA 900 170
VP-BKG 50 147
VP-BKH G4 1029
VP-BKI G4 1029
VP-BKK 125 25238
VP-BKP 501 555
VP-BKT G4 1074
VP-BKY 125 25150
VP-BLA 601 3013
VP-BLB 900 49
VP-BLD STR 5117/35
VP-BLF 501 679
VP-BLM 900 72
VP-BLN G3 402
VP-BLP 900 14
VP-BLV 500 344
VP-BMA AST 092
VP-BMD 125 257200
VP-BMF 50 206
VP-BMI 50 286
VP-BML 31A 140
VP-BMM 60 054
VP-BMR 400A RK-133
VP-BMS 90X 42
VP-BMX 31A 160
VP-BMY G3 463
VP-BND G2 199/19
VP-BNF 604 5332
VP-BNG 601 5119
VP-BNJ 900 120
VP-BNW 125 256057
VP-BNY G4 1208
VP-BNZ G3 452
VP-BOA 601 5114
VP-BOJ 125 257103
VP-BOK G3 390
VP-BOL 55 022
VP-BON AST 060
VP-BOR G3 484
VP-BOT G4 1212
VP-BPA 50 266
VP-BPE 125 257040
VP-BPI 900 149
VP-BPW 900 135
VP-BRF G4 1015
VP-BRJ 525 0351
VP-BRL STR 5155/32
VP-BRO 90X 13
VP-BSA 50 196
VP-BSF G4 1058
VP-BSH STR 5117/35
VP-BSI 125 258073
VP-BSK 900 125
VP-BSL 50 209
VP-BSM G5 555
VP-BSS G4 1001
VP-BST 50 258
VP-BTM 125 258233
VP-BTR 550 693
VP-BTZ 125 257109
VP-BUC 50 107
VP-BUL 560 0102
VP-BUS G4 1127
VP-BVV 550 307
VP-BWB 601 5151
VP-BWS 900 124
VP-BZA G4 1381
VP-BZE 50 144
VP-BZZ 525 0235

Cayman Islands
(see also VR-C)

VP-C 501 547
VP-CAI 560 5048
VP-CAM 601 5090
VP-CAN 604 5335
VP-CAP 501 583
VP-CAS 125 258167

VP-CAT 501 637
VP-CBB G4 1250
VP-CBD 900 16
VP-CBE 550 119
VP-CBM 550 729
VP-CBT 50 256
VP-CBW G4 1096
VP-CBX G5 511
VP-CCC 525 0040
VP-CCL 200 482
VP-CCM 550 310
VP-CCO 550 347
VP-CCP 550 0857
VP-CCR 601 5079
VP-CCV 560 0320
VP-CDE 125 258234
VP-CDM 501 463
VP-CDW 650 7034
VP-CED 550 0870
VP-CEF 50 283
VP-CEK 125 257175
VP-CEZ 50 138
VP-CFF 501 456
VP-CFG 501 577
VP-CFI 50 278
VP-CFL G4 1282
VP-CFP 525 0126
VP-CGA 2xx 100
VP-CGB 900 145
VP-CGE 650 7077
VP-CGP 50 204
VP-CHG 50 259
VP-CHH 500 083
VP-CHK 601 5102
VP-CHT 25B 075
VP-CHV 525 0264
VP-CIC 601 5011
VP-CID 900 130
VP-CIP G4 1371
VP-CIS 525 0252
VP-CJA 2xx 18
VP-CJB 501 564
VP-CJF 25B 075
VP-CJP 125 25258
VP-CJR 550 388
VP-CKG AST 096
VP-CKK 400A RK-200
VP-CKM 560 0413
VP-CLB 90X 34
VP-CLD 50 134
VP-CLE 601 3066
VP-CLN 50 251
VP-CMB 25B 118
VP-CMC 601 5044
VP-CMD 550 726
VP-CMF G4 1062
VP-CMG G5 519
VP-CMO 500 070
VP-CMZ 125 259021
VP-CNF 525 0153
VP-CNJ G3 426
VP-CNM 550 0857
VP-CNM 560 5070
VP-CNP G3 496
VP-COJ 601 5152
VP-COJ 604 5367
VP-COM 500 318
VP-CON 500 238
VP-CPA G2 204
(VP-CPC) 700 9005
VP-CPO 601 5165
VP-CPT 125 259004
VP-CRA 125 257118
VP-CRB 60 125
VP-CRT 50 88
VP-CRX 601 3052
VP-CRY G4 1176
VP-CSC 560 0439
VP-CSM STR 5092/58
VP-CSN 560 0401
VP-CSP 500 165
VP-CTA 525 0172
VP-CTB 501 432
VP-CTE 550 716
VP-CTF 550 716
VP-CTJ 550 068
VP-CTS 125 25243
VP-CTT 900 161
VP-CUB G2 207/34
VP-CUT AST 080
VP-CVK 601 5049
VP-CVL 45 059
VP-CWI 50 159
VP-CWM 550 667
VP-CWW 525 0124
VP-CXX 125 259032
VP-CYK 750 0097
VP-CYM G4 1090

Zimbabwe
(see also Z-)

VP-WKY 25B 160

Swaziland
(see also 3D-)

VQ-ZIL 125 25080

Bermuda
(see also VP-B)

(VR-B) 125 258182
VR-B 50 175
(VR-B) 50 231
(VR-B) 50 66
VR-BAA 601 5156
VR-BAB G3 373
VR-BAC 604 5309
(VR-BBP) 600 1073
VR-BBY 501 433
VR-BCC 601 5162
VR-BCF 125 257214
VR-BCF 23 038
VR-BCG 20 3/403
VR-BCH 10 70
VR-BCI 601 5193
VR-BCJ 20 55/410
VR-BCY 560 0376
VR-BDC G4 1183
VR-BDK 20 198/466
VR-BEM 25C 098
VR-BES AST 017
VR-BFF 10 7
VR-BFR 36 012
VR-BFV 25C 094
VR-BFW 10 54
VR-BFX 35 054
VR-BGB 650 0077
VR-BGD 125 25157
VR-BGF 25C 098
(VR-BGL) G2 124
VR-BGO G2 124
VR-BGS 125 256011
VR-BGT G2 211
VR-BHA 604 5307
VR-BHA G2 45
VR-BHB 36 007
VR-BHC 24X 267
VR-BHD G2 231
VR-BHE 125 257020
VR-BHF STR 5062/12
VR-BHG 550 273
VR-BHG G4 1017
VR-BHH 125 257140
VR-BHI 501 664
VR-BHJ 10 104
VR-BHJ 900 138
VR-BHL 20 429
VR-BHR G2 165/37
VR-BHV 55 045
VR-BHW 125 257209
VR-BHX 50 140
VR-BHY 200 496
VR-BHZ 200 492
VR-BIZ 550 469
VR-BJA 50 110
VR-BJA 900 154
VR-BJB 20 244
VR-BJD 36 008
VR-BJD G2 219/20
VR-BJD G4 1134
VR-BJE G3 347
VR-BJG G2 112
VR-BJH STR 5215
VR-BJI STR 5149/11
VR-BJJ 20 401
VR-BJJ 50 228
VR-BJK 501 372
VR-BJN 501 532
VR-BJO 36 008
VR-BJQ G2 140/40
VR-BJS 650 0119
VR-BJT G2 137
VR-BJV G2 186
VR-BJW 501 674
VR-BJX 900 4
VR-BJY 650 0040
VR-BJZ G4 1005
VR-BKA D1A A058SA
VR-BKB 35A 370
VR-BKE G4 1037
VR-BKG 50 147
VR-BKH 20 237/476
VR-BKI G4 1029
VR-BKJ 600 1016
VR-BKK 125 25238
(VR-BKL) G4 1048
VR-BKN 125 25240
VR-BKP 501 555
VR-BKR 20 133
VR-BKS G3 390
VR-BKT G4 1074
VR-BKU G4 1046
VR-BKV G4 1055
VR-BKY 125 25150
VR-BKZ 125 257199
VR-BLA 601 3013
VR-BLB 900 49
VR-BLC G4 1093
VR-BLD 600 1035
VR-BLF 501 679
(VR-BLG) 400 RJ-22
VR-BLH G4 1008
VR-BLJ G2 40
VR-BLL 50 136
VR-BLM 900 72
VR-BLN G3 402
VR-BLO G3 390
VR-BLP 125 258139
VR-BLQ 125 258175
VR-BLR G4 1127
VR-BLT 900 88
VR-BLU 35A 389
VR-BLV 500 344
VR-BLW 501 442
VR-BMA 601 3012
VR-BMB 125 25240
VR-BMD 125 257200
VR-BME AST 041
VR-BMF 50 206
VR-BMG 650 0185
VR-BMK 601 5029
VR-BML G2 70/1
VR-BMN 24X 267
VR-BMO 500 083
VR-BMQ G2 42/12
VR-BMT 500 083
VR-BMY G3 463
VR-BNB 125 257002
(VR-BND) 125 258164
VR-BND G2 199/19
VR-BNE G2 51
VR-BNF 601 5069
VR-BNG 601 5119
VR-BNI 35A 620
VR-BNJ 900 120
VR-BNO G3 308
VR-BNT 10 73
VR-BNV 400 RJ-36
VR-BNW 125 256057
VR-BNX G3 320
VR-BNY G4 1208
VR-BNZ G3 452
VR-BOA 601 5114
VR-BOB G3 375
VR-BOB G4 1120
VR-BOJ 125 257103
VR-BOK G3 390
VR-BOL 55 022
VR-BON AST 060
VR-BOS G2 13
VR-BOT G4 1212
VR-BOY G4 1009
(VR-BPA) 125 258139
(VR-BPB) 125 258175
VR-BPE 125 257040
VR-BPF 550 599
VR-BPG 125 258165
VR-BPI 900 149
VR-BPM 125 258186
VR-BPN 125 258239
VR-BPT 125 257109
VR-BPW 900 135
VR-BQA 601 5130
VR-BQB 560 0301
VR-BQF 55 039
(VR-BQG) STR 5155/32
(VR-BQH) 125 258233
VR-BRF G4 1015
VR-BRJ 20 275
VR-BRL STR 5155/32
VR-BRM G2 194
VR-BRM G2 91
VR-BRS 125 256004
VR-BSH STR 5117/35
VR-BSI 125 258073
VR-BSK 900 125
VR-BSL G3 304
VR-BSS G4 1001
VR-BST 60 035
VR-BTM 125 258233
VR-BTQ 500 340
VR-BTR 550 693
VR-BTT 50 32
VR-BTZ 125 257109
VR-BUB 500 345
VR-BUC 50 107
VR-BUL 560 0102
VR-BUS G4 1127
VR-BVI 125 25278
VR-BVV 550 307
VR-BWB 601 5151
VR-BWS 900 124
VR-BYE 550 599
VR-BZE 50 144

Cayman Islands
(see also VP-C)

(VR-C) 20 150/445
(VR-C) 35A 356
VR-CAC WWD 285
VR-CAD 35A 432
VR-CAD WWD 276
VR-CAE 50 228
VR-CAG G2 231
VR-CAR 20 440
VR-CAR 601 3017
VR-CAS 125 258167
VR-CAS G2 4/8
VR-CAT 501 637
VR-CAU WWD 72
VR-CAW STR 5133
VR-CBB G4 1250
VR-CBB WWD 350
VR-CBC G2 167
VR-CBD 125 256041
VR-CBK WWD 285
VR-CBL 50 95
VR-CBL G4 1243
VR-CBM 550 729

VR-CBM	G2	34
VR-CBO	50	98
VR-CBP	600	1067
VR-CBR	50	9
VR-CBT	20	237/476
VR-CBU	35A	396
VR-CBW	G4	1096
VR-CCC	650	0023
(VR-CCC)	STR	5006/40
VR-CCE	550	441
VR-CCF	20	285/504
VR-CCH	25B	091
VR-CCI	550	046
VR-CCL	200	482
VR-CCN	G3	345
VR-CCP	500	083
VR-CCQ	200	515
VR-CCQ	50	208
VR-CCQ	50	73
VR-CCR	601	5079
VR-CCV	560	0320
VR-CCV	601	5075
VR-CCX	125	258214
VR-CCY	STR	5085
(VR-CDA)	400A	RK-25
VR-CDB	20	305
VR-CDE	125	258234
VR-CDF	50	111
VR-CDG	125	256013
VR-CDH	25D	213
VR-CDI	35A	264
VR-CDK	55C	138
VR-CDM	501	463
VR-CDN	525	0085
VR-CDT	20	341
VR-CEB	500	094
VR-CEE	S65	465-22
VR-CEG	601	5104
VR-CEJ	125	258021
VR-CES	900	140
VR-CEZ	50	138
VR-CFG	501	577
VR-CFI	50	176
VR-CFL	G4	1282
VR-CGB	900	145
VR-CGD	25B	075
VR-CGP	50	204
VR-CGP	50	63
VR-CGS	31A	040
VR-CHA	601	5153
VR-CHB	551	559
VR-CHC	200	515
VR-CHF	501	637
VR-CHH	500	083
VR-CHJ	31A	040
VR-CHK	601	5102
VR-CHT	25B	075
(VR-CIA)	501	577
VR-CIC	601	5011
VR-CID	900	130
VR-CIL	WWD	289
VR-CIM	650	7035
VR-CIT	550	407
(VR-CJA)	55	033
VR-CJB	501	564
VR-CJJ	601	5142
VR-CJP	125	25258
VR-CJR	550	388
(VR-CKC)	601	5073
VR-CKK	600	1033
VR-CKP	125	257159
VR-CLA	100	203
VR-CLD	50	134
VR-CLE	601	3066
VR-CLI	600	1054
VR-CLN	50	251
VR-CMC	601	5044
(VR-CMC)	G3	423
VR-CMF	G3	374
VR-CMF	G4	1062
VR-CMG	AST	034
VR-CML	55	033
VR-CMO	500	070
VR-CMS	501	511
VR-CMZ	125	259021
VR-CNJ	G3	426
VR-CNM	STR	5229
VR-CNS	560	0177
VR-CNV	50	224
VR-COG	400A	RK-7
VR-COJ	601	5043
VR-COJ	601	5104
VR-COJ	601	5152
VR-COM	500	318
VR-CPA	G2	204
VR-CPO	601	5165
VR-CPT	125	259004
VR-CQZ	50	168
VR-CRT	50	88
VR-CSA	900	61
VR-CSF	125	256065
VR-CSM	STR	5092/58
VR-CSP	500	165
VR-CSS	551	030
VR-CTA	900	16
VR-CTA	G4	1278
VR-CTB	501	432
VR-CTE	550	716
VR-CTG	G3	450
VR-CTL	560	0023
VR-CUB	G2	207/34
VR-CUC	35A	203
VR-CVD	125	257107
VR-CVK	601	5049
VR-CVP	650	0210
VR-CWI	50	159
VR-CWM	550	667
VR-CWW	500	044
VR-CXX	125	259032
VR-CYM	G4	1090
VR-CYR	HFB	1057

Hong Kong
(see also B-H)

VR-HIM	125	257001
VR-HIN	125	257025
VR-HSS	125	257169

India

VT-AAA	**125**	**257161**
VT-EAU	125	258120
VT-EHS	**29**	**003**
VT-EIH	**29**	**004**
VT-ENR	**G3**	**420**
VT-EQZ	**125**	**25133**
VT-ERO	WWD	33
VT-ETG	**S550**	**0089**
VT-EUN	**550**	**393**
VT-EUX	**560**	**0299**
VT-KMB	**S550**	**0135**
VT-MPA	**125**	**257172**
VT-OAM	**400**	**RJ-38**
VT-OBE	**125**	**257215**
VT-OPJ	**525**	**0112**
VT-RHM	S550	0089
VT-SRR	125	257191
VT-SWP	25D	367
VT-TAT	**2xx**	**65**
VT-TEL	**400**	**RJ-46**
VT-TTA	**200**	**511**
VT-UBG	**125**	**25254**
VT-VPS	**550**	**269**

Antigua

V2-LSF	125	256065

Namibia

V5-CDM	**560**	**0151**
V5-KJY	24	165
V5-NAG	**31A**	**091**
V5-NAM	**900**	**103**
V5-NPC	**31A**	**138**

Brunei

V8-001	G5	509
V8-001	**G5**	**515**
V8-007	G3	436
V8-007	G4	1059
V8-007	G4	1109
V8-007	G5	515
V8-008	G4	1176
V8-009	G3	436
V8-009	G4	1150
V8-009	G4	1202
V8-009	G5	509
V8-A11	G3	436
V8-AL1	G4	1059
V8-AL1	G4	1109
V8-AL1	G4	1150
V8-HB3	G3	436
V8-MSB	G4	1202
V8-RB1	G4	1059
V8-SR1	G4	1059
V8-SR1	G4	1109
V8-SR1	G4	1150

Mexico

XA-	**125**	**25146**
XA-	**24**	**112**
XA-	24D	237
XA-	**500**	**210**
XA-	**550**	**268**
XA-	**650**	**0069**
XA-	**650**	**0073**
XA-	**75A**	**380-34**
XA-	**S60**	**306-128**
XA-	**T39**	**265-62**
XA-	**T39**	**276-25**
XA-	**T39**	**276-4**
(XA-)	125	257034
(XA-)	35A	077
(XA-)	560	0268
(XA-)	650	0078
(XA-)	G3	318
(XA-)	STR	5089
XA-AAA	**24B**	**208**
XA-AAP	**31**	**032**
XA-AAS	50	31
XA-ABA	**G2**	**136**
XA-ABB	24D	299
XA-ABC	G2	161
XA-ABC	S60	306-63
XA-ABH	25D	298
XA-ACC	24D	297
XA-ACC	35A	176
XA-ACC	STR	5212
XA-ACF	S60	306-12
XA-ACN	**125**	**256038**
XA-ADC	S60	306-6
XA-ADD	24D	298
XA-AGA	**501**	**469**
XA-AGL	125	256046
XA-AGN	**550**	**082**
XA-AHM	**G2**	**161**
XA-AIS	G4	1098
XA-ALE	35A	047
XA-APD	S40	282-123
XA-APD	S60	306-33
XA-APE	**900**	**178**
XA-ARA	**G2**	**79**
XA-ARE	S60	306-146
XA-ARE	S65	465-27
XA-ARG	23	068
XA-ARS	650	0156
XA-AST	**604**	**5357**
XA-ATA	35A	264
XA-ATC	S40	282-114
XA-ATE	**S60**	**306-123**
XA-AVE	**50**	**22**
XA-AVE	WWD	160
XA-AVR	G2	200
XA-AVR	S65	465-27
XA-BAF	S40	282-39
XA-BAL	G2	237/43
XA-BAL	G4	1114
XA-BAL	**G5**	**546**
XA-BBA	25D	223
XA-BBE	24D	255
XA-BCC	20	284
XA-BCC	CVT	36
XA-BEB	**STR**	**5132/57**
XA-BEG	50	224
XA-BEG	**90X**	**33**
XA-BEM	125	25068
XA-BNG	**400**	**RJ-33**
XA-BNO	**35A**	**336**
XA-BOA	501	607
XA-BOJ	125	25060
XA-BQA	WWD	276
XA-BRE	35A	373
XA-BRE	**60**	**058**
XA-BRE	G2	185
XA-BUX	35	020
XA-BUX	**35A**	**176**
XA-BUY	24D	270
XA-CAG	G4	1197
XA-CAH	125	256044
XA-CAP	24F	349
XA-CCB	S60	306-12
XA-CEN	**S60**	**306-26**
XA-CHA	75A	380-58
XA-CHP	**S60**	**306-22**
XA-CHR	G2	98/38
XA-CHR	G4	1195
XA-CIS	S60	306-63
XA-CLA	400A	RK-3
XA-CMN	S60	306-56
XA-COC	25B	194
XA-COL	125	25086
XA-CPQ	**G5**	**533**
XA-CPQ	S40	282-48
XA-CUR	**S60**	**306-127**
XA-CUZ	125	25279
XA-CZG	**35A**	**162**
XA-DAJ	500	241
XA-DAK	**25B**	**190**
XA-DAN	**S40**	**282-26**
XA-DAT	24D	322
XA-DAZ	25D	309
XA-DCO	S60	306-38
XA-DET	**24F**	**337**
XA-DGP	**525**	**0329**
XA-DIJ	**24D**	**269**
XA-DIN	125	25273
XA-DIN	31	026
XA-DIW	125	25226
(XA-DMS)	50	249
XA-DPS	G4	1227
XA-DSC	**S60**	**306-56**
XA-DUB	25D	306
XA-DUC	**20**	**269**
XA-EAS	25D	355
XA-ECM	S60	306-89
XA-ECR	200	513
XA-EEU	S40	282-54
XA-EGC	S40	282-61
XA-EKO	500	140
XA-EKT	**STR**	**5234**
XA-ELR	25D	290
XA-ELU	35A	261
XA-EMO	**STR**	**5140**
XA-EPM	75A	380-19
XA-ESQ	125	25028
XA-ESQ	25D	234
XA-ESR	S40	282-59
XA-ESS	23	037
XA-FCP	650	0165
XA-FES	STR	5155/32
XA-FEX	**90X**	**46**
XA-FHR	**G2**	**30/4**
XA-FHR	STR	5158
XA-FHR	STR	5231
XA-FHS	STR	5215
XA-FIR	**550**	**718**

XA-FIU 10 83
XA-FIU STR 5100/41
XA-FIW 24D 296
XA-FLM 20 364
XA-FMR 25D 274
XA-FMU 25D 249
XA-FNP S60 306-63
XA-FNY G2 175
XA-FOU G2 152
XA-FOU G3 449
XA-FRP 125 25185
XA-FTC 50 80
XA-FTN S40 282-80
XA-FVK 50 35
XA-FVK S65 465-27
XA-GAC G2 155/14
XA-GAE 900 137
XA-GAM 23 033
XA-GAN 650 0218
XA-GAP S65 465-8
XA-GBA 24D 260
XA-GCH 50 50
XA-GCH S40 282-115
XA-GDO 35A 449
XA-GDW T39 265-86
XA-GEO 24F 337
XA-GEO 601 5059
XA-GFB 125 258075
XA-GFC 50 80
XA-GGG 25B 147
XA-GHR 75A 380-58
XA-GIH S60 306-72
XA-GMD 31 005
XA-GME 601 5128
XA-GNI 2xx 60
XA-GNL 25D 329
XA-GOC 125 25107
XA-GRB 125 259021
XA-GRB 25D 309
XA-GRB 601 5149
XA-GRB 604 5375
XA-GTR 900 107
XA-GUB 125 25185
XA-GYR S40 282-6
XA-GZA STR 5100/41
XA-HEV 501 382
XA-HEW 20 250
XA-HFM 125 25107
XA-HGF 31 026
XA-HGF 50 236
XA-HHF 20 327
XA-HHR S60 306-6
XA-HNY STR 5162
XA-HOK S40 282-17
XA-HOO 500 175
XA-HOS 35 045
XA-HOS 35A 341
XA-HOU 125 25060
XA-HRM 31 026
XA-HRM 31A 044
XA-HRM STR 5066/46
XA-HYS 35A 243
XA-ICA 60 027
XA-ICK S60 306-86
XA-ICO 560 0461
XA-ICP 550 631
XA-IEM 501 384
XA-IIT 125 25152
XA-IIX 500 274
XA-ILV G2 195
XA-INF 650 0198
XA-INF S550 0010
XA-INK S550 0010
XA-ISR 600 1057
XA-JAX 25B 104
XA-JCE 501 544
XA-JCE S60 306-93
XA-JCG STR 5140
XA-JEL 500 250
XA-JEQ 125 256047
XA-JET 400A RK-163
(XA-JEW) 500 533
XA-JEX 500 530
XA-JEZ 550 140

XA-JFE 501 544
XA-JFE 601 5059
XA-JFE STR 5145
XA-JHR STR 5066/46
XA-JIK S60 306-130
XA-JIN 25D 210
XA-JIQ 24D 317
XA-JIX 125 257079
XA-JJA 400 RJ-33
XA-JJS 60 131
XA-JJS 601 5097
XA-JJS STR 5101/15
XA-JLV 24 136
XA-JLV 500 021
XA-JMD S60 306-119
XA-JML STR 5206
XA-JMN STR 5134/50
XA-JOC 25D 303
XA-JOV 500 035
XA-JPA 550 689
XA-JRF 125 25202
XA-JRF 125 256018
XA-JRF 125 257059
XA-JRF 550 642
XA-JRH 35A 609
XA-JRV 500 136
XA-JSC 24 123
XA-JSC 25XR 152
XA-JSO 24 123
XA-JUA 500 247
XA-JUD S40 282-43
XA-JUE S40 282-48
XA-JUZ 125 25014
XA-JYO 550 689
XA-KAC 125 257110
XA-KAH 500 289
XA-KAJ 28 004
XA-KCM 35A 418
XA-KEW 125 257096
XA-KEY 25XR 222
XA-KIM 601 3015
XA-KIQ 551 181
XA-KIS 125 257102
XA-KMX 550 247
XA-KOF 125 25065
XA-KON 125 257108
XA-KUG WWD 224
XA-KUJ 500 313
XA-KUT 125 256028
XA-LAN 35A 267
XA-LAP 25D 336
XA-LAR 23 074
XA-LEG 125 257046
XA-LEG 400 RJ-60
XA-LEG 75A 380-15
XA-LEG S40 282-100
(XA-LEI) S60 306-115
XA-LEL S40 282-68
XA-LEO 500 273
XA-LET 25D 244
XA-LFU 125 25112
XA-LGM 23 033
XA-LIJ WWD 285
XA-LIM 501 571
XA-LIO 10 40
XA-LIX S40 282-128
XA-LML 125 257076
XA-LML 35A 296
XA-LML S40 282-115
XA-LNK 24 174
XA-LOB 20 39
XA-LOF 25D 338
XA-LOH 50 9
XA-LOK 10 175
XA-LOQ S60 306-145
XA-LOR WWD 319
XA-LOT 550 244
XA-LOV 125 25283
XA-LRA 50 238
XA-LRA S60 306-63
XA-LRJ 25D 359
XA-LTH 550 462
XA-LTH 650 0101
XA-LUC S65 465-55

XA-LUD 500 587
XA-LUN 501 353
XA-LUV 500 598
XA-LUZ 25D 314
XA-LYM WWD 133
XA-LZZ G2 18
XA-MAH 125 256065
XA-MAK WWD 342
XA-MAK WWD 350
XA-MAL 25D 274
XA-MAL 501 373
XA-MAM 200 506
XA-MAR WWD 264
XA-MAZ STR 5079/33
XA-MBM 125 25030
XA-MDM 60 089
XA-MEX 400A RK-196
XA-MEY G3 252
XA-MHA 25XR 222
XA-MIC G3 323
XA-MII 400 RJ-58
XA-MIK STR 5066/46
XA-MIR 125 25068
XA-MIX G2 237/43
XA-MJG 31A 044
XA-MKI 601 5158
XA-MKY 601 5158
XA-MLG S65 465-48
XA-MMM 10 36
XA-MMO 25D 352
XA-MNA S40 282-115
XA-MPS 35A 460
XA-MSH 125 257128
XA-MSH 35A 380
XA-MUI WWD 160
XA-MUL S60 306-50
XA-MVR 50 94
XA-MVT 75A 380-42
XA-NAY 20 269
XA-NGS 125 258232
XA-NLA 24 180
XA-NLK 24 109
XA-NOG 25D 349
XA-NTE 125 256020
XA-NTE 125 257098
XA-OAC 400 RJ-29
XA-OAC 501 514
XA-OAC 550 297
XA-OAF 75A 380-55
XA-ODC 500 217
XA-ODC 550 553
XA-OEM G5 540
XA-OLI STR 5148
XA-OVR 50 88
XA-OVR 900 141
XA-OVR S60 306-130
XA-OVR S65 465-12
XA-PAX S60 306-123
XA-PAZ 25D 309
XA-PAZ 500 060
XA-PEI S60 306-20
XA-PEK S60 306-38
XA-PEN 31A 085
(XA-PEV) 501 607
XA-PFA 24E 329
XA-PFM 200 515
XA-PGO STR 5069/20
XA-PIC 31A 076
XA-PIC 500 141
XA-PIH S40 282-102
XA-PIJ 550 082
XA-PIL 55 014
XA-PIM 25D 368
XA-PIN 35A 201
XA-PIP 650 0146
XA-PIU 25D 293
XA-POG 25B 080
XA-POI 25XR 152
XA-POJ WWD 161
XA-PON 75A 380-39
XA-POO STR 5158
XA-POP 25D 324
XA-POQ 25D 351
XA-POR 550 273

XA-POR S60 306-49
XA-POS 24D 249
XA-POU STR 5053/2
XA-PRO 25D 216
XA-PSD G2 98/38
XA-PSD STR 5132/57
XA-PUE 20 393
XA-PUF WWD 153
XA-PUI 35A 277
XA-PUL STR 5151
XA-PUR S60 306-2
XA-PUV G4 1079
XA-PVR S65 465-12
XA-PYC 35A 336
XA-RAP 600 1057
XA-RAP S60 306-88
XA-RAQ 24E 329
XA-RAR 400 RJ-32
XA-RAV 35A 290
XA-RAX 25D 218
XA-RBS G2 14
XA-RCG 25D 330
XA-RCH 125 25101
XA-RDM 560 0342
XA-RDY 75A 380-60
XA-REA 24E 331
XA-REC S60 306-1
XA-RED S40 282-26
XA-REE 25D 314
XA-REG S40 282-130
XA-REI S60 306-20
XA-REK 24D 285
XA-REN 550 273
XA-REO WWD 124
XA-RET 125 258004
XA-RET WWD 409
XA-REY 20 127
XA-REY 20 393
XA-RFB S60 306-87
XA-RFS 31 005
XA-RGB 900 15
XA-RGB STR 5079/33
XA-RGC S40 282-39
XA-RGC S40 282-48
XA-RGC S40 282-61
XA-RGC S60 306-125
XA-RGG 125 259037
XA-RGS 650 0189
XA-RIA 36A 050
XA-RIC 24D 251
XA-RIH 75A 380-46
XA-RIL 125 25237
XA-RIN 25B 104
XA-RIR S60 306-36
XA-RIW WWD 86
XA-RIZ WWD 160
XA-RKE 200 508
XA-RKG S40 282-106
XA-RKH 560 0156
XA-RKP 25D 353
XA-RKX 560 0147
XA-RKY 35A 370
XA-RLE 501 544
XA-RLH S40 282-129
XA-RLI 25D 353
XA-RLL S60 306-83
XA-RLP 80A 380-4
XA-RLR 80A 380-50
XA-RLR S60 306-100
XA-RLS S60 306-57
XA-RLX 100 226
XA-RMA 20 39
XA-RMD STR 5228
XA-RMF 24D 290
XA-RMF 25D 308
XA-RMN 125 25185
XA-RMY 650 0179
XA-RNB 20 142
XA-RNE 400 RJ-61
XA-RNG 400 RJ-58
XA-RNK 31 021
XA-RNR S60 306-49
XA-ROC 25D 357
XA-ROD 80A 380-50

XA-ROF	STR	5133
XA-ROF	STR	5148
XA-ROI	G2	10
XA-ROJ	125	25206
XA-ROK	STR	5133
XA-ROK	STR	5148
XA-ROO	25D	227
XA-ROX	24D	260
XA-ROZ	25D	286
XA-RPS	S40	282-56
XA-RPT	**125**	**25161**
XA-RPV	25D	210
XA-RQB	**24X**	**150**
XA-RQI	25	032
XA-RQP	24	179
XA-RQT	WWD	124
XA-RRC	24D	259
XA-RRK	24D	307
XA-RSP	**125**	**25091**
XA-RSR	**125**	**25017**
XA-RSU	25D	363
XA-RTH	S60	306-39
XA-RTM	S40	282-39
XA-RTP	S60	306-110
XA-RTT	560	0092
XA-RTV	24	124
XA-RUD	550	631
XA-RUJ	24D	289
XA-RUQ	S60	306-15
XA-RUR	500	273
XA-RUS	G2	161
XA-RUU	**31**	**012**
XA-RUX	125	25101
XA-RUY	**125**	**258302**
XA-RUY	35A	373
XA-RVB	23	066
XA-RVB	35A	321
XA-RVG	STR	5139/54
XA-RVI	25D	286
XA-RVT	**S60**	**306-138**
XA-RVV	**50**	**213**
XA-RWN	125	25226
XA-RWY	S60	306-97
XA-RXA	**24B**	**197**
XA-RXB	25D	325
XA-RXO	560	0118
XA-RXP	S60	306-56
XA-RXQ	25D	342
XA-RXZ	50	168
XA-RYB	**125**	**259043**
XA-RYD	S60	306-72
XA-RYE	**500**	**068**
XA-RYH	**25D**	**334**
XA-RYJ	**75**	**370-5**
XA-RYK	125	256047
XA-RYN	24	164
XA-RYO	S65	465-55
XA-RYR	550	664
XA-RYW	125	25064
XA-RZB	550	654
XA-RZC	23	071
XA-RZD	**601**	**5087**
XA-RZE	25D	274
XA-RZG	400A	RK-36
XA-RZK	650	0204
XA-RZM	23	070
XA-RZQ	650	0126
XA-RZT	25D	330
XA-RZW	75	370-9
XA-RZY	25B	133
XA-RZZ	35A	485
XA-SAA	24D	306
XA-SAE	25D	341
XA-SAE	STR	5066/46
XA-SAG	**20**	**287**
XA-SAG	S40	282-111
XA-SAH	**S60**	**306-137**
XA-SAI	**125**	**256016**
XA-SAL	25B	121
XA-SAM	500	255
XA-SAR	**10**	**125**
(XA-SAR)	10	54
XA-SAR	10	96
XA-SAR	750	0119
XA-SAU	**125**	**257027**
XA-SAV	24D	306
XA-SBA	35A	380
XA-SBF	35A	376
XA-SBQ	STR	5124
XA-SBR	24	180
XA-SBS	S40	282-6
XA-SBV	**S60**	**306-109**
XA-SBX	S60	306-40
XA-SBZ	24D	251
XA-SCE	**24D**	**271**
XA-SCL	20	130
XA-SCN	S40	282-105
XA-SCR	**S65**	**465-65**
(XA-SCV)	WWD	122
XA-SCY	24D	324
XA-SDE	G2	18
XA-SDI	**501**	**395**
XA-SDK	50	224
XA-SDM	G2	237/43
XA-SDN	550	247
XA-SDP	23	066
XA-SDQ	25	005
XA-SDS	500	313
XA-SDT	**560**	**0162**
XA-SDU	**650**	**0052**
XA-SDV	550	037
XA-SDW	WWD	162
XA-SEB	75A	380-58
XA-SEC	G4	1172
XA-SEH	125	258004
XA-SEJ	560	0196
XA-SEN	500	060
XA-SEN	S40	282-7
XA-SEP	650	0076
XA-SET	550	458
XA-SEU	S40	282-104
XA-SEX	**550**	**642**
XA-SEY	**501**	**631**
XA-SFB	G2	79
XA-SFE	**500**	**125**
XA-SFP	50	22
XA-SFQ	**125**	**25273**
XA-SFS	WWD	13
XA-SGK	35A	380
XA-SGM	125	25283
XA-SGP	125	25114
XA-SGR	75	370-6
XA-SGU	24	101
XA-SGW	900	122
XA-SHA	WWD	86
XA-SHN	23	093
XA-SHO	500	111
XA-SHZ	601	3012
XA-SIF	50	231
XA-SIG	500	175
XA-SIM	50	215
XA-SIM	**900**	**114**
XA-SIM	S60	306-143
XA-SIN	STR	5005
XA-SIO	25B	121
XA-SIT	560	0218
XA-SIV	**125**	**258185**
XA-SJC	**560**	**0197**
XA-SJN	**25D**	**365**
XA-SJO	25D	370
XA-SJS	**25B**	**076**
XA-SJV	500	189
XA-SJW	500	169
XA-SJX	900	97
XA-SJZ	550	041
XA-SKB	**S60**	**306-111**
XA-SKE	125	25253
XA-SKH	125	256067
XA-SKI	STR	5124
XA-SKO	200	505
XA-SKW	525	0044
XA-SKX	560	0118
XA-SKZ	125	25121
XA-SLA	**560**	**0228**
XA-SLB	**650**	**0228**
XA-SLD	551	014
XA-SLH	S60	306-39
XA-SLJ	S60	306-125
XA-SLP	**125**	**256002**
XA-SLQ	500	111
XA-SLR	**125**	**25112**
XA-SMF	**S60**	**306-6**
XA-SMH	500	084
XA-SMP	S40	282-13
XA-SMQ	S40	282-50
XA-SMR	**S40**	**282-71**
XA-SMT	550	722
XA-SMU	**24D**	**255**
XA-SMV	550	720
XA-SND	S60	306-7
XA-SNG	G3	434
XA-SNH	125	256021
XA-SNI	S40	282-126
XA-SNM	31A	078
XA-SNN	125	257009
XA-SNO	25D	355
XA-SNP	**400A**	**RK-83**
XA-SNX	**560**	**0229**
XA-SNZ	24	157
XA-SOA	600	1063
XA-SOC	**STR**	**5152**
XA-SOD	D1A	A049SA
XA-SOK	650	7029
XA-SOL	50	116
XA-SON	**125**	**257079**
XA-SOR	**601**	**5147**
XA-SOU	525	0060
XA-SOX	500	217
XA-SOY	**STR**	**5142**
XA-SPL	25D	268
XA-SPM	50	242
XA-SPM	**S65**	**465-14**
XA-SPQ	**650**	**7028**
XA-SPR	31A	076
XA-SQA	**S40**	**282-125**
XA-SQQ	550	280
XA-SQR	550	464
XA-SQS	20	198/466
XA-SQU	G2	173
XA-SQV	**550**	**221**
XA-SQW	550	226
XA-SQX	501	428
XA-SQY	500	243
XA-SQZ	500	193
XA-SRB	500	197
XA-SST	**550**	**731**
XA-SSU	**24D**	**230**
XA-SSV	125	25187
XA-SSY	125	257199
XA-STG	STR	5206
XA-STI	**S60**	**306-89**
XA-STO	G2	79
XA-STT	500	310
XA-STU	S40	282-7
XA-STX	125	257186
XA-SUN	S60	306-143
XA-SUP	24X	319
XA-SUY	24D	324
XA-SVH	S60	306-97
XA-SVX	**35**	**012**
XA-SWC	20	21
XA-SWD	STR	5108
XA-SWF	35A	391
XA-SWK	125	256026
XA-SWM	650	7034
XA-SWP	G2	166/15
XA-SWX	25D	366
XA-SXD	25B	105
XA-SXG	25B	194
XA-SXK	75A	380-39
XA-SXY	25D	308
XA-SYS	S60	306-121
XA-SYY	**10**	**4**
XA-TAB	**100**	**204**
XA-TAL	125	25064
XA-TAM	25D	341
XA-TAN	20	272
XA-TAQ	25D	286
XA-TAV	**STR**	**5103**
XA-TAZ	STR	5103
XA-TBA	650	0019
XA-TBL	100	203
XA-TBV	25D	325
XA-TCA	**24B**	**224**
XA-TCB	125	257082
XA-TCI	**35A**	**349**
XA-TCM	550	717
XA-TCO	G3	403
XA-TCR	125	257102
XA-TCY	25	048
XA-TCZ	**650**	**7019**
XA-TDD	**50**	**252**
XA-TDG	**STR**	**5158**
XA-TDK	**G2**	**114**
XA-TDP	24	128
XA-TDQ	**80A**	**380-50**
XA-TDU	**2xx**	**29**
XA-TDX	**T39**	**276-27**
XA-TEL	550	275
XA-TEL	**900**	**168**
XA-TFC	T39	265-12
XA-TFD	T39	265-10
XA-TFL	**T39**	**265-48**
XA-TGA	**650**	**0036**
XA-TGK	125	259037
XA-TGO	**T39**	**276-6**
XA-THD	**35A**	**243**
XA-THF	**WWD**	**109**
XA-THO	**S550**	**0035**
XA-TIE	**25D**	**364**
XA-TII	**23**	**070**
XA-TIP	24B	227
XA-TIP	24D	293
XA-TIV	600	1057
XA-TIW	**T39**	**276-44**
XA-TIX	**T39**	**276-21**
XA-TIY	**T39**	**265-14**
XA-TJF	**AST**	**050**
XA-TJG	**900**	**131**
XA-TJU	**T39**	**276-8**
XA-TJV	STR	5130
XA-TJW	STR	5129
XA-TJY	**T39**	**276-39**
XA-TJZ	**T39**	**265-76**
XA-TKC	24	164
XA-TKQ	**125**	**258111**
XA-TKW	**S40**	**282-13**
XA-TKY	**501**	**411**
XA-TKZ	**560**	**0474**
XA-TLL	**S60**	**306-20**
XA-TLM	**601**	**5097**
XA-TMF	**S60**	**306-100**
XA-TMH	90X	33
XA-TMI	**S550**	**0080**
XA-TMX	**650**	**7069**
XA-TMZ	**650**	**0068**
XA-TNW	S60	306-73
XA-TNX	**125**	**256018**
XA-TNY	**125**	**25196**
XA-TOF	**500**	**345**
XA-TOM	**S65**	**465-55**
XA-TOO	G4	1114
(XA-TOT)	G3	302
XA-TPB	**125**	**258176**
XA-TPD	**STR**	**5134/50**
XA-TPJ	**STR**	**5231**
XA-TPU	**S60**	**306-143**
XA-TQA	**550**	**504**
XA-TRI	525	0060
XA-TZF	**60**	**088**
XA-TZV	**STR**	**5130**
XA-TZW	**STR**	**5129**
XA-UMA	35A	646
(XA-VAD)	G4	1227
XA-VEL	**S60**	**306-42**
XA-VER	**750**	**0072**
XA-VIG	**60**	**116**
XA-VIO	S60	306-34
XA-VIT	650	0020
XA-VIT	S60	306-50
XA-VTO	**900**	**129**
XA-VVI	24D	230
XA-VYA	**25D**	**336**
XA-VYF	500	265
XA-XET	125	256022
XA-XIS	**650**	**7032**

XA-ZAP	**35A**	**129**
XA-ZOM	S60	306-47
XA-ZTA	**60**	**134**
XA-ZTA	601	5158
XA-ZTH	**31**	**004**
XA-ZUM	S60	306-47
XA-ZUM	S65	465-15
XA-ZYZ	25	032
XA-ZYZ	25D	287
XA-ZZZ	**25D**	**287**
XB-AER	WWD	172
XB-AKW	125	25102
XB-ALO	20	287
XB-AMO	**500**	**152**
XB-APD	S60	306-33
XB-AQU	20	248/483
XB-AXP	125	25112
XB-AXP	125	25233
XB-BAK	10	65
XB-BBL	**S40**	**282-116**
XB-BEA	125	25068
XB-BIP	S60	306-63
XB-BON	**550**	**654**
XB-CAM	10	107
XB-CCM	125	25226
XB-CCO	500	175
XB-CUX	125	25262
XB-CXF	500	143
XB-CXK	125	257153
XB-CXO	STR	5141
XB-CXZ	125	25060
XB-CYA	CVT	36
XB-CYI	CVT	40
XB-DBA	500	067
XB-DBJ	STR	5145
XB-DBS	STR	5159
XB-DBT	STR	5156
XB-DKS	25D	309
XB-DLV	STR	5005
XB-DNY	WWD	183
XB-DSQ	125	25185
XB-DUH	STR	5157
XB-DUS	S40	282-106
XB-DVF	**500**	**587**
XB-DVP	75A	380-53
XB-DYF	500	313
XB-DZD	**24F**	**349**
XB-DZN	125	257158
XB-DZQ	**25D**	**332**
XB-DZR	**24D**	**273**
XB-EAL	125	25060
XB-EBI	**G2**	**96**
XB-ECR	200	513
XB-EDU	20	39
XB-EFR	500	090
XB-EGP	25B	194
XB-ELU	501	544
XB-EPB	20	127
XB-EPM	75A	380-19
XB-EPN	500	241
XB-EQR	S40	282-82
XB-ERN	125	25148
XB-ERU	75A	370-7
XB-ERX	501	460
XB-ESS	**S40**	**282-123**
XB-ESX	**S60**	**306-47**
XB-ETE	500	274
XB-ETV	**S60**	**306-96**
XB-EWF	CVT	36
XB-EWQ	500	141
XB-EXJ	G4	1055
XB-EZV	S40	282-7
XB-FDH	400	RJ-54
XB-FDN	500	068
XB-FFV	125	25112
XB-FIS	125	25060
XB-FIS	STR	5033/56
XB-FJI	WWD	115
XB-FJO	MSP	005
XB-FJW	24	141
XB-FKT	**31**	**029**
XB-FKV	**WWD**	**137**
XB-FMF	125	256033
XB-FMK	**125**	**257068**

XB-FNF	35A	210
XB-FNW	**35A**	**255**
XB-FPK	500	084
XB-FQO	500	278
XB-FRP	125	25185
XB-FST	S60	306-63
XB-FSZ	S60	306-50
XB-FUZ	S60	306-63
XB-FVH	20	393
XB-FVL	G2	100
XB-FWX	10	107
XB-FXD	G3	434
XB-FXO	501	550
XB-GBC	24D	285
XB-GBF	**500**	**273**
XB-GBZ	WWD	133
XB-GCR	20	127
XB-GDJ	**500**	**598**
XB-GDR	25D	308
XB-GDU	T39	265-12
XB-GDV	T39	276-27
XB-GDW	T39	265-86
XB-GGK	125	25064
XB-GHC	125	25121
XB-GHO	**24**	**141**
XB-GJO	75	370-9
XB-GJS	24D	299
XB-GLZ	**550**	**281**
XB-GMD	S65	465-12
XB-GNF	**125**	**25283**
XB-GRE	501	550
XB-GRN	WWD	301
XB-GRQ	23	074
XB-GRR	23	068
XB-GSN	G2	161
XB-GSP	**75A**	**380-55**
XB-GVY	501	368
XB-GXV	650	0101
XB-HDL	**S60**	**306-7**
XB-HGE	**25D**	**325**
XB-HHF	S40	282-6
XB-HIZ	**G3**	**403**
XB-HJS	**S60**	**306-110**
XB-HND	**500**	**255**
XB-HRA	**20**	**127**
XB-JHE	**400**	**RJ-48**
XB-JMM	**S60**	**306-130**
XB-JMR	**S60**	**306-35**
XB-JOY	24D	263
XB-JTN	**125**	**257185**
XB-LAW	S60	306-100
XB-LHS	35A	255
XB-LHS	35A	648
XB-LRD	S60	306-21
XB-LTH	550	462
XB-LXP	125	25233
XB-MBM	125	25030
XB-MCB	75A	380-36
XB-MLC	**125**	**257171**
XB-MTS	560	0030
XB-MVG	**S40**	**282-134**
XB-NAG	24D	270
XB-NIB	S40	282-125
XB-NUR	24D	275
XB-OBE	500	273
XB-OEM	20	248/483
XB-OEM	50	80
XB-OEM	G4	1055
XB-PGR	G2	81
XB-PUE	125	25158
XB-PYC	560	0261
XB-QND	**S60**	**306-21**
XB-RDB	75A	380-55
XB-RGO	**S40**	**282-114**
XB-RGS	S40	282-114
XB-RSG	75A	380-60
XB-RTT	**560**	**0092**
XB-RYO	S65	465-55
XB-SBC	125	25068
XB-SHA	75A	380-60
XB-SII	10	4
XB-SOL	**50**	**116**
XB-SUD	24B	197
XB-UAG	**500**	**278**

XB-VIW	STR	5140
XB-VRM	20	248/483
XB-VUI	125	25068
XB-ZNP	**S60**	**306-63**
XB-ZRB	10	107
(XB-ZRB)	31	029
XB-ZUM	S60	306-47
XC-AA24	**36A**	**050**
XC-AA26	**S60**	**306-12**
XC-AA28	**23**	**037**
XC-AA51	**S40**	**282-130**
XC-AA60	**35A**	**321**
XC-AA63	24D	249
XC-AA70	**G2**	**18**
XC-AA73	**S40**	**282-105**
XC-AA83	25D	286
XC-AA84	25D	330
XC-AA89	**75A**	**380-46**
XC-AGR	25D	295
XC-ASA	500	061
XC-ASB	500	251
XC-AZU	24D	285
XC-BCS	550	268
(XC-BDA)	WWD	340
XC-BEN	500	243
XC-BEZ	500	072
XC-BIN	20	198/466
XC-BOC	500	169
XC-BUR	500	245
XC-CFE	G2	161
XC-CFM	25D	284
XC-CIR	501	466
XC-COL	**WWD**	**135**
XC-CON	500	169
XC-CUZ	**35A**	**213**
XC-DAA	25D	283
XC-DAD	25D	223
XC-DDA	**S60**	**306-34**
XC-DFS	29	002
XC-DGA	**500**	**010**
XC-DGA	HFB	1049
XC-DIP	**20**	**282**
XC-DOK	550	221
XC-DOP	24D	273
(XC-DUF)	550	206
XC-DUF	550	226
XC-FEZ	**500**	**596**
XC-FEZ	G2	161
XC-FIA	75A	380-53
XC-FIF	25D	332
XC-FIT	500	010
XC-FIU	500	012
XC-FIV	**500**	**013**
XC-FOO	550	249
XC-FVH	**20**	**393**
XC-GAD	500	061
(XC-GAM)	20	198/466
XC-GAW	**500**	**586**
XC-GII	24	179
XC-GNL	25D	329
XC-GOB	125	25216
XC-GOV	500	189
XC-GOW	500	193
XC-GOX	500	197
XC-GOY	500	243
XC-GTO	**500**	**533**
XC-GUB	**25D**	**306**
XC-GUH	500	221
XC-GUO	500	201
XC-GUQ	500	143
XC-HAD	WWD	85
XC-HCP	WWD	230
XC-HDA	WWD	230
(XC-HDA)	WWD	339
XC-HEP	550	464
XC-HEQ	550	280
XC-HEY	S40	282-130
XC-HFY	75A	380-46
XC-HGY	**S60**	**306-38**
XC-HGZ	550	096
(XC-HGZ)	550	659
XC-HHA	550	185
(XC-HHA)	550	673
XC-HHJ	**35A**	**435**

XC-HHL	S60	306-12
XC-HIE	**29**	**002**
XC-HIS	**25D**	**312**
(XC-HIX)	20	111
XC-HIX	**20**	**248/483**
XC-IPP	**35**	**028**
XC-IPP	500	329
XC-IST	**29**	**001**
(XC-JAY)	550	505
(XC-JAZ)	550	602
(XC-JBQ)	550	497
(XC-JBR)	550	494
(XC-JBS)	550	666
(XC-JBT)	550	593
XC-JCC	**STR**	**5053/2**
XC-JCK	S40	282-1
XC-JCN	24D	299
XC-JDC	**S60**	**306-145**
XC-JOA	23	081
XC-MEX	G2	96
XC-NSP	**25B**	**194**
XC-OAH	S40	282-1
XC-OAH	S60	306-73
XC-ONA	75A	380-39
XC-PET	G2	173
XC-PGE	S40	282-130
XC-PGM	**550**	**644**
XC-PGN	650	0165
XC-PGP	**550**	**648**
XC-PGR	35A	460
XC-PMX	501	428
XC-PPM	500	329
XC-QEO	500	251
XC-ROO	550	249
XC-ROO	550	598
XC-RPP	**25D**	**236**
XC-SAG	24D	255
XC-SCT	500	010
XC-SCT	**550**	**153**
XC-SEY	**20**	**169**
XC-SKI	**STR**	**5124**
XC-SRA	S40	282-130
XC-SRH	STR	5154
XC-SUB	S40	282-114
XC-SUP	24X	319
XC-TIJ	HFB	1049
XC-UJC	75A	380-67
XC-UJD	**75A**	**380-68**
XC-UJE	**S60**	**306-139**
XC-UJF	**S60**	**306-144**
XC-UJG	S40	282-130
XC-UJH	125	25216
XC-UJH	S40	282-117
XC-UJI	S40	282-130
XC-UJK	G2	161
XC-UJN	**G3**	**352**
XC-UJO	**G3**	**386**
XC-UJP	23	037
XC-UJR	36A	050
XC-VSA	**28**	**002**
XC-ZRB	10	107

Burkino Faso

XT-	**550**	**0924**
XT-AOK	550	726

Cambodia (Kampuchea)

XU-008	**20**	**323/520**

Iraq

YI-AHH	20	337/529
YI-AHI	20	342/532
YI-AHJ	20	343/533
YI-AKA	STR	5233
YI-AKB	STR	5235
YI-AKC	STR	5237
YI-AKD	STR	5238
YI-AKE	STR	5239
YI-AKF	STR	5240

YI-AKG	125	257184
YI-AKH	125	257187
YI-AKI	G3	408
YI-AKJ	G3	419
YI-ALB	50	71
YI-ALC	50	101
YI-ALD	50	120
YI-ALE	50	122

Syria

YK-ASA	**20**	**328/522**
YK-ASB	**20**	**331/524**
YK-ASC	**900**	**100**

Latvia

YL-VIP	**125**	**257103**

Nicaragua
(see also AN-)

YN-BPR	125	256037
YN-BVO	35A	280
YN-BZH	20	128/436

Romania

YR-DSA	20	236
YR-DSB	20	242
YR-DVA	125	256024
YR-FNA	50	148

Yugoslavia

YU-BIA	500	031
YU-BIH	24D	320
YU-BJG	**25B**	**187**
YU-BJH	25B	186
YU-BKJ	25B	205
YU-BKR	**25D**	**221**
YU-BKZ	500	415
YU-BLY	75A	380-65
YU-BME	125	256048
YU-BML	500	554
YU-BNA	**50**	**43**
YU-BOE	S550	0045
YU-BOL	35A	618
YU-BPL	550	480
YU-BPU	551	144
YU-BPY	35A	173
YU-BPZ	**50**	**25**
YU-BRA	**25B**	**202**
YU-BRB	**25B**	**203**

Venezuela

(YV-)	550	0817
YV-	**400A**	**RK-142**
YV-01CP	23	040
YV-01CP	35A	157
YV-01CP	CVT	35
YV-03CP	**STR**	**5106/9**
(YV-04CP)	550	455
YV-05C	551	463
YV-05CP	551	018
YV-06CP	551	020
YV-07CP	10	47
YV-07P	500	253
YV-19P	500	253
YV-12CP	**55**	**031**
YV-15CP	23	047
YV-15CP	35A	342
YV-15CP	500	095
(YV-15CP)	35A	191
(YV-15CP)	35A	270
YV-17CP	10	100
YV-19CP	551	003
YV-21CP	**500**	**115**
YV-26CP	25C	098
YV-29CP	D1A	A049SA
YV-36CP	550	080
(YV-37CP)	WWD	193
YV-38CP	20	287
YV-41CP	55	019
(YV-41CP)	55	015
YV-43CP	500	284
YV-50CP	500	289
YV-52CP	**500**	**399**
YV-55CP	**500**	**215**
YV-58CP	WWD	172
(YV-60CP)	G2	163
YV-62CP	500	297
(YV-64CP)	S40	282-134
YV-65CP	35A	161
YV-70CP	10	66
YV-78CP	20	28
YV-79CP	501	397
YV-88CP	25	033
YV-89CP	36	002
YV-99CP	10	172
YV-100CP	**35A**	**083**
YV-101CP	10	47
YV-119P	WWD	184
YV-120CP	501	368
YV-123CP	WWD	16
YV-125CP	55	126
YV-126CP	20	30
YV-130P	25C	071
(YV-131CP)	35A	193
YV-132CP	25C	071
(YV-135CP)	501	384
YV-137CP	551	049
YV-140CP	551	014
YV-141CP	125	25195
YV-147CP	551	106
YV-151CP	550	016
YV-159CP	501	393
YV-160CP	WWD	211
YV-161P	36	002
YV-162CP	**550**	**332**
YV-163CP	MSP	103
YV-166CP	501	384
YV-169CP	551	018
YV-169CP	**560**	**0230**
YV-173CP	35A	163
YV-178CP	24F	342
YV-187CP	550	197
YV-187CP	STR	5107
YV-190CP	**WWD**	**219**
YV-200C	20	200
YV-203CP	**25C**	**061**
YV-205CP	551	024
(YV-209CP)	550	175
YV-210CP	WWD	308
YV-213CP	**550**	**076**
YV-221CP	10	47
YV-232CP	501	449
YV-253CP	501	418
YV-253P	501	418
YV-265CP	35A	247
(YV-269CP)	50	126
(YV-270CP)	35A	375
(YV-274CP)	D1A	A046SA
YV-276CP	550	385
YV-278CP	23	036
YV-286CP	35A	268
YV-292CP	55	052
YV-297CP	WWD	202
YV-298CP	550	175
YV-299CP	550	133
YV-300CP	551	172
YV-301CP	551	174
YV-301P	501	518
YV-309P	D1A	A049SA
(YV-325CP)	55	112
YV-326CP	35A	352
YV-327CP	35A	344
(YV-328CP)	35A	309
YV-332CP	**WWD**	**330**
YV-347CP	55	053
YV-370CP	500	171
YV-376CP	**550**	**637**
YV-387CP	WWD	306
YV-388CP	**HFB**	**1057**
YV-388CP	WWD	307
YV-393CP	WWD	262
YV-432CP	**35A**	**437**
YV-433CP	35A	431
YV-434CP	35A	422
YV-450CP	**50**	**219**
YV-451CP	WWD	343
YV-452CP	**50**	**4**
YV-455CP	**50**	**136**
(YV-553CP)	50	30
YV-572CP	CVT	17
YV-589CP	CVT	35
YV-601CP	10	73
YV-604P	550	385
YV-606CP	550	035
YV-625CP	500	210
YV-646CP	500	031
YV-662CP	550	682
YV-666CP	WWD	347
YV-678CP	551	106
YV-688CP	**501**	**524**
YV-701CP	**550**	**683**
YV-707CP	500	070
YV-713CP	**551**	**463**
YV-717CP	500	135
YV-735CP	125	258203
YV-737CP	400	RJ-6
YV-738CP	400	RJ-6
YV-757CP	AST	060
YV-770CP	WWD	258
YV-771CP	**AST**	**077**
YV-777CP	WWD	191
YV-778CP	**550**	**385**
YV-785CP	AST	057
YV-800CP	125	258209
YV-810CP	**550**	**467**
YV-811CP	**560**	**0134**
YV-814CP	125	258234
YV-815CP	125	25098
YV-824CP	**24**	**173**
YV-825CP	125	25175
YV-826CP	STR	5205
YV-838CP	400	RJ-6
YV-850CP	35A	596
YV-888CP	**550**	**235**
YV-900CP	**550**	**214**
YV-901CP	**500**	**058**
YV-909CP	550	317
YV-911CP	550	698
YV-940CP	500	299
YV-952CP	**31A**	**168**
YV-962CP	WWD	385
YV-997CP	35A	458
YV-999P	HFB	1037
(YV-1107)	550	449
YV-1111CP	125	25224
YV-1111CP	**600**	**1028**
YV-1478P	551	106
YV-2199P	AST	057
YV-2267P	500	052
YV-2295P	501	472
YV-2338P	**550**	**449**
YV-2426P	**551**	**300**
YV-2454P	**WWD**	**96**
YV-2477P	500	052
YV-2479P	500	035
YV-2482P	**WWD**	**172**
YV-2564P	**AST**	**057**
YV-2567P	551	200
YV-2605P	**501**	**518**
YV-2628P	**500**	**052**
YV-E-GPA	23	047
YV-O-CVG-1	WWD	308
YV-O-CVG-2	**551**	**020**
YV-O-CVG-3	**WWD**	**343**
YV-O-MAC-1	500	336
YV-O-MRI-1	35A	270
YV-O-MTC	550	251
YV-O-MTC-2	501	472
YV-O-MTC-20	550	251
YV-O-SID-3	501	397
YV-T-OOO	500	215
YV-T-AFA	500	115
YV-T-ASG	36	002
YV-T-AVA	20	287
YV-T-DTT	25C	071
YV-T-MMM	500	253

Zimbabwe
(see also VP-W)

Z-TBX	125	25067
Z-VEC	125	25215
Z-WKY	25B	160
Z-WSY	501	387

New Zealand

ZK-EUI	125	258058
(ZK-EUR)	125	258058
ZK-LJL	500	123
ZK-MAY	200	505
ZK-MAZ	100	213
ZK-MRM	125	258074
ZK-NLJ	650	0133
(ZK-RHP)	125	258088
ZK-RJI	125	258082
ZK-TCB	125	258001
(ZK-WNL)	10	50

Paraguay

ZP-	WWD	41
ZP-AGD	WWD	151
ZP-PNB	500	335
ZP-PNB	550	320
ZP-PUP	500	335
ZP-TCA	550	710
ZP-TNB	550	320
ZP-TWN	550	374
ZP-TYO	500	008
ZP-TYO	551	039
ZP-TYP	500	008
ZP-TZH	**500**	**185**
ZP-TZY	500	275

South Africa

ZS-ACT	125	259026
ZS-AGT	**31A**	**146**
ZS-AMB	500	071
ZS-ARG	**551**	**132**
ZS-AVL	125	259017
ZS-AVL	**604**	**5328**
(ZS-BAR)	45	007
ZS-BAR	**45**	**046**
ZS-BCT	AST	075
(ZS-BFB)	50	91
ZS-BMB	50	91
ZS-BPG	**125**	**258165**
ZS-BSS	525	0124
ZS-BXR	**25XR**	**141**
ZS-CAL	**125**	**25172**
ZS-CAQ	**50**	**133**
ZS-CAR	**S550**	**0078**
ZS-CAS	**50**	**91**
ZS-CAT	**25D**	**366**
ZS-CCT	125	259026
ZS-CCT	601	5176
ZS-CDS	**560**	**0414**
ZS-DCK	**125**	**258403**
(ZS-DCT)	31A	146
ZS-DCT	**45**	**052**
ZS-DDT	125	258465
ZS-DGB	604	5390
(ZS-DHL)	31A	170
ZS-DJB	35A	647
ZS-EAG	**31A**	**142**
(ZS-EFD)	35A	594
ZS-EHL	501	431
(ZS-FCB)	560	0503

ZS-FCB 560 5018
ZS-FSI 125 258078
ZS-FUN 24F 354
ZS-GLD 24D 291
(ZS-GSB) S40 282-53
ZS-IDC S550 0148
ZS-INS 35A 238
ZS-IYY 500 078
ZS-JBA 125 25259
(ZS-JBR) 45 007
ZS-JHL 125 256049
ZS-JIH 125 25260
ZS-JIS G2 136
ZS-JJO 24D 317
ZS-JKR 500 268
ZS-JOK 500 329
ZS-JOO 500 291
(ZS-JRM) 60 149
ZS-JRO 400A RK-101
ZS-JWC 23 030
(ZS-KGF) 501 538
ZS-KJY 24 165
ZS-KOO 550 154
ZS-KPA 501 567
ZS-LAL 20 228/473
ZS-LDK 550 310
ZS-LDO 501 652
ZS-LDV 500 656
ZS-LEE 550 380
ZS-LHP 501 667
ZS-LHT 550 439
ZS-LHU 550 179
ZS-LHW 550 416
ZS-LIG 550 474
ZS-LII 35 062
(ZS-LJM) 50 107
ZS-LLG 20 228/473
ZS-LLG 24B 210
ZS-LLO 550 235
ZS-LME 125 25242
ZS-LNP 550 560
ZS-LOW 501 514
ZS-LPE 125 25184
ZS-LPF 125 25269
ZS-LPH 500 402
(ZS-LRI) 25D 366
ZS-LTK 24 103
ZS-LUD 25D 295
ZS-LWU 24B 209
ZS-LXH 25D 206
ZS-LXT 501 622
ZS-LYB 500 278
ZS-MAN 125 25067
ZS-MBR 23 064
ZS-MBS 500 340
ZS-MBX 550 587
ZS-MCP 500 130
ZS-MCU 500 137
ZS-MDN 23 081
ZS-MGH 500 299
ZS-MGJ 24X 207
ZS-MGK 35A 357
ZS-MGL 501 384
ZS-MHN 400 RJ-59
ZS-MLN 551 266
ZS-MLS 550 621
ZS-MPI 500 334
ZS-MPN 501 393
ZS-MPT 560 0089
ZS-MTD 25B 160
ZS-MVV 560 0062
ZS-MVX 525 0010
ZS-MVZ 560 0064
ZS-MWW 35A 157
(ZS-MYN) 560 0064
ZS-MZM WWD 390
ZS-MZO 501 453
ZS-NAN 900 99
ZS-NAT 550 554
ZS-NDT 560 0160
ZS-NDU 560 0151
ZS-NDW 560 0166
ZS-NDX 560 0152
ZS-NER 600 1019
ZS-NEW 125 259017
(ZS-NEX) 35A 671
ZS-NFK 35A 671
ZS-NFL 550 697
(ZS-NFS) 35A 671
ZS-NGG 24X 280
ZS-NGL 560 0202
ZS-NGM 560 0201
ZS-NGR 500 080
ZS-NGS 560 0241
ZS-NHC 560 0203
ZS-NHD 560 0255
ZS-NHE 525 0033
ZS-NHF 500 296
ZS-NHL 125 259032
ZS-NHO 550 264
ZS-NID 35A 426
ZS-NII 550 184
ZS-NJF 25D 311
ZS-NJH 125 258224
ZS-NKD 601 5060
ZS-NMO G4 1129
ZS-NNF 2xx 2
ZS-NNV 560 0322
ZS-NOD 400 RJ-18
ZS-NPV 125 25215
ZS-NRZ 35A 077
ZS-NSB 35A 654
ZS-NTV 60 052
ZS-NUW 525 0150
ZS-NUZ 560 0398
ZS-NVV 560 0322
ZS-NYG 25C 098
ZS-NYV 31A 115
ZS-NZO 400A RK-57
ZS-OAM 500 077
ZS-OCG 400A RK-140
(ZS-ODP) WWD 171
ZS-OEA 24X 267
ZS-OFM 560 0467
ZS-OFW 31 031
ZS-OGS 500 260
ZS-OHZ 560 5079
ZS-OIE 550 480
ZS-OIF 125 25221
ZS-OIZ 45 006
ZS-OJO 31A 058
ZS-OLJ 45 046
ZS-OML 31A 170
ZS-ONE 500 002
ZS-ONG 50 287
ZS-ONL 601 3006
ZS-ONP 400A RK-157
ZS-PDB 400A RK-162
ZS-PMC 551 141
ZS-PNP 31A 202
ZS-PTJ S40 282-53
(ZS-PTL) 35A 594
ZS-PTL 45 046
ZS-RCC 500 106
ZS-RCS 550 065
ZS-RKV 550 060
ZS-SAB 750 0080
ZS-SEA 10 156
ZS-SES 35A 185
ZS-SGH 24B 187
ZS-SMB 560 0359
ZS-SMT 125 25128
ZS-SSM 25XR 022
ZS-TGG G2 8
ZS-TMG 500 149
ZS-TOW 35A 475
ZS-TOY 24B 219
ZS-ZBB 900 143

Macedonia

Z3-BAA 25B 205

Monaco

3A-MDB 125 25131
3A-MDE 125 25131
3A-MGR 20 473
3A-MGT 10 19
3A-MPP MSP 098
3A-MTB 501 482
3A-MWA 550 063

Mauritius

3B-GFI 600 1019
3B-NSY 50 230
3B-XLA 900 7

Swaziland
(see also VQ-Z)

3D-AAB 125 25080
3D-AAC G2 136
3D-AAC G3 354
3D-AAI G3 354
3D-ABZ 125 25242
3D-ACB 10 21
3D-ACQ 550 179
3D-ACR 500 268
3D-ACT 550 264
3D-ACZ 35A 238
3D-ADC 35A 475
3D-ADH 501 667
3D-ADR 100 202
3D-AEZ 25B 160
3D-AFH D1A A062SA
3D-AFJ 23 064
3D-ART 10 61
3D-AVH 550 341
3D-AVL 125 25254
3D-AVL 125 258025
3D-LLG 20 228/473

Guinea

(3X-GBD) G2 74
3X-GCI 10 89

Yemen

4W-ACA 125 25219
4W-ACE 125 257046
4W-ACM 125 257178
4W-ACN 125 258037

Israel

4X-AIP WWD 243
4X-CJA WWD 154
4X-CJB WWD 153
4X-CJC WWD 152
4X-CJD WWD 151
4X-CJE WWD 155
4X-CJF WWD 156
4X-CJG WWD 157
4X-CJH WWD 158
4X-CJI WWD 159
4X-CJJ WWD 160
4X-CJK WWD 161
4X-CJL WWD 162
4X-CJM WWD 163
4X-CJN WWD 164
4X-CJO WWD 165
4X-CJP WWD 166
4X-CJP WWD 376
4X-CJQ WWD 167
4X-CJR WWD 168
4X-CJR WWD 404
4X-CJS WWD 169
4X-CJS WWD 413
4X-CJT WWD 170
4X-CJU WWD 171
4X-CJV WWD 172
4X-CJW WWD 173
4X-CJX WWD 174
4X-CJY WWD 175
4X-CJZ WWD 176
4X-CKA WWD 177
4X-CKB WWD 178
4X-CKC WWD 179
4X-CKD WWD 180
4X-CKE WWD 181
4X-CKF WWD 182
4X-CKG WWD 183
4X-CKH WWD 184
4X-CKI WWD 185
4X-CKJ WWD 186
4X-CKK WWD 187
4X-CKL WWD 188
4X-CKM WWD 189
4X-CKN WWD 190
4X-CKO WWD 191
4X-CKP WWD 192
4X-CKQ WWD 193
4X-CKR WWD 194
4X-CKS WWD 195
4X-CKT WWD 196
4X-CKU WWD 197
4X-CKV WWD 198
4X-CKW WWD 199
4X-CKX WWD 200
4X-CKY WWD 201
4X-CKZ WWD 202
4X-CLA WWD 203
4X-CLB WWD 204
4X-CLC WWD 205
4X-CLD WWD 206
4X-CLE WWD 207
4X-CLF WWD 208
4X-CLG WWD 209
4X-CLH WWD 210
4X-CLI WWD 211
4X-CLJ WWD 212
4X-CLK WWD 213
4X-CLL WWD 214
4X-CLM WWD 215
4X-CLN WWD 216
4X-CLO WWD 217
4X-CLP WWD 218
4X-CLQ WWD 219
4X-CLR WWD 220
4X-CLS WWD 221
4X-CLT WWD 222
4X-CLU WWD 223
4X-CLV WWD 224
4X-CLW WWD 225
4X-CLX WWD 226
4X-CLY WWD 227
4X-CLZ WWD 228
4X-CMA WWD 229
4X-CMB WWD 230
4X-CMC WWD 231
4X-CMD WWD 232
4X-CME WWD 233
4X-CMF WWD 234
4X-CMG WWD 235
4X-CMH WWD 236
4X-CMI WWD 237
4X-CMJ WWD 238
4X-CMK WWD 239
4X-CML WWD 240
4X-CMM WWD 241
4X-CMN WWD 242
4X-CMO WWD 243
4X-CMP WWD 244
4X-CMQ WWD 245
4X-CMR WWD 246
4X-CMS WWD 247
4X-CMT WWD 248
4X-CMU WWD 249
4X-CMV WWD 250
4X-CMW WWD 251
4X-CMX WWD 252
4X-CMY 604 5388
4X-CMY WWD 253
4X-CMZ WWD 254
4X-CNA WWD 255
4X-CNB WWD 256

4X-CNC	WWD	257
4X-CND	WWD	258
4X-CNE	WWD	259
4X-CNF	WWD	260
4X-CNG	WWD	261
4X-CNH	WWD	262
4X-CNI	WWD	263
4X-CNJ	WWD	264
4X-CNK	WWD	265
4X-CNL	WWD	266
4X-CNM	WWD	267
4X-CNN	WWD	268
4X-CNO	WWD	269
4X-CNP	WWD	270
4X-CNQ	WWD	271
4X-CNR	WWD	272
4X-CNS	WWD	273
4X-CNT	WWD	274
4X-CNU	WWD	275
4X-CNV	WWD	276
4X-CNW	WWD	277
4X-CNX	WWD	278
4X-CNY	WWD	279
4X-CNZ	WWD	280
4X-COA	WWD	71
4X-COB	WWD	138
4X-COC	WWD	422
4X-COE	**604**	**5352**
4X-COJ	WWD	29
(4X-COK)	WWD	107
4X-COL	WWD	107
4X-COM	WWD	126
4X-CON	WWD	55
4X-COO	**S550**	**0086**
4X-COP	WWD	134
4X-COT	601	5032
4X-COV	**125**	**258283**
4X-COY	601	5154
4X-CPA	WWD	110
4X-CPB	WWD	113
4X-CPC	WWD	114
4X-CPD	WWD	130
4X-CPE	WWD	131
4X-CPF	WWD	139
4X-CPG	WWD	140
4X-CPH	WWD	141
4X-CPI	WWD	142
4X-CPJ	WWD	143
4X-CPK	WWD	144
4X-CPL	WWD	148
4X-CPM	WWD	149
4X-CPN	WWD	150
4X-CPO	WWD	414
4X-CQA	WWD	281
4X-CQB	WWD	282
4X-CQC	WWD	283
4X-CQD	WWD	284
4X-CQE	WWD	285
4X-CQF	WWD	286
4X-CQG	WWD	287
4X-CQH	WWD	288
4X-CQI	WWD	289
4X-CQJ	WWD	290
4X-CQK	WWD	291
4X-CQL	WWD	292
4X-CQM	WWD	293
4X-CQN	WWD	294
4X-CQO	WWD	295
4X-CQP	WWD	296
4X-CQQ	WWD	297
4X-CQR	WWD	298
4X-CQS	WWD	299
4X-CQT	WWD	300
4X-CQU	WWD	301
4X-CQV	WWD	302
4X-CQW	WWD	303
4X-CQX	WWD	304
4X-CQY	WWD	305
4X-CQZ	WWD	306
4X-CRA	WWD	307
4X-CRB	WWD	308
4X-CRC	WWD	309
4X-CRD	WWD	310
4X-CRE	WWD	311
4X-CRF	WWD	312
4X-CRG	WWD	313
4X-CRH	WWD	314
4X-CRI	WWD	315
4X-CRJ	WWD	316
4X-CRK	WWD	317
4X-CRL	WWD	318
4X-CRM	WWD	319
4X-CRN	WWD	320
4X-CRO	WWD	321
4X-CRP	WWD	322
4X-CRQ	WWD	323
4X-CRR	WWD	324
4X-CRS	WWD	325
4X-CRT	WWD	326
4X-CRU	WWD	327
4X-CRV	WWD	328
4X-CRW	WWD	329
4X-CRX	WWD	330
4X-CRY	WWD	331
4X-CRZ	WWD	332
4X-CTA	WWD	333
4X-CTB	WWD	334
4X-CTC	WWD	335
4X-CTD	WWD	336
4X-CTE	WWD	337
4X-CTF	WWD	338
4X-CTG	WWD	339
4X-CTH	WWD	340
4X-CTI	WWD	341
4X-CTJ	WWD	342
4X-CTK	WWD	343
4X-CTL	WWD	344
4X-CTM	WWD	345
4X-CTN	WWD	346
4X-CTO	WWD	347
4X-CTP	WWD	348
4X-CTQ	WWD	349
4X-CTR	WWD	350
4X-CTS	WWD	351
4X-CTT	WWD	352
4X-CTU	WWD	353
4X-CTV	WWD	354
4X-CUA	AST	004
4X-CUA	WWD	340
4X-CUA	WWD	392
4X-CUA	WWD	406
4X-CUB	WWD	341
4X-CUB	WWD	372
4X-CUB	WWD	384
4X-CUB	WWD	390
4X-CUB	WWD	408
4X-CUB	WWD	418
4X-CUC	WWD	385
4X-CUC	WWD	395
4X-CUC	WWD	411
4X-CUC	WWD	414
4X-CUC	WWD	423
4X-CUC	WWD	434
4X-CUD	AST	017
4X-CUD	WWD	367
4X-CUD	WWD	413
4X-CUD	WWD	416
4X-CUE	AST	019
4X-CUE	WWD	368
4X-CUE	WWD	386
4X-CUE	WWD	417
4X-CUE	WWD	436
4X-CUF	WWD	369
4X-CUF	WWD	375
4X-CUF	WWD	389
4X-CUF	WWD	399
4X-CUF	WWD	419
4X-CUF	WWD	426
4X-CUF	WWD	437
4X-CUG	AST	023
4X-CUG	AST	056
4X-CUG	AST	061
4X-CUG	WWD	370
4X-CUG	WWD	391
4X-CUG	WWD	404
4X-CUG	WWD	435
4X-CUG	WWD	439
4X-CUH	AST	025
4X-CUH	AST	057
4X-CUH	WWD	371
4X-CUH	WWD	376
4X-CUH	WWD	388
4X-CUH	WWD	403
4X-CUH	WWD	420
4X-CUH	WWD	432
4X-CUH	WWD	433
4X-CUI	AST	026
4X-CUI	AST	030
4X-CUI	AST	055
4X-CUI	AST	063
4X-CUI	WWD	355
4X-CUI	WWD	378
4X-CUI	WWD	422
4X-CUJ	AST	027
4X-CUJ	AST	034
4X-CUJ	AST	062
4X-CUJ	WWD	356
4X-CUJ	WWD	377
4X-CUJ	WWD	379
4X-CUJ	WWD	387
4X-CUJ	WWD	405
4X-CUJ	WWD	421
4X-CUJ	WWD	424
4X-CUJ	WWD	438
4X-CUJ	WWD	440
4X-CUK	AST	011
4X-CUK	AST	016
4X-CUK	WWD	357
4X-CUK	WWD	373
4X-CUK	WWD	393
4X-CUK	WWD	407
4X-CUK	WWD	425
4X-CUK	WWD	429
4X-CUL	AST	012
4X-CUL	WWD	358
4X-CUL	WWD	374
4X-CUM	AST	013
4X-CUM	WWD	359
4X-CUM	WWD	380
4X-CUM	WWD	394
4X-CUM	WWD	409
4X-CUM	WWD	430
4X-CUM?	WWD	409
4X-CUN	AST	014
4X-CUN	AST	032
4X-CUN	WWD	360
4X-CUN	WWD	397
4X-CUN	WWD	427
4X-CUN	WWD	431
4X-CUO	WWD	361
4X-CUO	WWD	381
4X-CUO	WWD	398
4X-CUO	WWD	409
4X-CUO	WWD	410
4X-CUO	WWD	428
4X-CUO	WWD	442
4X-CUP	AST	015
4X-CUP	AST	033
4X-CUP	WWD	362
4X-CUP	WWD	382
4X-CUP	WWD	400
4X-CUP	WWD	412
4X-CUP	WWD	441
4X-CUQ	WWD	363
4X-CUQ	WWD	383
4X-CUQ	WWD	401
4X-CUR	AST	018
4X-CUR	AST	021
4X-CUR	WWD	364
4X-CUR	WWD	396
4X-CUS	AST	020
4X-CUS	WWD	365
4X-CUS	WWD	402
4X-CUS	WWD	415
4X-CUT	AST	022
4X-CUT	AST	024
4X-CUT	WWD	366
4X-CUU	AST	087
4X-CUV	AST	076
4X-CUW	AST	071
4X-CUW	AST	075
4X-CUX	AST	079
4X-CUY	AST	080
4X-CVF	GXY	004
4X-CZM	**125**	**258279**
4X-FVN	WWD	134
4X-IGA	**GXY**	**003**
4X-IGB	GXY	005
4X-IGO	GXY	004
(4X-NOY)	WWD	213
4X-WIA	**AST**	**002**
4X-WIN	AST	001
4X-WIX	AST	073
Libya		
5A-DAC	23	074
5A-DAD	23	075
5A-DAF	20	128/436
5A-DAG	**20**	**143/442**
5A-DAJ	**STR**	**5136**
5A-DAR	STR	5221
5A-DCK	**CVT**	**38**
5A-DCM	**50**	**68**
5A-DCO	**SN**	**190/465**
5A-DDR	G2	240
5A-DDS	**G2**	**242**
5A-DGI	50	17
Cyprus		
5B-	**125**	**25088**
5B-CGB	20	32
5B-CGP	STR	5128/16
5B-CHE	**STR**	**5114/18**
5B-CHX	600	1028
5B-CIQ	550	660
5B-CIS	551	200
5B-CJG	**AST**	**099**
5B-CSM	650	0094
Tanzania		
5H-BLM	125	259027
5H-SMZ	125	257172
Nigeria		
(5N-)	125	256069
(5N-)	125	259016
(5N-)	125	259025
5N-AAN	**125**	**25125**
5N-AER	125	25099
5N-AET	125	25117
5N-AGU	125	25085
5N-AGV	**G2**	**177**
5N-AGZ	**125**	**258143**
5N-AKT	125	25117
5N-ALH	**125**	**25089**
5N-ALX	125	256012
5N-ALY	125	25106
5N-AMF	HFB	1028
5N-AMK	125	25010
5N-AML	G2	186
5N-AMM	80A	380-17
5N-AMN	G2	13
5N-AMR	550	045
5N-AMX	125	257115
5N-AMY	125	25227
5N-ANG	125	256050
5N-AOC	**25D**	**322**
5N-AOG	125	25143
5N-AOL	125	256050
5N-APN	**500**	**286**
5N-AQY	125	25231
5N-ARD	125	256030
5N-ARE	50	110
5N-ARN	125	256056
5N-ASQ	25D	344
5N-ASZ	125	25063
5N-AVJ	125	257118
5N-AVK	**125**	**257160**

5N-AVL	**501**	**651**
5N-AVM	**501**	**653**
5N-AVV	**125**	**25138**
5N-AVZ	125	25113
5N-AWB	125	25025
5N-AWD	125	25008
5N-AWJ	550	252
5N-AWS	125	256042
5N-AXO	125	257196
5N-AXP	125	257203
5N-AYA	**550**	**632**
5N-AYK	125	256060
5N-AYM	20	228/473
5N-AYN	20	427
5N-AYO	20	383/550
5N-BCI	**500**	**085**
5N-BUA	125	25178
5N-DNL	125	256052
5N-EAS	**125**	**25217**
5N-EMA	**125**	**256069**
5N-EPN	20	273
5N-EZE	WWD	141
5N-FGE	**900**	**96**
5N-FGO	**900**	**52**
5N-FGP	**G4**	**1126**
5N-FGR	**125**	**259018**
5N-IMR	560	0087
5N-IMR	G3	344
5N-MAY	**125**	**256062**
5N-NBC	125	256052
5N-NPC	**125**	**258109**
5N-NPF	125	258143
5N-NPF	**550**	**138**
5N-OIL	900	96
5N-OPT	125	256063
5N-RNO	**125**	**256054**
5N-WMA	**125**	**25178**
5N-YET	**125**	**256013**
5N-YFS	125	256054

Malagasy (Madagascar)

5R-MHF	**551**	**141**
5R-MVD	CVT	35
5R-MVN	CVT	16

Mauritania

5T-UPR	G2	175

Togo

5V-MBG	10	167
5V-TAA	G2	149
5V-TAC	G2	167
5V-TAE	10	167

Uganda

5X-AAB	WWD	134
5X-UOI	G3	345
5X-UPF	G2	133

Kenya

5Y-GEO	24D	273
5Y-HAB	550	028
5Y-MNG	**550**	**0876**
(5Y-TCI)	525	0217
5Y-TWE	**550**	**569**

Senegal

6V-AEA	CVT	8
6V-AFL	G2	136
6V-AGQ	G2	136

Yemen Republic

7O-ADC	**125**	**258037**

Malawi

7Q-YJI	125	257076
7Q-YLF	**550**	**706**
7Q-YTL	501	605

Algeria

7T-VCW	**125**	**257163**
7T-VHB	G2	230
7T-VHP	**STR**	**5233**
7T-VPA	**900**	**81**
7T-VPB	**900**	**82**
7T-VPR	**G4**	**1288**
7T-VPS	**G4**	**1291**
7T-VRB	G3	368
7T-VRC	G3	396
7T-VRD	G3	399
7T-VRE	20	156/448
7T-VRP	20	271/493
7T-VVL	**125**	**25131**

Barbados

8P-BAB	501	525
8P-BAR	501	525
8P-BAR	550	256
8P-BAR	WWD	396
8P-GAC	G3	355
8P-KAM	650	0119
8P-LAD	G2	210
8P-MAK	G4	1186
8P-MAK	**G5**	**537**

Croatia

(See also RC-)

9A-BLY	75A	380-65
9A-BPU	551	144
(9A-CAD)	525	0151
9A-CAD	525	0199
9A-CGH	525	0151
9A-CRL	10	173
9A-CRO	601	5067
9A-CRO	**604**	**5322**
9A-CRT	**601**	**5067**
9A-DVR	501	638

Malta

9H-ABO	S65	465-22
9H-ACR	**550**	**025**

Zambia

9J-ADF	24D	249
9J-ADU	500	153
9J-AED	25D	225
9J-AEJ	500	359
9J-EPK	125	25067
9J-RAN	125	25067
9J-RON	**601**	**3057**
9J-SAS	125	25067

Kuwait

9K-ACO	STR	5156
9K-ACQ	20	136/439
(9K-ACQ)	50	21
9K-ACR	125	25238
9K-ACT	35	025
9K-ACX	G2	164
9K-ACY	G2	4/8
9K-ACZ	125	256015
9K-AEA	125	25219
9K-AEB	G2	244
9K-AEC	G2	248
9K-AED	125	256054
9K-AEE	50	21
9K-AEF	50	40
9K-AEG	G3	408
9K-AEH	G3	419
9K-AGA	125	257184
9K-AGB	125	257187
9K-AJA	G4	1157
9K-AJB	G4	1159
9K-AJC	G4	1161
9K-AJD	**G5**	**560**
9K-AJE	**G5**	**569**
9K-AJF	**G5**	**573**

Sierra Leone

9L-LAW	75A	380-61

Malaysia

(9M-)	125	257001
(9M-)	125	258226
9M-ABC	**G4**	**1312**
9M-ARR	G2	116
9M-ATM	100	216
9M-ATM	400	RJ-22
9M-ATT	G2	131/23
(9M-AYI)	125	25015
9M-AZZ	**125**	**258219**
9M-BAB	**900**	**121**
9M-BAN	900	106
9M-BCR	**20**	**35**
9M-CAL	**60**	**034**
9M-DDW	125	258079
9M-DRL	125	258237
9M-FAZ	500	245
9M-FCL	**60**	**072**
9M-HLG	125	25257
9M-ISJ	**G4**	**1106**
9M-JJS	90X	5
9M-JMF	550	610
9M-NSA	**550**	**610**
9M-NSK	601	5166
9M-SSB	125	25215
9M-SSL	125	257112
9M-STR	125	257094
9M-SWG	601	5104
9M-TAA	550	671
9M-TAN	601	5154
9M-TRI	G4	1230
(9M-UEM)	550	610
(9M-VVV)	125	258337
9M-WAN	550	307
(9M-WCM)	125	258219

Democratic Republic of Congo

9Q-CBC	24D	248
9Q-CBS	601	5018
9Q-CBS	601	5061
9Q-CCF	125	25247
9Q-CFW	**125**	**256031**
9Q-CGK	50	177
9Q-CGM	125	25217
9Q-CGM	23	038
9Q-CHB	23	038
9Q-CHC	25	009
9Q-CHD	125	25217
9Q-CKZ	20	73/419
9Q-COH	125	25246
9Q-CPK	**50**	**177**
9Q-CPR	**125**	**25247**
9Q-CSN	125	25247
9Q-CTT	20	193

Burundi

9U-BTB	**50**	**66**

Singapore

9V-ATA	31	033
9V-ATB	31	034
9V-ATC	31	033A
9V-ATD	31	033B
9V-ATE	31	033C
9V-ATF	31	033D
9V-ATG	**45**	**029**
9V-ATH	**45**	**031**
9V-ATI	**45**	**033**
9V-ATJ	**45**	**035**
9V-BEE	STR	5011/1
(9V-PUW)	551	141

Rwanda

9XR-NN	50	6

Military Index

10	**CVT**	**10**
12	MSP	012
14	MSP	014
19	MSP	019
20	MSP	020
20-Q	MSP	020
22	**20C**	**22/404**
23	MSP	023
24	**MSP**	**024**
25	**MSP**	**025**
26	**MSP**	**026**
27	**50**	**27**
27	**MSP**	**027**
29	MSP	029
30	**MSP**	**030**
31	MSP	031
32	**MER**	**32**
32	**MSP**	**032**
33	**MSP**	**033**
34	**50**	**34**
34	**MSP**	**034**
34-Z	MSP	037
35	**MSP**	**035**
36	**MSP**	**036**
36	**50**	**36**
37	MSP	037
38	**MSP**	**038**
39	MER	39
40	**MSP**	**040**
41	MSP	041
41-A	**MSP**	**038**
41-AC	**MSP**	**057**
41-AR	MSP	019
41-AT	MSP	060
41-A	MSP	081
41-A	**MSP**	**054**
41-A	**MSP**	**059**
42	**MSP**	**042**
42-AP	**MSP**	**025**
43-BB	**MSP**	**034**
43-BL	**MSP**	**035**
43-B	MSP	045
44-CC	MSP	036
44	**MSP**	**044**
45	**MSP**	**045**
46	**MSP**	**046**
47	MSP	047
48	**20G**	**448**
48	MSP	048
49	**20**	**49/408**
51	MSP	051
53	MSP	053
54	**MSP**	**054**
56	**MSP**	**056**
57	**MSP**	**057**
58	**MSP**	**058**
59	**MSP**	**059**
60	MSP	060
61	**MSP**	**061**
62	**MSP**	**062**
65-EA	**20**	**260/488**
65-EB	**20**	**167/453**
65-EC	**20**	**342/532**
65-ED	**20**	**93/435**
65-EE	**20**	**238/477**
65-EF	**20**	**268/492**
65-EG	**20**	**291/505**
65-EH	**20**	**422**
65-KW	**MSP**	**024**
65-LB	**MSP**	**058**
65-LC	MSP	029
65-LD	**MSP**	**093**
65-LE	**MSP**	**071**
65-LF	**MSP**	**065**
65-LF	**MSP**	**070**
65-LG	**MSP**	**056**
65-LH	MSP	097
65-LI	**MSP**	**030**
65-LP	MSP	077
65-LU	MSP	096
65-LU	**MSP**	**091**
65-LV	**MSP**	**062**
65-LY	MSP	078
65-LZ	MSP	075
65-L	**MSP**	**082**
65-L	**MSP**	**094**
65	**20**	**465**
65	**MSP**	**065**
68	**MSP**	**068**
70	**MSP**	**070**
71	**MSP**	**071**
72	**20**	**472**
73	**MSP**	**073**
74	MSP	074
75	**MSP**	**075**
77	**20**	**477**
77	MSP	077
78	**50**	**78**
78	MSP	078
79	**20**	**79/415**
79	MSP	079
80	**20**	**480**
80	**MSP**	**080**
81	MSP	081
82	**MSP**	**082**
83	**MSP**	**083**
84	MSP	084
85	**MSP**	**085**
86	**20**	**86**
87	MSP	087
88	MSP	088
91	**MSP**	**091**
92	**MSP**	**092**
93	**20**	**93/435**
93	**MSP**	**093**
94	**MSP**	**094**
95	MSP	095
96	**20**	**96**
96	MSP	096
97	MSP	097
100	**MSP**	**100**
101	**MER**	**101**
101	MSP	101
104	**20**	**104/454**
113	**MSP**	**113**
113-CG	**MSP**	**034**
114	**MSP**	**114**
115	20A	115/432
115	**MSP**	**115**
115-ME	MSP	078
115-ME	**MSP**	**038**
116	**MSP**	**116**
117	**MSP**	**117**
118	**MSP**	**118**
118-DA	MSP	092
119	**MSP**	**119**
(120-FA)	20	49/408
124	**20**	**124/433**
129	**MER**	**129**
131	**20**	**131/437**
133	**MER**	**133**
133-CF	**MSP**	**059**
138	**20**	**138/440**
143	**MER**	**143**
145	**20**	**145/443**
154	20	154/447
167	**20**	**167/453**
182	**20**	**182/461**
185	**MER**	**185**
188	**20**	**188/464**
238	**20**	**238/477**
252	**20**	**252/485**
260	**20**	**260/488**
263	**20**	**263/489**
268	**20**	**268/492**
288	**20**	**288/499**
291	**20**	**291/505**
309	20	309/514
312-DF	MSP	014
314-D	**MSP**	**080**
314-DO	**MSP**	**062**
316-DH	MSP	036
316-DI	**MSP**	**045**
316-DL	**MSP**	**092**
330-DB	**MSP**	**001**
330-DC	MSP	051
330-DO	MSP	023
330-DP	**MSP**	**065**
339	**20**	**451**
339-JC	20	451
339-JE	**20**	**186/463**
339-JG	**20A**	**115/432**
339-JI	**20**	**483**
339-WM	20	186/463
339-WN	20	451
339-WP	20	309/514
342	**20**	**342/532**
375	**20**	**375/547**
422	**20**	**422**
463	**20**	**186/463**
483	**20**	**483**
DE	**MSP**	**080**
ELA61	MSP	081
G1-330	MSP	097
GE-316	**MSP**	**080**
MV	**CVT**	**1**
MW	**CVT**	**2**
MX	**CVT**	**10**
NB	**MSP**	**068**
NC	**MSP**	**083**
OD	MSP	053
F-FBLW	**MSP**	**024**
F-HAXA	**90X**	**12**
F-RABQ	MSP	020
F-RABZ	MSP	037
F-RAEA	**20**	**260/488**
F-RAEB	20	268/492
F-RAEB	**20**	**167/453**
F-RAEC	20	93/435
F-RAEC	20	291/505
F-RAEC	**20**	**342/532**
F-RAED	20	238/477
F-RAED	**20**	**93/435**
F-RAEE	**20**	**238/477**
F-RAEF	**20**	**268/492**
F-RAEG	20	342/532
F-RAEG	**20**	**291/505**
F-RAEH	**20**	**422**
F-RAFI	**50**	**5**
F-RAFJ	20	49/408
F-RAFJ	50	2
F-RAFJ	**50**	**78**
F-RAFK	**50**	**27**
F-RAFK	20	154/447
F-RAFK	20	268/492
F-RAFL	**50**	**34**
F-RAFL	20	167/453
F-RAFM	20	238/477
F-RAFN	20	93/435
F-RAFP	**900**	**2**
F-RAFQ	**900**	**4**
F-RAFU	20	309/514
F-RBL	MSP	095
F-RBL	**MSP**	**082**
F-RBL	**MSP**	**094**
F-RBLB	**MSP**	**058**
F-RBLC	MSP	029
F-RBLD	**MSP**	**044**
F-RBLD	**MSP**	**093**
F-RBLE	**MSP**	**071**
F-RBLF	**MSP**	**065**
F-RBLF	**MSP**	**070**
F-RBLG	**MSP**	**056**
F-RBLH	MSP	097
F-RBLL	MSP	081
F-RBLN	**MSP**	**026**
F-RBLP	MSP	077
F-RBLU	MSP	096
F-RBLU	**MSP**	**091**
F-RBLV	**MSP**	**062**
F-RBLW	**MSP**	**030**
F-RBLY	MSP	078
F-RBLY	**MSP**	**061**
F-RBLZ	MSP	075
F-RBQA	20	93/435
F-RCAL	20	422
F-RCAP	20	291/505
F-RHD.	**MSP**	**080**
F-RHDA	**MSP**	**092**
F-RHDD	MSP	053
F-RHDE	**MSP**	**027**
F-RHDF	MSP	014
F-RHFA	**20**	**49/408**
F-SCA	**MSP**	**054**
F-SCA	**MSP**	**059**
F-SCAC	**MSP**	**057**
F-SCAP	**MSP**	**025**
F-SCAR	MSP	019
F-SCAS	**MSP**	**038**
F-SCAT	MSP	060
F-SCB	**MSP**	**045**
F-SCBB	**MSP**	**034**
F-SCBC	**MSP**	**035**
F-SCCC	MSP	036
F-SDDB	**MSP**	**001**
F-SDDC	MSP	051
F-SDDO	MSP	023
F-SDIA	MSP	03
F-SDIB	MSP	001
F-SDIC	MSP	020
F-SEBH	CVT	19
F-SEBI	20	315/517
F-TEOA	20	49/408
F-UGWL	20A	115/432
F-UGWM	20	186/463
F-UGWN	**20**	**451**
F-UGWP	20	309/514
F-UKJA	**20**	**182/461**
F-UKJC	**20**	**451**
F-UKJE	**20**	**186/463**
F-UKJG	**20A**	**115/432**
F-UKJI	**20**	**483**
F-V10F	100	5
F-YCB.	MSP	031
F-YDJ.	MSP	012

Germany

1201	**601**	**3031**
1202	**601**	**3040**
1203	**601**	**3043**
1204	**601**	**3049**
1205	**601**	**3053**
1206	**601**	**3056**
1207	**601**	**3059**
1621	HFB	1058
1623	HFB	1060
1624	HFB	1061
1625	HFB	1062
1626	HFB	1063
1627	HFB	1064
1628	HFB	1065
(CA111)	HFB	1024
(CA112)	HFB	1025
(YA111)	HFB	1024
(YA112)	HFB	1025

Ghana

G.511	125	25028

Honduras

318	WWD	183

India

K2961	**G3**	**494**
K2962	**G3**	**495**
K2980	**G3**	**420**

Indonesia

A1645	STR	5059
A9446	STR	5046
T1645	STR	5059
T17845	STR	5011/1
T9446	STR	5046

Iran

5-2801	20	333/526
5-2802	**20**	**336/528**
5-2803	**20**	**340/531**
5-2804	**20**	**346/535**
5-3020	20	348/536
5-3021	**20**	**350/537**
5-4039	20	348/536
5-4040	20	350/537
5-9...	**50**	**101**
5-9...	**50**	**120**
5-9...	**50**	**122**
5-9001	**20**	**351/538**
5-9002	**20**	**353/539**
5-9003	**20**	**354/540**
15-2235	**20**	**333/526**
15-2533	**20**	**318/518**
1003	STR	5203
1004	**STR**	**5137**
901.	50	101
901.	50	120
901.	50	122

Ireland

236	125	25256
238	125	257082
239	125	256015
249	G3	413
251	**G4**	**1160**

Israel

027	WWD	185
029	WWD	152
031	WWD	186
035	WWD	152
064	WWD	107
927	**WWD**	**185**
929	**WWD**	**152**
931	**WWD**	**186**

Italy

(MM151)	50	151
MM577	808	501
MM578	**808**	**502**
MM61948	**808**	**506**
MM61949	808	507
MM61950	**808**	**508**
MM61951	808	509
MM61952	808	510
MM61953	808	511
MM61954	**808**	**512**
MM61955	808	513
MM61956	808	514
MM61957	808	515
MM61958	808	505
MM61959	808	516
MM61960	**808**	**517**
MM61961	**808**	**518**
MM61962	**808**	**519**
MM61963	808	520
MM62014	808	521
MM62015	808	522
MM62016	808	523
MM62017	808	524
MM62020	**50**	**151**
MM62021	**50**	**155**
MM62022	**G3**	**451**
MM62025	**G3**	**479**
MM62026	**50**	**193**
MM62029	**50**	**211**

Japan

9201	**36A**	**054**
9202	**36A**	**056**
9203	36A	058
9204	**36A**	**059**
9205	**36A**	**060**
9206	**36A**	**061**
05-3255	**G4**	**1359**
29-3041	**125**	**258215**
39-3042	**125**	**258227**
41-5051	**T1A**	**TX-1**
41-5052	**T1A**	**TX-2**
41-5053	**T1A**	**TX-3**
41-5054	**T1A**	**TX-4**
41-5055	**T1A**	**TX-5**
49-3043	**125**	**258242**
51-5056	**T1A**	**TX-6**
51-5057	**T1A**	**TX-7**
51-5058	**T1A**	**TX-8**
52-3001	**125**	**258245**
52-3002	**125**	**258247**
52-3003	**125**	**258250**
62-3004	**125**	**258268**
71-5059	**T1A**	**TX-9**
72-3005	**125**	**258288**
72-3006	**125**	**258305**
75-3251	**G4**	**1270**
75-3252	**G4**	**1271**
82-3007	**125**	**258306**
82-3008	**125**	**258325**
82-3009	**125**	**258333**
85-3253	**G4**	**1303**
91-5060	**T1A**	**TX-10**
92-3011	**125**	**258348**
92-3012	**125**	**258360**
92-3013	**125**	**258370**
95-3254	**G4**	**1326**

Jordan

122	20	255/487

Libya

001	STR	5136
0025A-DCO	**20**	**190/465**

Malawi

MAAW-J1	125	257076
MAAW-J1	**125**	**258064**

Malaysia

FM1200	125	25189
FM1201	125	25209
FM1801	125	25189
FM1802	125	25209
M24-01	125	25189
M24-02	125	25209
M31-01	600	1062
M31-02	600	1064
M37-01	**900**	**64**

Mexico

DN-01	STR	5144
ETE-1329	**500**	**090**
FAM	STR	5144
JS10201	**STR**	**5144**
MTX-01	**60**	**152**
MTX-01	24D	313
MTX-01	S60	306-34
MTX-02	24D	313
MTX-02	S60	306-34
MTX-03	**25D**	**339**
TP-04	G2	161
TP-06	**G3**	**352**
TP-07	**G3**	**386**
TP 101	S75	380-67
TP 102	**S75**	**380-68**
TP 103	S75	380-67
TP103	**S60**	**306-139**
TP104	35	028
TP 104	S75	380-68
TP104	**S60**	**306-144**
TP105	S40	282-130
TP105	S60	306-139
TP-105	36A	050
TP106	S60	306-144
TP107	S40	282-130
TP108	S40	282-117
TP108	125	25216
TP0206	125	25216

Morocco

CNA-NM	**ECM**	**165/452**
CNA-NV	**560**	**0025**
CNA-NW	**560**	**0039**

Myanmar

4400	**550**	**389**

Netherlands

V-11	**G4**	**1009**

Norway

041	**20**	**41/407**
053	**20**	**53/417**
0125	**ECM**	**125**

Oman

Oman 601	G2	214

Pakistan

0233	**560**	**0233**
J-468	**20**	**468**
J-469	**20**	**469**
J-753	**20**	**277/501**

Peru

300	**20**	**434**
FAP 522	**25B**	**159**
FAP 523	**25B**	**164**
524	**36A**	**051**
525	**36A**	**052**

Portugal

7401	50	195
7402	50	198
7403	50	221
8101	20	211
8102	20	215
8103	20	217
17101	20	211
17102	20	215
17103	**20**	**217**
17401	**50**	**195**
17402	**50**	**198**
17403	**50**	**221**

Russia

62 Black G2 62 or
62 Dark Blue G2 62

Saudi Arabia

101	STR	5129
102	STR	5130
103	G3	453
103	STR	5130
104	125	258115
105	**125**	**258118**
110	**125**	**258148**
130	**125**	**258164**

Seychelles

SY-001	560	003

South Africa

01	125	25181
02	125	25177
03	125	25182
04	125	25184
05	125	25259
06	125	25260
07	125	25269
(431)	20	41/407

Spain

01-405	**550**	**424**
01-406	**550**	**446**
01-407	**550**	**592**
45-01	**20**	**332/525**
45-02	**20**	**253/486**
45-03	**20**	**222/471**
45-04	**20**	**219/470**
45-05	**20**	**475**
45-20	**50**	**84**
45-40	**900**	**38**
45-41	**900**	**90**
401-02	20	253/486
401-03	20	222/471
401-04	20	219/470
401-05	20	332/525
401-09	50	84
403-11	**560**	**0161**
403-12	**560**	**0193**
T.11-5	**20**	**475**
T11-1	**20**	**253/486**
T16-1	**50**	**84**
T.18-1	**900**	**38**
T.18-2	**900**	**90**
TM11-2	**20**	**222/471**
TM11-3	**20**	**219/470**
TM11-4	**20**	**332/525**
TR.20-01	**560**	**0161**
TR.20-02	**560**	**0193**
U20-1	**550**	**424**
U20-2	**550**	**446**
U20-3	**550**	**592**

Sweden

86001	**S40**	**282-49**
86002	**S40**	**282-91**
102001	**G4**	**1014**
102002	**G4**	**1215**
102003	**G4**	**1216**
103001	**550**	**307**

Switzerland

J-4117	MSP	069
T-781	**35A**	**068**
T-782	35A	145
T-783	**50**	**67**

Thailand

60504	**35A**	**623**
60505	**35A**	**635**

Turkey

12-001	**550**	**502**
12-002	**550**	**503**
12-003	**G4**	**1163**
93-7024	**670**	**7024**
93-7026	**670**	**7026**
ETI-024	**670**	**7024**
ETI-026	**670**	**7026**

Uganda

UAF1	WWD	134

United Kingdom

9259M	**125**	**25012**
9260M	**125**	**25061**
XS709	**125**	**25011**
XS710	125	25012
XS711	**125**	**25024**
XS712	**125**	**25040**
XS713	**125**	**25041**
XS714	125	25054
XS726	125	25044
XS727	**125**	**25045**
XS728	**125**	**25048**
XS729	125	25049
XS730	**125**	**25050**
XS731	**125**	**25055**
XS732	125	25056
XS733	125	25059
XS734	125	25061
XS735	125	25071
XS736	**125**	**25072**
XS737	**125**	**25076**
XS738	125	25077
XS739	**125**	**25081**
XW788	125	25255
XW789	125	25264
XW790	125	25266
XW791	125	25268
XW930	125	25009
XX505	125	25252
XX506	125	25271
XX507	125	256006
XX508	125	256008
ZD620	**125**	**257181**
ZD621	**125**	**257190**
ZD703	**125**	**257183**
ZD704	**125**	**257194**
ZE395	**125**	**257205**
ZE396	**125**	**257211**
ZF130	**125**	**256059**

United States of America

01	G2	23
01	**G3**	**477**
USCG 160	WWD	160
USCG 519	500	019
USCG 2101	**HU25**	**374**
USCG 2102	HU25	386
USCG 2103	**HU25**	**394**
USCG 2104	**HU25**	**390**
USCG 2105	HU25	398
USCG 2106	HU25	402
USCG 2107	**HU25**	**409**
USCG 2108	HU25	405
USCG 2109	HU25	407
USCG 2110	**HU25**	**411**
USCG 2111	**HU25**	**413**
USCG 2112	**HU25**	**415**
USCG 2113	**HU25**	**417**
USCG 2114	HU25	418
USCG 2115	**HU25**	**419**
USCG 2116	HU25	420
USCG 2117	**HU25**	**421**
USCG 2118	**HU25**	**423**
USCG 2119	HU25	424
USCG 2120	**HU25**	**425**
USCG 2121	**HU25**	**431**
USCG 2122	**HU25**	**433**
USCG 2123	HU25	435
USCG 2124	**HU25**	**437**
USCG 2125	**HU25**	**439**
USCG 2126	**HU25**	**441**
USCG 2127	HU25	443
USCG 2128	HU25	445
USCG 2129	**HU25**	**447**
USCG 2130	HU25	450
USCG 2131	**HU25**	**452**
USCG 2132	**HU25**	**454**
USCG 2133	**HU25**	**456**
USCG 2134	**HU25**	**458**
USCG 2135	**HU25**	**459**
USCG 2136	**HU25**	**460**
USCG 2137	HU25	462
USCG 2138	HU25	464
USCG 2139	**HU25**	**466**
USCG 2140	**HU25**	**467**
USCG 2141	**HU25**	**371**

59-2868	**T39**	**265-1**
59-2869	T39	265-2
59-2870	T39	265-3
59-2871	T39	265-4
59-2872	T39	265-5
59-2873	**T39B**	**270-1**
59-2874	T39B	270-2
59-5958	STR	5010
59-5959	**STR**	**5026**
59-5960	STR	5028
59-5961	STR	5030
59-5962	**STR**	**5032**
60-3474	**T39B**	**270-3**
60-3475	T39B	270-4
60-3476	T39B	270-5
60-3477	T39B	270-6
60-3478	T39	265-6
60-3479	T39	265-7
60-3480	T39	265-8
60-3481	T39	265-9
60-3482	T39	265-10
60-3483	T39	265-11
60-3484	T39	265-12
60-3485	T39	265-13
60-3486	T39	265-14
60-3487	T39	265-15
60-3488	T39	265-16
60-3489	T39	265-17
60-3490	T39	265-18
60-3491	T39	265-19
60-3492	T39	265-20
60-3493	T39	265-21
60-3494	T39	265-22
60-3495	T39	265-23
60-3496	T39	265-24
60-3497	T39	265-25
60-3498	T39	265-26
60-3499	T39	265-27
60-3500	T39	265-28
60-3501	T39	265-29
60-3502	T39	265-30
60-3503	T39	265-31
60-3504	T39	265-32
60-3505	T39	265-33
60-3506	T39	265-34
60-3507	T39	265-35
60-3508	T39	265-36
61-0634	T39	265-37
61-0635	T39	265-38
61-0636	T39	265-39
61-0637	T39	265-40
61-0638	T39	265-41
61-0639	T39	265-42
61-0640	T39	265-43
61-0641	T39	265-44
61-0642	T39	265-45
61-0643	T39	265-46
61-0644	T39	265-47
61-0645	T39	265-48
61-0646	T39	265-49
61-0647	T39	265-50
61-0648	T39	265-51
61-0649	T39	265-52
61-0650	T39	265-53
61-0651	T39	265-54
61-0652	T39	265-55
61-0653	T39	265-56
61-0654	T39	265-57
61-0655	T39	265-58
61-0656	T39	265-59
61-0657	T39	265-60
61-0658	T39	265-61
61-0659	T39	265-62
61-0660	T39	265-63
61-0661	T39	265-64
61-0662	T39	265-65
61-0663	T39	265-66
61-0664	T39	265-67
61-0665	T39	265-68
61-0666	T39	265-69
61-0667	T39	265-70
61-0668	T39	265-71
61-0669	T39	265-72
61-0670	T39	265-73
61-0671	T39	265-74
61-0672	T39	265-75
61-0673	T39	265-76
61-0674	T39	265-77
61-0675	T39	265-78
61-0676	T39	265-79
61-0677	T39	265-80
61-0678	T39	265-81
61-0679	T39	265-82
61-0680	T39	265-83
61-0681	T39	265-84
61-0682	T39	265-85
61-0683	T39	265-86
61-0684	T39	265-87
61-0685	T39	265-88
61-2488	STR	5017
61-2489	STR	5022
61-2490	STR	5024
61-2491	**STR**	**5027**
61-2492	**STR**	**5031**
61-2493	STR	5034
62-4197	STR	5041
62-4198	STR	5042
62-4199	STR	5043
62-4200	STR	5044
62-4201	STR	5045
62-4448	T39	276-1
62-4449	T39	276-2
62-4450	T39	276-3
62-4451	T39	276-4
62-4452	T39	276-5
62-4453	T39	276-6
62-4454	T39	276-7
62-4455	T39	276-8
62-4456	T39	276-9
62-4457	T39	276-10
62-4458	T39	276-11
62-4459	T39	276-12
62-4460	T39	276-13
62-4461	T39	276-14
62-4462	T39	276-15
62-4463	T39	276-16
62-4464	T39	276-17
62-4465	T39	276-18
62-4466	T39	276-19
62-4467	T39	276-20
62-4468	T39	276-21
62-4469	T39	276-22
62-4470	T39	276-23
62-4471	T39	276-24
62-4472	T39	276-25
62-4473	T39	276-26
62-4474	T39	276-27
62-4475	T39	276-28
62-4476	T39	276-29
62-4477	T39	276-30
62-4478	T39	276-31
62-4479	T39	276-32
62-4480	T39	276-33
62-4481	T39	276-34
62-4482	T39	276-35
62-4483	T39	276-36
62-4484	T39	276-37
62-4485	T39	276-38
62-4486	T39	276-39
62-4487	T39	276-40
62-4488	**T39**	**276-41**
62-4489	T39	276-42
62-4490	T39	276-43
62-4491	T39	276-44
62-4492	T39	276-45
62-4493	T39	276-46
62-4494	**T39**	**276-47**
62-4495	T39	276-48
62-4496	T39	276-49
62-4497	T39	276-50
62-4498	T39	276-51
62-4499	T39	276-52
62-4500	T39	276-53
62-4501	T39	276-54
62-4502	T39	276-55
(62-12166)	STR	5025
(62-12167)	STR	5035
(62-12845)	STR	5071
83-0500	**G3**	**382**
83-0501	**G3**	**383**
83-0502	**G3**	**389**
84-0063	C21	509
84-0064	**C21**	**510**
84-0065	**C21**	**511**
84-0066	**C21**	**512**
84-0067	C21	513
84-0068	**C21**	**514**
84-0069	**C21**	**515**
84-0070	**C21**	**516**
84-0071	**C21**	**517**
84-0072	**C21**	**518**
84-0073	**C21**	**519**
84-0074	**C21**	**520**
84-0075	**C21**	**521**
84-0076	**C21**	**522**
84-0077	**C21**	**523**
84-0078	**C21**	**524**
84-0079	**C21**	**525**
84-0080	**C21**	**526**
84-0081	**C21**	**527**
84-0082	**C21**	**528**
84-0083	**C21**	**529**
84-0084	**C21**	**530**
84-0085	**C21**	**531**
84-0086	**C21**	**532**
84-0087	**C21**	**533**
84-0088	**C21**	**534**
84-0089	C21	535
84-0090	**C21**	**536**
84-0091	**C21**	**537**
84-0092	**C21**	**538**
84-0093	**C21**	**539**
84-0094	**C21**	**540**
84-0095	**C21**	**541**
84-0096	**C21**	**542**
84-0097	**C21**	**543**
84-0098	**C21**	**544**
84-0099	**C21**	**545**

84-0100	C21	546
84-0101	C21	547
84-0102	C21	548
84-0103	C21	549
84-0104	C21	550
84-0105	C21	551
84-0106	C21	552
84-0107	C21	553
84-0108	C21	554
84-0109	C21	555
84-0110	C21	556
84-0111	C21	557
84-0112	C21	558
84-0113	C21	559
84-0114	C21	560
84-0115	C21	561
84-0116	C21	562
84-0117	C21	563
84-0118	C21	564
84-0119	C21	565
84-0120	C21	566
84-0121	C21	567
84-0122	C21	568
84-0123	C21	569
84-0124	C21	570
84-0125	C21	571
84-0126	C21	572
84-0127	C21	573
84-0128	C21	575
84-0129	C21	576
84-0130	C21	577
84-0131	C21	578
84-0132	C21	579
84-0133	C21	580
84-0134	C21	581
84-0135	C21	582
84-0136	C21	583
84-0137	C21	585
84-0138	C21	574
84-0139	C21	587
84-0140	C21	588
84-0141	C21	584
84-0142	C21	586
85-0049	G3	456
85-0050	G3	458
86-0200	G3	465
86-0201	G3	470
86-0202	G3	468
86-0203	G3	475
86-0204	G3	476
86-0205	G3	477
86-0206	G3	478
86-0374	C21	624
86-0375	C21	625
86-0376	C21	628
86-0377	C21	629
86-0403	G3	473
87-0026	C21	280
87-0139	G3	497
87-0140	G3	498
88-0269	125	258129
88-0270	125	258131
88-0271	125	258134
88-0272	125	258154
88-0273	125	258156
88-0274	125	258158
89-0266	G2	45
89-0284	T1A	TT-5
90-0300	G4	1181
90-0400	400	
90-0400	T1A	TT-3
90-0401	T1A	TT-7
90-0402	T1A	TT-8
90-0403	T1A	TT-9
90-0404	T1A	TT-6
90-0405	T1A	TT-4
90-0406	T1A	TT-11
90-0407	T1A	TT-10
90-0408	T1A	TT-12
90-0409	T1A	TT-13
90-0410	T1A	TT-14
90-0411	T1A	TT-15
90-0412	T1A	TT-2
90-0413	T1A	TT-16
91-0075	T1A	TT-18
91-0076	T1A	TT-17
91-0077	T1A	TT-1
91-0078	T1A	TT-19
91-0079	T1A	TT-20
91-0080	T1A	TT-21
91-0081	T1A	TT-22
91-0082	T1A	TT-23
91-0083	T1A	TT-24
91-0084	T1A	TT-25
91-0085	T1A	TT-26
91-0086	T1A	TT-27
91-0087	T1A	TT-28
91-0088	T1A	TT-29
91-0089	T1A	TT-30
91-0090	T1A	TT-31
91-0091	T1A	TT-32
91-0092	T1A	TT-33
91-0093	T1A	TT-34
91-0094	T1A	TT-35
91-0095	T1A	TT-36
91-0096	T1A	TT-37
91-0097	T1A	TT-38
91-0098	T1A	TT-39
91-0099	T1A	TT-40
91-0100	T1A	TT-41
91-0101	T1A	TT-42
91-0102	T1A	TT-43
91-0108	G4	1162
92-0330	T1A	TT-44
92-0331	T1A	TT-45
92-0332	T1A	TT-46
92-0333	T1A	TT-47
92-0334	T1A	TT-48
92-0335	T1A	TT-49
92-0336	T1A	TT-50
92-0337	T1A	TT-51
92-0338	T1A	TT-52
92-0339	T1A	TT-53
92-0340	T1A	TT-54
92-0341	T1A	TT-55
92-0342	T1A	TT-56
92-0343	T1A	TT-57
92-0344	T1A	TT-58
92-0345	T1A	TT-59
92-0346	T1A	TT-60
92-0347	T1A	TT-61
92-0348	T1A	TT-62
92-0349	T1A	TT-63
92-0350	T1A	TT-64
92-0351	T1A	TT-65
92-0352	T1A	TT-66
92-0353	T1A	TT-67
92-0354	T1A	TT-68
92-0355	T1A	TT-69
92-0356	T1A	TT-70
92-0357	T1A	TT-71
92-0358	T1A	TT-72
92-0359	T1A	TT-73
92-0360	T1A	TT-74
92-0361	T1A	TT-75
92-0362	T1A	TT-76
92-0363	T1A	TT-77
92-0375	G4	1256
93-0621	T1A	TT-78
93-0622	T1A	TT-79
93-0623	T1A	TT-80
93-0624	T1A	TT-81
93-0625	T1A	TT-82
93-0626	T1A	TT-83
93-0627	T1A	TT-84
93-0628	T1A	TT-85
93-0629	T1A	TT-86
93-0630	T1A	TT-87
93-0631	T1A	TT-88
93-0632	T1A	TT-89
93-0633	T1A	TT-90
93-0634	T1A	TT-91
93-0635	T1A	TT-92
93-0636	T1A	TT-93
93-0637	T1A	TT-94
93-0638	T1A	TT-95
93-0639	T1A	TT-96
93-0640	T1A	TT-97
93-0641	T1A	TT-98
93-0642	T1A	TT-99
93-0643	T1A	TT-100
93-0644	T1A	TT-101
93-0645	T1A	TT-102
93-0646	T1A	TT-103
93-0647	T1A	TT-104
93-0648	T1A	TT-105
93-0649	T1A	TT-106
93-0650	T1A	TT-107
93-0651	T1A	TT-108
93-0652	T1A	TT-109
93-0653	T1A	TT-110
93-0654	T1A	TT-111
93-0655	T1A	TT-112
93-0656	T1A	TT-113
94-0114	T1A	TT-114
94-0115	T1A	TT-115
94-0116	T1A	TT-116
94-0117	T1A	TT-117
94-0118	T1A	TT-118
94-0119	T1A	TT-119
94-0120	T1A	TT-120
94-0121	T1A	TT-121
94-0122	T1A	TT-122
94-0123	T1A	TT-123
94-0124	T1A	TT-124
94-0125	T1A	TT-125
94-0126	T1A	TT-126
94-0127	T1A	TT-127
94-0128	T1A	TT-128
94-0129	T1A	TT-129
94-0130	T1A	TT-130
94-0131	T1A	TT-131
94-0132	T1A	TT-132
94-0133	T1A	TT-133
94-0134	T1A	TT-134
94-0135	T1A	TT-135
94-0136	T1A	TT-136
94-0137	T1A	TT-137
94-0138	T1A	TT-138
94-0139	T1A	TT-139
94-0140	T1A	TT-140
94-0141	T1A	TT-141
94-0142	T1A	TT-142
94-0143	T1A	TT-143
94-0144	T1A	TT-144
94-0145	T1A	TT-145
94-0146	T1A	TT-146
94-0147	T1A	TT-147
94-0148	T1A	TT-148
94-1569	AST	088
94-1570	AST	090
95-0040	T1A	TT-149
95-0041	T1A	TT-150
95-0042	T1A	TT-151
95-0043	T1A	TT-152
95-0044	T1A	TT-153
95-0045	T1A	TT-154
95-0046	T1A	TT-155
95-0047	T1A	TT-156
95-0048	T1A	TT-157
95-0049	T1A	TT-158
95-0050	T1A	TT-159
95-0051	T1A	TT-160
95-0052	T1A	TT-161
95-0053	T1A	TT-162
95-0054	T1A	TT-163
95-0055	T1A	TT-164
95-0056	T1A	TT-165
95-0057	T1A	TT-166
95-0058	T1A	TT-167
95-0059	T1A	TT-168
95-0060	T1A	TT-169
95-0061	T1A	TT-170
95-0062	T1A	TT-171
95-0063	T1A	TT-172
95-0064	T1A	TT-173
95-0065	T1A	TT-174
95-0066	T1A	TT-175
95-0067	T1A	TT-176
95-0068	T1A	TT-177
95-0069	T1A	TT-178
95-0070	T1A	TT-179
95-0071	T1A	TT-180
95-0123	560	0387
95-0124	560	0392
96-0107	560	0404
96-0108	560	0410
96-0109	560	0415
96-0110	560	0420
96-0111	560	0426
97-0049	G5	566
97-0101	560	0452
97-0102	560	0456
97-0103	560	0462
97-0104	560	0468
97-0105	560	0472
97-0400	G5	521
97-0401	G5	542
97-0402	G5	571
98-0006	560	0495
98-0007	560	0501
98-0008	560	0505
98-0009	560	0508
98-0010	560	0513
99-0100	560	0532
99-0101	560	0534
99-0102	560	0538
99-0103	560	0545
99-0104	560	0548
89001	STR	1002
150542	T39	277-1
150543	T39	277-2
150544	T39	277-3
150545	T39	277-4
150546	T39	277-5
150547	T39	277-6
150548	T39	277-7
150549	T39	277-8
150550	T39	277-9
150551	T39	277-10
150969	T39	285-1
150970	T39	285-2
150971	T39	285-3
150972	T39	285-4
150973	T39	285-5
150974	T39	285-6
150975	T39	285-7
150976	T39	285-8
150977	T39	285-9
150978	T39	285-10
150979	T39	285-11
150980	T39	285-12
150981	T39	285-13
150982	T39	285-14
150983	T39	285-15
150984	T39	285-16
150985	T39	285-17
150986	T39	285-18
150987	T39	285-19
150988	T39	285-20
150989	T39	285-21
150990	T39	285-22
150991	T39	285-23
150992	T39	285-24
151336	T39	285-25
151337	T39	285-26
151338	T39	285-27
151339	T39	285-28
151340	T39	285-29
151341	T39	285-30
151342	T39	285-31
151343	T39	285-32
157352	T39	282-46
157353	T39	282-84
157354	T39	282-85
158380	T39	282-95
158381	T39	282-93

158382	T39	282-92
158383	T39	282-96
158843	T39	306-52
158844	T39	306-55
159361	T39	306-65
159362	T39	306-66
159363	T39	306-67
159364	T39	306-69
159365	**T39**	**306-70**
160053	**T39**	**306-104**
160054	**T39**	**306-105**
160055	**T39**	**306-106**
160056	T39	306-107
160057	T39	306-108
162755	552	0001
162756	552	0002
162757	552	0003
162758	552	0004
162759	552	0005
162760	552	0006
162761	552	0007
162762	552	0008
162763	552	0009
162764	552	0010
162765	552	0011
162766	552	0012
162767	552	0013
162768	**552**	**0014**
162769	552	0015
163691	**G3**	**480**
163692	**G3**	**481**
165093	**G4**	**1187**
165094	**G4**	**1189**
165151	**G4**	**1199**
165152	**G4**	**1201**
165153	**G4**	**1200**
165509	**T39**	**282-9**
165510	**T39**	**282-81**
165511	**T39**	**282-29**
165512	**T39**	**282-2**
165513	**T39**	**282-66**
165514	**T39**	**282-30**
165515	**T39**	**282-72**
165516	**T39**	**282-90**
165517	**T39**	**282-61**
165518	**T39**	**282-77**
165519	**S40**	**282-19**
165520	**T39**	**282-32**
165521	**T39**	**282-94**
165522	**T39**	**282-28**
165523	**T39**	**282-20**
165524	**T39**	**282-60**
165740	**560**	**0513**
165741	**560**	**0524**

AMARC Codes

41-001	**HU25**	**443**
41-002	**HU25**	**424**
41003	**HU25**	**435**
41-004	**HU25**	**450**
41-005	**HU25**	**420**
41-007	**HU25**	**402**
41-009	**HU25**	**464**
41-013	**HU25**	**445**
41-015	**HU25**	**405**
7T-001	T39	285-3
7T-002	T39	277-10
7T-004	T39	285-12
7T-005	**T39**	**285-20**
7T-006	**T39**	**277-3**
7T-007	T39	285-7
7T-008	**T39**	**277-7**
7T-009	**T39**	**285-10**
7T-010	**T39**	**285-16**
7T-011	T39	277-8
7T-012	T39	285-13
7T-013	**T39**	**285-5**
7T-014	**T39**	**277-5**
7T-015	**T39**	**285-6**
7T-016	**T39**	**285-8**
7T-017	**T39**	**285-11**
7T-018	T39	285-29
7T-019	**T39**	**285-30**
7T-021	**T39**	**277-6**
7T-022	T39	285-14
7T-023	T39	285-15
7T-024	**T39**	**285-22**
7T-025	**T39**	**285-25**
7T-026	**T39**	**285-1**
7T-027	**T39**	**277-2**
7T-028	**T39**	**282-84**
7T-029	**T39**	**306-107**
7T030	**T39**	**306-69**
7T031	T39	306-52
7T032	**T39**	**306-66**
7T034	**T39**	**306-55**
CL002	STR	5043
CL003	STR	5034
CL004	STR	5024
CL005	STR	5044
CL006	STR	5017
CL006	STR	5022
CL007	STR	5041
CL008	STR	5045
TG002	**T39**	**276-10**
TG003	**T39**	**265-13**
TG004	T39	276-17
TG006	**T39**	**276-3**
TG007	T39	265-20
TG008	T39	265-14
TG009	**T39**	**265-19**
TG010	**T39**	**265-59**
TG011	T39	276-25
TG012	**T39**	**265-81**
TG013	**T39**	**265-8**
TG014	**T39**	**265-69**
TG015	**T39**	**265-5**
TG016	T39	265-10
TG017	T39	265-51
TG018	**T39**	**276-7**
TG019	T39	276-19
TG020	T39	276-21
TG021	T39	265-15
TG022	**T39**	**265-46**
TG023	T39	265-60
TG024	T39	265-12
TG025	T39	265-86
TG026	T39	265-62
TG027	T39	276-27
TG028	**T39**	**265-68**
TG029	T39	276-26
TG030	T39	265-28
TG031	T39	265-85
TG032	T39	265-65
TG033	**T39**	**265-2**
TG034	T39	265-61
TG035	**T39**	**265-40**
TG036	T39	265-44
TG037	**T39**	**265-27**
TG038	T39	265-76
TG039	T39	265-83
TG040	T39	265-54
TG041	T39	276-12
TG042	T39	265-36
TG043	T39	265-53
TG044	T39	265-57
TG045	**T39**	**265-45**
TG046	**T39**	**276-15**
TG048	T39	276-30
TG049	**T39**	**265-79**
TG050	T39	276-39
TG051	T39	265-71
TG052	T39	276-32
TG053	T39	276-50
TG054	T39	265-38
TG055	T39	276-36
TG057	**T39**	**265-21**
TG058	T39	265-17
TG059	T39	276-48
TG060	T39	276-4
TG061	T39	265-35
TG062	T39	265-18
TG063	T39	265-67
TG064	T39	276-22
TG065	T39	276-8
TG066	**T39**	**265-25**
TG067	T39	265-66
TG068	T39	276-33
TG069	T39	265-82
TG070	T39	276-53
TG071	T39	265-56
TG072	T39	265-24
TG073	T39	276-54
TG074	T39	276-42
TG075	T39	265-72
TG076	T39	276-46
TG077	T39	265-26
TG078	T39	265-50
TG079	T39	276-43
TG080	T39	276-51
TG081	T39	276-44
TG082	**T39**	**265-7**
TG085	**T39**	**265-9**
TG086	T39	265-42
TG087	**T39**	**265-55**
TG088	T39	265-70
TG089	**T39**	**265-39**
TG090	T39	265-74
TG091	T39	265-48
TG092	T39	276-2
TG093	**T39**	**265-29**
TG094	**T39**	**265-22**
TG095	T39	265-30
TG096	T39	265-41
TG-097	**T39**	**285-31**
TG098	**T39**	**270-4**
TG099	**T39**	**276-29**
TG100	**T39**	**276-16**
TG101	**T39**	**270-6**
TG102	**T39**	**270-5**
TG103	**T39**	**270-2**

Uruguay

500	35A	378

Venda

VDF-030	551	266

Venezuela

0002	**550**	**012**
0004	**G2**	**124**
0005	**G3**	**400**
0006	**24D**	**250**
0222	**500**	**092**
0442	20	235
1107	550	449
1650	**20**	**476**
2222	**550**	**251**
5761	**20C**	**23**
5840	20	216
FAV0013	**35A**	**270**

West Germany

1101	STR	5025
1102	STR	5121
1103	STR	5071
1601	HFB	1041
1602	HFB	1042
1603	HFB	1043
1604	HFB	1046
1605	HFB	1047
1606	HFB	1048
1607	HFB	1024
1608	HFB	1025
1622	HFB	1059
9825	HFB	1059
9826	HFB	1060
CA101	STR	5025
CA102	STR	5035
CA103	STR	5071
D9536	HFB	1024
D9537	HFB	1025

Yugoslavia

10401	25B	202
10402	25B	203
70401	25B	202
70402	25B	203
72101	**50**	**25**
72102	50	43

AIRCRAFT NOTED WHERE C/N IS NOT YET KNOWN

Reg'n	Type	Remarks
D-CARE	650	Seen at Le Bourget 11.4.00
D-ICAM	CIT	Seen at Le Bourget 2.3.00 - possibly c/n 501-0079, to be confirmed.
EC-HFA	CIT	Seen at Jersey 26.8.99 - possibly c/n 500-0209, to be confirmed.
EC-207	125	Reported at Koln/Bonn 13.11.88
EC-413	125	Reported at Palma, Mallorca, 27.3.90
EP-TFA	50	Noted at Tehran 1997 - c/n 101, 120 or 122?
EP-TFI	50	Noted at Tehran 3.2000 - c/n 101, 120 or 122?
HK-3452X	550	Registered to Aviaco Ltda - presumed ntu?
N5AF	G5	Seen at Long Beach 10.1.99 - possibly c/n 531 N531AF incorrectly painted.
N15EC	T39	Noted at Hanscom Field 13.8.95. May be c/n 276-22
N780JR	AST	Reported at Teterboro 30.6.93
N1015G	550	Noted at Wichita 5.8.92
N1123B	650	Noted at Wichita 21.1.97
N2808B	400	Noted at Beech Field, Wichita 28.5.91
N2810B	400	Noted at Beech Field, Wichita 1.4.93
N2826B	400	Routed St Johns-Reykjavik-Shannon-Ciampino 15.2.94, returned Ciampino-Shannon-Reykjavik 4.3.94
N5000E	31	Noted at Wichita 10.3.92, second use of marks
N5000E	31	Noted at Wichita 22.2.93, third use of marks
N5010U	31	Noted at Wichita 21.4.92, second use of marks
N5012G	31	Noted at Wichita 14.1.93
N5012H	31	Noted at Wichita 26.3.92, second use of marks
N5012K	31	Noted at Wichita 5.8.92
N5012K	45	Noted at Wichita 15.10.99
N5012Z	45	Noted at Tucson 1999, German flag, possibly c/n 45-044
N5013Y	31	Noted at Wichita 5.5.92
N5014E	31	Noted at Wichita 3.2.92
N5014E	60	Noted at Wichita 18.3.93
N5014F	35	Noted at Wichita 9.6.92
N5015U	60	Noted at Tucson 15.10.99
N5016V	31	Noted at Wichita 26.3.92, second use of marks
N5016V	31	Noted at Wichita 31.3.93, third use of marks
N5017J	31	Noted at Wichita 13.4.93
N5018G	31	Noted at Wichita 2.11.92
N5076K	560	Noted at Wichita 22.4.99
N5093D	560	Noted at Wichita 25.2.99
N5093L	550	Noted at Wichita 15.10.99
N5124F	525	Noted at Wichita 20.8.96
N5148B	550	Noted at Wichita 18.11.98
N5126L	525	Noted at Wichita 17.9.99.
N5163K	525	Noted at Wichita 16.10.98
N5200Z	560	Noted at Wichita 10.6.94
N5244F	525	Noted at Wichita 16.9.99
N5266F	550	Noted at Wichita 16.8.99
N40335	400	Noted at Beech Field, Wichita 5.8.93
N50111	31	Noted at Wichita 13.4.93, second use of marks
N50126	31	Noted at Wichita 17.9.91
N50126	35	Noted at Wichita 5.8.92
N50154	31	Noted at Wichita 19.11.91
N50157	31	Noted at Wichita 12.8.91
N50163	31	Noted at Wichita 20.7.92, second use of marks
N50163	45	Noted at Wichita 5.4.00
N51613	525	Noted at Wichita 27.2.97
N51983	560	An Excel, noted at Wichita 1.10.99
N82787	400	Noted at Beech Field, Wichita 13.2.94
OB-668	SLR	Registered in Peru, c/n quoted as '308-025'
PT-MMY	560	Reported at Wichita 5.5.97.
ST-PRE	JSR	Reported at Istanbul 15.6.96
XA-ADR	125	Reported at Miami 4.1.00.
XA-GGR	SLR	Reported at Toluca 13.12.99
XA-HEI	SLR	Reported at Mexico City 23.9.90
XA-PES	JSR	Reported at Toluca 22.3.00
XA-RLF	SLR	Reported at Mexico City in November 1991
XA-RMN	125	Reported at Orlando International 24.6.94
XA-TNP	SLR	Reported at Tucson 1999
XA-TQL	550	Reported at Phoenix Sky Harbor 22.11.99
XA-TRE	650	Reported at Toluca 22.3.00
XA-TRG	G2	Reported at Atlanta/Hartsfield 9.3.00, also quoted as a G3
XA-TRI	SLR	Reported at Toluca 22.3.00
XA-VYR	500	Reported at Dallas-Love Field
XB-GRN	650	Reported at Los Angeles International 3.3.00
XB-JHU	SLR	Reported at Toluca 2.8.95
XC-ASG	35	Reported At Mexico City 27.1.94
YV-94C	500	Reported at Fort Lauderdale Executive 12.9.93
ZC-PMC	550	Noted at Wichita 2.5.90 and later at Mexico City
9M-CHX	125	Reported at Kuala Lumpur 16.3.95
90-0400	400	Noted in USAF colours at Wichita 20.3.90 probably only painted as such for publicity purposes in connection with the TT-1 Jayhawk programme. Is possibly c/n RJ-45 - the marks are now genuinely allocated to c/n TT-3
MTX-04	SLR	Reported at Mexico City 12.6.99

See Master Index for type decode (SLR = Sabre)

CORPORATE AIRLINERS

Airbus A319CJ

C/n	Model	Regn
0910		A6-ESH
0913	132	G-OMAK
1002	112	Italy MM62173

Boeing BBJ

Line	C/n	Model	Registrations			
101	29102	737-73Q	N737BZ			
111	29441	737-79U	N1787B	N1779B	(N1101N)	N1011N
126	28581	737-75V	N1787B	N366G		
131	29024	737-72T	N50TC			
143	29054	737-73T	N1787B	N1780B	N6067E	N500LS
146	29273	737-72U	VP-BBJ	N1011N	VP-BBJ	
150	29251	737-7E0	A6-HRS			
158	28976	737-75U	VP-BRM			
167	29142	737-75T	N1787B	N700WH		
179	30076	737-7BJ	N374MC	D-AXXL	N737MC	
189	29139	737-74T	N1786B	N5573L	N73721	
197	29233	737-74U	N1786B	N4AS		
206	29135	737-74Q	N1786B	N777..	N60436	N737CC
217	29188	737-7P3	N1787B	HZ-TAA		
225	29136	737-74Q	N1787B	N1779B	N737GG	
234	29200	737-73U	N742PB			
241	29865	737-7AK	HB-IIO			
244	30070	737-7AV	N18NC			
251	30031	737-7AW	N1786B	VP-CBB	N73715	
265	29317	737-79T	N1787B	VP-BWR		
280	29268	737-7Z5	N1786B	A6-AIN		
301	30496	737-7BF	N224TA			
312	28579	737-75V	N367G			
323	29272	737-74V	N1786B	N737SP		
336	29791	737-73H	N348BA			
348	29149	737-7H3	TS-IOO			
356	30327	737-7BC	N127QS			
377	30328	737-7BC	N128QS			
384	30329	737-7BC	N129QS			
397	29274	737-7H6	9M-BBJ			
401	30751	737-7CG	N800G			
408	29866	737-7AK	HB-IIP			
415	30330	737-7BC	N130QS			
423	30547	737-7BQ	HZ-DG5			
432	29269	737-7Z5	A6-SIR			
445	29857	737-7Z5	N1795B	A6-LIW		
451	30752	737-7CN	N1026G	HB-IIQ		
456	29749	737-7AH	N73711	C6-TTB		
481	30753	737-7CP	N329K			
491	30752	737-7BC	N1005S	N171QS		
496	29979	737-7AF	N1787B	165829		
516	30754	737-7CJ	N1786B	N1055S	N349BA	
530	29858	737-7Z5	A6-UAE			
545	30755	737-7				
554	30772	737-7				
568	29980	737-7AF	For USN			
569	30756	737-7BC	N1..QS			
586	30782	737-7BC	N1..QS			

GRUMMAN G159 GULFSTREAM 1

C/n	Series	Identities
1		N701G ff 14Aug58 ZS-NVG (cargo aircraft)
2		N702G N1 N3 N3003 N40CE N42CE N40CE N116GA N39PP 86-0402 b/u 30Sep90
3		N703G CF-MAR C-FMAR b/u for spares Montreal, Canada
4		N704G N704HC N717 N99DE N89DE N371BG wfu 1985; b/u for spares 1985
5		N705G N601HK N606HP N700PR N43AS N9EB N159AJ N925WL N159AJ F-GFGT ZS-OOE
6		N2425 (VR-B) S9-NAU N221AP b/u Pal-Waukee A/P, IL, on 15Feb96
7		CF-LOO N5VX
8		N708G wfu for spares in 1985
9		N709G N43M N436M N436 N436M G-BNCE wfu Oct91 Aberdeen, UK due to corrosion; stripped for spares; canx 04May93
10		N1623 N1623Z XB-CIJ wfu 05Oct88 following landing accident
11		N650ST N650BT N100FL N100EL N7SL
12		N400P N166NK N91JR N8VB b/u for spares Dodson Aviation, Rantoul, KS circa Sep97
13		airframe not built
14		N714G N1607Z N723RA canx Nov88; b/u for spares 1988 Shreveport, LA
15		N715G N1501 N1501C N72EZ N26KW XB-ESO wfu 11Oct90 following landing accident
16		N716G N2998 N707WA N8001J N20NH N202HA N615C
17		N199M CF-TPC N9971F wfu 1985; b/u for spares 1986
18		N300UP N3UP N48PA
19		N80L N80LR N70LR N12GW PK-WWG N12GW b/u for spares Oct87; canx Sep89
20		N266P N227LS N227LA N250AL N5PC VR-CTN N732US F-GFMH
21		N721G N361G N361Q XC-BIO (N6653Z) b/u for spares 01Aug91 Savannah, GA; canx Nov95
22		N80G N8BG C-GKFG cx Feb97 as wfu
23		N1929Y N1929B OE-BAZ OE-HAZ N193PA N186PA
24		N1620 N1625 N1625B YV-P-AEA YV-09CP N713US HK-3315X HK-3315 w/o 06Feb90 El Salado Mt, nr Ibague, Colombia; canx 26Jun90
25		N725G (OE-) N725G (OK-NEA) N725G 4X-ARH
26		N726G N505S N120S N348DA YV-82CP N185PA
27	1C	N100P N1009 XB-FUB XB-VIW N2150M N80M N114GA N415CA N198PA
28		N900JL N9006L N666ES N11SX N118X N719RA wfu; a/c currently with Dodson Avn, KS, for spares use
29		N785GP N1844S N1845S N1925P N222SG N222SE N431G C- (marks cx Jun99)
30		N901G N961G wfu 01Apr89 for spares; canx Nov91
31		CF-JFC N715RA wfu; awaiting scrapping for spares by Intl Turbine Services, TX
32		N731G N734ET N734EB N733EB N297X N300MC canx Dec88; wfu
33		N126J N88Y N261L N295SA HR-IAJ TG-TJB (N23AH) N21AH 9Q-CBY
34		N620K N48TE HK-3634X N34LE 5Y-BLR
35		N735G XC-IMS XB-DVG XA-PUA N86MA 9Q-CBD
36		N131A N230E wfu 01Nov88 Detroit-Willow Run, MI
37		N130G N130B N716RD N20S N91G w/o 24Sep78 Houston, TX
38		ZS-AAC VQ-ZIP 3D-AAC N7001N N38JK N333AH N717RS
39		N40Y N39TG EC-376 EC-EVJ
40		N6PG N8ZA N40AG EC-493 EC-FIO
41		N7PG N9ZA N41TG EC-494 EC-EZO wfu Madrid, Spain
42		N366P N430H N888PR XA-MAS XC-AA61 ZS-OCA
43		N344DJ N140NT C-GNOR N39289 N716RA wfu for spares Jly88; canx Jan91
44		N285AA N121NC N717JF N717RW N717RD F-GFGV 5Y-JET
45		N745G N7788 N329CT N65CE
46		N746G wfu Oct86; used for spares
47		N747G N20CC N20HF b/u Oct86 Texas; canx Feb90
48		N748G VR-BBY N302K G-AWYF N213GA b/u Pal-Waukee, IL circa Apr97
49		N749G N456 F-GFIC
50		N80J N8BJ N6PA N3100E N8200E N820CE N28CG canx Jun90; to Schweizer Maintenance School, Elmira, NY by Aug91
51		N80K XC-HYC N90PM I-MGGG b/u 1994 Geneva, Switzerland
52		N752G VH-ASJ N3858H N18TF
53		N753G N700JW (N701JW) wfu 21Apr89; b/u for spares by White Industries, Bates City, MO; canx Jun94
54		CF-MUR C-FMUR N26AJ
55		N1234X N429X N429W N9MH N429W N27L N300PH VR-CAE N9446E N118LT b/u for spares 1986 Lawton, TX; canx Jly91
56		N756G N220B N510E YV-46CP N168PA
57		N757G I-CKET N66JD PK-TRM
58		N758G N358AA 5N-AAI N16776 N46TE N47TE XB-FLL
59		N759G N205AA N23D N11CZ HK-3316X HK-3316 w/o 02May90 Los Garcones A/P, Monteria, Colombia
60		C-FIOM PK-TRL
61		N761G N594AR N734HR N191SA b/u for spares Jun88 Wiley Post, OK; remains to Dodson Avn,KS
62		N205M w/o 25Jly67 New Cumberland, PA - but current as N400NL
63		N763G N144NK N580BC
64		N764G N466P CF-COL N49401 N64TG EC-460 EC-EXS wfu Madrid, Spain
65		N765G N345TW N340WB N641B N721RA canx Nov88; b/u for spares 1988
66		N766G N623W N65H N65HC N111DR XC-GEI wfu 04Sep86; b/u for spares
67		N767G N376 N48 N5241Z N806W
68		N768G N768GP N15GP N4765C N7ZA N68TG w/o 15Jly83 Tri-Cities A/P, Bristol, TN

GULFSTREAM I

C/n	Series	Identities
69		N769G N377 N47 N47R wfu 1986; to Votec School, Rexburg, ID; then to Pratt Community College, KS circa 1998 (still listed as current)
70		N770G N331H Parted out by Dodson Aviation, Ottawa, KS
71		N771G N530AA N60CR VR-BTI N222EF (N15SQ) N222EF F-GFIB XA-
72		N772G CF-NOC N743G (N93SA) N743G wfu 01Apr89; b/u for spares
73		N773G N773WJ N207M N720X canx Nov88; w/o pre Feb87 (buried by sand in Arizona Desert after drug running flight)
74		N774G N212H N5619D N701BN
75		N775G N304K PT-KYF
76		N776G N305K G-BRAL P4-JML
77		N777G N706G N73M N748M N748MN N748M 9Q-CFK G-BOBX wfu for spares 25Apr89
78		N1040 N778G N1040 N7040 N431H N33CP (PT-) HK-3681
79		N779G N190DM N79HS EC- (possibly EC-491 but was still painted as N79HS mid-Jly93); reported parted out 1993 Fort Lauderdale Intl, FL, still as N79HS
80		N780G N605AA N605AB N20GB N200GJ F-GGGY D2-EXC
81		N781G N22G N2PQ C-GMJS I-TASO 5Y-BMT+ 5Y-BMR +painted incorrectly c Oct97
82		N782G N798S N98R N798R N629JM (N801CC) SE-LFV SE-LDV N12RW
83	1C	N437A N117GA N245CA to White Inds, Bates City, MO for spares
84		N784G N362G N362GP N184K
85		N1150S XC-BAU (N66534) wfu 01Aug91; b/u for spares Savannah, GA; canx Nov95
86		N678RW N231GR N712MW N712MR N712MP N106GH N106GA N86JK N10TB
87		N787G N10VM N102PL N711BT N87CH N87CE (N87MK) N845JB wfu and scrapped; canx Sep97
88	1C	N788G N410AA N1M N357H N857H C-GPTN
89		N789G
90		N790G N4567 N18N N80R N41JK HK-3330X Remains with Dodson Aviation, KS Dec92
91		N791G USCG 1380 USCG 02
92		N710G NASA3 N3NA
93		N740AA N574DU N574K N674C N137C XA- N137C N197PA
94		N794G N8E
95		N795G N50UC N500RL N500RN
96		NASA1 N1NA N2NA
97		N797G N5152 N671NC N49DE YV-85CP N184PA
98		N708G NASA2 N2NA N29AY N98MK wfu Apr91; b/u for spares by White Industries, Bates City, MO
99		N709G N67B N102M N364G N364L N750BR w/o 13Nov88 nr Frankfurt, Germany; b/u; canx Dec89
100		N715G N166KJ N116K VH-FLO (ZK-) canx May95; wfu
101		N716G N222H N300SB F-GFGU 4X-ARV F-GNGU
102		N717G N621A N28CG N48CG N48CQ (N73CG) N48CQ HA-ACV C6-UNO N11UN
103		N718G N608RP N608R PT- XC-AA57
104		N719G C-FHBO
105		N702G I-TASB CofA expired 01Jun90; wfu Jly93 Milan-Linate, Italy; canx
106		N780AC N72X N72XL N38CG N64CG C-FAWG
107		N722G N34C N73B N7ZB N71CR N71CJ
108		N723G N1707Z N23UG b/u for spares late 1986; canx Feb90
109		N724G N1000 N823GA N2000C N1000 N1091 N804CC N307AT N109P reportedly scrapped
110		N727G N533CS C-GTDL canx May86; b/u for spares 1989
111		N728G N363G N3630 F-GJGC semi-derelict Oct91 Marseille, France
112		N729G N942PM N300PM N300PE (N300BP) N803CC wfu Mar89; canx Sep89; noted derelict Sep91 Detroit-Willow Run, MI with regn N803CC painted on a/c but covered over
113		not built
114		N712G N250M N705M N705RS N9300P VH-WPA N724RA wfu 01Mar88; b/u for spares by Intl Turbine Services, TX; canx Jan89
115		CF-ASC N61SB stored Dallas-Love Field, TX with engines removed
116	1C	N706G N26L N5400C N110GA N159AN N328CA to White Inds, Bates City, MO for spares
117		N710G N519M N23AK N41KD YV-08CP N167PA
118		N715G b/u for spares 1983; canx 1984
119		N734G YV-P-EPC YV-28CP N165PA
120		Greek P-9 wfu 1995; preserved Tatoi-Dekelia, Greece parked as "120" circa 1998
121		N732G N234MM wfu 1992; displayed Disney-MGM Studio Theme Park, Orlando, FL
122		N738G N153SR N152SR N707MP F-GFEF
123	1C	N736G N687RW N714MW N714MR N2602M N17CA to White Inds, Bates City, MO for spares
124		N737G N504C N725MK N476S ZS-NKT D2-EXD
125		N738G N205G N10NA N5NA N193PA
126		N739G N913BS N913PS N100TV N63AU N110RB
127		N741GA N500S N50LS N717JP XA-TDJ (not confirmed)
128		N122Y N516DM N910BS G-BMSR F-GIIX DBF 28Jun94 Lyon-Satolas, France; canx 04Aug94
129		N743G N770AC N770A N834H N812CC N113GA N129AF
130		N744G N902JL N3416 PK-TRO
131		N750G N730TL N730T N1TX N21TX C-FRTT 5Y-BLF
132		N120HC N944H N27G N154SR N154NS N154RH
133		N752G N2010 N7776 TU-VAC N33TF wfu; b/u for spares by White Industries, Bates City, MO
134		N754G N914BS N920BS G-BMPA (F-) 4X-ARF 3D-ARF 4X-ARF 3D-ARF ZS-ONO
135		N755G G-ASXT b/u Sep83 Denver, CO

GULFSTREAM I

C/n	Series	Identities
136		N756G XB-GAW XA-TBT
137		N757G CF-DLO N36DD N42CA (N811CC) noted 07Sep91 derelict Detroit-Willow Run, MI; marks N811CC not painted on a/c; canx Jun95
138		N758G N126K XA-ALK XA-RLK
139		N759G N42G N7972S N8500N N8500C N157WC N62J C-FRTU N196PA
140		N760G N300A N92K N92SA F-GFCQ
141		N762G N228H N800PA ZS-NHW
142		N764G N10ZA N142TG EC-461 EC-EXQ wfu Madrid, Spain
143		N720G N914P I-MDDD CofA expired 26Sep91; with Dodson Aviation, KS; canx
144		N766G N860E N70CR N70QR wfu 1986; canx Mar91
145		N767G N233U N149X N7FD N155T HK-3329X HK-3580W
146		N906F OE-GSN OE-HSN 001/4X-JUD Israeli AF N906F
147		N774G N861H w/o 11Jly67 Le Centre, MN
148		N775G N804CC N120S (N9036P) N107GH N1701L C-FWAM
149		N776G N636 N636G N400HT N684FM N192PA
150		N777G YV-121CP wfu Jun88 following landing accident
151		N741G NASA4 N4NA
152		N705G HP-799 OB-M-1235 N705G wfu 01May89; b/u for spares
153		N733G N733NM N80AC N153TG EC-433 EC-EXB
154		N267AA N736G N72B N800PM N800PD N802CC G-BNKO C-GNAK
155		N750G N992CP N22CP N24C N900PM N900PA N805CC G-BMOW 9Q-CJB
156		N737G N22AS N41LH
157		N741G N94SA canx Aug91; sale in Panama possible
158		N779G N679A N72CR N2NR N2NC 5Y-MIA not confirmed
159		N751G N287AA N940PM N200PM N200PF N809CC G-BNKN XA-RJB
160		N752G N3 N965CJ
161		N790G N307EL N925GC
162		N724G N547Q N547QR N547BN N547OR N31CN N300GP C-GPTA w/o 19Nov96 Lester B Pearson Airport, Toronto, Canada
163		N727G N618M N71CR w/o 11Jly75 Addison, TX
164		N738G N8PG N88PP N590AS N590AQ N290AS
165		N739G N75M N75MT N657PC N657P
166		N791G N67CR N20CR N76DM N725RA F-GKES (OO-IBG) HB-IRQ 4X-ARG D2-EXB
167		N794G N908LN C-GDWM N717RA
168		N754G N209T N722RA b/u for spares 1988; canx Nov88
169		N725HG N725HC N400WP N400WF N200AE
170		N790G N89K N189K YV-620CP
171		VH-CRA N171LS (N1PC) N728GM YV-621CP
172		N700DB N44MC N11NY N172RD TC-SMA
173		N360WT N944H N944HL N49CB I-TASC 5Y-BMT YV-988C
174		N774G N7004 N7004B N718RA wfu; b/u for spares by Intl Turbine Service, TX; canx Feb91
175		N795G N10CR N55AE N578KB YV-453CP N173PA
176	TC-4C	N798G US Navy 155722 preserved at Pensacola NAS, FL
177		N751G N307K N4PC OY-BEG N12GP G-BRWN PK-CTE
178	TC-4C	N778G US Navy 155723 w/o 16Oct75 Cherry Point, NC
179		N779G N1916M N61UT N60AC N60WK HK-3622 XC-AA53
180	TC-4C	N786G US Navy 155724 stored by Oct94 Davis-Monthan AFB; storage code 4G002
181		N759G N966H N966HL N25W N181TG w/o 01Jun85 Nashville, TN
182	TC-4C	N762G US Navy 155725 stored Davis-Monthan AFB
183	TC-4C	N766G US Navy 155726 stored Davis-Monthan AFB
184	TC-4C	US Navy 155727 stored by Oct94 Davis-Monthan AFB; storage code 4G004
185	TC-4C	US Navy 155728 stored by Oct94 Davis-Monthan AFB; storage code 4G003
186	TC-4C	US Navy 155729 stored by Oct94 Davis-Monthan AFB; storage code 4G001
187	TC-4C	US Navy 155730 stored by Apr95 Davis-Monthan AFB; storage code 4G005
188		N17582 HB-LDT C-FAWE
189		N776G C-GPTG
190		N1901W HK-3579X HK-4022X N190LE w/o 02Aug96 in Sudan whilst on delivery to Kenya as N190LE
191		N200XP N300P (N300XZ) G-BKJZ VH-JPJ PK-RJA
192		N712G N67H YV-76CP N171PA
193		N754G PK-TRN
194		N718G N6702 N702E N702EA N81T I-MKKK 4X-CST I-MKKK 5Y-BMS YV-989C not confirmed
195		N1900W N190PA
196		N728G N752RB N752R N93AC (N811CC) N93AC I-EHAJ N134PA N659PC
197		N385M N777JS (N725RB) (N811CC) N977JS (N385M) N20H N20HE N197RM N520JG
198		N740G N1902P N1902D N100C N80RD w/o 23Aug90 Houston Intercontinental A/P, TX; canx Oct91
199		N745G XA-RIV YV-83CP N183PA
200		N750G N255TK
322		N769G N90M N9QM N71RD
323		N900 N988AA N346DA S9-NAV N22320 "N900TT" +N980TT HI-678CA HI-678CT +painted incorrectly c Aug94

Production complete

Notes: The marks YV-78CP were reported as being carried by a Gulfstream 1 at Caracas on 02Dec90; could this be connected with c/n 117 YV-08CP, as these marks have also been reported on a PA-31T.

Marks YV-627C were reported for c/n 170 and YV-628C for c/n 171; previous marks of YV-620CP and YV-621CP are however reported as still being current. Details of any recent sightings would be most welcome.

G159 Gulfstream 1 Registration Cross-Reference

Note Current Registrations are in bold type

Canada

CF-ASC	115
CF-COL	64
CF-DLO	137
CF-JFC	31
CF-LOO	7
CF-MAR	3
CF-MUR	54
CF-NOC	72
CF-TPC	17
C-	**29**
C-FAWE	**188**
C-FAWG	**106**
C-FHBO	**104**
C-FIOM	60
C-FMAR	3
C-FMUR	54
C-FRTT	131
C-FRTU	139
C-FWAM	**148**
C-GDWM	167
C-GKFG	22
C-GMJS	81
C-GNAK	**154**
C-GNOR	43
C-GPTA	162
C-GPTG	**189**
C-GPTN	**88**
C-GTDL	110

Bahamas

C6-UNO	**102**

Angola

D2-EXB	**166**
D2-EXC	**80**
D2-EXD	**124**

Spain

EC-376	39
EC-433	153
EC-460	64
EC-461	142
EC-493	40
EC-494	41
EC-EVJ	**39**
EC-EXB	**153**
EC-EXQ	142
EC-EXS	64
EC-EZO	41
EC-FIO	**40**

France

(F-)	134
F-GFCQ	**140**
F-GFEF	**122**
F-GFGT	5
F-GFGU	101
F-GFGV	44
F-GFIB	71
F-GFIC	**49**
F-GFMH	**20**
F-GGGY	80
F-GIIX	128
F-GJGC	111
F-GKES	166
F-GNGU	**101**

United Kingdom

G-ASXT	135
G-AWYF	48
G-BKJZ	191
G-BMOW	155
G-BMPA	134
G-BMSR	128
G-BNCE	9
G-BNKN	159
G-BNKO	154
G-BOBX	77
G-BRAL	76
G-BRWN	177

Hungary

HA-ACV	102

Switzerland

HB-IRQ	166
HB-LDT	188

Dominican Republic

HI-678CA	323
HI-678CT	**323**

Colombia

HK-3315	24
HK-3315X	24
HK-3316	59
HK-3316X	59
HK-3329X	145
HK-3330X	90
HK-3579X	190
HK-3580W	**145**
HK-3622	179
HK-3634X	34
HK-3681	**78**
HK-4022X	190

Panama

HP-799	152

Honduras

HR-IAJ	33

Italy

I-CKET	57
I-EHAJ	196
I-MDDD	143
I-MGGG	51
I-MKKK	194
I-TASB	105
I-TASC	173
I-TASO	81

NASA

NASA1	96
NASA2	98
NASA3	92
NASA4	151

United States

N1	2
N1M	88
N1NA	96
(N1PC)	171
N1TX	131
N2NA	**96**
N2NA	98
N2NC	158
N2NR	158
N2PQ	81
N3	160
N3	2
N3NA	**92**
N3UP	18
N4NA	**151**
N4PC	177
N5NA	125
N5PC	20
N5VX	**7**
N6PA	50
N6PG	40
N7FD	145
N7PG	41
N7SL	**11**
N7ZA	68
N7ZB	107
N8BG	22
N8BJ	50
N8E	**94**
N8PG	164
N8VB	12
N8ZA	40
N9EB	5
N9MH	55
N9QM	322
N9ZA	41
N10CR	175
N10NA	125
N10TB	**86**
N10VM	87
N10ZA	142
N11CZ	59
N11NY	172
N11SX	28
N11UN	**102**
N12GP	177
N12GW	19
N12RW	**82**
N15GP	68
(N15SQ)	71
N17CA	123
N18N	90
N18TF	**52**
N20CC	47
N20CR	166
N20GB	80
N20H	197
N20HE	197
N20HF	47
N20NH	16
N20S	37
N21AH	33
N21TX	131
N22AS	156
N22CP	155
N22G	81
(N23AH)	33
N23AK	117
N23D	59
N23UG	108
N24C	155
N25W	181
N26AJ	**54**
N26KW	15
N26L	116
N27G	132
N27L	55
N28CG	102
N28CG	50
N29AY	98
N31CN	162
N33CP	78
N33TF	133
N34C	107
N34LE	34
N36DD	137
N38CG	106
N38JK	38
N39PP	2
N39TG	39
N40AG	40
N40CE	2
N40Y	39
N41JK	90
N41KD	117
N41LH	**156**
N41TG	41
N42CA	137
N42CE	2
N42G	139
N43AS	5
N43M	9
N44MC	172
N46TE	58
N47	69
N47R	69
N47TE	58
N48	67
N48CG	102
N48CQ	102
N48PA	**18**
N48TE	34
N49CB	173
N49DE	97
N50LS	127
N50UC	95
N55AE	175
N60AC	179
N60CR	71
N60WK	179
N61SB	115
N61UT	179
N62J	139
N63AU	126
N64CG	106
N64TG	64
N65CE	**45**
N65H	66
N65HC	66
N66JD	57
N67B	99
N67CR	166
N67H	192
N68TG	68
N70CR	144
N70LR	19
N70QR	144
N71CJ	**107**
N71CR	107
N71CR	163
N71RD	**322**
N72B	154
N72CR	158
N72EZ	15
N72X	106
N72XL	106
N73B	107
(N73CG)	102
N73M	77
N75M	165
N75MT	165
N76DM	166
N79HS	79
N80AC	153
N80G	22
N80J	50
N80K	51
N80L	19
N80LR	19
N80M	27
N80R	90
N80RD	198
N81T	194
N86JK	86
N86MA	35
N87CE	87
N87CH	87
(N87MK)	87
N88PP	164
N88Y	33
N89DE	4
N89K	170
N90M	322
N90PM	51
N91G	37
N91JR	12
N92K	140
N92SA	140
N93AC	196
(N93SA)	72
N94SA	157
N98MK	98
N98R	82
N99DE	4
N100C	198
N100EL	11
N100FL	11
N100P	27
N100TV	126
N102M	99
N102PL	87
N106GA	86
N106GH	86
N107GH	148
N109P	109
N110GA	116
N110RB	**126**
N111DR	66
N113GA	129
N114GA	27
N116GA	2
N116K	100
N117GA	83
N118LT	55
N118X	28
N120HC	132
N120S	148
N120S	26
N121NC	44
N122Y	128
N126J	33
N126K	138
N129AF	**129**
N130B	37
N130G	37
N131A	36
N134PA	196
N137C	93
N140NT	43
N142TG	142
N144NK	63
N149X	145
N152SR	122
N153SR	122
N153TG	153
N154NS	132
N154RH	**132**
N154SR	132
N155T	145
N157WC	139
N159AJ	5
N159AN	116

AIR-BRITAIN MEMBERSHIP

Membership of Air-Britain is open to all with an interest in aviation. The Association has almost 4,000 members in 48 different countries.

Membership Benefits

The annual subscription gives substantial savings on the cover prices of our magazines. for example, non-members would have to pay £45 per year for Air-Britain News whereas members obtain it for ony £33 and have four free Air-Britain Digests on top.

Some of the other benefits of membership include

- Discounts on Air-Britain books
- Access to branches and information services
- Air-Britain trips
- Photograph and slide sales libraries

House Journal All members are sent the Air-Britain house journal Digest and may elect to receive any or all of the three additional magazines News Aeromilitaria Archive.

The various combinations and costs are shown below

CAT	MAGAZINES	UK	EUROPE	OUTSIDE EUROPE
A	News	**£33**	£39	£44
B	Aeromilitaria	**£18**	£20	£23
C	Archive	**£18**	£20	£23
D	Aeromiltaria + Archive	**£26**	£30	£33
E	News + Aeromilitaria	**£40**	£47	£52
F	News + Archive	**£40**	£47	£52
G	News + Aeromilitaria + Archive	**£47**	£56	£60
L	Membership only	**£7**	£8	£9

To Join Air-Britain Please send your Name, Address and Category required to

Air-Britain Membership Secretary, Howard J Nash, "The Haven", Blacklands Lane, Sudbourne, Woodbridge, Suffolk, IP12 2AX, UK

E-mail: abms@sudbourne.demon.co.uk Fax +44 (0) 1394 450767

Payment can be made by using the following credit or debit cards: Visa, Mastercard, Switch, Visa Delta, Connect: Please include the full card name and number, expiry date (& Switch issue number if appropriate).

PLEASE NOTE: Membership runs from January to December. Back magazines are sent (where appropriate). A half year membership is available after 1 July to cover July - December inclusive at half the rates shown (new members only).